INDIA

Fodor's India

New — Twenty-Seventh Edition

[handwritten notes]

BAHAI Te
DIRLA
JAMA MASLI

PARI HILL
RAJGHAT
RAST- BHAVAN
DIWAN AEAN
Jam.
KUMAYI KNLB

FODOR'S TRAVEL PUBLICATIONS, INC.
New York & London

ISBN 0–679–02303–8

Fodor's India

Editor: Paula Consolo
Area Editor: Kathleen Cox
Contributors: Trevor Fishlock, Amy Hunter, Caroline Liou, Marcy Pitchard, Lisa Samson, Amit Shah
Drawings: Lorraine Calaora
Maps: C. W. Bacon
Cover Photograph: Kugler/FPG International

Cover Design: Vignelli Associates

Special Sales

Fodor's Travel Publications are available at special discounts for bulk purchases (100 copies or more) for sales promotions or premiums. Special editions, including personalized covers, excerpts of existing guides, and corporate imprints, can be created in large quantities for special needs. For more information, write to Special Marketing, Fodor's Travel Publications, 201 East 50th Street, New York, NY 10022. Inquiries from the United Kingdom should be sent to Fodor's Travel Publications, 20 Vauxhall Bridge Rd., London, England SW1V 2SA.

MANUFACTURED IN THE UNITED STATES OF AMERICA
10 9 8 7 6 5 4 3 2 1

CONTENTS

CONTENTS

SOUTHERN REGION

EASTERN REGION

NEPAL

SUPPLEMENTS

FOREWORD

The subcontinent of India offers the tourist a million miles of scenic natural wonders: some of the world's highest mountains; beautiful rivers and valleys; deserts, jungles, and wildlife. Everything seems to be on an epic scale. Five thousand years of continuous civilization have left a legacy of aesthetic grandeur in architecture, literature, music, and art. India's strongest attraction for the visitor lies in its interplay of contrasts. Nowhere do the past and present coexist in more colorful abandonment.

This edition includes a new section on Nepal, fabled for its mountain adventures, as well as for its spectacular Kathmandu Valley.

We wish to express our gratitude to the various offices of the Government of India Tourist Office in India for their invaluable assistance in the preparation of this guidebook, especially to Madhavrao Scindia, Minister of Civil Aviation and Tourism. Our thanks also to B.K. Goswami, Secretary of Tourism; Yogesh Chandra, Director General of Tourism; Renu Sahni Dhar, Additional Director General of Tourism; M. K. Lakanpal, Director of Hospitality; Dhiraj Bhalla, Assistant Director of Hospitality; and S. M. Gani, Regional Director (East and North East India), Government of India Tourist Office; and to the following officials for their assistance on the state and city levels: T. Stanley Babu, Andhra Pradesh; Bhudev Basumatari, Assam; R. Basu, M. Sahu, and Hemant Pradhan, Gujarat; Anoop Kannaw and Urgain Loondup, Jammu, Kashmir and Ladakh; B. K. Chauhan, Himachal Pradesh; Sudhakar Rao and C. R. V. Rao, Karnataka; T. Balakrishnan and A. K. Verghese, Kerala; K. K. Chakravarty, Madhya Pradesh; Dev Mehta, Maharashtra; V. S. Narasimhan, Meghalaya; S. K. Nanda, Orissa; Rajeeva Swarup and Rajendra Bhanawat, Rajasthan; Karma Gyatso Khangsarpa and Aungi Namgyal, Sikkim; C. K. Gariyali and V. Manimekalai, Tamil Nadu; Alok Sinha, Uttar Pradesh; T. D. Singh, Varanasi; and Roma Singh, Delhi.

We would also like to thank the Government of India Tourist Office officials in New York and Air India and Indian Airlines officials in New York and throughout India, as well as all the officials and guides from Rajasthan Tours who offered assistance in Rajasthan.

While every care has been taken to ensure the accuracy of the information contained in this guide, the passage of time will always bring change and, consequently, the publisher cannot accept responsibility for errors that may occur.

All prices and opening times quoted here are based on information supplied to us at press time. Hours and admission fees may change, however, and the prudent traveler will avoid inconvenience by calling ahead when possible.

Fodor's wants to hear about your travel experiences, both pleasant and unpleasant. When a hotel or restaurant fails to live up to its billing, let us know and we will investigate the complaint and revise our entries where the facts warrant it. Send your letters to the editors of Fodor's Travel Publications, 201 E. 50th Street, New York, NY 10022.

INTRODUCTION

by
TREVOR FISHLOCK

Journalist, author, and broadcaster, Trevor Fishlock in 1987 won the International Reporter of the Year prize in the British Press Awards. Five years earlier, while a staff correspondent in Delhi for The Times of London, *he won the David Holden Award for outstanding foreign reporting from India. He is now chief roving correspondent for* The Sunday Telegraph, London. *He visits India frequently and has had stints in Australia and the Soviet Union. His most recent books are* India File, The State of America, *and* Out of Red Darkness.

India will change you. It is not possible to be unmoved by it. For old hands already in its thrall and for new explorers about to set off, there is nothing quite so stimulating or sharpening as the prospect of India's immense drama. All journeys to this vast and varied land are adventures. It's very name stirs the imagination and holds out the promise of astonishments, great spectacles, and sudden challenges to preconceptions. It is neither bland nor always comfortable. It is not for everybody. Many of its sights, flavors, and evident contradictions are strong and sometimes provocative. There are subtleties and baffling complexities and opaquenesses not easily penetrated. But India pays large and enduring dividends to travelers who come with open minds, particularly those who take things in their stride and keep in their minds Rudyard Kipling's admonition, "A fool lies here who tried to hustle the East."

Nearly 2,000 years ago, the Greek geographer Strabo struck a cautious note when he wrote, "We must hear accounts of India with indulgence

1

for not only is it very far away, but even those who have seen it saw only some parts of it."

Modern transport has shrunk the distances, but Strabo's observation still has some validity. India's great size and variety mean that even today, most travelers may see only a small area of it. And it really is large. Walled off in the north by the massive bulwarks of the Himalayas, the source of the great rivers Indus and Ganges, India unrolls for more than 2,000 miles—over deserts and jungles, rain forests and well-tilled fields, and plains so vast they make your eyes ache—to the hot southern tip of Cape Comorin. It also spreads for 2,000 miles from the edges of Burma and China to a remote area of mudflats near the mouth of the Indus, the river, now mostly in Pakistan, from which India derives its name.

The peoples who came in waves through the mountain passes to conquer and to settle have created an amazingly complex society in a single country the size of Europe. India embraces great religions. Hinduism, which has its roots in the country's earliest history and remains one of the unifying elements, is the dominant faith. But Islam and Sikhism have helped to shape the country and are significant forces, part of India's fabric. The modern republic acknowledges 15 official languages, but there are hundreds of minor tongues. Among the 23 states and eight territories there are fierce regional loyalties. But in spite of the disparities, strains, and rivalries, the great bulk of Indians are loyal to the idea of India.

One of the keys to understanding today's India is to recognize that it is a country that exists in several centuries at once. India is, in part, a sophisticated and modern society, an industrial leader. It is also the home of primitive tribes, of millions of wretchedly poor people who live seemingly without hope. Between ancient and modern, rich and poor, lives a remarkable spectrum of humanity. The paradoxes of modern India can be seen in the existence of two important research centers: one for space, the other devoted to building a better bullock cart.

Cultures Meshed by Caste

The wonderful tapestry of cultures, languages, religions, diets, and costumes form a heterogeneity linked by the mesh of the caste system. This system has evolved over thousands of years, under racial, social, and religious pressures, as a way of ordering a huge mass of people in a large land area.

Caste provides people with an identity—the knowledge of where they stand in society and how they should live. It can provide security, govern a person's eating customs and other rituals, and determine the choice of a husband or wife (there is a widespread insistence on marriage within one's caste). India has more than 3,000 of these social divisions, from Brahmans to the untouchables.

Caste is so powerful a part of Indian life that it long ago penetrated the Moslem, Sikh, and Christian communities that are meant to be outside it. It is undoubtedly a force for stability in Indian life, strong and conservative, and possibly a defense against revolution. But it is one of the paradoxes of India in that it is also a cause of dissension and deadly rivalry. Caste prejudice, the labyrinth of petty apartheids, is one of the unpleasant facts of Indian life. The struggle of the lower castes and the untouchables to find justice and a decent life is enduring. Caste plays a significant part in the politics of the modern democracy because it is part of the very fiber of India, woven into Hindu ideas of life, rebirth, and predestination.

India is an ancient land, its roots going back 5,000 years. It is fabulous, intricate, and teeming. When, in 1947, the British bid farewell to the jewel in the crown of their empire, India had 350 million people. Now it has 850 million and is growing by more than a million a month. The government is trying to put the brakes on this phenomenal growth with a birth-control program. But nothing will stop India, the second most populous country on earth, from growing to a billion and beyond. It is expected to outstrip China as the world's giant early in the next century. Today, one person in every six in the world is an Indian.

Recent Impressive Advances

The pressures of population create enormous problems for the country's leaders. It is not just a matter of food. In a society with rising expectations, there is an ever-increasing demand for better education, health care, jobs, and housing, and these demands turn into political pressures.

India can point with pride to advances made in recent years. Improvements in public health and disease control have obviously been a big factor in the growth of the population. The years of appalling food shortages and the burden of having to import grain belong to the past. India has learned how to feed its swelling millions through its agricultural revolution, the investment in healthier and stronger crops and improved irrigation. People are manifestly better clothed, fed, educated, and housed. Huge sections of Indian society are moving up. In late 1991 and again in 1992, India's new prime minister and financial minister initiated sweeping reforms that liberalized the country's restricted economy. Privatization and international collaborations will mean India will use its vast resources more efficiently. The nation can feel justifiably proud of what has been achieved. But there is also a darker side. It is impossible to ignore the evidence of poverty and the fact that there are millions in want.

Indians take pride in their country's place as the largest democratic society on earth. In the postcolonial, post–World War II era, many newly independent countries pledged their devotion to the democratic ideal, only to retreat to old ways as traditions and enmities in their societies reemerged and took over. In India, the democratic ideal endures. It is a fact of modern history that sets India apart, and Indians are deeply conscious of it.

India is by far the giant of south Asia, its population, economy, and military strength dwarfing the surrounding countries of Pakistan, Nepal, Bangladesh, and Sri Lanka. Its population is three and a half times greater than the total population of all its neighbors, and its landmass is three times larger than all the others combined.

The political shape of the subcontinent in modern times was changed first by partition in 1947, when the two wings of Pakistan were carved out to create a Moslem homeland, and then by the war of 1971 in which East Pakistan broke away to become Bangladesh. The most important political matter in subcontinental relations is the enduring tension between India and Pakistan. This tension, whose roots are deep in historical rivalries and suspicions, is compounded by mutual mistrust and by the quarrel over the possession of Kashmir, the cause of two of the three wars the countries have fought since partition.

Diversity of People

It is hard to generalize about India and its people. One always runs into the exceptions and contradictions, for the diversity is astonishing. The people of Kashmir, Assam, and Nagaland are different from those of Kerala, Punjab, and Maharashtra. Languages, customs, traditions, histories, diets, and clothing are different, just as, in Europe, Norwegians are different from Spaniards. One has to keep in mind the sheer vastness of India.

Which brings us back to what the wise old geographer Strabo said about seeing only part of India. You can see some of the country by making the great triangular trip of Delhi-Agra-Jaipur. It is a familiar route for travelers and is not to be despised simply because it is well worn. Delhi is more than the capital. It is a repository of history and has been rebuilt several times. The Taj Mahal really is a marvel, well worth the trip, and Jaipur is a particular splendor. If you travel by road around these places, and pause often, you can see and learn much. But travelers do themselves and India an injustice if they do not get out of their comfortable hotels and walk in the streets and lanes and meet the people around them. They sell themselves short if they travel only on the jets of Indian Airlines and shut themselves away in luxurious lobbies and expensive restaurants.

Glamour and wealth are as much a part of the real India as anything else, even if the very rich are only a small minority. And in the smart hotels of great cities like Delhi, Bombay, Calcutta, and Madras, you can see the gatherings of tycoons, film producers, and other entrepreneurs and get a feeling of India's strong business tradition.

You can also see beautiful women, expensively dressed in saris or the long shirt and trousers favored by Punjabis, their bangles gently tinkling. In Bombay, particularly, you might think that these women are stars or starlets, part of the largest movie industry in the world. And you will probably be right.

Bustling City Life

Study the rush hour in any city for a while and you will get a good idea of India at work. One of the striking developments of recent times is the way cities and towns have swelled to create a large and important commercial and industrial population, a burgeoning middle class. The buses are crammed with office workers. Squadrons of bicycles weave to and fro. Young managers perch on motor scooters, often with a wife and children on board. Cars are expensive, but there are plenty of them, ranging from the veteran Ambassador—the great car of India based on a British 1950s design—to the newer Japanese models. And all the vehicles compete for road space with pony carts, rickshaws, camels, and elephants. The noise is tremendous.

Farming and the Monsoon

The great majority of Indians, however, live in rural areas. Nearly 75 percent of the people depend on farming. They live in 576,000 villages, some large and prosperous, some little more than poor hamlets. In many respects, the routines of their lives have changed little over the centuries. When you go to a village, you might imagine that here is the simplest of existences, but village life is a complex pattern of hard work, family problems, disputes, caste consciousness and rivalries, and religious rituals.

The rhythms of crop growing and the weather are central concerns. But the overriding concern is the monsoon—the wind that brings the annual rains—which plays a part in the politics of the country. Politicians and economists, as well as the millions who live off the land, wait anxiously and hopefully as the monsoon moves northward. Radio and newspaper reports are followed with keen interest. Everyone prays for a good monsoon. The air grows hot and the sky turns dark. Then the monsoon breaks with lightning and thunder. People dance in the heavy rain and give thanks. But, from time to time, the rains are scanty and the harvests are poor.

Farming Prospers in the North

The most prosperous farming region is Punjab, home of the "green revolution," which enabled India to feed itself. Punjabis are big, outgoing people, energetic and business minded. They have made Punjab the most prosperous state in the country. They are great farmers and took readily to mechanization, modern fertilizers, and new varieties of crops, the bases of the green revolution. Punjabis have spread throughout the north. Delhi has a strong Punjabi presence, and Punjabis are a major force in the film business in Bombay, India's Hollywood.

Punjab is also the home state of the Sikhs, perhaps the most distinctive Indians, who form over half the state's population. Sikhs are only about 2 percent of the Indian population, but their contribution to national life is in much larger proportion. They have a strong military tradition and retain an important presence in the army, navy, and air force. They are also big in medicine, engineering, and trucking. Sikhs are adherents of a religion founded in the 16th century, as an offshoot of Hinduism, and codified by 10 *gurus,* or teachers. To keep their unshorn hair tidy, Sikhs tuck it into a turban, their distinctive headgear (although other Indians also wear turbans).

The complex politics of the Sikhs and the fundamentalists' belief that their religion is in danger of being swallowed up by Hinduism are reasons for the troubles in Punjab. Hindus and Sikh Punjabis have traditionally lived in harmony, often worshiping in each other's temples. It was once common for one son in a Hindu family in Punjab to be raised as a Sikh. Sikh extremists, however, have been trying to drive a wedge between the two communities.

You will see a different style of turban in Rajasthan, the home of the Rajput people. The turbans here are big, bright edifices made out of 40 feet of muslin.

Bengalis are also distinctive. Their chief city is Calcutta, vigorous and teeming, with a strong cultural tradition. Bengalis are great debaters, poets, artists, and writers, and their politics are lively and contentious. Many Bengalis have names ending in *ji,* or *jee,* as in Chatterji.

Clothing, of course, is governed by the climate. Warm woolen jackets and shawls are worn in the north and cool sarongs are worn in the south. Although many men wear Western-style clothing (trousers and shirts or suits), most women wear the traditional sari or shirt and trousers, the trousers being baggy or narrow. The sari endures because it is graceful, cool, modest, and available in a vast array of patterns and colors.

Many men in the north favor the cool *kurta*—a long shirt and loose trousers, usually white. Also popular is the *dhoti,* the comfortable garment that is often worn loose and baggy or as a loincloth. Many Bengalis like wearing the dhoti, and you'll often see it worn in the countryside.

Land of Many Languages

The languages of India form part of its complexity. By and large, the country's political and regional boundaries are drawn on linguistic lines. With 15 major languages and hundreds of minor ones, as well as dialects, every state in the union is multilingual.

Each main language has an ancient literature and is spoken by millions of people. There is no majority language. Even Hindi, the main official language and the fifth major language of the world after Chinese, English, Russian, and Spanish, is not spoken by a majority. Only English is known throughout India, and only about three people in every hundred speak it. But this Anglophone minority has the greatest influence on running the country. They are the administrators, judges, industrialists, businessmen, leading politicians, and educators.

The languages of India are great unifiers within their home regions; but there are places where language is a sensitive—and political—issue.

Legacy of the Raj

The English language is one of the chief legacies of the British raj, and spoken English in India often has a distinctive and musical lilt. Many Indian words have entered English as part of the cross-fertilization: *bungalow, chintz, pajama,* and *calico* are familiar ones.

English was only one important legacy. A system of justice and the democratic ideal were others. And Indians from north to south love another legacy, the game of cricket. They are as devoted to it as any Englishman—more so, some would say. Listen to Indians discussing cricket, in any language, and you will hear something of the international cricket language: "sticky wicket," "keep a straight bat," and "well played, sir!" Test matches attract huge crowds, and employers complain about people taking the day off to attend. As you travel about, you can see even the poorest boys playing cricket in the dust or on a patch of grass, with makeshift bats and other gear, and dreaming of being cricket stars. The top players are national heroes. Cricket is one of the things that Pakistan and India have in common. When the two countries play each other, the crowds forget other rivalries and concentrate on sporting ones. When there was tension on the shared frontier in 1987, a cricket match defused it.

The British left little or no residue of bitterness when they quit India in 1947. The relations between the two countries have usually been cordial and remain special. Many Indians suffered during the years of the struggle for independence; Nehru and Gandhi were only two of the many thousands who were imprisoned for their activities against the British. But once independence was achieved, there was no attempt to erase the evidence of British management. Nehru, for example, always had a good relationship with the British, and many Indians look back with affection on their years in British schools and universities. India has done what it has usually done throughout history. It absorbed what the British had to offer and took it in its stride.

Traditional Values vs. Modern Cities

India respects its past and reveres old values and rituals, no more so than in the countryside. If you bear in mind that most of the people derive their living from the land, the social and family structures in the villages form a massive bedrock of stability. People live together in a joint family, an efficient way of sharing resources, work, and problems. Major decisions, such as a woman's wish to be sterilized in the birth-control program, may involve the whole family. For decisions affecting the whole community, villagers turn to the *panchayat,* the elected village council. This practice supervises development projects and lobbies the authorities for improvements like wells, irrigation pumps, and health facilities.

Although the countryside in many parts of India has a timeless appearance, with plodding oxen drawing carts and women balancing water jars on their heads, time does not stand still. Agricultural production has been modernized in many areas, new power stations drive irrigation pumps, most villages have electricity, and many villages now own a community television set. In some areas, you will be impressed by the sheer number of shiny new tractors. But bear in mind that these improvements and changes are based on centuries of tradition, of caste divisions and the close loyalties of the joint family—a strict social pecking order.

In the country in particular, you can plainly see that customs, religion, and economic demands put a heavy emphasis on the male. Men rule the roost. Couples fervently desire sons, and girls are often regarded as a burden. The birth of a son is always a matter of celebration; the birth of a girl is usually not. In general, boys in rural India get better treatment, food, education, and medical care. The life expectancy of women in the countryside is shorter than that of men.

It is a different story in the towns and cities whose populations are growing rapidly. It is difficult to observe caste barriers in crowded buses, trains, offices, factories, and restaurants. The rise of urban India has eroded caste differences. The extended family, with parents and sons and daughters-in-law all living together, is still important in the cities, as is the tradition of arranged marriages, with parents finding brides for their sons through personal contacts and newspaper advertisements. However, many young members of the middle class are opting for Western-style courtship and marriage.

It is in urban India that women are at their most emancipated and can compete as equals with men. Women are steadily advancing in medicine, education, law, science, civil service, commerce, and politics. And instead of being kept apart, many men and women in the cities get to know each other socially and professionally in universities and other places of work. The growth of the middle class in the cities is bringing about great changes in Indian life.

The cities are the dynamos, and people stream in from the countryside in search of the better life and more money. The result is that the cities have become overcrowded, and, in some places like Bombay and Calcutta, overcrowding creates a permanent and desperate crisis. In Bombay, for example, about half the city's 10 million people live in slums. Indeed, some of these shanty settlements are almost towns in their own right: the largest has a population of more than half a million. But people continue to pour in because they believe they will earn more than they can in the fields at home. And they are right. Even a lowly job in Bombay pays more than a laboring job in the country, enough to enable a man to send money back home. So many people, rich and poor, want to be in Bombay that property prices have soared to astonishing levels. Bombay's best areas have become as expensive as New York and Tokyo.

Since the early 1970s, the cities of India have grown by 40 percent and 12 cities now have populations of more than a million. Nearly a quarter of the Indians are town or city dwellers, and the migration into cities—with all the problems it creates—is one of the significant forces that is changing Indian life. It is shaping new attitudes and breaking ancient molds.

FACTS AT YOUR FINGERTIPS

THE LAND. Though you may think of India as a place that's hot and tropical, all of it is in the Northern Hemisphere. India is the seventh-largest country in the world, with a land frontier of 15,260 kilometers (9,425 miles), a total land area of about 3,287,000 square kilometers (1,261,000 square miles), and a coastline of 6,100 kilometers (3,535 miles)—approximately the cross-country distance of the United States. In the north, the Himalayas separate India from China. Situated between the two countries is Nepal; to its east is Bhutan, which is still closely connected to India by special treaty. All three countries lie along the chain of the Himalayas, and still more mountains separate India from Myanmar on India's eastern border. Also in the east lies Bangladesh, wedged between the Indian states of Assam, Meghalaya, Tripura, and West Bengal. In the northwest, Pakistan borders India and separates it from Afghanistan and the Confederation of Russian States.

Stretching southward, the country crosses the Tropic of Cancer, then tapers off into a peninsula with the Arabian Sea to the west and the Bay of Bengal to the east. Just off the eastern tip of the subcontinent lies Sri Lanka, separated from the mainland by a sliver of water, the Palk Straits. Sri Lanka, just 50 kilometers (31 miles) away, is an independent nation, whereas islands much farther away from India, such as the Lakshadweep Islands in the Arabian Sea and the distant Andaman and Nicobar Islands in the Bay of Bengal, are part of the Indian Union.

The mainland itself is a geographer's and geologist's paradise. The Himalayan range (*hima* = snow; *laya* — abode) is dramatically high, the altitude of the Indo-Gangetic Plain varies little from sea to sea, and the southern peninsula is a high plateau with coastal strips. The Karakoram Mountains and the Himalayas form a towering wall that is 3,200 kilometers (1,984 miles) long with a depth of 241 to 323 kilometers (150 to 200 miles), straddling Nepal and Tibet. Mount Everest, at 8,874 meters (29,108 feet), is undisputedly the highest peak in the world. Astronomers making calculations via satellite measurements in early 1987 claimed that K-2 in Pakistan was taller, but the dispute was resolved later in 1987 when an Italian expedition confirmed that Everest is still tops—256 meters (840 feet) higher than K-2.

The Garo, Khasi, and Jaintia hills in the northeast are tiny in comparison to their Himalayan neighbors. They run east-west to join the north-south Naga and Mizo hills that separate India from Myanmar.

The Indo-Gangetic Plain is probably the home of more people per square mile than any other spot on earth. The basins of the Ganges and the Brahmaputra make the land rich and productive. Between India's capital of Delhi and the Bay of Bengal, nearly 1,613 kilometers (1,000 miles), the elevation of the Gangetic plain drops only 213 meters (700 feet). Numerous plateaus are separated by mountain and hill ranges, among them the Satpura Hills and the Vindhya and Maikala ranges. The Eastern Ghats move down the peninsula and follow its contour, marking off a broad coastal strip between it and the Bay of Bengal, while on the opposite side of the peninsula, the Western Ghats define a narrower coast off the Arabian Sea. The two ranges meet near the southern tip of India in the Nilgiri Hills.

Geologically, the country has a three-part division: the Himalayas are formed by layers of marine deposits and were once covered by the sea; the soil of the Indo-Gangetic Plain comes from river deposits; and the rocks of the southern peninsula are among the oldest in the world. The Himalayan rivers are snow fed and flow continuously, often causing great floods during the monsoons; the Deccan rivers are rain fed and fluctuate greatly in volume; and the coastal rivers are short and drain little territory.

The Ganges is the mother of India's rivers, the bedrock of mythology and veneration. Its basin drains about a quarter of the country's entire area. The second-largest basin is that of the Godavari, which claims about 10 percent of the total landmass. The most important rivers are the Brahmaputra in the east, the Jamuna and Sutlej in the west, and the Krishna and Caveri in the south.

Basic Statistics for India

Land area: 3,287,000 square kilometers (1,261,000 square mi.)
Population: (1991 census) about 845 million
Population, average annual growth: 2.1 percent
Population, literate adults: 52 percent as per 1991 census
Average life expectancy: 58 years
Average per capita income (1991 estimate): $270 (in U.S. dollars)
Population of 18- to 25-year-olds: 80 million
Agriculture as a percentage of the gross national product (GNP): 41.9 percent (73 percent of the work force)
Industry as a percentage of the GNP: 22 percent
Religions (percentage of population):

Hindu	83.3
Muslim	11.0
Christian	2.6
Sikh	1.9
Buddhist	0.9
Other	0.3

Languages: Hindi is the official language, but English is spoken widely. Twenty-two states also use regional languages for administrative and educational purposes.

CURRENCY. The units of Indian currency are the rupee and paisa (a hundred paise equal one rupee). Paper money comes in the following rupee denominations: 1, 2, 5, 10, 20, 50, 100, and 500. Coins are in denominations of 5, 10, 20, 25, and 50 paise; and 1, 2, and 5 rupees. At press time, the rate of exchange was about U.S.$1 = Rs. 28; £ = Rs. 49.

In order to ensure the flow of hard currency into India and Nepal through tourism, foreigners are not allowed to bring Indian or Nepalese currency into either country. International airports in each country have currency exchange booths that are always open for arriving or departing flights. When you change your money, remember to get at least RS. 200 in small denominations for tips. Also, reject torn bills. Many merchants, hotels, and restaurants won't accept worn or tattered bills and it's a hassle to go to the *one* bank where you can get them exchanged.

Cash, bank notes, and traveler's checks up to U.S. $1,000 or equivalent don't have to be declared at the time of entry. Visitors in possession of more than that amount are required to fill out a Currency Declaration Form on arrival. This form allows you to exchange your unused currency (providing you've held on to your encashment slips) and lets you leave the country with your unchanged money. You receive an encashment slip every time you change money or checks. If you want to pay a hotel bill in rupees, you must have this slip. Foreigners and Indian residents abroad must also pay internal air-travel expenses in foreign currency, traveler's checks, or by credit card.

Traveler's Checks. American Express, Visa, and Thomas Cook traveler's checks are the international drafts of choice. Buy a fair percentage of them in small denominations for those times when you need instant cash and the banks are closed. Along with your traveler's checks, bring a list of foreign offices where you can get refunds if they're lost or stolen. And remember, though most hotels will gladly exchange your checks, they may give a lower rate than banks and exchange houses. Don't be tempted to change money on the black market, which gives a better rate of exchange; it is illegal.

Getting Money from Home. Currently, the only reasonable way to get money from home is to cash a personal check with an American Express or Visa card or, if you're a highly placed executive, with the Thomas Cook Carte d'Or at these companies' respective offices.

WHAT IT WILL COST. With a favorable exchange rate continuing to stretch the dollar's value, India remains a bargain destination and a shopper's dream.

Though rises in fuel costs are pushing up the fares for air and rail travel as well as for taxis, inland travel expenses are still low compared with other destinations. The cost of renting a car with driver, a good way to travel within each state, is about Rs. 4–Rs. 6 per kilometer, with a halt (stopover) charge of Rs. 50–Rs. 100 per night.

Good accommodations in Western-style hotels with air-conditioned rooms and deluxe hotel services can be expensive in the major cities of Bombay, Calcutta, Delhi, and Madras; but, throughout the country, fine hotels exist that will satisfy every budget. Dining is also economical, especially if you eat outside the hotels. Unless you order a feast, you'll find it hard to spend more than $10 per person for a hearty meal.

Visitors should also plan on paying an airport departure tax when they leave India. If you're heading for a neighboring country such as Nepal, the tax is Rs. 150; for all other international destinations the tax is Rs. 300.

CREDIT CARDS. In India and Nepal, Western-style hotels, restaurants, and fancier shops usually accept the following credit cards: American Express, Diners Club, MasterCard, and Visa. Throughout the book we use the following abbreviations: AE, DC, MC, V.

Planning Your Trip

Note: Because of continuing tensions and disturbances in Assam, Jammu, and Kashmir, the U.S. State Department at press time advises deferring travel to these states. Travelers to other parts of Northern and Eastern India, especially Punjab, should exercise caution. Special permits (see Restricted Area Permit, below) are required for many areas. Since sporadic incidents of violence due to political unrest can occur at any time throughout India, it is suggested that you call the U.S. State Department (tel. 202–647–5225) for its latest recorded travel advisory. Be prepared for a lengthy message, especially if your phone is not a touch-tone type. While in India, you are urged to contact the American Embassy in New Delhi or the American Consulates General in Bombay, Calcutta, and Madras for the latest information on the security situation in the area you are visiting or plan to visit.

India is one country where you should plan your trip in advance. It is too vast and complex a land to start organizing your itinerary after you arrive. Unless you are traveling on a package tour, with a fixed itinerary and schedule, read every possible brochure first and then settle on priorities.

Most first-time visitors to India try to pack in too many objectives. Distances are huge, traveling tiring, and sightseeing exhausting. Wise travelers plan a couple of days' complete relaxation, in a beach resort or mountain retreat, for every 7–10 days of touring, to digest all the wonders they have seen and to catch up on rest and laundry before the next phase of the trip.

The *Government of India Tourist Office* is one of the best of the national tourism-promotion organizations. Here, you will get informative leaflets covering the diverse attractions and regions of India. We hope you will find most of the planning information you need in this book, but public libraries will provide more in-depth information about social or political aspects. State-run tourist offices vary in reliability and information; some are informative about local events and some offer reasonably priced tour packages.

Major Government of India Tourist Offices are located at the following addresses:

USA: 30 Rockefeller Plaza, Room 15, North Mezzanine, New York, NY 10020, tel. 212–586–4901, fax 212–582–3274; 3550 Wilshire Blvd., Los Angeles, CA 90010, tel. 213–380–8855, fax 213–380–6111.

UK: 7 Cork St., London W1X 2AB, tel. 071–437–3677 or 78, fax 071–494–1048.

CANADA: 60 Bloor St. West, Suite 1003, Toronto, Ontario M4W3B8, tel. 416–962–3787 or 88, fax 416–962–6279.

AUSTRALIA: Level 5, 65 Elizabeth St., Sydney, NSW 2000, tel. 02–232–1600, fax 02–223–3003.

There are also overseas offices in Amsterdam, Bahrain, Bangkok, Dubai, Frankfurt, Geneva, Kuala Lumpur, Kuwait, Madrid, Milan, Paris, Singapore, Stockholm, and Tokyo. Visitors will find Government of India Tourist Offices in all the major towns of India; these offices will be even more helpful than the overseas branches because they have more detailed information pertaining to their own areas.

The services of Indian Airlines, the major domestic carrier, have improved greatly in recent years. Bookings can be made through Air India offices abroad, since Indian Airlines does not have overseas facilities. It is critical that you reconfirm all airline flights, domestic or international, throughout your stay in India. Train reservations and ticket purchases usually have to be made on the spot in each major city. Special lines for tourists are set up at major airports and railroad terminals. Indian railways are in the process of computerizing reservations and cancellations. This advancement has made rail travel much easier to organize.

The growth of major hotel chains in recent years has made advance booking much simpler, and accommodations for a complete tour itinerary can now be reserved through just one or two central reservations systems. Details of the major chains are given in the *Hotels* section of this chapter.

City sightseeing, car hire, and guide services can be easily arranged on arrival at each destination, either through hotel travel desks, the local Government of India Tourist Office, or the state tourist organization. The excursions and tours detailed in this section can also be arranged easily, but one should make airline reservations well in advance, especially during peak travel times.

The wise traveler to India builds in several reserve days in case of unexpected delays or the impulse to see more of a particular place. We would most strongly advise you not to try to work within a tight itinerary. Take it easy. Pick one major city, then concentrate on a particular region and enjoy it in depth. Come back again, as many do, to this fascinating land.

This book will help you to decide what you want to see in India. Study our maps of the tourist highlights, consult the list of itineraries appearing later in this chapter while building up your own itinerary, and then try to reconcile the itinerary you plan with the time at your disposal. Remember that airline schedules change slightly according to season, so be sure to check them.

TRAVEL DOCUMENTS. Travelers to India require a passport and a visa. **Americans** applying for a new U.S. passport must appear in person; renewals can be obtained in person or by mail (see below). First-time applicants should apply well in advance of their departure at a U.S. passport agency in Boston, Chicago, Honolulu, Houston, Los Angeles, Miami, New Orleans, New York, Philadelphia, San Francisco, Seattle, Stamford (CT), Washington, DC, or at their local county courthouse or certain post offices. Necessary documents include a completed passport application (Form DSP–11); proof of citizenship (birth certificate with raised seal or naturalization papers); proof of identity (driver's license, employee ID card, or any document with your photograph and signature); two recent, identical, two-inch-square photographs (black-and-white or color); $65 application fee for a 10-year passport (those under 18 pay $40 for a five-year passport). Passports are mailed to you in about 10 to 15 working days.

To renew your passport by mail, you'll need completed Form DSP–82; two recent, identical passport photographs; and a check or money order for $55.

British Citizens. Applications are available from travel agencies or a main post office. Send the completed form to your nearest regional passport office (locations include London, Liverpool, Newport, Peterborough, Glasgow, and Belfast). The application must be countersigned by your bank manager or by a solicitor, barrister, doctor, clergyman, or justice of the peace who knows you personally. In addition, you'll need two photographs and a £15 fee for the 32-page passport, £30 for the 94-page passport.

Canadian Citizens. Canadians can apply in person at regional passport offices in Edmonton, Halifax, Montreal, Toronto, Fredericton, Hamilton, London, Ott wa, Hull, Quebec, St. John's, Saskatoon, North York, Victoria, Windsor, Var ver, or Winnipeg. You can also send a completed application (available at office or passport office) to the Bureau of Passports, Suite 215, West To plexe Guy Favreau, 200 Réné Levesque Blvd., Montreal, Quebec, H clude $25, two photographs, a guarantor, and proof of Canadian citizenship. Passports are valid for five years and are nonrenewable.

VISAS

Citizens of all countries must have a valid tourist visa obtained from Indian consulates or high commissions (see list below). To get a visa, you need a valid passport and two passport-size photos. The tourist visa cost for Americans and Canadians is $5; for Britons, £23. The visa is good for 30 days, with a five-month extension possible. You must arrive in India within six months of the date your visa is issued. Individuals who need to extend their visas should visit the Foreigners' Regional Registration Office in New Delhi or Calcutta or at any of the offices of the Superintendent of Police in the various district headquarters. If you appear in person at an Indian consulate or high commission, your initial visa is usually granted within 48 hours. If you apply through the mail, allow a month and include a self-addressed and stamped envelope.

U.S. Citizens can apply to the following offices of the Consulate General of India: 3 E. 64th St., New York, NY 10021, tel. 212–879–7800; 150 North Michigan Ave., Chicago, IL 60601, tel. 312–781–6280; 540 Arguello Blvd., San Francisco, CA 94118, tel. 415–668–0662. You can also apply to the Embassy of India, 2107 Massachusetts Ave., Washington, DC 20008, tel. 202–939–7000.

British Citizens can apply to the India High Commission, India House, Aldwych, London WC2B 4NA; tel. 071–836–8484.

Canadians can apply to the Indian High Commission at 10 Springfield Rd., Ottawa, Quebec K1M 109, tel. 613–744–3751; or to the Consulates General at 2 Bloor St., Suite 500, West Cumberland, Toronto, Ontario M4W 3E2, tel. 416–960–0751; or 325 Howe St., Vancouver, British Columbia V6C 1Z7; tel. 604–662–8811.

RESTRICTED AREA PERMIT

At press time, a Restricted Area Permit was obligatory for Assam, Meghalaya, and Sikkim. You also need the permit to visit the Andaman Islands (a 30–day permit is available on arrival at Port Blair), Lakshadweep Islands (also easily obtained through the one resort open to foreigners), and Banni, an area in Gujarat's Kutch near Pakistan (easily obtained on arrival in Bhuj, the district capital). At press time, the government had just opened the districts of Spiti and Kinnaur, which are both in Himachal Pradesh. A Restricted Area Permit is required, and you must travel in a group of at least four people with a government approved travel agency. In most cases the agency will get your permit; otherwise, follow the advice given below for Assam and Meghalaya. Contact the Government of India Tourist Office abroad for the latest details. If you are told to apply to the Ministry of Home Affairs through a consular office or mission in your own country, don't. Follow the advice given below for Assam.

You can obtain an application for a Restricted Area Permit from any consular office abroad. With Sikkim, where permission for a 15–day visit is now easy to procure, send the permit application to the Sikkim office or any Indian mission. With Meghalaya, tight restrictions have been relaxed. Fifteen-day permits for parties of four or more travelers are now granted through these same Indian government offices. Currently, individual travelers were advised to send their permit to the Resident Commissioner at Meghalaya House (10 Aurangzeb Rd., New Delhi 110011), who will help expedite the process. Check with the Government of India Tourist Office for the latest details.

With Assam and Meghalaya, don't use the consular offices or missions to get permission, as many travel agents or even the Government of India Tourist Office will suggest. Send the permit application to the Ministry of Home Affairs, Government of India, Lok Nayak Bhavan, Khan Market, New Delhi 110003. Other offices are more likely to say "no" than go through the paperwork required to make your trip happen.

For all permits, you must be specific about your trip plans and provide a precise list of destinations within the state. For acceptable destinations, see the permit guidelines in each destination chapter. Also note the time restrictions and figure them into your itinerary. With Sikkim, you can also procure a permit from the following offices: the Sikkim Tourist Office in New Delhi; the Foreign Regional Registration offices in Delhi, Bombay, and Calcutta; and the Immigration Offices at airports in Delhi, Bombay, Calcutta, and Madras. With Meghalaya, you can also procure a permit from the Foreign Regional Registration offices.

With all destinations, except Sikkim and group permits into Meghalaya, allow three months for clearance. When you get your permit, make two copies and keep them with you when you travel. Travelers have recounted terrible stories in which they've either lost their only copy due to carelessness or had it inexplicably taken from them by the police at a checkpoint—which meant they couldn't proceed on their trip. The permit must be shown at various checkposts and to every hotel manager when you check in (or you won't be given a room).

Travelers can also visit most of these restricted areas as part of a tour group listed under each destination chapter and below under Tour Operators. Under these circumstances, the tour operator will help you secure the necessary permits.

TOUR OPERATORS. The first list of companies offers excellent tours to India and Nepal. A few of these companies also offer some outdoor adventures. We also indicate which of these companies will help travelers who want to see this area on their own and just need tickets, hotel reservations, or a hired car with driver. The second list of tour operators concentrates on outdoor adventures or unusual theme-oriented trips. In each list, we also include companies that operate in India (companies based in Nepal are listed in Before You Go in the Nepal chapter). Both countries have excellent agencies. Their prices can be competitive; their knowledge is comprehensive; and their service is reliable. Don't be afraid to give a call or send a fax. Most companies offer a two-tiered price structure, one with or without airfare from the West. If you choose a package based exclusively on land costs, you can arrive or depart according to your own schedule. With all recommended companies you can join a fixed departure tour, or you can ask for a more expensive custom-designed trip. Travelers who don't like group travel should consider a minitour that lasts for a week or less. This is one way to get into destinations that have group-travel restrictions. Finally, ask tour operators about expenses covered in the tour cost, such as supplementary insurance coverage. If your trip involves physical exertion, ask about the degree of difficulty and prior experience required.

General-Interest Tours. U.S. and Canada. *American Express* (3 World Financial Center, American Express Tower, New York, NY 10285–0230, tel. 212–640–5283, fax 212–619–9802) offers numerous tours and can also take care of all travel needs.

Cox & Kings Ltd. (Suite 335, 511 Lexington Ave., New York, NY 10017, tel. 212–935–3935 or 800–999–1578, fax 212–751–4791) provides a comprehensive range of tours and can take care of all travel needs.

Distant Horizons (679 Tremont St., Boston, MA 02118, tel. 617–267–5343 or 800–333–1240) offers excellent cultural tours in Nepal and India (Sikkim, northern West Bengal, Agra, and Rajasthan). Asian scholars will be your guide.

Mercury Travels (Suite 1302, 820 2nd Ave., New York, NY 10017, tel. 212–661–0380 or 800–223–1474, fax 212–983–5692) offers excellent cultural "theme" tours that focus on Buddhism, the life of Mahatma Gandhi, museums, and southern temple cities. It also sponsors some outdoor adventure trips, including skiing, rafting, trekking, and camel and wildlife safaris. It leads some trips to Nepal and can take care of all travel needs.

Sita World Travel (Indrama, Suite 1708, 501 5th Ave., New York, NY 10017, tel. 212–972–5500, fax 212–986–3511) is an excellent all-purpose agency that can take care of all travel needs. It offers numerous general and cultural-theme tours in India and Nepal.

Travel Corporation (India) (Suite 6E, 20 E. 53rd St., New York, NY 10022, tel. 212–371–8080, fax 212–759–9787) offers a full range of trips in India, including a special tour with overnights in palaces still owned by former maharajahs and a trip to the Andaman Islands. It can take care of all travel needs.

Zutshi's Travel World Service (71 Keystone Ave., Reno, NV 89503, tel. 702–323–0110, fax 702–323–6914) offers more than 40 trips to India, including comprehensive tours that highlight unusual destinations or take you off the beaten path. It also offers numerous trips to India's wildlife sanctuaries. Trips range from 3 to 22 days.

Britain. The following companies are the British-based offices of some of the agencies listed above: *American Express* (19–20 Berners St., London W1P 4AE, tel. 071–637–8600, fax 071–631–4803; *Cox & Kings* (St. James Court, 45 Buckingham Gate, London SW1F 6AS, tel. 071–931–9106, fax 071–630–6038); *Sita World Travels* (Naresh Chesham House, 136 Regent St., W1R 5FA, tel. 071–437–6900, ext. 233, fax 071–434–1255); and *Travel Corporation* (India) (Suite 3235, High Holborn House, 52–54 High Holborn, London WC1V 6RL, tel. 071–242–9930, fax 071–242–2838).

India. *RBS Travels* (Connaught Palace Hotel, 37 Shaheed Bhagat Singh Marg, New Delhi 110001, tel. 344952, fax 344952) can arrange customized trips to suit all budgets and interests: village visits in Rajasthan and Madhya Pradesh; Kerala, Goa, and Maharashtra beach excursions; religious pilgrimages. It also arranges mountaineering in Himachal Pradesh; trekking in Himachal Pradesh and Kashmir/Ladakh; and wildlife safaris in Uttar Pradesh and Rajasthan.

Four of the companies listed above also have offices in India: *Cox & Kings* (Indra Pl., H-Block, Connaught Circus, New Delhi 110001, tel. 332006, fax 3317373); *Mercury Travels* (Jeevan Tara Bldg., Parliament St., New Delhi 110001, tel. 312008, fax 351413); *Sita World Travel* (4 Nalcha Marg Shopping Center, Diplomatic Enclave, New Delhi 110021, tel. 3011122, fax 3010123); and *Travel Corporation of India, Pvt. Ltd.* (Chander Mukhi, Nariman Pt., Bombay 400021, Maharashtra, tel. 2021881, fax 2029424). Some of these companies have branches in other major cities in India; see Tour Operators under each chapter.

Special-Interest Tours. U.S. and Canada. *Above the Clouds Trekking* (Box 398, Worcester, MA 01602, tel. 508–799–4499 or 800–233–4499, fax 508–797–4779) sponsors treks throughout Nepal that range from easy to hard and from mini-trek length to a month-long trip. It also offers mountain biking, rafting, and wildlife safaris in Nepal. In India, it has a wildlife tour to Kerala with trekking in the Nilgiris and a visit to Karnataka's Nagarhole National Park. This outfit has established the Nepal Scholarship Fund for Nepalese students to pursue environmental degrees in the United States.

Archaeological Tours (Suite 1202, 30 E. 42nd St., New York, NY 10017, tel. 212–986–3054, fax 212–370–1561) sponsors excellent scholar-led tours in India, with a special emphasis on archaeology and history, such as an in-depth tour of south India's sacred and historic cities combined with stopovers at Goa and a wildlife sanctuary. It also offers a tour of Himachal Pradesh, Nepal, and Bhutan.

Asian Pacific Adventures (826 South Sierra Bonita Ave., Los Angeles, CA 90036, tel. 213–935–3156) offers two comprehensive combination vacations: a trekking, biking, and rafting trip in Nepal and a trip to India that includes biking, a camel safari, and visits to a wildlife sanctuary and to historically sacred cities in India. It also arranges customized bicycling trips and tours that focus on fine arts, wildlife, minority studies, Buddhism, and folk cultures.

Himalaya Trekking and Wilderness Expeditions (1900 Eighth St., Berkeley, CA 94710, tel. 510–540–8040 or 800–777–TREK, fax 510–644–1777) offers numerous miniexcursions to Goa, Varanasi, Khajuraho, Agra, Ellora, and Ajanta; a cultural and anthropological trip in south India; a trip from Ladakh to Manali via jeep and foot to search for leopards; and numerous other vehicular excursions. It also offers trekking in Himachal Pradesh, including a trip that follows the route of Gaddi nomads who travel with their sheep. In Nepal, it offers tours, treks, rafting, and biking.

InnerAsia Expeditions (2627 Lombard St., San Francisco, CA 94123, tel. 415–922–0448 or 800–777–8183, fax 415–346–5535) offers treks of varying difficulty, including rafting trips, wildlife safaris, and mountain climbing throughout Nepal. It also has a trip that coincides with the annual elephant polo championship at Tiger Tops. In India, it sponsors a trek from Dharamsala to Shimla in Himachal Pradesh, a trip to Rajasthan's Pushkar Cattle Fair, and biking in Rajasthan. It also offers a vehicular tour that includes Bhutan and India.

King Bird Tours (Box 196, Planetarium Station, New York, NY 10024, 212–866–7923) sponsors in-depth bird-watching tours in Assam, Rajasthan, Gujarat, Kerala, Tamil Nadu, and the Andaman Islands.

Lute Jerstad Adventures (Box 19537, Portland, OR 97219, tel. 503–244–6075, fax 503–244–1349), a small concern run by a Himalayan scholar, offers rafting and jungle safaris, treks in Nepal and India, especially in Ladakh and Himachal Pradesh. It also offers educational and cultural excursions in India, including a special tour that retraces the footsteps of Guru Padmasambhava in Nepal and Tibet, and a journey in India that focuses on the Age of the Moguls.

Mountain Travel-Sobek (6420 Fairmount Ave., El Cerrito, CA 94530–3606, tel. 510–527–8100 or 800–227–2384, fax 510–525–7710), a pioneer in outdoor adventure, offers treks, rafting and wildlife safaris, biking and mountain expeditions in Nepal, as well as eco-tours and medical tours that study mountain and wilderness illnesses. In India, it offers a camel safari in Rajasthan, treks in the Himalayas (including Sikkim and Ladakh), a Ganga River cruise, and wildlife safaris.

Nature Expeditions International (474 Willamette St., Box 11496, Eugene, OR 97440, tel. 503–484–6529) sponsors nature and culture tours led by anthropologists and biologists to some of India's best sanctuaries, including Kanha in Madhya Pradesh. It also has nature treks and tours in Nepal.

Overseas Adventure Travel (349 Broadway, Cambridge, MA 02139, tel. 617–876–0533 or 800–221–0814, fax 617–876–0455) offers numerous treks, rafting, and jungle safaris in Nepal. In India, it offers a trek through Zanskar in Ladakh and a trip to Varanasi, Khajuraho, Orchha, and Agra. More India trips are in the works. It also arranges "singles only" and family trips, cross-cultural exchanges for women, eco-tours, and budget trips. A percentage of all trekking fees goes to protect the environment.

Tiger Tops International (2627 Lombard St., San Francisco, CA 94123, tel. 415–346–3402, fax 415–346–8672) has pioneered many of the best treks and mountain expeditions in Nepal. The company also offers numerous treks in India, including the Garhwals in northern Uttar Pradesh, Himachal Pradesh, Ladakh and Zanskar, Darjeeling, and Sikkim. In addition, it sells a trek and a jeep safari into Himachal Pradesh's newly opened Spiti Valley. It also conducts wildlife safaris in their idyllic game-park retreats, and rafting trips.

Wilderness Travel (801 Allston Way, Berkeley, CA 94710, tel. 415–548–0420 or 800–247–6700) offers trekking, rafting, mountain biking, and jungle safaris in Nepal. In India, it sponsors treks (including a trek and vehicular journey that coincides with Ladakh's Hemis Monastery festival), camel safaris in Rajasthan (including a camel safari to the Pushkar Fair), and wildlife safaris.

Wildland Adventures (3516 NE 155th St., Seattle, WA 98155, tel. 206–365–0686 or 800–345–4453, fax 206–363–6615) promotes active participation in foreign cultures or in the protection of the environment. It offers year-round treks of varying difficulty all over Nepal. Some are theme-oriented, some include rafting and wildlife safaris. It also sponsors a novel heli-trek, for which you are flown into a remote area to trek. Another unusual trip in Nepal is the annual Buddha's Birthday Tree Trek, which coincides with the Buddha's birthday celebration at a monastery and includes planting trees in deforested areas. In India, it conducts treks in Sikkim, Himachal Pradesh, and Ladakh, as well as vehicular tours in Ladakh. A portion of the trip fee goes into the Earth Preservation Fund, which sponsors projects in Nepal, India, and other foreign destinations.

Womantrek (Box 20634, 1411 East Olive Way, Seattle, WA 98102, tel. 206–325–4772 or 800–477–TREK, fax 206–324–2514) offers treks for women in Nepal and India, with a special emphasis on cross-cultural appreciation and interaction. Groups are usually restricted to fewer than 15 women and attempts are made to design trips in remote areas where it is normally difficult for women to travel alone. Women guides from each region enable travelers to gain access to villages, where there is close contact with families.

Britain. *Exodus* (9 Weir Rd., London SW12 OLT, tel. 081–673–0859, fax 081–673–0779) offers jeep excursions in India's Ladakh, Himachal Pradesh, Darjeeling, Sikkim, Assam, Manipur, Nagaland, Rajasthan, and all over the south. It conducts comprehensive train trips in India; trekking in Sikkim, the Garhwals in Uttar Pradesh, and throughout Ladakh and Himachal Pradesh; and a cruise down the Brahmaputra River. In Nepal, it offers minibus tours with a wildlife safari, a mountain bike journey, and treks throughout the country.

ExplorAsia (13 Chapter St., London SW1P 4NY, tel. 081–630–7102, fax 081–630–0355) serves as a liaison for Tiger Tops and its subsidiaries and offers the same adventures listed above.

Sherpa Expeditions (131 A Heston Rd., Hounslow, Middlesex TW5 ORD, tel. 081–577–2717, fax 081–572–9788) specializes in treks to India's Ladakh and Zanskar, and to Lahaul in Himachal Pradesh (including a trip that follows a route of the Gaddi nomads), the Garhwals in Uttar Pradesh, and Sikkim. In Nepal, it offers numerous treks, river rafting, and wildlife safaris.

Trans Indus (Northumberland House, 11 The Pavement, Popes La., Ealing, London W5 4NG, tel. 081–566–2729, fax 081–566–1903) concentrates on India, with comprehensive tours in the south (some timed with festivals), numerous trips to Rajasthan, beach holidays, pilgrimage treks to sacred destinations, a tour by rail on the "Palace on Wheels," camel safaris in the Thar Desert, and wildlife tours. It also offers a trip to Darjeeling, Sikkim, and Orissa, and a few trips to Nepal's wildlife parks.

India. *Arventures Adventure Holidays* (Post Bag No. 7, Dehradun 248001, Uttar Pradesh, tel. 29172) creates every conceivable fixed or customized outdoor experience in the Himalayas: treks by elephant, bike, horse, jeep; wildlife safaris; and water-trips by *shikara* (Kashmiri gondola). It creates "theme" treks that focus on nature, photography, village life, or religion.

Empl Tours (108 Vishal Bhawan, 95 Nehru Pl., New Delhi 110019, tel. 6428310, fax 6428311) creates customized "adventure" trips throughout India. They offer hang gliding in Karnataka; numerous trips to sanctuaries, including elephant trips in Uttar Pradesh and Bandhavgarh National Park in Madhya Pradesh; horseback riding and camel trips in remote areas of Rajasthan with stays in the homes of former noblemen; treks in southern villages and the Himalayas; exotic boat cruises on the Ganges River in Uttar Pradesh, the Brahmaputra in Assam, and the Chambal in Rajasthan; catamaran trips in West Bengal; biking in Kerala, Tamil Nadu, and Karnataka; and jeep safaris to Spiti. Think of a destination and an adventure, and this company will create the trip.

Exotic Journeys (26 Sector 2 Market, R. K. Puram, New Delhi 110022, tel. 670221 or 6875320, fax 676377) offers elephant safaris in northern India; safaris in Gujarat's Rann of Kutch desert; biking in Rajasthan; bird-watching in the Himalayas; trekking in Tamil Nadu's Nilgiri Hills; plus photo safaris, educational tours, village stays, and a novel program called "Travel As You Like" where they supply a jeep, driver, and guide and create a trip through an Indian state or states, which can involve camping (equipment provided) or luxury hotel, palace, or inn stays.

Himalayan River Runners (188–A Jor Bagh, New Delhi 110003, tel. 4632180) is India's best rafting company, pioneering the latest runs in the Indian Himalayas with excellent personal attention and equipment. Fixed departures and customized trips are available. This company also runs a rafting-training camp in Rishikesh.

Mountain Travel India and *Tiger Mountain India* (1/1 Rani Jhansi Rd., New Delhi 110055, tel. 7533483, fax 777483) are the Indian-based offices for Tiger Tops and offer the same adventures listed above under Tiger Tops International.

Volunteer Vacations. If you'd like to do volunteer work in India, an excellent clearing house in New Delhi can help match your interest or skill with a worthwhile organization. Contact the **Gandhi Peace Foundation** (221/223 Deen Dayal, Upadhyaya Marg, New Delhi 110002, tel. 3317491 or 3317493). This foundation can place members of the medical or educational professions, agronomists, scientists, technocrats, or anyone interested in helping in rural or community projects designed to improve the well-being of the needy. There are no commitments regarding the minimum length of stay. Applicants should be 18 years old, but there is no upper-age limit.

Volunteers who would like to get immersed in Ladakh's Buddhist culture can help with farming and village-based projects designed to improve the living standards in this remote, high-altitude district. Contact the **Students' Educational and Cultural Movement of Ladakh** (SECMOL, Pharkey Labrang, Box 4, Leh 194101, Ladakh, Jamma and Kashmir, tel. 585).

In the United States, **Habitat for Humanity International** (121 Habitat St., Americus, GA 31709–3498, tel. 912–924–6935) sponsors housing projects in urban and rural areas of India. This organization, which subscribes to a Christian philosophy, counts former-President Jimmy Carter and his wife, Rosalynn, as active participants. It's open to anyone dedicated to hard work who can saw wood or use a hammer to pound nails.

To join a scientific or archeological expedition in India is more difficult. Although educational institutes and organizations sponsor projects around the world, there are few trips based in the subcontinent. You can try to find one by contacting the following organizations: **Earthwatch** (Box 403, 680 Mount Auburn St., Watertown, MA 02272, tel. 617–926–8200); **Foundation for Field Research** (Box 2010, Alpine, CA 92001–0020, tel. 619–445–9264); **University Research Expedition Programs** (University of California, Berkeley, CA 94720, tel. 415–642–6586); and **Cornell Adult University** (626 Thurston Ave., Ithaca, NY 14850, tel. 607–255–6260).

Special Tours for Special Needs. *Evergreen Travel Service* (4114 198th St., S.W., Lynnwood, WA 98036–6742, tel. 206–776–1184 or 800–435–2288, fax 206–775–6488) creates customized skiing and rafting trips and generalized tours for the handicapped traveler. Trekking is currently under study. No matter how severe your handicap, this well-run organization will find a way for you to enjoy India and Nepal.

TOURING ITINERARIES. In planning a trip to India your best bet is to concentrate on a particular region and keep inland flights, which are often delayed, to a minimum. This plan is particularly valid for brief visits of up to a week, such as might be undertaken by a business or transit traveler. The following tours will need Indian Airlines and Vayudoot timetables for detailed planning. Since plane service in India is often unreliable, we have indicated flights only between major cities. There are flights that can take you to most destinations, but these tours purposely concentrate on regions or themes to provide for an in-depth experience. Many of the tours also suggest good adventures that can add to your fun. While we suggest the optimum trip length, each itinerary can be easily reduced to fit your schedule.

Starting point: Delhi

Classic Subcontinent (October–April; 21 days). After arriving in Delhi, explore its old and new capitals. Don't miss the Red Fort, Jama Masjid, and be sure to wander through Chandni Chowk and visit the nearby Charity Bird Hospital. From Delhi, drive or take the express train to Agra. See its great Mogul architecture: the Taj Mahal, Agra Fort, Sikandra, and nearby Fatehpur Sikri. Drive to Gwalior, the capital of a former princely state, with stunning palaces and a fort. Take an optional excursion to Orchha, a 17th-century city of palaces. Drive to Khajuraho. See its exquisite temples and charming villages. Fly to Varanasi and take a peaceful morning cruise on the Ganges River. Visit its temples, silk emporiums, and Sarnath, imbued with Buddhist significance. Fly to Kathmandu. Explore the trio of monument-rich cities: old Kathmandu, Patan, and Bhaktapur. Take the memorable Himalayan morning flight and circle the majestic peaks of the Himalayas. Raft to Chitwan National Park and stay in a nearby lodge, where you can search for wildlife by jeep or elephant. Drive back to Kathmandu and fly back to Delhi.

Trains, Tigers, Tribes (October–April; 22 days). After exploring Delhi, take the train to Madhya Pradesh's city of Jabalpur, the gateway to Bandivgarh National Park, which is approachable by car. Spend time in a tented resort and go on a wildlife safari in this excellent sanctuary, which is known for its abundant tigers. Return to Jabalpur and take the train to Bhubaneswar in Orissa, with its architecturally unique temples. Wander through the city's old town and bazaars, where you can watch stonecutters at work. Go by car to Puri on the sea, a sacred Hindu destination with its famous Jagannath Temple. On the way, stop at Pipli's roadside market, known for its colorful patchwork-fabric products. Also visit Raghurajpur, a nearby village in the jungle that's populated by artisans. Stay at Toshali Sands, an ethnic-style village resort, just outside Puri, which has its own private beach. Trek inland and visit some of Orissa's most interesting tribal people. Return to Toshali Sands and relax before driving back to Bhubaneswar and flying to Delhi.

Rajput Odyssey (October–April; 25 days). After exploring Delhi, drive or go by train to Agra and Fatehpur Sikri. Drive or go by train to Gwalior. Drive to Sawai Madhopur's Ranthambhor Wildlife Sanctuary in Rajasthan. Stay in a former maharaja's hunting lodge and go on a jeep safari inside the park. Drive to Bundi, an old city with narrow lanes and palaces. Stay in a former maharaja's home in nearby Kota. Drive through Rajput Rajasthan—Chittorgarh, Udaipur, Ranakpur, and Jodhpur. By day, explore the cities with their medieval forts and palaces. At night, stay in hotels that were once hunting lodges, forts, or palaces of former maharajas. From Jodhpur, drive or travel by train in the former maharaja's saloon car to the golden city of Jaisalmer in the Thar Desert. Visit Jaisalmer's old *havelis* (mansions) and fort. Take a camel safari into the Thar Desert. Go by car or camel to Bikaner.

Stay in the former maharaja's quaint hunting lodge or mammoth palace. Drive through the Shekhavati district, an area strewn with old havelis covered with frescoes. Stay at Mandawa in an old castle or at an ethnic-style desert resort. In Dundlod and Nawalgarh (also in Shehavati), stay in hotels that are the homes of former Rajput noblemen. Drive to Jaipur, with its bazaars and pink-hued monuments. Stay in an old haveli or palace. Return to Delhi. Much of this trip through Rajasthan can also be done by bike or horse.

White Himalayas, White-Water, and Wildlife (December–March for skiing, November–mid-December and February–June for rafting; 17 days minimum, with three days rafting, three days skiing, three days on wildlife safari). After exploring Delhi, drive or fly to Dehra Dun in Uttar Pradesh. Drive to Mussoorie, a former British hill station in the Himalayas. Spend the night in an old château. Drive north to Auli, a modest but worthwhile ski resort in the Garhwal Himalayas. Rent good equipment and ski down slopes with memorable vistas. Drive to Uttar Pradesh's Himalayan foothills and raft six days from Rudraprayag down the Alakananda River to Rishikesh or three days from Deoprayag down the Ganges River to Rishikesh. Take a break at nearby Haridwar, a devout Hindu city. Enjoy the nightly Arti of the Ganga, a prayer service where floating candles light up the sacred river. Drive to Corbett National Park and stay at a forest rest house inside the sanctuary or at a classy resort on the park's perimeter. Go on the "hunt" for wildlife by jeep or elephant. Drive back to Delhi.

Essence of Hinduism (May–October; 18 days, without trekking). After exploring Delhi, drive to Haridwar in Uttar Pradesh. Visit this Art Deco Hindu pilgrimage center, with its colorful ashrams, which provide a good introduction to Hinduism. Attend a nightime Arti of the Ganga. Drive north to Mussoorie. Drive north to the Yamunotri Temple, near the source of the sacred Yamuna River and one of four revered Char Dhams (Hindu shrines) in the Himalayas. From here, trek or drive (with two obligatory day walks) to the Gangotri Temple, near the source of the sacred Ganges River and the home of interesting swamis and sadhus (Hindu holy men); to Kedarnath Temple, the abode of the god Shiva; and to the Badrinath Temple, the abode of the god Vishnu. A trek to these temples is sublime. A religious aura casts an additional spell over the regal Himalayas. Drive to Dehra Dun and fly back to Delhi.

Buddhist Realm of the Northwest (July–September or when the passes are clear of snow; 17 days, with no trekking). After exploring Delhi, drive or fly to Shimla, once a former British hill station and now the capital of the Himalayan state of Himachal Pradesh. Spend the night in a quiet inn. Drive through the mountain-backed Kullu Valley, where a raging river races through a gorge, to Manali. Spend two days in this little city to acclimatize if you intend to trek or one day if you take a jeep excursion. Choose an adventure: Take the jeep-able road over the nearby Rohtang Pass to Leh, the district capital of Ladakh (a three- to five-day journey, depending on stops) and explore Ladakh's great Buddhist monasteries. Take a jeep safari into the newly opened districts of Spiti and Kinnaur in Himachal Pradesh—a remote destination with spectacular vistas and monasteries. Take a trek through the lunar landscape of Ladakh or its adjoining Zanskar Valley, Lahaul, or Spiti. Return to Delhi by plane from Leh in Ladakh or from Bhuntar in Kullu near Manali.

Starting point: Madras

India's East: Beaches and Buddhism (September–May; 21 days). After arriving in Madras, see its picturesque bazaars and excellent silk emporiums, its colorful temples and British monuments. Drive to Kanchipuram, a city of silk weavers and the site of 124 temples. Proceed to Mahabalipuram, with its stone carvings and beach temples. Spend the night at Fisherman's Cove, a quiet beach resort. Return to Madras and fly to Port Blair in the Andaman Islands. Explore the islands that are open to foreigners. Go snorkeling or scuba diving along its coral reefs, rich with marine life. Enjoy the beaches. Fly to Calcutta. Visit its historic British monuments and Hindu and Jain temples. Walk through its Hindu and Moslem bazaars. Fly to Bagdogra in northern West Bengal and drive to Darjeeling, a former British hill station that is perched in the eastern Himalayas. Drive to Gangtok, the capital of Sikkim. Visit the Tibetology and nearby Buddhist monasteries. Take a five-day trek in western Sikkim or a two-day rafting run on the Teesta River. Drive to Kalimpong, another hill station in northern West Bengal, and see its monasteries. Drive to Bagdogra and fly to Delhi or Calcutta.

Starting Point: Cochin, Kerala

Beaches, Temples, Wildlife (November–April; 18 days). After arriving in Cochin, visit Kerala's harbor city, which has one of India's oldest Jewish settlements and its nearby antiques and handicrafts market. See a Kathakali performance, one of India's most striking dance forms. Fly to Agatti in the Lakshadweep Islands and take a 90–minute boat ride to Bangaram Resort, which is built on a coral atoll in the Arabian Sea. Snorkel, scuba dive, swim, or relax on an unspoiled beach. Return by boat and plane to Cochin. Take a backwater cruise through lush canals that thread through fishing villages from Alleppey to Kottayam or Cheriapalli. Drive up the Western Ghats to the Lake Periyar Wildlife Sanctuary. Take a boat cruise and search for elephants and other wildlife. Drive to Madurai in Tamil Nadu. See a "darshan" (prayer service) at the enormous Meenakshi Temple with its rich spiritual life. Comb the surrounding bazaars. Drive to Tiruchirapalli. Walk through Chinna Bazaar and climb up to the Rock Fort. See the Ranganatha Swamy Temple, a 156–acre complex that's a city within a city. Drive to Ooty, a former British hill station in the Nilgiri Range. Spend the night in the summer palace of the former Mysore maharaja or go to the nearby Mudumalai Wildlife Sanctuary or Bandipur Sanctuary. Search for wildlife. Drive to Karnataka's Mysore. Spend the night in the grand palace or in the more modest guest house of the former maharaja. Tour the princely city. Drive to Hassan and see two soapstone temples that are intricately chiseled with carvings at nearby Halebid and Belur. Drive to Mangalore, a city on the Arabian Sea. Take day trips north to beautiful beaches backed by traditional fishing villages. Fly to Bombay.

Starting point: Calcutta

Mysterious Northeast (September–June; 26 days). After arriving in Calcutta, explore the city. Fly to Guwahati in Assam. Take an eco-tour, which includes an indigenous boat trip down the Brahmaputra River, visits to tribal villages, cultural performances, fishing, bird-watching, and a stay at a resort near the Kaziranga National Park, the home of the one-horned Indian rhinoceros and the Karbi tribe. Return to Guwahati. Drive to Shillong, the capital of Meghalaya and a former British hill station. Golfers can try their luck on a hilltop course. Walk through the unusual bazaar, which is predominantly run by women. Drive to the jungle-lush Garo Hills and visit the Garo tribals who live in architecturally perfect bamboo villages. Drive back to Shillong and Guwahati. Fly to Bagdogra in northern West Bengal. Drive to Gangtok, the capital of Sikkim, and see its Buddhist monasteries. Drive to western Sikkim and visit more monasteries. Trek through peaceful villages and rhododendron forests. Drive to Bagdogra and fly to Delhi or Calcutta.

Starting point: Bhubaneswar, Orissa

Southern Heritage and Beaches (October–March; 23 days). After arriving in Bhubaneswar, explore the city. Drive to Konarak. See the Sun Temple on the shore. Head south to Puri, a sacred Hindu city with its Lord Jagannath Temple. Drive south to Gopalpur-on-Sea and stay at a lovely beach resort. Drive south to Andhra Pradesh's Visakhapatnam. Spend a day at its beaches or fly to Madras. See the city, then drive south to Fisherman's Cove, a resort on the ocean. Drive to Kanchipuram, the home of silk weavers and the site of 124 temples. Drive to Mahabalipuram, with its shore temples, stone carvings, and good beaches. Continue south to Pondicherry, a former French colony where you can still find excellent French food. Drive west to Tamil Nadu's four temple-strewn cities: Chidambaram, with South India's oldest temple built in the 5th century; Thanjavur, with its 10th-century temple; Tiruchirapelli, with its nearby Rangaganatha Swamy Temple, a gigantic complex within seven sets of walls; and Madurai, with its grand Meenakashi Temple. Fly to Madras.

Starting Point: Bombay

The Sublime and the Divine (September–April; 20 days). After arriving in Bombay, visit the cosmopolitan city with its old bazaars and fancy shops, its roadside stalls and classy restaurants. Take a boat cruise to the Elephanta Caves. Fly to Bhuj, the capital of Gujarat's Rann of Kutch, with its nearby salt flats. Visit artisan villages, where conical homes are covered with white mudwork and inlaid mirrorwork. Bargain for patchwork, embroidered-work, or mirror-work fabrics and leather sandals. Trek through the unusual Kutch, which is also the temporary home of migrating birds. Drive to the former princely state of Wankaner, southeast of Bhuj, and stay in the palace of the former maharaja. Visit the Little Rann of Kutch and go on a safari in search of the unique Indian wild ass. Drive south to Bhavnagar and stay in another converted palace. Take a day trip to Gujarat's Palitana, a hill covered with hundreds of temples. Return to Bhavnagar or proceed to Ahmedpur Mandvi and enjoy one of Gujarat's unspoiled beaches. Return to Bhavnagar and fly to Bombay. Fly to Aurangabad and see the majestic Ellora and Ajanta caves. Fly back to Bombay.

Silver Sands and Lost Empires (October–March; 20 days). After exploring Bombay, fly to Aurangabad. See the Ellora and Ajanta caves; then fly back to Bombay. Go by yacht or car along Maharashtra's coastline to Goa. This is a three- to seven-day journey, depending on your pace and the number of stops at enchanting tented beach resorts along the way. Visit Goa's Portuguese churches. Wander through a Lambani tribal market. Enjoy the beach resorts: snorkel, windsurf, go sailing. Drive inland to Karnataka's city of Hospet. Spend a day exploring nearby Hampi, the former seat of the Vijayanagar Empire. Drive south to Hassan. See the two 12th-century soapstone temples built by the Hoysala kings at nearby Halebid and Belur. Drive south to Mysore. Visit the famous palaces of the former maharaja. Explore the exotic markets. Drive south to Nagarhole, one of India's best national parks. Stay in a former maharaja's hunting lodge. Drive to Bangalore. Fly to Bombay.

WILDLIFE SANCTUARIES. Three percent of India's landmass or about 90,000 square kilometers (56,000 square miles) is protected wilderness. The country has 53 national parks and 247 sanctuaries, in which more than 350 different mammals and 1,200 bird species live. Many of these creatures are unique to the subcontinent: the white tiger, the Royal Bengal tiger, the Asiatic lion, the lion-tailed macaque, the Andaman teal, the great Indian bustard, and the monal pheasant.

Unfortunately, India did not always protect its wildlife. At one time wildlife "enthusiasts" indiscriminately hunted game on safaris sponsored by maharajahs and their English guests. They decimated the rich stock of wild animals from the Himalayas to the central grasslands, the sparsely forested south, and the marshes to the east. By 1952, 13 species were endangered, and today the list has multiplied to 70 species of mammals, 16 species of reptiles, and 36 species of birds. The snow leopard, male musk deer, desert fox, golden langur, sloth bear, and black-necked crane are all threatened.

Just as tragic is the wholesale destruction of India's forests. In the third-century B.C., the Ashokas banned the destruction of certain trees and declared that the forests under the emperor's domain were the exclusive refuge of saints and ascetics. In subsequent years, however, attitudes changed, as did the demands of the growing population. Today, only nine percent of India's land remains forested.

In 1972, the Indian government finally passed the Wildlife Act, which preserved natural parks and sanctuaries and provided protection of wildlife, particularly endangered species. Three years later, **Corbett National Park** became India's first tiger reserve, part of a large-scale enterprise, Project Tiger, cosponsored by India's Department of Wildlife and the World Wildlife Fund.

India is also attempting to re-cover a third of its landmass with forests—a daunting objective that requires more than saplings. The rural poor will need viable fuel sources to replace wood, and a humane initiative must be mandated to control the movement of foraging livestock, including the sacrosanct cow.

Still, for admirers of wildlife, India's parks and sanctuaries are enchanting. In addition to Corbett National Park in Uttar Pradesh, four special parks are well worth a visit. **Madhya Pradesh's Kanha National Park,** established in 1976, has the greatest abundance of wildlife in its vast plateaus of forests, meadows, and grasslands. Here, you can hope to spot tigers, barasingha (relative of the swamp deer), gaur (wild ox), dholes (wild dogs), leopards, sloth bear, hyenas, grey hornbills, black ibis, and white-necked storks.

Created in 1968, **Bandhavgarh National Park,** also in Madhya Pradesh, is set in sal forests and is rich in wildlife, including tigers, chinkaras (Indian gazelles), gaur, wild boar, jackals, Malabar hornbills, steppe eagles, and blue-bearded bee-eaters. You can also explore caves, a fourteenth-century fort, and other archaeological ruins.

Kazaranga National Park, in Assam, was declared a wildlife sanctuary in 1926. It is encircled by mountains and sliced by the Brahmaputra River. This is home to the prehistoric-looking one-horned Indian rhinoceros as well as wild buffaloes, tigers, wild elephants, wild boar, hog deer, leopards, crested serpent eagles, swamp partridges, and Bengal floricans.

Although the **Nagarhole Sanctuary** in Karnataka suffered from a devastating fire in 1992, the area around Kabini River Lodge was unaffected. Rich with teak forests and reservoirs, this sanctuary, established in 1954, is a prime stomping ground for wild elephants. You might also spot leopards, dholes, gaur, tigers, striped hyenas, sambar, barking deer, sloth bear, scarlet minavets, paradise fly-catchers, king vultures, and various species of eagles.

Every Indian state has booklets on its sanctuaries and parks, and the Government of India Tourist Office publishes a useful brochure on wildlife that highlights primary destinations. Also see each area chapter, including the Terai section of the Nepal chapter, which gives information on that country's excellent parks and re-serves.

THE CLIMATE. India's climate can be described as monsoon-tropical, in spite of such local variations as the winter rains in the northwest. Keep in mind that India is a subcontinent and make allowances for that fact in the following broad classification of the seasons: the cool weather lasts from October to the end of February, and the really hot weather from the beginning of April to the beginning of June, at which point the monsoon (rainy) season sets in until the end of September. The clear cool weather arrives again and moves gradually eastward and southward. The monsoon deserves special emphasis. This seasonal trade wind blows across the Arabian Sea and reaches India with almost mathematical regularity in May and traverses the country in June and July. It brings with it rain-laden clouds that water practically every part of India to some degree and return to the Arabian Sea in September and October. In the far north, the Himalayas, Nepal, Sikkim, and Kashmir can be extremely cold during winter, when many mountain passes and valleys are closed because of deep snow. The temperatures in these mountainous areas also vary a great deal, depending on elevation; evenings are generally cool.

Temperature and Rainfall Chart (Averages)

		Calcutta	Darjeeling	Delhi	Madras	Srinagar
Jan.	*	81	46	70	84	39
	†	0.37	0.53	0.99	1.41	3
Feb.	*	84	48	75	88	46
	†	1.17	1.19	0.83	0.41	3
Mar.	*	93	57	88	91	55
	†	1.36	1.88	0.51	0.29	—
Apr.	*	97	63	97	95	66
	†	1.75	4.14	0.33	0.61	—
May	*	97	64	106	100	77
	†	5.49	9.63	0.52	1.03	2
June	*	91	64	102	100	84
	†	11.69	24.18	3.03	1.86	—
July	*	90	66	97	97	88
	†	12.81	32.92	7.03	3.60	2
Aug.	*	90	64	93	95	86
	†	12.92	26.56	7.23	4.58	2
Sept.	*	90	64	93	90	82
	†	9.95	18.90	4.84	4.68	1
Oct.	*	90	61	93	90	73
	†	4.48	5.41	0.40	12.04	1
Nov.	*	84	54	84	84	61
	†	0.81	0.81	0.10	13.96	1
Dec.	*	79	48	73	84	48
	†	0.18	0.27	0.43	5.45	1

* Average maximum temperature in Fahrenheit.
†Average rainfall in inches.

WHEN TO GO. The peak tourist season runs from mid-September through March, but consider India a year-round destination. Just pick your climatic preferences. You can also plan a vacation around a spectacular festival, such as Dussehra in Himachal Pradesh, Wangala in Meghalaya, Carnival in Goa, Pongal in Kerala, or the fairs in Pushkar, Nagaur, or Jaisalmer in Rajasthan. If outdoor adventure is your objective, the time that it's offered will determine when you make your trip. During the winter months, for example, you can enjoy good skiing in the Himalayas at such places as Auli in Uttar Pradesh. Springtime in the Himalayas is spectacular, as orchards and hillsides come into bloom. In these regions, travel is best from April through October, though Manali in Himachal Pradesh is crowded in July.

Since India is such a vast land, additional information on the best times to visit is included in each chapter.

WHAT TO PACK. When you pack, remember to travel light and pay attention to the climate and pack accordingly. In India, delicate fabrics do not stand up well to laundering facilities except at deluxe hotels. Plain cottons or cotton/synthetic blends are the most practical and the coolest in summer. Synthetic materials that don't "breathe" should be avoided. Also refer to Customs and Culture, below, for additional advice on proper attire.

There is no difficulty in getting over-the-counter medicines in India, but if you take prescription drugs, bring along enough for your stay, and then some. Also bring the following necessities: sewing kit, fold-up umbrella if you're traveling during the monsoon, premoistened towelettes, high-power impact resistant flashlight, and spare batteries (unless they're a popular size).

Carry your passport and your money (most of it should be in traveler's checks) on your person. Keep multiple records of your checks and put a copy in each bag. Leave behind all your unnecessary credit cards.

Use good-quality soft luggage or well-made duffles that are waterproof, and keep them locked. Airlines will not accept untagged luggage. Add your destination address, with dates of arrival and departure, to luggage tags in case your bags go astray. Also put identification inside and remove all old tags.

While porters are available throughout India, it's a good idea to carry two small bags, to distribute the weight, rather than one large one. Indian Airlines allows two pieces of check-in luggage and one carry-on piece, per passenger. If the total weight of your check-in luggage exceeds 20 kilograms, you may be charged for excess baggage. The carry-on luggage cannot exceed 45 inches (length + width + height) and must fit under the seat or in the overhead luggage compartment.

HEALTH INFORMATION. For entry into India and Nepal from the U.S., Canada, or the U.K., no vaccination certificate or inoculations are required. Though immigration officials don't normally ask to see an International Health Certificate, this is one destination where it's smart to have one: The certificate contains invaluable information in case you need medical attention. See your doctor about obtaining one.

Three months before departure, talk to your doctor about protection against malaria, typhoid, cholera, tetanus, polio (a shot or booster), measles, mumps, rubella, and meningitis. To get the latest inoculation information and requirements, contact *U.S. Department of Health and Human Services,* Public Health Services, Centers for Disease Control, Center for Prevention Services, Division of Quarantine, Atlanta, GA; tel. 404–639–2572.

Warning: Japanese encephalitis, a mosquito-borne disease, occurs in epidemics during the summer months in some rural sections of India, Nepal, and Sri Lanka. The risks to travelers to urban centers is low, but precautions should be taken to guard against mosquito bites: sleep in screened quarters, wear protective clothing, and use insect repellents liberally. If you wish to inquire about a new investigational vaccine for Japanese encephalitis, contact the Division of Vector-Borne Viral Diseases in Fort Collins, CO (tel. 303–221–6429) or the American Embassies in India, Nepal, or Sri Lanka.

Food and Water Precautions. The biggest fear most people have about a trip to India is getting a bout of what is popularly called Delhi Belly, an upset stomach accompanied by diarrhea. Although the problem is common among foreigners, it *is* possible to avoid it if you are very careful about what you eat and drink. To be absolutely safe, don't drink tap water—ever. That means you should not brush your teeth with it, and you should avoid ice. If someone tells you the water that is about to be poured into your glass has been "filtered," kindly turn it down; water is often filtered to take out particles, but this doesn't mean it has been purified to kill off parasites. Buy bottled water from a reputable hotel or shop. Check the cap to make sure it has not been tampered with; bottles are sometimes refilled with tap water and sold to unknowing tourists.

Always keep at least one bottle of water in your hotel room for brushing teeth and late-night drinks. The heat can cause dehydration, and the dust may irritate your throat, so you will need to drink more liquids than usual. Dehydration will make you weak and more susceptible to other health problems, so when you're walking around town, remind yourself to stop for a drink. Hot tea, coffee, and bottled carbonated drinks are safe to drink. If you're trekking, bring bottled water and save the bottle and cap so that you can refill it with water that you prepare with purification tablets.

You should also avoid raw vegetables and fruit that has been peeled before it is brought to you. At many restaurant salad bars the vegetables are presoaked in an iodine solution to kill parasites, but be sure to ask the waiter about this before you indulge. When in doubt, eat something else. Peel your own fruit, choosing pieces with thick skins. Pork products should be avoided; make certain that other meats are thoroughly cooked. Some people find it best to stick to a vegetarian diet, but that would mean missing out on some very delicious dishes. Choose restaurants with care and eat hot foods while they're hot, and you should not have any trouble.

When choosing a restaurant keep in mind that very often the locally popular restaurant that looks worn around the edges offers the safest food. A small restaurant that can't afford refrigeration cooks food acquired that day. This isn't always true with the fancy hotel. Since electricity can be temperamental and the chef buys in bulk, the hotel's refrigerator can be a repository for more than foodstuffs. Keep in mind, however, that stomach upsets often are due as much to the richness of Indian food as to the lack of hygiene. If you have trouble with spicy food, ask the waiter which dishes are less spicy. Many hotel restaurants tend to cook with a lot of oil, which can trigger Delhi Belly. Ask the chef to use less oil. Fried foods from street vendors often look delicious, but check the oil: If it looks as old as the pot, it could be rancid and lead to trouble. It's safest to resist the temptation.

A little bit of personal hygiene can also go a long way in preventing stomach upsets: Remember to wash your hands before you eat anything, even snacks. Carry premoistened towelettes with you, and use them when soap and water are not available. They are also a welcome refreshment on hot afternoons.

Medical Precautions. It is advisable to bring a medical kit containing mosquito repellent with at least 95% deet (N. diethyl toluamide), adhesive bandages, plastic strip thermometer, water-purification tablets, aspirin or its equivalent, diarrhea medication, antibiotics, and an antiseptic skin cleanser. Treat any minor scratches, cuts, or blisters at once. India can be dusty, and dust carries infection. If you foresee the need for any prescription medication, ask your doctor to write a prescription beforehand, using the drug's generic name. Some doctors recommend taking daily multivitamin tablets, especially those with B-complex, while traveling in hot weather and when your diet is changed.

If you travel into forested areas during or right after the monsoon, protect yourself against leeches. Cover your legs and carry salt. Don't wear sandals. When a leech clings to your clothing or skin, dab it with a pinch of salt, and the leech will fall off. If itching persists, apply an antiseptic; infection rarely occurs. For bedbugs, buy a bar of Dettol soap (available throughout India and Nepal) and use it when you bathe. It relieves itching and discomfort.

The sun can be intense in India. Beware of overexposure even on overcast days. To avoid sunburn, use a sunscreen with a sun protection factor of at least 24. Play it safe and also wear a wide-brimmed hat. If you plan to travel higher than 3,048 meters (10,000 feet), also use zinc oxide or lip balm with sun block and keep your eyes protected behind sunglasses that block ultraviolet rays. And when you're in snow remember that UV rays reflect from below.

High-altitude sickness, an adverse reaction to low oxygen pressure, can be deadly. If your urine turns bright yellow, you're not drinking enough water. Eat foods that are high in carbohydrates and cut back on salt. Stop and rest immediately if you develop any of the following symptoms: nausea, loss of appetite, extreme head-ache or lightheadedness, unsteady feet, sleeplessness. If resting doesn't help, head for lower ground.

For an up-to-date directory of U.S. doctors who specialize in tropical illnesses, contact Dr. Leonard Marcus at the *American Society of Tropical Medicine and Hygiene,* 148 Highland Ave., Newton, MA 02160. Include a 9-×12-inch stamped envelope with $1 in postage.

The *International Association for Medical Assistance to Travelers* (IAMAT) is a worldwide association offering a list of approved doctors. For their directory, contact IAMAT at 417 Center St., Lewiston, NY 14092; in Canada: 40 Regal Rd., Guelph, Ontario NIK 1B5; in Europe: 57 Voirets, 1212 Grand-Lancy-Geneva, Switzerland.

For $4.95, the U.S. government offers an annual publication, *Health Information for International Travel.* Contact Superintendent of Documents, U.S. Government Printing Office, Washington, DC 20402, tel. 202–783–3238.

HINTS TO THE DISABLED. Most countries in Asia, including India, are not prepared for travelers who are disabled. There are no special boarding ramps in buses, trains, airplanes, on public sidewalks, or at museums or monuments. Disabled travelers must rely on careful preplanning and should have a companion to assist them. Wheelchair travelers should have a collapsible, easily folding, compact wheelchair with lightweight, sturdy wheels for city sidewalks. Also bring easily removable accessories since replacement will be difficult.

For more information, we advise that you contact the following organizations:

Society for the Advancement of Travel for the Handicapped (347 Fifth Ave., Suite 610, New York, NY 10016, tel. 212–447–7284, fax 212–725–8253) provides, free of charge, a list of travel agents who are experienced in handling itineraries for disabled travelers.

Information Center for Individuals with Disabilities (Fort Point Pl., 1st Fl., 27–43 Wormwood St., Boston, MA 02210, tel. 617–727–5540) also offers useful assistance and a list of travel agents that specialize in tours for the disabled.

Moss Rehabilitation Hospital Travel Information Service (12th St. and Taber Rd., Philadelphia, PA 19141, tel. 215–456–9603, TDD 617–456–9602) provides information on tourist sights, transportation, and accommodations for destinations around the world.

Mobility International (Box 3551, Eugene, OR 97403, tel. 503–343–1284) has information on accommodations and organized study around the world.

The Itinerary (Box 1084, Bayonne, NJ 07002, tel. 201–858–3400) is a bimonthly travel magazine for the disabled.

INSURANCE. We suggest that you be fully covered with theft, loss, and especially medical policies before your arrival in India. Review your existing health and home-owner policies; some health insurance plans cover health expenses incurred while traveling, some major medical plans cover emergency transportation, and some home-owner policies cover the theft of luggage.

Several companies offer policies that supplement existing health insurance for travelers and cover medical evacuations:

Carefree Travel Insurance (Box 310, 120 Mineola Blvd., Mineola, NY 11501, tel. 516–294–0220 or 800–323–3149).

International SOS Insurance (Box 11568, Philadelphia, PA 19116, tel. 215–244–1500 or 800–523–8930).

Travel Guard International (1145 Clark St., Stevens Point, WI 54481, tel. 715–345–0505 or 800–782–5151).

British travelers may apply to *Europe Assistance* (252 High St., Croydon, Surrey CR0 1NF, tel. 081–680–1234), which insures against sickness and motoring mishaps.

If your baggage disappears, report it to the police immediately. Airlines and many insurance companies insist that notification be made within 24 hours. Lost luggage is usually covered as part of a comprehensive travel insurance package that includes personal accident, trip cancellation, and sometimes default and bankruptcy insurance.

Several companies offer comprehensive policies:

Access America Inc. (Box 807, New York, NY 10163, tel. 800–851–280), a subsidiary of Blue Cross–Blue Shield.

Near, Inc. (1900 N. MacArthur Blvd., Suite 210, Oklahoma City, OK 73127, tel. 800–654–6700).

Travel Guard International (*see* above).

The Association of British Insurers (Aldermary House, Queen St., London EC4N 1TT, tel. 071–248–4477), which offers British travelers comprehensive advice on vacation insurance.

TRAVEL TO INDIA

BY AIR. Nonstop service to Bombay, Calcutta, Madras, and Delhi is available from Great Britain, Europe, Asia, and Australia. U.S. travelers can either take a direct flight with a stop in England or numerous countries in Europe or take a connecting flight involving two or more planes and two or more stops.

From North America. Flying time from New York is about 16 hours, not including stops. *Air India* (in New York, 800–442–4455; in Chicago, 800–621–8231; in Montreal, 800–268–9582; in Vancouver, 800–663–3433; in Toronto, 416–865–1033) offers a direct flight from Chicago or New York with a stop at London. *Delta* (tel. 800–241–4141) also has a direct flight from New York with a stop in Frankfurt. The following airlines offer connecting flights: *KLM,* tel. 212–759–3600; *Air Canada,* tel. 800–776–3000; *Air France,* tel. 800–237–2747; *Cathay Pacific,* tel. 800–233–2742; *British Airways,* tel. 800–247–9297; *Lufthansa,* tel. 800–645–3880; *Pakistan Airlines,* tel. 212–370–9157 in New York, in Chicago 312–263–3082, in Los Angeles 213–559–6409, in Montreal 514–626–5250, in Toronto 416–591–5490; *Gulf Air,* tel. 800–772–4642; *Thai Airways,* tel. 800–426–5204; *Royal Jordanian,* tel. 800–223–0470; *Singapore Airlines,* tel. 800–742–3330; *Air New Zealand,* tel. 800–262–1234.

Fares. Major airlines offer a wide range of ticket prices. As a rule, the earlier you buy the ticket, the lower the price and the greater the cancellation penalty (up to 100 percent).

An APEX (advance purchase) ticket on a major airline can be a good value if you can work around the restrictions: The tickets must be bought in advance, they restrict your travel time, and they include penalties for travel changes.

Charter flights offer the lowest fares but have limited departures, poor on-time records, and strict cancellation policies. Check with a travel agency about the charter flight packager's reputation. One popular charter operator is *Council Charter,* a division of the Council on International Educational Exchange (CIEE), 205 E. 42nd St., New York, NY 10017; tel. 212–661–1414.

Somewhat more expensive—but up to 50 percent less than APEX fares—are tickets purchased through consolidators that buy blocks of tickets on scheduled airlines and sell them at wholesale prices. You may lose all or most of your money if you change plans, but you will be on a scheduled flight with less risk of cancellation than a charter. Once you've made your reservation, call the airline to make sure you're confirmed. Two popular consolidators are *UniTravel,* tel. 800–325–2222, and *Access International,* 250 W. 57th St., New York, NY 10107, tel. 212–333–7280.

You can also join a travel club that offers its members special discounts, such as *Moments Notice,* 40 E. 49th St., New York, NY 10017, tel. 212–486–0503; *Discount Travel International,* 114 Forrest Ave., Narberth, PA 19072, tel. 215–668–2182; and *Worldwide Discount Travel Club,* 1647 Meridian Ave., Miami Beach, FL 33139, tel. 305–534–2082.

Student Travel. *Council Travel,* a CIEE subsidiary, is the foremost U.S. student travel agency, specializing in low-cost charters and serving as the exclusive U.S. agent for many student airfare bargains and student tours. CIEE's 80-page *Student Travel Catalog* and "Council Charter" brochure are available from any Council Travel office in the United States (enclose $1 if ordering by mail). In addition to the CIEE headquarters in New York (address above), there are offices in Berkeley, La Jolla, Long Beach, Los Angeles, San Diego, and San Francisco, CA; Chicago, IL; Amherst, Boston, and Cambridge, MA; Portland, OR; Providence, RI; Austin and Dallas, TX; and Seattle, WA.

From Britain. Flying time from London to Delhi is about nine hours, not including stops. *British Airways* (tel. 081–759–5511), *Air India* (tel. 071–491–7979), and *Thai Airways* (tel. 071–499–9113) have direct flights. *Lufthansa, Royal Jordanian, Gulf Air, Air France, KLM,* and *Emirates Airways* offer connecting flights.

Fares. There are no APEX fares between London and India, but there are some charters. Check with your travel agent. There are also some promotional excursion fares and beyond this, some undercutting by a few travel agents in conjunction with lesser-known airlines. We do not vouch for the legality of this practice, but we cannot ignore the fact that it occurs. A good place to look for budget fares is in the London weekly entertainment magazine, *Time Out,* and the national Sunday press.

OVERLAND. It is unfortunately not at present feasible to travel overland from Europe to India by successive local train and bus connections. We hope politics will allow one to undertake the journey again in the future. You would need time, patience, flexibility, and a certain amount of stamina, but this trip would be a memorable one.

CUSTOMS ON ARRIVAL. The foreigner who enters India for a period of up to six months as a tourist has a choice of two channels for customs clearance. The Green Channel is for passengers who don't have dutiable articles or unaccompanied baggage. The Red Channel is for passengers with dutiable articles, unaccompanied baggage, or high-value articles that must be entered on a Tourist Baggage Re-Export Form (TBRE). If you leave behind an item declared on the TBRE, you will have to pay duty on the missing item.

You can bring in the following duty-free articles: personal effects (clothes and jewelry), a camera with five rolls of film, binoculars, a portable musical instrument, a radio or portable tape recorder, a tent and camping equipment, sports equipment (fishing rod, a pair of skis, two tennis rackets), 200 cigarettes or 50 cigars, .95 liters of liquor, and gifts not exceeding a value of Rs. 500 (about $18). You may not bring in dangerous drugs, gold coins, gold and silver bullion and silver coins not in use, or live plants.

AIRPORT TOURIST OFFICES. All major Indian airports have a tourist office or desk, usually open until late at night, where useful general information may be obtained. Some also have a hotel accommodation booking service (no commission) for those without confirmed reservations.

AIRPORT-TO-TOWN TRANSPORTATION. Transportation is plentiful, but if you take a taxi or auto rickshaw to your hotel or to the center of the city, be sure that the meter is working or agree on a price beforehand. Fares will vary from Rs. 60 to Rs. 300, depending on where you are and how far you must travel. Buses, operated by ex-servicemen's organizations, are run from some airports into city centers or to major hotels. The schedule is usually well timed with arriving flights, though not always with departures, and tickets cost Rs. 20–Rs. 30. Prepaid taxi counters are available at Bombay, Delhi, and Madras. You pay a rate in advance based on your destination and are assigned a taxi; the fixed price takes care of the problem of bargaining. In Calcutta, bargain hard or wait for a metered taxi.

Staying in India

HOTELS AND OTHER ACCOMMODATIONS. The greatest single advance made by the tourism industry of India in the past decade has been in providing new and renovated hotels. In the cities and the major tourist centers, including beach and hill resorts, these hotels are well up to international standards, yet the prices are lower (except for rooms in Bombay) than similar hotels elsewhere. The need for hotel rooms is great, since India's tourist traffic (foreign and domestic) is now close to 2 million visitors each year.

The following list describes the range of accommodations that are available within India. If you decide to book accommodations in advance, remember to check carefully for what is included in the quoted room price. Also follow this advice once you arrive in India. Ask, in particular, about service charges and taxes, which are frequently revised and vary from place to place.

Western-style Hotels. These hotels, which are the most expensive and accept credit cards, are much like their American and European counterparts. Many have little local ambience, but deluxe hotels do offer a full array of services for the business traveler: secretarial services; access to copiers, computers, fax machines, and conference rooms; and executive suites. The following abbreviations for credit cards are used: AE, American Express; DC, Diners Club; MC, MasterCard; V, Visa.

Indian-style Hotels. An Indian-style hotel is less fancy, less costly, and often comes with a bathroom that has a shower instead of a shower/bathtub. Rooms have the basic necessities, including air-conditioning, but no opulent appointments. Some Indian-style hotels accept credit cards; some take traveler's checks; all take rupees.

Inns and Lodges. The traveler with an old-fashioned notion of class and charm should stay in any of the recommended inns and lodges. Some are rustic properties tucked away in the mountains; others are in hill stations and are elegant down to the sterling silver tea service that appears with breakfast and afternoon tea. Pampering is part of the experience. The cost is reasonable and meals are usually included. Some of these establishments accept credit cards or traveler's checks, but many only take rupees. Make your reservation well in advance.

Heritage Hotels. The Hotel Classification Committee of the Government of India has just initiated an excellent incentive program that encourages owners of palaces and forts to convert their properties into hotels or to make restorations on already-converted properties to bring them up to government standards. These hotels are called Heritage Hotels. Contact the Government of India Tourist Office abroad for a list of hotels that have already been approved. Room prices range from inexpensive to deluxe.

Houseboats. Unfortunately, these are exclusive to Kashmir, now a troubled state. If the tensions quiet down, don't miss this idyllic experience. For details, see the Accommodations section in the Kashmir chapter, and reserve before you arrive.

Camping. Some areas, such as the beautiful Maharashtra coastline, have camping sites, set up with roomy safari-style tents, available at nominal cost. You can also rent equipment from private companies or some state tourist departments.

Government Lodging. The Government of India and individual state governments, the Public Works Department (PWD), and the Forestry Department provide inexpensive accommodations throughout India. Some government tourist bungalows are fine; others provide a dreary ambience. PWD and Forest Department Inspection bungalows are usually rustic—small lodges or cabins set in secluded areas. Circuit Houses, originally built by the British, are also occasionally available and some continue to evoke the spirit of the Raj. Staying in PWDs, Forest Department Inspection Bungalows, or Circuit Houses can be difficult; priority is given to Indian government employees.

Ratings. The ratings in this guide are based on double occupancy, excluding taxes and service charges. At press time, the rate of exchange was Rs. 28 to U.S. $1; or Rs. 49 to the U.K. pound sterling. For all accommodations, we use the following price categories: *Deluxe* over Rs. 2,000; *Expensive,* Rs. 1,200–Rs. 2,000; *Moderate,* Rs. 500–Rs. 1,200; *Inexpensive,* under Rs. 500.

At press time, the central government announced a new policy that will affect the cost of accommodations. Rooms that are priced above Rs. 1,200 will be subject to an "expenditure tax" that will increase the base tariff. For this reason, many hotels in the moderately priced range may choose to lower their tariff to escape the tax and protect their business. The fluctuation of the rupee has also prompted many hotels to set their tariffs in U.S. dollars to protect their profits.

GROUP HOTELS

Booking hotels has been simplified because of the number of hotel chains that cover important cities and popular tourist destinations in India. Some of the major hotel groups are listed below.

ASHOK GROUP (INDIA TOURISM DEVELOPMENT CORPORATION).

ITDC covers most key tourist destinations with properties ranging from five-star luxury hotels, such as the Ashok in Delhi and an ex-maharajah's palace in Mysore, to simple and inexpensive lodges for travelers in places of pilgrimage, hill stations, and major archaeological sites. ITDC also operates a nationwide travel agency, restaurants, duty-free shops at airports, city sightseeing tours in many major tourism centers, and sound and light shows.

Reservations. In the U.S., contact *Ashok Hotels Central Reservations,* Golden Tulip World-Wide Hotels, 437 Madison Ave., New York, NY 10022; tel. 212–838–6554 or 800–333–1212. In England, tel. 081–847–3951. In India, contact Hotel Sales Division, Hotel Samrat, Chanakyapuri, New Delhi 110021, tel. 603030, fax 360233.

CENTAUR GROUP. A subsidiary of Air-India with four hotels—two in Bombay, one in Delhi, and one in Srinagar.

Reservations. Information about reservations may be obtained from Air-India offices in India. In the United States, reservations may be made through Air-India for any of these hotels, provided one is traveling on Air-India.

CHOICE HOTELS INTERNATIONAL. Formerly called Quality International, this chain includes Comfort Inns and Quality Inns located in India.

Reservations. In the U.S., contact *Choice Hotels International,* 10759 Columbia Pike, Silver Spring, MD 20901, tel. 800–221–2222, fax 301–681–7478. In Canada, contact *Choice Hotels International,* 4174 Dundas St. West, S-301, Toronto, Ont., M9X1X3, tel. 800–638–2657, fax 416–236–3631. In Britain, contact *Choice Hotels International,* 2 Valentine Pl., London SE1 8QH, tel. 071–928–3333, fax 071–928–4762. In India, contact *Quality Inns India,* A-51 Vasant Marg, Vasant Vihar, New Delhi 110057, tel. 675347 or 671327.

CLARKS GROUP. One of the older chains of good-quality deluxe hotels, with more modest rates. Clarks hotels are located in Agra, Jaipur, Lucknow, and Varanasi.

Reservations. *U.P. Hotels Ltd.* 1101 Surya Kiran, 19, Kasturba Gandhi Marg, New Delhi 110 001; tel. 331–2367, fax 3312990 or, in Bombay, 103 Embassy Center, Nariman Point, Bombay 400 021; tel. 2851721, fax 2872155.

OBEROI GROUP. This chain should take the credit for raising the standards of luxury-grade hotel accommodations in India. The rates are at the top of the scale, but their services and comprehensive range of facilities are excellent.

Reservations. In the U.S. and Canada, contact *Oberoi,* tel. 800–6–OBEROI or 212–682–7655, fax 212–983–5692. In Britain, contact *Oberoi,* tel. 081–788–2070, fax 081–789–5369. In India, contact *Oberoi Central Reservations Service,* The Oberoi, New Delhi, 110003, tel. 4363030, fax 4360484.

TAJ GROUP. Superb luxury hotels and resorts in key tourist areas offer the finest-quality facilities and services. This chain has started to open less luxurious hotels, usually called "gateways," that offer very good service and lower priced rooms.

Reservations. Contact the worldwide offices of *Utell International* or *Taj Hotels:* in the U.S., Utell tel. 800–448–8355, fax 402–398–5484 or Taj tel. 800–458–8825 or 212–972–6830, fax 212–687–0743; in Canada, Utell, tel. 800–668–8355, fax 416–480–2770 or Taj, use the same numbers and fax for U.S.; in Britain, Utell tel. 081–995–8211, fax 081–9952474, or Taj tel. 0800–282699 or 071–828–5909, fax 071–8348629. In India, use *Central Reservation Service,* Taj Mahal Hotel, Bombay, tel. 2023366, fax 2872711.

WELCOMGROUP. One of the newest hotel groups, about 20 years old, its rates are at the top end of the scale, and the services are excellent.

Reservations. For Sheraton hotels, contact ITT Sheraton: in the U.S. and Canada, tel. 512–440–8285 or 800–325–3535, fax 416–947–4874 (in Canada) and 512–835–2349 (in U.S.); in Britain, tel. 071–0800–353535, fax 071–731–0532.

For other Welcomgroup hotels, contact ITC International in the U.S. and Canada, tel. 201–379–7773, fax 201–379–1473. At press time, ITC had no office in Britain. In India, you can reserve any Welcomgroup hotel through Welcomgroup Maurya Sheraton Hotel and Towers, Diplomatic Enclave, New Delhi 110021, tel. 3010101, fax 3012892.

In addition to the major groups listed above, privately operated hotels may be booked direct, or reservations may be made through hotel counters in many of the major airports in India on arrival. During peak seasons, especially in Delhi, it is best to arrive with hotel reservations.

BEACH HOLIDAYS. With a 6,100-kilometer (3,535-mile) coastline and separate island territories, India has fantastic beaches. You can easily spend an entire vacation on the sea—whether at a classy hotel or resort, at a modest bungalow, or in an ethnic-design village or charming safari-style tent.

In the southwest, Goa and Kerala's Kovalam Beach have a well-developed tourism infrastructure with accommodations to suit every budget and preference. You can rent equipment for all watersports, and you can take lessons.

Port Blair, in the Andaman Islands, and Bangaram, a coral atoll in the Lakshadweep Islands, have limited facilities, but that means they also have fewer tourists, which adds an air of exclusivity, especially at Bangaram. At either destination, you can scuba dive and snorkel in extensive coral reefs that are crowded with marine life.

The Maharpshtra coastline, north of Goa, also has tented beach resorts that face the Arabian Sea. Some are along natural harbors; others are clustered in palm groves; one overlooks an historic fortress built on an island off the shoreline.

Gujarat's vast coastal area is just being developed. Although the Samudra Beach Resort in Ahmedpur Mandvi is already in operation, the state's best escape is north of the sleepy city of Mandvi in the district of Kutch, especially near Sutri village. You won't find any hotel; but you can tent with permission, easily obtained on arrival.

Karnstaka also has a little-known stretch of beach south and north of the port city of Mangalore. Simple accommodations are available, but you can also stay in Mangalore and take day trips here. One exquisite hideaway is at Kaup, just north of the city. A narrow road heads to the coast and passes through quaint fishing villages that face the sea before the one-lane thoroughfare ends at a spit just below the small city of Malpe. Except for fisherfolk, the shore is nearly deserted, and you're never far from the shade of coconut trees.

In India's east, the beaches at Diamond Harbor, south of Calcutta, provide a chance to unwind from the city's fast pace. South of West Bengal, Orissa's sacred city of Purl has quiet beaches on either edge of the town, and nearby Toshali Sands Resort shuttles its guests to a private cove. Near Orissa's southern border, Oberoi Hotels has a small resort with a British-style bungalow that faces the ocean at Gopalpur-on-Sea. From Tamil Nadu's Madras, you can drive south to the Fisherman's Cove Resort in Covelong, which is nestled in a tiny inlet, or continue to the historic village of Mahabalipuram. Here, resorts on the water are a short walk from ancient shore temples and rock-cut sculptures. The union territory of Pondicherry, a former French colony below Mahabalipuram, also has pearl-white beaches, with hotels that front the sea.

MEETING THE PEOPLE AT HOME. Although there are enough museums, scenery, historic sites, and artistic monuments in India to keep the average tourist on the run, many travelers want to penetrate the surface to learn what Indian people are like in their own homes. The government tourist bureaus and the ITDC offices in Delhi, Bombay, Madras, and Calcutta have lists of families who board international visitors as part of an organized Meet-the-People project. Rajasthan has also introduced a reliable system of Paying Guest accommodations in major cities within the state. See the Rajasthan chapter for details.

ROUGHING IT. This means hitchhiking, moving about the country in the cheapest-class trains or on buses, carrying your luggage on your back and sleeping in youth hostels or pilgrim accommodations. A number of specialized student-travel guidebooks and a few general guidebooks are now available for this particular kind of travel. Those who tour this way should gather material from various sources—guidebooks, local tourist centers, and meetings with people who have gone on similar trips. For further material on youth hostels, write *American Youth Hostels*, Box 37613, Washington, DC 20013; or call your local chapter. In Canada, write *Youth Hostels Association*, 1600 James Naismith Dr., Gloucester, Ontario

K1B 5N4. In England, write *Youth Hostels Association,* 14 Southampton St., London WC2E 7HA. In India, contact *Youth Hostels Association of India,* 5 Nayaya Marg, Chanakyapuri, New Delhi 110021, tel. 3016285; *World University Service,* Community Center, University of Delhi, Delhi 110007, tel. 2518022. A free Youth Hostel directory listing 16 places in the four regions of India is available from the YHA. In addition to maintaining hostels throughout India, the YHA sponsors cultural programs and organizes treks.

DINING OUT. When you visit India, mealtime can mean a delectable adventure with cuisines encompassing all of Asia, the Middle East, and the West. Indian dishes, which vary from region to region, are elevated to high art. Meats, fish, vegetables, lentils, and grains proliferate in splendid combinations—subtle and enticing.

Just as the cuisines are numerous so are the ambiences in places where you can eat. Hotel restaurants with live music create an elegant tone. Local restaurants, always ethnic, offer great meals at bargain rates in a setting that makes you feel far from home. Street stalls, cooking up simple specialties, can satisfy an eating urge at almost no cost.

Most restaurants don't have a dress code; casual, neat attire is fine. Unless you arrive with a large party, reservations are rarely required. But it is advisable to reserve to avoid disappointments. In major cities, restaurants normally stay open until 11 P.M. or midnight. In other areas expect an earlier dinner unless you're staying in a Western-style hotel. Visitors should also be aware that some Indian states also observe a weekly meatless day, when no slaughtering is done and no red meat is sold or served in most restaurants.

Spirits and Beverages. Indian beer, which is good and plentiful, costs about Rs. 80–Rs. 120 per bottle at hotel bars, Rs. 50 in shops. Imported beer is usually unavailable. Imported whiskey and gin are expensive. Indian whiskey, vodka, gin, and rum are good and cost Rs. 80–Rs. 160 per bottle outside hotels. Prices vary from state to state. Sikkim makes good rum and brandies; Goa has tasty sweet wines and *feni* (a potent liquor made from cashew nuts).

Gujarat observes prohibition, but foreign travelers may apply to the Gujarat Tourism Development Corporation for a permit that allows them to buy liquor in the state. The Government of India Tourist Offices in the United States also issue a three-month liquor permit allowing you to carry liquor into the state. Elsewhere, most localities have two "dry" days per month: the first and seventh days of the month.

Indian coffee has a caramel tang and is inexpensive. Tea is excellent and inexpensive, although those who take it black or without sugar should indicate so, since it is frequently brewed Indian-style with milk and sugar. India has a tremendous variety of good soft drinks that cost Rs. 4, and recently some delicious bottled fruit juices, including a refreshing mango fruit drink, costing Rs. 4.

Ratings. Restaurants in this guidebook are classified by price categories. Prices are per person and include a first course, main course, and dessert, but exclude costs for beverage, taxes, and tips. At press time, the rate of exchange was Rs. 28 to U.S. $1; or Rs. 49 to the U.K. pound sterling. The price categories are: *Deluxe,* over Rs. 300; *Expensive,* Rs. 200–Rs. 300; *Moderate,* Rs. 100–Rs. 200; *Inexpensive,* under Rs. 100.

TIPPING. Most major hotels include a service charge of about 10 percent on your bill, but waiters, room service, housekeepers, porters, and doormen all expect to be tipped, as they do in the rest of the world. You won't go wrong if you tip Rs. 10 per night to your room waiter. Bellboys and bell captains should be paid Rs. 5 per bag. If you are staying in a private home, it is customary to tip the domestic workers. Taxi drivers do not expect tips unless they go through a great deal of trouble to get you to your destination. However, tip a hired driver Rs. 25 for a half day's trip and Rs. 50 for a full day's trip. It is also customary to give a hired driver money for his meals if you are on a day trip.

There are no service charges at government-run houses, bungalows, or hostelries. Tip individuals according to the rates just cited. Railroad porters should be given Rs. 5 per bag. Set the rate before he picks up your bags. Unusually heavy luggage should be tipped at a higher rate. When you arrive at the airport in Delhi, Bombay, Calcutta, or Madras, you can get your own baggage cart and wheel your luggage. If you opt for a porter, bargain the price to Rs. 5 per bag.

TOUR-GUIDE SERVICES. English-speaking guides may be arranged in advance by your travel agent or by the agent's correspondent in India, but it is easier to get suitable services locally through *Government of India Tourist Offices* or through regional state-level tourist offices. Guides who are fluent in French, Italian, German, Russian, and Japanese will cost more. Local sightseeing guides for a group of four or fewer will cost about Rs. 80–Rs. 100 for a half day, Rs. 100 for a full day.

Inquire at *Government of India Tourist Offices* about overnight, long-distance travel guides. Tipping and paying for meals is customary. Numerous state tourist departments also have guides available at similar rates. Contact each department when you arrive. The *Archaeological Survey of India* has authorized guides, wearing green identification badges, at many national monuments. This service is free and saves you the problem of having to determine the level of competence of the many "guides" who throng tourist sites.

FESTIVALS AND SEASONAL EVENTS. India, one of the world's great spiritual sanctuaries, holds religious celebrations year-round, along with numerous fairs, cultural festivals, and sporting events. Since the specific dates of many celebrations each year are determined by the lunar calendar, check with the Government of India Tourist Office or your travel agent for details. Also refer to the individual state chapters for additional festivals and seasonal events.

January. *Pongal Festival.* This harvest festival in Kerala shows off the culture of South India with music, dancing, and tasty regional food.

January 15. *Republic Day.* India celebrates the adoption of its Constitution. A festive day everywhere, with a big parade in Delhi.

January. *Vasanta Panchami.* This Hindu festival is devoted to Saraswati, Goddess of Wisdom and Learning. In Bengal, her images are carried in a procession to bathe in the rivers. Kite flying is also associated with this festival.

January–February. *Desert Fair.* Five days of traditional dances and music at Jaisalmer, in Rajasthan. This is becoming one of India's most popular events.

February. *Surajkund Crafts Mela.* Some of India's finest artisans set up "shop" for a week to demonstrate their skills and sell their products in an ethnic-style village near Delhi.

February. *Losar.* This festival, which celebrates the Buddhist New Year, is especially big in Sikkim, where costumed *lamas* (monks) perform dances.

February. *Tirumala Nayak.* The great southern temple city of Madurai holds a spectacular procession of floats in temple tanks, with music and dancing—extremely colorful.

February/March. *Maha Shivaratri.* This celebration, honoring the Hindu god Shiva, is held at all Shiva temples. It's especially interesting at Guwahati, Mandi, Baijnath, Khajuraho, Konarak, Chidambaram, and Varanasi.

February/March. *Holi.* On the first night of this festival of spring, Hindu devotees light a bonfire in which a demoness goes up in flames, demonstrating the destruction of evil. On the second day, kids throw colored water on each other and you. Dress in dispensable clothes; you'll be a favorite target.

February/March. *Kumbh Mela.* The largest religious festival in India, celebrating immortality, is held once every three years in one of these four sacred cities: Allahabad, Haridwar, Nasik, or Ujjain.

February/March. *Festival of Dances.* India's best dancers perform regional dances at the Khajuraho Temples in Madhya Pradesh.

March/April. *Carnival.* Goa's fabulous Mardi Gras features masked dancers, floats, and good eating.

April. *Baisakhi.* All of India celebrates the Hindu solar New Year with ritual bathing and visits to temples. This day is also important to Sikhs, who hold a spectacular festival in Amritsar in honor of Guru Gobind Singh, who founded the Khalsa.

Mid-April. *Rongali.* This week-long festival celebrates the advent of spring and the Assamese New Year, with traditional dancing and singing in ethnic costumes—a fabulous event.

April/May. *Id-ul-Fitr.* This Moslem holiday signals the end of Ramadan, a month-long period of daytime fasting to commemorate the descent of the Quran from heaven. Alms are given to the poor, prayers are offered, and there is much feasting and rejoicing—big in Kashmir.

April/May. *Meenakshi Kalyanam.* Goddess Meenakshi's wedding is celebrated for 10 days in Madurai, with a huge procession in which vast chariots carry temple images through the streets to musical accompaniment.

April/May. *Puram.* During Kerala's most spectacular temple festival, decorated elephants carry images of Shiva in a colorful procession followed by fireworks.

May. *Buddha Jayanti.* Buddhists celebrate the birthday of Sakyamuni (Historic Buddha), his enlightenment, and death with rituals and chantings at monasteries. Special celebrations are held at major centers of Buddhist pilgrimage, such as Sarnath near Varanasi and Bodhgaya in Bihar.

June/July. The *Hemis Festival* in Ladakh honors the birthday of Guru Padmasambhava with masked lamas and musicians performing ritual *chaams* (dances).

June/July. *Rath Yatra.* The most spectacular temple festival in Puri, Orissa honors Lord Krishna with a procession of huge chariots.

July/August. *Muharram.* Shiite Moslems commemorate the martyrdom of Mohammed's grandson, Hussain, who died at the battle of Karbala, with all-night chanting and intense self-flagellation—big in Kashmir, Hyderabad, and Lucknow.

August. *Raksha Bandhan.* During this festival for brothers and sisters, girls tie decorative threads around a boy's wrist and receive a gift in return.

August 15. *Independence Day.* Special commemorative celebrations mark the country's independence from British rule in 1947.

August. *Bakrid* or *Id-ul-Zuha* celebrates the sacrifice of Harrat Ibrahim (who willingly killed his son at the behest of God) with animal sacrifices. This solemn festival concludes with a feast and joyous celebration—big in Kashmir.

August. *Janmashtami.* On Lord Krishna's birthday, people flock to temples to see dance dramas enacting scenes from his life.

August/September. *Ganesha Chaturthi.* This festival honors Ganesha, the popular elephant-headed god of good fortune. In Bombay, his image is carried in processions and immersed in the sea.

August/September. *Pang Lhabsol* offers thanks to Mount Kanchenjunga, Sikkim's guardian deity. Stately dances are performed in monasteries by costumed lamas.

August/September. *Onam.* Kerela celebrates this harvest festival with feasting, dances, and boat races by "snake" boats with up to 100 paddlers.

September/October. *Dussehra* or *Durga Puja.* This 10-day festival honors the Hindu goddesses Durga, Lakshmi, and Saraswati and commemorates the victory of Rama, who represents the force of good, over the force of evil, represented by the demon Ravana. This is one of India's most colorful celebrations, with the classic Ramayana enacted throughout the country. In West Bengal, Calcutta turns into one giant festival. Dussehra in Kullu Valley is the most famous event in Himachal Pradesh; also big at the Kamayaka Temple in Assam.

October 2. *Gandhi Jayanti.* On Mahatma Gandhi's birthday, pilgrims from all over India pay respect at the Raj Ghat in Delhi, where Gandhi was cremated.

October/November. *Diwali.* This festival, also called the Festival of Lights, is the most important Hindu celebration in India. Diwali signals the New Year and celebrates the day the hero Rama ended a 14-year exile. Oil lamps flicker in most homes. Celebrations are also held in many temples dedicated to Lakshmi and Kali.

November. *Shillong Tourist Festival.* Meghalaya's celebration coincides with Ka Pamblang Nongkrem, a five-day knock-out Khasi ceremony with colorful tribal dances.

November. *Guru Purab.* This major Sikh festival marks the birthday of Guru Nanak, the founder of the religion—especially festive in Amritsar and Patna.

November. *Pushkar Fair.* In a small village near Ajmer, in Rajasthan, tribal folk assemble with their camels for one of the world's most spectacular fairs and a pilgrimage to a nearby lake.

November. *Konark Festival.* This festival, held near the famous Sun Temple, highlights Orissa's culture, especially the Odissi dance form.

November/December. *Wangala.* Also called the Hundred Drums Festival, this four-day tribal celebration in Meghalaya is important to the Garos, who dress in traditional costumes and dance for days to musical accompaniment—an amazing affair.

BUSINESS HOURS AND HOLIDAYS. India has numerous government holidays, when the commercial world shuts down, and Sunday is the weekly day off.

On workdays, shops are generally open 10 A.M.–7 P.M. Small traders stay open longer. Office hours are usually 10 A.M.–1 P.M. and 2 P.M.–5 P.M. Monday–Friday; Saturdays 10 A.M.–noon. State-run banks are normally open 10 A.M.–2 P.M. Monday–Friday; Saturdays 10–noon. Some foreign banks have extended hours, and international airports, some domestic airports, and a couple of luxury hotels have 24-hour money-changing facilities. They're noted in the appropriate chapter. Post offices are generally open 10 A.M.–4:30 P.M. Monday–Saturday. Most museums are closed on Mondays and Site Museums (set near archaeological monuments) are normally closed on Fridays. All museums close for government holidays.

Try to get your business done in offices and banks as early in the day as possible. The afternoon lunch hours can extend into the late afternoon, especially in government offices. Carry business cards. Indians are conscious of this protocol.

MEASUREMENTS. India has fully adopted the metric system. The kilometer is 0.62 mile, and an easy rule of thumb is that 8 kilometers equal 5 miles. There are 1,000 meters in a kilometer, and 100 centimeters in a meter. A meter is just over 3 feet in length and a centimeter is about four-tenths ($\frac{4}{10}$) of an inch.

Temperature in India is now measured by the Centigrade system. Water boils at 100 degrees Centigrade, which is 212 degrees Fahrenheit. Water freezes at 0 degrees Centigrade and at 32 degrees Fahrenheit. To convert to Fahrenheit, multiply Centigrade by nine-fifths ($\frac{9}{5}$) and add 32. To convert to Centigrade, subtract 32 and multiply Fahrenheit by five-ninths ($\frac{5}{9}$). There are 2.2 pounds in every kilogram, but we doubt that you will be buying anything in terms of weight here.

When you hire a car and buy gasoline (petrol), you should remember that four liters are slightly over a U.S. gallon and just under a British imperial gallon.

Indians refer to large numbers with two words peculiar to the country. You will often read in English-language newspapers and magazines about a *crore* of rupees and a *lakh* of people. Crore is 10 million; lakh is 100,000.

ELECTRICITY. Electric voltage is 220 volts, 50 cycles. If you have appliances that adapt to this voltage, bring converters with two-pin round-headed plugs.

TIME ZONES. Indian Standard Time is 5½ hours ahead of Greenwich Mean Time and 10½ hours ahead of the U.S. Eastern Standard Time. Thus, noon in India is 2:30 A.M. in New York. Nepal has recently stopped adhering to the ancient sundial and is now 15 minutes ahead of Indian Standard Time.

POSTAGE AND MAIL. Domestic and international mail delivery is reliable in India. The cost of an airmail letter (weighing 10 grams) to England, Europe, Canada, and the United States is Rs. 11. Aerograms cost Rs. 6.50; airmail postcards, Rs. 6.

The easiest way to receive mail in India is through a local office of American Express. Mail is held for 30 days before it's returned to the sender. It can also be forwarded for a nominal fee. To get your mail you show your American Express card or American Express traveler's checks, plus one piece of identification, preferably a passport. It's a free service to American Express traveler's check or card holders.

If you need to send a package that has to get to Europe or North America in 1–3 days, you can use a courier service. In most major cities, you'll find DHL International, Skypak, Overseas Express, and Blue Dart. Inquire at your hotel.

TELEPHONES, FAXES, AND TELEXES. International telecommunications can be subject to long delays outside of major cities, but most hotels, airports, and post offices are connected to the computerized International Subscriber Dialing (ISD) system, which eliminates the need to book a call through an operator. With ISD, you just dial 00, followed by the country code, the area code, and the number. There is no surcharge for using the ISD system, but some hotels will add their own surcharge. To avoid this, make your calls at ISD/STD offices, which are easily spotted by their bright yellow signs.

AT&T's USA Direct service is now available in India. Dial 000–117 to access an AT&T operator, who will place your call; you can either charge the call to an AT&T credit card or call collect.

International fax service is available for a fee at most major hotels and at a mushrooming number of private companies that provide fax, telephone, and computer services at reasonable rates. To send a telex or telegraph, head to the central post office in a major city (some hotels also provide these services).

Domestic long-distance calls can be made quickly through a similar computer system called Subscriber Trunk Dialing (STD), which is usually available in hotels and through specially designated public phones.

If you are unable to find an ISD or STD facility, you must book long-distance calls through an operator: To place an international call, dial 186; to call within India, dial 180.

A local phone call in India costs a rupee when made from a pay phone. To use these, dial the number, then deposit the money once the connection has been made. Keep in mind that throughout India and even within cities, the number of digits in a phone number varies. Also, numbers change frequently as the telephone system is modernized. We have supplied the most up-to-date numbers available at press time; be aware that some numbers will have changed by the time this book reaches the stores.

To call India from abroad, you must use the country code, 91, followed by the city code (without the first zero) and the local number. To place a long distance call from one Indian city to another, dial the city code (including the first zero) and the local number. Following are some important city codes in India:

Agra: 0562	Gangtok: 03592	Ootacamund (Ooty): 0423
Ahmedabad: 0272	Guwahati: 0361	Panjim: 0832
Allahabad: 0532	Gwalior: 0751	Patna: 0612
Alleppey: 0477	Haridwar: 01334	Pondicherry: 0413
Amritsar: 0183	Hubli: 0836	Porbandar: 0286
Aurangubad: 02432	Hyderabad: 0842	Port Blair: 03192
Bangalore: 0812	Imphal: 0385	Pune: 0212
Bardez: 832	Indore: 0731	Puri: 06752
Bhopal: 0755	Jaipur: 0141	Quilon: 0474
Bhubaneswar: 0674	Jaisalmer: 02992	Rajkot: 0281
Bhuj: 0283212	Jammu: 0191	Ranchi: 0651
Bikaner: 0151	Jodhpur: 0291	Salcette: 8342
Bogmalo: 8345	Kalimpong: 03552	Salem: 0427
Bombay: 022	Kanchipuram: 04112	Shillong: 0364
Calcutta: 033	Kodaikanal: 04542	Shimla: 0364
Calicut: 0495	Kottayam: 0481	Siliguri: 0353
Chandigarh: 0172	Lucknow: 0522	Srinagar: 0194
Cochin: 0484	Madras: 044	Thanjavur: 04362
Coimbatore: 0422	Madurai: 0452	Tiruchirapalli: 0431
Covelong Beach: 041	Mahabalipuram: 04113	Trivandrum: 0471
Cuttack: 0671	Mangalore: 0824	Udaipur: 0294
Darjeeling: 0354	Mathura: 0565	Ujjain: 0734
Dehra Dun: 0135	Mussoorie: 01362	Vadodra (Baroda): 0265
Delhi: 011	Mysor: 0821	Varanasi: 0542
Ernakulam: 0484	Nainital: 05942	Vishakhapatnam: 0891
Gandhinagar: 02712	Nasik: 0253	

LAUNDRY AND DRY CLEANING. In deluxe and expensive hotels in India, you can get your laundry or dry cleaning done within a day or even faster if you pay a nominal surcharge. Outside these places, or at some resort areas, you must wait two days to have it done. Laundry methods in Asia differ from those of local laundromats in the United States and the United Kingdom. Mark Twain meant it when he said that the Indian *dhobi* (washerman) breaks stones with people's shirts. Ordinary cottons and linens are safely turned over to the dhobi, and will cost a fraction of what you are accustomed to paying. Washing machines, however, are beginning to put the dhobi out of work. Dry cleaning chemicals can be harsh, so you should not entrust delicate fabrics to the ordinary establishment. At higher-priced hotels, you can expect the standards of both services to be up to those of North America or Europe.

No matter how you are traveling, deluxe or budget, it's a good idea to carry a small container of laundry detergent to wash out clothes. Except for the monsoon seasons, light cottons or cotton blends will dry in one's bathroom overnight.

CUSTOMS AND CULTURE. Within India and Nepal, expect to find numerous distinct cultures and religions, along with an intense regional pride. Come prepared to respect mores that are often quite different from your own. Both of these countries are essentially conservative. What is acceptable in the West isn't necessarily acceptable in the East. Only children should wear short shorts. A T-shirt is not offensive, but the topless look should be left to the wandering sadhu (Hindu holy man). Women should wear knee-length skirts or slacks. Going braless is mindless. And any woman dressed in a scooped or plunging neckline must be prepared to accept wandering eyes and unflattering remarks.

Travel in a Moslem area calls for even more discretion. Women should consider wearing a *salwar kameez*, the local long blouse and loose trousers, which is inexpensive and quite comfortable. Bathing suits should be conservative. Topless and nude bathing have become a serious problem, especially in India, and not just for the women who leave themselves exposed. Many men now assume that all foreign women, irrespective of their swimming attire, are fair game for aggressive pursuit.

Grass, hash, heroin, and other recreational drugs are illegal in India and Nepal. Unfortunately, many visitors willingly indulge in the practice, and the number of addicts has increased significantly in both India and Nepal. Keep yourself out of it. Pay heed to the popular refrain: Say no to drugs.

When you visit holy places in India and Nepal, try to remember these general rules: remove your shoes before entering shrines, temples, monasteries, and mosques, even if they seem in ruins (in some places, such as the Taj Mahal, cloth overshoes are provided for a small charge); do not smoke or drink alcoholic beverages, such as beer, on temple grounds; be restrained while photographing holy places (much as you would be in a cathedral or a synagogue). Many inner sanctums of Hindu temples are off-limits to non-Hindus, and some temples are entirely off-limits. Most temples have signs in English telling you so or guards at the entrance. Many Hindu and Jain temples and *gurudwaras* (Sikh temples) do not allow any leather to be worn inside—shoes, belts, handbags, or camera cases. Remember to walk clockwise around Buddhist structures, both inside and out. Also remove your hat and lower an umbrella within the confines of a monastery. This courtesy is also observed in the presence of a lama (Buddhist monk). When a woman enters a mosque, she should cover her head. In some shrines, the sexes are also separated. Look around before you sit, and let the situation govern what you do.

Photographers should carry some change for those people who demand money for the privilege of taking their picture. Most Indians are good-natured about posing for a picture, but Moslem women and tribal people may object. Out of respect, ask before you click. Military installations, airports, bridges, railway stations, and trains may not permit photographs for security reasons.

Those who trek should be sure to pack out their garbage; don't leave anything behind. Also use a trekking agency that carries kerosene for cooking. The deforestation of the Himalayas and all the subcontinental mountains is threatening the habitat of precious wildlife and vegetation and the survival of the people who live in these areas. Remember that the roar of a tiger is more valuable than a roaring campfire.

There's no denying the presence of beggars in this part of the world. On the whole, begging is a racket. Unfortunately for the traveler with a pocketful of just-converted currency, it's hard to resist a plea, especially from a child. But remember, charity that turns children into beggars, dependent on the beneficence of foreigners, is misdirected. Travelers are encouraged to visit a local school or medical clinic and make a contribution to a responsible adult.

You can also give a much appreciated donation to indigenous organizations that will put the money to good use. Among these are:

Chipko Movement (Naveevan Ashram, Post Office Silyara, Tehri-Garhwal, Uttar Pradesh, India), which is dedicated to the environmental preservation of the Himalayas.

Indian National Trust for Art and Cultural Heritage (71 Lodi Estate, New Delhi 110003, India), which is working to protect India's environment and culture.

Students Educational and Cultural Movement of Ladakh (Pharkey Labrang, Leh 194101, Jammu & Kashmir, India), which sponsors worthy projects to protect Ladakh's culture.

Child Workers in Nepal (Box 4374, Kathmandu, Nepal), which rehabilitates homeless children.

The Himalayan Trust (Box 224, Kathmandu, Nepal), which is an organization started by Sir Edmund Hillary to help the Nepalese.

MUSEUMS AND GALLERIES. India has superb museums, especially for history, archaeology, and art. In addition to the large-scale museums in most cities, you will find smaller ones close to most major archaeological sites that can give much greater meaning to the study of the ruins themselves.

Most museums, galleries, and historical sites have a modest entrance fee, usually Rs. 1–Rs. 10, and charge extra for photography, when it is allowed (some require that you check your camera before entering and retrieve it at the end of your visit). Tourist information counters have local listings of museums and their hours. Temples that are open to non-Hindus usually do not charge admission, but donations are customary. They will charge for photography, whenever it's allowed (some will not allow you to photograph in the inner sanctum). Entrance fees, ranging from Rs. 1–Rs. 20, are charged at forts and other monuments. Many locations charge neither for entrance nor photography.

HINTS TO PHOTOGRAPHERS. Color and black-and-white film is available in larger towns and cities, made locally or imported from eastern Europe or Japan. A roll of 35 mm, 36-exposure film will cost about Rs. 80–Rs. 120.

Normally, five trips through modern airport scanners won't affect film; six or more trips, and the film could be damaged. In many airports you can avoid the scanner by showing your camera to the security-check officials. Some officials will demand that you disassemble your camera and remove the lens and all batteries. If you don't trust scanners, bring special lined film-protection bags. Dust is a problem throughout India; buy an inexpensive skylight filter to protect your lens and keep your camera under wraps when it's not in use.

SHOPPING. India is an unbeatable destination for the shopper and the bargain hunter. Many products combine good design, marvelous color, and elegant usefulness; others may look perfect in a romantic moonlight-on-the-Ganges-type setting, but not quite so well on your hall table. We have no warnings to offer; we just suggest that before you buy some irresistible object, picture it in its eventual setting—you will come away with the best India has to offer!

State-run emporiums sell good-quality, regional crafts at fixed prices. You will find these handloom-handicraft emporiums in most cities and tourist centers. For "local color" and some bargaining, visit the bazaars, where silversmiths, goldsmiths, gem-cutters, enamelers, and copper beaters work and sell in tiny shops.

Street peddlers usually ask for about three times the price they hope to get. Decide how much the coveted object is worth to you and remember that the vendor has been at the game much longer than you have.

Artisans in Agra create exquisite marble inlay work. Jewels are sliced petal thin and embedded in the marble with such precision that you cannot see the joints even with a magnifying glass. This craft goes back to the days of the Moguls.

Genuine pieces of the Pallava, Chola, or even Vijayanagar period bronzes are usually not obtainable on the market. You will be lucky if you get a good imitation at a reasonable price. Genuine antiques need export permits, which are only granted for select pieces. The antiques and curio shops that are listed in the area chapters are reliable, and you can find some stunning treasures.

Take a look at India's hand-loomed rugs. It is India, not Iran, that has the world's largest rug industry. And India's products are close in design to their Persian counterparts and were introduced by the Moguls. More than a simple souvenir, an Indian rug is an attractive investment. And in Delhi and many of the Himalayan towns, where there are groups of Tibetan refugees, you will find superb rugs and other craft objects in an entirely different and attractive artistic tradition.

If you are interested in pocket-size items, there are enchanting terra-cotta or brightly painted wooden toys for children and for grown-ups. For something less breakable, there is metalwork like the jet and silver *bidriware* and the wares of Moradabad, which combine bright enamel and brass. You can also pick up attractive and simple souvenirs made of more unpretentious materials such as pottery, hand-painted tiles, ceramics, and cane or bamboo ware.

If you want to brighten your wardrobe and express your personality, you might choose a pair of embroidered slippers or gilt sandals that look spectacular and are extremely comfortable. You will be dazzled when confronted with bags, belts, scarves, shawls (like the Kashmiri "Paisley" ones, recently put back into the high-fashion category), and all sorts of costume jewelry.

If you can resist buying a sari—or at least an embroidered silk shawl or scarf—you will be one of the very few women of cast-iron willpower in the Western world. Indian textiles have a variety and beauty unmatched anywhere else—you can have the fiber, the color, and the texture you choose. The south specializes in heavy silks and brilliant contrasting colors. Uttar Pradesh is famed for its *chikan* embroidery on white voile and Varanasi for its brocades. Bengal offers off-white shot with gold, while the Deccan provides a choice of summer saris. The Chanderi cottons have tiny floral motifs in gold, while their first cousins of Maheshwari prefer interesting variations in texture to a pattern. True Oriental splendor is attained in the Jamdani muslins—as costly as they are beautiful, since eight men may spend all day weaving a single inch—and in the Baluchar saris of eastern India, whose intricate designs are woven by a secret process handed down from generation to generation. Rajasthan introduces a bright and gay note in its saris made by the "tie and dye" method, which results in startling patterns.

Indian women manage to wear their saris with spectacular grace—but, of course, they have been doing so for several millennia. If you feel bound to imitate them, then you will need a *choli* (blouse) and a long skirt petticoat, threaded through the top like men's pajamas, a draping lesson, and a good memory (or a notebook) to avoid tying yourself up in knots. So try draping your sari once, and if you feel utterly unself-conscious, wear it that way. You can also buy most fabrics by the meter.

Particular handicraft emporiums, shopping streets, and bazaar areas are listed under each town heading in the regional sections of this guide, together with particular local specialties.

A word of warning: Be alert when shopping. Bargain hard and generally do not trust shopkeepers' descriptions of age or quality. Check goods after paying, and count your change. Do *not* let taxi drivers take you to their favorite shops—you will pay much more.

NIGHTLIFE. India's nightlife is tame in comparison to that of other Asian capitals. Delhi, Bombay, Madras, Calcutta, and major resorts have a handful of discos and sedate dinner dances and floor shows, but generally most Indians entertain at home. What the cities offer most at night are cultural shows of outstanding Indian music, dance dramas and recitals, folk theater, and regional-language theater. Philharmonic orchestras can be heard in Bombay. See the area chapters for detailed information on regional highlights, including India's wonderful festivals.

Traveling in India

BY AIR. Since India is more of a continent than a country, good internal air transportation has proved to be as vital to India's development as a nation as it is to you, the tourist. The state-owned *Indian Airlines* serves over 73 cities, and *Vayudoot*, a feeder airline with mostly 19-seat Dornier 228s, operates over 45 routes out of major and regional airports throughout India. Domestic flights between major cities usually operate on a daily basis, but flights to remote destinations and small cities are less frequent, the aircraft smaller, and there are more delays or cancellations. At press time, a move was underway to partially denationalize the airlines and open up the domestic skies to air-taxis and more charters. Contact your travel agent or the Government of India Tourist Office to get updated information. For flights on Indian Airlines or Vayudoot, get your tickets when you purchase your international ticket to the subcontinent. In the winter, some tickets are hard to get once you've arrived.

Warning: If you purchase an Indian Airlines or Vayudoot ticket in advance and the fare increases before your flight, you must pay the difference in foreign exchange or rupees (you'll need a valid encashment certificate). Indian Airlines will also accept major credit cards; Vayudoot does not.

It is vital to reconfirm your flights at least 72 hours before departure. Check in no later than 60 minutes before domestic flights and two hours before international flights. Even on domestic flights there is advance seat selection and rigid check-in procedures. Expect tight security at all airports. Do not pack a pocketknife in your hand luggage. Even golf clubs are not allowed as hand luggage. Remove the batteries from your camera and pack them in your checked luggage. For most flights, checked-in baggage also must be identified on the tarmac, next to the aircraft, before boarding. This careful security has led to a high safety rate on these airlines.

Also, plan on paying an airport tax of Rs. 300 for overseas flights and Rs. 150 for flights to neighboring countries. There is no airport tax on domestic services.

Fares. A sample of one-way fares: Delhi-Bombay, $115; Delhi-Calcutta, $132; Delhi-Madras, $162; Delhi-Srinagar, $77; Delhi-Agra, $23; Delhi-Jaipur, $28; Calcutta-Madras, $139; Calcutta-Point Blair, Andaman Islands, $134; Calcutta-Bagdogra, Darjeeling, or Sikkim, $50; Bombay-Madras, $110; Bombay-Trivandrum, $124. At press time, the government announced that fares will be increased. Expect a 25 percent hike.

Special concessional fares are available on Indian Airlines, such as "Discover India," which allows unlimited travel for 21 days within India for $400. Another good promotion is "India Wonderfare," which allows a week of travel within the north, east, west, or south of India for $200. There's a surcharge of $100 for Port Blair in the Andaman Islands if you choose the east or south sector. Payment must be made in foreign currency. A special fare ticket can be purchased (and reservations made) when you book your trip to India, or on arrival, but in the latter instance it must be bought in foreign currency. These fares will also be subject to a rate hike.

Students aged 12 to 26, with valid student identity card, qualify for a 25 percent concession (payable in foreign currency) on Indian Airlines flights. A child under age 2 who sits on your lap pays 10 percent of the adult fare. Children aged 2 to 12 pay 50 percent. *Perfect Media* is a handy monthly updated guide to all schedules and fares and provides airport information. It costs Rs. 22 at bookstores and newspaper stands. Indian Airlines and Vayudoot offices in all sectors also have free information.

On arrival, you can expect to wait 15 to 20 minutes for your baggage. Use this time to visit the airport tourist desk, hotel accommodations desk, or attend to banking. Hang on to your baggage tags since you may need to show them before you will be permitted to leave the airport with your belongings. Although early morning mist can cause delays at certain times of the year, most flights depart more or less on schedule, even during the stormy monsoon. High-season "extra" flights are more frequently delayed, sometimes for hours.

If you take a coach from the city air terminal, it will usually be timed to arrive two hours before departure. In the larger centers, ex-servicemen's organizations run the town-to-airport transport service. Indian Airlines and local tourist offices do the job in smaller places, but there are seldom any buses for flights departing early in the morning. Coach fares usually range from Rs. 15 to Rs. 30, depending on the distance. Taxi fares should be based on the meter or set in advance. A couple of larger airports have a pre-paid taxi counter where you pay the fare beforehand and are assigned to a taxi. Taxi fares are usually two to three times the coach fare, and are a good value for two or more persons traveling together.

BY TRAIN. India's first passenger train ran in 1853, from Bombay to Thana—a distance of 35 kilometers (21 miles). In the following year, the line from Calcutta (Howrah) to Raniganj was opened, and by 1880, all the major cities of India had been connected. The present railway system covers 67,000 kilometers (41,540 miles).

Classes of Accommodations and Trains. Unlike trains in the U.S. and Europe, Indian trains have numerous classes of accommodations: first-class air-conditioned (private compartments with two or four sleeping berths), ordinary first-class (non-air-conditioned private compartments with two or four sleeping berths), second-class air-conditioned sleeper (only available on some trains), second-class two-tier sleeper (padded berths), second-class three-tier sleeper (usually unpadded berths), and ordinary second class (always crowded and rarely comfortable). Many new trains designated "Superfast" have "air-conditioned chair cars" where the seats recline.

Most major cities are linked by "Mail" trains, which, except for the special Express and Superfast trains, are the fastest and should be your choice in travel if time is a factor. "Passenger" trains, which usually offer only second-class accommodations, make numerous stops and are always crowded. Trains that run on broad gauge tracks are much faster than those on meter gauge or narrow gauge tracks.

Itineraries and Reservations. Indian Tourist Offices abroad and the International Tourist Guide facilities at the offices of the Western and Central Railways in Bombay, the Eastern Railway in Calcutta, and the Northern Railway in Delhi can help you plan your trips by train. Try to obtain the *Tourist Railway Timetable,* available from any overseas Government of India Tourist Office; Thomas Cook's *International Railway Timetable;* and the *All India Railway Timetable* and *Perfect Media,* which are available in India.

Given the popularity of train travel in India, prior reservations are essential for all Mail, Superfast, and Express trains. You must also reserve a sleeping berth for overnight travel or you could be put off the train. Your best bet is to make your reservations through a travel agent before you arrive in India. If your trip plans are flexible, you can also try to get reservations once you arrive. Use a local agent, who may need to borrow your passport, or head to the railway station and make the arrangements yourself. If you find that the train you want is already fully booked, go see the head stationmaster. Often he or she will have extra tickets available for foreign tourists, especially for the more popular trains. If you're in a major city with more than one station, the local tourist office or your hotel concierge can tell you which station has reservation facilities for the particular train that you want to take.

When you travel by train, be sure you arrive at the train station with enough time to find your seat—the sleeper and seat numbers are displayed on the platform and on each carriage, along with a list of passengers' names and seat assignments. If you need help, speak to the station superintendent.

Special Express Trains. The *Taj Express,* which travels daily between Delhi and Agra, takes about three hours and allows nine hours for sightseeing before returning to Delhi. The *Pink City Express,* which travels daily between Delhi and Jaipur, takes about five hours and allows for about six hours of sightseeing before returning to Delhi. Numerous trains also provide express service (about 3½ hours) between Bombay and Pune. Good Superfast trains are the *Rajdhani Express* (linking Calcutta, New Delhi, and Bombay) and the *Shatabdi Express,* which covers three different routes: between Delhi and Kanpur in Uttar Pradesh via Lucknow; between Delhi and Chandigarh; and between Delhi and Bhopal via Gwalior, Agra, and Jhansi.

Hill Trains. India continues to maintain some of the old British Victorian trains that run on meter-gauge or narrow-gauge tracks which wind their way up to hill stations. The deisel-hauled Kalka–Shimla train starts from Kalka and climbs 4½ hours to Shimla, a distance of about 97 kilometers (60 miles), through 103 tunnels and over numerous bridges in the northwestern Himalayas. The *Darjeeling Himalayan Toy Train,* connecting West Bengal's New Jalpaiguri and Darjeeling in about seven hours, is steam operated and has ingenious reversing stations and the double loop by which the railway gains height through the northeastern Himalayas. From New Jalpaiguri, the train climbs to 2,294 meters (7,400 feet) at Ghoom, the highest altitude attained by any railway in the subcontinent, before dropping down to 2,108 meters (6,800 feet) at Darjeeling. The deisel-powered Matheran Line begins in Neral, not far from Bombay, and makes a winding two-hour journey up to Matheran, a tiny hill station. The Nilgiri Hill Train begins at Mettupalayam in Tamil Nadu's Nilgiri foothills and chugs 46 kilometers (29 miles) up to Ootacamund in about 4½ hours. Coonoor, a station on this line, was featured in the movie *Passage to India.*

Palace-on-Wheels. One of the most exclusive rail-travel experiences available in India, if not in the world, is the *Palace-on-Wheels,* which uses luxurious coaches for a seven-day all-inclusive package tour from Delhi to major tourist destinations in Rajasthan and to Agra in Uttar Pradesh. You travel and live in glorious style, with sightseeing side trips arranged in such places as Jaipur, Agra, Jaisalmer, Udaipur, and Jodhpur. For information and bookings, contact the Central Reservation Office, Rajasthan Tourism Development Corporation, Chandralok Building, 36 Janpath, New Delhi 1100001; tel. 3321820. The fare, based on double occupancy in a cabin, is $200 per person per night from October to March and $175 per person

per night in April, August, and September. You can also book your trip through a travel agent, but expect the fare to be higher.

At press time, India also announced plans to launch a similar deluxe tour train through Karnataka and Goa. Contact the Goverment of India Tourist Office in your home country for details.

Fares and Distances. All fares are calculated on a kilometer basis, but they become cheaper when greater distances are traveled. Air-conditioned classes are obviously the most expensive. At press time, the approximate fares range from Rs.90 (second-class) to Rs. 300 (air-conditioned first class) for 200 kilometers (124 miles); Rs. 260 to Rs. 1,050 for 1,000 kilometers (620 miles); Rs. 360 to Rs. 1,400 for 1,500 kilometers (930 miles); and from Rs. 420 to Rs. 1,700 for 2,000 kilometers (1,240 miles).

Sample Fares from second class to air-conditioned first and distances: Delhi–Agra (199 kilometers [123 miles]) from Rs. 37 to Rs. 291; Delhi–Bombay (1,542 kilometers [956 miles]) from Rs. 154 to Rs. 1,542; Delhi–Jaipur (308 kilometers [191 miles]) from Rs. 55 to Rs. 420; Bombay–Pune (192 kilometers [119 miles]) from Rs. 37 to Rs. 287; Madras–Cochin (709 kilometers [440 miles]) from Rs. 100 to Rs. 813.

The *Rajdhani Express,* which includes bedding, meals, and the reservation fee, has a special fare: Bombay–Delhi, Rs. 1,690 (AC sleeper), Rs. 975 (Two-tier), Rs. 480 (AC chair); Calcutta–Delhi, Rs. 1,725 (AC sleeper), Rs. 995 (Two-tier), Rs. 490 (AC chair). In addition to the fare for any ticket, expect to pay a nominal fee for reservations and a nominal supplement charge for all Superfast trains.

Rail Passes. The Indrail Pass is good value for the visitor wishing to make an extended rail tour of India. It is sold only to foreign nationals who reside outside India. It entitles the holder, within the period of validity, to travel by all trains, including the Superfast trains, throughout India. Holders are not charged the fast train supplement or reservation fees and are entitled to free meals on the *Rajdhani Express.* Rates are calculated in U.S. dollars, but may be purchased abroad in other approved foreign currencies, including pound sterling.

The fares, which range from second class to air-conditioned first class have just been increased. If there is another hike, it should be marginal. The Indrail Pass for one day is $12 to $65; seven days, $55 to $220; 15 days, $65 to $270; 21 days, $75 to $330; 30 days, $90 to $410; 60 days, $135 to $600; and 90 days, $175 to $800. Fares for children under 12 are about half the above rates.

To purchase the Indrail Pass outside India, contact your travel agent or the Government of India Tourist Office in your country for the name of the designated General Sales Agent. You can also purchase the pass in India at railway offices in major cities and towns, international airports, and through government-recognized travel agents in Bombay, Calcutta, Delhi, and Madras. Under these circumstances, however, the pass must be purchased in U.S. dollars or U.S. dollar traveler's checks. If you wait until you arrive in India, confirmation of seats can be risky. Try to purchase the pass in your home country at least two months before your journey. Include a complete list of your railway itinerary to insure seat confirmation before you depart.

Note: Travel by rail is not recommended during the summer months, when the heat is the most oppressive and trains are overcrowded.

BY CAR. *Hertz* and *Budget* rental cars are now available for hire in India's major cities, including Bombay, Delhi, Hyderabad, and Madras. Potential drivers should remember, however, that cities are congested and traffic in India moves on the left side of the road. Hiring a car with driver or a tourist taxi is a better alternative and is reasonably priced. Hire a car or tourist taxi only from a government-approved and licensed operator. For reliable companies, consult the listings in each chapter. You can also hire a car through your travel agent. Make arrangements in advance if you plan to visit any area during its peak season. Rates vary from state to state and sometimes within a state. See each chapter for details. Also expect to pay an added Rs. 50–Rs. 100 halt charge per night on the road.

Rules of the Road. Traffic keeps to the left and is supposed to pass on the right, as in the British system. Subject to local regulations, tram cars can be passed on either side. There is no general speed limit for cars apart from the 30 MPH limit in the cities. In rural areas, slow-moving cyclists, bullock carts, and occasional camels or elephants share the road with daredevil long-distance trucks and buses. Speeds vary according to road conditions. The horn is used as a warning before a vehicle passes. It's also used to warn pedestrians who are on the road. In fact, the horn can create a deafening racket. Bring ear plugs! Remember that for Hindus, cows are considered sacred; for them or any other animals on the road, slow down and use your horn; bypassers will help to shoo them off the road. In a rural society, the loss or damage of any livestock can bring economic hardship, and the driver of a vehicle who hits such an animal typically flees for his life.

Roads. Main trunk roads are generally good, but secondary roads can be a mess, especially during monsoons. In addition to other drivers (of whatever transportation) and animals, one may encounter rural roads that are used as a novel extension of farms, with food grains laid out to dry or sisal rope strung over the pavement so that passing vehicles can tamp it down.

The present national highway system includes roads whose total length is 31,000 km (approximately 20,000 miles).

Monsoons usually play havoc with roads and bridges, and it is advisable before you set out for a long car trip to consult one of the following automobile associations (AAs) that periodically issue regional motoring maps, excellent road information, and detailed charts:

A.A. of Eastern India, 13 Promothesh Barua Sarani, Calcutta 700 019

A.A. of South India, 38-A Mount Rd., Madras 600 006

A.A. of Upper India, Lilaram Building, 14–F, Connaught Pl., New Delhi 110 001

A.A. of Uttar Pradesh, 32–A, Mahatma Gandhi Marg, Allahabad 211 001.

A.A. of Western India, L.N. Memorial Building, 76 Veer Nariman Rd., Bombay 400 020

Gasoline (Petrol) costs, at the time of writing, are about Rs. 14.65 per liter. The government controls the price, which changes every year during March when the central government releases the annual budget figures.

Driving License and Insurance. An International Driving License is recognized in India. In case of loss, one of the automobile associations will issue a replacement license on presentation of your national driving permit. Third-party insurance is compulsory and must be obtained locally; international motor insurance is not acceptable in India.

BY SHIP. There are a number of ways to travel by ship around the coasts of India. It is possible to sail from Madras or Calcutta to Port Blair in the Andaman Islands. See the Andaman and Nicobar Islands chapter for details.

Except during the monsoon, a luxury yacht sails between Bombay and Goa. See the Bombay chapter for details.

At the time of writing, ferry service between Rameshwaram and Sri Lanka's southern port of Talaimannar had been suspended. Inquire at the Government of India Tourist Office in Madras for current information on this service.

Cabins are available for the ship to the Andamans, but conditions are not those of a luxury cruise ship. Ask beforehand if you must provide your own food. The yacht that sails between Goa and Bombay also has cabins and supplies meals on board.

Departing from India

CUSTOMS. If you enter India with any sophisticated *foreign-made* articles that are subject to duty, such as cameras, video equipment, computers, or other expensive electronic equipment, it is wise to put with your travel documents the receipt from the retailer or some other evidence that the item was bought in your home country. If you bought the article on a previous holiday abroad and have already paid duty on it, carry the receipt for it. These items will be listed in your passport when you arrive. You must take them out of the country or you'll be required to pay an exorbitant duty.

CONTINUATION ON SAME SCALE

CHINA

BHUTAN

BANGLADESH

BURMA

PAKISTAN

NEPAL

Ledo
Tezpur Jorhat
Guwahati Kohima
Shillong
Silchar Imphal
Agartala

Srinagar Kargil
Leh
Gulmarg Pahalgam
Jammu
Pathankot Chamba
Amritsar Manali
Kullu
Bhakra Dam Shimla
Ambala Chandigarh Mussoorie
Kurukshetra Dehra Dun
Lansdowne
Nainital
Bikaner DELHI Bareilly
Mathura Lucknow
Jaisalmer Jaipur Agra Kanpur
Jodhpur Ajmer Gwalior Kasia
Bundi Jhansi Allahabad
Chittorgarh Kota Orchha Khajuraho
Abu Rd Udaipur Sanchi Jabalpur
Modhera Indore Bhopal
Bhuj Ahmedabad Mhow
Rajkot Vadodara Mandu Nagpur
Porbandar Gir Jalgaon
Somnath Surat Ajanta Sevagram Wardha
Nasik Ellora
Aurangabad
BOMBAY
Pune
Mahabaleshwar Warangal
Solapur Secunderabad
Bijapur Hyderabad
Aihole Guntur
Belgaum Hampi
Panaji Guntakal
(Goa) Karwar
Nellore
Mangalore Hassan Bangalore MADRAS
Mercara Mysore Mahabalipuram
Ootacamund Salem Pondicherry
Coimbatore Chidambaram
Ernakulam Thanjavur
Cochin Tiruchirapalli
Madurai Rameshwaram
Trivandrum Tirunelveli
Kovalam Talaimannar
Kanya Kumari

Pokhara
Gangtok
KATHMANDU
Lumbini Darjeeling
Patna
Varanasi
Bodhgaya
Ranchi
Rourkela CALCUTTA
Raipur
Bhubaneswar
Konarak
Berhampur Puri
Gopalpur on Sea
Visakhapatnam
Rajahmundry
Vijayawara

ARABIAN
SEA

BAY OF BENGAL

SRI
LANKA

Colombo

N

ROAD MAP
OF INDIA

0 m   100   200   300   400
0 km 100 200 300 400 500
━━━━ NATIONAL HIGHWAYS
──── OTHER ROADS

	2.	The Italian Marco Polo visits South India; Guru Nanak, first Sikh teacher; Ramanuja and Madhava, mystic philosophers
15th–16th century	1.	Three Moslem Dynasties; Lodis in Delhi, Brahmanis in the Deccan, Adil Shahis at Bijapur. The Portuguese arrive in South India
	2.	Flowering of Hindu and Bengali literature
16th–17th century	1.	Mogul Dynasty (Babur, Humayun, Akbar, Jahangir, Shah Jahan, Aurangzeb)
	2.	Reigns over North and Central India; Akbar brings Hindus and Moslems together, epoch finds expression in architecture and Mogul and Rajput miniature painting
17th century	1.	Establishment in the South of British East India Company, followed by Dutch and French; emergence of two Indian military powers: Marathas under Shivaji and Sikhs in Punjab
18th century	1.	See-saw wars all over India; British tighten their hold (Clive); Nadir Shah sacks Delhi
1857	1.	First stirrings of Indian nationalism: Sepoy Rising
1858	1.	British Crown takes over from East India Company
Second half of 19th century	2.	Hindu religious reform movements: Arya Samaj, Brahmo Samaj, Ramakrishna Mission
1885	1.	Establishment of Indian National Congress
1913	1.	Rabindranath Tagore wins Nobel Prize for literature
1915	1.	Mahatma Gandhi returns from South Africa to lead struggle for emancipation and independence
	2.	Excavations culminate in Archaeological Survey of India; Bengal school of modern painting
1930	2.	Chandrasekara Vekata Raman wins Nobel Prize for physics
1947	1.	Independence and partition of subcontinent into India and Pakistan (predominantly Moslem)

Post-Independence:

1948	January, Assassination of Mahatma Gandhi
1950	January 26, India declared a Republic, with its own constitution
1951	First General Election. Nehru confirmed as Premier
1954	Repossession of Pondicherry, from the French
1961	Annexation of Goa, taken back from Portuguese
1962	November–December. War with China over northern border disputes
1964	Death of Jawaharlal Nehru
1965	War between India and Pakistan over Kashmir
1966	January. Mrs. Gandhi becomes Prime Minister
1971	Second major war with Pakistan. Bangladesh becomes separate state
1974	India explodes first nuclear device in Rajasthan desert
1975	June. Declaration of "State of Emergency" by Mrs. Gandhi
1977	March. General Election, Mrs. Gandhi out, Mararji Desai becomes Prime Minister
1980	January. Mrs. Gandhi returned to power
1981	June. India launches communications satellite
1984	Mrs. Gandhi assassinated. Rajiv Gandhi elected Prime Minister by largest post-independent majority
1984	Dec. 3. Methyl isocyanate gas escapes from tank owned by Union Carbide in Bhopal. Worst industrial accident in history of technology

1987	Peace accord signed by governments of India and Sri Lanka aimed at ending the communal conflict between the central government and the Tamil separatist fighters in the northern and eastern provinces of Sri Lanka.
1989	Vishwanath Pratap Singh elected Prime Minister in a coalition of minority parties called the National Front.
1990	Moslem extremists in Kashmir resort to terrorism in their demands to quit India and form their own Islamic state.
1991	Assassination of Rajiv Gandhi
1991	Narasimha Rao elected Prime Minister when the Congress party resumed power.
1992	Hindu extremists dismantled a mosque at Ayodhya said to have been built on a Hindu holy site. This touched off riots throughout India. At press time, the government was still trying to restore order.

RELIGIONS BLEND
WITH CULTURE

by
TREVOR FISHLOCK

Religion is a dominant force in India and plays an integral part in everyday life. Its influence and symbolism are pervasive, and visitors will soon see that they have come to a deeply religious society.

On city pavements, devotees create small religious paintings out of chalk, colored powder, and petals. There are shrines in the streets, where people offer *puja,* or homage. The dashboards of taxis are decorated with pictures of gods. Many homes contain a niche to hold a sacred picture or idol. There is a large number of wandering religious men, or *sadhus,* dressed in saffron robes, their bodies smeared with ash, who carry their worldly possessions—a bowl, a staff, and a blanket—with them. Some are silent; some preach and sing religious songs.

The greatest inspiration for India's architecture has come from the various religions of the country. India has marvelous temples built by Hindus, Buddhists, and Jains. These temples are encrusted with carvings of gods, animals, plants, and religious motifs. There are wonderful temple complexes as well. The important Jain temple city of Shatrunjaya Hill, in Gujarat, contains 863 lavishly decorated temples.

There are innumerable religious festivals and rites, in addition to small celebrations, associated not only with gods and goddesses, but also with water, animals, the planets, the sun, and the moon. The visitor should try to be present at one of these occasions because they are a lavish spectacle.

Of the 850 million people who live in India today, roughly 82.7 percent are Hindus, 11.2 percent are Moslems, 2.6 percent are Christians, 1.9 percent Sikhs, .7 percent are Buddhist, .5 percent are Jains, and .3 percent are Zoroastrians.

Hinduism Allows Liberties

Hinduism is one of the world's most powerful religious and social forces. A Hindu's religion rules his or her whole life, from the ceremonies performed at birth to food, clothing, employment, marriage, and death. Hinduism provides a means of supporting and improving one's existence in the world, and the religious part of the system is no more important than the social. The whole provides a framework for dealing with all manner of superstitions and beliefs.

Hinduism is not dogmatic, and although there is a belief in the power of the Supreme Being, it is not the central focus. Millions of gods are admitted to the Hindu pantheon, allowing great freedom of worship. Indeed, Hindus often have a businesslike arrangement with their gods. They offer sacrifices and gifts when prayers are answered, but shout abuse at them when things do not go according to plan.

For simplicity, Hindus have assigned the major attributes of the Deity to a trinity of principal gods: Brahma, the creator; Vishnu, the preserver; and Shiva, the destroyer. Brahma is often shown with four heads, each holding sway over a quarter of the universe. The four *Vedas* are believed to have emanated from his heads, and he is therefore the god of wisdom. His bride, Saraswati, is the goddess of learning. Vishnu is the highest of the gods, who periodically visits the world to destroy evil and preserve truth. His incarnations as Rama and Krishna have inspired great fervor among Hindus. Rama is the hero of the great epic, the *Ramayana*, which is staged annually all over India. Krishna is represented as a handsome youth, holding or playing a flute. The Krishna cult is Hinduism's expression of human love. Krishna has inspired much of India's art.

Shiva is the terrible god of destruction, and he controls war, pestilence, famine, and death as well as related calamities like floods and drought. His consort, Parvati, is benevolent and affectionate, but she can take on the form of Durga, goddess of battle. She can also become Kali, the black goddess who has conquered time.

Ganesh, the son of Shiva and Parvati, wears an elephant's head; he is the god of luck and success. Hanuman, the monkey who, according to the *Ramayana*, helped Rama construct a bridge between Ceylon and India, is worshiped as a god in some parts of India.

The Hindu code for living is based on *dharma*, doing one's duty, as dictated by conscience, custom, and social background. Dharma is linked to *karma*, the belief that present actions affect future existence. The soul is eternal and goes through a cycle of births, deaths, and rebirths. Hindus believe that present difficulties are caused by the sins committed in a former life. The future may be improved by a series of selfless actions. If one's motives are truly altruistic, they can lead to a state of *moksha*, or serene peace and liberation from the pain and problems of the world. Many techniques are prescribed for the attainment of moksha: pilgrimages, yoga, ascetic practices, and the following of a *guru*, or spiritual teacher.

The Western notion is that the most profound part of Hinduism is an esoteric religious experience. But Hindus say that this mysterious aspect, the harnessing of forces through meditation and yoga, is not the most important. Hinduism is realistic; it provides a way of living in the real world

The people show a great flair for cultural expression, which illustrates the richness and variety of their cultural heritage. Tradition is evident, in spite of India's rapid modernization.

Since independence, Indians have become increasingly keen to promote their sense of national identity, and there has been a revival of interest in Indian art, music, and dance. The successful Festival of India in 1985 was the most extensive series of cultural events ever to be staged in several cities in Britain, France, and the United States.

A brief survey of the main elements of Indian culture follows. Many specialist publications are available for those who want to gain greater knowledge of a particular aspect.

Architecture

Indians take great pride in their ancient civilization. Archaeological research has revealed that the roots of Indian life can be traced back almost 5,000 years to the settlements in the Indus valley. The Indus and Harappa civilization, with its great cities of Mohenjo-Daro and Harappa, lasted from the third to the middle of the second millennium B.C. Mohenjo-Daro and Harappa had two main intersecting streets, and houses constructed from sun-dried bricks and wood. The streets had drainage systems, and the houses had wells.

The Vedic Aryan and Buddhist period, from about 1400 B.C. to A.D. 300, saw the beginning of the fashioning of *stupas* (shrines) and pillars. The earliest Aryans were content with a simple wooden railing enclosing their idols, but later the style became far more elaborate. Caskets containing precious metals or bones, ashes, golden leaves engraved with prayers, beads, and coins were placed just below the summit of the stupa. On top, a square enclosed by a railing represented the heaven from which the gods governed the world.

The Hindu civilization, from about A.D. 400, saw stone coming into its own for whole buildings. The constructions are large, with thick walls, sturdy pillars, heavy lintels and ceiling slabs, corbeled arches and domes. Some of the carvings were erotic, symbolizing, in Hindu eyes, the sanctity of the creative force.

The Islamic civilization, from the twelfth century, endowed India and Pakistan with some of their most beautiful buildings. The Moslems built mosques, forts, gardens, and tombs. The early Mogul emperors were cultivated men, patrons of art, architecture, and literature. Akbar encouraged artists and poets, and the deserted city of Fatehpur Sikri, an important tourist attraction, was his capital for 12 years. The mausoleum of Empress Mumtaz Mahal—the Taj Mahal—was built by Emperor Shah Jahan in memory of his wife, who died in childbirth in 1630.

The Mogul style of architecture was regal and imperial, worthy of the wealthy, refined rulers. The most important buildings were constructed in white marble, sometimes encrusted with semiprecious stones, while others were built of red sandstone.

The European colonizers brought their architectural styles with them. The Portuguese built their towns on the west coast in late Renaissance and baroque styles, and the French introduced Louis XVI architecture in the eighteenth century.

The architecture of British India shows that there was constant experimentation with different building styles. One of the grandest edifices is the Victoria railway terminus in Bombay. It is an architectural sensation, the finest Victorian Gothic building in India. Bombay glories in other Gothic Revival buildings, while in Calcutta there are many decaying buildings

HINDU and BUDDHIST ARCHITECTURAL MOTIFS

STUPAS
NEPAL

GUJARAT

BUDDHIST
SANCHI

KASHMIR

DRAVIDIAN MADURAI

NEPAL

ORISSAN
BHUBANESWAR

MYSORE

NORTH INDIAN
KHAJURAHO

KERALA

INDO-ISLAMIC ARCHITECTURAL STYLES (12th to 18th C)

MAMLUK

GUJARATI

KHILJI

EARLY MOGUL

TUGHLUQ

MIDDLE MOGUL

LODI & SUR

DECCANI

LATE MOGUL

in the English Classical style. On a smaller scale, vice-regal lodges, hotels, and churches abound, and an Englishman can usually find something architecturally familiar in an Indian city.

The grandly imperialistic city of New Delhi was designed by Sir Edwin Lutyens in the 1920s to make an emphatic statement about the grandeur of empire. It was the new capital of British India. Some of its landmarks are Rashtrapati Bhavan, the official residence of India's president, which was the former Vice-Regal Lodge; India Gate; Parliament House; and Connaught Circus.

Sculpture and Painting

The fact that India has an ancient tradition of sculpture has been known in the West since the thirteenth century, but no real understanding or appreciation of it existed until the nineteenth century. Before that, it was dismissed as the product of bizarre religions and as having no aesthetic value.

But the study of excavated Indian antiquities by the British and other Europeans slowly changed intellectual attitudes. As people began to understand Indian religions, they came to appreciate Indian sculpture.

The earliest examples of Indian sculpture date from the Harappan period. The objects are assured and mature. Artists depicted animals—the mythical unicorn, revered throughout ancient Asia, being one of the most popular. The elegant figure of a dancing girl from Mohenjo Daro is world famous.

After the founding of Buddhism in the sixth century B.C., much sculpture became Buddhist in feeling, and artists sought to express the eternal and the infinite. The Buddha represented one of the highest aspirations of human thought and art.

During the reign of the emperor Ashoka (268–232 B.C.), about 84,000 stupas (the emperor converted to Buddhism) were erected. Ashoka ordered his philosophy and edicts to be carved on stone pillars throughout India. Sculpture of the time showed the glory of ancient India, covering every aspect of life.

The fourth century A.D. marked the rise of the classical phase of Indian sculpture. The centuries of the Gupta dynasty (320–600) produced sculptors who excelled not only in stone but also in metal casting by the technically advanced cire perdue process. Unfortunately, much of this sculpture was destroyed by Moslem invaders.

During the medieval period, different styles of sculpture evolved in different parts of India. The work is unrivaled for sheer exuberance, and its vibrancy leaves no aspect of life unexplored. Gods with attendant dancers festooned with jewelery were given the full baroque treatment. At Bhubaneswar, in Orissa, sculptors carved lithe figures representing traditional ideals and at Konarak, also in Orissa, a temple to Surya, the sun god, takes the form of a giant chariot, covered with erotic sculptures depicting a variety of sexual postures. Other temples were covered with figures of loving couples, heavenly beings, deities, and animals. They are all a lasting testament to the vigor of Indian sculptors.

Indian painting can be traced back to the beautiful work found in the Ajanta caves. About 200 B.C., artists were producing work of lyrical beauty, naturalism, and grace. This rhythmic line formed the basis of Indian painting through the ages. The Ajanta paintings had a wide influence on Indian art.

India is renowned for the scope of its large murals—and for its long tradition of painting in miniature. Walls of palaces and temples were decorated with scenes from Buddhist, Hindu, and Jain religious teachings. The majority of these murals have disappeared, but miniature paintings are more accessible. The earliest are the Buddhist religious texts painted on palm leaves.

Under the Moguls, miniature painting flourished. Akbar encouraged painting and installed more than 100 artists, mostly Hindus, at Fatehpur Sikri, to work under two Persian masters, Abdus Samad and Mir Sayyid Ali. The paintings reflected the exuberance of their patron.

Other schools of painting were developing in India at the same time. In Rajasthan, the miniatures showed happy people in bright clothing and had a wider appeal than the courtly scenes of the Moguls.

As the power of the British grew, Western ideas and values became popular among fashionable and wealthy Indians. As a result, traditional painting became less appealing. Many Indian artists switched to painting the sort of subjects and scenes that the British liked—costume, occupations, festivals, flowers, birds, and animals.

Later, Indian artists, reacting against foreign domination, began a revival of interest in the traditional folk art of their ancestors. Nevertheless, the great figures in Indian art in this century belong to the international tradition, although their Indian roots can be seen. Some of the most original current work creates a dynamic synthesis between the Indian past and Western materials and techniques.

Music

The music of India is the result of a sophisticated and ancient tradition. Music and dance are all pervading, bringing vitality to festivals and ceremonies. The beginnings of Indian music can be traced to the Vedas, and music has developed definite laws of theory and practice. There are many legends—the notes of the scale and basic rhythms are said to have come from the Lord himself.

Music developed as an adjunct to worship, and temples became the most important repositories of music and dance. It is the logical development of a long historical process that is a distinctive and integral part of Indian history and culture. Music should not be judged in Western terms; time and perseverance are needed to appreciate it.

Indian music is broadly divided into two forms—Carnatic in south India and Hindustani in the north—both having a common heritage and philosophy. North Indian music uses a wide range of beautiful instruments like the sitar and the flute. In the south, the forms of music are stricter, with little improvisation. In general, the composition of Indian music is lyrical and exciting and offers the Western ear a new dimension in musical appreciation.

There has been a growing interest lately in all kinds of Eastern music among the young in North America and Europe. Some of this interest is faddish, but there are musicians who are genuinely experimenting. Renowned masters like Yehudi Menuhin are working out ways of collaborating with Indian musicians, while Indian artists like Ravi Shankar tour the West with great success.

Dance

Indian dance has a rich and varied background. Folk dances derive from various sources, but the origin of all the classical systems is the temple, where they were conceived and attained their full stature. Dance formed an intrinsic part of worship. Indian dance demands a spirit of devotion and surrender because it is believed that a high spiritual experience can be gained from a sincere practice of the art.

Dancing is mentioned in the Vedas, and there are references to it in the great epics, the *Ramayana* and the *Mahabharata*. There are several well-defined dance forms, each from a different part of the country. The four main ones are Bharata Natyam in the south, particularly in Tamil Nadu; Kathakali in Kerala; Manipur in the northeast; and Kathak in the north.

Bharata Natyam is a dynamic, precise dance style. The dancer wears anklets of bells that emphasize the rhythm. In many south Indian temples, one can see Bharata Natyam dance poses in sculpture.

Kathakali is one of the most popular dance forms. It developed during the sixteenth and seventeenth centuries and was inspired by the heroic myths and legends of Hindu religious writings, with gods, warriors, demons, wise men and villains. Boys aged 12–20 are trained for six years in this dance form. Kathakali makeup is an elaborate process, the characters being classified into distinct types according to the color of their make-up and costumes. Performances are held all over Kerala in temple courtyards, clubs, and open spaces.

Manipur dances are vigorous when performed by men and lyrical when performed by young women. They revolve around episodes in the life of Vishnu. The women's costumes are picturesque and richly embroidered.

Kathak is exciting and entertaining—the most secular of all the dance forms. The footwork is complicated, and long strings of bells adorn the dancers' ankles.

There has recently been a revival of interest in Indian classical dance, and artists have traveled to the West. In spite of some experiments, dance remains close to its traditional form and does not portray contemporary themes.

Literature

The great tradition of Indian writing centers on the epic, romantic dramas and poems. The *Ramayana* and *Mahabharata,* like the great Homeric epics, take their place among the great literature of the world. They are available in English translation and help the reader to understand the rich traditional background that has inspired India's creative arts.

Poetry has grown and flourished, and the Bengali poet, Rabindranath Tagore, who won the Nobel Prize for Literature in 1913, is ranked among the great poets of the world. Sri Aurobindo, who was born in Calcutta in 1872, spent much of his youth in England, and English was his mother tongue. His poem, *Savitri,* is an epic. He founded the famous *ashram* (retreat) in Pondicherry.

British rule meant that English became the common language, and a number of Indian authors have written in English. However, over the past 50 years, several have developed a style and approach that is quintessentially Indian. R. K. Narayan, who began writing in 1930, delights his readers with scenes from Indian middle-class life. Raja Rao and Kamala Markandaya use social and political themes.

An excellent way to get the authentic feel of the country is to read the autobiographies of India's famous creative citizens. Mahatma Gandhi and Jawaharlal Nehru both wrote fascinating books. Ved Mehta, a regular contributor to *New Yorker* magazine, gives vivid accounts of his experiences during partition and as a student in the United States. V. S. Naipaul, who was born in Trinidad in 1932, analyzed the Indian scene brilliantly in such books as *India, A Wounded Civilization.* More recently, Salman Rushdie's *Midnight's Children,* which won the Booker Prize, was hailed as a masterpiece. The work of Anita Desai has also received critical acclaim.

A number of English authors have written fascinating accounts of India as they experienced it. Rudyard Kipling was the first. E. M. Forster produced the classic *A Passage to India,* and Paul Scott wrote the superb *Raj Quartet.*

The Mass Media

For most Indians, movies are an accessible form of entertainment. India's film industry, centered in Bombay, is the largest in the world, making about 700 features a year, most of them very long. The majority of the movies fulfill a need for escapism, romance, drama, and color. They follow a set formula: a love story, a battle between good and evil, a lot of action, a little comedy, and breaks in the action when the stars sing a song. Happy endings are almost compulsory. Social issues are explored, but the audience prefers the filmmaker not to dwell too long on them.

In addition, a number of high-quality films are being made by idealistic filmmakers like Satyajit Ray and Mrinal Sen. Their work is strong and original.

Radio and television are government controlled and the programs are, for the most part, dull and unimaginative. One listener threatened to put a bomb in his local radio station because the programs were so boring. Many other listeners sympathized with him!

The government says that radio and television should educate and enlighten and not be a forum for political controversy. Many of India's radio sets are communally owned and listened to by entire villages. All-India Radio broadcasts in many of India's languages and dialects. Television is slowly growing more important, and Indian-made soap operas are becoming popular. But those who can afford to do so buy video equipment and watch Western programs, pirated or otherwise.

Newspaper and book publishing are growing industries. The circulation of newspapers is about 40 million, the highest ever, and in some regions sales of the vernacular press are larger than that of the English-language newspapers. Indians feel proud that their country has a free press, although some, especially politicians, argue that India is "not ready" for it.

NORTHERN REGION

DELHI

India's Capital—Ancient and New

by
KATHLEEN COX

Kathleen Cox, author of Fodor's The Himalayan Countries, *writes for numerous publications and is currently under contract to write two books on India. A former columnist for* The Village Voice *and* Playboy, *she is also the writer and coproducer of the documentary comedy,* Gizmo! *She lives in New Delhi.*

In the mid-1600s, when Bombay and Madras were trading posts and Calcutta a village of mud flats, Delhi flourished in a state of magnificent pomp and glory—the 450-year-old capital of a string of empires. First it served the various Hindu and Moslem dynasties, then the powerful Moguls who ruled India until the 1800s,when the British wheedled their way in. One after another, each new power created its own new Delhi, with each successive capital city (there are eight) pushing farther north until the British came along. While building their predominantly residential district called Civil Lines on this northerly route, the British hit marshy flood-prone land that forced them to stop. Years later, they changed the course of development and built the bulk of their capital, the Imperial City, to the south.

Although the needs of the postindependence population—over 9 million people live in Delhi—have squeezed new neighborhoods into every available pocket of Delhi, fusing all the capital cities into one, celebrated monuments remain—especially the 18 tombs or mausoleums of various emperors—that attest to the significance of Delhi's political heritage. Even Mahatma Gandhi's *samadhi* (place of cremation) lies here.

Delhi's massive collection of monuments—there are more than a thousand—began in earnest when Qutab-ud-din Aibak, an Afghan and follower of Islam, defeated the Hindu Chauhan dynasty in the late twelfth century. He declared himself sultan and founded the Sultanate of Delhi. After a parade of Turkish and Afghan rulers, Babur, the first great Mogul, seized power in 1526. But he loathed Delhi and moved his capital to Agra, where the Moguls continued to rule until Shah Jahan controlled the empire in 1650. He switched the capital back to Delhi.

This Mogul emperor, who possessed an exquisite artistic eye, especially in architecture, created the seventh city (much of it still stands in Old Delhi) and, in the process, brought about Delhi's glorious renaissance. But Shah Jahan was not destined to rule long. In 1658, his son, Aurangzeb, who was anxious for the throne, deposed his father, imprisoning him in the Agra Fort, where he died. After 20 years, Aurangzeb grew sick of Delhi. He moved his capital to the Deccan plateau, where he kept himself busy waging a series of military campaigns.

With Aurangzeb's departure, the fortunes of Delhi began to decline. First, the emperor of Persia, Nadir Shah, sacked the city in 1739. Then Ahmad Shah Abdali, an Afghan, swept in and wreaked havoc in 1757. By 1803, Delhi's position of eminence was shattered; chaos ruled better than any leader. The British-owned East Indian Company, actively expanding its power over the subcontinent, grabbed hold of Delhi in 1803. Although the British agreed to protect and support the remnants of the Mogul dynasty, they were propping up a hollow regime—a frail vestige of former glory.

Then Delhi suffered through the Indian Mutiny of 1857 (a four-month-long savage battle pitting the British against their subjects, considered India's first struggle for independence). The outcome essentially put an end to the age of the Moguls. The victorious British may have proclaimed the withering Bahadur Shah "the Emperor of Hindustan," but the conquering forces were clearly in charge and the so-called emperor died in exile in Burma.

For the next 54 years, Delhi ranked second to Calcutta, the British chosen seat of power. But in 1911, King George V announced the transfer of the capital back to the once-powerful city. With this decision, Sir Edwin Lutyens, the king's architect, and Lutyens's colleague, Sir Herbert Baker, set in motion the construction of the eighth city—New Delhi. A firm believer in the empire and all it represented, Lutyens designed an Imperial City that verged on grandiosity; palatial-sized buildings set amid broad tree-lined avenues punctuated by Mogul-style gardens, complete with fountains and shallow pools. He intended to use marble on many of the facades, but the cost forced him to use less-ostentatious sandstone.

In about 20 years, Lutyens's capital was completed. But the British hardly finished decorating the vast interiors when they had to pack up and ship out. In 1947, England relinquished the subcontinent, the largest chunk of its empire. India won its independence and Lutyens's Imperial City now served the proud leaders of a young democracy.

RAS BIHARI MARG

To Amritsar

BAHADURGARH RD

GURU GOVIND SINGH MARG

BASTION ROAD

QUTB ROAD

GARSTIN BASTION MARG

VIVIKANANDA MARG

ORIGINAL RD

ARYA SAMAJ RD

FAIZ

DESH BANDHU GUPTA RD

SADAR THANA RD

RANI JHANSI MARG

CHITRA GUPTA RD

CHELMSFORD RD

2

PLACE SADHU VASWANI MARG

LINK RD

GANGA RAM HOSPITAL ROAD

SHANKAR ROAD

PUNCHKUIN RD

PAHARGANJ

Connaught Place

Lakshmi Narayan Temple

MANDIR MARG

SHANKAR ROAD

MARKET ROAD

BHAGAT SINGH MARG

KAROL BAGH SINGH MARG

ASHOKA ROAD

13

PARLIAMENT STREET

JANPATH

5 KASTURBA

4

K.S. KRISNAN RD.

BABA KARAK SINGH MARG

TALKATORA

15

RAISINA RD

RIDGE ROAD

UPPER

CRESCENT RD

Parliament House

PARLIAMENT ROAD

Dr. RAJENDRA PRASAD RD

6

RAJPATH

Rashtrapati Bhavan

NORTH AV

7

8

MAULANA AZAD RD

DALHOUSIE RD

SOUTH AV

TYAGARAJA MG

DUPLEX RD

MENON MARG

MOTILAL NEHRU

AKBAR RD

KUSHAK RD

MURALI MARG

TEES JANUARY MG

11

TIN MURTI MG

WILLINGDON

PANCHSHEEL MG

CHANDRAGUPTA MG

AURANGZEB RD

CLUB RD

SAFDARJANG RD

TUGHLAK RD

PRITHVIRAJ ROAD

AMRITHA SHERG MG

SARDAR PATEL ROAD

NYAYA MARG

SHANTI PATH

NITI MARG

VINAY MARG

AUROBINDO MARG

LODI

To Indira Gandhi International Airport & Jaipur

Diplomatic Enclave

Race Course

Safdarjang Tomb

JOR BAGH ROAD

Moti Bagh

Safdarjang Airport

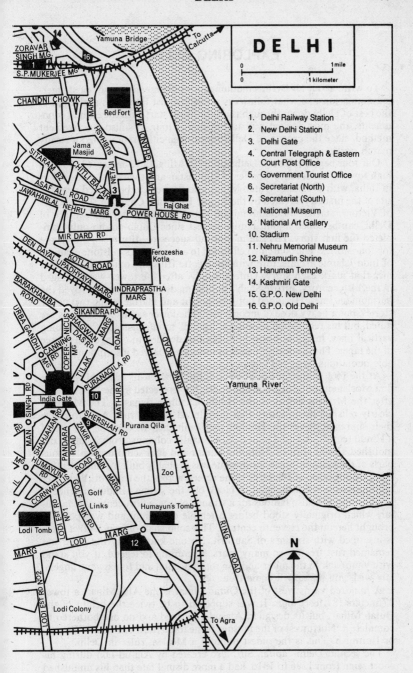

DELHI

0   1mile

0   1 kilometer

1. Delhi Railway Station
2. New Delhi Station
3. Delhi Gate
4. Central Telegraph & Eastern Court Post Office
5. Government Tourist Office
6. Secretariat (North)
7. Secretariat (South)
8. National Museum
9. National Art Gallery
10. Stadium
11. Nehru Memorial Museum
12. Nizamudin Shrine
13. Hanuman Temple
14. Kashmiri Gate
15. G.P.O. New Delhi
16. G.P.O. Old Delhi

Yamuna River

Yamuna Bridge

To Calcutta

ZORAVAR SINGH MG.

S.P. MUKERJEE MG.

CHANDNI CHOWK

Red Fort

Jama Masjid

SITARAM B.

CHITLI BAZAR

ASAF ALI ROAD

JAWAHARLAL NEHRU MARG

MIR DARD RD.

DEN DAYAL UPADHYAYA MARG

KOTLA ROAD

Raj Ghat

POWER HOUSE RD.

Ferozesha Kotla

INDRAPRASTHA MARG

BARAKHAMBA ROAD

SIKANDRA RD.

URBA GANDHI MG.

CANNING MG.

COPER-NICUS MG.

BHAGWAN DAS RD.

TILAK MARG

PURANAQILA RD.

MATHURA ROAD

India Gate

MAN SINGH RD.

SHAHJAHAN RD.

SHERSHAH RD.

PANDARA ROAD

ZAKIR HUSSAIN MARG

10

9

Purana Qila

HUMAYUN RD.

CORNWALLIS RD.

LODI EST RD. NO.1

TOGF LINK RD.

Golf Links

Zoo

Humayun's Tomb

Lodi Tomb

LODI EST RD NO.2

LODI MARG

MARG

12

Lodi Colony

Ring Road

To Agra

MAHATMA GHANDI MARG

SUBHASH MARG

NETAJI

3

16

1

14

N

EXPLORING DELHI

To write about all Delhi's monuments would create a guide of stagger-
ing dimensions, so what follows is a selective list that gives a glimpse of
the best of Delhi down through the ages. We'll start with the earliest monuments, the most logical way to organize a tour. It's also a convenient
method, since the growth of Delhi's first seven cities represented a steady
march north.

Our tour begins in South Delhi at Qutab Minar, a 73-meter- (234-foot-)
high tower—the seventh wonder of Hindustan and the tallest stone tower
in India, with 376 steps. Qutab Minar also happens to be located near the
site of the first city, created by the Rajput Prithviraj Chauhan. This Tower
of Victory, started by Qutab-ud-din Aibak in 1193 after his capture of
Delhi, can be called a joint family project since Qutab-ud-din only completed the first story. His son-in-law and successor, Iltutmish, added the
top four stories. The combined effort led to a handsome sandstone example
of Indo-Islamic architecture with terra-cotta frills and outbursts of balconies that mark each story. Unfortunately, after the tower was damaged
in the 14th century, Firoze Shah Tughlak made repairs that destroyed the
harmonious lines. He added not only height and marble to the two upper
stories, but a heavy dose of incongruity. The lower sandstone sections are
fluted, but his renovation adopted a "round" motif. Instead of continuing
vertical lines, he chose horizontal. He also decided to change the degree
of the taper. The decorative bands of intricately carved inscription are Arabic quotations from the Quran.

At the foot of the Qutab Minar lies the Quwwat-ul-Islam Masjid, the
first Moslem mosque in Delhi and India. It was erected in the 12th century
after the Moslem defeat of the Hindu Chauhan dynasty. The Moslems
clearly relished their victory that introduced Islamic rule. As if to prove
their supremacy over the Hindus, they built their mosque on the site of
a Hindu temple and used materials, especially columns, from 27 other demolished Hindu shrines. Note the Hindu and Jain sculptures in various
parts of the mosque. Since the mosque was probably built by Hindu craftsmen, the presence of the large stone screen across the front of the prayer
hall may have been intended to block out the strong Hindu influence.

The mosque is also famous for a strange object, a fifth-century Iron Pillar, which originally stood before a temple of Vishnu and was possibly
brought here in the eleventh century. This solid shaft of iron, 24 feet high,
is inscribed with six lines of Sanskrit. No one knows why the pillar has
remained rust free for so many years. According to legend, if you stand
with your back to the pillar and can reach around and touch your fingers,
any wish you make will come true.

A hundred yards west of the Qutab Minar is the Alai Minar, a tower
27 meters (87 feet) high. It was supposed to be twice the height of the
Qutab Minar, but its designer, Ala-ud-Din, died and no one bothered to
complete it. Northwest of the mosque is the tomb (now roofless) of Emper-
or Iltutmish. This is the oldest tomb of a Moslem ruler in Delhi.

The second Delhi capital, Siri, also created by Ala-ud-Din during his
short reign from 1296 to 1316, had a more dismal fate than his unfinished
tower. His seat of power, almost completely ravaged by the passage of
time, was also a coveted building site for Ghiyas-ud-din Tughlak, who ultimately created the third Delhi capital, Tuglakabad.

Tughlakabad

Nine kilometers (five miles) east of the Qutab Minar, Tughlakabad served as the hill fortress-palace-town of this first Tughlak king, a soldier of fortune and the founder of the Tughlak dynasty (1320–1400). The extensive city, with its vast number of mosques, palaces, and residences set behind 11 kilometers (seven miles) of heavy battlements and inwardly sloping walls, was built in a speedy two years that was nearly mirrored in its similarly quick demise. In five short years, Tughlakabad turned into an Indian ghost town. One legend claims that a Sufi saint put a curse on the village. Another attributes the hasty decline to a guilty conscience. When the king returned victorious from battle, a newly erected pavilion, which just happened to be built by his own son, proved to be more perilous than any military campaign. It collapsed on top of Ghiyas-ud-din, putting an unexpected end to the celebration, not to mention his life. His son, Muhammad Shah, the successor, fled the royal headquarters.

Despite the disposable nature of Tughlakabad, the actual ruins have managed to survive on an impressive scale. Stark walls stand out on the landscape, and the fortress remains still provide a sense of the city within the enclosure. You can imagine the lay of the streets and the series of structures and even see the large stone-lined reservoir that supplied the water to this capital and the remnants of an ingenious network of underground passages. Facing the ruins of the fort, its founder's tomb, a small, solid pentagonal mausoleum, has remained miraculously intact. The structure is made of red sandstone with a marble dome, the first of its kind in India. By a quirk of fate, this tomb also contains the remains of Muhammad-bin-Tughlak, the patricidal son.

About three kilometers (two miles) south of Tughlakabad on the road to Badarpur, you'll find Suraj Kund, a sacred tank that is the largest Hindu monument around Delhi, built in the 11th century by a Rajput king. It is believed that a Sun temple, one of the few in India, once stood here, its steps leading down to the rock-cut pool that is shaped like an amphitheater.

Little remains of the fourth city, Jahanpanah, created by Muhammad-bin Tughlak and his successor, Firoze Shah Tughlak, who decided in 1351 to shift the capital closer to the Yamuna River. With the move, the capital acquired a new name, Firozabad, in tribute to himself ("bad" means city).

Lodi Gardens

On your way to Lodi Gardens, visit Hauz Khas Village, a new attraction that celebrates Indian village life. Set behind walls, this artists' colony has boutiques, cafés and restaurants, and art galleries.

In the intervening years leading up to the creation of the sixth capital in the 1500s, Delhi went through a terrible phase. After Timur (Tamerlane) ransacked the city at the end of the fourteenth century, he ordered the massacre of the entire population—just retribution, he thought, for the murder of some of his soldiers. As if in subconscious response to this mournful period, the subsequent Lodi dynasty built no city, only mausoleums and tombs.

A visit to Lodi Gardens, which contains the fifteenth- and sixteenth-century tombs of the Lodi rulers, offers a peaceful stroll along winding walks that cut through landscaped lawns with flowers and trees. See, especially, the dignified tomb of Mohammad Shah, the third ruler of the Lodi dynasty—a tomb that also houses the graves of various other members of the ruling family. The octagon rises up near the southern entrance. Also see the imposing octagonal tomb of Sikandar Lodi, set in the northwest corner. Delhi is a city of gardens, and Lodi Gardens is one of the best.

The Mogul Monuments

Delhi's sixth capital rests on the site of the Purana Qila, an old fort near the Delhi Zoo. This area of Delhi was the scene of a fierce sixteenth-century power struggle between the Afghan Sher Shah and the Mogul Emperor Humayun. In the 1530s Humayun began to build his own capital, Dinpanah, on these grounds, but Sher Shah defeated him in 1540. After destroying the Moguls' fledgling city, Sher Shah constructed his own city, Shergarh, over the remains, only to have Humayun strike back 15 years later and seize control.

Unfortunately, once you enter the massive Bara Darwaza (western gate), only two buildings remain intact: the Kila Kana Masjid, Sher Shah's private mosque, an excellent example of Indo-Afghan architecture with lovely proportions; and a two-story octagonal red sandstone tower, the Sher Mandal, which ultimately became Humayun's library. This small building also served as Humayun's deathtrap a few years later. Hearing the call to prayer, Humayun started down the steep steps, slipped, and fell—so much for Humayun. This untimely accident leads us to a magnificent structure just south of the zoo: Humayun's tomb, built by his grieving widow, Hameda Begum, who is also buried inside.

Humayun's Tomb

This tomb, erected in the middle of the sixteenth century, marks the beginning of a new architectural era that culminated in the glorious Mogul masterpieces at Agra and Fatehpur Sikri. The Moguls, who brought to India their love of gardens, fountains, and water, produced sublime structures, such as this mausoleum, which combines severe symmetry with Oriental splendor.

Built in a style reminiscent of Persian architecture, the tomb stands on a raised platform set amid spacious gardens enclosed by walls, the first "tomb-in-a-garden" complex in India. The color effect of Humayun's Tomb—a soothing blend of red sandstone and white, black, and yellow marble—is stunning. The marble dome, a lovely departure from former heavy domes, is India's first example of the dome within a dome (the interior dome is set inside the soaring larger dome seen from the exterior), a style that is also used in the Taj Mahal.

Many other notable Moguls are buried here, including the builder and possibly Humayun's barber, who is supposedly entombed inside the blue domed, square structure. Finally, as you enter or leave, stand a moment in the gateway. Notice how the entire monument is framed in the arch; this, too, happens again at the Taj Mahal. And, as you contemplate the serene setting, consider that many of the dead buried inside were murdered princes, victims of foul play.

Shahjahanabad—Lal Qila (Red Fort)

After you pass through Delhi Gate, you soon see the silhouette of the massive outer walls of the Lal Qila (Red Fort) just ahead on the right. Lal Qila is the greatest wonder of all the cities of Delhi, even outdoing Lutyens's Imperial City. Here is Shah Jahan's symbol of Mogul power and elegance, built behind red sandstone walls that gave the fort its name.

It's easy to imagine imperial elephants swaying by with their *mahouts* (elephant drivers) or any conceivable vestige of Shah Jahan's pomp.

The formerly unobstructed view of the main entrance, called the Lahore Gate, flanked by semioctagonal towers and facing Chandni Chowk, is blocked by a barbican (a kind of gatehouse), which the paranoid Aurangzeb added for greater security—much to the grief of Shah Jahan, his father. From his prison, where he was held captive by his power-hungry son, Shah Jahan wrote, "You have made a bride of the palace and thrown a veil over her face."

Once you enter the main gate, continue along a vaulted arcade, Chhatta Chowk, originally the shopping district for the royal ladies and now a bazaar selling goods of significantly lower quality. The arcade leads to the Naubat Khana (Imperial Bandstand), the main gateway of the palace—a red sandstone structure, where music was played five times daily. Beyond this point, everyone but the emperor and princes had to proceed on foot, a rule that was observed until 1857. A spacious lawn, once a courtyard serving as the boundary where all but the nobility had to stop, leads to the great Diwan-i-Am, the Hall of Public Audience.

Now, you've entered the seventh city of Delhi, the Delhi of Shah Jahan. Marble dominates. Seen against a background of green grass and blue sky, the hall, raised on a platform and open on three sides, evokes a time of irretrievable glory—like the moment described by Bernier, a seventeenth-century French traveler, who was overwhelmed by the hall's magnificence. Here the emperor sat on a royal throne, set in a marble alcove in the center of the back wall—a throne studded with decorative panels that sparkled with countless inlaid precious stones. These panels, stolen by British soldiers after the Indian Mutiny of 1857, were restored 50 years later by Lord Curzon. It was here that the emperor listened to and judged the plight of subjects brought before him in full view of the throngs of people who watched from the courtyard below. The rest of the hall, Bernier explained, was reserved for rajahs and foreign envoys, all standing with "their eyes bent downwards and their hands crossed." High above them, under a pearl-fringed canopy resting on golden shafts in the royal recess, "glittered the dazzling figure of the Grand Mogul, a figure to strike terror, for a frown meant death." Facing the emperor's throne is the marble seat of the prime minister.

Behind the Diwan-i-Am stands a row of palaces that overlook the not-too-distant Yamuna River. To the extreme south is the Mumtaz Mahal—now the Red Fort Museum of Archaeology, with relics from the Mogul period and numerous paintings and drawings. The next palace is the Rang Mahal (the Painted Palace), which used to be richly decorated. The hall, which had a silver ceiling until the treasury ran too low, may have been a sitting room for the royal ladies. It contains a marble basin constructed into the center of the floor (the bottom is carved in the shape of a lotus), with a water channel—called the Canal of Paradise—running through this palace and many of the others.

The third palace is the Khas Mahal, the exclusive palace of the emperor, divided into three sections: the sitting room, the dream chamber (obviously for sleeping), and the prayer chamber, with lavishly decorated walls and painted ceilings still intact. The lovely marble screen contains the carved Scale of Justice—two swords and a scale that symbolize punishment and justice. From the attached octagonal tower, Muthamman Burj, the emperor, would appear before his subjects every morning. He also came here to watch elephant fights held in the fields.

The next palace is the famous Diwan-i-Khas (Hall of Private Audience), the most exclusive pavilion. Here Shah Jahan consulted with his ministers and held private meetings. He would sit on his famous solid-gold Peacock Throne, which was inlaid with hundreds of stones. Back then, its value was 12 million pounds sterling, or $19.8 million at today's rate of exchange. It was too precious, too beautiful! When Nadir Shah sacked Delhi in 1739, he hauled the throne to Persia. A Persian couplet written in gold above an arch sums up Shah Jahan's sentiments about his city: If there be a paradise on earth/It is this! It is this! It is this!

Finally, you reach the Royal Hammams, exquisite Mogul baths with inlaid marble floors. Imagine the self-indulgence as you wander through the three rooms. There's a fountain that supposedly had rose-scented water, and a state-of-the-art hot steam bath. No wonder Shah Jahan called his city paradise.

From here, a short path leads to the Moti Masjid (the Pearl Mosque), designed by Aurangzeb for his personal use and the use of the royal ladies. Once the ceiling was copper plated. The prayer hall is inlaid with *musalla* (prayer rugs) outlined in black marble. Though the mosque has the purity of white marble, some claim the excessively ornate style reflects the decadence that set in before the end of Shah Jahan's reign.

Jama Masjid

Looming majestically on a high platform across the street stands an exquisite statement in red sandstone and white marble: the Jama Masjid, India's largest mosque, completed in 1656 by Shah Jahan. Broad steps lead up to the double-story gateways and a magnificent courtyard (where thousands still gather to pray), which is enclosed by pillared corridors with domed pavilions in each corner. The best time to visit is Friday, the holy day; the exact hour is tricky. Check beforehand to be certain you'll be able to go inside. For a small fee, you can also climb to the top of a minaret (however, a woman must be escorted by a "responsible" male). From here, you have an extended view of Old Delhi.

The mosque, with its onion-shaped dome and tapering minarets, is characteristically Mogul. But Shah Jahan added an innovation. Note the novel stripes running up and down the well-proportioned marble domes. Just standing in the courtyard, you are engulfed in the quiet power of Islam; tranquillity prevails, enhanced by the architecture. Each dome, portico, and minaret of this mosque is subordinated to the whole, producing an overal impression of harmony.

Inside the prayer hall (entered by the devout after a ritual washing in the big water basin—a symbolic purification), the pulpit is carved from a single slab of marble. In one corner of the hall is a room where Shah Jahan installed the footprints of Hazrat Muhammad, the Holy Prophet.

The northern gate of the mosque leads into Chandi Chowk, the former imperial avenue, down which Shah Jahan would ride at the head of a lavish cavalcade. Today, everything rushes indiscriminately into the congested avenue—bullock carts, wandering cows, limousines, taxis, private cars, dogs, auto rickshaws, bicycles, bicycle rickshaws, horse-drawn tongas, and crowds of pedestrians. It's a great place to explore (see the section on Delhi markets and bazaars).

As we move toward the twentieth century, two other monuments should be seen, built during the decline of the Mogul period.

Jantar Mantar and Safdarjang's Tomb

The first monument is on Parliament Street near Connaught Place (the center hub of New Delhi); the Jantar Mantar (observatory) built by Maharajah Jai Singh II of Jaipur in 1725. This astronomer-king, who left five similar structures in India, created precise masonry instruments that look as if they stepped out of science fiction. The largest structure is a huge right-angle sundial, the Samrat Yantra (supreme instrument). Next, head south to the tomb of Safdarjang, one of the last prime ministers of the Moguls in Delhi. Erected in 1754 by Nawab Shuja-ud-Daula, the son of Mirza Shuja-ud-Daula, it is also the last Mogul mausoleum built in this city.

Now, leap to the twentieth century. . . .

The Imperial City and Modern Delhi

Start at the War Memorial Arch, better known as India Gate: a memorial to the Indian Army dead of the First World War, modeled along the lines of the Menin Gate in Belgium. The names of the dead, all 90,000, are inscribed on the arch. Majestic Raj Path—the broadest avenue of Delhi and the scene of the yearly parade on Republic Day (January 26)— heads west to the sight of the eighth and last capital of Delhi: Sir Edwin Lutyens's Imperial City. As you move up the avenue, you come first to the enormous Secretariat buildings that face one another on Raj Path. Identical in design, the two buildings have 1,000 rooms and miles of corridors. Directly behind the North Secretariat is the Sansad Bhavan (Parliament House), a huge circular building in red and gray sandstone with an open colonnade that extends around the circumference. Proceedings in the two houses of Parliament—Lok Sabha (House of the People) and the Rajya Sabha (Council of States)—are in Hindi, the national language, or English.

Continue up Raj Path to Rashtrapati Bhavan, the Presidential Palace. Though built in the twentieth century, its daunting proportions seem to come from an earlier and more lavish time. The Bhavan contains 340 rooms and its grounds cover 330 acres. The shape of the central brass dome, the main feature of the palace, copies a Buddhist *stupa* (shrine). A majestic courtyard bearing the Jaipur Column leads to the yawning Greek portico of the building. The overall effect is nearly overwhelming, with the building practically spilling over the small Raisini Hill.

A newer part of Delhi is the Diplomatic Enclave to the south, where a few excellent examples of modern architecture can be seen in the residences and office buildings of the diplomatic corps assigned to the Indian capital.

Our tour of Delhi concludes with a stop at a hospital across from the Red Fort. This is no ordinary hospital for humans; it is a bird hospital— the Charity Bird Hospital run by Jains for over 35 years. Vegetarian birds (and rabbits) are treated inside, and nonvegetarian birds and animals are treated in the courtyard. Bathed, fed, and given vitamins, the healthy birds refuse to leave. That's how you can spot the building—flocks of birds fly over its roof. Visiting hours, unlike most hospitals, are liberal, and donations are welcome.

Delhi's Markets and Bazaars

If you were born to shop or if you just like to wander through markets and bazaars, Delhi will keep you happy for days. After a brief introduction to the Old Delhi markets, especially Chandni Chowk, you'll find a list of other shopping districts, some where you can barter or just gaze. For those who don't like to shop or for those who are stuck with a long list and too little time, the best bet is a single trip to the Central Cottage Industries

Emporium on Jan Path near Connaught Place. Here, you'll find all India's handicrafts under one gigantic roof. But no bartering; prices are fixed.

Old Delhi and Chandni Chowk

Chandni Chowk, that perpetually congested avenue heading west from the Red Fort, is the best way to get into Old Delhi, with its twisting lanes, small streets, and crowded bazaars. As in the days of the Moguls, astrologers set up their booths on the narrow pavement. Shoemakers squat outside and repair sandals, blithely ignoring the human swirl around them. If you peer through a portico, you may see men getting shaved, silver being weighed, plus every other conceivable form of commerce, while outside, a cow sits complacently in the street.

If you visit the old town on an auspicious day, you will meet wedding processions with bridegrooms dressed like princes—their turbans flashing with cut-glass jewels—astride white horses. The groom is accompanied by relatives and friends and colorful brass bands that demonstrate the exuberance and the importance of this cavalcade. Often such processions take place at night, with portable chandeliers held high like torches.

Strange aromas fill the air, the pungent odor of Oriental spices and the overwhelming smell of garbage. Cattle stroll in the middle of the road, chewing some grocer's vegetables or abandoned refuse. Jewelry, delicate ivory carvings, and rich silks and brocades are exhibited in closely packed profusion. Medicine booths conceal doctors taking care of patients, who sit in open-air waiting rooms. Old Delhi is nothing if not super-Oriental—the glory and the guile, grandeur and grime, of the fascinating and slowly changing East. Chandni Chowk is a place in which to wander, to lose yourself, for you're never really lost.

Around Connaught Place

The sorrowfully neglected Connaught Circus, which encircles a park in the central hub of New Delhi, is another shopper's mecca, with fixed prices, for the most part. A little sprucing up of the facades would improve the atmosphere, but once you step inside the fancier shops (like the Ivory Palace or Banaras Silk House), the former elegance takes over.

Built underneath a portion of the green park is Palika Bazaar, India's bad idea of a modern market. Entering this underground shopping arcade is like descending into the Times Square subway station—dreary, dirty, and crowded. But Palika Bazaar has a lot to offer. Every imaginable item is in this bazaar if you can tolerate hunting through dingy surroundings.

Also visit Shankar Market, northwest of the Block of the Outer Circle of Connaught Place. If you don't see signs for this market, ask. Here you can buy great fabrics, especially cottons—handblocked and superfine. Often the merchant doubles as a tailor.

Finally, browse along Jan Path. At the southern end, you'll find the Tibetan Market. Sometimes a careful search can turn up a Tibetan treasure. But basically, buy what you like; most of the "antiques" are brand-new. Besides, you can't take any article out of India if it's 100 years old or more.

PRACTICAL INFORMATION FOR DELHI

WHEN TO GO. Delhi is at its best between October and April, and the choice months are November–March. At this time, there's a minimum of rainfall, the countryside is green, the gardens in bloom, and the climate is agreeable. A coat is recommended for evening wear from mid-December to February. The big event of the year is the Republic Day Parade on January 26. Visitors are advised to make their hotel bookings for this date well in advance. October and November are good months for the festivals—*Dussehra* and *Diwali.*

HOW TO GET THERE. By Air. For information on flights from the United States or Britain to Delhi's Indira Gandhi International Airport, see *Facts at Your Fingertips.* *Indian Airlines* also has international flights between Delhi and the following cities in neighboring countries: Kathmandu (Nepal), Kabul (Afghanistan), Lahore and Karachi (Pakistan). Indian Airlines also flies from the nearby National Airport (Air Bus terminal or Boeing terminal) to all important destinations in India. *Vayudoot* feeder airline connects small cities in India, including Chandigarh, Dehra Dun, Dharamsala, Jaisalmer, Jodhpur, Kanpur, Kullu, Lucknow, Ludhiana, and Shimla. For information, contact Indian Airlines (tel. 141 general inquiries; tel. 144 reservations; tel. 143 flight information) and Vayudoot (tel. 3295311 or 3315768). *Jagson Airlines,* an independent carrier, has commenced flights between Delhi and Kullu and Delhi and Shimla. Other destinations may be added. It also offers a Sunday sightseeing flight called Himalayan Darshan, which leaves Delhi and circles around major peaks, weather permitting. Contact Jagson Airlines, 12 E, Vandana Bldg., 11 Tolstoy Marg, New Delhi 110001; tel. 3324693. Other carriers could be in operation soon. Contact your travel agent before you depart. All terminals are about 15 km (9 mi.) from the center of New Delhi. Remember to confirm your ticket 72 hours before departure and arrive at the terminal an hour before flight time.

By Bus. Every day, deluxe buses from Haryana, Himachal Pradesh, Jammu and Kashmir, Uttar Pradesh, and Rajasthan—all with their videos blaring—come rolling into the *Inter State Bus Terminus* at Kashmiri Gate, 8 km (5 mi.) north of Connaught Place. For information and details, call the following numbers: ISBT general inquiry, tel. 2519083, open 24 hours; Haryana, 2521262, open: 6 A.M.–noon and 1–9 P.M.; Himachal Pradesh, 2516725, open 7 A.M.–7 P.M.; Jammu and Kashmir, 3324422 or 2524559, open 10 A.M.–5 P.M.; Rajasthan, 2522246, open 6 A.M.–10 P.M.; Uttar Pradesh, 2518709, open 6 A.M.–8 P.M. Deluxe buses to Jaipur (Rajasthan) also leave daily from Bikaner House, near India Gate.

By Train. Some of India's best trains roll through Delhi. The Delhi Railway Station is 7 km (4⅓ mi.) north of Connaught Place and the New Delhi Railway Station is about 1 km directly north of Connaught Place. Most trains leave from the New Delhi Railway Station; but check before you set out. For tickets and information, foreigners should contact the International Tourist Guide, New Delhi Railway Station, Platform No. 1 (open 7:30 A.M.–5 P.M., closed Sunday; tel. 3352164). At this window (for foreigners only), tickets must be paid in foreign currency, usually dollars or sterling, unless you have a valid encashment slip. If you don't have an encashment slip, you can purchase a ticket in rupees at the general counter at the same location (open daily, 9:30 A.M.–8 P.M.). Before you board any train, you must have a confirmed ticket, and if you travel at night, a reservation for a sleeper and a berth.

By Rented Car with Driver. Hire a car with driver from one of the recommended tour operators listed below. Expect fares to be about Rs. 6–Rs. 7 per km, including a halt charge of Rs. 50–Rs. 100 per night. Delhi is 200 km (120 mi.) from Agra, 249 km (149 mi.) from Chandigarh, 261 km (162 mi.) from Jaipur, 586 km (363 mi.) from Jammu, 569 km (353 mi.) from Lucknow, 368 km (228 mi.) from Shimla, 765 km (474 mi.) from Varanasi. Although renting a car with a driver in Delhi costs slightly more than in most other areas in India, it's still an economical way of getting around if you have the money to spare and really want to see the area.

TOURIST INFORMATION. Lots of information is available in Delhi on every site in India as well as nearby countries for that matter. The Government of India Tourist Office is usually crowded, but the staff is helpful and has good current information. Some of the separate state offices are better than others, with Jammu and Kashmir and Kerala outshining the rest.

Government of India Tourist Office, main office: 88 Jan Path; tel. 3320005 or 3320008; open Mon.–Fri. 9 A.M.–6 P.M., Sat. 9 A.M.–1 P.M. They have an excellent map of Delhi plus information on most of India. The International Airport counter is open for flight arrivals, and railroad stations have counters that are open around the clock.

State Tourist Offices. Go to the Chandralok Building at 36 Jan Path, New Delhi and you'll find the following offices: Rajasthan (tel. 3322332), Uttar Pradesh (tel. 3321068), Haryana (tel. 3324911), and Himachal Pradesh (tel. 3325320). At Kanishka Plaza, 19 Ashok Rd., you'll find Bihar (tel. 311087), Punjab (tel. 3323055), Jammu and Kashmir (tel. 3325373), Kerala (tel. 3316541), and Madhya Pradesh (tel. 3321187). The Andhra Pradesh office is at Ashok Road (tel. 382031). Goa is at Goa Sadan, 18 Amrita Shergill Marg (tel. 692065). Offices for the other states are located at the State Emporia Complex on Baba Kharak Singh Marg: Assam (B–1; tel. 343961), Gujarat (A–6; tel. 3532107), Karnataka (C–4; tel. 343862), Manipur (C–7; tel. 344026), Orissa (B–4; tel. 344580), Tamil Nadu (C–1; tel. 344651), and West Bengal (A–2; tel. 353840). Sikkim's office is located at New Sikkim House, 14 Panchsheel Marg, Chanakyapuri (tel. 3015346). The office for Andaman and Nicobar Islands is at F–105 Curzon Road Hostel, Kasturba Gandhi Marg (tel. 387015). Maharashtra's office is at the Government of India Tourist Office on Jan Path (same phone and hours; see above). In general, the other state offices are open Monday-Friday, 10 A.M.–5 P.M., and most Saturday mornings.

FOREIGN CURRENCY EXCHANGE. Most of the Western-style hotels have money-exchange counters that will cash your traveler's checks with twice the speed and half the hassle as banks. *American Express* (at Wenger House, Connaught Place, tel. 3712513 or 3324149) and *Thomas Cook Pvt. Ltd.* (Hotel Imperial, Jan Path, tel. 350404) will cash their own traveler's checks. American Express is open daily, except bank holidays, 9:30 A.M.–7:30 P.M. You can also cash checks at the following banks: *Bank of America,* Hansalaya Bldg., Barakhamba Road, tel. 3315101; *Citibank,* Jeevan Bharti Bldg., 124 Connaught Circus, tel. 3328989; *ANZ Grindlays Bank,* H Block, Connaught Circus, tel. 3319643; *Reserve Bank of India,* 6 Parliament Street; *State Bank of India,* SBI New Bldg., Parliament Street. The *Central Bank of India* (Hotel Ashok, Chanakyapuri) is open 24 hours. Other banks are open Monday–Friday 10 A.M.–2 P.M., Saturdays till noon.

ACCOMMODATIONS. Delhi has luxurious Western-style hotels, moderately priced hotels, and even some lovely guest houses that are cozy and a real bargain. Book reservations early if you want to stay at a fancy Western-style hotel. Unless noted, all hotels have these amenities: shops, swimming pool, TV, restaurants galore, baby-sitters, international communication setups, foreign-exchange and travel counters, and business centers. Bedrooms have low-key modern decor; all have well-appointed bathrooms. Prices are based on double occupancy and exclude taxes and service charges: *Deluxe,* over Rs. 2,000; *Expensive,* Rs. 1,200–Rs. 2,000; *Moderate,* Rs. 500–Rs. 1,200; *Inexpensive,* under Rs. 500.

Deluxe

Ashok Hotel. 50–B, Chanakyapuri, New Delhi 110021; tel. 600121. 10 km (6 mi.) from the airport. 575 rooms. Ashok's palatial red-and-white sandstone exterior benefits India's first national hotel, still run by the government and popular with visiting VIPs. The rooms are a bit worn around the edges, but they are spacious and clean. Ashok has several restaurants, a shopping plaza, and a 24-hour bank. AE, DC, MC, V.

Holiday Inn Crowne Plaza. Barakamba Ave., Connaught Pl., New Delhi 110001; tel. 3320101 or, in U.S. and Canada, 800–HOLIDAY; in London, tel. 071–722–7755, fax 3325335. 24 km (15 mi.) from airport. 500 rooms. Delhi's newest luxury hotel has a high-tech, vaguely art-deco atrium lobby with a waterfall. It also features a no-smoking floor and wheel chair accommodations. AE, DC, MC, V.

Hyatt Regency. Bhikaiji Cama Pl., Ring Rd., New Delhi 110066; tel. 6881234 or 800–233–1234 in U.S., fax 6886833. 8 km (5 mi.) from the airport. 535 rooms. Superposh, this hotel even has a micro-waterfall in the lobby. Make sure your room doesn't face the noisy parking lot or the shantytown out back. AE, DC, MC, V.

Le Meridien. Windsor Place, New Delhi 110001, tel. 3710101, in U.S. and Canada, tel. 800–543–4300; in Britain, tel. 071–439–1244, fax 3714545. 18 km (11 mi.) from the airport. 358 rooms. Sleek and modern, with an interior atrium and glass elevators, this 20-story hotel is near the heart of the city. AE, DC, MC, V.

Oberoi. Dr. Zakir Hussain Marg, New Delhi 110003; tel. 4363030, fax 4360384. 18 km (11 mi.) from the airport. 350 rooms. A marble high rise with black-marble floors and bouquets of flowers in the lobby, the Oberoi is Delhi's most elegant hotel. Best rooms overlook the pool. AE, DC, MC, V.

Taj Mahal Hotel. 1 Mansingh Rd., New Delhi 110011; tel. 3016162, fax 011/3017299. 18 km (11 mi.) from the airport. 350 rooms. This white-marble hotel has an appealing fancy glitz. In the beamed ceiling lobby, reminiscent of Mexico, you might catch sight of a lavish wedding. You can also visit the resident astrologer. AE, DC, MC, V.

Taj Palace Inter-Continental. 2 Sardar Patel Marg, Diplomatic Enclave, New Delhi 110021; tel. 3010404, fax 011/3011252. 12 km (7 mi.) from the airport. 504 rooms. If the Taj Mahal Hotel is booked up, try its other hotel. Expect the same fine service, just less razzle-dazzle. AE, DC, MC, V.

Welcomgroup Maurya Sheraton Hotel and Towers. Diplomatic Enclave, New Delhi 110021; tel. 3010101, fax 011/3010908. 6 km (4 mi.) from the airport. 500 rooms. Another marble monolith, its good restaurants make this a popular choice. AE, DC, MC, V.

Expensive

Claridges Hotel. 12 Aurangzeb Rd., New Delhi 110011; tel. 3010211, fax 011/3010625. 12 km (7 mi.) from the airport. 167 rooms. This is an old British staple where the primary aim is pleasing the guest with great service. There are also appealing outdoor areas in which to relax. AE, DC, MC, V.

Hotel Imperial. Janpath, New Delhi 110001; tel. 3325332, fax 011/3324542. 23 km (14 mi.) from the airport. 230 rooms. This British Raj hotel and Delhi landmark is ragged around the edges, but its location in the heart of New Delhi makes it popular. Good ambience for the nonflashy traveler. AE, DC, MC, V.

Hotel Samrat. Chanakyapuri, New Delhi 110021; tel. 603030. 10 km (6 mi.) from the airport. 269 rooms. This Ashok group hotel adjoins the Hotel Ashok. Less fancy, its rooms are spacious and attractive. Ask for a room overlooking the swimming pool. AE, DC, MC, V.

Moderate

The Connaught Palace. 37 Shaheed Bhagat Singh Marg, New Delhi 110001; tel. 344225, fax 011/310757. 23 km (14 mi.) from the airport. 80 rooms with bath. This new hotel doesn't have a swimming pool, but rooms are extremely clean with an attractive modern decor. Best views overlook the stadium. Good value and good service. AE, DC, MC, V.

Hans Plaza. 15 Barakhamba Rd., New Delhi 110001; tel. 3316868, fax 011/3314830. 20 km (12 mi.) from the airport. 67 rooms. You won't find a swimming pool, but this newish Western-style hotel in the center of New Delhi has attractive clean rooms. AE, MC, V.

Inexpensive

The following three guest houses in Sunder Nagar, 16 km (10 mi.) from the airport, are quiet havens with attractive lawns and clean air-conditioned rooms that add up to a terrific bargain. All rooms are quite pleasant, with modern decor, TV, and Western-style bathrooms. Unless noted, they lack a dining room but offer multicuisine room service.

Jukaso Inn. 50 Sunder Nagar, New Delhi 110003; tel. 692137. 50 rooms. This inn also has an interior courtyard with a cozy restaurant. AE.

Kailish Inn. 10 Sunder Nagar, New Delhi 110003; tel. 617401. 16 rooms. This inn offers car-rental arrangements. AE, MC, V.

Maharani Guest House. 3 Sunder Nagar, New Delhi 110003; tel. 693128. 25 rooms. AE, DC, MC, V.

YMCA Tourist Hostel. Jai Singh Rd.; Box 612, New Delhi 110001; tel. 311915. 14 km (7 mi.) from the airport. 123 rooms. This hostel offers simple, clean rooms (some are air-conditioned). It also has a multicuisine restaurant, tennis courts, swimming pool, and fitness center. AE, DC, V.

DINING OUT. Delhi is cosmopolitan, with cosmopolitan tastes and international cuisines. Delhi dry days are strictly observed—no alcohol available on the first and seventh days of the month and national holidays. The law that restricted liquor to hotel restaurants has been changed; many private restaurants now have bars or at least serve beer and wine.

Although we have included only the best options, most accommodations listed above also have restaurants. Breakfast is usually served 8–10:30; lunch, 12:30–3; dinner, 8–11. The restaurants listed below are informal and unless noted are open for all three meals and don't require reservations. Prices are based on one person eating a three-course meal, excluding taxes, tip, or beverage: *Deluxe,* over Rs. 300; *Expensive,* Rs. 200–Rs. 300; *Moderate,* Rs. 100–Rs. 200; *Inexpensive,* under Rs. 100.

MULTICUISINE

Expensive–Deluxe

Cafe Prominade. Hyatt Regency, Bhikaiji Cama Pl., Ring Rd.; tel. 6881234. This airy restaurant, spilling into a downstairs lobby, serves the best buffet in Delhi, with imported cheeses, cold cuts, a well-stocked salad bar, and tasty desserts. You can also order à la carte. At night, you often have to contend with a rock band. This café also has a monthly foodfest that highlights a foreign cuisine. Open 24 hours. AE, DC, MC, V.

Moderate–Expensive

La Brasserie. Le Meridien, Windsor Pl.; tel. 3710101. Enclosed behind brass-trimmed glass partitions in the hotel lobby, this bustling café, with lots of marble and muted pink pillars, has a menu that features numerous cuisines and includes sizzlers, club sandwiches, and salads. It occasionally sponsors international food festivals. Open 24 hours. AE, DC, MC, V.

Moderate

The Host. F–8 Connaught Pl.; tel. 3316381. Mirrors are set in arches in the walls of this Victorian-style restaurant, where taped Indian music creates a quiet ambience. Choose from Chinese, Continental, and Indian dishes, including a good selection of tandoori items and Indian breads. Open 10 A.M.–midnight. AE.

Inexpensive–Moderate

Farm House Restaurant. Delhi Tourism Complex, Qutab Minar, tel. 650045. You can either eat inside or enjoy your meal at a table on the lawn with the Qutab Minar as a backdrop. The Farm House has a multicuisine menu, but don't miss its tandoori dishes. Try the unusual chicken *dharyali* (chicken pieces marinated in spinach), tandoori garlic chicken kebab, or *aachan gosht* (mutton kebab). Open 11 A.M.–11 P.M. AE.

Janpath Food Plaza. Hotel Janpath, Janpath; tel. 3320070. On the lawn behind the hotel and away from the bustle, this refuge offers a great opportunity to try a selection of cuisines from Delhi's best restaurants. Wander from stall to stall and place your order. A waiter will serve you at a table. Try the grilled prawn from Crazy Corner, the pepper chicken *chitinad* (spicy bits of chicken) from Coconut Grove, the dry chili chicken from Mandarin, and *makke ke roti* with *sarson ka saag* (flat bread served with mild spinach curry) from Bhojan. At night, there's a Western band. Open noon–midnight. Rupees only.

INDIAN

Deluxe

Bukhara. Welcomgroup Maurya Sheraton, Diplomatic Enclave; tel. 3010101. This extremely popular restaurant has a handsome copper and wood decor. It emphasizes superb northwest frontier specialties: leg of lamb, tandooris, and kebabs. There are tables outside. Reservations advised. Open 12:30 P.M.–2:30 P.M. and 8 P.M.–midnight. AE, DC, MC, V.

Dum Pukht. Welcomgroup Maurya Sheraton, Diplomatic Enclave; tel. 3010101. Heavy brocade fans and Nawabi costumes adorn the walls here, where the menu is printed on silk and set in silver. The cuisine, *Dum Pukht* (aromatic Indian dishes cooked in sealed pots), originated with the Moslem nawab rulers. Splurge and have a feast—*Dumpukht Asafjahi* or *Dumpukht Wajid Shahi,* meals named for two nawabs in Uttar Pradesh. Reservations advised. Open 12:30–3 P.M. and 8–12 P.M. AE, DC, MC, V.

Haveli. Taj Mahal, 1 Mansingh Rd.; tel. 30161447. Chandeliers, Indian paintings, and a bank of latticed windows create the aura of an elegant *haveli* (mansion). At night, ghazal singers and instrumentalists entertain. The menu features north Indian cuisine, especially tandoori items: *kakori* kebab (lamb) and *murg mirch tikka* (boneless chicken flavored with green chilis). Dinner reservations advised. Open 12:30–3 P.M. and 7:30–midnight. AE, DC, MC, V.

Moderate

Chor Bazarre. Hotel Broadway, 4/15A Asif Ali Rd.; tel. 3273821. Expect a 1927 Fiat roadster for a salad bar, a spiral staircase that leads nowhere, and an eclectic mix of tables and chairs collected from *chor* (thieve's) bazaars. Also expect north Indian cuisine, especially Kashmiri dishes. The chef serves good *ghazab ka tikka* (tandoori cooked chicken coated with cheddar cheese), *sharabi kababi tikka* (chicken cooked in tomato and onion and served with flaming brandy), or *rohgan josh* (mutton cooked in spicy gravy). Dinner reservations advised. Open 12:30 P.M.–3:30 P.M. and 8 P.M.–midnight. AE, DC, MC, V.

Dhaba. Claridges Hotel, 12 Aurangzeb Rd., New Delhi; tel. 3010211. Dhaba refers to a curbside truck stop that serves inexpensive meals. That's the motif in this popular restaurant, which has long wooden tables in numerous small rooms, and an actual truck body set into a back wall. Try chicken *tikka* (chicken pieces cooked before your eyes) or *balti* meat (mutton prepared in a big dhaba-style vessel). Open noon–2:30 P.M. and 8–11:30 P.M. AE, DC, MC, V.

Gulati Restaurant. 6 Pandara Rd. Market; tel. 388839. In this small, usually crowded restaurant, you can hobnob with politicos and eat Mughlai servings and try a variety of different *dahls* (lentil dishes). Open noon–midnight, closed Mon. MC.

Inexpensive–Moderate

Coconut Grove. Ashok Yatri Niwas, 19 Ashok Rd.; tel. 3713052. This attractive restaurant has cane chairs, bamboo trim, lots of plants, subdued lighting, and taped south Indian classical music. It offers the cuisines of Kerala and the southern coastal regions, including *konju thenga* curry (prawns cooked in mildly spicy coconut sauce) and pepper chicken *chitinad* (spicy chicken cooked in a thick pepper gravy). You can also enjoy an outdoor barbecue that features south Indian grilled specialties. Dinner reservations advised. Open noon–5:30 P.M. and 7 P.M.–11 P.M. AE.

Karim Hotel. Gali Kababian, Jama Masjid, Old Delhi; tel. 3269880. This extremely simple restaurant is an Old Delhi institution that offers an ethnic ambience and Mughlai cuisine. Open 10 A.M.–midnight. Rupees only.

Karim's Nemat Kada. 168/2 Jha House, Hazrat Nizamuddin West, near the police station; tel. 698300. This attractive restaurant in an Islamic neighborhood has a welcoming ambience and serves very good Mughlai dishes. Open noon–midnight. Rupees only.

Inexpensive

Kake da Hotel. 74 Outer Circle, Connaught Pl. (between L and M blocks); tel. 3316580. The best butter chicken in town is served here. Bring handiwipes or wear old clothes; napkins are scarce. Expect a crowd and a steal of a meal. Open 11 A.M. until the chicken is gone, closed Sun. Rupees only.

CHINESE

Expensive–Deluxe

Taipan. Oberoi, Dr. Zakir Hussain Marg; tel. 4363030. This elegant rooftop restaurant, with Chinese watercolors on the walls, handsome smoked-glass and brass lanterns, and polished teak lattice screens, serves Szechuan cuisine. Try the spinach in hot sesame oil and chili sauce, the steamed chicken in lotus leaves, or tasty king prawns in garlic. Dinner reservations advised. Open 12:30–3 P.M. and 8–midnight. AE, DC, MC, V.

Tea House of the August Moon. Taj Palace, Sardar Patel Marg, Diplomatic Enclave; tel. 3010404. Dine in a "tea house" complete with goldfish pond, bridge, bamboo grove, and dragons on the wall. The chef serves good Cantonese, Szechuan, and dim sum. Try the king prawns pepper salt (crispy fried prawns tossed with salt, red pepper, and onion) or smoked lamb sesame seed; or ask for the assorted vegetables in hot garlic sauce, which is not on the menu. Dinner reservations advised. Open 12:30–2:45 P.M. and 7:30–11:45 P.M. AE, DC, MC, V.

Moderate

Berco's. E–8 Connaught Pl.; tel. 3323757. In this coffee shop–style restaurant, you get fast service but not fast-food fare. Choose from good spicy and nonspicy Chinese (also Japanese and Indian) dishes. There's always a crowd at 2 P.M. Open noon–11 P.M. Rupees only.

The Great Wall of the Village. Bistro Complex, 94 Hauz Khas Village, near Deer Park; tel. 6853857. This intimate upstairs restaurant has rough white-stucco walls and a hint of China in its decor, as well as a red-silk scroll menu. Try the Szechuan chili chicken, the prawns in hot garlic sauce, or the crispy vegetables coated in salt and pepper. There's a Western band nightly, except Tuesday. Dinner reservations advised. Open noon–3:30 P.M. and 7:30 P.M.–midnight. AE, DC, MC, V.

Zen. B–25, Connaught Pl.; tel. 3310077. This handsome new restaurant is decorated with cedar paneling, etched-glass partitions between booths, and Zen sculptures mounted on black silk and affixed to the walls. Crowds come for a good selection of Szechuan and Cantonese cuisines, and a few Japanese dishes. Try the paper-wrapped chicken (chopped chicken and prawns cooked in their juices in tinfoil), the spicy pepper prawns, or Peking duck served with sweet bean sauce and pancakes. Dinner reservations advised. Open 12:30 P.M.–3 P.M. and 7 P.M.–11:30 P.M. Snacks are available 3 P.M.–7 P.M. AE, DC, MC, V.

THAI

Deluxe

Silk Orchid. Holiday Inn, Barakhamba Ave.; tel. 3320101. A rooftop restaurant with panoramas of Delhi, the Silk Orchid's subdued lighting creates a romantic setting. Try the *tom yam goong* (spicy prawn soup), *goong mae nam tord krathiem prik Thai* (fried prawns in pepper garlic), and *kaeng kiew warn kai* (chicken cooked in green curry paste). There's a nightly dance band. Dinner reservations advised. Guests under 18 not allowed. Open 12:30 P.M.–3 P.M. and 8:30 P.M.–1 A.M. AE, DC, MC, V.

JAPANESE

Expensive

Tokyo Restaurant. Ashok Hotel, Chanakyapuri, New Delhi; tel. 600412. Japanese paper lanterns hanging from the ceiling, delicate bamboo screens, and taped Japanese music get you into the mood for the Tokyo's good Japanese cuisine. Specialties include tempura, *kappa-maki* (cucumber sushi roll), *yakitori* (barbecued chicken), or *yaki-udon* (noodles with pork and vegetables). Open 12:30–3 P.M. and 7:30–11 P.M. Reservations advised. AE, DC, MC, V.

CONTINENTAL

Deluxe

The Grill Room. Holiday Inn Crowne Plaza, Barakhamba Ave.; tel. 3320101. Come to this rooftop restaurant for the views of Delhi as well as the grilled Continental dishes and a selection of Western appetizers and desserts. To start, try the crabmeat and lobster salad, then go for the seafood mixed grill or the chateaubriand with bearnaise sauce. Reservations advised. Open 12:30 P.M.–3 P.M. and 7:30 P.M.–midnight. AE, DC, MC, V.

Orient Express. Taj Palace, 2 Sardar Patel Marg, Diplomatic Enclave; tel. 3010404. The decor here befits its name—you step aboard a fancy dining car on the *Orient Express.* Attentive waiters dressed in formal black help you select from a large assortment of Continental dishes that are as appealing to the eye as to the taste. The price for the meal is fixed and steep—but worth it. The Orient is considered one of the world's best restaurants. Dinner reservations advised. Open noon–3 P.M. and 7:30–11:30 P.M. AE, DC, MC, V.

Valentino's. Hyatt Regency, Bhikaiji Cama Pl., Ring Rd.; tel. 6881234. This restaurant has an Art Deco decor, with roses etched in glass panels, mirrored pillars, and early twentieth-century reproductions of well-known paintings. It serves a variety of fresh pastas with a choice of nonvegetarian or vegetarian sauces, and a popular Dutch veal loin served with morrel cream sauce. You can order imported appetizers: mozzarella, mortadella, smoked salmon. There's a nightly dance band, except Mondays. Dinner reservations advised. Open noon–2:30 P.M. and 8–midnight. AE, DC, MC, V.

SWEETS AND TREATS. Don't be put off by the shabby appearance of the rooftop *Coffee House* on top of Mohan Singh Place Building on Baba Khara Singh Marg, across the street from the state emporia complex. This is a Delhi landmark and a favorite hangout that serves good snacks and, yes, great coffee. Open 8 A.M.–10 P.M.

Bengali Sweet Centre, tucked in the corner of South Extension I Market, off Ring Rd., sells fabulous sweets. Try their *kulfi* (Indian ice cream), *kaju burfee* (pure cashew sweet), *kalakand* (hardened milk sweet), *samosa* (fried vegetable dumplings), and *aloo chat* (spicy cold "potato salad"). Open 10 A.M.–10 P.M.

Sweets Corner at Sunder Nagar Market, a good shopping area near the Oberoi Hotel, also has a similar range of great snacks. Open 7 A.M.–7 P.M. daily.

HOW TO GET AROUND. From the Airports. It's approximately 18 km (11 mi.) to the center of New Delhi from either airport. Numerous hotels provide airport pickup service. You can also take the airport bus (Rs. 15 from the national airport, Rs. 20 from the international airport), which runs frequently to major hotels and the center of town. Taxis are also available. Don't try to hail one yourself, but go to the Prepaid Taxi counter; your destination determines the exact rate. Don't give the driver your payment slip until you arrive. If he demands more rupees, complain to the hotel doorman. A taxi from the airport to the center of New Delhi should cost about Rs. 150.

Once you're in Delhi, you've arrived in an enormous sprawl of a city, with numerous neighborhoods that have restaurants, monuments, and parks that appeal to tourists. There are a few good ways to get around the city.

By Taxi. Taxis are Rs. 5.80 for the first km, Rs. 3.60 per additional km.

By Auto Rickshaw. This is the best way to scoot around town. The driver can be surly, can claim that the meter is broken, and can rig the meter to go faster than the scooter. But still, they're the most fun and they're cheap. Auto rickshaws charge Rs. 3.50 for the first km and Rs. 1.80 per additional km.

By Bus. Forget the bus, unless you're good at catching fast-moving vehicles and like top-heavy tilters.

By Bike Rickshaw. In Old Delhi if you're not up to walking, this is the best alternative. A real bargain. It should be cheaper than the auto rickshaw.

By Diesel Rickshaw (twice as big as an auto rickshaw). From behind Palika Bazaar, you'll find these oversized rickshaws that will take you to fixed points at set fees. Slow-moving, although faster than a bus.

TOURS. Numerous companies offer the following fixed-departure tours by bus (guide included): half-day tour of Old Delhi, Rs. 55, half-day tour of New Delhi, Rs. 55; Delhi by Evening tour, Rs. 55, and day tour to Agra, Rs. 325.

Delhi Tourism Development Corporation (DTDC, Bombay Life Building, N–Block, Connaught Circus, tel. 3313637) offers the tours listed above by non-air-conditioned coach.

Ashok Travels and Tours (ITDC, L-Block, Connaught Pl., tel. 3320331, with counters at all Ashok hotels) offers the same tours by air-conditioned buses at a slightly higher price.

The tour operators listed below can also arrange similar tours.

To hire your own guide in Delhi, contact the Government of India Tourist Office (see *Tourist Information* above).

TOUR OPERATORS. For all travel needs, including renting a car with driver, contact any of these reliable agencies: *American Express,* Wenger House, A-Block, Connaught Pl., New Delhi 110001, tel. 3324119, fax 3321706; *Cox & Kings,* Indra Pl., H-Block, Connaught Pl., New Delhi 110001, tel. 332006, fax 3317373; *Thomas Cook,* Yogeshwar Bldg, 4th Floor, M–2, Connaught Circus, New Delhi 110001, tel. 350404; *Mercury Travels,* Jeevan Tara Bldg., Parliament St., New Delhi 110001, tel. 312008, fax 351413; *RBS Travels,* Connaught Palace Hotel, 37 Shaheed Bhagat Singh Marg, New Delhi 110001, tel. 344952, fax 344952; *Sita World Travel,* 4 Nalcha Marg Shopping Center, Diplomatic Enclave, New Delhi 110021, tel. 3011122, fax 3010123; *Travel Corporation,* TCI, Hotel Metro, N–49, Janpath, tel. 3315181, fax 3316705. You can also arrange for a car or tours through Ashok Travels and Tours (address above). Most of these companies provide services around the clock.

SEASONAL EVENTS. Lots of events happen regularly in Delhi. Just let a foreign dignitary arrive and advance preparations have truckloads of workers planting flowers, hanging posters, spiffying up the city. The specific dates for many events each year are determined by the lunar calendar; consult the Government of India Tourist Office for details.

January 26. *Republic Day Parade.* You need a ticket to see this event on Raj Path, and tickets go from the ordinary to the VVIP. Lots of military hoopla, floats from each state with great cultural highlights: dancers, musicians, planes flying overhead. **Cameras not allowed,** nor conspicuous handbags of any kind. The entire week is a celebration including festivals held in various auditoriums and hotels.

February 1–15. *Surajkund Crafts Mela.* In an ethnic village, set up at Hotel Raj Hans, 8 km (5 mi.) south of Delhi in neighboring Haryana, master craftsmen show how they create their terrific handicrafts, which you can also buy. Dancers, musicians, magicians, and village gymnasts perform. Lots of fun.

March. *Holi.* This festival marks the start of spring and marks you as the target for water bombs filled with red color (permanent or washable)—stay indoors or wear old clothes.

May (full moon). *Buddha Jayanti.* The birth, enlightenment, and death of the Buddha are celebrated with prayer meetings at Ladakh Buddha Vihara (Bela Road).

August. *Raksha Bandhan.* Once, according to Hindu mythology, Indra, the king of the heavens, warred with demons and his consort tied a silk amulet around his wrist to help him win back his kingdom. Now, sisters and brothers pledge their love to one another and the sister ties a silk string around the brother's wrist. That explains all the stalls you'll see selling glittery paper wrist bands.

Aug. 15. *Independence Day.* Lots of speeches, and that's about it.

October 2. *Gandhi Jayanti.* This day honors the birthday of Mahatma Gandhi, with special singing and ceremonies at the Raj Ghat.

October. *Dussehra.* This 10-day celebration with plays and music recitals of *Ramlila* recalls the mythological victory of Rama over evil. The most spectacular rendering is held at the Delhi Gate (performances for one month). On the 10th day, an elaborate procession heads to the Ram Lila grounds, where enormous effigies of the demon Ravana, his brother, and son (all stuffed with firecrackers) are exploded before a crowd of people.

October/November. *Diwali.* The Festival of Lights and start of the Hindu New Year is celebrated with thousands of candles lit at night on balconies of houses. The city crackles with the explosion of fireworks. Lots of fun.

HISTORIC SITES. Entrance to most temples and monuments is free or extremely inexpensive; where a donation is asked, a few rupees will suffice. Important sites are open daily sunrise to sunset, unless noted below.

Baha'i Temple of Worship. On Kalkaji Hill, near Nehru Pl., it's open 9:30 A.M.– 12:30 P.M. 2–5 P.M. every day, except Mondays. On Saturdays, Sundays and public holidays, hours are extended until 7 P.M.

Firozabad. 3 km from Connaught Pl., near Delhi Gate. See the Kotla Firoze Shah (the remains of Firoze Shah Tughlak's palace), with its third-century Ashoka pillar mounted on the top. Also see the partially ruined Jami Masjid—the largest mosque from the Tughlak era and still a Moslem religious shrine.

Hazrat Nizamudin Aulia. 4.8 km (3 mi) from Connaught Pl., near Humayun's Tomb. Shrine of Sheikh Nizamuddin Chisti, fourth in the line of Chisti saints, and an important place of Moslem pilgrimage. Chisti died in 1325. Many other notables are buried nearby, including Jahanara, Shah Jahan's daughter.

Humayun's Tomb. 4.8 km (3 mi) from Connaught Pl. in Nizamuddin. Built in the mid-sixteenth century by Haji Begum for her husband (she's also buried here), the tomb represents a new architectural era that culminated in Agra and Fatehpur Sikri. Definite Persian influences include the first "tomb-in-a-garden" complex in India.

Jama Masjid. In Old Delhi. Built of red sandstone and marble in 1656 by Shah Jahan. The largest mosque in India and the last building constructed by Shah Jahan. Some areas within the mosque are restricted to non-Moslems. Check with tourist department for the appropriate visiting hours, which vary.

Jantar Mantar (Observatory). 0.4 km from Connaught Pl. Scientific instruments built by the astronomer-king Maharajah Jai Singh II of Jaipur in 1725. Accurate instruments that measure celestial movements act as a sundial.

Lakshmi Narayan Temple. 2 km from Connaught Pl. Built in 1938 by the industrialist Birla Mandir in the Orissan style. Contains the deities of Narayan, Lakshmi, Durga, and Shiva. Remove your shoes once you enter the courtyard.

Lal Qila (Red Fort). Across from Jama Masjid. The site of the seventh capital of Delhi begun by the Mogul Emperor Shah Jahan around 1638. Built of red sandstone (Lal Qila); inside are a series of beautiful buildings in red sandstone and marble. *Son et lumiere* show is held nightly. Hours frequently change; check with your hotel or call 3274580 for details.

Lodi Tombs. 4.8 km from Connaught Pl. on Lodi Rd. Fifteenth- and 16th-century tombs of the rulers of the Sayyid and Lodi dynasties: Mohammad Shah and Sikander Lodi. Also some believe that within the Bara Gumbad Mosque lie the remains of the unknown architect.

Lutyens's Imperial City. Near Lodi Tombs. See particularly the Sansad Bhavan and the Rashtrapati Bhavan (Presidential Palace). Entrance into the Rashtrapati requires permission (hard to get) from the Government of India Tourist Office.

Purana Qila. 3.2 km from Connaught Pl., off Mathura Rd. The ruins of this fifteenth-century fort constructed by the Afghan Sher Shah contain three imposing gateways. Inside is the octagonal red sandstone tower (Sher Mandal) that the Mogul Emperor Humayun used as his library, with the steep steps that became the instrument of his death—he slipped, fell, and died. Also see the Qila-i-Kuhna Masjid (Sher Shah's private mosque) built in Indo-Afghan style.

Qutab Minar. 14.4 km (9 miles) from Connaught Pl. in South Delhi. Construction of this 234-foot tower was begun in 1193 by Qutub-ud-din Aibak, was finished by his son-in-law, then redesigned in the 14th century by Firoze Shah TughlaK. Also see the Quwwat-ul-Islam Masjid nearby, the first Moslem mosque in Delhi and India, erected in the 12th century, with its Iron Pillar.

Raj Ghat. 4 km from Connaught Pl. on the banks of the Yamuna River. A square platform of polished black marble that marks the site where Mahatma Gandhi was cremated on Jan. 31, 1948.

Safdarjang's Tomb. 4.8 km (3 mi) from Connaught Pl. on Aurobindo Marg. The last Mogul mausoleum built in Delhi, constructed in 1753 by Nawab Shuja-ud-Daula for his father, Mirsa Shuja-ud-Daula (Safdarjang).

Tughlakabad. 5 km (3 mi) east of Qutab Minar. The ruins of Delhi's third capital begun in 1320 by Ghiyas-ud-din Tughlak. Thirteen gates of the fortress still guard the remains and the landscape; you can see the tomb of the capital's founder.

MUSEUMS AND GALLERIES. Crafts Museum. Bhairon Rd.; tel. 3317641. Terrific examples of traditional Indian crafts—folk and tribal arts from all over India. The museum spreads over an eight-acre complex and includes a crafts demonstration complex plus 15 structures that represent the village dwellings of various states in India. Inside these huts are the day-to-day cultural objects from the specific areas. The museum is open daily 10 A.M.–6 P.M.

Gandhi Museum. Opposite Raj Ghat; tel. 3310168. A display of some of Gandhi's personal possessions, plus a library. Open 9:30 A.M.–5:30 P.M.

National Gallery of Modern Art. Jaipur House India Gate, former residential palace of the Jaipur maharajah; tel. 382835. Exhibits the work of modern Indian artists: paintings, graphics, and sculpture. Open 10 A.M.–5 P.M., closed Mondays.

National Museum. Jan Path; tel. 3019538. Wide-ranging collection of India's and central Asia's artistic treasures, art and archaeology, anthropology, decorative art, calligraphy, and textiles. Among the Indian collections are 5,000-year-old relics of the Indus Valley civilization (Mohenjo-Daro, Harappa, and so forth). Brahmanical, Jain, and Buddhist sculptures in stone, bronze, and terra cotta of the early and medieval periods of Indian history. Good minatures of the Mogul, Rajput, Deccani, and Pahari schools, as well as earlier work. Among the old manuscripts, you can see the famous Gita Govinda and the profusely illustrated *Mahabharata;* the *Bhagavad Gita,* written and illuminated in golden ink; the miniature octagonal *Koran* and Mogul Emperor Babur's *Babarnama* in his handwriting. Temple hangings and brocaded saris, costumes from different parts of India, beautifully worked weapons, set with precious stones from the Mogul and earlier periods, ancient jewelry, and painted pottery are part of the collection. In addition, the Aurel Stein collection of antiquities he recovered during his explorations in central Asia and the western borders of China includes mural paintings from Buddhist shrines (some of the few examples removed from that area), silk paintings, and sculpture. Open 10 A.M.–5 P.M.; closed Mondays.

Nehru Memorial Museum. Teen Murti House on Teen Murti Marg; tel. 3015333. Official residence of Nehru, preserved as it was when he lived there—books, mementos, and pictures. 10 A.M.–5 P.M.; closed Mondays.

Rail Transport Museum. Shanti Path, Chanakyapuri; tel. 601816. A must for railway buffs. 26 vintage locomotives and numerous old carriages and saloon cars on 10 acres of track. A lot of fancy forms of transport that no longer race along the rails. Open 9:30 A.M.–5:30 P.M.; closed Mondays.

Red Fort Museum of Archaeology. Red Fort; tel. 3273703. Small historical collection devoted to the Mogul period. Exhibits consist of old arms, dresses, paintings, documents, and seals. Open 9 A.M.–5 P.M.; closed Fridays.

Tibet House Museum. Institutional Area, Lodi Rd.; tel. 611515. Open 10 A.M.– 5 P.M.; closed Sundays.

PARKS, GARDENS, ZOOS. Delhi has numerous lovely parks and gardens in which you can sit and watch the passing sights after too much big-city running around. They're open every day between sunrise and sunset, except when noted. Here are some of the best:

Children's Park, near India Gate, has nice walkways and good play equipment for the kids.

Deer Park, in the Chinkara complex near Hauz Khas, features deer and peacocks. It is a pleasant place to stop after seeing Qutab Minar.

Mughal Gardens, located in the Rashtrapati Bhavan estate, has red stone paths, fountains, and a lovely rose garden. This garden is open to the public only in February and March, when the flowers are in bloom. For permission to visit at that time, contact the Government of India Tourist Office.

Nehru Park, comprises 85 acres of walks and landscaping with rocks inscribed with remembered words of Jawaharlal Nehru. There are lots of birds and many lovely places just to sit.

Yamuna Waterfront, has Mogul-style gardens near the Raj Ghat, where Gandhi was cremated; the Shanti Vana, where Nehru was cremated; and the Vijay Ghat, where Prime Minister Shastri was cremated.

Delhi Zoo. Not a great modern zoo with lots of freedom for the animals, but, set against the Purana Qila (old fort), you get some pleasure just in walking around. Open 9:30 A.M.–4:30 P.M., closed Fridays.

PARTICIPANT SPORTS. Golf. Play golf against a backdrop of ancient monuments at *Delhi Golf Club,* Zakir Hussain Marg. Open 6 A.M.–3 P.M.; tel. 699239 or 362727 for reservations and details.

Horseback Riding. *Delhi Riding Club,* Safdarjang Road. For details, tel. 3011891.

Swimming. All deluxe and expensive hotels have swimming pools. Check hotel listings. The Imperial Hotel (tel. 3325332) allows nonguests to use its pool for a small fee.

SPECTATOR SPORTS. Delhi is a **polo** town, and just by virtue of its existence as capital of India, you'll find a **cricket** match somewhere almost anytime. For details about polo, call *Delhi Polo Club,* President's Estate, Rashtrapati Bhavan; tel. 3015604. For cricket matches, check the newspapers. Tickets may be hard to come by for some games at which the rivalry is intense.

THEATER, DANCE, MUSIC. For serious cultural events, Delhi is rich. Just open up the newspaper and find out what's happening where. Numerous auditoriums put on cultural events and many hotels have performers. Or just contact the Government of India Tourist Office to see what's doing. This is a great city in which to see good dance and theater and to hear some of India's finest musical performers.

RECOMMENDED READING. *Delhi Diary* (Rs. 5), a weekly small magazine available free in many hotels and at most newsstands, is excellent. It tells you what is happening; lists restaurants, hotels, shopping information; and has a handy, albeit limited, map in the back. It's small enough to fit in your pocket. If you're into shopping (and Delhi is a great shopping city), try to find a copy of *Explore and Shop in the Delhi Markets* by Colette Galas (about Rs. 60). The best bookstores (in the Connaught Pl. area): *Book Worm,* B–29 Connaught Pl.; *New Book Depot,* B–18, Connaught Pl.; *Oxford Book and Stationery Co.,* N-Block, Connaught Pl., excellent for books on India; *Piccadilly Book Stall,* Shop No. 64, Shankar Market, deceptive tiny-sized stall crammed with treasures, many out of print, on the occult, India, and neighboring countries. These bookstores are generally open 10 A.M.–6 P.M., closed Sundays.

SHOPPING. Delhi is the marketplace for all of India; shopping can be fun, and bargaining is the rule, except at fixed-price shops. Go for a 30–50 percent reduction from the first price they give you. Walk away. Let them chase after you. It's part of the game. Besides the *Central Cottage Industries Emporium,* on Janpath (open 10 A.M.–6 P.M.; closed on Sundays), which has every handicraft of India somewhere under its roof, also visit the *State Emporia,* a string of shops on Baba Kharak Singh Marg. The state shops are also closed on Sundays and take a lunch break usually 1:30–2:30 P.M. The better shops on Connaught Place take a lunch break during that time and observe Sundays as a day of rest. Also visit the new boutiques in *Hauz Khas Village* (open 10:30 A.M.–6 P.M., closed Sundays). Central Cottage Industries Emporium, some of the State Emporia, and many fixed-price stores accept credit cards.

Another extremely good shopping area in Delhi is *Sunder Nagar Market* (closed Sundays), near Oberoi Inter-Continental. In particular, visit these shops:

The Studio (4 Sunder Nagar) sells excellent contemporary silver jewelry.

Ladakh Art Gallery (10 Sunder Nagar) has a great collection of old silver jewelry.

Padma Gems Jewellers (9–A Sunder Nagar) sells exquisite gold and silver jewelry, including semiprecious and precious stones.

Kumar Gallery (11 Sunder Nagar) specializes in original tribal statues, old dhurries and Tibetan carpets, miniatures, Tanjore and Mysore paintings, and temple art.

Also visit these other reputable stores in Delhi:

For silk: *Banaras House Limited,* N–13 Connaught Pl., and *Handloom House* (government run), 9–A Connaught Pl.; both shops close for lunch and close on Sundays.

For handmade shoes: Don't be lured by the shops on Connaught Pl.; Mr. Lee's your man to see—*K.K. Lee,* 30–B, Khan Market. He's reliable and honest; closed Sundays.

For the best *kurtas* and *chikan* work (hand embroidery): *Lal Behari Tandon,* 20 Palika Bazar (central hall); closed Sundays.

For silver jewelry, *Silver Moon,* 59 Palika Bazar, just behind the Central Hall; closed Sundays.

For tempting pure essence, *Jain Super Store,* 172 Palika Bazar, just off the Central Hall; closed Sundays.

For proenvironment products, including cleverly designed T-shirts, *People Tree,* 8 Regal Bldg., Parliament St.; closed Sundays.

For interesting ready-made clothes, from antique saris to exquisite sequin work: *Once Upon a Time,* 12 Hauz Khas Village; closed Sundays.

Wild Orchids, W/53 Greater Kailash II, sells classy salwar kamaz (blouses and pants) in a variety of silks and cottons. This shop can also design outfits for you. Closed Sundays.

NIGHTLIFE AND BARS. Delhi is a good place to see Indian classical dance or music. Regional dances are performed daily at *Parsi Anjuman Hall,* Bahadur Shah Zafar Marg, Delhi Gate. Shows start at 6:30 P.M. For details, call tel. 3275978 or 3317831. Also check with your hotel or the tourist office for other special performances. All the major hotels have bars; check listings under *Hotels.* The classiest of these are at the *Oberoi;* sedate and elegant. Most hotel bars are open from lunch until late at night.

THE PUNJAB AND HARYANA

Sikhs, Hindus, and Mountain Shrines

by
KATHLEEN COX

Note: Because of sporadic incidents of political violence in the Punjab, the U.S. State Department advises Americans to exercise special caution in the state; especially avoid traveling by bus or train to or through the Punjab.

For centuries, the Punjab, the northwest border state of India, has been the scene of communal strife pitting Moslem against Hindu. In the mid-1500s, around the time of Babur, a new movement began that initially gave rise to the hope of a peaceful future. A Punjabi Hindu, Baba Nanak, began to preach a new gospel—a fusion of the best of Hinduism and Islam—a gospel that spurned the notion of castes and the worship of idols. Nanak developed a following, a title—Guru (*gu:* one who dispels darkness, by teaching enlightenment: *ru*)—and numerous disciples called Sikhs. By 1708, the Sikhs had their own city, Amritsar, with its beautiful Golden Temple, their headquarters.

Unfortunately, communalism flared up anew. As the relationship between Islam and Sikhism soured, the Sikhs turned militant. Communalism continued into the twentieth century, erupting finally into a wholesale slaughter of Hindus, Sikhs, and Moslems during the post–World War II partitioning. As Hindus and Sikhs tried to flee Moslem Pakistan for India

95

and Moslems tried to flee India for Pakistan, an estimated 500,000 were killed.

The Punjab still suffers from religious intolerance. Only now, instead of Hindus and Sikhs against Moslems, the hostility rages between Hindus and Sikhs—with disastrous consequences. The Golden Temple was stormed and seriously damaged, Indira Gandhi was assassinated, and relations between Pakistan and India were strained (India considers Pakistan a training ground and refuge for Sikh terrorists). Fear grips the people who are caught in the struggle of the Sikh extremists, who want their people, a minority, to have their own Sikh state called Khalistan.

For all these reasons, travel to the Punjab is ill advised. For a vicarious trip under these circumstances—or if differences between the groups are settled—the following information can serve as your guide.

The Golden Temple of Amritsar

Amritsar was founded in 1579 by Ram Das, the fourth teacher (guru) of the Sikh religion (the Sikhs have had 10 gurus), as a central place of worship for the followers of his faith. He constructed a pool, the "Pool of Nectar" (which is what Amritsar means) and planned the temple that his son and successor expanded.

Known as the Golden Temple (Darbar Sahib), it is the glory of Amritsar and the nucleus of Sikh worship. The pool is surrounded by a pavement of white marble, and the temple itself is reached by a marble causeway. Its bronze plates, heavily covered with pure gold leaf, burn in the tropical sun and flash their light in piercing gleams while their reflection in the still waters leaps up at you. Over the whole there reigns a stillness, a power of peace that seems to stem from that uplift that inhales the cosmic *prana* (breath) of the universe. The Sikhs believe that prana is expressed through the environment of the physical world, and the serenity that permeates the temple feeds the adept with the celestial food they need to conquer doubt, disease, and even death. In the Sanctuary, under a canopy, lies the *Granth Sahib,* the sacred book of the Sikhs, which is read from time to time by a priest to the accompaniment of devotional music.

The buildings around the Sacred Tank shelter pilgrims who come to worship from distant places. The Akal Takht (the Immortal Throne) is the supreme seat of Sikh religious authority and contains several relics. Incidentally, the only restriction imposed on those who visit these sacred places is that they must remove their shoes. As is the way with mosques and shrines, slippers are provided, but here no charge is made and no donation is accepted. The gardens that surround the Baba Atal Tower— richly painted with frescoes depicting scenes from the life of Guru Nanak—are of a strange and wistful beauty. The whole is impregnated with an energy that typifies the soul of the Sikh.

Haryana

Haryana has a minimal share of attractions, but it has roadside tourist conveniences (à la Howard Johnson motels) that put the state ahead of the rest of the country.

Take the Grand Trunk Road from Delhi, the start of a journey north to Chandigarh, the joint capital of the Punjab and Haryana. The first point of interest is Panipat, a sprawling industrial city with numerous architectural reminders of decisive battles that changed the fate of India. Just outside the city, you can see the Kabuli Bagh Mosque, built by Babur to commemorate his victory in 1526 over Ibrahim Lodi, king of Delhi—a victory that gave birth to the Mogul Empire. You can also visit the tomb of the vanquished Lodi, who lost his life as well as his kingdom during the decisive battle.

The next attraction on the road is Kurukshetra, where the epic battle described in the *Mahabharata* was supposedly fought. Another legend claims that under an ancient spreading banyan tree, Krishna delivered his sermon of Bhagavad Gita. And, finally, a dip in Kurukshetra's sacred tank, especially during a solar eclipse, has an unbelievable redeeming effect, or so it is claimed.

Chandigarh, a few miles north, is either an urban planner's dream or a futuristic blight, depending on your point of view. An old city it is not! In fact, if you've traveled through India for a few weeks before arriving here, Chandigarh is bound to astonish you. Where are the bullock carts, roadside stalls, and bustling produce markets? You might even think, Where is India? But it's right before your eyes. Chandigarh is always described as Le Corbusier's city (Le Corbusier contributed to the design of the United Nations), but Chandigarh is more accurately the creation of Nehru. At the time of partition, when the greater part of the Punjab, including its graceful capital Lahore, fell to Pakistan, a new capital had to be found—or created. A site was chosen under the Siwalki Hills, with two small rivers flowing on either side. This site was Chandigarh, and, according to an enthusiastic Nehru, who was prime minister at the time, the new capital would be "a new town, symbolic of the freedom of India, unfettered by the traditions of the past."

The city is divided into 47 sectors. Each one is 800 by 2,200 meters (2,640 by 7,260 feet)—a self-contained unit for living with housing, marketing, schools, and banks. It's all there. Building height, population density, traffic flow—all have been considered. To some visitors this may sound like a vision out of *Brave New World*, but Chandigarh must be viewed within the context of India. It is, and should be, a source of pride—living evidence that India doesn't see itself confined to confusion, poverty, crushing crowds, heartwrenching contrasts, and improvised solutions that often characterize urban life in many of its great cities. In this sense, Chandigarh is as much a symbol as a specific place. And though living life in a symbol may not be everyone's dream, Chandigarh is well worth visiting and knowing.

A few of the specifics about Chandigarh: Get yourself a map from the tourist office. Sector 1 is the Capital Complex, featuring Secretariat, Assembly, High Court, and Open Hand Monument (which resembles Picasso's dove of peace). Because of political tensions, entry into the buildings is restricted. Sector 10 is the Museum and Art Gallery, with a good collection of contemporary Indian art. Sector 14 is the Punjab University campus. The Gandhi Bhawan here is perhaps the most elegant building in the city. Designed by Pierre Janerat, Le Corbusier's cousin, it is a gem of a building, small and shaped like an open lotus blossom. Sector 16 is the Zakir Rose Garden, supposedly the largest such garden in all Asia, extending over 30 acres with 1,500 varieties of roses.

Nek Chand's Rock Garden

It's ironic and wonderful that Chandigarh, the totally planned city, should have spawned this spectacular homage to imagination and intuitive construction—the Rock Garden located on the edge of Sector 1. Some 30 years ago, Nek Chand (the name means "benign moon") was a Public Works Department official whose job was to inspect roads and write maintenance reports. As he went about his work, he began collecting rocks, stones, and refuse that people dumped along the roadside. Soon, he began assembling his bits of junk—tiles, torn clothes, broken bangles, shards of glass, electric and plumbing fixtures—into a vision, his "kingdom of the gods and goddesses." Without the knowledge of any of Chandigarh's city planners, Nek Chand's Rock Garden took shape on the edge of the city. Chand had absolutely no artistic training when he embarked on his project, and, even today, he shrugs when the discussion turns to art. Yet, Nek Chand's talent was recognized early by the Indian government. Land was set aside for his project, and he was given several assistants to help bring his dream to life.

Visiting the Rock Garden today, you'll enter a low Alice-in-Wonderland entranceway ("it is good to bow down when you enter the kingdom of the gods and goddesses") and walk along a winding path through a series of environments. You'll see waterfalls, pools, imaginary forests, and miniature villages. You'll go up steps, around corners, and stoop under several more arches. Wherever you go, you'll be in the midst of hundreds of delightful figures—humans and animals—fashioned from recycled junk. Americans who are acquainted with the work of Red Grooms will have an idea of what to expect. But whereas Red Grooms is a sophisticated self-conscious artist using the idiom of naif art, Nek Chand is the real McCoy.

That the Rock Garden is in a state of perpetual expansion seems altogether appropriate. The garden is so filled with the energy of life that it does one good to know that it is alive and growing. Nek Chand has been honored throughout the world (including a Fantasy Garden in Washington D.C., which he supervised), but in all likelihood, he'll be in the Rock Garden when you visit. His office is a cozy rock grotto that any Hobbit would gladly call home. You might think Nek Chand is a simple man, but once you've seen his elaborate fantasy kingdom, you'll realize that he's a man with a vision—and the skill and perseverance to execute it. He is a rare individual who gave Chandigarh a gift that neither Nehru nor Le Corbusier could provide—a spirit of gaiety, surprise, and love—a testament of faith in the uniqueness and eccentricity of human beings. Nek Chand gave India's determinedly modern city a bit of personality.

PRACTICAL INFORMATION FOR
THE PUNJAB AND HARYANA

WHEN TO GO. October–March is the time to visit the Punjab and Haryana. They're both *very hot* in the summer.

HOW TO GET THERE. To travel through Haryana to Chandigarh, you can go by air, train, bus, or car. Travel through the Punjab in a train or bus, however, is risky. These vehicles are the frequent target of terrorists.

By Air. *Indian Airlines* has four weekly flights to Chandigarh from Delhi, Jammu, and Srinagar, and two weekly flights from Leh. Vayudoot has 24 weekly flights to Chandigarh from Delhi, a daily flight from Kullu, four weekly flights from Shimla, and three weekly flights from Dharamsala. For information, contact Indian Airlines (tel. 28722) and Vayudoot (c/o Shivalik Travel, tel. 44996).

By Car. Chandigarh is 248 km (154 mi) from Delhi by very good roads; 380 km (236 mi) from Jammu; and 119 km (74 mi) from Shimla. Figure about Rs. 5 per km and a night halt charge of Rs. 50–Rs. 100. Use a tour operator recommended in the Delhi, Jammu and Kashmir, and Himachal Pradesh chapters.

TOURIST INFORMATION. Tourists are advised to go to one of the following tourist departments on their arrival in Chandigarh to get a good map and information.

Chandigarh Tourist Office (General Bus Stand, Sector 17; tel. 22548) has good information on Chandigarh.

Haryana Tourism (No. 17–18–19, Sector 17–B, Chandigarh, 160017, tel. 21955) also has good information on its state. Offices are open Mon.–Fri., 10 A.M.–5 P.M. and Sat., 10 A.M.–1 P.M.

FOREIGN CURRENCY EXCHANGE. Most Western-style hotels have money-exchange counters, as do branches of the *State Bank of India,* open Mon.–Fri. 10 A.M.–2 P.M., Sat. 10 till noon.

ACCOMMODATIONS. Chandigarh has adequate hotels; however, most have a dreary mall setting: large buildings that front a parking lot. The rest of Haryana has numerous roadside stops (named after birds) that offer travelers rest and relaxation. These modern facilities, run by Haryana Tourism, are extremely good value. Expect a spacious, clean room with a contemporary decor, a multicuisine restaurant, and room service. The better-quality rooms have TV and air-conditioning. Additional amenities are noted in each listing. Prices are based on double occupancy and exclude taxes and service charges: *Moderate,* Rs. 500–Rs. 1,200; and *Inexpensive,* under Rs. 500.

CHANDIGARH

Moderate

Hotel Chandigarh Mountview. Sector 10, Chandigarh 160010; tel. 45882. 33 rooms with bath. This three-story Western-style hotel has an attractive lawn and spacious modern rooms. Amenities include air-conditioning, TV, room service, multicuisine restaurant/bar, foreign-exchange counter. AE, DC, MC, V.

Hotel President. Madhya Marg, Sector 26, Chandigarh 160022; tel. 40840. 20 rooms with bath. Despite its dreary shopping-mall environment, this Western-style hotel has modern rooms that are spacious and clean. Air-conditioning, TV, room service, multicuisine restaurants, bar, health club, foreign-exchange and travel counters, secretarial service. AE, DC, MC, V.

Quality Inn Mehfil. Block 10, Sector 17, Chandigarh 160017, tel. 43501. 120 rooms with bath. Scheduled to open in 1993, this new high rise, set on spacious grounds, will have good-size rooms with air-conditioning and a contemporary decor. TV, room service, multicuisine restaurants, bar, swimming pool, health club, foreign exchange and travel counters. AE, DC, MC, V.

Except for the hotel in Surajkund, the following Haryana Tourism hotels are *Inexpensive.*

AMBALA
55 km (34 mi.) from Chandigarh

Kingfisher. District Ambala, Haryana; tel. 58352. 12 rooms with attached bath. The Kingfisher has a health club, swimming pool, and bar. Rupees only.

BADKHAL LAKE
32 km (20 mi.) from Delhi

Badkhal Lake. Badkhal Village, District Faridabad; tel. 26900. 29 rooms with bath and 8 camper huts with bath. This lake-side complex is 5 km (3 mi.) from the Delhi-Agra Highway, with a swimming pool, steam bath, massage, boating, and fishing. Rupees only.

HODAL
92 km (57 mi.) from Delhi

Dabchick. Hodal, District Faridabad; tel. 91. 8 rooms with bath in a motel and 8 rooms in cottages. This complex on the Delhi-Agra Highway has a bar as well as camel, horse, and elephant rides, plus a snake charmer. Rupees only.

PINJORE
22 km (14 mi.) from Chandigarh

Yadavindra Gardens. District Ambala; tel. 2855. 19 rooms with bath. This complex, near the Mogul-designed Pinjore Gardens, is on National Highway No. 22. It has a bar, shops, bank, minizoo, children's park, Japanese gardens, and camel rides. Rupees only.

SULTANPUR
46 km (29 mi.) from Delhi

Sultanpur Bird Sanctuary. District Gurgaon; tel. 42. Two rooms and eight huts with bath. This complex, near National Highway No. 8, has a bar and is ideal for bird-watching. Rupees only.

SURAJKUND
8 km (5 mi.) from South Delhi

Hotel Rajhans. District Faridabad; tel. 6830766. 76 rooms with bath. The Rajhans has a health club, along with swimming pool, golf course, tennis court, horseback riding, cycling, and a lake. MC, V. *Inexpensive–Moderate.*

UCHANA
124 km (77 mi.) from Delhi

Karna Lake. District Karna; tel. 4279. 19 rooms with bath. This complex on National Highway No. 1 has a bar, shop, and facilities for boating and fishing. Rupees only.

DINING OUT. Since most people pass through Haryana on their way to another destination, this state has wisely chosen to provide excellent eateries along the national highways that lead from Delhi to Agra, Jaipur, Chandigarh, and farther north. These Indian-style Howard Johnsons are open until very late or 24 hours. The multicuisine food and service are good; prices, per person for a three-course meal, excluding taxes, tip, or beverage, are *Inexpensive,* under Rs. 100. Payment is in rupees. In Chandigarh, the best meals (less than Rs. 200) are served in the hotels. Breakfast is usually served 8–10:30 A.M.; lunch, noon–3 P.M.; and dinner, 7:30–10 P.M.

SWEETS AND TREATS. In Chandigarh, stop at the **Indian Coffee House,** Sector 22, for good south Indian snacks and coffee. **Sindhi Sweets** (two shops in Sector 17) creates a vast array of desserts and milk drinks. Try Karachi halwa, made of *ghee* (clarified butter), nuts, and arrowroot. It has the color and consistency of apricot taffy—delicious! Or try *keser milk badam* (ice-cold milk laced with crushed cashews, pistachios, and seasonings).

HOW TO GET AROUND. From the Airport. Unmetered taxis charge Rs. 100–Rs. 150 between the Chandigarh airport and the city. Bargain!
By Taxi. Unmetered taxis charge a flat fee (about Rs. 40) from one sector of the city to another.
By Auto Rickshaw. Auto rickshaws are metered. Fare: about Rs. 3 for the first 1.5 km and Rs. 1 for every part thereof, with a waiting charge of 50 paise for every eight minutes; plus a 7 percent surcharge on the overall meter reading.

By Cycle Rickshaw. Cycle rickshaws will also pedal you around Chandigarh. Fares: negotiable, with a minimum sector-to-sector fare of Rs. 2.

By Bus. Due to the communal problems in Haryana and the Punjab, buses have become a dangerous way to travel.

TOURS. *Chandigarh Tourism* conducts tours in deluxe buses and eight-seater Matador vans in and around Chandigarh and Haryana. For details contact them at Hotel Chandigarh Mountview, Sector 10 (tel. 45882), or *Chandigarh Tourist Information Office,* General Bus Stand, Sector 17 (tel. 22548). The following tours are available at reasonable rates: Local sightseeing; Chatbir Zoo; Pinjore Gardens; Pinjore Gardens via Mansa Devi; Pinjore Gardens via Nada Sahib; Mansa Devi; Bhakra Dam, Nagal, Gobind Sagar Lake, Ropar Boat Club, and Anandpur Sahib shrine.

TOUR OPERATORS. For all travel needs, including a car with driver, use an agency recommended in the Delhi chapter, above.

SEASONAL EVENTS. Feb. 1–15. *Surajkund Crafts Mela.* This two-week fair at an ethnic village in Surajkund, 8 km (5 mi.) from South Delhi, brings together some of India's finest artisans, who sell their products and show you how they're created. You can also see dance and music performances. A wonderful event! **February–March.** *Rose Festival.* The Zakir Rose Garden in Chandigarh holds an annual two-day rose festival. Contact the tourist department for the exact date.

HISTORIC SITES. Important monuments and temples in Punjab and Haryana are generally open daily from sunrise to sunset. Entrance is usually free; where a donation is requested, a few rupees will suffice.

Amritsar. *Darbar Sahib* (Golden Temple). Founded in 1579, this marble temple is the most important Sikh shrine in India. Remember to remove your shoes before entering.

Panipat. *Kabuli Bagh Mosque.* Built by the Mogul Emperor Babur, this mosque commemorates a victory that launched the Mogul era in the subcontinent.

Kurukshetra. At Jyotisar under a banyan tree, the Hindu god Krishna supposedly delivered the sermon of the Bhagavad Gita.

MUSEUM AND GALLERY. Chandigarh. *Government Museum and Art Gallery* (Sector 10, tel. 25568) has an excellent collection of contemporary paintings and sculpture, plus old miniature paintings from the Kangra, Rajasthani, and Mogul schools. Open 10 A.M.–4:30 P.M., closed Monday. Nominal entrance fee.

PARKS AND GARDENS. *Leisure Valley* in Chandigarh is a 300-acre sprawl that runs through the length of the city and is filled with untouched greenery and gardens. The most famous is the Zakir Rose Garden, named after the late President Zakir Hussain. Located in Sector 16, the garden is the biggest in Asia, with 1,500 varieties planted over 30 acres. *Rock Garden* is the creation of Nek Chand, built out of rocks and whatever refuse he found. The garden covers six acres and is still a work in progress. Entry fee: Rs. 1. Summer: 9 A.M.–1 P.M.; 3–7 P.M. Winter: 9 A.M.–1 P.M.; 2–6 P.M.

The Pinjore (Yadavindra) Gardens are the former great Mogul gardens designed by Nawab Fidai Khan, the architect for Emperor Aurangzeb in the 17th century. Open every day. Motel accommodations are available.

ZOO. *Chattbir Zoo,* on the Chandigarh-Patiala Road, has Bengal tigers, Himalayan black bears, and birds galore. Open every day. Entry fee: Rs. 1.

SPORTS. Fishing on Sukhna Lake, Chandigarh. Rs. 3 per day. Contact Lake Club, Sector 1 (tel. 26661). You can **golf** at Haryana Tourism's nine-hole course at Hotel Raj Hans, Surajkund, 8 km (5 mi.) south of Delhi. Call tel. 6830766.

BARS. Most of the hotels have bars, but the *Suroor Bar* at the Hotel Pankaj, Sector 22, is probably the closest you'll come to visiting a downtown New York City bar. Everything is modern, minimal, and carefully lighted. Where else, but in Le Corbusier's city of tomorrow?

UTTAR PRADESH

Abode of the Gods

by
KATHLEEN COX

Although smaller in size than Britain, the state of Uttar Pradesh has 20 million more inhabitants. Before Independence, *Zamindars,* absentee landowners, lorded over the peasantry, usually exploiting them mercilessly. Former tenant-farmers are now small landholders, but they still have to cope with the lack of equipment, enormous families, and sometimes unsympathetic officials. They find solace in religion; two of the holiest rivers meet at Allahabad—the Yamuna (or Jumma) and the Ganges (or Ganga). At the *sangam*—their confluence—India's biggest religious bathing festival, the Magh Mela, is held each spring. Every twelfth year, on an auspicious date that is chosen by astrologers, millions converge on the riverbanks in Haridwar and Allahabad to join in the Kumbh Mela, an even more important ritual to the devout.

It was along the Ganges and Yamuna that the first Aryans made advances into India, calling their newly won territory Aryavarta ("Land of the Aryans"). It was the kings of this valley who fought in the Great Battle recorded in the *Mahabharata.* It was in the foothill area (in present-day Nepal) that Siddhartha Gautama, a prince of the Sakyamuni clan and the man who became the Historic Buddha, was born.

The Gangetic plain served as a pivot to the Mauryan Empire, whose most outstanding figures were Chandragupta and Ashoka. Harsha of

Kanauj made himself master of northern India in the seventh century, and the region remained Hindu until Mahmud of Ghazni invaded and captured the imperial city in 1019. For at least 500 years, Moslem dynasties ruled over north India. Then, in the eighteenth century, when the Mogul Empire began its decline, the British East India Company—with Calcutta as its base—moved to expand its control, which finally led to the battle of Buxar (1764). The work of British conquest was now under way and a few months later when Robert Clive, founder of British India, returned to India, he reported: "It is scarcely a hyperbole to say that tomorrow the whole Mogul empire is in our power."

EXPLORING UTTAR PRADESH

Leaving Delhi, bypass Meerut, a small city known as the cradle of that memorable insurrection, the Indian Mutiny of 1857–58, commonly referred to as India's First War of Independence. The British governor-general's order of 1856 that all units were liable for overseas service upset the Indian troops, since, by Hindu religious law, those who leave their native land become outcasts. The Indians, especially the sepoy regiments, predominantly high-caste Rajputs, were offended by the British blunder and interpreted it as a deliberate act of religious intolerance.

Just a spark would trigger the move for sedition. This the British government provided the next year; it rearmed the troops with a new rifle that required a greased cartridge. The grease was rumored to be cow's fat, defiling the Hindu who touched it. The grease was also rumored to be pig's fat, which outraged Moslem soldiers. Insubordination burst into open rebellion at the Meerut garrison. The Indians shot their officers and then marched on Delhi to transfer their allegiance to the Mogul emperor's descendant, who still kept his court and imperial title. This revolt, which can be regarded as the initial stirring of a nationalist movement, lasted several months. Although it didn't spread beyond the confines of northern India, it resulted in grim battles and the liquidation of the East India Company. The British Crown took over, but the mood was never again the same.

ALIGARH, KANAUJ, AND KANPUR

For centuries a Rajput fortress, Aligarh lost its independence to the Moguls at the beginning of the sixteenth century. Then, in the middle of the eighteenth century, Afghans, Jats, and Marathas fought over Aligarh. In 1803, during the Maratha occupation, the Aligarh fort was reputed to be impregnable. Finally, in the second Maratha War, Aligarh was captured by the British. The massive fort, heavily involved in these events, lies four kilometers (2½ miles) north of Aligarh.

Today a small town on the Ganges, Kanauj was for many centuries the Hindu capital of northern India—a city of wealth and beauty, of fine temples and shining palaces. Its prestige remained until the Moslem invasion of the eleventh century. Ransacked and ruined, Kanauj passed into oblivion. Little remains of its ancient glories, except the melancholy ruins of a few ramparts and temples.

Some 81 kilometers (50 miles) farther is Kanpur—the Pittsburgh of India—one of India's great industrial cities, created by trade and manufacturing. Tragic events took place here at the time of the 1857 Indian Muti-

UTTAR PRADESH

0　　miles　　50

0　　km　　50

HIMACHAL
PRADESH

CHINA

HARYANA

Yamunotri

Mussoorie

Dehru Dun

Rishikesh

Haridwar

Gangotri

Kedarnath

DELHI

Badrinath

RAJASTHAN

Ganges River

Joshimath

Corbett National Park

Mathura

Nainital

Fatehpur
Sikri

Agra

Bareilly

Gwalior

Ganges River

Dudhwa
National
Park

N

NEPAL

Sitapur

Kanpur

Lucknow

Sravasti

Ayodhya

Gorakhpur

Allahabad

Kasia

Sarnath

Varanasi

MADHYA
PRADESH

Ganges
River

BIHAR

ny—the equally heroic exploits of Tantia Topi, the Indian fighter, and the defense of Wheeler's entrenchment, which ended in the massacre of British citizens.

LUCKNOW

Far less industrialized than neighboring Kanpur, Lucknow has a population of more than a million, including a good portion of Shiite and Sunni Moslems living among Hindu neighbors. Lucknow is the eighteenth-century capital of the Persian sheiks, called Nawab Wazirs, who originally arrived in Avadh (Lucknow and surrounding territory) during Emperor Akbar's reign in the 1500s. Over time, successive Mogul rulers, whose own fortunes were on the decline, granted the nawabs more and more power.

For a time, the nawab capital was in Faizabad, but around 1775, Asafud Daula, the fourth nawab, shifted his seat of power to Lucknow. His charity and perhaps megalomania endowed Lucknow with some of the best of its architecturally rich and sometimes outlandish structures, which are located near the left bank of the River Gomti in the northern part of the capital. Asaf's munificence was real and ingenious.

Bara Imambara

In 1784, after a year of life-threatening famine that affected everyone regardless of status, Asaf began the construction of the Bara Imambara, his relief project. He divided the starving into two distinct work forces: the poor who built by day and the rich who destroyed by night. Obviously, this arrangement retarded forward momentum. But the nawab wanted to extend the time of employment to keep paying the poor. Besides, the poor outnumbered the formerly rich and the rich weren't such hot demolition experts.

The Imambara stands directly behind two elaborate gateways. The outer gate, where musicians used to play, is on the opposite side of the public road, which unfortunately cuts the original perspective; the inner gate is purely for symmetry. Once you enter the second gate, Asaf's mosque, with its 47-meter (152-foot) minarets, stands to the right; a row of cloisters that supposedly conceals a bottomless well is on the left.

The Imambara (tomb) is built with clay and brick—no cement or iron; and wood is used in the interior only for decoration. The walls are 5 meters (16 feet) thick but of hollow construction, and the roof is 3 meters (10 feet) thick. Throughout the structure, there are no supporting beams or pillars. An ingenious distribution of weight holds up the ceiling on each floor.

The ground floor is divided into three halls. To the extreme left is an octagonal chamber of Chinese design. Its Chinese saucer-shaped ceiling has a 67-meter (216-foot) dome that extends up to the third floor. The priest sat on his throne (the original, which was of gold and sandalwood, was stolen and replaced with silver) in this room and addressed his devotees. The middle chamber features a ceiling whose shape is an inverted boat. Measuring 50 meters (162 feet) long, 16 meters (53 feet) wide, and 16 meters (50 feet) high, this hall is the largest in the world. A gallery extends around the upper story from which the harem viewed the events below. The nawab and the Imambara's architect are buried in the center of the room. The numerous mirrors are collected from assorted nawab palaces. The chamber to the right is of Indian design.

As you leave the Imambara, notice on the left a small paper replica of a shrine (*tazia*), made and replaced annually for the woman who, reported-

ly, on receiving the word from God, gave the land to the nawab who had
been badgering her for years to sell it. She relented, but only on condition
that he construct this tazia in her honor. No one knows her name or what
happened to her. Originally, tazias were constructed of wax that mysteriously refused to melt after hours in the sun. Now only one man understands this delicate craft, but he, too, is awaiting the word of God before
he reveals his secret.

From outside the Imambara, a set of stairs leads up to an extraordinary
labyrinth called Bhul Bhulaiya, which came about as a result of the building design required to support the ceilings. Try to find your way around.
Every 20 steps or so leads to an intersection with four choices, three of
which lead nowhere (here's a secret: think right). Guides do a brisk "es-
cort" business. From the rooftop there's a great view of Lucknow.

Chhota Imambara

The Chhota Imambara, or Hussainabad Imambara, was built in 1836
by the Muhammad Ali Shan, the eighth nawab, as his burial place. A fish
as a weathervane, just inside the gate, may seem odd, but the fish is auspicious in Hindu and Moslem mythology; its presence is a good omen. The
chain that leads to the statue of the woman, at the left of the entrance,
is no act of whimsy either. It served then and now as a lightning rod to
protect the statue and the building from storms.

The tiny mosque on the right was for women. The next building on the
right as you walk along the channel that leads to the Chhota is a burial
tomb for the nawab's daughter, Zinat Asuja, and is a miniature replica
of the Taj Mahal. The building directly across from it, which holds her
husband's remains, was originally planned for symmetry.

The Chhota, with its gilded dome and vast number of turrets and minarets, is almost baroque. Its handsome black-and-white facade is, in fact,
a vast collection of verses from the Quran. Inside, you are confronted by
a dazzling collection of mirrors, chandeliers, and lamps. The tall red-and-
white lamp near the middle of the floor, with its 500 moving pieces, was
purchased by the nawab in 1836. The center chandelier in the entry room
has 1,000 moving pieces. Here, too, you'll see a vast collection of tazias.
Also on the left-hand wall, as you face the entrance, you'll see an extremely
old print in blue lettering on white; it contains the entire Quran.

Jama Masjid, Picture Gallery

To the west of the Chhota is the elegant Jama Masjid, started by Muhammad Ali Shah and completed after his death. This royal mosque of
the nawabs, closed to non-Moslems, is a lovely long building crowded by
three onion-shaped domes and flanked by two lofty minarets.

For a glimpse of the fancy men who ruled over Lucknow, visit the Picture Gallery (originally a building built by Muhammad Ali Shah), reflecting into a pool of water and surrounded by a grove. It's a portrait gallery
that could be called the Nawab Hall of Fame.

The Residency

Toward the heart of Lucknow stands the Residency, the battle-scarred
remains of Asaf-ud Daula's other elaborate architectural contribution.
Originally conceived as a pleasure house with a network of underground
chambers that provided relief from the summer heat, it was acquired by
the British when they annexed the province and deposed and deported

the last nawab, Wajid Ali Shah. That act sealed the fate of this building. During the 1857 Indian Mutiny, British inhabitants crowded into the elegant building, which then became the scene of some of the fiercest fighting. For 87 days, the British held out until Sir Colin Campbell broke through the Indian lines and relieved the half-starved defenders. Of the 3,000 troops and noncombatants who had refused to surrender, fewer than 1,000 staggered out. Although the marks of cannon shots gouge every remaining wall, the surrounding gardens and lawns are kept in order. Peace and goodwill prevail; unpleasant memories lie buried with the past.

Tombs

In the center of Lucknow are the perfectly proportioned tombs of Nawab Saadat Ali Khan and his wife, Begum Mursheedzadi, built in the beginning of the nineteenth century. The Kaisar Bagh adjoining the tombs contains rows of apartments that housed the ladies of the royal harem. Near the river is Shahnajaf Imambara, which derives its name from Najaf, a city in Iraq. It is the early nineteenth century tomb of Nabob Ghazi-ud-din Haider and his wives, including Mubarak Mahal (a European). This building, constructed in 1814, was a stronghold for independence fighters in 1857. Like the Residency, what you see today—its low frontage and large flattened-out dome—defuses an atmosphere of great turmoil.

La Martiniere

On the outskirts of the city, in a park close to a small lake, rises a Rococo structure built in 1795, not by a nawab but by a Frenchman, Claude Martin, during the reign of Asaf-ud Daula. Nothing is missing in this compendium of styles; gargoyles rub shoulders with Corinthian columns and Roman arches are next to Oriental turrets. This fantastic hodgepodge was designed as a boys' school, with Kipling's protégé for *Kim* a student.

Chowk

The Chowk is the bazaar in the old city of Lucknow, where the Moslem servants of the nawabs originally lived. Note the architectural detail of many of the buildings: stone lacework along the upper stories, later 1920s and '30s style facades that add up to a curious blend. Once you enter the main gate, you hit the bustle of the bazaar—rows and rows of silver and jewelry merchants, shops and stalls selling hand-embroidered *chikan* work. The former haunt of the nawab feudal aristocracy, ancestral dwellings abound, some still inhabited by old-time families. Here, gracious nawab manners still persist, and you sense the eighteenth-century charm that existed when Lucknow was the center of culture and refinement.

ALLAHABAD

In ancient times Allahabad, which is at the confluence of the Ganges and Yamuna rivers, was known as Prayag. It was and still is an important place of Hindu pilgrimage. By the end of the twelfth century, Prayag fell under Moslem rule and in 1584 was given its new name.

The Patal Puri Temple lies underneath an enormous fort built by the Mogul Emperor Akbar. Descending a long sloping passage, you see a tree in the dim square-shaped hall. This tree, watered continuously by the priests, was mentioned by the Chinese traveler Hsuan Tsang in 640 and is known as Akshaya Batt, the Undying Banyan Tree. Another shrine of tremendous importance to Hindus is Bharadwaja. Named after the great sage who occupied a hermitage on the high bank overlooking the place where the waters meet, it is mentioned in the *Ramayana*. Bharadwaja had 10,000 pupils, and, as the head of a clan, he provided his students with free board and lodging. His *ashram* became a cross between a seat of learning and a welfare institution. Now Allahabad University occupies this site.

Akbar's Fort and Mogul Monuments

Akbar's Fort is an impressive work of masonry. It houses an Ashoka Pillar, a single shaft of polished sandstone 35 feet high. Its capital disappeared during its 2,200 years of existence, but it still shows some of the edicts the emperor inscribed around its base—even though Jahangir's inscriptions of his family tree partially obliterated them. The mausoleum of Prince Khusrao, Emperor Jahangir's eldest son, is covered with paintings and a Persian verse that ends with a chronogram giving the Moslem year of 1031 (A.D. 1622) as the date of his death.

If you're in Allahabad during the Magh Mela, held each spring at the confluence of the two rivers, don't miss the ceremonies. Bundle-laden pilgrims in the thousands arrive each day, setting up tents and makeshift huts. Holy men lie on beds of nails or read out scriptures to worshipers before they take the ritual plunge. Rows of barbers shave the heads of pilgrims to comply with orthodox precepts that bald is the beatific best. Hindu women throw rose petals and marigolds into the holy river as offerings. Improvised stalls sell food, souvenirs, and images of deities. There are no bathing *ghats* (riverbank steps), and most pilgrims are rowed by innumerable boats into mid-river to perform their immersion.

Allahabad is famous for its literary traditions. The Sahitya Sammalan is a pioneer institution for the study of the Hindi language. Outside the city, the ancestral home of the late Jawaharlal Nehru, called Anand Bhavan (Place of Joy), is now a museum set up in his memory. Next to it stands Swaraj Bhavan (House of Freedom), which he donated to the nation in 1930 as a children's home.

FAIZABAD AND AYODHYA

On leaving Lucknow, go due east and you will arrive at Faizabad, capital of the nawabs of Avadh before they switched to Lucknow. Of its numerous monuments, the mausoleum of Behbu Begum is the finest in the region. Adjoining Faizabad is Ayodhya, principal city of the ancient kingdom of Kosala. Revered by Hindus as the birthplace of Lord Rama, Ayodhya is a center of tension between Moslems and Hindus. The Hindus claim that centuries ago Moslems destroyed a temple to Ram and replaced it with a mosque. At press time, militant Hindus had destroyed the 16th-century mosque, touching off riots throughout India. Siddhartha Gautama (Historic Buddha) supposedly traveled extensively in these parts, and Hsuan Tsang, that tireless seventh-century tourist, reported glowingly of the place.

SARNATH: CRADLE OF BUDDHIST FAITH

Sarnath, 11 kilometers (six miles) from Varanasi, is the center of the Buddhist world, just as Varanasi is the spiritual center for Hindus. At Sarnath, Siddhartha Gautama preached his first sermon more than 2,500 years ago. Here, he revealed the Eightfold Path that leads to the end of sorrow, the attainment of inner peace, enlightenment, and ultimate nirvana. Here, he established his doctrine of the Middle Way, the golden path between extremes of asceticism and self-indulgence.

Two hundred years later, Ashoka arrived—the Mauryan emperor who was the greatest convert to Buddhism. He erected a pillar at Lumbini on the Nepalese border where the Historic Buddha was born. In Sarnath, he built several *stupas* (shrines) and another pillar with the famous lion capital that symbolizes the ideals of peace and righteousness—adopted by India as the state emblem. You can see it in the excellent Sarnath Archaeological Museum. Six hundred years after that, under the Gupta dynasty, Sarnath reached its zenith. Back then, the Chinese traveler Fa Hsien claimed, 1,500 priests sat every day around the banyan tree close to the Vihara Temple. This tree is supposedly the actual Bo-Tree under which Gautama Siddhartha meditated for years before he realized enlightenment.

The twelfth century marked Sarnath's decline, with the devout Queen Kumaradevi building a large monastery: the final tribute, before Varanasi rulers dismantled the stupas for building materials. In the sixteenth century, the Moslem Emperor Akbar built a brick tower on top of some of the most sacred remaining stupas to commemorate his father's visit some years earlier. The demise continued until 1836, when Sir Alexander Cunningham started extensive excavations. First, a stone slab was discovered with an inscription of the Buddhist creed; then numerous other relics were found.

Five great monuments remain: The Dhamekh Stupa (A.D. 500) is the largest survivor, with geometric ornaments on its walls. This stupa supposedly marks the location where the Buddha set the Wheel of Law in motion, although excavations have unearthed the remains of an even earlier stupa of Mauryan bricks of the Gupta period (200 B.C.). The second monument is the Dharamrajika Stupa, set up by Ashoka to contain the bodily relics of the Buddha. It's basically in ruins, thanks to the eighteenth-century king, Jagan Singh, who decided he had a better use for the construction materials. Also see the main shrine where Ashoka used to sit in meditation with the Ashoka pillar in front, and the Chankama, which marks the sacred promenade along which Buddha paced while preaching.

In recent years, Sarnath has undergone a revival. Near the Dhamekh Stupa and joining the old foundations of seven monasteries is a new temple, Mulagandha Kuti Vihara, built in 1931 by the Mahabodhi Society. The walls of the temple are decorated with frescoes depicting scenes of the Buddha's life, painted by a Japanese artist, Kosetsu Nosu. The temple also contains a fine collection of Buddhist relics and a rare collection of Buddhist literature. On the anniversary of the temple's foundation—the first full moon in November—an assembly of monks and lay devotees from all parts of Asia come together. Also visit the Chinese temple, which contains an attractive marble image of the great teacher. Before you leave, buy carrots (one rupee) and feed the deer in the nearby park.

VARANASI

Varanasi, or Kashi ("resplendent with divine light"), as it was called in the twelfth century B.C., has been the religious capital of the Hindu faith since recorded time and is a microcosm of Indian life. No one knows the date of Varanasi's birth. When the Buddha came here around 500 B.C., he encountered an ancient settlement. Contemporary with Babylon, Nineveh, and Thebes, Varanasi is one of the oldest cities in the world, a hub of firmly rooted traditions.

VARANASI
(BENARES)

0 miles
0 km 2

● Ghat □ Temple ▣ Mosque

to Sindhora   to Azamgar

to Babatpur Airport

to Jaunpur

to Sarnath

MAQBUL ALAM RD

RAJA BAZAR RD

Varuna River

Queens College Rd

Varanasi City Stn

GRAND TRUNK RD

Raipur Road

Cantonment Stn

Kashi Stn

THE MALL

VIDYAPEETH ROAD

GRAND TRUNK

Cantonment Stn. Road

CHAITGANG RD

KASHI ROAD

AURANGABAD RD

RAJA MOTICHAND RD

Sheopurwa Road

LUXA ROAD

Manikarnika Ghat

DURGAKUND ROAD

MADANPURA ROAD

Manduadih Stn

Dasaswamedh Ghat
Boats leave for
morning tours

N

Sonapura Rd

Asi Rd

RIVER GANGA

1 Clark's Hotel
2 I.T.D.C. Varanasi Hotel
3 Hotel de Paris
4 Tourist Office
5 Taj Hotel
6 General Post Office
7 Aurangzeb's Mosque
8 Viswanatha Temple
9 Durga Temple

PANCH KOSHI RD

HINDU
UNIVERSITY

Ramnagar
Fort & Palace

Every devout Hindu wants to visit Varanasi once in a lifetime to purify the body and soul in the Ganges, to shed all sin, and, if possible, to die here in old age and find release from the cycle of rebirth, which is the ulti- mate goal of the Hindus. This release means eternal unity with Brahma: "sinless, stirless rest, that change which never changes." Descending from the Himalayas on its long trek to the Bay of Bengal, each drop of the Ganga—as the Hindus call it—is august and propitious; the waters hold the powers of salvation, and the main sanctuary is Varanasi. Every year, the city welcomes millions of pilgrims, a lengthy trail many of them never retrace.

The old city of Varanasi (800,000 inhabitants) is a maze of small streets and alleyways, hiding in disorderly array no less than 2,000 temples and shrines. Domes, minarets, pinnacles and towers, and derelict eighteenth- century palaces dominate the sacred left bank of the river. The streets are noisy; color is rife. The air hangs heavy, as if in collaboration with the clang of temple gongs and bells. Some houses have simply decorated en- trances; other buildings are ornate (notice the Indian-style gingerbread on balconies and verandas). You'll see marriage processions and funeral pro- cessions and cows grabbing big flower necklaces destined for the gods, and you'll probably be hounded by phony guides and assertive hawkers.

For all its variety of sacred spots, Varanasi is really one big shrine dedi- cated to Shiva. Shaivism, the worship of Shiva, is one of the oldest forms of cult worship, and was practiced in the Indus Valley thousands of years ago. Legend recounts how the Ganges was created. The water goddess Ganga was ordered to redeem the souls of some humans of great merit. But the fall of such a quantity of water would cause great damage to the world, so Shiva caught the goddess in his hair and let her seep out slowly to wash the ashes of the worthy mortals, and their souls ascended to heaven.

Along the Ganges

Along a seven-kilometer (four-mile) stretch of the Ganges, you see steps called *ghats* that lead down from the steep city bank to the sacred river. These stone steps (there are about 70 sets of them) wed the great Hindu metropolis to the Ganges. The numerous *linga* (phallic-shaped stones) set on most terraces emphasize this religious connection.

The best time to visit the ghats is at early dawn, when residents of the city shake off sleep and proceed down to the river. A solemn multitude of people and even animals—thousands of spots of color, lit by the sun's first rays—all move in one direction, bent on immersion in the holy stream.

If you decide to hire a boat, which is not expensive, go to the Dasash- wamedh Ghat, the main ghat. As you slowly move along the river, you'll be drawn in by what you witness. Young men perform vigorous Hatha Yoga exercises; older men sit cross-legged in the lotus position, eyes closed in deep meditation. Brahmin priests sit under huge umbrellas offering prayers. Devotees drink from the polluted water. A carcass may even float by. Women glide in and out of saris with such perfect finesse that they reveal nothing and you don't think to avert your eyes. Others beat and swoosh linen against the stone, purifying the clothes they wear.

Thin blue smoke twists up to the sky from the burning ghat, the Mani- karnika, the chief cremation center of Varanasi (the other smaller crema- tion ghat is called Harish Chandra Ghat). Corpses wrapped in silk or linen—traditionally white for men and red for women—are carried on bamboo stretchers to the smoking pyres, where they are deposited and wait their turn: first an immersion into the Ganges, then, after a short wait, placement on the pyre for the ritual that precedes the cremation. These funeral ghats cannot be photographed; but you are allowed to watch.

Monuments Along the River

In the seventeenth century, the Mogul Emperor Aurangzeb pulled down the Vishveswara Temple and erected the Gyanvapi Mosque on its site. The foundation and rear of the mosque still reveal parts of the original temple. The tallest of its minarets, dominating the skyline of the holy city, collapsed during the great flood of 1948.

North of the Gyanvapi Mosque and also on the river is another of Aurangzeb's creations—the Alamgir Mosque—an odd blend of Hindu and Moslem design. Aurangzeb destroyed the seventeenth-century Beni Madhav ka Darera, which was dedicated to Vishnu, and replaced it with the mosque. The lower portions and wall are Hindu, the mosque is Islamic.

Ramnager Fort

Due south, on the opposite side of the Ganges, is the residential palace of the former maharajah of Varanasi. Called the Ramnager Fort, the Durbar Hall (Public Audience) and the Royal Museum have interesting collections that are open to the public. The palace was built to resist the floods of the monsoon, which play havoc with the city side of the river.

The Inner City

Start your tour of the old city with a visit to the Kashi Vishwanath Temple, dedicated to Shiva. The temple is located back from the Ganges in between the Dasashwanedh and Manikarnika ghats. Follow narrow streets crowded with animals, people, and little shops crammed with customers bargaining back and forth—often for the world-famous silver and gold brocades, for the appropriate wedding ornament, or even for a cremation cloth.

The most sacred shrine in all Varanasi, which is off-limits to non-Hindus, is the Kashi Vishwanath. It is best seen from the top floor of the opposite house (pay a small fee to the owner). You'll see men and women making flower offerings to the lingam in the inner shrine. The present temple was built by Rani Ahalyabai of Indore in 1776 near the site of the original shrine destroyed by Aurangzeb. The spire is covered with gold plate, a gift from the Maharaja Ranjit Singh in 1835.

NORTHERN UTTAR PRADESH

Uttar Pradesh is a state of extremes—Mogul architecture at its best in Agra, Hindu reverence at Varanasi, and spectacular scenery and outdoor adventure in its northern expanse. Start your tour at Bareilly, 100 kilometers (62 miles) northwest of Lucknow, now an important rail and industrial center and formerly the chief city of the Rohillas, a marauding Afghan tribe that provoked a short but bloody war (1773–74) with the nawabs of Avadh and the British. The Khandan Mosque here has some Persian inscriptions that date from the thirteenth century.

Thirty-three kilometers (20 miles) west, you'll find the ruins of the fortress city Ahich Chatra, excavations of which have yielded sculptures, pottery, and Buddhist stupas ranging from the third century B.C. to A.D. 900. Not far from Ahich Chatra, you'll get your first glimpse of the distant Himalayas that divide India from Tibet and Nepal. Almost immediately, the road narrows and winds into the Himalayan Foothills, the favorite area of Mahatma Gandhi. Finally, you'll enter the Lake District of the Kumaon Hills and arrive at Nainital, 1,981 meters (6,500 feet) above sea level.

Nainital

Divided into Malli Tal and Talli Tal (upper and lower lake), Nainital is a base for forays into the Kumaon Hills, including a long climb to the top of Naina Peak, with its view of the Himalayas and Nainital. The name of this town—the summer capital of the state until 1947—comes from an old temple of Goddess Naina Devi that stands on the shore of the lake. Naina Devi is the presiding deity of the hill people, who consider the lake to be sacred. Other nearby lakes are the Bhim Tal and Naukutchia Tal (the nine-cornered lake), only a short distance away.

Almora and Pindari Glacier

From Nainital, head north to Almora, surrounded by the Himalayas. Set on a hill where Vishnu supposedly stayed, Almora was founded in the sixteenth century as the chief city of the Chand rajahs who ruled in this area. The Gurkhas of Nepal also had a fling of power here, until the British seized control during the Gurkha War in 1815. Almora, compact and picturesque, is perched on a ridge with each surrounding hill topped by a temple. A small hill station with a distinct air of antiquity, it offers numerous walks leading to exquisite views.

To the west is another tiny hill station, Ranikhet (queen's field, for the queen who supposedly came and never left). A visit to the Pindari Glacier, due north, is a journey controlled by weather conditions; it will take about six days on foot to cover a circular route that begins about 80 km (50 mi) north of Almora. The trek takes you through dramatic scenery and leads to the very shadow of the snow-covered Himalayas. You proceed stage by stage, with well-equipped bungalows at frequent intervals. At each level, the tree line thins until the pines cease, and you see the extensive glacier backed by mighty mountains.

Corbett National Park

India's oldest wildlife sanctuary (started in 1935), Corbett National Park is named after the fearless hunter and generous wildlife pioneer Jim Corbett, author of *Man-Eaters of Kumaon.* Corbett grew up in these westernmost hills, and the local people, a number of whom he saved at the risk of his own life, held him in high esteem. But it wasn't until his death in Kenya in 1957 that India honored him by renaming the Hailey National Park for this well-liked man.

The park, with elephant grass, sal forests, and the Ramganga River covering its entire length, extends over an area of 520 square kilometers (125 square miles). From the back of an elephant, from inside a car, or from the height of a stationary watchtower, you may see elephants, tigers, leopards, black bear, wild boar, deer, snakes (including the python and king cobra), crocodiles, and birds and more birds. This is a *great* park, well worth a visit. The best time is from December to May; the park is closed during the monsoon (May to October).

HARIDWAR

Back in Ramnagar, travel northwest, hugging the edge of the mountains until you reach Haridwar, a sacred city of pilgrimage on the bank of the Ganges. Haridwar has the religious fervor of Varanasi, but its mood is joyous, not solemn. Here, King Bhagirath brought the Ganges down from heaven to provide a path of salvation for his ancestors. Here, the three supreme deities—Brahma, Vishnu, and Shiva—left their mark. In fact, a set of Vishnu's footprints is supposedly embedded in an upper portion of the wall of Haridwar's most important ghat, Har-ki-pauri. You see *swamis* (monks or teachers), *sadhus* (wandering holy men), devotees, over 150 *ashrams* (spiritual retreats) and *dharmshalas* (religious guest houses), temples, statues of deities, and numerous ghats set against the Ganges canal and river. The bustling scene serves as a constant reminder of Haridwar's importance in Hindu mythology. Religious strictures have also made Haridwar "dry" and strictly vegetarian—even eggs are taboo.

One of the earliest names of this ancient city was Gangadwara, which means the Gate of the Ganges. A gate it is—sitting at the mouth of a gorge in the Shivalik Mountains where the fast-moving Ganges rushes out, then slows dramatically as it enters the plains on its seaward course toward the Bay of Bengal. The devout believe that to bathe here once means salvation, and all along the banks, you'll see faithful bathers congregating. At sunrise or at sunset, you must witness the celebration of *puja* (the offering of prayers to the Ganges) held at the Har-ki-pauri Ghat.

Moti Bazaar and Arti of the Ganges

The most festive puja is at evening and is called Arti of the Ganges. The event is heavily attended, so leave early and allow at *least* an hour just to walk through the part of the city that hugs the Ganges canal and takes you to the Har-ki-pauri Ghat. Here, every ashram and dharmshala is bathed in a tropical hue often outlined in contrasting trim. There's a vague aura of old Miami Beach. Many of the buildings were built in the 1920s and '30s and are distinctly Art Deco.

Start your walk at the Lalto Rao Bridge by the Bhola Giri Temple and Ashram, done up in the shade of natural terra cotta with its dharmshala set off by light blue trim. Next, as you head northeast along Jodhamal Road, is the Chiniot Bhawan, a yellow temple with lacy stone trim. Step inside and see ornate marble gods and goddesses dressed in their festive clothes.

Move along Jodhamal to the Moti Bazaar—pleasantly congested and busy, yet not overwhelming. Ayurvedic medicine shops sell *jalzeera* (Indian spice powder for stomachaches); religious shops sell small polished stones (omens and lingams) and beads of coral or sandalwood for devotees to hold while saying mantras. Stalls sell fresh pickle chutneys, shawls, and saris.

At the end of the bazaar, the narrow street spills into a large square, where open-air stalls sell *dias*—leaves woven together like little boats and filled with fresh flowers and thimble-sized clay bowls and wicks. These beautiful vessels are set afloat on the Ganges during Arti. Men sell enormous balloons and boys sell wooden whistles and pipes. There's a carnival air. You've arrived at Har-ki-pauri Ghat surrounded by a complex of temples—mostly new except for the sixteenth-century Shri Ganga Mandir.

A short bridge leads to the Pant Dweep (tiny terraced island), the best vantage point. If you can, sit on the top ghat step. The preliminary show is as fascinating as Arti, with all India walking by: Rajasthanis in colorful turbans and wild mustaches, Sikhs, Nagas, sadhus, and swamis. People bathe, and many set off their dias in hasty anticipation.

A few minutes before Arti begins, temple bells ring and priests from surrounding temples descend the steps of the ghat—each carrying bells and a large brass lamp filled with oil. The priests ignite the lamps—the start of Arti. Flames rise up as they hold the vessels over the Ganges. Bells ring continuously. The priests swing the vessels up and down across the surface of the water. The fragrance of *dwoop* (incense) circulates. Chants, barely audible, silence the throngs. Burning dias flicker away on their downward journey along the swift-moving Ganges. Within 15 minutes, Arti is over.

In Haridwar, the temples aren't old, but they're always festive, and some are erected on mythologically important sites. See the Daksh Mahadev Temple and Sati Jund in Kankhal, a part of Haridwar, with yellow stone lions at the entrance. Here, the father of Sati (Shiva's first wife) performed a sacrifice and neglected to invite Shiva. Sati was so insulted that she arrived uninvited and performed her own sacrifice—throwing herself into the fire at Yagva Kund now inside the Deksh Mahadev. A large statue of the devoted Nandi (Shiva's bull) stands outside. There are other temples in this complex. One contains a Shiva lingam surrounded by a copper cobra, with the water dripping down on the stone; another shows this goddess in all her manifestations. There is also a ghat for devotees to step down to the Ganges to bathe.

For a good view of Haridwar, visit the Mansa Devi Temple dedicated to the goddess Mansi, which stands on the top of one of the nearby Shivalik Hills. You can go by cable car or on foot.

Pawan Dham

Pawan may mean "holy" and *Dham* may mean "house," but once you step inside the Pawan Dham Ashram, constructed in 1970 by Swami Vedanta Maharaj, you almost need sunglasses, and you can't help but smile. No wonder this swami had such a large following. The gigantic building is pure religious fun. Most walls are covered with elaborate mythological frescoes made of inlaid and painted glass. Ceilings dazzle with more colored glass. The few walls without a fresco have mirrors—perhaps so devotees see themselves as part of the Hindu pantheon. Step close to one of the numerous cubicles that contain gaily decorated marble gods and goddesses. Now look into the mirrored side walls inside the chamber. The statue appears in infinite reflection. The crowning *piéce de kitsch* is a large freestanding inlaid glass chariot drawn by horses, with Krishna and Arjun inside and Hanuman, the monkey god, riding on top of a stanchion. His weight kept the heavenly chariot earthbound.

RISHIKESH

Rishikesh, 24 kilometers (15 miles) north of Haridwar, is a busy, new city. It may be another city of religious significance tied to the Ganges and it may have important ashrams, but Rishikesh also pays homage to concrete and dust.

For hundreds of years, Rishikesh has been an important retreat for those on the spiritual path. There are over 100 ashrams here, including Maharishi Mahesh Yogi's Transcendental Meditation Center, which once hooked the Beatles, Swami Sivananda's Divine Life Society, and the Yoga Sadhan Ashram.

Triveni Ghat, with its sprawling terrace, is Rishikesh's main bathing ghat. Each evening, from 5 to 6 P.M., a local swami comes down to preach, his service followed by a small-scale Arti. The fish, considered sacred in this part of the river, seem to understand their peculiar status. Over the years, they've become so tame that they swarm to the surface to catch daily offerings.

Two mythological stories are connected to Rishikesh and commemorated by temples. Supposedly, Lakshman (a brother of Lord Rama) stood on one foot in the middle of the Ganges and meditated for 100 years as an act of penance for killing his guru—an unfortunate event that occurred while he was attempting to help his brother, Rama. A suspension bridge, the Laxmanjhoola, crosses the Ganges where Lakshman evidently did his prolonged act of physical balance. The Bharat Temple is connected to Bharat, another brother of Rama, who also did penance in Rishikesh during the same period as did Lakshman and for the same approximate duration. He had committed no sin, however; his motivation was self-purification.

DEHRA DUN

Dehra Dun, 42 kilometers (26 miles) from Rishikesh, is the largest Uttar Pradesh city in the lower Himalayan foothills. It's an important government administration center, home of the superexclusive Doon School (Rajiv Gandhi was one of its alumni), and the location of Asia's largest forest research institute, with museums open to the public. Dehra Dun is no great beauty of a city, thanks to unregulated limestone quarrying. But it's a good stopover for those heading north, and it offers two nearby diversions to break up a long ride.

Visit the Tapkeshwar Cave Temple, set in the woods along a stream. To the sound of piped religious music, you descend a stone staircase with pesky monkeys lying in wait, pass under a natural rock ledge with mossy grass hanging down, and reach a series of caves. Inside are shrines with small statues of Nandi, Ganesh, Hanuman and, in the main cave, a Shiva lingam set on a copper base—all tended by a gregarious *pujari* (priest). If you have a translator, this is one time to believe the stories. The pujari will explain that the temple is at least 5,000 years old and recount how the water that used to drip steadily from the roof of the cave onto the lingam has decreased over the years with each disaster: the two world wars; the Chinese invasion of Tibet; the deaths of Mahatma Gandhi, Nehru, and Indira Gandhi; and a famine. Now you're lucky if you see much more than a droplet or two.

You can also cool yourself at Sahastradhara, where sulfur springs tumbling down from the mountains form a natural pool in which people can bathe. It's open from sunrise to sunset. There's a limited-menu Indian café and a temple on the side of the hill that leads up to yet another cave with another Shiva lingam. This time plenty of water drenches the sacred stone.

Mussoorie

Mussoorie, 2,005 meters (6,576 feet) above sea level, rises on a horseshoe-shaped foothill that overlooks the Ganges River, sluggishly moving through the plains on one side and the vibrant silhouette of the lower Himalayas on the other.

At first glance, Mussoorie looks like another former British hill station turned "honeymoon retreat," where the emphasis is on short walks and relaxation. You're bombarded with billboards that advertise hotels and see cars loaded with young couples. But then something happens. Tucked away here and there, some of that grand old elegance peeks out. Some of it is a bit musty around the edges and some of it even totters on old Victorian legs, but it's there and it's holding its own in a way that makes this particular hill station still special.

Stop at Hakman's Hotel and have a drink for old time's sake. As you sit and look around, it's as if time stood still—when the stiff, upright British got up and left. Check the artwork on the walls and the old telephones. Walk through the former cabaret theater and linger a moment in the grand yet bizarre entrance to the hotel. For another trip into nostalgia—this one quite elegant—visit the châteaulike Hotel Savoy, a sprawl of Victorian charm sitting on a hill all its own.

While in old Mussoorie, walk west along Charlesville Road to Happy Valley, a Tibetan township where Buddhist flags wave in the breeze and small restaurants entice you with good Tibetan cooking. At the other end of Mussoorie, you'll find bazaars. Stroll through the Mall to Kulri, set up for tourists, and the more interesting Landaur Bazaar. It's an ethnic market with a lengthy string of tiny shops built along a narrow, winding ridge. Wherever you walk—along the Mall, up to Camel's Back Road, or Gun Hill—the views explain why British Captain Young decided that this particular ridge was an ideal retreat for his countrymen back in 1827.

Mussoorie is also a great base for day excursions. Visit Kempty Falls (15 km [9 miles]), a short drive to the north that ends at appealing falls that spill into a refreshing pool of water with an unassuming café set up alongside. Go east to Dhanolti (24 km [15 miles]) along a narrow road that climbs and winds, passing men leading pack horses that are laden with pails of collected milk. Occasionally, you will see tiny shrines mounted with flags erected along the road, terraced fields of wheat, small villages with simple stone or sod houses linked together, foot paths, and potato fields. This rugged terrain brings you to a tiny village set in a pine forest: Dhanolti. There's a new hotel under construction and an Uttar Pradesh Tourist Bungalow, which serves food and supplies an outdoor map that points the way to good walks.

Mussoorie is also the "gateway" to Yamnotri and Gangotri—two essential goals of pilgrimage that mark the source of the Yamuna and Ganges rivers. The shrines here draw thousands of devotees to this part of India, which is also scenically beautiful—reason enough to make the trip.

Yamnotri

Yamnotri is 140 kilometers (87 miles) almost due north of Mussoorie. The road, which takes you to Hanumanchatti within 13 kilometers (8 miles) of the temple, is Himalayan beautiful, with the Yamuna River escorting you on the left. You'll pass through tiny villages like Barkot, encircled by pine forests, with stunning snow-clad peaks forming a picturesque backdrop. Walking sadhus share the road. Once the road ends and you start out for the temple, you'll come to Jankibaichatti, a good overnight halt, with rest houses and hot-water springs.

Yamnotri itself is huddled against the western bank of the snow-covered Banderpunch (6,423 meters [20,720 feet] above sea level). Here, an ancient Hindu sage is said to have built his hermitage and bathed daily in the Yamuna and Ganges. When old age prevented more treks to the Gangotri, a stream of the Ganges emerged from the Yamnotri rocks. Yamunaji Temple, dedicated to the goddess Yamuna, nearby hot springs gushing out of the mountain (the Surya Kund is considered the most sacred), and a rock

(Divya Shila) are revered by Hindus, who flock here from May to November to offer prayers.

Gangotri

The Gangotri Temple, built in the eighteenth century and dedicated to the goddess Ganga, commemorates the source of the Ganges. Here, too, pilgrims flock during the season to pay respect to this shrine and their holiest river. The scenery on the way to Gangotri is magnificent, with canyons, cascades, and rushing rivulets at each turn of the way. At an elevation of 3,100 meters (10,000 feet), Gangotri shows off its famous temple on the right bank of the river. On the opposite bank are a few huts, inhabited by sadhus who have settled here: some mere escapists from the turmoil of the world; others inflamed by zeal. You can also continue on from Gangotri, traveling by foot or pony, to the Gaumukh Glacier, a distance of about 20 kilometers (12 miles), where you can offer tribute to that exact starting point of the river.

Kedarnath and Badrinath

Hindu pilgrims also hope to visit two other important shrines in this northern area of Uttar Pradesh—Kedarnath and Badrinath, the assumed abodes of Shiva and Vishnu, set over 3,100 meters (10,000 feet) up in the mountains.

Instead of taking the direct route to Kedarnath, try to go via Deoprayag, a charming Indian village built into the slope of a hill at the confluence of the Bhagirathi and Alakandanda rivers. You can even spend a night in the minimal but clean tourist bungalow. Deoprayag (God's place) is the site of the ancient and recently renovated Raghunath Temple, which commemorates the spot where Rama supposedly came to meditate. It is also in Deoprayag that the merging rivers assume the known name River Ganges. The whitewashed old village, connected to the new part of town by a pedestrian-sized suspension bridge, is filled with local *pandits* (priests), who lead visiting Hindus in their prayers on the bathing ghat that provides access to the river. As you walk through the narrow lanes, there's an abundance of charm in the architecture and hillside setting and a prevailing sense of tranquillity, with the dominant sound that of the river thrashing along on its course.

On leaving Deoprayag, you'll find that the road narrows and winds. Occasionally, you'll see distant pastoral hamlets in which life moves to a quiet rhythm. At Gaurikund, with hot-water springs and a temple, the road ends. From here, you'll go by foot or pony (there are rest huts along the way) on a 15-kilometer (9-mile) journey near glaciers and waterfalls. You'll clomp through rocky forests until just after you cross a narrow bridge above a village, where you'll see a simple gray stone temple standing on a raised platform guarding the dwellings in Kedarnath. The temple, snowbound and closed from November to May, stands on the banks of the Mandakini. A statue of Nandi, Shiva's mount, is in the courtyard. Several holy bathing spots are around the temple, and inside the simple shrine are beautiful carvings of Shiva, Parvati, and the five *pandavas* (legendary rulers), who built this temple as atonement for the sins they committed during the Great Battle, recorded in the *Mahabharata*.

To get to Badrinath, return to Rudraprayag and take the road passing through the Alaknanda valley and the village of Karnaprayag, a busy meeting place for the surrounding hill people. Then, you enter the Pipalkoti Valley, with its important township, Joshimath, which is also the winter seat of the Badrinath shrine. Here, you come across the Buddhist Bhutias, an Indo-Mongoloid people whose lifestyle underwent severe change when trade with Tibet became impossible. Their greatest possession is the yak, their beast of burden that also provides milk, butter, and meat. To the east, the steep Nanda Devi Summit (7,952 meters [25,650 feet]) appears like a pyramid. Snow, blown by the winds, gives the impression of smoke blowing over gray rock; the locals call it the Nandi Devi, "kitchen of their deity."

In the winter, skiers can check out Joshimath's nearby Auli, India's newest ski resort. A 3-kilometer (2-mile) run is in operation, and a 32-kilometer (20-mile) run is under construction. When that run is completed, the trail will be one of the longest in the world.

The brightly painted Badrinath Temple, 52 kilometers (32 miles) north of Joshimath, is dedicated to Vishnu and also figures in Buddhist mythology. Hindus claim that a sage chastised Vishnu for indulging in earthly pleasure—allowing his consort, Lakshmi, to rub his feet. Vishnu fled to this valley and meditated in a posture associated with the Buddha, who also happens to be the ninth incarnation of this deity. Over time, Lakshmi found Vishnu and begged him to give up this un-Vishnu-like pose. He agreed, but only if Badrinath remained a valley of meditation.

Much of the Badrinath Temple has been enlarged; only the inner sanctum has escaped alteration. The main shrine has a *mandapa* (pavilion) and an inner sanctum, with a black stone idol of Vishnu that sits under a gold canopy. The main temple is surrounded by shrines, dedicated to Lakshmi and Hanuman (the monkey god), and numerous sacred *kunds* (tanks). Try to attend an evening prayer service; it's a highly charged event.

PRACTICAL INFORMATION FOR

UTTAR PRADESH

WHEN TO GO. For the non-Himalayan areas (the plains region): This part of Uttar Pradesh has a variable climate. It can be very hot and dry in summer and fairly cool in winter. From November to February, the maximum temperature rarely exceeds 65°F in daytime; at night, it falls to 45°F. The main tourist season for the plains lasts from October to March. For the Himalayas: The best visiting seasons are from May to July and mid-September to early November. Temperatures are pleasant during the day and cool by night. The Valley of Flowers bursts into bloom in July and August, which is the time of the monsoon. Corbett National Park is open from mid-November to mid-June, with the best viewing time from March to June.

HOW TO GET THERE. By Air. *Indian Airlines* makes nine weekly flights into Lucknow from Delhi and three weekly flights from Patna, Calcutta, and Bombay. Indian Airlines makes daily flights to Varanasi from Agra, Delhi, Kathmandu, and Khajuraho, four weekly flights from Bhubaneswar, and three weekly flights from Calcutta and Jaipur. *Vayudoot* makes six weekly flights from Delhi to Dehra Dun and Lucknow. For Indian Airlines information, call 64146 in Lucknow; 43746 in Varanasi. For Vayudoot information, call 26608 in Dehra Dun; 235409 in Lucknow.

By Bus. The *Uttar Pradesh State Road Transport Corporation* (UPSRTC) runs deluxe interstate buses from Delhi and other large northern cities, including Shimla and Chandigarh; it also provides excellent and frequent service between most areas in the state that are of interest to the tourist. For fares and details: in Delhi, call 2518709, 6 A.M.–8 P.M. at *Interstate Bus Terminus,* Kashmiri Gate; in Lucknow, call

Kaiserbagh Bus Station, 242503 or Charbagh Bus Station, 50988. At press time, the number in Varanasi for UPSRTC was about to be changed. Contact the tourist department (see Tourist Information, below).

By Train. Uttar Pradesh is well covered with railroad tracks. You can get to most important cities (Lucknow, Allahabad, Dehra Dun, and Varanasi) from either Delhi or Calcutta. Keep in mind, however, that some of these journeys are overnight. When you reserve a sleeper (first- or second-class and air-conditioned), you must also reserve a berth, or you could be asked to leave the train. For train information in Lucknow, call 131 or 132; for reservations, call 51833 or 51383. In Varanasi, call 131 for inquiries and 43520 for reservations.

By Rented Car with Driver. Delhi is 497 km (308 miles) from Lucknow, 710 km (440 miles) from Varanasi (Calcutta is 681 km (422 miles) from Varanasi). Heading toward the Himalayas, Delhi is 222 km (138 miles) from Haridwar, 322 km (200 miles) from Nainital, 255 km (158 miles) from Dehra Dun, and 278 km (172 miles) from Mussoorie. The cost of renting a car is about Rs. 5 per km, plus halt charges of Rs. 50–Rs. 100 per night.

TOURIST INFORMATION. Uttar Pradesh tourist departments are extremely helpful, offering brochures and maps. For information, contact the government-run tourist agency, UPTOURS, Hotel Gomti, 6 Sapru Marg, Lucknow 226001; tel. 232659, fax 0523/232659. It's open daily 10 A.M.–5:30 P.M. Uttar Pradesh tourist offices are also located in the following important destinations. Most offices are open 10 A.M.–5 P.M., closed Sundays.

Allahabad. Tourist Bungalow, 35 Mahatma Gandhi Rd.; tel. 601873.

Almora. Holiday Home; tel. 2180.

Dehra Dun. Hotel Drona, 45 Mahatma Gandhi Rd.; tel. 23217. In June, open daily 9 A.M.–7 P.M.

Haridwar. Lalta Rao Bridge, Station Rd.; tel. 427370. Also, Information Counter, Railway Station; tel. 427817; open daily 6 A.M.–1:30 P.M.

Joshimath (on the way to Badrinath and Kedarnath). Tourist Bungalow; tel. 81.

Lucknow. 10/4 Station Rd., tel. 246205; and Tourist Reception Center, Railway Station, Charbagh; tel. 52533; open daily 10 A.M.–5 P.M.

Mussoorie. The Mall; tel. 2863.

Nainital. The Mall; tel. 2337.

Pauri (Garhwal). Tourist Bungalow; tel. 2241.

Rishikesh. Railway Rd.; tel. 209.

Srinagar (Garhwal). Tourist Bungalow; tel. 10.

Uttarkashi. Tourist Bungalow; tel. 190.

Varanasi. Tourist Bungalow, Parade Khothi; tel. 43486 or 42018. Tourist Information Counter, Cantonment Railway Station; tel. 46376; open daily 8 A.M.–8 P.M. Also visit the Government of India Tourist Office, 15–B, The Mall, Cantonment; tel. 43744; open Mon.–Fri., 9 A.M.–5:30 P.M. and Sat., 9 A.M.–1 P.M. It also has a counter at the airport that is open for arrivals.

For information about Corbett National Park, contact the Field Director, Corbett National Park, Ramnagar 244715, tel. 850819; or the Chief Wildlife Warden, 17 Rana Pratap Marg, Lucknow 226001; tel. 246140.

FOREIGN CURRENCY EXCHANGE. Most Western-style hotels have money-exchange counters. Otherwise, go to a branch of the *State Bank of India;* open Mon.–Fri. 10 A.M.–2 P.M., Sat. till noon.

ACCOMMODATIONS. Uttar Pradesh has some Western-style hotels in the major cities and a few charming old-fashioned guest houses. For some areas of the state—Badrinath, Kedarnath, Gangotri, and Yamunotri—the choice is limited. Most accommodations in this area are listed below under Tourist Rest Houses and Safari-Style Tents. Despite the lack of choice accommodations, don't avoid this part of Uttar Pradesh. All government-run facilities can be reserved in advance through the Uttar Pradesh State Tourism Development Corporation (UPSTDC), Chanderlok Bldg., 36 Janpath, New Delhi 110001; tel. 3322251 or 3711286, fax 011/3711296. You can also reserve a room through the manager of each individual unit. Include a 50 percent deposit of the room rate. No room is more than Rs. 500 per double per night. Prices are based on double occupancy and don't include taxes or service charges: *Deluxe,* over Rs. 2,000; *Expensive,* Rs. 2,000–Rs. 1,200; *Moderate,* Rs. 500–Rs. 1,200; *Inexpensive,* under Rs. 500. Most Western-style hotels take major credit cards.

ALLAHABAD

Moderate

Hotel Presidency. 19–D, Sarojini Naidu Marg, Allahabad 211001; tel. 624097. 10 air-conditioned rooms with bath. This intimate hotel has a nice ambience and good management. Air-conditioned rooms have Western-style decor. TV, room service, multicuisine restaurant, swimming pool, foreign-exchange counter, doctor. DC, V.

Hotel Yatrik. 33 S.P. Marg, Allahabad 2110011; tel. 601509. 34 rooms with bath. This is Allahabad's best hotel, and it's set in a quiet part of the city. The rooms are spacious and modern. The best have air-conditioning and overlook the pool. TV, room service, multicuisine restaurant, bar, swimming pool, travel agency, secretarial services. MC, V.

BADRINATH

Inexpensive

Hotel Devlok. Reservations: Manager, Hotel Devlok, Badrinath Distt. Chamoli; tel. 12. 30 rooms with attached bathrooms. This government-run hotel, within walking distance of the famous temple, offers Western-style rooms, with clean, warm bed comforters. Best rooms are called "deluxe" and "executive." There is a lounge and a vegetarian restaurant. Rupees only.

CORBETT NATIONAL PARK

Deluxe

Tiger Tops Corbett Lodge. Reserve through Tiger Tops India, 1/1 Rani Jhansi Rd., New Delhi 110055; tel. 771055, fax 011/777483; or through Tiger Tops offices abroad (see Special-Interest Tours in *Facts at Your Fingertips*). 24 rooms with bath. This new luxury resort on the banks of the Kosi River near the park has an exquisite two-story lodge made of marble, stone, and slate. Each room has white-washed adobe and stone walls and its own balcony overlooking mango groves, the river, and a swimming pool. Nearby is a circular lounge. Activities include nature walks, elephant and jeep safaris, pony rides, village and temple visits, and fishing. There's an off-season discount from June 30 to November 14. Meals and most activities are included. AE.

Expensive

Quality Inn Corbett Jungle Resort. Reserve through Quality Inn, 51 Vasant Marg, Vasant Vihar, New Delhi 110057; tel. 675347 or 671327; or through Quality Inn abroad (see Group Hotels in *Facts at Your Fingertips*). 18 rooms with bath and some tents with shared bathrooms. Also outside the park and on the banks of the Kosi River, this new resort features stone cottages with interior wood-paneling and a fireplace. There's also a complex of safari-style tents, as well as a lodge for eating and a cocktail lounge. Activities include elephant and jeep safaris, swimming, fishing, and tennis. An off-season discount is offered from June 30 to November 1. Meals and most activities are included. AE, DC.

Inexpensive

For all reservations in the park, contact: Field Director, Corbett National Park, Ramnagar 244715, tel. 850819 or the Chief Wildlife Warden, 17 Rana Pratap Marg, Lucknow 226001, tel. 246140.

Bijrani, Dhela, Jhuna, Kalagarh, and Sarpduli Rest Houses. Each rest house has about four to six rooms, with simple bath. Set into the forest and not convenient to the complex's restaurant, all rooms are rustic, have no-frills kitchens, and are private. Bring a sleeping bag and provisions. Very inexpensive (under Rs. 250). Rupees only.

Dhikhala Forest Rest House Complex. This facility, inside the park, has simple, clean rooms with bath. The old lodge has better ambience than the new lodge. You can also rent a cabin for more privacy or a tent (bring a sleeping bag). Multicuisine restaurant and a reception center. Rupees only.

DEHRA DUN

Moderate

Hotel Madhuban. 97 Rajpur Rd., Dehra Dun 248001; tel. 24097, fax 0135/23181. 42 rooms and cottages with bath. You can stay in the Western-style hotel with modern furnishings or in a cottage where the interiors are done up in different Indian state decors. Air-conditioning, TV, room service, multicuisine restaurant, bar, swimming pool, foreign-exchange counter, secretarial services, doctor. AE, DC, MC, V.

Hotel Nidhi. 74–C Rajpur Rd., Dehra Dun 248001; tel. 24611. 24 rooms with bath. This multistory hotel is attractive and modern. Air-conditioned rooms have a Western-style decor. TV, room service, multicuisine restaurant, doctor, foreign-exchange counter. AE, DC.

Inexpensive

Hotel Drona. 45 Gandhi Rd., Dehra Dun 248001; tel. 24371. 78 rooms with bath. This Western-style hotel, run by the government, offers a variety of rooms. The best rooms are "deluxe," with air-conditioning and TV. Room service, multicuisine restaurant, tourist office, shops. Rupees only.

DHANOLTI

Inexpensive

Dhanolti Tourist Bungalow. Reservations: Manager of Tourist Complex, Dhanolti, tel. 2, or Tourist Department in Mussoorie, tel. 2863. 5 rooms with bath. This rustic government-run bungalow has clean, spacious rooms with working fireplaces. Bathrooms have Indian-style toilets; hot water is available by bucket. Simple meals are available at nominal cost. Rupees only.

HARIDWAR

Moderate

Hotel Surprise. Haridwar-Delhi Rd., Jwala Pur, Haridwar 249021; tel. 1146 or 1148. 55 rooms with bath. This mini high rise has the upscale traveler in mind. The lobby is an overstatement in marble with an enormous chandelier; but rooms are pleasantly unpretentious. Deluxe rooms have TV and air-conditioning. It's 1½ km (1 mi.) from Haridwar to get beyond the vegetarian limits. Room service, multicuisine restaurants, foreign-exchange desk, travel agency, swimming pool, shopping arcade, doctor. AE, DC, MC, V.

Inexpensive

Haridwar Tourist Bungalow. Haridwar 249021; tel. 426379. 22 rooms with bath. A government facility, this bungalow is within walking distance of the center of Haridwar and faces the Ganga Canal. Rooms have minimal furnishings; ask for an air-cooled room. There is a vegetarian restaurant, with room service. Rupees only.

LUCKNOW

Deluxe

Taj Palace. Vipin Rd., Gomtinagar, Lucknow 226016. No phone at press time. Reserve through the Taj Group of Hotels (see Group Hotels in *Facts at Your Finger-*

tips). 112 rooms with bath. Scheduled to open by March 1993, this swank hotel, which blends the Raj and the East, faces the Gomti River. Sure to have elegant rooms, the hotel will offer the standard Taj amenities, including a swimming pool and business center. AE, DC, MC, V.

Expensive

Clarks Avadh. 8 Mahatma Gandhi Marg, Lucknow 226001; tel. 240131, fax 0522/236507. 98 rooms with bath. This Western-style "luxury" hotel has attractive air-conditioned rooms with a subdued contemporary decor. Ask for a river view. TV, room service, multicuisine restaurants, bar, foreign-exchange and travel counter, secretarial services, golfing arrangements. AE, DC, MC, V.

Pushpa Akbar Continental Hotel. City Center, Gomtinagar, Lucknow 226016; tel. 39192. 100 rooms with bath. Also scheduled to open by March 1993, this modern high rise will offer Western-style, contemporary rooms, with air-conditioning. TV, room service, restaurants, bar, business center, foreign-exchange and travel counter, shops. AE, DC, MC, V.

MUSSOORIE

Moderate–Deluxe

Savoy. The Mall, Mussoorie 248179; tel. 2010 or 2620. 121 rooms with bath. The château-style Savoy, located on a hill overlooking the mountains, opened in 1902 when no road led to Mussoorie. Queen Mary stayed in these grand rooms when she was the Princess of Wales; so did Nehru and the Dalai Lama. The Victorian mood is deliberate, the owner and his wife are refined, but expect some tarnished edges and old-fashioned simplicity to the decor. Request a deluxe suite, if you can afford it (also deluxe prices), or an upstairs double off the veranda. Restaurants, room service, beer garden, bar, laundry, doctor, foreign-exchange and travel counter, hiking, horseback riding and fishing arrangements, and post office. Meals included. AE, DC, MC, V.

Moderate

Carlton's Hotel Plaisance. Happy Valley Rd., Mussoorie 248179; tel. 2800. 10 rooms with bath. If cozy elegance appeals to you, stay in this small bungalow built by an English barrister in the early 1900s. The dining room and parlor have handsome antiques, hunting trophies, and family memorabilia. Bedrooms are modest, yet comfortable. Gracious hosts cater to your needs. No Himalayan views; you're nestled in an orchard. No bar. Discount mid-Nov.–Mar. Room service, car rentals, horseback riding arrangements. AE, DC.

NAINITAL

Moderate

Arif Castles. Nainital 263001; tel. 2801. 66 rooms with bath. This hotel, just outside the downtown area, is Western-style and has spacious rooms with a modern decor. Included are air-conditioning, TV, room service, multicuisine restaurants, bar, health club, billiards, foreign-exchange and travel counter. Off-season discount: July 16–Sept. 15; Nov. 1–Dec. 15; and Jan. 5–Apr. 15. AE, DC, MC, V.

Inexpensive

Swiss Hotel. Nainital 263001; tel. 2603. 18 rooms with bath. A chalet-style exterior, a rose garden, and good views are offered at the Swiss. Rooms have a simple Western-style decor and fireplaces; some rooms have TV. Unfortunately, service can be indifferent; don't hesitate to complain. Room service, multicuisine restaurant, foreign-exchange counter, sailing and bird-watching arrangements, doctor. AE, DC.

RISHIKESH

Moderate

Hotel Ganga Kinare. 16 Veer Bhadra Rd., Rishikesh 249021; tel. 566. 34 rooms with bath. This Western-style hotel on the Ganga River has a back lawn and terrace with steps that lead down to the water for a holy dip. The modern rooms are attractive, with air-conditioning and TV; best rooms have a river view and no view of dusty Rishikesh. Vegetarian restaurant, foreign-exchange and travel counter, yoga meditation center. AE, DC, MC, V.

Hotel Natraj. Dehra Dun Rd., Rishikesh 249021; tel. 1099. 75 rooms with bath. A three-story stucco-and-marble hotel, the Natraj's rooms have a quietly elegant, contemporary decor. Best rooms are on the upper floor. TV, air-conditioning, multicuisine vegetarian restaurants, health club, yoga, shopping arcade, swimming pool, free airport transfer, foreign-exchange and travel counter, secretarial services. AE, DC, MC, V.

Inexpensive

Inderlok Hotel. Railway Rd., Rishikesh 249021; tel. 555. 50 rooms with bath. In the heart of Rishikesh, this well-managed, modest Western-style hotel offers clean air-conditioned and fan-cooled rooms. Room service, multicuisine restaurant, tour and yoga instruction arrangements, terrace. DC.

Rishikesh Tourist Bungalow. Tourist Complex, Rishilok; Munikireti 249021; tel. 373. 48 rooms with bath (Indian-style toilet). Located near interesting ashrams, this bungalow-style hotel, run by the government, has lovely grounds and offers spacious, clean rooms. Rooms are fan-cooled, and room service is provided. There is a multicuisine vegetarian restaurant. Rupees only.

VARANASI

Deluxe

Hotel Taj Ganges. Nadesar Palace Grounds, Varanasi 221002; tel. 42495, fax 322067. 130 rooms with bath. This Western-style high rise has a large lobby and spacious modern rooms. Best rooms are on its renovated floor. Air-conditioning, TV, room service, multicuisine restaurants, bar, foreign-exchange and travel counter, doctor, swimming pool, tennis court, secretarial services, shopping arcade. AE, DC, MC, V.

Expensive

Hotel Clarks Varanasi. The Mall, Varanasi 221002; tel. 46771, fax 42947. 136 rooms with bath. A modern Western-style hotel, Clarks offers large air-conditioned rooms with a contemporary decor and TV. Best rooms overlook the pool. Room service, multicuisine restaurant, bar, foreign-exchange and travel counter, yoga center, swimming pool. Indian classical dance and music performances are presented on request. AE, DC, MC, V.

Hotel Hindusthan International. C-21/3, Maldahia, Varanasi 221002; tel. 57075, fax 55359. 51 rooms. This four-year-old property is closer to the ghats than Varanasi's top hotels, but it is smaller and books a lot of groups so you may have trouble getting a room here. We have not stayed overnight at the Hindusthan, but we have inspected rooms, which are clean, modern, and air-conditioned. If you have problems here, let us and the management know. Multicuisine restaurant, bar, swimming pool, banquet, conference rooms. AE, MC, V.

Moderate–Expensive

Hotel Varanasi Ashok. The Mall, Varanasi 221002; tel. 46020. 85 rooms with bath. A long landscaped driveway leads to this multistory Western-style hotel, just outside the madness of downtown Varanasi and right next door to the Clarks. Air-conditioned rooms have simple, contemporary furnishings and balconies, with the best views overlooking the pool. The Ashok is smaller than the Clarks and the Taj Ganges, so it feels more personable. TV, room service, multicuisine restaurant, bar, foreign-exchange and travel counter, swimming pool, secretarial services, shopping arcade. AE, DC, MC, V.

Inexpensive

Hotel India. 59 Patel Nagar, Varanasi 221002; tel. 44401. 33 rooms with bath. Recently renovated and under new management, this Western-style hotel provides rooms with TV and a pleasant, though simple, decor. Some rooms are air-conditioned. Room service, fans, multicuisine restaurant, bar. AE, DC, MC, V.

Hotel Pradeep. Jagatganj, Varanasi 221002; tel. 44963. 30 rooms with bath. A small hotel, the Pradeep has clean rooms with modest, Western-style furnishings and overhead fans. Some rooms are air-conditioned. Multicuisine restaurant, room service, travel agency, doctor. Rupees only.

TOURIST REST HOUSES AND SAFARI-STYLE TENTS. In Uttar Pradesh the government has constructed simple yet basically clean tourist rest houses and a couple of safari-style tent facilities. They're very inexpensive (under Rs. 350 per room), accept only rupees, and should be reserved in advance through the address listed above under Accommodations or through the manager of each individual unit. They can also be reserved through the Manager, Drona Travels, GMVN, 45 Gandhi Rd., Dehra Dun 248001; tel. 26894 or 24371. The Tourist Rest Houses usually offer a range of rooms. For an attached bathroom, request a deluxe or executive room with two twin beds or a family suite with four beds. Other options are ordinary double or a dormitory with a shared bath. Most bathrooms have an Indian-style toilet and simple shower, most often with hot water available by bucket. A *chawkidar* (caretaker) will fix a simple meal (called catering) for a nominal fee. Bring a sleeping bag or a sleeping-bag sheet, a towel, a bar of soap, and a roll of toilet paper.

These accommodations are located in the following areas: Auli (Distt. Chamoli; no phone); Barkot (Distt. Chamoli; tel. 36); Bhojwasa (Distt. Uttarkashi; no phone); Chandra Puri Tent Camp (Distt. Chamoli; no phone); Chopta (Distt. Chamoli; no phone); Deoprayag (Distt. Tehri; tel. 33); Gangotri (Distt. Uttarkashi; no phone); Jankichatti (Distt. Uttarkashi; no phone); Joshimath (Distt. Chamoli; tel. 18); Kedarnath (Distt. Chamoli; no phone); Pauri (Distt. Pauri; tel. 159); Srinagar (Alakanda, Distt. Pauri, tel. 99); and Uttarkashi (Distt. Uttarkashi; tel. 171).

DINING OUT. Except for the big cities and Mussoorie, eating well can't be considered a major draw in Uttar Pradesh. Breakfast is usually served 8–10:30; lunch, noon–3; and dinner, 7:30–10. Payment is normally in rupees unless the restaurant is connected to a Western-style hotel. The restaurants listed below are informal and, unless noted, are open for all three meals and don't require reservations. Prices are based on one person eating a three-course meal, excluding taxes, tip, or beverage: *Expensive,* Rs. 200–Rs. 300; *Moderate,* Rs. 100–Rs. 200; *Inexpensive,* under Rs. 100.

DEHRA DUN

Inexpensive–Moderate

Vatika. Hotel Madhuban, 97 Rajpur Rd.; tel. 24094. This cheery restaurant, with lots of windows, serves Continental and Indian cuisines, including especially good Mughlai dishes. At night you're entertained by live Indian *ghazals* (musicians). Dinner reservations advised. Open 7 A.M.–midnight. AE, DC, MC, V.

HARIDWAR

All food in Haridwar is vegetarian. It you want meat or even eggs, try Hotel Surprise, outside Haridwar's city limits.

Moderate

Hotel Surprise. Haridwar-Delhi Rd., Jwala Pur; tel. 1146. The decor at the air-conditioned **Gazal** restaurant is Western and the food is nonvegetarian Continental or Chinese. You can also dine outside at **Barbeque for South Indian** for tandoori items or at the **Rooftop Restaurant** for grilled specialties, with good views in either place. Gazal is open 8–11 A.M., noon–3 P.M., and 7–midnight. Barbeque and Rooftop are open 6–10 P.M. AE, DC, MC, V.

Inexpensive

Chotiwala Restaurant. Next to Har-ki-Pauri ghat, no phone. Eat outside or in a simple room crowded with tables. While a radio plays Hindi music, diners eat ample portions, Indian fashion, with the right hand. Friendly ambience. Open 7 A.M.–11 P.M. Rupees only.

LUCKNOW

Inexpensive

Ritz Continental. 7 Sapur Marg (opp. Jawahar Bhavan); tel. 240686. Exclusively vegetarian, this modern restaurant has white brick walls, mirrors, tiles, and overhead fans. Although the chef serves some Continental dishes, the most frequently requested cuisine here is Indian. Try Ritz special *sahi paneer* (cheese cooked in white gravy and coconut) or *navratan curry* (numerous vegetables cooked in a spicy gravy). Open 10:30 A.M.–10:30 P.M. Rupees only.

Shekhawat Kabab Corner. Near Triveni Lodge, behind the Gymkhana Club, Kaiserbagh; no phone. This tiny stall serves the best mutton kebabs and mutton *biryanis* (rice dishes) in Lucknow. Expect simplicity—sit on chairs inside or outside by the narrow road. Lots of fun! Open 5 P.M.–9 P.M., or until the food runs out; closed Tuesday.

Spicy Bite. Tulsi Theatre Bldg., 12 Rani Laxshmi Marg; tel. 245050. Artificial plants, an aquarium, and Formica tables and cane chairs fill up this cozy restaurant, along with a crowd of patrons. The menu features Continental dishes, such as pizzas and burgers, but the Chinese cuisine is the draw. Try the chicken spring rolls and various rice dishes. Open 11 A.M.–11 P.M. DC, MC, V.

MUSSOORIE

Moderate

Carlton's Hotel Plaisance. Happy Valley Rd.; tel. 2800. Meals are served in a family dining room or on the enclosed porch of this attractive inn. Tasty Indian and Continental cuisines. Reservations required. Open 1–2:30 P.M. and 8–10 P.M. AE, DC.

The Savoy. Tel. 2010 or 2620. The interior of this restaurant can feel cavernous unless it's high season and there's a crowd. Your best bet is to eat in the enclosed front terrace or outside gazing at the mountains. The menu includes a good selection of Chinese, Continental, and Indian cuisines. Open 7:30–10 A.M., 12:30–2:45 P.M., 7:30–10 P.M. AE, DC, MC, V.

Inexpensive

Jungli Murgi Restaurant. Roselynn Estate Hotel, The Mall; tel. 2201. The decor here is "woodsy" informal, and the menu offers good Indian and tandoori food. Open 9 A.M.–9 P.M. Rupees only.

RISHIKESH

Like the neighboring city of Haridwar, Rishikesh is devoutly "dry" and only strictly vegetarian foods—not even eggs—are served.

Moderate

Kautilya. Hotel Natraj, Dehra Dun Rd.; tel. 1099. This upstairs restaurant has an elegant modern decor, with fine linen on the tables. The chef creates very good Indian, Chinese, and Continental vegetarian dishes. Try *natraj au gratin* (vegetables baked in a cream sauce). Dinner reservations are advised. AE, DC, V.

Inexpensive

Anjali Restaurant. Railway Rd.; no phone. This popular in-town restaurant is always crowded with patrons enjoying Indian and Chinese food. The chef serves a popular thali with small portions of fresh vegetables. Open 8 A.M.–9 P.M. Rupees only.

Indrani Restaurant. Inderlok Hotel, Railway Rd.; tel. 555. This small hotel has a delightful, informal restaurant. You can choose between Continental and Indian cuisines. Open 8 A.M.–10 P.M. DC.

VARANASI

Expensive

Amrapali. Clarks Varanasi, The Mall; tel. 46771. Come to this spacious restaurant, with wood paneling and subdued lighting, when you're in the mood for Continental cuisine. The sizzlers are especially popular, but you can also order Indian and Chinese dishes. Dinner reservations advised. Open 7 A.M.–9:30 A.M., 12:30–3 P.M., and 7:30–10:30 P.M. AE, DC, MC, V.

Mandap. Hotel Taj Ganges, Nadesar Palace Grounds; tel. 42495. Brass temple bells hang from the ceiling, and a bank of windows overlook a pool and terrace. You can expect live Indian music nightly, except Thursday. Although the menu offers multicuisine fare, the Indian dishes are the most popular. Try *murg tikka lababdar* (chicken cooked in a tandoori oven, then simmered in a tomato-and-onion gravy) or *kadhai paneer* (cheese and green pepper cooked in a coriander-and-tomato gravy). Dinner reservations advised. Open 12:30 P.M.–3 P.M. and 7:30 P.M.–11 P.M. AE, DC, MC, V.

Moderate

Atithya. Hotel Varanasi Ashok, The Mall; tel. 46020. This restaurant lives up to its name, which means the "art of hospitality." Indian classical performers entertain patrons nightly in the high season. Choose from Chinese, Continental, and Indian cuisines. Try the tandoori items, or ask about the special Chinese dishes. Dinner reservations advised. Open 6 A.M.–11 A.M., noon–3 P.M., and 7 P.M.–midnight. Snacks are available during the afternoon. AE, DC, MC, V.

SWEETS AND TREATS. Lucknow. *Thandai ki Dookan,* a one-of-kind Lucknow institution, is nothing more than a stall opposite Gol Darwaza (the gate that leads into Chowk), not far from the Police Station. Try their famous *thandai,* a delicious concoction of milk, dry fruits, pistachios, and spices—an Indian milk shake—for about Rs. 10. Open 8 A.M. to late at night.

HOW TO GET AROUND. For some inexplicable reason, although Uttar Pradesh does very well at getting people from town to town by bus, train, and airplane, local transportation is sloppily controlled—or not controlled at all.

From the Airport. Allahabad. A taxi is your best bet; figure about Rs. 75 into the city. **Dehra Dun.** An airport bus (Rs. 20) meets each plane and goes to Dehra Dun, where you can get a taxi for Mussoorie for Rs. 400–Rs. 500 (the trip takes about 3 hours). Taxis from the airport to **Mussoorie** cost Rs. 600, or to **Haridwar** or **Rishikesh** about Rs. 250–Rs. 350 (the trip takes about 90 minutes). **Lucknow.** A taxi is best; figure about Rs. 175 into the city. **Varanasi.** An airport bus will take you into town for about Rs. 30; a taxi will take you directly to your hotel for about Rs. 210.

By Plane. Indian Airlines has three weekly flights between Varanasi and Lucknow. For information, call 64146 in Lucknow and 43746 in Varanasi.

By Train. Numerous tracks connect the major cities in Uttar Pradesh: Allahabad, Lucknow, Haridwar, and Varanasi. Contact the tourist department in each city for fares and details.

By Bus. UPSRTC has a network of buses running throughout the state. For routes and schedules, contact the tourist office in each city.

By Rented Car with Driver. This is the best way to tour this state, especially the Himalayan region. Rates are about Rs. 5 per km, with a halt charge of Rs. 50–

Rs. 100 per night. Hire a car from one of the recommended tour operators listed below. It's best to book in advance.

By Taxi. Rates are about Rs. 4.50 per km. Bargain.

By Auto Rickshaw. This should be cheaper than a taxi. Beware of the drivers in Varanasi—they're often cheats. Fares are normally determined by destination, with an Rs. 5 minimum charge. Set the price in advance.

By Bike Rickshaw. This is the best way to get around the congested cities. Figure about Rs. 20 per hour.

TOURS. Contact the local tourist offices about the following inexpensive bus tours (prices were under review at press time):

Dehra Dun. Daily city tour, including Malsi Deer Park, Tapkeshwar Temple Cave, and Sahastradhara (sulfur spring). Subject to enough passengers. For further details, call 23217.

Lucknow. Local sightseeing tours by UPSTDC (tel. 246205 or 248349), plus longer tours to Dudhwa National Park.

Mussoorie. Kempty Falls tour (peaceful bathing spot) daily. Dhanolti, scenic pine forest with good views of the Himalayas, and Surkhanda Devi Temple, on a hill with more good views. Subject to enough passengers. Tel. 2863.

Nainital. Numerous tours run by *Kumaon Division Development Corporation;* tel. 2656. Local sightseeing, two-day tour to Corbett National Park, four-day tour to Badrinath.

Rishikesh. Four-day tour from Rishikesh to Badrinath; seven-day tour to Badrinath and Kedrinath; four-day tour to Yamunotri, Gangotri, Kedarnath, and Badrinath; seven-day tour to Yamunotri and Gangotri; seven-day tour to Valley of Flowers, Hemkund, and Badrinath. Contact the Yatra Manager, Yatra Office, GMVN, Muni-ki-reti, Rishikesh 249201; tel. 372.

Varanasi. Two tours: Ganges River trip, temples, and Benaras Hindu University; and Sarnath and Ramnagar. Call 43486 or 42018 for fares and details.

You can also take a private boat cruise on the Ganges River. Figure about Rs. 30 per hour for a small boat. Cruises depart from the Dasaswamedh Ghat.

TOUR GUIDES. In most important destinations, you can hire a good guide through the tourist department. In Varanasi, contact the Government of India Tourist Office (see Tourist Information, above). For one to four people, rates are about Rs. 80 for four hours and Rs. 100 for eight hours.

TOUR OPERATORS. In Uttar Pradesh, adventure travel is on the rise, with the variety of opportunities expanding each year. Here are a few reliable outfits that offer terrific trips (also see this category in *Facts at Your Fingertips*) and make all arrangements in advance:

Arventure Adventure Holidays. Box 7, Dehra Dun; tel. 29172. Arranges treks galore, mountaineering, wildlife safaris, and biking led by an experienced staff.

Himalayan River Runners. 188–A, Jor Bagh, New Delhi; tel. 4632180. This is the best rafting company, offering good trips on all of Uttar Pradesh's white-water rivers.

GMVN. Trekking and Tour Executive, Mountaineering Division, Munkireti, Rishikesh; tel. 373. This government undertaking offers inexpensive treks and mountaineering, skiing packages, biking near Corbett, and fishing.

For all travel needs, contact these agencies:

UPTOURS. (see Tourist Information, above).

SITA. Shri Das Foundation Bldg., The Mall, Varanasi 221002; tel. 43421.

TCI. Shri Das Foundation Bldg., The Mall, Varanasi 221002; tel. 43096.

SEASONAL EVENTS. Since the lunar calendar determines most dates, contact the Government of India Tourist Office for details.

February. *Lucknow Festival.* Classic Indian culture displayed on a grand scale for over a week: theater, music, and dance, including the *kathak,* one of India's four classical dance forms, which has its home in this region. From a temple dance, it developed under the patronage of Moslem rulers into a court dance with a different gesture code and foot technique. The knotted Hindu draperies are replaced by tight-fitting pajamas and loose tunics made of heavy brocades.

Mid-February. *Shivratri* at Dehra Dun. Shiva's birthday is celebrated with a fair at Tapkeswar Cave Temple.

Spring. *Magh Mela* held at the confluence of the Ganges and Yamuna, in Allahabad. An amazing spectacle of thousands of Hindu devotees undergoing a sacred immersion.

May. *Buddha Purnima,* Sarnath. Birthday of Gautama Siddhartha, the Historic Buddha. A large fair with a procession of his relics. Very big occasion.

May. Mahashivratri celebrates the opening of the *Kedarnath Temple;* Akhand Jyoti Darshan celebrates the opening of *Badrinath Temple;* Akshayata-Tritaya the opening of *Yamunotri* and *Gangotri* temples. Temple priests make offerings to temple idols. Big events.

June/August. *Id-ul-Fitr,* Lucknow. Moslem celebration marking the end of Ramadan (month of fasting). Religious; big splash of festivity.

July. *Rath Yatra.* Held at Ramnagar Fort, Varanasi. Festive celebration in honor of Lord Jagannath, the Lord of the Universe, attracts big crowds. Temple "chariot" procession with sacred deities in seats of honor.

September–October. *Dussehra,* Varanasi. Big Hindu festival commemorating the victory of Lord Rama over Ravana. Enactments of *Ramila* held all over the city. At Ramnagar, elephants are available for hire and on the tenth day, a large procession culminates with the burning of effigies and a big fireworks display. In Varanasi proper, deities are taken in procession to be immersed in the Ganges.

October. *Muharram,* Lucknow. Moslem commemoration of the martyrdom of the grandson of the Prophet Mohammed Imam Hussain. Procession of beautiful tazias and illumination of the two Imambaras.

Once every 12 years (next time, 1998) *Kumbh Mela* is observed in Haridwar. *Sadhus* (devotees) fill up the city to have a sacred dip in the Ganges. Fakirs and yogis practice their amazing acts. Very religious, very festive. India's biggest festival—possibly the biggest in Asia. *Ardh Kumbh* is held every few years (next time, 2000). Half as big as Kumbh Mela, but still amazing. These same events are held in Allahabad.

HISTORIC SITES. Entrance to most places is generally free; where a temple donation is requested, a few rupees will suffice. Historic sites are open daily sunrise to sunset unless noted below.

AYODHYA

This is the principal city of the ancient kingdom of Kosala and the birthplace of Lord Rama, hero of the *Ramayana.* It is one of India's seven most sacred places. See *Hamuman Temple* and *Kanak Vhavan Temple,* mentioned in writings that go back to the seventh century.

ALLAHABAD

Akbar's fort sits atop the *Patal Puri Temple* with a tree that is continuously watered by Hindu priests. The tree is called the Undying Banyan Tree (Akshaya Batt) and is mentioned in writings that go back to A.D. 640. Unfortunately, the rest of the fort is off-limits.

BADRINATH

A colorfully decorated temple with stone carvings is believed to be Vishnu's former abode. In the inner sanctum is a black stone deity of Vishnu. The temple is closed during the winter months, usually late October until May. During the season, the inner sanctum is open 4:30 A.M.–1 P.M. and 3–9 P.M. Evening *arti* (prayer service) is 6–7.

DEHRA DUN

Tapkeshwar Caves (5½ km from Dehra Dun) are shrines, dedicated to Shiva, that are claimed to be 5,000 years old. In a delightful pastoral setting.

DEOPRAYAG

Ancient *Raghunath Temple,* dedicated to Vishnu, commemorates the spot where Rama (avatar of Vishnu) supposedly came to meditate. Very simple structure of granite, the temple was recently renovated.

FAIZABAD

In this ancient capital of the nawabs, there's a lovely *mausoleum* of Behbu Begum, one of the best in Uttar Pradesh.

GANGOTRI

The temple is closed during the winter months, usually late October until May. During the season, the inner sanctum is open 6 A.M.–noon and 2–9 P.M. Morning *arti* (service) begins at 6 and evening arti is at 6–7.

HARIDWAR

Har-ki-Pauri Ghat is where Vishnu left a set of his footprints—hard to see—but it *is* the most sacred ghat and backed by temples. See arti at sunset, a beautiful prayer offering to the Ganges, which concludes with hundreds of little flower boats lit with candles set loose on the river. Visit the *Daksh Mahadev Temple,* dedicated to Shiva, and *Sati Kund* in Kankhal (part of Haridwar). Go up to the *Mansa Devi Temple,* dedicated to the goddess Mansi, an avatar of Durga, from which you get a good view of Haridwar. Also see three ashrams on the northern edge of Haridwar: *Pawan Dham Ashram,* built in 1970, a sort of a Hindi psychedelic show—wonderful fun; *Parmarth Ashram,* more subdued; and *Sapt Rishi Ashram,* downright solemn in comparison.

KEDARNATH

In this supposed abode of Shiva is a simple gray temple on a raised platform set against the banks of the Mandakini, with a Nandi statue standing in the courtyard. A visit here represents an extremely important pilgrimage to be approached on foot or pony (15 km [9 miles] from the road). The temple is closed during the winter months, usually late October until May. During the season, the inner sanctum is open 4:30 A.M.–1 P.M. and 2–9 P.M. Morning arti begins at 6 and evening arti is at 6–7.

LUCKNOW

Bara Imambara was built by Asaf-ud-Daula as his burial place in 1784 after a year-long famine. The project created "relief work" for the rich and poor—it contains neither cement nor iron. There are three interior chambers in different styles (from left to right after you enter): Chinese, Persian, and Indian. Find your way through the Bhul-Bhulaiya maze upstairs. Open 6 A.M.–5 P.M.

Rumi Darwaza, beyond the outer gate of Imambara, was built in 1784 by Asaf-ud-Daula as another relief project. It is a facsimile of a gate in Constantinople.

Chhota Imambara was built in 1836 by Muhammad Ali Shah as his burial place. Two miniature replicas of the Taj Mahal are just inside the gate and contain the tombs of his daughter, Zinat Asuja, and her husband. In the Imambara is a dazzling display of chandeliers, lamps, and *tazias.* Open 6 A.M.–5 P.M.

Residency is the remains of Asaf-ud-Daula's pleasure house, which was taken over by the British and subsequently became the scene of fierce fighting during the 1857 Indian Mutiny. If you want to go into the hall, called the Model Room (Rs. 2), entrance time is 8 A.M.–5 P.M. No restrictions to visit the rest of the Residency.

Also in the center of town, see the tombs of *Nawab Saadat Ali Khan* and his wife, Begum Mursheedzadi, constructed in the nineteenth century. Nearby are the *Kaisar Bagh,* rows of apartments that housed the ladies of the royal harem.

Shahnajaf Imambara is the tomb of Nawab Ghazi-ud-din Haider and his wives. Built in 1814, it became a stronghold for Indians during the 1857 Mutiny. Open 6 A.M.–5 P.M.

La Martiniere was built in a jumble of styles by Claude Martin in 1795. An architectural compendium dedicated to whimsy, it is now a school.

RISHIKESH

Important Hindu ashrams that can be visited here: *Swami Sivananda's Divine Life Society; Maharshi Mahesh Yogi's Transcendental Meditation Center;* and *Triveni Ghat,* the main sacred ghat and scene of a miniarti performed each evening.

SARNATH

At this center of the Buddhist world, 6 km (4 miles) from Varanasi, Buddha preached his first sermon 2,500 years ago, in which he revealed the Eightfold Path leading to enlightenment. Ashoka is responsible for the construction of many of the third-century stupas. Sarnath reached its zenith under the Gupta dynasty in the sixth century. It's a lovely, peaceful place with new Buddhist temples.

VARANASI

Dasashwamedh Ghat is the main ghat to visit here. *Manikarnika Ghat* and *Harish Chandra Ghat* are the cremation ghats. You can watch cremations at no cost, but photographs are forbidden.

Gyanvapi Mosque is Aurangzeb's seventeenth-century creation erected on the site of the Vishveswara Temple, which he destroyed.

Alamgir Mosque. After Aurangzeb destroyed a temple—the Beni Madhav Ka Darera, which was dedicated to Vishnu—he put up this mosque with an odd fusion of the abhorred Hindu (lower portion) and Moslem (upper portion) designs.

Ramnagar Fort is the former residential palace of the ex-maharajah of Varanasi; approached by boat, most of it is now a museum.

INNER CITY OF VARANASI

Kashi Vishwanath Temple, dedicated to Shiva, is in between the Dasashwamedh and Manikarnika ghats. It is off-limits to non-Hindus, but pay a small fee and see the interior from the house opposite. Watch morning or evening prayers—flower offerings given to the lingam. The temple was constructed in 1776, with its spire covered in gold plate—a gift from Maharajah Ranjit Singh in 1835.

Durga Temple, dedicated to Durga, consort of Shiva; this eighteenth-century construction is located due west of Asi Ghat. The *shikara* (spire) is formed on top of five lower spires—a convergence that is a visual symbol of the belief that all five elements of the world merge with the Supreme. Durga is also called the Monkey Temple; the pests are everywhere and they'll steal anything.

Bharat Mata Mandir, on Vidya Peeth Road, is a temple inaugurated by Mahatma Gandhi and dedicated to India. Inside is a large relief map of India carved of marble.

YAMUNOTRI

The temple is closed during the winter months, usually late October until May. During the season, the inner sanctum is open 6 A.M.–noon and 2–9 P.M. Evening arti is 6–7.

MUSEUMS AND GALLERIES. Museums are free or a nominal fee is requested. In Allahabad, *Allahabad Museum,* Alfred Park, has terra cottas, good Rajasthani miniatures, and modern paintings. Open generally 10 A.M.–6 P.M. Closed Mondays. *Anand Bhavan* (Place of Joy) is the former home of Jawaharlal Nehru and contains personal momentos of this freedom fighter/politician. Open 10 A.M.–1 P.M. and 2 P.M.–5 P.M. Closed Mondays.

In Lucknow, *Archaeological Museum,* Kaiserbagh, contains archaeological finds, with a heavy concentration from Uttar Pradesh. Open 10 A.M.–5 P.M.; Rs. 0.50. *Picture Gallery,* between the two Imambaras, was built by Nawab Mohammad Ali Shah. Kind of a *Who's Who* portrait gallery of the megalomanical *nawabs* (provincial governors). Open 8 A.M.–5 P.M.

State Museum, Banarsi Bagh, is a general all-around museum with paintings and artifacts. Open 10 A.M.–5 P.M., closed Mondays.

In Sarnath, *Archaeological Museum* contains great Buddhist treasures. Open 10 A.M.–5 P.M., closed Fridays.

In Varanasi, *Bharat Kala Bhavan* (Art Gallery) at Banaras Hindu University has a good collection of paintings and art objects. Closed Sundays and university holidays. Open 9:30 A.M.–4:30 P.M.; in summer, 8 A.M.–noon.

In Ramnagar, *Fort Museum* houses a fine collection of palanquins, furniture, arms, weapons, and costumes. Open daily 9 A.M.–noon; 2–5 P.M.

GARDENS AND ZOOS. Dehra Dun. *Forest Research Institute Botanical Garden* and *Malso Deer Park* are both open sunrise to sunset. Free.

Lucknow. Lucknow is a city of lovely gardens. See in particular *Zoological Garden of Lucknow* in the Banarasi Bagh (*bagh* means "garden"), founded in 1921 as a memorial to a visit by the Prince of Wales, open 5 A.M.–7 P.M.; *Sikandar Bagh* (open 6 A.M.–5 P.M.), site of fierce fighting in 1857; gardens under the management of the National Botanical Research Institute; *Nehru Bagh;* and the *Gautama Buddha Park,* a delightful park for children.

SPORTS AND OUTDOOR ADVENTURES. Uttar Pradesh is an adventure state. Boating, fishing, skiing, trekking or wonderful walks, and white-water rafting are all here to be experienced in beautiful surroundings. What follows is a partial list. Contact the Uttar Pradesh tourist departments for the current range of possibilities.

Boating. Mussoorie and Nainital. Sailing down the Ganges.

Bicycling. Contact the Tour Operators above for bicycling trips near Corbett National Park.

Fishing. *Corbett National Park* (see Wildlife Sanctuaries, below). *Dehra Dun.* For details and permit, contact Divisional Forest Officer (East), Dehra Dun 248001. *Mussoorie.* For details and permits, contact Divisional Forest Officer, Yamuna Division, Mussoorie 248179.

Rafting. You can raft one to three days (Oct.–mid-Dec. and Feb.–June) on the Ganga from Deoprayag to Rishikesh; take a six-day run (Nov.–mid-Dec. and Feb.–Apr.) on the Alakananda from Rudraprayag to Rishikesh; or run the Bhagirathi from Tehri to Rishikesh, the greatest challenge (Nov.–mid-Dec. and Feb.–Apr.). Make arrangements in advance; tel. 373.

Skiing. Auli, near Joshimath, will have a chair lift in operation by 1993. This is a brand-new and developing resort. GMVN runs ski courses from January to March for 5, 10, and 15 days. They will supply the skiing equipment. For further details, reservations, and cost, contact GMVN in Dehra Dun (74–1 Rajpur Rd., Dehra Dun 248001; tel. 26817). This resort will be spectacular once it's in full operation. For now, just to ski it's an inexpensive treat.

Trekking. Here are some of the most popular possibilities in Uttar Pradesh:

Rudraprayag to Badrinath via Chamoh–Pipalkou–Gulabkoti–Joshimath (by bus). On foot: Joshimath–Pandukeshwar (13 km or 8 mi.)–Badrinath (18 km or 11 mi.). Elevation 1,829–5,564 meters (6,000–10,250 feet). At all these stages there is a Public Works Department (P.W.D.) Inspection Bungalow. Reservations authority: Executive Engineer. P.W.D. Pauri. A three- to four-day hike.

Rudraprayag to Kedarnath via Kakaragad (last bus stop)–Gupta Kashi (6 km or 4 mi.)–Phata (14 km or 9 mi.)–Gauri Kund (13 km or 8 mi.)–Kedarnath (11 km or 7 mi.). Elevation 914–3,567 meters (3,000–11,700 feet). Reservations authority for accommodations along this route: Secretary, District Board, and Executive Engineer, both at Pauri. A two-day hike. Hire porters at Rudraprayag.

Kedarnath to Chamoli via Gauri Kund–Phata–Nalapatan–Ukimath–Tungnath–Gopeshwar–Chamoli (total 80 km or 50 mi.). Elevation 914–3,567 meters (3,000–11,700 feet). P.W.D. Inspection Bungalow at all stages. Reservations authority: Executive Engineer, P.W.D., Pauri. Four days or less.

Almora to Pindari Glacier, by bus to Kapkot (where you must wait for ponies and porters)–Lharkhet (16 km or 10 mi.)–Dhakuri (9 km or 6 mi.)–Khati (9 km or 6 mi.)–Dwali (11 km or 7 mi.)–Phurkia (5 km or 3 mi.)–Pindari Glacier (5 km or 3 mi.). P.W.D. Bungalows at all stages. Reservations authority: P.W.D., Bageshwar. Bring a tent for camping at Martoli, near the glacier. Elevation 1,067–3,354 meters (3,500–11,000 feet). Sundardhhunga and Kaphini Glaciers can be visited en route.

A trip to Pindari Glacier is well within the capacity of any hiker, and the effort involved is amply rewarded by the views en route as well as by the magnificence of the glacier itself. Six or seven days are required for this trek. The best time to visit is May 14–June 15, when the flowers are in bloom and the snow bridges have not melted away, or Sept. 15–early October, when the air is free from haze and the Trail Pass is still negotiable. The glacier is three miles from Phurkia, and the trek involves a climb of 762 meters (2,500 feet). An early start enables you to spend some time on the glacier and to take in its grandeur and beauty. The return journey can be shortened by halting only at Dwali, Dhakuri, and Kapkot.

Mussoorie to Chakrata via Saingi (14 km or 9 mi.)–Lakhwar (11 km or 7 mi.)–Nayhtat (9 km or 6 mi.)–Chorani (14 km or 9 mi.)–Chakrata (11 km or 7 mi.). Dak Bungalows at all stages. Reservations not necessary but accommodations are usually primitive.

Chakrata to Himachal Pradesh boundary (toward Shimla) via Desban (11 km or 7 mi.)–Mandali (19 km or 12 mi.)–Kalhyan–Tinuni (19 km or 12 mi.)–Arakot (14 km or 9 mi.). Elevation: 884–2,134 meters (2,900–7,000 feet). Forest Rest Houses at all stations. Reservations authority: District Forest Officer, Chakrata.

WILDLIFE SANCTUARIES. *Corbett National Park,* 320 km (199 mi.) from Delhi, is India's oldest sanctuary and one of its best. From the back of an elephant, inside a jeep, or waiting patiently in a *machan* (watch tower), you may see elephants, tigers, leopards, black bear, wild boar, deer (numerous species), snakes (including the python and king cobra), crocodiles, and birds. The park is open November–mid-June. The main entrance is at Dhikala, and you must arrive before dark. At press time, the cost of admission was under review. It will be reasonable. At Dhikala, you can also arrange for elephant or jeep rides and guides. Daylight photography only is allowed. Fishing is currently banned to increase the stocks.

During the park season, GMVN operates a three-day tour (Fri.–Sun.) from New Delhi. For details, contact UPSTDC, Chandralok Building, 36 Janpath, New Delhi; tel. 3322251 or 3711286.

SHOPPING. The main shopping areas are in the cities of Lucknow and Varanasi, two places where it's hard to say no. The main shopping bargains are, of course, the exquisite Varanasi silks, brocades, and saris. Lucknow's gold and silver and white embroidery (called *chikan*), table covers, and silverware, and Mirzapur's carpets. Brassware and lacquered toys complete the list. In the Himalayan area, look at handwoven products made of Garhwal wool: shawls, hats, and gloves. The main centers of shopping at Allahabad are the Civil Lines, Johnstonganj, and the Chowk (bazaar). In Lucknow, fixed-price shopping is concentrated at Hazratganj. Aminabad (a market area) is the place to go for perfume essences (attars). The following three cities have great chowks:

In Lucknow, the *Chowk* is great for browsing and getting a sense of lively Lucknow. Lots of special hand-embroidered chikan work. The best shops are *Lal Bihari Tandon,* Gota Bazar, Chowk, and *Delux Kurta Industry,* 11 Gota Bazar, Chowk, which has great *dhotis* (skirtlike garments) for babies and small children. Also visit the Nazirabad area in Aminabad, which sells chickan work. Shops in the Chowk are generally closed on Thursday. For Lucknow essence (natural perfume), head to Sugandhco at Habibullah Estate, Hazratganj, or at D–4 Janpath Market. Each shop is open 11 A.M.–7:30 P.M.; closed Sundays.

In Haridwar, *Moti Bazaar* is a delightful, manageable size, with medicine shops and religious stalls. Fun; mostly for browsing.

Varanasi has three good shopping areas: *Chowk, Godowlia,* and *Vishwanath Lane.* If you want to buy silk, play safe so you won't get stuck with shoddy goods. Get a list of approved shops from the Uttar Pradesh Tourist Department. Good-quality silk costs money. If you get a steal, you're the one who's probably been robbed. The following are reputable shops: *Brij Raman Das & Sons,* K37/32, Golghar, open Mon.–Sat., 9 A.M.–8 P.M. (rupees only); and *The Silk Corner,* Mint House Motel, near Taj Ganges, open daily 9:30 A.M.–8 P.M. (AE, DC, MC, V).

BARS AND NIGHTLIFE. Don't expect too much nightlife in Uttar Pradesh, but most of the hotels have bars where you can enjoy an afternoon cocktail or a pleasant evening. Bars generally are open 11 A.M.–3 P.M. and 6–11 P.M. or midnight. A selection includes the *Polo Bar* in the Hotel President, Dehra Dun, which is in a cozy downstairs room. Also in Dehra Dun, the subdued lighting in the *Madhushala,* Hotel Madhuban, gives the feeling of intimacy. In Lucknow, the new bar at the Taj will probably be best. To reminisce about the Raj era, have a drink in the Victorian barroom of *Hakman's Hotel* or try the comfortable cocktail lounge in the *Savoy,* which has a pleasant ambience. In Varanasi, the *Kambari* in Clarks Varanasi is an attractive and quiet place.

AGRA AND FATEHPUR SIKRI

The Road into the Past

by
KATHLEEN COX

As distances go, the trip from Delhi to Agra is not more than a stone's throw—200 kilometers (124 miles) by car from the capital of modern India to the former seat of the Mogul Empire. But few trips in India—or anywhere else in the world—offer such an extensive journey into history and ethereal historic beauty. This is the royal road of the Mogul emperors established in the sixteenth and seventeenth centuries, when their capital fluctuated between Delhi and Agra. Today, Delhi reigns over India, but Agra still reigns over that unforgettable past created by warriors as skilled in art and architecture as they were on the battlefield.

A trip to Agra should include Fatehpur Sikri, the abandoned capital of Akbar the Great, and extend farther south to Jhansi, home of Lakshmi Bai, India's Joan of Arc, and to Gwalior and Shivpuri, which are in neighboring Madhya Pradesh.

Vrindaban

When you enter Vrindaban, 131 kilometers (82 miles) south of Delhi, it's like entering holy ground. This is a city of 1,000 shrines, the biggest being Gobind Deo. Erected to Hindu glory, with the encouragement of the tolerant Mogul Akbar, the temple suffered a dismal reversal during

135

the reign of one of Akbar's descendants. The continual glare of a giant oil lamp burning from an upper story so annoyed Aurangzeb that he over-reacted and lopped off the entire top half of the shrine. The site of a walled-in garden, Nikunja Ban, Vrindaban is also significant to the Hindu pilgrim. Here, Krishna, the most popular of the incarnations of Vishnu, the pre-server, supposedly appeared before his worshipers. In fact, almost every step you take in this city follows the path of this adored god, as does the road that takes you to Mathura, about 10 kilometers (six miles) south.

Mathura

Mathura, situated on the west bank of the Yamuna River, which flows from Delhi to Agra, is supposedly the birthplace of Krishna. Hindu pil-grims the world over visit a shrine in a part of the city called Katra. Origi-nally the site of a Hindu temple, it, too, was destroyed by the intolerant Aurangzeb, who built a mosque in its place. But the basement of the origi-nal Kesava Deo remains, as does a sign proclaiming that Krishna was born here.

The holiness of Mathura is all pervasive—drawing worshipers of Vishnu the way that Varanasi draws the adorers of Shiva, the destroyer. Even the Hare Krishnas are headquartered here. Just as the followers of Shiva flock to the Ganges, pilgrims to Mathura are drawn to the Yamuna—in particu-lar to the Vishram Ghat. Here Krishna supposedly rested after killing the tyrant Kansa (in whose prison he is believed to have been born). Religious ceremonial acts on the Yamuna are less intense than those on the Ganges: at sunset, hundreds of flickering oil lamps are launched on the river. But rites are performed, and they are worth seeing.

Mathura is one of the oldest cities of India, far older than Agra, with a history that goes back to before the Maurya dynasty, which ruled India from 325 to 184 B.C. This explains why the government museum has such an accumulation of artistic wealth left behind by foreign conquerors, in-cluding the Parthians and the Greeks. This also explains the flowering of Mathura sculpture, which started in the first century A.D. and lasted for a startling 1,200 years, going into decline when sculptors gave up sacred Buddhist and Hindu subjects to turn their chisels to the frivolous figures of full-bosomed dancing girls. Unfortunately, much of the grandeur of Mathura suffered the wrath of its conquerors, and few Hindu monuments remain.

Sikandra: Akbar's Tomb

Ten kilometers (six miles) down the royal road, you'll come to the glori-ous introduction to Agra: Sikandra, named after Sultan Sikander Lodi of the dynasty conquered by the Moguls. Sikandra is the site of the tomb of Akbar, the great Mogul emperor (1542–1605) who planned its design and began its construction in 1602. The tomb was finally completed by his son Jahangir in 1613.

A model of symmetry, built out of red sandstone and marble, the mau-soleum stands in the center of a huge garden. The entrance is through an imposing, two-story gateway, 23 meters (75 feet) high, with exquisite mo-saic and inlay work, and is topped by four slim marble minarets that rise up from each corner.

The main tomb is a fusion of Hindu and Moslem styles, as if reflecting the religious tolerance of Akbar, who dreamed of peaceful coexistence be-tween the two religions. Each floor of the five-story structure has a series of arcades, tapering to a marble cloister that seems to float on the top of the cloister beneath it.

A narrow passageway leads to the cryptlike grave, now dimly lit by a hanging lamp (the gift of Lord Curzon). A replica of the white marble cenotaph rests precisely above it on the upper floor so no one can ever walk on Akbar's resting place. This identical crypt is inscribed with the 99 names attributed to Allah, plus the phrase "Allah-o-Akbar" (God is Great) at the head; and the phrase "Jalla Jalalahu" (Great Is His Glory) at the foot.

AGRA

Akbar the Great made Agra great. The city's origins before the Mogul conquest are dim: The conquering Babur, Akbar's grandfather, practically founded the ultimately important Moslem center. And, by some strange process of mutation, the warlike Moguls—Babur was a descendant of the wicked Tamerlane of central Asia—were transformed into the most civilized and refined rulers of their day, revering the arts and thirsting for learning with a tolerance seldom found in history. The pitifully short golden age of Agra came to an end with the seventeenth-century reign of Shah Jahan, but it had an unforgettable climax in the Taj Mahal.

Not much happened in Agra before the Moguls and not much has happened since. Sacked by the Jats and occupied by the Marathas, the city entered a peaceful slumber in 1803, when it fell into the hands of the British. Today, its population has reached 1.2 million, but it is still a small city by Indian standards. The surrounding countryside of sandy stretches somehow produces a rice crop, cultivated by patient and hardworking farmers.

To the lover of art and to the traveler seeking the wonders of the world, Agra is the goal of a pilgrimage to the creative best: the Agra Fort and the Taj Mahal.

The Fort and Its Palaces

At the Agra Fort, the story of that portion of the Mogul Empire extending from Akbar to his son Jahangir to Shah Jahan is recorded in stone: the rusty-red sandstone of forbidding walls raised by Akbar, the shimmering white marble of palaces built by Shah Jahan. The fort, which is open from sunrise to sunset, is an excellent introduction to Agra. It took centuries for the castles of Europe to evolve from stern medieval citadels to graceful Renaissance palaces. At Agra, this process of evolution took place within the span of these three generations.

No one would question the fort's indomitable appearance. It stands on the banks of the Yamuna, surrounded by a wall 22 meters (70 feet) high, which guards a 12-meter (40-foot) moat with another 22-meter wall behind it. These double walls, pierced with slits and loopholes, seem capable of barring anyone from an inner paradise whose towers can only be glimpsed from the outside. Luckily, this daunting mass can be penetrated for the price of admission at the Amar Singh Gate, where visitors usually enter the fort.

In all, the walls around the Agra Fort measure 1½ miles in circumference. The original military structure was begun by Akbar, who is believed to have demolished an ancient castle on the site. He completed the fort eight years later, then built the palace called the Jahangiri Mahal, the first of the many interior constructions—built with the simpler architecture and intricate decoration so typical of the Mogul era.

AGRA

| 0 miles | ½ | 1 |
| 0 meters | 800 | 1600 |

1. Agra University
2. Tourist Bungalow
3. Jama Masjid Mosque
4. Bus Station
5. General Post Office
6. Tourist Information (Govt. of India)
7. Tourist Bureau (U.P. Govt.)
8. Central Telegraph Office

Jahangiri Mahal

Once you enter the Amar Singh Gate, to the north is the biggest private residence inside the Agra Fort, the Jahangiri Mahal (palace), supposedly built by Akbar for his son (Akbar's Palace, closer to the entrance, is in ruins). Here, you see a striking example of Akbar's ability to blend Hindu architecture with the style imported by the Moguls from Central Asia. The palace is huge, measuring about 76 by 93 meters (250 by 300 feet). You enter through a hall leading to a courtyard surrounded by columns. The central court of the palace is lined by two-story facades bearing remnants of the rich gilded decorations that once covered a great deal of the structure. On one side of the court is a hall known as Jodh Bai's dressing room (Jodh Bai was the Hindu mother of Jahangir), with a ceiling supported by serpents carved in stone. Also leading into the court is a hall known as Jodh Bai's reception room and a series of rooms, one of which is known as the library and is remarkable for its Mogul decoration. Most likely, these rooms were used both by Jahangir's mother and his empress, Nur Jahan (meaning light of the world).

Jahangir loved wine and the arts almost as much as he loved his wife. Nur Jahan attempted to convince him to settle down to the serious occupation of ruling an empire, but, finally, she had to do the job for him—sitting by his side in their palace in the Agra Fort, dispensing imperial justice. She was a strong-willed woman and made short shrift of anyone who stood in her way. One favorite method she employed was dropping rivals into a pit that conveniently led to the Yamuna River (the grim underground chambers near this pit are still intact).

Nur Jahan is also given credit for the discovery of distilling the attar of roses. After a quarrel with Jahangir, she went off to brood in the palace courtyard, where she noticed that, in the heat of the sun, rose petals floating in a pond oozed an oily substance. The fragrance was overwhelming. With a clever daub of this new perfume, she returned to Jahangir, who found her irresistible.

After Jahangir's death in 1628, Shah Jahan (whose mother was one of the other wives of Jahangir) assumed the throne and started his own collection of buildings inside the fort, some of them architectural pearls.

Shahjahani Mahal

The building known as Shahjahani Mahal is actually the remodeled northern part of Jahangiri Mahal; three rooms and a corridor enhanced by a tapering tower gallery topped with a pavilion bearing a spike. From this imperial vantage point, Shah Jahan watched elephant fights. In more tranquil moments, he received instruction from a Hindu holy man who was carried up in a litter.

Khas Mahal

Shah Jahan outdid himself in the Khas Mahal (the Private Palace), built in 1637: three pavilions overlooking the Yamuna with a fountain tank opposite the central pavilion. This white marble building follows the Mogul pattern in style: three arches on each side, five in front, and two turrets rising out of the roof. Once flowers created with precious stones were encrusted in its walls, but the jewels were looted in the eighteenth century. Of the other two pavilions, one is of white marble and is supposed to have been decorated with gold leaf, while the other is made of redstone. In one part of the Khas Mahal, a staircase leads down to the "air-conditioned" quarters of the palace, cool underground rooms that were probably inhabited during the scorching heat of summer.

Sheesh Mahal

On the northeastern end of the courtyard of the Khas Mahal stands the Sheesh Mahal (Palace of Mirrors), built in 1637. This building was the bath of the private palace and the dressing room of the harem, with each of the two chambers containing a bathing tank that was once fed by marble channels. In its glory, small mirrors that covered the ceilings and walls caught the sunlight and turned the interior of the Sheesh Mahal into a dazzling vision of brilliance. Cleanliness was evidently a greater concern to the Moguls than to their contemporary counterparts who lived in seventeenth-century castles and palaces in Europe (where fountains were only for show).

Anguri Bagh

A rectangle in front of the Khas Mahal bears the mysterious name of Anguri Bagh (Vineyard Garden), but no one has ever found any trace of the grapevines. This was apparently a Mogul garden, with fountains and flowerbeds on a marble-paved platform divided by stone partitions. Apartments that might have been used by members of the emperor's harem surround three sides of the garden. Below the terrace, a marble cistern leads to the platform.

Diwan-i-Am

To the people of the empire and to the European emissaries who came to see this powerful monarch, the most impressive part of the fort was the Diwan-i-Am (Hall of Public Audience), set within the large quadrangle. A huge low structure, it rests on a stage four feet high, with nine cusped Mogul arches held aloft by rows of slender supporting pillars. There is considerable disagreement about which of the three Mogul emperors—Akbar, Jahangir, or Shah Jahan—built this hall, but none at all about the creator of its throne room. Only Shah Jahan could have conceived this alcove with its inlaid mosaics, one of the marvels of Mogul art. Here, the emperor sat and dispensed justice to his subjects, rich and poor alike. Below the throne, his *wazir* (prime minister) sat on a small platform with a silver railing, where he received the petitioners as they came in.

The petitioner bowed three times before he reached the wazir, never daring to raise his eyes to the Grand Mogul, while a herald proclaimed that the poor mortal stood in the presence of the "Sun of the World." Bernier, a French traveler of the day, dared to lift his gaze on the ruler, however, and recorded what he saw: "The monarch, every day about noon, sits upon his throne with some of his sons at his right and left, while eunuchs, standing about the royal persons, flap away flies with peacock tails, agitate the air with large fans or wait with profound humility to perform the different services allotted to them."

Unlike the contemporaries of the Moguls, you get to wander freely through the palace that was once reserved for the private life of the emperor and his courts. For example, not far from the public audience hall lies what is believed to have been the Inner Mina Bazaar, where ladies of the court shopped for jewelry or silks. Sometimes, too, the Grand Mogul and his intimates played store—a game in which the wives of noblemen acted as vendors while the emperor amused himself by haggling. The exact location of this regal shopping center is unknown; it may have been in the Macchi Bhavan.

In the Macchi Bhavan (Palace of Fish), gaily colored fish danced through water channels for the amusement of the court. Evidently, this was one part of the fort in which the emperor and his harem could escape all the inhibitions of pomp and ceremony.

Diwan-i-Khas

Contrasted with the Hall of Public Audience is the Diwan-i-Khas, or Hall of Private Audience, built by Shah Jahan in 1636–37. Here, the emperor received foreign ambassadors or dignitaries of his kingdom. The Diwan-i-Khas, which is due east of the Diwan-i-Am, contains two halls connected by three arches. White marble covers their red sandstone walls and lavish carvings can still be seen at the base of the columns that support the arches. Outside this light structure is the famous throne terrace with its pair of black-and-white thrones. The black throne was carved from a single block of marble and stands on a marble platform overlooking the Yamuna. A low railing of white marble contrasts with the black throne. According to the inscriptions found on it, this seat of power was apparently made for Jahangir. The white throne, consisting of several blocks of marble, was installed for Shah Jahan, who is said to have relaxed here by fishing below the terrace or by watching the magnificent elephant fights staged in the fort.

Musamman Burj

Near the Diwan-i-Khas is the tall Musamman Burj, originally built by Shah Jahan for Mumtaz Mahal, his wife, who is buried in the Taj Mahal. It is an octagonal tower with a courtyard on the lower floor paved with octagonal marble slabs. Here, too, are those delicate lattices of marble, no doubt used as screens to enable the ladies of the court to look out on the fort without being seen. In the center of the tower is a beautifully carved fountain. But all this beauty turned into the setting for a tragedy: Shah Jahan died here in 1666, after seven years as a prisoner of his own son, Aurangzeb. Here, he breathed his last, looking out at the Taj Mahal. Only his devoted daughter, Jahanara, remained with him during his final days.

The Mussamman Burj is another of the exceptional monuments left by Shah Jahan. One writer compared it to "a fairy tower hanging over grim ramparts." Unfortunately, only the barest trace still exists of the decorative designs that once adorned this tower: plunderers removed all the precious stones in 1761.

Nagina Masjid

To the northeast of the Diwan-i-Khas, you'll find the white marble Nagina Masjid, a private mosque raised by Shah Jahan with typical cusped arches. Walled in on three sides, it has a marble courtyard for worshipers and three graceful domes. This mosque was probably used by the royal ladies or by those seeking audience with the emperor.

Moti Masjid

A short distance away stands the Moti Masjid, a pearl mosque built in white marble by Shah Jahan and considered ideal in its proportions. The beauty of the Moti Masjid hits you suddenly—it's not at all evident from the outside. But a marble courtyard with arcaded cloisters on three sides unfolds before your eyes (the fourth side on the west has a place for the leader of the worshipers). Marble screens conceal what may have been the section reserved for women. Seven archways support the roof of this mosque, which bears three handsome domes. Over the arches of the prayer chamber, a Persian inscription compares the mosque to a pearl and states that as ordered by Shah Jahan, it took seven years to build. Unfortunately, as of this writing, the Moti Masjid is temporarily closed for renovations.

Also of interest are the two main gates, the Amar Singh and Delhi Gates, a pavilion known as Salim's Fort near the entrance, and the intriguing Hauz-i-Jahangiri. The Hauz-i-Jahangiri is a bath carved out of a huge block of stone five feet high and 25 feet in circumference that, according to the inscription, connects it to Jahangir. There are many theories regarding its purpose: some insist that Akbar ordered it carved to celebrate Jahangir's birth; others say it was Jahangir's wedding present to Nur Jahan in 1611.

Finally, just who is Lieutenant Governor Colvin, whose tomb is in the fort? The unfortunate soldier died here during the Indian Mutiny of 1857, when the fort was under siege.

THE TAJ MAHAL—MONUMENT TO LOVE

To some, the Taj Mahal is overrated. To others, it's a sublime experience to be ranked with the Pyramids of Egypt, the Palace of Versailles, or the Parthenon of Athens as the aesthetic epitome of a civilization. To still others, it simply represents the greatest love story ever told. This should make it clear that the Taj Mahal, despite the imposing dimensions of its architecture and all the good and bad literature it has inspired, is very much a matter of taste.

One other preliminary word: give the Taj Mahal a chance. It speaks a different language when seen by moonlight, through the shimmer of dawn, in the bright light of midday, and at sunset. Although a full moon brings out its distinct and heavenly beauty, it also brings out the crowds who destroy the serenity and stately aura. So, taking everything into consideration, probably the best time to see the Taj Mahal is in the early morning when it emerges from the night ahead of the sun, whose first pale rays give a soft luster to the marble, which glistens in a coat of pink, blue, or even mauve. And the surroundings at this time of day are calm and peaceful—nothing upstages its grandeur.

You can't experience the Taj Mahal if you don't know its story. Nearly all the world's great monuments were the product of the religious fervor of a people or the vanity of a king. But the Taj Mahal is an exception; it was built as a monument to love.

Arjuman Banu, the niece of Jangir's queen, Nur Jahan, was the second wife of Emperor Shah Jahan, the artist among the Mogul builders. In 1612, at the age of 21, she married him and took on the names that have passed down through time: Mumtaz Mahal, the Exalted of the Palace, and Mumtazul-Zamani, the Distinguished of the Age. Numerous tales speak of her generosity and her wisdom, both as a household manager and as an adviser to her imperial husband, but even these qualities were overshadowed by the love that bound her to Shah Jahan. She bore him 14 children, and it was in childbirth that she died in 1630 at Burhanpur, where her husband was waging a military campaign.

When she died, Shah Jahan was grief stricken. His hair supposedly turned gray within a few months, and it is said that he put aside his royal robes for simple white muslin clothes. A huge procession brought her body from Burhanpur, where it had been temporarily buried, to Agra six months after her death. Shah Jahan vowed to build her a memorial surpassing anything the world had ever seen in beauty and in wild extravagance. He brought in skilled craftsmen from Persia, Turkey, France, and Italy. He put a huge army of 20,000 laborers to work, building a whole new village (Taj Ganj, which still stands) to house them. The cost of reproducing the Taj Mahal today has been estimated at nearly $70 million, but who would try?

A Masterpiece in Marble

The Taj Mahal lies on the banks of the Yamuna River, where it can be seen, like a fantastic mirage, from the nearby Agra Fort. Construction began in 1632; although no one knows who drew up the actual plans, Shah Jahan's chief architect, Ustad Ahmad Lahori, was clearly involved. Some people accuse the Taj Mahal of architectural exaggeration and coldness (not so inappropriate for a mausoleum), but no one has ever denied its perfect proportions. This huge mass of white marble resting on red sandstone is a jewel, fashioned over 17 years. The work ended on the exact anniversary of the Mumtaz Mahal's death.

Glimpsed from the enormous main gateway inscribed with verses of the Quran (the entire Quran is said to be reproduced on its walls), the Taj Mahal reveals itself with the suddenness of a jewel box opened before your eyes. This gate leads you inside a walled garden—and there, the magic spell is cast. A rectangular pool (unfortunately with too-shallow water), bordered by cypresses, catches the shimmering image of the tomb.

In the Agra Fort, virile red sandstone and elegant white marble symbolize different periods of Mogul architecture in a juxtaposition wrought by time. But here, the two materials have been brought together with deliberate effect. The Taj Mahal is built on two bases, one of sandstone and, above it, a marble platform measuring 97 meters (313 feet) square and worked into a black-and-white chessboard design. A slender marble minaret stands at each corner of the platform; these towers blend so well into the general composition that it's hard to believe their 40-meter (130-foot) height. Each one is also purposely constructed at a slight tilt away from the tomb (in case of an earth tremor, they'd fall away from the beautiful building).

In the mausoleum itself, the easy curves of pointed Mogul arches on the facade set off the square corners of the building. The entrance to the tomb is an archway soaring more than 28 meters (90 feet) high and inscribed with more verses from the Quran. Mogul inlay work, used so lavishly throughout the Taj Mahal, is carefully worked into the entrance. Notice the tiny, intricate flowers—the detailed stonework on each petal and leaf. Shine a flashlight and see the delicate translucence of some of the stones. Feel the perfectly smooth surfaces. Step inside and succumb to the pull of another dimension that draws your gaze to the graceful curve of the dome, a marble sky that is actually a dome within a dome. The dome seen from the exterior is above the dome you now see inside.

The Royal Tombs

Directly under the dome lie the tombs of Mumtaz Mahal and Shah Jahan, but they aren't immediately visible. The Taj Mahal plays a tantalizing game of illusion, revealing its treasures one by one. Originally, the tombs were surrounded by a barrier of gold encrusted with precious stones, but this barrier was apparently removed by Shah Jahan's rupee-pinching son Aurangzeb, who replaced it with a marble screen that is the height of a man. Carved from a single block of stone, the screen is a lattice-work as intricate as lace.

The tomb of Mumtaz Mahal is in the center of the enclosure behind the screen: diminishing rectangles leading up to what looks like a coffin. In fact, both Mumtaz Mahal and Shah Jahan are buried in a crypt below these tombs in obedience to a tradition that no one should ever walk over their graves. Supposedly, Shah Jahan originally planned to build a black marble mausoleum for himself on the other side of the Yamuna, linking it by bridge to the Taj. But Aurangzeb had other ideas, which explains why the emperor is buried next to his wife. It was most likely done as another money-saving measure—an ironic postscript to the munificence of Shah Jahan.

The cenotaph of Mumtaz Mahal bears this Persian inscription: "The illustrious sepulcher of Arjuman Banu Begum, called Mumtaz Mahal. God is everlasting, God is sufficient. He knoweth what is concealed and what is manifest. He is merciful and compassionate. Nearer unto him are those who say: Our Lord is God."

The epitaph of the builder of the Taj Mahal reads: "The illustrious sepulcher of His Exalted Majesty Shah Jahan, the Valiant King, whose dwelling is in the starry Heaven. He traveled from this transient world to the World of Eternity on the twenty-eighth night of the month of Rajab in the year of 1076 of the Hegira [February 1, 1666]."

Inlay Work and Marble Screens

The inlay work of the Taj achieved unrivaled grace with the tomb of Mumtaz Mahal. Designs, executed in jasper, agate, lapis lazuli, carnelian, and bloodstone, are rendered with such skill that neither your sense of touch nor a magnifying glass can detect breaks between two stones. For example, one flower that measures only a square inch contains 60 different inlays. There is less unanimity over the tomb of Shah Jahan, which dwarfs that of Mumtaz Mahal and has been called pompous and out of proportion. But maybe it's fitting that he should lie for eternity next to his favorite wife, and the romantically inclined give Aurangzeb credit for bringing the two together.

More than just the tombs of these royal lovers is under the dome of the Taj Mahal. In each corner of the mausoleum, small domes rise over round chambers about 9 meters (30 feet) in diameter. Light from these rooms filters into the chamber through marble screens. The play of light within the entire Taj is fascinating. Precious stones inlaid in the tombs, in the screens surrounding them, and in the walls glow against the background of white marble.

So fantastic is the decoration of the Taj that it inspired the imagination of marauders who raided the mausoleum in 1764 and managed to stagger off with two silver doors that once served as an entrance. Thieves also made away with the gold sheets that formerly lined the burial vault below the tombs. But they never got around to plucking out the pietra dura inlay work—probably because they didn't believe it was real.

Outside the mausoleum stand a pair of red sandstone mosques, one on each end. Much simpler than the central building, they frame the Taj from the river.

It is easy to leave the Taj Mahal with a sense of disbelief. Somehow, the wealth of marble and precious stones (35 different varieties of carnelian can be counted in a single carnation leaf on the tomb of Mumtaz Mahal) seems disassociated from the airy dream you first envision from a distance. But then, outside the gateway to the garden, where fountains used to play, look again. The Taj is real—a vivid, real dream.

OTHER AGRA LANDMARKS

Agra offers several other landmarks that would probably be far better known if it weren't for the illustrious Taj Majal and the Agra Fort.

Another beautiful mausoleum, in a more subdued key than the Taj, is the tomb of Itmad-ud-Daula, father of Queen Nur Jahan and grandfather of Mumtaz Mahal. Though small, this monument (about five kilometers, or three miles, north of the Taj on the left bank of the Yamuna) is wonderfully proportioned; some say it is more pleasing than the Taj. Through a gate near the river, you enter a garden with a two-story tomb of white marble standing on a plinth of red sandstone. Almost the entire surface is covered in mosaics inlaid with semiprecious stones: geometrics, flowers, and typically Persian designs. Four small minarets rise up from the corners of the lower story. Within the sepulchral chamber, light penetrates through more screens of marble latticework. Actually, the tomb, a forerunner of the Taj, is the first Mogul building of all white marble, with designs even more delicate than those of the Taj Mahal.

The Chini-ka-Roza, or China Tomb, lies half a mile north of the tomb of Itmad-ud-Daula. Its name apparently comes from the brilliant glazed tiles used in its mosaics. Allama Afzel Khal Mullah Shukrullah, the prime minister of Shah Jahan and a Persian poet, and his wife are buried here. Not far from this tomb is the Ram Bagh (originally Arambagh, Garden of Leisure), designed by the Mogul Babur, according to one version of its origin. Babur's body was taken here before it was removed to Kabul. The Ram Bagh is supposed to be India's first Mogul garden.

Finally, mention should be made of the Jama Masjid, the huge congregational mosque of Agra built in 1648 by Shah Jahan's daughter, Jahanara.

Fatehpur Sikri, the Ghost City

Thirty-seven kilometers (24 miles) southwest of Agra lies an imperial capital frozen in time. When Elizabethan Englishmen came to Fatehpur Sikri in 1583 to meet the great emperor Akbar, they were amazed. Here was a city exceeding London both in population and in grandeur. They lost count of the rubies, the diamonds, and the plush silks. Today, Fatehpur Sikri is deserted, left in solitude to reminisce over its past.

The history of the city began when Akbar, desperate because he had no heir, decided to visit a Moslem holy man, Salim Chisti, who lived in a small village. Chisti blessed Akbar, and, in turn, the emperor was blessed with a son, whom he named Salim in honor of the holy man. Salim later took the throne as Jahangir. The grateful Akbar decided to move his capital to the village, where he died in 1569.

FATEHPUR SIKRI

(NOT TO SCALE)

1. KWABGAH
2. CHESSBOARD
3. DIWAN-I-KHAS
4. ANKH MICHAULI and
   ASTROLOGER'S SEAT
5. PANCH MAHAL
6. MARIAM'S HOUSE
7. JODH BAI'S PALACE
8. BIRBAL'S PALACE
9. LADIES MOSQUE
10. BULAND DARWAZA
    (GATE OF VICTORY)
11. SALIM CHISTI'S TOMB
12. COURT POETS' PAVILIONS

WELL   BATH

NAHABAT KHANA

AGRA

MINT

TREASURY

WATER TANK

DIWAN-I-AM

PACHCHISI COURTYARD

HIRAN MINAR

ELEPHANT GATE

BASTION

CARAVAN SARAI

STABLES

RUMI SULTANA

AGRA

LIBRARY

WATER TANK

N

JAMI MASJID

STONECUTTERS MOSQUE

Fatehpur Sikri lies on a rocky ridge about three kilometers (two miles) long and 1½ kilometers (one mile) wide. But this ridge was no problem to the Mogul emperor, who simply sliced off the top to find room for his city. At the foot of the ridge, he waved his hand once more and created an artificial lake measuring 33 kilometers (20 miles) around. The lake formed one side of the city; the three others were protected by massive walls pierced by nine gates. In all, the circumference of the capital was about 12 kilometers (seven miles). Here, as at the Agra Fort, you'll find the same specialization of buildings with impressive public halls and a delightful private residence under separate roofs. But there is more unity in the architecture of Fatehpur Sikri.

Momentos of Mogul Power

For miles around, you can see the victory gateway, Buland Darwaza, rising above the capital. This massive triumphant portal, which sums up Mogul power, was built by Akbar after he conquered Gujarat. Its dimensions are in keeping with its purpose: 42 meters (134 feet) high over a base of steps that climb another 11 meters (34 feet). Beware of the bees that have their own fortifications here and the phony guides who badger and bluff.

Jama Masjid

Probably the greatest structure in the city is the Jami Masjid, the imperial mosque built around 1575 and designed to hold 10,000 worshipers. Although not as sophisticated as the Jama Masjid of Delhi, it excels in its symmetry and in the geometric inlay designs that cover its interior. Note the deliberate use of Hindu elements in the design (especially the decorations on the pillars)—more examples of Akbar's wish for religious harmony so frequently mirrored in his architecture. The courtyard of the mosque contains a mausoleum that, paradoxically, is the most living part of the city. Here, behind walls of marble lace, lies the tomb of Salim Chisti under an elaborate canopy inlaid with mother-of-pearl. Every year, thousands of childless women (Moslem and Hindu) come to pray at the tomb of this Mohammedan saint for the same blessing he conferred on the emperor four centuries ago.

Diwan-i-Am

The other main public building of Fatehpur Sikri is the Diwan-i-Am (Hall of Public Audience), more than 350 feet (92 meters) long, which consists of cloisters surrounding a courtyard that contains the Hall of Judgment. Here, Akbar sat on a throne flanked by marble screens and handed down his decisions as the chief justice of his subjects. Those who were condemned to die were supposedly impaled, hanged, or trampled under the feet of an elephant. In a lighter vein, Akbar played pachisi (early form of Parcheesi) with slave girls as living pieces in the courtyard behind the Diwan-i-Am.

Diwan-i-Khas

The Hall of Private Audience (Diwan-i-Khas) has an unimpressive exterior; but inside the hall, divided by galleries, stands a strange stone column blossoming into a flat-topped flower. Elaborate designs on the column sweep up to the top, which served as Akbar's throne, used when he was receiving ambassadors or nobles. Four stone bridges connect the top of the pillar to the surrounding galleries. The intent behind such a lofty seat is not clear, but apparently it enabled the emperor to receive visitors without having to mingle with them.

Though small in size and not much more than a summer house in appearance (it is open and covered with an umbrella), the Astrologer's seat near the Diwan-i-Khas was an important cog in the Mogul empire. Open-minded Akbar was so intrigued by the trust his Hindu subjects placed in astrologers that he, too, consulted an astrologer. The astrologer determined what color the emperor wore each day (Akbar's favorite colors were yellow, purple, and violet).

Ankh Michauli

Nearby is the Ankh Michauli (its name means blindman's bluff). Supposedly, Akbar loved playing this "grope-and-feel" game inside this building with the ladies of his harem. Fantasy and whimsy prevail in the decorative stone monsters who were supposed to frighten thieves away from the crown jewels believed to have been kept in secret niches carved into the walls.

Jodh Bai's Palace

A feminine touch exists in the Jodh Bai Palace, built for Akbar's Hindu wife. Moslem and Hindu architecture blend together once again: the sculpture found inside the rooms is Hindu, while Mogul domes extend above the top of the palace. Living quarters and bathrooms were located around a large interior court. An upper-story room, walled in by a red sandstone screen, is called the "Palace of Winds," the coolest vantage point from which the ladies of the court could watch what was happening without being seen.

Joan of Arc—India-Style

Fatehpur Sikri can be the end of your trip or the starting point for an excursion south to Jhansi. Here, the Rani of Jhansi, Lakshmi Bai, began her career as the Joan of Arc of India. The widow of the Rajah of Jhansi, she decided to succeed her husband as the head of his tiny state after he died in 1853, leaving no male heir. Unfortunately, the British had just proclaimed a new policy of taking over princely states whose rulers had left no son. They pensioned off the young widow rani, still in her twenties.

The rani joined the Indian Mutiny in 1857. In April 1858, a British general captured Jhansi, but the rani slipped through his lines. After a wild ride on horseback, she reached Kalpi and joined another rebel leader, but their troops were defeated on May 22. The rani and her followers moved into Gwalior Fort, which was immediately attacked by the British. On June 17, 1858, the rani rode out of the fort, holding the reins of her horse in her teeth, and took the offensive: wielding her sword with both hands. Dressed as a man like the Maid of Orleans, she was shot and sliced by a saber. She slumped to her death clutching her horse. Her room in the old fort of Jhansi is now a shrine of Indian independence.

The medieval city Orchha is about 12 kilometers (seven miles) south of Jhansi. Built by the Bundela Rajputs, it has a fortress with some exquisite palaces; most noteworthy is the seventeenth-century Jahangir Mahal, built by Bir Singh Ju Deo, friend of Prince Salim, the future Mogul Emperor Jahangir. Murals in the Lakshmi Temple are fine examples of Bundela art.

Deogarh and Shivpuri

Another different style of architecture is at Deogarh, 110 kilometers (66 miles) south of Jhansi and 13 kilometers (eight miles) east of the famed Dasavatara Temple. Built 1,500 years ago, this temple is a classic of Gupta art, with its tapering tower and its four portals standing majestically over stone steps. Otherwise, you might prefer to stick to the main road and head west from Jhansi to Shivpuri, 53 kilometers (32 miles) away, the one-time summer capital of the Majarajah of Gwalior. Here, the beauty is natural.

Shivpuri, on a cool, wooded plateau at an altitude of 434 meters (1,400 feet), is on the edge of a national park where you may encounter tigers or other wild animals. About 22 kilometers (13 miles) before Shivpuri on the Jhansi road stands a ruined village, Surwaya, with an old Hindu monastery. But Shivpuri is far better known for relaxation than history. In the park, outside town, a silvery lake (Sakhya Sagar or Chandpatha), with 12 kilometers (seven miles) of shoreline, is inlaid in Mogul fashion against a green setting of wooded hills. From Shivpuri, a delightful road or a toy-like railway leads to Gwalior; then it's almost a straight line back to Delhi.

PRACTICAL INFORMATION FOR AGRA

WHEN TO GO. The best time to visit is from mid-October to March. The mornings and evenings are cool, the days warm and sunny. From early March to the end of May, it's hot. Temperatures in the day can soar to over 100°F. Visitors are advised to sightsee in the early morning or late afternoon. Between mid-June and early July, the monsoon arrives, lasting until the end of September.

HOW TO GET THERE. By Air. *Indian Airlines* flies daily to Agra from Delhi, Khajuraho, and Varanasi. This airline also makes five weekly flights into Gwalior from Bhopal, Delhi, Indore, and Bombay. For information in Agra, call 360948.

By Bus. Numerous tour operators in Delhi provide inexpensive bus tours to Agra. (*See* the Delhi chapter, above, for details.)

By Train. From Delhi, take the *Taj Express,* which runs daily, leaving in early morning and returning that evening (about a three-hour journey). The *Taj Express* and numerous other trains continue from Agra to Gwalior (for inquiries, call 72515; for reservations, call 63787). Once you arrive at the train station in Agra, you can take a day tour to the Agra monuments and Fatehpur Sikri conducted by Uttar Pradesh State Road Transport Corp. (a deluxe bus with guide, fare: about Rs. 75). Tour begins at 10:15 A.M. from the Agra Cant. Railway Station and returns in time for the *Taj Express* departure to Delhi.

From Jaipur, take the *Jaipur Agra Fort Express.* Inquire at the Jaipur Railway Station, tel. 131.

By Car. Agra is 203 km (126 miles) from Delhi; 232 km (144 miles) from Jaipur; and 118 km (73 miles) from Gwalior. The roads are good from any direction. The round trip from Delhi to Agra (including Fatehpur Sikri) via hired car and driver is about Rs. 4–Rs. 5 per km.

TOURIST INFORMATION. In Agra, two good sources of information offer brochures: *Uttar Pradesh State Tourist Office,* 64 Taj Rd. (tel. 360517) and a counter at the Agra Cant. Railway Station (tel. 66438); and the *Government of India Tourist Office,* 191 The Mall (tel. 72377), which also has a counter at the airport that is open for arrivals. The Government of India has the best map of Agra. It's wise to come armed with your own detailed information on the monuments if you want to get into the nitty-gritty of the architecture. Guides can be good, but their speil has a worn-out and overused, superficial edge. The Uttar Pradesh State Tourist Office is open Monday–Saturday, 10 A.M.–5 P.M., closed Sunday and the second Saturday of each month. The Government of India Tourist Office is open Monday–Friday, 9 A.M.–5:30 P.M. and till 1 P.M. Saturday.

In **Jhansi,** the *Uttar Pradesh Tourist Bureau* is at Hotel Virangana, tel. 1267.

FOREIGN CURRENCY EXCHANGE. Most Western-style hotels have exchange counters. Otherwise, go to Agra's *State Bank of India* on Mahatma Gandhi Rd. or the *Canera Bank* at Sadar Bazaar. The banks are open Monday–Friday, 10 A.M.–2 P.M.; till noon Saturday.

ACCOMMODATIONS. The full range of accommodations is available in Agra, which is a convenient base for excursions to Fatehpur Sikri and Mathura. Room rates are based on double occupancy and don't include taxes or service charges: *Deluxe,* over Rs. 2,000; *Expensive,* Rs. 1,200–Rs. 2,000; *Moderate,* Rs. 500–Rs. 1,200; *Inexpensive,* under Rs. 500. During peak season (mid-October to March), book early at better hotels.

AGRA

Deluxe

Hotel Clarks Shiraz. 54 Taj Rd., Agra 282001; tel. 361421, fax 361428. 147 rooms with bath. 100 more rooms are under construction. A sprawling white high rise set on eight acres with extensive gardens, the Clarks Shiraz evokes the 1960s, not the age of the Moguls. Rooms have a subdued contemporary decor. Some rooms offer a view of the Taj. Multicuisine restaurants, bar, room service, TV, air-conditioning, foreign-exchange and travel counter, swimming pool, minigolf course, tennis, badminton, shops, doctor. AE, DC, MC, V.

Taj View Hotel. Taj Ganj, Fatehabad Rd., Agra 282001; tel. 361171, fax 361179. 100 rooms with bath. The Taj View may lack architectural inspiration, but it offers good service and spacious, modern air-conditioned rooms with TV. Best rooms offer a view of the Taj. Multicuisine restaurants, bar, room service, foreign-exchange and travel counter, doctor, swimming pool, health club, shops, astrologer. AE, DC, MC, V.

Welcomgroup Mughal Sheraton. Taj Ganj, Agra 282001; tel. 361701, fax 361730. 300 rooms with bath. Winner of the Aga Khan Award for excellence in architecture, this stunning hotel, done up in brick and marble, is the class act in Agra. Spacious rooms have a low-key modern decor, accentuated by soft-white walls and handsome dark-wood trim. Some rooms offer a view of the Taj. Be aware that the Sheraton has no elevators; rooms are spread out on just two floors, so steps are few, but the walk from the front desk to your room may be longer than you expect. There are multicuisine restaurants, room service, bar, TV, air-conditioning, foreign-exchange and travel counter, swimming pool, tennis courts, croquet, minigolf course, health club, camel and elephant rides, astrologer, shops. AE, DC, MC, V.

Expensive

Hotel Agra Ashok. 6B, The Mall, Agra 282001; tel. 361223. 58 rooms with bath. This attractive Western-style hotel is also inspired by Mogul architecture: lots of marble, lattice trim, and an interior fountain. Spacious rooms have a modern decor, TV, and air-conditioning. Some offer a view of the Taj. Amenities include coffee shop and multicuisine restaurant, bar, room service, foreign-exchange and travel counter, swimming pool, shops, doctor, puppet show, palm reader. AE, DC, MC, V.

Moderate

Hotel Mumtaz. Fatehabad Rd., Agra 282001; tel. 361771. 40 rooms with bath. This Western-style hotel has simply decorated, modern rooms with air-conditioning and TV. Multicuisine restaurant, bar, room service, foreign-exchange and travel counter, swimming pool, doctor, shops, palm reader. AE, DC, MC, V.

Inexpensive

Mayur Tourist Complex. Fatehabad Rd., Agra 282001; tel. 360310. 30 cottages with bath. Nestled around a landscaped lawn, this delightful enclave offers rooms in cottages done up in an ethnic decor. Some rooms are air-conditioned. Multicuisine restaurant, rooftop barbecue, room service, TV, children's playground, doctor. AE, V.

New Bakshi House. 5 Laxman Nagar, Agra 282001; tel. 361292. 6 rooms with bath. If you'd like to stay in a typical Indian middle-class neighborhood, this guest house is perfect. Each room is cozy and clean. In the restaurant you can choose between home-cooked Indian and Continental meals. Amenities include free pick-up and transfer service, doctor, and travel arrangements. Rupees only.

JHANSI

Inexpensive

Jhansi Hotel. Shastri Marg, Jhansi; tel. 1360. 25 rooms with bath. This simple Western-style hotel is the best option in Jhansi. Clean rooms have a modest contemporary decor. Some rooms are air-conditioned and have TV. Multicuisine restaurant, bar, room service, car rental, foreign-currency exchange, doctor. MC.

DINING OUT. Many accommodations listed above have restaurants, some of which are included here. Breakfast is usually served 7–10; lunch, noon–3; dinner, 7:30–11. The restaurants listed below are informal and, unless noted, are open for all three meals and don't require reservations. Prices are based on a three-course dinner for one person, excluding beverage, tip, and taxes: *Deluxe,* over Rs. 300; *Expensive,* Rs. 200–Rs. 300; *Moderate,* Rs. 100–Rs. 200; *Inexpensive,* under Rs. 100.

AGRA

Expensive

Bagh-e-Bahar. Mughal Sheraton, Taj Ganj; tel. 361701. This sumptuous garden restaurant serves good Continental cuisine and provides music to dance to at night. Open 7:30–11 P.M. Reservations advised. AE, DC, MC, V.

Mahjong Room. Mughal Sheraton, Taj Ganj; tel. 361701. Enjoy excellent Chinese dishes in this darkly lit, intimate restaurant with an elegant Oriental decor. Open 12:30–3 P.M. and 7:30 P.M.–midnight. Dinner reservations advised. AE, DC, MC, V.

Mughal Room. Clarks Shiraz, 54 Taj Rd.; tel. 361421. This handsome rooftop restaurant is done up in pinks and reds, with a twinkling-star ceiling. At night enjoy live performances of Indian *ghazals* (musicians). You can choose from good Indian, Chinese, and Continental cuisines. Open 7:30–11:30 P.M. Reservations advised. AE, DC, MC, V.

Nauratna. Mughal Sheraton, Taj Ganj; tel. 361701. Come to this intimate restaurant with an opulent Mogul decor that includes lots of marble for Mughlai and nawab specialties. During lunch, expect Indian classical music performances, and at night, ghazals. Open 12:30–3 P.M. and 7:30 P.M.–midnight. Dinner reservations advised. AE, DC, MC, V.

Moderate

Sonam. 51 Taj Rd.; tel. 361039. Set in an old British bungalow, the Sonam has a weathered patina; there's linen on the tables, a gigantic chandelier, a working fireplace in winter and air-conditioning in summer. You can also eat at tables set up on the spacious lawn. The multicuisine food and ambience are reliably good. Try *murg samandar* (whole chicken for two cooked with cardamon) or *dum-e-ran* (leg of lamb curry). Open 6 A.M.–midnight. Rupees only.

Sonar Restaurant. 25 Mall Rd., Phool Sayad Crossing; tel. 361144. This informal restaurant, crowded with tables, has a no-frills decor. Tables are also set up on its pleasant lawn. Chef serves good multicuisine meals, especially tasty chicken dishes. Open 6 A.M.–11 P.M. Rupees only.

SWEETS AND TREATS. For excellent Indian sweets and snacks, head for **Brijwasi**, D–2, Shopping Arcade, Sadar Bazar. The pastry shop is downstairs, while upstairs you can relax in a charming coffee shop with tile-and-mirror walls. It's very popular. Open 7:30 A.M.–10:30 P.M. Rupees only.

HOW TO GET AROUND. From the Airport. Taxis run about Rs. 100 to most main hotels and Agra.

By Tourist Taxi. These Ambassadors don't have meters. Rates are determined by destination. Figure about Rs. 4–Rs. 5 per km. Set the fare in advance. You can also hire a tourist taxi from one of the recommended tour operators listed below.

By Auto Rickshaw. Unfortunately, they're unmetered in Agra. Use Delhi rates as your guide (see the Delhi chapter) and bargain hard!

By Bike Rickshaw. This pleasant option, also good in Agra, should cost no more than Rs. 30 per hour.

JHANSI

By Tourist Taxi. Unmetered; fix the rate in advance. Figure about Rs. 4–Rs. 5 per km.

By Tonga (horse-drawn carriage). Cheap and a good way to get around.

TOURS. *Uttar Pradesh State Road Transport Corporation* (96 Gwalior Rd., tel. 72206; and Platform No. 1, near Enquiry Window, Agra Cant. Railway Station) offers a daily bus tour with guide of Fatehpur Sikri, Agra Fort, and Taj Mahal. Rs. 75 per person. Call for booking and further details.

Uttar Pradesh State Tourism Development Corporation (Taj Khema, tel. 360140, or Raja-ki-Mandi, tel. 72123) offers three tours: Taj Mahal, Agra Fort, Fatehpur Sikri. Daily 10:15 A.M.–6:30 P.M.; Fatehpur Sikri. Daily 10:15 A.M.–2 P.M.; and Sikandra, Fatehpur Sikri, Taj Mahal, Agra Fort. Daily 9 A.M.–7 P.M. At press time, fares were under review. They will be reasonable. Call for details. All tours start and end at the Agra Cant. Railway Station.

Excellent guides are available from the *Take-A-Guide Office* (opposite Taj View Hotel, Fatehabad Rd., tel. 360209.). For up to four persons, half-day charges are Rs. 80; full-day charges are Rs. 100. The office is open 9 A.M.–6 P.M. daily.

TOUR OPERATORS. For all travel needs, including a rented car with driver, contact the following agencies: *Ashok Travels and Tours*, Hotel Agra Ashok, The Mall, tel. 76223; *Travel Bureau*, Fatehabad Rd., near Taj View Hotel, Agra 282001, tel. 360118, fax 0562–360006; *Travel Corporation India*, TCI, Hotel Clarks Shiraz, 54 Taj Rd., Agra 282001, tel. 361121. In peak season, book a rented car with driver in advance.

SEASONAL EVENTS. The specific dates for many events are determined by the lunar calendar; consult the Government of India Tourist Office for details.

February/March. *Holi.* During this exuberant spring festival, the women of Barsana (near Mathura, the legendary home of Radha, Krishna's consort) hold colored-water throwing contests with the men of nearby Nandgaon (Krishna's home). If you plan to watch, wear old clothes.

August/September. *Ganmashtami.* Lord Krishna's birthday is celebrated with nightlong prayers and temple festivities in Agra and Mathura.

October/November. In Mathura, *Diwali* marks the start of the Hindu New Year, most festive of Indian festivals. Thousands of candles, and flickering lights illuminate the city, homes, and public buildings. A noisy, firecracker good time.

In Mathura, see a *puja* (prayer service) held every evening at the Vishram Ghat on the Ganges. A beautiful ceremony that ends with the release of flickering oil lamps into the holy river.

HISTORIC SITES. All historic monuments are open sunrise to sunset, except for the Taj Mahal, which is open sunrise to 7:30 P.M. Entrance fee for foreigners to the Taj Mahal was under review at press time. It could be steep, but it's worth it! Other entrance fees are nominal (under Rs. 10). *Agra Fort.* Construction on the red-sandstone fort and white-marble palaces started with Akbar in 1565 and continued through the next two generations (Jahangir and Shah Jahan). Enter via the Amar Singh Gate, then follow the extensive description in the chapter essay. If you hire a guide, make sure he's been approved by the government.

Chini-ka-Roza (China Tomb) is a half mile north of Itmad-ud-Daulah's tomb. Constructed as a memorial to Allama Afzel Khal Mullah Shukrullah of Shiraz, who was the prime minister of Shah Jahan and a Persian poet, the building is sadly neglected.

Itmad-ud-Daulah's Tomb. Built in 1622–28 by the Empress Nur Jahan, the tomb of Nur Jahan's father is 5 km (3 mi.) north of the Taj on the left bank of the Yamuna. Her mother is also buried here. This is the first Mogul structure constructed entirely of marble.

Jama Masjid. The congregational mosque of Agra was built in 1648 by Shah Jahan's daughter, Jahanara Begum.

Ram Bagh, near China Tomb. This is the earliest example of a Mogul garden, designed by the Emperor Babur in 1526. Unfortunately, it's not well maintained.

Akbar's Mausoleum is in Sikandra, 12 km (7 miles) from Agra. Designed and begun by the emperor in 1602 before his death, it was completed by his son Jahangir in 1613. Its graceful red sandstone and marble construction represents a fusion of Hindu and Moslem architecture.

Taj Mahal. This memorial tomb, created by Shah Jahan for his queen, Mumtaz, was started in 1632 and completed around 1653. Once you enter this architectural masterpiece of red sandstone and marble, follow the description in the chapter essay under *Taj Mahal: Monument to Love.*

Fatehpur Sikri. After a sixteenth-century mystic, Salim Chisti, blessed the Mogul Emperor Akbar with a much-wanted male heir, Akbar built his capital in the mystic's tiny community, 37 km (24 mi) west of Agra. He constructed his impressive city on a rocky eminence, enclosing three sides with walls, the fourth protected by a lake.

MUSEUMS. Agra. *Taj Mahal Museum,* within the Taj Mahal, contains a collection of findings from the Mogul period and a history of the Taj. **Jhansi.** The *Archaeological Museum,* Rani Mahal, is the former home of the heroine Rani Lakshmi Bai. Here you see a good collection of sculptures from the ninth to the twelfth centuries. Open 8 A.M.–5 P.M. Free. **Mathura.** The *Government Museum,* Dampier Park, is one of India's best museums, with a great collection of sculpture going back to the fifth century B.C., beautiful sculptures of the Mathura school that flourished in the region, and the art of the Kushan period (the most comprehensive collection in existence); plus good bronzes and terra cottas. Closed Monday and official holidays. Open July 1–April 15 (10:30 A.M.–4:30 P.M.); April 16–June 30 (7:30 A.M.–12:30 P.M.). Guides can be arranged at the museum for a nominal fee.

SHOPPING. In Agra, look for good bargains in hand-knotted carpets and *dhurries* (rugs), precious and semiprecious stones, inlaid marble work, and brass statues. Visit the following reliable shops:

Chirali, Fatehabad Rd. (near Hotel Amar), sells high-quality precious and semiprecious stones and beautiful *zari* (embroidery work). It also designs jewelry on order. Open 9:30 A.M.–7:30 P.M. AE, DC, MC, V.

Cottage Industry, 18 Munro Rd., sells good dhurries and carpets. Open 10 A.M.–7 P.M. AE, DC, MC, V.

Ganesha, also at 18 Munro Rd., has new and old curios in brass, copper, and bronze. Open 7 A.M.–9 P.M. AE, DC, MC, V.

Jewel Palace, Pertappura, is a high-quality shop selling precious and semiprecious stones. It also designs jewelry on order. Open 8 A.M.–8 P.M. AE, DC, MC, V.

Oswal Emporium, 30 Munro Rd., produces excellent marble inlaid items. Prices range from Rs. 125 to over a million. Open 9:30 A.M.–7 P.M. AE, DC, MC, V.

NIGHTLIFE AND BARS. In Agra, bars in all the better hotels usually serve until 11 P.M. Otherwise, nightlife in this area is rather sedate.

RAJASTHAN

Shrine to Chivalry

by
KATHLEEN COX

Desert with dunes, scrub, cactus, and rock, fertile green tracks, hills, ravines, enchanting lakes, and jungles—all exist in Rajasthan, the second-largest state in India. Here, the Aravalli Mountain Range cuts the state into two distinct regions: northwestern and southwestern, with the western part (the Thar Desert) only sparsely populated.

Rajasthan is also rich in history, legend, and lore. Formerly called Rajputana ("Abode of Kings") the area was originally made up of at least 22 princely states, each ruled by a proud *Rajput* (prince). From the earliest centuries, the conflict for control over northern India between the Hindu Rajput rulers, who were (and still are) great horsemen, and the powerful Moslems was passionately contested in a series of military campaigns and intrigues—some of them downright sneaky. One story has an eleventh-century Hindu guide, supposedly in league with an invading Moslem army, generously helping the soldiers get lost in the desert where they nearly died of thirst. Or consider the exploits of the seventeenth-century Mogul Emperor Akbar, whose "strategy" was the reverse of divide and conquer. To expand his empire, he took a Rajput princess of Jaipur as one of his wives (his son and successor Jahangir was the product of this union). And several of Akbar's most trusted generals were Rajputs who had previously fought against him. One of them, Man Singh, was even appointed governor of a great imperial province.

Whatever the outcome of a battle, the Rajputs were masterful warriors who held on to an unwavering sense of honor and pride in a tradition that decreed, when the battle went against them, that they had to make the supreme sacrifice. Clothed in saffron robes of immolation, they went to battle and died. If the sign of defeat was displayed on the battlefield, the women in the fortress performed the rite of *sati,* the Hindu act of throwing oneself into a flaming pyre—far superior to the indignity of capture. The Rajputs, who claim direct lineage with Hindu divinities and the heroes of India's great epic poems (the *Ramayana* and the *Mahabharata*), are in a class by themselves in world history.

Even when these independent rulers were forced to merge after independence, each one kept title to an impressive accumulation of palaces, private lands, jewels, and miscellaneous mind-boggling possessions and, of course, none gave any thought to compromising his princely lifestyle. To compensate each ruler for the loss of control over his state and subjects, the maharajah also received a "privy purse," which was paid out annually until 1973, when then-prime minister Indira Gandhi decided that the princes had been paid enough. Mrs. Gandhi also cut off many of the royal privileges.

Without the stipend, some of the maharajahs proved they were poor businessmen and nearly went broke (many had to sell their palaces and live off their horded wealth). The elimination of pomp and privileges reduced them all to a humbler status; some turned their exclusive estates into fancy hotels catering to the upper crust.

In spirit, however, Rajasthan is still the legendary land of the Rajput. Forts and palaces, lakes and gardens—all steeped in romance and chivalry—bear witness to a history of conquest and power. Here, the best martial qualities of a race are linked to the refinements of courtesy and an elegant culture. Nowhere else can you see people more intrinsically Indian and more true to their heritage than in Rajasthan.

EXPLORING RAJASTHAN

JAIPUR

Encircled on all but the southern side by the rugged Aravalli hills with numerous peaks crowned by imposing forts, Jaipur, the capital of Rajasthan, still looks cradled and well protected. Jaipur takes its name from Maharajah Jai Singh II, who, in the early 1700s, became king of Amber at the age of 13. Precocious and inquisitive, the young king soon proved to be such a distinguished scholar and diplomat that Aurangzeb, the reigning Mogul emperor, called him Sawai (One-and-a-Quarter), his way of claiming the young boy's superiority over all his Rajput predecessors. History proved him right.

At that moment, the Mogul Empire was approaching dissolution. With the milder rule from Delhi, it was no longer necessary for the Rajputs to bury themselves in mountain fortresses. They could now come down to the fertile plains with impunity. So, not long after Jai Singh came to the throne, he realized the need to shift the capital from Amber, the ancient rock-bound stronghold of his ancestors, down to the new site in the adjoining valley.

In no time, Sawai Jai Singh could add architect and astronomer to his list of credentials. In 1727, he conceived and designed the bulk of his new

RAJASTHAN

0 miles 50

0 km 50

PUNJAB

PAKISTAN

Thar Desert

Ganganagar

HARYANA

UTTAR PRADESH

Delhi

Mathura

Fahtepur Sikri

Jhunjhunu

Mandawa

Bikaner

Gajner

Kolayat

Alwar

Deeg

Sikar

Bharatpur

Agra

Jaisalmer

Pokaran

Nagaur

Makrana

Amber

Keoladeo Ghan Bird Sanctuary

Jaipur

Van Vihar Wildlife Sanctuary

Pushkar

Ajmer

Tonk

Barmer

Jodhpur

Gwalior

Marwar

Sawai Madhopur (Ranthambhor Wildlife Sanctuary)

Bundi

Kota

Ranakpur

Chittorgarh

Jhalawar

Guna

Mt. Abu

Abu Road

Udaipur

Jaisamand

MADHYA PRADESH

Ahmedabad

Indore

GUJARAT

MAHARASHTRA

Bombay

capital, with its exquisite buildings of rose-colored terra-cotta described in historical writings as the "tone of the autumn sunset." Although the Sawai's city is dusty and crammed with camels, horses, dogs, and people, and is reminiscent of a gold-rush frontier town in its heyday, it remains an astonishing model of city planning. Enclosed inside fortified walls 6 meters (20 feet) high and guarded by eight gates, every aspect—the streets, sidewalks, height of the buildings, number and division of blocks—was based on geometric harmony, sound environmental and climatic considerations, and the intended use of each zone within the city. No detail escaped the sawai's attention. With pink and orange the dominant colors, the effect is magic at dusk even if the city is not kept up as it was in his time.

City Palace

Enter the City Palace complex through the Sireh Deorhi Gate, the principal entrance on the east. This complex, with its numerous pavilions, courtyards, chambers, and palace, was begun by the sawai, with further additions made by later maharajahs. Once you're inside the outer courtyard, the building directly in front is the Mubarak Mahal (guest pavilion), built by Maharajah Madho Singh II fewer than 100 years ago. This marble and sandstone building, with its delicate marble lacework, surrounds the original guest pavilion built earlier by the sawai. It now houses the textile and costume museum, which displays a collection of brocades, silks, and handblocked traditional royal garments and robes, plus musical instruments (all donated by the royal family). Some of the exhibits go back to the seventeenth century. Also visit the armory in the northwest corner of the courtyard. You'll see one of India's best collections of arms and weapons, including an 11-pound sword belonging to the Rajput General of Akbar.

Proceed to the inner courtyard (through the gateway guarded by two stone elephants) and enter the art gallery housed in the Diwan-i-Am (Hall of Public Audience). The building, constructed by another descendant, Pratap Singh, in the late 1700s, is gorgeous—huge—with rows of massive gray marble columns, the second-largest chandelier in India, and a magnificient painted ceiling (painted in the 1930s for the maharajah's second marriage). The art gallery contains an extensive collection of miniatures from the Mogul and various Rajput schools, rare manuscripts, and gigantic carpets form the 1600s that were originally on the floors of the Amber Palace.

In the center of the inner courtyard, you'll notice a pair of mammoth silver urns inside the Hall of Private Audience, a raised platform with beautiful marble pillars. This building was used for formal banquets and ceremonial occasions. When Maharajah Madho Singh II sailed to England to attend the coronation of King Edward VII, these solid silver urns carried water from the Ganges (the only water the devout Hindu would drink)—a seemingly inefficient yet ostentatious method of hauling water.

From the inner courtyard, enter the Zanana courtyard on the left. Here you'll see the famous Chandra Mahal, or Moon Palace, with its seven stories that tower above the other structures. Built by Sawai Singh II, the lovely cream-hued building is still the official residence of the present Maharajah "Bubbles," or, more formerly, Lieutenant Colonel Sawai Bhawani Singh, who lives in the upper stories. The ground floor is also exquisite, with sumptuous chandeliers, murals, and a quasi-three-dimensional painting of an old maharajah.

Adjoining the palaces are the Jai Niwas gardens (off limits to the paying public), which offer the romantic prospect of splashing fountains and ornamental water. A legend claims that the Rajah Jagat Singh, oppressed by the heat of the palace, frequently escaped into some shady corner of this greenery. From here, he supposedly amused himself by exchanging love letters with his *zenana* (harem)—the letters dutifully carried back and forth in the mouth of his favorite dog. A monument to this trusty hound stands in the garden—his reward for his services as "post dog."

Jantar Mantar

Not content with designing this famous palace, Jai Singh also supervised the design and construction of five remarkable observatories in northern India. The largest and best preserved—the Jantar Mantar—is in Jaipur near the entrance to the City Palace. Built of masonry, marble, and brass, it is equipped with gigantic, futuristic scientific instruments, called *yantras,* each one designed by the Sawai "Newton of the East," who was well aware of European developments in this field and wanted to create observatories that would outdo anything already in existence—an attitude befitting this maharajah.

Abstract and weirdly beautiful, each yantra is uncannily accurate in measuring various celestial data. Samrat Yantra, a 28-meter- (90-foot-) high right-angle triangle, is a sundial that tells local time that is accurate to within a few seconds. The *dhruva,* a peculiar brass slab, determines the position of the North Star at night. Numerous other yantras determine celestial latitude and longitude, and serve as alternative sundials (some relating to the zodiac). Of course, Jai Singh provided himself with an observer's seat from which he supervised his scientific calculations.

Hava Mahal—"Palace of Winds"

Also worth a visit in the old city is the Hawal Mahal (Palace of Winds), a landmark built by Maharajah Sawai Pratap Singh in Jaipur in 1799. The Hawa Mahal is located on the bustling commercial thoroughfare called Siredeori Bazaar (directly after Johari Bazaar heading north). The curious five-story structure, which gets its name from the westerly winds that send cool breezes through the windows, is elaborate and fanciful. Constructed of pink sandstone, its delicate honeycomb design glows in the evening light. Every story has semioctagonal overhanging windows, each with a perforated screen, from which the ever-discreet women of the court could view the activities on the street below. The roof is curvilinear, with domes and finials, which adds to the general effect of lightness and delicacy.

Ram Niwas Garden and the Albert Hall Museum

Outside the walled city, relax in quiet at the Ram Niwas Garden, then see the strange Albert Hall Museum located on the beautiful grounds. The sandstone and marble building, constructed in the Indo-Saracenic style in the late 1800s, contains eclectic displays, not your ordinary run of paintings and sculpture. Many of the unexpected exhibits offer convenient cultural explanations for the curious foreigner. Look at the one devoted to *Mehendi,* the Indian art of decorating hands and feet with henna, and the one that identifies the folk instruments you may have heard and dances you may have seen in Rajasthan. Upstairs you'll find a table display of numerous clay models that demonstrate the vast range of yoga positions mastered by the physically agile yogi.

Amber Palace

For six centuries, the capital of Rajasthan and the nucleus of Rajput history, Amber is now little more than a deserted palace, surrounded by majestic ramparts. The construction, started by Maharajah Man Singh in the early 1700s and completed 100 years later, is a blend of Rajput and Mogul influences. The palace, which rises on the slopes of a steep hill behind the Maota Lake, retains an aura of great beauty. As soon as you enter the Valley of Flowers and pass through the pink gate, Amber Palace glows with variegated colors and nobility.

To get to the palace, you can either walk or arrive, pompously enough, on the back of a gaily caparisoned elephant. This archaic means of transportation explains the unusual height of the palace gateways. Inside the palace, the principal hall, known as the Hall of Victory, presents a galaxy of decorative art—panels of alabaster with fine inlay work of the tenderest hues, together with every kind of workmanship for which Jaipur is famous. And, typical of the Mogul period, the rooms are essentially small and intimate, while the successive courtyards and narrow passages are particularly Rajput.

Each room shows some vestige of its former glory, especially the Sheesh Mahal (Chamber of Mirrors). When you step inside, close the doors, strike a match, and watch the ceiling twinkle and glow. Numerous narrow flights of stairs lead up to the royal apartments that provide the best views of the valley, the lovely palace courtyards, the formal gardens abutting an octagon pool that edges the lake, and the ancient fortress (the Jaigash Fort) that stands guard from the crest of the hill above you. Vast and somber, its vaults still hide the treasures of Jaipur—or at least that's the rumor.

Alwar, Deeg, and Bharatpur

Continuing northeast, the next place of interest is Alwar, built into the jagged Aravalli hills. Alwar, founded in 1771, is dominated by its medieval fort, which crowns a conical rock. Once the capital of the princely state of the same name, Alwar contains a city palace (Vinai Vilas Mahal) that was constructed in the late 1800s. The palace is separated from the hill by the Sagar Tank (an artificial water tank). The upstairs is a museum devoted to manuscripts (over 7,000, the most notable being an illuminated copy of the Quran in Arabic with Persian translation in red lettering) and paintings, including a rare collection of Mogul and Rajasthani miniatures. An armory contains the personal weapons of Akbar, Jahangir, Shah Jahan, and Aurangzeb, with hilts of gold studded with jewels.

Also visit Gunijankhana, the feudal academy of arts, and see excellent examples of the Alwar School of painting. Unlike conventional Rajput paintings, the pictures here of dancing girls do not conceal the limbs and sensuousness of Rajput women. Also see the marble mausoleum of Bakhtawar Singh (1781–1815)—an excellent example of Indo-Islamic architecture—south of the Sagar Tank. Another spot to visit is the Purjan Vihar, a public park on the outskirts of town, with its renowned Summer House.

Siliserh Lake, about 13 kilometers (eight miles) from Alwar, is fringed by a dense forest and adorned with *chhatris* (domed cenotaphs). A magnificent former hunting lodge, built by a nineteenth-century maharajah for his queen, and now converted into a hotel, is nestled in the hills and overlooks the lovely lake. Travel another 29 kilometers (18 miles) to Sariska, a tiger reserve surrounded by the Aravallis. Here, too, you'll find a royal hunting lodge, the Sariska Palace (now a hotel), set on the edge of the sanctuary.

Continuing east from Alwar you'll reach Deeg, renowned for its massive fort and pleasure palaces (built by Badan Singh in the 1700s), surrounded by sumptuously laid-out gardens, tanks, and fountains, added by his son, Suraj Mal. Richly carved columns, cornices, and eaves are arranged with an exquisite sense of balance; kiosks are scattered about like sentinels, giving the palace an air of mystery and romance. The largest of the palaces, Gopal Bhavan, contains a curious marble swing. Originally the property of the nawabs of Oudh, this eccentric plaything was carried off to Deeg by Maharajah Jawahar Singh. (Indeed, a good portion of the gorgeous inlaid marble you see here was stolen from Mogul palaces in Agra and Delhi.) Among the other buildings are the Suraj Bhavan, built of marble and ornamented with semiprecious inlaid stones; the Nand Bhavan, the big hall of audience; and the Macchi Bhavan, a decorative pavilion surrounded by fountains and ornamental ponds.

Bharatpur, capital of the former state of the same name and one of the chief cities of Rajasthan, is some 35 kilometers (22 miles) farther south. Founded by Suraj Mal, considered an outstanding military figure of the eighteenth century, Bharatpur is famous for its Lohagarh (Iron Fort), which successfully repulsed numerous Mogul and British attacks. No wonder—Suraj Mal's fortifications were an ingenious design: two massive mud ramparts, each encircled by a moat of formidable dimensions (over 47 meters [150 feet] wide and about 16 meters [50 feet] deep), which surrounded the central fortress built of solid masonry that had yet another ditch around it filled with water. Cannon balls stuck in the mud walls and caused no damage to the stone bastions of the inner fort. To get a better idea of the scale of the fortification, keep in mind this fact: The outer mud rampart, which is now demolished, had and 11-kilometer (seven-mile) circumference. The inner fortress, which was octagonal in shape, had two gates, both trophies of war captured from Delhi. The central and most important tower of the fort, set up in 1765, commemorated the successful assault on the Mogul capital. The museum contains sculptures and other testimonies to the art and culture of the region.

Shekhavati

From Bharatpur, head back to Jaipur, then travel northwest to Sikar, about 97 kilometers (60 miles) from Jaipur. From here, give yourself a day or two to take a picturesque excursion through an area called Shekhavati, named after the fifteenth-century King Shekha of Amarsar. First, head northeast to Nawalgarh, about 29 kilometers (18 miles) away—a beautiful village with hundreds of *havelis* (traditional Rajput homes with interior courtyards). Many of the older havelis have colorful frescoes covering the exterior and interior walls. You have now entered the land of the wealthy Marwaris, successful merchants on this formerly important and historic caravan route and great patrons. From the nineteenth-century houses that remain, the Marwaris were obviously devoted to the visual arts—recording contemporary world events and their passions on the walls of their homes. Go farther north to Dundlod village, with its lovely palace-hotel, and then on to Mandawa, with its giant medieval fort, and spend a night as the guest of the maharajah in his well-appointed seventeenth-century castle/hotel, with its stunning views. See more havelis and then continue in your leisurely pace to Fatehpur, a small city. All along the route you will pass through villages with color and fanciful art.

Bikaner

About 160 kilometers (100 miles) due west of Fatehpur is Bikaner. Founded at the close of the fifteenth century by Rao Bika, a descendant of Jodhai, the founder of Jodhpur, Bikaner stands aloof on high ground surrounded by walls and the Thar Desert. Visit the sixteenth-century Junagarh Fort built by Raja Raj Singh, an outstanding general of the Mogul Emperor Akbar. Within this massive edifice (located in the heart of the city), protected by a moat, are housed some of the rarest gems of Rajput architecture. Especially beautiful are the ancient palaces of sandstone and marble, including the Chandra Mahal (Moon Palace) and the Phool Mahal (Flower Palace), with lavish mirror work, carvings, and paintings. There are also temples, a mosque, and Har Mandir, a handsome chapel in which royal weddings and important births were celebrated. Also visit Durbar Hall, built in the Mogul style and lavishly decorated with paintings. Floral bouquets, set in red and gold borders, gilded leaf work, and vases are the leading motifs. Two or three stories high, with slender columns, cusped arches, and intricate screens, palaces rise on all sides. The zenana is separated by a broad court with paneled niches. Gilt reliefs, glass mosaics, and lacelike mirrors adorn graceful and intimate apartments.

Bikaner is also the home of the famous Camel Corps, still useful in desert warfare. Outside the city are other palaces and temples—imposing edifices of carved red sandstone. Jain temples and monasteries abound in this city and neighborhood. Most of them early sixteenth century, they are rich in carvings. Eight kilometers (five miles) away are the chhatris of the rulers of Bikaner.

For a squeamish experience, visit the Karni Mata Temple in Deshnok, about 32 kilometers (20 miles) from Bikaner, on the road to Jodhpur. This temple devoted to Karni Mata, an incarnation of Durga, is also the home of hundreds of rats, which are considered sacred and roam freely inside the temple. It is said that if a rat touches you or, better still, jumps on you, you'll be blessed with a lifetime of good luck (not rabies).

Jaisalmer: Island in the Sand

Some 484 kilometers (300 miles) in a southwesterly direction is the ancient city of Jaisalmer, founded by Rawal Jaisal in 1156. Lying at the extreme edge of Rajasthan, Jaisalmer is a tiny jewel in the heart of the Thar, the great Indian desert. Once the capital of the Bhati Rajputs, the medieval city rises in a sea of sand on a low range of hills surrounded by a stone wall three miles around—a towering vision in delicate yellow hue—only infrequently broken by green oases.

Your first sighting of Jaisalmer sets off an ethereal vision, but one that is slightly seamy when you examine its past. Jaisalmer started out as an important caravan center—remnants of caravansaries still exist (some of them converted into hotels). Right through the eighteenth century, rulers amassed their wealth from taxes levied on those passing through. Jaisalmer was also a smuggler's paradise, with opium the longtime best-seller.

Two great gateways, from east to west, pierce the towered battlements of the twelfth-century citadel. Inside are numerous Jain and Hindu temples, palaces, and more charming havelis. It's a walker's utopia, with tiny lanes and visually rich rewards. Most of the buildings, especially the facades, are exquisitely carved with elaborate workmanship, frequently filigreed like lace. Don't miss these gems: The seven-story palace built by

Maharawal (1763–1820)—a conglomeration of buildings crowned by a vast umbrella of metal, mounted on a stone shaft. Notice the historic spot, Satiyar-ka-Pagthiya, just before the palace entrance. Here, the royal ladies performed seti, the act of self-immolation when their husbands were slain, at the fall of the fortress in 1294. Also, see the eight Jain temples and four Hindu temples built in the fifteenth and sixteenth centuries. The Jain temples, dedicated to Rikhabdevji and Sambhavnathji, are filled with thousands of deities and dancing figures in mythological settings. The Gyan Bhandar (Jain library) inside the Jain temple complex contains over 1,000 old manuscripts—some of them dating from the twelfth century and written on palm leaf in black ink with painted wooden covers. The library also has a good collection of Jain, pre-Mogul, and Rajput paintings.

Outside the fortress, walk through the narrow lanes with more of the delicate, lacy architecture that shimmers in soft yellow. See the Patva Havelis—a string of five connected havelis built by the Patva brothers in the 1800s. Two of the five are now owned by the government and are open to the public. It's also possible to visit the interior of the others; offer a small fee (not more than Rs. 50) to the current residents. Next, visit the Nathamal Ki Haveli, flanked by stone elephants, built by two brothers. Instead of working in tandem, each brother concentrated exclusively on the left or right side. Although the result is harmonious, look carefully. You'll see subtle differences in the windows and carvings. Here, too, a courteous request may get you inside. The interior of Salim Singh's haveli is in sad disrepair. Perhaps that's a fitting denouement. Salim Singh, financier for Jaisalmer, nearly bankrupted the state with his excessive extortion. He also went overboard when he committed a series of murders to avenge the murder of his father. The exterior six-story eighteenth-century haveli, however, is still lovely, with 38 balconies and elaborate carvings.

Jodhpur

Once the capital of the state of Marwar, Jodhpur, about 210 kilometers (130 miles) southeast of Jaisalmer, tumbles down a low sandstone hill on the edge of the Thar Desert. Today, remnants of an immense fortification wall, nine kilometers (six miles) in circumference, with eight gates facing various directions, guard the old city from the sand that surrounds the Thar Desert. At the summit of the hill soars the majestic Meherangarh Fort, built in 1459 by Rao Jodha when he shifted his capital from Mandore. Standing above a perpendicular cliff, the fort looks impregnable—an imposing landmark, especially at night when it is bathed in yellow light.

The walls of the fort enclose a variety of handsome, red sandstone buildings, palaces, barracks, temples, and havelis. The Victory Gate, leading up from the city to the fort, was erected by Maharajah Ajit Singh to commemorate his military successes over the Moguls at the beginning of the eighteenth century. Seven other gateways stand in honor of other victories—internecine—involving warfare among the various Rajput princes. On the walls of the final gate of entry are the palm marks of Rajput widows who immolated themselves on flaming pyres after their husbands were defeated in battle.

Delicately latticed windows and pierced screens worked in sandstone are the surprising motifs inside the rugged fort. The palaces—Moti Mahal, Phool Mahal, Sheesh Mahal, and the other apartments—are exquisitely decorated, with paintings still gracing some of the ceilings and walls. Outside the fort are more interesting old buildings and temples, such as the Jaswant Thada, a royal crematorium in marble, built in 1899 for Maharajah Jaswant Singh II. Also visit the Umaid Bhawan Palace, built from

1929 to 1942 by the Maharajah Umaid Singh. This sandstone palace has been partially converted into a deluxe hotel. The Umaid Bhawan also houses the Government Museum, with its fancy collection of royal finery, local arts and crafts, and miniature paintings. You might also catch a glimpse of the family of the current maharajah, who live in their accustomed splendor in one extensive wing of the palace.

While in Jodhpur, also wander through the Girdikot and Sardar markets, crowded with fruit and vegetable stalls and tiny shops, and noisy with the day-to-day bustle of a typical Indian market. Don't be surprised if you see some of the local folk wearing those favored equestrian pants, jodhpurs; they originated here.

About eight kilometers (five miles) to the north are the Mandore Gardens, the site of the ancient capital of the State of Marwar. Here, surrounded by lovely gardens and mischievous monkeys, you'll find the *devals,* or cenotaphs, of the former royalty.

Mount Abu—Hill Station

Situated on lush, verdant hills about 1,219 meters (4,000 feet) above sea level, Mount Abu, with its famous Dilwara Jain temples, is a hill resort endowed with antiquity. To reach Mount Abu, a place of pilgrimage for Jains, take the road that heads almost due south from Jodhpur. Originally a center of the cult of Shiva, Mount Abu became the Jainist religious stronghold by the eleventh century. Abu (a shortened form of Arbuda) was known in Hindu legend as the son of the Himalayas. This son, supposedly a serpent, rescued Shiva's sacred bull Nandi when it fell into a chasm. Here, too, Vasishta, the great sage of the epic period, established his *ashram*—something between a hermitage and a seat of learning. The four fire-born Rajput clans claim they were created from his sacrificial fire.

High in the steep valleys between the rocky peaks are five Jain shrines. For ornamental skill in intricate stonework and as pieces of architectural virtuosity, the Vimal Vasashi and the Tejpal temples stand out in the history of stone carving. The Vimal Vasashi was built in 1031 and is dedicated to Adinath, the first Jain Tirthanka. Composed of pure white marble, its exterior is deceptively simple, giving no hint of the wealth of ornamentation and sculpture hidden inside.

A procession of marble elephants leads up from the pavilion to the domed porch. On the backs of the carved animals sit the founder, Vimala, and his family. The central courtyard is surrounded by a high wall enclosing some 50 cells, each one enshrining its saintly image. In the central shrine, laden with jewels, sits the figure of Adinath. The octagonal dome, decorated with finely carved human and animal shapes and processions, is supported by eight sculptured pillars. The ceiling is a mass of intricate fretted marble lacework.

The second temple of major importance was built 200 years later. Here, exuberance knows no bounds, reaching the zenith of Indian inventive genius in decorative art. The most striking feature is the pendant of the temple's dome. To stimulate their talent, the carvers were supposedly offered rewards in silver equal in weight to that of the marble filings. Not content with this, Tejpal, the lavish founder, offered the weight in gold of any further filings that could be pared off after work was completed. Whatever the truth, there's no doubt that the proportion of perspiration to inspiration was clearly well balanced.

Ranakpur

About 160 kilometers (100 miles) northeast of Mount Abu is Ranakpur, a famous Jain temple, nestled in a lovely glen. As at Mount Abu, the shrine is dedicated to Adinath and dates from the beginning of the fifteenth century. Despite its current state of tranquillity, *dacoits* (Indian bandits) formerly used the sacred shrine as their headquarters. They were finally ejected about 25 years ago, when the temple was cleaned up and restored to its impeccable condition.

Inside the temple are 29 halls supported by 200 different pillars, plus subsidiary shrines, in the shape of side altars, that face all four directions. A wall, about 62 meters (200 feet) high, encircles the entire structure. Its inner face contains a quantity of elaborately sculptured cells, each adorned with a graceful spire. Embedded in this galaxy of spires rise the central shrines; 20 domes constitute the complex roofing of the pillared hall. Intricate carvings, friezes, and sculptured figures in close formation adorn the ceilings of all these structures. And beneath the floor are hidden meditation chambers. In front of this temple are two more Jain shrines and a temple dedicated to the sun god (displaying erotic sculpture).

Udaipur

Udaipur, southeast of Ranakpur, is called the City of Dreams; its ruler, the maharana, the "Sun of the Hindus," a descendant of the highest ranking "Solar" Rajputs. The maharana's island palaces sparkle in post and pinnacles of colored glass, amber, and pale jade. The gray waters of the Pichola Lake—the artificial creation of a fourteenth-century fantasy—reflect the famous eighteenth-century Jag Niwas Lake Palace (now a hotel), which seems to float on the water's surface. Not far from the Lake Palace is the smaller, equally lovely seventeenth-century Jag Mandir.

Udaipur, originally the capital of the state of Mewar, takes its name from Maharana Udai Singh, who founded the city in the middle of the sixteenth-century after fleeing the third Moslem attack on the city of Chittaur. Although his act didn't live up to the Rajput code of bravery to the deadly finish, it brought about Udaipur and its gorgeous palaces, which everyone now enjoys.

Another legend claims that Udai Singh chose this location for Udaipur after a wandering holy man (*sadhu*) told him that if he built his capital on the edge of the lake, it would never be captured. Given the maharana's predilection for staying alive, he readily took the sadhu's advice. Unfortunately his son, Maharana Pratap Singh, attempted a surprise victory over the Delhi Moslem Empire and succeeded. His success was short-lived. In 1615, his successor, Amar Singh, was forced to sign a conditional submission to the Emperor Jahangir in Delhi. So much for the sadhu's promise.

The maharana's City Palace stands on the crest of a ridge overlooking the lake, an imposing structure and the largest palace in Rajasthan. Built at various periods, it still preserves a harmony of design, enhanced by massive octagonal towers surmounted by cupolas.

In its sumptuous apartments, decorated by multicolor mosaics, mirror work and inlaid tiles abound on all sides, together with some fine paintings and historical relics. Roof gardens afford a wide panorama below. The later island palaces rival the ancient palace on the mainland. Almost in the middle of the lake, Jag Nivas (Lake Palace) consists of apartments, courts, fountains, and gardens. On another island at the southern end, Jag Mandir Palace, started in the seventeenth century, was added to and embellished during the next 50 years. Three stories high, of yellow sandstone with an inside lining of marble, it is crowned by an imposing dome. Its interior is decorated with arabesques of colored stones. It was to Jag Mandir that Sharja, son of Emperor Jahangir, came to hide after leading an unsuccessful revolt against his father.

Other lakes in the immediate neighborhood, all artificial like Pichola, are joined to it by canals. Sahelion-Ki-Bari Park, at a two-kilometer (1½-mile) distance, is a good example of this Hindu art of landscape gardening on a princely scale. It was laid out by Maharana Sangram Singh. A good road snakes its way along the shores of Fatehsagar Lake. Close below the embankment is the Sahelion-ki-Bari, the "Garden of the Maids," designed for the special use of the maharana's ladies, who arrived in a bunch from Delhi as a peace offering from the emperor. Ornamental pools, with finely sculptured cenotaphs of soft black stone surrounded by a profusion of fountains, are the main decor.

Udaipur's Environs

Sixty-five kilometers (40 miles) north is Rajsamand, an artificial lake of considerable size possessing a masonry embankment, entirely paved with white marble, constructed by Maharana Raj Singh in 1660. Broad marble steps lead down to the water, while three delicately carved marble pavilions jut into the lake. Cut into the stones of the embankment is the longest Sanskrit inscription known in India, a poem, etched into 25 slabs, that recounts the history of Mewar.

About 52 kilometers (32 miles) southeast of Udaipur lies Dhebar, or Jai Samand Lake, one of the largest artificial sheets of water in Asia, created by a dam almost a quarter of a mile across and over 31 meters (100 feet) high—no small engineering feat considering it was built in the seventeenth century. A temple of Shiva, flanked by six cenotaphs with a carved elephant in front of each, stands on the embankment. Bhils tribesmen still inhabit the islands in the lake.

All around Udaipur, you'll come across lake and shrine, temple and cenotaph—a wealth of white marble overlooking calm waters and interspersed with trees. Not all are monuments of victory or relics of peace and splendor. Sati stones commemorate the self-sacrifice of women who hurled themselves into raging fires while their husbands, pledged to death, fought against the overwhelming odds of invading hordes.

Twenty-two kilometers (14 miles) north of Udaipur is Eklingji, a tiny temple complex with 108 shrines that are dedicated to Shiva, the deity of the rulers of the Mewar. The present building, standing on the site of the original fifteenth-century edifice, is of late-eighteenth-century construction. Like most sacred buildings in this region, it's entirely of white marble. The roof is decorated by hundreds of circular knobs and crowned by a lofty tower. In the inner shrine is a four-faced black marble image of Shiva. Outside is the statue of Nandi, his sacred bull. At a short distance, Nagda, now in ruins, bore the brunt of too many Moslem invasions. One of the most ancient places in Mewar, it has two temples dating from the eleventh century, both ornamented with interesting carvings.

Continuing north, you'll arrive at Nathdwara and a famous temple of Krishna that draws pilgrims in the thousands from all parts of India. The image, supposedly dating from the twelfth century, was rescued from the destructive hands of the Moslems and brought here in 1699. A legend claims that when it was carted away, the chariot sank suddenly at the site of the present temple. It couldn't be budged or removed, so here it stayed.

About 66 kilometers (41 miles) from Udaipur is the historic pass of Haldighati. Here the valiant Maharan Pratap defied the might of Akbar, described then as "immeasurably the richest and most powerful monarch on the face of the earth." Outnumbered 100 to one, the Rajputs stood their ground until they all died except Pratap, who managed to escape on his horse, Chetak. From his outpost in the hills, he slowly won back all his strongholds except Chittaur.

Chittorgarh—Cradle of Rajput Courage

Due east of Udaipur is Chittorgarh, a city steeped in heroism. The ancient capital of Mewar State, this city and its ruins represent the origin of Rajput courage. The foundations of the fort of Chittaur are traditionally linked to the seventh century, and it remained the capital until 1567.

The glory of Chittorgarh is the Tower of Victory, set up by Rana Kumbha in the middle of the fifteenth century to commemorate his triumph over the Moslem kings of Gujarat and Malwa. Kumbha, like all the Rajput rulers, was a direct descendant of Bappa Rawal, that great chieftain who reigned in Chittaur in the eighth century. Supposedly, Boppa was "a giant who stood 20 cubits" (the best part of 30 feet!), whose spear no mortal man could lift. Since the start of the dynasty, 59 princes, descendants of this man of mythical dimensions, have assumed the throne of Chittaur.

The front of Chittorgarh presents a battered appearance. Built on the precipitous edge of a hill, the gigantic fort is over 11 kilometers (seven miles) in circumference. Inside are ruins of temples, palaces, and tanks, ranging from the ninth to the seventeenth century, and the almost-intact Tower of Fame, a Jain structure of the twelfth century.

Chittaur was sacked three times: the first was in 1303, when Allauddin Khilji, a Moslem ruler, attempted to abduct the Rani Padmini, considered the most beautiful woman in the world. The women of Chittaur matched the courage of their men. When the battle on the field went against them, a funeral pyre was lit in a vault. The Rajput women, decked in their bridal robes, plunged into the flames, singing their way to death. When the last warrior had died "for the ashes of his fathers and the temples of his gods," all the conqueror found inside the city was a wisp of smoke rising from the vault.

The second sack was in 1535 by Sultan Bahadur Shah of Gujarat. Once more, the Rajputs, realizing an impending defeat, accepted death. After the queen mother arranged for the safe escape of her infant son, the future Maharana Udai Singh, she led the women into the furnace. Thousands of women died in the flames, while many more men were killed on the field. The third sack took place in 1567, this time at the hands of Akbar, the great Mogul. The two commanders, Jaimal and Patta, who led the defense of the fort, so impressed Akbar that he erected statues of them on elephants and had them set up at the entrance to his palace in Agra.

Kota—Bundi

Kota, Rajasthan's industrial center, is about 184 kilometers (114 miles) northeast of Chittorgarh. Former capital of Kota state, the city is on the right bank of the Chambal River, with an imposing fort standing sentinel over the valley. Inside you can visit the old palace, which now contains the Maharana Madho Singh Museum, with an exquisite collection of Rajput miniatures of the Kota school, sculptures, frescoes, and superb antiques.

North of Kota is Bundi, embedded in a narrow and picturesque gorge, where time moves at a slower pace and history itself seems to have lingered. The old city is enclosed in huge walls, fortified by four gateways. The Chittar Mahal (Palace of Towers), set atop a hill, consists of acres of stone-built structures, one opening out from another. Gardens galore rise up in terraces on the hillside. The palace is covered with spy holes and mysterious foliage-shrouded windows. Even the garden terraces have trapdoors under your feet that presumably served as dungeons in less peaceful times. Shields, swords, and daggers hang on the walls, as well as the martial family portraits of men with inordinately long mustaches brushed up to fall back like cat's whiskers. Those glory days have passed. But within the charming walkable city, you still find hints of those former times, when Rudyard Kipling stayed at Bundi, while tigers lurked in the nearby forests, and crocodiles teemed in the Mej River.

Since those days, a new palace, the Phool Sagar, has been constructed on the lakeside, still in Rajput style with banquet rooms and halls decorated with hunting trophies. And, in the streets of old lovely Bundi, Rajput men with bright turbans and Rajput women, their multicolored skirts flashing in the sun, crowd the dusty roads. With shiny pots on their heads and a child in their arms, they sail by with a smile, accompanied by the jingle of their jewelry.

Before you leave Rajasthan, head back toward Jaipur, by way of Ajmer and Pushkar, northwest of Bundi.

Ajmer and Pushkar

Situated at the foot of a hill, Ajmer is an ancient city (founded in the seventh century) and an important place of pilgrimage for Moslems—a curious anomaly in the land of Hindu Rajputs, an anomaly that also explains its stormy past. The Hindu Chauhans who created Ajmer remained in power until the late twelfth century, when Mohammed Ghori grabbed the city for himself. Then Ajmer changed hands repeatedly. In 1556, it was annexed by Akbar, who made it his royal residence, building the fort that still dominates the city. From here, he could command the main routes from the north. Ajmer also served as his key to the conquest of Rajputana and Gujarat. After the death of the great Moslem saint, Khwaja Muin-ud-Din Chisti, who preached here in the thirteenth century, a tomb, Dargah, was created in his honor. During his reign, Akbar visited once a year and supposedly walked from Agra to the saint's mausoleum, a distance of about 322 kilometers (200 miles). Frequented later by Shah Jahan, it owes its beautiful marble pavilions to his tender care.

All year long, and especially in January during the six-day Urs Mela celebration, this tomb draws Moslems from all over India and Pakistan. Even the Mogul Emperor Akbar made the journey many times. Today, as you walk up the bazaar to the holy site, you'll feel the emotional intensity as throngs press forward, carrying gifts. Inside the religious complex, Moslems throw money and food into two large caldrons placed on platforms. Each day the money is removed and the food is cooked and served to the people who congregate in the surrounding courtyards.

Close to Ajmer, at the foot of Taragarh Hill, stands a rare specimen of architecture, Adhai-din-Ka-Jhonpra, a mosque supposedly built in 2½ days by Mohammed Ghori on the former site of 30 Hindu temples. James Tod, in his standard work of 100 years back, waxed eloquent about its "gorgeous prodigality of ornament, richness of tracery, delicate sharpness of finish, laborious accuracy of workmanship." Two short minarets with inscriptions were added later.

Ajmer also has a refreshing artificial lake, Anasagar, created in the first half of the twelfth century by the Rajput King Anaji, who raised a vast embankment between two hills. The Mogul emperors were so entranced by this landscape that one after another, they embellished it with gardens, a long parapet, and five elegant pavilions of polished white marble created by Shah Jahan.

Pushkar lies a few kilometers north of Ajmer. Here, during Kartik Poornima (October or November), vast crowds of devout Hindus and tourists assemble at the water's edge, where the devout take a ritual dip. This religious festival is also the occasion for a lively camel market, which turns Pushkar into a festive city. According to sacred scripts, Brahma—first of the Hindu trinity—on passing this place let a lotus flower slip from his hand. Water sprang from the spot where the petals fell. The lake was formed and called Pushkar, which means lotus. Many ashrams and temples surround the holy lake—one of them dedicated to Brahma.

PRACTICAL INFORMATION FOR RAJASTHAN

WHEN TO GO. The tourist season runs from September to April, when temperatures are in the 70s and 80s in daytime and in the 60s at night—ideal weather, thanks to the absence of dampness. But Rajasthan is probably at its best during the monsoon (July–September), when the mountains and hills are covered with greenery and there's plenty of water in the lakes. Rainfall is light—from 12 to 24 inches per year, depending on the region. In the hot season, from the end of March to July, temperatures can rise above 100° F.

HOW TO GET THERE. By Air. From Delhi, *Indian Airlines* has two daily flights to Jaipur and Udaipur, and 11 weekly flights to Jodhpur. From Bombay, Indian Airlines has three daily flights to Jaipur, two daily flights to Udaipur, and 11 weekly flights to Jodhpur. From Aurangabad, it has a daily flight to Jaipur, Jodhpur, and Udaipur. Call for information in Jaipur (tel. 550519 or 550222); in Jodhpur (tel. 3310071); in Udaipur (tel. 3952). *Vayudoot* has a weekly flight that connects Delhi with Jaipur, Bikaner, Jodhpur, Kota, and Jaisalmer. Call for information in Jaisalmer (tel. 2406).

By Bus. Daily buses to Jaipur from Delhi are clean and cheap, and take about 5 hours. In Delhi, call for details; *Rajasthan Roadways* (tel. 2522246). From Jaipur you can get deluxe buses to nearby states. Call Central Bus Station, tel. 75834 or tel. 66579. This is also true in Udaipur (tel. 27191).

By Rented Car with Driver. Good roads connect Jaipur with Delhi and Agra. Car rental with driver costs about Rs. 4 per km, plus night halt charges (Rs. 50 per night). Hire a car from a recommended tour operator (see below or in the Delhi and Agra chapters).

By Train. From Delhi, the daily *Pink City Express* (five hours, Delhi–Jaipur) enables you to visit the city within a day, which is not enough time and only recommended to those who have no alternative. Other trains are the *Ahmedabad Express,* which leaves at 9:30 A.M.; the *Chetak Express,* which leaves at 1 P.M.; (each takes 22 hours to Udaipur), and the *Ahmedabad Mail,* which leaves at 10 P.M. and gets to Jaipur after dawn and to Abu Road (for Mount Abu) at teatime. The *Jodhpur Mail* covers the distance from Delhi in 12 hours, as does the *Bikaner Mail.* From Bombay, there are excellent trains that stop at Kota, Sawai Madhopur, and Ahmedabad. In Rajasthan, there are good rail connections throughout the state. For tickets and information in Delhi, contact the *International Tourist Guide,* New Delhi Railway Station, Platform No. 1; open 7:30 A.M.–5 P.M. (closed Sun.); tel. 3352164. In Jaipur, tel. 131.

TOURIST INFORMATION. The *Government of India Tourist Office* in Jaipur and the *Rajasthan Tourist Offices* throughout the state have excellent brochures on cities and special interests (wildlife, crafts), with comprehensive information and maps. The Government of India Tourist Office (State Hotel, Khasa Kothi, Jaipur 30200, tel. 72200) is open Monday–Friday, 9 A.M.–6 P.M., and Saturday till 2 P.M. The Rajasthan Tourist Offices are open 10 A.M.–5 P.M.; closed Sunday, unless noted otherwise. They are located in the following destinations:

Ajmer. Khadim Tourist Bungalow, Savitri Girls College Rd.; tel. 21626.

Alwar. *Information Center,* Near Purjan Vihar Garden; tel. 21868.

Amber. Near elephant stand; tel. 86264.

Bharatpur. Saras Tourist Bungalow, Agra Rd.; tel. 3700.

Bikaner. Junagarh Fort, Poonan Singh Circle; tel. 5445.

Bundi. Circuit House; tel. 2697.

Chittorgarh. Janta Avas Grih Station Rd.; tel. 2009.

Jaipur. Paryatan Bhawan, Government Hostel Campus, Jaipur 302016; tel. 70180 or 76362; Central Bus Stand, Sindhi Camp (no phone), open 6 A.M.–8 P.M. daily; and Railway Station (tel. 69714).

Jaisalmer. Moomal Tourist Bungalow, tel. 2406; open 8 A.M.–noon and 3 P.M.–6 P.M., closed Sunday.

Jhunjhunu. Hotel Shiv Shekhawati, Khemi Sati Rd.; tel. 2651.

Jodhpur. Ghoomar Tourist Bungalow, High Court Rd; tel. 45083.

Kota. Chambal Tourist Bungalow; tel. 27695.

Mount Abu. Opposite Bus Stand; tel. 3151.

Sawai Modhopur. Project Tiger Office; tel. 223.

Udaipur. Kajri Tourist Bungalow, Shastri Circle, tel. 29535; Dabok Airport, open at arrivals; Counter at Railway Station, open 8 A.M.–noon.

FOREIGN CURRENCY EXCHANGE. Most Western-style hotels have money-exchange counters. Otherwise, banks are open Monday–Friday, 10 A.M.–2 P.M.; Saturday till noon. In Jaipur, the *State Bank of Bikaner and Jaipur* (M.I. Rd., opposite G.P.O.) is open Monday–Friday 2:30–6:30 P.M.

ACCOMMODATIONS. Spending a night in Rajasthan frequently conjures up an interlude in a former raja palace. Sometimes the old castles/hunting lodges are great; sometimes they're a great disappointment, with character exchanged for amenities and a modern decor; and at an awful cost—both in terms of what is lost and what it costs to stay there. Nonetheless, *Rajasthan Tourism Development Corporation* (RTDC), a state-run organization, provides a good range of facilities to meet every budget. Prices are based on double occupancy and exclude taxes and service charges: *Deluxe,* over Rs. 2,000; *Expensive,* 1,200–Rs. 2,000; *Moderate,* Rs. 500–Rs. 1,200; *Inexpensive,* under Rs. 500.

AJMER-PUSHKAR

Moderate

Hotel Mansingh Palace. Vaishali Nagar, Ajmer 305001; tel. 30855. 60 rooms with bath. This new hotel, on the edge of Anasagar Lake, is designed to resemble a Rajput fortress, with sandy-brown exterior and parapets. Air-conditioned rooms have marble floors, an attractive contemporary decor, and TV. Room service, multicuisine restaurant, bar, foreign-exchange counter, shops, and cultural entertainment on request. AE, DC, MC, V.

Inexpensive

Sarovar Tourist Bungalow. Pushkar; tel. 40. 40 rooms with bath. Set on the banks of Sarovar Lake, this lovely older RTDC bungalow has pleasant grounds and simple, clean rooms with an institutional decor. Best rooms are air-conditioned and have balconies overlooking the lake or garden. All rooms have fans. Vegetarian Continental- and Indian-cuisine restaurant and room service. Rupees only.

During the **Pushkar Festival,** RTDC constructs a memorable tented tourist village in the *mela* (fairground). Accommodations are ordinary and deluxe tents, Rs. 1,000, and superdeluxe cottages, Rs. 2,500; vegetarian meals are included. The fair is held around November (see *Festivals and Seasonal Events in Facts at Your Fingertips*). At least two private companies now set up their own tented villages, but the

RTDC camp is your best bet. Book your tent well in advance through Central Reservation Office, Rajasthan Tourism Development Corporation, Ltd.; Chanderlok Building, 36 Jan Path, New Delhi, 110001 or through your travel agent.

ALWAR
(All three facilities listed here are near Siliserh Lake or in or near Sariska Tiger Preserve)

Deluxe

Taj Ramgarh Lodge. Alwar. Reservations through Ramgarh Lodge, Jamuva Ramgarh, Jaipur 303109; tel. 521241, fax 0141/521098. 11 rooms with bath. This attractive two-story retreat overlooks Ramgarh Lake and is 30 km (19 mi.) from Sariska. Rooms have a modern decor. Indian- and Continental-cuisine restaurant, room service, car-rental service, tennis, billiards. Meals included. AE, DC, MC, V.

Moderate

Sariska Palace Hotel. Sariska District, Alwar; tel. 222. 33 rooms with bath. This former palace and royal hunting lodge on the edge of the Sariska Tiger Preserve has a rustic, old-time ambience. Bedrooms and suites are gigantic and clean. Public rooms still evoke the past—wicker chairs and bits of Victoriana. Some air-conditioned rooms, room service, Indian- and Continental-cuisine restaurant, foreign-exchange counter, doctor, jeep safaris. AE, DC.

Inexpensive–Moderate.

Lake Palace Hotel. Siliserh; tel. 22991. 10 rooms with bath. Set on a hill overlooking Silisar Lake, this former palace, now an RTDC hotel, looks palatial and has stunning views. Rooms, however, are modest with a simple, Western-style decor. Some rooms (moderately priced) are air-conditioned and have TV. Room service, multicuisine restaurant, bar, boating, safaris. Rupees only.

BHARATPUR

Moderate

Bharatpur Forest Lodge. Bharatpur 321001; tel. 2760. 17 rooms with bath. Set in the bird sanctuary, this modest Ashok bungalow offers clean, comfortable rooms, some with decorative interior swings and air-conditioning. All rooms have balconies. Indian- and Continental-cuisine restaurant, room service, foreign-exchange counter, boating, doctor. Off-season discount April–August. AE, DC, MC, V.

BIKANER–GAJNER

Moderate

Gajner Palace Hotel. Gajner Wildlife Sanctuary. Reservations: Lallgarh Palace, Bikaner 334002; tel. 3263, fax 0151/5963. 23 rooms with bath. Set on a lake, this former hunting lodge of a maharajah is built in sandstone and has lovely grounds, its own temple, and a Rajput-Victorian ambience. Bedrooms are "comfy," with simple period decor. Room service, Indian- and Continental-cuisine restaurant, boating. Rupees only.

Lallgarh Palace Hotel. Bikaner 334001; tel. 3263, fax 0151/5963. 42 rooms with bath. This red sandstone turn-of-the-century former palace of the Bikaner maharajah is imposing: an Indo-Saracenic architectural tour de force on majestic lawns on the edge of the city. Rooms, however, are modest, with simple period furnishings, and are either air-conditioned or air-cooled. Indian- and Continental-cuisine restaurant, room service, billiards, swimming pool; Rajasthani cultural programs on request. Rupees only.

CHITTORGARH

Inexpensive

Hotel Castle Bijaipur. Bijaipur, Dist. Chittorgarh; tel. 1. Reservations: Managing Partner, Hotel Pratap Palace, Opp. Head Post Office, Chittorgarh 312301; tel. 2099. 9 rooms with bath. This seventeenth-century Rajput castle, set inside a fort, has just been converted into a hotel. Spacious bedrooms have simple period decor. The management treats you like family. Room service, Mewari-regional-cuisine restaurant, gardens, tribal tours, trekking, camel, jeep, and horse safari arrangements. Rupees only.

JAIPUR

Deluxe

Taj Jai Mahal Palace. Jacob Rd., Civil Lines, Jaipur 302006; tel. 73215, fax 141/65237. 102 rooms with bath. A former palace, the Taj Jai has a white-marble exterior and its grounds are regal, with a replica of the first Mogul garden built by Emperor Babur and a giant chessboard with plaster-of-paris pieces. Rooms are modern, with a distinct Western touch, with air-conditioning and TV. Room service, multicuisine restaurants, bar, cultural shows, doctor, foreign-exchange and travel counter, swimming pool, health club, yoga, shopping arcade. AE, DC, MC, V.

Taj Rambagh Palace. Bhawani Singh Rd., Jaipur 302005; tel. 75141, fax 141/521098. 110 rooms with bath. Jaipur's most famous palace hotel is classy, right down to the peacocks that strut across its perfect lawns. If you want a regal ambience, request a bedroom in the original palace. You'll be surrounded by original furnishings. The new wing is done up in a contemporary decor. Amenities include TV, air-conditioning, room service, multicuisine restaurants, bar, indoor swimming pool, health club, tennis, foreign-exchange and travel counter, baby-sitters, cultural entertainment, astrologer, shopping arcade. AE, DC, MC, V.

Welcomgroup Rajputana Palace. Atal Ban, Kaiser-i-Hind Rd., Jaipur 302017; tel. 64613. 220 rooms with bath. Designed as an enormous *haveli* (mansion), this new hotel will open in late 1992. Contemporary-style rooms will overlook a series of courtyards. Air-conditioning, TV, restaurants, bar, room service, doctor, foreign-exchange and travel counter, swimming pool, shopping arcade. AE, DC, MC, V.

Expensive

Hotel Clarks Amer. Jawaharlal Nehru Marg, Box 222, Jaipur 302017; tel. 550701, fax 141/550013. 202 rooms with bath. This seven-story high rise on the outskirts of Jaipur has rooms with an unassuming modern decor. TV, air-conditioning, room service, multicuisine restaurants, bar, swimming pool, cultural shows, minicoach shuttle to Jaipur, foreign-exchange and travel counter, shopping arcade. AE, DC, MC, V.

Hotel Jaipur Ashok. Jai Singh Circle, Bani Park, Jaipur 302016; tel. 75121. 98 rooms with bath. The hotel's exterior is delightful—red sandstone and marble covered with vine. Recently renovated, rooms are modern and decorated in soft pastels. They have TV and air-conditioning. Room service, multicuisine restaurants, bar, doctor, swimming pool, foreign-exchange and travel counter, shopping arcade. AE, DC, MC, V.

Moderate

Samode Haveli. Samode House, Gangapole, Jaipur 302002; tel. 42407. 18 rooms with bath. This pristine maharajah's haveli in the old city is dedicated to the preservation of old Rajasthani elegance, seen in its dining room as well as in its deluxe bedrooms, which have fresco-covered walls, pillars, and ceilings. All rooms are immaculately clean. Numerous terraces and courtyards, room service, Indian-buffet restaurant, foreign-exchange and travel counter, cultural performances on request. AE.

Samode Palace. Samode, District Jaipur; tel. 34 or, in Jaipur 302017, tel. 42407. 30 rooms with bath. Set on a bluff at the end of a golden-hued village (45 km [28 mi.] from Jaipur), this summer palace of Jaipur's former maharajah is idyllic. Though the towering structure is lavish, with painted walls and carved marblework, bedrooms are simple and have original Victorian furnishings. Suites are best, with lots of maharajah mementos. Room service, Indian- and Continental-cuisine restaurant, bar, occasional cultural performances. In the area, expect more peacocks, doves, and monkeys than people. Rupees only.

Inexpensive

Bissau Palace. Outside Chand Pole, Jaipur 302016; tel. 74191. 30 rooms with bath. Recently renovated, this maharajah's two-story bungalow is filled with mementos, paintings, and artifacts—in its lounge, library, and intimate dining room. Most rooms have interior pillars and Rajasthani touches. They're all neat and clean. Small swimming pool, spacious lawns, verandas, air-conditioning, room service, multicuisine restaurant, foreign-exchange and travel counter, shop, cultural performances on request. AE, MC, V.

Hotel Mandawa House. Sansar Chandra Rd., Jaipur 302001; tel. 75358 and 65498. 18 rooms with bath. Interior renovations are planned for this maharajah's home, where each room is named after a family member or ancestor and will be decorated in the style of the era in which that relative lived. Numerous terraces, courtyards, resident parakeet, multicuisine restaurant, air-conditioning, room service, foreign exchange and travel counter, doctor. AE.

Narain Niwas Palace Hotel. Kanota Bagh, Narain Singh Rd., Jaipur 302004; tel. 563448. 22 rooms with bath. Time stands still in this modest, former palace. Public rooms and higher-priced bedrooms (still inexpensive) are charming, with objets d'art, mementos, portraits, wall frescoes, and eccentric Victoriana. The less-interesting standard rooms and garden-cottage rooms have simple furnishings. Air-coolers, room service, multicuisine restaurant, attractive lawns, swimming pool, doctor, car-rental service, foreign-exchange counter, shops. AE, DC, MC, V.

JAISALMER

Deluxe

Gorbandh Palace. Amar Sagar Rd., Jaisalmer 34501; tel. 2749. 67 rooms with bath. Opening in early 1993, this two-story hotel is a golden sandstone jewel, built in haveli style, with modern Rajasthani decor and an interior courtyard with fountain and skylight. An additional section of ethnic-village-style cottages (inexpensive) will be constructed in late 1993. Air-conditioning, TV, room service, multicuisine restaurant, bar, shops, swimming pool, foreign-exchange and travel counter, doctor. AE, DC, MC, V.

Moderate

Nerayan Niwas Palace. Near Malka Prol, Jaisalmer 342006; tel. 2408, fax 22374. 38 rooms with bath. A former caravansary, this appealing hotel offers perfect rooms for a desert city—unassumingly modern and comfortable. Some rooms are air-conditioned; others are air-cooled. Its interior courtyard has the appeal of a modest oasis. Included are room service, multicuisine restaurant, bar, foreign-exchange and travel counter, doctor, shops, and camel safari and trekking arrangements. AE, DC, MC, V.

Inexpensive

Moomal Tourist Bungalow. Jaisalmer; tel. 2392. 50 rooms with bath. The rooms in this two-story building are drab, but the sheets are clean and the price is right. Some rooms have air-conditioning (although the electricity sometimes shuts off); others have ceiling fans. If you don't need air-conditioning, ask for one of the thatch-roof bungalows. Restaurant, bar, travel counter. Rupees only.

JODHPUR

Deluxe

Welcomgroup Umaid Bhawan Palace. Jodhpur 342006; tel. 22316, fax 22374. 100 rooms with bath. This turn-of-the-century pink sandstone palace-hotel, which is still the home of Jodhpur's former maharajah, is an architectural dream that dominates the landscape. The exterior, public rooms, and grounds are lavish. Bedrooms, while not opulent, have some period decor. They're extremely spacious and have air-conditioning and TV. There are multicuisine restaurants, room service, bar, indoor swimming pool, health club, tennis, billiards, squash, foreign-exchange and travel counter, doctor, shops, museum. Golf, village safari, and camel rides on request. Hotel guests can also arrange for an overnight train trip to Jaisalmer in the maharajah's private saloon car. AE, DC, MC, V.

Moderate

Ajit Bhawan Palace. Near Circuit House, Jodhpur, Rajasthan 342006; tel. 20409. 50 rooms with bath. If you want an abundance of charm and less regal display, stay in this enchanting smaller palace and village complex, designed and owned by the maharajah's uncle. Each bungalow is decorated in its own Rajasthani motif. The grounds are delightful, with paths that wind through greenery and over little bridges. Stay an extra day so that you can join one of the hotel's village tours. Multicuisine restaurant, room service, bar, foreign-exchange and travel counter, doctor, shops, cycling, horseback riding. AE, DC, MC, V.

Hotel Karni Bhawan. Defence Laboratory Rd., Ratanada, Jodhpur 342006; tel. 32220. 15 rooms with bath; 14 more under construction. This sandstone Rajput home has Western-style rooms and rooms with Gujarati furniture. It serves special Rajasthani food under huts on its peaceful back lawn. Room service, outdoor restaurant, garden, terraces, swimming pool, foreign-exchange counter, tour arrangements, doctor. AE, DC, MC, V.

KHIMSAR

Expensive

Welcomgroup Royal Castle. Box Khimsar, District Nagaur; tel. 28. 14 rooms with bath. This great escape hotel is set in a fifteenth-century palace. Best rooms have furnishings from the 1920s. Multicuisine restaurant, room service, barbecue, sightseeing, desert tour, camel safari arrangements. AE, DC, MC, V.

KOTA

Moderate

Briraj Bhawan Palace Hotel. Civil Lines, Kota; tel. 23071. 7 rooms with bath. Don't expect a posh palace; but do expect gracious service here. You stay in a sprawling Victorian home filled with mementos of the former maharaja. The drawing room and dining room are especially quaint. Bedrooms are old-fashioned and simple, with air-cooling. There is room service from a fixed-menu Indian and Continental restaurant. Rupees only.

MOUNT ABU

Moderate

Connaught House. Rajendra Marg, Mt. Abu 307501, tel. 3360 or reserve through General Manager, Umaid Bhawan Palace, Jodhpur 342006, tel. 20941, fax 291/22374. 15 rooms with bath. Stay in the English-style, Victorian cottage surrounded by gardens rather than in the annex, which was built in 1987 and has simple Western rooms—although these do have good views of the valley. Room service, multicuisine restaurant. Rupees only.

Palace Hotel. Bikaner House, Delwara Rd., Mount Abu 307501; tel. 3121. 38 rooms with bath. This former summer palace of the Bikaner maharajah is palatial in size but modest in decor. Photos and simple Victorian furnishings adorn public rooms. Everything is immaculate, with modernization kept to a minimum. The management treats you with care. Suites (also moderate) are gigantic; doubles are large. All bedrooms have unpretentious original furnishings. Room service, fixed-menu Indian and Continental restaurant, billiards, tennis courts, spacious lawns, pony rides arranged on request, foreign-exchange counter. AE, DC, V.

Inexpensive

Hotel Hilltone. Box 18, Mount Abu 307501; tel. 3112. 46 rooms with bath. This Western-style, rambling hotel has a cozy lobby and pleasant gardens. Bedrooms are simply decorated and clean. Cottage suites offer good privacy. Multicuisine restaurant, room service, bar, doctor, swimming pool, health club, shop, foreign-exchange counter. AE, DC, MC, V.

NAGAUR

Expensive

Nagaur Fort. Nagaur. Reservations: General Manager, Umaid Bhawan Palace, Jodhpur 342006; tel. 20941, fax 291/22374. 12 tents with separate baths (hot water by bucket). Stay in a spacious royal tent, with hand-blocked designs printed on the interior, set in an enormous fort constructed from the fourth to sixteenth centuries. Meals are served in a marble pavilion in a Mogul garden. At evening, entertainers perform in another pavilion. Open year-round. Book at least 60 days in advance. Rupees only.

NEEMRANA
122 km. (76 mi.) from Delhi

Moderate–Deluxe

Neemrana Fort-Palace. Off National Highway No. 8, Neemrana, tel. 8. Reservations: A-58 Nizamuddin East, New Delhi 110013; tel. 616145, fax 4621112. 27 rooms with bath. This gem of a 14th-century fort, perched on a hill, is half-way between Jaipur and Delhi. Newly restored and refurbished, each room is furnished with antiques and decorated with Rajput mementos and indigenous handicrafts. The Eastern-palace architecture is characterized by latticed wooden windows or *jalis* (perforated stone screens), cusped arches, gleaming pillars, squinches, and various-sized niches that contain stunning objects. Swatches of the original royal blue white-wash have been left untouched, showcased like minimalist paintings. Recovered decorated lintels are mounted on walls. Forget about room telephones or televisions. Plan to explore the nearby traditional Rajasthani village, or simply relax and watch preening peacocks and swooping parrots from private terraces, balconies, courtyards, in gardens, or from under a 12-column pavilion. Breakfast and morning tea included. Indian and French fixed meals are served by candlelight. At press time the hotel had applied for a liquor license and credit card plates.

POKARAN

Moderate

Fort Pokaran. Pokaran; tel. 274, or reserve through Pokaran House, P.W. D. Rd., Jodhpur 342001, tel. 320614. 14 rooms with bath. The men's private quarters in this fourteenth-century fort, with an excellent museum, have just been converted into a hotel. Some rooms offer period decor; others have simple Western furnishings. Multicuisine restaurant, room service, air-cooling, arrangements for meals on sand dunes and safaris. Rupees only.

RANAKPUR

Moderate

Maharani Bagh Orchard Retreat. Ranakpur; tel. 51 or 55, or reserve through General Manager, Umaid Bhawan Palace, Jodhpur 342006, tel. 20941, fax 291/22374. 11 rooms with bath. The retreat of the former Jodhpur maharani, this nineteenth-century cottage complex nestled in a mango orchard has air-cooled Western rooms. Room service, outdoor restaurant serving Rajasthani specialties and Continental cuisine, swimming pool, cultural performances on request. Rupees only.

Narlai-Gah. Near Ranakpur. Reservations through Ajit Bhawan, Jodhpur 342006; tel. 20409. About 12 rooms with bath. This modest old fort, owned by the uncle of Jodhpur's former maharajah, is in the Aravali hills. It is scheduled to open at the end of 1992. Each room will incorporate a special Rajasthani theme. Activities will include trekking, jeep safaris, and horseback riding to temples and villages in the hills. Room service, restaurant, bar, foreign-exchange and travel counter. AE, DC, MC, V.

SARDARSAMAND LAKE

Deluxe

Sardarsamand Lake Resort. Reserve through General Manager, Umaid Bhawan Palace, Jodhpur 342006; tel. 20941, fax 291/22374. 10 rooms with bath; more under renovation. This hunting lodge of Jodhpur's former maharajah is now a resort. Built in 1933, with Art Deco furnishings in the rooms, the sandstone and granite lodge is set on a lake that is popular with migrating birds from October to March. Rooms have verandas with a view of the lake and plains. Air-cooling, room service, Indian and Continental restaurant, swimming pool, tennis court, cultural performances on request. Rupees only.

SAWAI MADHOPUR

Deluxe

Taj Sawai Madhopur Lodge. Ranthambhor National Park Rd., Sawai Madhopur; tel. 2541, fax 141/521098. 16 rooms with bath. About 12 km (7.5 mi.) from the park, this former hunting lodge of the Jaipur maharajah was built in the 1930s. It has a cozy sitting room and an intimate dining hall. Its sweeping veranda overlooks an expansive lawn and separate guest cottages, constructed in 1960 for Queen Elizabeth II. Its simple Western rooms are impeccably clean. There are also some spacious tents, with shared bathrooms. Indian- and Continental-cuisine restaurant, room service, swimming pool, car-rental service. AE, DC, MC, V.

Inexpensive

Castle Jhoomer Baori Forest Lodge. Sawai Madhopur; tel. 2495. 12 rooms with bath. This former maharajah's hunting lodge and home for his harem is now an RTDC hotel about 11 km (7 mi.) from Ranthambhor National Park. The nineteenth-century four-story limestone building, perched on a bluff, has simply decorated bedrooms and common rooms with Rajasthani touches. Room service, multicuisine restaurant, bar, roof terraces, garden, jungle safaris. Rupees only.

SHEKHAVATI AREA

Moderate-Expensive

Castle Mandawa. Mandawa, District Jhunjhunu 333702; tel. 224 or 271. 47 rooms with bath. This eighteenth-century castle, now a popular hotel, is still owned by the descendants of the local *thakur* (king). All rooms are different and have period furniture. The suites and some rooms are opulent and spacious. There is an Indian- and Continental-cuisine restaurant; room service; bar; doctor; gift shop; camel, horse, and jeep safari arrangements; cultural shows. AE, DC, MC, V.

Moderate

Dera Dundlod Kila. Dundlod, District Jhunjhunu 333702; tel. 98. Reservations: Dundlod House, Civil Lines, Jaipur 302006; tel. 66276, fax 141/73921. 25 rooms with bath. This eighteenth-century fort, still owned by the descendants of the former thakur, has a stunning *Diwan-e-Khas* (public room), with original wall frescoes and Louis XIVth furniture. Fastidiously clean bedrooms have painted walls; but they're not opulent. A suite is also available. Under great management, amenities include room service; Continental- and Indian-cuisine restaurant; bar; nearby swimming; doctor; palmist; and jeep, horse, and camel safari arrangements. Rupees only.

Desert Resort. Mandawa, District Jhunjhunu 333702, tel. 224 or 271. 18 cottages with bath, and 10 rooms with bath. Set on a sand dune and modeled after a typical Rajasthani village, this terrific resort features clay and brick huts with delightful exterior paintings and thatched roofs and clay rooms in a lodge surrounding a courtyard. Interiors, with stone floors, are impeccably clean, with local handicrafts and a modern desert decor. Its dining room twinkles with mirror work and cowrie shells imbedded in clay walls. Indian- and Continental-cuisine restaurant; room service; bar; doctor; foreign-exchange counter; swimming pool; cultural shows; and camel, horse, and jeep safari arrangements. AE, DC, MC, V.

Roop Niwas Palace. Nawalgarh, District Jhunjhunu 333702; tel. 2008 or, in Jaipur, 62987. 22 rooms with bath. A mix of Rajput and European architecture, this former palace is on the outskirts of one of the most interesting Shekhavati villages. While the hotel is far from grand, the owners—descendants of the former thakur—aim to please. Rooms are modest but clean, the dining room is Rajput-quaint, and the grounds are lovely. Room service, Indian- and Continental-cuisine restaurant, limited bar, doctor, billiards, swimming pool, cultural programs, and horse and camel safari arrangements. Rupees only.

UDAIPUR

Deluxe

Taj Lake Palace Hotel. Pichola Lake, Udaipur 313001; tel. 23241, fax 294/25804. 85 rooms with bath. This famous 250-year-old marble palace sits like a vision in Pichola Lake. Interior public rooms are elegant. Spacious bed-sitting-rooms (the most costly) have lake views; less grand "superior" bedrooms, some with balconies, also offer lake views. Some of the "ordinary" rooms (least costly) have views of the lily pond or courtyard. All rooms have a contemporary decor, air-conditioning, and TV. If you want palatial furnishings, splurge on a suite. Multicuisine restaurants, room service, bar, foreign-exchange and travel counter, shopping arcade, small swimming pool, cultural programs, and horseback riding and boating arrangements. Reserve well in advance. AE, DC, MC, V.

Moderate-Deluxe

Shivniwas Palace. City Palace, Udaipur 313001; tel. 28239, fax 294/23823. 31 rooms with bath. This former palace, part of the City Palace complex, is also the current home of the Udaipur maharajah. It offers great privacy and excellent views of Pichola Lake. Air-conditioned rooms have a contemporary decor, but the sumptuous suites (deluxe price) have a regal appearance. Room service, multicuisine restaurant, swimming pool, tennis, billiards, boating, health club, foreign-exchange and travel counter. AE, DC, MC, V.

Expensive

Hotel Shikarbadi. Goverdhad Vilas, Udaipur 313001; tel. 83200, fax 294/23823. Just outside the city, this former hunting lodge of the Udaipur royal family is a lovely, rustic retreat. Air-conditioned rooms are attractive, with tiled ceilings and stone walls. Deer and monkeys come nearly to the door. Multicuisine restaurant, room service, TV, foreign-exchange and travel counter, bar, swimming pool, horseback riding, cultural performances on request. AE, DC, MC, V.

Inexpensive

Lake Pichola Hotel. Outside Chandpole, Udaipur 313001; tel. 29197. 20 rooms with bath. This lovely old palace on the banks of the lake has a pleasant old-time ambience and charming Rajasthani decor in its modest bedrooms. All rooms have marble balconies with a lake view. Room service, multicuisine restaurant, bar, car-rental service, foreign-exchange counter, puppet show, boating. Good value. AE, MC, V.

Paying Guest Accommodations. The Government of Rajasthan has set up paying guest accommodations in Jaipur, Jodhpur, and Udaipur. All homes have been inspected and the hosts' guest preferences (nationality, couples or families, age restrictions, etc.) are described in directories available at Government of India Tourist Offices abroad or through the Department of Tourism, Paryatan Bhawan, Government Hostel, M.I. Rd., Jaipur 302016; tel. 76362 or 70180. This is an excellent opportunity to meet the people, and room prices are usually inexpensive.

DINING OUT. In Rajasthan, you can explore Indian vegetarian dining—*thalis, domas, paneer* (cheese), butter *masalas,* and other exotic dishes. You can also find a nonvegetarian, Indian, Continental, or Chinese meal—at least in the bigger cities or at hotels. While we include only the best options, most accommodations listed above also have restaurants. Breakfast is usually 8–10:30; lunch, noon–3; dinner, 7:30–10. Payment is normally in rupees unless the restaurant is connected to a Western-style hotel. The restaurants listed below are informal and, unless noted, are open for all three meals and don't require reservations. Prices are based on one person eating a three-course meal, excluding taxes, tip, or beverage: *Deluxe,* over Rs. 300; *Expensive,* Rs. 200–Rs. 300; *Moderate,* Rs. 100–Rs. 200; *Inexpensive,* under Rs. 100.

AJMER-PUSHKAR

Due to Pushkar's religious sanctity, all Pushkar restaurants serve vegetarian cuisine and alcohol is prohibited.

Moderate

Sheesh Mahal. Hotel Mansingh Palace, Vaishali Nagar, Ajmer; tel. 30855. Influenced by Mogul architecture, this handsome restaurant has delicately mirrored ceilings and white walls with inset arches. The chef serves Continental and especially good Mughlai dishes. Try *murgh tikka masala* (spicy boneless chicken) or *macchhi chutneywali* (marinated pomfret cooked in the tandoor). There are live Indian *ghazels* (musicians) at night. Dinner reservations advised. Open 6:30–10 A.M., 12:30–3 P.M., and 7:30–11 P.M. AE, DC, MC, V.

Inexpensive

R.S. Restaurant. Shri Brahma Temple, Pushkar; no phone. This delightful, open-air restaurant serves good vegetarian Indian and Continental dishes. Open 7 A.M.–10 P.M. Rupees only.

Sobhraj Restaurant. Near the Delhi Gate, Ajmer; tel. 20640. This restaurant, set in Ajmer's oldest hotel, provides a quiet escape from the crowded bazaar. Tables have linen, and ceiling fans whir overhead. Choose from Indian or Continental cuisine. Open 7 A.M.–10:30 P.M. Rupees only.

Sun Set Cafe. Next to the Sarovar Tourist Bungalow, Pushkar; no phone. This open-air restaurant, on a lawn facing the lake, serves good Chinese, Continental, and Indian vegetarian fare. Open 6 A.M.–11 P.M. Rupees only.

JAIPUR

Expensive

Suvarna Mahal. Rambagh Palace, Bhawani Singh Rd.; tel. 75141. Once the maharajah's royal banquet hall, this stunning room has handsome drapes, tapestry-covered walls, and high, painted ceilings. Piano music is performed at lunch and in the evening. You can choose from Continental, Chinese, and Indian cuisines, including regional dishes such as *murg tikka zaffrani* (chicken marinated in yogurt and saffron and cooked in the tandoor) or *dahi ka mass* (lamb cooked in a yogurt-based curry). Dinner reservations advised. Open 6–9 A.M., 12:30–2:30 P.M.; 7:30–10:30 P.M. AE, DC, MC, V.

Moderate

Niros. M.I. Rd.; tel. 74493. Established in 1949, this Jaipur institution, with marble floors and handsome mirrors set into the walls, serves the best nonvegetarian Chinese, Continental, and Indian dishes in town. It also has reliably good vegetarian fare. Specialties include *rashmi kebab* (skewered boned chicken), *panir tikka* (cottage cheese with skewered tomatoes, onions, and capsicum), or mutton *tikka masala* (tandoor-cooked lamb simmered in a spicy tomato-and-butter sauce). Dinner reservations advised. Open 10 A.M.–11 P.M. AE, DC, MC, V.

Shivir. Mansingh Hotel, Sansar Chandra Rd.; tel. 78771. Jaipur's only rooftop restaurant offers a city view, live Indian ghazals at lunch and dinner, and a subdued modern decor. The menu features Indian cuisine, with the popular choice Mughlai or tandoori specialties. Dinner reservations advised. Open 12:30–2:30 P.M. and 7:30–11:30 P.M. AE, DC, MC, V.

Inexpensive

Chanakya. M.I. Rd.; tel. 78461. Subdued lighting, table linen, and taped Indian classical music create an appealing ambience in which to enjoy terrific vegetarian meals: Indian, Continental, Chinese. Start with *jal jeera,* an unusual spicy beverage. Follow it with the Chanakya special (a tasty mixture of dried fruits, cottage cheese, vegetables, and spices, topped with edible pure silver) or the Rajasthani special called *gatta* (a spicy dish of gram flour rolled in herbs and spices and cooked in tasty tomato sauce). Open noon–11 P.M. AE, DC, MC, V.

Chokhi Dhani. Tonk Rd. (22 km [14 mi.]) from the city; no phone. This evening excursion takes you to an ethnic village complex, where you sit inside a lantern-lit hut and eat Rajasthani vegetarian dishes served on a leaf. Also enjoy typical cultural performances—dances, singing, puppet shows—or take a ride on a camel. Open 5 P.M.–11 P.M. Rupees only.

JAISALMER

Moderate

The Trio. Mandir Palace, near Gandhi Chowk, tel. 2733. Eat upstairs under the open sky or a Rajasthani canopy surrounded by ethnic decor. This popular restaurant serves multicuisine dishes, including unusual local fare: *kadi pakora* (rolled lentil balls cooked in gram flour and yogurt) and *ker sangri* (desert beans and capers prepared in a mildly spicy sauce). Local performers entertain at night. Open 7:30 A.M.–10:30 P.M. AE, DC, MC, V.

JODHPUR

Expensive

Marwar Hall. Umaid Bhawan Palace; tel. 22316. A gorgeous palace dining room, Marwar Hall has huge chandeliers hanging from its vaulted ceiling. The chef prepares very good Continental and Indian dishes, including tasty Mughlai and regional Marwari dishes. Dinner reservations advised. Open 5:30 A.M.–9 A.M., 1 P.M.–3:30 P.M., and 7:30–10 P.M. AE, DC, MC, V.

Inexpensive

Midtown Vegetarian Restaurant. Hotel Shanti Bhawan, Station Rd.; tel. 21689. Right in town, this unpretentious yet superclean Rajasthani-decor restaurant serves a good range of South Indian and Rajasthani dishes and some Chinese and Continental fare. Try the Midtown specials: a *dosa* (Indian-style crepe), filled with potato, cheese, and cashew nuts; or the *thali* (assorted portions of unusually prepared vegetables). It also has a salad bar. Open 8 A.M.–11 P.M. Rupees only.

MOUNT ABU

Moderate

Takshashila Restaurant. Near the taxi stand; tel. 3173. This reliable restaurant, with mirrored walls and marble floors, draws a crowd. The chef serves good vegetarian Continental, Indian, and Chinese cuisines. Open 8–11:30 A.M., noon–3 P.M., and 7–10:30 P.M. Rupees only.

Inexpensive

Angan Dining Room. Near the taxi stand; tel. 3173. With lots of green marble and a mirrored ceiling, this restaurant looks like an old-fashioned dining hall. It offers an excellent all-you-can-eat Gujarati thali. Come hungry! Open 11 A.M.–2:30 P.M., and 7–9:30 P.M. Rupees only.

Saraswati Hotel Restaurant. Opposite the taxi stand; tel. 317. Another popular all-you-can-eat Gujarati thali restaurant, it's extremely simple, with wooden tables and overhead fans. Food is delicious. Open 11 A.M.–1:30 P.M. and 6:30–8:30 P.M. Rupees only.

UDAIPUR

Deluxe

Neelkamal. Lake Palace Hotel; tel. 23241. Subdued and elegant, with views of the lake, this restaurant features Continental and Indian cuisines, including Rajasthani specialties. Nonhotel guests must call in advance to see if they can be accommodated; the room is small. Open 12:30–2:30 P.M. and 7:30–10:30 P.M. AE, DC, MC, V.

Moderate

Heritage. Hospital Rd.; tel. 23368. This restaurant, with taped Indian classical music and tapestry-covered and hand-carved chairs, is extremely appealing. The tasty cuisine is "nouvelle" Indian vegetarian, including delicious ice creams with no artificial ingredients. Try *makai masala* (fresh corn simmered in a creamy sauce) and *dum tarkari* (baked vegetables in creamy saffron and cardamom). Open 10:30 A.M.–10:30 P.M. Rupees only.

SWEETS AND TREATS. Bikaner. Try some of the popular *rasgulla* (syrupy milk-based sweet balls) at Chhoto Motu Jhosi Hotel, a local favorite on Station Rd. Open 7 A.M.–7 P.M. **Jaipur.** You can't beat the local ambience and vegetarian snacks and sweets in the restaurant at **LMB Hotel** at Johari Bazaar. Sample their *chaat* (Indian potato salad) with *LMB Bahar* (a combo drink of fresh fruit juices). Also try their sweet Rasmalai special. Open 8 A.M.–11:30 P.M.

Jodhpur. Midtown Vegetarian Restaurant (address above) has homemade ice cream and numerous fresh fruit drinks and shakes. This is a great place to sample an exotic Indian fruit. Open 8 A.M.–11 P.M.

HOW TO GET AROUND. From the airports. At Jaipur, a taxi costs about Rs. 150 into the city. At Jodhpur, the taxi fare is about Rs. 100 into the city. At Udaipur, the taxi fare is Rs. 185 into the city.

How you decide to get from city to city within Rajasthan depends on your budget and your time. It's a big state with a lot of territory between major attractions.

By Air. *Indian Airlines* has daily flights that connect Jaipur, Jodhpur, and Udaipur. *Vayudoot* has a weekly flight between Jaisalmer and Jodhpur. For information, see How to Get There, above.

By Bus. Good, inexpensive deluxe coach services connect most major cities. In Jaipur, call the Central Bus Stand (tel. 75834) for deluxe buses.

By Train. Trains are slower than the buses, but they will get you to most cities. In Jaipur, call 131.

By Rented Car with Driver. Figure about Rs. 4 per km for an Ambassador with driver, plus Rs. 50 per night halt charges. With trips around Mount Abu, the cost is about Rs. 5 per km. Hire a car with driver from one of the tour operators listed below.

By Taxi. Taxis are the same price as a rented car with driver. Set the rate before you start.

By Auto Rickshaw. Rates are about Rs. 3.50 per km for this convenient way to get around any crowded city. Again, set the fare before you depart.

The following destinations offer additional alternatives.

BIKANER

By Bike Rickshaw. Establish fares in advance. This is the cheapest way to get around.

JAIPUR

By Bike Rickshaw. This should be cheaper than an auto rickshaw. Bargain.

JAISALMER

This is a walk-around town as far as the old city is concerned.

By Camel and Camel Cart. Lots of fun, but some discomfort. Call the tourist office (tel. 2406), tour operators (see below), or arrange for service through your hotel.

By Bike. Bikes can be rented at shops near the fort for about Rs. 25 daily.

JODHPUR

By Bike Rickshaw and Horse Tonga. Fix the rate in advance. Bargain.

KOTA

By Bike Rickshaw. Cheap, but fix the fare in advance.

MOUNT ABU

By Tonga or Pony. Haggle, and set the fare in advance.

UDAIPUR

By Tonga. Set the fare in advance. Bargain.

TOURS. At press time, the Rajasthan Development Tourism Corporation (RTDC) was redesigning its network of state and city tours. Contact the New Delhi office of the RTDC (Chandralok Bldg., 36 Janpath, tel. 3321820) or the Jaipur RTDC (Hotel Swagatam Campus, Near Railway Station, Jaipur 302006, tel. 60586 or 79252) for latest details on package tours by luxury bus or minibus from Delhi. RTDC also offers horse or camel safaris that take you to some of the state's best fairs. Travelers planning to visit Rajasthan should also consider taking the luxurious *Palace-on-Wheels* (week-long train excursion); see *Facts at Your Fingertips* (Traveling in India by Train) for details.

Within the state, RTDC will also offer city tours and nearby excursions in Chittargarh, Jaipur, Jodhpur, and Mt. Abu. Contact the local tourist office or the head office in Jaipur (see address, above).

Mr. Saroop Singh, the owner of Ajit Bhawan and uncle of Jodhpur's former maharajah, offers a daily 6- to 7-hour jeep safari to nearby villages of artisans. In his company, you'll be warmly welcomed by the villagers and learn all about Rajasthani culture and handicrafts. Contact Ajit Bhawan, tel. 20409. Rs. 400 with snacks. AE, DC, MC, V.

Guides are also available at most destinations. Contact the Government of India Tourist Office in Jaipur (see *Tourist Information,* above) or any of the Rajasthan state tourist offices. For one to four persons, figure Rs. 80 for a half day and Rs. 100 for a full day, plus Rs. 50 for lunch.

TOUR OPERATORS. For good tours and all your travel needs, including hired car with driver, contact *Rajasthan Tours.* Its head office is at Rambagh Palace Hotel, Jaipur, Rajasthan; tel. 521041 or 521784. Open 9 A.M.–6 P.M. daily. It also has branches at Bikaner (tel. 4834), Jodhpur (tel. 27464), Jaisalmer (tel. 2561), and

Udaipur (tel. 23030). It accepts AE, DC, MC, V. You can also arrange for a car with driver through many of the hotels listed above and through RTDC.

Rajasthan Mountain Sports Association provides horseback riding and polo lessons in Jaipur; elephant, horse, and camel day trips in major cities; and extended tours throughout Rajasthan in fancy horse-drawn carriages, on the back of a horse, camel, elephant, or inside a jeep. Many of their trips include stays at palaces and forts. Contact in advance: Rajasthan Mountain Sports Association, c/o Dundlod House, Hawa Sarak, Civil Lines, Jaipur 302006; tel. 66276, fax 141/73921. Rupees only.

Royal Safaris offers a range of camel, horse, camel-cart, and jeep safaris and treks in the popular areas surrounding Bikaner, Jodhpur, and Jaisalmer. It also features unusual destinations rarely visited in this popular state: visits to ethnically pure villages, homes of craftspeople, little-known fairs and ashrams. It can custom-design any trip at any time of the year. Contact in advance: Royal Safaris, Nachna Haveli, Gandhi Chowk, Jaisalmer 345001; tel. 2538. AE, DC, MC, V. Also check *Facts at Your Fingertips* for tour operators who offer trips to Rajasthan.

SEASONAL EVENTS. Since the lunar calendar determines most dates, contact the Government of India Tourist Office before setting out for any event.

January. *Urs Mela.* For six days in Ajmer, Moslems flock to the tomb of their revered Saint Khwaja Muin-ud-Din Chisti to honor his death. *Desert Festival.* Jaisalmer's gala event includes traditional Rajasthani music; a display of desert handicrafts, camel caravans, camel races, and turban-tying competitions. Don't miss it if your Rajasthan trip is planned around this time. Book rooms well in advance. You can also arrive astride a camel on a safari that takes you through the Thar Desert. Contact RTDC for details (see Tours, above).

January/February. *Baneshwar Fair.* During this solemn event, Bhil tribals immerse the ashes of their recently departed in a holy confluence of three rivers at Baneshwar (70 km [43 mi.] south of Udaipur). Do not take photos. *Naguar Fair.* Nagaur (135 km [84 mi.] from Jodhpur) holds an enormous cattle, camel, and horse fair—a popular event with cultural programs and camel races. If you want to arrive by camel, contact RTDC (see Tours, above).

February. *Hadoti Festival.* In Kota, musicians and dancers celebrate the Hadoti culture.

March. *Holi* or *Brij.* On the eve of this festival that heralds the arrival of spring, Rajasthanis have processions with music and dancing. Expect to be doused with colored water. Jaipur also holds an *Elephant Festival,* with richly dressed elephants paraded through the streets. *Gangaur Festival.* This festival in Udaipur and Jaipur honors the goddess Parvati, with festive processions of young girls and this deity, who is the symbol of marital bliss.

June. *Summer Festival.* Mount Abu celebrates the season with folk music and Rajasthani dance performances.

July/August. *Naag Panchami.* This festival in Jodhpur is dedicated to the 1,000-headed mythical serpent, Sesha. Huge cloth *naags* (cobras) are displayed in a festive fair. *Teej Festival.* This festival, dedicated to Parvati, celebrates the beginning of the monsoon. Rajasthani women take to swings hanging from trees and have swinging contests. Procession of the goddess Parvati involving elephants, camels, and dancers. A big event in Jaipur.

October/March. *Shilp Darshan Mela.* At a delightful complex in Udaipur, set up with typical village homes from Rajasthan, Gujarat, Goa, Maharashtra, and Madhya Pradesh, master craftspeople from these states show how they create award-winning handicrafts, which are also for sale. Dancers and musicians perform daily. Don't miss this wonderful ongoing event.

October/November. *Pushkar Festival.* Rajasthan's amazing festive and religious event has a carnival atmosphere. Gaily festooned cattle and thousands of people gather for a sacred dip at dawn in the holy waters of the lake. Book a tent or room well in advance through RTDC (see Tours, above) or your travel agent. You should also inquire about RTDC's new horse safari: a great way to arrive at the fair.

November. *Bikaner Festival.* During this festival in Bikaner there is folk music and dance, culminating in a fire dance, with men jumping in and out of flames.

December. *Shekhavati Festival.* This festival highlights the old frescoes on Shekhavati's *havelis* (mansions) and celebrates the local arts, traditional music and dance, and cuisine. Another good event!

HISTORIC SITES. Entrance to most places is generally free; where a donation is requested, a few rupees will suffice. Most monuments and historic sites are open daily, sunrise to sunset, unless noted below.

AJMER-PUSHKAR

Adhai-Din-Ka-Jhonpra. In 1193 after Muhammed Ghori destroyed an ancient Sanskrit college and 30 Hindu temples, he construed this mosque of Indo-Islamic style on the temple ruins supposedly in 2½ days. The mosque stands on the pillars, each different, of these temples.

Anasagar. An artificial lake built in the twelfth century by Anaji Chauhan and added to by Jahangir. Shah Jahan built the *Baradari* (pavilions).

Dargah. Tomb of the Sufi saint Khwaja Muin-ud-Din Chisti (1142–1246). Here, Akbar sought the blessings of a son. Open sunrise until 10 A.M. and from 4 until about 7 P.M.

Nasiyan (Red Temple). Jain temple built in the nineteenth century with a two-story hall containing gilt representations of Jain mythology. Open 8 A.M.–4 P.M.

ALWAR

Alwar Fort. A medieval fort, in which Babur hid treasures for his son Humayun. Jahangir stayed here three years. The fort was eventually conquered by Maharajah Pratap Singh in 1775. Gigantic citadel towering on a hill; 15 large and 51 small towers with 446 holes for muskets. Several gates—Jai Pol, Suraj Pol, Laxman Pol, Chand Pol, Hrishan Pol, Andheri Gate. See the remains of Jai Mahal, Nikumbh Mahal, Salim Sagar Pond, Suraj Kund, and numerous temples. Great view of city.

Vinay Vilas Mahal (City Palace). Built in the late eighteenth century in a Rajput and Moghal blend of architecture. Behind the Vinay Vilas, you can see temples and a cenotaph of Maharajah Bakhtawar Singh built by Maharajah Vinay Singh in 1815. Unusual Bengali roof and arches.

BHARATPUR

Jawahar Burj. Old fort built in 1726 by Suraj Mal to commemorate his victories over the Moguls and later the British. Coronation ceremonies of Jat rulers of Bharatpur took place here.

Lohagarh Fort (Iron Fort). Designed in the early eighteenth century by Maharajah Suraj Mal, the founder of Bharatpur, the fort held off numerous British attacks. See Kishori Mahal, Mahal Khas, Kothi Khas. Open 9 A.M.–5 P.M.

Palace. A blend of Rajput and Mogul architecture. Magnificent apartments with beautifully designed floor tiles.

BIKANER AREA

Bhanda Sagar Jain Temple (five km from Bikaner). A sixteenth-century Jain temple, dedicated to the twenty-third Teerthankar Parsvanathji. Open 6 A.M.–11 A.M. and 7 P.M.–10 P.M.

Devi Kund (eight km from Bikaner). Royal crematorium with a number of cenotaphs belonging to former rulers of the Bika dynasty. The *chhatri* of Maharajah Surat Singh is white marble with Rajput paintings adorning the ceiling.

Junagarh Fort. Built in the sixteenth century by Raja Raj Singh, an outstanding general of Mogul Emperor Akbar. Encircled by a moat with numerous red sandstone and marble palaces. Suraj Pol (Sun Gate) is the main entrance. Weddings and births were celebrated in Har Mandir (chapel). Numerous palaces are adorned with columns, arches, and graceful screens. Open 10 A.M.–5 P.M.

Karni Mata Temple (in Deshnok, 33 km [20 mi.] from Bikaner). Dedicated to Karni Mata, an incarnation of Durga. The rats that crawl around here are sacred. Maharajah Ganga Singh donated the massive silver gates.

Lalgarh Palace (Red Fort). Built by Maharaja Ganga Singh in the nineteenth century. Red sandstone with terrific carvings. In the banquet hall, see the collection of old photographs and trophies.

BUNDI

Chitter Mahal (Palace of Towers). Massive gates surround an enormous collection of stone buildings built by successive rulers starting in the 1600s. The palace is covered with spy holes and mysterious windows. Visit the Naubat Khana, the Hathi Pol (curious water clock that formerly struck each half hour), the Diwan-i-Am. Also see the Chitra Shala, built by Rao Rajah Shatroo Salji in the 1600s. Terrific Bundi mural paintings that adorn the walls and ceilings were added much later.

Naval Sagar, an artificial lake with a temple of Varuna (Aryan god of water) in the center.

Phool Sagar. A twentieth-century palace and present home of the Durbar (former ruler of Bundi). Also known as the Flower Palace, the magnificent home has banquet rooms, numerous halls, plus an intriguing collection of murals created by Italian prisoners of war. To visit, permission is required; call the secretary, tel. 1, 34.

Taragarh (Star Fort). Built in 1372, the fort with an enormous tank (originally the palace reservoir) provides a commanding view of Bundi.

CHITTORGARH

Chittorgarh Fort. Foundations attributed to the seventh century. Beyond the first gate, Padal Pol, a tablet marks the spot where Prince Bagh Singh died during the second attack on Chittorgarh. Between the second gate (Bhairon Pol) and the third gate (Hanuman Pol) are two *chattris* (tombs) where Jaimal of Badnore and Kalla were killed by Akbar in 1567. Near the main gate (Ram Pol), there is another chattri for Patta of Kelwa, a 15-year-old fighter who died here. The fort is 11 kilometers (seven miles) in circumference and contains some great Rajput architecture. See the *Vijay Stambh* (Victory Tower), nine stories high, and covered with secular sculpture. Built by Maharana Jumbha to celebrate his victory over the Moslem rulers of Malwa and Gujarat in 1440. Kirti Stambh ("Tower of Fame"), built by a Jain merchant in the twelfth century and dedicated to Adinathji (the first of the Jain tirthankaras). The tower is covered with figures from a Jain pantheon. Padmini's Palace, supposedly for Queen Padmini, overlooks a pool. Within the walls, a battle occurred between Allauddin Khilji and Rana Ratan Singh that ended with the death of Padmini. Meera and Kumbha Shyam Temple, built in the Indo-Aryan style and associated with the mystic poet-wife of Bhojraj, the eldest son of Rana Sanga. Kalika Mata Temple was initially built in the eighth century as Surya (Sun Temple) and later converted into Kalika Mata, or a mother goddess temple, in the fourteenth century.

Nagari (14 km [9 mi.] north of Chittorgarh). Ancient town that flourished from the Maurya to the Gupta era. Interesting archaeological sites with a distinct connection to Buddhism and Hinduism.

DEEG

Former summer resort of the rulers of Bharatpur (32 km [20 mi.] from there). Numerous forts, palaces, and gardens. See *Ghopal Bhavan* and *Suraj Bhavan,* built of marble. Open 8 A.M.–noon; 1–6 P.M. Much of the inlaid marble on these buildings was stolen from Mogul palaces in Agra and Delhi.

JAIPUR

Amber Palace and Fort (11 km [7 mi.] from Jaipur). Construction begun by Maharajah Man Singh in early 1700s, completed 100 years later: an excellent blend of Rajput and Mogul influences. See the Hall of Victory, with panels of alabaster and inlay work; *Sheesh Mahal* (Hall of Mirrors)—step inside, close doors, strike a match—the ceiling glows. Rooms are small; typical of Mogul period. Courtyards and narrow passages: typical Rajput. Above the palace is the Jaigash Fort (supposedly still contains hidden treasures of Jaipur). Open: 9 A.M.–4:30 P.M.

City Palace and Museum. Begun by Sawai Jai Singh in the 1700s, with further additions by later maharajahs. Open: 9:30 A.M.–4:45 P.M.

Gaitor (eight km from Jaipur). Royal cenotaphs of kings at the foot of the Nahar-garh hills. The cenotaph of Sawa Jai Singh II is of white marble, with intricate carv-ings over the dome, supported by 20 pillars. Other cenotaphs are for Madho Singh, Ram Singh, and Partap Singh.

Govind Devji Temple. Temple of Lord Krishna facing the City Temple complex. From here you can get a good view of the City Palace, Chandra Mahal.

Hawa Mahal. (Palace of Winds). Built in 1799 by Maharajah Sawai Pratap Singh. Located on the Johari Bazaar heading north. A five-story building with a pyramidal facade. Overhanging windows with latticed screens, domes, spires. Open: 10 A.M.–5 P.M. Closed Fridays.

Jantar Mantar (Observatory). Built before the city of Jaipur in 1726. Located southeast of Chandra Mahal within the city palace complex. Largest and best pre-served of the five astronomical observatories built by Sawai Jai Singh. Open: 9 A.M.–5 P.M.

Nahargarh Fort (15 km [nine mi.] from Jaipur). Originally called Sudarshangarh Fort, it was built in 1734 by Sawai Jai Singh. The upper floor was constructed by Sawai Ram Singh II in 1868–69; more apartments were added in 1902–03 by Sawai Madho Singh II. Great view of Jaipur from here. Open: 10 A.M.–5 P.M.

Sisodia Palace and Garden (eight km [five mi.] from Jaipur). Built by Maharajah Sawai Jai Singh in 1770 for his queen, Sisodia. Central room with galleries on three sides surrounded by terraced gardens with fountains, pools, and sculpture.

JAISALMER

Citadel. Constructed by Rawal Jaisal in 1156 on Trikuta hill surrounded by high golden walls. Inside are Jain temples dedicated to Rikhabdevji and Sambhavnathji, constructed from the twelfth to the fifteenth century. Filled with deities and mytho-logical carvings. *Gyan Bhandar* (library), part of the Jain temple complex, contains some of the oldest manuscripts in India.

Havelis: Salim Singh Ki Haveli built by Salim Singh in the seventeenth century. Narrow dimension from ground floor widens at the top, with balconies jutting out. In sad disrepair within; a courteous request (or a few rupees) should get you inside. *Nathmal Ki Haveli* built in the nineteenth century by two architect brothers. The structure is flanked by stone elephants. Look carefully, they are not identical—just harmoniously in tune. Again, a courteous request or a small donation may get you inside. *Patva Havelis*—a string of five havelis built by the Patva brothers. Two of the five are owned by the government and are open to the public (inquire at the tourist department for the times). Handsome carved pillars. Painted murals on some of the interior walls. The other three are accessible, with a small donation, if the owner is in the mood.

JODHPUR

Jaswant Thada. Royal crematorium built in 1899 for Maharajah Jaswant Sinbgh II near the Meherangarh Fort. A white marble structure housing the portraits of past rulers. Plus other cenotaphs, also in marble, to commemorate acts of bravery and generosity of successive rules. Open: 8 A.M.–6 P.M.

Mahamandir Temple (two km from Jodhpur). Temple with 100 pillars. Richly ornamented with figures in various yoga postures.

Meherangarh Fort. Overlooking Jodhpur and constructed by Rao Jodha in 1459. Seven gates lead into the fort. Numerous interior palaces and temples and an excel-lent museum. Open 6 A.M.–6 P.M. (Apr. 1–Oct. 30); 9 A.M.–4:30 P.M. (Nov. 1–Mar. 31).

Umaid Bhawan Palace. Built by Maharajah Umaid Singh 1929–42. Also known as *Chhitar Palace* because of the sandstone that was used.

KOTA AREA

Baroli (40 km [25 mi.] from Kota). One of the oldest temple complexes in Raja-sthan, constructed in the ninth century. Built in the Panchaytan (group of five) style, some still with rich carvings.

Jhalra Patan (60 km [37 mi.] from Kota). "City of Bells," with the Jhalra patan, one of the best sun temples in India located within this ancient city. Also see old Jain temples, plus the ruins of Buddhist cave temples recently excavated.

MOUNT ABU

Adhar Devi Temple. Chiseled out of a rock, and dedicated to the goddess Durga. *Dilwara Jain Temples.* Constructed from the eleventh to the thirteenth century. Open: noon to 6 P.M. for non-Jains.

RANAKPUR

Chanmukha. Jain temple constructed in the fifteenth century and dedicated to Adinathji. Great sculpture throughout interior and on the 1,444 pillars. Open from noon to 5 P.M. for non-Jains.

SHEKHAVATI DISTRICT

The following towns and villages are worth visiting to see the art of frescoes created in the mid-nineteenth century. The frescoes cover the facades and interiors of havelis of former Marwari merchants. Originally, the themes were religious, then moved to ornamental motifs. In the 1900s, painters called *chitera* began imitating British lithographs and etchings. First, only natural pigments were used; then, around 1890, a gradual switch was made to chemical dyes. The towns are located in this district, which lies between Delhi and Jaipur. Visit Sikar (the old quarter), Mandawa, Fatehpur Sikri, Khetri, and Nawalgarh.

UDAIPUR

City Palace. Begun in the 1600s by Udai Singh and constructed of granite and marble. The main entrance is via the triple gate, Tripolia, with eight carved marble arches. Inside are numerous palaces: Suraj Gokhada (Sun Balcony), Badi Mahal (Garden Palace), Sheesh Mahal, Bhim Vilas, Chini Chitrasala, Mor Chowk (Peacock Courtyard). This is one place where it's worth having a guide. Open: 9 A.M.–4:30 P.M.

Eklingji (22 km [14 mi.] from Udaipur). The main temple was built in 1734. Ornate pillared hall under a huge pyramidical roof. The important temples are open daily 4–7 A.M., 10 A.M.–1 P.M., and 5–7 P.M.

Jagdish Temple. Built in 1651 by Maharana Jagat Singh I. Largest temple in Udaipur, with good sculptures and carvings. Offers a great view of Udaipur.

MUSEUMS AND GALLERIES. Practically every city and town in Rajasthan—besides being a museum in itself—contains a museum with centuries-old art objects and artifacts. Some of the buildings housing the museums are sights to behold, from palaces to forts. Entrance fees are nominal.

AJMER

Government Museum. Akbar's palace and royal quarters filled with Rajput and Mogul armor and regional sculptures. Open 10 A.M.–5 P.M.

ALWAR

Government Museum (second floor of City Palace). Great collection of Mogul and Rajput paintings from the eighteenth and nineteenth centuries and ancient manuscripts in Urdu, Sanskrit, and Persian. Good collection of armor. Open 10 A.M.–5 P.M.; closed Fridays and official holidays.

BIKANER

Ganga Golden Jubilee Museum. One of Rajasthan's best museums, with a good collection of artifacts from the pre-Harappan civilization and the Gupta and Kushan era, including terra cotta, pottery, paintings, sculpture, armor, and coins. A separate collection of local arts and crafts. Open 10 A.M.–5 P.M.; closed Fridays and holidays.

Sadul Museum. Inside Lallgarh Palace. Houses memorabilia of the former local maharajah. Open 10 A.M.–5 P.M.; closed Wednesdays.

CHITTORGARH

Government Museum (former Fateh Prakesh Palace). Collection of sculptures from temples and other buildings in the fort. Open 10 A.M.–5 P.M.; closed Fridays and official holidays.

JAIPUR

Albert Hall Museum, in Ram Niwas Garden. Eclectic displays from clay models showing yoga postures to carpets and displays of folk instruments and Rajasthani culture. Beautiful building. Open 10 A.M.–5 P.M.; closed Fridays and holidays.

City Palace Museum. Collection of royal garments, textiles, carpets, armor, and miniature paintings. Open 9:30 A.M.–4:45 P.M.

Hawa Mahal Museum. Open 10 A.M.–5 P.M.; closed Fridays.

JODHPUR

Government Museum, in Umaid Public Garden. Collection of armor, textiles, local arts and crafts, miniatures, portraits, and manuscripts. Open 10 A.M.–5 P.M.; closed Fridays.

Meherangarh Fort Museum. Within various apartments and palaces of the regal fort are palanquins, howdahs, royal cradles, miniatures, folk instruments, costumes, and furniture. Open 8 A.M.–6 P.M. (Apr. 1–Oct. 30); 9 A.M.–4:30 P.M. (Nov. 1–Mar. 31).

Umaid Bhawan Palace Museum. Former possessions of the maharajah. Many clocks. Open 10 A.M.–5 P.M.

KOTA

Government Museum. Old coins, Hadoti sculpture. Open 10 A.M.–4:30 P.M.

Maharana Madho Singh Museum. Set in old palace. Rich collection of Rajput miniatures in Kota school, sculptures, frescoes, weapons, and other antiques. Open 11 A.M.–5 P.M.

UDAIPUR

Ahar Museum. Standing in the remains of the old city; royal cenotaphs of the maharanas of Mewar. Open 10 A.M.–5 P.M.

Bharatiya Lok Kala Museum. Indian folk art museum. Folk dresses, ornaments, puppets, masks, dolls, instruments, and paintings. Puppet show can be arranged on request. Open 9 A.M.–6 P.M.

City Palace Museum. The only way to see this palace and its museum is with a guide. Open 10 A.M.–5 P.M.

GARDENS AND ZOOS. Alwar. *Purjan Vihar* (Company Garden), designed in 1868 by Maharajah Shiv Dhan Singh, has a lovely collection of ferns in an area called Simla. This is a great place for getting away from the heat.

Bundi. *Kohaksar Bagh,* near Shikar Burj (Royal Hunting Lodge), is an old garden surrounding the cenotaphs of former Bundi kings and queens.

Jaipur. *Ram Niwas Garden and Zoo.* The garden was designed in 1868 by Sawai Ram Singh II. The zoo has a number of birds and animals, plus a crocodile and python breeding farm. *Sisodia Garden and Palace* was built by Maharajah Sawai Singh in 1770 for his queen, Sisodia. A central room of the palace has galleries on three sides surrounded by terraced gardens with fountains and pools. *Vidyadharji Ka Bagh* was built by Vidyadhar, chief architect of Sawai Jai Singh II, with terraced gardens, fountains, and pools.

Jaisalmer. *Bada Bagh,* 6 km (4 mi.) from Jaisalmer, surrounds the royal ceno-taphs, some of which are elaborately carved with sculptures of former rulers on horseback.

Jodhpur. *Mandore Gardens,* 9 km (6 mi.) from Jodhpur, is set at the ancient capi-tal of Marwar, with the "Hall of Heroes"—16 Hindu and folk deities carved out of one rock, plus royal cenotaphs of the Maharajah Jaswant Singh and Maharajah Ajit Singh. Ornate cenotaphs are built atop plinths with exquisite sculpture.

Udaipur. *Gulab Bagh,* a rose garden designed by Maharana Sijjan Singh, contains a lovely building with a library. Children can ride the *Aravalli Express,* a minitrain. *Saheliyon Ki Bari* is the garden of the maid of honor, constructed for the use of the royal ladies. It has ornate pools with delicately carved kiosks and elephants in marble. Fountains surround a lotus pool, marble throne, and sitting room.

SPORTS AND OUTDOOR ADVENTURES. Bicycling. Check Special-Interest Tours in *Facts at Your Fingertips* for companies that offer biking in Rajasthan.

Bird-watching. King Bird Tours (see Special-Interest Tours in *Facts at Your Fin-gertips*) offers a good trip in Rajasthan for bird enthusiasts.

Camel, Elephant, and Horse Safaris. Contact the recommended tour operators listed above, or see those listed under *Facts at Your Fingertips,* for memorable safaris through the desert. Some trips coincide with wonderful festivals.

Polo. During Jaipur's polo season (mid-March–March 31 and mid-October–October 31), tournaments are held at the *Rajasthan Polo Club* near the Rambagh Palace. Don't be surprised if you also witness competitions between elephants, cam-els, and bikes. For details, contact the Rambagh Palace or Jaipur Polo Club, tel. 69235. You can also learn to play polo; contact Rajasthan Mountain Sports Associ-ation (see Tour Operators, above).

Trekking. Royal Safaris (see Tour Operators, above) creates good treks in the Thar Desert, including trips to remote villages and little-known fairs. All arrange-ments should be made in advance.

Wildlife Sanctuaries. Remember, you must arrive at all parks before they close at sunset. Also expect to pay nominal charges for entrance and often camera charges. All fees are paid at the park entrances.

Alwar. *Sariska Tiger Reserve.* The closest sanctuary to Delhi, this Project Tiger reserve is open September–June, with the optimum time to visit starting in Febru-ary. It's also home to leopards, wild dogs, deer, wild boars, jackals, langurs, and numerous birds, including peacocks. Jeep safaris are available and good lodges are near the reserve (see accommodations, above).

Bharatpur. *Keolodeo Ghana National Park.* The best time to visit this water-bird sanctuary is October–February. The park, which has recorded over 350 species of birds and some wild animals, was the former hunting preserve of the royal family of Bharatpur. You can stay in a forest lodge (see Accommodations, above). Try renting a bike or hiring a bike rickshaw. The drivers are good amateur ornitholo-gists.

Jaisalmer. *Desert National Park.* In this vast expanse of sand dunes, you can ride camels and see desert foxes, cats, hares, lizards, sand grouse, the great Indian bustard breeding ground, cranes, eagles, and falcons. The best time to visit is September–March, and the ideal way to travel is by camel. Either camp in the desert or stay in a Jaisalmer hotel (see Accommodations, above).

Sawai Madhapur, 162 km (100 mi.) from Jaipur. *Ranthambhor National Park.* This famous tiger reserve is also home to deer, wild boars, langurs, leopards, jackals, hyenas, panthers, crocodiles, jungle cats, and numerous birds. There are many lakes, an old fort built in 944, and an eighth-century Ganesh temple. The park is closed July–September. During the rest of the year, it's open 7 A.M.–10 A.M. and 2:30 P.M.–5:30 P.M. The best way to see the park is to hire a jeep. Numerous lodges and a fancy hotel are nearby (see Accommodations, above).

SHOPPING. Rajasthan's craftsmen have been famous for centuries for stonecut-ting, enameling, setting precious stones, tie-dying textiles, block printing silks and muslins, creating blue pottery, and lacquer and filigree work. If you want to avoid shops and middlemen, contact the tourist department for the addresses of craftspeo-ple and visit them where they live and work. This is an educational and money-saving way to buy handicrafts. The Rajasthan Government also has emporiums (called *Rajasthali*) in the following cities: Jaipur, Jaisalmer, Mt. Abu, and Udaipur. Also just take walks and browse, even buy, in the local bazaars. They're always fun; always interesting. And if you want something, remember to bargain, always! Jaipur and Jodhpur are the two big shopping cities.

JAIPUR

When shopping in Jaipur, beware of guides and drivers. They often insist that they know the best shops and bargains, but they usually get a commission on all purchases, which often increases the price of your "bargain." Also, "government approved" are two meaningless words easily painted over any shop door. The following shops are reliable, provide good service, and sell excellent merchandise:

P. M. Allah Buksh and Son, M.I. Rd., was established in 1880 and still sells the finest hand-engraved, enameled, or embossed brassware, including oversize old trays and historic armory. Open 9:30 A.M.–8 P.M.; closed Friday. AE, MC, V.

Gem Palace, M.I. Rd., has the best gems, jewelry, and a small collection of museum-quality curios. Their list of royal clientele (Princess Diana and Prince Charles recently paid a visit) also makes Cartier seem third-rate. They guarantee all purchases and will design (quickly) on order. *Note:* Make sure you find the right place; stores with similar names (there's a Gem Plaza across the street) don't necessarily have similar merchandise. Open daily 10 A.M.–7 P.M. AE, DC, MC, V.

Manglam Arts, Amber Palace Rd., has rooms full of exquisite old and new fine art, including Hindu *pichwies* (cloth temple hangings), Jain temple art, tantric and folk art, plus terra-cotta sculptures, silver furniture, handwoven *dhurries* (rugs), wood carvings, and wonderful old fabrics. There's also a branch in Udaipur and Agra. Open daily 10:30 A.M.–7 P.M. AE, DC, MC, V.

Channi Carpets and Textiles, Mount Rd., Opp. Ramgarh Rd., sells handwoven merino wool carpets, cotton dhurries, and handblocked cotton and silk fabrics: linen, clothes, pillow cushions. It can also make clothes for you in six hours. Open daily 9:30 A.M.–7 P.M. AE, DC, MC, V.

Bhorilal Hanuman Sahar, Shop 131, Tripoliya Bazar, sells old brass, copper, and bronze by the weight. Plan to poke through burlap bags of rescued treasures. Open 11 A.M.–7:30 P.M.; closed Sunday. Rupees only.

For good handblocked fabrics, visit these villages: Sanganer, 10 km (6 mi.) from Jaipur on Kota Rd., and Bagru, 30 km (18.5 mi.) from Jaipur on Ajmer Rd. Nearly every family is involved in this craft. Rupees only.

Also visit *Tilak Gitai,* E–5, Gokhle Marg, Ashok Nagar, who is a master craftsman creating miniature paintings on antique paper: Moghul, Rajput, and Pahari styles. Rupees only.

Finally, wander through Kazana Walon ka Rasta in the old city and watch stonecutters create wonderful art in marble. Closed Sundays. Rupees only for most shops and workrooms.

JAISALMER

This town is shopping heaven. Stop at the government-run *Rajasthali* first to get an idea of what things cost. It's near Gandi Chowk.

Damoder Handicraft Emporium, near Rang Prol in the fort, has an excellent selection of local handicrafts, especially good old textiles. Open 7:30 A.M.–9 P.M. Bargain. V.

Take a two-day excursion to Chohtan, Barmer, Dhanau, and Samva, 233 km (145 mi.) from Jaisalmer. The people from these villages are artisans creating embroidered, mirror-work textiles and camel-hair and sheep wool-dhurries and carpets. You can see them work and buy direct. Just bargain. Rupees only.

JODHPUR

Abani Handicrafts (Anand Bhawan, High Court Rd., near Ghoomer Tourist Bungalow) has a wide selection of old and new wood carvings, curios, brass, silver, copper, paintings, and textiles: the Rajasthani works! Open daily 9 A.M.–8 P.M. AE, DC, MC, V.

Bunakar Moti Bhagwan Pargabatri (in nearby Salawas) is an award-winning master craftsman who creates beautiful silk and wool handwoven dhurries. You can visit his home from morning until evening. Rupees only.

MOUNT ABU

Chacha Museum (in the center of town) sells good Rajasthani and Gujarati handicrafts. Open daily 10–10. AE, DC, MC, V.

UDAIPUR

Manglam Arts, Sukhadia Circle, is described under Jaipur, above. Same hours.

NIGHTLIFE AND BARS. Most of the better Western-style hotels in Rajasthan provide cultural programs for their guests—dances, singing, and puppet shows.

Hotel bars in Rajasthan are normally open 11 A.M.–2:30 P.M. and 6–10:30 P.M. Three, in particular, offer great ambience:

Jaipur. At the *Polo Bar* in the Rambagh Palace, you'll be surrounded by exquisite marble and a collection of trophies won by the maharajah's polo team. An indoor fountain adds to its appeal. Open 10:30 A.M.–2:30 P.M. and 6:30 P.M.–10:30 P.M.

Jodhpur. The *Trophy Bar* at Umaid Bhawan Palace has an unquestionable regal aura. Open 11 A.M.–3 P.M. and 7 P.M.–midnight.

Udaipur. Hotel guests at the Lake Palace can enjoy the *Amrit Sagar Bar* and gaze out at the dreamy lake. Nonguests should call (tel. 23241) in advance to see if they can be accommodated.

HIMACHAL PRADESH

Mountains, Vales—Unspoiled Serenity

by
KATHLEEN COX

Flanked by the lofty mountains of Jammu and Kashmir in the west, the Garhwal Himalayas of Uttar Pradesh in the east, and the rugged Tibetan mountains in the north, Himachal Pradesh, with its own towering peaks and romantic vales, is an enchanting state too often overlooked by Western tourists traveling in India. Every road in this state seems to bend, climb, and descend with few breaks of a straight stretch. The air, no matter the time of the year, is invigorating—a healthy relief from the plains. And, except for the occasional city, like Shimla or Mandi, the preferred pace of life remains slow and pastoral.

Villages mean a small huddle of shops and stalls supplying necessities and few luxuries, at least for the people who live here. But for foreigners who have the time to linger, Himachal Pradesh offers a hefty dose of outdoor sports at their best—treks, fishing, walks, even rafting and skiing. Its heady vistas change with the terrain, from snowcapped green mountains, to fertile valleys, to barren somber peaks where the monsoon never penetrates. And its people—Sikhs, Hindus and Buddhists—are culturally diverse and wear distinct styles of dress. Himachal Pradesh is also an important haven for Tibetan refugees; it's the present home of the Dalai Lama.

Shimla, the capital of Himachal Pradesh, set atop a 10-kilometer- (six-mile-)long winding ridge at an altitude of 2,171 meters (7,238 feet), was

190

originally part of the kingdom of Nepal. In the 1800s, after the Gurkas of Nepal established one too many forts in their attempt to usurp new territory, the British East India Company finally intervened and defeated them in the Gurka War of 1819. During the fierce fighting, a British lieutenant just happened to stumble across the thick wooded perch with its stunning vistas and ideal climate, a place already known for its temple dedicated to the goddess Shyamla (another Kali, the goddess of wrath, incarnation). The lieutenant decided this oasis was the ideal place to pitch the tents of the battle-fatigued British.

Three years later, a second British officer, Major Kennedy, constructed the first year-round residence (the house still stands; it serves as the seat of various Himachal Pradesh government offices). But decades still had to pass before Lord Lawrence, the British viceroy, finally adopted the hilltop ridge as his undeclared summer capital in 1864. Only then did Shimla make the grand leap in status, becoming the premier British hill station, with Lord Curzon adding the pièce de résistance when he ordered the construction of the Kalka–Shimla narrow-gauge train in 1902 and inaugurated it two years later. This diesel train, still running today, is a great way to begin your exploration of Shimla and Himachal Pradesh.

EXPLORING HIMACHAL PRADESH

Shimla

The old-fashioned train—and don't think posh—chugs its way along a five-hour, 96-kilometer (60-mile) journey, passing through 103 tunnels and forests of flowering rhododendrons, slowly winding into the mountains and only occasionally coming to a halt at a Swiss-chalet-style railway station (a deliberate Lord Curzon touch), one of many that dot the line. This is a nonhurried journey that slows you down, almost too much. For the new Shimla of independent India has changed, stepped up its tempo, making it more city than hill station.

Shimla's old Victorian face is tarnished. Paint is peeling and mortar is crumbling. New buildings have squeezed out lawns, gardens, and the genteel air that came with exclusivity. But democratic Shimla still has the Mall—now crowded with shops, walks, horses, and monkeys—the ridge, all those zigzag up-and-down streets open only to pedestrians, and those views into the surrounding valleys and distant mountains that are still serene.

Although Shimla is no longer the Shimla of Kipling, who set so many of his stories here, or the former viceroy's idea of a peaceful getaway, give it a chance. Let the new mood grow on you. Besides, a few buildings still try hard to remind you of their time of pomp and glory. See the former Viceroy's Lodge, now the Indian Institute of Advanced Studies. You can't go inside, but the grounds are lovely, the views are terrific, and the exterior of the main lodge is an English Renaissance (Elizabethan) treat. The building was constructed by Lord Dufferin between 1884 and 1888 out of Himalayan gray stone transported to Shimla by mules. At that time, the English thought it was built in too much of a hurry, which was reflected in the constant need for repair. Also, see the Kennedy house, the first house built in Shimla (across the street from the Shimla Railroad Station).

Then, after resting over espresso at the Indian Coffee House, walk up to the Ridge and the Christ Church, supposedly the second-oldest church in northern India, consecrated in 1857. The women who attended this modest-size church were supposedly lectured in a sermon to cut back on the size of their crinolines, which took up too much room. The women responded by going to church the next Sunday in their riding habits. From here, head up to Jakhu Hill (two kilometers or 1¼ mile), the highest peak, offering the best nearby view. On the top is a Hanuman Temple, dedicated to the monkey god, and appropriately guarded by a vigilant band of monkeys. Beware! They're always on the watch for an edible offering.

For the true Indian experience, explore those crooked alleys in the Middle and Lower Bazaar. The mix of people brings you back to the heart of Asia—tall, stately Punjabs; hill tribes in homespun cloth; Tibetans; and an occasional lama with his prayer wheel, tender, and flint.

Shimla is an ideal base for sports and outdoor enthusiasts who are looking for a mountain to climb or a slope to ski down. Within minutes, hills, mountains, peace, and rural simplicity become the pervasive themes.

Take the winding road northeast to Narkanda (65 kilometers [40 miles]). You pass through villages, then scattered dwellings built into the hillsides, and then occasional terraces of wheat and potato fields, usually bordered by pine forests. Snowcapped mountains gleam in the distance. Narkanda offers great views, walks, and treks into the inner Himalayas.

Naldehra, 22 kilometers (14 miles) northeast of Shimla, has a nine-hole golf course—India's oldest, which Lord Curzon helped design. The spectacular scenery is enough of a diversion to wreak havoc with your score. This is also a great place for walks and picnics. If you're in the area in June, don't miss Naldehra's Sipi Fair, a gay, colorful festival at which costumed villagers from all over the state sell their handicrafts.

Nirath, Rampur, Sarahan, and Kinnaur

Proceed northeast from Narkanda until you reach the small village of Nirath (approximately 121 kilometers [75 miles] from Shimla). Here you can visit an eighth-century *shikara*-style Hindu temple, dedicated to the sun god Surya. The temple is decorated with wooden walls and contains a *mandapa* (entrance hall), recently restored with a typical Himachal Pradesh blue slate roof.

Farther north is the town of Rampur, with tiers of houses that rise against the banks of the Sutlej River. At the lovely monastery, you begin to see the influence of Buddhism in the region. Rampur, the commercial center of the area, is the site of a November Lavi—one of the state's largest trade fairs, which draws thousands of local villagers in colorful traditional dress.

Northeast of Rampur is Sarahan (174 kilometers, or 108 miles, from Shimla), located high above a valley, with exquisite views of snowcapped mountains and rolling fields. Atop a peak called Srikand (elevation 5,679 meters or 18,626 feet) is a stone image of Shiva, known as Srikand Mahadev. Worshipers offer their blessings by placing a cup of *charas* (a form of hashish) in front of the image. The charas is ignited and reduced to ashes. Other offerings are placed under stones.

In the village of Sarahan, visit the 200-year-old Bhimakali Temple set in a courtyard—an exquisite temple complex that combines Hindu and Buddhist architecture. Much of the detail of this serenely situated structure is magnificent. Note the elaborate silver doors made by Kinnauri silversmiths at the turn of the century during the reign of Maharajah Sir Padum Singh. Inside the rectangular towers at one end of the courtyard is the Hindu temple, which is served by Brahman priests. The inner sanctum contains Hindu and Buddhist bronzes, numerous masks, and an image of the Bhimakali goddess 80 cm in height.

At press time, the prohibition on travel by foreigners into the district of Kinnaur was just removed. Bordering Tibet and sliced by the Sutlej River, Kinnaur is unspoiled, with an unending vista of towering peaks. Life is hard for the Kinnors, who live in high-altitude isolation, but they are known for their singing, dancing, and great festivals. Even legends and epics refer to them as the "celestial musicians."

Chail

Chail (45 km, or 28 miles, southeast of Shimla) is a mountain village and resort developed by maharajah Bhupinder Singh (the maharajah of Patiala). He was so dashing and handsome that he charmed the British ladies and enraged their jealous husbands, who made him feel less than welcome in Shimla. The maharajah vowed to stay away from the fusty British and put his energy and money into creating his own classy retreat that would put Shimla in its place.

At an altitude of 2,161 meters (7,054 feet), Chail rests on three hills, with the former palace of the maharajah (the Chail Palace Hotel) a sprawl atop Rahgarh Hill. The surrounding forests—the palace is situated on over 600 acres—are the home of barking deer, monkeys, occasional leopards, and numerous species of wild birds. Relax in the quiet of an elegant stretch of lawn, walk for hours along well-marked paths that pass by orchards, gardens, and deep-green woods. Chail also boasts a well-kept cricket field, India's highest and possibly the highest in the world.

Bilaspur

Northwest from Shimla, the road circles through forests, valleys, and mountains at times so rocky that the road seems scooped out of stone. You enter the Arkai Range and Arki, a tiny village with an old yellow stone palace perched on the edge of a hill overlooking a splendid green and yellow valley—the dominant spring colors. Moving on, you reach Bilaspur and a small café that overlooks the Gobindsagar Lake, a strange sight that reveals an odd partnership between art and nature. There, in the small lake (not much larger than a pond) are a slew of 200-year-old Hindu temples. This is actually the site of the old city of Palampur, submerged by the construction of the Bhakra Dam. During high season (the monsoon months of July–October), only the spires peek above the water. The rest of the year, as the water recedes, some of the simple stone temples become completely clear of the lake, as though built on the water's edge.

Mandi—Gateway to Kullu Valley

On the left bank of the Beas River, Mandi at first glance looks like a New England mill town, with rickety houses packed tight along the river's edge. Mandi is a pleasing city with temple spires poking up everywhere. (There are over 100.) Many temples are of recent construction and brightly painted. Others are simple dark granite and date from the sixteenth and seventeenth centuries, built in an odd blend of Mogul and Hindu styles. The latter have a faintly mausoleum exterior shape, but inside they typify Hindu style, with carved square pillars and an inner sanctum.

Visit in particular the sixteenth-century Panchvaktra on the right side of the riverbank, not far from the bridge leading into the city. Inside the temple, a monolithic and benign granite Nandi faces, not the expected *lin-*

gam (phallic symbol), but an unusual five-faced Shiva sitting in his medita-tion pose. To the left of the inner sanctum is a stone replica of the deity that sits inside. Also, visit the Bhutnath, set on the river's edge in the heart of the city near a series of colorful new Shiva temples. This time Nandi stands outside the temple facing a small lingam in the inner sanctum. The temple is stark and has few exterior carvings. All the sculptured emphasis is on the double archway entrance, as if drawing our attention to Shiva's symbol. Finally, see the Trilknath Temple, another old temple set back from the river. In February or March, Mandi's Shivratri Fair, which pays homage to Shiva, turns the Bhutnath temple and the city itself into one big party. Devotees carry deities on temple chariots (small gaily dressed palanquins); folk dances and folk music brighten the mood.

All year round, the inner city markets and bazaars are a walker's treat. Take an evening stroll (shops close at 8 P.M.). Every lane is narrow and cobbled and lined with tiny shops or stalls, often with dark rough wood interiors; an occasional temple; a moss-covered slope; and even a hearty tree that sneaks its roots into the crowded area. The architecture is stone and bare (or paint faded) wood. Sloping roofs overhang second stories fre-quently fronted by verandas, balconies, and push-open French-style win-dows. The overall effect is of an Italian hill town gone Asian. Also, while walking up and down these skinny streets that so often lead ultimately to the river, try to find Ravi Nagar, a pleasant spot, with its spacious rec-tangular garden and quiet communal courtyard.

Rewalsar Lake

If time permits, visit Rewalsar Lake, 24 kilometers (15 miles) southeast of Mandi. Rewalsar is the resting place of departed saints and the birth-place of the Indian mystic, Padmasambhava (Guru Rimpoche), who spread the Buddhist faith. The drive is beautiful, winding into mountains that overlook terraced fields of wheat and modest square houses of wood or sod with carefully checkered slate roofs that flicker in the sun. Rewalsar Lake is tiny and famous for its floating reed islands. The power of prayer or a minuscule breeze can set them in motion (more often in the eyes of the believer). Three shrines for the three different faiths—Buddhist, Sikh, and Hindu—dot the edge of the water. The Buddhist complex dominates. Prayer flags rise from courtyards. Prayer wheels encircle the exterior walls of the monastery. Inside sits a golden Buddha surrounded by numerous prayer stalls in which monks read scrolls.

Kullu Valley

From Mandi, the Kullu road proceeds for 40 kilometers (25 miles) through the Mandi-Larji Gorge along the Beas River. The narrow road, blasted through solid rock, has left eerie precipices that tower overhead, while down below, the raging torrent rushes by. At Aut, you turn north along the river and head up the Kullu Valley, which hugs the Beas—80 kilometers (50 miles) long and, when the vista opens up, just barely more than two kilometers (1.2 miles) at its broadest. Idyllic, yet wild and domi-nant. No wonder this valley is known as the Abode of the Gods.

In March, apricot and apple trees burst into pink and white blossoms. On the higher slopes, giant rhododendrons with crimson flowers give the appearance of trees decked out in small lanterns. Early in June, horse chestnuts are in flower, swarms of wild bees humming around them. By July masses of blue and purple irises are splashed over the hillside. Butter-cups range in color from the familiar golden yellow to pink-red. The fall brings on an explosion of bright colors. With winter, the vista turns white except for the stately green forests of pine and cedar.

Manikaran

At Bhuntar, about 70 kilometers (43 miles) north of Aut, take the turn east across the bridge for an hour-long memorable trip to Manikaran (Jewel of the Ear). The road, winding along the Parvati River, is hardly wide enough for the public bus that makes the daily journey between Manikaran and Mandi. At intervals along the way, you'll see homes of mud and stone with straw roofs, as well as fog-hugging snowcapped mountains.

Manikaran is a spiritual center. Here Parvati and Shiva, on a journey through the Himalayas, stopped and meditated by the hot and cold streams for 1,000 years. Here, Parvati dropped a jewel from her earring into the river, where it was devoured by the Serpent King, Shesh Nag. Shiva prayed for its return with such power that the world shook and Shesh Nag hissed up Parvati's jewel, creating the bubbling springs. Along with her jewel thousands of others shot out, until 1905, when an earthquake put an end to the bounty.

In the Sri Ramchandra Temple, built in the fifteenth century, Vishnu sits in the inner sanctum below an electric clock. The famous Dussehra festival, now held at Kullu, was once held here. Also see the old Sir Raghunath Temple, dedicated to Vishnu, across from the Tourist Complex. Then head to the river and the little white, new Himachal Pradesh temple, dedicated to Shiva and the nearby Gurdwara Sri Guru Nanak Dev Ji Hari Har Ghat, built in the 1940s. You'll walk through waves of blinding white steam, passing rectangular hot-water pits where there are pots of food cooking. You'll enter a hall with chambers here and there, the steam rising up. Inside one, the devout sit in the heat and pray. Inside, other pilgrims purify themselves in bathing tanks. Another room is set up for free tea and meals (although a donation is welcome); there are rooms in which to spend the night at no charge. Upstairs is the sacred room, gaily decorated, where services are held periodically (evening and early morning). All are welcome.

Every temple has sacred bathing tanks, and all the streets and lanes have gurgling hot pits where clothing is washed and food is cooked. The pace of life nearly stops here: a few tourists, the chatter of crows, the lowing of a cow. It's a place in which to walk, relax, and enjoy natural beauty in an almost primeval state. Footpaths or friendly villagers gladly show you the way up and up into serene, heavenly peaks. And by all means, refresh yourself in a hot-spring bath set up in the new tourist complex; it's clean and revitalizing—a rare treat.

Kullu

Just before you enter the bustling little city of Kullu, you'll pass a large grass square on your right, called the Dhalpur Maidan, and a stadium on your left. This is the site of Himachal Pradesh's famous annual fair, the Kullu Dussehra, which celebrates the victory of good over evil. The October Dussehra is the most important gathering in Himachal Pradesh. To the accompaniment of drums and bells, deities from neighboring village temples are carried down to Kullu in an evening procession of decorated palanquins that marks the start—the Vijay Dashmi—of the festival. Once the deity arrives at Dhalpur Maidan, it is placed before the supreme deity, Raghunathji, the presiding god of Kullu Valley, who sits in his honored position under a festive tent. The maidan is covered with booths, ringed with crowds, and alive with folk dances, music—the full spectrum of Himachal Pradesh village culture. Dussehra ends on an electric yet squeamish note—the sacrifice of a bull and small creatures as gifts to the gods.

Every year on April 28–30, Kullu also holds a cattle fair on the same popular maidan. People from surrounding villages arrive to buy and sell their livestock. The spirit here is also festive, with folk dances and local cultural events the prime attraction.

While in Kullu, see the Raghunathji Temple, the shrine of the supreme deity, and the Vaishno Devi Temple, involving a delightful walk to a small cave that enshrines an image of the goddess Vaishno. Drive to the foot of Bijli Mahadev Shrine and spend a day climbing 11 kilometers [7 miles] to an altitude of 2,400 meters (8,000 feet). Besides panoramic views of the entire valley, you'll see a remarkable temple, the Bijli Mahadev. The temple is also called the Temple of Lightning because of a curious phenomenon: its 19-meter (60-foot) staff that glistens in the sun supposedly attracts divine blessings in the form of lightning. When lightning strikes, it shoots down the staff and shatters the Shiva lingam. Every year, this supposedly happens and every year the priests restore the image, putting it back together with butter and then awaiting the annual recurrence of the "miracle."

Also, in the small city of Kullu, spend time wandering through the Akhara Bazaar, a great place to buy Kullu handicrafts—shawls, *pattus* (bolts of cloth), *toppis* (Himachal Pradesh caps), and *pullans* (like bedroom slippers).

Naggar

Two roads lead to Manali. Take the less traveled one, which means turning right at Katrain, 20 kilometers (12 miles) north of Kullu, and crossing over to the right side of the Beas River. Before heading north, see Naggar, the former capital of the rajas of Kullu, and a sleepy village, with its door just slightly open to tourism. Perched on a mountainside, the 400-year-old castle, built of weathered wood and stone, is now a renovated tourist hotel with minimal amenities but breathtaking views from its veranda. At its feet rests a tiny village with a slew of cozy wooden homes knit together by narrow lanes and paths. Orchards and fields of seasonal crops tumble down the slope to the river.

Naggar is peaceful and friendly. Walk through the narrow lanes to the old stone temple, dedicated to Shiva with Nandi nearby. Here boys play cricket in the temple courtyard and girls play jacks with red-clay stones, while a priest, oblivious to all the activity, prays quietly near the idol in the inner sanctum. Stop at a tea stall, where a kettle simmers over a fire. Meander along footpaths that take you into backyards and by wooden huts filled with white rabbits whose angora fur is a precious commodity. Climb to the nearby Tripura Sundari Temple, with its pagodalike appearance and intriguing wood carvings. Walk, relax, and, above all, give in to Naggar's timelessness and that rare chance to discover beauty at every turn.

Manali

From Naggar, stay on the right side of the Beas River and continue north 12 kilometers (seven miles) until you reach Jagatsukh, another small village that was a former capital of Kullu and the site of ancient temples: The Shikhara-style Shiva temple and the nearby old Devi Sharvali Temple, dedicated to the Goddess Gayatri (a sister of Durga). Up ahead is Manali, set against towering snowcapped peaks, many of them unscaled and unnamed. Unfortunately, this mountain town, situated at an altitude of 1,800 meters (6,000 feet), has been overwhelmed by too many new hotels and swarms of tourists.

While in Manali do visit the peaceful 600-year-old Hadimba Devi Temple with a four-tiered pagoda-shaped roof, a somber wooden shrine set in a cedar grove. The temple is dedicated to a wife in the legendary Pandava family, who figures prominently in the Hindu epic *Mahabharata*. Legend claims that the artist who created the pretty shrine with its exterior and door covered with handsome carvings received a dubious token of gratitude from the king. He was so enamored with the results that he cut off the artist's hand to prevent him from duplicating another temple that might rival the Hadimba. Undaunted, the artist used his left hand and created a finer temple at Chamba (the Triloknath Temple). Again his work was so admired, no rival was wanted. This time they cut off his head.

Also visit the small village of Vashisht, on the right bank of the Beas. Just off the road in an interior courtyard is another lovely pyramidal stone temple, recently restored. Inside is a granite idol of Vashista with haunting silver eyes. A Shiva lingam sits in the corner and wooden carvings adorn the interior pillars. Vashisht is another source of sulfur springs; near the shrine are two sacred tanks (one for men, the other for women) where devotees purify themselves. The Himachal Pradesh Tourist Department has also set up a complex of hot sulfur baths that are clean and refreshing.

The influx of Tibetan refugees in Manali has left its stamp on the town. The new Tibetan Monastery, in an area called Model Town, and the adjoining Tibetan Bazaar are examples. You'll have to look hard to find anything ethnic. The emphasis is on "West is best," no matter how shoddy.

Farther north from Manali is Kothi, a quiet village at the foot of the Rohtang Pass, offering views of massive snow-covered peaks. From Kothi, it's three kilometers to the Rahla Falls that shoot water from the Beas into a deep gorge. Solang Valley is Himachal Pradesh's ski resort, with good runs at an unbelievably low price that includes all necessary equipment. And here, year-round, the Himalayas will catch hold of you. Continue north another 38 kilometers (24 miles) to the Rohtang Pass, at an altitude of 3,978 meters (13,050 feet), where you'll see the twin peaks of Geypan and the Sone Pani glaciers. This is the gateway to the next set of valleys—the remote Lahaul, Spiti, and Kinnaur. Nearly indomitable, the pass is open only from July to September, a little earlier for the trekker.

Lahaul, Spiti, and Kinnaur

To the uninitiated, Lahaul and Spiti mean little more than barren rocks, raging torrents, perilous mountain paths, and glaciers unrelieved by ordinary creature comforts. But to anyone who wants a profound confrontation with nature, these valleys on the Indo-Tibetan border represent an unforgettable experience. Here, the Himalayas assume their wildest and most uninhabitable stance. And here, all but the cynical adventurer will feel that dimension of glory that approaches the mystical.

For a trek into the Lahaul Valley and excursions into newly opened Spiti, cross the Rohtang Pass. Once you enter the bleak and windswept Khoksar, the first village in the valley, you've also entered that serene realm of Tantric Buddhism, the religion of Tibet. Lahaul reminds us vividly and often of its culture. Prayer wheels, *chortens* (stupas), prayer flags, gompas (monasteries)—they're all here in the valley, as are perpetual repetitions of mantras, which seem to beckon us to continue on.

Summers in Lahaul are cool and pleasant. Like Ladakh, no monsoon unleashes its fury here. The height of the mountains keeps out the rain clouds. Keylong, the capital of Lahaul, is 117 kilometers (73 miles) from Manali—set in a green valley with fields of barley and buckwheat, an oasis surrounded by somber brown hills and massive snowy peaks. The Kardong Gompa, overlooking Keylong from the top of a hill across the river, has exquisite frescoes and murals and an enormous prayer drum with numerous strips of paper, each inscribed with the sacred mantra: *Om Mani Padme Hum* (Hail to the Jewel in the Lotus).

Spiti is now open to foreigners who travel with a government-recognized agency and obtain a Restricted Area Permit. A motorable road leads from Lahaul's Batal village, over the Kunzum Pass (5,000 meters or 16,400 feet) to Kaza village, Spiti's district headquarters. Nearby, set above the raging Spiti River, is the Key Gompa, the most important Mahayana Buddhist monastery in the entire Himalayas. Due north is Kibber village, at 3,900 meters (13,000 feet) one of the world's highest inhabited areas. From here, you can proceed to the Dhonkar and Lahlung gompas, cross the Pin Parvati Pass (4,803 meters or 15,573 feet) and enter the Pin Valley. The final important destination is the Tabo Gompa, a 1,000-year-old monastery that adheres to an otherwise defunct Buddhist sect in Tibet.

The men that you see in Spiti wear a long double-breasted woolen gown, reinforced by a long woolen rope wrapped around the waist in multiple coils. This belt provides warmth and turns the upper part of the gown into an ample blouse in which all kinds of articles are stored, including a Buddhist prayer wheel; a silver bowl for water, tea, or liquor; a spare garment; or a newly born lamb. The women grease their hair with butter and wear it in numerous thin plaits that are then woven with yak's tailhair to increase the length. Their hairdo resembles a net of black strands that spreads down the back, often hanging to the knees.

Since food is scarce and arable land is limited, the people of Spiti have evolved a scheme to ward off the dangers of overpopulation; the eldest son inherits the land, while the younger sons are sent off to a local lamasery, where they take a vow of celibacy. Women who fail to find husbands often enter convents. Monogamy is the general rule, but both polygamy and polyandry occur occasionally. If the eldest son dies, a younger brother quits the lamasery and takes over the deceased brother's land, his widow, and the children.

At press time, the government had just opened the northeastern frontier district of Kinnaur, south of Spiti and bordering Tibet. Kinnaur, sliced by the Sutlej River, is set in the towering Kinner Kailash mountains, a part of the Himalayas. Legend claims that the the people of Kinnaur were the celestial musicians who entertained the gods; to this day, they are known for their exquisite singing and dancing. Trips to Kinnaur include visits to Kalpa, the capital of the district, which was a favorite haunt of Lord Dalhousie. Travel in this high-altitude area is demanding. There are few roads, and those that do exist are usually dirt tracks. You will camp; there are no accommodations except for a couple of government bungalows, which are normally reserved for government officials. The best way to visit Kinnaur is on foot. Foreigners must follow the same guidelines provided above for trips to Spiti.

Baijnath

Passing through the Kangra Valley, first stop is Baijnath, with its important Hindu temple, constructed in the Shikara style with a low pyramid-shaped roof. This is considered the oldest Shiva shrine in India, built possibly by the legendary Pandavas. Like most stone temples in Himachal Pradesh, the Baijnath is not massive, sitting on the crest of a low mountain above the Binwakund River. Set against the backdrop of the Himalayas and nestled within the relatively tall stone wall of its courtyard, the overall effect accentuates its contained and diminutive size. The Baijnath is quite a contrast to the Dravidian temples of South India, with their soaring towers that humble you before you set foot in the shrine. The four thick pillars supporting the Baijnath have handsome carvings, including an unusual composite image of Vishnu and Lakshmi. Inside, the inner sanctum is a Shiva lingam (called the Vaidyanath), one of 12 natural lingams worshiped in India.

Dharamsala

Dharamsala is a former British hill station (40 kilometers, or 25 miles, from Kangra), spilling off a spur of the Dhauladhar range and surrounded on three sides by snowcapped peaks. When the white shrouded mountains first come into view, the rugged slopes appear black and foreboding, but as you draw nearer, the bleak mass softens to green and the white tops shimmer. Even Dharamsala, devastated by an earthquake in 1905, has a gentle aura, befitting the recent influx of Buddhist refugees who, along with their spiritual leader the Dalai Lama, fled Tibet after the Chinese invasion.

Dharamsala is broken into two distinct parts. In Lower Dharamsala, you'll find the Kotwali Bazaar, schools, businesses, government offices, and a feel that's distinctly Indian and Hindu in character. Upper Dharamsala at Mcleod Ganj (10 kilometers, or six miles, away), on the far side of an Indian army base and just beyond St. John's Church in the Wilderness, is decidedly Tibetan and Buddhist. Throughout tiny Mcleod, you'll see European and American students of Buddhism, many with heads shaven, wandering about, discussing their texts.

Visit the Namgyal Monastery, where hundreds of purple-robed monks (men and women) gather inside their new temple and pray, sometimes for hours, reading from scrolls and sitting beneath an enormous golden image of the Buddha that towers over them from the front of the shrine. Non-Buddhists can enter the interior of the shrine from a side entrance, where they can see more large statues. Remove your shoes! Also inquire about Tibetan cultural performances at the Tibetan Institute of Performing Arts, perched on the top of a hill. You may be lucky and see great dancing, hear music, or witness a Tibetan opera.

While in Upper Dharamsala, also visit one special monument that survived the earthquake and remains a stalwart reminder of the days of British rule: St. John's Church in the Wilderness (set not in the wilderness but in a cozy pine grove), built in 1860. The stained-glass windows of this church are treasures; inside is a monument to Lord Elgin, a British viceroy originally from Scotland, who asked to be buried in this church, dedicated to the patron saint of Scotland.

Jwalamukhi Temple

From Dharamsala, take a delightful 53-kilometer (33-mile) trip south to the Jwalamukhi Temple in Kangra Valley. You'll pass mango, banana, bamboo, and pine groves and charming farming villages with wheat fields that stretch back to the mountains. The Jwalamukhi Temple, a complex of tiny shrines, is the scene of an ongoing festival and one of the most important Hindu pilgrim centers in northern India. Here Hindus celebrate a mysterious, perpetually burning flame that is revered as the manifestation of the Goddess Parvati. The Mogul Emperor Akbar tried and failed to smother the flame and left behind a solid gold umbrella, which still remains. The huge brass bell inside the mandapa was a gift from the king of Nepal.

Dalhousie

Dalhousie, the gateway to Chamba Valley (the vale of milk and honey), is set on five different hills rising from the main ridges of the Dhauladhar. Dalhousie is another former British hill station, named after a former British viceroy, Lord Dalhousie, who, weary from one too many battles, sought peace and quiet here. Today, the small village and all the hotels have seen far better days. There's a seedy neglect to many of the old Victorian structures. The effect is dismal and depressing; not even the panorama of spectacular snowcapped peaks justifies much more than the briefest visit. Many of the hoteliers are also gougers, so watch out!

Chamba

After you reach the crest of the mountain, the road begins its slow descent to Chamba, winding continuously while hugging the edge of the mountain that slopes down to the near-dry Ravi River. The closer you get to the valley basin, the more terraced the land becomes. Still, the road seems untraveled; the chosen course appears to be dusty foot paths that race up and down the hills.

Just when you're lost in the peace and quiet, you round a bend, and there's Chamba, sprawling on the mountainside. Even the Ravi comes alive, with the water rushing now. This mountain village/city (with 5,000 people) is the center of the valley and is rich in ancient stone temples.

Walk into the center of town and see the Lakshminarain temple complex, with three shrines dedicated to Vishnu and three dedicated to Shiva (the earliest of the six stone temples built in the tenth century and the last constructed in 1828). The temples follow two distinct architectural trends. The Vishnu temples are of the Shikara type, with two overhead "parasol" roofs that are intended to drain off snow; the others are indigenous hill style. Also visit the Bhuri Sing Museum, with its excellent collection of miniature paintings from the Kangra and Basoli schools. As you walk down Museum Street, note the shoe stalls. Chamba is a big sandal town, and this is where you buy this footwear.

Take a lazy walk on the Chaugan, a grassy public promenade (maidan), above the river and near the center of town. This park often turns into an impromptu trading center for villagers who come in from the surrounding hills. The Chaugan is also the site of the colorful week-long Minjar Fair held annually in August or September at the time of the corn harvest to invoke the rain gods.

Chamba is no great beauty of a city, nor does it require much time to explore. It's very much the local business district. But go in any direction and you'll be surrounded by serenity and Himalayan magic. And this makes Chamba a good walking and trekking base. See Sahoo, a charming hill village where the Gujjars (seminomadic Moslems) live six months a year. In the winter, they migrate with their families and buffalo to the plains of the Punjab. The people are tall and tend to dress in dark, muted clothes; the men wrap thick turbans around their heads, and the women adorn themselves with heavy jewelry. While in Sahoo, also walk to the old Shiva temple with a lingam sitting on a copper base inside the inner sanctum. This walk means an idyllic stroll through green fields into the village proper—into pure village life Himachal Pradesh–style—even if some of the residents live here only half the year.

Bharmour

From Chamba, one beautiful drive should not be missed. Go east from Chamba 65 kilometers (40 miles) to Bharmour. This is Shiva territory, and occasionally you'll pass three-pronged staffs called Trisuls (the three vertical prongs are the symbol of Shiva) stuck into the earth or small lingams set in tiny shrines—tributes to the favored god. This is also Gaddi territory, although you'll still see many Gujjars traveling through. Like the Gujjars, the Gaddi shepherds are seminomads who move their flocks of goats and sheep down from Bharmour in the cold months to warmer Dharamsala and the Kangra Valley. Or they used to. Today, many Gaddi families stay put around Bharmour, where they're developing cash crops: wheat, walnuts, almonds, maize, and apples. Gaddi men wear handwoven beige coats that flair out and end at mid-thigh with rope belts coiled around the waist. The women wear patterned long skirts, heavily gathered at the waist.

For most of your journey, the road stays narrow but essentially level as it hugs the Ravi River flowing along the base of the valley. High rugged peaks crowd in from the other side of the road: thick jagged rock that remains about an arm's length away. The water of the Ravi is cold and a vivid green. Mountain streams splash down the precipice and across the road. Gorges with small rivulets racing to meet the Ravi slice open the rocky border, revealing a quick glimpse of the sky. Footpaths crisscross the difficult slopes and lead to isolated simple houses of wood or stone. Suspension bridges carry animals and villagers back and forth across the river.

You take a sharp turn and leave the Ravi, following the narrower Buddhal. Up ahead are snow-covered mountains, dominated by the not-too-distant Kailash Peak, which extends across the panorama. Minutes later, you arrive in Bharmour, an ancient quiet haven with 84 temples (many of them small structures with simple lingams), nestled in a beautiful courtyard called Churasi (84 in Hindi).

Look at the wooden Laxshna Devi, erected in the seventh century; the stone Narsingh Temple constructed in the tenth or eleventh century, one of the few dedicated to Vishnu with a lionesque idol in the inner sanctum; and the stone Manimahesh, built in the seventh century. Sit in the peaceful courtyard and watch the people—so many of them Gaddis. Take in the views that unfold all around. This is nature and life at its best.

Pangi Valley

From Chamba, you can head north for the rugged Pangi Valley, a dry, cold region about 2,400 meters (8,000 feet) above sea level. In the midst of wild hills, the Chenab River (Chandra Bhaga) flows in a deep, narrow gorge where it lashes against rugged cliffs. This area is a trekker's paradise; the valley stays dry during the monsoon, and numerous peaks that tower to a level of 6,600 meters (22,000 feet) are still the challenge of mountaineers. Every village and hamlet has its own temple; the most important are Mindhal Vasni, about 15 kilometers (nine miles) from Killar, and the Purthi, about 30 kilometers (19 miles) from Killar.

Killar, 137 kilometers (85 miles) northeast of Chamba (a trekking route), lies in a valley set in a deep, narrow gorge of the Chenab River in the high Himalayas. Grand, majestic! From Killar, you can trek north-west to Kishtwar in Jammu and Kashmir, turn east halfway to Kishtwar, and cross the Umasi La Pass into the Zanskar Valley. You can trek south-east to Keylong and Mandi, or trek from Killar to Lahaul, which will land you in Purthi and a convenient rest house on the bank of the Chandra Bhaga.

As is so often true in Himachal Pradesh, the Pangi Valley shows off northern India at its best: unspoiled, less traveled, and with nature clearly in charge. Days spent here are indelible, touching the soul. Time stops. Greater forces have more power.

PRACTICAL INFORMATION FOR

HIMACHAL PRADESH

WHEN TO GO. While Himachal Pradesh—except for Lahaul and remote areas—is accessible year-round, the state is loveliest in spring and fall when flowers are in bloom; nights are crisp and cool, and days are warm. Bring warm woolens. Hotels do their best to supply heat, but you may find that their best is not sufficient.

Chamba and surrounding hill districts: the best seasons are April–mid-July and mid-September–December. The monsoon (July–September) brings rain and mist, but not continuous torrents.

Kangra Valley (Dharamsala area): the best seasons are March–June, September–November. If the monsoon with its periodic rain doesn't bother you, the summer months are fine.

Kullu Valley and Manali: April–mid-November—the lush months—show off Kullu at its colorful best. Manali is unbearably crowded during May and June. Plan your visit for other months, including the winter, when you can ski at nearby Solang Resort.

Lahaul, Spiti, and Kinnaur: To get to these areas, you'll be at the mercy of the weather. Roads are generally clear of snow July–October. The days can be warm, but the nights are cold.

Mandi: Approachable year-round, but the best time is April–November.

Shimla, Chail, and nearby points: Year-round resort. July–August brings the monsoon, but not constant rain. Winter also turns Shimla into a snowy getaway, with nearby winter sports and white Himalayan views.

RESTRICTED AREA PERMIT. At press time, foreigners traveling in a group of four with a recognized travel agency could visit the districts of Spiti and Kinnaur for up to 15 days. Most travel agencies will help you get the required permit. If you must get it yourself, follow the advice for obtaining the Restricted Area Permit given in *Facts at Your Fingertips*.

HOW TO GET THERE. By Air. For visits to Shimla and southern Himachal Pradesh, *Vayudoot* flies daily from Delhi and Chandigarh into Jubbarhati Airport (23 km, or 14 mi., from Shimla). *Indian Airlines* also makes numerous daily flights between Delhi and Chandigarh (117 km, or 73 mi., from Shimla). From Chandigarh, regular bus service and fixed-rate taxis (about Rs. 1,200) fly back and forth between Shimla. For other Himachal destinations, Vayudoot flies from Delhi, Chandigarh, and Shimla into Bhuntar Airport (10 km, or 6 mi., from Kullu; 52 km, or 32 mi., from Manali). Vayudoot also has three weekly flights connecting Delhi and Chandigarh to the new Gaggal Airport in Kangra Valley, 15 km (9 mi.) from Upper Dharamsala. For Vayudoot information, contact HPTDC in Shimla (tel. 78311) or in Kullu (c/o Ambassador Travel, tel. 2296). *Jagson Airlines* (12 E, Vandana Bldg., 11 Tolstoy Marg, New Delhi 110001, tel. 3324693) also has flights between Delhi and Shimla and between Delhi and Kullu. All flights should be booked in advance, and passengers must confirm their tickets 72 hours before departure and arrive at the terminal an hour before the flight.

By Bus. *Himachal Pradesh Tourism Development Corporation* (HPTDC) runs air-conditioned deluxe coaches between Delhi and Shimla, Delhi and Manali, and Shimla and Manali. The fare from Delhi to Shimla is Rs. 200 and the trip takes about 10 hours; from Delhi to Manali the fare is Rs. 300 and the trip takes 16 hours; from Shimla to Manali the trip costs Rs. 125 and takes about nine hours. These buses run from April to July and September to November. Himachal Pradesh Road Transport Corporation (HPRTC) runs deluxe buses from Delhi to most major cities in Himachal and within the state, including Keylong in Lahaul. For routes and schedules, call 2516725 in Delhi; in Himachal, check with the tourist departments (see below under Tourist Information).

By Train. Frequent train service is available from Delhi and Chandigarh to Kalka (90 km, or 56 mi., from Shimla). The *Himalayan Queen,* which departs late at night from the New Delhi Railway Station, reaches Kalka in time for the morning departure of the British-built *Toy Train,* a narrow-gauge diesel that winds for five hours through the mountains to Shimla. You'll sit on a wooden bench, but the trip is scenic and fun. Book your ticket in advance: first class (air-conditioned or non-air-conditioned) or second class (air-conditioned). Reserve a sleeper and berth. In Delhi, call *International Tourist Guide,* tel. 352164, 10 A.M.–5 P.M.; in Shimla, tel. 72915. Travelers heading to Dharamsala can go by train from Delhi to Pathankot (90 km, or 56 mi., from Dharamsala). There are no other convenient train stations in or near Himachal.

By Rented Car with Driver. From Delhi to Shimla (370 km or 230 mi.), a four-hour ride on a dusty highway through the Indian state of Haryana leads to a scenic climb through the mountains to Shimla. Total trip time is about seven hours. In Delhi, hire a car from a recommended travel agency and figure Rs. 5 per km with a halt charge of Rs. 50–Rs. 100 per night. Within the state, a hired car with driver is a good way to travel. You can stop when you want and take any road that appeals to you. To hire a car in Shimla, contact HPTDC, the Mall, tel. 78311 or 77646; *Vishal Union Service,* tel. 5123 or 77645; or *Kalka Taxi Union,* tel. 78225. In other important destinations, use a recommended travel agency. Shimla is about 240 km (149 mi.) from Kullu and 280 km (174 mi.) from Dharamsala. Most roads are fairly well maintained but narrow and slow-going.

TOURIST INFORMATION.
Himachal Pradesh is an outdoor state, and its tourist department is an excellent source of what to do: where, when, and how. These offices also have excellent general information on hotels, sightseeing, and travel. Most tourist offices are open Monday–Saturday 9 A.M.–6 P.M., except where noted. In Delhi, you can contact the *Himachal Pradesh Tourist Office,* Chandalok Building, 36 Janpath, New Delhi 110001; tel. 3325320.

In **Shimla,** contact the Himachal Pradesh Tourist Office or HPTDC at the Mall, Shimla 171001, tel. 78311 or 77646. Open April 1–July 15, 9 A.M.–7 P.M. daily and July 15–March 31, 10 A.M.–5 P.M. daily, except January–March, when the office is closed on Sundays. A second tourist office is at Victory Tunnel. Open 10 A.M.–5 P.M., closed Sundays. Government tourist offices are also in the following cities:

Dalhousie. Tourism Information Office, tel. 2136.

Dharamsala. Tourist Information Center, tel. 3163 and 3107.

Kullu. Tourist Information Office, tel. 2349.

Manali. Tourist Information Office, tel. 2325 or 2360. Open April–October, 8 A.M.–midnight daily; November–March, 9 A.M.–5 P.M. daily.

Most HPTDC tourist bungalows also have free brochures and maps at a nominal cost.

FOREIGN CURRENCY EXCHANGE.
Most Western-style hotels have money exchange counters. Otherwise, go to a branch of the *State Bank of India,* open Monday–Friday 10 A.M.–2 P.M.; Saturday till noon.

ACCOMMODATIONS.
Himachal Pradesh has some Western-style hotels in the more established tourist areas and some charming old-fashioned guest houses, many of them former private homes. Throughout the state, you'll find dependable adequate facilities—many run by the state government—with clean rooms, decent bathroom facilities, and simple restaurants. The government-run stopovers are moderate to inexpensive, so don't expect more than the minimal extras. But given

the mood of Himachal Pradesh—an adventure-oriented, undervisited state for travelers who want to get off the beaten path and be close to the best of nature—the accommodations are appropriate. What follows is a list of hotels, guest houses, and some government bungalows in major scenic areas. This list is supplemented with a second list of rest houses that are suitable for trekkers or travelers going the remote route. Rates are based on double occupancy and exclude taxes and service charges: *Deluxe,* over Rs. 2,000; *Expensive,* Rs. 1,200–Rs. 2,000; *Moderate,* Rs. 500–Rs. 1,200; *Inexpensive,* under Rs. 500. Many Western-style hotels accept traveler's checks and credit cards.

BAIJNATH

Moderate

Palace Motel. Taragarh, Kangra Valley 176081; tel. (Baijnath) 34. 14 rooms with bath. Built in the 1930s, this former palace of a nawab has been converted into a hotel by its new owners, a member of the Kashmir Hindu royalty. Secluded grounds are lovely. Rooms aren't posh, but they have a homey, old-fashioned ambience. Best rooms are on the ground floor and are spacious, with furniture from the 1940s and 50s and pictures of the current owner's family and the Hindu pantheon. There's a charming family dining room with a fixed, multicuisine menu. Facilities include an old-fashioned TV lounge, swimming pool, tennis court, horseback riding, and trekking and tour arrangements. Meals included. Rupees only.

CHAIL

Moderate

Chail Palace Hotel. Reservations: Manager, Chail Palace Hotel, Chail, Dist. Solan; tel. 8337 or 8343. 19 large rooms with tubs in the hotel; 10 rustic and private cottages with 1–4 bedrooms. Although the palacelike exterior of this HPTDC hotel is decidedly Victorian, rooms are unpalatial and have simple furnishings. Upper-floor rooms, however, are quiet and spacious. Cottages offer privacy and rustic charm, especially the Honeymoon Cottage with its copy of the *Kama Sutra.* Room service, TV in larger rooms, multicuisine restaurant, bar. Rupees only.

CHAMBA

Inexpensive

Hotel Iravati. Chamba, tel. 2671 or reserve through Area Manager, HPTDC, Dalhousie; tel. 2136. 12 rooms with bath. This new Western-style HPTDC hotel has spacious rooms with overhead fans. Some rooms have balconies. There is a multicuisine restaurant with room service. Rupees only.

DALHOUSIE

As of this printing, it's difficult to recommend more than one hotel in this hill station. Your best bet is to stay in Khajjiar (see below).

Inexpensive

Aroma 'n Clair's. Court Rd., The Mall, Dalhousie; tel. 2199. 20 rooms with bath. The best part of this hotel, which has a lovely location, is its 1930s kitsch. Individual rooms, though large, offer minimal-to-bleak decor. Some amenities are available: TV, multicuisine restaurant, library, bank, shops, tour arrangements. Off-season rates August and mid-November–March 31. AE, MC, V.

DHARAMSALA

Inexpensive

Hotel Bhagsu. Mcleod Ganj, Dharamsala; tel. 3191. 20 rooms with bath. Within walking distance of the prime attractions, this HPTDC bungalow is on a pleasant lawn in Upper Dharamsala. All rooms are clean, with a simple modern decor. "Deluxe" rooms are more spacious and also have TV. Multicuisine restaurant and room service. Traveler's checks accepted.

Hotel Dhauladhar. Dharamsala; tel. 2107. 21 rooms with bath. Rooms in this HPTDC bungalow, which is in Lower Dharamsala and 10 km (6 mi.) from Mcleod Ganj, are clean, with a simple modern decor and private balconies. Best rooms have a valley view. Multicuisine restaurant, room service, terrace, bar. Traveler's checks accepted.

JWALAMUKHI

Inexpensive

Hotel Jwalaji. Jwalamukhi, Dist. Kangra 176081; tel. 80. 25 rooms with bath. Within walking distance of the temple, this two-story HPTDC hotel offers spacious rooms with simple, modern decor. Best rooms are air-conditioned. Room service, good vegetarian restaurant. Rupees only.

JUBBAL

Jubbal Palace Guest House. Reservations: Chapslee Inn, Lakkar Bazaar, Shimla; tel. 77319 or 78242. Set on the grounds of the palace of the rajah of Jubbal, this new guest house and inn is slated to open mid-1993. The architecture is grand, with carved-wood ceilings and fine details. The setting is serene, encircled by the Himalayas. Rates were unavailable at press time.

KATRAIN

Expensive

Welcomgroup Span Resorts. Kullu-Manali Highway, Katrain, Kullu; tel. 38. 24 rooms with bath. Just acquired by Welcomgroup at press time, there could be changes at this fancy resort, which is nestled on the Beas River, 15 km (9 mi.) from the heart of Manali and offers Western-style cottages with modern rooms. Multicuisine restaurants, bar, room service, travel counter, doctor on call, gift shop; fishing, croquet, table tennis, and miniature golf facilities. Meals are included. AE, DC.

KEYLONG

Inexpensive

Keylong Tourist Home. Keylong, Lahaul. Reservations: Tourist Information Office, Manali 175131, tel. 2325 or 2360. 3 rooms with bath; tents available with shared bath. This bungalow has clean rooms and safari-style tents with cots. Simple meals are catered on request. Closed mid-October–mid-June or when the pass is not cleared of snow. Rupees only.

KHAJJIAR

Inexpensive

Hotel Devdar. Reservations: Area Manager, HPTDC, Dalhousie; tel. 2136. 11 rooms with bath. This recently renovated HPTDC bungalow has modest, clean rooms that are perfect for its idyllic setting on a hill overlooking a pond. Simple restaurant, room heaters, room service, horseback riding. Open mid-April–November. Rupees only.

KUFRI

Expensive

Kufri Holiday Resort. Shimla Hills 171012; tel. 8300 or 8341. 30 rooms with bath. This complex, which sits on a bluff, has a Western-style lodge and separate cottages. Cottages offer more privacy, but all rooms have good views and a contemporary decor. Numerous amenities include TV, multicuisine restaurants, room service, pickup service from Shimla, foreign-exchange and travel counter, skiing, yak and pony rides, meditation groves, cultural performances on request. AE, MC, V.

KULLU

Inexpensive

Hotel Sarvari. Kullu; tel. 2488 or reserve through Tourism Development Officer, Kullu; tel. 2349. 8 rooms with bath. Set on a hill, this one-story HPTDC bungalow has modestly decorated Western-style rooms with overhead fans. Simple restaurant, bar, room service, garden, TV lounge, tourist office. Rupees only.

Hotel Silver Moon. Kullu; tel. 2488 or reserve through Tourism Development Officer, Kullu; tel. 2349. 6 rooms with bath. On a hill on the edge of Kullu, this pretty two-story HPTDC bungalow has impeccably clean rooms with lots of charm. There are an attractive old-fashioned TV lounge, an intimate restaurant, and a pleasant garden. Room service. Rupees only.

MANALI

Expensive

Johnson's Lodge. Reservations: Johnson's Orchard, The Mall, Manali 175131; tel. 2303. 4 apartments with bath. Built in the 1920s, this stylish bungalow with a sweeping back veranda offers apartments that are a blend of elegant and rustic. Each has two bedrooms, drawing room, dining room, and kitchen for preparation of your own meals. Perfect for families. Book well in advance. TV, travel and outdoor-adventure assistance. Rupees only.

Moderate

Hotel Woodrock. Reservations: Amar Anand Resorts, P.O. Himalayan Chalet, Manali 175131; tel. 2244 and 2344. 20 rooms with bath. Expect a Swiss-chalet exterior and modern, Western-style rooms with pine ceilings and lots of pine trim. Each room also has a private balcony. Library, room service, restaurant, bar. DC, MC, V.

Inexpensive–Moderate

May Flower Guest House. Manali 175131; tel. 2104. 16 rooms with bath. Up the road from central Manali is this charming inn that steals your heart once you step inside. The family-style dining room sets the tone: everything comfortable and orderly. A new wing has spacious rooms with front verandas and enclosed back balconies. Every room has a fireplace, and you're treated with care. Book well in advance. Room service, restaurant, travel and outdoor-adventure assistance. Meals included. Open March–November 15. Rupees only.

Inexpensive

John Banon's Guest House. The Manali Orchards, Manali 175131; tel. 2335. 10 rooms with bath. Though this isn't Manali's most beautiful lodge, there's a garden and an orchard, and the owner is a delightful person who ensures a pleasant stay. Cozy rooms have fireplaces, upstairs rooms open onto a veranda. The mountains and town center are a short walk away. Room service, travel and outdoor-adventure assistance. AE, DC, MC, V.

Thakur's Rahul Hotel. Manali 175131; tel. 2180. 17 rooms with bath. On a quiet side street near the other inns, this small hotel has spacious grounds for relaxing and offers clean, simple rooms with knotty-pine trim. Room service, restaurant, outdoor-adventure assistance. Rupees only.

MANDI

Inexpensive

Hotel Mandav. Mandi; tel. 2123. 7 rooms with bath. On a hill just outside the city, this old two-story HPTDC bungalow has clean, simple rooms that are slightly worn around the edges. The best rooms are upstairs off the veranda. Bar, room service, multicuisine restaurant. Rupees only.

MANIKARAN

Inexpensive

Hotel Parvati. Manikaran; tel. 235. 10 rooms with bath. This two-story HPTDC hotel set on the Parvati River has simple Western-style rooms. Ask for a river view. Multicuisine restaurant, room service, terraces, sulfur baths. Rupees only.

NAGGAR

Inexpensive

Castle Hotel. Reservations: Tourist Office, Naggar, Kullu; tel. 2349. 12 rooms, some with attached bath. This renovated HPTDC palace-hotel, set on a bluff with a lovely veranda and terrace courtyard overlooking Kullu Valley, has simply furnished, rustic rooms. The older rooms, with fireplaces and attached bathrooms, have more charm; newer rooms have a shared bath. Multicuisine restaurant, outdoor cafeteria, two tiny museums, temple. Rupees only.

NALDEHRA

Inexpensive

Hotel Golf Glade. Naldehra. Reservations: HPTDC, Tourist Information Office, The Mall, Shimla 171001; tel. 78311. 5 rooms and numerous rustic huts, all with bath. This clean, well-run HPTDC facility, near a golf course, has modestly furnished, comfortable rooms, a multicuisine restaurant, and golf course. Rupees only.

PARWANOO

Moderate

Timber Trail Resort and **Timber Trail Heights.** Parwanoo 173220; tel. 2340. 20 rooms with bath; 10 tents with shared bath. Across the border from Haryana, this unusual resort is divided into two sections, one on a mountain and the other at the base. You reach the mountaintop site via a ropeway that runs from sunrise to sunset. All rooms are modern and attractive, but the mountaintop retreat offers spectacular views. There are good multicuisine restaurants, attractive gardens, bar, room service, TV, billiards, table tennis. AE.

RENUKA LAKE

Inexpensive

Hotel Renuka. Renuka Lake; tel. 41 or reserve through Manager, Hotel Yamuna, Panota Sahib; tel. 41. 4 rooms with bath. This HPTDC facility has modestly furnished Western-style rooms, with a simple restaurant and lakeside café. Rupees only.

SARAHAN

Inexpensive

Hotel Shrikhand. Reservations: HPTDC, Tourist Information Office, The Mall, Shimla 171001; tel. 78311. 15 rooms with bath. A new HPTDC bungalow, the Shrikhand offers attractive rooms with a modest contemporary decor, terrific views from private balconies, a restaurant, and lounge. Rupees only.

SHIMLA

Deluxe

Chapslee. Lakkar Bazar, Shimla 171001; tel. 77319 or 78242. 6 rooms with bath. Chapslee is the height of understatement. Its lawn is modest, its exterior far from grand; but step inside this private home of a *kanwar* (prince) and his wife and you're surrounded by sumptuous antiques. Forget about Western amenities; this is Indian class, with a hot-water bottle slipped into your bed at night, afternoon tea, a library with old books. The Pink Suite is gorgeous and has three fireplaces. Gourmet meals included. Reserve well in advance. Closed January–mid-March. AE, DC, MC, V.

Expensive–Deluxe

Woodville Palace Resort. Himachal Bhawan Rd., Shimla 171001; tel. 6422 or 72763. 12 rooms with bath. This stately 1930s villa, owned by a *kanwar* (prince) and converted into a hotel, offers grand living. The rooms have original Victorian and Art Deco decor. Hollywood stars spent (and spend) time here, no doubt, carousing and playing billiards and croquet. Multicuisine restaurant, gardens, billiard room, car-rental arrangements. Meals included. Reserve well in advance. Rupees only.

Expensive

Oberoi Cecil. The Mall, Shimla 171001; tel. 6041-3. 80 rooms with bath. Under renovation at press time (projected reopening: 1993), this fortress-style hotel has a very grand four-story atrium lobby. Rooms are elegant, with Victorian furnishings. Room service, TV, multicuisine restaurant, bar, foreign-exchange counter, travel desk, car-rental service. Meals included. AE, DC, MC, V.

Oberoi Clarkes. The Mall, Shimla 171001; tel. 609-5. 39 rooms with bath. Shimla's oldest hotel, Clarkes has a slate-blue and white chalet-like exterior. Rooms are cozy and nicely furnished but not grand. Ask for a room with fireplace and good views. TV, room service, foreign-exchange desk, travel desk and car-rental service, multicuisine restaurant, bar. Meals included. AE, DC, MC, V.

Moderate

Springfield. Chota Shimla, opp. Tibetan School, Shimla 171001; tel. 3609. 8 rooms with bath. On a ridge removed from the city bustle, this old English bungalow with separate cottage has a spacious lawn and gardens, and serene Himalayan vistas. Rooms are large, with unpretentious, Western-style furnishings. The best rooms have a private balcony. Family-style dining room, sitting room, doctor, travel and trekking arrangements. Reserve well in advance. AE, V.

Moderate–Inexpensive

Hotel Wildflower Hall. Chharabra, Shimla 171001; tel. 8–212. 38 rooms with bath and 12 cottages. This former residence of Lord Kitchener, who also landscaped the gardens, is now an HPTDC hotel. Located 13 km (8 mi.) from Shimla, the Wildflower sports an attractive two-story exterior with an upper-story veranda and gables. Appealing cottages are rustic. Interiors of all rooms are simple yet clean and spacious. Multicuisine restaurant, bar, room service, outdoor café, beautiful grounds, car-rental arrangements, doctor. DC, V.

REST HOUSES AND CIRCUIT HOUSES. Throughout Himachal Pradesh, there are basic yet adequate forest rest houses (sometimes called tourist huts), which are often located in sublime rustic settings, and circuit houses, which are often love-ly holdovers from the grand Victorian era. Fees for rest houses—very spartan but clean linen, private rooms and bathrooms—are about Rs. 40 per double, and for circuit houses—quality varies but can be the best in town—Rs. 75 per double. Un-fortunately, government officials get first preference at the circuit house. Inquiries should be made via the H.P. Tourist Office (see Tourist Information, above). The rest houses are usually managed by the Public Works Department and the circuit houses by the General Administration Department. Take your chances and book well in advance, or have an alternative booking and check the circuit house on your arrival. Circuit houses are in Chamba, Mandi, Solan, Kasauli, Bilaspur, Dharams-ala, Narkanda (near Shimla), Kullu, Manali, and Keylong. Rest houses are numer-ous, tucked here and there; just write and inquire.

DINING OUT. Except for Shimla and Manali, anticipate only simple—yet good—meals in Himachal Pradesh. Breakfast is usually served 8–10:30; lunch, 12:30–3; and dinner, 7:30–10. Payment is normally in rupees only unless the restau-rant is connected to a Western-style hotel. Most of these hotels also accept credit cards. The restaurants listed below are informal and unless noted are open for all three meals and don't require reservations. Prices are based on one person eating a three-course meal, excluding taxes, tip, or beverage: *Deluxe,* over Rs. 300; *Expen-sive,* Rs. 200–Rs. 300; *Moderate,* Rs. 100–Rs. 200; *Inexpensive,* under Rs. 100.

MANALI

Almost all the best meals are served in private lodges, where the dining room is restricted to guests. Here is one exception.

Inexpensive

Mount View Restaurant. The Mall, across from the bus station; no phone. This simple restaurant is crowded with booths; music plays unobtrusively; a photo of the Dalai Lama smiles down from the wall. The Buddhists who run this restaurant provide Tibetan, Chinese, Indian, and Japanese meals. Open 8 A.M.–11 P.M. Rupees only.

SHIMLA

Expensive

Chapslee. Lakkar Bazar; tel. 77319 or 78242. This home-turned-inn is filled with antiques and elegance, and the fixed-menu meals match the ambience. There is Indi-an cuisine at lunch, Continental at dinner. The formal dining room can only accom-modate about 12 people. Open 1–2:30 and 8–9:30. Reservations required. Closed January–March 15. AE, DC, MC, V.

Oberoi Clarkes. The Mall; tel. 6091. Low-key decor and lovely mountain views accompany the Continental, Chinese, and Indian food (including Himachali cui-sine) served at Clarkes. Try the popular chicken imperial (chicken with mushroom sauce) and *kadai* mutton (mutton pieces in thick gravy). There may be an evening dance band in May, June, and during Christmas week. Open 7–11 A.M., 1–3 P.M., and 8–11 P.M. Reservations advised. AE, DC, MC, V.

Woodville Palace Resort. Himachal Bhawan Rd.; tel. 6422 or 72763. Shimla's other culinary treat, this villa has an interior dining room filled with antiques. The chef offers Chinese, Continental, and Indian dishes, with especially tasty kebabs. Open 1–3 P.M. and 8–10 P.M. Reservations required. Rupees only.

Inexpensive–Moderate

Ashiana. The Ridge; tel. 78464. Shimla's former bandstand is now an informal restaurant. You can choose from Chinese, Continental, and Indian cuisines. Also ask about the regional Pahari dishes, such as *kamod* (mutton cooked in a spicy curd gravy) and *sepurbadi* (steamed lentils fried in spinach). Meals served 9–11 A.M., 12:30–3:30 P.M., and 7:30–10 P.M. Snacks are served during nonmeal hours. Rupees only.

Fascination. The Mall; tel. 72313. This informal upstairs restaurant has two cozy rooms with good views. The chef serves good Indian, Continental, and Chinese meals, including tasty chili chicken. Open 9 A.M.–11 P.M. Snacks are served during nonmeal hours. Rupees only.

SWEETS AND TREATS. Chamba. *Cafe Ravi View.* On the river's edge, this simple café offers good tea and snacks and a pleasant ambience. Open 9 A.M.–9 P.M.

Manali. *Delhi Chat Bhandar,* almost opposite the Taxi Stand, serves a sweet and spicy *papri chat* (gooey mix of pastry, potatoes, and yogurt covered in a sweet-and-sour sauce), and a "special veg. chilla" (stuffed and fried Indian crepe). Each is a bargain for about Rs. 5. Open 10:50 A.M.–9:50 P.M. daily.

Mandi. Stop at the *Indian Milk Bar,* 8 km (5 mi.) from Mandi on the road to Sundernagar. Its signboard is in Hindi, so look for a small building with brightly painted stones on the exterior. For about Rs. 5, you can enjoy a great chocolate milk shake.

Shimla. Visit the *Indian Coffee House* on the Mall, near Evening College. The old eatery looks run-down; but waiters serve you in fancy Indian attire, as you relax over coffee and snacks and let the charm slip through. Open 8:30 A.M.–9 P.M.

HOW TO GET AROUND. Figure all taxi fares are about Rs. 4.50 per km. Bus fares are always inexpensive. **Chamba. Taxis** and HPRTC **buses** are available. Contact the reception desk at Hotel Iravati (2136), or the HPRTC bus stand (tel. 2210).

Dharamsala. From Gaggal Airport, a bus (Rs. 15) or taxi (Rs. 100) will take you to Dharamsala (15 km or 9 mi.). Buses and taxis are available at the bus stand (tel. 2243) or the local tourist office (tel. 3163 or 3107).

Kullu and Manali. From Bhuntar Airport (52 km, or 32 mi., from Manali), HPRTC buses go to Kullu and Manali (about Rs. 10). The bus ride to Kullu is about 15 minutes; the trip to Manali takes about 90 minutes. Taxis are plentiful: Kullu (Rs. 80) or Manali (Rs. 300). In Manali, private taxis are available for hire from the Taxi Operators Union (tel. 2135 or 2450). Rates are fixed according to destination. Ask to see the posted list. HPTDC (Transport Wing, tel. 2116) also has cars and jeeps with drivers for hire. HPTDC buses are available at the bus stand. Contact the tourist office (tel. 2325) for rates and schedules.

Mandi. Buses and taxis are available in Mandi at the HPRTC bus stand (tel. 2403) or the local tourist office (tel. 2575).

Shimla. From Jubbarhati Airport, you can go to Shimla by bus or taxi. The *Airport Coach Service* (Rs. 25) takes an hour, stops on the Ridge and at the Holiday Home Hotel. For pickup locations back to the airport, contact HPTDC, Shimla (tel. 78311 or 77646). A taxi (about Rs. 200) will take you to your hotel in about 45 minutes. HPRTC (tel. 3566) provides local bus service in and around Shimla. Taxis and cars for hire are available through the *Kalka Taxi Union* (tel. 78225). and the *Vishal Taxi Union* (tel. 5123 or 77645). The Mall and the Ridge are strictly prohibited to vehicles; but you can hire a bicycle rickshaw. Set the fare before you start; it should be less than a taxi.

TOURS. HPTDC and the private sector don't sponsor scheduled-departure state-wide tours; but HPTDC does offer day-long tours by bus and private car in and around Dalhousie, Manali, and Shimla. Contact the tourist department in each area for details and reservations.

TOUR OPERATORS. Himachal offers numerous outdoor adventures. Contact the following specialized tour packagers for a memorable experience. Also see *Facts at Your Fingertips* for a list of Tour Operators who offer special trips in Himachal Pradesh.

Himalayan Adventurers Pvt. Ltd. (Manali 175131; tel. 104) and *Manoo's Mountain Adventures* (Thakur's Hotel, Rahul, Manali 175131; tel. 180) sponsor excellent treks off the beaten path (including into newly opened Spiti and Kinnaur), skiing trips, jeep safaris (including the trip from Manali to Leh), and some white-water rafting.

Himalayan River Runners (188-A, Jor Bagh, New Delhi 110003; tel. 4632180) offers excellent rafting runs, including jeep excursions with hikes and rafting in Spiti.

HPTDC (Ritz Annexe, Shimla 171001; tel. 3249) organizes good, inexpensive tours, treks, hang gliding, and ski courses. They can also help with all travel needs, including arrangements for a car with driver.

The *Mountaineering Institute of Manali and Allied Sports Complex* (Manali 175131; tel. 2342) organizes courses in high-altitude trekking, mountaineering, rock climbing, and outward-bound-type courses for preteens. They also provide porters and guides for treks.

From March to December, you can also experience Himachal's princely past and go on a *Royal Circuit Tour* that features overnight stays in the homes of former maharajahs and *kanwars* (princes), fortress complexes from the 1700s, elegant manor homes from the 1880s, and turn-of-the-century palaces. For complete details, contact Kanwar Ratinjit Singh, Chapslee, Shimla 171001; tel. 78242 and 77319.

SEASONAL EVENTS. Himachal puts on some big shows that draw crowds: Hindu festivals, such as Dussehra; Buddhist celebrations, such as Sisu; and gigantic fairs, such as the Lavi Mela. The lunar calendar determines most dates; consult the Government of India Tourist Bureau for details.

February. Manali and Kufri (near Shimla) hold a week-long *Winter Sports Carnival.*

February/March. The week-long *Shivratri Mela* (religious festival), held in Mandi and at the Baijnath Temple near Palampur, starts with a jubilant procession of temple deities accompanied by chanting and drumming.

March/April. The *Sisu Fair* at Lake Rewalsar honors the Indian mystic, Guru Padmasambhava, who introduced Buddhism to Tibet.

July/August. During Chamba's week-long *Minjar Harvest Festival,* hill people appease their rain god with an exuberant procession and offerings.

August/September. A pilgrimage to Lake Manimahesh from Bharmour near Chamba takes thousands of Hindus to purify themselves in frigid waters.

October/November. The world-famous nine-day *Hindu Dussehra Festival* in Kullu celebrates the victory of good over evil with elaborate parades of deities, dances, music, and animal sacrifices performed around a gigantic bonfire. This is the most famous festival in Himachal.

November. The *Lavi Mela,* on the banks of the Sutlej River in Rampur near Shimla, is one of India's largest fairs. Hill people come to dance and sing.

November. The *Renuka Fair* commemorates the sacrifice of Mother Renuka with the annual immersion of temple deities.

HISTORIC SITES. There is generally no charge for entry, but when donations are requested, a few rupees will suffice. Historic sites are generally open daily, sunrise to sunset, unless otherwise noted.

BHARMOUR

There are 84 temples nestled in a courtyard named after *churasi* (yogis) who came here to meditate centuries ago. *Laxshna Devi* is a wooden temple dedicated to Shiva that was built in the seventh century. *Nargingh Temple* is dedicated to Vishnu and is from the tenth or eleventh century. *Manimahesh Temple* is dedicated to Shiva and was built in the seventh century.

CHAIL

Chail Palace, former summer capital of the maharajah of Patiala, was built after World War I. Now a state-run hotel, it has great grounds with good walks and pleasant views.

CHAMBA

Lakshminarain is a stone temple complex, with three shrines dedicated to Shiva and three to Vishnu. The earliest was built in the tenth century, the last was constructed in 1828. Vishnu temples are of the Shikara type, with two overhead roofs; the others are in indigenous hill style.

DHARAMSALA

St. John's Church in the Wilderness, built in 1860, contains beautiful stained glass windows and a monument to Lord Elgin, the British viceroy who was originally from Scotland and asked to be buried in this church dedicated to the patron saint of Scotland.

Namgyal Monastery, a new Buddhist monastery with a towering golden image of Buddha, is the current seat of the Dalai Lama, the spiritual leader of Tibet, who fled Tibet after the Chinese invasion. It has daily ceremonies, open to the public, usually at 5 or 6 A.M. and 5 or 6 P.M.

JWALAMUKHI

Jwalamukhi Temple, dedicated to the "Flaming Goddess," is an important northern pilgrimage center, with its flame kept perpetually burning by priests. The golden dome over the temple was a gift of Mogul Emperor Akbar.

KANGRA

Baijnath Temple (A.D. 800), a Shikara-style stone temple with a low pyramid-shaped roof, is possibly the oldest Shiva shrine in India, conceivably constructed by Pandavas. Handsome carvings adorn interior pillars, including an unusual composite image of Vishnu and Lakshmi.

KEYLONG

Kharding Gompa is the largest monastery in Lahaul, with colorful frescoes and murals and an enormous prayer drum containing strips of paper with the sacred mantra written a million times. It formerly was the capital of Lahaul.

KULLU

Bijli Mahavev Temple has a 19-meter- (60-foot-) high spire that supposedly attracts lightning—divine blessings—which then shatters the Shiva lingam contained inside the temple. The priests reassemble the sacred symbol and wait for the miracle to occur all over again.

Basheshwar Mahadev Temple (in Bajaura, 15 km [9 mi.] from Kullu) is a ninth-century pyramidical granite temple dedicated to Shiva and covered with exquisite stone carvings and sculptural detail, some of which was destroyed in the late 1700s.

Raghunathji Temple, built in the seventeenth century, houses the presiding deity of Kullu Valley.

MANALI

Hadimba Devi Temple, 600 years old, is a wooden shrine with a four-tiered pagoda-shaped roof. The temple is dedicated to the goddess Hadimba.

Vashisht Rishi and *Lord Rama* temples (in Vashisht, three km from Manali) are pyramidical stone temples, with sacred sulfur springs and temple baths.

MANDI

Panchvaktra Temple is of the Shikara style, with an unusual five-faced Shiva sitting in the meditation pose.

Bhutnath Temple, also of Shikara style, with a small lingam in the inner sanctum, is situated by the river in the old city.

MANIKARAN

Sri Ramchandra Temple was built in the sixteenth century and dedicated to Vishnu. *Sri Raghunath Temple* is also dedicated to Vishnu. All Manikaran, with its bubbling sulfur springs and legends connecting it to Shiva and Parvati, who supposedly meditated in Manikaran for 1,000 years, is imprinted with a sense of spiritual history.

MANIMAHESH

Manimahesh Temple (a 34-km [21-mi.] trek from Bharmaur), constructed in the Shikara style, is one of the oldest and most beautiful temples in Himachal Pradesh.

SARAHAN

Bhimakali Temple is sacred to Hindus and Buddhists. Visitors should not turn their backs on the inner sanctum's sacred idol, Bhimakali. Cameras are also not allowed inside the temple that leads to this sacred chamber.

SHIMLA

Institute of Advanced Studies, former Viceregal Lodge, was constructed in 1884–88 during the time of Lord Dufferin. Sitting atop Summer Hill, the structure was built of Himalayan gray stone in English Renaissance (Elizabethan) style. No entrance is allowed without prior permission from the secretary of the institute; but enjoy the beautiful grounds and views of Shimla.

Wildflower Hall (13 km [8 mi.] from Shimla), former residence of Lord Kitchener built in 1903, is now a state-run hotel. Kitchener landscaped the present gardens, with their lovely grounds and walks.

MUSEUMS AND GALLERIES. *Bhuri Singh Museum,* Chamba, has an excellent collection of miniature paintings from the Kangra and Basoli schools, and the rescued murals from nearby Rang Mahal Palace, which suffered a fire years ago. Open 10 A.M.–5 P.M.; closed Mondays and official holidays.

Roerich Art Gallery, Naggar, houses a collection of paintings of the Russian artist Nicholas Roerich. Check with the tourist information office in Kullu (tel. 2349) for the hours.

Himachal State Museum, near Chaura Maidan, Shimla, contains "hill" art and cultural art of Himachal Pradesh, including Pahari (mountain) and other miniature schools, of painting, sculpture, bronzes, costumes, textiles, and jewelry. Open 10 A.M.–1:30 P.M.; 2–5 P.M. Closed Mondays and official holidays.

SPORTS AND OUTDOOR ADVENTURES. Himachal Pradesh does its best to keep the sports enthusiast happy, with new adventures offered each season.

Climbing and Mountaineering. Test your courage on 6,000-meter (19,680-foot) mountains near Manali and in Lahaul. The climbing season is July–September. Arrange in advance with the Indian Mountaineering Federation (Headquarters Complex, Benito Juarez Rd., Anand Niketan, New Delhi 110021, tel. 6883412). Once you've chosen your challenge, send three copies of the completed application, along with the appropriate fee to book the peak and expedition to the Honorary Secretary of the Federation. Allow at least six months for processing. The Mountaineering Institute of Manali and Allied Sports Complex (Manali 175131; tel. 2342) offers courses in mountain climbing.

Fishing. Fish for trout in the Pabar River near Rohru, a day-long excursion from Shimla, and in the Beas River near Manali. Try for *mahseer* (Himalayan river fish) on the Beas near Dharamsala. For more details and the required license, contact the District Fisheries Officer for each district. In Manali, contact the Tourist Department.

Golfing. Naldehra, 23 km (14 mi.) from Shimla, has a nine-hole course, with available equipment. The season runs from May to November. For details and reservations, contact the HPTDC in Shimla; tel. 78331 or 77646.

Hang Gliding and Para-gliding. At Billings, you can soar in the Kangra Valley from March to April and mid-August to November. Bring your own equipment. Contact HPTDC (see Tourist Information, above) about scheduled international competitions.

Hot Springs. Manikarin. Hotel Parvati has 14 hot-spring baths set up in individual, clean cubicles. Contact HPTDC (tel. 35) for details and reservations. Nominal charge. **Tattapani.** Regular bus service from Shimla goes to Tattapani (51 km or 32 mi.) and popular sulfur springs that emerge from the Sutlej River. Private cubicles are available; reservations are not necessary. Contact HPTDC for further details; tel. 78331 or 77646. **Vashisht.** HPTDC has eight sulfur baths set up in private cubicles inside a small complex just outside Manali. An adjoining café serves tea and beverages. Open 7 A.M.–10 P.M. daily. Make reservations at the Manali Tourist Office (tel. 2325). Nominal charge.

Ice Skating. Shimla's Skating Rink is open from November to February. Nominal charge. Rent reasonable skates from Capital Boot House on The Mall.

Jeep Safaris. You can head from Manali to Leh in Ladakh and travel through this remote, "lunar" terrain. If you obtain a Restricted Area Permit, you can also go into newly opened Spiti by jeep. All these excursions can be made from July to September or when the passes are cleared of snow. Arrangements must be made in advance. Contact the *Tour Operators* listed above or check the listings in *Facts at Your Fingertips.*

Rafting. Himalayan River Runners (see Tour Operators, above) sponsors whitewater runs north of Shimla on the Sutlej River (November to mid-December and February to April) and is currently studying a new three-day run on the Spiti River in Spiti (mid-July to September). Arrangements must be made in advance. Himalayan Adventurers (see Tour Operators, above) offers a one-day run on the Beas River in Kullu Valley (mid-May to mid-July and mid-August to mid-September).

Skiing. Himachal's skiing facilities aren't sophisticated, but the vistas are lovely, and the price is low, including the cost of good equipment. At **Narkanda** (near Shimla), where the slopes aren't challenging, the season runs from January to mid-March. Contact HPTDC, Shimla (tel. 78331 or 77646) for details. **Solang Valley,** 13 km (8 mi.) from Manali, is Himachal's premier resort. The season runs from December to March. The Mountaineering Institute and Allied Sports Complex (see Tour Operators, above) offers comprehensive skiing courses. You can also combine trekking with skiing and extend the season to June. Arrange in advance with Himalayan Adventures (see Tour Operators, above).

TREKKING. No matter where you travel in Himachal Pradesh, there's spectacular trekking. For Manali, Kullu Valley, environs around Shimla, Chamba, and Kangra valleys, the best time to trek is May–June and September–mid-October, although there are some treks that are possible in the summer months. The trekking season in Lahaul (June–October) is determined by snow, and treks are strenuous; you're rarely below 3,600 meters (12,000 feet). Trekkers should have a guide and should make arrangements in advance. Contact the Tour Operators listed above or a recommended Tour Operator in *Facts at Your Fingertips.* Trekkers can also rent camping equipment or hire porters and guides from Himalayan Adventurers and the Mountaineering Institute (addresses above). There are so many good treks in Himachal that we highlight only a few of the best, rated by degree of difficulty.

Trek 1. Naggar (south of Manali) to Malana; 28 km (17 mi.) of rugged climbing up to this secluded mountain village, where the Malanas have their own language and customs. Follow local customs: don't bring or wear any leather in the village—hide your shoes in a bush—walk on the right side of any path, and don't touch any person or building. Three or four days. Moderately difficult.

Trek 2. Jubbal to Hari-ki-Toon Valley. From Jubbal, 100 km (62 mi.) northeast of Shimla, you can go by foot or pony along the Toms River through forests, fields of wildflowers, and remote hamlets to the Hari-ki-Toon Valley. For details, contact Chapslee Inn (Lakkar Bazar, Shimla 171001; tel. 77319 or 78242). Three to five days. Moderate.

Trek 3. Bharmour to Lake Manimahesh. Take the 37-km (23-mi.) Hindu pilgrimage (August or September) from the temple town of Bharmour in Chamba Valley to the Shiva Temple at Lake Manimahesh, and if you dare, take a holy dip in the frigid sacred lake, near a revered peak where Shiva supposedly meditated. You'll follow a meandering stream into the mountains, walk through alpine meadows, and finally ascend a steep path to a rocky ridge. The area is home to the Gaddi and Gujjar nomads. During the pilgrimage, tea and snack stalls are set up along the route. Ponies and porters are available for hire at Bharmour, and tented accommodations are available through HPTDC in Shimla (see Tourist Information, above). Before or after the pilgrimage, a guide is advised. Six days. Moderate.

Trek 4. Pangi Valley to Lahaul or Ladakh. From Chamba Valley, you'll head north 137 km (85 mi.) to the dry, rugged Pangi Valley beyond the Sach Pass (4,428 meters or 14,523 feet). The Chenab River (Chandra Bhaga) lashes through a deep, narrow gorge. Numerous high-altitude peaks challenge mountaineers. Every village and hamlet has its own temple. When you reach Killar, you can turn east on the way to Kishtwar in Kashmir and cross the Umasi La Pass into Ladakh's Zanskar Valley. You can also trek southeast to Keylong and on to Manali or from Killar through Lahaul to Purthi and a convenient rest house on the banks of the Chandra Bhaga. This entire area is rarely explored and offers numerous routes rated short to long, easy to difficult. This trek, which is offered by Himalayan Adventures and Manoo's Mountain Adventures (see Tour Operators, above) can be done from June to September. Plan at least eight days. Treks range from easy to difficult.

Trek 5. Manali to Bir. This trek takes you from Kullu Valley into Kangra Valley along a lesser-known high-altitude route. From Manali, you'll follow icy streams, enter evergreen forests and alpine meadows, and catch great views of Kullu Valley along the way. You'll cross the Kaliheyni Pass (4,500 meters or 15,500 feet), where the landscape changes to patches of snow and glacier moraines, and see distant views of Buddhist Lahaul. You'll head into Sunni River valley, with its meadows and gorges. A snow bridge leads to forests and finally to the isolated valley home of Gaddi shepherds in Barabangal village. The next destination is the base of Thamser Pass (4,725 meters or 15,750 feet). From here, you'll pass through meadows, by lakes, and waterfalls until you enter Kangra Valley and another home of the Gaddi in Bir village. This 10-day trek, which is offered by Himalayan Adventures and Manoo's Mountain Adventures (see Tour Operators, above) is best from June to September. Moderate to difficult.

SHOPPING. In Shimla and especially Kullu and Manali, you can buy wonderful handknit or handloomed woolen goods: shawls, sweaters, hats, jackets, gloves. In Manali and Dharamsala, you can also buy beautiful Tibetan handicrafts, clothing, and carpets. In Upper Dharamsala, visit the *Charitable Trust Handicraft Emporium and Bookstore* and the *Showroom of Tibetan Handicraft Production* (both located in the McLeod Ganj bazaar). They're open 9 A.M.–6 P.M., closed Mondays. Chamba is known for its durable and inexpensive leather sandals. In Shimla, look for fine carved walking sticks; and if you're interested in rare books on India and the Himalayas or old etchings, visit *Maria Brothers,* No. 78, The Mall, tel. 5388; open 10:30 A.M.–1 P.M. and 5–8 P.M. Rupees only. In Manali, two good shops sell Tibetan products: *Tibetan Carpets and Handicrafts Emporium* (The Mall), open Monday–Saturday, 9:30 A.M.–8:30 P.M., rupees only; and *Himalayan Heritage* (The Mall, opp. Nehru Park), open Monday–Saturday, 9 A.M.–9:30 P.M. and Sunday, 3 P.M.–9:30 P.M., rupees only.

NIGHTLIFE AND BARS. In **Dharamsala,** inquire at the Tibetan Information Office (tel. 2343 or 2457), near the monastery, about Tibetan music and dance performances at the *Tibetan Institute of Performing Arts.* Starting the second Saturday in April, the institute usually puts on a 10-day festive Tibetan opera. In **Shimla,** the old *Gaiety Theater* still has occasional summer productions. The best public bar in Shimla is at Oberoi Clarkes, open 12:30–2:30 P.M. and 7–11 P.M.

KASHMIR, JAMMU, AND LADAKH

A Glimpse of Heaven

by
KATHLEEN COX

Note: Due to increased political unrest in Kashmir and Jammu, the U.S. State Department urges extreme caution in traveling in this part of India. Furthermore, the department at press time (late 1992) advised postponement of travel to the following areas until further notice: Srinagar, Kashmir Valley and surrounding areas (excluding Jammu, Udampur, and Kathwa districts). Check with the department before making final plans.

"Kashmir—only Kashmir!" These were the Emperor Jahangir's final words. To see his summer playground one last time; to die here, surrounded by the mighty Himalayas; to see again the stately Chenars that edged the emerald green lakes; to sit within his treasured gardens, lightheaded with the fragrance of spectacular flowers and mesmerized by the play of his exquisite marble fountains.

But the Mogul's final wish wasn't granted. On his last annual pilgrimage that took him from the heat and dust of the plains to his enchanted vale, Jahangir died. Satraps, nobles, and his imperial court hovered over him on his death bed and begged to know his last request. All he whispered was, "Kashmir."

This Oriental super-Switzerland has lost little of the original charm that first attracted the Moguls. Just a breath of the invigorating air and you'll succumb to the spell of this conspiracy between mountain and nature—India's jewel of the East.

In the third century B.C., Kashmir formed part of Ashoka's far-flung Mauryan Empire. After Akbar grabbed it in 1587, the Mogul emperors never stopped paying lengthy visits, escaping from the unpleasant summer on the plains and taking refuge in this idyllic vale where they laid out, at lavish expense and with impressive technical ingenuity, their elegant "pleasure gardens." It's no surprise that the appeal of this valley survived the fall of the Moguls, also entrapping the British, who flocked to Kashmir during the last decades of their rule in India.

In those days, since only the upper echelons could afford the time and expense involved in making the difficult journey, Kashmir never became an official hill station. A semiautonomous state ruled by the maharajah of Kashmir and Jammu, it also remained a specifically restricted "Kashmiri" homeland, with the maharajah shrewdly passing an edict that prevented foreigners from owning land in his state. This edict gave rise to the houseboat—a Britisher's novel solution to the unfortunate restriction. This boat, aptly called "Victory," offered such an attractive alternative that in no time a flotilla of posh floating homes—each one outfitted in Victorian splendor—sat moored in Dal Lake.

Kashmir—slightly smaller than Great Britain, with under 6 million inhabitants—is in the heart of Asia. Few realize that it's farther north than Tibet. For thousands of years, caravans carrying precious merchandise passed from China and elsewhere through Kashmir on their way to the plains of India. This international flavor continues today. Here, you'll find a variety of races, national costumes, and traditions. The Kashmiri *pandit* (man of letters) forms the Hindu leading minority (Nehru was a Kashmiri pandit, as was his daughter, Indira Gahdhi). The Kashmiri Moslems, representing about 90 percent of the population, are extremely devout, industrious, and hardworking. Their daily chanting bears witness to a strong brotherhood—a communal feeling—both joyful and profound.

In late 1989, Moslem factions that periodically called for secession renewed their demand. Some of these secessionists claim Kashmiri Moslems should form their own independent country; others would like to see Kashmir join Pakistan. In the meantime, their demands have led to violence, which in turn has led to a firm response from the central government in Delhi, which insists that Kashmir is an integral part of India. At press time, peace in the valley remained illusive; an acceptable solution will be difficult to find.

EXPLORING KASHMIR AND JAMMU

As soon as you enter the Jammu region from Pathankot, you catch sight of the snowcapped peaks of Kashmir, the Pir Panjal range. Jammu splits up naturally into three tracts—the mountainous, the submontane, and the plains. The inhabitants of these three divisions have their own dialects, customs, and dress. The Dogras inhabiting the plains speak Dogri, a mixture of Sanskrit, Punjabi, and Persian. The inhabitants of the "middle-mountains" are called Paharis and occupy themselves in agriculture and cattle breeding. Like the Kashmiris, they are hearty travelers and can cover long distances without fatigue. The Gujjars are seminomadic herds-

Vale of Kashmir & Ladakh

■ Monastery

0 miles   25   50   75
0 km   40   80   120

to Karakoram Pass

R. Shyok

to Manali

(Khardung La 18,380')
Tiskey
Leh
Hemis
Upshi
Spitok
Fiang

Khalse
Lamayaru
R. Zaskar
Padam
Fatu La 13,432'
Namika La 12,200
Mulbekh
Podkharbu
Rangdoom
Marul
Kargil
L A D A K H

R. Indus
R. Suru

Nun Kun 23,410'

N

Drass
Amarnath Cave
Kishtwar
Baltal
Panjtarni
Vaojan
Zoji La 11,580
R. Sind
Chananwari
Pahalgam
Kolahoi 17,839'
Nichnai
Sonamarg
Lidarwat
Aarau
Martand
Banihal Pass
Kangan
L. Mansar
L. Tar Sar
Anantnag
R. Lidar
Gangabal
Tilail Khal
Kishan Sar
V'ishan Sar
Ganderbal
Dal
Shalimar
Awantipur
R. Jhelum
VALE OF KASHMIR
Nara Nag
Haramuk 16,015'
SRINAGAR
Pampur
Khasbal
L. Anchar
Sangram
Baramula
L. Wular
L. Achabal
Tosha Madan
Gulmarg
Tangmarg
Khilanmarg
Buna Darwas
Laipathar

men. In summer, they drive their cattle or goats into the high mountains and make temporary flat-topped mud huts for themselves and their livestock; in the winter, they return to the lowlands.

Jammu, known as the "City of Temples," has long been a center of Indian culture in which the arts have flourished. For centuries, the Pahari painters have been well known for their lovely miniatures that show a dexterity of line and a matchless blend of color. Before independence, Jammu, unlike Kashmir, was a private domain that the maharajah kept to himself—and the British raj, wisely enough, made no effort to prevent this. No European was allowed to enter without a government permit. Each winter, the maharajah moved down from the snowy heights of Kashmir and retired to his palace in Jammu, which enjoys the winter climate of the plains, standing 310 meters (1,000 feet) above sea level.

Although Jammu is primarily a transit stop to and from Kashmir, try to visit the multitowered Raghunath Temple, the largest temple complex in northern India. Located in the heart of the city and surrounded by numerous other temples, Raghunath, constructed over a 25-year period beginning in 1835, is dedicated to Lord Rama (a Vishnu incarnation). A good portion of the interior is covered in dazzling gold leaf. Also see the Ranbireswar Temple, built in 1883 and dedicated to Lord Shiva, with its 12 large crystal lingams and the Dogra Art Gallery, which houses a lovely collection of miniatures. You can also visit the sacred cave of the goddess Vaishno Devi, an important Hindu shrine on a hill in Katra, 50 kilometers (31 miles) from Jammu, that contains a hilltop cave high above the Jammu plains. The cave is supposedly where Vaishno Devi took shelter after killing a demon.

Srinagar, Capital of Kashmir

About 112 kilometers (70 miles) beyond the Banihal Pass, the gateway to the Vale of Kashmir, lies Srinagar, the capital of the state, nestled in the mountainous walls of the Himalayas at the center of the famous vale. This is the Venice of the East—a "Venice" ensconced miraculously in the midst of an Eastern-style Switzerland (or is it Amsterdam?). Set against the winding Jhelum River with Dal Lake sweeping off to the east and the Himalayas rising up in the distance, Srinagar brings to mind many water-based cities, while retaining a Moslem character completely its own.

Eyes linger on the tall riverside wooden houses, with their intricately carved verandas and balconies jutting precariously over the Jhelum—majestic homes that frequently have their own private *ghats* (front steps) that lead down to the water. Many homes are old and weatherworn, but some still have brightly painted shutters and trim, and always you see that carefully worked Kashmiri gingerbread on the verandas.

Then there's the river, unfortunately muddy and polluted. *Dongas,* large flat-bottom vessels on which entire families live, compete for space on this waterway with lumber-laden barges, houseboats, ducks, swimming children, and *shikaras* (small boats with canopied roofs and fluttering curtains used as water taxis). You could spend days just watching the flow of life that moves back and forth throughout Srinagar.

Take a walk through the old city, giving yourself plenty of time to meander and follow on whim the narrow, winding streets that often lead to a dead end or the river, the focus of life. Men in fur caps and women in dark *pherans*—their heads covered in bright-colored scarves or mysteriously veiled in black—walk along the crowded streets. Horsedrawn *tongas* (carts) prance by—the animals robust and jaunty, with the string of bells jangling around their necks adding to the festive air. Old men, frequently smoking their "hubbly-bubbly" (the Kashmiri hookah) sit inside small shops or open-air stalls that display all the artistry of Kashmir: furs and embroidered leather or fabrics, carved woodwork, papier-mâché objects, copper or silver urns and pots, shawls, and magnificent carpets.

Apart from the attractions of the old city and the river still spanned by some original wooden bridges, Srinagar has numerous landmarks. Early one morning, climb the stone steps that lead to the Shankaracharya Temple (built by a Hindu during the tolerant reign of Jahangir) at the top of a 310-meter (1,000-foot) hill on the southeastern edge of Srinagar. You can still see parts of an original temple that existed here (the low enclosing wall and the plinth), believed to have been constructed by the son of Ashoka around 200 B.C. The existing temple provides a striking panorama, well beyond the city to the configurations of the Jhelum River and the adjoining Dal Lake.

There are also great views from the Hari Parbat Fort on top of a hill that is sacred to Hindus—Sharika Hill. Although the fortress dates from the eighteenth century, the wall around Hari Parbat was built by Akbar in the late 1500s. If you want to go inside, get permission from the State Archaeological Department in Srinagar.

Srinagar, a predominantly Moslem city, also has its hefty share of historic mosques. See the Jamia Masjid, the largest in India. First built by Sultan Sikander in the thirteenth century and destroyed three times by fire, the last construction—maintaining the original design—was supervised by the Mogul Emperor Aurangzeb in 1674. An attractive example of Indo-Saracenic architecture, its vast interior contains 400 cedarwood pillars, each made from a single tree trunk. Also, see the Pather Masjid, built entirely of limestone by Jahangir's wife, Nur Jahan, in 1620. And visit the pagodalike Shah Hamdan Mosque, one of the oldest mosques in the city (first constructed in the late fourteenth century) and also destroyed by fires and rebuilt, the last time in 1732—without a single nail or screw. The walls and ceilings are covered with delicate painted woodwork. Unfortunately, only Moslems are allowed inside. Finally, visit the Hazratbal on the western shore of Dal Lake, a new modern shrine that contains a sacred hair of the Prophet Mohammed, which is shown to the public on religious holidays.

Dal and Nagin Lakes

For most, a visit to Srinagar means a vacation, however short, on a legendary houseboat. Although it's possible to book your boat in advance (in high season this is advised), you can also wait and make a reservation at the Tourist Reception Center in Srinagar. But before you make your choice, it's wise to hire a shikara to see your boat first. The houseboats are moored on Dal and Nagin lakes, and on the Jhelum River. If you want peace and quiet, choose the Nagin or the remote end of Dal. If you're after the hustle and proximity of the city, stay on the southern end of Dal or right on the busy Jhelum—but be ready for noise!

Houseboats come in all sizes and price ranges, but the aura of most of them is genteel elegance. Even the new boats continue the original design—lovely, fragrant carved walls and ceilings of cedar, a formal dining room, a handsome sitting room, and bedrooms, a sun deck on the roof, plus a cozy veranda from which you can watch the sun rise or set, depending on your location. A word of caution: Staying on a houseboat sets you up as easy prey for the small tradesmen—touts—who paddle out in their shikaras transformed into floating stores—wide-eyed hawks casing the joint. Before you unpack, you'll be besieged with everything available in

Kashmir, from a fresh cutting of local flowers (which is quite pleasant) to razor blades and mineral water. Prices can be exorbitant, so bargain for anything you want. And when you've had enough of the handicrafts, salespeople, and tailors, just say "no" with authority and send them away.

Mogul Garden

No trip to Srinagar is complete without a tour of the waterside Mogul gardens—a trip that should be made by shikara. Each small boat for private hire takes up to four passengers, but with two passengers, it constitutes the height of pampered luxury. Once you've stretched out on the comfortable cushions under the shelter of the fringed canopy, you understand why this boat is dubbed the "gondola" of Kashmir. Your boatsman, with his heart-shaped paddle, glides you soundlessly over the calm water. You pass by ingenious floating vegetable gardens; stop, if you're in the right season, and snap off a gorgeous lotus bloom; follow the swooping course of an electric kingfish, and always remind yourself that this heaven is real.

At intervals all around the 19-square-kilometer (12-square-mile) surface stand the stately *chenars,* giant plane trees, which turn fire red in the autumn. The chenars, which were favorite trees of the Moguls, who first planted them in Kashmir, form the backdrop to the first garden you'll visit: the Shalimar Bagh (Garden of Love), laid out in the early 1600s by Jahangir for Queen Nur Jahan—four terraces of lawns and flower beds rising one above the other. A shallow water channel runs down the middle—typical Persian quadrant style—and on the top terrace, reserved for the royal women, is a black-marble pavilion, secluded and elegant. From May to October, you can watch an evening sound-and-lumiere show here.

A TOUR OF THE LAKES AND VALLEYS

Gulmarg

Gulmarg, the meadow of flowers, 56 kilometers (32 miles), northwest of Srinagar, was a favorite vacation spot of the Moguls and later of the British. At an elevation of 2,460 meters (8,200 feet), this bowl-shaped valley, set high in the mountains and encircled by fir- and pine-covered slopes, is not just a convenient base for numerous treks; it is an up-and-coming year-round resort. You can play golf in the warm months on one of the world's highest courses (originally developed by the British). You can sled (called "sledging") or ski in winter on assorted slopes with T-bar, puma, and chair lift, or trek with a *sherpa* up four kilometers (2¼ miles) to Khilanmarg, with its breathtaking view and memorable run (a gondola will soon replace this novel, rigorous uphill climb). Although Gulmarg, with its snug circle of rustic hotels, is more like a frontier town than another Sun Valley or Chamonix, it is one of the best skiing bargains in the world. Lessons, lift tickets, and all equipment (fairly up-to-date, with outdoor clothes included) cost just a few dollars a day.

Gulmarg is also the place for invigorating walks and spirited pony rides. From its 11-kilometer (seven-mile) long Circular Path, which takes you through pine forests, you'll have a magnificent view of the entire valley of Kashmir, including Srinagar. You can also see the distant Nanga Parbat, over 7,800 meters (26,000 feet). This giant, whose name means naked mountain, dominates the landscape for miles in every direction.

Wular and Manasbal Lakes

From Gulmarg, head northeast to Sangrama and then continue northeast until you reach Wular Lake, the largest freshwater lake in India. Set in magnificent, high mountains, the Wular, which is the color of soft jade, is another popular vacation haunt. One legend claims that the Wular was formerly a city of such decadence that the mountains released a deluge that swallowed it up; when the water is low, you can see the remaining ruins, it is said. The Wular has evidently claimed so many lives that the deepest area is known as Mota Khon (Gulf of Corpses).

Just a few miles beyond the Wular is Lake Manasbal, a bird-watcher's paradise (30 kilometers, or 18 miles, from Srinagar). The deepest lake in Kashmir, Manasbal is famous for its lotus blossoms, which spread across the water in the summer.

Take the road that branches to the left at Ganderbal and head into the Sindh Valley, one of the most famous in Kashmir. As you travel along the sinuous terrain, the mountains come down precipitously on both sides, covered with that particular Kashmiri pine known as the budle tree. The average specimen stands over 30 meters (100 feet) tall.

Pahalgam and Lidder Valley

Sixty miles southeast of Srinagar is the Lidder Valley, with majestic mountain scenery. As you enter the valley via Baltal, you can take a day-long trek to a height of 3,900 meters (13,000) feet to the sacred cave of Amarnath, believed to be the former abode of Shiva. The pilgrim's rough-hewn treck, steps cut out of rock, leads straight to the object of worship—a stalactite, shaped like a lingam, hanging from the roof of the cave. At the year's most auspicious moment for worship—the night of the full moon between July and August, when Shiva supposedly explained the secret of creation to Parvati—pilgrims pour in from every corner of India to offer their prayers to the god.

The Kolahoi Glacier

Lucky the traveler who takes the three-day trek from Pahalgam (equipment, porters, ponies, and guides are available here) up to the Kolahoi Glacier, the Matterhorn of Kashmir. This popular and moderate trek offers some of the most inspiring scenery in Kashmir. Besides seeing great panoramas, you'll also witness the agility of the nomadic Gujjar, who move their herds with sublime grace and speed. The actual journey that leads to the glacier takes you first to Aru, a tiny village situated at the foot of a meadow—a convenient stopping place. On the second day, you'll come to Lidderwatt, a camping site in a meadow forded by two small streams and surrounded by mountains. Here the sun pours down from a subtropical sky, while the encircling pines hold on to night well beyond daybreak. The third day takes you through a pine forest, then the view bursts wide open at Satlanjan. Here you'll cross more narrow streams and finally see the milky green Kolahoi—craggy and daunting.

Snow Bridges

A word of warning for anyone who follows this enchanting village to the watershed: Beware of leaving too late in the year, when melting snow can be dangerous. Up to the end of May or the beginning of June, you can rely on the snow bridges; after that, they can be deadly. And in its early phase, what is termed a snow bridge in Kashmir is just barely a bridge. During the winter, the ravines fill in and bridge over with snow, while the mountain torrent continues to force its way through a tunnel underneath. Until the thaw sets in, you can walk up and down these precipitous gorges on top of the snow, with the river crashing its way through beneath, unseen and frequently unheard. But once the snow starts to melt, these bridges become so slender at the middle of their arches that they can snap at any moment, which can mean a drop of 4.5 to 6 meters (15 to 20 feet). Or, the snow bridge may already have broken up in the middle, leaving a gap of two or three feet, which you then have to jump across. The safest trip is across the giant snow bridge at Chananwari, a six-kilometer (10-mile) pony trek from Pahalgam.

EXPLORING LADAKH

One of the prime adventure opportunities in India is remote and rugged Ladakh, lying between the two highest mountain ranges in the world: the Himalayan and the Karakoram. Ladakh can be approached by road, or you can fly straight to Leh, the capital. However, if you've got the time, the drive is the only way to go. The territory of Ladakh, about twice the size of Switzerland, represents 70 percent of the total area of Jammu and Kashmir and is one of the highest regions on earth—a good portion of it over 2,700 meters (9,000 feet) above sea level. With a total population of only 150,000, Ladakh has one of the lowest population densities in the world (two–three people per square mile). For the most part inhospitable and craggy, the otherworldly terrain is arid beyond belief, with mountain peaks soaring three to four miles high. The joint effects of elevation and isolation amid snowy mountains produce the most unusual climate in the world—a weird combination of desert and arctic. Burning heat by day is followed by piercing cold at night, with everything parched by the extreme dryness of the air. The annual rainfall rarely exceeds three to four inches; few rain clouds get over the prohibitive peaks. As you travel up and down the arid, windswept mountains for miles and miles, you'll see deserts of granite dust, bare crags, and mountains of different hues. Ladakh is rightly called the "moonland."

In spite of the harsh landscape, Ladakh offers a wealth of environmental intrigue. Pink granite contrasting with a deep blue sky, brisk sunshine, pure air, and green valleys ingeniously irrigated in a vast desert. There are wild yak, the elusive snow leopard, the docile marmot, and blue sheep. But the greatest draw in Ladakh is the chance to witness a rich Buddhist culture firmly rooted in the majority of the people who live here, a culture that's fascinating to ponder. *Gompas* (monasteries) sit perched on high cliffs. *Chortens* (stupas) and *mani walls* (sacred stone walls) keep evil spirits from entering a village; prayer flags flap in the cold, strong wind.

Ladakh is connected with Kashmir Valley by a black-topped road that usually remains open from the end of June to mid-October, depending on the snowfall. The road passes through picturesque villages on the banks of the Sindh River, leaving the valley at Sonamarg. The first pass you'll cross to reach Ladakh is Zoji La (3,473 meters, or 11,578 feet, above sea level). On the other side starts the Drass Valley. Each side of the pass provides a startling contrast. You'll leave behind your last glimpse of forest-clad hills and suddenly stare into a vast mountainous landscape that's predominately stark, arid, and stony.

Kargil District

Kargil, with a population of about 5,000 predominately orthodox Shiite Moslems, is the second-largest town in Ladakh and the headquarters of the Kargil district. Situated in the Suru Valley at the junction of the Drass and Suru rivers, Kargil's elevation of only 2,700 meters (9,000 feet) is low for Ladakh; reduced snowfall and greater warmth have produced fertile fields that are rich in barley, wheat, and vegetables; rows of flourishing poplars and willows, and successful orchards. Kargil is famous for its mulberries and apricots.

Long ago, Kargil, the halfway point to Leh, used to be an important junction on the Asian trade route. Hundreds of caravans from China, Afghanistan, Turkey, and India laid over here, conducting intense bartering in the process—a heavy exchange of silk, jewels, ivory, and carpets. Now tourists who come overland to Leh often opt to stop here. Flanked by Shiite tombs (*Imambaras*) and mosques (over 400 years old), the ancient bazaar is crammed with local handicrafts (traveling hookahs, metalware, jewelry).

After crossing the Suru River, the road follows the Wakha Chu stream. Shergole, a tiny village 10 kilometers (16 miles) from Kargil, is your gateway to Buddhist Ladakh. There, built into a cliff and perched halfway up the mountainside, is a gompa containing some beautifully painted interior walls. Check to see if the lamas are present; it's worth a visit if they're around to let you in. Here, too, you'll begin to see the traditional prayer flags waving from the roofs of houses and handsome women decked out in their traditional Tibetan costumes.

Mulbekh

From Shergole, it's a few miles to Mulbekh and its gompa, with an enormous Buddha carved into rock. Inside the gompa are some beautiful frescoes, statues, and relics.

Indus Valley

Once you leave Mulbekh, the road climbs to the top of the 3,660-meter (12,200-foot)-high pass; the Namika-La. You'll wind your way back down to a valley and then proceed up and up again until you reach Fota La, the highest point on the Srinagar-Leh road: 4,083 meters (13,609 feet) above sea level. The wind whips around stark, craggy peaks and across barren plateaus, rustling prayer flags mounted atop *chortens* (Tibetan stupas) constructed by Buddhists who have successfully negotiated the treacherous and lonely pass. As you head down to the Indus Valley, you'll execute one particularly sharp bend in the road. Suddenly you'll see the distant whitewashed Lamayuru Gompa—Ladakh's oldest monastery and the welcome green oasis of an old sleepy village.

Lamayuru Gompa

This was formerly a large monastery with numerous buildings, all constructed in the eleventh century by the Gelug Sect, which follows the teachings of the Dalai Lama. In the fifteenth century it was taken over by the Kargyu (Red Hat Sect). Today, Lamayuru has only one remaining intact structure. The biggest prayer hall is filled with statues, *thangkas* (Tibetan cloth paintings), and elaborately painted wood cubbies that hold the Holy Books. Also worth seeing are the mani walls built into the surrounding slopes—each stone carried and put into place by a Buddhist pilgrim. Note the mantra carved into the rocks: *Om Mani Padme Hum* (Hail to the Jewel in the Lotus). More than religiously significant, these walls protect the village from avalanches.

Alchi and Spitok Gompas

Near the village of Saspol, take the turn that leads to the eleventh-century Alchi Gompa, with five important and exquisite structures. You'll see an imposing collection of gigantic painted clay statues of various Buddhas, ornately carved arches and doors, and hundreds of handsome small paintings, 1,000 years old, crammed onto many of the interior walls. Alchi is also unusual in that it is set in the lowlands, rather than on top of a hill.

About five miles from Leh is another important monastery, the Spitok Gompa, built 500 years ago on top of a hillock overlooking the Indus River. This monastery, the seat of the head lama of Ladakh, now contains a new gompa within its walls, plus exquisite thangkas, and a separate chamber farther up the hill that pays tribute to Mahakala, "the Black One." The numerous faces on the statue remain veiled except for one day of festive celebration in January. This chamber also contains an exceptional collection of old masks. Unfortunately, some rooms in the Spitok are now off-limits to tourists.

Leh—From Buddhist to Military

Your next stop is Leh, seen first from a distance huddling in a narrow valley at the base of snow-covered peaks (part of the Karakoram Mountain range). By the third century B.C. Leh (at 3,450 meters, or 11,500 feet, above sea level) was an important Buddhist center; later, it became a major commercial center on the silk route in central Asia. Now the twentieth century has forced Leh to assume an infinitely less glamorous role as an important Indian military base. Even with the army, Leh has remained an isolated, compact town, with its 12,000 inhabitants trying hard to hold on to their original culture.

The most striking buildings in Leh are the sixteenth-century Leh Palace and Temple of the Guardian Deities, both unfortunately in a state of decay and still owned by the Ladaki royal family, perched on a mountain towering over the palace, as if asserting the supremacy of the spiritual realm. Large and rambling, this gompa contains a solid gold statue of the Buddha (weighing just over a ton), painted scrolls, ancient manuscripts, and crumbling wall paintings.

The Leh bazaar may not offer great bargains (prices are better elsewhere), but it has much in the way of local color. Also, within the bazaar, see the Shiite Mosque, a good example of Turkish and Iranian architecture, built in 1594 by a son (Singe Namgyal) for his mother. Finally, just wander into the labyrinth of streets and alleys that take you through the old town on the lower slopes that lead up to the palace. On the plain below is the newer part of town.

Gompas around Leh

Leh is an excellent base for excursions to several nearby monasteries and other worthwhile points of interest. Most of them are located on the road that heads southeast to the largest Buddhist gompa i̶ ̶ ̶ ̶ ̶ ̶ ̶ ̶
Hemis Gompa, 16 kilometers (25 miles) from Leh. ̶ ̶ ̶ ̶ ̶ ̶ ̶
route is the Tibetan R̶e̶f̶ ̶ ̶ ̶ ̶
fled Tibet afte ̶ ̶ ̶ ̶
lishing a n̶ ̶ ̶

At Sh̶ ̶ ̶
belongs to ̶ ̶
tall, copper-g̶ ̶ ̶
(Lord Buddha). ̶ ̶
in pure gold.

The next attractio̶ ̶
offering a panoramic vie ̶ ̶ ̶ ̶ ̶ ̶ ̶ ̶ ̶ ̶ us
chambers, including one ha ̶ ̶ ̶ ̶ ̶ ̶ int-
ed clay statue of Maitreya in ̶ ̶ ̶ ̶ ̶

Last, but in no way least, is t̶ ̶ ̶ ̶ ̶ ̶ ̶ 600s by
King Singe Namgyal, this monaster̶ ̶ ̶ ̶ ̶ al tour de
force—one that hits you suddenly. Pra̶ ̶ ̶ ̶ tall pillars
in the courtyard wave you forward. If pos̶ ̶ ̶ isit during the
Hemis Festival (usually in June or July), w̶ ̶ ̶ the birthday of
Guru Padmasambhava. This colorful event feat̶ ̶ masked dancers gy-
rating slowly to loud music (the forces of good) to fight off the demons.
Hemis also has statues of gold, stupas studded with precious stones, and
a great collection of tankas, including one claimed to be the largest in existence, exhibited once every 11 years (the next viewing is 2000).

Zanskar Valley, the New Frontier

Zanskar Valley, stretching out from a noble height of over 3,900 meters
(13,000 feet), is for adventurous, intrepid travelers who are willing to exchange comfort for a journey into a remote area where the ancient Buddhist culture is still largely intact. This district—a collection of isolated
hamlets with magnificent gompas lying between the two branches of the
Zanskar River—is well guarded by snowcapped peaks.

The climate is severe. A warm day can suddenly turn cold as ice. Win-
ters are harsh, yet not totally unkind. With the cold, the normally endless
trip into Leh for the people who live here is dramatically shortened. Once
the Zanskar is frozen, they simply walk across, lopping off a good portion
of a circuitous trek. "Fair Weather" roads in Zanskar are always difficult,
even during fair weather. Still, if you want to see a place that is untouched
and remote, go. Zaskar feels cut off from the world and from the rush of
time.

To begin your journey through Zanskar, start from Kargil and head
south through the Suru Valley, a fertile area with astonishing beauty. Pass
the distant Nun (at 7,023 meters or 23,410 feet) and Kun (at 6,966 meters
or 23,219 feet), Zanskar's two highest peaks. Continue to follow the river
until you reach Rangdum, an isolated hamlet with a seventeenth-century
gompa set into the hills. Wind your way up to the Pensa La Pass—4,332
meters (14,440 feet) above sea level—where unexpected hot springs gurgle
not far from the summit. A legend claims that these springs gave rise to
the ancestor of the famous Zanskar stallion, now declared a protected animal.

Finally you'll reach Padam, the district headquarters and a tiny village. Be certain to visit the Karsha gompa, the largest and wealthiest monastery in Zanskar, with excellent chambers filled with statues and ancient frescoes. From Padam, the adventurous can also trek to Manali in Himachal Pradesh.

When you return to Kargil, take a dirt road at Tungri and walk up to Dzongkhul, a cave monastery attributed to the tenth-century Indian mystic Naropa, who spent years here in meditation. The monastery contains his supposed footprints, his staff, and numerous small shrines.

PRACTICAL INFORMATION FOR

JAMMU AND KASHMIR

WHEN TO GO. Winter is for skiing and snow-related adventures in Kashmir. Spring and early autumn represent a panorama of beautiful color, with ideal temperatures an extra dividend. In April/May, the snows in the upper reaches usually start to melt and the willows turn green. Almond trees bloom and flowers carpet the landscape. In September, autumn's dahlias and cosmos are in full bloom. The days are pleasant and the nights are cool. Summer is the time to trek, to ride horseback, to go rafting, to bike, to fish—the time to explore the remote magnificence of Ladakh. The passes here remain closed from sometime in October until May or June because of snow.

HOW TO GET THERE. By Air. *Indian Airlines* flies to Jammu, Srinagar, and Leh in Ladakh—even in winter, although flights are often delayed or canceled because of inclement weather. From Delhi, Indian Airlines makes a daily flight to Jammu, 12 weekly flights to Srinagar, and a daily flight to Leh in Ladakh. From Chandigarh, there are four weekly flights to Jammu and Srinagar and two weekly flights to Leh. Within the state, Indian Airlines flies three times weekly between Jammu and Srinagar and three times weekly between Srinagar and Leh. On arrival, foreigners must register at the Foreigners' Regional Registration Office inside each terminal. Flights should be booked well in advance and passengers must reconfirm their tickets 72 hours in advance and should arrive at the terminal 90 minutes before flight time. Call for information: in Jammu (tel. 77825 or 42735); in Srinagar (tel. 72270); and in Leh (tel. 3522).

By Bus. *Jammu and Kashmir State Road Transport Corporation* (J&KSRTC) shuttles deluxe buses from Delhi to Jammu. Buses leave Delhi from Ashok Yatri Nivas Hotel, 19 Ashok Rd. Buses also go from Delhi to Jammu and Srinagar, leaving at 4:30 P.M. and arriving the next day at 5:30 P.M. In Delhi, the firm is at 218 Kanishka Shopping Plaza, 19 Ashok Rd.; tel. 3324551 (ask for J & K Roadways). In Srinagar, call 72698. The fare to Srinagar from Delhi is Rs. 250; to Jammu, Rs. 150. A daily bus also runs between Srinagar and Leh, with an overnight halt in Kargil, when the pass is open (summer until early autumn).

By Train. From Delhi, the daily *Shalimar Express* to Jammu Tawi (no railway into Srinagar or Ladakh) takes 22 hours, and the faster *Himsagar Express* runs five times weekly. The *Jammu Tawi Express* runs to Jammu daily from Calcutta and twice-weekly from Bombay. From Jammu to Srinagar, you can take the bus (numerous runs daily) or go by taxi. A fixed-rate taxi costs Rs. 800 and can be shared by four people.

By Rented Car with Driver. From Jammu or Srinagar, the cost to rent a car with driver should be approximately Rs. 8 per km, with a halt charge of Rs. 50–Rs. 100 per night. In Leh, the cost of renting a jeep with a driver is approximately $80 to do one day of local sightseeing. A jeep that carts you around all Ladakh can be costly. Delhi is 587 km (364 miles) to Jammu and 876 km (538 miles) to Srinagar; Srinagar is 434 km (269 miles) to Leh.

By Taxi. A taxi is good for long hauls to popular destinations. Before hiring a taxi, however, get the legal rate from the tourist department. Jammu to Srinagar should be about Rs. 8 per km; from Srinagar to Leh should be about Rs. 4,500 for taxi or jeep. You can share the cost with other travelers.

TOURIST INFORMATION. The *Jammu & Kashmir Tourist Department Corporation (J&KTDC)* is one of the best. They are out to please and have current information covering nearly every conceivable area of interest to the tourist. If you're in Delhi before you head up to Kashmir, you'd be wise to check into the J&K tourist office, 202–203 Kanishka Shopping Plaza, 19 Ashok Rd.; tel. 3325373. It's an example of efficiency and gracious service that you can expect in most of the big offices once you head north. The department has offices in major cities in India.

Tourist Reception Centers are in Srinagar (Shervani Rd., tel. 72449 or 77305, open 24 hours), Jammu (Veer Marg, tel. 48172 or 44359, open 8 A.M.–10 P.M.), and Leh (tel. 497, open 8 A.M.–8 P.M.). Following is a list of other offices in the state. *Batote,* 113 km (70 mi.) from Jammu, tel. 42; *Gulmarg,* tel. 99; *Kargil (Ladakh),* tel. 29; *Katra,* 45 km (28 mi.) from Jammu, tel. 3 and 5; *Kud,* 105 km (65 mi.) from Jammu, tel. 7; *Pahalgam,* tel. 24; *Ramban,* 148 km (92 mi.) from Jammu (no phone).

FOREIGN CURRENCY EXCHANGE. Most of the Western-style hotels have money-exchange counters. Otherwise, head for a branch of the *State Bank of India* or *Jammu and Kashmir Bank,* open Monday–Friday, 10 A.M.–2 P.M.; Saturdays, 10 A.M.–noon. The State Bank of India also has a branch (open weekdays, 4–7 P.M.) in the Srinagar Tourist Reception Center.

ACCOMMODATIONS. At press time, some hotels in Gulmarg, Pahalgam, and Srinagar were closed due to political problems. Check with your travel agent or the tourist department before you depart. In more stable times, you have a wide range of possibilities in the Jammu and Kashmir states—from fancy to rustic minimal. You also have the famous houseboats, which run from grand to just barely seaworthy. But, as with the other Himalayan states, a visit should be for the adventure and the ethereal beauty of it all. Some of the most exquisite and remote areas offer few creature comforts (certainly no TV)—but what memories and what breathtaking views! Prices are based on double occupancy and exclude taxes and service charges: *Deluxe,* over Rs. 2,000; *Expensive,* Rs. 1,200–Rs. 2,000; *Moderate,* Rs. 500–Rs. 1,200; *Inexpensive,* under Rs. 500. Most of the Western-style hotels take major credit cards. Kashmir is popular—all of it—so book early. Government-run huts, especially in Gulmarg and Pahalgam, should be reserved two to three months in advance to play it safe.

GULMARG

Expensive

Hotel Highlands Park. Gulmarg 193403; tel. 207. 39 rooms with bath. Old hunting trophies hang in this château-style hotel's lobby. Air-conditioned, pine-paneled rooms are comfortable and have ample heat in the winter. Multicuisine meals are included. Foreign-exchange and travel counter, room service, health club, restaurant, bar. Closed Nov.–Dec. 10. AE, DC.

Inexpensive

J&K Tourist Department Huts. J&K Tourist Department, Reception Center, Srinagar 190001; tel. 72499 or 77305 or, in Gulmarg, tel. 239. 14 huts with bath. These small, very popular wood cottages dot the slopes of the valley. They're not ornate, but with a fireplace in each bedroom, they're just right for Gulmarg. Bring your own sleeping bag, or rent linen at a nominal cost. Reserve two months in advance in the summer. Rupees only.

JAMMU

Moderate

Hotel Asia Jammu Ashok. Jammu Tawi, Jammu 180001; tel. 43127. 48 rooms with bath. Across from the Amar Mahal Palace, this government hotel is modern and has pleasant rooms. There are a swimming pool, bar, multicuisine restaurant, coffee shop, shopping arcade, TV, foreign-exchange and travel counter, doctor on call. AE, DC, MC, V.

Hotel Asia Jammu Tawi. Nehru Market, Jammu 180001; tel. 49430. 44 rooms with bath. This is a Western-style hotel about 1½ km (1 mi.) from the center of town, with reasonably attractive air-conditioned rooms and, best of all, a swimming pool. Also included are a health club, room service, restaurant with live music, bar, foreign-exchange and travel counter, shopping arcade, doctor on call. AE, DC, MC, V.

KARGIL (LADAKH)

Inexpensive

Hotel Broadway. *Suruview.* Kargil 194105; tel. 103. 40 rooms with bath. This excellently managed hotel off the main street has a plain lobby and clean, sparsely decorated rooms. The best rooms overlook the Suru River. There's an excellent multicuisine restaurant and room service. Transport and trekking arrangements can be made. AE, DC, MC.

Hotel Carvan Sarai. Kargil 194105; tel. 79. 40 rooms with bath. Perched above the center of Kargil, this simple, clean hotel, built in tiers, has a Middle-Eastern ambience. Upper floor rooms have a great river view. There is a multicuisine restaurant. Rupees only.

Hotel Siachen. Kargil 194105; tel. 22. 27 rooms with bath. On the banks of the Suru River and off the main street, this excellently managed, popular hotel has clean, simple rooms with verandas and a garden in its parking lot. Room service, doctor on call, foreign-exchange and travel counter, excellent multicuisine restaurant. DC.

J&K Government Tourist Bungalows. J&K Government Tourist Information Center, Tourist Office, Kargil 194105; tel. 29. About 12 rooms with bath. The better of these two bungalows is on a hill and has spacious rooms. The other bungalow is near the Suru River. In summer reserve well in advance. Rupees only.

KATRA

Moderate

Asia Vaishnodevi Katra. Katra, Jammu; tel. 161. 37 rooms with bath. This clean, Western-style hotel with simply decorated rooms is a short walk from the bus stand. Included are a vegetarian restaurant, health club with sauna and massage, *puja* (prayer) room, travel counter, barbershop, and room service. DC, V.

LEH (LADAKH)

Deluxe

Ladakh Sarai. Reservations: Mountain Travel India, Pvt. Ltd. 1/1, Rani Jhansi Rd., New Delhi 110055; tel. 771055, fax 011/777483, or through any Mountain Travel office. 15 tents. Here you'll stay in a *yurt* (tent) in a meadow below the Stok Gompa, 15 km (nine mi.) from Leh. Large, lantern-lit circular tents are attractively furnished. Toilets and solar-heated showers are in separate tents. The lobby, also separate, is Ladakhi-style with comfortable low platforms and a little shrine. Multicuisine meals (for staying guests only) are normally eaten outside. Meals and sightseeing are included. Closed October 15–April 15. AE, DC, MC, V.

Hotel Highland. Stok, Leh 194101. Reservations: c/o EMPL Tours, 108 Vishal Bhawan, 95 Nehru Pl., New Delhi 110019; tel. 6428310, fax 011/6428311. 12 rooms with bath. Near the Stok monastery, this new two-story hotel, with a lovely back lawn, has a Ladakhi-style exterior (white with black-and-red trim) and modern, comfortably furnished rooms. Multicuisine restaurant serving fixed-menu meals with some Ladhakhi dishes, bar, arrangements for trekking, rafting, and cultural performances on request. Meals, airport transfer, and mountain bikes are included. Closed December–May. AE, DC, MC, V.

Hotel Lha-Ri-Mo. Leh, Ladakh 194101; tel. 301. 30 rooms with bath. A short walk from all markets and nestled behind an attractive garden, this is the loveliest hotel in Leh. The restaurant is especially charming, with intricately hand-painted beams. The rooms are simple but pleasing. There is an excellent multicuisine restaurant (for hotel guests only) as well as a travel agent and a doctor on call. Meals are included. Closed November–May. AE.

Hotel Shambha-la. Skara, Leh 194101; tel. 267, or, in Delhi, 6867785. 26 rooms with bath. On the outskirts of Leh, this spacious Ladakhi-style hotel offers lots of tranquillity—on the extensive grounds and in the upstairs sitting room, which has Buddhist wall hangings and murals. The lobby and dining-room decor follows the same theme. Rooms, however, have simple, Western decor; upstairs rooms have good views. Multicuisine restaurant, room service, beer bar, library, doctor, courtesy jeeps into Leh, travel arrangements. Closed November–May. AE.

PADAM (ZANSKAR, LADAKH)

Inexpensive

Padam Tourist Bungalow. J&K Tourist Officer, Kargil 194105; tel. 29. 5 rooms with a bath. If you can get a room in this government bungalow, you'll need a sleeping bag. Linen is clean and there are blankets, but the simple rooms get cold. The restaurant serves good Indian and Continental meals. Some tenting is allowed on the spacious lawn. Reserve well in advance. Rupees only.

PAHALGAM

Expensive

Pahalgam Hotel. Pahalgam; tel. 26. 46 rooms with baths. Set on the main street, this wonderful lodge has been renovated and offers Western-style amenities and attractive, centrally heated rooms. The best rooms have a river view. Multicuisine meals are included. Restaurant, room service, TV, heated swimming pool, health club. Discount December–January. AE, DC.

Moderate

Hotel Woodstock. Pahalgam; tel. 27. 50 rooms with bath. This weathered gray lodge has spacious, carpeted rooms that are centrally heated and have a rustic decor. The best rooms have a view of the river. TV, bar, multicuisine restaurant, doctor on call, room service, car rental, health club, shopping mall. Discount November–March. AE, DC.

Plaza Hotel. Pahalgam; tel. 39. 30 rooms with bath. This attractive lodge, enclosed by a pleasant garden, is well managed. It's not fancy, but it's also not expensive and its rooms have a cozy charm. Indian and Continental meals are included. Restaurant, bar. Closed mid-November–mid-March. Rupees only.

Inexpensive

J & K Government Tourist Bungalow and Huts. Reservations: J&K Tourism Department, Tourist Reception Center, Srinagar 190001; tel. 72449 or 77305. 7 rooms with bath in the bungalow, 57 huts with bath, and safari-style tents (very inexpensive) with shared bath. These accommodations are a bargain. The stone bungalow is old, with clean, spacious rooms. The huts are charming: little stone dwellings with ample rooms and verandas. Restaurant, bar. In summer reserve well in advance. Rupees only.

SRINAGAR

Deluxe

Oberoi Palace. Gupkar Rd., Srinagar 190001; tel. 71241. 101 rooms with bath. This was the former home of the maharajah; its beautiful lawns and six-hole golf course overlook Dal Lake. Its spacious rooms need refurbishing, however. Ask for an upper-floor, lakeview room. The hotel is a distance from the road and Srinagar.

Excellent multicuisine restaurant, room service, bar, TV, shopping arcade, badminton, travel and foreign-exchange counter. AE, DC, MC, V.

Expensive

Centaur Lake View Hotel. Chesmeshahi, Srinagar 191001; tel. 75631. This gigantic hotel on Dal Lake has modern rooms and multicuisine restaurants, bar, room service, swimming pool, health club, tennis court, shopping arcade, and travel and foreign-exchange counter. AE, DC, MC, V.

Moderate

Lake Isle Resort. Reservations: Naseem Bagh, Srinagar, 190001; tel. 78446; or BGA Corporation, 790 Shirley Dr., Tipp City, OH 45371, tel. 513–667–8071. 11 rooms with bath. Set on a secluded island in Nagin Lake, this 50-year-old two-story bungalow with spacious front lawns and great views is a delight. The rooms are in Kashmiri decor. An upstairs library is perfect for reading. Multicuisine meals are included. Restaurant, bar, sightseeing arrangements, badminton, boating and fishing, room service. Closed mid-November–April. AE, MC, V.

Inexpensive

Cheshma Shahi Hutments. J&KTDC, Tourist Reception Center, Srinagar, 191001; tel. 72449 or 77305. About 12 huts with bath. On a hill overlooking Dal Lake, near the Cheshma Shahi Mogul Garden, these charming new government-run cottages are spacious, economical, and popular, with restaurant, bar, and room service. In summer reserve well in advance. Rupees only.

Hotel Akbar. Box 95, Srinagar 191001; tel. 74547. 24 rooms with bath. This new, rambling, multistory structure with lovely gardens is on an island near Dal Gate. Rooms are attractive with carved-wood ceilings and simple furnishings. Good multicuisine restaurant, room service, outdoor adventure arrangements. AE, DC, MC, V.

HOUSEBOATS. Houseboats moored to the banks of Dal and Nagin lakes are 25–39 meters (80–125 feet) long and 3–6 meters (10–20 feet) wide. An average-size houseboat has a dining room, living room, one to three bedrooms with attached baths, and, in most cases, hot and cold running water. Most of the houseboats have terraces for sunbathing and lovely verandas. They are electrified and usually nicely furnished. Many kinds of houseboats are available. The approximate costs, which includes meals: *Deluxe Class,* Rs. 700 per double; *A Class,* Rs. 430 per double; *B Class,* Rs. 360 per double. There are lots of houseboats—lots of steal-you-blind houseboats as well as lots of houseboats surrounded by congestion and noise.

The following houseboat operators will give you the houseboat stay you've imagined: gracious service and relative peace and quiet. They'll pick you up at the airport and put together all your excursions, from fishing and trekking to traveling around by car. You can rent the entire boat or just a bedroom and share, but given the intimacy of a boat, sharing is an important consideration. To play it safe, stick to the Deluxe, A, or B category.

Butt's Clermont Houseboats (G. M. Butt & Sons, Clermont Houseboats, Dalgate, Srinagar 191001; tel. 2175–4337) has deluxe-class boats on Dal Lake near the Hazratbal Mosque. The best boats are old and have two bedrooms; you're surrounded by beautiful furnishings and memorabilia. Newer boats with two or three bedrooms are fancy and come with the same classy service. AE, DC, MC, V.

Reshu Boktoo & Sons (Dal Gate, Box 95, Srinagar 191001; tel. 74547) has deluxe and Class A boats on the western side of Nagin Lake. Their classiest boat is the *Golden Lotus.* Nice two-bedroom boats are also available. The owners supervise excellent treks in Kashmir and Ladakh and know the best fishing spots. AE, DC, MC, V.

Abdud Rashid Major & Bros (Nagin Lake, Srinagar 191001; tel. 74850) has two small, one-bedroom boats, the *H.P. Peony* and *Young Peony,* set on the eastern side of Nagin. When you step aboard, you'll feel as if someone's grandmother supervised the decorating. They're a real bargain. Rupees only.

TOURIST HUTS AND BUNGALOWS. The J&KTDC maintains other inexpensive tourist huts and bungalows throughout this part of the state.

Jammu. *Mansar Lake,* 80 km from Jammu, tourist bungalow and huts; and *Surinsar Lake,* 42 km from Jammu, tourist bungalow.

For reservations, contact the Tourist Reception Center, Jammu 181001; tel. 48172 or 44359.

Kashmir. *Achabal,* former pleasure retreat of Empress Nur Jahan, now a camping ground, 58 km (36 mi.) from Srinagar, tourist bungalow and huts; *Aharbal,* 51 km (32 mi.) from Srinagar, near a beautiful waterfall, tourist bungalow; *Daksum,* 85 km (53 mi.) from Srinagar, a forest retreat surrounded by mountains, tourist bungalow; *Kokarnag,* 70 km (43 mi.) from Srinagar, botanical garden and hot springs high up in the mountains, tourist bungalow and huts; *Lake Manasbar,* 32 km (20 mi.) from Srinagar, tourist bungalow; *Sonamarg,* 83 km (51 mi.) from Srinagar, in a valley way up in the mountains, tourist bungalow and huts; *Verinag,* 80 km (50 mi.) from Srinagar, Mogul ruins and hot springs, tourist bungalow; *Yusmarg,* 40 km (25 mi.) from Srinagar, lovely valley in the hills of the Pir Pangal range, tourist huts.

For reservations in all of these huts and bungalows, contact the Tourist Reception Center at Srinagar 190001; tel. 72449 or 77305.

Ladakh. Simple, sparsely furnished bungalows are located in Drass, Mulbek, and Saspol. Sleeping bags are advised. For reservations, contact the Tourist Department in Leh 19401; tel. 497.

There is also an inexpensive Public Works Department Rest House in **Khalsi.** For reservations: Superintendent Engineer, Public Works Department, Leh 19401.

DINING OUT. In Kashmir, there is a strong hint of Middle Eastern cooking, and *kebabs* (small pieces of chicken, mutton, or balls of minced meat threaded on a skewer and cooked or fried) are great favorites. *Biryanis,* typically Moslem dishes whose pedigree goes back to the Great Moguls, are prepared on all festive occasions. They are made from pigeons, chicken, or mutton with plenty of rice and butter and some spices. Other Kashmiri Mughlai dishes to tickle your palate: *gustava,* a meatball curry cooked in a gravy of yogurt and spices; *rista,* a beaten spicy lamb; *rogan josh,* a mutton cooked on the bone in a spiced curry; and if you're lucky you'll find some chef who can prepare fried spinach cooked in mustard oil, tumeric, and aromatic water in which dried cockscomb flowers have been soaked. After your meal, have sweet Kashmiri tea. Most good restaurants are in the better hotels and are mentioned under Accommodations, above. Lunchtime is 12–3; dinnertime is 7:30–10. Dress is casual. Reservations are advised in all hotel restaurants.

Prices are based on one person eating a three-course meal, excluding taxes, tip, or beverage: *Deluxe,* over Rs. 300; *Expensive,* Rs. 200–Rs. 300; *Moderate,* Rs. 100–Rs. 200; *Inexpensive,* under Rs. 100.

JAMMU

Inexpensive

Cosmo Bar and Restaurant. Hotel Cosmopolitan, Veer Marg; tel. 47561. This unpretentious, air-conditioned restaurant has good local ambience and serves tasty Indian, Mughlai, Chinese, and Continental food. Open noon–10 P.M. DC, V.

KARGIL (LADAKH)

Inexpensive–Moderate

Naktul Chinese Restaurant. On the road to the lower tourist bungalow; no phone. This small, friendly eatery serves large portions of Chinese food. Open 7 A.M.–10 P.M. Rupees only.

LEH (LADAKH)

Inexpensive

Dreamland Restaurant. Fort Rd.; no phone. Small and informal, Dreamland is often crowded with young Ladakhis chattering with foreigners and eating good Tibetan and Chinese meals. Open 8 A.M.–10 P.M. Rupees only.

Mentokling Restaurant. Near the police station, no phone. This informal, outdoor restaurant with simple tables and awnings offers a relaxing ambience. It serves good soups and multicuisine dishes. Open 8 A.M.–10 P.M. Rupees only.

SRINAGAR

Moderate

Adhoo's. Residency Rd.; tel. 72593. Usually crowded, this simple restaurant has a terrace out back and offers Kashmiri specialties. Open 9 A.M.–11 P.M. Rupees only.

Lhasa. Boulevard Lane; tel. 71438. If you like Tibetan and Chinese food, eat in Lhasa's supercasual candle-lit garden. Open noon–11 P.M. Rupees only.

Mughal Darbar. Shervani Rd.; no phone. This upstairs restaurant serves big portions of Kashmiri, Indian, and Chinese food in a crowded, dimly lit room. Open 9 A.M.–11 P.M. Rupees only.

SWEETS AND TREATS. Punjabi Vegetarian Roadside Stall. Khalsi (141 km, or 87 mi., from Kargil, Ladakh). Look for the sign and two benches by the road and have delicious *chana masala* (tomato curry with potato), *chappati* (unleavened bread), rice, and tea for under a dollar. Open 5:30 A.M. until the electricity shuts off.

Mama Mia's Hotel and Restaurant. On Nagin Lake, Srinagar. This is a houseboat moored to the western bank serving espresso from the supercasual sundeck. Nice ambience; great views. Open all day.

HOW TO GET AROUND

JAMMU

From the Airport. The airport is a short hop to downtown Jammu. A taxi ride should cost about Rs. 40.

By Taxi. Taxis are available, but drivers hate to use their meters. Bargain, using Delhi rates: Rs. 5.80 for the first km, Rs. 3.60 per additional km.

By Auto Rickshaw. The most fun and cheaper than taxis. Just make certain the driver uses the meter.

By Bus. *J & K State Road Transit Corporation (J&KSRTC)* has minibuses running regularly throughout the city. Contact the Tourist Reception Center (tel. 48172 or 44359) for routes and fares.

By Rented Car with Driver. Contact the Tourist Reception Center for a list of approved car-rental agencies; tel. 48172 or 44359. Figure Rs. 5–Rs. 6 per km, plus Rs. 100 for night-halt charges.

LEH

From the Airport. Taxis and jeeps into Leh are available for about Rs. 50. J&KSRTC has buses making local runs to many nearby destinations, but they're crowded and slow. At the taxi stand near the Tourist Bungalow, you can hire an unmetered taxi or jeep for excursions. Get a list of reasonable fares from the tourist department.

SRINAGAR

From the Airport. An airport bus takes you to the Tourist Reception Center in the heart of Srinagar for about Rs. 15. By taxi, figure about Rs. 80 into Srinagar or Rs. 150 for Nagin Lake, the location of the best houseboats.

By Taxi. At about Rs. 5–Rs. 6 per km, this is the least sensible way to travel if you plan to stay in the city, but it's okay for excursions around Dal Lake.

By Auto Rickshaw. Drivers here have the same reluctance to use the meter as elsewhere. Auto rickshaws should be much cheaper than taxis.

By Shikara. (lovely Kashmiri gondola). This is the only way to travel here. Although rates are supposedly fixed, no *shikara* owner will agree to them. Negotiate in advance and figure on about Rs. 40 per hour. No more than five passengers are allowed in a shikara. Ideally, they are best for two stretched out in pampered style. They're slow, but who cares? For complete rates for various shikara trips, check at the Tourist Reception Center.

By Tonga. This is another nice alternative. Robust horses with bells around the neck take you around town in two-wheel vehicles. Less expensive than the rickshaw. Haggle, but then enjoy yourself.

By Rented Car or jeep with Driver. Good and possibly necessary (if you can afford it) for long excursions. Contact the Tourist Reception Center in Tourist Information, above) to rent a car for about Rs. 5–Rs. 6 per km (overnight halt charges, Rs. 100). It can also supply a list of reliable private agencies that rent cars and jeeps with drivers.

TOURS. The *Special Tourist Taxi Association* (Jammu Tourist Reception Center, Veer Marg. tel. 49554 or 47366) provides a tour to Amar Mahal Palace Museum, Dogra Art Gallery, Ranbireshwar Temple, Raghunath Mandir, and Bahur Fort (about Rs. 140 per person).

The *Srinagar Tourist Reception Center* (Shervani Rd., tel. 72449 or 77305) runs bus and shikara tours to Shankaracharya Temple, Charchinari, Chashma Shahi, Nishat, Harwan, and Shalimar, with refreshments and lunch (7:30 A.M.–2 P.M., Rs. 75); and to Harwan, Shalimar, Nishat, Charchinari, and Chashma Shahi (2:30–9:30 P.M., about Rs. 100); plus day trips to Gulmarg, Pahalgam, Sonamarg, Wular Lake, and Verinag. Each day trip costs about Rs. 70. Times vary with the season.

The *Students' Educational and Cultural Movement of Ladakh* (SECMOL) (Pharkey Labrang, tel. 585) has excellent guides for tours to monasteries, palaces, and even private homes. Charges are based on your itinerary and are reasonable.

TOUR OPERATORS. Srinagar is the starting point for a lot of wonderful adventures. Like houseboat *wallahs,* there are good and bad private outfits ready to take you boating and trekking into the wilderness. Many are really just out to take you for a ride. Here is a list of really good packagers, who will give you a memorable, *good* time (check *Facts at Your Fingertips* for additional tour operators).

Reshu Boktoo & Sons, (Travel & Tour Operators, Box 95, Dal Gate, Srinagar 191001, tel. 74547) has good treks through Kashmir and Ladakh; jeep "treks" (week-long excursions from Srinagar via jeep to Leh and Ladakh); and Shikara water treks. The company will also arrange for duck shooting in winter and trout fishing the rest of the year. It can take care of all travel needs (including car or jeep with driver). Personal attention.

Himalayan River Runners (188-A Jor Bagh, New Delhi 110003, tel. 4632180) runs excellent rafting trips on the Zanskar River in Ladakh.

SEMCOL (Pharkey Labrang, Box 4, Leh 194101, tel. 585) has excellent guides for tours in Ladakh and arranges inexpensive treks with a special emphasis on the Ladakhi culture and the district's unique ecology. Contact well in advance.

SEASONAL EVENTS. The three areas of Jammu, Kashmir, and Ladakh are each influenced by three specific religions: Jammu, Hindu; Kashmir, Islam; and Ladakh, Buddism. Each year, these areas observe the traditional cycle of festivals and religious observances that are celebrated throughout India. The following additional festivals are special to this state:

June *Hemis Festival.* Ladakh's biggest monastery is the site of a two-day festival commemorating the birthday of Guru Padmasambhava, with masked dancers and eerie music. It's an intensely devout and culturally rich Buddhist festival, heavily attended. Contact the tourist department for details.

July/August. During the full moon, thousands of Hindu devotees trek three–five days to Amar Nath, about 48 km (30 mi.) from Pahalgam and supposedly the abode of Shiva, where they pray before the sacred lingam.

September. *Thikse Festival.* At the Thikse Gompa near Leh, lamas perform ritual *chaams* (dances).

HISTORIC SITES. Entrance to most places is generally free; where a donation is requested, a few rupees will do. Entrance to monasteries is from Rs. 10 to Rs. 20. Important sites are open daily from sunrise to sunset, unless noted below.

JAMMU AREA

Bahu Fort. The oldest building in Jammu, constructed over 3,000 years ago; the interior temple is dedicated to Kali.

Raghunath Temple, dedicated to Lord Rama (Vishnu avatar). Largest temple complex in Northern India, it was started in the nineteenth century and took 25 years to complete. Much of the interior is covered in gold leaf. The surrounding temples are dedicated to other gods and goddesses associated with the *Ramayana.*

Ranbireswar Temple, Jammu, constructed in 1883 by Maharajah Ranbir Singh, dedicated to Shiva. It has 12 crystal Shiva lingams.

Vaishno Devi. A 14-km (9-mi.) hike from Katra leads to this important Hindu shrine, a cave dedicated to the goddess Vaishno Devi. The long, narrow cave has three rock formations covered with gold canopies, representing the three divine aspects of the goddess Kali, Lakshmi, and Saraswati. An important pilgrimage site for Hindus.

LADAKH AREA

Alchi Gompa, 135 km (84 mi.) from Leh, 5 km from Saspol. Six separate structures with a collection of gigantic painted clay statues of the Buddha, carved arches and doors, and hundreds of small paintings (1,000 years old).

Dzongkhul, a cave monastery near Padam, is attributed to the tenth-century Indian mystic who spent years here in meditation. The monastery contains small shrines and sacred idols, and supposedly Naropa's sacred staff and footprints.

Hemis Gompa, 49 km (30 mi.) from Leh. Ladakh's biggest monastery built in the 1600s by King Singe Namgyal. Filled with gold statues, stupas studded with precious stones, and a great collection of *tankas,* including one claimed to be the largest in existence, exhibited once every 11 years.

Karsha Gompa, in Padam, Zanskar. The largest and wealthiest monastery in Zanskar, with 500-year-old frescoes.

Lamayuru. Ladakh's oldest monastery, built in the eleventh century. Formerly numerous structures existed; now only one remains. Inside the biggest prayer hall is a cave with a statue of Naropa, an Indian mystic who created the monastery.

Leh Khar Palace and Temple of the Guardian Deities, both in ruins, set above the city. The temple still houses a towering Chamba statue of Buddha carved into the face of an enormous rock.

Mulbekh Gompa and a statue of Avalokitesvara (Buddha of Compassion), with 1,000 eyes and numerous heads. 40 km (25 mi.) from Kargil. Gompa contains beautiful frescoes and statues.

Sankar Gompa, 3 km from Leh, has an excellent collection of miniature gold statues and paintings.

Shey Palace and Gompa. Built in the 1600s on the ruins of another fort, this palace is in decay, but there's a magnificent two-story, copper-gilt statue of a meditating Sakyamuni, called Shey Thubha (Lord Buddha). The gompa contains beautiful frescoes. The Victory Stupa is Ladakh's largest, crowned in pure gold.

Spitok Gompa, 5 km from Leh, was built 500 years ago. The current seat of the head lama of Ladakh, it has exquisite thankas and a separate chamber that pays tribute to Mahakala, "the Black One." Her face is unveiled only one day in January.

Thikse Gompa, 12 km (7 mi.) from Leh, is 800 years old. One chamber contains an enormous statue of Maitreya (Future Buddha) in the meditation pose.

SRINAGAR AREA

Achabal, 58 km (36 mi.) from Srinagar. A former Mogul garden, designed by a daughter of the Mogul Emperor Shah Jahan and the favorite retreat of Empress Nur Jahan. Now a grove with water cascades and fountains, a pleasant place to visit.

Amar Nath, 47 km (29 mi.) from Pahalgam. A cave that was supposedly the abode of Lord Shiva, with a stalactite in the shape of a lingam created by water dripping through the limestone roof of the cave.

Char Chenar. Shah Jahan's mogul garden is on an island in Dal Lake with a pavilion and three *chenars* (fire trees). There used to be a fourth.

Chasma Shahi (Royal Spring). The smallest Mogul garden, designed by Shah Jahan in the 1630s. Beautiful pavilions, illuminated at night.

Hari Parbat Fort. Built in the eighteenth century by Atta Mohammad Khan, an Afghan governor; the surrounding wall was built by Mogul Emperor Akbar in the late 1500s. Among the numerous ancient structures are a temple dedicated to Parvati, a Moslem shrine and mosque, and a Sikh *gurdwara* built to commemorate the visit of Har Govind Singh to Kashmir. Permission to enter must be obtained from the State Archaeological Department, Lalmandi Square, Srinagar. The fort, however, is poorly maintained; it's the exterior views that make a visit worthwhile.

Harwan, 6 km (4 mi) from Srinagar. Ruins of a Buddhist monastery dating back to the third century.

Hazratbal. White marble shrine built recently contains a sacred hair of Prophet Mohammed shown to the public on certain days.

Jamai Masjid is the largest mosque in Kashmir. First constructed by Sultan Sikander in the thirteenth century, it was destroyed three times by fire. The last construction was in 1674 by Aurangzeb in Indo-Saracenic architecture and laid out in the style of a Persian court mosque, with 400 cedarwood pillars, each from one tree.

Nasim Bagh (Garden of the Morning Breeze) is a Mogul garden of chenars originally laid out by Akbar in the early 1600s.

Nishat Bagh (Garden of Pleasure) is a Mogul garden designed by Asaf Khan, brother of Nur Jahan, in 1633. Ten terraces, formal gardens, a water channel with polished marble stepping-stones, fountains, and pavilions. Persian in style.

Shah Hamdan Mosque. First constructed in fourteenth century, suffered three fires. The last construction was in 1732 with no nails or screws used. Lovely carved windows and entrances. Only Moslems can go inside.

Shalimar Bagh (Garden of Love). Mogul garden constructed by Emperor Jahangir for his Nur Jahan in 1619. Four terraces with a water channel running from level to level. Typical Persian quadrant style. The black-marble pavilion on top exclusively used by royal women. Sound-and-light show.

Shankaracharya Temple. The present temple was built during the reign of Jahangir by an unknown Hindu. It sits on the site of a temple originally constructed around 200 B.C. by a son of Ashoka. The low enclosing wall and plinth belong to the ancient temple.

MUSEUMS AND GALLERIES. Expect to pay a nominal entrance fee at all the following. *Amar Mahal Palace Museum,* Ram Nagar, Jammu, has an interesting collection of Pahari miniature paintings in a former palace designed like a French château. Open 10 A.M.–noon and 3–5 P.M. in winter; 3–7 P.M. and Sun., 10 A.M.–noon in summer. Closed holidays.

Dogra Art Gallery, Gandhi Bhavan, Jammu, houses nearly 600 miniatures from Basholi and Kangra schools; plus sculptures, terra-cotta pieces, murals. Open 11 A.M.–5 P.M. in winter; 7:30 A.M.–1 P.M. in summer. Closed Monday and holidays.

Shri Partap Singh Museum, Lal Mandi, Srinagar, was started by the maharajah of Jammu and Kashmir. Archaeology, natural history, and products of Kashmiri arts and crafts. Particularly interesting are the finds from Harwan, a Buddhist site of the third century. The collections of coins, carpets, embroideries, and textiles are all from the state. Open 10 A.M.–5 P.M.; closed Wednesdays and holidays.

Stok Palace Museum, Stok, 17 km (11 mi.) from Leh, contains precious stones, thankas, ceremonial dresses, coins, and prayer instruments. Open 7 A.M.–6 P.M.

SPORTS AND OUTDOOR ADVENTURES. Bicycling. The Srinagar Tourist Reception Center (tel. 72449 or 77305) rents 10-speed bikes. You can also rent bikes in Leh from SECMOL (see address above).

Climbing and Mountaineering. Many mountains throughout the region are open to expeditions, with the season extending from mid-May to mid-October. Climbing a mountain demands advance planning and prior permission from the Indian Mountaineering Foundation (Benito Juarez Rd., Anand Niketan, New Delhi 110021, tel. 6883412). It can take months to get a climb approved. You can also join one of the organized expeditions offered by tour operators in *Facts at Your Fingertips.*

Fishing. Acclimatized varieties of trout attain greater size and are more plentiful here than in their original European or North American habitats. Sturdy equipment is therefore required for fishing in Kashmir's fast waters. The trout fishing season is March–October, and the mahseer fishing season, August-September. Licenses are available from the *Directorate of Fisheries,* Tourist Reception Center, Srinagar (tel. 72449) and at Jammu, Nowabad Canal Road (tel. 47804). Both are open 10 A.M.–2 P.M. Monday–Saturday. Licenses are issued for a maximum of three days at Rs. 75 per rod per day.

This same office periodically publishes maps showing beats and the routes leading to them. It's not necessary to bring your own equipment; rods, reels, lines, and lures may be hired locally. Fishing in the Sindh and Liddar rivers is usually poor from mid-May–mid-July due to the cold water.

Golf. There are excellent golf courses in Srinagar, Gulmarg, and Pahalgam. *Srinagar Golf Club's* links: nine holes and double-flag 18 holes. *Gulmarg Golf Club's* course is good; it was redesigned to fill international standards and is probably the world's highest at 2,697 meters (8,700 feet). Spring and autumn tournaments are held both in Srinagar and in Gulmarg (June and September). For details, contact the Tourist Reception Center, Srinagar; tel. 72449 or 77305. Contact *Kashmir Government Golf Club,* Maulana Azad Rd., Srinagar (tel. 76524) for reservations and temporary membership details; Rs. 40 per day.

Gulmarg Golf Club has temporary membership available; tel. 39 for details. *Pahalgam Golf Club* also has temporary membership available; tel. 51, for details.

Horseback Riding. Contact the tourist departments in Gulmarg, Pahalgam, and Sonamarg to arrange rides. You can also go by pony for up to a week on the Amar Nath Pilgrimage (see Trekking, below).

Rafting. In Zanskar, Ladakh, experienced rafters can make a six-day run from Padam to the Indus River (mid-July–mid-September). Arrange in advance through Himalayan River Runners (see Tour Operators, above).

Skiing. This is a popular sport in Gulmarg from December to March, when the meadow is covered by a thick blanket of snow 2–3 meters (6–10 feet) deep. The annual skiing competition is held in three stages during this period. There are now several ski lifts, and all equipment can be hired. Skiing courses are run by the Indian Institute of Skiing and Mountaineering. Information is available from any Government of India Tourist Office or from Commissioner of Tourism, J & K Government, Srinagar. An enjoyable winter holiday with lodge-style hotels, but don't expect European standards for skiing facilities—at least not yet.

Trekking. The soaring heights and scenic grandeur of the Inner Himalayas can best be viewed by hiking. Starting points of the treks indicated here (and there are many more) can be reached in comfort by bus or taxi. Guides, supplies, ponies, and *mazdurs* (porters) are available at all these points. Since good tents are for hire at several places in Kashmir and Leh, we suggest that you carry tents even if there are tourist lodges and forest rest houses along the route. In this way, you will be completely independent. Light double-fly tents of medium size are recommended; they can be easily carried by pack ponies or porters and offer adequate resistance to hazardous weather.

For a list of reliable tour operators who'll give you a great personalized trek, see Tour Operators, above or in *Facts at Your Fingertips.* The tourist department will be able to help you arrange ponies and porters and will advise you about hiring charges, which should be fixed before you start. The best time to trek in Jammu and Kashmir is April–November; in Ladakh, July–September.

You are well advised to contact the tourist offices in Srinagar, Gulmarg, Pahalgam, Sonamarg, Kargil, Padum, or Leh to get a thorough briefing on the latest conditions of the routes, the location of potentially dangerous streams and snow bridges, and other details before setting out. Carry all the food you need. You'll find little to buy. Also, if you're trekking above 3,100 meters (10,000 feet), pay attention to the warning about high-altitude sickness (see *Facts at Your Fingertips*). Here are some of the more popular trek routes, rated by degree of difficulty.

JAMMU AND KASHMIR

Trek 1. Amarnath Cave. This strenuous trek (July or August) starts at Pahalgam, near Srinagar, and ends at the sacred Amar Nath Cave. Bring tenting gear. You'll follow the Lidder River, pass flower-strewn meadows, cross the Mahagunus Pass, then wait with thousands of chanting devotees to see the revered lingam. Children under 12 are not allowed. To go by pony, arrange in advance with the Tourist Reception Center in Srinagar (address above). Five to seven days. Moderately difficult.

Trek 2. Vaishno Devi. Make a 13.5-km (8-mi.) trek to the venerated cave that honors three Hindu goddesses. This is a spiritually charged excursion that begins at Katra, near Jammu. One day. Easy.

Trek 3. Kishtwar to Lehinvan or Srinagar. From Kishtwar near Jammu, you'll head over the Margan Pass into the remote Marwa and Warvan valleys, with their gorges, rivers, glaciers, rice paddies, flowering meadows, and orchards. You'll share the trail with mule trains and shepherds. Relax in hot springs in Totawoin village; get a close look at Himalayan peaks. You can extend this trek to 25 days and go through Ladakh's Zanskar Valley across windswept passes to Leh. At least nine days. Difficult.

LADAKH

Ladakh has extensive possibilities of high and difficult trekking and challenging climbing. There are innumerable towering peaks, most of them unnamed and unclimbed. The Suru and Zanskar valleys are excellent areas for trekking in the shadow of the high peaks of Nun and Kun. The Zanskar Valley can be approached from Kargil in about a week's trekking. The 4,340-meter (14,000-foot) high pass of Penzi-La has to be crossed to reach the valley. There is a "jeep-able" road following the River Suru up to Rangdoom Gompa, about 130 km (81 mi.) from Kargil. It is necessary to take all equipment, which can be hired in Srinagar, Manali, or Leh. Here are the more popular possibilities:

Trek 1. Around Leh. Trek to Lamayuru, Shey, Hemis, and Thikse monasteries and hike through Ladakh's mountaintop landscape of sand dunes surrounded by snow-covered peaks. Five to seven days. Moderately easy.

Trek 2. Zanskar to Leh. From Zanskar Valley, you can do a tough, high-altitude trek from Padam, the district headquarters. You'll cross a rope bridge; wind through gorges; climb up steep ridges and over passes; and, if you're lucky, see wild animals. You'll meet Tibetans, Ladakhis, and yak herders. You can also go from Zanskar to Manali via Lahaul. 12 to 14 days. Difficult.

Wildlife Sanctuaries. *Dachigam National Park,* 21 km (13 mi.) from Srinagar. This former royal game preserve belonging to the maharajah is now a protected sanctuary and is home to leopard, Himalayan black bear, brown bear, hangul (Kashmir stag), musk deer, and numerous birds. The best time to visit is June–October. Tourists need a special permit from the Chief Wildlife Warden, J & K Government, Tourist Reception Center, Srinagar; tel. 75411.

Hemis High Altitude National Park, 35 km (22 mi.) from Leh, is the natural habitat of ibex, snow leopard, rare bharal sheep, great Tibetan sheep, and high-altitude birds, including the Himalayan snow cock. Best viewing season is September–May. For passes or permission to camp, contact the Wildlife Warden, Tourist Reception Center, Leh; tel. 497.

Kishtwar High Altitude Park near Jammu has musk deer, Himalayan black and brown bear, and 50 species of birds. Best viewing season is March–May. No pass is required.

SHOPPING. Carpets, woodwork, and shawls take pride of place among the handicrafts of Kashmir. From Ladakh come soft, snug *pashmina* tweeds and shawls made of the belly-wool of the Himalayan goats, and Tibetan-style jewelry of jade and turquoise, set in beaten silver. The Kashmir Valley craftspeople produce decorative articles in papier-mâché in three grades. In the first, pure gold leaf is used; it is rarely exported due to high customs rates. Here is your chance to buy on the spot at reasonable prices bowls, boxes, and trays of amazing richness of detail and beauty of Oriental design. Other products worthy of attention are *gaba* and *numda* rugs. Gaba are thin and light and can be hung up on the wall like tapestries. Numda are made of thick, light-colored felt with embroidered flower designs. Also good are embroidered wall hangings and fashion fabrics, leather and fur coats, bags, Kashmir silk, and carvings in walnut wood. Time and again you will be accosted by hawkers; first make sure they have a Tourist Department registration card, then start your bargaining session.

NIGHTLIFE AND BARS. Due to the political unrest in Srinagar, bars have been closed. In the rest of the state, the best bars are in the hotels and serve liquor 11 A.M.–3 P.M. and 6–11 P.M.

WESTERN AND CENTRAL REGION

BOMBAY

City on the Move

by
KATHLEEN COX

Razzle-dazzle Indian style—that's Bombay, the country's most trendy city. Its superb harbor provides the city with the country's busiest port. Its airport is also India's most active for international arrivals and departures. And Bombay is not only the financial hub of India, it is one of the largest manufacturing centers in the East.

The capital of Maharashtra rests on the Arabian Sea, an island set off from the rest of India by a winding creek. Perhaps it's this separation that sets Bombay's culture apart from that of the rest of India. Bombay's culture is new, vibrant, and often aggressive, reflecting the affluence and energy of a busy city of 9 million people. People often compare this city with New York and insist that, like New York, it's a place you either love or hate. Bombay hits you with that kind of intensity. Its streets are crowded with traffic; Bombay has its share of gridlock. It can also be Manhattan-style expensive.

But in many ways, Bombay is a city unto itself. It's distinctly tropical, with pockets of palm trees and warm, salty breezes that keep you aware of the Arabian Sea. Its weathered Victorian mansions, some still privately owned, and grand public buildings, many beautifully lit at night, stand as a lingering reminder of the days of the British Raj. Then there's the presence of wealthy Arabs in elegant white robes who come to this city—their favorite playground—especially on weekends. Bombay, or "Bollywood" (a sobriquet it achieved when it surpassed Hollywood as the world's largest movie production center), *is* a great playground—a great city to explore and a walker's delight, with miles of shorefront promenades.

While emperors, rajahs, and foreign invaders were warring along the river valleys and plains of India, the marshland islands (initially Bombay consisted of seven) remained untouched for many centuries by any but the fishing tribes. Yet the Arabian Sea connected these tribes—along with the inhabitants of the rest of India—to Africa. It was the sea that brought trade to the subcontinent even before the days of the Roman Empire and the sea that brought Europeans who first conquered, then modernized. The sea, in fact, created Bombay.

The first people known to have taken an interest in Bombay's harbor were the Portuguese in the early 1500s. (Vasco da Gama arrived at Calicut, farther south, in 1498.) Bom Bahai (Bombay) was ceded to the Portuguese in 1534 by the sultan of Gujarat in a treaty that was meant to keep them at bay. Some time later, had it not been necessary to add to the desirability of a royal princess, Bombay's destiny would have been different: Bombay or Mumbai or Mumbadevi—no one knows the exact derivation—was given as a dowry to Charles II of England in 1661, when he married Catherine of Braganza.

The British occupied the islands, began to join them, and established a fort and trading post. Around this time a young Marathi leader, Shivaji, was amassing power and his own kingdom in the nearby Western Ghats. An astute guerrilla-style fighter, he made some raids on the British and used the booty to fight his wars with the Mogul Emperor Aurangzeb. Although British-held Bombay was within his territory, Shivaji was too occupied with the Great Mogul—chasing and being chased—to prevent the British from growing in strength. Eventually Indians, who saw opportunities for trade and shipping, came to Bombay. The city grew in importance as other towns faded.

After many years of intrigue, betrayals, and mismanagement, the territory Shivaji had governed fell under the British. The *Peshwas,* the ministers who took over the rule of Maharashtra from the royal line, lost the Fourth Maratha War in 1818. The pride the British had in Bombay and their power over the western region are symbolized in Bombay's most celebrated landmark near Shivaji's statue, the Gateway of India, built to commemorate George V's visit in 1911.

An interplay of favorable circumstances made Bombay into India's industrial metropolis and one of Asia's busiest seaports. When the menace of Maratha sea raiders was finally broken, the East India Company's ships began to call at Bombay. Weavers from Surat settled there and, by 1850, the first cotton mills made their appearance. The outbreak of the American Civil War gave a further boost to this industry, as did a major land reclamation project in 1862 that joined the seven small islands into one. Soon coastal steamer services were started, followed in 1869 by the opening of the Suez Canal, which revolutionized Bombay's maritime trade with Europe. Since then, this go-ahead city never looked back, and today Bombay claims 15 percent of all factories in the country and its textile industry accounts for 40 percent of the country's total.

In the past few decades, there has been a lot of reshuffling. In 1956, the Bombay State created at independence was enlarged to include other Marathi- and Gujarati-speaking areas. Such a mammoth territory meant there were 48 million people talking in the main two languages, administered by one roster of government officials. A good deal of energy was wasted on linguistic controversy. Eventually the whole area was reorga-

Race Course

Haji Ali's Tomb

Mahalakshmi
Temple

KESHAVRAO KHADE MARG

Golf Course

LALA LAJPATRAI MARG

Tardeo

3

BELLASIS

FALKLAND

BHADKAMKAR ROAD

Dr. A. PREMJI MARG

ROAD

MAULANA SHAUKATALI

TARDEO ROAD

Dr. GOPALRAO DESHMUKH MARG

ALTAMOUNT ROAD

BHULABHAI DESAI (WARDEN ROAD)

AUGUST KRANTI MARG

Arabian Sea

GIRGAUM ROAD

4

PATEL RD

VITHALBHAI PATEL RD

SARDAR

LAXMIBAI JAGMOHANDAS MARG

BAL GANGADHAR KHER MARG

WALKESHWAR ROAD

CHARNI RD

SHANKAR SHET RD

5

Chowpatty

13

M KARVE RD

NETAJI SUBHASH RD (MARINE DRIVE)

Back Bay

Walkeshwar
Temple

11

6

Nariman
Point

1. Victoria Gardens & Zoo	9. Churchgate Station
2. **Victoria Terminus**	10. Town Hall
3. Central Station	11. Raj Bhavan
4. Hanging Gardens & Towers of Silence	12. Hutatma Chowk (Flora Fountain)
5. Jain Temple	13. Aquarium
6. **MTDC**	14. St. Thomas Cathedral
7. General Post Office	15. Foreigner's Registration Office
8. Government Tourist Office	

BOMBAY

0 500 1000 Yards

0 500 1000 Meters

Jacob Circle

COM. BABURAO JAGTAP MARG

N.M. JOSHI MARG

ROAD

MAULANA AZAD

CLARE RD

Museum and Zoo

1

Gloria Church

MOTISHAH ROAD

NESBIT ROAD

S CHAPSI MARG

Mazagon Garden

WADI BUNDER RD

ROAD

ROAD

PAREL ROAD

BABULANATH RD

JAIL RD

Round Temple

C.P. TANK ROAD

SARDAR PATEL ROAD

DONGRI ROAD

NANDLAL JANI RD

D'MELLO ROAD

Mumbadevi Temple

MOHAMED ALI ROAD

ABDUL REHMAN ST

KALBADEVI ROAD

CARNAC RD

N

Cross Island

15

PALTAN ROAD

M. KARVE ROAD

LOKMANYA TILAK MG

Municipal Corporation

2

Harbour

H. SOMANI MG

MAHATMA GANDHI RD

DADABHOY NAOROJI RD

7

MINT RD

8

9

14

Ballard Pier

VEER NARIMAN RD

Cricket Stadium

12

Rajabai Tower

10

Museum

MADAM CAMA RD

GEN. BHONSLE MARG

N PAREKH MARG

SHAHID BHAGAT SINGH RD

Gateway of India Apollo Bunder

to Elephanta Caves

nized into Maharashtra and Gujarat states. The population of the state has grown rapidly since its reorganization, and the region is now among the most prosperous in India.

Exploring Bombay

Not far from the Gateway, beyond the Colaba market, is a village of the Kolis, one of the original fishing tribes. Although one word has a *c* and the other a *k,* you can see the connection. They speak Marathi, but they have their own ways. No one disputes a Koli woman's place in the bus line. The Koli women carry their fish all over town, walking with a fine stride, saris worn, Marathi fashion, skintight between their legs, and their hair, slicked back, with flowers. They do the marketing of the fish, and they keep the money. The men master the waves and bring home the fish. They are a sociable group, spending lavishly on weddings and dancing and playing games all night on festive occasions.

The southern tip of the island is held by the Army and Navy. Within the military area is St. John's Church, called Afghan, because it was built to commemorate soldiers killed in the nineteenth century Afghan campaigns. Its spire can be seen from all over Bombay. Gravestones that once crowded cemeteries near churchyards used to tell the gruesome story behind Britain's attempts to maintain its hold on India: cholera, plague, and malaria hit the families as soon as they entered the harbor.

In contrast to this part of the city is Churchgate, named for the gate in the old fort wall nearest St. Thomas's Cathedral. This area is all reclaimed land. The Mantralaya (State Secretariat), which houses some important government offices, faces an inlet of the sea. Here also is the new, acoustically perfect Tata Theater (National Center for the Performing Arts), which holds regular performances of Indian classical music and dance. At Nariman Point is a rising modern complex of skyscrapers, housing offices, and hotels. Included are the Air India Building, with the country's only rooftop helipad, and a luxurious penthouse atop the Express Towers that the late Indian press baron Ramnath Goenka called home.

Marine Drive

Between here and Hutatma Chowk (Flora Fountain)—Bombay's hub— are some of the city's most interesting institutions; the Indo-Saracenic Prince of Wales Museum and the nearby Jahangir Art Gallery; University Hall and the Rajabai Tower, which commands a panoramic view of the commercial heart of Bombay. Close to the harbor are the Mint, which you can visit by special arrangement, and the Town Hall, with its wide sweep of steps.

Skirting along Back Bay is Marine Drive, famous as the Queen's Necklace, which can be seen at night from Malabar Hill's Hanging Gardens. Every evening strollers walk on the extensive promenade parallel to the drive where coconut hawkers from Kerala, wearing ankle-length white cloths wrapped around the waist, sell their refreshing drink and *kulfiwallahs;* their baskets of Indian ice cream covered in a red cloth offer another popular treat.

Chowpatty Beach, with its statue of Tilak, a great political leader of this century, is Bombay's political nerve center. There are other places for big meetings in Bombay, but this site on the sea, accessible to thousands streaming in from all parts of the city and traditionally used for big festivals, gives a particular significance to any statement or decision made there.

This is where millions teem on big days such as Ganesh Chaturthi, when rich and poor, frail and hearty move to the sea with clay or plaster or even silver or gold representations of Ganesh, the elephant-god. On any evening of the year, Chowpatty is busy; yogis bury themselves in the sand, fishermen haul in their nets, children romp, and hungry working people flock to the stalls for *bhel-puri* (a popular snack) and colored drinks.

Not far from Chowpatty, at 19 Laburnum Rd. (off Pandita Ramabai), is Mani Bhavan, a private home that Mahatma Gandhi visited occasionally. Today, the building is preserved as a national memorial and museum, containing a pictorial exhibit and a library, as well as a glassed-in preserved room where the Mahatma studied and slept.

Farther north, at the end of a causeway that leads out to the Arabian Sea, is the lovely white Haji Ali Shrine, built in honor of this Moslem saint who drowned here years ago. You can only visit the mosque and his tomb at low tide. Nearby is Bombay's oldest Hindu temple, the Mahalakshmi Temple, which is dedicated to Lakshmi, the goddess of wealth. Inside the inner sanctum, the images of three goddesses—Mahalakshmi, Mahakali, and Mahasaraswati—are appropriately adorned with gold jewels and pearls.

Malabar Hill

The east side of Malabar Hill, which you see from Chowpatty, is covered with greenery topped by the Kamala Nehru Park. Up on Malabar Hill and below it on the west side by the sea are the mansions of wealthy industrialists who made their fortunes mainly in textiles. (Cotton grows in many places just north of Bombay and in what is now the state of Gujarat.)

B. G. Kher Road runs along the top of Malabar Hill. It leads past steep roads winding down to the Arabian Sea; many movies set in Bombay find a place for a car chase on these curving streets. On the hill is "Varsha," the residence of the chief minister of the state. Also on Malabar Hill is the Walkeshwar Temple, dedicated to Shiva. Legend claims that Lord Rama stopped here on his way to Sri Lanka to search for his consort, Sita. To retrieve her, he was told to worship Shiva, so he built a symbolic lingam of sand (*walaka*) on this hill.

Bombay's Parsees

The greenery on the left as you go beyond the gardens is part of the Parsee Towers of Silence, the place where the Parsees dispose of their dead. (There is a model of the towers in the Prince of Wales Museum.) A park surrounded by a high wall nearly conceals these bastions. Even relatives of the deceased are not allowed to go beyond a certain point within the enclosure, but stay in the park where they can sit and meditate. Bearers carry the body to the top of one of these cylindrical towers, where it is laid out and devoured by waiting vultures. The skeleton—after a few days' exposure to the elements—is then thrown down the tower's well, where it returns to dust.

This strange method of disposal has a twofold explanation. The Zoroastrian religion—of which the Parsees are the last surviving community—respects the earth and the fire too much to pollute them with the bodies of the dead. Another tenet declares that rich and poor must unite in death.

Originally, the Parsees were from the city of Pars in Persia. About 1,300 years ago they fled their homeland to escape Moslem persecution. Today, they represent a small minority of Bombay's population; but their economic and cultural influence is considerable. Largely responsible for building up the city's trade and industry, many of India's leading businessmen and philanthropists are members of this community.

A World of Markets

Bombay, like most cities in India, has numerous shopping haunts waiting to be explored. Visit early one morning the Mahatma Jyotiba Phule Market (formerly Crawford Market), at the junction of Dadabhoy Naoroji Road and L. Tilak Road, and walk through Bombay's fresh-produce emporiums. If it's late spring or early summer, treat yourself to a delicious Alphonzo mango, a food worthy of the gods, and, anytime of the year, have fresh sherbet or *faluda* (an Indian milk shake) at the famous Badshah Cold Drink Depot and Annexe. From here, wander into nearby Jhaveri and Dagina bazaars, Bombay's crowded jewelry markets, where shops are filled with fabulous gold and silver in every conceivable design.

Chor Bazaar's Mutton Street near the Kutbi Masjid is a narrow thoroughfare lined with stores that are crammed with antiques—clocks, victrolas, brass, and glassware. Allow yourself plenty of time to poke through the shops. Finally, if you want to add to your Western wardrobe, go to Fashion Street (on M. G. Road, opposite the Bombay Gymkhana Club). Here, open-air stalls feature the latest styles at give-away prices.

Environs of Bombay

If you arrive in Bombay by air, Juhu beach is the first strip of land you'll see as the plane descends. A glimpse is all you get, but you must return to Juhu later. On the way, you'll cross the Mahim Creek. In this fishing village at low tide you can study the heavy ancient boats designed for the rough seas. Juhu, once a secluded spot, is now crowded on weekends because of its good resorts and beaches. When the tide turns, the undertow can become hazardous for the unwary.

Those who are interested in historical ruins should plan a day trip north of Bombay to the Kanheri Caves, 42 kilometers (26 miles), and Fort Bassein, 76 kilometers (47 miles). The Kanheri Caves, comprising 100 caves cut into the top of a hill, are one of the largest groups of Buddhist underground chambers in western Indian. The earliest caves were created in the second century, with many of them simple cells that were occupied by Buddhist monks for over 1,000 years. A few of the caves have interesting pillars, sculptures, and interior stupas. The fifteenth-century Bassein Fort was ceded to the Portuguese in 1534 by Gujarat's Sultan Bahadur. This fortified town remained in their hands for 205 years, when it was conquered by the Marathas. British bombardment in 1780 damaged it heavily, but you can still see the civic and ecclesiastic vestiges of this once-prosperous Portuguese city. The *Porta do Mar* (Sea Gate) near the fort commands a splendid view of the sea.

During this excursion, you can also visit the Lion Safari Park, near the Kanheri Caves. Here you can see the Indian lion, roaming free, while you travel around in small buses.

The Elephanta Caves

Elephanta Island, one of Bombay's major tourist attractions, as well as a reminder of India's past glories, is an hour's launch ride from the Gateway of India. Exactly who carved the cave temples on the island, originally called Gharapuri, or when, is not known. It is known, however, that the

Portuguese renamed the island Elephanta after a large stone elephant found near the landing place. (The figure collapsed in 1814 and was subsequently moved to Victoria Gardens and reassembled.)

Shortly before the time of Elephanta's excavation (between the sixth and eighth centuries) Bombay had experienced the Golden Age of the late Guptas, during which the talents of artists had a free scope. Sanskrit had been finely polished, and Kalidasa and other writers—under the Court's liberal patronage—had helped to bring about a revival of Hindu beliefs. It is the worship of Shiva, or Shaivism, that inspired these temples. That Shiva was well loved and the many ramifications of his personality well understood is shown by the polish and refinement of the artwork in the caves.

Crossing Bombay harbor on the way to Elephanta, you'll see centuries of India's life literally sailing before your eyes. The fishing sailboats in the harbor seem as much a part of the picture as do the modern liners. Tankers come full to Butcher Island, to the left of Elephanta. Their oil goes to Bombay's refineries. Behind them are the Tata electricity plant and the institute connected with atomic energy.

A flashlight and a knowledgeable guide on the island will help you to sort out the figures shown in the sculptures. You would have to be thoroughly familiar with Hindu mythology to fully understand each detail. But you cannot mistake the expressions on Shiva's faces, nor their intent. The powerful representations of strength, love, and spiritual peace at first seem buried in the dark halls. As you stay longer, they appear to grow and the walls to vanish, and you see them as a world in themselves. Part of the impression conveyed at Elephanta is the unity of dissimilar things, and likewise the differentiation one personage can undergo. Shiva gives good scope for such a portrayal.

The sculptures are great art, not only in the sense that they are beautifully executed, with a secure knowledge of the subject and a superb technique of the chisel, but also because they show things we don't ordinarily think of as being there and combine apparently independent parts into new entities.

The outside of the main cave consists of a columned veranda 9 meters (30 feet) wide and four meters (six feet) deep, approached by steps flanked by sculptured elephants. At each end of the façade is a pillar projecting from the wall, carved in the shape of a *dwarapala* (doorkeeper). The entire temple is 40 meters (130 feet) square. The main sculptures are on the southern wall at the back. Three square recesses contain giant figures of dwarapalas. The panel to the left shows a manifestation of Shiva combining the male and female forms, while on the right panel you'll see the figures of Shiva and his consort, Parvati. The central recess in the hall contains the most outstanding sculpture, the unusual *Mahesamurti,* the Great Lord Shiva, a 6-meter (18-foot) triple image. The three faces represent three aspects of Shiva as the creator on the right, the preserver in the center, and the destroyer on the left. The multiheaded deity is a composite of the stern, just, loving, father figure, an expression of the monotheistic tendency of Hinduism. On either side of the recess are pilasters carved with gigantic dwarapalas.

Other sculptures at the doorways and on side panels show Shiva's usefulness. Shiva brought the river Ganga (Ganges) down to earth—the story says—letting it trickle through his matted hair. The facts of the universe are played with in wild delight, represented through this god's acts. Shiva is also depicted as Yogisvara, lord of yogis, seated on a lotus, and as Nataraja, the multiarmed cosmic dancer. The beauty of this sculpture lies in the grace, balance, and sense of relaxation conveyed in spite of the multiple action.

The fact that these sculptures were, in many cases, damaged by the Portuguese soldiery does not detract from their beauty. The serenity of facial expressions triumphs over the loss of arms and legs. In the magnificently fierce scene of Shiva destroying the demon Andhaka—he seems to be emerging from clouds in which his legs are hidden—one overlooks the broken rocks, so powerful is the remaining portion.

PRACTICAL INFORMATION FOR BOMBAY

WHEN TO GO. The best time to visit Bombay is November to April. For the next few months, the city turns very hot. In August and September the monsoon brings lots of rain and humidity.

HOW TO GET THERE. By Air. Numerous international carriers fly in and out of Bombay, including *Air India,* Air Canada, Air France, British Airways, Delta, KLM, Lufthansa, Swiss Air, and Royal Nepal. *Indian Airlines* connects Bombay with all major cities, including daily flights from Ahmedabad, Bangalore, Bhopal, Calcutta, Calicut, Cochin, Coimbatore, Delhi, Goa, Hyderabad, Indore, Jaipur, Jodhpur, Madras, Mangalore, Trivandrum, Udaipur, and Vadodara. There are also occasional flights every week from Bhubaneshwar, Bhuj, Gwalior, and Lucknow. *Vayudoot* has occasional flights every week from Goa, Patna, Ranchi, Varanasi, and Indore. For information in Bombay, call Air India (tel. 2024142), Air Canada (tel. 2027632), Air France (tel. 2025021), Delta (tel. 2029020), KLM (tel. 2211185), Lufthansa (tel. 2020887), Swiss Air (tel. 2870122), Indian Airlines (tel. 2876161), and Vayudoot (tel. 2048585).

By Bus. *Maharashtra State Road Transport Corporation* runs deluxe buses to Bombay from Goa, Bangalore, Mangalore, Indore, Baroda, and Hyderabad. For details and tickets, visit the MSRTC counter at the Central Bus Stand, Bombay Central, or Parel Depot. For information, contact the Central Bus Stand (tel. 3095424).

By Train. Regular trains connect Bombay with Agra, Ahmedabad, Bangalore, Bhopal, Bhubaneswar, Calcutta, Cochin, Delhi, Goa, Gwalior, Hyderabad, Indore, Jaipur, Jodhpur, Madras, and Trivandrum. Contact *Western Railway,* Churchgate, tel. 4933535 (arrival information), tel. 291952 (first-class reservations), tel. 375986 (second-class reservations); or *Central Railway,* Victoria Terminus Station, Bori Bunder, tel. 2043535.

By Ferry. At press time, the overnight ferry service between Bombay and Goa had been resumed. For details and booking, contact the *Maharashtra Tourism Development Corporation* (MTDC), address below.

By Rented Car with Driver. Fairly good roads connect Bombay with the following major cities: Vadodara (Baroda), 432 km (268 mi.); Ahmedabad, 545 km (338 mi.); Panaji, Goa, 597 km (370 mi.), and Hyderabad, 711 km (441 mi.). If you choose to travel by road from Bombay, hire a car with driver from one of the recommended tour operators listed below. Figure about Rs. 5–Rs. 6 per km and a halt charge of Rs. 50–Rs. 100 per night.

TOURIST INFORMATION. You can contact these two good sources of information on Bombay: The *Government of India Tourist Office* (123 Maharshi Karve Rd., Churchgate, tel. 293144) is open 8:30 A.M.–6 P.M., closed Sundays. Every second Saturday of the month, it also closes at 2:30 P.M. You'll also find a counter at both airports. The *Maharashtra Tourism Development Corporation,* or MTDC (C.D.O. Hutments, opposite L.I.C. Bldg., Madam Cama Rd., tel. 2026713 or 2027762), is open 9:45 A.M.–5:30 P.M., closed Sundays and the second and fourth Saturdays of every month. Its bus tour and hotel and resort bookings counter (same location) is open daily 9:45 A.M.–5:30 P.M.

FOREIGN CURRENCY EXCHANGE. Most Western-style hotels have money-exchange counters. Otherwise, try *ANZ Grindlays',* 90 Mahatma Gandhi Rd., tel. 275367; *American Express,* Regal Cinema Bldg, near Council Hall, Colaba, tel. 2048291; *Thomas Cook,* D. Naoroji Rd., tel. 2048556; or a branch of the *State Bank of India.* The banks are open Monday–Friday, 10 A.M.–2 P.M.; Saturday, till noon. American Express is open Monday–Friday, 9:30 A.M.–7:30 P.M.; Saturday and Sunday, 9:30 A.M.–5:30 P.M.

ACCOMMODATIONS. Hotels in Bombay range from compact places with the barest essentials to grand and luxurious structures catering to the visitor's every need. Many new hotels have been built in the main city, but one should book well in advance for these, especially in the winter season, November–February. Prices are based on double occupancy and exclude service charges and taxes: *Deluxe,* over Rs. 2,000; *Expensive,* Rs. 1,200–Rs. 2,000; *Moderate,* Rs. 500–Rs. 1,200; *Inexpensive,* under Rs. 500. Most Western-style hotels take major credit cards.

Deluxe

The Leela Kempinski. Sahar, Bombay 400059, tel. 6363636, fax 6360606; in the U.S., tel. 800–426–3135; in Britain, 0800–898580. 430 rooms with bath, including 8 rooms for the handicapped. Close to the airports and 25 km (16 mi.) from the city, this is a stylish hotel with 9 acres of gardens that include a small waterfall. In the huge lobby water cascades down to the lower level. Modern, spacious rooms have TV and air-conditioning. Ask for a view of the pool. The hotel has restaurants, bars, room service, shops, health club, swimming pool, tennis court, foreign-exchange and travel counter, business center, free shuttle to airports and city. AE, DC, MC, V.

The Oberoi. Nariman Point, Bombay 400021; tel. 2025757, fax 2043282. 350 rooms with bath. This elegant sky rise has a marble high-tech atrium lobby where musicians frequently play classical music. Air-conditioned rooms are modern with an understated contemporary decor and TV. Ask for a room with an Arabian Sea view. Besides a floor butler for each floor, the Oberoi has room service, numerous restaurants, health club, swimming pool, foreign-exchange and travel counter, shopping arcade, business center, doctor. AE, DC, MC, V.

The Oberoi Towers. Nariman Point, Bombay 400021; tel. 2024343, fax 2043282. 650 rooms with bath. Less sumptuous than the Oberoi, but still modern and elegant, this high rise adjoining it is also less pricey. Even-numbered rooms have an Arabian Sea view; odd-numbered rooms have a distant harbor view. All rooms are air-conditioned and furnished in a quiet, modern decor. The same services are available as at the Oberoi (above), except no floor butlers. AE, DC, MC, V.

Taj Hotel President. 90 Cuffe Parade, Colaba, Bombay 400005; tel. 4950808 or 800–458–8825 in U.S., fax 2151201. 319 rooms with bath. This Western-style high rise has a spacious marble lobby. Air-conditioned rooms, done up in a modern decor, offer panoramic views as well as TV and room service. There are multicuisine restaurants, bar, health club, swimming pool, foreign-exchange and travel counter, business center, and shopping arcade. AE, DC, MC, V.

Taj Mahal Hotel. Apollo Bunder, Bombay 400039; tel. 2023366 or 800–458–8825 in U.S., fax 2872711. 347 rooms with bath. This Victorian beauty was constructed at the turn of the century. Its white-trimmed, granite exterior faces Bombay's harbor and commands great views. Each floor opens onto an interior veranda that draws your eyes to the handsome central dome and skylights. Air-conditioned rooms are spacious, with a contemporary decor. The best rooms have a harbor view. Included are TV, room service, multicuisine restaurants, bar, pool, health club, business center, doctor, bank, foreign-exchange and travel counter, and a shopping arcade. AE, DC, MC, V.

Taj Mahal Intercontinental. Same address, phone, and fax as above. 303 rooms with bath. This 24-floor high rise adjoins the Taj Mahal Hotel and offers less expensive, but still very deluxe-priced, air-conditioned rooms that are spacious and have contemporary decor. Ask for a harbor view. Amenities include the same services available at the Taj Mahal Hotel. AE, DC, MC, V.

Expensive

The Ambassador. Veer Nariman Rd., Churchgate, Bombay 400020; tel. 2041131, fax 204004. 127 rooms with bath. The old-fashioned lobby to this 1940s high rise is charming, with lots of marble, pretty chandeliers, and antiques. Air-conditioned rooms are simply furnished, but they're spacious. Included are TV, room service, multicuisine restaurants, bar, foreign-exchange and travel counter, shop, secretarial services. AE, DC, MC, V.

Hotel Natraj. 135 Netaji Subhash Rd., Bombay 400020; tel. 2044161, fax 2043864. 83 rooms with bath. Facing the Arabian Sea, this Western-style high rise has a comfortable, small lobby and air-conditioned rooms that are adequately furnished but not fancy. Ask for a deluxe room that overlooks the water. The Natraj offers TV, room service, multicuisine restaurant, bar, foreign-exchange and travel counter, bookshop. AE, DC, MC, V.

Moderate

Garden Hotel. 42 Garden Rd., Colaba, Bombay 400039; tel. 241476, fax 2871592. 32 rooms with bath. A pleasant marble lobby distinguishes this intimate Western-style hotel. Air-conditioned rooms are clean, small, with modest furnishings and tiny balconies. TV, room service, multicuisine restaurant. Good value. Rupees only.

Hotel Godwin. 41 Garden Rd., Colaba, Bombay 400039; tel. 241226. 48 rooms with bath. Another small hotel, the Godwin has an inviting lobby and spacious airconditioned rooms that are also very moderately priced and clean. TV, room service, roof garden with squawking geese, multicuisine restaurant. Good value. AE, DC, MC, V.

Ritz Hotel. 5 Jamshedi, Tata Rd., Bombay 400020; tel. 220141. 74 rooms with bath. The lobby is unpretentious; the location is central. This 45-year-old hotel was once owned by an Italian who added minor streamlined art deco details to the architecture. Rooms are clean and have simple Western furnishings. TV, room service, restaurants, bar, foreign-exchange counter, travel assistance, shops. Good value. AE, DC, MC, V.

Inexpensive

Chateau Windsor Guest House. 86 Veer Nariman Rd., Churchgate, Bombay 400020; tel. 2043376. 40 rooms with bath. Don't be put off by this hotel's location on an upper floor of an older high rise. The lobby is modest, and the rooms are simply furnished but clean, quiet, and have private balconies. The management also aims to please. Some rooms are air-conditioned. TV, room service, doctor, travel agent. Rupees only.

BOMBAY SUBURBS

Bandra

Deluxe

Welcomgroup Searock Sheraton. Land's End, Bandra, Bombay 400050; tel. 6425454, fax 6408046. 400 rooms with bath. Set on a rocky beach, this modern high rise has a spacious white-brick lobby and air-conditioned rooms with handsome contemporary furnishings. Best rooms overlook the swimming pool and sea. The beach, however, is too rocky for bathing. TV, room service, multicuisine restaurants, bar, swimming pool, tennis, health club, yoga and aerobics, foreign-exchange and travel counter, business center, doctor, shopping arcade, golf on request, free shuttle to city and airports. AE, DC, MC, V.

Juhu Beach
About 20 km (12 mi.) from Bombay Center

Expensive–Deluxe

Centaur Juhu Beach. Juhu Tara Rd., Juhu, Bombay 400049; tel. 6113040, fax 6116343. 366 rooms with bath. This gigantic Western-style high rise is set on the beach but feels like a city hotel inside. Air-conditioned rooms have a contemporary decor, with no sense of the tropics. Best rooms offer a beach view; only deluxe-priced suites face the sea. Numerous multicuisine restaurants, bar, TV, room service, secretarial service, swimming pool, health club, good swimming beach, foreign-exchange and travel counter, shopping arcade, free airport shuttle service. AE, DC, MC, V.

Holiday Inn. Balraj Sahani Marg, Juhu, Bombay 400049; tel. 6204444, or 800–HOLIDAY in U.S., fax 6204452. 210 rooms with bath. This Western-style high rise has a spacious lobby and modern air-conditioned rooms decorated with splashes of red. Best rooms offer a partial beach view; only deluxe-priced suites face the sea. Room service, multicuisine restaurants, bar, TV, health club, two swimming pools, tennis and squash courts, good beach with windsurfing, foreign-exchange and travel counter, business center, shops, free shuttle to Bombay center. AE, DC, MC, V.

Ramada Inn Palm Grove. Juhu Beach, Bombay 400049; tel. 6147466, or 800–2–RAMADA in U.S., fax 6113682. 114 rooms with bath. The lobby of this Western-style high rise has lots of marble and etched glass. Air-conditioned rooms are spacious, with a subdued decor. Best rooms offer a limited view of the beach; only deluxe-priced suites and executive rooms face the sea. Room service, multicuisine restaurants, bar, TV, health club, swimming pool, good beach with windsurfing, business center, foreign-exchange and travel counter. AE, DC, MC, V.

Expensive

Hotel Sea Princess. Juhu Beach, Bombay 400049; tel. 6122661, fax 6113973. 72 rooms with bath. This attractive, modern high rise has a pleasant, small lobby. Air-conditioned rooms are cheery and simply decorated in contemporary decor. Best rooms offer a partial beach view; only expensive-priced suites face the sea. Multicuisine restaurants, bar, room service, TV, swimming pool, good beach, foreign-exchange and travel counter, shops. AE, DC, MC, V.

Moderate

Sun 'n' Sand. 39 Juhu Beach, Bombay 400049; tel. 6201811, fax 6202170. 119 rooms with bath. A great tropical ambience is offered at this Western-style hotel, with an intimate lobby that leads out to a garden terrace overlooking the beach. Air-conditioned rooms are newly renovated with a modern decor. Best rooms offer a view of the beach; only expensive-priced rooms face the sea. Multicuisine restaurants, room service, bar, TV, swimming pool, good beach, health club, foreign-exchange and travel counter, shops. Good value. AE, DC, MC, V.

DINING OUT. In Bombay, you can expect great meals and a wide choice of cuisines: Continental, Chinese, and numerous regional Indian dishes, including Mughlai, Goan, Gujarati, Rajasthani, and Maharashtra's own Malwani. Many restaurants tend to be pricey, but some tasty bargains will leave you and your wallet quite satisfied. While we include only our selection of the best restaurants, many hotels also have restaurants. Breakfast is usually 8–10:30; lunch, 12:30–3; and dinner, 8–11:30. The restaurants listed below are informal and, unless noted, are open for all three meals and don't require reservations. Prices are based on a three-course dinner for one person, excluding beverage, tip, and taxes: *Deluxe,* over Rs. 300; *Expensive,* Rs. 200–Rs. 300; *Moderate,* Rs. 100–Rs. 200; *Inexpensive,* under Rs. 100.

Deluxe

Kandahar. The Oberoi, Nariman Point; tel. 2025757. Featuring tasty, robust North West Frontier cuisine, this elegant restaurant with quiet decor has a view of the sea and a glass-enclosed tandoori kitchen. Try the tandoori *khinga* (king-size prawns marinated in yogurt and spices, then cooked in a tandoor), *kebab-e-chandni* (deboned chicken drumsticks stuffed with minced chicken, chilies, and cheese), or the special flavored *parathas* (layered flat bread). Reservations advised. Open 12:30–3 P.M. and 8–midnight. AE, DC, MC, V.

Mewar. Oberoi Towers, Nariman Pt; tel. 2024343. *Gumbaz* (domes) and *jhakoras* (windows) are covered with embroidered silk; paintings of Rajasthani maharajahs adorn the walls; *santoor* and sitar performers entertain nightly, except Tuesday. The cuisine is Indian in this regal ambience. Try *ker sangri* (exotic cactus and vegetables stir-fried in mustard oil), *murgh makhmali kebab* (boneless chicken coated with cheese and cream), or *jhinga pardanashin* (prawns with mustard seed cooked in a coconut shell). Reservations advised. Open 12:30–3 P.M. and 8–midnight. AE, DC, MC, V.

Tanjore. Taj Mahal International, Apollo Bunder; tel. 2023366. This Indian restaurant, with lots of marble, serves tasty tandooris and north Indian dishes on beautiful silver-plated, banana-leaf-shaped plates. At dinner, you can also enjoy Indian classical dance performances. Specialties include *thalis* (assorted dishes served on a platter), *rann-e-Kabul* (leg of lamb marinated in chili, ginger, and garlic and cooked slowly), and *achaari jheenga* (prawns marinated in yogurt and spices and cooked in a tandoori oven). Reservations required. Open 12:30–3 P.M. and 7:30–11:45 P.M. AE, DC, MC, V.

Zodiac Grill. Taj Mahal International, Apollo Bunder; tel. 2023366. This Continental cuisine restaurant is Western-style elegant, with subdued lighting, handsome chandeliers, captains in black jackets, waiters in black or white (including white gloves), and a pianist playing softly in the background at dinner. Specialties include lobster *chambery* (lobster pieces cooked inside puffed pastry with a mustard-cream sauce) and *camembert dariole* (cheese soufflé). Also enjoy a bottle of imported wine. Reservations required. Open 12:30–3 P.M. and 7:30 P.M.–midnight. AE, DC, MC, V.

Expensive

Copper Chimney. Dr. Annie Besant Rd., Worli; tel. 4924488. Murals of exotic birds, brass planters hanging from the ceiling, and subdued lighting set an elegant tone at this popular Indian-cuisine restaurant. The tandooris are excellent, especially *reshmi kebab* (mildly spiced and barbecued boneless chicken). Reservations advised. Open 11:45 A.M.–3:45 P.M. and 6:45 P.M.–midnight. AE, DC, MC, V.

Gaylord Restaurant. Mayfair Bldg., Veer Nariman Rd., Churchgate; tel. 221259. This 40-year-old institution, which serves Continental and Indian cuisines, has an Anglo ambience—upholstered chairs, Victorian mirrors, small crystal lamps, marble floors, and a handsome upstairs balcony. Try the lobster Newburg or *murg makhani* (boneless chicken cooked in tomato curry with cream). Gaylord's also has café seating out front. Reservations advised for indoor restaurant. Café open 10 A.M.–11:30 P.M. Restaurant open 12:30–3:15 P.M. and 7–11:30 P.M. AE, DC, MC, V.

Khyber Restaurant. 145 Mahatma Gandhi Rd.; tel. 273227. This is one of Bombay's most attractive restaurants, with six delightful rooms done up in a North West Frontier decor—terra-cotta urns, copper trays, handsome murals. The waiters, dressed in Pathan tribal garb, serve delicious Mughlai and North Indian food, including pomfret green masala (fried pomfret stuffed with tangy green chutney and scallions) and *Khyber raan* for two (leg of lamb marinated overnight, then roasted in a clay oven). Very popular. Reservations advised. Open noon–4 P.M. and 7:30–midnight. AE, DC, MC, V.

Ling's Pavilion. 19/21 K.C. College Hostel Bldg., Lands Downe Rd.; tel. 2850023. Entering this elegant new restaurant is like walking into a Chinese watercolor. Recessed ceiling lights duplicate a nightime sky; and there's a perfect tree, a bridge, and a pond, as well as numerous wall murals. Waiters dressed in Chinese finery serve the mainly Cantonese cuisine, with the accent on fresh seafood. Reservations advised. Open 12:30–3 P.M. and 7–11:30 P.M. DC, MC, V.

Society. Ambassador Hotel, Veer Nariman Rd., Churchgate; tel. 2041131, ext. 504. If you're in the mood for Continental cuisine and want a good steak, visit this cozy Victorian restaurant, with parquet floors, mirrors, and deep-red-velvet decor. Their best steak is named after a former maître d'—Steak à la Fernandes—and it's cooked at your table. You can also get good flambés. Reservations advised. Open 12:30–3 P.M. and 7:30–11:45 P.M. AE, DC, MC, V.

Moderate

Chetana Vegetarian Restaurant and Bar. 34 K. Dubash Marg, Kala Ghoda; tel. 222514. Chetana's Rajasthani decor—handblocked fabrics on the ceiling and traditional torans on the walls—provides a cozy ambience in which to enjoy tasty Gujarati *thali* (small portions of assorted regional dishes) at lunch and delicious Rajasthani cuisine at dinner. Sample these Rajasthani dishes: *daal bati* (lentils), *ker sangri* (cooked cactus), *kadhi* (curd curry), *gatteka saag* (cooked vegetable and gram flour dish), and *mint raita* (curd and mint salad). There is great service, with more waiters than tables. Reservations advised. Open noon–3:30 P.M.; 3:30–6:30 P.M. for snacks, and 7–11 P.M. Rupees only.

Goa Portuguesa. Mili Bldg., Kataria Rd., opposite Mahim Head Post Office; tel. 454776. Designed like a modern Goan cottage, this charming restaurant serves such Goan dishes as spicy *rechiad* fish (pomfret stuffed with red Goan masala) and prawn *balchao with pao* (pickled prawns prepared in a curry with palm vinegar). Every night except Tuesday and Thursday, you're serenaded with live Goan music. One of Bombay's hot spots; reservations are advised. Open noon–3:30 P.M. and 7–midnight. AE, DC, MC, V.

Kamling Chinese Restaurant. 82 Veer Nariman Rd., Churchgate; tel. 2042618. This spacious restaurant with traditional Chinese decor—red-enamel pillars and lanterns—serves fine Cantonese cuisine. Specialties include chicken Peking style (fried with spring onions and soy sauce) or prawns Manchurian style (fried prawns with garlic, ginger, and chili). Dinner reservations advised. Open noon–11:30 P.M. DC, MC, V.

Inexpensive

Hotel Sindhudurg. Sita, R.K., Vaidya Rd., Dadar; tel. 4301610. The signboard is in Marathi, not English. This simple ethnic eatery has three small rooms filled with booths and patrons. It serves Maharashtran Malwani cuisine—tasty non-vegetarian and vegetarian thalis. Open 11:30 A.M.–3 P.M. and 7–11:30 P.M. DC.

Wayside Inn. 38 K. Dubash Marg, Kala Ghoda; tel. 244324. Plants lined up on open windows, whirring overhead fans, and the owner's collection of crockery and mugs on walls and in sideboards create an inviting casual atmosphere. On Tuesday, Thursday, and Saturday, enjoy Parsi cuisine, such as *dhansak* (brown rice cooked with meat or chicken and ground vegetables) or pomfret stuffed with chutney and cooked in a banana leaf. On other days, try the popular pomfret and chips. Open 9 A.M.–7 P.M. Rupees only.

SWEETS AND TREATS. *Bhel-puri* (a delightful concoction of rice, dahl, and chutneys served with puffed fried bread) is a popular snack available throughout Bombay, especially at the beaches. Follow this hearty, inexpensive meal with mixed *kulfi* (five-flavored Indian ice cream), usually available from the same vendor. One especially good stand is at Chowpatty Beach, next to the Mafatlal Swimming Pool.

For good Bengali sweets, join the crowd at *Brijwasi Sweet Shop* at Churchgate (near Ambassador Hotel). Try *gulab jam* (sweet balls in sugary syrup) or *malai* sandwiches (a milk-and-sugar-based sweet with heavy-duty calories). Make a special trip to *Badshah Cold Drink Depot and Annexe* (Umrigar Bldg., opposite Mahatma Phule Market, i.e., Crawford Market) and have some memorable fresh ice cream, sherbet, and *faluda* (milk shake) in yummy original flavors. Open 7:15 A.M.–11 P.M. daily.

HOW TO GET AROUND. From the Airports. The *Airport City Coach Service* will take you to Bombay's Nariman Point on the hour 2–5 A.M. and 7 A.M.–11 P.M. from the international airport (Rs. 30) and every hour on the half hour 2:30–5:30 A.M. and 7:30 A.M.–11 P.M. from the domestic airport (Rs. 25). A taxi from the airports to Nariman Point will cost about Rs. 200. Try to get the driver to use his meter, and once you arrive at your destination ask to see the tariff card, which is used to convert the meter amount into the revised rate; otherwise set the fare before you depart.

By Bus. Buses are cheap, but they're slow going in Bombay's traffic.

By Train. Bombay city is interlinked with an extensive local electric train network. Rates are determined by the distance to the destination. At every station, the train stops for only 15 seconds. To avoid traffic jams and for economic traveling, use local trains, which are the best alternative, although they tend to get overcrowded during rush hours. Trains start for western suburbs from Churchgate and for eastern suburbs from Bombay Victoria Terminus.

By Rented Car with Driver. Rates vary with the make of the car. A non-air-conditioned Ambassador (cheapest) should run about Rs. 5–Rs. 6 per km, with an 80 km (50 mi.) minimum. Use one of the tour operators listed below.

By Taxi. Taxis should cost about Rs. 7 for the first km, then per tariff card for each additional km.

By Auto Rickshaw. Since Bombay traffic can be slow going, these small three-wheeled vehicles are often the best way to get around. Rates are Rs. 4.50 for the first km, then the meter fare is calculated by the latest tariff card.

TOURS. *India Tourism Development Corporation* (ITDC) and *Maharashtra Tourist Development Corporation* (MTDC) offer city bus tours (9 A.M.–1 P.M. and 2–6 P.M., except Mondays) that include the Gateway of India, Aquarium, Prince of Wales Museum, Hanging Gardens, Jain Temple, and Kamla Nehru Park. ITDC tours depart from Nirmal Building, Nariman Point (tel. 2023343 for details). MTDC also offers a suburban tour (10 A.M.–7 P.M. daily) that includes Juhu Beach and Kanheri caves; and a boat cruise to Elephanta Caves with guided tour (9–1, 10–2, 11–3, and 2:30–6:30). Contact MTDC for departure points for bus tours (address and phone under Tourist Information, above). The MTDC launch to Elephanta leaves from the Gateway to India. Many tour operators, listed below, also offer similar tours to these destinations.

Private Guides. The Government of India Tourist Office (address above) can arrange for an excellent guide. For 1–4 persons, figure Rs. 125 (half day) or Rs. 175 (full day).

TOUR OPERATORS. The following reliable agencies can take care of your travel needs, including a rented car with driver: *Cox and Kings* (272 D. Naoroji Rd., Bombay 400001, tel. 2043065); *Jetair Tours* (41–42 Maker Chambers III, Nariman Pt., Bombay 400021, tel. 223275); *Travel Corporation India* (TCI, Chander Mukhi Bldg., Nariman Pt., Bombay 400021, tel. 2021881); *Tradewings* (30 K. Dubash Marg, Bombay 400023, tel. 2443340); and *Sita World Travel* (Atlanta Bldg., Nariman Pt., Bombay 400021, tel. 240666).

Odyssey Tours (1307 Everest Apt., J.P. Rd., Versova, Andheri [W], Bombay 400061, tel. 6271690, fax 6271691) in collaboration with MTDC is trying to establish four- and eight-day luxury cruises by yacht (20-passenger capacity) between Bombay and Goa, with stops along Maharashtra's coastline. These cruises will hopefully run between October and April. Contact Odyssey or MTDC for details.

SEASONAL EVENTS. The specific dates for many events are determined by the lunar calendar; contact the Government of India Tourist Office or MTDC for details. The following festivals take place throughout Maharashtra, exclusively in Bombay, or in some other state destination.

January. *Makar Sankranti.* During this festival, which marks the passing of the sun from Dhanu to Makar, sweets are exchanged.

February. *Elephanta Festival of Music and Dance.* Wonderful cultural shows are performed for three nights in this annual festival held at the famous caves. A beautiful event.

February/March. *Holi.* On this day that marks the start of spring, wear old clothes. Celebrants throw colored water on anything that moves.

February/March. *Shivratri.* This Hindu festival honors Shiva with special celebrations at important Shiva temples.

March. *Ellora Festival of Classical Music and Dance.* For three nights, India's best performers entertain under the moonlight, with the historic Kailas Temple as a backdrop.

March/April. *Gudhi Padva.* This is the Maharashtrian New Year; *gudhis* (bamboo staffs), symbolic of victory and achievement, are erected and worshiped to ensure a good year.

July/August. *Narali Pournima.* This festival celebrates the full moon of Shravana. Fishermen decorate their boats, sing and dance, and offer coconuts to the sea to ensure their safety during the upcoming fishing season.

July/August. *Gokul Ashtami.* On Krishna's birthday, men and boys form human pyramids, then attempt to break money- and curd-filled earthen pots strung across the streets.

July/August. *Pola.* During this harvest festival, the invaluable bullock is bathed, decorated, then paraded through rural villages to the accompaniment of traditional music and dancing.

August/September. *Nag Panchami.* On this day, live cobras, venerated by Hindus, or their images are worshiped. In Battis Shirale, a village near Sangli, devout

Hindus show no fear—catching cobras, which they caress and worship, then release. This is also a good time to see Maharashtrian folk dances, especially in the countryside.

August/September. *Ganesh Chaturthi and Festival.* This 10-day festival marks the birthday of the Hindu's elephant-headed god. Elaborately crafted clay images of Ganesh are paraded through streets, installed on platforms and worshiped. On the 10th day, they're carried in enormous processions and immersed in the ocean or the nearest lake. This is an especially big event in Pune and Bombay, where some of the clay images are 9 meters (30 feet) tall. Pune events also include music and dances, bullock cart races, and foodfests.

September/October. *Navaratri and Dussehra.* Navaratri, meaning "nine nights," is a big celebration that precedes Dussehra, which honors the Hindu goddess Durga's victory of good over evil. Expect a lot of noise from fireworks and numerous fairs.

October. *Diwali.* On the Hindu New Year, nighttime candles and lamps light up homes to welcome Lakshmi, the Hindu goddess of wealth. There are numerous cultural events.

HISTORIC SITES. Entrance to most sites is generally free or costs a nominal fee; when a donation is requested, a few rupees will suffice. Historic sites are open daily sunrise to sunset, unless noted otherwise below.

Bassein Fort (north of Bombay) was built in the fifteenth century by Bahadur Shah Sultan of Gujarat. He ceded it to the Portuguese in the sixteenth century, when they ruled over the northern coast.

Elephanta Caves, off the Bombay coast, contain seventh-century temples that are dedicated to Shiva. The most important sculpture is the three-faced Shiva called Maheshamurti. The island is accessible by launch; MTDC offers an excellent tour (see Tours above).

Gateway of India, at Chhatrapati Shivaji Marg, is the landmark of Bombay, a 26-meter (85-foot)-high stone archway, designed by Wittett in the sixteenth century in Gujarati style and built to commemorate the visit of King George and Queen Mary to India in 1911. An equestrian statue of Chhatarapati Shivaji and a statue of Swami Vivekanand have been installed here.

Haji Ali Shrine, at the end of a causeway off Lala Laipaitra Marg, honors a Moslem saint who drowned here while on a pilgrimage to Mecca. When a casket containing the mortal remains floated and came to rest on a rocky bed in the sea, devotees constructed the tomb and mosque at this spot. It can be visited only during the low tide.

Jain Temple, B. C. Kher Marg on Malabar Hill, was built in 1904. The marble shrine is dedicated to Adinath, the first *tirthankara* (perfect soul). Interior recesses contain statues of the 24 tirthankaras of the Jain religion. Its walls have dazzling paintings that depict incidents in their lives. The ceiling shows the different planets as personified in the mythology.

High Court, at K. B. Patil Marg, is an attractive building constructed in early Gothic style. The central structure rises 54.2 meters (179 feet) and is surrounded by a statue representing justice and mercy. It was completed in 1878.

Kanheri Caves, 42 km (26 mi.) north of Bombay, has over 100 caves cut into rock, most of them created in the second century by Hinayana Buddhist monks who also lived here. Caves 1, 2, and 3 are especially noteworthy: massive pillars, sculptures, and stupas.

Mahalakshmi Temple, near Lala Laipaitra Marg, is dedicated to Lakshmi, Vishnu's consort and the Hindu goddess of wealth.

Mumbadevi Temple, near Jhaveri Bazaar, is dedicated to the Goddess Mumbai (Mother Earth). The original eighteenth-century Hindu temple was destroyed and replaced, years back, with this structure built by Koli fishermen. Tuesday is a big day of worship.

Municipal Corporation Building, at Mahapatra Marg, is the V-shaped building standing opposite Victoria Terminal. It is designed in early Gothic style, blended with Indian motifs. The dome, its chief architectural feature, is 71.5 meters (234 feet) from the ground.

Prince of Wales Museum, Mahatma Gandhi Marg, was built in 1911 and is named after Britain's King George, who laid the cornerstone in 1905. Its Indo-

Saracenic architecture, with a magnificent dome copied after the Gol Gumbaz in Bijapur, is one of Bombay's finest Victorian buildings.

Rajabhai Tower, located at K. B. Patil Marg, is 79 meters (261 feet) high. Its university clock tower also houses the university library. Built in nineteenth-century Gothic style, it commands a fine view of the city.

Royal Asiatic Society, Horniman Circle, was once the Town Hall. Now it houses the Asiatic Society Library, one of the oldest and largest in the city, and statues of former British rulers.

St. John's Church, Malabar Hill, was built in 1857 and is dedicated to the British soldiers who fell in the Sind and Afghan campaigns of 1838 and 1843.

Surya Narayan Temple, Surajwadi, Panjiapol Lane, Bhuleshwar, was constructed in 1899 of white stone in honor of the sun god, Surya Narayan. The celestial gatekeepers, Jiy and Vijay, guard its entrance. In the inner sanctum, Surya Narayan sits on a one-wheel chariot drawn by a horse with seven heads and flanked by his two wives.

Towers of Silence, Malabar Hill, is a solemn area with three platforms on which the Parsees leave their dead. It's strictly off-limits.

Victoria Terminal, Dadabahai Noroki Marg, is one of the largest buildings in Bombay. Combining Indian and Gothic architecture, it was completed by the British in 1888. The imposing dome has a life-size statue of Queen Victoria and statues of peacocks, snakes, monkeys, and rats (all auspicious symbols). Its entrance is guarded by two stone lions.

Walkeshwar Temple, Walkeshwar Road, is a Hindu temple dedicated to Shiva, with a lingam supposedly created from *waluk* (sand) in its inner sanctum. Nearby is the Banganga Tank, where devotees purify themselves.

MUSEUMS AND GALLERIES. Entry fees are nominal. *Mani Bhavan,* Laburnum Road, a private home that the great leader Mahatma Gandhi visited, has been converted into a museum with an interesting collection of Gandhi memorabilia. Open 9:30 A.M.–6 P.M.; closed Sundays and Monday afternoons.

Nehru Planetarium and Science Museum, Lala Lajpat Rai Marg, has science exhibits and programs on astronomy (in English 3–6 P.M.). Open noon–7 P.M.; closed Mondays.

Prince of Wales Museum. Bombay's principal museum, located at Mahatma Gandhi Road. It is divided into three sections: art, archaeology, and natural history. The Tata family collection forms part of the archaeology and art sections. The natural history section was started with part of an admirable collection of the Bombay Natural History Society. The picture gallery contains, in addition to ancient Indian paintings, works by European and contemporary Indian artists and copies of Ajanta paintings. There is also a large collection of jade, crystal, china, lacquer, and metal objects, both ancient and modern. There are some excellent dioramas in the natural history section. The museum has an interesting collection of exhibits from the Maratha period. Open October–June, 10 A.M.–6:30 P.M.; July–September, till 6; closed Mondays.

Victoria and Albert Museum, situated in Byculla, is the oldest museum in Bombay. The three principal sections are those of natural history, archaeology, and agriculture. There is also a small collection of miscellaneous art objects. Most of the exhibits in the museum relate to Bombay and western India. There are displays of archaeological finds, maps, and photographs of Bombay's history. Open 10:30 A.M.–5 P.M. Mondays, Tuesdays, Fridays, and Saturdays; 10 A.M.–4:45 P.M. Thursdays; 8:30 A.M.–4:45 P.M. Sundays; closed Wednesdays.

Jahangir Art Gallery, near the Prince of Wales Museum at Mahatma Gandhi Road, is Bombay's main art gallery. In the same building is Pundole Art Gallery. Most galleries are open 10 A.M.–7 P.M.

PARKS AND GARDENS. *Ferozshah Mehta Gardens* (Hanging Gardens) at Bal Gangadhar Kher Marg, was laid out in 1881 on top of a reservoir that supplies water to many areas. A special feature of this garden is its topiary hedges that are pruned into animal shapes. A flower clock can also be seen here.

Veermata Jijabai Bhonsle Udyan, Victoria Gardens at Dr. B. Amdeker Rd., has a clock tower, ornamental gates, a varied collection of more than 300 wild plants and trees, and a sun dial, all adding to the beauty of the place, at a bandstand. From time to time, musical programs are performed. Elephant, camel, and pony rides are available for children. Open 8 A.M.–6 P.M.; closed Wednesdays.

Kamala Nehru Park at B. G. Kher Marg, was laid out in 1952. It is mainly an amusement park for children, named after the wife of the first prime minister of India. Civic receptions are also held here. On the slopes of Malabar hills, it offers a panoramic view of Marine Drive and Chowpatty Beach. It is illuminated on the Republic and Independence days.

Lion Safari Park, 38 km (23 mi.) from Bombay, gives visitors an opportunity to watch the Indian lion from special closed vehicles provided by the park. Open 9 A.M.–5 P.M. Closed Mondays and Tuesdays.

Taraporewala Aquarium, Marine Drive, contains interesting specimens of marine life as well as freshwater fish. Open Tuesday–Friday, 11 A.M.–8 P.M.; Saturday–Sunday, 10 A.M.–8 P.M.

SPORTS AND OUTDOOR ADVENTURES. Beaches. Bombay beaches in the main city are no longer clean or maintained properly by the authorities. They are rather crowded and dirty. Suburban beaches are a better alternative.

Chowpatty Beach, at the end of Marine Drive, is a popular beach in the center of the city, where the celebration of festivals such as Ganesh-Chaturthi immersion takes place. It is crowded most of the time, surrounded by kiosks and hawkers selling Bombay special snacks. The beach has become more of a venue for political meetings and gatherings than a place for swimming. The water is too polluted for that, anyway.

Juhu Beach, 21 km (13 mi.) from Bombay center, is a long stretch of beach fringed with palm and coconut trees. A popular beach for all, it has a number of hotels, cottages, and restaurants. MTDC and the YMCA run a water-sports center that offers windsurfing, sailing, water scooters, and speedboats. Horse, camel, and pony rides are also available. You can swim from October until May.

South of Bombay, MTDC is developing delightful tented beach resorts along its unspoiled and beautiful coast. See the Maharashtra chapter for details.

Horse Racing. Bombay's race course is one of the finest in the East. The racing season is November to April, Saturday and Sunday.

Sailing. Members of any yachting association affiliated with the Royal Bombay Yacht Club can charter a boat for local sailing. For rates and details, contact the club (Apollo Bunder, Bombay 400039, tel. 2021880).

SHOPPING. Bombay is a great place for shopping, with a diversity of options from bargain bazaars and open stalls to trendy boutiques and government-run emporiums. Shops are closed on Sundays unless noted otherwise. Here are some best bets:

Ensemble, Great Western Bldg., 130/132 Shahid Bhagat Singh Marg, sells exquisite designer *salwar kameez* (loose blouse and pants), antique scarves, handbags, and Western-style clothes for men and women. Very pricey, very beautiful. Open 11 A.M.–8 P.M. AE, V.

Kaysons Sari Shoppe, Stadium House, Veer Nariman Rd., sells high-quality silk by the meter, salwar kameez, and gorgeous silk scarves and stoles. Open 11 A.M.–8 P.M. AE, DC, MC, V.

Kala Niketan Silk and Saris, 95 Queens Rd., and neighboring stores also offer a wide range of silk from all over India, scarves, and stoles. Open 9:30 A.M.–7:30 P.M. AE, V.

Ajmal & Sons Perfumers, Shop No. 1, Cecil Court, Lands Downe Rd., behind Regal Cinema, has a wide range of pure essences from flowers, which is poured into small vials and boxed like precious jewelry. It's sold at very reasonable prices. Try morning breeze, lotus, night queen, and the heavenly pure white musk. Open 10 A.M.–7 P.M. Rupees only.

Phillips Antiques, Madam Cama Rd., opposite Regal Cinema Museum, has the best old prints, engravings, and maps in Bombay. This store also sells many treasures originally left behind by the British—Staffordshire and East India Company china, old jewelry, crystal, lacquerware, sterling silver. Open 9 A.M.–1 P.M. and 2:30–6:30 P.M. AE, DC, MC, V.

Natesan's Antiqarts, Jahangir Art Gallery and Taj Intercontinental Hotel, sells high-quality, guaranteed subcontinental antiquities: wood carvings, sculptures, and paintings, plus wonderful new artifacts. Can also export. Open 10 A.M.–7 P.M. daily. AE, DC, MC, V.

A. K. Essajee, Suleman Chambers, Side Street, opposite Cottage Industry, sells handsome old and new Indian curios and handicrafts: carved doors and chairs, old perfume bottles, jewelry, Rajasthani chests, Tanjore and Mysore paintings, old silver jewelry, silver, bronze, and Islamic artifacts. Also ships. Open 9 A.M.–7 P.M. AE, MC, V.

Tribhovandas Bhimji Zaveri, 241–43, Zaveri Bazaar, has fabulous gold jewelry and diamonds, plus other precious and semiprecious stones. It's crowded with merchandise and customers. Open 11:30 A.M.–7:30 P.M. AE, MC, V.

Ramesh Art Emporium and Pukhraj Jawanmal Surana, 47 and 48 Dagina Bazaar, Mumbadevi Rd., near the temple and Zaveri Bazaar, sells top-quality old and new silver jewelry, including good tribal pieces, and silver curios. Bargain. Open 9 A.M.–8 P.M. Rupees only.

MCS (Mehra Carpet Showroom), Crystal, 79 Dr. Annie Besant Rd., Worli, has an excellent selection of Indian carpets and *dhurries* (rugs). Open 10 A.M.–7 P.M. AE, MC, V.

Central Cottage Industries Emporium, 34 Chhatrapati Shivaji Maharaj Marg, by the Gateway, is a great place to pick up good gifts from all over India at fixed prices. Open 10 A.M.–7 P.M. AE, MC, V.

Also visit these good bazaars:

Fashion Street, opposite Gymkhana Club on M. G. Rd., is a row of stalls selling good Western clothes. Open 10 A.M.–8 P.M. daily. Bargain. Rupees only.

Chor Bazaar, Mutton Street near Kutbi Masjid, has numerous shops that sell antiques and curios, especially old phonographs, chandeliers, clocks, nautical instruments, brass and glassware. Open 10 A.M.–7 P.M. Rupees only.

NIGHTLIFE AND BARS. Check the daily newspaper for a listing of ongoing cultural performances. Since this is the world's largest film-producing country, Bombay certainly has its share of movie houses as well as actors and actresses. Indian films generally are extravaganzas, containing a bit of everything from romance and music to drama and suspense. Such films are called *masala,* after the all-purpose word for spices that are added to practically every dish. Few of the Indian-made films are in English, but some have subtitles. There are also some cinemas, such as the Foreign Film Theatres, that show films made in the United States or England.

Every Saturday (8 P.M.–midnight) and Sunday (4 P.M.–midnight) at the *Tourist Plaza* near the Prince of Wales Museum (K. Dubash Marg), you can watch Indian street performers, from acrobats to pop singers; have your hands decorated with henna; get your fortune told; and sample a range of cuisines.

Bombay's hotel bars are usually open 11:30 A.M.–3 P.M. and 6 P.M.–midnight or later. *Bayview Bar* in the Oberoi Hotel at Nariman Point is one of the prettiest—you sit in Art Deco surroundings and have a breathtaking view of the Arabian Sea. At night, you can dance to a live band (Sun.–Thurs. until midnight and on Fri. and Sat. until 1:30 A.M.).

MAHARASHTRA

Beaches, Forts, Sacred Caves

By
KATHLEEN COX

After a tour of fast-paced Bombay, you'll find Maharashtra's tempo much slower. Travel just a short distance and you'll escape the commercial world. You can head south along the coastline, where unspoiled beaches, backed by palm groves and dotted with delightful tented resorts, extend to Goa. Travel inland to the Western Ghats and you can relax in former British hill stations or explore old forts that still reign over their strategic locations. Go north and northwest and wander through cave temples, including the famous Ellora and Ajanta caves, where man's artistry became an epiphany in stone.

The area around Bombay is called the Fort Country of Maharashtra and was a stronghold of the legendary Shivaji, a great warrior. In the seventeenth century, Shivaji consolidated the power of the Marathas, who inhabited this region. Drawing inspiration from Hindu religious tales, he was fired by the idea of liberating his country from the grip of the Moslems. The tools were all there: a frugal, sturdy race of men and the hilltops of the Deccan Plateau, which could with little effort be made into impregnable small forts, excellent for highly mobile guerrilla warfare. The men under Shivaji were dedicated. They could scale the forts on these hills. They and their ponies could go where the elaborate Moguls could not.

There is the story of a Maharashtrian milkwoman who, after the gates of one of Shivaji's forts were closed, climbed down a supposedly unscalable wall to return to her baby at home. Shivaji rewarded her and reinforced the defenses. In 1680 he died, leaving behind a new, powerful nation. The Maratha influence spread all over central India and became all-encompassing.

EXPLORING MAHARASHTRA

About 74 kilometers (46 miles) north of Bombay, you'll begin to move toward Kalyan and Ambernath. The eleventh-century Ambernath Temple, covered with beautiful designs, is one of the best examples of Deccan temple architecture. A little difficult to find, the temple is in a valley between small hills, and there is a river running along the temple-compound wall; a grove of trees completes this hidden, contemplative site. Constructed in 1060 to commemorate a king of the Silhara dynasty and used for the worship of Shiva, this temple of exposed black rock has none of the commercial atmosphere of the paint and plaster city temples. Highly imaginative carvings, playful and spiritual, cover the temple inside and out. Though the hall is not big, the sculptured dome makes it seem spacious. The *lingam* (phallus) shrine is in a crypt, which you climb down into. For worship, flowers are thrown onto the lingam, and at intervals a temple priest throws water that flows out as holy water.

The next stop should be Nasik, 145 kilometers (90 miles) north of Bombay, one of the holy cities of the Hindus, who believe that Lord Rama, hero of the epic *Ramayana,* spent the major part of his exile here. Set on the banks of the Godavari, a sacred river, Nasik is also the site of the Kumbh Mela (held every 12 years), when pilgrims by the thousands come for a purifying dip that celebrates an old legend.

Long ago, the gods and demons discovered the existence of a *kumbh* (pitcher) that rested at the bottom of the sea. This kumbh contained a nectar that would make anyone who drank it immortal. During a 12-day battle over its possession, which resulted in Vishnu grabbing the kumbh on behalf of the gods, four drops of nectar fell—one each upon Nasik, Ujjain, Haridwar, and Allahabad. Since a day in heaven, the scene of the battle, equals a year on earth, each of these four cities, in rotation, now has a Kumbh Mela to celebrate this event.

Although this city figures prominently in Hindu mythology, its man-made treasures celebrate the Buddhist faith. Eight kilometers (five miles) southeast of Nasik are 23 rock-cut caves that were executed in the first century A.D. by members of the Hinayana sect, who were prohibited from creating the Buddha's image. A throne, a footstool, or footsteps symbolized his presence. Called the Pandu Lena caves, many of them were laid out as one-story *viharas* (monasteries) and their setting is unusual and impressive—chiseled out of a conical peak at the end of the Trimbuk Mountain. Caves 3, 8, and 18 are the best. In Cave 3, you'll find a *stupa* (reliquary mound), and in Cave 18, you can see a *chakra* (wheel)—both are important Buddhist symbols. The images of the Buddha were added later.

Matheran

Matheran, 105 kilometers (65 miles) north of Bombay, is a resort whose name means "woodlands overhead." The hill is an island of trees in an almost treeless plain. The approach to the town is in itself delightful. From

ISLAND of BOMBAY

Krishnagiri Nat. Park

DRAVI
Mandapeshwar Caves

Bassein

Borivli

Manor Beach

Kanheri Caves

Thana

Bhiwandi

Kalyan

Mumbra

Jogeshwari Caves

L.Tulsi

L.Vehar

SALSETTE

Juhu Beach

Airport

TROMBAY

Mahim Creek

BOMBAY

Belapur

Panvel

Elephanta Island & Caves

Uran

to Ahmedabad

to Nasik & Agra

Bassein

Bhiwandi

R. Kalu

Thana

Kalyan

Ambernath

Belapur

Neral

Panvel

Matheran

BOMBAY

Uran

Revas

Karnala Funnel

L.Shiravata

Karla Caves

Alibag

Pen

Khandala

Lonavla

Bhaja Caves

Cheul

Lohghand

Visapur

Pala

L.Mulshi

Pune

Kirkee

Mula

Khadakvasla

Murud

L.Kharakvasla

Simhagad

Janjira

Raigarh

Purandhar

Bhor

R. Nira

Mahad

Old Mahabaleshwar

Bankot

Mahabaleshwar

Wai

Pratapgarh

Panchgani

Wathar

Satara

R. Krishna

Anjanwel

Koyna Reservoir

Chiplun

to Kolhapur

Patan

ARABIAN SEA

Bombay Region

0 Miles 10 20 30 40

0 km 5 15 25 35 45 55 65

■ Temple □ Fort ⌂ Caves

Bombay, you can take a train to Neral, two hours out, where you'll see tiny, toylike trains that will take you to Matheran. The narrow-gauge railway of short, brightly painted wagons climbs leisurely through thickening woods and tunnels around sharp bends that wind into the hills.

An Englishman, Hugh Mallet, collector of Thane, built this little town. Before he arrived in 1850, there were three tribes who lived on the hill. The tribes are still here, but, like everyone else, they have adapted themselves and now benefit from the tourists who come here.

Varieties of tall trees, some moss- and orchid-covered, shade you as you walk. From the tops of Louisa and Echo Points to the west, you can see Bombay, its oil refineries, the Elephanta caves, Karnala funnel—a 47-meter (150-foot) pillar rising from a much-fought-over fort—and the sea. To the west of the hill is Parbal, which has a ruined fort. Between the hills roam panthers and wild boar. A path leading from One-Tree-Hill to the valley is named after Shivaji, who came to arrest an unworthy subordinate and stopped to worship at Matheran. Near the path is a Hindu shrine, from which three lingams are supposed to have emerged naturally from the rock.

The Karla and Bhaja Caves

Soft rolling hills quickly pass as the road levels out to the open planes between steep ranges. The solid black rock of the plateau, in some places 3,049 meters (10,000 feet) deep, is the home of many caves and forts. Just beyond Lonavla, 120 kilometers (74 miles) west of Bombay, is a turning point to the left for Karla Caves, created in the first century A.D. by Hinayan Buddhist monks, of the same sect that carved Kanheri. The main cathedral cave at Karla is the largest in the region. The sun window at the entrance was designed to slant the rays through its latticework toward the *stupa,* a dome-shaped focus of worship at the end of the prayer hall.

Before the caves were rediscovered and protected by the British, wild animals had possession. The Peshwas had taken advantage of the holy site to put up a temple just outside the entrance, and there are small Hindu shrines tucked in along the ledge of the hill for good measure.

A fairly rough road leads to the nearby Bhaja Caves. These 18 caves, in a lusher atmosphere than Karla, were probably meant for nuns and, created in the second century B.C., represent the earliest examples of rock-cut shrines in India. To the west of the caves is Longhand Fort. It was originally a Moslem fortification that Shivaji took twice but lost again. Behind and above Bhaja Caves is Visapur Fort.

Pune

Pune, in the Sahyadri Hills 163 kilometers (101 miles) from Bombay, makes a wonderful base for a trekking holiday. The former capital of the Peshwa administrations (1750–1817) and known until recently as Poona, the city was the capital of the powerful Maratha empire and is closely associated with the great warrior King Shivaji (1630–80).

On the south edge of town is Parvati Temple, a white building prominent on a hilltop among smaller shrines. Easily climbed stairs lead up to it. From here you can view the valley stretching to the first of the four ghats to be crossed on the way to Mahabaleshwar. It is said that after the defeat of the Marathas by Ahmed Shah Durrani at Panipat (1761), Balaji Bajirao was so heartbroken that he retired to Parvati Hill and died there.

Nonetheless, Pune recovered much of its former glory under Nana Peshwa in the latter part of the century. The saying *Jab tak Nana, tab tak Pune* (as long as Nana lives, Pune will live) expressed its faith in him. But the last year of the empire was filled with strife, and in 1817 Pune finally fell to the British at the Battle of Kirkee. Under them, the city developed into the "monsoon capital" of Bombay Province and became a large military center.

Today, Pune is distinctly divided into the spacious cantonment and the crowded old city, where localities have been named after days of the week. Pune is also the home of the Osho Commune International, whose guru was Bhagwan Shree Rajneesh who once had his ashram in Oregon and who prior to his death took to calling himself Osho. Today, visitors who have an obligatory white robe and have test results that prove that they're AIDS-negative and who also leave behind their drugs, cigarettes, and cameras, are welcome to attend a nightly meeting where they can supposedly still feel Osho's presence as they pray before his empty white throne.

Fort Country

Four forts in the vicinity of Pune are worth an excursion. Ahmadnagar, a historical Moslem city 82 kilometers (51 miles) to the north, is named after Ahmed Nizam Shah, founder of the Nizam Shahi dynasty, who built the city in 1490. Sixty years later, its main landmark, the fort, was erected by Hussain Nizam Shah. This battle-scarred citadel lies behind 2½ kilometers (1½ miles) of walls. It gained notoriety when the British used it as a prison for Boer War captives in 1901, and in 1942 for Indian nationalist leaders, including Nehru. The Moslems also left behind other monuments, including Chand Bibi, the tomb of a royal minister, and the Alamgir Dargah, the tomb of Emperor Aurangzeb, who died at Ahmadnagar at age 97 in 1707 (his body was later removed to Aurangabad). Shivneri, farther north, is the birthplace of Shivaji and the site of the impressive Shivneri Fort.

Heading south to Mahabaleshwar, you should visit the Sinhagad and Purandhar forts, 25 kilometers (16 miles) and 38 kilometers (24 miles) respectively from Pune. Also connected to this great Maratha warrior, these elaborate forts once had stables for horses (and often for elephants), caches for hiding treasures and men, extensive underground tunnels, outlandishly high and thick walls, semicircular towers, and access that was purposely steep and difficult that usually led to gateways that were hidden from view.

Mahabaleshwar

Winding roads lead through the ghats to Maharashtra's most popular hill station, Mahabaleshwar, 120 kilometers (74 miles) from Pune. As you climb the last ghat, the valley below seems significant. On the right, just before the little city of Panchgani, is a promontory called Harrison's Folly. Farther away is another outreach of land, Sidney Point. From here, you can look up to the top of Krishna Valley, marked by a cone-shaped hill.

Finally you'll reach Mahabaleshwar, a tiny village with many hotels. As in so many hill stations, here you'll find crowds of tourists, horses galore to ride, and numerous good views of the surrounding valleys. You can also find some unexpected treats: fresh strawberries and fresh rose petal and strawberry ice-cream, available in season. You can also use Mahabaleshwar to see two more forts that figure into Shivaji's military exploits: nearby Pratapgarh Fort, which was built in 1656, and Raigarh Fort, 80 kilometers (50 miles) away.

Aurangabad

Aurangabad, 375 kilometers (233 miles) northwest of Bombay, takes its name from the Emperor Aurangzeb, the last of the great Moguls, who made it his capital. Here, since time immemorial, the sounds of history have thundered. And in the numerous fine monuments that lie in the region, you can see the influences of various empires, religions, and philosophies. Here lie the seventh-century Aurangabad cave temples—the historic medieval fortress of Daulatabad, with its miles of forbidding ramparts, once, oh so briefly, the capital of Hindustan.

Aurangabad today is a ghost town of legends, with its alleyways steeped in lore. It is the gateway to Ajanta and Ellora and is the most convenient headquarters for a trip there. And as a city in its own right, Aurangabad has many places of interest that will captivate the tourist. It is better to visit the caves here before visiting Ajanta and Ellora, for anything after them might well seem to be an anticlimax.

First there is the Panchakki. This pre-Mogul (seventeenth-century) monument is a mill where water was harnessed to turn large stones to grind flour. It serves as the tomb of a Moslem saint, Baba Shah Musafir, who was buried there in 1624. Baba Shah Musafir lies in a simple grave surrounded by gardens, fountains, basins, and an artificial waterfall.

Just three kilometers (about two miles) from the city center is a far more grandiose affair—the Bibi-ka-Maqbara, the mausoleum built in 1679 by Aurangzeb for his wife, Rabia-ud-Daurani. It is a rather pale imitation of the Taj Mahal, the masterpiece of his father, Shah Jahan, but it's impressive if you haven't seen the Taj. The exterior lacks symmetry and balance, and its interior decoration has nothing comparable with the wonder at Agra. Yet this royal resting place has its own splendor and grace.

Also nearby are Daulatabad and the Aurangabad caves. Daulatabad, a medieval fortress on a pyramid-shaped hill 15 kilometers (nine miles) from the city, was originally known as Devagiri, the "Hill of the Gods." During the fourteenth century, it was renamed Daulatabad, the "City of Fortune," by the sultan of Delhi, Muhammad Tughlak, who decided to move his capital there, 1,129 kilometers (700 miles) away. He moved the whole population of Delhi, too, but after thousands died on this forced march, he ordered the survivors to march back to Delhi. Daulatabad remained. The fort is surrounded by five kilometers (three miles) of walls, and a visit here means a climb to the top of the rock, 183 meters (600 feet) high. When you get there, you are greeted by a huge cannon, six meters (20 feet) long, which somehow got there in the seventeenth century. One feature of the climb through the citadel is a spiraling tunnel 46 meters (150 feet) long near the top. Its upper entrance is crowned by an iron lid where defenders lighted a fire of hot coals to scorch besiegers in the tunnel. The Chand Minar pillar at the base of the fort was built as a victory column.

And then there are the Aurangabad caves, of which Caves 6 and 7 have the best sculptures. The other caves are separated by hills. At Aurangabad, the caves reproduce two forms of religious structures: the place of worship, or chaitya, and the monastery, or vihara. Carved out during the seventh century, the caves are later forms in Mahayana style. This style can be seen in such temples as Cave 1, with a Buddha on a lotus seat supported by snake-hooded demigods; or Cave 2, where a huge Buddha sits with his feet on a lotus; or Cave 3 with 12 carved pillars and another seated Buddha in front of his shrine. In the second group, which is a mile away, Cave 7 is interesting, with its huge figure of Bodhisattva Padmapani. (A Bodhisattva is a near-Buddha and one of the forms through which Buddha passed before he achieved enlightenment; *padmapani* means lotus-in-hand.) He is praying for deliverance from eight fears that are illustrated dramatically in stone: fire, the enemy's sword, the chains of slavery, shipwreck, attacks by a lion, snakes, a mad elephant, and death portrayed as a demon.

Ellora and Ajanta Caves

Long forgotten and rediscovered by chance in 1819, the cave temples of Ajanta and Ellora rank among the wonders of the ancient world. Here, over a period of 1,400 years—between the second century B.C. and the fifth century A.D.—great armies of monks and craftsmen carved cathedrals, monasteries, and whole cities of frescoed sculpted halls into the solid rock faces. Working with the simplest tools and an ingenious system of reflecting mirrors to provide them with light, they cut away hundreds of thousands of tons of rock to create the cave temples. The precision of their planning, their knowledge of rock formations, and the delicacy and profusion of their art have been called an art form "worthy of the Renaissance," created by a religious fervor as intense as that of medieval Europe. Between them, the cave temples span three great religions—Buddhism, Hinduism, and Jainism.

First came **Ajanta.** It is believed that a band of wandering Buddhist monks first came here in the second century B.C. searching for a place to meditate during the monsoons. Ajanta was ideal—peaceful and remote from civilization. The setting was spectacular: a sharp, wide horseshoe-shaped gorge that fell steeply to a wild mountain stream flowing through the jungle below. The monks carved crude caves into this rock face for themselves, and a new temple form was born.

Over seven centuries, the cave temples of Ajanta evolved into a work of splendid art. Today, there are 29 caves in all; some of them were once monasteries, others were *chaityas,* or Buddhist cathedrals. All of them are intricately and profusely decorated with sculptures and murals depicting the many incarnations of Buddha.

Here, as a flickering light shines on the massive murals in the darkness, fables from the Buddhist texts come alive: Princes and princesses go about the splendid ritual of their lives; dancers perform to the sounds of a silent lute; richly caparisoned elephants and horses prance; celestial musicians play their instruments; great scenes of drama are enacted in courts, palaces, and bazaars; and a whole era comes to life again. But everywhere, at all times, spirituality flows deep and quiet below the surface.

Despite their age, some of the paintings have retained their freshness and vivid detail wrought in rich earth colors, lampblack, and lapis lazuli. The paintings depict the life and teachings of the Buddha. A large segment, including some of the most exquisite paintings, is devoted to the Buddha's earlier life as a prince surrounded by beautiful women, luxurious settings, and details of court life.

The Ajanta caves are like chapters of a splendid epic in visual form. Natural light brightens the caves at different times of the day, and structural engineers are awestruck by the sheer brilliance of those ancient masters who, undaunted by the limitations of seemingly crude implements and tools, material, and labor, created this marvel of art and architectural splendor.

As at Ellora, monumental façades and statues were chipped out of hard rock. But Ajanta was given an added dimension by its unknown creators, a dimension expressed in India's most remarkable examples of cave paint-

AJANTA

CAVE TEMPLES

(2ND c BC TO 7TH c AD)

W - A - G - H - O - R - A   R - I - V - E - R

ings. The artists lovingly told the story of the Buddha and, at the same time, portrayed the life and civilization they knew. Time has damaged some of these masterpieces, but the vivid colors and the flowing lines that remain continue to astound experts. True, this was religious art, but it was living art as well. When the electric spotlights flicker onto the paintings, the figures seem to come alive. Life was good then, and love was open. Modern art never succeeded in paying tribute to woman in the way it has been done at Ajanta.

There are 29 caves in all, but they are much smaller than those at Ellora, because the sculptors had to work on a much smaller site. The caves here have no courtyards; instead they were originally carved with steps leading to the river below. Only four caves are chaityas, while the rest are viharas. The best paintings are to be found in Caves 1, 2, 16, 17, and 19, and the best sculptures are in Caves 1, 4, 17, 19, and 26.

The paintings at Ajanta are called frescoes, although they were not executed in the true fresco technique developed in Italy. Here, a rough rock wall was covered with a plaster made from clay and cow dung mixed with chopped rice husks in a layer about a half-inch thick. On top of this layer, a smooth coat of lime was applied, and then the painter began his work. First, the composition was outlined in red and then an undercoating was applied. All the colors used at Ajanta were of local origin: red ocher, burnt brick, copper oxide, lampblack, and dust from green rocks that had been crushed. The outline was accentuated and highlights were added before the surface of the mural was polished to a shine.

The life of the Buddha and the illustration of tales from Buddhist fables, or *jatakas,* are the two main themes of the caves at Ajanta. The total effect is that of a magic carpet transporting you back into a drama played by nobles, wise men, and commoners. The caves are numbered from west to east, not in chronological order.

The earliest cave, which dates from 200 B.C., is Cave 13. However, it is only from A.D. 100 that the exquisite brush and line work begins. Caves 9 and 10 have a chaitya in a hall filled with Buddhas, dominated by an enormous stupa. In breathtaking detail, the *Shaddanta Jataka,* a legend about the Buddha, is depicted in a continuous panel in Cave 10.

Opinions vary as to the most exquisite of the Ajanta caves. Most popular are those in Cave 1, of the Bodhisattva Avalokitesvara and Bodhisattva Padmapani. Padmapani, or the "one with the lotus in his hand," is credited by the sculptures as being the alter ego of the Lord Buddha and who assumed the duties of the Buddha when he disappeared. The Avalokitesvara is the most esteemed of the Bodhisattvas and is known as the Sangharatna, or "jewel of the order." Padmapani is depicted with his sinuous-hipped wife, one of the most widely reproduced figures of Ajanta. The painting has been compared in technique with the work of Michelangelo and Correggio.

Cave 2 is remarkable for its ceiling decorations and its murals relating the birth of the Buddha. The Buddha's mother, Queen Maya, dreams that an elephant with six tusks has entered her body. This dream is interpreted to mean that she is to bear a great son. In one panel, you see the birth of the Buddha and the newborn child walking over lotus flowers with the king of gods, Indra, holding an umbrella over his head.

In Cave 4, sculpture is the main interest. It is the largest vihara in Ajanta, and depicts a man and a woman fleeing from a mad elephant, and a man giving up his resistance to a tempting woman. Cave 10 is believed to be the oldest cave at Ajanta, going back to the second century B.C.

The mystical heights attained by the artist-monks reach their zenith in Caves 16 and 17, where the viewer is released from the bondage imposed by time and space. Transcending these barriers, one is faced by a continuous narrative that spreads horizontally and vertically, evolving into a panoramic whole—at once logical and stunning. There is an excellent view of the river from Cave 16, which may have been the entrance to the entire series of caves. One painting here is riveting. Known as *The Dying Princess,* it is believed to represent Sundari, the wife of the Buddha's half brother, Nanda, who left her to become a monk. You can almost see the princess's eyes cloud over in death. One agrees with the art critic who said, "For pathos and sentiment and the unmistakable way of telling its story, this picture cannot be surpassed in the history of art."

Cave 17 possesses the greatest number of pictures undamaged by time. Luscious heavenly damsels fly effortlessly overhead, a prince makes love to a princess, and the Buddha tames a raging elephant—all on the portico of the cave.

Another mural tells how Prince Simhala conquered Ceylon (now Sri Lanka), an island of beautiful ogresses who trapped the prince and his 500 companions. The captivity was a merry one, but Simhala sensed the trap and fled on a winged white horse with an ogress in pursuit. This beauteous witch enticed the king of Simhala's country into marriage and ate her husband for their wedding banquet. But Simhala drove out the ogress and conquered her island of Ceylon. Next to this painting is the scene of a woman applying lipstick.

Another favorite is the painting in Cave 17 of a princess performing *sringar* (toilet). For its sheer exuberance and joie de vivre, the painting in Cave 2 of women on a swing is judged the best.

A number of unfinished caves were abandoned mysteriously, but even these are worth a visit. A steep climb of 100 steps takes you to the caves. You may also take the bridle path that is a gentler ascent, with a crescent pathway running alongside the caves. From here there is a magnificent view of the ravines of the Waghura River.

In the seventh century, for some inexplicable reason, the focus of activity shifted from Ajanta to a site 123 kilometers (76 miles) to the southwest—to a place known today as **Ellora.** The cave temples of Ellora, unlike those at Ajanta, are not solely Buddhist. Instead, they trace the course of religious development in India—through the decline of Buddhism in the latter half of the eighth century, the Hindu renaissance that followed the return of the Gupta dynasty, and the Jain resurgence between the ninth and eleventh centuries. Of the 34 caves, the 12 to the south are Buddhist, the 17 in the center are Hindu, and the 5 to the north are Jain.

At Ellora, only 30 kilometers (19 miles) from Aurangabad, the cave paintings of Ajanta give way to sculpture, which often covers the walls in an exquisitely ornate mass. In the Buddhist caves, the carvings present a serene reflection of the Buddhist philosophy. But in the subsequent Hindu caves, they acquire a certain exuberance, a throbbing vitality. Gods and demons do fearful battle, Lord Shiva angrily flails his eight arms, elephants rampage, eagles swoop, and lovers intertwine.

Unlike Ajanta, where the temples were chopped out of a steep cliff, the caves at Ellora were dug into the slope of a hill in a north–south direction (they face the west and could receive the light of the setting sun). Many of the caves date from the seventh century, when Buddhism started its gradual decline; that is why elements of Hinduism and Jainism can be found incorporated in the cave sculptures. A description of the most eye-catching caves should serve as a good introduction to what you can expect when you visit Ellora.

The largest of the Buddhist caves is Cave 5, which is 36 meters by 17 meters (117 feet by 56 feet). It was probably used as a classroom for young

ELLORA CAVE TEMPLES

(5TH C TO 8TH C AD)

monks, and its roof is supported by 24 pillars. Since everything was carved out of the mountain, the word "supported" is more a way of expressing an optical illusion. Working their way down, sculptors first "built" the roof before they "erected" the pillars.

Cave 6 is unusual. It contains a statue of the Hindu goddess of learning, Saraswati, in the company of Buddhist figures. Cave 10 is the "Carpenter's Cave," where Hinduism and Buddhism meet again. Here, the stonecutters reproduced the timbered roofs of their day over a richly decorated façade that imitates masonry work. Light comes into the cave through an elaborate horseshoe window over a porch. Inside this chaitya, the only Buddhist chapel at Ellora, the main work of art is a huge image of Buddha. Despite this image and a number of Buddhist figures on a frieze over the pillars of the temple, this cave is dedicated to Viswakarma, the architect of the Hindu gods and the patron saint of Indian craftsmen.

Cave 11 (two stories) and Cave 12 (three stories) are remarkable for having more than one floor. The two caves comprise a monastery behind an open courtyard that leads to its façade, which looms nearly 15 meters (50 feet) high. Although this façade is simple, the interior is lavish. This block of rock was gouged into a ground-floor hall, a shrine on the story above it, and another hall on the top story with a gallery of Buddhas seated under trees and parasols.

The immediate successors to the Buddhist caves are the Hindu caves, and a step inside them is enough to pull the visitor up short. It's another world—another universe—in which the calm contemplation of the seated Buddhas gives way to the dynamic cosmology of Hinduism, in which mythical gods seemingly come alive from stone. These sculptures are estimated to have been created around the seventh and eighth centuries.

Transfixed, the visitor watches the "action" as goddesses battle; Shiva flails the air with his eight arms; elephants big as life groan under their burdens; boars, eagles, peacocks, and monkeys prance around what has suddenly turned into a zoo; and lovers strike poses that leave the imagination somewhere far behind.

Ellora is dominated by the mammoth Kailasa temple complex, or Cave 16. Dedicated to Shiva, the complex is a replica of his legendary abode at Mount Kailasa in the Tibetan Himalayas. The world's biggest monolithic structure, approximately twice the area of the Parthenon in Greece and $1\frac{1}{2}$ times as tall, the Kailasa, one of India's finest monuments, reveals the genius, daring, and skill of its artisans.

To create the complex, an army of stonecutters started at the top of the cliff, where they removed 930,000 cubic meters (three million cubic feet) of rock to create a vast pit with a free-standing rock left in the center. Out of this single slab, 86 meters (276 feet) long and 48 meters (154 feet) wide, they created Shiva's abode, which includes the main temple, a series of smaller shrines, and galleries (small rooms) built into a wall that encloses the entire complex. Nearly every surface is exquisitely sculpted with epic themes.

As you walk through the extensive portals that lead to the courtyard, you are immediately flanked by a heavenly world dominated by sculptures of important Hindu gods and goddesses, including Ganesha (the elephant-headed god), who is the son of Shiva. The main sanctuary, which stands in the courtyard, rests on a base eight meters (25 feet) high that is supported by friezes of elephants. The sanctuary, which has an outer pavilion and a huge lingam or phallus (the symbol for Shiva) in its inner-sanctum, is covered by a three-story tower that reaches nearly 31 meters (100 feet) in height.

Walk around the courtyard and examine the numerous friezes that illustrate the legends of Shiva and stories from the great Hindu epics, the *Mahabharata* and the *Ramayana.* One interesting panel on the eastern wall relates the origin of the symbol for Shiva, the lingam or phallus, which was the result of a contest over supremacy between the two Hindu gods, Brahma and Vishnu. While they argued over who was more powerful, an enormous burning pillar emerged in their midst. Astonished, the two gods tried to measure its length. Vishnu turned into a boar and burrowed into the earth to locate the pillar's base. Brahma turned into a swan and flew toward heaven to find the top. But the pillar kept growing and their quest failed. When the two gods returned, Shiva materialized from the flaming pillar. The two gods fell at Shiva's feet and acknowledged his supremacy. The pillar, represented by the lingam (Shiva's creative energy), became Shiva's symbol of veneration.

Another famous frieze on the outer wall of the main sanctuary in the southern side of the courtyard shows the demon Ravana shaking Mount Kailasa, a story from the *Ramayana.* Through incredible artistry, this single panel evokes a wealth of emotion as Ravana decides to show his strength by lifting Mount Kailasa on his head. The mountain appears to tremble; a fearful Parvati, Shiva's consort, clings to the god's arm; gana figures (dwarfs) crouch down in terror. But Shiva remains unperturbed and merely puts the big toe of one foot down on the ten-headed Ravana.

PRACTICAL INFORMATION FOR MAHARASHTRA

WHEN TO GO. The best time to visit is October–March. In April the temperature climbs and Maharashtra gets hot. During the monsoon (usually June–September), the area around Aurangabad becomes lush green and many claim this is an ideal time to visit the Ellora and Ajanta caves. The best viewing time at Melghat Tiger Reserve and Nawegaon National Park is January–April.

HOW TO GET THERE. By Air. *Indian Airlines* has 10 weekly flights to Aurangabad from Bombay and a daily flight from Delhi, Jaipur, Jodhpur, and Udaipur. It also has three weekly flights from Bhopal to Aurangabad. Indian Airlines connects Pune with a daily flight from Delhi and three weekly flights from Madras and Bangalore. To get to Nagpur, the gateway to Melghat Tiger Reserve and Nawegaon National Park, Indian Airlines flies daily from Bombay and Delhi and has three weekly flights from Bhubaneshwar, Calcutta, and Hyderabad. *Vayudoot* has 16 weekly flights to Pune from Bombay and three weekly flights from Ahmedabad, Vadodara (Baroda), Hyderabad, and Goa. For Indian Airlines information, call 4864 in Aurangabad; 28179 in Pune; and 28841 in Napgur. For Vayudoot information, call 659120 in Pune.

By Bus. *Maharashtra State Road Transport Corporation* (MSRTC) runs deluxe buses from Bombay to major destinations in the state. For details and tickets in Bombay, visit the MSRTC counter at the Central Bus Stand, Bombay Central, or Parel Depot. *Maharashtra Tourism Development Corporation* (MTDC, address below under Tourist Information) also runs buses to Aurangabad (daily), Panchgani (daily), Mahabaleshwar (no service in the monsoon season), Gantatipule (no service in the monsoon season), and Nasik (daily). ITDC (address below under Tours) also has bus service between Bombay and Aurangabad.

By Train. A broad-gauge train now runs daily between Aurangabad and Bombay. Soon it will connect to other major cities. There's also excellent train service from Bombay to Pune, including express trains that make better time than going by car. For train information in Bombay, see the Bombay chapter. For train information in Pune, call 667333 and 667340. In Aurangabad, call 24815.

By Rented Car with Driver. Fairly good roads connect major destinations in Maharashtra with these out-of-state cities: Ahmedabad, Vadodara (Baroda); Panaji (in Goa); and Hyderabad. If you choose to travel by road from Bombay, hire a car with driver from one of the tour operators recommended in that chapter. Rates are about Rs. 5–Rs. 6 per km, with a halt charge of Rs. 50–Rs. 100 per night.

TOURIST INFORMATION. *MTDC* is extremely helpful, with good brochures on major destinations. The head office is in Bombay, C.D.O. Hutments, opposite L.I.C. Bldg., Madam Cama Rd.; tel. 2026713 or 2027762. It also has offices in these locations:

Aurangabad. MTDC Holiday Resort, Station Rd., Aurangabad 431001; tel. 24259. Open 7 A.M.–8 P.M. daily. There's also an airport counter.

Nagpur. Sanskrutik Bachat Bhavan, near Laxsmi Talkies, Normal School Area, Sitabuldi, Nagpur 440012; tel. 533325. Open 10 A.M.–5:45 P.M.; closed Sundays and second and fourth Saturdays.

Pune. I Block, Central Bldg., Pune 411001; tel. 668867. Open 10 A.M.–5:45 P.M.; closed Sundays and second and fourth Saturdays. Counters at the airport and railway station are open 8 A.M.–8 P.M. daily.

For good information in Aurangabad, also visit the *Government of India Tourist Office,* Krishna Vilas, Station Rd.; tel. 4817. Open 10 A.M.–5:30 P.M.; closed Sundays and second and fourth Saturdays.

FOREIGN CURRENCY EXCHANGE. Most Western-style hotels have money-exchange counters. Otherwise, go to a branch of the *State Bank of India;* open Monday–Friday, 10 A.M.–2 P.M., Saturdays till noon. In Aurangabad, the Ashok Hotel bank is open Monday–Saturday, 5 P.M.–8 P.M. MTDC Holiday Resort will have a bank in 1993 that will exchange foreign currency 8 A.M.–10 A.M. and 5–8 P.M. Monday–Saturday.

ACCOMMODATIONS. Aurangabad, Pune, and Mahabaleshwar offer a range of hotels to fit all budgets. Other places, such as the beautiful coastline and sanctuaries, have limited options. Some coastal areas now have MTDC tented beach resorts with walk-in two- and four-bed tents. These attractive tents have windows, front and back entrances, and plenty of space for walking around. They come with comfortable cots, clean linen, electricity, fans, and filtered drinking water. Each tented resort also has separate bathrooms and shower facilities, a delightful thatch-covered restaurant usually serving Indian and limited Continental cuisines, and an unspoiled beach. The tented resorts are closed June 15–Oct. 1. For advance booking at a tented resort or any MTDC facility (unless noted otherwise below), contact MTDC, Tours Division and Reservation Office, opposite L.I.C. Bldg., Madam Cama Rd., Bombay, Maharashtra; tel. 2026713. For tented resorts, include a full deposit (Rs. 250 per night per double occupancy); meals are included. Tents are restricted to couples or families. The deposit amount for other MTDC facilities is listed below. Prices for all accommodations are based on double occupancy and exclude taxes and service charges: *Expensive,* Rs. 1,200–Rs. 2,000; *Moderate,* Rs. 500–Rs. 1,200; *Inexpensive,* under Rs. 500. Most Western-style hotels take major credit cards.

AURANGABAD

Expensive

Welcomgroup Rama International. R-3 Chikalthana, Aurangabad 431210; tel. 83467. 100 rooms with bath. This attractive two-story hotel has a white exterior with red bands of elephants chiseled on its facade. The modern lobby is lavish. Air-conditioned bedrooms are modern and have TV. Multicuisine restaurant, room service, swimming pool, health club, tennis, minigolf, foreign-exchange and travel counter, doctor, astrologer, shopping arcade. AE, DC, MC, V.

Moderate

Ambassador Ajanta Hotel. Chikalthana, Aurangabad 431210; tel. 82211. 125 rooms with bath. Sweeping lawns and a circular drive lead up to this marble hotel.

Its lobby is filled with lovely Indian antiques; spacious, air-conditioned bedrooms have a Western decor with TV. Best rooms overlook the pool. Multicuisine restaurant, room service, Gujarati-decor bar, swimming pool, gardens, tennis, foreign-exchange and travel counter, doctor, shopping arcade. AE, DC, MC, V.

Aurangabad Ashok. Dr. Rajendra Prasad Marg, Aurangabad 431001; tel. 24520. 67 rooms with bath. This yellow two-story bungalow has a spacious lobby. Air-conditioned rooms are simply decorated and have TV. Ask for a room with a tub. Room service, multicuisine restaurant, bar, swimming pool, foreign-exchange and travel counter, bank, doctor, shopping arcade. AE, DC, MC, V.

Quality Inn Vedant Aurangabad. Station Rd., Aurangabad 431210; tel. 26785. 100 rooms with bath. This modern high rise is scheduled to open in 1993. It will have air-conditioned rooms with a modern decor. TV, room service, multicuisine restaurant, swimming pool, health club, foreign-exchange and travel counter, doctor, shopping arcade. AE, DC, MC, V.

Inexpensive

MTDC Holiday Resort. Reservations: Manager, Station Rd., Aurangabad; tel. 24259. 62 rooms with bath. This complex of two-story bungalows offers clean, functional rooms with a plain decor. Some rooms are air-conditioned; all rooms have fans and mosquito netting. There is a simple but decent multicuisine restaurant; also room service, bar, tourist office, handicrafts shop, small garden. For advanced booking, include a full deposit of Rs. 250 per night per double room. Rupees only.

BHATYA BEACH
365 km (226 mi.) from Bombay

Inexpensive

MTDC Tented Resort. Bhatya, Dist. Ratnagiri 415713. Reservations: MTDC, tel. 2026713. 20 tents with shared bath. This complex is on a sandy hill overlooking a secluded beach near coconut groves. Thatched-hut restaurant. Rupees only.

BORDI BEACH
165 km (102 mi.) from Bombay

Inexpensive

MTDC Tented Resort. Bordia, Dist. Thane, tel. 243. Reservations: MTDC, tel. 2026713. 5 tents with shared bath. Tents are set on an isolated stretch of beach backed by tropical trees. Small multicuisine restaurant, boating facilities. Rupees only.

CHIPLUN

Moderate

Taj Gateway Riverview Lodge. Village Dhamandivi, Taluka Khed, District Ratnagiri; tel. 2853 via Lote. 37 rooms with bath. This new three-story bungalow, with tiered gardens and a sweeping view of the Vishista River and valley, is six hours from Bombay en route to Goa. It's peaceful, with spacious Western-decor rooms that have balconies. Room service, Indian- and Continental-cuisine restaurant, bar, doctor, foreign-exchange counter, and arrangements for trekking and river excursions in typical wooden fishing boats. Rupees only.

GANPATIPULE BEACH

Because this is also an important Hindu pilgrimage site, 375 km (233 mi.) from Bombay, no liquor is available in either of the facilities listed below.

Inexpensive

Courtesy Hotel. Reservations: Courtesy Hotels, 5 Dhanashri Nanda Patkar Rd., Vile Parle (East), Bombay; tel. 6123094. 24 rooms with bath. Under construction at press time, this Western-style hotel on a hill above a beautiful beach is scheduled to open in early 1993. Rooms have a streamlined modern decor and sea views; fans or air-conditioning, room service, multicuisine restaurant, foreign-exchange counter. Rupees only.

MTDC Cottages and Tented Resort. Reservations: MTDC, tel. 2026713. 4 cottages and 45 tents. Nestled in a coconut grove on the edge of a cove, this complex also offers exceptionally good Chinese, Indian, and limited Continental dishes in its thatch-covered restaurant. Rupees only.

HARIHARESHWAR BEACH
200 km (124 mi.) from Bombay

Inexpensive

MTDC Tented Resort. Reservations: MTDC, tel. 2026713. 30 tents. In this delightful complex, set in an inlet and backed by hills, tents are located near two beaches. The more secluded beach is preferable. Rupees only.

KARLA CAVES

Moderate

Fariyas Holiday Resort. Frichley Hill, Lonavla 410401; tel. 2701, fax 022/2871441. 90 rooms with bath. 10 km (6 mi.) from the caves. Lovely terraced gardens, a sleek modern lobby, and a gigantic indoor swimming pool are highlights at this hilltop Western-style hotel. Air-conditioned rooms have a lackluster contemporary decor, but they're spacious and have private balconies. Included are TV, room service, multicuisine restaurants, bar, health club, sightseeing arrangements, foreign-exchange counter, shops. AE, DC, MC, V.

Inexpensive

MTDC Karla Holiday Resort. Karla; tel. 30. 64 rooms with bath. Very near the caves. In a secluded area back from the road, this complex offers two good bargain-priced options: air-conditioned suites with two bedrooms and sitting room; and recently renovated "A-type" old-fashioned bungalows with one bedroom, pitched tile roofs, and verandas. Limited room service, Indian- and Chinese-cuisine restaurant, bar, boating, nice grounds. For advanced booking, include a full deposit of Rs. 400 per night for suites and Rs. 150 for bungalows. Rupees only.

KIHIM BEACH
136 km (84 mi.) from Bombay

Inexpensive

MTDC Tented Resort. Reservations: MTDC, tel. 2026713. 40 tents. In a coconut grove on the edge of a beach, the best located tents in this five-acre complex have an unobstructed beach view and are positioned away from the bathroom facility. For optimum privacy, avoid the weekends. Rupees only.

MAHABALESHWAR

Moderate

Hotel Anarkali. Kasim Sajan Rd., Mahabaleshwar 412806; tel. 336. 35 rooms with bath. The best modern Western-style hotel in this hill station, Anarkali offers a good location and spacious, contemporary-decor rooms with TV and room service. Indian- and Chinese-cuisine restaurant, bar, car-rental service, horse rides. 50 percent discount during off season (usually October–March). DC.

MELGHAT TIGER PROJECT

Inexpensive

MTDC Resort. Chikhaldara, District Amravati; tel. 34. 30 rooms with bath and some tents with shared bath. Here, concrete cottages with basic but clean furnishings are set on a hill in the forest. A new lodge, 3 km (2 mi.) away, has a good view of the valley; its rooms have clean Western furnishings. Included are simple catering, elephant safaris, and regional folk dances on request. For advance bookings, include a full deposit of Rs. 150 per night per room. Rupees only.

MURUD-HARNAI
247 km (153 mi.) from Bombay

Inexpensive

MTDC Tented Resort. Tal. Dapoli, Dist. Ratnagiri 415713. Reservations: MTDC, tel. 2026713. About 20 tents with shared bath. This new complex, set on a palm-fringed beach, offers good local Konkan cuisine. It's scheduled to open in early 1993. Closed April–September. Rupees only.

NAWEGAON NATIONAL PARK

Inexpensive

MTDC Nawegaon Forest Lodge and Tents. Reservations: MTDC, tel. 2026713. About 15 units and 15 tents. Set on stilts in a forested area on the edge of a lake, "Sanjay Kutir A-Type" rooms have slatted wood exteriors and rustic but very clean interiors with attached baths. There's no electricity; lanterns light your way. You can also stay in safari-style tents (shared bathrooms) that are located deeper into the forest. There are also simple, catered meals on request, elephant safaris, rowboats, fishing (bring your own equipment). For advance bookings, include a full deposit of Rs. 200 per night for a room; Rs. 100 for tents. Rupees only.

PUNE

Moderate–Expensive

Blue Diamond. 11 Koregaon Rd., Pune 411001; tel. 663775, fax 212/666101. 114 rooms with bath. A Western-style high rise with an attractive lobby, Blue Diamond offers expensive-priced deluxe rooms that are very spacious and elegant, and moderate-priced executive and economy rooms (least expensive and a good bargain) that are slightly smaller but well appointed. Best rooms face the pool. Air-conditioning, TV, room service, multicuisine restaurants, bar, business center, swimming pool, health club, foreign-exchange and travel counter, bank, sightseeing, golf, yoga, and bird-watching arrangements. AE, DC, MC, V.

Moderate

Executive Ashok. 5 University Rd., Shivajinagar, Pune 411005; tel. 57391. 71 rooms with bath. This Western-style hotel has a modern lobby and rooms with a modern decor. The best rooms overlook the pool. Air-conditioning, TV, room service, multicuisine restaurants, bar, doctor, business center, foreign-exchange and travel counter, swimming pool, health club, shops. AE, DC, MC, V.

Kohinoor Executive. 1246 Apte Rd., Deccan Gymkhana, Pune 411001; tel. 58938. 42 rooms with bath. This new Western-style hotel is in a quiet yet centrally located neighborhood. Its modern lobby is intimate, with a small fountain. Air-conditioned rooms have pretty contemporary furnishings and TV. Room service, multicuisine restaurants, bar, foreign-exchange counter. Good value. DC, MC, V.

Hotel Sagar Plaza. 1 Bund Garden Rd., Pune 411001; tel. 661880. 80 rooms with bath. Another new deluxe hotel, Sagar Plaza has an atrium lobby with a glass elevator. Modern, air-conditioned rooms are done up in pretty pastels and have

TV. Multicuisine restaurants, room service, bar, business center, foreign-exchange and travel counter, small swimming pool, bookshop. AE, V.

Inexpensive

Hotel Amir. 15 Connaught Rd., Pune 411001, tel. 661840, fax 212/444253. 100 rooms with bath. Amir, a Western-style hotel, has a friendly ambience and provides good service. Deluxe rooms (also inexpensive) are the best option—spacious and clean, with a modern decor and a painted mural of a Pune scene on one wall. Excellent multicuisine restaurants, air-conditioning, TV, room service, bar, shops, health club, foreign-exchange and travel counter, Indian Airlines office. AE, DC, MC, V.

TARKARLI BEACH
546 km (338 mi.) from Bombay

Inexpensive

MTDC Tented Resort. Dist. Sindhudurg. Reservations: MTDC, tel. 2026713. About 20 tents with shared bath. This new complex, scheduled to open in early 1993, will have a pristine beach, with tents nestled in a palm grove. The thatched-hut restaurant will serve Konkan specialties. Rupees only.

DINING OUT. Except for Aurangabad and Pune, your eating options in Maharashtra are limited. Breakfast is usually served 8–10; lunch, noon–3; dinner, 7:30–10. The restaurants listed below are informal and, unless noted, are open for all three meals and don't require reservations. Prices are based on a three-course dinner for one person, excluding beverage, tip, and taxes: *Deluxe,* over Rs. 300; *Expensive,* Rs. 200–Rs. 300; *Moderate,* Rs. 100–Rs. 200; *Inexpensive,* under Rs. 100.

AURANGABAD

Expensive

Madhuban. Welcomgroup Rama, R 3, Chikalthana; tel. 82241. This elegant restaurant has a marble fountain and live Indian instrumental music at night. The chef serves Continental, Chinese, or Indian dishes, with especially good tandoori items. You can sample all three at a luncheon or dinner buffet, or eat à la carte. Dinner reservations advised. Open 6:30–10 A.M., 12:30–2:45 P.M., 7:30–10:30 P.M. AE, DC, MC, V.

Moderate

Angeethi. Mehar Chember, 6 Vidya Nagar, Jalna Rd.; tel. 27966. Cozy Angeethi has brick-and-tile walls and upholstered chairs. The chef serves Indian, Continental, and especially popular Chinese dishes. Try the chicken Manchurian or fried fish with lemon sauce. Open for buffet lunch noon–3 P.M., and à la carte dinner 7–11 P.M. Rupees only.

Minglinghs. Hotel Rajdoot, Jalna Rd.; tel. 25991. When you enter this large old-fashioned restaurant, you'll walk past "waterfalls" into a sea green room with a fountain centerpiece. The menu offers Indian, Continental, and Chinese dishes. Go for the Chinese. Try Minglingh special prawns or the ginger chicken. Open 11 A.M.–3 P.M. and 7–midnight. Rupees only.

Shaolin Chinese Restaurant. Pawandeep, Kushalnagar, Jalna Rd.; tel. 27291. Judging by the name of this Oriental-decor restaurant, you may expect only Chinese cuisine, but the menu also features Indian dishes. Specialties include chicken *tangri kebab* (drumsticks cooked in a tandoor) or chicken à la Canton. Open 10 A.M.–3 P.M. and 7 P.M.–midnight. Rupees only.

Tandoor Restaurant and Bar. Shyam Chambers, Bansilal Nagar, Station Rd.; tel. 8482. At this popular restaurant with brown tiled walls, plants, and subdued lighting that highlights an understated Egyptian motif, very good Chinese and Indian dishes are served. Tandoori items are delicious. Dinner reservations advised. Open 11:30 A.M.–11:30 P.M. Rupees only.

Inexpensive

Bhoj Restaurant. Printravel Hotel, Dr. Ambedkar Rd.; tel. 28481. This cheery restaurant with bright-yellow walls and a Rajasthani mural serves very good Indian vegetarian fare (South Indian and Punjabi cuisines). Sample the *thalis* (numerous small portions served on a platter). Open 6 A.M.–11 P.M. Rupees only.

PUNE

Expensive

Ashvamedh. Hotel Blue Diamond, 11 Koregaon Rd.; tel. 663775. A rustic decor—handsome wooden pillars and trim—and live Indian instrumental music at night add up to an attractive ambience here. The chef serves Continental and Indian dishes; the tandooris are especially good. Dinner reservations advised. Open 12:30–2:30 P.M. and 7:30–11:30 P.M. AE, DC, MC, V.

Moderate

Golden Arch. Executive Ashok, 5 University Rd.; tel. 57391. Scheduled for renovation, Golden Arch continues to serve Continental, Chinese, and Indian cuisines. Indian and Continental are best. The good tandoori mixed grill and *macchi amritsari* (marinated pomfret in garlic and ginger paste served in a spicy red gravy) are recommended. Dinner reservations advised. Open 12:30–2:30 P.M. and 7:30–11 P.M. AE, DC, MC, V.

Haveli Bar and Restaurant. 7 Dr. Coyaji Rd. (East St.); no phone. While you can eat indoors, this delightful restaurant with Haveli palace decor has an enchanting courtyard with a *shamiana* (canvas roll-up roof) overhead and a narrow canal with fountain in the center. The chef serves good Indian cuisine, including tasty tandoori items. Among the specialties are *jal tarang* (stuffed pomfret marinated with mint chutney, then cooked in a tandoor) and *begum bahar* (chicken pieces cooked in gravy with bran). Open noon–3 P.M. and 7–11 P.M. Rupees only.

Kapila Garden Restaurant. Dhole Patil Rd.; tel. 666902. In this open-air garden, you eat at informal tables under small thatch-covered huts, seated on plastic chairs. No beef and pork are served, but you'll find good chicken, fish, and vegetables prepared in Indian and Continental dishes. The butter chicken (curried chicken) is extremely popular. Reservations advised. Open 7–11 P.M. Rupees only.

Kebab Korner. Amir Hotel, 15 Connaught Rd.; tel. 661840. This outdoor restaurant has an Indian-village decor: thatched huts, a small waterfall, red lights set into a brick wall, and a "bangle-wallah" creating pretty bangles (for sale) in a corner. Live Indian *ghazals* are performed on Wednesday nights. The excellent Indian cuisine matches the charming ambience. Try the delicious butter chicken and tandoori items, such as the pomfret or rolled minced mutton, with Kashmiri *pillau* (vegetable and dried-fruit rice dish). Reservations advised November to March. Open 7:30–11:30 P.M. DC, MC, V.

Portico. J.M. Road, Deccan Gymkhana; tel. 55503. An antique car (Austin) stands guard at the entrance to this handsome modern restaurant done up in black and white. You can choose from Continental and Indian cuisines. There's also a salad bar. A specialty is chicken Portico (minced chicken and mutton prepared in a gravy with dried fruit, boiled eggs, and cream). Reservations advised. Open noon–3 P.M. and 7–12 A.M. AE, DC.

Suzie Wong. Amir Hotel, 15 Connaught Rd.; tel. 661840. This open-air restaurant, with simple Oriental touches—pavilion and red-cane chairs and tables—serves Chinese cuisine. Popular choices are the mildly spicy fried Mandarin pomfret, *sun tung mein* noodles (minced chicken and peas cooked in soy sauce and served with soft noodles), or Chinese sizzlers (spicy-hot dishes). Reservations advised November to March. Open noon–3 P.M. and 7–12 P.M. DC, MC, V.

Inexpensive

Shabree Restaurant. Hotel Parichay, 1199/2 A.F.C. Rd.; tel. 59901. Extremely informal and popular, this restaurant serves one meal: a Maharashtrian vegetarian *thali*. Come with a big appetite and be prepared to eat Indian style with your right hand. Waiters will offer an unending series of dishes. Say *"ho,"* and you'll be served;

"noko" means "no thanks." Lots of fun and very inexpensive. Open 11 A.M.–3 P.M. and 7–11 P.M. Rupees only.

SWEETS AND TREATS. Aurangabad. For good Indian and Continental snacks and tasty sweets, including ice cream and milk shakes, drop in at *Food Wala's Fast Food Centre* (Denshaws Ice-Cream Parlour, Nirala Bazaar). You can also get fresh fruit juices here. Open 9 A.M.–10 P.M.

Mahabaleshwar. Just outside Mahabaleshwar on the road to Pune, stop at a roadside stall—some are vine-covered, with tables and chairs set underneath—and have freshly made strawberry or rose ice cream (complete with crushed rose petals), shakes, and juices. Available March to June.

Pune. Don't miss a visit to *Badshah Cold Drink Annexe and Snack Bar,* 7 Dr. Coyaji Rd.—also called East St. Arrive hungry, and try the vegetarian South Indian snacks or pizzas and the exquisite fresh fruit juices, fruity milk shakes (rose, raspberry, and "chikoo" are sublime), and then make room for the excellent *kulfi* (Indian ice cream). The pretty outdoor terrace, covered with woven bamboo, and the downstairs interior room, with mirrored walls and fresh-fruit display, are both open 7:30 A.M.–12:30 P.M.; the air-conditioned upstairs family room is open 4 P.M.–midnight. At *Karachi Sweet Mart,* 562 Sachapir St., you'll find the best north Indian sweets, created by a family in this business for over 100 years. Order the *badam pak* (a little square of milk, Kasmiri saffron, cashews, almonds, and pistachios), *kaju roll* (sugar and crushed cashews rolled in edible silver), or *rosmalai* (a fried milk, refined wheat, and sugar ball served in sugary syrup). Open 8 A.M.–8 P.M. daily. At *Chitale Bandhu Mitaiwale* on Bajirao Rd., join the crowd and try Maharashtrian sweets, such as *ba sundi* (ice milk), *mango barfi* (a curd-and-sugar, mango-flavored sweet), or *shrikand* (pudding of curd, sugar, saffron, and nutmeg). Open Tuesday–Sunday, 8 A.M.–1 P.M. and 3:30–8:30 P.M.; Monday, till noon.

HOW TO GET AROUND. From the Airports. Most airports are within 10 km (6 mi.) of the city. Taxis should cost about Rs. 60; auto rickshaws, when available, should cost about Rs. 20–Rs. 30.

By Hired Car with Driver. This is the best way to see the Maharashtra coastline and for getting from Aurangabad to the Ellora and Ajanta caves. If you plan to fly into Nagpur to visit the sanctuaries, a car with driver is also recommended. Hire a car from a tour operator listed in the Bombay chapter. For trips in areas outside Bombay, rates are about Rs. 5–Rs. 6 per km, with a halt charge of Rs. 100 per night.

By Taxi. Throughout Maharashtra, a taxi for local trips should cost about Rs. 7 for the first km; Rs. 3.50 per additional km. In Aurangabad, a taxi to and from Ellora should cost about Rs. 350; and to and from Ajanta should cost about Rs. 700.

By Auto Rickshaw. Good for short trips, especially in congested areas, these three-wheel vehicles charge about Rs. 4.50 for the first km and Rs. 2.50 for each additional km.

TOURS. *MTDC* conducts package bus tours from Bombay to places within the state. For details and bookings, contact Tours Division and Reservation Office (MTDC, address above in Tourist Information). Here are some of the best tours:

Aurangabad Tour via Nasik to Ellora and Ajanta. Four days and three nights; daily departures. Stay in MTDC Holiday Resort or in a choice of hotels.

Ganpatipule Holiday at MTDC Tented Beach Resort. Three days and two nights; departures Oct. 15–June.

Harihareshwar Holiday at MTDC Tented Beach Resort. Same trip length and departures as the Ganpatipule tour, above, but to MTDC tented resort in Harihareshwar.

Kihim Holiday at MTDC Tented Beach Resort. Three days and two nights; departs Monday, Wednesday, and Friday. This trip involves a pleasant journey by boat.

Melghat Tiger Safari. Five days and four nights. Weekly departures.

Tarkali Beach Holiday at MTDC Tented Beach Resort. This new package trip runs on demand.

Vidarbha (Darshan and Jungle Safari). Highlights include visits to Vidarbha Temple and Nawegaon National Park. Six days and five nights. Weekly departures.

Indian Tourism Development Corporation also offers deluxe bus tours from Bombay to Aurangabad. In Bombay, contact ITDC, Nirmal Towers, Nariman Point, Bombay; tel. 2026679 or 2023343. In Aurangabad, ITDC is at Hotel Aurangabad Ashok, Dr. Rajendra Prasad Marg; tel. 24520.

Ellora and Ajanta Conducted Tour from Aurangabad. Daily bus tour to Ellora, 9:30 A.M.–5:30 P.M., and Ajanta, 8 A.M.–5:30 P.M. Reservations are required, contact MTDC, Holiday Resort, Station Rd.; tel. 24259.

ITDC also has similar tours. Reservations required; contact ITDC in Aurangabad (address above).

Pune. MTDC offers a four-hour bus tour of local sights, including Shaniwar Wada (old palace ruins), Kelkar Museum, Agha Khan Palace (Gandhi National Memorial), and Shinde's Chhatri. Departs at 8 A.M. and 2 P.M. For details and reservations, contact MTDC in Pune (address above) in Tourist Information.

Private Guides. The *Government of India Tourist Office* has good private guides available for visits to the Ellora and Ajanta caves. You can hire them at an office near the ticket windows at the sites or make arrangements in advance through MTDC or the Government of India tourist offices in Aurangabad (addresses above). For one–four people, a guide should cost about Rs. 125 for a half day and Rs. 175 for a full day.

TOUR OPERATORS. For all travel needs, including a hired car with driver, use a reliable agency listed under this category in the Bombay chapter. Also see Special-Interest Tours in *Facts at Your Fingertips* for the names of India-based agencies that can create a special trip in Maharashtra.

SEASONAL EVENTS. See the Bombay chapter for a list of important seasonal events in Maharashtra.

HISTORIC SITES. Entrance to most places is generally free or nominal; where a donation is requested, a few rupees will suffice. Historic sites are open daily sunrise to sunset, unless noted otherwise below.

CAVES

Ajanta Caves (approached from Aurangabad). These caves are famous for their exquisite murals and rock-cut carvings of Buddhist origin. Five of the caves, nos. 9, 10, 19, 26, and 29 are *chaityas* (halls) for group worship; the others are *viharas* (monasteries).

Bedsa Caves (near Lonavala). The most interesting second-century B.C. rock-cut cave has a main cathedral hall that is similar to the cathedral hall at Karla. Inside are pillars with good carvings.

Bhaja Caves (near Lonavala). Built in the second century B.C., Cave No. 12 has a handsome vault; the last cave to the south has good sculptures, including a prince on an elephant, a prince on a horse, and a dancing couple.

Ellora Caves (approached from Aurangabad). These renowned rock-cut caves are more than 10 centuries old. Of the 34 caves, 12 are of Buddhist origin, 17 are Hindu, and 5 are Jain. Among the Buddhist caves, nos. 5, 10, 11, and 12 are outstanding. Of the Hindu caves, nos. 16, 21, and 29 stand out. No. 16, Kailasa Temple, is an intricately hewn monument that is perhaps the world's largest monolith. Of the Jain group, nos. 32 and 34 should be seen.

Karla Caves (near Lonavala). The Buddhist rock-cut temples date from the second century B.C. The main cathedral, one of the finest Buddhist caves in India, has beautiful pillars with *mithuna* (copulating) couples and capitals with delicately wrought elephants.

Pandu Lena Caves (Nasik). These 23 caves, built in the first century A.D., were predominantly built as one-story monasteries. The best caves are nos. 3, 8, and 18.

FORTS

Ahmedanagar Fort (north of Pune). This fort was built in the 1500s by Hussain Nizam Shah and was used as a prison by the British.

Daulatabad Fort (near Aurangabad). An imposing structure, with novel architectural tricks to confuse and thwart an attacking force, this fort was captured in the fourteenth century by the Sultan of Delhi, who turned it into his second capital.

Purandhar Fort (south of Pune). Once the capital of the Maratha Kingdom, Purandhar is one of the most imposing forts in Maharashtra.

Raigad Fort (south of Pune). This fort was Shivaji's capital from 1664 to 1680.

Sinhagad Fort (south of Pune). Called the "Lion Fort," this edifice on top of a sheer-sided hill was captured in the 1600s by one of Shivaji's most trusted warriors, Tanaji Malasure, whom he called "the lion"; the battle also claimed the lion's life.

Shivneri Fort (north of Pune). This fort is set above the old city where Shivaji was born.

MUSEUMS AND GALLERIES. Entrance to the following places is free or a nominal fee is charged.

Pune. *Raja Dinkar Kelkar Museum* ("Kamal Kunj," Raja Kelkar Museum St., Natu Baug) contains the excellent collection of this raja—instruments, cloth paintings, terra-cottas, saris, wooden carvings and doors, brasswork, plus the palace of his favorite Moslem dancing girl. Open daily 8:30 A.M.–12:30 P.M. and 3–6 P.M.

SPORTS AND OUTDOOR ADVENTURES. Beaches. Backed by coconut groves and palm trees, great beaches extend from Bombay to Goa. You won't find resort hotels yet, but this is expected to change soon. Already, many idyllic coves and harbors have tented beach resorts run by MTDC (see above under Accommodations). Here are some of the best stretches with good surf and sand: *Kihim,* 136 km (84 mi.) from Bombay; *Murud-Harnai,* 247 km (153 mi.) from Bombay; *Bhatya Beach,* 365 km (226 mi.) from Bombay; Ganpatipule, 375 km (233 mi.) from Bombay; and *Tarkali Beach,* 546 km (338 mi.) from Bombay.

Camping. MTDC rents tents and sleeping bags that you can pitch in Maharashtra. Nominal fees. Contact any MTDC office. You can also use a tent at their beach resorts.

Fishing. Permits are not necessary. Bring your own equipment and plan to fish at Chiplun or Nawegaon National Park. You can also fish in the sea or lagoon at MTDC's tented resort at Ganpatipule, where equipment is available.

Rock climbing. From November to February, MTDC runs a rock and fort climbing course that teaches rock climbing and includes some trekking around Karla. Contact MTDC in Bombay.

Watersports. At MTDC's Panshet Resort, 45 km (28 mi.) from Pune, you can kayak, wind-surf, and zoom around on a waterscooter on Panshet Lake.

Wildlife Sanctuaries. *Melghat Tiger Reserve* covers 1,571 sq. km (607 sq. mi.) of forest area and is home to tigers, bison, panthers, sambar, and flying squirrels. You can also visit the historic Gawilgarh Fort. *Nawegaon National Park* has a lovely lake with good fishing. The best time to visit both parks is January–April. The best approach is from Nagpur, 260 km (161 mi.) from Melghat and 150 km (93 mi.) from Nawegaon. See the MTDC tours, listed above, that can take you on trips to discover these sanctuaries.

Yoga. *Romani Iyengar Memorial Yoga Institute* (1701-B/1, Shivaji Nagar, Pune; tel. 58134) has courses available to individuals who are already familiar with his technique.

SHOPPING. Aurangabad is famous for its *bidriwork* (gun metal inlaid with intricate bits of silver) and *himroo* shawls made of silk and cotton. Visit these two excellent shops: *Aurangabad Himroo Factory's Handicrafts Emporium* (Shahganj, opposite Gandhi Statue), which has authentic handwoven himroo and beautiful pure silk shawls. Open daily 8 A.M.–8 P.M. Rupees only. *Ajanta Agate Handicrafts* (Ajanta Rd., Harsul) has excellent-quality bidriwork and a selection of semi-precious stones set in jewelry or worked into statues and other small items. Open daily 10 A.M.–8 P.M. Rupees only.

In Pune, you can bargain for inexpensive Western-style clothes at open-air stalls on M. G. Road. Along Mal Dhakka Mangalwarpeth, stalls sell old curios, including brass and glassware, every Wednesday and Sunday; bargain! Rupees only.

NIGHTLIFE AND BARS. Your best bet is to have your nightcap in your hotel. Bars are generally open 11 A.M.–2:30 P.M. and 6:30–11 P.M.

GUJARAT

Salt Marshes, Lush Lands, and Lions

by
KATHLEEN COX

In Gujarat, India's westernmost state, salt flats of the Indian subcontinent meet with the monsoon lands of peninsular India. Here you'll find India's largest marshland and its only sanctuary of Asiatic lions.

Gujarat's lakes are mostly man-made for irrigation. Its forests give shelter to thousands of birds. In spring, fragrant flowers bloom across the landscape. In winter, mist rises from rivers that empty into the Arabian Sea. India's 5,000–kilometer (1,524–mile) coastline begins in Gujarat and runs 1,650 kilometers (503 miles)—the longest coastline of any state in India. The hills, low and forested, rise gently to 1,000 meters (305 feet). In upland hamlets are bred India's finest cattle, making Gujarat the home of India's dairy industry.

Women, in swirling skirts and blouses of heavy black and red fabric embellished with mirrors and rich embroidery, reflect Gujarat's passion for the bright and colorful: bounteous greens, earthy reds, deep maroons, light saffrons, and sapphire blues suffuse Gujarat's handicrafts and textiles, its folk dances, and its festivals. Even the Hindu temples, Jain shrines, Moslem mosques, and secular palaces are adorned with Gujarati ornamentation that sets them apart from monuments in the rest of India.

The northwestern border of Gujarat forms part of India's international frontier with Pakistan, while Rajasthan adjoins Gujarat on the northeast,

Madhya Pradesh on the far east, and Maharashtra on the south. The state has a population of 34 million. Of the original inhabitants, only the Bhil and about a dozen subtribes have survived. After the fall of the Ashoka empire, various local dynasties ruled in different parts of Gujarat until the Moslem conquest of the entire area. When the British came in 1856, Gujarat and Maharashtra formed one huge bilingual state; in 1960, the two were divided.

With a large Jain population, the people of this state are largely vegetarians. Masters of vegetarian cooking, Gujaratis make a variety of mouthwatering dishes out of the simplest lentils and vegetables. The Gujarati *thali* (vegetarian) meal is an endless procession of savory vegetables cooked in aromatic spices, supported with a variety of crisply fried snacks and delicious confections made from sweetened, thickened milk or thick cold curd mixed with nuts. The farmhouse dinner is a Gujarati innovation. It consists of crisp hot *rotis* (flat unleavened bread) made from *jawar,* or millet flour, huge dollops of butter, a pungent garlic chutney, and fresh vegetables steamed in an earthen oven. It is washed down with thick, sweetened milk flavored with sliced nuts and saffron.

The Gujaratis are, however, better known for their sharp business acumen exemplified by the citizens of Ahmedabad, the former state capital of Gujarat. The new capital, Gandhinagar, is 30 kilometers (19 miles) away on the banks of the Sabarmati River.

Some festivals of Gujarat are unique; others are slightly different from those in other states. (See Seasonal Events in Practical Information for Gujarat, below.)

Gujarat offers a scintillating range of fabrics. Textile weaving, vegetable-dye painting, tie-and-dye work, gold and silver thread work (*zari*), intricate silk embroidery, and patola- and tanchoi-type saris have been Gujarat's pride for centuries. The lacquered furniture of Sankheda, the mirror works of Kutch, bead-encrusted artifacts from Rajkot, and fine wood carvings from the vicinity of Ahmedabad have become popular with tourists, as have experimental paintings and murals at roadside art shows, the main markets, and the emporiums at Ahmedabad, Jamnagar, Surat, and Vadodara (Baroda).

Exploring Gujarat

Just over the state line, going from Bombay to Ahmedabad, is Sanjan, where a masonry flame-topped pillar marks the landing place of the Parsis in A.D. 745 after they had spent 19 years in Diu, an island south of Saurashtra (the former name of peninsular Gujarat). Why they left Diu is not known, but they set off in the same ships that had brought them from Persia. They had to keep moving the sacred fire for protection, and it was only after 700 years that they set it up permanently at Udvada, a little north of Sanjan. Now there are Parsi groups in almost every Gujarati town, and many of their last names are derived from the names of these towns.

Along the palm-fringed coast sliced by frequent banyan-lined rivers running into the Gulf of Cambay are many ancient ports, including Surat, at the mouth of the Tapti River. By the fourteenth century, Surat, which was founded by a Hindu Brahman, was the most important port on India's west coast. This city became a flourishing international trade center; and over the years, the Moguls, Portuguese, Dutch, French, and English envied its prosperity.

Surat's fortress-castle was built in 1546 and it changed hands repeatedly, indicative of the port's value. After the sixteenth century Mogul Emperor Akbar captured it from the Portuguese, it became a gateway for Mecca. About a 100 years later, the Maratha-ruler Shivaji raided Surat four times; the size and elaborateness of the Dutch and English tombs indicate the amount of wealth the Europeans were anxious to defend.

Today, most of Surat's population is still engaged in three of its oldest enterprises: diamond cutting and polishing, the creation of zari (gold and silver thread work), and textile production.

Due south of Surat is Saputara, or the "abode of serpents," a hill resort set on the second-highest plateau of the Sahyadri Range. From here, you can visit the Mahal Bardipara Forest Wildlife Sanctuary and Gira waterfalls.

Vadodara (Baroda)

About 113 kilometers (70 miles) south of Ahmedabad lies the "garden city" of Vadodara, which has boulevards lined with flaming gulmohar trees. Once a princely capital, it acquired its original name, Vadodara ("In the Heart of the Banyan Trees") because of the profusion of banyans.

The reign of the family that governed Vadodara until independence started in the early eighteenth century. Damaji Gaikwar was the son of a Maratha general in the Peshwa's army. He was allowed to levy one-fourth of the income of certain areas conquered by the army. Damaji II, along with the Peshwa, took Ahmedabad in 1753, ending Moslem rule in the region. The victors then divided the country. After Damaji II returned from the Battle of Panipat (against the Afghans), which destroyed much of the Peshwa's power, he chose Anhilwad Patan as his capital. His area dwindled in the course of controversies. By 1802, for receiving British help, he had to cede further land to the British, retaining small segments throughout Gujarat and Saurashtra.

Lakshmi Vilas Palace, an architectural blend of the occidental and Oriental and a conglomeration of domes, towers, and spires set in a beautifully landscaped garden, is still the personal residence of the former royal family and not open to the public. Though the museum of armor and sculpture on this estate is supposedly accessible, it's hours are extremely erratic. You can visit the Oriental Institute, with its rich collection of ancient Sanskrit manuscripts, including a historic copy of India's great epic, *Ramayana*. You can also enjoy two good museums. The Baroda Museum and Art Gallery, set in a lovely park, contains good Mogul miniatures and European paintings. Nearby is the Maharajah Fateh Singh Museum, with more paintings by European masters and numerous Oriental and Indian exhibits.

Some of the royal family's treasures, including the famous jewel "Star of the South," are at the Nazarbagh Palace, one of the spacious old dwellings of former times. In the collection is an embroidered cloth laid with stones, originally intended for the Prophet's Tomb. Two other palaces with well-kept gardens are the Pratap Vilas and Markarpura, which is south of the town. Also inquire about performances at Baroda Gharana, an important school of Indian classical music.

At the Dabhoi Fort ruins, 27 kilometers (17 miles) southeast of Vadodara, you can see the remains of walls, temples, and especially gates that are fine examples of the Gujarat style of Hindu military architecture. The Malika Mata (Kali) Temple, built in the shape of a Greek cross, is covered inside with fine carvings.

Nearby, farmers dressed all in white and women in flared red skirts can be seen tending the fertile fields. Abutting these fields is the busy town of Anand. Much of India's milk and butter comes from this cooperative dairy organization, which is helped by Danish experts and equipment supplied by UNICEF.

Modhera

The sun temple of Modhera, 97 kilometers (60 miles) northwest of Ahmedabad, claims its place among India's most significant monuments. Built in A.D. 1026–27 on an exceptionally high plinth, it is designed to let the sun's rays penetrate the shrine. Full of grandeur and balance, its lines are enhanced by a wide bank of steps descending to a tank. A pillared dancing hall leads to the Assembly Hall and shrine. Such is the design of the shrine that the Surya (Sun God) image—now missing—would be highlighted by the rising sun and the equinoxes.

On the road to Saurashtra is Sarkhej, once a deserted country retreat of sultans. Here are the tomb and mosque of Mahmud Begara, whose name, Begara, came from his enormous mustache shaped like the curved horns of a bullock. Among this group of buildings is the tomb of Ganj Bakash, a saint and spiritual guide of Begara. Sarkhej's monuments, although Moslem, are almost purely Hindu inspired.

About 30 kilometers (18 miles) northeast of Modhera is Patan, famous for its Patola silk saris, made from an intricately dyed yarn that when woven reveals exquisite geometric patterns. Above all, Patan is noted for the Rani Vav step-well. Found almost exclusively in Gujarat, these architectural marvels were gigantic, elaborately carved stone staircases with various levels of subterranean wraparound corridors and a well at the bottom—all of which offered water and shade from the sun.

Named after the Mahatma, Gandhinagar, on the west bank of Sabarmati, is the new capital of Gujarat. Government buildings, children's gardens, a thermal power house, legislative assembly, and Sarita Garden are some of the places worth a visit in this new capital.

Echoes of Ancient Egypt

Travel 76 kilometers (47 miles) south of Ahmedabad to a place called Lothal, where archaeologists have uncovered the earliest-known urban civilization of the subcontinent. This site is, in fact, an extension of the Harappan civilization that is found at Mohenjo-Daro and Harappa (now in Pakistan). Here, archaeologists have excavated part of an ancient port, complete with dockyard, streets, houses, underground drains, and a wall. Lothal was probably one of ancient India's important ports having maritime connections with Mesopotamia and Egypt.

Among the interesting discoveries at this site is a terra-cotta that represents a joint burial of a man and a woman. It is probable that when Mohenjo-Daro and Harappa fell into decadence, Gujarat continued to preserve the same civilization for several centuries until it merged into the all-assimilating culture of the Aryans.

The peninsula of Gujarat, formerly named Saurashtra, which means a hundred kingdoms, is a region draped in romance and valor. In every city of Saurashtra, its rulers have left behind palaces, temples, mosques and museums, gardens, and sun-sparkling fountains. Parrots, which form the favorite motif of interior decoration and paintings of the region, flock by the thousands and feed on wild berries. Peacocks spread out their tails in the well-kept gardens.

From the centrally located university city of Rajkot, where Mahatma Gandhi spent his childhood, Saurashtra's many tourist destinations can be covered in day trips. The 50-year-old Watson Museum in Rajkot has numerous antiques—furniture, crystalware, carpets, bronzes, hunters' trophies, and jewels.

About 48 kilometers (30 miles) north of Rajkot is the former kingdom of Wankanar, with its ornate palace, built early in this century by the then maharajah. Farther north is the Rann of Kutch, a vast salt flat that also happens to be the last remaining outpost of the Asiatic wild ass and the world's largest flamingo breeding ground. Within the Kutch, you can visit old walled cities, such as Bhuj, and an area called Banni, with its mud-hut villages. Throughout the Kutch, you can also find some of India's best handicrafts: locally embroidered and mirror-worked fabrics, bandanna tie-dye fabrics, and exquisite silverwork. This is a rarely traveled yet fascinating part of Gujarat.

The city of Junagadh, at the foot of the sacred Girnar Mountain, is a few hours' drive south of Rajkot. Junagadh has many venerated Hindu and Jain temples; an Ashoka edict inscribed on a rock; an important Moslem mausoleum, Maqbara, which contains the remains of illustrious nawabs; and the Darbar Museum, an alabaster-white palace with a collection of Continental crystalware, chandeliers, and furniture upholstered with silver- and gold-encrusted brocades.

Atop Girnal Hill, you can see the beautifully carved Neminath Temple, one of five marble Jain shrines that overlook the city. This is also the site of a Hindu temple dedicated to Shiva and the tomb of a Moslem saint. Also visit Upar Kot, a historic fort on the eastern side of the city that has impressive gates, some walls 228 meters (70 feet) high, and an interior mosque. *Junagadh* means "old fort" and owes its name to this massive structure. Near Upar Kot are some interesting Buddhist caves with good carvings.

Sasan Gir, a forest preserve 54 kilometers (33 miles) from Junagadh, is the only remaining home of the majestic Asian lion. Here, in forest clearings or at its vast Kamleshwar Lake, you'll have a good chance of sighting the royal beast in its natural habitat. Within the park, also visit villages that are home to the Sidis, a tribal group that came back from Africa more than 200 years ago.

Southward from Junagadh lie the port town of Veraval and the sacred temple of Somnath at Prabbas Patan. Sacked and pillaged seven times and each time built anew to greater glory, the Shiva temple at Somnath, looking west to the Arabian Sea, is a magnificent edifice eulogized by the great historian-astronomer-mathematician Abu Raithan Al-Beruni. The museum reassembles the saga of the temple's destruction and rededication. Nearby is Bhalka Tirth, believed to be the place where Lord Krishna breathed his last. Coastal ships are built at Veraval.

Gujarat's Historic Coastline

Northwest of Somnath is Porbandar, a small port town and the birthplace of Mahatma Gandhi. Its narrow lanes are flanked by residential quarters with antique charm. Kirti Mandir, Gandhi's ancestral home, is open to the public. The exterior is attractive and the procession of pilgrims coming to honor him is touching, but the interior is spartan. A *swastika* (Sanskrit for "doing good for all") marks the spot where he was born. In another room, you can see a photo exhibit of the important events in his life. Gandhi's wife was born next door.

As the Saurashtra Peninsula narrows northward into a small strip at Dwarka, you'll approach one of the most sacred Hindu shrines, the Krishna Temple, with its spire supported by 60 pillars. Dwarka is believed to have been the kingdom of Lord Krishna. Over 2,000 generations have chanted hymns in this shrine. Among the other temples at Dwarka, the most beautiful is dedicated to Rukmani, Krishna's consort. Close to the port city of Okha on the Bet Dwarka islands are the Pat Rani temples. Lord Krishna supposedly lived on Bet Dwarka.

Just inland from Dwarka is Jamnagar, founded in 1540 by Jam Raval. An industrial town, it is also a good place to pick up tie-dye fabrics. Places of interest include the city lake with its historic Lakota Fort that is now a museum.

On the other end of the Saurashtra Peninsula is Palitana, 217 kilometers (134 miles) from Ahmedabad. On the hills of Shatrunjaya that rise over the little city are 863 Jain shrines that have been called the "Abode of the Gods." Their construction began in the eleventh century and continued over a period of 900 years. Their finely carved spires and towers glisten in the sunlight. Their exteriors are covered with friezes and sculptures; interiors are filled with statues of their *tirthankars* (perfect souls) who are the apostles of their faith. The entire hilltop seems a prayer in stone, a feeling emphasized by the presence of devout Jain *sadhus* (holy men) and *sadhivs* (holy women) dressed in crisp white.

Ahmedabad

Ahmedabad quietly blends the glorious past and a vibrant present. For architects, it is a remarkable repository of distinctive architectural styles— from the early Indo-Saracenic of the fifteenth century Moslem sultans to the experimental modern form of the legendary Le Corbusier. Rich detail, delicate tracery, and ornamental minarets impart a very Indian character to what had originally been foreign concepts.

Founded in A.D. 1411 by the Moslem Sultan Ahmed Shah, Ahmedabad flourished under the Gujarat dynasty and subsequently became the seat of the Mogul governors of Gujarat—Jahangir, Shah Jahan, and Aurangzeb, all of whom later became emperors.

At one time it was said that Ahmedabad hung on three threads: gold, silk, and cotton. Today, the city is once again the Manchester of the East, with about 40 mills that employ thousands and produce about one-third of India's total textiles.

In Ahmedabad, more than anywhere else in India, you can see the strong Hindu and Jain influences on Moslem forms. While Ahmedabad was a center of Moslem power and splendor and the home of a rich Islamic military official elite and of skilled Moslem weavers, its wealth came from trade and industry, which were largely controlled by Hindu and Jain merchants and bankers. When the city was a major center on the important trade routes, they controlled Ahmedabad's export trade in textiles and the import trade in luxuries for the courts, collected revenue for the state, and financed princes and armies.

From the second quarter of the seventeenth century, the city fell into a century-long decline. A terrible famine struck from 1630 to 1632. When the British took over the city, it was a desolate sight. Empty buildings were filled with rubbish and weeds. Wild animals roamed around broken-down city walls.

A quiet corner in Ahmedabad marks the city as the home of Mahatma Gandhi, the apostle of peace and nonviolence. In 1915 Gandhi set up a simple retreat, or "Insistence for Truth," north of the city, on the Sabarmati River. It became Satyagraha Ashram, the nerve center of India's freedom movement. From here, he also started the famous Dandi March to the sea in protest of the British-imposed salt tax, an event that launched the "Quit India" movement that brought about the end of British rule.

Bhuj and the Rann of Kutch

The Rann of Kutch and its district capital, Bhuj, 411 kilometers (255 miles) northwest of Ahmedabad, was built by Rao Khengar (1548–85). Its seventeenth-century fort was added by his successors, who ruled over Kutch until its merger with India in 1948. Once a walled-in city, it had five huge gates that were locked at night. Iron spokes on their exterior kept out invading forces and their elephants. After nightfall, only those visitors who approached a small window in one gate and knew the king's password could get inside.

Today, much of the wall and some of the gates are gone, but the old city remains a maze of homes and bazaars where merchants sell famous Kutch products: tie-and-dye, mirror-work, embroidery, and patchwork fabrics; beadwork; painted wooden toys and furniture; unusual cutlery; and leather shoes.

From Bhuj you can take an 80-kilometer (50-mile) day excursion to Dhordo and Hodka, two of the 40 villages open to foreigners (a permit is required) in the Banni area in the Rann of Kutch. Set amid salt flats, these villages are a testament to traditional artistry and a powerful example of the will to survive. At one time most of the people here were nomads who moved with their camels, cattle, and goats in search of water because of insufficient rain. Now many of these settlements are permanent, and the villagers survive on the meager income from handicraft sales. Modernization is slowly under way, but most of the homes are *bhungas,* round clay-and-dung huts with conical straw roofs that are held up by painted bamboo slats, which form a colorful, pointed ceiling. The window frames of the bhungas are decorated with white mudwork inlaid with mirror; colorful paintings cover the walls. The villagers, Hindus and Moslems, create all the products for sale in Bhuj.

PRACTICAL INFORMATION FOR GUJARAT

WHEN TO GO. The best time to visit Gujarat is October to March, when the temperature ranges between 55° and 85° F. From July to September, Gujarat can be hot and uncomfortable.

RESTRICTED AREA PERMIT. At press time, foreign visits to the Banni area in Kutch required a permit, which is free and can be obtained in about two hours from the Collector's Office in the Umed Bhavan Complex in Bhuj, open 10:30 A.M.–6:10 P.M., closed Sunday and second and fourth Saturdays. Visitors must list specific villages. Dhordo, Dumado, and Hodka villages specialize in embroidery and leatherwork. Ludia village has beautiful traditional round huts with exterior paintings. At press time, this permit requirement was under review. Check when you arrive in Bhuj.

HOW TO GET THERE. By Air. From London and New York, *Air India* makes a weekly flight to Ahmedabad, which has an international airport. From Delhi, *Indian Airlines* has two daily flights to Ahmedabad and a daily flight to Vadodara (Baroda). From Bombay, Indian Airlines has 16 weekly flights to Ahmedabad; a daily flight to Bhavnagar, Rajkot, and Vadodara; and five weekly flights to Bhuj and Jamnagar. From Goa and Indore, it has two weekly flights to Ahmedabad. From Madras, it has five weekly flights to Ahmedabad. *Vayudoot* has three weekly flights from Pune and Hyderabad to Porbander and six weekly flights to Rajkot. For Indian Airlines information, call 353333 in Ahmedabad; 63868 in Vadodara;

and 23350 in Rajkot. For Vayudoot information in Ahmedabad, contact Express Travels, tel. 448602; in Porbander, contact Vayas Travel, tel. 22141.

By Bus. Deluxe buses from Bombay make frequent runs to Ahmedabad and Vadodara. There's also frequent bus service to Ahmedabad from Pune in Maharashtra and Ajmer, Udaipur, and Mount Abu in Rajasthan.

By Train. Ahmedabad and Vadodara are well connected with Bombay and Delhi by train. Among many good trains are the *Sarvodaya Express, Delhi-Ahmedabad Express, Karnavati Express,* and the *Gujarat Express.* You can also reach Ahmedabad by meter-gauge lines from Rajasthan and Agra. Remember, if you travel overnight, you must reserve a sleeping berth or you could be booted from the train. For reservations and information in Bombay or Delhi, see those chapters. In Ahmedabad, call 131; in Vadodara, call 557575 or 327979.

By Hired Car with Driver. Ahmedabad and Vadodara are on National Highway 8, which connects Bombay and Delhi. From Ahmedabad, Bombay is 510 km (316 mi.); Delhi, 886 km (549 mi.); Jaipur, 625 km (388 mi.); Ajmer, 561 km (348 mi.); Udaipur, 287 km (180 mi.); Mount Abu, 222 km (138 mi.); Bhopal, 571 km (354 mi.). From Vadodara, Bombay is 425 km (264 mi.); Delhi, 995 km (617 mi.); Jaipur, 725 km (450 mi.); Udaipur, 370 km (229 mi.); Bhopal, 515 km (319 mi.); Indore, 348 km (216 mi.). In Gujarat, hire a car from one of the tour operators listed below. Figure Rs. 4 per km, with a 250-km (155-mi.) daily minimum charge.

TOURIST INFORMATION. For information on Gujarat, contact the *Tourist Corporation of Gujarat* (TCG). Offices are open 10:30 A.M.–6 P.M., closed Sundays and second and fourth Saturdays. The head office is at H. K. House, off Ashram Rd. (behind Jivabhai Chambers), Ahmedabad 390009; tel. 449683, 460533, and 449172. Other offices are in the following cities:

Rajkot. Bhavnagar House, Jawahar Rd. (behind State Bank of Saurashtra), Rajkot 360001; tel. 31616.

Surat. 1/847 Athugar St., Nanpura, Surat 395001; tel. 26586.

Vadodara. Narmada Bhavan, C-Block, Indira Ave., Vadodara 390001; tel. 540797 or 65088.

Bhuj. There is a Tourist Information Office at Aina Mahal Trust, near Mahadeo Gate; open 9 A.M.–noon and 3 P.M.–6 P.M., closed Saturday.

FOREIGN CURRENCY EXCHANGE. Most Western-style hotels have money-exchange counters, as do branches of the *State Bank of India,* open Monday–Friday, 10 A.M.–2 P.M.; Saturdays till noon.

ACCOMMODATIONS. While good Western-style hotels exist in Ahmedabad, Vadodara, and Surat, and some lovely palace-hotels provide comfortable stays in a few remote destinations, much of Gujarat offers only simple accommodations. Arrive with the proper expectations. Be aware that Gujarat is a dry state. Liquor permits must be obtained from your hotel or from the Government of India Tourist Office in your home country before you depart. This permit allows you to purchase liquor from hotel-permit rooms for consumption in your room. Prices of hotels are based on double occupancy and exclude taxes and service charges: *Deluxe,* over Rs. 2,000; *Expensive,* Rs. 1,200–Rs. 2,000; *Moderate,* Rs. 500–Rs. 1,200; *Inexpensive,* under Rs. 500. Some Western-style hotels take major credit cards.

AHMEDABAD

Expensive

Quality Suites Shalin. Gujarat College Rd., Ellisbridge, Ahmedabad 380006; tel. 446767, fax 460022. 70 rooms with bath. This is a new hotel that caters to the business person. Its sleek lobby has large banks of windows that overlook a small garden and lawn. Suites are modern, with TV and air-conditioning. Pool-facing rooms have the best view. Room service, restaurants, permit room, small swimming pool, foreign-exchange and travel counter, doctor. DC, MC, V.

Cama Hotel. Khanpur, Ahmedabad 380001; tel. 25281. 55 rooms with bath. This well-run hotel has an attractive lobby, with lots of marble and plants. It also has a quiet back lawn and spacious air-conditioned rooms with contemporary furnishings and TV. Higher-priced doubles (still moderate) have balconies. Ask for a river view. Room service, permit room, multicuisine restaurants, doctor, foreign-exchange and travel counter, swimming pool, attractive lawn. AE, DC, MC, V.

Hotel Karnavati. Ashram Rd., Ahmedabad 380009; tel. 402161. 48 rooms with bath. This four-story Western-style hotel has an enormous lobby, with a display of old torans (embroidered decorations and a symbol of welcome) hung from the ceiling. Large air-conditioned rooms have a simple, modern decor and TV. Corner rooms, called deluxe but moderately priced, offer the best view. Room service, multicuisine restaurants, permit room, foreign-exchange and travel counter, doctor. AE, DC, MC, V.

Hotel Riviera. Khanpur, Ahmedabad 380001; tel. 24201. 69 rooms with bath. This Western-style hotel has good rooms with modern decor, air-conditioning, and TV. Multicuisine restaurant, room service, permit room, doctor, foreign-exchange and travel counter. AE, DC, MC, V.

AHMEDPUR MANDVI

Inexpensive

Samudra Beach Resort. Ahmedpur Mandvi via Una, Dist. Junagadh 362510; tel. 2216. 15 cottages with bath. You enter this delightful government-run resort, converted from a former royal retreat, through a *haveli* (mansion) gate and stay in attractive clay-covered cottages. Verandas have traditional Gujarati swings; interiors are tastefully decorated in Gujarati decor. There are overhead fans, room service, multicuisine restaurant, 6-km (4-mi.) swimming beach, water sports. Rupees only.

BHAVNAGAR

Moderate

Welcomgroup Nilambag Palace. Bhavnagar 364002; tel. 24340. 14 rooms with bath. 55 km (34 mi.) from Palitana. This lovely, yet not grand, turn-of-the-century palace is now an excellent hotel. Belongings of its former maharajah still adorn interior rooms. Bedrooms are gigantic, with handsome furnishings. There's a pretty garden and a pool. Room service, Indian- and Continental-cuisine restaurant, library, tennis, swimming pool. AE, DC, MC, V.

BHUJ

Expensive

Toran Rann City. Reservations: Tourism Corporation of Gujarat, H. K. House, off Ashram Rd., Ahmedabad 390009; tel. 449683. 5 huts with baths. This is a delightful new complex of traditional *bhungas* (round clay-and-dung huts with conical roofs), which have the typical Kutch interior: window trims with inlaid mirrors and white mudwork, and wall paintings. Each hut has simple, clean furnishings and its own bath. There's an outdoor eating area serving Kutch specialties, along with room service. Meals included. Closed mid-June–mid-October. Rupees only.

Inexpensive

Hotel Prince. Station Rd., Bhuj, Kutch 370001; tel. 20370. 26 rooms with bath. This Western-style hotel has very clean rooms with a simple decor. Some rooms are air-conditioned; others have overhead fans. Room service, TV, multicuisine restaurant, travel arrangements. Rupees only.

CHORWAD

Inexpensive

Beach Palace Resort. Via Gadu, Chorwad, Dist. Junagadh 362510; tel. 96. 12 rooms with bath in palace; 18 rooms with bath in palace annex. This twentieth-century palace of a former nawab, now a government-run hotel, is in an idyllic setting facing the sea. Unfortunately, while rooms are palatial in size, furnishings are clean but worn in the palace and very modest in the annex. At the abutting beach, the current is too swift for swimming, but you can swim a few kilometers away. Overhead fans, room service, multicuisine restaurant. AE, DC.

JAMNAGAR

Inexpensive.

Hotel President. Teen Batti, Jamnagar 361001; tel. 70516. 26 rooms with bath. This small Western-style hotel has clean, modest rooms. Those called super deluxe and deluxe (all inexpensive) are best—with air-conditioning, carpets, and TV. All rooms have overhead fans and room service. Multicuisine restaurant, foreign-exchange counter, car-rental service. DC, MC, V.

PORBANDAR

Inexpensive

New Oceanic Hotel. Chowpatty, Villa No. 8, Porbandar 360575; tel. 20717. 4 rooms with bath. Facing the ocean, this small Western-style hotel has air-conditioned rooms with plain furnishings; but they're very clean. Vegetarian Indian- and Continental-cuisine restaurant, TV lounge. Rupees only.

Toran Tourist Bungalow. Chowpatty, Porbandar 360575; tel. 22745. 20 rooms with bath. This government-run "no-frills" bungalow faces the sea. Western-style rooms, with individual terraces, are clean. Best rooms are air-conditioned. Overhead fans, room service, vegetarian multicuisine restaurant, TV lounge. Rupees only.

RAJKOT

Inexpensive

Galaxy Hotel. Jawahar Rd., Rajkot 360001; tel. 31781. 36 rooms with bath. This Western-style hotel is on the upper floors of a shopping complex. Some rooms have Gujarati laquered-wood furnishings; others have a simple but modern decor. If you want air-conditioning ask for it; some rooms are only air-cooled. TV, multicuisine restaurant, library, shops, foreign-exchange counter. AE, DC, MC, V.

SASAN GIR

Inexpensive

Lion Safari Lodge. Sasan Gir 394720; tel. 21. 24 rooms with bath. This government-run Western-style bungalow is set on the edge of the Gir Sanctuary. Rooms are clean, with plain modern decor and balconies that overlook a river. Some rooms are air-conditioned; all rooms have fans. Included are room service and a simple restaurant. Rupees only.

SURAT

Moderate

Rama Regency. Near Bharti Park, Ambica Niketan, Athwa Lines, Surat 395007; tel. 666565, fax 667294. 140 rooms with bath. This modern, multistory hotel is near the river. Its rooms have a contemporary decor, and those facing the pool have the best view. Room service, multicuisine restaurants, permit room, TV, health club, swimming pool, foreign-exchange counter, shopping arcade, doctor. AE, DC, MC, V.

VADODARA

Expensive

Welcomgroup Vadodara. R. C. Dutt Rd., Vadodara 390005; tel. 323232. 102 rooms with bath. A three-story luxury hotel, this place offers attractive rooms with a contemporary decor, air-conditioning, and TV. Ask for a room with a pool view. Multicuisine restaurants, room service, permit room, swimming pool, health club, foreign-exchange and travel counter, secretarial services, shopping arcade. AE, DC, MC, V.

Express Hotel. R. C. Dutt Rd., Vadodara 390005; tel. 323131. 64 rooms with bath. This Western-style high rise has a small, modest lobby and pleasant, modern rooms with air-conditioning and TV. Room service, multicuisine restaurants, permit room, foreign-exchange and travel counter, secretarial services, free airport shuttle. AE, DC, MC, V.

Inexpensive

Surya Palace Hotel. Opposite Parsi Agyari, Sayajigunj, Vadodara 390005; tel. 329999, fax 325668. 80 rooms with bath. This new multistory high rise has a marble lobby and spacious contemporary-decor rooms with air-conditioning and TV. Room service, multicuisine restaurants, permit room, swimming pool, health club, doctor, secretarial service, foreign-exchange and travel counter, free airport shuttle, shopping arcade. AE, DC, V.

WANKANER

Expensive

The Palace. Wankaner 363621, 38 km (24 mi.) from Rajkot; tel. 324. 20 rooms with bath. Still maintained by the former maharajah of Wankaner, this castle on a quiet hill has rooms in the Royal Guest House, which adjoins the sumptuous main residence (built in 1901), and in nearby Oasis, a bungalow fronted by a courtyard and near an orchard by a river. The Oasis has an indoor swimming pool and an exquisite old step-well. Four rooms have Art Deco furnishings. Other rooms in both facilities have older furnishings that aren't particularly ornate. The hosts here are delightful. All meals are served in the main palace dining room. There are overhead fans, room service, fixed-menu Indian- and Continental-cuisine meals, a private museum, horseback riding, land-boat arrangements in nearby salt flats, jeep excursions to wildlife sanctuaries. Folk-dance performances can be arranged with advance notice. Meals included. Rupees only.

DINING OUT. Gujaratis, predominantly vegetarians, have created a wonderful regional cuisine with delicate flavoring. The best way to sample Gujarati dishes is to order a *thali*—a variety of dishes (dry-cooked vegetables, cooked vegetables in gravy, lentils, yogurt) served in small metal bowls on a metal platter. Many restaurants offer a limited or an unlimited thali. Unlimited means come hungry and let them keep refilling your plate. Breakfast is usually served 7:30–10; lunch, 12:30–2:30; and dinner, 7:30–10:30. Most restaurants take only rupees unless they are connected to a Western-style hotel. The restaurants listed below are informal and, unless noted, are open for all three meals and don't require reservations. Prices are based on a three-course dinner for one person, excluding beverage, tip, and taxes: *Expensive,* Rs. 200–Rs. 300; *Moderate,* Rs. 100–Rs. 200; *Inexpensive,* under Rs. 100.

AHMEDABAD

Moderate

Aab-o-Daana. Cama Hotel, Khanpur; tel. 25281. This attractive Mogul-influenced restaurant has lots of marble and lattice screens. Expect local entertainment nightly: ghazals, sitar, or Western band. The chef serves Indian, Continental, and Chinese meals. Try the chili fried chicken or *kachar gosht* (pickled mutton)—a spicy delicacy. Open 7:30–10 A.M., 12:30–2:30 P.M., 7:30–10:30 P.M. AE, DC, MC, V.

Patang. Ashram Rd.; tel. 77708. Ahmedabad's loveliest restaurant revolves atop a modern building. The decor is stylish Gujarati—brass ceiling, rough-stone interior walls. Live Indian classical music is played nightly. The chef prepares good Indian, Continental, and Chinese dishes. Specialties include assorted kebab platter, chicken *kadai* (chicken in a spicy brown gravy cooked and served in a special kadai dish), or vegetarian *paneer pasand kadai* (cottage cheese in a spicy tomato gravy garnished with cashews). There's a buffet at lunch and dinner. Reservations advised. Open 12:30–2:45 P.M. and 7–10:30 P.M. DC, MC, V.

Thikana. Trade Center, near Stadium Admedabad; tel. 464794. Connected to the upstairs of Angeethi (see below), this small new restaurant has upholstered booths and chairs. Subdued lighting and soft Indian music (taped) add to the intimate ambience. Its extensive menu features Nawabi *dum pukht cuisine:* The food is sealed in aluminum foil while it's cooked in special pots to keep in subtle aromas. Try *murgth kesar badam* (boneless chicken) or *gosht Asafjahani* (mutton pieces). Each dish is marinated in special spices and cooked in different almond-based gravies that impart their own flavor. Dinner reservations advised. Open noon–3 P.M. and 7 P.M.–11 P.M. AE, DC.

Moderate

Angeethi Restaurant. Trade Center, near Stadium Ahmedabad; tel. 464794. This delightful eatery has a café ambience—tile floor, red-and-white checkered placemats—and an upstairs balcony with a hideaway dining nook for couples. Punjabi, Continental, and Chinese meals are served; ask about the daily specials. Open 12:30–3 P.M. and 7–11 P.M. AE, DC.

Inexpensive

Garden Cafe. Ashram Rd.; tel. 77708. On the second-story terrace of a modern complex, this outdoor café, with plants surrounding fountains and small pools, plays piped-in Western music. It serves good multicuisine meals—tandooris, fresh *chats* (cold mixed vegetables), pizzas, and sandwiches. Open 6 P.M.–11:30 P.M. DC, MC, V.

Riwaaz. Riviera Hotel, Khanpur; tel. 24201. At press time, this restaurant was under renovation, with plans calling for a terrace extension. Come here for good tandoori items and butter chicken (curried chicken). You can also order Chinese and Continental dishes. Open 7–11 A.M., noon–3 P.M., and 7–11 P.M. AE, DC, MC, V.

Toran Dining Hall. Opposite Sales India, Ashram Rd.; tel. 462197. The decor here is sleek—soft gray walls with marble trim, recessed lighting, and dark mirrors inset in pillars—but the food is traditional Gujarati thali. Come hungry and your platter will be filled and refilled with freshly prepared delicacies. Save room for the unusual sweets. This is thali raised to haute cuisine. Open 10:30 A.M.–3 P.M. and 6:30 P.M.–10 P.M. Rupees only.

Vishalla. Opposite Vasana Tol Naka; tel. 403357. A few kilometers outside the city center, this excellent outdoor restaurant serves a delicious Gujarati thali in purely ethnic surroundings. You eat with your right hand off a banana leaf under charming thatched huts. While you wait for your meal, you can visit its Gujarati handicrafts museum or watch an evening performance of traditional entertainment. The manager will help you decipher the menu board. Open 11 A.M.–1 P.M. and 7–11 P.M. Rupees only.

PORBANDAR

Inexpensive

Swagat Dining Hall. M. G. Rd.; tel. 20246. This upstairs restaurant, with booths and Formica tables, serves tasty vegetarian dishes—Indian, Continental, and Chinese. Try the popular *dosas* (vegetable-stuffed crêpe). There is taped music and courteous service. Open 9 A.M.–3 P.M. and 5–10 P.M. Rupees only.

RAJKOT

Inexpensive

Bhabha Dining Hall. Panchnath Rd., near Alfred High School; no phone. Too bad you can't make reservations; this tiny, popular restaurant draws a crowd. It serves one dish: Gujarati thali. Here, the unlimited thali is called the "special." Arrive good and hungry. Open 10:30 A.M.–3 P.M. and 7–10 P.M. Rupees only.

SURAT

Inexpensive

Dhawalgiri Restaurant. Dhawalgiri Guest House, Dhawalgiri Apartment, opposite Collector's Bungalow, Athwalines; tel. 40040. This very good restaurant serves excellent multicuisine vegetarian dishes that are supposed to promote good health. Open 10 A.M.–10 P.M. Rupees only.

VADODARA

Expensive

Ruchika Restaurant. Welcomgroup Vadodara, R. C. Dutt Rd.; tel. 323232. In an elegant contemporary decor, tasty Mughlai cuisine and especially good tandoori items are offered. Dinner reservations advised. Open 12:30–3 P.M. and 7:30–11 P.M. AE, DC, MC, V.

Inexpensive

Mandap. Express Hotel, R. C. Dutt Rd.; tel. 323131. If you're in the mood for a good Gujarati thali, this informal restaurant will satisfy your craving. Open 11 A.M.–3 P.M. and 7–10 P.M. AE, DC, MC, V.

SWEETS AND TREATS. Ahmedabad. For good ice cream, Western snacks, and good coffee, drop in at *Hasty Tasty,* Anand, near Municipal Market, Navrangpura; open 11:30 A.M.–11 P.M. For delicious Western pastries, cakes, pizzas, and even tacos, visit the *Bakery Cafe,* near Stadium Crossroads, Trade Center, Navrangpura; open 8 A.M.–11 P.M. For good Indian sweets, go to *Rajbhog,* opposite Urja House, near Swastik Cross Rd., open 10:30 A.M.–11 P.M.

HOW TO GET AROUND. From the Airports. Ahmedabad. The airport is 10 km (six mi.) from the city. *Ahmedabad Municipal Transport Service* (AMTS) runs buses from the airport to the city for Rs. 3. You can also go by taxi for about Rs. 120. **Vadodara.** The airport is 6 km (four mi.) from the city. You can take a taxi (about Rs. 60) or an auto rickshaw (about Rs. 30). From the other airports, your choice is also taxi or auto rickshaw.

By Plane. *Indian Airlines* has a daily flight between Ahmedabad and Vadodara, and five weekly flights between Jamnagar and Bhuj. *Vayudoot* has three weekly flights between Ahmedabad and Vadodara.

By Bus. *Gujarat State Road Transport Corporation* buses tend to be crowded and slow going, but they do go to every place in the state. In Ahmedabad, for schedules and reservations, contact the Central Bus Station, Geeta Mandir; tel. 344764. In Vadodara, contact the Central Bus Station, near Railway Station; tel. 327000.

By Train. From Ahmedabad, you can go by train to Bhavnagar, Vadodara, Surat, Junagadh, Veraval (near Somnath), Jamnagar, Porbandar, Rajkot, and Bhuj. For information and reservations in Ahmedabad, contact *Ahmedabad Junction Railway Station;* tel. 131. In Vadodara, contact *Railway Station, Sayajigunj;* tel. 557575, 63535, or 327979. If you travel at night, remember to reserve a sleeping berth.

By Rented Car with Driver. From Ahmedabad, Vadodara is 113 km (70 mi.); Surat, 120 km (74 mi.); Lothal, 84 km (52 mi.); Rajkot, 216 km (134 mi.); Porbandar, 394 km (244 mi.); Palitana, 217 km (134 mi.); and Bhuj (in Kutch), 411 km

(255 mi.). With reasonably good roads throughout Gujarat, this is a good way to explore the state. The cost of a car is about Rs. 4 per km, with a 250 km (155 mi.) minimum charge per day. Hire a car from one of the recommended tour operators listed below.

By Taxi. Tourist taxis are usually available at city railroad stations and airports. They charge by the hour, with a minimum tariff. For short hops, it's cheaper to use an auto rickshaw.

By Auto Rickshaw. Auto rickshaws should cost about Rs. 2.25 per km. Make sure the driver uses his meter; or negotiate before you start up.

TOURS. Tourist Corporation of Gujarat (TCG) offers two economical five-day bus tours that depart from Ahmedabad. For details and booking, contact TCG at H. K. House, off Ashram Rd., Ahmedabad; tel. 449683, 449172, or 460533.

Saurashtra Darshan Tour includes Rajkot, Jamnagar, Dwarka, Porbandar, Somnath, Sasan Gir, Junagadh, Veraval, Palitana, Velavadar, Lothal. It departs each Friday.

North Gujarat and Rajasthan Tour includes Udaipur, Chittorgarh, Mount Abu, Ambaji, Khumbharia, Modhera, Bahucharaji. It departs first and third Saturdays.

Ahmedabad Municipal Corporation (AMC) conducts two local bus tours of Ahmedabad. For details and booking, contact AMC, tel. 365610.

Morning Tour: Sidi Saiyad, Hutheesing Jain Temple, Sardar Patel Museum, Calico Museum, Dadahari step-well, Lake Kankaria, Geeta Mandir, Shah Alam Mosque.

Afternoon Tour: Gandhi Ashram, Vechaar Utensils Museum, Snake Farm, Municipal Museum.

Vadodara Municipal Corporation (VMC) conducts three afternoon bus tours of sites around Vadodara. For details and booking, contact VMC, tel. 329656.

Tour 1: EME Temple, Sayaji Garden, Kirti Mandir, Geeta Mandir, Baroda Dairy, Fatehsinh Museum, Aurobindo Society. Offered on Tuesday, Wednesday, and Friday.

Tour 2: Nimeta (picnic spot), Ajwan (Brindavan pattern garden). Offered July–September on Saturday, Sunday, and Monday.

Tour 3: Both above tours combined. Offered October–June on Saturday, Sunday, Monday (tour lasts until 9 P.M.).

A five-day *South Gujarat, Ajanta, and Ellora Tour* leaves on demand.

TOUR OPERATORS. For all travel needs, including rented car with driver, contact the following dependable agencies:

Travel Corporation of India, near Natraj Theatre, behind Handloom House, Ashram Rd., Ahmedabad 380001; tel. 407601. *TCI* also has cars available for hire.

Exotic Journey (26 Sector 2 Market, R. K. Puram, New Delhi; tel. 670221) sponsors good safaris into the Rann of Kutch Desert. Also see Special-Interest Tours in *Facts at Your Fingertips* for names of other India-based agencies that can create a special trip in Gujarat.

For excellent hikes or camel safaris in the Rann of Kutch, contact this erudite guide in advance: D. R. Rathora, Primary Teacher, Baladia, Bhuj-Taluka, Bhuj 370001. He can organize a 10- to 15-day trip through the salt flats or marshlands (frequented by flamingos) or to villages where artisans create the famous Kutch products. The best time is from November to February.

SEASONAL EVENTS. Since most of the events are determined by the lunar calendar, contact the tourist offices for the exact dates. Fairs, which may be rooted in religion to commemorate events in honor of gods or goddesses, are truly secular social events in which all are invited to participate.

January. *Makar Sankranti.* During this festival, which marks the passing of the sun from Dhanu to Makar, sweets are exchanged and kite-flying contests fill the skies, especially in Ahmedabad from Janaury 13 to 15, during its International Kite Festival. There are regional, state, and international contests and demonstrations. An extravagant affair!

January/February. *Bhavnath Fair.* This five-day event is held during Mahashivatri at the foot of Mount Girnar. After a holy dip in the Mrigi Kund, pilgrims offer prayers at the temple. An awe-inspiring midnight ritual is a *Mahapu-*

ja, in which holy men from all over the country ride about the fair on caparisoned elephants to the reverberating accompaniment of musical instruments. Great folk dancing!

February/March. *Rannotsav.* Organized by Gujarat Tourism, this four-day festival in Bhuj celebrates the Kutch culture. Folk artists sing, dance, and play local musical instruments; artisans sell their crafts and give demonstrations; local food is served. Lots of color, with some events occurring in nearby villages.

February/March. *Holi.* On this day, marking the start of spring, wear old clothes. Celebrants throw colored water on anything that moves.

March/April. *Rathyatra.* This is by far the biggest festival in Ahmedabad, with a day-long procession of thousands of devotees walking behind temple chariots accompanied by adorned elephants, camels, and trucks carrying mythological tableaux. The procession commemorates the visit of Krishna and Balram to Mathura.

August. *Gokulashtami.* Krishna's birthday is celebrated as a joyous festival, with feasting and merrymaking. Large fairs are held in Dwarka. Gujaratis perform the Ras, a folk dance supposedly introduced by Krishna.

August/September. *Tarnetar Fair.* This three-day tribal fair takes place at the Trineshwara (three-eyed) Temple. One ongoing event involves the "hunt for a husband," with marriageable young girls eyeing eligible young boys and sometimes finding a match. Colorful costumes, good folk dances, and music.

September/October. *Vadodara International Navratri Festival.* During these nine nights of music and dancing devoted to the nine forms of the mother goddess Durga, the entire city holds dance, singing, and music competitions. Vadodara is illuminated at night for festive prayer services. Navaratri is a big event in all of Gujarat.

November. *Diwali.* Candles adorn practically every house at night; firecrackers go off in every village and city. The day preceding Diwali is celebrated as the new year, believed to be an auspicious day to enter any business transaction.

HISTORIC SITES. Entrance is usually free; where a donation is requested, a few rupees will suffice. Monuments are open sunrise to sunset, unless noted otherwise below.

AHMEDABAD ENVIRONS

Ahmed Shah Mosque, southwest section of Bhadra, was built for the founder of Ahmedabad. Originally a Hindu temple, it was ransacked and rebuilt as a mosque.

Hutheesing Jain Temple, outside Delhi Gate, was built in 1850 and is dedicated to Dharmanath, the 15th Jain tirthankar. The white-marble structure is surrounded by 52 small shrines.

Jama Masjid, one of the largest Indian mosques, was built in 1423. It has 300 pillars that divide the huge prayer hall into 15 large squares, each one surmounted with a dome.

Sidi Sayyid Masjid, Relief Rd., near the river, is a mosque, built in 1572, that is famous for its latticed windows carved in single-stone panels. The pattern of one window is an exquisite rendering of the Tree of Life.

Siddi Bashir Mosque, the architectural marvel of Gujarat, rises above the Sarangpur Gate. The mosque has two delicately carved, three-story minarets, with balanced stone balconies wrapped around each story. Gently push one minaret and both shake in unison. Across the railway line, Raj Bibi Mosque also had a pair of shaking minarets before the British demolished one to unravel its mystery. You are forbidden to shake the one that remains.

Ranki Vav in Patan, 125 km (77 mi.) from Ahmedabad, is one of the finest stone step-wells in Gujarat, with subterranean sculptured corridors and steps leading to a well.

OTHER GUJARAT SITES

Ambaji, Arasur Hill near Mount Abu, 194 km (120 mi.) from Ahmedabad, is dedicated to the worship of Shakti and is one of the most important Hindu pilgrimage centers in Gujarat. Gujarat Bhavai, a folk drama, is often staged in the temple complex.

Dwarka, where Lord Krishna supposedly established his kingdom, is one of the four most sacred Hindu pilgrimage centers in India. Archaeological excavations show that present-day Dwarka is the sixth city on this site; the others were reclaimed by the sea. The five-story Dwarkadhish Temple, said to be over 2,500 years old, is supported by 60 columns and is crowned by a soaring, elaborately carved spire. Also see the nearby Rukmani Temple, dedicated to one of Krishna's consorts, and Nageshwar Mahadev and Gopi Talav Teerth, two other important shrines near Dwarka. Krishna's actual residence is said to be on nearby Bet Dwarka Island, approached by public boat launch. Here the Hindu god Vishnu supposedly killed the demon Shankhasura.

Modhera Sun Temple is one of the finest examples of Indian architecture of its period. Built in 1026 during the reign of King Bhimdev I of the Solanki dynasty, the temple is dedicated to the sun god Surya and stands high on a plinth overlooking a deep stone-stepped tank. Every inch of the edifice, both inside and outside, is magnificently carved with gods and goddesses, birds, beasts, and flowers. The inner sanctum, which housed the presiding deity, was so designed that the first rays of the rising sun lit up the image of Surya.

Palitana, a picturesque temple city atop the holy Shatrunjaya Mountain, is dedicated to Shri Adhishwara, the first Jain trithanker. Every Jain dreams of walking up the hill to build a temple, adding to the 900-plus shrines already at the bejeweled crest. The fantastic collection of temple jewels can be seen by special permission of the Hill Inspector or Manager of Anandji Kalyanji Trust in Palitana or during deity-adorning ceremonies at Shri Adishwara Temple. Photos are not permitted.

Somnath, one of India's 12 most sacred Shiva temples and called a Jyotorlinga, is a majestic seashore monument. It was ransacked and destroyed repeatedly by Moslem invaders, then rebuilt. It is believed that the temple was first built of gold, then silver, wood, and finally stone. The present temple is a twentieth-century reconstruction. The shrine's gates were carried away by Mahmud of Ghazni in 1026. Suraj Mandir, near the shrine, is also a sun temple. A museum housed in the temple contains relics of the old Somnath shrine. Also see Bhalka Teerth, near Somnath, where Lord Krishna, mistaken for a deer, was wounded by an arrow; and Dehotsarga at Triveni Ghat, also nearby, where Krishna was cremated.

MUSEUMS AND GALLERIES. Gujarat has several museums worth visiting, notably in Ahmedabad, Bhuj, and Vadodara. Entrance is usually free or costs a nominal fee.

AHMEDABAD

Calico Museum of Textiles (Sarabhai House in Shahi Bagh) is considered one of the finest textile museums in the Far East. Its rare collection of fabrics dates to the seventeenth century. Included are Patola fabrics from Patan and south India, temple cloths, textiles from the Mogul period, handwoven cloths, brocades, and wooden blocks showing the Portuguese influence. A museum shop sells reproductions of some of the pieces on display, as well as cards and books. Open 10:30 A.M.–12:30 P.M. and 2:30–5:30 P.M.; closed Wednesdays.

N. C. Mehta Museum of Miniatures (L. D. Institute of Indology, University Area) houses rare Indian miniatures, a collection amassed by a philanthropist who donated them to the museum. Other paintings are also on display. Open 9–11 A.M. and 4–7 P.M.; closed Mondays.

Sabarmati Ashram (Sabarmati River) was Mahatma Gandhi's headquarters for 15 years. Many of Gandhi's historical events, such as the Dandi March, commenced here. The ashram was founded in 1915 and today houses many of Gandhi's personal effects. It still makes handicrafts, handmade paper, and spinning wheels. Open 8:30 A.M.–6:30 P.M. daily. On Sundays, Tuesdays, Thursdays, and Fridays, at 8:30 P.M., there is a son-et-lumiere show in English, with a small admission fee.

Shreyas Folk Museum is in the sloping green woodland that makes up the Shreyas Foundation. The museum has a fine collection of folk art and objects that illustrate the culture of Gujarat. On display are exquisite embroideries; unusual pots, pans, and other utensils; handicrafts; weapons; and bullock and camel carts. The museum also has a children's section that displays costumes, folk art, puppets, coins, and legends of various Indian states. Open afternoons only; call 78295 for details.

BHUJ

Aina Mahal Museum, in Darbargadh, contains the former maharajah's private collection of costumes, antiques, and paintings. Open 9 A.M.– noon and 3 P.M.–6 P.M., closed Saturday.

Bhartiya Sanskruti Darshan, on College Road, near Umed Bhawan, is a new re-creation of a Kutch village and is scheduled to open in late 1992. Call 1518 for hours.

Prag Mahal Palace Museum, in Darbargadh, was the residence of the former maharajah. You can visit the Durbar hall and his private rooms. Open 9 A.M.–noon and 3 P.M.–6 P.M., closed Saturday.

VADODARA

Baroda Museum and Art Gallery, in Sayaji Bagh, was founded in 1894 and has sections on art, archaeology, ethnology, geology, and natural history. The art gallery, in an adjoining building, contains Indian and European paintings. Open daily 9:30 A.M.–4:30 P.M.

Maharaja Fateh Singh Museum, Nehru Road, has a unique collection of art treasures of the former rulers of Baroda. Also on display are the works by Murillo, Raphael, and Titian, as well as modern European and Indian paintings and sculptures and a fine collection of Chinese and Japanese art. Open daily except Mondays 9 A.M.–noon and 3–6 P.M. July–March, 4–7 P.M. April–June.

PARKS AND GARDENS. Ahmedabad. *Deer Park,* next to Sarita Udyan in Gandhinagar, is a sprawling reserve for deer.

Sundervan Snake Garden, off M. Dayanand Road, has snakes from all over India. There is also a daily show that includes demonstrations with live snakes. For the less queasy, the garden is inhabited by freely roaming tame ducks and rabbits. And there's even a puppet show in the evenings!

SPORTS AND OUTDOOR ADVENTURES. Beaches. Gujarat's relatively unexploited coastline is gradually being developed into resorts, each with its own features, unique identity, and attraction.

Ahmedpur-Mandvi is an untouched beach located in Saurashtra and near the Union Territory of Diu. The beach has palm trees of a unique variety not generally found in India. The government-run Tourist Village resort is an attractive place in which to stay.

Mandvi, in Kutch, is a sleepy village on the coastline, 60 km (37 mi.), from Bhuj. It has a good white-sand beach that continues north to the sand dunes at Sutri village, about 50 km (31 mi.) away. If you want to tent, inform the Deputy of Road and Buildings (State), Mandvi, tel. 306 or Executive Magistrate, Mandvi, tel. 11.

Treks and Camel Safaris. You can arrange to hike or go by camel through the Rann of Kutch from October to February. This area is unspoiled, rarely traveled, and offers adventure, wildlife, and a glimpse into one of India's most artistically rich cultures. See Special-Interest Tours in *Facts at Your Fingertips* or in Tour Operators, above.

Land Yachts. You can arrange to skim across the Kutch salt flats on these novel land-based crafts. Contact Wankaner Palace (see Accommodations, above).

Wildlife Sanctuaries. *Sasan Gir Forests.* Asiatic lions, those increasingly rare beauties, can be spotted at close range in this sanctuary, the last major stronghold of the beasts. Also in the 800-square-kilometer (500-square-mile) forest are leopards, antelope, sambars, varieties of deer, and wild boar.

The best time to visit is March–May, when you'll have a chance to see the animals lazing near water holes. The forest is closed mid-June–mid-October. Jeep safaris are available.

Little Rann of Kutch Sanctuary. The only home of the rare wild ass and the world's largest flamingo breeding ground, this wide salt-flat area is just a few feet above sea level and is completely dry November–June, when you can drive through by jeep. The best time to visit is December–May.

Valvadar Sanctuary. This grassland preserve is home to the exquisite black buck, one of nature's swiftest animals. The best time to visit is October–June and on moonless and full-moon nights.

SHOPPING. Gujarat offers a scintillating range of fabrics, including woven textiles, tie-and-dye work, gold and silver thread work (*zari*), silk embroidery, and various styles of saris. Also popular and lovely are mirror work on cloth, bead-encrusted artifacts from Kutch, lacquered furniture from Sankheda, and wood carvings from Ahmedabad and Kutch.

In Ahmedabad, visit the following reliable fixed-price shops:

Banjara, 2 and 3 Ground Floor, Jasmine, Khanpur, sells custom-designed leather goods from caps to footwear and luggage. Open 9 A.M.–8 P.M., closed Sunday. Rupees only.

Handloom House, Ashram Rd., has beautiful Gujarati textiles, plus a good sampling of Indian handicrafts. Open 10 A.M.–7 P.M., closed Sunday. AE, DC.

Gujari, Ashram Rd., a government-run emporium, has delightful Gujarati handicrafts and textiles (hand-embroidery, mirror work, patchwork, rabira embroidery, tanka stitchery, block printing). Also visit *Garvi,* the companion store in the back of the same building. Here you'll find more beautiful Gujarati fabrics and excellent readymade clothes, wall hangings, bedspreads, cushion covers, and *dhurries* (rugs). Both shops are open 10:30 A.M.–2 P.M. and 3–7 P.M., closed Sunday. AE, DC.

Mintissa, Ratnam Bungalow, Stadium Rd., sells beautiful silk and cotton *salwar kameez* (long blouse and loose pants)—readymade and to order. Open 10 A.M.–12 P.M. and 4–6 P.M.; closed Sunday. Rupees only.

Avni Boutique, near H. L. Commerce College, Navrangpura, and *Bandhej,* opposite L. D. Commerce, University Area, also sell exquisite *salwar kameez*—readymade and to order. Open 10 A.M.–7 P.M.; closed Sunday. Rupees only.

If you're prepared to bargain, or just like to browse, also visit these two fascinating bazaars. *Manek Chowk* in the old city. Here you can find beautiful Gujarati textiles by the meter. One must-stop is *Gamthiwala* (Rani's Hajira Naka, 1st Shop) Open 10 A.M.–7 P.M., closed Sunday. Rupees only.

Law Garden Bazaar is a delightful nighttime bazaar where Gujarati products are set up on the sidewalk and sold. Examine items carefully. Some fabrics are hand-embroidered, but many items are embroidered by machine. Bargain! Rupees only.

In Bhuj, visit the old city and these shops for delightful Kutch handicrafts (bead and button work) and a good selection of fabrics, wall hangings, cushion covers and bedspreads, and traditional clothing:

Kachchh Darshan Handicraft Industries, Shroff Bazaar, is one of the oldest shops. It is run by Mr. Ashok Khatau, who knows his merchandise. Open Monday–Saturday, 9:30 A.M.–8:30 P.M. and Sunday, 10 A.M.–1 P.M. Rupees only.

Kala, Waniawad, is open 9 A.M.–1 P.M. and 3 P.M.–8:35 P.M., closed Sunday. Rupees only.

In Vadodara, the best shopping area is *Leheripura Mandir Bazaar,* with its many shops dealing in fabrics, jewelry, and curios. In the *Fine Arts Faculty Building* of Baroda University a wide selection of pottery—from antiques to newly made pieces—can be found.

NIGHTLIFE AND BARS. Gujarat is a dry state; all alcohol must be consumed in your room. Most permit rooms are open 10:30 A.M.–6:40 P.M. In Ahmedabad, enjoy good cultural performances at Vishalla under the stars. See Dining Out, above.

MADHYA PRADESH

India's Heartland

by
KATHLEEN COX

A journey into the heart of India carries you back to historic moments of valor, glory, passion, and divinity. Madhya Pradesh's life is etched in stone—arrested by the chisels of master craftsmen. This lovely state is also studded with meandering rivers, extensive lush forests, hills and ravines, and some of the rarest species of birds and beasts, including the exquisite and elusive tiger. Conservationists have rated the Kanha and Bandhavgrah National parks, with their undulating meadows and abundant wildlife, the finest in the country. Indeed, Madhya Pradesh is the original Kipling country, the hunting grounds of Akela the wolf, Kaa the python, and Sher Khan the tiger.

Long before the written word, the magic of this central state was inscribed in colors that defied time, remaining as permanent reminders inside nearly 500 labyrinthine caves of Bhimbetka. On the caves' walls, a series of prehistoric paintings in vivid and panoramic detail sweep you back to at least 8000 B.C. In fact, you can call this entire state a museum without walls—one that contains over 1,800 man-made monuments, including some of the world's finest. Here, you can visit the *stupa* (shrine) at Sanchi, purportedly the best example of Buddhist architecture in India; the Bhimbetka rock shelter paintings that date from the Mesolithic period (approximately 8000 B.C.); and the Gwalior Fort, which Babur called "the pearl in the necklace of Indian forts." You can also see the beautifully preserved medieval town of Orchra; Mandu, a city built for joy by the Moslems in the fifteenth and sixteenth centuries about which the Emperor Jahangir wrote, "Of all places in Hindustan none is more beautiful than Mandu after the rains"; and, of course, the unforgettable temples at Khajuraho, where the ecstasy of passion has been immortalized in stone.

The Historic Record

When the great Ashoka ruled over the Maurya Empire in the third century B.C., he laid the foundation of the great stupa at Sanchi. Shortly after his death, his empire collapsed and the Sungas took over, followed by the Guptas (A.D. 300–500), whose reign is referred to as the Golden Age. Repeated invasions of the Huns from central Asia finally led to triumph over the splendor of the Guptas' Malwa Empire. The Huns, in turn, were defeated early in the seventh century by the famous Hindu emperor Harsha, who supposedly put 60,000 war elephants and 100,000 horses on the battlefields to achieve his conquest. Despite the fear this man inspired on the battlefield, Harsha did have a benevolent streak. Every five years he distributed to the poor all his accumulated riches until finally he was reduced to begging.

The close of the tenth century witnessed a period of confusion from which emerged the Paramara dynasty with the great king Bhoja, a renowned Sanskrit scholar. The succeeding Chandellas created the magnificent temples at Khajuraho. The first Moslem invasions in the eleventh century ushered in a 400-year period of constant skirmishing between Moslems and Hindus—the latter reasserting themselves each time the Delhi sultanate showed any weakness; then, the stake in the battle was usually the fabled city of Mandu. The last of the great Mogul emperors, the fanatic Aurangzeb, managed to extend his rule through this part of India, but at such tremendous financial cost that his empire collapsed with his death. Next came the Marathas, who started life as peasants skilled in guerrilla warfare. They reigned over Malwa until the advent of the British at the close of the eighteenth century.

EXPLORING MADHYA PRADESH

Bhopal and the Narmada River

Unfortunately, Bhopal is known primarily for the catastrophic Union Carbide gas-leak tragedy in 1984, which killed thousands who lived under the shadow of the plant. But Bhopal is much more than this now-closed industrial complex; it's a lovely city in India's heartland. Nestled in rich foliage, it's half hidden among mountains. A myriad of lights from houses are reflected in the placid waters of a pretty lake. Tall minarets and mosques stand majestically against the backdrop of shimmering city lights.

It was in the eleventh century that the legendary Raja Bhoj (1010–53), fond of lakeside views, created a lake around which grew a sprawling city, Bhopal, named after him. Soon more lakes and gardens, parks and ponds were constructed, but succeeding battalions of invaders seemed determined to erase it from the face of the earth, and Bhopal went into oblivion.

For a long while, Bhopal remained silent. But with the coming of the extravagant Moguls in the fourteenth century, the city was reborn.

The Afghan general of the Moguls, Dost Muhammed Khan, came here and was taken by its natural beauty. He set out a plan, and the new city of Bhopal began to take life on the ruins of the old city. Soon, the city, with its lakes, parks, gardens, and broad avenues, became a popular retreat. The Moguls made it a refuge for artists and musicians and a city of monuments and mausoleums. Their influence still lingers. Amuse yourself by watching a man, late in the night, with a *paan* in his mouth, an exquisitely carved silver purse in his hand, humming the lines of a poem. He has just come out of a *mushaira,* a symposium of poets.

Khan started the trend of creating picturesque lakes and raising beautiful monuments, with each ruler being more ambitious than his predecessor. Centuries have passed, rulers have come and gone, but the monuments are still under construction. The sprawling Taj-ul-Masajid,, started by Begum Shah Jahan in the 1800s, still incomplete, consists of an impressive main hall with an interarched roof, a broad facade, and a wide courtyard. Other monuments include the Jama Masjid, built by Kudsia Begum, which has tall dark minarets crowned with glittering golden spikes. The famous Moti Masjid is patterned on Delhi's Jama Masjid.

An outstanding feature of Bhopal, of course, is its two picturesque lakes. An overbridge divides one lake into two—Upper Lake and Lower Lake. The Upper Lake is over two square kilometers in size. From Idgah and Shamla Hills you'll get a fabulous view of the sunset and the twinkling city lights on the lakes.

Bhojpur is renowned for the remains of its magnificent Shiva temple and of two huge dams. The eleventh-century temple, known as the Bhojeshwar Temple, was constructed in a simple square plan, with each wall measuring 20 meters (66 feet)—an unusual design for such buildings. Its richly carved dome, though incomplete, has a magnificent soaring strength of line and is supported by four pillars. These pillars, like the dome, are massive, but because of their tapered form they retain a remarkable elegance.

Richly carved above, the plain doorway is a sharp relief from the two exquisitely sculpted figures that stand on either side. On the temple's other sides are balconies, each supported by massive brackets and four intricately carved pillars. The lingam in the sanctum rises to an awe-inspiring height of 2 meters (7½ feet) with a circumference of 6 meters (18 feet). Set on a massive platform 7 meters (21½ feet) square and composed of three superimposed limestone blocks, the architectural harmony of the lingam and platform creates a superb synthesis of solidity and lightness. The temple was never completed, and an earthen ramp used to raise stones to dome level still stands.

A vast lake once lay west of Bhojpur, but nothing remains today except the ruins of two huge dams that contained the lake's waters. The lake was destroyed by Hoshang Shah of Malwa (1405–34), who cut through the lesser dam, either intentionally or in a fit of destructive rage, and added an enormous fertile area to his possessions. According to a Gond legend, it took an army three months to cut through the dam and three years to empty it; then its bed was not habitable for 30 years. The climate of Malwa was considerably altered by the removal of this vast sheet of water.

Surrounded by the northern fringe of the Vindhyan ranges, Bhimbetka lies 40 kilometers (25 miles) south of Bhopal. In this rocky terrain of dense forest and craggy cliffs, over 700 rock shelters were recently discovered, extending back to the Neolithic Age. Hundreds of paintings in the caves depict the life of the prehistoric cave dwellers, making the Bhimbetka group an archaeological treasure, an invaluable chronicle of the history of humanity.

Executed mainly in red and white with occasional greens and yellows and with themes taken from the everyday events of aeons ago, most scenes depict hunting, dancing, music, horse and elephant riders, animal fights, honey collection, decoration of bodies, disguises, and household scenes. Animals, such as bisons, tigers, lions, wild boar, elephants, deer, antelopes, dogs, monkeys, lizards, and crocodiles, are also shown in abundance. In some caves, popular religious and ritual symbols occur frequently. The superimposition of paintings indicates that the same canvas was used by different people at different times.

Sanchi

Sanchi, 46 kilometers (29 miles) from Bhopal, sits on a hill crowned by a group of stupas and pillars that represent the peak of perfection in Buddhist art and architecture. This holy site occupies a unique position in the history of Buddhism. It was originally consecrated by the Kushan rulers in the first century A.D. Emperor Ashoka sought to give permanence to the site by replacing the original wooden structures and railings with perfectly wrought stone embellished in forms and symbols that expressed Buddhist teachings. After he constructed eight stupas at Sanchi, he built a nunnery for his queen, who came from Vidisha, espoused Buddhism, and entered the holy order of nuns. Meanwhile his son, Mahendra, went to Sri Lanka and spread the faith to that island.

The glory that was Sanchi, seat of Buddhist learning and place of pilgrimage during the third century B.C., can still be experienced in the site's serene complex of structures. Every form of Buddhist architecture found expression here: stupas, temples, pillars, monasteries, and four magnificent *toranas,* or gateways, which were added in the first century B.C. and face the Great Stupa No. 1. The master builders and carvers of these stupendous portals made of buff sandstone taken from the mines in Raisen drew inspiration from the *Jataka* tales (stories about the previous lives of the Buddha). The carvers, by trade silversmiths from Vidisha, brought to fruition on stone all the intricate, detailed skill of design and pattern consistent with their jeweler's art. The profuse carvings on the gateways depict the Buddha's incarnations and all the great moments in his life, which, in dramatic sequence, reveal the intense faith and supreme artistry of the creators of Sanchi.

After the decline of Buddhism in India, Sanchi went into oblivion. In 1818, Sir John Marshall, the director general of the Archaeological Survey of India, rediscovered the numerous remains. The architectural pieces and sculptures displayed here include the Ashoka pillar and images of the Buddha and Kushan.

At Sanchi, be certain to see the following:

Great Stupa No. 1. 36.5 meters (120 feet) in diameter and 16.4 meters (54 feet) high, this magnificent commemorative structure is a landmark in Buddhist architecture. Its construction was started during the reign of Emperor Ashoka but was completed by his successors in the second and first centuries B.C. The present stupa is a superstructure with a hemispherical dome that contains Buddhist relics built over the original earthen mound. It surmounts a high circular dome with a railing around its base. The railing encompassing the dome has four elaborately carved toranas that are among the finest examples of Buddhist art.

Gateways. Each portal is comprised of two square pillars that are decorated on top with sculptures of either lions, elephants, or dwarfs. Each set of pillars supports three horizontally placed columns (an architrave) that are elaborately carved. Bas-reliefs on the toranas depict tales of the

SANCHI
(3rd c BC – 10th c A D)

1. GREAT STUPA NO. 1
2. EASTERN GATEWAY
3. NORTHERN GATEWAY
4. WESTERN GATEWAY
5. SOUTHERN GATEWAY
6. STUPA NO. 2
7. STUPA NO. 3
8. ASHOKA PILLAR
9. GUPTA TEMPLE
M = MONASTERIES

Buddha's previous incarnations and main events in his life in symbolic form—footprints, the Bodhi tree, the Wheel of Law, and the stupa motifs. The eastern gateway depicts the departure of Gautama (who eventually became the Buddha) from his father's place, his mother's dreams before his birth, and the miracles of Gautama as the Buddha. It also has a panel with animals that surround their adored Buddha, which illustrates Buddha's respect for all life. One of its most elaborate panels on the northern gateway is on the lowest column of the architrave. Before Prince Guatama attained enlightenment, he and his family were banished from their kingdom by his father because Gautama gave away their miraculous elephant, which could and *did* bring rain to the draught-stricken kingdom of Kalinga. The panel shows the intercession of the gods pacifying the king's anger and the son and his family's return to the kingdom. The western gateway shows the seven incarnations of the Buddha. This architrave exhibits the preachings of the Buddha's first sermon in the Deer Park at Sarnath. One of the important panels on the southern gateway represents the birth of Gautama, with his mother, standing by the side of a lotus flower, flanked by two elephants pouring water over her head.

Stupa No. 2. On the western slope of the hill, this shrine dates from the second century B.C. It's surrounded by a well-preserved balustrade.

Stupa No. 3. Built 150–140 B.C., this stupa, north of the Great Stupa, has a hemispherical dome surmounted by an umbrella. In the chambers of this stupa were found the relics of Sariputra and Maudgalyayana, two of the Buddha's most important disciples.

Ashoka Pillar. Adjoining the southern gateway, the fragments on the Ashoka column depict an inscription in Brahman characters instructing Buddhists to avoid schism. An outstanding feature of this pillar is its lustrous polish, dating from the third century B.C. The Republic of India adopted the lion motif on the pillar as its state emblem.

Gupta Temple. Near the Great Stupa, this is one of the earliest known structural temples in India. Dating from the fifth century A.D., it's built of dressed stone slabs and has a flat roof.

The Caves at Udaigiri

A group of two Jain and 18 Hindu caves are at Udaigiri, 13 kilometers (seven miles) from Sanchi. Hindu authorities regard the carvings of the boar incarnation of Vishnu in Cave No. 5 as the ultimate representation of the triumph of good over evil. Vishnu, with the head of a boar, is shown supporting Prithvi, the earth goddess he has rescued from the clutches of a snake demon. With self-assured poise, Vishnu stamps on the snake while rows of angels and demons look on.

Cave No. 7 was excavated on Chandragupta II's orders for his personal use. Cave No. 19 is the largest and the one with the most carvings. Cave No. 20 is unique because it is entered from below ground level and none of its compartments is high. The other caves are not as impressive and hardly merit a visit, unless you are a serious history buff.

Shivpuri

Steeped in royal legacies of the past, Shivpuri, former summer capital of the Scindia rulers of Gwalior, is 112 kilometers (69 miles) from Gwalior on the Agra-Bombay Highway. A charming town, with palaces and artificial lakes, Shivpuri's fabled *chattries* (cenotaphs) are a reminder of former glory. These memorials to the Scindia dynasty are unique for their delicate filigree and inlaid marble work and their fusion of Hindu and Moslem architecture. Even before Shivpuri was a royal summer capital, its dense forests were the hunting grounds of the Mogul emperors, including Akbar, who captured great herds of elephants for his stables. Much later, tigers roamed the wooded hills, and royal *shikaris* (hunters) bagged many a magnificent beast. Shivpuri was also a natural choice for the summer resort capital. Shivpuri's royal ambience lives on in the exquisite palaces and hunting lodges and the graceful, intricately embellished marble chattries erected by the Scindia princes.

A sanctuary for rare wildlife and avifauna, Shivpuri is best known for its Madhav National Park. Driving through the park's 156 square kilometers (61 square miles) of jungle may offer a glimpse of deer, black buck, wild boar, and a variety of rare birds. The park, open throughout the year, is equally rich in waterfowl. An artificial lake, Chandpata, is the winter home of migratory geese, pochard, pintail, teal, mallard, and gadwall. The point where the forest track crosses the wide rocky stream that flows from the Waste Weir provides a good site for bird-watching. Species that frequent this sport are redwattled lapwing, large-pied wagtail, pond heron, white-breasted kingfisher, cormorant, painted stork, white ibis, lagger falcon, purple sunbird, paradise flycatcher, and golden oracle.

The cenotaphs of the Scindias are set in a Mogul garden, with quiet nooks under flowering trees intersected by pathways with ornamental balustrades, illuminated by Victorian lamps. The chattries of Madho Rao Scindia and Maharani Sakhya Raje Scindia, the dowager queen, face each other across a water tank. With their shikhara-type spires and Rajput and Mogul pavilions, they synthesize the architectural idioms of the Hindu and Islamic styles. The white marble surface of Madho Rao Scindia's cenotaph follows the pietradura style, with lapis lazuli and onyx creating a spectacularly rich effect that is heightened by the delicacy of the trellis work on the sides. The dowager queen's cenotaph has a noble dignity of line and superb structural harmony. Both memorials contain life-size images of the Scindias, which ceremonially dressed retainers bless with flowers and incense each day. Each evening, classical ragas break the stillness that envelops the statues.

Rising from a natural eminence is Madhav Vilas Palace, the elongated rose-pink summer palace of the Scindias that was built on truly royal proportions. A fine example of colonial architecture, the "Mahal," as it is called, has remarkable marble floors, iron columns, graceful terraces, and a Ganapati *mandapa* (pavilion). From the turrets, the view of Shivpuri and the park beyond is spectacular.

At the highest point, deep within the forests of the park, is the turreted George Castle, built by Jiyaji Rao Scindia, that offers a lovely view of the lake. The best time to visit the castle is at sunset when the lake mirrors the changing hues of the day. Edging the forests of the Madhav National Park is the Sakhya Sagar Lake, habitat of a variety of reptiles, including marsh crocodile, or mugger; Indian python; and the monitor lizard. Bhadaiya Kund nearby is a scenic picnic spot at a natural spring, whose water is rich in minerals that supposedly have curative powers.

Gwalior Fort

About 112 kilometers (69 miles) from Shivpuri is Gwalior—and yet another chapter in Indian history—where the Moguls only played a minor part near the end of a long drama.

Gwalior is practically synonymous with its fort, one of the oldest in India (it is mentioned in an inscription dated A.D. 525). According to a legend, Suraj Sena, a local leader suffering from leprosy, met a Hindu saint, Gwalipa, on the rocky hill where the fort now stands. Gwalipa offered him a drink of water from Suraj Kund, a sacred pool. The drink cured the leper. Gwalipa then told Suraj Sena to build a fort on the hill (the derivation of the name Gwalior) and to use the name of Pal if he wanted his dynasty to survive. Suraj Pal's family flourished until one cynic refused to obey the tradition. Naturally, that was the end of the kingdom.

The grandeur of Gwalior dates from another dynasty, the Tomars, who established their rule in the fourteenth century. A Tomar king, Mansingh (1486–1516), built the Man Mandir, a six-towered palace that forms the eastern wall of the fort. About 93 meters long and 25 meters deep (300 feet by 80 feet), it is decorated with perforated screens, mosaics, floral designs, and moldings in Hindu profusion. Beneath it, two underground floors were burrowed into the 93-meter-(300-foot-)high hill of the fort, serving as air-conditioned summer quarters for Mansingh—and dungeons for the prisoners of the Moguls who, under the rule of Akbar, seized the fort.

Captured by the Marathas in 1784, Gwalior Fort became the scene of fierce fighting again in 1857, when it was the base for 18,000 Indians who rose up against the British in the Sepoy Revolt (Indian Mutiny), the beginning of India's struggle for independence. Under Tantia Topi and a woman hero, Rani Lakshmi Bai of Jhansi, the Indians made a valiant last stand. The rani's cenotaph is in Gwalior.

Mansingh also built the Gujari Mahal, a turreted palace of stone—now the home of an archaeological museum. This palace was also built for love. The king met a Gujar maiden, Mrignayani (the "Fawn Eyed"), famed for her skill as a slayer of wild animals. She agreed to marry him only if he brought the waters of the Rai River, the secret source of her strength, into the fort. For the sake of his bride, Mansingh built the Gujari Mahal and an aqueduct linking it to the Rai.

A visit to the Gwalior Fort requires an arduous climb up to the gates (elephants, bearing royalty, once used the road, which is too steep for cars). The fort contains a mosque on the site of the shrine of Saint Gwalipa; Chaturbhuj Mandir Temple housing a four-armed idol of Vishnu; and five groups of gigantic Jain sculptures carved out of rock walls. The biggest, the image of the first Jain pontiff, Adinath, is 17 meters (57 feet) high with a foot measuring about three meters (nine feet). It was constructed in 1440.

Vishnu also reigns in eleventh-century temples known as Sas Bahu (the mother-in-law and daughter-in-law temples). Another temple, the ninth-century Teli Ka Mandir, with its 30-meter (100-foot) tower, is the highest building in the fort. This temple is an interesting blend of Dravidian architecture from south India, typified by the spire, with Indo-Aryan decoration on its walls. Finally, visit the Suraj Kund, the oldest Gwalior shrine, the pond that cured Suraj (Sena) Pal.

Outside the fort, Gwalior offers the tomb of Muhammad Ghaus, a Moslem saint worshiped by the Moguls, and the tomb of Tansen, one of Akbar's court musicians, which is still venerated by musicians. Lashkar, a mile from the fort, is a "modern" city built in 1809 on the site of an encampment. There you can visit two palaces, the Jai Vilas and the Moti Mahal, and a picturesque bazaar, the Inderganj Chowk. Gwalior is an ideal departure point for many other destinations within the state.

Other Sites Out of Gwalior

The medieval township of Orchha has hardly been touched by the hand of time. Lying 120 kilometers (74 miles) from Gwalior on the road to Khajuraho, Orchha is famous for its palaces and temples, built in the seventeenth century. Orchha was once the capital of the Bundela Rajputs, later under Mogul rule, and some of its palaces contain murals of the Bundela school. Particularly worth seeing is the Jahangir Mahal, a rectangular palace with eight minarets, which the Bundela raja, Bir Singh Ju Deo, built to commemorate the Emperor Jahangir's visit in the seventeenth century. See three important temples: the Chaturbhuj, Ram Raja, and Laxminarayan mandirs. The Laxminarayan Mandir has exquisite paintings that adorn the ceilings and walls of three corridors. Vibrant in color and stylization, the paintings are in an excellent state of preservation and express religious themes and historical events. The exterior of this temple is an interesting combination of temple and fort architecture.

The Madhya Pradesh State Tourism Development Corporation has converted the Sheesh Mahal into a hotel unit, giving visitors to Orchha the unique opportunity of experiencing the bygone splendor of this ancient city.

Datia, 69 kilometers (43 miles) from Gwalior, is a town whose antiquity can be traced to the *Mahabharata*. It is a town of great historic significance, highlighted by a seven-storied palace built entirely of stone and brick by Raja Bir Singh Ju Deo in 1614. The palace is considered one of the finest examples of Bundela architecture in the country. Within it are some fine wall paintings of the Bundela school. The Mogul frescoes in Datia's other attraction, the imposing Gopeshwar Temple, also reveal an interesting blend of cultures.

Surrounded by forested hills and lakes, Chanderi is a craft center famous for its saris and brocades. This city, 239 kilometers (148 miles) from Gwalior, has been influenced in its architecture by the Bundela Rajputs and the sultans of Malwa. The Koshak Mahal, built on the orders of Mohammed Khilji of Malwa in 1445, has an architectural style similar to the Jahaz Mahal in Mandu. The Jama Masjid and Shahzadi Ka Rouza were also built by the Malwa sultans, as was the Battisi Bandi built in 1485 by Sultan Ghyasuddin Shah. Northwest of Chanderi is the picturesque tank and temple complex of Parameshwar Tal, built by the Bundela kings. The old city of Chanderi, which has Jain temples of the ninth and tenth centuries, remains an important center of pilgrimage.

Narwar was once the capital of Raja Nal, whose love for Damyanti has been the theme of many legends and folk songs. Narwar lies 122 kilometers (76 miles) from Gwalior. Like Gwalior, it is dominated by a magnificent fort, standing on a hill overlooking the town. The fort and Narwar's palaces are typically Rajput in style, with flat ceilings, fluted columns, and multifoil arches. Glass beads are an interesting interior embellishment.

Known as Padmavati in ancient times, Pawaya is a fascinating complex of ruins, 68 kilometers (42 miles) from Narwar on the Gwalior-Jhansi road. Pawaya's ruins still bear testimony to the days when it was the capital of the Nag Kings in A.D. 3. Particularly noteworthy is the life-size statue of Chaksha Manibhadra of A.D. 1. The ruins of the medieval fort built by the Paramars and the nearby Dhoomeshwar Mahadeo Temple are Pawaya's other attractions.

Indore

Indore, India's fourth-largest textile center, with a population of over 1 million, is a newcomer among cities in India. The area was given to Malhar Rao Holkar in 1733 by the Marathas Peshwas for whom he fought. While Holkar was away fighting, he left the affairs of state to his widowed daughter-in-law, Ahalyabai, whom he had saved from being a *sati*. Since her son, who was insane, died young, she became the ruler. At a time when all other states were floundering, her reign was a model of good administration.

Indore's outstanding temple is the Jain Kanch Mandir, or Glass Temple, built from 1882 to 1922. Every inch of its surface is inlaid with mother-of-pearl and Italian cut glass. Huge crystal chandeliers add glitter; glass-and-beaded paintings depict Jain iconography and cosmology—the dreadful punishments visited on sinners, the world of mortals, and the celestial realm of the gods.

Nearby, the Lal Baug Palace, constructed by the Holkar dynasty from 1885 to 1925, is an architectural blend of the East and the West. Its exterior resembles an Italian villa, and most of the interior rooms resemble Versaille, but at least two rooms are decorated in the Indian Mogul tradition.

Ujjain

Ujjain, with a population of over 350,000, was described by Chandragupta II's court poet, Kalidasa, as "the town fallen from heaven to bring heaven to earth." Kalidasa also found "its palaces like mountains and its houses like palaces." Though the Gupta capital was Patiliputra, this was the city from which the emperor ruled for long periods. When Buddha was born, Ujjain was already a thriving city and the capital of a kingdom called Avanti. Legend has it that Shiva lived here after destroying a demon and thus Ujjain was born.

One of the four drops of heavenly nectar from the kumbh seized by Vishnu also supposedly dropped on Ujjain. Once every 12 years, millions of Hindu devotees congregate to celebrate the Kumbh Mela, the most sacred festival in the Hindu calendar. The last Kumbh Mela was January 1992.

Ujjain's literary, scientific, and religious life continued for centuries, and it was hundreds of years later that another poet was captivated enough to see it as "the very home of the golden age; paved with jewels, full of romance, with dancing girls in the temples and love in everyone's hearts." Politically, Ujjain went through swift transitions, from the hands of the Rajputs and the Moslems to the Marath Scindias of Gwalior.

The Scindias rebuilt the Mahakaleshar, the main temple, and dedicated it to Shiva, on the ruins of an earlier one destroyed by the Moslems. To the south is Bade Ganeshki Ka Mandir, a temple dedicated to the elephant-headed god. Set in lovely seclusion is Navagraha Mandir (Temple of Nine Planets), on the road to Indore at the confluence of the Shipra and two other rivers.

According to Hindu geography, the first meridian passes through Ujjain. A legend claims that the moon and Mars were born here. Ujjain's scientific work was done in an observatory built in the eighteenth century by Sawai Jai Singh of Jaipur. It was called the Jantar Mantar. Also see Kaliadeh Palace, surrounded by the Shipra River and built in 1458, with its Persian-style central dome; and the nineteenth-century Gopal Mandir, a temple dedicated to Krishna, with a beautiful silver image of this god in its inner sanctum.

Mandu

Mandu is a celebration in stone, of life and joy, of the love of the poet-prince Baz Bahadur for his beautiful consort, Rani Roopmati. Balladeers of Malwa still sing of the romance of these royal lovers. High up on the crest of a hill, Roopmati's pavilion continues to look down on Baz Bahadur's palace—a magnificent expression of Afghan architecture.

MANDU FORT
(NOT TO SCALE)

HILL
RIVER
ROAD
RAMPART
WATER TANK

GATE

TOURIST BUNGALOW

CHISTI KHANS PALACE

RAMPOL GATE

DELHI GATE

ALAMGIR GATE

BHANGI GATE

UJALA BAOLI

JAHAZ MAHAL

TAWELI MAHAL

LAIKOT

SURAJ TALAO

HINDOLA MAHAL

MUNJA TALAO

HOSHANG'S TOMB

LOHANI GATE

JAIN MANDAR

EK THAMBA

CHOR KOTO

RAM MANDAR

ASHRAFI MAHAL

JAMA MASJID

CHHAPPAN MAHAL

DARYA KHAN'S TOMB

HATHI MAHAL

LAL SARAI

MALIK MUGHITH'S MOSQUE

BAIHAN KA MAHAL

ODAI KA MAHAL

ECHO POINT

LAL BUNGALOW

SAGAR TALAO

NILKANTH

JALI MAHAL

BAZ BAHADUR'S PALACE

BHAGWANIYA GATE

RUPMATIS PAVILION

REWA KUND

SONGARH

TARAPUR GATE

N

Perched along the Vindhyan ranges, at an altitude of 610 meters (2,000 feet), Mandu, with its natural defenses, was originally the fort-capital of the Paramar rulers of Malwa. Later, toward the end of the thirteenth century, it came under the sway of the sultans of Malwa, the first of whom renamed it Shadibad, "the city of joy." And indeed, this was the pervading spirit of Mandu, with its rulers building exquisite palaces like the Jahaz and Hindola mahals, ornamental canals, and graceful baths and pavilions. Each of Mandu's structures is an architectural gem; some are outstanding, like the massive Jama Masjid and Houshang Shah's Tomb, which inspired the builders of the Taj Mahal centuries later. Under Mogul rule, Mandu was a pleasure resort, its lakes and palaces the scenes of splendid and extravagant festivities. The glory of Mandu lives on, in its palaces, mosques, legends, and songs chronicled for posterity.

Twelve gateways punctuate the 45-kilometer (28-mile) parapet of walls that encircle Mandu. Most notable of these is the Delhi Darwaza, the main entrance to the fortress city, approached through a series of well-fortified gateways with walled enclosures and strengthened by bastions, such as the Alamgir, Kamani, Bhangi Barwaza, and Gadi gates, through which the present road passes.

Those with an appetite for royal architecture can feast on the following:

Jahaz Mahal. This 120-meter (394-foot)-long "ship palace," built between the two artificial lakes, Munj Talao and Kapur Talao, is an elegant two-story palace. It was probably built by Sultan Ghiyas-ud-din Khalji for his large harem. With its open pavilions, balconies overhanging the water, and open terrace, the Jahaz Mahal is an imaginative re-creation in stone of a royal pleasure craft. Viewed on moonlit nights from the adjoining Taveli Mahal, the silhouette of the building, with the tiny domes and turrets of the pavilion gracefully perched on the terrace, is an unforgettable spectacle.

Hindola Mahal. An audience hall also from Ghiyas-ud-din's reign, this structure derives the name of "Swinging Palace" from its sloping sidewalls. Superb and innovative techniques are also evident in its ornamental facade: delicate trelliswork in beautifully molded sandstone columns. To the west of Hindola Mahal stand several unidentified buildings that still bear traces of past grandeur. Note the elaborately constructed wall called Champa Baoli, which is connected to underground vaulted rooms in which cold and hot water were once available. Other places of interest in this enclave are Dilawar Khan's mosque, the Nahar Jharokha (tiger balcony), Taveli Mahal, and two large wells called the Ujali (bright) and Andheri (dark).

Ashrafi Mahal. This "palace of gold coins," which faces the Jama Masjid, was built by Hoshang Shah's successor, Mahmud Shah Khilji. Conceived as an academic institution (*madrassa*) for young boys, the study cells still remain in a fair state of preservation. In the same complex, Khilji built a seven-story tower to celebrate his victory over Rana Khumba of Mewar; only one story survives. The tomb, intended to be the largest structure in Mandu, is also in ruins.

Baz Bahadur's Palace. Built in the sixteenth century, the palace's unique features include a spacious courtyard surrounded by halls and high terraces that afford a superb view of the surrounding countryside.

Nilkanth Mahal. This palace, which belongs to the Mogul era, was constructed as a pleasure resort for Akbar's Hindu wife. On the walls are inscriptions, written during Akbar's time, that refer to the futility of earthly pomp and glory.

Hoshang Shah's Tomb. India's first marble edifice is a refined example of Afghan architecture. Examine the magnificently proportioned dome, marble latticework of remarkable delicacy, and porticoed courts and towers that mark each corner of the rectangle. Shah Jahan sent four of his greatest architects to study the tomb's design. Among them was Ustad Hamid, who has been linked with the construction of Shah Jahan's Taj Mahal.

Jama Masjid. The great mosque of Damascus inspired the Jama Masjid, conceived on a grand scale with a high plinth and a huge domed porch projecting into the center. Similar imposing domes with seemingly innumerable domes filling the intervening space dominate the background. Most visitors are immediately struck by the vastness of the building and the simplicity of its construction. The great court of the mosque is enclosed by huge colonnades with a rich and pleasing variety of arches, pillars, number of bays, and domes above.

Roopmati's Pavilion. This graceful pavilion was originally built as an army observation post and later served as a retreat for the queen. From its hilltop perch, the queen could see Baz Bahadur's palace and the Narmada flowing through the Nimar plains far below.

Hathi Mahal, Darya Khan's Tomb, Dai ka Maha, Malik Mughith's Mosque, and Jali Mahal are some of Mandu's other fascinating monuments. Also visit Echo Point, the Delphic Oracle of Mandu, where a shout reverberates some distance and is clearly heard back.

The Lohani caves and temple ruins, not far from the royal enclave, also merit a visit. While you are there, pause at Sunset Point, in front of the caves. From here, you'll have a panoramic view of the surrounding countryside.

Omkareshwar

Omkareshwar, the sacred island, is shaped like the holiest of all Hindu symbols, *Om,* and has drawn a hundred generations of pilgrims. Here, at the confluence of the rivers Narmada and Kaveri, the devout have gathered to kneel at the temple of Shri Omkar Mandhata. And here, as in so many of Madhya Pradesh's sacred shrines, the works of nature complement those of man to provide an awe-inspiring setting.

Shri Omkar Mandhata Temple stands on a small island that has been formed by the fork of the Narmada. Constructed of pliant soft stone, the temple is exquisitely carved. Note especially the friezes on the upper portion of the roof. Encircling the shrine are verandas with columns that are carved in circles, polygons, and squares.

The Siddhnath Temple is a fine example of early medieval Brahmanic architecture. Its unique feature is a frieze of elephants, carved on a stone slab, at its outer perimeter. Twenty-four Avatars, a cluster of Hindu and Jain temples, is remarkable for the skillful use of varied architectural modes.

Maheshwar

Called Mahishmati when it was King Kartvirarjun's capital, Maheshwar, 91 kilometers (56 miles) from Indore, was a glorious city in the dawn of Indian civilization. This temple town on the banks of the Narmada was mentioned in the *Ramayana* and *Mahabharata.* Revived to its ancient position by the Holkar queen Rani Ahilyabai of Indore, Maheshwar's temples and mighty fort complex stand in quiet beauty, mirrored in the river below.

A life-size statue of Rani Ahilyabai sits on a throne in the Rajgaddi within the fort complex. This is the right place to begin a tour of Maheshwar, for this pious and wise queen was the architect of its revived importance. Other fascinating relics and heirlooms of the Holkar dynasty can be seen in rooms that are open to the public. Within the complex is an exquisite small shrine that is the starting point of the ancient Dussehra ceremony still enacted today.

Peshwa Ghat, Fanase Ghat, and Ahilya Ghat line the river Narmada. Their steps lead down from the sandy banks to the river. Throughout the day, you can see a kaleidoscope of rural India in the pilgrims and holy men who sit at the ghats in silent meditation, in the rows of graceful women who carry gleaming brass pots down to the holy (life-giving) river, and in the ferry loads of villagers who cross and recross these surging waters. Lining the banks, too, are poignant stone memorials to the *satis* of Maheshwar, who perished on the funeral pyres of their husbands.

Crowned by soaring spires, the many-tiered temples of Maheshwar are distinguished by their carved overhanging balconies and their intricately worked doorways.

Maheshwari saris are renowned throughout India for their unique weave, introduced 250 years ago by Rani Ahilyabai. Woven mostly in cotton, the typical Maheshwari sari has a plain body and sometimes stripes or checks in several variations. The mat border designs have a wide range in leaf and floral patterns.

Jabalpur and Marble Rocks

A pleasure resort and the capital of the Gond Kings during the twelfth century, Jabalpur, in the center of the state, was later the seat of the Kalchuri dynasty. The Marathas held sway over Jabalpur until 1817, when the British wrested it from them and left their impression on the spacious cantonment with its colonial residences and barracks.

From Jabalpur, it's 23 kilometers (14 miles) to the Marble Rocks, which soar 30 meters (100 feet) on either side of the Narmada River, creating a scene of cool serenity. Here, the Narmada makes its way through the rocks, narrows down and then plunges in a waterfall known as Dhuandhar, or the smoke cascade. The Chausath Yogini Temple, situated atop a hillock and approached by a long flight of steps, offers the best view of this natural display. Dedicated to the goddess Durga, this tenth-century temple has exquisitely carved stone figures of deities belonging to the Kalchuri period.

Wildlife Sanctuaries

Jabalpur is also the departure point for two excellent national parks: Kanha, 173 kilometers (107 miles), and Bandhavgarh, 194 kilometers (120 miles). Kanha, the setting for Kipling's *Jungle Book,* was declared a park in 1955; it ranks as one of India's finest sanctuaries, with 940 square kilometers (582 square miles) of forests and grasslands threaded with rivers. More than 22 species of mammals roam the vast territory, including the striped hyena, leopard, jungle cat, wild pig, Indian bison, barking deer, mouse deer, swamp deer, and black buck. You're also apt to spot an array of birds: the hoopoe, shrike, stork, heron, and painted snipe. There are two main entrances, connected by a 30-kilometer (19-mile) dirt road. The state tourism corporation has built a lodge and offers four-wheel-drive and elephant safaris near each entrance.

Bandhavgarh, established in 1968, is a smaller park (105 square kilometers, or 65 square miles), but here you also have a good chance of sighting a variety of wildlife within the forests, swamps, and grassy meadows. This park has more tigers than any other Indian sanctuary. It is also home to the Indian fox, sloth bear, gray mongoose, blue bull, wild pig, Indian bison, and the elusive striped hyena and leopard. You may also see vultures, ibis, and spoonbills among its 100 recorded bird species. There's a lodge set up by the state tourism corporation, and jeep and elephant trips are offered. You can also visit the 2,000-year-old Bandhavgarh Fort within the park.

Satpura Mountain Range Retreat

Pachmarhi, 210 kilometers (130 miles) from Bhopal and set in the Satpura Mountains, is Madhya Pradesh's premier hill station. Don't expect big crowds or an abundance of hotels; this little village is still a quiet getaway, with hikes that lead to waterfalls as well as the historic Pandav Caves, where the five Pandava brothers of the *Mahabharata* epic supposedly spent some time, and numerous cave shelters filled with old paintings.

PRACTICAL INFORMATION FOR
MADHYA PRADESH

WHEN TO GO. The temperature and weather are ideal for visits from mid-October to mid-March. The monsoon brings heavy rain from mid-June to September. The best viewing time in the national parks is February–June; they're closed from July to Oct. 31.

HOW TO GET THERE. By Air. From Bhubaneshwar, *Indian Airlines* has three weekly flights to Raipur. From Delhi, Indian Airlines has five weekly flights to Bhopal, Indore, and Gwalior. From Bombay, Indian Airlines flies daily to Bhopal, Indore, and Raipur; and has five weekly flights to Bhopal, Gwalior, and Khajuraho. From Aurangabad, it has three weekly flights to Bhopal. From Ahmedabad, it has two weekly flights to Raipur. From Calcutta, it has three weekly flights to Raipur. For information, call 61633 in Bhopal; 21568 in Gwalior; and 21211 in Indore.

By Bus. Deluxe buses connect Bombay to Indore and Bhopal. They also connect Gwalior with Delhi, Agra, and Jaipur. See those chapters. For bus information in Bhopal, contact Bhopal Bus Stand, tel. 540841; in Indore contact Sarvate Bus Stand, tel. 65788; in Gwalior, contact MPSTDC, tel. 21568.

By Train. Bhopal and Gwalior are on the Bombay–Delhi and Madras–Delhi line of the Central Railway. They're easily accessible from Bombay and Delhi. *Shatabdi Express* is your best bet from Delhi. *Punjab Mail, Dadar Express,* and *Jhellum Express* are the best options from Bombay; they're also good for Delhi. The best train to Indore from Bombay is the *Avantika Express;* the best from Delhi is the *Malway Express.* From Jabalpur (the gateway to the national parks), the best train is the *Mahakaushal Express,* which originates in Delhi. For train information and reservations in Bombay or Delhi, see those chapters. In Bhopal, contact Bhopal Railway Station, tel. 73275; in Gwalior, contact MPSTDC, tel. 25168; in Indore, contact Indore Railway Station, tel. 23284 for inquiries or tel. 36185 for reservations; in Jabalpur, contact MPSTDC, tel. 322111. If you travel overnight, remember to reserve a sleeping berth.

By Rented Car with Driver. Bhopal is on National Highway 12. Here are some important distances from Bhopal: Delhi, 741 km (459 mi.); Bombay, 789 km (489 mi.): Hyderabad, 813 km (504 mi.); Ahmedabad, 571 km (354 mi.). Gwalior is on National Highway 3 and is 119 km (74 mi.) from Agra, 321 km (199 mi.) from Delhi, and 338 km (210 mi.) from Jaipur. Indore is on National Highways 12 and 3 and is 602 km (373 mi.) from Bombay, 806 km (500 mi.) from Delhi, and 803 km (498 mi.) from Hyderabad. Hire a car from one of the tour operators recommended below or in the appropriate chapter. In Mahya Pradesh, a rented car with driver should cost about Rs. 4 per km, with a halt charge of Rs. 50–Rs. 100 per night.

TOURIST INFORMATION. *The Madhya Pradesh State Tourism Development Corporation* (MPSTDC) is extremely helpful and has excellent brochures and maps. The head office is in Bhopal 4th Floor, Gangotri, T. T. Nagar, Bhopal 462003; tel. 554340–3; open 10 A.M.–5 P.M., closed Sundays. MPSTDC also has offices in the following destinations (same hours):

Gwalior. Hotel Tansen, 6 Gandhi Rd.; tel. 21568.
Indore. Tourist Bungalow, behind Rabindra Natya Griha; tel. 38888.
Jabalpur. Railway Station; tel. 322111.
Jhans (in nearby Uttar Pradesh). Railway Station; no phone.
Pachmarhi. Amaltas, near Tehsil; tel. 2100.
Raipur. Railway Station; tel. 524363.
Satna. Railway Station; tel. 3223.
Ujjain. Railway Station; tel. 29240.

FOREIGN CURRENCY EXCHANGE. Most Western-style hotels have money-exchange counters. Otherwise, go to a branch of the *State Bank of India,* open Monday–Friday, 10 A.M.–2 P.M.; Saturday, till noon. In Bhopal, the State Bank of India in New Market is also open Monday–Saturday, 3:30–8 P.M.

ACCOMMODATIONS. While only the big cities and a few smaller destinations in Madhya Pradesh have private hotels, MPSTDC does have a network of extremely nice accommodations that are also good value. To reserve a room more than five days in advance, contact Central Reservations, MPSTDC in Bhopal (address above). Less than five days in advance, contact the manager of each unit. Include a 50 percent deposit (about Rs. 200 per double per night). Prices are based on double occupancy and exclude taxes and service charges: *Deluxe,* over Rs. 2,000; *Expensive,* Rs. 1,200–Rs. 2,000; *Moderate,* Rs. 500–Rs. 1,200; *Inexpensive,* under Rs. 500. Some Western-style hotels take major credit cards.

BANDHAVGARH

Deluxe

Bandhavgarh Jungle Camp. Reservations: Tiger Tops India, 1/1 Rani Jhansi Rd., New Delhi 110055; tel. 771055, fax 777483; or through Tiger Tops abroad. 8 tents with shared bathrooms. On the edge of the park and on the grounds of a former maharajah's hunting lodge, this resort has fancy safari-style tents with cots and small tables. Meals are served in a thatched-roof *gol ghar* (round house), and drinks are served at a separate bar. Guests participate in elephant and jeep safaris. Price includes everything but drinks and laundry. Closed mid-May–Oct. AE, DC, MC, V.

Inexpensive

White Tiger Forest Lodge. Bandhavgarh National Park. Reservations: MPST-DC; tel. 554340–3 in Bhopal. 26 rooms with bath. This thatch-roofed lodge, set on pillars and resembling *machans* (wildlife-viewing towers), is adjacent to the park. Ethnic-style interiors have clay walls, tile floors, and modern furnishings. All rooms are extremely clean and have fans. Some rooms are air-conditioned. Room service, Indian- and Continental-cuisine restaurant, jeep and elephant safaris. Closed July 1–Oct. 31. Rupees only.

BHOPAL

Moderate

Hotel Lake View Ashok. Shamla HIlls, Bhopal 462013; tel. 541600, fax 553399 (Attn: HLVA). 45 rooms with bath. This Western-style hotel, with a red stone exterior, is jointly run by Ashok and MPSTDC and sits on a hill overlooking the lake.

Air-conditioned spacious rooms have a modern decor and private balconies that offer good views. TV, room service, multicuisine restaruant, bar, baby-sitters, doctor, secretarial service, shopping arcade, foreign-exchange and travel counter. Good value. AE, DC, MC, V.

Jehan Numa Palace Hotel. Shamla Hills, Bhopal 462013; tel. 540100, fax 551912. 60 rooms with bath. Once the secretariat of a Moselm nawab, this lovely two-story palace, with a new wing that fits in architecturally, is now a hotel. The marble lobby (with a stuffed tiger) opens into an interior courtyard. The two upper-floor rooms are best, with spacious private verandas and period furnishings. In the other rooms, which have modernish furnishings, you'll lose all sense of the palace once you close your door. TV, air-conditioning, room service, multicuisine, restaurants, bar, foreign-exchange and travel counter, gift shop. AE, DC, MC, V.

Inexpensive

Hotel Palash. Near 45 Bungalows, T. T. Nagar, Bhopal 462003; tel. 553006. 33 rooms with bath. This new MPSTDC Western-style hotel has a spacious lobby and clean rooms with modern decor and balconies. Best rooms are air-conditioned; all rooms have overhead fans. TV, room service, multicuisine restaurant, bar, car-rental service. MC, V.

GWALIOR

Expensive

Welcomgroup Usha Kiran Palace. Jyendraganj, Lashkar, Gwalior 474009; tel. 23453. 27 rooms with bath. The former guest house of the Gwalior maharaja is now an appealing hotel, with his stylish furnishings still adorning the rooms. Don't think grand, but do expect comfort. Some rooms are air-conditioned; all rooms have fans. Room service, multicuisine restaurant, bar, billiards, buggy rides, elephant rides and golfing on request, foreign-exchange and travel counter. AE, DC, MC, V.

Inexpensive

Hotel Tansen. 6A Gandhi Rd., Gwalior 474002; tel. 21568. 36 rooms with bath. A modern two-story MPSTDC hotel, the rooms are spacious and clean, with Western-style decor. All rooms have fans; some are air-conditioned. Room service, TV, multicuisine restaurant, bar, doctor, car-rental service, MPSTDC office. Rupees only.

INDORE

Inexpensive–Moderate

Indotels Manor House. A.B. Rd., Indore 452008; tel. 32121, fax 491501. 66 rooms with bath. The lobby of this hotel has lots of marble. Deluxe and executive rooms (moderately priced) are more spacious than the ordinary doubles (inexpensive); all have a contemporary decor. Air-conditioning, TV, room service, multicuisine restaurants, bar, secretarial service, foreign-exchange and travel counter, doctor. AE, DC, MC, V.

Inexpensive

President Hotel. 1 R.N.T. Marg, Indore 452001; tel. 432860, fax 32230. 65 rooms. This new five-story hotel has a spacious lobby with lots of marble and sitting areas that are well lit by large banks of windows. Executive Deluxe rooms are larger than Super Deluxe rooms, but they all have a modern decor. Air-conditioning, TV, room service, multicuisine restaurants, bar, secretarial services, health club, doctor, foreign-exchange and travel counter. Good value. AE, DC, MC, V.

Hotel Surya. 5/5 Nath Mandir Rd., Indore 452001; tel. 431155. 28 rooms with bath. This small high rise has an intimate lobby and offers air-conditioned VIP rooms in various decors that range from garish, with lots of chrome and leather, to quietly modern. Other air-conditioned rooms have a subdued contemporary decor and balconies with street views. Both options provide TV. Ordinary rooms are not air-conditioned. Room service, multicuisine restaurant, bar, travel assistance, doctor. Good service. DC, MC, V.

JABALPUR

Inexpensive

Hotel Kalchuri. Near Circuit House No. 2, Jabalpur; tel. 327411. 30 rooms with bath. This new MPSTDC Western-style hotel has clean, spacious rooms with a modern decor. Some rooms are air-conditioned; all rooms have fans. Room service, Indian- and limited Continental-cuisine restaurant, bar, car-rental service. Rupees only.

KANHA NATIONAL PARK

Inexpensive

Baghira Log Huts. Kisli, Kanha National Park; no phone. 16 rooms with bath. Surrounded by dense forest and near the Kisli Entry Gate, this cluster of rustic MPSTDC log huts, with thatched-roofs, is perfect for its location. Rooms have stone and wood walls and modern, clean furnishings; they offer good privacy. There are overhead fans, room service, Indian- and limited Continental-cuisine restaurant, jeep and elephant safaris. Closed July 1–Oct. 31. Rupees only.

Kanha Safari Lodge. Mukki, Kanha National Park; no phone. 30 rooms with bath. Set on the Banzar River, near the Mukki Entrance Gate, this two-story MPSTDC facility is less remote; rooms have ethnic-style woven matting on the walls and modern furnishings. Some rooms are air-conditioned; all rooms have overhead fans. Room service, Indian- and limited Continental-cuisine restaurant, bar, jeep and elephant safaris, river swimming and fishing (bring your own equipment). Closed July 1–Oct. 31. Rupees only.

MANDU

Inexpensive

Tourist Cottages. Roopmati Rd., Mandu; tel. 235. 10 cottages; each has 2 units with attached bath. These MPSTDC cottages, set on nice grounds, offer privacy and clean, large rooms with a Western-style decor. Some rooms are air-conditioned; all rooms have fans. There is also a pleasant and informal open-air restaurant with Indian and limited Continental cuisines, room service, and a bar. Rupees only.

Traveller's Lodge. Mandu; tel. 221. 8 rooms with bath. Consider this older two-story MPSTDC bungalow the second option in Mandu. Air-cooled rooms are clean, with Western-style decor. An Indian- and limited Continental-cuisine restaurant provides room service. Rupees only.

ORCHHA

Inexpensive

Sheesh Mahal. Orchha; tel. 224. 8 rooms with bath. This MPSTDC hotel is part of an impressive medieval palace complex set on a bluff. The furnishings are very simple, but the rooms are clean and spacious, with delightful Mogul touches in the architecture. Upper-floor rooms, including the suite, have spectacular views of the quiet, monument-strewn village. Room service, Indian- and limited Continental-cuisine restaurant. Rupees only.

PACHMARHI

Inexpensive

Satpura Retreat. Pachmarhi; tel. 2097. 6 rooms with bath. This former British bungalow, now an MPSTDC hotel, has a tile roof and sweeping verandas that offer good mountain views. Air-cooled rooms are spacious, with simple period furnishings. The sitting room and dining room are also old-timey and delightful. Room service, Indian- and limited Continental-cuisine restaurant, jeep-rental service. Rupees only.

SANCHI

Inexpensive

Tourist Cafeteria. Sanchi; tel. 243. 2 rooms with bath. This new MPSTDC set-up, near the monuments, has clean, air-cooled rooms, with simple modern decor. Room service, Indian- and limited Continental-cuisine restaurant. Rupees only.

Traveller's Lodge. Sanchi; tel. 223. 8 rooms with bath. Also run by MPSTDC, this older bungalow has clean, spacious rooms with Western-style decor that open onto a courtyard. Some rooms are air-conditioned; all rooms have overhead fans. Room service, Indian- and limited Continental-cuisine restaurant. Rupees only.

SHIVPURI

Inexpensive

Tourist Village. Near Bhadaiya Kund, Shivpuri; tel. 2600. 20 cottages with bath. This delightful MPSTDC complex has an attractive reception and dining hall, and pleasant grounds next to the Madhav National Park and a small lake. You'll stay in immaculate cottages with red-tile roofs and a modern ethnic decor: simple *dhurris* (rugs) and bamboo rugs, jute and bamboo chairs, electric lanterns. All cottages have overhead fans, good views, and privacy; some cottages have air-conditioning. Room service, multicuisine restaurant, TV lounge. Rupees only.

UJJAIN

Inexpensive

Shipra Motel. Ujjain; tel. 28262. 30 rooms with bath. This new MPSTDC Western-style motel offers modern-decor rooms. Some rooms are air-conditioned; all rooms have overhead fans. Room service, Indian- and limited Continental-cuisine restaurant, bar, car-rental service. Rupees only.

DINING OUT. Good private restaurants are rare in Madhya Pradesh; the best places to eat are in the hotels. While we include only the best options, most of the accommodations listed above have restaurants. Breakfast is usually served 7:30–10; lunch, noon–3; and dinner, 7–10. The restaurants listed below are informal and, unless noted, are open for all three meals and don't require reservations. Prices are based on one person eating a three-course meal, excluding taxes, tip, or beverage: *Expensive,* Rs. 200–Rs. 300; *Moderate,* Rs. 100–Rs. 200; *Inexpensive,* under Rs. 100. Most Western-style hotels accept credit cards.

BHOPAL

Expensive

Garden Barbecue. Jehan Numa Palace Hotel, Shamla Hills; tel. 540100. Sit surrounded by a marble fountain, towering mango tree, and flowers in this courtyard restaurant. You can choose from Continental, Chinese, or Indian cuisines. Try the chicken Bhopal *rizali* (chicken cooked in melon seeds and garnished with coriander) or barbecue items. Open 7:30–10:30 P.M.; closed during the monsoon season. Reservations advised. AE, DC, MC, V.

Moderate

Kinara. Hotel Lake View Ashok, Shamla Hills; tel. 541600. In this modern-decor restaurant, with a bank of windows overlooking the lake, you can enjoy Continental and Indian cuisines, including princely dishes from Madyha Pradesh. Try the *mans* *ka soola* (beaten and marinated mutton cooked in a tandoor) or the *kebab-e-murgh* (whole chicken with the breast stuffed with coriander, fruit, and chilies, then cooked in the tandoor). Dinner reservations advised. Open 7–10 A.M., 1–3 P.M., and 7:30–10:30 P.M. AE, DC, MC, V.

Inexpensive

Manohar Dairy and Restaurant. 6 Hamidia Rd., no phone. Hindi film songs play in the background as you sit at Formica tables in this popular restaurant, cooled by overhead fans. Try a smorgasbord of Indian dishes that are all extremely low priced: *cholla bhatura* (fried puffed bread with lentils), *cholla tikiya* (fried mashed potatoes with lentils), *dahi papdi* (puffed chips in yogurt and chutney), and for dessert, *kala kand* (hardened milk sweet with pistachios). Open 6 A.M.–11 P.M. Rupees only.

INDORE

Moderate

Three Seasons. Indotels Manor House, A.B. Rd.; tel. 32121. Renovations are planned for this restaurant, but expect a modern look and candlelight dining at night. The chef serves Continental, Chinese, and Indian dishes. Try the Szechuan smoked chicken with red peppers, the tandoor items, or *navratan* curry (nine vegetables cooked in a coconut-flavored curry). Open noon–3 P.M., and 7–11:30 P.M. AE, DC, MC, V.

Inexpensive

Apsara. Rabindra Natya Griha; tel. 23026. There is both outdoor and indoor seating at this popular, strictly vegetarian multicuisine restaurant. Try the *paneer butter masala* (cheese in a spicy tomato gravy) or the *basan* special (roasted gram cooked in water). Open 8 A.M.–10:30 P.M. Rupees only.

SWEETS AND TREATS. Bhopal. Indore. For regional Malwa snacks, go to *Jain Bhutta Kees,* Hemington Rd.; open 4 P.M.–7 P.M. For *kulfi* (Indian ice cream), stop at *Mhowke Lala Agrawala,* Sikh Mohalla Main Rd., near Kothari Market; open 11 A.M.–9 P.M.

HOW TO GET AROUND. From the Airports. The Bhopal and Gwalior airports are 11 km (7 mi.) from the city. The Indore airport is 9 km (6 mi.) from the city. Take a taxi (Rs. 3.50 per km) or auto rickshaw (Rs. 3 per km). Bargain!

By Plane. From Bhopal, *Indian Airlines* flies five times a week to Gwalior and Indore and three times a week to Khajuraho. From Gwalior, Indian Airlines flies five times a week to Bhopal and Indore. From Indore, Indian Airlines flies five times a week to Bhopal and Gwalior.

By Bus. MPSTDC runs deluxe air-conditioned buses between Bhopal and Indore twice daily for Rs. 150. Other buses travel throughout the state. For bus information in Bhopal, contact Bhopal Bus Stand, tel. 540841; in Indore, contact Sarvate Bus Stand, tel. 65788; in Gwalior, contact MPSTDC, tel. 21568.

By Rented Car and Driver. Fairly good roads run through Madhya Pradesh. Here are some important distances from Bhopal: Sanchi, 60 km (37 mi.); Indore, 186 km (115 mi.); Ujjain, 189 km (117 mi.); Mandu, 290 km (180 mi.); Khajuraho, 387 km (240 mi.); Gwalior, 422 km (262 mi.); Kanha, 540 km (335 mi.). In Madhya Pradesh, a rented car with driver should cost about Rs. 4 per km, with a halt charge of Rs. 50–Rs. 100 per night. Hire a car from one of the tour operators listed below.

By Taxi. Taxis should cost about Rs. 3.50 per km. If there's no meter, set the fare beforehand.

By Auto Rickshaw. Figure about Rs. 3.40 for the first km, 50 paisa per additional km.

TOURS. MPSTDC offers comprehensive bus tours of Madhya Pradesh that start in Calcutta, Bangalore, Nagpur, Bombay, and Delhi, with arrival in Madhya Pradesh by train. Contact MPSTDC in Bhopal (tel. 554340) for details. MPSTDC also offers numerous tours within the state.

TOUR OPERATORS. For all your travel needs, contact *Travel Bureau* (Van Vihar Rd., Bhopal 462002; tel. 540470, fax 360006) or *MPSTDC* (see Tourist Information, above). *Flightline* (8/8 Shriram Apt., 6 Malviya Nagar Rd., Bhopal 462013; tel. 534787, fax 551912) offers two good combo adventure tours that include bicycling and short river cruises in wooden boats. Expect to tent near remote villages, attend colorful bazaars, and see the weaving of this state's beautiful textiles. Also see Special-Interest Tours in *Facts at Your Fingertips* for the names of India-based agencies that can create a special trip in Madhya Pradesh.

SEASONAL EVENTS. Since the lunar calendar determines most events, contact the Government of India Tourist Office for exact dates.

January–February. *Vasant Panchami.* This festival honors Saraswati, the Hindu goddess of learning, with lots of kites flying in the air. It's also a popular time for marriages.

February–March. *Bhojpur Festival.* This three-day festival at the historic Bhojeshwar Temple in Bhojpur includes a crafts fair and regional tribal and folk performances.

February–March. *Shivratri.* Hindu devotees worship Shiva and sing sacred songs in important Shiva temples.

February–March. *Holi.* During this boisterous festival that celebrates the start of spring, people throw red colored water on everyone. Wear old clothes.

April. *Orchha Festival.* For three days, this medieval city turns festive with regional performances.

September. *Malwa Festival.* This 10-day fair in Indore, Ujjain, and Mandu includes local tribal and classical dances, music, stalls with Malwa handicrafts, a regional food festival, archery competition, and even a vintage-car display.

September–October. *Dussehra.* This 10-day event celebrates the victory of good over evil and honors Durga, the Hindu goddess. On the 10th day, effigies of Ravana, the demon and embodiment of evil, are ignited.

October–November. *Diwali.* This festival marks the start of the Hindu New Year. Candles, welcoming the goddess Lakshmi (Goddess of Wealth), light up most homes. Lots of firecrackers.

December. *Tansen Samaroh Music Festival.* Gwalior honors Akbar's great musician, Miya Tansen, with days of wonderful music performances by India's top talents. A great treat!

HISTORIC SITES. Entrance to monuments is generally free or nominal in cost; where a donation is requested, a few rupees will suffice. Historic sites are open daily sunrise to sunset. For more details about Mandi and Sanchi, refer to the introductory essay above.

BHOJPUR

Bhojeshwar Temple, an exquisite eleventh-century shrine dedicated to Shiva, contains numerous Shiva images and temples built into its walls. The Shiva linga in the inner sanctum is carved from one stone.

BHOPAL

Taj-ul-Masajid was built in 1868–1901 and is one of the largest mosques in India, with an impressive main hall, broad facade, and courtyard.

Jama Masjid, with lovely gold spires, was built in 1837 by Kudsia Begum, supposedly on the site of a former twelfth-century temple.

Shaukat Mahal, at the Chowk entrance, is the palatial whimsy of a Frenchman, who incorporated numerous architectural styles: Occidental, post-Renaissance, and Gothic.

Sadar Manzil, also at the Chowk entrance, was the Hall of Public Audience of the former Bhopal rulers.

GWALIOR

Gwalior Fort, one of the largest Indian forts, was built in the fifteenth century by Raja Mansingh Tomar and contains numerous monuments:

Gujari Mahal was built for his queen, Mrignayani. Its beautiful interior now houses the architectural museum.

Sas Bahu Ka Mandir is an eleventh-century temple dedicated to Vishnu.

Teli Ka Mandir is a ninth-century temple dedicated to Vishnu, with a Dravidian roof and an Indo-Aryan, northern India decorative exterior.

Suraj Kund is the site of the pond where Suraj Sena was cured by Saint Gwalipa, who set in motion Gwalior's illustrious history.

INDORE

Jain Kanch Mandir, a dazzling glass temple constructed from 1882 to 1922, celebrates this religious sect in sparkling detail. Open 9 A.M.–5 P.M. daily.

Lal Baug Palace, built from 1885 to 1925 by the Holkar kings, is a blend of architectural styles: Italian, French, and Indian. It has collections of paintings, sculptures, and tribal art. Open 10 A.M.–6 P.M.; closed Monday.

JABALPUR

Madan Mahal Fort, overlooking the city, was built by Raja Madan Shah in 1116.

MANDU

This historic pleasure resort of Hindu and Moslem rulers, with 12 gateways, is strewn with monuments. Here are the best.

The Tomb of Hoshang Shah (1405–1435), India's first marble edifice, is a superb example of Afghan architecture, with an exquisite dome, marble latticework, and delicate courtyards and towers. The Mogul Emperor Shah Jahan sent his builders to analyze its construction before he built the Taj Mahal.

Jami Masjid, inspired by the great mosque at Damascus, was started by Hoshang Shah and completed by Mahmud Khiki in 1454. It's considered Mandu's most impressive structure, with a huge domed porch, beautifully decorated entrances and a roof with 61 domes.

Asharfi Mahal, facing the Jami Masjid, was called the "palace of gold coins." Now in ruins, it was once a college for young Moslem boys.

Rewa Kund, built by Moslems, is a holy lake for Hindus.

Baz Bahadur's Palace, built in the 1500s, was a pleasure retreat, with rooms on four sides of a courtyard with a beautiful cistern.

Roopmati's Pavilion was originally an army observation post before it became a retreat for Queen Roopmati.

Nilkanth Mahal, built on the site of a Hindu shrine dedicated to Shiva, was a palace built for Akbar's Hindu wife. It offers one of the best views of Mandu.

Hindola Mahal, also known as the Swinging Palace because of sloping walls that create the illusion of a swaying building, was probably constructed in the fifteenth century.

Jahaz Mahal, called the ship palace, is set between two artificial lakes. The Mogul Emperor Jahangir and his wife, Nur Jehan, used to stay in this two-story architectural marvel, which was probably built in the late 1400s.

OMKARESHWAR

Shri Omkar Mandhata Temple, set on an island and dedicated to Shiva, is a unique example of early medieval Brahmanic architecture.

Twenty-four Avatars is a complex of Hindu and Jain temples in various architectural styles.

ORCHHA

Jahangir Mahal, a rectangular palace with eight minarets, was built in the seventeenth century to commemorate a visit by this Mogul emperor.

Ram Raja Temple, a palace-turned-temple, has soaring spires and grand architectural detail. It's the only temple in India where Rama (Vishnu) is worshipped as a king.

Laxminarayan Temple. This fort-style temple has exquisite Bundela paintings covering the walls and ceiling of three halls.

Chaturbhuj Temple. Set on a massive platform, this shrine is dedicated to Rama.

SANCHI

Great Stupa No. 1 was started during Ashoka's reign, but was completed in the second and third centuries B.C. It has four gateways that represent some of the finest Buddhist sculpture in India.

Stupa No. 2 dates back to the second century B.C. and has a well-preserved balustrade.

Stupa No. 3, a hemispheric dome surmounted by an umbrella, was built 150–140 B.C.

Ashoka Pillar dates from the third century. Only a fragment remains.

MUSEUMS AND GALLERIES. Entrance is free or nominal in cost.

Bhopal. *Roopanker Museum of Fine Arts* and the *Modern Art Center* (both in the Bharat Bhawan complex) house paintings, sculptures, and a good collection of folk and tribal art. Roopanker arranges special exhibitions, seminars, artist camps, lectures, and orientation courses in art. Open February–November, 2–8 P.M. November–February, 1–7 P.M.; closed Monday throughout the year.

Gwalior. *Gujari Mahal Archaeological Museum* has good collections of sculpture, inscriptions, metal images, terra-cotta objects and archaeological pieces, including those recovered at the ancient sites of Besnagar, Pawaya, and Ujjain. It also contains an interesting collection of coins, paintings, among them copies of frescoes from the Bagh Caves (Buddhist caves from the sixth and seventh centuries). Open 10 A.M.–5 P.M., closed Mondays.

Jivaji Rao Scindia Museum, in the Jai Vilas Palace, includes the treasures of the former maharajah displayed in ornate rooms. Open 10 A.M.–5 P.M.; closed Mondays.

Sanchi. *Archaeological Museum* has antiquities recovered from ongoing excavations. Open 9 A.M.–5 P.M.

SPORTS AND OUTDOOR ADVENTURES. Organized adventures are just developing in Madhya Pradesh, but you can consider a bike or river cruise (see Tour Operators, above). Also check Tour Operators in *Facts at Your Fingertips.* **Wildlife Sanctuaries.** *Bandhavargh National Park* lies in the Sal Forest in the heart of the Vindhyan Mountain range. It has a variety of wildlife, including tigers, panthers, spotted deer, sambar, barking deer, wild boar, and bison. There are also the archaeological remains of the Kalchuri period; adjacent to the remains are a large number of prehistoric caves. Vehicles and elephants are available at the Forest Lodge for touring the park. The park is closed Fridays and during the monsoon season (July–October).

Kahna National Park can be reached by a regular bus service from Jabalpur. Considered one of India's best parks, Kahna is the natural habitat of a large variety of wild animals, including tigers, panthers, sambar, cheetahs, black bucks, and barking deer. Vehicles and elephants are available at either tourist lodge for touring the park. The park is closed during the monsoon season (July–October).

SHOPPING. There are lots of good handicrafts in Madhya Pradesh, where craftsmen have kept alive skills and traditions that go back hundreds of years. Small shops in bazaars and government-operated stores are located in practically every city and town, displaying handwoven brocades of Chanderi and Naheswar and *kosa* silks of Raigarh, along with leather toys and exquisitely wrought metal bells. Other specialties include silver jewelery, lacquer bangles, golden-thread embroidery, marble ashtrays and boxes, and beaded tapestries of gods and goddesses.

Bhopal has a fascinating old *Chowk* (bazaar), where you can look for interesting silver tribal jewelry and lovely handlooms. Rupees only. Bargain! Bazaars are open 9:30 A.M.–7:30 P.M.; closed Sundays. Also visit *Mrignayani*, 9 New Market, T. T. Nagar, the government-run emporium, which has all of the state's handicrafts under its roof. Open March–November, 10 A.M.–8 P.M. (lunch break: 1:30–3:30 P.M.) and December–February, 10:30 A.M.–7:30 P.M. (lunch break: 1:30–2:30 P.M.); closed Thursday all year.

Indore, a cotton textile center, has a colorful bazaar called Cloth Market, where you can buy locally woven Maheshwari and Chanderi textiles in cotton and silk. Open 9 A.M.–8 P.M.; closed Sunday. Also visit these two shops, which specialize in these fabrics:

Menka International, 498 M. G. Rd., open 10 A.M.–8 P.M.; closed Sunday. Traveler's checks.

N. Jankilal Bhaiya, 505 M. G. Rd., open 9 A.M.–8 P.M.; closed Sunday. Rupees only.

If you're in Mandu on a Tuesday, be sure to stroll through the weekly village market, about 8 km (5 mi.) from the historic city. It's a must stop for taking photos. Open 8 A.M.–6 P.M.

NIGHTLIFE AND BARS. Bhopal. The best place to have a nightcap is at Ripples (Hotel Lake View Ashok), which overlooks the lake. Open 11 A.M.–3 P.M. and 7 P.M.–11 P.M. Most bars in the state follow these hours.

THE TEMPLES
OF KHAJURAHO

by
KATHLEEN COX

Above, half seen, in the lofty gloom,
Strange works of a long dead people loom,
What did they mean to those who now are dust,
These rioting figures of love and lust?
The Garden of Kama

America wouldn't be discovered for 500 years; the groundwork for Chartres Cathedral wouldn't be laid for a hundred years, but in the year 1000, Central India was in its grand ascendancy, especially the region of Khajuraho, under the rule of the Chandella Rajputs. The Chandellas, like so many other Rajputs, traced their lineage back to the lunar god Chandra.

Chandra noticed Hemavati, the beautiful daughter of a Brahman priest, while she bathed in a moonlit pool. Hemavati's indiscretion led to her seduction, with the child of this unexpected alliance none other than Chandravarman, founder of the Chandella dynasty. Many years later, when Chandravarman came to power, his mother supposedly visited him in a dream. Build temples, she said—and build them he did, as did subsequent rulers.

During this time (A.D. 950–1050), India was the Asian Eldorado. People were rich, the land was fertile, life brimmed with pleasure. *Purdah* (the seclusion of women) hadn't yet cast its inhibiting pall on all the joy. Everyone lived the tenth-century-style good time: trooping off to fairs, feasts, hunts, dramas, music, and dancing.

All this untroubled abundance provided the perfect climate for creativity, with temple building emerging as the major form of expression. No strict boundaries existed between the sacred and the profane. The temple was the house of god, meeting hall, neighborhood social club, and gossip center. Offerings of the faithful filled the Rajput's coffers, and he, in turn, provided for his people, overseeing the construction of more temples—a happy, nonvicious cycle that led to the creation of 85 temples in a hundred years. And everyone of them was built at a time when architects and sculptors had passed through the classic and mannerist stages into the flamboyant baroque, the zenith of artistic power under the Chandellas.

What did these sculptors choose to represent on the temples that clustered around the now-tranquil village called Khajuraho? God, as the Hindu understands him—Shiva, Vishnu, Brahma—and the Jainist saints who are all lavishly honored. But despite the interest in heaven, the real focus was more earthbound, rooted in the facts of life.

And not just the hunt and war, feasting, music, and dancing, but the side of life that many Westerners discuss only in whispers. Here, portrayed with no false modesty and even less prudery, virile men and voluptuous women, immortalized in stone, cavort in the most intimate and extraordinarily erotic postures. To call these sculptures pornography is irrelevant. Although some of the decorative sculpture might be too revealing for the excessively innocent or too titillating for the sexually adventurous, most adults will be fascinated by what they see. Here is the best of Hindu sculpture: sinuous, twisting forms—human and divine—throbbing with life, tension, and conflict. Here every carving exudes consummate skill.

EXPLORING KHAJURAHO

The small village of Khajuraho is in the Chattarpur district of Madhya Pradesh in north-central India. It's hard to imagine that this rural area was ever politically important. The only significant river is some distance away, and the village itself seems far removed from any kind of substantial economic activity. Yet in this remote area, the Chandellas placed their temples—some monumental, some small. Over their small corner of rich civilization, in which people adored the gods and the gods showered their blessings on people, this dynasty reigned for five centuries until history, which rarely shows any regard for human happiness, intervened. The Chandella kingdom, which gave all its energies to enjoying life, succumbed to invaders of a stronger moral fiber. In the year 1100, Mahmud the Turk began the Holy War against the "idolaters" of India. By 1200, the sultans of Delhi ruled over the once-glorious Chandella domain.

The Khajuraho Temples

When you face the entrance of any of the 22 remaining Khajuraho temples, the row of ascending and separate finials looms upward like a series of mountain peaks. The analogy is deliberate; these temples represent a highly imaginative rendering of the Himalayas, the legendary abode of the sacred gods who are worshiped within. The obvious upward movement also represents the Hindu path toward heavenly nirvana: one first fulfills

TO LALGUAN
MAHADEVA

PARVATI

TO CIRCUIT HOUSE
AND RAJNAGAR

CHITRAGUPTA
DEVI JAGDAMBE
MAHADEVA
KANDARIYA MAHADEO
LAKSHMANA
MATANGESVARA

VISHWANATH
NANDI

VARAH

TO CHATRAI

VAMANA

JAVARI

BRAHMA
MUSEUM

KHAJURAHO

CHAUSATH YOGINI

GHANTAI

ADINATH

**WESTERN
GROUP**

SHIVSAGER
TANK

PARSVANATH
SHANTINATH

**EASTERN
GROUP**

TO BAMITHA

DULADEO

TO BENIGANJ

River KHUDDAR

**SOUTHERN
GROUP**

JATKARI

CHATURBHUJ

TO RAJGARH

N

**KHAJURAHO
TEMPLES**

material obligations (the lowest peak), then social obligations, and then religious ones until one finally reaches the highest station and total peace, or nirvana. Also notice the placement of exterior carvings. That, too, is intentional. Human forms dominate the lower half, with abstract design—god's play—relegated to the celestial top.

The Khajuraho temples are of the Indo-Aryan type and are generally classified as *Nagara*, or North Indian. But they have definite features that set them apart; indeed, no others like them exist in any part of India. Though dedicated to different deities (Shiva, Vishnu, or the Jain tirthankaras—"perfect souls"), the general outline remains the same.

Each temple stands on a high platform and without the customary enclosure. The larger shrines (at least one in each group) have a central sanctuary for the honored god and one more at each corner for the lesser deities. The floor plan is divided into five distinct sections (three in the smaller temples). The appearance resembles a cross with two sets of arms. The visitor enters through the portico (*ardhamandapa*) into the assembly hall (*mandapa*), which leads to the sanctum where the idol is enshrined. There is a vestibule (*antarala*) to cross and then finally the *garbhagriha*, or cell-shaped sanctum. Around this shrine is the ambulatory or processional passage (*pradakshinapatha*). The smaller temples omit this last feature and the assembly hall. But the most noteworthy aspect of the Khajuraho temple is the *shikhara* (spire) surrounded and flanked by countless sister towers that push each other heavenward.

Although the floor plan and the silhouette of the temples are unique and noteworthy, the eye rightfully focuses on the soaring vertical lines that are beautifully balanced by two or three horizontal bands covered with hundreds and hundreds of sculptured figures—gods and goddesses, celestial nymphs and handmaidens (*asparas* and *surasundaris*), bold serpents and leonine beasts, and the array of human females (*nayikas*), usually made more sexy and alluring than their heavenly counterparts. And, of course, the major theme, which has given Khajuraho its reputation: the *mithuna* couples, "these rioting figures of love and lust," which, oddly enough, account for only 3–4 percent of the carvings.

How to interpret this preoccupation with the erotic? One explanation is rooted in religion, specifically the Tantric doctrine that was popular in the Chandella period. This cult, the antithesis of asceticism, emphasized the female as the dominant force of creation and taught that the senses are the equal of the spirit. The gratification of earthly desires is a step toward the attainment of nirvana. Another explanation is that the sculptors wanted to exhibit the full range of human life, which they certainly did. However, while many of the mithuna groups are explicitly carnal, others portray a wide spectrum of human emotion: jealousy, fear, modesty, and the tenderness and tranquillity of love fulfilled.

Tour of the Temples

The three groups of temples cover an area of about eight square kilometers (three square miles). The Western Group is the largest and most important (the Khajuraho Archaeological Museum is located here, too). It includes the oldest (Chausath Yogini); the largest (Kandariya Mahadeo); plus the Devi Jagdambe, particularly "mithunaised." The Eastern Group, which is close to Khajuraho village, contains the Brahman and Jain shrines. The Southern Group is about two kilometers (one mile) south of the village and has only two temples, but they should be seen.

Western Group

Begin your tour with the Chausath Yogini Temple on the west side of the Shivsager Tank. The oldest temple at Khajuraho (some date it as early as A.D. 820 but 900 seems closer), it is dedicated to Kali, the goddess of wrath. Chausath means 64, which equals the number of female nymphs serving the fierce goddess. This temple is built of granite (all the others are a pale, warm-toned sandstone) and is the only one oriented northeast–southwest instead of the usual north–south. It was once surrounded by 64 roofed cells for the figures of Kali's attendants, of which only 35 remain. Different in material and design, it is one of two temples at Khajuraho that do not follow the typical style.

Lalguan Mahadeva stands about a half kilometer (a third of a mile) from Chausath Yogini. This Shiva temple is in ruins and the original portico is missing, but it is of historical interest, since it is built of both granite and sandstone and represents the transition from Chausath Yogini to the later temples.

Kandariya Mahadeo is to the north of Chausath Yogini. This is the biggest and, by common consent, the best temple at Khajuraho and one of the best in India, representing the Indian "Golden Age" of temple art. Built in the typical Hindu five-shrine design, this temple is dedicated to Shiva; the inner sanctum houses a marble lingam with a four-foot circumference. The entrance archway is decorated with statues of musicians, lovers in fond embrace, crocodiles, and flying gods and goddesses. The ceilings, circles set in a square, are carved with scrolls and scallops; the pillars are ornamented with beasts and grotesque dwarfs; and flowers and pennants decorate the lintels and doorjambs of the sanctum. Outside, the three bands of sculpture around the sanctum and transept bring to life the whole galaxy of Hindu gods and goddesses, mithuna couples letting loose with every fantasy, celestial handmaidens, and lions. One art historian counted 872 statues—226 inside and 646 outside. This temple, with its imposing size, fine proportions, and inexhaustibly rich sculpture, is a high point of the Khajuraho tour.

Mahadeva Temple, also dedicated to Shiva, shares its masonry terrace with the Kandariya and the Devi Jagdambe. Although mostly in ruins, the temple still boasts a remarkable freestanding statue in the portico of a man caressing a lion.

Devi Jagdambe Temple was dedicated successively to Vishnu, Lakshmi, and then, because the sacred image of the goddess is black, Kali (the goddess of wrath). It is of the three-shrine design and, from the inside, seems shaped like a cross. The third band of sculpture has a series of mithuna themes of uncensored erotica. The ceilings are similar to those of the Kandariya, and the three-headed, eight-armed statue of Shiva is one of the best cult images at Khajuraho. Above the entrance to the sanctum is a carving of Vishnu.

Chitragupta Temple lies slightly north of the Devi Jagdambe and resembles it in construction. Facing east toward the rising sun, the presiding deity is Surya, the sun god, who finds his most grandiose tribute at Konarak. The temple cell contains his five-foot-high image with his chariot and seven horses that carry him away at dusk. He is also depicted above the doorway. In the central niche to the south of the sanctum is an image of Vishnu shown with 11 heads. The central head is his own, while the others represent his numerous incarnations. A profusion of sculpture—scenes of animal combats, royal processions, masons at work, and joyous dances—depict the lavish country life of the Chandellas.

The Vishwanath and Nandi temples face each other on a common terrace to the east of Chitragupta and Devi Jagdambe. There are two staircases: the northern flanked by a pair of lions and the southern, by a pair of elephants. Since it is an important Shiva temple, the Vishwanath has a simpler extra shrine to house the god's mount, the massive and richly harnessed statue of the sacred bull Nandi. It also supposedly had two original lingams (stylized phallic symbols)—one of pure emerald, the other of simpler stone. Only one, unfortunately the less valuable, remains. The Vishwanath is similar in dedication and floor plan to its larger sister, the Kandariya, but, unlike the latter, two of the original corner shrines remain. On the outer wall of the corridor surrounding the cells is an impressive image of Brahma, the three-headed Lord of Creation, and his consort, Saraswati. On all the walls, the form of the woman dominates, portrayed in all her daily tenth-century occupations: writing a letter, holding her baby, studying her reflection in a mirror, applying makeup, or playing music. The nymphs of paradise are voluptuous and provocative; the sexy scenes, robust. An inscription states that the temple was built by Chandella King Dhanga in 1002.

Parvati Temple, near Vishwanath, is a small and relatively unimportant shrine originally dedicated to Vishnu. But the original idol was supposedly replaced by the goddess Ganga standing on a crocodile. The name Parvati (wife of Shiva) is a misnomer.

The Lakshmana Temple, though dedicated to Vishnu, is almost in all respects similar to the Vishwanath. It is also a perfect example of the fully developed five-shrine Khajuraho style, since all four shelters for the minor gods are undamaged. The ceiling of the hall is charmingly carved in shell and floral motifs. The highly decorated lintel over the entrance to the main shrine shows Lakshmi, goddess of wealth and consort of Vishnu, with Brahma, Lord of Creation (on her left) and Shiva, Lord of Destruction (on her right). The planets are depicted on a frieze above the lintel. The relief on the doorway illustrates the scene of the gods and demons churning the ocean in order to obtain a pitcher of miraculous nectar from the bottom. The gods won the ensuing 12-day battle over the pitcher, drank the nectar, and gained immortality. Another doorway relief shows Vishnu in his nine incarnations. The idol in the sanctum with two pairs of arms and three heads represents the same god in his lion and boar incarnations. Outside, two (not the usual three) sculptured bands display boar hunting, elephants, horses, soldiers, and—on the upper one—celestial maidens and some of those famous mithunas absorbed in their erotic pleasure.

Matangesvara Temple, south of Lakshmana, is the only "living temple," with worship taking place in the morning and afternoon. Its square construction and simpler floor plan is exceptional for Khajuraho. The temple has oriel windows, a projecting portico, and a ceiling of overlapping concentric circles. An enormous lingam, nearly 3 meters (8½ feet) tall, is enshrined in the sanctum.

Varah Temple, in front of the preceding shrine, is dedicated to Vishnu's Varaha-Avatar, or Boar Incarnation. The huge boar, snouty and stolid, is swathed and ringed with more than 600 carvings of gods and demons.

The Archaeological Museum is across the street from the Matangesvara Temple. Three separate galleries contain interesting sculptures and stone panels salvaged from ruined temples.

Eastern Group

This group lies close to the village and includes three Hindu temples (Brahma, Vamana, and Javari) and three Jain shrines (Ghantai, Adinath,

and Parsvanath). This proximity of the cults attests to the religious tolerance of the times in general and of the Chandella rulers in particular.
About halfway between the western group of temples and the village is
a modern building housing a tenth-century idol of Hanuman, the monkey
god.

Vamana Temple is northernmost and is dedicated to Vishnu's dwarf
incarnation. The idol in the sanctum, however, looks more like a tall, sly
child than a dwarf. The hall, a squat, heavily adorned pile of masonry and
sculpture, contrasts strongly with the relatively plain-ribbed shikhara. The
sanctum walls show total tolerance—almost all the major gods appear
with their consorts in attendance. Vishnu appears in many of his forms,
with even a Buddha thrown in. Outside, two tiers of sculpture are mainly
concerned with the nymphs of paradise, who strike charming poses under
their private awnings. The sculptors obviously enjoyed lavishing their energy on so many full-blown female bodies, so many ornaments, and so
many handsome coiffures. Here, too, you see the unexpurgated mind at
work.

Javari Temple is just to the south. It is small and of the simplified three-
shrine design, but well proportioned and lovely. The two main exterior
bands again boast hosts of heavenly maidens.

Brahma Temple is slightly to the south and opposite the Javari. Made
of both granite and sandstone, it is considered one of the earliest temples.
Its general outline, particularly that of the spire, suggests some other style
of Indian temple. It was originally dedicated to Shiva, but the idol in the
shrine was miscalled Brahma, and the name stuck.

The Jain temples are to the south of this group, beginning with a little
gem, the Ghantai. This open-colonnaded structure is only the shell of what
was once a complete temple, but it is still one of the most attractive monuments at Khajuraho. Note the classicism and detail of the pillars. These
slender columns seem decorated with French *passementerie*—bugles,
braid, and bell-like tassels hang in graceful patterns. Adorning the entrance are an eight-armed Jain goddess riding the mythical bird, Garuda,
and a relief illustrating the 16 dreams of the mother of Mahavira, the
greatest religious figure in Jainism and a contemporary of the Buddha.

Adinath Temple, a minor shrine, is east of Ghantai. Its porch is a modern addition, as is the statue of Tirthankara (perfect soul) Adinatha. The
shikhara and its base are richly carved.

Parsvanath Temple, to the south, is the largest and finest of the Jain
temples and probably the best construction, technically speaking, in all
Khajuraho. Although Kandariya may have the best design, Parsvanath
makes up for its lack of size and architectural perfection with marvelous
sculpture. Its unrelievedly chiseled facades, turrets, and spires demand
close inspection. The sanctum has a carved bull (Adinatha's emblem)
standing on a pedestal. In 1860, another image was installed, that of Parsvanath. The outer walls have excellent statues of sloe-eyed beauties in nat-
uralistic poses, occupied in feminine pursuits with children, cosmetics, and
flowers. A statue of Shiva and Parvati is almost the epitome of love: her
breast cupped in his hand, they regard each other with tenderness and desire. Almost all the exterior offers some of the best Hindu art in India.
There is another temple in this group, the Shantinath, which is modern
but does contain some ancient Jain sculpture.

Southern Group

There are only two temples in this group. Duladeo Temple, south of
Ghantai Jain Temple, though built in the customary five-shrine style,

looks flatter and more massive than do the typical Khajuraho shrines. Attributed to the 12th century and one of the last temples erected in Khajuraho, the Duladeo Temple lacks the usual ambulatory passage and crowning lotus-shaped finials. Its decoration is still graceful and well executed, particularly the multiple-figure bracket capitals inside and the flying wizards on the highest carved band outside. Here, too, in this temple dedicated to Shiva, eroticism works its way in.

Chaturbhuj Temple is nearly two kilometers (one mile) farther south of Duladeo. Small, but with an attractive colonnaded entrance and a nice feeling of verticality, it enshrines an impressive large, four-handed image of Vishnu. The exterior sculpture, with a few exceptions, falls short of the Khajuraho mark.

Intermission

Although the temples are Khajuraho's major attraction and the compelling reason for any visit, lovely nearby respites from the intense concentration of sculpture do exist. See the Eastern Temples at sunset. Sit on the steps of the Vamana and watch the villagers come home from working the fields or fill their brass vessels at the nearby well. Walk into the adjacent Khajuraho village and meander around the streets crowded with boar, goats, buffalo.

One afternoon, take a five-kilometer (three-mile) ride by rickshaw to the tiny village of Rajnagar, with the maharajah's former fortress now a school set on the crest of a hill. Roam the narrow, winding streets lined with charming whitewashed houses and shops. Also visit a new sanctuary, Panna National Park (40 kilometers [25 miles] south of Kujaraho), which is the habitat of tigers and other wildlife and fauna.

PRACTICAL INFORMATION FOR KHAJURAHO

WHEN TO GO. Avoid May through August, when the thermometer climbs over 100°. Rainfall in July and August is also heavy. The best time to visit is from October to the end of March; by then the rainy season has ended and the temperature is generally delightful.

HOW TO GET THERE. By Air. The best way is the morning *Indian Airlines* flight, daily throughout the year, from Delhi (1½ hours) and Agra (40 minutes). Indian Airlines also flies daily from Varanasi and makes three weekly flights from Bombay, Aurangabad, and Bhopal. For information in Khajuraho, tel. 35. If you're in a rush, you could cover Khajuraho in a day, leaving Delhi or Agra in the morning and flying back early the same afternoon. But that's the speed demon's pace, which gives about five hours in Khajuraho, barely enough time to fly through the important temples. The best plan is to stay overnight. Take in the temples in the gentler light of later afternoon or early morning. Khajuraho can get hot by midday.

By Train. Trains are impractical; the nearest station is 70 km (43 mi.) away.

By Bus. At press time, MPSTDC was planning to run daily deluxe air-conditioned buses between Jhansi and Khajuraho (projected cost: about Rs. 150). Contact MPSTDC (see address below). Public buses also connect Khajuraho with Agra, Bhopal, and Indore. Contact the Government of India Tourist Office (see address below).

By Rented Car with Driver. Good roads lead to Khajuraho. Here are some important distances: Agra, 395 km (245 mi.); Allahabad, 285 km (177 mi.); Bhopal, 372 km (231 mi.); Varanasi, 415 km (257 mi.); Lucknow, 287 km (178 mi.); Delhi, 598 km (371 mi.). Hire a car from one of the tour operators listed below or in the appropriate chapter.

TOURIST INFORMATION. Two separate tourist departments offer different information on Khajuraho. Both are helpful and worth a visit or telephone call. *Government of India Tourist Office,* opposite the Western Temple Complex, tel. 2047, is open Monday–Friday, 9 A.M.–5:30 P.M. and Saturday 8 A.M.–noon. There's also a counter at the airport that is open when planes arrive. *Madhya Pradesh State Tourism Development Corporation* (MPSTDC) has an office at the MPSTDC Tourist Bungalow, tel. 2051; open 10 A.M.–5 P.M., closed Sundays.

FOREIGN CURRENCY EXCHANGE. Most Western-style hotels have money-exchange counters. Otherwise, go to the *Canara Bank* in Hotel Khajuraho Ashok; open Monday–Tuesday and Thursday–Friday, 10 A.M.–2 P.M., Saturday till noon.

ACCOMMODATIONS. Khajuraho has a limited number of hotels in all price ranges. Prices are based on double occupancy and exclude taxes and service charges: *Deluxe,* over Rs. 2,000; *Expensive,* Rs. 1,200–Rs. 2,000; *Moderate,* Rs. 500–Rs. 1,200; *Inexpensive,* under Rs. 500. Some Western-style hotels take major credit cards. Peak season (October–end of March) can be busy, so book in advance.

Deluxe

Jass Oberoi. By-Pass Rd., Khajuraho 471606; tel. 2085. 54 rooms with bath; 50 under construction. This is Khajuraho's most elegant hotel. Its marble lobby has lovely Indian curios and a circular staircase covered by a dome. Best rooms overlook the pool. All rooms have balconies and handsome furnishings and are air-conditioned. TV on request, room service, multicuisine restaurants, bar, swimming pool, tennis courts, health club, foreign-exchange and travel counter, cultural entertainment, shopping arcade. AE, DC, MC, V.

Taj Hotel Chandela. Khajuraho 471606; tel. 2054. 102 rooms with bath. A two-story deluxe hotel, the Taj Chandela has lovely lawns and a marble lobby with a small fountain. Best rooms open onto a courtyard and pretty pool. All rooms are air-conditioned and spacious, with a modern decor. Multicuisine restaurants, room service, bar, swimming pool, health club and yoga, minigolf course, tennis court, foreign-exchange and travel counter, doctor, shopping arcade, cultural entertainment. AE, DC, MC, V.

Moderate

Hotel Khajuraho Ashok. Khajuraho 471606; tel. 2024. 38 rooms with bath. This two-story Western hotel has been renovated, but there's still a strong smell of pesticide. Some rooms, however, do offer a view of the temples. The decor is Western modern. Air-conditioning, room service, multicuisine restaurant, bar, swimming pool, foreign-exchange and travel counter, bank, shopping arcade. AE, DC, MC, V.

Inexpensive

Hotel Jhankar. Khajuraho 471606; tel. 2076. 19 rooms with bath. This new MPSTDC one-story hotel offers clean, spacious rooms with modern decor. Some rooms are air-conditioned; others have fans. Room service, multicuisine restaurant. Rupees only.

Hotel Payal. Khajuraho 471606; tel. 2076. 25 rooms with bath. This pleasant MPSTDC hotel has rooms that open onto an interior courtyard with a lawn and gardens. Rooms, some air-conditioned, are spacious and clean, with Western decor and balconies. Room service, multicuisine restaurant. Good value. Rupees only.

DINING OUT. The restaurants listed below are informal and, unless noted, don't require reservations. Prices are based on one person eating a three-course meal, excluding taxes, tip, or beverage: *Expensive,* Rs. 200–Rs. 300; *Moderate,* Rs. 100–Rs. 200; *Inexpensive,* under Rs. 100. Most Western-style hotels accept credit cards.

Expensive

Apsara. Jass Oberoi, By-Pass Rd.; tel. 2085. In this attractive restaurant, with teak lattice screens and silk bird paintings, the chef prepares good Continental and Indian dishes. Try the chicken *korma* (boneless chicken cooked in an onion and tomato curry) with Kashmiri pilaf (rice prepared with dried fruit and cashews).

From 6:30 to 7:30 P.M., you'll be entertained by local performers. Dinner reservations advised. Open 7–10:30 A.M., noon–3 P.M., and 7:30–10:30 P.M. AE, DC, MC, V.

Rasana. Taj Hotel Chandela; tel. 2054. One wall of this intimate restaurant has Rajasthani jewelry sewn into bright textile hangings. At night, candles add a romantic touch. Choose from Continental, Chinese, or Indian cuisines. The chef creates especially good tandoori dishes. Dinner reservations advised. Open noon–2:30 P.M. and 7:30–10:30 P.M. AE, DC, MC, V.

Inexpensive

Raja Cafe. Opposite the Western Temple group; no phone. At this popular, informal eatery, you can eat inside, on the terrace, or on the roof. Although the chef also prepares Chinese and Indian dishes, repeat customers go for Continental favorites, especially the southern fried chicken and macaroni. Open March–November, 7 A.M.–10:30 P.M.; otherwise, 8:30 A.M.–9 P.M. Rupees only.

Tourist Village Restaurant. Tel. 2128. Set in the MPSTDC Tourist Village, this open-air restaurant in the style of a *dhaba* (diner) has a bamboo and Indian-tile roof, brick floor, and hanging lanterns. You can choose from Indian and limited Continental dishes. Open for meals 6–10 A.M., noon–2 P.M., 7–10 P.M.; snacks available during nonmeal hours. Rupees only.

SWEETS AND TREATS. Just beyond Madla village, 24 km (15 mi.) from Khajuraho, is the *Tree House*, located on a riverbank at the end of a dirt tract to the left of the main road. After swimming or boating in the river, enjoy a cool drink in India's only tree deck, a cleverly designed oasis built into the branches. Open all the time.

HOW TO GET AROUND. From the Airport. The airport is six km (four mi.) from the temples. A taxi should cost about Rs. 50.

By Taxi. Private taxis are good for excursions beyond Khajuraho. Rates are about Rs. 4 per km. You can also engage a taxi for about Rs. 100 for four hours of local sightseeing. Set the fare before you depart.

By Bicycle Rickshaw. Once you're in the small village, this is the best way to get around. Drivers are supposed to follow fixed rates, but they like to keep this fact a secret. Negotiate hard or check with the Government of India Tourist Office (across from the Western Temple complex); an outside board lists the rates. Once you've seen the Western Temple complex, the other temples are spread around Khajuraho. Hire a rickshaw for a few hours (Rs. 50 per four hours) and have the driver take you from temple to temple, to the old village, and to your hotel.

SEASONAL EVENTS February/March. *Shivratri Mela.* Villagers hold a large fair in Khujaraho, with lots of stalls selling local products. On the Hindu sacred day of Shivratri, devotees pray at the Matangeshwar Temple and take a holy dip in the nearby pond.

March. The *Khajuraho Dance Festival* is a week-long opportunity to see numerous forms of classical Indian dance performed by India's best dancers on an outdoor stage with the temples as a backdrop. Contact tourist offices for specific details and buy tickets in advance. *Lok Ranjan Festival.* During the dance festival, also attend free nightly performances of tribal and folk dances as well as regional music held at MPSTDC's Tourist Village.

TOURS. From Bangalore, Bombay, Calcutta, and Delhi, MPSTDC offers year-round tours in Madhya Pradesh that include Khajuraho. Once in Khajuraho, you can hire an excellent guide from the *Government Tourist Office* or at Raja Cafe (two–four hours; about Rs. 80; four–eight hours, Rs. 150). Many of the guides are fluent in German, Japanese, Italian, English, and French. Don't get taken in by those who pose as guides inside the temple complex. They'll talk your head off, but the facts they tell are their own. Audio tapes may also be available in 1993. Contact the Government of India Tourist Office.

TOUR OPERATORS. For all travel needs, including a car with driver, contact Orient Express (Hotel Taj Chandela, tel. 2049) or Khajuraho Tours (Old Memorial Bldg., tel. 2033), open daily, 10 A.M.–6 P.M.

HISTORIC SITES. See all the 20 remaining tenth- and eleventh-century temples and their fabulous carvings. The best times of day to view the temples are early morning and late afternoon, when the light is soft and shadows highlight the delicate carvings. They are in three main groups, those of the west being generally acknowledged to be the best. Close to Khajuraho village is the Eastern Group, while three miles from there stands the Southern Group. Of these 20 temples, five are easily accessible—Kandariya Mahadeo Temple is by far the largest and the finest, the others being Lakshmana, Visvanatha, Chitragupta, and Devi Jagdambe. These temples are found in a group close to each other and make an imposing picture with their elegant spires against the sky. Temples are open from early morning to sunset. Western Complex, Rs. 1; others, free.

MUSEUMS. The *Archaeological Museum* near the Western Group of temples has three galleries: Jain, Buddhist, and miscellaneous, essentially sculptures collected on the temple sites. Tickets for the Western Group also include entry to the museum. Open 10 A.M.–5 P.M.; closed Fridays. Nominal entry charge.

The *Jain Museum,* near the Jain temples, has artifacts from the Eastern Group of temples. Open daily 9 A.M.–5 P.M. Nominal entry charge.

SPORTS AND OUTDOOR ADVENTURES. Wildlife Sanctuaries. Panna National Park, 20 km (12 mi.) from Khajuraho, was established in 1981. Within its 543 square kilometers (337 square miles) of grasslands and forests, visitors are apt to see blue bulls, bison, the elusive tiger, and numerous species of birds. Guides and jeep and elephant safaris are available at the Hinota and Mandla gates. The park is open sunrise to sunset. The best viewing time is February–June. The park is closed July–October.

SHOPPING. Opposite the Western Group of temples is a square with numerous carts of so-called curios—most of which are new. Buy what you like and bargain hard. Also visit these two good shops:

Mrignayni Emporium, opposite the Archaeological Museum and run by the Handicraft Board of Madhya Pradesh, sells tribal art, textiles, and local handicrafts. Open 10 A.M.–6 P.M.; closed Tuesdays. Rupees only.

Karan Jewelers, in the bazaar opposite the Western Group of temples, has good bronzes, paintings, and jewelry; and semiprecious and precious stones, especially diamonds that are mined nearby. AE, MC, V.

NIGHTLIFE AND BARS. The Chandela Cultural Center sponsors folk and tribal dances daily (6:30 P.M.–7:30 P.M. and 8:30 P.M.–9:30 P.M.); admission $5 per show. Contact MPSTDC, tel. 2051. Bars are open 10 A.M.–midnight. The best bar is the *Temple Bar* at Jass Oberoi, which quietly reflects Khajuraho's historic legacy and offers an elegant ambience.

SOUTHERN REGION

MADRAS AND TAMIL NADU

Glories of Dravidian India

by
KATHLEEN COX

In almost any country, the south has a personality of its own, and India is no exception. The pace of living in this sun-drenched state is more leisurely and traditional than in the rest of the country.

The region covers the State of Tamil Nadu and some of its environs, along the coast of the Bay of Bengal on the east and the Western Ghats on the west. It was formerly a number of separate princely states that were amalgamated, for linguistic reasons, after independence.

The land of Tamil, founded by Dravidians over 5,000 years ago, is primarily agrarian. It has frequent lush green vistas, charming narrow waterways, vast groves of coconuts, bananas, and sugarcane, and innumerable tiny villages with huts of thatch, wood, mud, or brick—well-tended homes that are pleasingly neat and tidy. Throughout the region, you'll see colorful drawings on the ground or pavement in front of each dwelling. Each morning the woman of the house, using her imagination, and white or colored powder, creates *kolams* (or *rangolis*) in intricate geometric or floral designs. Traditionally, the powder was made from rice and the design was then eaten by insects or birds. In this way the woman pleased the gods by starting her day with an act of charity. Even Madras, the capital, offers glimpses of the traditional way of life that has all but vanished in many other cities of India. And when Madras becomes too hot, the southern hill stations and the beaches offer a great escape.

TAMIL NADU

0 — miles — 100

0 — km — 100

🐘 Wildlife sanctuaries

🛕 Temples

N

ANDHRA PRADESH

KARNATAKA

Bangalore

Madras

Vellore
Kanchipuram

Covelong Beach

Mahabalipuram (Mamallapuram)

Tiruvannamalai

Tindivanam

Yercaud

Pondicherry

← Ootacamund (Ooty)

Bay of Bengal

Coimbatore

Chidambaram

Kaveri R.

Tranquebar

Tiruchirapalli (Tiruchi)

Thanjavur (Tanjore)

Kodikkarai (Point Calimere)

Kodaikanal

Madurai

Vaigai R.

KERALA

Ramanthapuram

Rameswaram

Dhanushkodi

Tambraparni R.

SRI LANKA

Kanya Kumari (Cape Comorin)

Padmanabhapuram

INDIAN OCEAN

The difference between South India and the rest of the country is much greater than a few degrees on a thermometer. The south has been relatively unaffected by the waves of invasion that shaped India for centuries, even though it was the starting point of the last invasion of all—that of the Europeans. Alien empire builders either never reached the south during the long centuries of Indian history or their fury and zeal were spent by the time they got here.

The result is a fascinating survival of ancient India in its purest form. Nowhere else is classical dancing performed on the scale of the Bharata Natyam dances of Madras and other, smaller cities. Nowhere else can you experience the exuberance of medieval India as you can in old Madurai or Tiruchirapalli. The temples of South India can't be classified according to the dictates of Western architecture and esthetics. Their *gopura* (towers) are massive, and some—especially the more recent ones—have colors in combinations that no Westerner sees outside Miami Beach. But as expressions of traditional India, the ancient temples are the heart and soul of any trip.

EXPLORING TAMIL NADU

MADRAS

Madras is the fourth-largest city in India—outranked by Delhi, Bombay, and Calcutta for the dubious distinction of cramming as many people as possible into one place. Fortunately, you don't feel the density in Madras. The sprawling city, which is divided in two by the Cooum River, has few tall buildings to mar the impression of an easygoing market town. The welcome sense of spaciousness is enhanced by Madras's waterfront on the Bay of Bengal, one of the world's largest and most attractive beaches set in the heart of a city.

In spite of its large population, currently over 4 million, this city has a gentle pace and is made for people watching. The southerners are different from their northern counterparts, having the poise and self-assurance that comes from carrying the civilization of thousands of years. Saris aren't worn in the same manner as in northern India, and though some men dress in the elegant white *dhotis* of the north, they often wear brightly colored *lungis* (cloth draped around the waist and worn long or pulled up between the knees).

That gracefulness is present in Madras in such liberal quantities is appropriate. In the Government Museum, you can see the famous bronze of the Chola period (tenth century) of Nataraja-Shiva in the cosmic dance pose. This beautifully executed two-foot-high statue, which seems to be constantly moving, has rightfully become the symbol of Indian art that is recognized all around the world.

No visitor should leave Madras without seeing a performance of the Bharata Natyam. Many of these dance recitals are about Krishna, the most popular of Vishnu's nine incarnations, symbol of the ideal man. As they dance, the women appear to express their infatuation with the god, described in one prayer as "Lord Krishna, with eyes like lustrous pearls, head bedecked with peacocks' feathers and body of the hue of Heaven." The dancers exhibit perfect control over each muscle in their bodies, while executing intricate movements with clockwork precision. Once you've seen a Bharata Natyam dancer move her neck while keeping her head still, you'll respect the artistry and skill behind this classical Indian dance form.

MADRAS

0 _____ 1 mile
0 _____ 1 kilometer

1. General Post Office
2. Central Railway Station
3. Stadium
4. Egmore Railway Station
5. Government Tourist Office
6. St. George's Cathedral
7. Aquarium
8. Connemara Hotel
9. Chola Sheraton Hotel
10. Taj Coromandel Hotel
11. National Art Gallery and Museum

Paradoxically, this least Westernized of India's Big Four cities is also its oldest European settlement. The written records trace the first European foothold in Madras 500 years to the Portuguese, but the Portuguese were only latecomers. Legend claims that Thomas the Apostle ("Doubting Thomas") came here as a missionary from Palestine and was martyred while praying in front of a cross engraved in stone on St. Thomas Mount (near the Madras Airport) in A.D. 72. This stone, called the Bleeding Stone because it supposedly sheds blood on December 18 (the day of St. Thomas's death), is now installed behind the high altar inside the lovely sixteenth-century Church of Our Lady of Expectation, erected on the foundation of an earlier church that St. Thomas is said to have built. His revered name has also survived in St. Thomé, a pleasant seaside residential section of southern Madras, while his body is believed to be entombed in the center of the San Thomé Cathedral Basilica, a handsome neo-Gothic structure with elegant arches and a 56-meter (180-foot) steeple, built in 1896. Inside, notice the image of Christ standing on a lotus flower (a typical Hindu pose).

From here, wander into the nearby inland district called Mylapore, the home of Tiruvalluvar, the Tamil poet who lived in the second century and wrote the *Kural,* the greatest of all works in the Tamil language. It's still recited reverently in South India. In Mylapore, you must visit the Kapaleeswarar Temple dedicated to Kapaleeswarar (Shiva). This structure offers an impressive contrast to the European architecture found in the cathedral. The sawed-off pyramid of its recently renovated *gopuram* (tower entrance) shatters the horizon far more violently than does the slim spire of San Thomé. This typical Dravidian temple, which was rebuilt in the sixteenth century, is covered with brightly painted sculptures. Although non-Hindus can't enter the sanctum sanctorum (inner shrine), they can enter the outer courtyard.

Fort St. George, the Original Madras

Strickly speaking, the history of Madras began with the history of the British in India. In 1639, 25 years before the British reached Bombay and 50 years before they arrived in Calcutta, the Raja of Chandragiri gave Francis Day a lease to open a trading post for the British East India Company on the site of Madras, then known as Madraspatram. The following year, work began on Fort St. George, which was finished in 1653. From this stronghold, Britain held Madras until India achieved independence, with the exception of a two-year period beginning in 1746, when Dupleix took it for France only to lose it again in 1748. Fort St. George is tightly interwoven with the swashbuckling story of the struggle for India in the eighteenth century. Here, Robert Clive arrived in 1743 as a modest clerk for the East India Company. When Fort St. George surrendered to the French, Clive escaped and became an officer in the army of the East India Company. By the time he was 30, he had become governor of Madras and was well launched on his meteoric career, which saw him preserve India for Britain only to die by his own hand in disgrace back in his native England.

Modern Madras has grown around Fort St. George, and the old fortress, which now houses the Tamil Nadu State Legislature and other political offices, is a good place to start a tour of this part of the city.

Its 6-meter (20-foot) walls still guard the center of Madras and its busy commercial artery, Anna Salai (Mount Road). Inside the walls, you can stroll through the pages of history. Clive's house is still here, and Colonel

Wellesley, who later became the Duke of Wellington, lived in another old home, which can also be seen within the fort.

Inside Fort St. George, visit the oldest Anglican church in India, St. Mary's Church, consecrated in 1680. The records show that one of its most generous benefactors was Elihu Yale, the Boston-born English merchant who also showed his generosity to the university that now bears his name. Yale, too, was a governor of Madras, although his term in office is not as memorable as that of Clive. The roof and walls of St. Mary's are five feet thick and bombproof, which probably explains why the French ransacked the sacred interior and committed the profane: They turned the building into a military fortification. Finally, look at the Fort St. George Museum, once used as an exchange by the merchants of the East India Company and now containing interesting relics from that era.

George Town, the original Madras, lies north of the fort. Its streets still bear such names as China Bazaar Road, Evening Bazaar, Portuguese Church Street, and Armenian Street, all reminiscent of the four-century history of Madras as a center of international trade. On Armenia Street, notice the fine old Armenian Church, originally built in 1620. It subsequently became the cornerstone of the influential Armenian community. And don't miss the great Evening Bazaar (also called Parrys—pronounced Paris—after the former British confectionery factory that made Parrys Sweets, those candies you get on Indian Airlines). Evening Bazaar (which is in high gear all *day*) is located near Broadway and Nataji Subhash Chandra Bose Road (known as NSC Bose Road to taxi drivers). Produce fills the narrow streets and the senses. The odors change from street to street in this photographer's haven—a wholesale emporium of countless open stalls, selling fruit, vegetables, pastries, flowers, colorful paper ornaments, bangles—a thoroughly fascinating bustle of bartering and noise.

Marina Beach and Other Sights

South of Fort St. George along the Bay of Bengal, Madras puts on its elegant face. South Beach Road runs past Madras University, the Senate House, the Chepauk Palace (the nawabs of the Carnatic once held court in this Moorish-style structure, now a government building). This is the Marina, the shore drive that every Madras citizen proudly tells you is the second-longest beach in the world. The Marina has an elegant promenade with flowerbeds along its lane and a glistening sand beach that is never crowded—at least not with swimmers: The waters off the Marina are infested with sharks. As a consolation, there's a swimming pool on the Marina, next to the dreary Madras Aquarium.

Near this aquarium is another memento of East India Company days, an old building known as the Ice House. The Ice House was used to store ice brought all the way from New England by Yankee seafarers for the benefit of sunbaked businessmen in the pre-air-conditioned age. Also visit the Anna Samadhi, burial place of and shrine for Dr. C. N. Annadurai, the great orator and revered leader of Tamil Nadu, who died in 1969. The true "sight" here are the ordinary people who pay homage to one of the great heroes of their culture. It is said that when Dr. Annadurai died, a number of devoted followers committed suicide. Come in the evening when families visit the beach to relax in the cooling breeze that floats off the Bay of Bengal.

Madras has two good museums: the Government Museum and the National Art Gallery (both on Pantheon Road). The Government Museum has a vast collection of the best South Indian bronzes (see the famous Cosmic Dancer), plus wonderful archaeological remains from excavations at the Amravati Buddhist stupa, part of which was constructed in the first and second centuries. The National Art Gallery has a good collection of ancient and modern Indian art.

At the headquarters of the Theosophical Society, which was started at the turn of the century to encourage the comparative study of religion, philosophy, and science while promoting a universal brotherhood without regard to race, creed, or sex, you'll find an excellent library with old palm-leaf manuscripts and rare books. The grounds of the society, just over Elphinstone Bridge on the Adyar River, also have one of India's oldest banyan trees. This tree is mammoth—500 people can stand under its branches, which offer 12,400 square meters (40,000 square feet) of shade.

Also in Adyar, visit the Kalakshetra School, where classical dance, as well as other important South Indian art forms, is taught. You can also see the ancient designs of Indian textiles reproduced anew.

The Madras Snake Park and Conservation Center, situated in beautiful Guindy Deer Park in Madras, was founded by Romulus Whitaker, an American who settled in India. The park gives the public a chance to see, photograph, and touch the common snakes of India (over 500 species), most of which are housed in an open "pit." Other reptiles—crocodiles, alligators, monitor lizards, and chameleons—also call the park home. Over a half million people visit the park each year. The entrance fees, apart from covering the cost of maintaining the park, are used for various wild-life projects and relevant surveys. The Snake Park has received numerous grants and the continued support of the World Wildlife Fund. While you're here, ask how the snake's skin is removed to make those articles that are hawked in abundance. You may decide to do without them.

MAHABALIPURAM

Madras's southern border extends 59 kilometers (37 miles) to Mahabalipuram, on the Bay of Bengal. There's a good road between the two cities, and no visit to the capital of South India should omit this monument to the glory of the Pallava emperors. This city was once the main harbor and naval base of the great Pallava empire, the capital of which was in Kanchipuram. Although the reign of the Pallavas waned some 1,200 years ago, its gifts still stand on and near the shore of this "city of the seven pagodas," its European designation. Tiny Mahabalipuram, with its 4,000-plus population, offers a breathtaking display of masterful sculpture carved out of solid rock. In fact, the Pallavas developed four distinct kinds of sculpture: *rathas* (temple chariots), bas-relief sculptural panels, rock-cut caves, and freestanding temples. Here, humans worked nature into sublime art, although nature is now taking its revenge: The salt spray of the bay is carving the rock temples all over again.

The Five Rathas

The so-called pagodas of Mahabalipuram are actually seventh-century rathas, although to a Western eye they resemble small pyramid-shaped temples cut off by flat roofs. The walls of these freestanding, monolithic temples—each chiseled from a single rock—are a picture book of Hindu mythology. The five rathas, also known as the Pancha Pandava Rathas after the heroes of the *Mahabharata,* a Hindu epic, are dedicated to Durga, Shiva, Vishnu, and Indra. Near these delicate temples, life-size stone statues of an elephant, a lion, and a bull mount guard. These rathas, which are not overpowering in size, are well proportioned even though they are all unfinished, as the finials are not in place.

MAHABALIPURAM
(Mamallapuram)
City of the Seven Pagodas

Seventh c. A D

to Salivankupam

to Kovalam

I.T.D.C.
'Temple Bay'
Resort

BUCKINGHAM CANAL

Mathurangam
Bridge

from
Madras

Tirumurti
Temple

Pidari
Ratha

Krishna's
Butterball

Post
Office

Koneri
Mandapam

Ganesa
Ratha

Museum

Koneri Tank

Naraha Cave
*Arjuna's Penance

Bus
Station

Mahishasura
Rock

Krishna
Mandapam

Dolotsava
Mandapam

Shore

Vishnu
Tank

Temple

P.W.D.
Rest
House

Bengal

Mahismardini Mandapam

Old
Lighthouse

New
Lighthouse

Archaeological
Office

Adivaraha

Carved Rocks

Bay of

N

- Temple
- Mandapam
- Ratha
- Carving

GROUP
OF
FIVE
RATHAS

0 Feet   500   1000
0 Meters   100   200   300

*also known as
"Penance of Bhaghirata"

Rock-Cut Caves

In the nine rock-cut caves, you'll find some of India's most animated Hindu sculptures. Visit the seventh-century Mahishasura Mandapam and see the sculptural relief of the goddess Durga, riding a lion in her struggle against evil, which is represented by the image of Mahishasura, the buffalo-headed demon. Another bas-relief shows the god Vishnu in his cosmic sleep, lying on the coils of a serpent. Pastoral scenes from the life of Krishna are carved into the Krishna Mandapam cave temple.

Bas-Relief

The pièce de résistance at Mahabalipuram is the "Penance of Arjuna," the world's largest bas-relief and a masterpiece of composition: carved on two gigantic boulders (31 meters [100 feet] long with an average height of 16 meters [50 feet]) that lie side by side. This bas-relief, with its nearly 100 figures of gods, demigods, people, animals, and birds—almost every real and mythological form of creation—has been called a fresco in stone, and its vitality makes its figures lifelike. The most prominent of its myriad characters is the group of elephants, one of them 5 meters (17 feet) long, and Arjuna, his emaciated figure standing on one leg and doing penance—praying to Lord Shiva for a powerful weapon to destroy his enemies. All creation is witness to his act.

Shore Temple

On the shore stands one of South India's oldest temples, surrounded by a row of bulls carved out of solid rock and now protected against erosion by a stone wall. Built by King Rajashimha in the eighth century, the temple, which has two shrines—one to Vishnu and the other to Shiva, is a good example of the first phase of Dravidian temple architecture. Surrounded by a row of bulls carved out of solid rock, the Shore Temple stands with its back to the sea, rising up against blue waters with a white wreath of foam. There were once two or three more temples along the shore, but only one has withstood time and the sea for 12 centuries.

Mahabalipuram also has a fine beach and several good resorts; it's a relaxing, slow-tempoed place to stay.

KANCHIPURAM

From the Pallavas' port to their capital at Kanchipuram—one of India's holiest cities—is an easy 64-kilometer (40-mile) trip inland. On the way, stop at Thirukkalikundram, 13 kilometers (eight miles) west of Mahabalipuram, where a small temple stands atop a hill. There, every day just before noon, a priest feeds two white kites—birds that the faithful believe are the spirits of two saints. In the village at the foot of the hill, there is also a Pallava rock temple dedicated to Shiva. And, along the route, notice more of those kolam (or rangoli) drawings on the ground in front of each Tamil Nadu dwelling.

The Golden City of Temples, Kanchipuram—also a must-see for those touring South India—is currently a charming, bustling village with numerous whitewashed homes featuring open porches stretched across the front with all the trim brightly painted. Kanchipuram contains no less than 124 shrines and is sacred to both Shiva and Vishnu, which makes it an important stopping place for Hindus making their rounds of the seven holy cities of India (the other six are Haridwar, Ujjain, Varanasi, Mathura, Ayodhya, and Dwarka). Kanchipuram is the Varanasi of the South, and its religious architecture is a treat.

Kanchipuram's Pallava temples were built by its kings, who also founded Mahabalipuram. The kings patronized not only architecture and sculpture but all the arts, transforming their capital into one of India's greatest centers of learning. Hindu and Buddhist philosophies flourished here side by side. Since you would need a lifetime to visit and examine all the temples, here are a few of the best:

Kailasanatha Temple

The first temple built in Kanchipuram was the Kailasanatha Temple constructed in the early eighth century by King Rajashimha. A smaller temple built by his son, Mahendra, stands in the east end of the courtyard. Dedicated to Shiva, these sandstone temples are considered the finest examples of Pallava architecture. They are adorned with excellent sculptures—a big *nandi* (bull-headed god) on a raised platform, other nandis everywhere, and images of Shiva galore—as well as many lovely paintings on the walls. Note, too, the unusual tiny shrines built around the courtyard, each with its own shrine and pillared pavilion—58 exquisite monuments of fastidious labor.

Vaikunthaperumal Temple

Built by King Nandivarman a few years after the Kailasanatha Temple, the Vaikunthaperumal, with its three-story *vimana* (tower over the central temple), is dedicated to Lord Vishnu, who is shown repeatedly: sitting, standing, and reclining—the figures often appearing one on top of another. Notice the sculptured panels of the *mandapa* (pavilion in front of the central temple); they recount the history of the Pallavas, including their battles with the Chalyukas. At that time, such nonreligious subject matter in a temple was unusual, possibly a first. In many ways, this temple, with its colonnade of lion pillars, marks the next stage in the development of Dravidian architecture. On its walls, you can also see more surviving Hindu murals.

Ekambareswara Temple

Although originally constructed by the Pallavas, this temple's most significant feature—its 61-meter (196-foot) *goporum* (tower entrance), with more than ten stories of intricate sculpture—was the result of a sixteenth-century addition by the Vijayanagar kings. This temple, which has just been renovated, is also dedicated to Shiva, who appears in the form of earth, one of Hinduism's five sacred elements. Inside the courtyard is a mango tree that is supposedly 3,500 years old. It is said that each of its four main branches bears fruit with a different taste and that each branch represents one of the four Hindu *Vedas* (sacred texts). Of the original 1,000 pillars that once stood in the mandapa, only about 600 remain.

Sri Varadaraja Temple

The 31-meter (100-foot) goporum of the Varadaraja Temple was originally built in the eleventh century but overhauled by the Vijayanagar kings 500 years later. Also known as the Devarajaswamy Temple, this edifice is dedicated to Vishnu, and its 100-pillared mandapa—all of it exquisitely carved—is one of the best. Be certain to see the massive chain carved from one stone, as well as the handsome pillars standing in the courtyard.

Sri Kamakshi Temple

In the heart of the old town, the Sri Kamakshi, with its fancy gold-plated goporum, is dedicated to the goddess Kamakshi (Parvati). This temple is the site of an annual winter car festival, when numerous small deities from nearby temples are pulled by wooden temple cars in a procession, led by an elephant. The colorful event draws huge crowds.

Although Kanchipuram is most famous for its temples, it's also well known as a silk-weaving center. "Connjeevaram sari" (what the English formerly called Kanchipuram) is still synonymous with the best in Indian silk saris, as well as silk by the meter.

Vellore

About 56 kilometers (35 miles) to the west of Kanchipuram is Vellore, on the banks of the Palar River. The heart of Vellore is its fort, built in the thirteenth century and still an excellent example of military architecture, despite a long and bloody history of battles. The last siege of Vellore occurred in 1806 during a sepoy mutiny caused by military grievances, antedating the great upheaval of the Indian Mutiny of 1857 by 51 years.

Across a moat, impressive gates lead into the fort. Inside there's an exquisite temple of Shiva, probably built in the fourteenth century, that was not in use until a *lingam* (phallic symbol) was installed in 1981. Attractive sculpture adorns the temple's ceiling and pillars.

Thiruvannamalai

From Vellore, head south to Thiruvannamalai and one of South India's largest temples. Sprawling over 25 acres, the Arunachala Temple is dedicated to Tejo Lingam (Lord Shiva in his fire incarnation—one of the five elements he represents). Here a goporum rises 62 meters (200 feet), with 11 sculptured stories. Behind it in the temple grounds is a magnificent pavilion of a 1,000 pillars.

The Arunachala Temple lies at the foot of a hill that bursts with celebration during the Karthikai Deepam festival during the full moon around the end of November. A huge bonfire, ignited on top of the hill and visible for miles, guides pilgrims to the shrine of a Hindu saint, Sri Ramana Maharisha, who spent much of his time here.

Pondicherry

Head east to Tindivanam, then south to Pondicherry. The atmosphere of a sleepy French provincial town has been struggling to survive since this former tiny enclave was returned to Indian administration in 1954 after 250 years of French rule. Near its handsome Government House by the sea was a statue of Dupleix, the unsuccessful rival of Clive, who governed Pondicherry for 40 years in the eighteenth century. Ghandi's statue has taken its place. The French touch is now maintained by a statue of Joan of Arc.

Another influence that has begun to change Pondicherry was started by Sri Aurobindo, philosopher, poet, and patriot, who withdrew to Pondicherry in 1910 after a political trial that lasted two years. With the help of a French woman, called "Mother," he founded the ashram that bears his name. His ideal, a superman who surpasses his fellowmen in the things of the spirit, is the antithesis of Nietzsche's; and his humanism is distinctly different from the philosophy of modern Western thinkers. The residents of the ashram (spiritual retreat), which can be visited, are supposed to be living according to the Master's (and Mother's) teachings—he died in 1950, she died in 1973—in a rarefied atmosphere of *sachidananda* (pure spirit). But the ashram and nearby Auroville, "the City of Dawn," an international commune of sorts, launched in 1968 by Mother, are embroiled in nonspiritual bickering. Much of Pondicherry's economy is Aurobindo-oriented. At Auroville, you'll see stabs at futuristic architecture in settlements called Aspiration and Revelation, in 17 different types of windmills, and in the Matri Mandir, a humongous sphere (an intended meditation hall) that has been under construction since 1971.

Chidambaram

Continuing south, you'll enter the South Arcot district—the southern India rice bowl—vibrant green with paddies where men lead water buffalo back and forth through lush, fertile fields. After about 64 kilometers (40 miles) you'll reach Chidambaram. Chidambaram is the site of the oldest temple in South India, the Nataraja Temple, conceivably (no one knows for sure) built in the fifth century by a Chola king. Suffering from leprosy, according to legend, the king took the advice of a resident saint, bathed in a sacred tank, and recovered. Supposedly he showed his gratitude by building the earliest stages of this temple (the sacred tank is inside) erected over a span of centuries. The Nataraja is dedicated to Shiva in various aspects, including the cosmic dancer prancing on the remains of evil and ignorance.

In the Chit Sabha (the inner sanctum) covered with gold plate, the presiding deity is identified by one of the five elements (all of which Shiva represents): air, known as the Akasa Lingam. What you see is a black curtain, standing for ignorance, that is raised three times daily. There are four other halls: the Nritta Sabha, Deva Sabha, Kanaka Sabha, and Raja Sabha. The Kanaka, also covered in gold plate, houses the famous Nataraja image of Shiva, the cosmic dancer cast in an alloy of five metals. The Nritta Sabha, the Hall of Dance, has over 50 pillars depicting dancing figures. Representing a heavenly chariot carved in stone, it contains an image of Shiva engaged in a dance contest with the goddess Kali. Shiva won. Deva Sabha is the Hall of Festivals, where all the processional deities are kept. Then there's the Raja Sabha. At 105 by 59 meters (340 by 190 feet) and with 1,000 pillars, some call it the most spectacular. Here the Pandyas and Cholas celebrated their victories. Two of the temple's four goporums of granite are covered with sculptures illustrating the 108 dance positions of Bharata Natyam. No one knows how the granite reached Chidambaram; there's none within an 80-kilometer, or 50-mile, radius

Vishnu is also worshipped at Chidambaram, although his Govindaraja temple is overshadowed by the shrine of Shiva. This temple is a more recent work, but it has an excellent statue of Lord Vishnu lying on a bed of snakes. The shrine closes at 11:30 A.M.

If you are lucky enough to be at Chidambaram in the early evening, visit the Siva-Sakthi Music and Dance School at 123 East Car Street. Inside this elegant old building with massive stone pillars, you might see a class of poised, talented girls learning the Bharata Natyam. Their instructress is a former dancer, regal, with perfect grace. The effect as she provides the beat with a slap of her hands against a pillar and the girls move with stunning grace is magical, memorable. A small donation would be an appropriate gift in return, although it's not required.

An interesting side trip from Chidambaram is the old Danish trading port and town of Tranquebar, with its well-preserved fort and sleepy old colonial air. This town was Denmark's major Asian holding from 1620 until 1840, when the whole settlement was sold to the British. Still well preserved are the fort, Dansborg Castle, two churches, and the houses of colonial administrators and merchants.

Thanjavur: Showplace of Chola Architecture

Not far from Kumbakonam is Thanjavur (Tanjore), lying at the foot of what has been called India's greatest temple, the Brahadeeswarar Temple, dedicated to Shiva. Thanjavur was the capital of the Chola Empire from the tenth to the fourteenth centuries. A Chola king, Raja Raja Chola, who held the throne from 985 to 1016, built the greatest of the empire's 74 temples: the Brahadeeswarar, with its soaring tower (vimana) over the inner sanctum. This tower rises more than 62 meters (200 feet). On its dome rests a single block of granite weighing 80 tons. The enormous hulk was inched up to the top along an inclined plane that began in a village six kilometers (four miles) away, a technique used by the Egyptians to build the Pyramids. This is also the first of four Chola temples in Tamil Nadu to have a vimana soaring over the goporum.

The main shrine of the temple lies at the end of a paved courtyard and houses a huge lingam. This courtyard is guarded by another goporum tower. As you near the inner shrine of Brahadeeswarar, you will encounter India's second largest statue of Nandi the bull (the biggest is at Lepakshi near Anantapur). Five meters (16 feet) long in black granite, Nandi is the mount of the god Shiva. Other sculptures inside the temple draw upon Vishnu and Buddhism as well as Shiva for their subjects. The walls of the inner courtyard of the temple are covered with excellent frescoes of the Chola and the Nayak periods. For a long time, the earlier and more interesting Chola frescoes lay hidden under the upper layer of the Nayak paintings. Only when the modern archaeologist was able to expose the bottom layer did art historians realize the existence of an excellent school of painting in the Chola period, comparable to the famous frescoes in the Ajanta cave shrines.

Near the temple is a vast palace built by the Nayak and Maratha dynasties. Although much of the palace is in ruins, it does contain the celebrated Saraswathi Mahal Library, with 30,000 volumes (8,000 of these are manuscripts written on palm leaves). Written in Tamil, Sanskrit, Marathi, Telugu, and a number of European languages, the manuscripts cover subjects from dancing to astronomy. The palace also has a superb collection of bronzes, poorly displayed in an old audience hall.

At Thanjavur also see the Schwartz Church built by a raja in 1779 to express his friendship for a Danish missionary, Rev. C. V. Schwartz, and the nearby Shiva Ganga Tank, known for its sweet water. Close to Thanjavur lies Thiruvaiyar, the nineteenth-century home of Sri Thyagaraja, saint and composer. He wrote more than a thousand songs in Carnatic (southern Indian) music. A major music festival is held here every January in his honor.

Tiruchirapalli

West of Thanjavur and 56 kilometers (35 miles) by road, you'll leave the "rice bowl" and enter the ancient Cauvery delta town of Tiruchirapalli

(Tiruchi), built up by the Nayaks of Madurai. Tiruchi has always been a seat of power in South India and it bears the scars of wars fought to control it, particularly by the French and English.

The military and architectural heart of Tiruchi is its famous Rock Fort, rising 105 meters (300 feet) over the city on the banks of the Cauvery River. A staircase with 434 steps out into the rock, some of them tunneled, leads up to the summit and a temple dedicated to Lord Vinayaka (closed to non-Hindus). Along the way are various landings and shrines: an ancient temple dedicated to Ganesh (the elephant-headed god), a Shiva temple (called Thayumana Swamy Temple) with its hundred-pillared hall (also off-limits to non-Hindus), and cave temples cut into the rock—the two biggest were executed by Pallava sculptors who placed seven pillars across the facade and a square shrine at one end of a hollowed-out wall. Finally at the top, you are rewarded with a breathtaking view of the city and the countryside below.

Below the rock at the base of the fort, a "must" walk is through Chinna Bazaar, the Big Bazaar, and down the interesting narrow side streets—all of which make up the heart of the Old City. You'll share the streets with crowds of people and the typical Indian array of animals, including donkeys. Have a "yard of coffee," so named for the way it is poured at a yard's length from the cup, at any of the *bhavans,* "French cafes"—Tamil-Nadu style.

Tiruchi has several other points of interest, including St. Joseph's Church, with its lovely Our Lady of Lourdes Parish, all done up in warm tropical colors and a gorgeous sandlewood altar. Also see the eighteenth-century Christ Church built by the Danish missionary, Reverend Schwartz; and the Teppakalum, a large tank, surrounded by a flower market and open-air stalls. Tiruchi is a busy place, industriously turning out hand-loomed cloth, cigars, mats, textiles, and several kinds of artificial diamonds.

Five kilometers (three miles) to the north, though, the glory of religious India explodes again on Srirangam, an island in the Cauvery linked to the mainland by a bridge with 32 arches. Here, worshipers of Vishnu come to one of India's largest temples dedicated to their god—the Ranganatha Swamy Temple built between the fourteenth and seventeenth centuries. The people of Srirangam and the town itself exists primarily inside this 156-acre temple, which has seven sets of walls. It's a fascinating, bustling complex. The temple itself really begins when you reach the mandapa behind the fourth wall. This is another of those 1,000-pillared halls (although only 940 remain). There are 22 towers around the temple, with the intended tallest nearing completion. This is very much a "living temple." Pilgrims from all over India come here every year in January for the Vaikunta Ekadasi festival. It is then that Heaven's Gate is opened and the idol of Ranganatha is brought into the mandapa from the inner shrine under a golden dome. This temple also houses a beautiful collection of jewelry.

Another smaller temple is about two kilometers (one mile) to the east: a shrine of Shiva. Here, in the Mambukeswaram pagoda, Shiva's lingam, or phallus, is submerged in water, one of the five elements that he represents. This temple is also called Thiruvanaikkaval after the legendary elephant that once worshiped the lingam.

The water surrounding Srirangam island is not only holy but useful. In the eleventh century, a Chola ruler built a stone dam below the island to harness the Cauvery River. He built it so well that you can still see it today, a sturdy, long wall serving the same purpose today as before.

Madurai

In Madurai, 128 kilometers (79 miles) from Tiruchi, you'll throw out all your points of reference and bases of comparison. Here, architecture and sculpture are not passive monuments but living backdrops for scenes that must have been enacted in the cathedral cities of the Middle Ages. Although Madurai is not a pretty city, it's the beating heart of the land of the Tamils and the high point of a journey south from Madras.

Madurai was thriving when Augustus took the throne of Rome (coins found here point to the existence of trade with Rome). Until the fourteenth century, it was the capital of the Pandya rulers of South India, who made it the mother city of Tamil literature with their generous patronage of poets and academics. Then the Nayaks ruled Madurai from the middle of the sixteenth century to 1743 and their majestic imprint is still fresh. The 10 tall goporums of the Meenakshi Temple raised during their dynasty are your first glimpse of Madurai, whether you arrive by car, train, bus, or airplane.

From the air, though, you can also see the two hills of rock marking boundaries between the "sweet place" (the meaning of "Madurai") and its surrounding green paddy fields. They are known as Yanai Malai and Naga Malai (the elephant hill and the snake hill). Three kilometers (two miles) long, the Yanai Malai of gray and pink granite does seem to resemble a recumbent elephant. The sweetness of Madurai comes from the nectar that fell from the hair of the god Shiva on the city.

It is Shiva and his consort, Meenakshi, who are honored in Madurai's greatest landmark, the Meenakshi Temple. This, incidentally, is the first big Indian temple whose towers are being restored to their original polychrome colors. Concrete moldings and bright fresh paint have replaced the gentle pastels and crumbling stones of weathered Hindu sculpture. The result is fascinating. A few hundred leering incarnations of deities from the Hindu pantheon are not something you'll forget in a hurry. The goporums are lavishly covered with brilliant carvings of gods, goddesses, animals and mythical figures.

Rich Pandemonium

The temples are a city within a city that includes a fascinating bazaar, bustling from dawn to nightfall. As you set out to visit the Meenakshi Temple, you will find yourself in a human tide on which the southern women float gracefully, flowers in their jet-black hair and bright saris draped around their straight bodies.

Although there are four entrances to the Meenakshi Temple, enter through the eastern entrance and stop, for a moment, to notice the mural on the upper right in the entrance mandapa. In 1923, when paintings were added, the Indian artist included an image of Mahatma Gandhi. When the British insisted on its removal, the artist simply turned Gandhi into a holy man with long hair. He cleverly used watercolor that eventually disappeared, revealing Gandhi as a young man—hands held together in the traditional *namaste* greeting.

The swirling life of the Meenakshi Temple never seems to stop. However, the temple is closed to devotees from 12:30 to 4 P.M.—a time when visitors are allowed to take photographs. Too bad, for then the temple seems dead. Madurai is known as the "city of festivals" and there seems to be one just about every day. Trumpets, drums, and religious chanting constantly fill the air but do not seem to disturb pilgrims taking a quick snooze under shady arcades.

Although nonbelievers are denied access to the two sanctuaries where Meenakshi and Shiva, in his incarnation as Sundereswarar, are enshrined, they can visit the rest of the temple quite freely. Hindus have no corporate worship and perform the *puja* (worship of the gods) either themselves or through the intermediary of a priest. It used to be possible to climb to the top of one of the goporums, from which the panorama over the city of temples is extraordinary, but bomb threats have entered the arena and the goporums were temporarily closed at this writing.

A legend says that this temple was founded by Indra, the Hindu god of thunder, who found a lingam in the jungle and ordered his builders to house Shiva's symbol in a temple. When Indra set foot in the temple, he found that its tank was filled by some miracle with golden lilies. You can see this tank, surrounded by a colonnade (from which you get an excellent view of the goporums as well). Worshipers bathe in the tank of the Golden Lily, where women perform some marvelous sleights-of-hand that enable them to change saris without ever appearing to be undressed. In the past, a bath in the lily tank served another purpose: tradition has it that a Tamil author's works were judged here by the simple expedient of placing his manuscript on the water. If it stank, it sank.

The high point of the Meenakshi Temple, however, is its Hall of a Thousand Pillars. Here, again, the figure is an approximate one; the exact number of pillars is 985. This hall was built around 1560 and is as great a work of structural engineering as it is of art. The pillars are a picture book in stone that run the gamut of human expression from stateliness and grace to lusty humor and ribaldry. It has been said that visitors can wander through these pillars—which represent a grove of a thousand palm trees where a god was once found—and see something new no matter how often they return. Baroque is about the only European style approaching the exuberance of this Dravidian temple.

Outside the Hall of a Thousand Pillars are more pillars. But these are the famous "musical pillars" of the Meenakshi Temple, and they play musical notes when they are struck. The temple also contains a hall known as the Kambatti Mandapam, where Shiva in all of his various manifestations is represented on sculptured pillars.

At any time, this temple of Shiva and his consort is filled with worshipers pouring oil on minor gods, depositing flower offerings, and going through pujas in front of their deities. But its greatest day comes around the end of April during a festival celebrating the marriage of the sacred couple. The wedding is reenacted in the temple and then the images are paraded through the streets of Madurai. In all, the festive proceedings last three days. During the celebrations of the Tamil New Year (mid-April), the evening processions have a particular charm.

Once outside the majestic entrance goporums of the temple, see another example of the architectural mastery of the Nayaks. This is the palace or *mahal* of Tirumala Nayak, a blend of Hindu and Saracen architecture. Its curved dome, which soars without any visible support, is quite an accomplishment. In the evening, it is the location for an impressive son-et-lumiere presentation.

The modern city of Madurai lives side by side with its traditions. Spinning and weaving mills turn out some of the best cloth in all South India, and the city is an educational center as well. One of its two colleges was founded by an American Protestant mission (Madurai was the headquarters for missionaries as early as the seventeenth century, when an Italian Jesuit came here and learned Tamil). Also, plan time to visit the Gandhi

Museum, a display of many of Gandhi's possessions that is touching in its simplicity and understatement.

Five kilometers (three miles) outside Madurai is the famous Teppakulam (tank), with an island temple. It's a peaceful place, away from the hubbub and bustle. Eighteen kilometers (11 miles) away is Azhagarkoil, with some excellent sculpture in the hall of a temple, dedicated to Lord Azhagar (Vishnu). Azhagar is the brother of Meenakshi in Hindu mythology.

Rameswaram

This side trip from Madurai can be the jumping point from South India to Sri Lanka. The sacred island of Rameswaram, said to be in the shape of Lord Vishnu's conch, is about 160 kilometers (100 miles) south from Madurai, with Sri Lanka only 74 kilometers (46 miles) away on the other side of Palk Strait. This sliver of land, separating the Bay of Bengal in the north from the Indian Ocean, is one of the main goals of Hindu pilgrims who come here to pay tribute to Rama, the hero of the epic *Ramayana*. Rama came here in search of his wife, Sita, who had been kidnapped. Rama is one of the ten incarnations of Vishnu, and to many pilgrims, Rameswaram is as holy as Varanasi. The Ramanathaswamy Temple is built on the site where Rama worshipped Shiva to do penance for killing Ravana, the 10-headed demon king of Lanka. Rama wanted to set up a lingam to honor Shiva, so he told the monkey god, Hanuman, to find one by a certain hour, which he was unable to do. Sita, Rama's wife, made one of sand; that explains the lingam in the principal sanctum. When Hanuman returned with a second lingam, Rama saw the monkey god's disappointment and installed this lingam, too. That in turn explains the lingam in the northern sanctum. Rameswaram is so intimately linked with Rama that to the Hindus every grain of sand is considered sacred.

The Ramanathaswamy Temple, rising above a lake as a vast rectangle about 310 meters (1,000 feet) long and 202 meters (650 feet) wide, is one of the most beautifully sculptured in India. It dates from the twelfth century, although the process of building it took 3½ centuries, with the inspiration for its construction coming from one of the princes of Sri Lanka.

Here you'll find a nine-story goporum, typical of Dravidian temples. But the corridors of the temple are unique. They surround the rectangle, stretching out over a distance of 1,240 meters (4,000 feet). Through occasional apertures, light filters into these corridors and flits over the carved pillars lining every foot on both sides. Each pillar is an individual composition carved out of solid granite—one of an army—and the total effect of the two ranks standing watch on the sides of the corridors is stunning. Leading authorities call this the most evolved of all Dravidian temples.

Also try to visit the Kothandaramasamy Temple near the southernmost tip of the island. This temple marks the location where Vibishana, the kidnapper of Sita and brother of Ravana, surrendered to Rama. It is the only structure on Dhanushkodi (the tip) that survived a devastating cyclone in 1964.

Kanya Kumari (Cape Comorin)

At Dhanushkodi, two seas meet; at Kanya Kumari (Cape Comorin) at the southernmost part of India, the Bay of Bengal, the Arabian Sea, and the Indian Ocean all flow together. It was known to the ancients, too; Ptolemy called it *comaria akron* on his maps and Marco Polo knew it as Comori.

If time is a premium, this southern tip of India is overrated—crowded with too many tourists and hustling hawkers selling junk. The distance from Madurai to the cape is a good 193 kilometers (120 miles) or more, depending on the number of side trips. One possible stop is Courtallam, which lies in the Western Ghat mountain range. Its main claims to fame are the 93-meter (300-foot) waterfalls of the Chittar River and a small temple dedicated to Shiva. The falls have a local reputation as a spa—bathing in them is supposed to invigorate a worn-out body. From here, it's a four-hour drive to Kanya Kumari.

To the southeast, also on the sea, is Tiruchendur, with a seashore temple dedicated to Subrahmanya. After driving through the Tirunelveli district, considered one of the oldest centers of civilization in India (prehistoric burial urns have been discovered here), you'll reach Kanya Kumari. Here the Western Ghats, which begin in Mysore, run into the sea, creating an obstacle course of jagged rocks that make the cape dangerous for ships. According to legend, this is where Shiva married the goddess Parvati, daughter of King Himalaya. The seven varieties of rice thrown at the wedding were transformed for eternity into the seven-colored sands of Kanya Kumari: red, brown, yellow, silver, orange, dark blue, and purple, as they have been preserved by Varuna, god of the sea.

The Kanya Kumari Temple, erected on a promontory of the cape, is revered by Hindus. Offshore lie the two rocks where Swami Vivekanda sat overnight in meditation before dedicating himself to improving the prestige of Hinduism by visiting America to expose Westerners to his faith. Also visit the Mahatma Ghandhi Memorial, constructed on the spot where the urn containing Gandhi's ashes was relinquished to the sea. The building was specifically designed so that on his birthday—October 2—at noon, the sun's rays fall through openings in the roof and shine directly on the center of his memorial. Then, for a quiet walk, meander through the fishing village near the Catholic church. The tiny community has an appealing quasi-Portuguese feel.

Not far from Kanya Kumari is the Suchindram Temple, with its seven-story goporum and exquisite oversize water tank. This is one of the few temples that worship the trinity of Shiva, Vishnu, and Brahma. Non-Hindus can't enter the inner sanctum; the lingam inside is made up of three parts: The top represents Shiva, the middle represents Vishnu, and the bottom represents Brahma. The rest of the temple area (not off-limits) is colorfully decorated and has musical pillars, which produce different tones when tapped, and an enormous statue of Hanuman.

Padmanabhapuram

Continue northwest to Padmanabhapuram, the ancient seat of the rulers of Travancore, who trace their ancestry to A.D. 849. The Padmanabhapuram Palace, with its steep tiled roofs, white walls, wood carvings, glossy black floors made from a crazy concoction including ash and egg white, and small courtyards, has an elegant pagodalike beauty that is reminiscent of Japanese domestic architecture. The palace also contains a museum with excellent old murals. In the adjoining Ramaswamy Temple, beautiful carved panels portray scenes from the *Ramayana*. From here, you can head back to Madurai or continue up the Malabar Coast into Kerala. (See *Kerala* chapter).

Kodaikanal and the Nilgirl Hill Stations

Tamil Nadu also has gentle, wooded hills framing a lake or two, which offer cool nights and a rest from temple-city intensity. Within the borders of this state are three of India's hill stations: Kodaikanal, only a short distance from Madurai; Ootacamund (Ooty) and other delightful resorts in the Nilgiri Hills farther north; and Yercaud (east of Ooty) in the Salem district.

Kodaikanal is 121 kilometers (75 miles) from Madurai via a scenic road that runs through coffee plantations and forests as it climbs up through the Western Ghats to Kodai, at an altitude of over 2,134 meters (7,000 feet). Europeans first discovered this spot in the Palni Hills in 1821. Fifteen years later, the collector of Madurai (the equivalent of a district governor) built a house that was soon followed by a rush of imitations. The descendants of these nineteenth-century Europeans still flock to Kodaikanal for the holiday seasons (April–June and September–October), when vacationers can count on the cooperation of the climate and sun.

It's not just the weather that brings people to Kodaikanal; the ride *is* gorgeous. A wise man, Sir Vere Levenge, put a finishing touch on the hill resort landscape by damming a stream to form a lake, with a three-mile walkway and riding trail around it. Boating on the lake is one of the popular pastimes in Kodaikanal. There are also tennis and golf clubs and numerous walks you can take, but no elegant old-fashioned hotels.

The Queen of Hill Stations—Ooty

The Queen of South India's hill stations is Ootacamund, "Snooty Ooty," the capital of a chain of resorts in the Nilgiris or the Blue Hills (*nila* means "blue" and *giri* means "hill") on the northern edge of Tamil Nadu.

With its green downs, gentle rains, and temperatures ranging between 50 and 60 degrees Fahrenheit most of the time, Ootacamund was adopted as a summer home away from home at an early date by British officials and planters in South India. After a few tentative attempts to penetrate the Nilgiris, whose scenic beauties were previously enjoyed only by the aboriginals, a collector of Coimbatore named John Sullivan went up to Ootacamund in 1819. Sullivan liked it so much that he became the first European to build a house there. By 1824, other English people were settling in the hills, and they were followed by Indian maharajahs. Then, the British governors of Madras made Ooty their summer resort and built the Government House there. One of them, the duke of Buckingham, brought his English penchant for gardening with him, making life hell for the workers laying out the gardens of Government House. One morning, informally unshaven and dressed in old clothes, he started to give advice to one of the gardeners, who didn't recognize him. The gardener finally had enough. He turned to him in disgust and said, "The way you go on, man, it would seem you was the duke himself."

The Todas and other hill people encountered by Sullivan in 1819 would never recognize their Ootacamund today. Thousands of summer houses are scattered over the hills, with the owners busy playing golf and tennis or shopping on Charing Cross, the heart of Ooty. The town boasts botanical gardens, an annual flower show, a number of hotels, and a select circle of clubs where "snooty" of Ooty fulfills its name.

The downs of Ootacamund might well be in Devon or Yorkshire. There are 80 kilometers (50 miles) of them, fortunately served by excellent roads, and they offer golf, hunting, or just walking. Nearby are the 110-year-old Government Botanical Gardens, with more than 650 varieties of plants. An artificial lake, conceived by Sullivan in 1823, gilds the lily of Ooty's natural beauty. It's small, but it offers pleasant boating and good fishing. Near the shore of the lake is Hobart Park, where weekly horse races are run in season.

Ooty is also a good starting point for short and medium-length side trips into the hills. The biggest of these is Doddabetta, 2,634 meters (8,640 feet) high (most of it is done by car). Snowdon and Elk Hill (with its rock temple) are the two runners-up in size, though heavily wooded Cairn Hill is certainly the most beautiful.

Mukurthi Peak, a drive of 26 kilometers (16 miles) down the picturesque Mysore Road, is the Todas' gateway to heaven. In days when female infanticide still prevailed among them, the condemned babies used to be taken to this hill to be done away with. Unlike the other Nilgiri tribes, these handsome people did not turn to agriculture or handicrafts; they still preserve their ancient way of life as herdsmen of the hills. Barely a thousand of them, they are recognizable by their flowing beards and long toga-like robes.

About 64 kilometers (40 miles) from Ooty is the Mudumalai Game Sanctuary, with a full roll call of Indian wildlife.

Besides Ooty, there are two other hill stations in the Nilgiris. Kotagiri is 1,981 meters (6,500 feet) above sea level and 19 kilometers (12 miles) from Ooty, while Coonoor is 29 kilometers (18 miles) down the mountain railway line at an altitude of only 1,707 meters (5,600 feet). The climate here is somewhat warmer than at Ooty. Coonoor is surrounded by tea plantations and has a shady park (Sim's Park) and some pleasant walks for hikers. Kotagiri is an island of green fields (including a golf course) surrounded by thick forests. It's one of the quietest spots in the Nilgiris and in all of South India.

Yercaud—the Jewel of the South

Northeast of Ooty is Yercaud, a quiet resort in the Servaroyan Hills (Sheraroy Range), about an hour's drive beyond Salem. At an elevation of 3,048 meters (5,000 feet), the climate is inviting year-round. Yercaud has appealing vistas, gardens, waterfalls, and a lake. You can also arrange a trip to the Servaroyan Temple stop, the third-highest peak in the Sheraroy Range. During the annual festival in May, hundreds of tribal people from the Yercaud area arrive at the temple area, a festive and colorful event. Yercaud is also the least expensive hill station in Tamil Nadu, and the least "discovered."

PRACTICAL INFORMATION FOR TAMIL NADU

WHEN TO GO. This is a place to visit during winter. Here the thermometer never falls below 70° F but often rises to 90° F between November and February, and humidity can be high. When it's overcoat weather in Delhi (December–February), you can lie on the beach in Tamil Nadu. Summer (April–June) is forbidding, except in hill resorts like Ootacamund or Yercaud. The beach resorts of the South, like Mahabalipuram, are fun all year long, since you've got the water to cool off from the heat. Festivals, especially the spectacular "car" processions in major temple towns, are found year-round, but most frequently in March–April. The best months for the hill stations are April–June and September–October.

HOW TO GET THERE. By Air. The following cities in India have direct daily *Indian Airlines* flights into Madras: Bangalore, Bombay, Calcutta, Cochin, Delhi, Hyderabad, and Trivandrum. It also connects Madras with six weekly flights from Cochin; five weekly flights from Ahmedabad; four weekly flights from Goa, Mangalore, Port Blair, and Vishakhapatnam; and three weekly flights from Bhubaneshwar and Pune. Madras is also an international airport connecting the city to Colombo in Sri Lanka (*Indian Airlines* and *Air Lanka*), to Penang and Kuala Lumpur in Malaysia (*Malaysian Airlines, Air India,* and *British Airways*), to Paris (*Air India*), to London (*British Airways* and *Air India*), to New York (*Air India*), and to Singapore (*Singapore Airlines, Indian Airlines,* and *Air India*). *Vayudoot* has six weekly flights to Madras from Bangalore; four weekly flights from Tirupathi; three weekly flights from Belgaum, Cochin, and Pondicherry; and a weekly flight from Hyderabad. *Indian Airlines* also has three weekly flights from Bangalore to Tiruchirapally and a weekly flight from Colombo to Tiruchirapally. Vayudoot also has three weekly flights from Bangalore, Madras, and Puttaparthi into Pondicherry; and three weekly flights from Agatti (Lakshadweep Islands) to Coimbatore and Madras. For *Indian Airlines* information, call 141 in Madras (for general inquiry and 144 for reservations); 22795 in Madurai; and 41343 in Tiruchirapally. For Vayudoot information, in Madras call 478174.

By Bus. *The Thiruvalluvar Transport Corporation* (TTC) operates daily express deluxe coaches from Madras to Bangalore, Ernakulam (Cochin), Hyderabad, Mysore, Pondicherry, Trivandrum, and other important southern Indian cities. As with most deluxe buses running throughout India, these buses are usually rolling television sets: Hindi movies blaring from the first kilometer to the last. So be prepared. Otherwise, the buses are more efficient, cleaner, cheaper, and faster than any train. For details, fares, and reservations, call *Express Bus Services,* Parrys Bus Stand, tel. 561835/36 in Madras. Its ticketing office is open daily 7 A.M.–9 P.M.

By Train. Some fast trains head from India's principal cities to the Madras Central Station: the daily *Tamil Nadu Express* and the *Grand Trunk Express* from Delhi (both take about 30 hours); the daily Bombay–Madras Mail from Bombay (about 27 hours); and the daily *Coromandal Express* from Calcutta (about 27 hours). For railway information, contact Madras Central (tel. 131 for inquiries and tel. 132 for reservations). Remember that on every train that involves an overnight ride, you must pay for a sleeper and *reserve* a berth. Otherwise, you might find yourself off the train. And always check to see if your class sleeper supplies bedding (usually only first class is air-conditioned). Sometimes you can rent bedding for the night.

By Rented Car with Driver. You can reasonably drive to Madras from the following cities: Bangalore, 334 km (207 mi.); Pondicherry, 162 km (100 mi.); Mysore, 465 km (288 mi.); and the Periyar Wildlife Sanctuary, 554 km (343 mi.). Hire a car from one of the tour operators listed below or listed in the chapter that covers the state from which you depart. Rates are about Rs. 3–Rs. 4 per km, with an Rs. 50–Rs. 100 halt charge per night.

TOURIST INFORMATION. When you get to Madras, visit the *Tamil Nadu Government Tourist Office* at 143 Anna Salai, Madras 600002 (tel. 840752, open 10 A.M.–5:45 P.M., closed Saturdays and Sundays). There's also a Tamil Nadu Information Counter at the domestic airport (tel. 2340569), open daily 6 A.M.–9:30 P.M.; and at the international airport (tel. 2341260), open daily 10 P.M.–6 A.M. and during all morning flights; and another branch at the Central Railway Station Counter (tel. 563351), open 7 A.M.–7 P.M., and at the Egmore Railway Station (tel. 8252165), open Monday–Saturday, 7 A.M.–9 P.M. and Sunday, 2 P.M.–9 P.M. Also contact *Tamil Nadu Tourism Development Corporation* (TTDC), at 143 Anna Salai (tel. 830498 and 830390), to arrange for low-budget tours or to book government-run accommodations and a car with driver. Open daily, 24 hours for tour bookings and Monday–Saturday, 9:45 A.M.–5:45 P.M. for hotel reservations. You can also contact the *Government of India Tourist Office* at 154 Anna Salai, Madras 600002 (tel. 869685; open 9 A.M.–5:30 P.M.; closed Sundays). It also has a counter at the international airport (tel. 2340386), open around the clock.

These bureaus have excellent information and maps on Madras and the rest of Tamil Nadu. They also offer excellent guides and can give you information about Tamil Nadu sightseeing tours. You'll also find Tamil Nadu Tourist offices or counters in the following cities and areas. Most of them are open 10 A.M.–5:45 P.M., Monday–Friday.

Chidambaram. Railway Feeder Rd., tel. 2739.

Coimbatore. Railway station, no phone.

Kanya Kumari (Cape Comorin). Beach Rd., tel. 276.

Kodaikanal. Township Bus Stand, no phone.

Madurai. Hotel Tamil Nadu Complex, West Veli St. (near Central Bus Stand), tel. 22957; at the Railway Junction, tel. 24535; and at the Madurai Airport, no phone.

Mahabalipuram. Covelong Rd., tel. 232.

Ootacamund. Super Market Bldg., Charing Cross, tel. 3977.

Pondicherry. Tourism Information Bureau, Directorate of Tourism, 19 Goubert Ave., Pondicherry 605001, tel. 24575. Open Monday–Friday, 8:45 A.M.–5:45 P.M. and Saturday, 8:45 A.M.–1 P.M., closed Sundays.

Rameswaram. 14 E. Car St., tel. 371 and at the railway station, tel. 373.

Salem. (near Yercaud) Tel: 66449.

Thanjavur. Central Theater Complex, Jawan's Bldg., no phone.

Tiruchirappalli. No. 1 Williams Rd., Cantonment, tel. 40136. Information also at airport and railroad station.

FOREIGN CURRENCY EXCHANGE. Most Western-style hotels have exchange counters. In Madras, ANZ Grindlays (3A Padmanabha Nagar, Adyar) is open Tuesday–Saturday, 8:30 A.M.–12:30 P.M. and Sunday, 8:30 A.M.–10:30 A.M. Citibank (803 Anna Salai) and Bank of America (41 Anna Salai) are open Monday–Saturday, 10 A.M.–2 P.M., closed Sunday. At press time, American Express was planning to open a branch office by 1993. In the rest of the state, go to a branch of the *State Bank of India,* open Monday–Friday, 10 A.M.–2 P.M.; Saturdays till noon.

ACCOMMODATIONS. Hotel and guest-house accommodations in Tamil Nadu run the gamut from deluxe to cheap. Madras, in particular, has numerous hotels, but many are substandard and offer shoddy service, especially the hotels in the inexpensive range. The hotels we list offer courteous service and clean rooms. To reserve a room in any Hotel Tamilnadu, contact the head office of TTDC in Madras (address under Tourism Information, above) or through the manager of the individual unit. Include a full deposit (about Rs. 300 per double per night). From November to March, reserve rooms in advance in popular destinations: Madras, Covelong, Madurai, and Mahabalipuram. Prices are based on double occupancy and exclude taxes and service charges: *Deluxe,* over Rs. 2,000; *Expensive,* Rs. 1,200–2,000; *Moderate,* Rs. 500–Rs. 1,200; *Inexpensive,* under Rs. 500. Most Western-style hotels take major credit cards.

CHIDAMBARAM

Inexpensive

Hotel Tamilnadu. Railway Feeder, Chidambaram 608001; tel. 2323. 23 rooms with bath. This modest, government-run hotel offers clean, simple rooms with fans. Some rooms are air-conditioned and have TV. Room service, a multicuisine restaurant, bar, foreign-exchange and travel counter, doctor. Rupees only.

COIMBATORE

Moderate

Hotel Surya International. 105 Race Course Rd., Coimbatore 641018; tel. 37751, fax 32010. 44 rooms with bath. A Western-style hotel, its air-conditioned rooms have a simple, near-dreary decor and TV. Multicuisine restaurant, bar, room service, foreign-exchange and travel counter. AE, DC, MC, V.

Inexpensive

Hotel Tamilnadu. Dr. Nanjappa Rd., Coimbatore 641018; tel. 36311. 49 rooms with bath. This government-run facility offers clean Western-decor rooms with fans; some rooms are air-conditioned and have TV. Multicuisine restaurant and bar. Rupees only.

COVELONG BEACH
32 km (20 mi.) from Madras

Expensive–Deluxe

Taj Fisherman's Cove. Chingleput District 603112; tel. 2304, fax 282150. 80 rooms with bath. This resort, set in a cove, offers modern air-conditioned rooms in a high rise or in cottages close to the water. Cottages, with tile floors and cane furnishings, offer more privacy. All rooms overlook the sea and have TV. Multicuisine restaurants, bar, room service, foreign-exchange and travel counter, swimming pool, tennis, bikes, backwater boating, catamarans, baby-sitters, doctor, shops. AE, DC, MC, V.

KANCHIPURAM

Inexpensive

Hotel Baboo Soorya. 85 East Raja Veethi, Kanchipuram 631502; tel. 3575, fax c/o Sentinel Hotel Reservation System 473084. 38 rooms with bath. Tucked back from the main street, this new four-story hotel has lots of red granite and marble in its modern lobby. Extremely clean rooms have a Western-style decor and TV. Some rooms are air-conditioned. Room service, Indian vegetarian-cuisine restaurant, bar, foreign-exchange and travel counter. Multicuisine nonvegetarian-cuisine restaurant ready by 1993. Excellent value. AE, DC, MC, V.

Hotel Tamilnadu. Kamatchi Sannathi St., near Railway Station, Kanchipuram; tel. 2561. 18 rooms with bath. This new government-run hotel has clean, modestly furnished, air-conditioned rooms. Multicuisine restaurant, room service. Rupees only.

KODAIKANAL

Expensive

Carlton Hotel. Lake Rd., Kodaikanal 624101; tel. 561, fax 42570. 91 rooms with bath. On a lovely lawn overlooking a lake, this Western-style hotel has spacious modern rooms with TV. Multicuisine restaurant, bar, room service, golf and tennis arrangements, boating, shopping arcade, health club, travel agency, foreign-exchange and travel counter. Meals included. AE, DC, MC, V.

MADRAS

Deluxe

Taj Connemara Hotel. Binnys Rd., Madras 600002; tel. 860123, fax 860193. 150 rooms with bath. The city's prettiest Western-style hotel, it's also centrally located and has a lovely lobby and numerous quiet lounges and garden areas. The old wing has deluxe rooms that have contemporary furnishings. Best rooms in this class have private terraces leading to the pool. Standard doubles (in the new wing) are also attractive. Ask for a river view. Air-conditioning, TV, multicuisine restaurants, bar, room service, swimming pool, baby-sitters, doctor, foreign-exchange and travel counter, shopping arcade, business center. AE, DC, MC, V.

Taj Coromandel Hotel. 17 Nungambakkam High Rd., Madras 600034; tel. 474849, fax 470070. 240 rooms with bath. Centrally located, this high rise was scheduled for renovations at press time. Its lobby will be elegant, with teak pillars and teak set in the ceiling. The air-conditioned rooms will have a contemporary decor. The best rooms will overlook the pool. TV, room service, multicuisine restaurants, bar, swimming pool, health club, doctor, foreign-exchange and travel counter, business center, shopping arcade. AE, DC, MC, V.

The Trident. 1/24 G.S.T. Rd., Madras 600027; tel. 2344747, fax 2346699. 166 rooms with bath. Located near the airport and 10 km (six mi.) from the city, this new Western-style hotel, affiliated with the Oberoi chain, has an attractive lobby with an enclosed interior garden and water cascade. Spacious, air-conditioned rooms are elegant, with a decor that incorporates Indian fabrics. Best rooms overlook the pool. TV, room service, multicuisine restaurants, bar, swimming pool, health club, foreign-exchange and travel counter, business center, courtesy airport shuttle, shopping arcade, 12-hour room rate (half price) for transit travelers. AE, DC, MC, V.

Welcomgroup Chola Sheraton. 10 Cathedral Rd., Madras 600086; tel. 473347, fax 478779. 100 rooms with bath. This hotel is also centrally located. Rooms are air-conditioned and spacious, with a contemporary decor. Best rooms overlook the pool. TV, room service, multicuisine restaurants, bar, foreign-exchange and travel counter, health club, swimming pool, golfing arrangements, bank, business center, shopping arcade. AE, DC, MC, V.

Welcomgroup Park Sheraton. 132 T.T.K. Rd., Box 1453, Madras 600018; tel. 452525, fax 455913. 160 rooms with bath. A centrally located, modern monolith, the Park Sheraton has a marble lobby that is lavish and spacious. The air-conditioned rooms are done up in soft hues, including satin print curtains and bedspreads, and have TV. Multicuisine restaurants, bar, room service, swimming pool, health club, foreign-exchange and travel counter, shopping arcade, business center. AE, DC, MC, V.

Expensive

Ambassador Pallava. 53 Montieth Rd., Madras 600008; tel. 868584, fax 868757. 120 rooms with bath. This centrally located, Western-style hotel has been renovated. A former maharaja's chariot stands in its lobby. Spacious rooms have a simple Western decor. Best rooms have balconies that overlook the pool. Air-conditioning, TV, room service, multicuisine restaurants, bar, swimming pool, health club, business center, foreign-exchange and travel counter, shopping arcade. AE, DC, MC, V.

Moderate

Breeze Hotel. 850 Poonamallee High Rd., Madras 600010; tel. 6413334. 60 rooms with bath. This new four-story hotel has an attractive lobby with a polished red granite floor. Rooms are fair-size, with rough stucco walls and an uninspired but clean Western decor. TV, air-conditioning, room service, multicuisine restaurants, bar, foreign-exchange and travel counter, doctor, baby-sitters, secretarial services. AE, DC, MC, V.

Dee Cee Manor. 87 G. N. Chetty Rd., T. Nagar, Madras 600017; tel. 881145. 64 rooms with bath. This new hotel has a small modern lobby with a water fountain. Rooms have simple modern furnishings. TV, air-conditioning, room service, multicuisine restaurants, bar, doctor, foreign-exchange and travel counter. AE, DC, MC, V.

Quality Inn Aruna. 144/145 Sterling Rd., Madras 600034; tel. 471841, fax 863212. 98 rooms with bath. This new hotel is scheduled to open in 1993. It will offer centrally air-conditioned rooms with a modern decor. TV, room service, multicuisine restaurants, bar, health club, swimming pool, foreign-exchange and travel counter, shopping arcade, business center. Excellent value. AE, DC, MC, V.

The Residency. 49 G. N. Chetty Rd., T. Nagar, Madras 600017; tel. 8253434, fax 8250085. 99 rooms with bath. This new 10-story hotel has a large lobby with a waterfall. Air-conditioned rooms have a contemporary decor. Corner rooms offer the best views. TV, room service, multicuisine restaurants, bar, foreign-exchange and travel counter, doctor. Good value. AE, DC, MC, V.

Sindoori Hotel. 24 Greams Lane, off Greams Rd., Madras 600006; tel. 471164. 84 rooms with bath. This new Western-style hotel is centrally located and has a pretty marble lobby. Spacious doubles have contemporary furnishings and are air-conditioned. TV, room service, multicuisine restaurants, bar, foreign-exchange and travel counter, business center, doctor, shopping arcade. Good value. AE, DC, MC, V.

Inexpensive–Moderate

Hotel Shrilekha Inter-Continental. 564 Anna Salai, Teynampet, Madras 600018; tel. 453132. 180 rooms with bath. This modern high rise offers air-conditioned rooms with TV. Inexpensively priced rooms are not air-conditioned and don't have

TV. All rooms are clean, with a simple Western-style decor. Room service, vegetarian multicuisine restaurant, bar, foreign-exchange counter, doctor, shop. AE, DC, MC, V.

MADURAI

Expensive

Taj Garden Retreat. Pasumalai Hill, Madurai 625004; tel. 88256. 15 rooms with bath. Set on a hill, this handsome bungalow, once the private home of an Englishman, has a sweeping veranda that overlooks Madurai. It also has a separate annex. All rooms have an elegant, contemporary decor; but rooms in the bungalow offer the best view. Air-conditioning, TV, room service, multicuisine restaurant, bar, swimming pool, tennis courts. AE, DC, MC, V.

Moderate

Madurai Ashok. Alagarkoil Rd., Madurai 625002; tel. 42531. 43 rooms with bath. A Western-style, two-story bungalow, the Madurai Ashok has a swimming pool and modestly decorated rooms that are spacious and air-conditioned. There's also a lovely lawn. TV, room service, multicuisine restaurant, bar, foreign-exchange counter, doctor. AE, DC, MC, V.

Pandyan Hotel. Race Course, Madurai 625002; tel. 42470. 57 rooms with bath. This Western-style hotel has reasonably attractive, air-conditioned rooms with balconies and an inviting lawn. Ask for a temple view. TV, room service, multicuisine restaurant, bar, foreign-exchange and travel counter, shopping arcade. AE, DC, MC, V.

MAHABALIPURAM

Inexpensive–Expensive

Silver Sands. Covelong Rd., Mahabalipuram 603104; tel. 228, fax 280. Reservations also available through Transit House, 26 Venkatraman St., T. Nagar, Madras 600017; tel. 887346. 75 rooms with bath. Silver Sands has a whimsical ethnic decor and rustic ambience. Accommodations include villas (expensive) with beach views, TV, and music systems; beachfront rooms (moderately priced) with a sitting room, interior swing, and veranda overlooking the ocean; deluxe rooms (also moderate) without an ocean view but with a sitting room and swing; air-conditioned standard rooms (low end of moderate) with interior swings but no sea view. All rooms are air-conditioned. Open-air, multicuisine restaurants, bars, room service, excellent beach, swimming pool, minigolf, fishing and cultural program arrangements, disco, yoga, free shuttle into Mahabalipuram, foreign-exchange and travel counter, bikes for rent, shops. Off-season discount May–October. AE, DC, MC, V.

Moderate

Temple Bay Ashok Beach Resort. Mahabalipuram 603104; tel. 251. 23 rooms with bath. Overlooking the ocean, this complex offers rooms in the main building and in cottages (two doubles per unit). Air-conditioned cottages have beach views and cane and wicker furnishings. TV, room service, multicuisine restaurant, bar, swimming pool, good beach, foreign-exchange and travel counter. AE, DC, MC, V.

Inexpensive

Hotel Tamilnadu Beach Resort Complex. Mahabalipuram 603104, tel. 235. 45 rooms with bath. This TTDC complex is set in a grove by the sea. The best rooms are in brick cottages with air-conditioning, TV, and Western decor. Room service, multicuisine restaurants, bar, swimming pool, beach, bike rentals, foreign-exchange and travel counter, doctor. V.

Ideal Beach Resort. Covelong Rd., Mahabalipuram 603104; tel. 240, fax 243. 23 rooms with bath. A personalized beach resort, Ideal Resort features a Sri Lankan touch, with lush green gardens decorated with sculptures. The best rooms are upstairs in deluxe, air-conditioned cottages, with marble floors, Western decor, and a veranda offering an ocean view. Room service, multicuisine restaurant, swimming pool, cultural programs and South India tour arrangements on request, horseback riding, foreign-exchange and travel counter. AE, MC, V.

MUDUMALLAI WILDLIFE SANCTUARY

Moderate

Bamboo Banks Farm Guest House. Masinigudi, Nilgiris 643223; tel. 222 via Ooty. 6 rooms with bath. Located on the edge of the sanctuary, this modest resort with lush grounds offers simple-decor rooms in a spacious guest house and private cottages. There is a multicuisine buffet-style restaurant, horseback riding, swimming, bird-watching, and wildlife safaris by jeep or elephant. Meals are included. AE, DC, MC.

Jungle Hut. Masinigudi, Nilgiris 643223; tel. 240 via Ooty. 12 rooms with bath. Also on the edge of the sanctuary, this resort offers rooms featuring exposed-brick and stone walls and cane furnishings—lots of bamboo and handlooms. Meals are included. Multicuisine buffet meals, room service, jeep and elephant safaris, swimming, trekking; fishing trips and elephant safaris available on advance notice. Traveler's checks or rupees.

OOTACAMUND

Expensive

Taj Fernhill Palace. Ootacamund 643004; tel. 3910. 50 rooms with bath. Just taken over by the Taj chain, this Victorian palace, once the summer home of the former Mysore maharaja, is scheduled for a face-lift that could make it one of India's loveliest hotels. It sits on a secluded bluff surrounded by spacious grounds. The exterior has charming gingerbread details; public rooms are sumptuous; and bedrooms are spacious, with original furnishings. Working fireplaces, room service, TV, multicuisine restaurant, bar, foreign-exchange and travel counter. AE, DC, MC, V.

Taj Savoy Hotel. 77 Sylks Rd., Ootacamund 643001; tel. 4142. 40 rooms with bath. Set on a bluff with lovely gardens, this yellow-stucco bungalow is well appointed with reminders of the Raj. Separate bungalows have an understated Victorian decor. All rooms have working fireplaces. TV, room service, multicuisine restaurant, bar, doctor, car-rental service, foreign-exchange counter, tennis, billiards, golfing, trekking, horseback riding, and fishing arrangements. AE, DC, MC, V.

PONDICHERRY

Moderate

Pondicherry Ashok. Chinahalapet, Pondicherry 605014; tel. 463. 20 rooms with bath. Set on a beautiful beach, this new two-story hotel has spacious, air-conditioned rooms done up in a modern decor. All rooms face the sea and have verandas. TV, multicuisine restaurant, bar, doctor, foreign-exchange counter, shops. AE, DC, MC, V.

Inexpensive

Park Guest House. Goubert Salai, Pondicherry 605002; tel. 24412. 80 rooms with bath. This well-maintained Western-style hotel, set on the beach and run by the Sri Aurobindo Ashram, is a bargain as long as you don't mind pictures of ashram figures on the walls. Clean rooms have fans, a modest modern decor, and overlook a garden with sculptures and the beach. Upstairs rooms have verandas. No smoking or drinking permitted. Only breakfast and snacks available. Bike rentals available. Rupees only.

RAMESWARAM

Inexpensive

Hotel Tamilnadu. Rameswaram 623526; tel. 277. 26 rooms with bath. This beach-front government-run hotel offers clean, simple rooms with fans and balconies that overlook the ocean. Some rooms are air-conditioned; TV, restaurant, room service. Rupees only.

THANJAVUR

Moderate

Hotel Parisutham. 55 G. A. Canal Rd., Thanjavur 613001; tel. 21466, fax c/o 20355. 52 rooms with bath. This Western-style hotel, set on a pleasant lawn, has very clean modern rooms with fans or air-conditioning. Upstairs rooms have balconies. Best rooms face a back garden. TV, multicuisine restaurants, bar, room service, foreign-exchange and travel counter, secretarial services, shops, cultural programs and tours on request. AE, DC, MC, V.

Inexpensive

Hotel Tamilnadu. Gandhi Rd., Thanjavur 613001; tel. 57. 31 rooms with bath. This government-run hotel has a simple Western-style decor, but fan-cooled rooms are clean. Best rooms open onto an upstairs veranda overlooking an interior courtyard. Multicuisine restaurant, bar, TV, room service. Rupees only.

TIRUCHIRAPPALLI

Moderate

Hotel Sangam. Collectors Office Rd., Tiruchirapalli 620001; tel. 44700. 58 rooms with bath. A Western-style hotel, set on a lawn, Sangam offers reasonable rooms with a modern decor, air-conditioning, TV, and room service. Multicuisine restaurants, bar, foreign-exchange and travel counter, doctor, shops, swimming pool by 1993. AE, DC.

Inexpensive

Femina Hotel. 14–C Williams Rd., Cantonment, Tiruchirappalli 620001; tel. 41551, fax 40615. 115 rooms with bath. This modern high rise has an enormous lobby and offers air-conditioned deluxe rooms and executive club rooms that are spacious, with a Western-style decor. All rooms have balconies. Best rooms offer a fort view. TV, room service, multicuisine vegetarian restaurants, secretarial services, foreign-exchange and travel counter, shops, doctor. AE, DC, MC, V.

Ramyas Hotel. 13–D/2 Williams Rd., Tiruchirappalli 620001; tel. 41128, fax 42750. 80 rooms with bath. This modest Western-style hotel offers clean rooms with balconies and a simple contemporary decor. Some rooms are air-conditioned. TV, room service, multicuisine restaurants, bar, foreign-exchange and travel counter, doctor. Good value. AE, DC, MC, V.

YERCAUD (SALEM)

Inexpensive

National Hotel. Omalur Rd., Salem 636009; tel. 54100. 105 rooms with bath. This Western-style complex offers modern rooms in the main building and rooms in pleasant cottages. Best rooms in both facilities are air-conditioned. Multicuisine restaurant, room service, travel counter. V.

DINING OUT. South India's curries, mixed with coconut milk, are hotter than those in the north but not as rich; instead of fat, only a light oil is used in most dishes. Since many South Indians are vegetarians, you'll find a wide variety of tasty vegetable dishes. Some of the best—and least expensive—meals are found in simply decorated *bhavans* (Indian-style coffee shops) that serve delicious coffee and *thali* (named after the metal plate on which the meal is served). Thali is an epicurean's delight: generous servings of numerous tasty items (curried vegetables, rice, *dhal,* curd, *poori*). Sometimes the meal is served on a clean banana leaf. Bhavans also serve traditional *dosas, pakora, idli,* and vegetable cutlets. We list some excellent bhavans, but if you see a crowded restaurant, its popularity is a good indication that the food is good.

Also keep in mind that many accommodations listed above also have restaurants. Breakfast is usually 8–10; lunch, noon–2:30; dinner, 7:30–10. Payment is normally in rupees unless the restaurant is connected to a Western-style hotel. The restaurants listed below are informal and, unless noted, are open for all three meals and don't require reservations. Prices are based on one person eating a three-course meal, excluding taxes, tip, or beverage: *Deluxe,* over Rs. 300; *Expensive,* Rs. 200– Rs. 300; *Moderate,* Rs. 100–Rs. 200; *Inexpensive,* under Rs. 100.

CHIDAMBARAM

Inexpensive

Anu Pallavi Restaurant. Hotel Saradha Ram, 19 V.G.P. St.; tel. 2966. This restaurant, with a large fan-cooled front room and a dimly lit air-conditioned back room, draws crowds, especially at lunchtime, when there's an unlimited vegetarian thali. Also available are vegetarian and non-vegetarian dishes, including *murgh makkani* (boneless chicken cooked in cream and tomato). Open 11 A.M.–3 P.M. and 7 P.M.–11 P.M. Rupees only.

KANCHIPURAM

Inexpensive

Sri Rama Cafe. 20 Nellukkara St.; tel. 3995. Always crowded, this typical South Indian café, a small air-conditioned room with booths and an adjoining sweet shop, serves a hearty vegetarian thali and good South Indian dishes. Open 5 A.M.–10 P.M. Rupees only.

MADRAS

Deluxe

The Patio. Taj Coromandel Hotel, 17 Nungambakkam High Rd., tel. 474849. This new pool-view restaurant, a formal dining room in the English style, has etched glass and teak pillars, and except on Wednesday, a pianist to entertain you. The cuisine is Continental. At lunch, choose from a menu of assorted hors d'oeuvres and desserts. Dinners are more elaborate, with chateaubriand for two, lobster, tiger prawns, and grilled dishes. Children under 18 are not allowed, nor are jeans and T-shirts. Reservations required. Open 12:30 P.M.–3 P.M. and 7:30 P.M.–11:30 P.M. AE, DC, MC, V.

Peshawri. Welcomgroup Chola Sheraton, 10 Cathedral Rd.; tel. 473347. Peshawri's Pathan decor—rough stone walls, copper plates, and soft lighting—is handsome. The Indian Northwest Frontier cuisine, with an emphasis on tandooris, is popular in Madras. Among the specialties are *murgh malai kebab* (boneless chicken marinated in cheese, cream, and lime juice) and *kadak seekh reshmi* (crispy rolled chicken cooked over a grill). Dinner reservations advised. Open 12:30–3 P.M. and 7:30–midnight. AE, DC, MC, V.

Dakshin. Welcomgroup Park Sheraton, 132 T.T.K. Rd.; tel. 452525. A handsome restaurant, with Tanjore paintings, South Indian statues, and brass lanterns shaped like temple bells, Dakshin features the cuisines of India's southern states. Meals are served on a banana leaf set in a silver thali dish. Every night, except Thursday, there's an Indian flutist. The nonvegetarian or vegetarian thali gives a taste of all the cuisines; or try Tamil Nadu's *dakshin yera* (fried prawns marinated in ginger, chili, and garlic) or Andhra Pradesh's spicy *mirupakaikodi* (sautéed chili chicken). Dinner reservations advised. Open 12:30–3 P.M. and 7:30–midnight. AE, DC, MC, V.

The Rain Tree. Taj Hotel Connemara, Binnys Rd.; tel. 860123. This outdoor restaurant is in a delightful garden with delicate lights strung in the trees. It offers a Bharata Natyam dance recital and an Indian flute performance, and tasty Tamil Nadu *chettinad* cuisine served on a banana leaf set in a copper plate. Specialties include *vathal kozhambu* (sun-ripened berries cooked in a spicy chettinad gravy) and *yera varuwal* (prawns marinated in chettinad masala, then deep-fried). Dinner reservations advised. Open 7:30–midnight. AE, DC, MC, V.

Shanghai. The Trident Hotel, 1/24 GST Rd., near the airport; tel. 434747. Pretty upholstered chairs, lacquered black lattices, paintings of emperors, and a good view of an enclosed interior garden and water cascade add up to an appealing ambience for Chinese fare. Try the lotus chicken (chicken wrapped in lotus leaves, which is marinated and steamed) or jumbo king prawns cooked in garlic sauce. Dinner reservations advised. Open 12:30–2:45 P.M. and 7:30–11:45 P.M. AE, DC, MC, V.

Moderate

Cascade. Kakani Towers, 15 K.N.K. Rd., near Taj Cormandel Hotel; tel. 472514. This pleasant restaurant, run by a professor, has some mirrored walls, a chipped marble fountain, and a white- and silver-blue decor. Quiet Chinese taped music creates the right mood for tasty Chinese, Malaysian, Japanese, and Thai cuisines. Specialties include golden basket (a variety of minced preparations served in a rice flour basket), chili crab, and Szechuan *sapo* (prawns, chicken, fish, or lamb marinated in five-spice powder, then cooked and served in a sapo dish). Don't overorder; portions are large. Dinner reservations advised. Open 12:30 P.M.–3 P.M. and 7:30 P.M.–midnight. AE, DC, MC, V.

Chinatown. 74 Cathedral Rd.; tel. 476221. An upstairs restaurant, Chinatown has soft lighting and a bright red and black Oriental decor in its three adjoining rooms. The Chinese food is tasty, including fried crab in green pepper or chicken in oyster sauce. Dinner reservations advised. Open noon–3 P.M. and 7–midnight. AE, DC, MC, V.

Haveli. 74 Cathedral Rd.; tel. 475770. Expect subdued lighting in this intimate restaurant with reproductions of Indian miniatures set in mirrors on the walls. The menu features Continental and Indian cuisines, with a good selection of tandoori items and sizzlers. Open noon–3 P.M. and 7 P.M.–midnight. AE, DC, MC, V.

Inexpensive

AVM Dasa. 806 Anna Salai, no phone. This spacious informal restaurant, with a high ceiling, attractive cedar gazebo, lattice screens, and Tiffany-style lamps, is cosmopolitan chic. The food is vegetarian—Indian and Continental. There's also a salad bar, ice creams, and fresh-fruit drinks. At lunch, a pianist plays Western standards. Open noon–3 P.M. and 7–midnight. DC, V.

Hotel Hari Nivas. 168 Thambu Chetty St., near High Court Bldg.; tel. 582121. This 55-year-old Madras institution is in an old hotel in a crowded bazaar. Have fun while you eat vegetarian Indian food served on a banana leaf if it's the set meal, on a metal plate if it's a snack. For snacks, you can eat in a fan-cooled lunch hall or in an air-conditioned side room with an illuminated shrine to Krishna. For a set meal, you can eat in an air-conditioned room with a shrine to its owner. Lunch rooms are open 8 A.M.–7 P.M. Set meal rooms are open 10 A.M.–3 P.M. and 6–9 P.M. Rupees only.

Kaaraikudi Chettinad Restaurant. 84 Dr. Radhakrishnan Salai; tel. 869122. Statues of guardian deities watch over the entrance of this establishment; the wooden pillars and marble tiles were brought from an old house in Kaaraikudi near Thanjavur. The cuisine of this region is served at tables on the lawn and inside, in a simple space with Kaaraikudi ethnic touches. Try the chicken *kaaraikudi* (spicy roasted chicken leg) or *kola urundai* (deep-fried minced mutton paddies). Weekend dinner reservations advised. Open 11 A.M.–3 P.M. and 7 P.M.–11:30 P.M. DC, MC, V.

New Madurai Restaurant. 21 Subba Rao Ave., off College Rd., tel. 474635. Enjoy a meal on a wooden table outside or eat in any of the simple air-conditioned rooms, where pictures of Hindu gods and a large painting of Vishnu adorn the walls. The chef serves Chinese and Indian dishes, including locally popular South Indian dishes, such as spicy Madurai special chicken curry and spicy fish fry. Open 11 A.M.–3 P.M. and 7 P.M.–11 P.M. Rupees only.

MADURAI

Inexpensive

New Arya Bhavan. 241–A West Masi St.; tel. 34577. This bhavan, a 35-year-old Madurai institution, specializes in North Indian vegetarian fare, such as cooked *paneer* (cheese) items, mixed vegetable curries, tandoori *rotis* (puffed fried bread), and fresh *kulfi* (Indian ice cream), but you can also order South Indian vegetarian meals and eat off a banana leaf. It is immaculately clean. The downstairs hall has overhead fans and wooden booths; air-conditioned upper rooms are modern and glitzy, with their jazzy black-and-white decor. Open 6:30 A.M.–10:30 P.M. Rupees only.

MAHABALIPURAM

Moderate

Ideal Beach Resort. Covelong Rd.; tel. 240. Eat in a pretty garden or in a simple interior restaurant with Sri Lankan murals and sculptures. The chef serves Indian, Continental, and Sri Lankan items, such as Sri Lankan rice and curry or Sri Lankan fish curry. Follow your meal with *vatil appam* (custard). Open 7 A.M.–10 P.M. AE, MC, V.

Seafront Restaurant and **Whispering Woods.** Silver Sands Covelong Rd., tel. 228. At Seafront, sit under a thatched roof on the beach. At Whispering Woods, sit at tables in a pine grove out of sight but not sound of the beach. Both places serve Chinese, Continental, and Indian dishes, including fresh seafood. Seafront is open 24 hours. Whispering Woods is open 10 A.M.–11 P.M. AE, DC, MC, V.

Inexpensive

Sunrise Restaurant. Shore Temple Rd.; tel. 336. Newly renovated, this cozy thatched hut (no ocean view but cool tropical breezes) has red table cloths and a canvas cloth ceiling. It serves Indian, Continental, and Chinese dishes. Order the masala fried fish, the grilled lobster, jumbo prawns, or the special nonvegetarian thali, which gives you a taste of everything. Open 6:30 A.M.–11 P.M. or until the last guest is fed. Rupees only.

PONDICHERRY

Moderate–Expensive

Grand Hotel d'Europe. 12 Rue Suffren; no phone. The chef in this hotel dining room prepares excellent French food. There is a fixed menu. You must stop by in advance for lunch or dinner, noon–3 and 7:30 P.M.–10 P.M. The dining room is extremely small. Rupees only.

Le Club. De L'Alliance Française, 33 Rue Dumas; tel. 29745. This upstairs restaurant, with two rooms inside and a rooftop terrace, serves French cuisine in a tropical atmosphere: candlelit tables, lots of plants everywhere, and a thatched ceiling in one room. You can choose from assorted steaks, including *bavette à l'echalotte* (steak with shallot cream sauce); grilled delicacies; and fresh seafood, such as *poisson au poivre vert* (fish fried with butter, then fried in cream, wine, green pepper, and herbs); or the daily specials. Dinner reservations advised. Open 7 A.M.–9 P.M., noon–2 P.M., and 7 P.M.–10 P.M. Rupees only.

THANJAVUR

Inexpensive

Sri Venkata Lodge. 84 Gandhiji Rd.; tel. 20556. This 40-year-old institution has two rooms: one air-conditioned; the other fan-cooled. It serves a popular South Indian breakfast of *rava pongal* (spicy wheat porridge), a lunchtime thali on a banana leaf; and Chinese and Indian vegetarian minimeals for dinner. Open 5 A.M.–10 P.M. Rupees only.

Thevar's Biriyani. 74/36 Gandhiji Rd.; tel. 20248. This small informal restaurant, crowded with booths, serves nonvegetarian Indian dishes. The *biriyani* (rice with chicken or mutton) is the house speciality. Open noon–3:30 P.M. and 6:30 P.M.–10:30 P.M. Rupees only.

TIRUCHIRAPPALLI

Inexpensive

Amaravathi. Ramyas Hotel, 13–D/2 Williams Rd.; tel. 41127. Pictures of palm trees and lots of soft green and white in the decor establish a tropical ambience. The chef offers Chinese, North Indian, and Andhra Pradesh cuisines. Try the vegetarian meal on a banana leaf, crispy vegetable balls, or the tandoori items. Open 11 A.M.–3 P.M. and 7 P.M.–11 P.M. AE, DC, MC, V.

Woodlands. Femina Hotel, 14–C Williams Rd., Cantonment; tel. 41551. The decor is Western modern: white walls with bare wood trim, soft lighting, and upholstered booths and chairs. But Indian instrumental music plays softly in the background and the vegetarian cuisines are Eastern: Chinese and Indian. Try the *dosas* (stuffed Indian-style crepes) or the thali. Weekend dinner reservations advised. Open 11 A.M.–3 P.M. and 7 P.M.–11 P.M. AE, DC, MC, V.

SWEETS AND TREATS. Madras. After visiting the National Gallery, walk to nearby Alsa Mall and its downstairs *Hot Bread Bakers and Confectioners* and adjoining coffee shop. You'll find Danish pastries, pizzas, doughnuts, cookies, ice cream, and even curry in a bun. Open 5:30 A.M.–10 P.M. Next door is *Chappan Bhog,* which serves Indian sweets and snacks. Try *silver badam barfi* (almond milk sweet) or vegetable *samosas.* Open 9:30 A.M.–9 P.M. Another good choice is the popular *Woodland's Drive-In Restaurant,* 29/30 Cathedral Rd. (It's name is a misnomer.) Choose from numerous eating halls surrounded by gardens; then choose from a large selection of Indian sweets and snacks. Open 6 A.M.–9 P.M.

Madurai. *New Arya Bhavan,* 241–A West Masi St., has tasty sweets, snacks, and excellent coffee; open 6:30 A.M.–10:30 P.M.

Tiruchirapalli. In Chinna Bazaar, relax at *Impala Sweet Restaurant,* 3/4 N.S.B. Rd., and have delicious coffee and snacks; open 7 A.M.–9:30 P.M.

HOW TO GET AROUND. From the Airport. Madras. The Meenambakkam National Airport is about 15 km (nine mi.) from the center of Madras. The Aviation Express offers an airport minicoach service to most hotels. (Rs. 20; tickets issued on the coach). Service runs with flight arrivals and departures. You can also get into Madras in a prepaid taxi. Head to the prepaid taxi counter in either airport terminal. Rates are about Rs. 90, plus a Rs. 5 flat charge for luggage. **Madurai.** A taxi (about Rs. 60) will take you the 10 km (six mi.) into the city. **Tiruchirappalli.** A taxi (about Rs. 60) is also your best bet.

By Plane. *Indian Airlines* flies daily between Madras and Madurai, Madras and Tiruchirappalli, and Madras and Coimbatore. It also has three weekly flights from Madurai to Tiruchirappalli and six weekly flights from Tiruchirappalli to Madurai. *Vayudoot* has a daily flight between Madras and Coimbatore.

By Train. Good trains connect Madras with most important Tamil Nadu cities. Trains depart from either Madras Central (tel. 131 for inquiries and tel. 132 for reservations) or Madras Egmore (tel. 563545 for first-class inquiries and reservations, otherwise tel. 135). In Madurai, contact the *Madurai Junction Railway Station,* West Pell St. (inquiries: tel. 37597; first-class reservations, tel. 23535; second-class, tel. 33535. Reservations are open 7 A.M.–1 P.M. and 1:30–8 P.M.).

By Bus. *Thiruvalluvar Transport Corporation* has state-run buses that travel throughout the state, but they're always crowded. For bus information in Madras, contact *Parry's Bus Stand,* Esplanade; tel. 561835.

By Rented Car with Driver. This is the best way to see Tamil Nadu. Here are some important distances from Madras: Coimbatore, 492 km (305 mi.); Madurai, 461 km (286 mi.); Mahabalipuram, 58 km (36 mi.); Pondicherry, 162 km (100 mi.);

Rameswaram, 613 km (380 mi.); Salem, 326 km (202 mi.); Tiruchirapalli, 319 km (197 mi.). Hire a car from a recommended agency listed under Tour Operators, below. Figure about Rs. 3–Rs. 4 per km and a halt charge of Rs. 50–Rs. 100 per night.

By Taxi. A good way to see sights around major cities, a taxi costs a minimum of Rs. 10 or Rs. 3 per km. Make sure the driver uses his meter or set the fare in advance.

By Auto Rickshaw. In congested cities and small towns, this is an economical and fast alternative. The minimum charge is Rs. 4.40 or Rs. 2 per km.

By Bike Rickshaw. In temple cities and villages, this is a leisurely, pleasant way to travel, and it's cheaper than an auto rickshaw. But remember, pedaling in the heat is rough. Set the fare in advance.

TOURS. *The Tamil Nadu Tourism Development Corp. Ltd.,* (TTDC) at 143 Anna Salai, VST Motors Bldg., Madras, 600002 (tel. 830390 or 830498), sponsors a series of inexpensive Tamil Nadu deluxe bus tours with guides. Departures are from the Central Railway Station parking area and the TTDC office (address above).

Madras City Sightseeing Tour. Daily 7:30 A.M.–1:30 P.M. and 1:30–6:30 P.M. Full-day tour: 8 A.M.–7 P.M. Rs. 60 (half day); Rs. 105 (full day).

Sakthi Temple Tour to Thiruverkadu, Melmaruvathur, and Mangadu. Tuesdays, Fridays, and Sundays. 6:30 A.M.–5 P.M. Rs. 85.

Mahabalipuram Tour (Kanchipuram-Crocodile Bank-Mahabalipuram). Daily, 6:20 A.M.–7 P.M. Rs. 135.

Tirupati Tour (Andhra Pradesh Temple). Tirupati-Tirumala-Tiruchanur. Daily 6 A.M.–7 P.M. Rs. 250.

Tamil Nadu Weekend Package Tour (Thanjavur, Velankanni, Nagore, Tirunallar, Poompuhar, Vaitheeswaran Koil, Chidambaram, Pitchavaram, Pondicherry). Late Friday–Sunday. Rs. 350.

Tamil Nadu Eight-Day Package Tour (Highlights: Chidambaram, Pondicherry, Tiruchirapalli, Kodaikanal, Madurai, Kanyakumari, Suchindram, Tiruchendur, Rameswaram, Thanjavur). Leaves Saturday and returns the next Saturday. Rs. 1,950.

TTDC also offers a seven-day *East–West Coast Tour* covering major destinations in Kerala and Tamil Nadu; a 14-day *Sunny South Tour* covering Tamil Nadu, Kerala, Pondicherry, and Bangalore in Karnataka; a five-day *South India Tour* of Tamil Nadu and Karnataka; a weekend *Arupadal Veedu Tour* to important Tamil Nadu temples; a five-day *Mookambika Tour* to Karnataka; and a seven-day *Mantralayam–Goa Tour* of Karnataka and Goa. Contact TTDC for details. *India Tourism Development Corporation* (29 Victoria Crescent, Commander-in-Chief Rd., Madras 600105 (tel. 474216) offers similar tours. Tickets are also available at the ITDC counter in the Government of India Tourist Office at 154 Anna Salai Rd.; tel. 478884.

The *Pondicherry Tourism Development Corporation* offers a sightseeing tour of Pondicherry that departs from the Tourist Information Bureau in Pondicherry (address under Tourist Information, above). Daily 9 A.M.–1 P.M. Rs. 20.

If you wish to hire a guide, the best-trained and most knowledgeable are available through the Government of India Tourist Office (address under Tourist Information, above) and the Tamil Nadu Tourist offices throughout the state. General rates: four hours for four people, about Rs. 80; eight hours for four people, about Rs. 100 plus an Rs. 60 lunch allowance.

TOUR OPERATORS. The following agencies can take care of all travel needs, including car with driver (also see the listings under Special-Interest Tours in *Facts at Your Fingertips* for adventures offered in this state):

India Tourism Development Corporation (ITDC), 29 Victoria Crescent, Commander-in-Chief Rd., Madras 600105; tel. 478884.

Tamil Nadu Tourism Development Corporation (TTDC), 143 Anna Salai, Madras 600002; tel. 830498.

Sita World Travel, 26 Commander-in-Chief Rd., Madras 600105, tel. 478861.

Mercury Travels, 191 Anna Salai, Madras 600006; tel. 869993.

Most offices are open daily 9 A.M.–5:30 P.M.

SEASONAL EVENTS. The specific dates for many events each year are determined by the lunar calendar; consult the India Tourist Office for details.

January. *Pongal.* This colorful three-day festival that gives thanks to the rain god, the sun god, and the cow is held at the close of the harvest season. This is Tamil Nadu's best festival, with bonfires, and bulls and cows fancied up with beads and garlands, games, and dancing.

January/February. *Madurai Float Festival.* During the Vandiyur Mariamman Teppakulam (temple) annual festival, decorated floats carry the sacred deities around the temple tank. This is a beautiful and interesting event.

February/March. *Natyanjali Festival.* This two-day event in Chidambaram celebrates Shiva, "The Cosmic Dancer," with performances by India's best classical dancers. A great event!

March. *Arupathumoovar.* This 11-day religious festival is held at the Kapaleeswarar Temple in Mylapore, Madras. The 11th day is the grand moment, with over 60 sacred deities taken out in an elaborate procession.

March/April. *Pondicherry Carnival.* The former French colony celebrates its heritage during a carnival and parade with costumed participants and bands.

April/May. *Chitra Festival.* This spectacular 10-day festival at Madurai's Meenakshi Temple celebrates the marriage of goddess Meenakshi to Lord Shiva. Numerous deities are carried around in a chariot procession that also includes lots of traditional devotional music. A fascinating fair; heavily attended.

May. *Kanchipuram Temple Festival.* During this 10-day festival in Kanchipuram, deities from the nearby temples are carried through the city. The procession occurs on the third day and is declared an official city holiday, so every local resident gets to attend, along with all the people who come to see the event.

May. *Servaroyan Temple Festival.* In Yercaud, nearby tribal people celebrate their heritage with a festival.

August/September. *Ganesh Chaturthi.* Celebrated throughout Tamil Nadu, this festival involves Ganesh, the elephant-headed god, with processions and ritual baths of the deity in rivers.

September/October. *Navaratri.* This 10-day festival is observed throughout Tamil Nadu, honoring the Hindu goddesses Durga, Lakshmi, and Saraswati.

October/November. *Deepavali.* A two-day festival throughout Tamil Nadu, with fireworks and lots of raucous celebrating.

December/January. *Madras Music and Dance Festival.* A three-week festival of music and dance in Madras is presented by the Indian Fine Arts Society, with great dance and music performed by India's best. At about the same time in Tiruchirapalli, the *Vaikunta Ekadesa* festival is another procession and deity celebration, held at the Srirangam Temple.

HISTORIC SITES. Entrance to most places is generally free; where a donation is requested, a few rupees will suffice. Historic sites are open sunrise to sunset unless noted otherwise below.

Madras. *Church of Our Lady of Expectations* was built in the sixteenth century on the foundation of a church built by St. Thomas in the second century. The "Bleeding Stone" on which a cross is engraved is supposed to shed blood on December 18, the day that marks St. Thomas's death.

San Thomé Cathedral Basilica, Madras, is a structure with a neo-Gothic 56-meter (180-foot) steeple erected in 1896. The interior has an interesting image of Christ standing on a lotus flower (Hindu pose).

Kapaleeswarar Temple in Mylapore is typically Dravidian. Dedicated to Shiva, it was built in the 1500s. Painted in terrific bright colors. Non-Hindus can enter the courtyard, but only Hindus can enter the inner sanctum. Open 5 A.M.–noon; 4–8:30 P.M.

Parthasarathy Temple in Triplicane, eighth century, dedicated to Vishnu, was originally constructed by the Pallavas and rebuilt by the Vijayanagar kings in the seventeenth century. Open 6:30 A.M.–noon; 4 P.M.–8 P.M. Non-Hindus can enter the courtyard but not the inner sanctum.

Fort St. George, Madras, was built in 1640 by Francis Day for the East India Company. It now houses the Tamil Nadu State Legislature, offices of the ministry and secretaries to the government. See St. Mary's Church, consecrated in 1679, the oldest Anglican church in India.

Chidamburam. *Nataraja Temple,* dedicated to Shiva, is the oldest temple in South India. It was built in the fifth century by a Chola king and covers 40 acres. The roof of the sanctum sanctorum is covered with gold plate.

Kanchipuram. *Kailasanatha Temple* was built in the early eighth century by Pallava King Rajasimha. The smaller temple at the east end of the courtyard was built by his son. Dedicated to Shiva, sandstone temples are excellent examples of Pallava architecture.

Vaikunthaperumal Temple, Kanchipuram, was built in the eighth century by the Pallava King Nandivarman and dedicated to Vishnu. Unusual three-story vimina (tower over the central temple).

Ekambareswara Temple, Kanchipuram, was originally constructed by the Pallavas in the seventh and eighth centuries. The sixteenth-century Vijayanagar kings added the 10-story, intricately carved goporum (tower entrance). Dedicated to Shiva, the nearby mango tree is supposedly 3,500 years old.

Kanya Kumari. *Kanya Kumari Temple,* Kanya Kumari, is dedicated to the virgin goddess Kanniyakumari, who protects the country. The eastern gate facing the Bay of Bengal is opened only five times a year, and a ritual bath at the Kumari ghat is considered sacred. Temple open 4:30–11 A.M.; 5:30–9 P.M.

Gandhi Memorial, Kanya Kumari, was constructed on the spot where the urn with Gandhi's ashes was kept on public view until relinquished to the sea. The building was designed so that on Gandhi's birthday, October 2, a ray of sun falls on the spot where the urn was kept.

Vivekananda Rock Memorial, Kanya Kumari, was built in 1970 to commemorate the spot where Swami Vivekananda meditated before dedicating his life to spreading the ideals of Hinduism. A blend of all temple architectural styles in India. Ferry services to the memorial, 7–11 A.M.; 2–5 P.M. Nominal fee.

Suchindram Temple (13 km [8 mi.] north of Kanya Kumari) has inscriptions dating from the ninth century. One of the few temples to worship the trinity of Shiva, Vishnu, and Brahma. Exquisitely carved seven-story goporum, lovely musical pillars, and a huge Hanuman (monkey god) statue, plus an enormous bathing tank. Very pretty. Non-Hindus can enter the courtyard but not the inner sanctum.

Padmanabhapuram Palace (45 km [28 mi.] north of Kanya Kumari) was the ancient palace of the rulers of Travancore until A.D. 1333. Palace (open 9 A.M.–5 P.M., closed Mondays and holidays; Rs. 0.50) contains excellent murals and stone sculptures.

Madurai. *Meenakshi Temple* is dedicated to Shiva and is one of the biggest temple complexes in India. Most of the current structure was erected between the twelfth and the eighteenth centuries, but references to the temple date from the seventh century. Open 4:30 A.M.–12:30 P.M.; 4 P.M.–9:30 P.M. Photography, however, is permitted only after an Rs. 10 payment and during the hours the temple is closed: 12:30–4 P.M.

Tirumalai Nayak Palace, Madurai, was built in Indo-Saracenic style in the seventeenth century by Thirumalai Nayak. Beautiful courtyard surrounded by an arcade supported by vast pillars. All that's left of the once-enormous complex are two royal residences. Used to have quarters for the harem, relatives, a theater, a pond, and a garden. Open 8 A.M.–noon; 1–5 P.M. Rs. 0.40. Sound and light show every evening on the life of this Nayak king: 5:45 P.M. in winter; 6:30 P.M. in summer. Rs. 1–3.

Mahabalipuram. *Rock-cut Caves,* Mahabalipuram, are of seventh-century Pallava construction. The Mahashasuramardhini mandapam has a sculptural relief of the fight between the goddess Durga and Mahishasura, the buffalo-headed demon and the bas-relief of Vishnu in his cosmic sleep. In the Krishna mandapam are excellent scenes depicting the life of Krishna. The bas relief—the world's largest (31 meters [100 feet] long with an average height of 16 meters [50 feet])—is also a Pallava construction.

Shore Temple, at Mahabalipuram has two shrines, one dedicated to Shiva and the other dedicated to Vishnu. Built by the Pallava king, Rajashima, in the eighth century, it is an excellent example of Dravidian architecture.

Pondicherry. *Auroville* is an international commune started by a French woman, now deceased, called "Mother," who was involved with Sri Aurobindo. Futuristic architecture can be seen here, especially the *Matri Mandir* meditation hall, a gigantic sphere under construction since 1971.

Rameswaram. *Ramanathaswamy Temple* was built over a 300-year period starting in the twelfth century. An excellent example of Dravidian architecture, with the longest pillared temple corridor in all India.

Srirangam. *Rangagantha Swamy Temple* was built between the fourteenth and the seventeenth centuries. A temple town with seven sets of walls leading to the most sacred areas. There are 21 towers. A fascinating complex teeming with life.

Thanjavur. Brahadeeswarar Temple, dedicated to Shiva, was constructed between 985 and 1016 by Raja Raja Chola. The first of four Chola temples in Tamil Nadu to have a vimana soaring over the goporum. The vimana is constructed from one single granite block.

Thiruvannamalai. *Arunachala Temple* sprawls over 25 acres. It is one of South India's largest. Dedicated to Shiva in his fire incarnation, the goporum is 11 stories high. The exact date of its construction is unknown; parts existed as early as the seventh century.

MUSEUMS AND GALLERIES. Most museums are free or have a nominal entrance fee; some accept a small donation. Listed here are some of the more important museums in the state.

MADRAS

The Fort Saint George Museum. South Beach Rd. Featured here are costumes, prints, and paintings of the British in India. Open 10 A.M.–5 P.M.; closed Fridays.

The Government Museum and National Art Gallery. Pantheon Rd., Egmore. Established in 1857, it has one of India's best all around art collections, including Hindu, Buddhist, and Jain sculptures from Tamil Nadu, Andhra Pradesh, and Mysore, with sculptures from the Buddhist site of Amaravati (first century B.C.), the earliest surviving sculptures from the south. In the galleries devoted to metalwork are South Indian lamps; objects connected with household and temple worship; and images in bronze, including the famous Nataraja. Also see the collection of wood carvings from processional temple cars. The contents of the Arms Gallery are mostly from the palace at Thanjavur and Fort St. George, and those of the prehistoric gallery include antiquities from the Iron Age sites of Adichannallar and Perumbiar. The Bronze Gallery contains some of the best of India's ancient icons and some excellent modern bronzes. Open 8 A.M.–5 P.M., closed Fridays.

The National Art Gallery. Pantheon Rd., Egmore. Set in a beautiful Indo-Saracenic building, the gallery houses an excellent collection of old and new art, including rare Rajput and Mogul miniatures, exquisite tenth–thirteenth-century bronzes, and twelfth-century Indian handicrafts. Open 8 A.M.–5 P.M., closed Fridays.

MADURAI

The **Gandhi Museum** has a picture gallery and some of Gandhi's personal possessions. Open 9 A.M.–1 P.M.; 2–5:30 P.M.; closed Wednesdays.

The **Meenakshi Temple Art Museum** in the 1,000-pillared hall contains temple art and architecture. Open daily 7 A.M.–8 P.M.

PONDICHERRY

The Government Museum is a celebration of Pondicherry history, starting with Chola bronzes and sculptures, moving to French cultural artifacts and ending with traditional Indian handicrafts. Open 10 A.M.–5 P.M.; closed Mondays.

THANJAVUR

The **Tanjore Art Gallery,** Palace Buildings, contains ancient Chola statues in bronze and granite. Open 9:30 A.M.–1:30 P.M. and 2:30–5:30 P.M.; closed Fridays.

GARDENS. Madras. *The Gardens of the Horticultural Society,* established in 1835 next to Saint George Cathedral on Cathedral Rd., is open 8 A.M.–12 P.M. and 1:30–5:30 P.M.; closed Thursday. *Children's Park and Deer Sanctuary,* eight km (five mi.) from the heart of Madras in Guindy, has a large number of Indian antelope and numerous other animals, including monkeys and reptiles. The best time to visit is early morning or early evening. Open 8:30 A.M.–5:30 P.M.; closed Thursdays. *Snake Park,* in Guindy, is home to numerous reptiles. Good demonstrations on the hour start at 10 A.M. daily. Open 9 A.M.–6 P.M.

Ootacamund. The *Botanical Gardens,* established in 1847 by the Marquis of Tweedale, contains exotic and ornamental plants. Children's *Lake Garden* has flowers and musical lights. Both open sunrise to sunset.

Pondicherry. The *Botanical Gardens,* planted in 1826, contains exotic plants from all over the world, and an aquarium. Open sunrise to sunset.

Thanjavur. *The Children's Park* has a small diesel train for children that operates on Sundays. Open sunrise to sunset.

SPORTS AND OUTDOOR ADVENTURES. Beaches. You can swim at: *Covelong,* 38 km (24 mi.) south of Madras—a lovely fishing village with a resort; *Pondicherry;* and *Mahabalipuram,* which boasts beautiful stretches of sand with temples on the shore. *Rameswaram* has many good beaches, but watch the current. At *Kanya Kumari* beaches, also watch the current; it's rugged!

Biking. You can rent bikes in Mahabalipuram and Pondicherry. Rs. 20–30 per day.

Boating. You can do backwater boating near Chidambaram. Inquire at the local tourist department. You can rent boats on the lakes in Kodaikanal, Ootacamund, and Yercaud.

Fishing. Go on a sea cruise in Pondicherry and look for dolphins or deep-sea fish. Equipment is available. The cruise costs Rs. 250 per hour. Book through the Tourist Information Bureau (see Tourist Information, above). You can fish for trout in Ootacamund. To get a license, contact the Assistant Director of Fisheries (tel. 2232).

Golfing. You can golf in Kodaikanal and Ootacamund. Equipment is available at each.

Horse Races. The season at the Guindy Race Course in Madras is November–March. Call the Madras Race Club (tel. 2345514) for details. In Ootacamund, the course is active April–June. Contact the Ooty Race Club (tel. 3943) for details.

Trekking. For information about treks around Kodaikanal and Ootacamund, contact the Tamil Nadu Tourist offices (see addresses under Tourist Information, above).

Wildlife Sanctuaries. Anamalai Wildlife Sanctuary. Coimbatore District. Open all year, the best time to view the elephants, bison, tigers, wild boar, and crocodiles is October–April. You can go through the sanctuary on an elephant or in a van. Lodging is available.

Mudumalai Wildlife Sanctuary. Nilgeris (60 km or 37 mi. from Ootacamund). Open all year, the best season is February–May. This park is home to deer, bison, elephants, gaur, monkeys, and reptiles, including pythons and crocodiles. Elephant rides for viewing animals are available, as is lodging.

Point Calimere Wildlife Sanctuary. Thanjavur District. Open all year, the peak season is November–January, when the migratory birds are in the park. By April–June many birds have moved on. You can also see deer and wild boar.

Mundanthurai Tiger Sanctuary. Tirunelveli District. The peak season in this park is January–September. The forest department provides tours, and lodging is available in simple rest houses.

Vedanthangal Water Birds Sanctuary. (70 km or 43 mi. from Madras). One of India's major bird sanctuaries, this is where most birds congregate from October to March. Peak time is usually December–January; but the bird population always depends on the monsoons. Check with the tourist office before you visit. Species include cormorants, egrets, storks, and herons. Rudimentary accommodations are available.

For more details and lodging reservations at these sanctuaries, contact the State Wildlife Warden, Forest Department, Administrative Office Building, Teynampet, Madras 600020; tel. 413947.

SHOPPING. Madras. The four best markets are *Jam Bazaar,* junction of Pycroft's and Triplicane roads (bustling fruit and vegetable market); *Evening Bazaar* (also called Parrys) near Broadway and N.S.C. Bose Road (wholesale markets); *Burma Bazaar* at the eastern end of N.S.C. Bose Road along the harbor (best visited at night); and Pondy Bazaar in T. Nagar. You may not want to buy anything, but they're fun for browsing. If something strikes your fancy, haggle. Also visit these good shops:

Aparna Art Gallery (5 Bawa Rowther Rd.) sells excellent old and new curios in wood and bronze, Tanjore and Mysore paintings, and miniatures. Open 9 A.M.–6 P.M., closed Sundays. It also has a shop at 781 Anna Salai in the Rayala Building; open 10 A.M.–5 P.M., closed Sundays. Both shops accept AE, DC, MC, V.

G. R. Thanga Maligai (104 Usman Rd., T. Nagar) sells excellent gold and silver. Open 9:30 A.M.–8:30 P.M., closed Tuesdays. AE, DC, MC, V.

Shreenivas Silks and Sarees (77 Sri Thyagaraya Rd., Pondy Bazaar, T. Nagar) has fabulous Kanchipuram silks in which old temple and artisan designs are woven into the fabric. Open 10 A.M.–9 P.M., closed Tuesdays. AE, MC, V.

Nalli Chinnasami Chetty (9 Nageswara Rao Rd., T. Nagar) has two floors filled with silks (including the beautiful Kanchipuram silk) and handlooms. Open 9 A.M.–9 P.M., closed Sundays except during festival times. DC, MC, V. *Kumaran Stores* (61 Usman Rd., T. Nagar) is another excellent silk emporium. Open 9 A.M.–9 P.M., closed Sundays. DC, MC, V.

Shilpi (Shop No. 1, Gee Gee Minar Bldg., 23 College Rd.) sells exquisite handlooms by the meter and handloom products, lovely salwar kameez (loose blouse and trousers), skirts and blouses, shawls, handbags, linen. Open 10 A.M.–8 P.M., closed Sundays. AE, DC, MC, V.

Poompuhar Sales and Show Room (818 Anna Salai) has a good selection of Tamil Nadu handicrafts: brass, wood, papier-mâché sculptures, handlooms. Open 10 A.M.–7:30 P.M., closed Sundays. AE, DC, MC, V.

Kanchipuram. This city of weavers makes some of India's finest silk. Buy only from government-approved shops; however, *Sreenivas Silk House* (17-A, T. K. Nambi St.) is one of the best and sells handloomed, handwoven, and hand-printed silk and cotton by the meter, as well as readymade clothes, silk ties, and scarves. Open daily 9 A.M.–9 P.M. AE, MC, V.

Madurai. For excellent Madurai cotton handlooms, visit *Handloom Society Hall* (24 West Chitrai St.). Open daily 7 A.M.–9 P.M. Rupees only. Also wander around the temple complex. You'll find rows and rows of men sitting behind sewing machines sewing up readymade items in minutes and stalls with all kinds of merchandise. It's fun just to watch.

Thanjavur. For good curios visit *V.R. Govindarajan,* 31 Kuthiraikatti St., Karanthal, tel. 20282. You can spend hours poking around the numerous rooms here filled with Tanjore paintings, brass and copper artifacts, wood carvings, and glass. Open 24 hours daily. Rupees only.

Subhashini Arts (1680 Krishnan Koil 2nd St., M. Chavady) sells exquisite Tanjore glass painting by an award-winning Indian artist, R. Eswarlal. Open 10 A.M.–1 P.M. and 2–6 P.M. Rupees only.

Tiruchirapalli. Visit *Chinna Bazaar* and *Big Bazaar* near the base of the fort.

NIGHTLIFE AND BARS. Don't leave Tamil Nadu without seeing a performance of the *Bharata Natyam*—the purest and in some ways the most beautiful classical dance form in India. In Madras, check the newspaper, *Hindu,* or call the Government of India Tourist Office (tel. 869685), which keeps a list of current cultural events. The following theaters and halls also have cultural events with some frequency:

Kalaivanar Arangam, Government Estate, Wallaja Rd., tel. 565669; *Rajah Annamalai Hall,* Esplanade, tel. 561425; *Rani Seethai Hall,* 603 Anna Salai, tel. 474863; *Music Academy,* 115 East Mowbray's Rd., tel. 475619.

In the last week of December, the Siva-Sakthi Music and Dance School, 123 East Car Street, Chidambaram, holds a formal Bharata Natyam program with its students. The students are young and talented. The building is old, with pillars, perfect for this classic dance form.

In Madras, the best bars are in the luxury hotels. Bars throughout the state are generally open 11 A.M.–11 P.M.

KERALA

Palm-Fringed Paradise

by
KATHLEEN COX

Just around the corner of Kanya Kumari (Cape Comorin), the southern-most tip of India, begins a strange land of paradox. Kerala is one of India's most progressive regions, but it has all the ingredients of a tropical paradise, right to the palm trees waving over sandy beaches. A thin strip along the southwest coast, isolated by the wall of the Western Ghats, Kerala is unbelievably cosmopolitan, with a heritage of 3,000 years of relations involving the rest of the world. Phoenicians, Arabs, Jews, Chinese, and Europeans came by boat to do heavy trading in this rich land that still raises its valuable cash crops: tea, rubber, cashews, teak, and a wide assortment of spices, including "black gold" (pepper). Yet Kerala moves at a leisurely pace, like the slow-moving boats that float through its network of canals and backwaters.

Kerala isn't for the hurried tourist, eager to chalk up a city a day. Forget the airline ticket to Cochin, with a quick hop to Trivandrum and the beach. Plan to travel into the Western Ghats—winding roads that take you by tea plantations and palm and rubber trees. Arrange for a languid cruise through the stunning backwaters. The state is small, but there's a lot to do.

Kerala didn't exist on the map until 1956, when it became one of India's smallest states, created out of Travancore-Cochin and the Malabar Coast district of Madras State. The result of this redrawing of the map of India is a slender but picturesque wedge along the Malabar Coast, which faces the Arabian Sea, with forest-clad mountains that rise as high as 1,550 meters (5,000 feet) at its back. Twenty-four million people live within this state that is slightly smaller than Switzerland. Though there isn't much room for newcomers, the population of Kerala has increased 20 percent over the past decade.

Despite Kerala's brief existence, it soon made a name for itself, becoming the first place in the world to adopt a communist regime in a free election: a political event that caused tremendous discussion and speculation, since Kerala also happens to be the most educated state in India. With a near-70 percent literacy rate (against a national rate of 36 percent), nine out of 10 children attend school, a startling figure anywhere in Asia. Although the communists lost control a few years back, they still carry some influence.

The scenery of Kerala is shaped by a partnership of geography and history. At least a quarter of its area is covered by forests that contain 600 varieties of trees, which makes timber an important industry—one in which woodsmen still use elephants as bulldozers. Up in the mountains are vast plantations of tea and cardamom (its name came from the Cardamom Hills of Kerala). Down below, pepper, coffee, rubber, cocoa, ginger, and turmeric—an essential spice in curry—grow in wild profusion. The mountains lord over a contrasting landscape of coconut trees and gray farmhouses built under palm-thatched roofs.

At times, when you travel through Kerala, it's hard to realize where you are. Towns and villages are heavily sprinkled with well-built churches, and one-quarter of the state's population is Christian. But nestling next to a church might be a house under a Chinese roof, gracefully bowed in the center with carved woodwork below the pointed ends. Or, at Cochin, you can even wander into a Jewish synagogue.

This human kaleidoscope developed over thousands of years. Behind the ramparts of the Western Ghats—there are only 16 passes through these mountains and none of them is easy—the Malabar Coast escaped domination by successive waves of empire builders who conquered ancient India by land. Long before Vasco da Gama, the Phoenicians came here to trade for spices, ivory, and sandalwood. Around 1000 B.C., King Solomon's ships visited biblical Ophir, supposedly the village of Poovar, south of Trivandrum, the present capital of Kerala.

The spice treasure of Kerala, especially pepper, lured fortune seekers from a good many European countries. The Dutch preceded the Portuguese, although their stay was short. In 1516, the Portuguese signed a treaty with the rani of Quilon (wife of the raja) and clung to it even though Arab traders, jealous of competition, talked the rani into harassing the encroachers. The Portuguese did some harassing themselves. When they discovered that the Christians, who were sharing this part of India with them, had never heard of the pope, these pious Catholics persecuted the "heretics."

In 1602, the Dutch, under the banner of the Dutch East Indian Company, reappeared and succeeded in forcing out the Portuguese in 1663 through skillful public relations with local chieftains. Still, the European procession was far from over. The British East India Company (on the Malabar Coast since 1684) opened its first settlement at Anjengo, south of Quilon. In the eighteenth century, the British won over the raja of Travancore. By 1795, the Dutch were down and out. (Travancore was originally known as Thiruvazhum Kode, an alluring name that meant "the abode of prosperity," but the British had difficulty with the pronunciation and solved the problem by substituting their corrupted phonetic version: Travancore.)

Kerala's Diverse People

The people of Kerala who speak Malayalam seem unaffected by the Europeans' unending game of monopoly. One of the most important Hindu castes of Kerala, the Nairs (or Nayars), were traditionally governed by the matriarchal system under which property was inherited through the female side of a family. Though the matriarchal system is on the wane, Nair women maintain a proud position in Kerala society. In the past, though, the Nair male was quite a warrior—Nairs only gave up dueling under British pressure. The Nair family is a huge unit. Their ancestral home is known as the *tarawad,* and some Nair tarawads are handsome structures with rich carvings on their heavy wooden doors and door frames.

Kerala's Brahmans, the Namboodiris, have another unique family system. Until recently, only the eldest son was allowed to take a wife from his own caste (the others had to marry Nairs who are Kshatriyas, and their children had no right to the family's heritage).

Because there weren't enough Brahman eldest sons to go around, many Namboodiri women went through life unmarried. Now most Namboodiris marry within their own community, and the old system has died out. Another Hindu community, the Ezhavas, produced a great religious teacher, Narayan Guru Swami, who preached the revolutionary notion of one caste, one god.

Hindus, Christians, Jews, and Moslems, all form part of the human flow of Kerala. Most of the men dress in impeccable *dhotis* (white wraps around the waist) or *lungis* (colorful wraps), and the women wear multicolored saris. Soon, you even get used to the rather incongruous sight of the ever-present black umbrella held over the head to ward off the equally everpresent sun or the occasional shower that strikes unexpectedly.

The people of Kerala are worth watching when they relax, too. The Kathakali dance drama is one of India's most electric dance forms, and it originated here in this tropical state. Festivals crop up at regular intervals—with the most picturesque, Onam, a four-day harvest celebration (August or September) that ends with races of exotic giant snake boats manned by 100 oarsmen.

EXPLORING KERALA

There's no fixed itinerary for visiting Kerala, but for convenience, we've arranged the main points of interest south to north.

Trivandrum and Environs

Trivandrum, built on seven hills, offers proud buildings that overlook quiet valleys. The main architectural landmark of Trivandrum is the Padmanabhaswami Temple, dedicated to Vishnu, a handsome example of South Indian temple architecture with a seven-story *goporum* (tower). No one knows the date of construction. One legend traces it to 3000 B.C., but everyone knows how it was built. Four thousand masons, 6,000 laborers, and 100 elephants did the job in six months. In the main courtyard, the

Kulasekhar Mandapam, there is some intricate granite sculpture; more sculpture can be appreciated on nearly 400 pillars supporting the temple corridor. Only Hindus may penetrate the sanctuary itself.

If you're an Indian art buff, visit Trivandrum's Museum and the Sri Chitra Gallery. The latter has a good collection of paintings as eclectic as Kerala itself. On its walls hang examples of the Rajput, Mogul, and Tanjore schools; copies of the Ajanta and Sigirya frescoes; and works from China, Japan, Tibet, and Bali, along with canvases by modern Indian painters. At a more earthy level, see the wonderful display of local arts and crafts in the museum, housed in a rambling palace with a Cubist pattern of gables. For travelers who want their nature in easily digested form, there's a zoo and an excellent aquarium (also used by marine biologists and fishery experts). To see what life was like here before modern India, visit the Kaudiyar Palace, the residence of the maharaja of former Travancore-Cochin.

Trivandrum, the state capital and once a sedate city, now boasts an international airport that has brought an influx of tourists. Many of these recent arrivals spend languorous days on Kovalam beach, 16 kilometers (10 miles) south of Trivandrum. Here you can take long walks on beautiful sandy beaches lined with palm-fringed lagoons and rocky coves. Or just laze around and watch lungi-clad fishermen as they drag in nets filled with the day's catch, then push their slender wooden fishing boats out again with a Malayalam "heave-ho" chant.

Trivandrum to Quilon

Once you've experienced Kovalam, head north 52 kilometers (32 miles) to Varkala, a seaside town set against a backdrop of red cliffs with mineral water springs spurting down to the beach. Varkala is the goal of Hindu pilgrims bound for its Janardhana Temple, reputed to be 2,000 years old.

Varkala is also where Narayana Guru Swami, one of modern India's greatest Hindu religious reformers and saints, entered into *samadhi* (contemplative retirement) in 1928. Instead of the bewildering pantheon of Hindu gods, he preached a simple faith: "One Caste, One Religion, and One God." It's appropriate that this movement should have sprung up in tolerant and progressive Kerala. Now it's carried on by a brotherhood of Swami's disciples. Their message is that of their leader: "Man must improve, whatever his religion."

Not far from Varkala lies a more mundane historical spot, Anjengo, where the British East India Company opened its first trading post on the Malabar Coast. You can visit the remains of an old fort built by these seventeenth-century merchants.

Nineteen kilometers (12 miles) north, you'll reach Quilon, one of the oldest ports along the Malabar Coast. The ancients reached it long before, though: Phoenician, Persian, Greek, Roman, and Arab vessels all traded here. The most industrious were the Chinese. During the T'ang dynasty (seventh to tenth centuries), China established trading posts in Quilon and, under the reign of Kubla Khan (thirteenth century), it exchanged envoys with this prosperous Indian city state (it became part of Travancore only in 1742).

To the visitor, Quilon offers its vista on Ashtamudi Lake, indented by red capes jutting from a shoreline of palms. Along the shore stand the Thevally Palace and Government House. Three kilometers (two miles) from Quilon, you can wander through Thangassery, with its lighthouse, ruined forts, and slumbering Portuguese, English, and Dutch cemeteries.

American Express offers Travelers Cheques built for two.

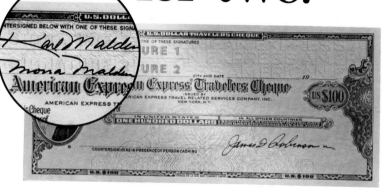

American Express® Travelers Cheques *for Two*. The first Travelers Cheques that allow either of you to use them because both of you have signed them. And only one of you needs to be present to purchase them.

Cheques *for Two* are accepted anywhere regular American Express Travelers Cheques are, which is just about everywhere. So stop by before your next trip and ask for Cheques *for Two*.

Travelers Cheques

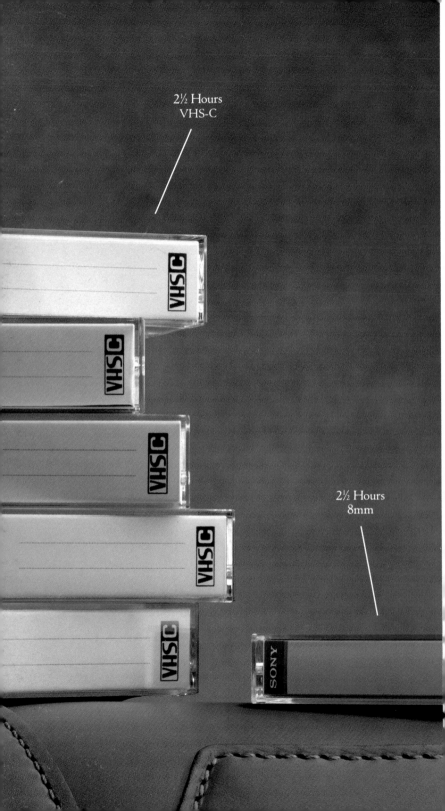

2½ Hours
VHS-C

VHS**C**

VHS**C**

VHS**C**

VHS**C**

VHS**C**

2½ Hours
8mm

SONY

SONY

PACK WISELY.

Given a choice, the seasoned traveler always carries less.
Case in point: Sony Handycam® camcorders, America's most
popular. They record up to 2½ hours on a single tape.
VHS-C tapes record only 30 minutes.* And why carry five tapes
when you can record everything on one? Which brings us
to the first rule of traveling: pack a Sony Handycam camcorder.

Over 1500 Great Weekend Escapes...

in Six Fabulous Fodor's Guides to
Bed & Breakfasts, Country Inns, Cottages,
and Other Weekend Pleasures!

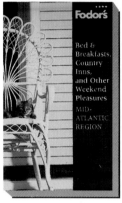

The
Mid-Atlantic
Region

The
South

New
England

The
West Coast

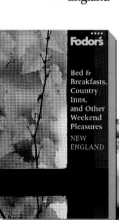

England
and
Wales

Canada

Quilon is also the starting point of a beautiful stretch of inland water-ways—83 kilometers (53 miles) of backwaters, called *kayals,* that snake through canals frequently shaded by the leaves of coconut palms. It's a lazy, calm voyage that takes you all the way to Alleppey. You can go by public boat, which is very cheap but takes about a day. Or you can hire a launch for around $100 and make the journey in half the time. In either case, you'll travel by hidden villages and lush vegetation—a panorama of rural/waterside life Kerala style.

Alleppey

When you arrive in Alleppey, a waterborne city (a miniature Cochin), you will find its canals teeming with numerous straw-roofed country boats introduced by the Chinese. Alleppey is a busy place. From coconut husks, it makes coir rope (the leading industry) and carpets (mats). It also thrives on the production of black pepper.

Also in Alleppey, as in Cochin, you can see Chinese "fishing machines," immense contraptions consisting of a huge net lowered into the water on the end of a pole poised on a fulcrum. Once a catch has been lured into its meshes by a lantern on top of the "machine," it takes a half-dozen men on the other end of the pole to lift the haul out of the water. The boats, *wallams,* which serve as water trucks for the Kerala countryside, are Chinese in design. Flat-bottomed and built of planks stitched together with cords, they are about 12 meters (40 feet) long and carry nearly 20 tons. Like ferries, they are double-ended, some with beautiful scrollwork on their bows. Cargo is carried under a roof of woven coconut fronds aboard these wallams. Although motor launches ply the backwaters of Kerala for tourists and travelers in a hurry, the wallam is still man powered. Its two-man crew drives it by punting, planting their long poles in the bottom at the bow and then walking a bit to propel their boat, just as bargemen (not gondoliers) still do on the canals of Venice. If you visit in August, you may just get to witness the Nehru Trophy Boat Race—a competition with those exotic snake boats.

Kottayam to Lake Periyar

From Alleppey, head for Kottayam. This small city has always been a busy base for Christian missionaries, and it boasts a number of old churches, including its Syrian church: the Cheria Palli, with colorful murals and numerous carved altars. From Kottayam, turn inland toward the east—the start of a beautiful side trip that takes you into a swift change of scenery and ultimately to the Periyar Lake Wildlife Sanctuary (115 km, or 71 mi.). At first, you run through lush vegetation and palm-thatched villages dominated incongruously by churches built in an exuberant Portuguese colonial style.

After passing through low-lying palms and paddies, the road begins to wind up the Ghats, lined with prosperous tea plantations where plants are carefully pruned to a four-foot height (any higher, their leaves are no longer tender). These tea plantations, established early in the century by the British and now mainly under Indian management, are a flourishing industry. The picking of the tea by nimble-fingered women goes on for most of the year; then the baskets of young leaves go to factories for drying, rolling, fermenting, and sifting the leaves. About 80 kilometers (50 miles) from Kottayam, the road passes through Peermade, a hill station, and then it reaches Thekkady, close to Periyar Lake.

Periyar Game Sanctuary

The lake is a human-made touch added to the natural beauty of the Western Ghats: a reservoir created by a dam on the Periyar River. This lake, with its many fingers that wind around capes and hills, some rising 914 meters (3,000 feet) above its surface, is the heart of the 777-square-kilometer (300-square-mile) wildlife sanctuary.

Periyar offers one of the most sybaritic ways of seeing big game. Here, forget exhausting treks or long safaris. You lounge in a motor launch as it drifts around a bend and comes into sight of elephants or deer or bison stopping at the shores of the lake for a drink. During the dry season, when waterholes in the forest are empty, leopards and tigers also pad up to the water. One word of advice: Either bribe all the Indian kids to be quiet— they love to scream and shout at a sighting—or hire a private launch.

Shooting, of course, is prohibited, but the hunter's loss is the photographer's gain. Elephant herds are so accustomed to *quiet* visitors drifting next door in launches that they hardly notice the intrusion. This is no place to be caught short of film, and specially built tree perches provide good observation posts. Elephants with their young graze beside deer, gaur (wild oxen) and sambar (large Asiatic deer); you may even glimpse tigers and bears. Of course, all the jungle's smaller creatures are photo material.

Cochin

Although Cochin is not a pretty city, it is one of those rare places where the twentieth century and ancient civilizations exist side by side. Cochin's past is so rich that it has a valid claim as a museum city. Cochin is also one of the three biggest ports on the west coast of India and the biggest in Kerala, handling over 5 million tons of cargo in a year, and a prosperous center of the coir industry. Stroll through the streets behind the docks lined with old merchant houses, *godowns* (warehouses), and open courtyards heaped with betel nuts, ginger, peppercorns, and hanks of coir. The air is filled with the smell of spices and the shouts of men pushing heavy carts. This Eastern scene has changed little over the centuries.

Cochin manages to pursue its various lucrative trades in its setting of wooden islands and canals winding past houses on stilts. Both in the past and in the present, Cochin has displayed a lively blend of people and architecture that is worth seeing. It's one of the few places in the world where you can visit a Jewish synagogue, Portuguese churches, Dutch buildings, and a couple of mosques and Hindu temples and see Chinese fishing nets all in the same day.

We use "Cochin" as a handy name for a cluster of islands and towns. Over on the mainland, three miles from the harbor but linked by bridges and ferries, lies Ernakulam, once the capital of the former state of Cochin. If you arrive by air, your terminal will be on Willingdon Island, a human-made island (it consists of material dredged in an ambitious harbor-deepening operation). On Vypeen Island, facing the sea, fishermen still use their Chinese cantilever contraptions. The coir makers work on Gundu Island in a cooperative where excellent samples of their products are on display, although businessmen dealing in coir make their homes in the residential quarter of Fort Cochin, where, in tropical India, you stumble onto an English village green, pseudo-Tudor houses, lawns, a club, and a perfect replica of a prosperous London suburb—except that palms betray where you are. Bolghatty Island is the most beautiful of the lot, and its colonial mansion, formerly used by the Dutch governor and later by the British resident, is now a hotel. Finally, there is Mattancheri, southwest of the harbor: the home of a dwindling Jewish community. History at Cochin is found in the most abundant quantities here and at Fort Cochin.

Fort Cochin is believed to be the oldest European settlement in India. It first saw the Portuguese flag in 1500; three years later, Alfonso de Albuquerque came with half a dozen ships bearing settlers and built Fort Cochin. He also brought five friars who built the first European church in India in 1510, still standing in Fort Cochin as St. Francis Church. Vasco da Gama first arrived in Cochin in 1502. He returned again in 1524 as Portuguese viceroy of the Indies. He died here and was buried in St. Francis Church. You can still visit his gravestone, but his remains were shipped back to Portugal in 1538 (he's buried in Lisbon). St. Francis Church, the oldest European church in India, reflects the colonial struggle for India. It was a Dutch Reformed church from 1664 to 1804, an Anglican church from 1804 to 1947, and now it's part of the Church of South India. The giant fans in the nave are operated from outside. The church contains Dutch gravestones and has the *Doop Book,* a register of baptisms and marriages from 1751 to 1894. You can look at a photographic reproduction of the vital statistics (the original is too fragile).

St. Francis is a sedate church in the Spanish style, but not nearly as flamboyant as the Santa Cruz Cathedral in Fort Cochin, which verges on the gaudy. The Santa Cruz was completed in 1904.

The White Jews of Cochin

Fort Cochin may be old, but compared with Mattancheri, it's an upstart. The first emigration of Jews to Kerala supposedly took place in the sixth century B.C., followed by a much bigger wave in the first century A.D., when Jews fleeing Roman persecution in Jerusalem came to Cranganore and settled there. One of the most impressive sights in the synagogue of Mattancheri are the copper plates presented to the Jewish community in the fourth century A.D. by King Bhaskara Ravi Varma, who awarded them the village of Anjuvannam, a name meaning "five castes" (the Jews were considered the lords of five castes of artisans). Incidentally, both Jews and Christians have always been considered of high caste in Kerala. The plates state that Anjuvannam shall be the hereditary possession of Joseph Rabban and his descendants "so long as the world and moon exist."

The king's word was good, and the Jewish colony flourished, serving as a haven to Jews from the Middle East and, in later centuries, Europe. The Portuguese put an end to this state of affairs. When Albuquerque discovered the Jews near Cochin, he requested permission from his king to "exterminate them one by one" and destroyed their city at Cranganore. Moslem anti-Semitism flared up, too. It was with the arrival of the Dutch that the Jews of Cochin were able to live without fear once more—as they always had in India.

The synagogue in Mattancheri's Jewish colony was built in 1568 after the expulsion of the Jews from Cranganore. It was considerably embellished in the mid-eighteenth century by Ezekiel Rahabi, who build a clock tower and paved the floor of the synagogue with hand-painted tiles of willow pattern (each one different), brought all the way from Canton in China. Indeed, the entire synagogue is beautiful, and the elder loves to show his visitors around.

Sadly, though, the congregation has almost vanished; and, as an active synagogue, its days are probably numbered. Few of the pale, blond white Jews of Cochin are left (unlike the "black Jews" from the mainland of India, who are a mixture of Jewish and Hindu stock). Many of the white

Jews emigrated to Holland and to England in the past two centuries, and others have gone to Israel.

Mattancheri also offers Cochin's other most interesting building—the "Dutch" Palace—built by the Portuguese (hence the quotation marks) in the middle of the sixteenth century. The Dutch Palace was taken over by the Dutch, who added some improvements before presenting it to the rajas of Cochin, who used it as a palace. The rajas, in turn, made more improvements, notably some excellent mythological murals. In one room, you can see the entire story of the *Ramayana* on the walls. The palace also contains a rare example of traditional Keralan flooring, which looks like polished black marble but is actually a subtle mix of burned coconut shells, charcoal, lime, plant juices, and egg whites. Both the synagogue and the palace are within easy walking distance of the boat jetty at Mattancheri.

While in Cochin, you must see a Kathakali dance drama. There are many dance companies, and you can also attend a "short" two-hour performance at the Gurukalam Kathakali Yogam in Ernakulam, a tiny theater (bring mosquito repellent) that is weirdly magical. The dancers wear fantastic makeup and spectacular costumes. When the show begins, the stylized movements are larger than life—eerie, and wondrous—and an unequivocal delight. No surprise, since the performers begin rigorous training to master control of the eyeballs, neck, toes, fingers, and cheek muscles at age five.

From Cochin to Trichur

After Cochin, the pace slows down again. Sixteen kilometers (10 miles) north is industrial Alwaye, the "Ruhr of Kerala." Here Travancore made a successful stand against Tipu Sultan, an invader from neighboring Mysore who came storming into Alwaye in 1790. Actually, Travancore was helped by a flood on the Periyar River, which forced Tipu to cancel his plans. Alwaye is also the home of the Union Christian College, one of the few started in India by Indians instead of foreign missionaries. But the main reason to visit is that Alwaye is on the route to Kaladi, birthplace of Sankaracharya. Sankaracharya was an eighth-century saint and philosopher, the father of the *Advaita* doctrine of Hindu philosophy and one of the first of the monotheists who seem to flourish in Kerala—whether as Hindus, Christians, Jews, or Moslems.

Along the shore north of Alwaye, you reach old Cranganore, now known as Kodungalloor. The Cheraman Perumals, the early rulers of this part of the Malabar Coast, had their capital here, and an old building known as Cheraman Parambu is said to have been their palace. Kodungalloor was not always a drowsy seaside town. It was the first of Kerala's international harbors, and the heritage of its history includes a Portuguese fort, a number of Hindu temples (the best-known are the Thiruvanchikulam and the Bhagavathi), and India's first mosque. Nearby Kottappuram adds a Christian touch: Here St. Thomas the Apostle is said to have landed in India, and a church is dedicated to him.

Back inland once more, the main road and rail line run from Alwaye to Trichur, which has a zoo (with quite a collection of snakes), an art exhibition in its town hall, an old palace, and a fort. Trichur is a must-see if you happen to be in Kerala during its Pooram festival, an annual affair occurring in April or May. This is one of South India's biggest shows, complete with processions, huge fireworks displays, and elephants decked out regally.

Kozhikode (Calicut)

The landscape reverts once more to coconut palms, tea, rubber plantations, and groves of tropical fruit trees as you head toward the sea from Trichur north to Kozhikode (Calicut). Kozhikode is rather remote from the rest of Kerala and, prior to 1956, it was not in the same state.

Long ago, it was a center of power of the Malabar Coast under its rulers, the Zamorins, a name meaning lords of the sea. The lovely city is noted for its block-printed cotton cloth and is the origin of the word *calico*.

The city, which has a large Moslem population, has always been a major port of the Malibar Coast, with its glory days as a trading center beginning when Vasco da Gama landed here on May 20, 1498, after rounding the Cape of Good Hope. The English first appeared in Kozhikode in 1615, and the British East India Company gained control of the city in 1792 following a treaty with Tipu Sultan.

Lakshadweep Islands

India's smallest Union Territory lies off the coast of Cochin in the Arabian Sea: the Lakshadweep Islands, 36 coral atolls, some of which have been inhabited for centuries by devout Sunni Moslems. To protect the people and the fragile island ecology from the impact of tourism, the government has judiciously opened up just Bangaram, an uninhabited island, to foreigners. You fly to Agatti, then take a 90-minute boat trip through coral-rich waters to the one rustic resort, on a pearly white beach surrounded by lagoons. Here, on this remote landfall, you can relax and swim, scuba dive or snorkel over its extensive coral reefs. If you visit Bangaram, admire the marine life and coral; but don't leave with any coral souvenirs. Foreigners need an entry permit to visit; it's easily arranged when you book into the one resort.

PRACTICAL INFORMATION FOR KERALA

WHEN TO GO. Kerala's peak season is October–March, when the weather is warm and pleasant. From March to September, it grows hot and steamy, with heavy rain beginning in June. From September until December sporadic light showers turn Kerala a lush green. The best season for Lakshadweep is October–May.

HOW TO GET THERE. By Air. Trivandrum has international flights to and from Columbo and the Maldive Islands. *Indian Airlines* has daily flights to Cochin from Delhi, Bombay, and Goa. It has six weekly flights from Bangalore and Madras. It has daily flights to Trivandrum from Bombay, Delhi, and Madras; and four weekly flights from Bangalore. It has a daily flight between Calicut and Bombay. *Vayudoot* also has three weekly flights connecting Cochin with Madras and Coimbatore. It has three weekly flights connecting Agatti (Lakshadweep Islands) with Coimbatore and Madras. For Indian Airlines information, call 353901 in Cochin; 66370 in Trivandrum; 55233 in Calicut. For Vayudoot information, call 69613 in Cochin.

By Bus. Various luxury coaches connect Kerala with important South Indian cities: Bangalore, Kanya Kumari (Cape Comorin), Madras, Madurai, Mangalore, Pondicherry, and so on. If you don't mind the near-constant blare and glare of video, buses are usually clean, and cheap, and much faster than the train. For details, contact: *Kerala State Road Transport Corporation* (KSRTC) in Ernakulam

(Cochin), Bus Terminus, tel. 352033. In Trivandrum, call KSRTC, Central Bus Station, Thampanoor, tel. 63886.

By Train. Good rail connections link Cochin and Trivandrum with Bangalore, Bombay, Cannanore, Delhi, Madras, and Mangalore. For details, call Ernakulam (Cochin) Rail Station, 353100; from Trivandrum, call 62966 (days); 63066 (evenings).

By Rented Car with Driver. To Cochin from Bangalore, 565 km (350 mi.); Ootacamund, 312 km (193 mi.); Madurai, 324 km (201 mi.); Madras, 694 km (430 mi.); Mysore, 424 km (263 mi.). To Trivandrum from Bangalore, 712 km (441 mi.); Madras, 784 km (486 mi.); and Madurai, 307 km (190 mi.). Kerala has some of the best and most scenic roads in India.

TOURIST INFORMATION. The Department of Tourism in Kerala has good, basic tourist information on Kerala, including maps and brochures. Contact its head office before you visit: Department of Tourism, Government of Kerala, Park View, Trivandrum 695033; tel. 61132. Kerala Tourism Development Corporation (KTDC), Mascot Sq., Trivandrum 695033; tel. 68476, fax 65347 offers statewide tours, reasonably priced accommodations, and tourist taxis. On arrival, contact the following offices:

Kozhikode (Calicut). Kerala Reception Center, KTDC Corner; tel 76101. Open daily 9 A.M.–6 P.M.

Cochin. *Government of India Tourist Office,* Willingdon Island, Cochin 340352; tel. 6045. Open 9 A.M.–5 P.M., closed Saturdays and Sundays.

Kerala Tourism Information Counter, Old Collectorate Bldg., Park Ave., Ernakulam; no phone. Open 10 A.M.–5 P.M., closed Sundays and second Saturdays.

Kerala Tourism Information Counter, Airport; no phone. Open at flight arrivals.

KTDC, Tourist Reception Center, Shanmughom Rd., Ernakulam, Cochin; tel. 353234. This office handles bookings for government-run tours, tourist taxis, and accommodations. Open daily 9 A.M.–6 P.M.

Trivandrum. *Kerala Tourist Information Center,* Department of Tourism, Park View; tel. 61132. Open 10 A.M.–5 P.M. Monday–Saturday.

Kerala Tourist Information Counter, Central Bus Station, Thampanoor; tel. 67224. Open 24 hours.

Kerala Tourist Information Counter, Railway Station, Thampanoor; no phone. Open 24 hours.

Kerala Tourist Information Counter, Trivandrum Domestic Airport; tel. 71085. Open at flight arrivals.

Government of India Tourist Information Office, International Terminal; no phone. Open at flight arrivals.

KTDC Reception Center, Station Rd., Thampanoor; tel. 75031. Open daily 9 A.M.–6 P.M.

FOREIGN CURRENCY EXCHANGE. Most Western-style hotels have money-exchange counters. Otherwise, go to a branch of the *State Bank of India,* open Monday–Friday, 10 A.M.–2 P.M.; Saturdays till noon.

ACCOMMODATIONS. In major tourist destinations, you can find a good range of hotels to suit all budgets. The rest of the state has limited but adequate options. In the peak season (October–March), book your room early. All KTDC hotels can also be reserved through the KTDC offices listed above. Taj Kerala Hotels and Resorts (TKHR), a new joint collaboration between the Taj Group of Hotels and KTDC, can be booked through any Taj Hotel or through its overseas offices (see Group Hotels in *Facts at Your Fingertips*). Prices are based on double occupancy and exclude taxes and service charges: *Deluxe,* over Rs. 2,000; *Expensive,* Rs. 1,200–Rs 2,000; *Moderate,* Rs. 500–Rs. 1,200; *Inexpensive,* under Rs. 500. Most Western-style hotels take major credit cards.

ALLEPPEY

Inexpensive

Alleppey Prince Hotel. A.S. Rd., N.H. 47, Alleppey 688007; tel. 3752. 36 rooms with bath. This Western-style hotel has spacious air-conditioned rooms that are scheduled for renovation by 1993. Expect a modest modern decor. Best rooms will overlook the pool. Multicuisine restaurant, bar, TV, room service, swimming pool, backwater cruise arrangements, foreign-exchange counter. DC, MC, V.

COCHIN

Deluxe

Taj Malabar Hotel. Willingdon Island, Cochin 682009; tel. 340010, fax 340297. 100 rooms with bath. This resort, with good privacy and sea views, has a pleasing lobby with lots of carved dark wood and Kerala-style furnishings. It offers two choices of air-conditioned rooms. If you want antiquity and handsome, older furnishings, ask for a room with wooden floors in the old wing. Rooms in the new wing have a modern decor. In the entire hotel, best rooms have a seaside view; the next best have garden views. Multicuisine restaurants, bar, TV, room service, swimming pool, doctor, foreign-exchange and travel counter. AE, DC, MC, V.

Moderate–Expensive

TKHR. Ernakulam. 108 rooms with bath. Unnamed at press time, this new high rise, scheduled to open by 1993, faces the harbor. The best of the contemporary-decor rooms will have a sea view. TV, air-conditioning, room service, multicuisine restaurants, bar, business center, foreign-exchange and travel counter, shops, swimming pool by 1994. AE, DC, MC, V.

Moderate

Casino Hotel. Willingdon Island, Cochin 682003; tel. 340221, fax 340001. 70 rooms with bath. This handsome Western-style hotel offers excellent value and privacy. Its lobby is cozy, with cane furnishings. Air-conditioned rooms are spacious with a contemporary decor. Best rooms overlook the lawn and swimming pool. TV, room service, multicuisine restaurants, bar, foreign-exchange and travel counter, local tours, backwater trip arrangements, swimming pool, doctor, shop. AE, DC, MC, V.

KOVALAM

Expensive–Deluxe

Surya Samudra Beach Resort. Pulinkudi, Mullur, Trivandrum 695521; tel. 413, fax c/o Surya Samudra 77702. 12 rooms with bath. Overlooking the sea and 10 km (6 mi.) south of Kovalam, this resort on eight acres is secluded, with an exquisite beach. Fastidiously designed, it offers a range of accommodations from simple cottages with immaculate interiors that blend modern and ethnic touches and have a shared bath to stunningly restored Kerala-style wooden homes, called nallakettus, with intricate carvings on the exterior and domed wooden ceilings and pleasing, understated modern decor. All cottages offer privacy and ocean views. Multicuisine restaurant, ayurvedic massages, backwater cruise and tour arrangements, fishing trips, cultural programs on request, foreign-exchange counter. Seawater swimming pool by 1993. Book well in advance. Off-season discounts. Traveler's checks.

Expensive

Kovalam Ashok Beach Resort. Kovalam Beach, Trivandrum 695527; tel., fax 62522. 125 rooms with bath. Built in tiers into a bluff overlooking the Arabian Sea, this resort lacks great character and warmth; but it has a good beach. Rooms in the main block have modern furnishings and private verandas. Ask for an unobstructed sea view. Cottages, with tiled floors and a cozier feel, offer sea views and privacy. Air-conditioning, TV, room service, multicuisine restaurants, bar, swimming pool, health club, tennis court, foreign-exchange and travel counter, shopping arcade. AE, DC, MC, V.

Moderate

Hotel Samudra. Samudra Beach, Kovalam, Trivandrum 695527; tel. 62089. 50 rooms with bath. At press time, the Hyatt Hotel chain was scheduled to take over this KTDC resort. Contact your travel agent for latest details. Currently, the best rooms in this modest complex are air-conditioned, have a TV, and are set in cottages with views of the beach. All rooms have plain, clean furnishings and private verandas overlooking the ocean. Room service, multicuisine restaurant, bar, ayurvedic massages, bank, foreign-exchange and travel counter. Off-season discounts. AE, DC, MC, V.

Inexpensive

Hotel Rockholm. Light House Rd., Vizhinjam (Kovalam), Trivandrum 695527; tel. Vizhinjam 306. 17 rooms with bath. The Rockholm's exterior is modest, but its superb location on a bluff overlooking the sea and its good service make this hotel popular. The small lobby is filled with reading material. Rooms are extremely clean, with modest contemporary furnishings and verandas. Upper-floor rooms are best. Fans, room service, multicuisine restaurant, good beach nearby, car-rental and backwater cruise arrangements, foreign-exchange counter. AE, DC, MC, V.

KOZHIKODE (CALICUT)

Moderate–Expensive

TKHR. About 80 rooms with bath. This new modern high-rise hotel, scheduled to open in 1993 and unnamed at press time, is in the city. Rooms will have a contemporary decor, with the best view of the sea and coconut groves. Air-conditioning, TV, room service, multicuisine restaurants, bar, business center, foreign-exchange and travel counter, shops. Reserve through any Taj Hotel. AE, DC, MC, V.

KUMURAKOM
30 km (19 mi.) from Kottayam

Moderate–Expensive

TKHR Baker's Estate. 30 rooms with bath. Formerly Kerala's first rubber plantation, this two-story dwelling will be operating as a hotel by 1993. Room decors will feature a sedate mix of the old and the new. TV, room service, multicuisine fixed-menu meals, bar, water sports. Reserve through any Taj Hotel. AE, DC, MC, V.

LAKE PERIYAR

Deluxe

Hotel Lake Palace. Thekkady, Idukki District; tel. Kumily 2023. 8 rooms with bath. This KTDC facility, a former maharaja's hunting lodge, is set on an island inside the sanctuary. Scheduled for renovation by 1993, it will recapture its original, old-fashioned charm. Most rooms will open onto a sweeping porch with good views. The ambience is idyllic. Multicuisine fixed-menu restaurant, boating, trekking. Meals included. AE, DC, MC, V.

Expensive

Spice Village. Kumily, Thekkady Rd., Thekkady 685536; tel. 92314. fax 340001 or reserve through Casino Hotel (see Cochin, above). 37 rooms with bath. This new resort on the edge of a small village and just outside the sanctuary features thatched-roof cottages that are clustered atop small hills. Interiors are "rustic" modern: lots of knotty pine furnishings and trim, white walls, red-tile floor, plaid upholstery and bedspreads. Lush plantings, including spice trees, add fragrance and privacy. Limited room service, fans, multicuisine fixed-menu restaurant, foreign-exchange counter, swimming pool, jungle treks, boat safaris and plantation visits, doctor. V.

Moderate–Expensive

TKHR. Just outside the sanctuary, this new resort will open by mid-1993. Set on nearly seven acres, it will have a rustic, Kerala-style ambience. Contact the Taj Group for latest details.

Moderate

Aranya Nivas. Thekkady, Idukki District 685536; tel. Kumily 2023. 30 rooms with bath. This old British lodge, with granite exterior, is a KTDC hotel and is scheduled for renovation by 1993. Some rooms will keep the original furnishings; other rooms will have a more modern decor. The best rooms overlook the lake. Room service, multicuisine restaurant, bar, car-rental service, foreign-exchange counter, boating, bank, shop. AE, DC, MC, V.

LAKSHADWEEP ISLANDS

Deluxe

Bangaram Island Resort. Lakshadweep. Reservations: Casino Hotel, Willingdon Island, Cochin 682003; tel. 340221, fax 340001. 30 double rooms with bath. Set on an island dotted with lagoons, coconut groves, and beautiful beaches, this new resort is an oasis. You stay in simple thatched cottages (two or four rooms to a unit), with terra-cotta floors and pleasant modern furnishings. The emphasis is on the preservation of the environment, with minimal construction. The resort will help you procure the obligatory permit and book your Vayudoot flight and 90-minute boat ride. Multicuisine restaurant, room service, bar, wind-surfing, kayaking, snorkeling, scuba diving, glass-bottom boats, fishing trips. Meals included. Off-season discount Apr. 1–Oct. 1. AE, DC, MC, V.

MADUKA KUNNU
(30 km from Kottayam)

Deluxe

Estate Bungalow. Tel. 232. Reserve through Casino Hotel (see Cochin, above). 5 rooms with bath. No signs point the way. Your driver will know the gate house that leads to this estate on a rubber plantation with pineapple and spice trees. You can stay in the main house or in an old wooden Kerala-style dwelling with wrap-around verandas. Expect peace and privacy, hospitality, and opportunities to discover plantation life. Malayalee-cuisine restaurant, bar, fans. AE, DC, MC, V.

TRIVANDRUM

Moderate

Mascot Hotel. Mascot Sq., Trivandrum 695033; tel. 68990. 42 rooms with bath. A former British bungalow, this KTDC hotel was under renovation at press time. Spacious rooms will have a modern decor, but much of the original grandeur will be restored. The best rooms will overlook the swimming pool. TV, air-conditioning, room service, multicuisine restaurants, bar, foreign-exchange and travel counter, tour arrangements, swimming pool, health club, shop. AE, DC, MC, V.

VARKALA
(40 km from Trivandrum)

Moderate–Expensive

TKHR. 30 rooms with bath. This two-story half-moon-shaped hotel, with a good beach, is scheduled to open in early 1993. Facing the sea, rooms will have a contemporary decor with Kerala-theme touches. Air-conditioning, TV, room service, multicuisine restaurants, bar, foreign-exchange and travel counter. AE, DC, MC, V.

DINING OUT. For beef lovers, Kerala has the real thing. It also has great seafood and southern Indian vegetarian cuisine. In fact, this is a state—like Goa—that offers good eating; both Indian and non-Indian. Besides some of the best options listed here, many accommodations listed above also have restaurants. Breakfast is usually 8–10:30; lunch, noon–3; dinner, 7:30–10. Payment is normally in rupees unless the restaurant is connected to a Western-style hotel. The restaurants listed below are informal and, unless noted, are open for three meals and don't require reservations. Prices are based on one person eating a three-course meal, excluding taxes, tip, or beverage: *Deluxe,* over Rs. 300; *Expensive,* Rs. 200–Rs. 300; *Moderate,* Rs. 100–Rs. 200; *Inexpensive,* under Rs. 100.

ALLEPPEY

Moderate

Vembanad Restaurant. Alleppey Prince Hotel, A. S. Rd.; tel. 3752. Vembanad's decor is simple—a few oars tacked on one wall, fresh flowers, crisp linen. The accent is on good food: Continental, Chinese, and Indian cuisines, including Kerala dishes. Try *kozhi olath* (diced chicken cooked with coconut chips) or, if you can order in advance, fish *vevichathu* (deep-fried sailfish coated in hot spices). At lunch, sample the good Kerala *thali* (assorted regional dishes served on a platter). Portions are large. Open 7–11 A.M., noon–2:30 P.M., and 7–10:30 P.M. DC, MC, V.

COCHIN

Expensive

Fort Cochin. Casino Hotel, Willingdon Island; tel. 340221. Enjoy the day's catch in an attractive Kerala-style cottage with subdued lighting. The chef is terrific and can cook up your choice to your specifications, from simple to grand, with delectable sauces. Reservations advised. Open 7 P.M.–midnight. AE, DC, MC, V.

Rice Boats. Taj Malabar Hotel, Willingdon Island; tel. 340010. Expect to eat inside one of two traditional Kerala wooden boats under a woven bamboo awning. The lighting is subdued, oars and bamboo hats adorn the walls, and a country-western guitarist entertains nightly. The chef prepares seafood specialties, including *karimeen grandeur* (fresh local sea fish marinated in subtle spices and shallow-fried), and lobster and prawn dishes. Reservations advised. Open 7:30 P.M.–midnight. AE, DC, MC, V.

Moderate

Regency. Hotel Abad Plaza, M. G. Rd.; tel. 361636. This handsome restaurant with dark-wood pillars inlaid with mirrors offers Continental, Indian, and Chinese dishes. Specialties are spicy Szechuan deep-fried prawns and island chicken curry served in a pineapple. You can also enjoy great seafood. No liquor is served, but at night you're entertained by performers singing Indian ghazals. Dinner reservations advised. Open 12:30 P.M.–3 P.M. and 7:30–11 P.M. AE, DC, MC, V.

Inexpensive

Frys Village Restaurant. Chittoor Rd., next to Mymoon Cinema; tel. 353983. Somehow this city restaurant—four pavilions with bamboo curtains—screens out the surrounding bustle. It also serves the typical Kerala set meals (thalis): fish *molly* (fillet in a sweet green curry with coconut), fish curry (spicy hot), or the very inexpensive *kadala* (Kerala plain curry) with *puttu* (steamed rice and coconut cake) for under Rs. 5. Open 12:30–3 P.M. and 6–11:30 P.M. Rupees only.

Pandhal. M. G. Rd., opposite Grand Hotel; tel. 367759. This modern multicuisine restaurant with rough white stucco walls, pine ceiling, and small waterfall serves an excellent Kerala thali and a variety of seafood. Its Chinese cuisine and steaks are especially popular. The place is usually crowded. Dinner reservations advised. Open noon–3 P.M. and 7–midnight. AE, DC, MC, V.

KOVALAM BEACH

Moderate

Rockholm Hotel Restaurant. Light House Rd.; tel. 306. While you can eat indoors, the best ambience here is on the delightful terrace set on the bluff with the ocean pounding below. Kovalam's best chef prepares excellent multicuisine dishes, including the day's catch. Try the seasonal fish dishes, such as grilled pomfret, fried mussels, or prawns served Kerala style. Dinner reservations suggested. Open 7 A.M.–9:30 P.M. AE, DC, MC, V.

Surya Samudra Beach Resort Restaurant. Pulinkadi, Mullur; tel. 413. Eat in this delightful open-sided, octagon-shaped restaurant with a Kerala-style double-dome ceiling. Set on a bluff overlooking the ocean, beautiful vistas and stone carvings surround you. You hear the sound of the surf and classical music. The chef prepares Indian and Continental dishes, with fresh food bought daily and no preservatives. Even the ice cream is homemade. Try the lobster *crème de la mer* (de-shelled lobster boiled in cream with mild spices and sherry) or shark *puttu* (half boiled, then crumbled shark, fried again with ginger and spices). Save room for freshly baked cake and bread. Reservations a must. Open 7:30 A.M.–9:30 P.M. Rupees only.

TRIVANDRUM

Moderate

Marthanda. Hotel Pankaj, opposite Secretariat, M. G. Rd.; tel. 76667. This cozy restaurant, with soft lighting and stylish paintings and murals, offers Chinese, Continental, and Indian dishes, including regional specialties. Try the diced chicken Szechuan or ask for the popular fish *Malabari* (fish curry cooked with coconut) or beef *Travancore* (cubed beef fried in spicy masala gravy). Neither of these dishes is on the menu. Reservations advised. Open 7–10 A.M., noon–3 P.M., and 7–11 P.M. AE, DC, MC, V.

Inexpensive

Nalukettu. Opposite Trivandrum Club, Vellayambalam; tel. 69287. This 70-year-old traditional Nair family house with a pitched tile roof has numerous dining rooms; the air-conditioned one is best, but walk around and see the interior *naluket-tu* (courtyard). You can also eat outside at night. The chef prepares multicuisine dishes, including Kerala items. Try the mutton or chicken coconut fry (curry dish prepared with chopped coconut, coconut milk, and masala spices). Reservations advised. Open 11 A.M.–11 P.M. AE, DC, MC, V.

SWEETS AND TREATS. Cochin. You can escape the crowds and have good vegetarian Indian snacks and sweets (*barfi* and *pedas,* made from a sugary milk paste) in tiny *Mezbaan,* 38/1278 M. G. Rd., Padma Junction; open daily 9 A.M.–8 P.M. For Western or Indian snacks and sweets, including good ice cream, go to *Pandhal,* M. G. Rd. Snacks are served daily 3 P.M.–7 P.M.

Trivandrum. Head for the cozy *Snoozer Ice Cream Parlour* (Press Rd.) and choose from 87 different ice-cream concoctions. Open 11 A.M.–8 P.M.

HOW TO GET AROUND. From the Airport. Cochin. City buses run regularly between the airport and Cochin (Rs. 1). A taxi to your hotel should cost about Rs. 40–Rs. 80; bargain! **Trivandrum.** A taxi into Trivandrum is your best bet and should cost about Rs. 60–Rs. 100; to Kovalam Beach, Rs. 80–Rs. 100. Bargain.

By Plane. *Indian Airlines* flies three times a week between Cochin and Trivandrum. *Vayudoot* flies three times weekly between Cochin and Agatti, the gateway to Bangaram Island. It also flies three times a week to the Lakshadweep Islands from Calicut and Cochin.

By Bus. Buses ply the streets, but they're crowded. For bus information in Cochin, call 352033; in Trivandrum, call 63886.

By Train. You can travel Cochin–Kottayam–Quilon–Trivandrum–Kozhikode (Calicut) via train. In Cochin, for train information and reservations, call 353100; in Trivandrum, call 62966 (days) and 63066 (evenings).

By Tourist Taxi. Comfortable tan or white Ambassadors, the best way to get around Kerala, are available for hire at most good Western-style hotels and through travel agencies listed below under Tour Operators. Rates are about Rs. 3–Rs. 3.50 per km, with a halt charge of Rs. 50 per night. Minimum change is Rs. 25. If you travel one-way to a remote destination, you will probably be charged for the return journey to cover fuel costs.

By Taxi. Yellow-topped taxis are available in most cities, but they're usually more expensive than tourist taxis.

By Boat. In **Kerala**, ferries cruise along a network of backwater canals that provide a lazy way to get from city to city.

Alleppey. You can take a public ferry backwater day-long trip to Quilon for less than Rs. 40. For departure times, inquire at the District Tourism Promotion Council, Jetty Rd., tel. 62308. You can also hire a lovely old wooden boat with a captain and do the trip in grand, leisurely style (Rs. 100 per hour for the entire boat). Arrangements can be made through *Vembanad Tourist Service,* Akkarakalam Building, near Bus Stand, Jetty Rd., Alleppey 688010; tel. 60395. You can also go by public ferry or luxuriously in a Vembanad boat to Changanacherry. This is an extremely scenic five-hour ride through narrow canals and past temples and quaint villages. From Changanacherry, you can proceed to Lake Periyar.

Cochin. Frequent ferry service runs from early morning until about 10 P.M. There are ferries from Fort Cochin, Ernakulam, Mattancherry, Willington Island, plus numerous other runs. Ask at your hotel for specifics, or contact the local tourist office.

Kottayam. This is a convenient starting and ending point for a backwater trip to Alleppey. Inquire at the boat jetty.

Quilon. From here you can take the day-long public ferry that weaves through the backwaters to Alleppey. Go to the boat jetty for information. You can also do shorter trips and rent a boat for the day.

By Auto Rickshaw. This is the cheapest and most convenient way to travel in Trivandrum and Cochin. Rates are about Rs. 1 per km. Minimum charge is Rs. 4.

TOURS. KTDC offers three novel "Body, Mind, and Soul" Tours: a 7- or 14-day package "age halt" health tour with yoga, ayurvedic massages, special diets, and herbal treatments, sightseeing, and cultural programs; a nine-day "calm balm" tour of Kerala's scenic destinations; and a seven-day "soul stir" tour to Kerala's temples, with evening lectures and cultural programs. Contact the head office of KTDC (address above under Tourist Information). **Alleppey to Quilon.** You can join a fixed-departure, eight-hour boat tour for each direction that includes a guide and makes interesting stops along the way. For these tours, contact the District Tourism Promotion Council (Jetty Rd., Alleppey, tel. 62308; or Guest House Complex, Ashramam, Quilon, tel. 79654). Boats run August–May and seats can be booked on arrival. Boats depart from Alleppey on Tuesday and Friday; from Quilon on Monday and Thursday; Rs. 70 each way. Bring your own lunch. *Vembanad Tourist Service* (address above) offers boat tours that allow you to explore backwater life all around Alleppey. Trips last from an hour to overnight. For tours exceeding a day, contact in advance. Expect to pay about Rs. 100 per hour per boat.

Cochin (Ernakulam). KTDC (Tourist Reception Center, Shanmugham Rd., Ernakulam, tel. 353234) conducts the following inexpensive deluxe bus and boat tours (bus tours depart from the Tourist Reception Center): *Boat Sightseeing Tour of Cochin.* Two daily three-hour tours; departures 9 A.M. and 2 P.M. from the Boat Jetty in front of Sealord Hotel; Rs. 30. *Cochin–Thekkady.* Two-day weekend bus tour to Periyar Wildlife Sanctuary; departs 7:30 A.M. Saturday and returns Sunday night; Rs. 175, excluding food and accommodation. *Cochin–Velankanni.* Three-day bus tour, including Periyar Wildlife Sanctuary and Tamil Nadu temple cities of Madurai, Tiruchi, and Thanjavur; departs every second Friday and returns Monday morning; Rs. 400, excluding food and accommodation.

KTDC also offers a sunset cruise, which departs from the Sealord Jetty at 5:30 P.M.; Rs. 15. It also offers a backwater cruise (four hours) in an indigenous country boat that travels in tiny canals through hidden villages. The cost is $20 for up to four people to cover vehicular charges to and from the jetty. Contact KTDC one day in advance. Taj Malabar Hotel (see *Accommodations,* above) offers a series of luxurious crusies aboard a yacht for trips from two hours to overnight journeys ($50–$375 per person).

Trivandrum. KTDC (Tourist Reception Center, Station Rd., Thampanoor, tel. 75031) conducts a series of bus tours: *Trivandrum Tour,* full-day tour departs at 8 A.M. except Mondays; Rs. 50. *Kanyakumari Tour* (Cape Comorin) is a full-day trip, starting at 7:30 A.M. daily; Rs. 100. *Ponmudi Tour* (Hill station) departs daily at 7:45 A.M. *Lake Periyar Wildlife Sanctuary* (two-day tour) departs Saturdays 6:30 A.M. on all but the last Saturday of each month; Rs. 50. *Kodaikanal Tour* (Tamil Nadu hill station) is a three-day trip starting 6:30 A.M. on the last Saturday of each month; Rs. 250.

Private Guides. The *Government of India Tourist Office* in Cochin and the *Tourist Information Center* in Trivandrum can supply good guides. For one to four people for four hours, Rs. 65; for eight hours, Rs. 120.

TOUR OPERATORS. The following full-service agencies can handle all your travel needs, including car with driver:

KTDC (addresses above under Tourist Information).

Sita World Travel, M. G. Rd., Cochin; tel. 353012.

Travel Corporation of India, M. G. Rd., Ernakulam, Cochin; tel. 351646.

For special outdoor adventures in Kerala, also check in the listings under Special-Interest Tours in *Facts at Your Fingertips.*

SEASONAL EVENTS. Since the lunar calendar determines most events, contact the Government of India Tourist Office for details.

April/May. *Pooram.* Kerala's most spectacular temple festival takes place in Trichur. Elephants, sporting gorgeous gold-plated mail, carry Brahmans with ceremonial umbrellas and the temple deity, Vadakkunathan (Shiva), in a procession accompanied by the beat of temple drums. Great festivities and fireworks.

August. *Nehru Trophy Boat Race.* On the second Saturday of August, snake boats compete at Alleppey for the Nehru Trophy. Big tourist draw.

August/September. *Onam,* Kerala's biggest festival, celebrates the harvest season. Lasting three days, it features dancing, singing, and exotic snake boat races at Alleppey, Aranmula, and Kottayam. Boats of all descriptions—beak-shaped, kite-tailed, curly-headed—and lots of hoopla!

December/January. *Makaravilakka Festival.* This important Hindu pilgrimage to the Ayyappa Temple at Sabarimala (180 km [112 mi.] northeast of Trivandrum) is held November–January. The procession involves only men and prepubescent and postmenopausal women. The arrival of the devotees, who come from all over India, is supposed to coincide with the conclusion of a 60-day fast. Many just make a five-km trek from the sacred Pampa River.

HISTORIC SITES. Entrance to most places is generally free; where a donation is requested, a few rupees will suffice. Monuments are open sunrise to sunset unless noted otherwise below.

Dutch Palace in Mattancheri (eight km [5 mi.] from Ernakulam) was built by the Portuguese and given to the maharaja in 1555. It's called Dutch because the Dutch later renovated it. The center of the building contains a large coronation hall, and seventeenth-century murals tell the entire story of the *Ramayana.* Three temples are dedicated to Vishnu, Shiva, and Pazhavayannoor Bhagavathi. Open 10 A.M.–5 P.M., closed Fridays.

Cochin Synagogue, Mattancheri, was originally constructed in 1568 and rebuilt in the late 1600s and 1700s after partial destruction. Beautiful Chinese floor tiles—no two alike—were added in 1762 by Ezekiel Rahabi, who also built the clock tower. The Cochin maharaja gave the synagogue the great scrolls of the Old Testament and copper plates. The entire building is a treasure vault. Open 10 A.M.–noon and 3–5 P.M., closed Saturdays.

St. Francis Church, Fort Cochin, was the first European church built in India, constructed in 1510. Vasco da Gama was buried here. You can see his gravestone, but his remains were shipped back to Portgual. Sedate, stark architecture.

Valiapalli, Kottayam, is a ninth-century Syrian church that supposedly contains a cross brought from a church in Kodungalloor (Cranganore) that was established by St. Thomas.

Janardhana Temple, Varkala, 54 km (33 mi.) north of Trivandrum, is claimed to be 2,000 years old. A famous pilgrimage center for Hindus, the temple is dedicated to Vishnu.

MUSEUMS AND GALLERIES. Entrance is usually free or there is a nominal fee. **Trivandrum.** *Napier Museum* and *Chitralayam Art Gallery,* within the Museum

Complex, have eclectic collections of bronzes and Kerala artifacts, and paintings, including Rajput, Mogul, and Far Eastern art. Open 10 A.M.–5 P.M.; closed Mondays.

Cochin. *Parishath Thampuran Museum,* Darbar Hall Rd., Ernakulam. Emphasis here is on archaeology, models of temples, sculptures, and old photography, old paintings, and antiques from the nineteenth century. Open 9:30 A.M.–12:30 P.M. and 3–5:30 P.M., closed Mondays and holidays.

Hill Palace Museum, Tripanithura (13 km or eight mi. south of Cochin), which belonged to the former Cochin maharaja, has royal costumes, coaches, old weapons, and coins, sculptures, and paintings. Open 9 A.M.–5 P.M., closed Mondays.

Kozhikode (Calicut). *Pazhassiraja Museum,* East Hill, five km from Calicut, has copies of ancient mural paintings, antique bronzes, old coins, archaeological findings. Open 10 A.M.–5 P.M., closed Mondays.

SPORTS AND OUTDOOR ADVENTURES. Kerala is just developing its outdoor-adventure possibilities. At press time, KTDC and the Kerala Tourism Department were considering treks, bike trips (some combined with backwater cruises), and boat cruises along the sea. Contact the head offices (see Tourist Information, above) for latest details. **Beaches.** Kerala is aware of its prize beaches—palm-fringed with towering cliffs and coves; but bad zoning policies could destroy their beauty.

Kovalam Beach. 18 km (11 mi.) from Trivandrum. Lovely beaches backed by cliffs; but the "hippies" and their drugs have also made this beach their home.

Lakshadweep. The one island open to foreigners in this gorgeous archipelago with lagoons and coral reefs requires a permit and an expensive yet delightful stay at the one resort (see Accommodations, above). It's an ideal place for swimming, boating, and snorkeling.

Golf. You can golf at the *Trivandrum Golf Club.* Equipment is available. Call 68034 for details.

Wildlife Sanctuaries. *Lake Periyar Wildlife Sanctuary* surrounds a large artificial lake. Inexpensive boat trips are available, but fellow passengers tend to squeal at the slightest sign of distant movement. Splurge and get a boat for yourself (Rs. 200). You can see elephants, maybe leopards, tigers, langur, wild boar, deer, and numerous birds. You can also hire a guide and hike; there are lookouts to climb. Best time to visit is October–May. For hiking information, contact the Divisional Forest Officer, Thekkady 685536; tel. 2027.

Parambikulam Wildlife Sanctuary is set around three dams, 48 km (30 mi.) from Pollachi northeast of Trichur. Elephants, tigers, deer, gaur, otters, bears, and crocodiles abound. For details about forest-rest-house accommodations, contact the Divisional Forest Officer, Thunakkadavu, P.O. Parambikulam, Palkat Dist.; tel. 23.

SHOPPING. In Kerala, you can buy wonderful handicrafts in natural fibers (palm, screw pine, banana leaf, bamboo) as well as sandalwood and rosewood products, great papier-mâché masks, brass-bell metalwork, and, in Cochin and Trivandrum, old curios.

Cochin. *Kairali* (M. G. Road, Ernakulam), a government-run shop, has a good collection of Kerala handicrafts and curios. Open 9 A.M.–8 P.M., closed Sundays. AE, DC, MC, V.

Surabhi (M. G. Road, Ernakulam), run by the state's Handicrafts Cooperative Society, also has a good selection of locally made products. Open 9:30 A.M.–1:30 P.M. and 3:30–7:30 P.M., closed Sundays. Rupees only.

Indian Arts and Curios (Jew Town) is the oldest and most reliable shop on this curios- and antiques-laden street. The shop has two outlets, each filled with brass and wood items and Tanjore glass paintings. Open 8:30 A.M.–5:30 P.M. AE, MC, V. Also visit *Monalisa.* Open 9:30 A.M.–5 P.M. MC, V. Bargain. In all the shops in this area, buy what you like, but not for investment. Often "old" means no more than 24 hours old.

Trivandrum. *Natesan's Antiquarts* (M. G. Rd. and Kovalam Ashok Beach Resort) sells lovely old and new curios, including statues and paintings from South India. Extremely reliable. Open 10 A.M.–8 P.M., closed Sundays. AE, DC, MC, V.

Lawrence Handicrafts (M. G. Rd. and Kovalam Ashok Beach Resort) sells a similar range of curios. Open 10 A.M.–7 P.M., closed Sundays. AE, V.

Gifts Corner (M. G. Rd.) is a great place to poke around for old and new curios. They also have two warehouses that they'll take you to visit. Open 10 A.M.–8 P.M., closed Sundays. AE, MC, V.

S.M.S.M. Institute (Central Handicrafts Emporium, Puthenchanthai, behind the Secretariat) sells good Kerala curios. Open 9 A.M.–8 P.M., closed Sundays. AE, DC, MC, V.

Kottayam. Make a 40 km (25 mi.) excursion to Aranmula, via Chenannur, and visit the *Viswatharathy Handicrafts Center.* This is one of the only family-operated places still creating metal mirror products, an unfortunately dying art form, which turns bronze into mirror. You can buy exquisite compacts, hand mirrors, and other items at reasonable prices. The best selection is available November–January. Open daily 10 A.M.–8:30 P.M. Rupees only.

ENTERTAINMENT. A trip to Kerala must include seeing a performance of the Kathakali dance form. *Katha* means "story"; *kali* means "play," and that's what you see: a story/dance form over 400 years old—Indian pantomime performed in painted face and with great costumes. The performers start training at a very young age, learning how to control every muscle in their bodies and toes. Traditional performances can run for hours; but you can see an abridged version and a demonstration of the intricate application of the makeup. These shows are wonderful, even for the young. Call for reservations and details.

Cochin. *Art Kerala,* Chittoor Rd., Ernakulam, tel. 366238. Daily performance is 7–8:30 P.M. *Cochin Cultural Center,* Manicketh Rd., Ernakulam; tel. 367866. Daily 6:30–8 P.M. *Gurnkulam Kathakali Yogam,* Kalathiparambil Lane, Ernakulam; tel. 369471. This delightful theater has daily shows from 7–8:30 P.M. *Indian Performing Art Center,* Bolgatty Palace; tel. 355003. Daily 6:30 P.M.–8 P.M. You can also watch performances of Kerala's traditional martial art form, Kalari Payat, at *Arjuna Kalari Samgham;* tel. 360980. Daily 5 A.M.–9 A.M. and 5 P.M.–9 P.M..

Trivandrum. At *Trivandrum Kathakali Club, Drisyavedi,* and *Margi,* regular Kathakali programs are organized. Inquire at the Tourist Information Center for details. On Saturday at 7 P.M. October–March), the Department of Tourism sponsors free classical Indian dance performances at the Nishagandhi Theater (Kanakakunnu Palace, Museum Rd.).

Bars. The best bars are in the better hotels. KTDC has inexpensive beer parlors in major tourist destinations where you can enjoy beer at a discount. All drinking establishments are generally open 10 A.M.–10 P.M.

GOA

Tropical Gold Coast

by
KATHLEEN COX

If you think every paradise in the world is first discovered then ruined by the discoverers, go to Goa. No bigger than a thumbprint on the Malabar Coast map, this former Portuguese territory—the home of about 1 million easygoing, hospitable people, both Hindu and Christians—is in India but not entirely of it.

The climate and scenery are resort perfect. With the exception of the monsoon season (June to September), which affects most of India, the temperature and weather stay high and dry. Most who visit Goa dream of becoming marooned in a charming village where the silvery sands of some of the world's most beautiful beaches are never more than a few steps away. The palm-bordered rivers move wide and lazily down to the Arabian Sea, while the towns are a pleasing blend of Portuguese and Indian. Houses gleam with a light wash of color set off by brightly painted pillared front porches and trim. Goa appears to be the epitome of well-cared-for tropical suburbia.

In the not-too-distant past, Goa was like an Asian Tangiers, with connections to Europe as well as the East. A constant flow of European products (legal and illegal) were uncrated in Goa's ports. Yet after four centuries of heavy-handed Portuguese Catholicism, somehow only about 30 percent of the people became Christian. It also seems that the somewhat

GOA

0 miles	5	10	15	20	
0 km	5	10	15	20	25	30

◉ Temple ◻ Fort ✝ Church ▽ Bathing Beach

MAHARASHTRA

from Ratnagiri

Terekhol River

Pernem

Chapara River

Macasana

Sinquirvale

Colvale

Assonora

Chorlem

Parvar

Vagator Beach ▽

Cunchelim

Mapusa ✝

Bicholim ◉

Gonteli

Tanem

Queigate

Pandava Caves

Aravalem Waterfalls

Onda

Baga Beach ▽

Calangute Beach

Betim

Old Goa

Valpoi

Caranzol

Fort Aguada Beach ▽

Birondem

from Belgaum

Gaspar Diaz Beach ▽

PANAJI ◉

✝

Agassaim

Mangest

Bamboi

Dona Paula Beach

Sancordem

from Black Rock

Mormugao

Vasco da Gama

Cortalim

Ponda

Durbat

Molem

DABOLIM AIRPORT ☆

Ambora

olem

Dudhsagar Waterfall

Kalay

Margao

Sanvordem

Sanguem

Digui

Colva Beach ▽

Quepem

Viliena

Matto

Rivona

Galiem

Cupa

Cabo da Rama ▽

Netorlim

Chauri

Shri Math

Cotigao

Maxem

Polem

to Karwar

to Cochin

ARABIAN SEA

KARNATAKA

puritan atmosphere of India proper had trouble penetrating the borders. So most Goans remained much more liberated and better off materially than did their neighbors in the rest of India.

The Portuguese were entrenched in Goa for 451 years, but they were ousted by India in a quick, nearly bloodless operation in 1961—leaving behind a ghost town studded with Baroque churches and a thriving if artificial, economy. Today Goa has changed. There are now many more schools, doctors, ever-present cows, the great novelty of a free press, free elections, and the pride of self-rule in a democracy.

Naturally, the Goans have suffered growing pains. Chief among them is the complicated and tedious unraveling of the colonial economy. Goa struggles to produce enough food to feed itself, and some whitewashed villages are almost deserted, with many able-bodied men seeking work in Bombay. But iron mines produce high-grade ore for export; delicious tinned prawns and shrimp sail off to the supermarkets; and conscientious agrarian and environmental planning is beginning to pay off with the occasional model farm and forward-thinking reforestation project. Although tourism also plays a growing role in reviving the economy, the state seriously attempts to keep an eye on Goa's beauty, holding back hoteliers who see rupee signs in architectural plans for mammoth resort monstrosities that would destroy the quaint, peaceful charm.

A lively and unfortunately volatile topic among Goans is language: Should they speak Konkani, the traditional tongue, or Marathi, spoken next door, which would pave the way for absorption by the larger, more powerful Maharashtra? Goans are fiercely loyal to their state (there are more than 300 Goan village clubs in Bombay); India takes second place in their hearts.

A Historic Review

Early Goan history is a hazy maze of Hindu dynasties and subdynasties until the Middle Ages, when the Hindus stopped fighting each other and banded together to fight off the Moslems. Suddenly, everyone wanted a foothold on the Malabar Coast—the great source of spices and the important link in the Arabian trade routes. The Portuguese were the first Europeans to appear on the scene. Alfonso de Albuquerque arrived in 1510, fighting until he controlled the coast and had established a formidable and wealthy trading power. Silks and spices, porcelains and pearls, passed in and out of Goa's harbors until she rivaled Lisbon itself. "Golden Goa" was well known to the rest of the world.

Thirty years after Albuquerque came the most famous figure in Goan history, seeking not spices but souls: St. Francis Xavier. Born in a Spanish castle, and a doctor at the University of Paris, Francis left for Goa with a new title—apostolic nuncio to the East—when the king of Portugal requested missionaries for his overseas territories. With no possessions but a breviary and a crucifix, Francis transformed Goa by his preaching and his example before moving on to more distant lands. Ten years later, he died on the threshold of China, but his body was eventually returned to Goa, where it can be seen in a state of eerie quasipreservation in the Bom Jesus Basilica.

At the end of the sixteenth century, life turned precarious for the Portuguese. They had to fight off newcomers, of which there were many—Hindu, Moslem, Dutch, and British. By 1750, the proud Baroque capital of Velha Goa (Old Goa) was battle scarred and plague ridden, so the population moved downriver to Panaji. The Portuguese methods of rule degenerated as badly as did the buildings, with Goans suffering from the

Inquisition, set up after Francis Xavier's death. This horrendous tool of injustice finally gave up the ghost in 1812. And the viceroyship, which was a political plus that enriched its possessor, did little for the Goans. Throughout the nineteenth and early twentieth centuries abortive revolts sprang up—fragile sparks of rebellion that were ruthlessly quelled by the Portuguese. In December 1961, India put a stop to what from her point of view was an intolerable situation. Operation Vijaya brought Goa back to India after a 451-year absence.

Daman and Diu, two other Portuguese vest-pocket enclaves, fell to India at the same time. Daman (56 square kilometers, or 22 square miles), north of Bombay, and Diu (38 square kilometers, or 15 square miles), across the Gulf of Cambay, share Goa's character, religions, and rural pursuits.

EXPLORING GOA

If you're in Goa, it's partially for the sun, sand, and surf; Goa has 132 kilometers (82 miles) of coastline plus deep river estuaries, so you'll have quite a choice of public beaches. Closest to Panaji, the capital, are Miramar (Gaspar Dias) and Dona Paula beaches. At Miramar, closer of the two, the swimming is marred by a strong undertow and the view is marred by an unfortunate stretch of architectural eyesores. The Dona Paula Beach is palm fringed and commands a fine view of the Mormugao Harbor. Across the Mandovi River from Panaji is gorgeous Calangute Beach. This "queen of Goan beaches" is 16 kilometers (18 miles) in length, with Baga, Anjuna, then Vagator, cloistered in dramatic rocks and cliffs—a spectacular place to watch the sun disappear over the water. Another good public beach is the Colva, on the south coast near Margao. Here the nomadic Lambanis, who travel the western states of India, set up shop on portable blankets cluttered with great handicrafts, jewelry, embroideries, and quilts.

Panaji, a pleasant whitewashed city, was only a sleepy village before the Portuguese transferred their capital closer to shore. The most important monument dating from the precapital days is the Secretariat Building—once a Moslem palace, then a Portuguese fort. Near the building stands the statue of the Abbé Faria, priest and hypnotist, portrayed in the act of mesmerizing a female patient. The best view of Panaji is from the Church of Our Lady of the Immaculate Conception or, if you're lucky, from the Portuguese-style villa of a Goan host who happens to live on the hillside. You can also get a good sense of Panaji from the banks of the wide Mandovi, where slow-sailing craft journey up and down the gray water.

The scenery around the capital is lush, with rice paddies, palms, groves of mango, and jackfruit. But plan for a leisurely pace, because of the number of linking ferries, usually crowded but still offering an easygoing, enjoyable ride. One easy excursion is to Velha Goa. The sixteenth-century Portuguese capital is a study in splendor and decay. Go by boat if you can, so that after you disembark you can drive or walk through the Viceregal Arch, as each viceroy had to do before taking possession of his office. This arch, where Vasco da Gama gazes out from his niche in full regalia, was the symbolic entry to the city, as well as the gateway from the harbor.

The tiny city was once the greatest commercial center east of Suez, rivaling Lisbon in grandeur. "Whoever has seen Goa, need not see Lisbon" was no careless boast. Now the great square, the site of the trials of the Inquisition, is little better than a neglected field.

The following is a convenient order for a tour of Velha Goa:

St. Cajetan, an Italian and contemporary of St. Francis Xavier, lent his name to this handsome church and convent of the Theatin Order. Constructed in the seventeenth century, the church was modeled after St. Peter's Basilica in Rome. The facade is neoclassic, with twin towers flanking the great dome, but the interior decoration is pure, unrestrained baroque. The main altar soars nearly to the top of the edifice, the patron saint's altar is adorned with twisted columns, and the pulpit is an exercise in delicate carving. A large arched window, whose tiny panes are made of seashells, is interesting. In the crypt are the tombs of generations of Portuguese rulers.

Another curious feature is the tank, or well, located beneath the raised platform, the present site of the altar. Its presence has led many to believe that this was the site of a temple tank, meaning that this church replaced a former Hindu shrine. Many of the paintings that adorn the walls were brought from Europe in the fifteenth century; others were done locally.

The Se Cathedral, the largest church in Velha Goa, is an imposing white structure constructed between 1562 and 1652. Unfortunately, its facade became lopsided after the collapse of the north tower in 1776. The cathedral's tiny congregation seems out of proportion to its 71-meter (230-foot) length and the magnificence of its decoration. The bell in the existing tower is referred to as the "Golden Bell" because of its rich tone, immortalized in a Portuguese poem. Notice also the Chapel of the Blessed Sacrament, the third chapel on your left as you face the altar. The closed blue doors combine three schools of art: the bottom panel is characteristically Hindu, the middle panel is Moslem, and the top panel below the arch is Greek. The main altar, dedicated to St. Catherine, is simple in shape, with classical arches and Corinthian columns; richly gilded scenes in deep relief portray episodes in the saint's martyrdom. In the left nave are the chapels of St. Joseph, ornamented on every possible surface, St. George, and Our Lady of Necessity.

On the right is the chapel of the Holy Spirit, with its lovely altarpiece showing Mary surrounded by the black-bearded apostles on the day of Pentecost. Other chapels on this side are dedicated to St. Bernard, St. Anthony, and the Holy Cross. Almost hidden in this last chapel in the Mauresque style is a cross on which a vision of Christ is said to have appeared in 1919.

St. Francis of Assisi Church and Convent (built in 1661) is easily the best example of Portuguese religious art in Old Goa. The Franciscan Order was the first to arrive in Goa, even though nearly everyone thinks of Francis Xavier and the more spectacular results of the Jesuits in connection with Goa. True to the humility of their founder, the Franciscans went straight to the poor and downtrodden, whereas the Jesuits allied themselves with the resident Brahmans. The Franciscan church is simple and handsome, spacious and harmonious. The portal is pure Manueline style; inside, this theme is developed in rich stucco ceilings and a profusion of carvings. High above the main altar, a crucified Christ is shown with his right arm detached from the cross in order to embrace St. Francis. In the convent next door, visit the museum and gallery, with portraits of 16 Franciscan martyrs.

The Chapel of St. Catherine is an endearing little Renaissance church, one of the first erected by Albuquerque in 1510 to celebrate his arrival in Velha Goa on St. Catherine's Day.

The Bom Jesus Basilica took 10 years to build and is a striking example of Jesuit architecture. The interior is perhaps the richest of the churches in Old Goa, highly and heavily decorated, yet admirably proportioned. Built in the sixteenth century, the basilica is sacred to the Infant Jesus, but the infant's statue is dwarfed by that of Ignatius of Loyala, founder of the order of Jesuits, which stands above the gilded high altar.

Most will visit Bom Jesus not for its size or its style but for the relic on display. Here, in a splendor he constantly refused during his lifetime, lies the body of St. Francis Xavier. The body traveled after death almost as much as the saint had done in life, but in spite of each transfer (at least four) to this final resting place, the body resisted damage. Indeed, the deceased Francis suffered more from piety than from anything else—both of his big toes were bitten off by female fanatics and an arm was severed at the request of a pope and carried off to Rome.

St. Francis owes his opulent casket to the generosity of the duke of Tuscany, who received the saint's pillow as a relic and sent the Florentine tomb in exchange. The entire chapel is covered with marble, inlaid with semiprecious stones, and decorated with paintings portraying the life of the saint. In recent years, the casket was cut open. Now, the curious or the worshiping can have a grisly glimpse of the head and shoulders of Francis.

Walk up the road from Bom Jesus to the Monte Santo or Holy Hill. Here you can see a number of other remnants of Portuguese glory. The most interesting is the Convent and Church of Santa Monica, which once housed more than 100 nuns, then slowly dwindled in importance until the last nun died in 1885. The church is refreshingly simple, in the Doric style, and contains a supposedly miraculous cross in one chapel. Its building is massive, more like a fortress than a nunnery.

Also on the Monte Santo are other churches, most of them ruined; and, on a less saintly level, a black stone whipping post where prisoners were given the Portuguese third degree. The best preserved of the group of churches is the little chapel of St. Anthony. Because St. Anthony is the patron saint of soldiers, the saint's image used to receive an annual salary from the commander of the army. One ill-advised general, who considered this a wasteful expense, cut off the payment. He died from a fall on the saint's feast day. The next general restored Anthony's stipend.

Despite the number of Christian churches, Goa is 68 percent Hindu and just 30 percent Christian. If there are few temples in proportion to the Hindu population, it's partially because the first wave of Portuguese destroyed them. The temples were rebuilt, but inland, at a safe distance from the foreign colonizers. In and around Ponda, there are seven temples within a five-kilometer (three-mile) radius. The most interesting is the small but lovely Shri Manguesh, set on a lush green hill. Dedicated to Shiva, the temple has an air of tropical elegance, with its blue pillars, tiles on the wall, old locally made crystal chandeliers, and large silver idols. The special Shri Mahadeva at Tambdi Surla, 66 kilometers (41 miles) from Panaji, in the foot of the ghats is the only example of Kadamba temple architecture (the Kadambas ruled from the eleventh to the thirteenth century) remaining in Goa. Built of basalt stone, the temple is in a tranquil setting on a riverbank and site on a simple plinth with intricately carved pillars in the *mandapa* (pavilion). There is no use of mortar anywhere in the structure—stone is hammered into stone.

Dozens of mosques once dotted the countryside, but the Portuguese, who showed no favoritism, pursued their policy of destruction and quickly demolished them. The only remaining mosque of any historic importance dates from 1560 and is known as the Safa Shahouri Masjid, built by Ibrahim Adilshah of Bijapur. Unfortunately, an extensive garden with fountains that surrounded the mosque succumbed to the wrath of the marauding Portuguese.

Today, Old Goan homes are splendid sites, both inside and out. Some of them are open to the public. Contact the Government of India Tourist Office when you arrive.

PRACTICAL INFORMATION FOR GOA

WHEN TO GO. Goa can be lovely during the monsoon season from June to September. There are periodic downpours, but Goa will be tropically lush. Otherwise, temperatures average 79°F. December, January, and February are great (a light wool sweater might be good to have in the evening). Because of various festivals, Goa is very crowded from December to February. Book accommodations well ahead.

HOW TO GET THERE. By Air. *Indian Airlines* has daily flights into Goa from Bombay, Delhi, and Cochin. It has four weekly flights from Bangalore and Madras and two weekly flights from Ahmedabad. *Vayudoot* has three weekly flights from Pune, Hyderabad, and Bombay. For information in Goa, contact Indian Airlines (tel. 43826) and Alcon (tel. 45197) for Vayudoot.

By Bus. Buses can get you to Goa, but they're usually crowded.

The *Kadamba Transport Corporation Ltd.* (KTC, a government of Goa undertaking), the *Karnataka State Road Transport Corporation* (KSRTC), *Maharashtra State Road Transport Corporation* (MSRTC), *Maharashtra Tourism Development Corporation,* and numerous private buses can take you to and from the major destinations. Consult the appropriate chapter for details. In Panaji, Goa, contact KTC Bus Terminus, tel. 43334; KSRTC Bus Terminus, tel. 45126; and MSRTC Bus Complex, tel. 44363.

By Hired Car with Driver. Most drives from the major cities—Bangalore, Bombay, Mangalore, and Mysore—are long trips. Although the roads are good (by Indian standards), they are unlit and narrow. Rates are about Rs. 4.50 per km, with a halt charge of Rs. 50–Rs. 100 per night. Make arrangements before you depart with one of the agencies listed below under Tour Operators.

By Train. The train is more complicated to take than the bus and goes slower. However, long-distance trains do provide an alternative to planes, and by traveling on the ground you see more. From Bangalore, you can take the *Vasco Mail* (a direct train), the *Kittun Express* or *Mandovi Express,* all of which involve a change of trains. From Delhi, you can take the *Jhelum Express, Sahyadri Express,* or *Mandovi Express.* From Bombay, take the *Miraj Express, Gomantak Express, Sahyadri Express,* or *Mandovi Express.*

TOURIST INFORMATION. Goa is a well-organized state when it comes to tourism. The *Government of India Tourist Office* has information on almost every topic of interest to the traveler. *Goa Tourist Directory,* a free brochure published by the Goa Tourist Department, supplies basic information about what to do and minimal information on sights to see in Goa. Here's a list of department offices:

Main offices. Government of India Tourist Office, Communidade Bldg., Church Sq., Panaji 403001; tel. 43412. Open Monday–Friday, 8:30 A.M.–6 P.M. and Saturday, 8:30 A.M.–1 P.M. Directorate of Tourism, Government of Goa, Tourist Home, Pato Bridge, Panaji 403001; tel. 45715. Open 9:30 A.M.–5:45 P.M., closed Saturdays and Sundays.

Dabolim Airport. Tourist Information Center; tel. 42644. Open during plane arrivals.

Interstate Bus Terminus. Tourist Information Counter, No. 5; tel. 45620. Open 9:30 A.M.–4 P.M., closed Sundays.

Margao. Tourist Information Center, Tourist Hostel; tel. 225134. Open 10 A.M.–5:30 P.M., closed Sundays.

Vasco da Gama. Tourist Information Center, Tourist Hostel; tel. 2673. Open 9:30 A.M.–5 P.M., closed Sundays.

FOREIGN CURRENCY EXCHANGE. Most Western-style hotels have money-exchange counters. There's a *State Bank of India* opposite Hotel Mandovi, Panaji, and a branch in Calangute, Mapusa, Margao, and Vasco da Gama. Hours are Monday–Friday, 10 A.M.–2 P.M., and Saturday till noon.

ACCOMMODATIONS. Goa has a great assortment of beach resorts to fit all budgets. Some of the best accommodations in terms of seclusion and ambience are extremely low priced. Most hotels also offer discounts after the peak season (December–January). Inquire when you book. During the peak season, you must book you room months in advance. Prices are based on double occupancy and exclude taxes and service charges: *Deluxe,* over Rs. 2,000; *Expensive,* Rs. 1,200–Rs. 2,000; *Moderate,* Rs. 500–Rs. 1,200; *Inexpensive,* under Rs. 500. Most Western-style hotels take major credit cards.

Deluxe

Majorda Beach Resort. Majorda, Salcette 403713; tel. 20266, fax 20212. 120 rooms with bath. Facing Majorda Beach, this resort with a modern Portuguese influence offers air-conditioned rooms in its main redstone building that are spacious, with cane furnishings and seaside verandas. Best rooms are upstairs, with garden and ocean views. You can also stay in villas (up to four units per villa) that have a similar decor, plus a veranda or porch. Best rooms face a well-landscaped garden. TV, room service, multicuisine restaurants, bar, baby-sitters, two swimming pools, tennis, windsurfing, water scooter, health club, foreign-exchange and travel counter, doctor, shopping arcade, airport shuttle service. AE, DC, MC, V.

Oberoi Bogmalo Beach. Bogmalo 403806; tel. 2191, fax 2510. 121 rooms with bath. This high rise has an elegant open-air lobby with refreshing tropical breezes. Air-conditioned rooms have rough stucco white walls, handsome furnishings, and individual sea-facing verandas with cane swings. Multicuisine restaurants, TV, room service, bar, health club, swimming pool, speedboats, water scooters, windsurfing, waterskiing, para-sailing, tennis, tour arrangements, foreign-exchange and travel counter, shopping arcade, airport shuttle service. AE, DC, MC, V.

Ramada Renaissance Resort. Colva Beach, Varca Village, Salcette 403713; tel. 5200, fax 5225. 128 rooms with bath. Near the beach, this new resort, with a large lobby, offers rooms in its main building and in its villas (two units per villa). Ask for a sea view if that's your preference. Rooms are sleek and modern, with Indian artifacts. TV, air-conditioning, room service, multicuisine restaurants, bar, swimming pool, six-hole golf course, tennis courts, water sports, health club, jogging track, business center, foreign-exchange and travel counter, shopping arcade. AE, DC, MC, V.

The Leela Beach Goa. Cavelossim, Salcette 403731; tel. 6363, fax 6352. 164 rooms with bath. Adjacent to a beach, this posh resort has peach-hued villas (four units per villa) on 60 acres, with lagoons that are crossed by bridges. Its vast lobby, with lots of marble, has a water channel that flows around the exterior. Squawking geese parade around the landscaped grounds. Rooms, with verandas overlooking the lagoon, are large and have contemporary furnishings. TV, air-conditioning, room service, multicuisine restaurants, bars, gigantic swimming pool, tennis and squash courts, jogging track, health club, outdoor amphitheater, business center, foreign-exchange and travel counter, baby-sitters, doctor, shopping arcade, airport shuttle service. Extremely deluxe. AE, DC, MC, V.

Taj Aguada Hermitage. Sinquerim, Bardez 403515; tel. 87501, fax 7733. 15 rooms with bath. This secluded resort, a cluster of Goan-style, air-conditioned villas, is set on a hill overlooking Sinquerim Beach. Each unit offers individual veranda and garden and a modernized Goan interior in the living room, adjoining dining area, and bedroom. A regular car service shuttles you to their nearby Taj Fort Aguada Beach Resort, which offers numerous amenities (see below). AE, DC, MC, V.

Taj Fort Aguada Beach Resort. Sinquerim, Bardez 403519; tel. 87501, fax 7733. 130 rooms with bath. Built within the ramparts of a seventeenth-century fort, the hotel consists of a posh main building with contempory-style rooms with views of the nearby ocean, and intimate, tile-roofed cottages (two units per cottage) that offer more privacy. Air-conditioning, TV, room service, multicuisine restaurants, bar, foreign-exchange and travel counter, doctor, baby-sitters, shopping arcade, swimming pool, health club, tennis, sailing, waterskiing, windsurfing, boating, parasailing, airport shuttle service. AE, DC, MC, V.

Taj Holiday Village. Sinquerim, Bardez 403519; tel. 832/87514, fax 832/7733. 144 rooms with bath. Designed like a ritzy Goan village, this delightful tropical resort features tile-roofed cottages scattered around gardens and extensive lawns that face Sinquerim Beach. Air-conditioned and non–air-conditioned rooms have a modern decor. Multicuisine restaurants, TV, room service, bars, baby-sitters, foreign-exchange and travel counter, tours, tennis, squash, volleyball, waterskiing, para-sailing, windsurfing, boating, health club, airport shuttle service. AE, DC, MC, V.

Expensive

Averina Beach Resort. Mobor, Cavelossim 8342/403731; tel. 6303, fax 8342/23815. 144 rooms with bath. A new resort, it has an open-air lobby with cane furniture and many plants. Rooms, with modern furnishings and verandas, offer a partial sea view. TV, air-conditioning, room service, multicuisine restaurants, bar, swimming pool, health club, beach, foreign-exchange and travel counter, tours, shopping arcade. DC, MC, V.

Moderate–Expensive

Comfort Inn Whispering Palms Beach Resort. Candolim Beach, Bardez 403515; tel. 8324/6140, fax 8324/3231. 54 rooms with bath. A small resort with an intimate lobby, it has good-size modern rooms with balconies in eight blocks of two-story cottages. Upper floors offer the best sea views. The beach is a short walk away. TV, air-conditioning, room service, multicuisine restaurants, bar, foreign-exchange counter, swimming pool, airport shuttle service. AE, DC, MC, V.

Dona Sylvia. Cavelossim Beach, Salcete 403731; tel. 832/6321, fax 832/3231. 140 rooms with bath. Another new resort set near a beach, it features a cluster of cottages (two or four rooms per unit) and an open lobby with tropical cane furnishings. Rooms, with verandas, are done up in a slightly nautical theme and have a modern decor. Some rooms are air-conditioned. Rooms on the upper floor have a sea view. Fans, room service, multicuisine restaurants, bar, swimming pool, foreign-exchange and travel counter, shops, airport shuttle service. AE, DC, MC, V.

Moderate

Prainha Cottages by the Sea. Dona Paula Beach 403004; tel. 832/4004, fax 832/3433. 27 rooms with bath. This complex, set in a palm-backed harbor facing the beach, offers a peaceful ambience. Stay in the main building or in a room in a row of attached two-story cottages. Immaculately clean, air-conditioned rooms have tiled floors, a streamlined modern decor, and a veranda. Best rooms are on the upper floors. Multicuisine restaurant, room service, bar, baby-sitters, doctor, foreign-exchange counter, tour arrangements; car, motorcycle, and bike rentals. DC, MC, V.

Vagator Beach Resort. Vagator, Bardez 403522; tel. Siolim 241. 83 rooms with bath. Secluded and very moderately priced, this Goan-style complex offers two options. Nestled in a palm grove facing the beach, brick and tile-roofed cottages (two units per cottage) have a private veranda and simple, clean furnishings. Chapora Fort cottages, set on a hill and a short walk to the beach, offer similar furnishings, private porches or veranda, and sweeping views. Multicuisine restaurants, bars, room service, swimming pool at Chapora Fort, lovely gardens, foreign-exchange counter, taxi service, boutique, surfboards. Good value. Rupees only.

Inexpensive

Estrela Do Mar Beach Resort. Cobrawado, Calangute, Baga 403516; tel. 6014. 12 rooms with bath. If you want seclusion and beautiful gardens within walking distance of a beach, stay here. The main bungalow is especially charming, with a red and yellow exterior. Best rooms offer ocean views. All rooms are simply decorated and have ceiling fans and private verandas. Open-air multicuisine restaurant, room service, bar, bike rentals. Rupees only.

DINING OUT. Portuguese dishes have been adapted with a Goan zest: a healthy pinch of red chili tempered with coconut milk. Sample Goa's excellent seafood—like pomfret *recheiado* in a red or green sauce or tiger prawns *baffad* (spicy Goan style). Try squid, sardines, and stuffed fried oysters. Also, try *Feni,* the local brew, but watch out! It packs a punch. Prices depend on what you choose to eat. Shrimp is expensive; other fish dishes are not.

While we include only the best options, many accommodations listed above also have restaurants. Breakfast is usually 7:30–10; lunch, noon–3; dinner, 7:30–10. Payment is normally in rupees only unless the restaurant is connected to a Western-style hotel. The restaurants listed below are informal and, unless noted, are open for all three meals and don't require reservations. Prices are based on one person eating a three-course meal, excluding taxes, tip, or beverage: *Deluxe,* over Rs. 300; *Expensive,* Rs. 200–Rs. 300; *Moderate,* Rs. 100–Rs. 200; *Inexpensive,* under Rs. 100.

Expensive

Banyan Tree. Taj Holiday Village, Sinquerim, Bardez; tel. 87514. You'll walk over a small footbridge to enter this Thai-style restaurant, where you can eat on the tile-covered veranda or inside an air-conditioned Thai-decor central room. Subdued lighting and taped Thai music accompany the Thai and Chinese cuisines. Specialties include *gari goong* (prawns cooked in green curry) and *padd Thai* (noodles tossed with bean sprouts and garnished with peanuts). Open 12:30–2:45 P.M. and 7:30–10:30 P.M. Dinner reservations advised. AE, DC, MC, V.

Casa Portuguese Restaurant and Bar. Baga, Bardez; no phone. This lovely old Portuguese-Goan home with whitewashed walls, vaulted ceilings, elegant dark-wood trim, and hand-carved wooden chairs serves tasty Goan and Portuguese dishes. The ambience is romantic, with softly lit wall sconces and a guitarist who serenades at night. Try *peixe em alhos* (catch-of-the-day fish grilled in garlic), *postas de salmao* (fried salmon), or the daily special. You can also eat on the veranda or in the garden. Open 6:30–11:30 P.M., closed second day of each month. Rupees only.

Haystack. Arpora, Bardez; no phone. Set in a simple stucco building with a tile roof, this restaurant serves a great Goan buffet, or you can order à la carte selections. Expect a crowd and a great ambience, with Goan dances and music. Open only Friday nights 7–midnight. Rupees only.

The Only Place. Carmona; no phone. On Saturday night, eat inside an old Goan home and choose from a buffet that includes Goan and Portuguese dishes, then watch Goan folk dances performed outside. The rest of the week, eat outside by candlelight under mango trees and select from a menu that changes frequently. Open November–May, 7 P.M.–11 P.M. Rupees only.

Moderate

Coconut Inn. Candolim, next to Shanta Durga Temple; tel. 6169. This Goan house, now a restaurant, is nestled in palm trees and lush green gardens. Eat on a softly lit veranda surrounded by antiques or in a garden with lovely Indian statues. The chef serves Goan- and Continental-style dishes, including fresh seafood. Its menu changes frequently. Open 8 A.M.–12 P.M. and 6–11 P.M. Rupees only.

O Pescador Restaurant. Dona Paula; tel. 4255. Overlooking Dona Paula Bay, this restaurant serves good Polynesian food. The interior room has a simple decor, with the emphasis on the views. You can also eat outside. Try their popular creamed-prawn curry or *bandu lagoon* prawns (prawns in the shell cooked in a spicy sauce). Open noon–3 P.M. and 7–11 P.M. Rupees only.

Inexpensive

Martin's Beach Corner. Caranzalem Beach; tel. 4357. Don't leave Goa without enjoying at least one meal at this place. You won't find better seafood or prices. The owner, Martin, is the chef, and his restaurant is Goan simple—three thatched huts overlooking the beach. You name the dish, he'll prepare it. His fried mussels are exquisite, as are the crab chili fry and the tiger prawns. If your hotel tells you that Martin's is closed, don't believe it. Hotels are jealous of his popularity and prices. Dinner reservations advised. Open 11 A.M.–3 P.M. and 7–11 P.M. Rupees only.

SWEETS AND TREATS. For delicious sweets, go to *A Pastelaria,* Mandovi Hotel, Panaji. Sample the cashew nut slices, chocolate walnut roll, or Goan *bebinca* (cake made with coconut juice and eggs). Open 9 A.M.–9 P.M.

HOW TO GET AROUND. From the Airport. Dabolim Airport is 29 km (18 mi.) from Panaji. Many hotels offer free shuttle service. The airport coach to Panjim costs Rs. 15 and runs frequently. Taxis cost Rs. 150 to Panjim. Once you're in Goa, take advantage of the state's greatest natural resource: water.

By Ferry. Until the new bridge opens in 1993, free ferries cross the Mandovi River between Panaji and Betim. They're usually crowded and slow paced, but picturesque and relaxing. Most of these ferries also carry cars for a nominal charge.

By Bus. KTC buses run between the main towns. In Panjim, call 43334.

By Taxi. Yellow-topped, metered taxis are available in most central areas and from most hotels. Figure about Rs. 4.50 for the first km; Rs. 3.50 per additional km.

By Tourist Taxi. Luxury cars can be hired from most hotels or from tour operators listed below. Figure about Rs. 4 per km.

By Auto Rickshaw. Goa also has the metered auto rickshaw. Fare: about Rs. 2.50 for the first km; Rs. 2 per additional km.

By Motorcycle Taxi. Unique to Goa, this transportation is perfect for the solo traveler. Rate: Rs. 5 for 3 km in the cities. To go to distant villages, you must negotiate, especially if the driver has to return without a fare.

TOURS. The *Goa Tourism Development Corporation* (GTDC) conducts inexpensive deluxe-bus sightseeing tours. For reservations, contact the head office, Trionara Apt., Panaji, tel. 46515, or its counters at the tourist hostels in Panaji, Margao, Vasco, Mapusa, Calangute, Colva, and Farmagudi.

North Goa Tour. Daily 9 A.M.–6 P.M. from Panaji. Rs. 45.

South Goa Tour. Daily 9:30 A.M.–6 P.M. from Panaji. Also departs daily from Tourist Hostels in Mapusa and Calangute at 8:30 A.M. Rs. 45.

GTDC also conducts wonderful hour-long **boat cruises** with cultural programs on Mandovi River. All cruises start from the Steamer Jetty: *Sunset Cruise* at 6 (Rs. 50); *Sundown Cruise* at 7:15 (Rs. 50); *Full Moon Cruise* at 8:30–10:30. Dinner is optional (Rs. 65).

Seagull Cruises and Tours, Leela Beach Goa, tel. 6363, ext. 886 or tel. 3640 after 8 P.M., conducts excellent day tours and cruises that provide a good introduction to Goa's history and culture. Rs. 500–Rs. 650.

Private Guides. The Government of India Tourist Office (see address under Tourist Information, above) has guides for hire. For one–four people, Rs. 80 half day; full day, Rs. 150, including lunch.

TOUR OPERATORS. The following agencies can take care of all travel needs, including hired car with driver:

Goa Tours, 2 May Fair Apartments, Dr. Dada Vaidya Rd., Panaji; tel. 43277.

Alcon International, Hotel Delmon, Caetano Albuquerque Rd., Panaji; tel. 45197.

Seagull Cruises and Tours (see address under Tours, above) can arrange trips to nearby islands, fishing excursions, day hikes, and water sports with 48-hour notice.

Trade Wings, 6 Mascareenhas Bldg., Mahatma Gandhi Rd., Panaji; tel. 44235.

You can also hire a car and driver from:

Goa Tourism Development Corporation (address under Tours, above).

SEASONAL EVENTS. A religious feast is usually a great excuse to sing, dance, and hold a village fair. Goa also holds many *jatras,* where a Hindu idol is removed from a temple and paraded through the nearby village. Since the lunar calendar determines many events, contact the Government of India Tourist Office for details. What follows is a list of Goa's unusual festivals:

January. *Feast of the Three Kings* at Reis Magos, Cuelim and Chandor. Big processions!

February/March. *Carnival,* held three days before Lent, is Goa's best party, with costumes, floats, music, and dancing.

March. A popular *jatra* takes place at the Shri Damodar Temple at Panti (22 km or 14 mi. from Margao).

March. *Shigmotsav.* Goa celebrates its annual spring festival with processions and floats that depict Hindu mythology.

March/April. *Procession of All Saints of the Franciscan Third Order,* held the fifth Monday in Lent, is another colorful procession of 40 statues of saints paraded through Goa Velha. It is the only such procession held outside Rome.

May. Another colorful jatra, this one features night-long fire-walking by devout Hindus who have undergone penance. This unusual event occurs at the *Shri Lairai Temple* in Sirigao.

August. During the *Festival of Novidades,* Christians gather at chapels in fields and offer the first sheaves of the rice crop to dignitaries.

August/September. *Ganesh Chaturthi,* a festive celebration of the birthday of Ganesh, the elephant-headed god.

November/December. The International Seafood Festival is held at Miramar Beach near Panaji, with three to five days of good eating, music, and Indian, Western, and local folk dances.

December. The *Feast of St. Francis Xavier,* patron saint of Goa, is celebrated with mass and a big fair in Old Goa.

December. The *Feast of Our Lady of Immaculate Conception* at Panaji and Margao features mass and a big fair.

December 25. Christmas festivities all over Goa.

HISTORIC SITES. The Government of India Tourist Office has a list of old Goan houses with antique furniture and objets d'art that are privately owned but available for viewing on request. Contact the main office when you arrive (see address under Tourist Information, above). Ask in particular to see Menezes Braganza in Chandor near Margao. If the cultural mood takes over suddenly, you can see the following churches and temples, at almost any time, surise to sunset.

Old Goan Churches. *Basilica of Bom Jesus* (sixteenth century), with the remains of St. Francis Xavier. *Se Cathedral* (1562–1652), dedicated to St. Catherine and the largest of the old churches. Richly embellished interior. *Church of St. Francis of Assisi* (1661), simple harmonious structure. Exquisite carvings and paintings. *Chapel of St. Catherine* (1510), constructed by Albuquerque to commemorate his arrival in Old Goa. *St. Cajetan Church* (seventeenth century), modeled on the design of St. Peter's Basilica in Rome.

Temples. *Shri Manguesh* (22 km from Panaji) in Ponda. Dedicated to Shiva; colorful interior. *Shri Mahalsa* (one km from Manguesh) The deity worshiped is Mohini, a reincarnation of Vishnu. *Shri Mahadeva* at Tambdi Surla (66 km, or 41 mi. from Panaji) in the foot of the Ghats. Only thirteenth-century temple remaining in Goa.

Mosque. *Safa Shahouri Masjid,* at Ponda, built in 1560.

MUSEUMS. Goa is not a museum-rich state, unless you define the term loosely and include the old churches and temples. But while seeing the churches, visit the *Archaeological Museum and Portrait Gallery* in Old Goa. The museum contains numerous sculptures of the early and late medieval periods collected around Goa, including friezes depicting self-immolation. The Portrait Gallery displays the portraits of the Portuguese rulers. There are also religious paintings on canvas and wood. Open 10 A.M.–noon; 1–5 P.M.; closed Fridays. Free.

SPORTS AND OUTDOOR ADVENTURES. Beaches. At *Miramar* (Gaspar Dias), close to Panaji, watch the stiff undertow and avoid looking at the backdrop of concrete high rises. *Dona Paula,* also near Panaji, is palm-fringed with fine views of Mormugao Harbor. *Calangute Beach,* across the Mandovi River in the Bardez district, is the "Queen of Goa Beaches," with 16 km (10 mi.) of sand. It includes the Baga, Anjuna, and Vagator beaches (each progressively farther north). The northern end of Goa is backed by dramatic cliffs for great sunset viewing. *Colva Beach,* south of Panaji and directly west of Margao, has long stretches of beautiful sand.

Bicycling. Bikes are for rent in most villages. Rs. 20 per day.

Hiking. The Government of India Tourist Office (see address under Tourist Information, above) and Seagull Cruises and Tours (see address under Tours, above) can provide guides for inland hikes. An especially good day walk is around Dudhsagar Waterfalls.

Water Sports. You can windsurf, waterski, parasail, scuba dive, go snorkeling, fishing, surfboarding, or have fun in a canoe, banana boat, dingy sailboat, catamaran, motor boat, or water scooter. Plan to take lessons or just rent the equipment. Contact the following companies:

Aqua Sports, 5th Floor, Nizari Bhavan, Menezes Braganza Rd., Panaji; tel. 46584.

Dominic Watersports, Sinquerim Beach, Bardez; no phone.

Ramada Renaissance, Varca, Salcete; tel. 23611.

Water-Sports Goa, Bogmalo Beach, Bogmalo; tel. 2489.

Wildlife Sanctuaries. There are three sanctuaries in Goa, all providing a day away from too much sand and surf. The *Bhagwan Mahavir Sanctuary* is the biggest (240 sq. km or 149 sq. mi.) in Molem about 35 km (22 mi.) due east of Margao. This thick forest with bison, cobra, python, deer, langurs (monkeys), and the elusive panther (don't expect to see one) is also populated by a rich variety of birds (crested serpent eagle, brown fish owl, green pigeon, shrike).

The Bondla Sanctuary is also a jungle resort (20 km [12 mi.] northeast of Molem). A great sanctuary for kids or the "kid" in all of us, with minizoos, a deer park, wilderness trail, and elephant ride. Closed Thursday.

The Cotigao Wildlife Sanctuary is on the southeastern edge of Goa. Set in a hilly, forested terrain, it protects the same animals as does the Bhagwan Mahaver Sanctuary.

SHOPPING. While Goa isn't a great area for shopping, some stores do offer a good selection of handicrafts.

Enrico's Indian Art and *Khazana* (opposite Taj Holiday Village, Sinquerim, Bardez) have good selections of Rajasthani, South Indian, and Goan handicrafts and jewelry. Open 9 A.M.–9 P.M. AE, DC, MC, V.

Also visit *Goa Handicrafts* (Tourist Hotel, Panjim), a government-run shop that sells Goan products: wooden curios, crochet lacework, terra-cotta. Open 10 A.M.– 1 P.M. and 2–7 P.M., closed Sundays. Rupees only. *Terra-cotta Pottery Center* (Bicholim, Shed No. D-7, Industrial Estate) is another state-run company that sells excellent wares. Open 9 A.M.–6 P.M., closed Sundays. Rupees only.

Near Colva Beach and next to the Colva Beach Resort, wander through the *La-mani Bazaar,* operated by Karnataka tribals from September to May. They sell love-ly mirror work and cowrie-shell-covered hats, belts, bags of all sizes, wall hangings, bedspreads—created from their traditional fabrics, plus tribal jewelry. Bargain. Rupees only. In Mapusa's market, the local people sell their own products, from food to handicrafts, every Friday. The best time to attend is in the morning.

NIGHTLIFE AND BARS. The bar at *Casa Portuguesa Restaurant* (Baga, Bardez, no phone) is cozy—one table and five chairs at the bar. The house is charm-ing. Open 6 P.M.–midnight, closed second day of each month. Any other good bar is at *Martin's Beach Corner* (Caranzalem Beach, tel. 4357). There is no music, just the sound of pounding surf. Open 11 A.M.–3 P.M. and 7–11 P.M.

BANGALORE AND KARNATAKA

Oriental Splendor and Hindu Rococo

by
KATHLEEN COX

Within the borders of Karnataka (formerly Mysore), you can find the most colorful and fascinating aspects of India, plus an occasional high level of comfort that can be Orientally sumptuous and Occidentally efficient. Although the lowlands can be hot in the summer, the plateau of Karnataka is situated where two mountain ranges converge into the beautiful Nilgiri Hills. One visit to this part of the state explains why Karnataka is called the emerald land. It's green and gorgeous, with lush rice paddies and gently sloping hills. The hill climate is pleasant and warm—in some places bracing—and even the rains that start in May are not the nonstop torrents experienced elsewhere but quick showers that are immediately followed by blue skies. There are rivers and waterfalls, forests filled with wild game and precious woods (such as teak, ebony, and sandalwood), and flowers everywhere. At a superficial glance, much of the northern areas of Karnataka seem right out of the American West—scrubby, near-barren land, studded with enormous boulders and dramatic craggy hills. However, your first sighting of a historic temple, tomb, or ancient fort reminds you that this is the exotic Indian subcontinent.

Karnataka, the size of New England, probably has been inhabited as long as anywhere else on earth. Thousand-year-old Hindu temples, decorated with carvings of amazing virtuosity; grandiose Moslem monuments; remains of lost civilizations; and some excellent modern city planning are just a few of the reasons to visit.

The scenes of village life are bound to linger. The 42 million people of Karnataka, called Kannadigas after their language, known as Kannada, are sinewy and robust. Colorfully dressed women wait patiently to fill their jugs with water at the village well, which is also the social center.

The men, often scantily dressed in *lungi* (colorful wraps) and *dhotis* (white wraps), work in the fields, walking slowly behind buffalo dragging plows that have not changed much in 3,000 years. In Karnataka, the climate makes it possible to live perpetually outdoors—the huts in the villages are often of rudimentary construction, and people think nothing of setting up their beds outside. Throughout much of the central and northern part of this exotic state, you'll encounter the delightful tribal nomads, the Lambanis—the women strutting their hips and wearing brightly layered, mirror-covered, bejeweled skirts and blouses, and heavy silver jewelry on their ears, necks, fingers, arms, feet, and ankles.

The simplicity of the country is one extreme balanced by another: the grand palaces and formal gardens; the splendor of such festivals as Dussehra; and the relics of centuries of royal living—Hindu and Moslem. Scattered throughout the state in places like Belur, Halebid, Hampi, Aihole, Pattadakal, and Badami, you'll find some of the best religious monuments in India.

Parts of Karnataka are geologically among the oldest formations in the world. People have lived here for at least 10,000 years, probably longer. And, because they have had little geographic possibility or incentive to move beyond their frontiers, they've remained faithful to the traditions of their forefathers. The state's history is intimately entwined in the great epic, the *Ramayana*. After India's first great emperor, Chandragupta Maurya, embraced Jainism, he retired to Shravarabelacola, renouncing all worldly possessions, including his empire. Many of the great names of India's early history, such as the Cholas and the Gangas, ruled parts of Karnataka. Saints and philosophers followed each other on this auspicious soil. The Hoysala dynasty (A.D. 1000–1345) was the first to control all of what is now modern Karnataka. The people of Karnataka were great builders, creating the magnificent temples at Somnathpur, Belur, and Halebid. The Moslem hordes swept in here, too, with the Hoysala capital at Dwarasumudra (the modern Halebid) sacked by Malik Kafur in 1310 and again by Mohammed-bin-Tughlaq in 1327.

Power continued to swing back and forth between the Hindus and the Moslems. Vijayanagar, whose ruins are at Hampi, was Hindu; other places, such as Bijapur, remained resolutely Moslem. Taking advantage of the general chaos, Hyder Ali, an adventurous commander in chief of the army, engineered a successful coup d'etat in 1761 and seized control. Then he and his son, Tipu Sultan, humbled the British who had their own expansionary plans. The two men added to the province (with the help of the French) and ruled it from Sriangapatna. In 1799, the British bounced back with a vengeance. Taking control, they eventually returned sovereignty to the old Hindu dynasty in the person of Sri Krishnaraja Wadiyar III, ancestor of the last maharaja, who set up his capital in Mysore City. This family provided an unbroken line of enlightened rulers who made modern Karnataka a model state. The last maharaja was so popular that the new Republic of India retained him as the state's governor.

EXPLORING KARNATAKA

Bangalore

Bangalore is a flourishing city of over 3 million inhabitants, capital of the state, an industrial center, and a garden spot. Bangalore is a relatively new city; at the end of the 1500s, nothing was there but a mud fort and a small bull temple, both built by a chieftain and the founder of Bangalore, Kempe Gowda. The bull temple is reminiscent of the Dravidian style and contains a gigantic monolith of Nandi (5 meters [15 feet] high and 6 meters [20 feet] long). The mud fort was rebuilt in stone by Hyder Ali in the 1700s. It's in ruins today.

With the city and suburbs well planned in advance, Bangalore feels orderly, serene, and regal. Vidhana Soudha, on the northern boundary of Cubbon Park, a sprawling white granite structure built in the neo-Dravidian style in 1956, houses the State Legislature and the Secretariat. Permission is required to go inside. Bangalore is also the site of the prestigious Indian Institute of Science, established with the philanthropy of the Tata family (India's Rockefellers). In short, Bangalore is a snazzy city where Western-style luxuries such as a drive-in movie, 15 flavors of ice cream, and video-game arcades exist, but with an Eastern flair.

Bangalore's charm peeks through tree-shaded gardens, manicured lawns, and ever-blooming fragrant flowers. The beautiful botanical Lal Bagh Gardens, designed by Hyder Ali and Tipu Sultan, are landscaped with a variety of centuries-old trees, fountains, lotus pools, terraces, a Japanese garden, and an assortment of tropical and subtropical herbs and plants spread out over several acres. The huge Glass House at Lal Bagh is also the delightful arena for special exhibits.

Nandi Hills

The Nandi Hills, 59 kilometers (37 miles) from Bangalore, witnessed numerous savage battles for centuries. Now it's a health and pleasure resort. Two 1,000-year-old Shiva temples grace the charming landscape: one at the foot and the other at the top of the hill, and four rivers have their source here. Back in the 1700s, Tipu Sultan made these hills the site of his summer palace. Take a walk to Tipu's Drop, a 609-meter (2,000-foot) sheer cliff. Here, condemned criminals met a grisly fate—they were pushed over the edge.

Mysore

An excellent 137-kilometer (85-mile) road leads from Bangalore to Mysore, the city of palaces. On the way, you'll pass through country strewn with strangely shaped boulders and pass near Ramnagar, the site of an experimental center for rural health, and Channapatna, which produces lacquered toys and spun silk. Finally, you'll reach the city of palaces, gardens, and Oriental splendor.

Mysore, no longer the official capital, still survives as the principal residence of the former royal family. Beautifully planned and executed, the city gives little evidence of the crushing poverty so often associated with India. When you see what the maharajas accomplished in the way of pub-

KARNATAKA

0 miles 100

0 km 100

N

MAHARASHTRA

Solapur

Bidar

Gulbarga

TO HYDERABAD

Bijapur

Badami

Aihole

Pattadakal

Belgaum

GOA

Dharwar

Hampi

Hospet

Karwar

Magod Falls

Gokarna Beach

Kumta

Harihar

Chitradurga

Jog Falls

Coondapur

Sringeri

Belur

Nandi Hills

TO MADRAS

Malpe

Halebid

Hassan

Mangalore

Mercara

Sravanabelagola

Srirangapatna

Bangalore

Somnathapura

Mysore

Sivasamudram

Talkad

Nagarhole

Arabian Sea

KERALA

Bandipur

Coimbatore

TAMIL NADU

ANDHRA PRADESH

lic service, you will understand why his highness was appointed the first governor of Karnataka.

Maharaja's Palace

By far the most impressive Mysore building is the Maharaja's Palace, a massive edifice that took 15 years to build (starting in 1897, on the site of the former wooden palace, which was destroyed by a fire). Here the Oriental decorative imagination runs wild. The palace, one of the biggest of its kind in India, is in the Indo-Saracenic style—a gigantic synthesis of Hindu and Islamic architecture. Entrance gateways, domes, arches, turrets, colonnades, lovely Hoysola-like carvings, glittering chandeliers, and etched windowpanes—are all in magnificent profusion. On Sundays and holidays, the palace is illuminated with thousands of tiny lights that turn the palace into a glittering statement of wealth.

Inside the palace, you can see a few of the royal family's private rooms, plus the impressive Durbar Hall (*Durbar* is a feudal term for receiving the nobility). This hall is an elegant preservation of history, with its ornate ceilings and huge "grandstand" awning that overlooks the great court. The Kalyana Mandap (Marriage Hall), where the women sat behind screened balconies, has lifelike paintings of the Dussera procession, and in the museum is the solid gold *howdah* (elephant throne) that the maharaja used during the festivals and other ceremonial occasions.

Public Buildings

Everything in Mysore seems palatial, even if the building in question turns out to be the Maternity Hospital, the Technical Institute, or even the Railway Office. The city's central square—Statue Square—just across from the palace, houses the marble effigy of the last maharaja's grandfather and predecessor, standing beneath a golden domed canopy.

Mysore also has an enjoyable wholesale bazaar (Devraja Market) near Krishnaraja Circle—a covered market of manageable size, with rows of hanging bananas, displays of other fruit, vegetables, and flowers galore, plus all the other foodstuffs India offers. It's bustling, noisy, and lots of fun.

Lalitha Mahal

As you head out of the center of Mysore toward Chamundi Hill, you'll see a dignified white edifice called the Lalitha Mahal, built in 1921 by the Wadiyars to house distinguished foreign guests. The palace has now joined the legion of those royal residences that have been converted into hotels, a second life that allows the mere ordinary Indian or foreigner to taste some of that grandeur earlier reserved for royalty. These palaces are usually in superb locations, and the Lalitha Mahal is no exception. The interior has a magnificent, lofty dining hall with a stained-glass dome.

Chamundi Hill

Continue to Chamundi Hill, named after the royal family's patron goddess, Chamundeswari (Parvati). A good road leads to the top, but you can also climb the thousand steps (three centuries old). About two-thirds of the way up is a 5-meter (16-foot) Nandi (Shiva's holy bull), constructed in the 1600s from a single piece of granite, including the garlands and bell around his neck.

The view from the top of the hill is superb: a beautiful panorama of all Mysore and the surrounding hills, lakes, and turrets of temples and churches. The Sri Chamundeswari Temple is dedicated to the royal Wadiyar family's titular deity. The base of the temple, dating from the twelfth century, was supposedly built by the founders of Mysore; the ornately sculptured pyramidal tower was constructed in the 1800s. Next to the temple is the giant statue of the demon Mahishasura (Mysore is named after him), who was killed by the goddess Chamundeswari, bringing peace to the country. Here he stands, built in mortar about 35 years ago, with sword and snake held aloft in each hand.

If possible, time your visit to Mysore to coincide with the 10-day Dussera festival (September/October). The city is at its best, clothed in color, light, and joy. This is the same major Hindu festival celebrated under different names all over India, but here it is a royal as well as a popular festival. The pomp, grandeur, and ceremony are not to be missed. Until 1974, the late maharaja sat on his jeweled throne every night of Dussera; on the tenth day, he left the palace in a royal procession seated in his golden howdah atop a magnificently caparisoned elephant. The maharaja's son does not take part in the parade. Instead the family idol, Chamundeswari, is taken from the temple and put in the elephant's howdah. The torch- and daylight parades are unique. *Theppotsava,* the worship of deities on decorated barges afloat in a floodlit lake, is magical.

Brindavan Gardens

Only 19 kilometers (12 miles) northwest of Mysore are the Brindavan Gardens, which extend in terraces beneath the Krishnarajasagar Dam. The place started life functionally—as an irrigation dam at the confluence of three rivers. The dam is two kilometers (1¼ miles) long and forms an enormous lake. It is constructed entirely in stone and crushed bricks and is ornamented with parapets and a niche for the river goddess. Even though the dam is one of the biggest in India, it commands only slight attention next to the gardens, exquisitely designed and alive with bright flowers and silvery fountains. An excellent time to go is at night, when the gardens, hundreds of fountains and pools of all colors, sizes, and shapes are illuminated.

Srirangapatna

Srirangapatna is an island fortress between two branches of the Cauvery River and the former capital of the Mysore rajas from 1610 to 1799. Hyder Ali and Tipu Sultan were its most famous residents. The battle for control of this area of India lasted 180 years. The first to succeed were the British, on the fourth try in 1799, when Tipu Sultan lost his life in the skirmish.

Visit the fort and its imposing surroundings. The Moslems lived cheek to jowl with two Hindu temples, one of which, the Sri Ranganathaswamy, is about 1,000 years old. Here you can see the dungeons in which captured British officers were imprisoned. The "Breach" marks the place where the British finally smashed through the fortifications and entered the town; the Water Gate was Tipu's last stand. See the ruins of Tipu's fortified palaces near the old parade grounds and the sultan's favorite mosque, the Jamiad-e-Tipu Sultan, with its twin minarets. The top of the minarets offer a good view of the fort and also a glimpse of Mysore.

Without doubt, the best monuments are outside the fort: Tipu's summer pleasure palaces (he indulged himself) and his mausoleum, the Gumbaz.

Daria Daulat Bagh

Set in a charming garden, the Daria Daulat Bagh Palace doesn't look so impressive from the outside, but once inside you'll think otherwise. There are carved ornate arches, liberally gilded wall panels, eighteenth-century colored frescoes. On the right of the entrance, you'll see Hyder Ali and Tipu riding at the head of their troops. On the left there's a vain reminder of the victorious first battle against the British. All along the walls, in tiered bands, are scenes from the happy lives of the ruling Moslem nawabs obviously enjoying the comfort of their palaces, holding court, or simply looking important. The Duke of Wellington also used this palace as his residence after the British seized power in 1799.

Gumbaz

Two kilometers (one mile) from the palace is the Gumbaz, a beautiful mausoleum for the Moslem rulers, who also took their eternal rest in lavish style. In the center of a garden stands the cream-colored Gumbaz on its black-marble pillars. The pillars support the lowest tier of the monument: a balconylike wall, delicately and minutely carved, surmounted at the four corners by miniature minarets. Above the veranda is another tier, ornamented with arches and a carved plinth that in turn supports a third tier, repeating the theme of the first on a larger scale—the whole crowned by a bulbous dome.

The interior of the mausoleum is lacquered with Tipu Sultan's tiger-stripe emblem, and the doors are of ebony inlaid with ivory. Next to the elegant Gumbaz is a prayer hall in the same style.

Karapur Forest and Nagarhole National Park

An infamous event occurred in Karnataka in years past called *Khedda,* or "Operation Wild Elephant." The big pachyderms of Karnataka, considered the handsomest and strongest of the breed, were in great demand by maharajas and princes who could afford them, circuses, zoos, and people wanting efficient working animals for construction projects. The arena for these roundups was in the Karapur forest, 79 kilometers (49 miles) south of Mysore, with the opponents—swarms of skilled tribesmen—against a herd of trumpeting mammoths.

Much of this area has now been flooded by a new dam, and kheddas have stopped. But in their time, they provided one of the most overwhelming spectacles in India. Hundreds of forest tribesmen would stalk the elephants. To the frenzied commotion of villagers beating bamboo poles against empty tins, drums, or gongs and with clouds of thick smoke billowing around them, the elephants would become dazed and frightened, moving unknowingly toward the trap set for them in the Kabini River. Once captured, they were trained.

Today, instead of the sight of animals in terror, you can watch wild elephants—untrapped and untamed—moving in peaceful security around the same forests. Kabini River Lodge, operated by Jungle Lodges and Resorts of India and the government of Karnataka, is a terrific resort at Karapur. Visitors stay in the renovated Victorian hunting bungalows of the maharaja of Mysore and the British viceroy. Excellent game-viewing tours by jeep take you through the Nagarhole National Park, with Colonel Wakefield and his staff skillful at stalking the wild beasts. Here you're likely to spot the rare Indian gaur (wild ox), wild boar, sambar, barking deer, families of elephants (mothers, calves, "aunt" elephants, and tuskers), and maybe a leopard or tiger. You'll also have the unusual chance to paddle along the waterways in a *coracle,* a round, basket-shaped boat lined with buffalo hide. Coracles are so slow and quiet that you can approach very close to the families of wild animals and the abundance of birdlife (over 225 different species).

Sravanabelgola

About 84 kilometers (52 miles) north of Mysore is Sravanabelgola, presided over and dominated by the colossal statue of the Jain saint Gomateshwara. His monolithic image, 18 meters (57 feet) tall, watched over pilgrims for 1,000 years, ever since the time of the Ganga kings under whose patronage Jainism flourished. The religion has declined now in numeric importance, but the statue reminds us of its principles: Gomateshwara's nakedness suggests renunciation of all worldly things, and the still posture indicates perfect self-control. The gigantic image rises atop one of Sravanabelgola's two hills, Indragiri, where many smaller statues and a beautiful temple also stand. A rock-hewn stairway of 614 steps leads to the summit and the monolith, which is 8 meters (26 feet) across the shoulders and sports a 3-meter (10-foot) waistline, and 3-meter (9-foot) long feet. As one critic said: "There is nothing grander or more imposing anywhere out of Egypt, and even there, no known statue surpasses it in height." Every 12 years, Jains from all over India gather here for the spectacular bathing festival in which priests clamber up specially built scaffolding to pour hundreds of pots of 16 substances over Gomateshwara's head—including milk curds, honey, rice, fruit, and even gold and silver coins and precious jewels. The next festival will be in 1993.

Belur

Between Sravanabelgola and Hassan, 56 kilometers (35 miles), there is grassland and woodland that will make any New Englander or Englander feel right at home. From Hassan, it is only 35 kilometers (22 miles) through lush tropical landscapes to Belur, a city that flourished under the Hoysala kings during the twelfth century. The frontier-style town boasts only one reminder of that splendid time—but what a reminder! The Belur Temple of Lord Channakeshava, still a functioning temple dedicated to this Vishnu incarnate, stands almost as perfectly preserved as it did the day it was completed. (Started in 1116 by the Hoysala King Vishnuvardhana, it was completed 103 years later.) Legend claims that when Moslem conquerers came to Belur to destroy the temple, they left it alone, awed by its magnificence.

Carved of soapstone, the Belur temple is like Somnathpur in design: star-shaped, with the squat temple set on a platform. It is also flat on top, without Somnathpur's suggestion of a spire. Superbaroque Belur is a contemporary of Chartres, with more in common than meets the eye. In both cases, the patience of the anonymous artisans seems infinite. Although each monument serves a different religion, they both share the desire to instruct the faithful through the only means open to them at the time: the image. At Belur we find gods and goddesses in all their varied aspects and incarnations and scenes from the great Indian religious epics. Perhaps because the Indian's natural state is more religious, and there is less separation between religion and the realities of life, we also find hunters, dancers, musicians, and beautiful women dressing and adorning themselves.

Except at the bottom of the temple, the friezes are not as long and continuous as those of Somnathpur, and a series of semidetached pillars and ornamented porches lend greater variety to the facade. The plan of the temple is the traditional porch-vestible-shrine. The shrine has three doorways on the east, south, and north, with the eastern the loveliest of all. A railed parapet sculpted with eight exquisite friezes runs along the side of this doorway. On the rail to the right of the door are epic scenes and tiny musicians seated here and there. Above these ornamental rails are about 20 pierced stone windows showing a variety of scenes or geometric designs. The jambs of the northern doorways are carved with female bearers, and to the northeast is a chain of destruction: a double-headed eagle attacking a mythical beast, that is going for a lion, that is clawing an elephant, that is seizing a snake, that is swallowing a rat—followed by a sage pondering the entire spectacle. The southern doorway is crowded with gods, demons, and animals. Beyond the railed parapet are about 80 fine-chiseled separate images of goddesses. Each entrance is flanked by two pavilions with carved figures, and at the sides, the crest of the Hoysalas: Sala, their ancestor, stabbing a stylized tiger.

Back in the center of the temple, notice the domed ceiling supported by four pillars—a majestic lotus bud with depictions of scenes from the *Ramayana*. Notice, too, the sculptures of the women at the top of the four pillars. Some of the jewelry they wear can be moved: the bracelets on an arm and a head ornament. The women are beautiful, voluptuous, full-breasted, and full-hipped, taking any number of graceful poses beneath the intricately pierced, scrolled, and scalloped stone canopies.

The nineteenth-century architect and critic James Fergusson summed up Belur in this way: "These friezes . . . carved with a minute elaboration of detail . . . are one of the most marvelous exhibitions of human labor to be found even in the patient East. Here the artistic combination of horizontal with vertical and the play of outline and of light and shade far surpass anything in Gothic art." South of the main temple, a smaller shrine built over a period of 250 years, the Channigaraya Temple, is worth a good look. The other remaining Hoysala temple (Viranarayana) has rows of very fine images on its outer walls.

Halebid

Near Belur is its sister temple at Halebid. The Hoysaleswara Temple was started in 1121 after Belur by the same king but left uncompleted after 180 years of labor. It, too, is a star-shaped plan, but a double-shrine temple. At Halebid the sculptor's virtuosity reaches its peak—one can't "explain" this carving, but it is possible to say that these artists were able to treat stone like wood or ivory. One reason, apart from patience and talent, was that they worked in soft soapstone, which hardens with time. The friezes are breathtaking; first comes a row of elephants for stability, then one of lordly lions, then convoluting scrolls of swift horses. Above more scroll work are scenes from the religious epics that not only present philosophical ideas but mirror the living conditions of the time. Mythical beasts and swans follow. The largest frieze is also the most exuberant; based on a heavenly theme, it gives heavenly results. Here are the *apsarasis*, or "celestial maidens," clothed in jewels, with bracelets on each arm—sometimes they have as many as six arms. Sitting or standing in graceful postures under pierced canopies, the maidens are eight centuries old yet eternally young. The walls are also graced by small turrets, beadwork cornices, columns and by what many consider to be Halebid's pièce de résistance: the entire Hindu pantheon brought to life in stone. Many of these carvings are on the west facade and include not only the gods and goddesses but many of their incarnations and such curious deities as Ganesh, the elephant god, with his papal-like tiara. There are 280 figures, mostly feminine, that rival the best in Gothic art.

Also take a look at the smaller Kedareswara Temple, whose friezes are similar to those of the others and are executed with equal finesse. There is, in addition, a relatively unadorned early Jain temple, dedicated to Parsvanatha, whose finely polished pillars serve as fancy mirrors.

Sringeri

From Halebid, either head straight for the ancient temple city of Hampi, or take a "beach-break" and visit the seashore near Mangalore (see below) or head to Sringeri, situated on the bank of the Tunga River. Sringeri is also an important pilgrimage center. Here St. Sankaracharya established a monastery to protect Hinduism (from the advance of Islam) and to help establish the Vijayanagar empire. In the lovely fourteenth-century Vidya Shankara Temple, 12 zodiac pillars are arranged so that the sun's rays fall on the pillar that corresponds to that month. And the statuesque stone lions have stone balls inside their mouths that can be rotated but never removed.

Mangalore and Karnataka's Beaches

Mangalore, on Karnataka's coast, is the world's principal cashew-nut port and a thriving maritime city. But Mangalore feels languid, with simple fishing trawlers and small wooden sailboats moving slowly down the Gurpur River to the Arabian Sea. Palm trees rustle above tile-roofed bungalows, old churches, temples, and mosques. Near Mangalore, you'll find important Hindu pilgrimage centers, such as Dharmasthala, Udipi, and Kollur. Mudbidri and Karkala, an hour's drive northeast of Mangalore, are important Jain destinations, with remarkable Jain carvings and giant stone images.

There's Dharmasthala (74 kilometers or 46 miles), which promotes charity and offers free food to all who arrive, and Udupi (60 kilometers or 37 miles), which celebrates the Dwaitha philosophy. Northeast of Mangalore, visit Moodabidri (35 kilometers or 22 miles), with its Jain temple, constructed in 1430, that has 1,000 monolith pillars, and Karkala (52 kilometers or 32 miles), where a 13-meter (42-foot) statue of Gomateswara, a Jain tirthankara, was erected in 1432.

From Mangalore, you can also head to "undiscovered" beaches. One of the prettiest stretches begins at Kaup, 46 kilometers (28 miles) north of Mangalore. Starting at this fishing village, with a lighthouse, the road meanders north about 10 kilometers (six miles) hugging the coastline, which has silvery sand and good swimming. You'll see no cars, just people on bikes or walking, mending fishing nets, working on their wooden boats. The road ends at the end of a spit. Across the way is Malpe, where you can hire a small fishing craft from local villagers, who will take you five kilometers (three miles) to St. Mary's Island, a beautiful hideaway with great rock foundations.

Hampi

Across the center of Karnataka, northeast toward Hampi, is a different kind of tranquillity—the tranquillity of departed spirits. If you like ruins—

not the battered fort or the tottering temple or even the Pompeii-like state of suspended animation—but real desolation, then see Hampi.

In this once-proud city of the Vijayanagar empire, the vista of extensive plains is interrupted by red hills with craggy boulders, precariously balanced. But in all other respects the story is the same: Hampi is the shell of a colossal empire. The brilliance of Vijayanagar from the fourteenth to the mid-sixteenth century accentuates the debacle. Travelers then found it "as large as Rome" and "the best provided city in the world." And so well protected—surrounded by the turbulent Tungabhadra River and rocky ridges. Most notable of its rulers was Krishnadeva Raya (1509–29), whose military prowess, lavish hospitality, and love for the arts made him known beyond the confines of India.

Unfortunately, the reigning rajas were continually at war with the Moslem sultanates of the Deccan, who eventually combined against the Hindu kingdom. Enormous armies clashed in 1565 north of the capital. A few hours of fighting was enough to destroy the place. Ramaraja, the last of a great dynasty, was decapitated. The city lost its life, too.

Plan at least a day to wander through Hampi. The vast ruins include temples, palaces, baths, and pavilions. All of Hampi's architecture is in perfect harmony with its natural surroundings, blending into the hills, rocks, caves, and rivers. The most sacred buildings are on either side of the Tungabhadra River or on the peaks of the surrounding hills.

The Virupaksha Temple

The Virupaksha Temple, dedicated to Virupaksha (an aspect of Shiva) and now considered the most sacred structure in Hampi, is still active—active with monkeys, too. When the bells are rung early in the morning and in the evening, the critters race into the interior courtyard for food. The temple, completed in the sixteenth century, has a nine-story goporum at one end of the formerly world-famous Hampi Bazaar that once sold heaps of precious jewels and diamonds. At the opposite end of the bazaar is a pavilion containing a destroyed Nandi.

On the surrounding hills are more temple complexes, including the Matanga Hill Temple, dedicated to a ferocious aspect of Shiva. This hill gives a good view of the original Hampi layout. Just below the hill and on the riverbank is the Kodandarama Temple, which contains an image of Rama and is considered to be the most sacred bathing ghat on the Tungabhadra.

Vithala Temple Complex

The most famous and imposing single complex, to be saved for a lingering visit at sunset, is the Vithala Temple complex, the highest glory of Vijayanagar architecture. Constructed in the sixteenth century and dedicated to Vishnu, the walled rectangular courtyard contains the renowned chariot with lotus-shaped wheels: the entire vehicle intricately carved from a single granite stone.

Notice, too, the Vithala Temple, with the elephant balustrades, and horses on the entrance columns, and its exquisite hall of imaginatively carved musical pillars, each hewn from a single stone. With a tap of the hand, each pillar duplicates the sound of a specific instrument. Music once filled the temple, with singing and dancing at sunrise and sunset. The sacred dancing was performed in the other detached hall in the southern part of the courtyard, its numerous columns all intricately carved.

Hazara Rama Temple Complex

This other interesting temple complex takes you away from the sacred center of Hampi to the royal center, farther away from the river. This temple, in a rectangular compound, is called the Hazara Rama and is also dedicated to Vishnu. The Hazara Rama was for the private worship of the king. Surrounding this temple are the ruins of numerous civic buildings, royal residences, wells, aqueducts, and gigantic tanks. Of these, don't miss the Lotus Pavilion, the Queen's Bath, and the Elephant's Stables (still in a reasonable state of repair).

As you leave Hampi and head for the bustling little city of Hospet, keep in mind as you enter the level plains that you have also entered the suburban area of the former empire. Little remains of this area—most of the dwellings for the common folk were built of wood, mud, or other perishable materials. Only a few temples have survived.

Aihole, Badami, and Pattadakal

A group of three villages—Aihole, Badami, and Pattadakal, the two successive capitals and coronation ground, respectively, of the Chalukyan dynasty that honor the glories of post-Gupta architecture (fifth to eighth centuries)—lie northwest of Hampi on the road to Bijapur. These temple hamlets take you through simple yet exquisite villages that are the epitome of pastoral. The only activity occurs at the occasional "shandy" (market), usually held once a week on the outskirts of a tiny town. Stop if you see one in progress, and wander among the villagers, who come miles to sell livestock, fruit, vegetables, clay pots, dried fish, colorful powders and spices, soaps, and incense. They're lots of fun.

Aihole

The 125 temples in Aihole are the oldest and date from A.D. 450 to 750, revealing the genesis of Hindu medieval art, which was initially influenced by Buddhist temple architecture, then slowly developed into its own rich style. In an enclosure surrounding a tank, you'll find the Durga, the largest and most elaborately carved temple. Notice its U-shape, which mirrors the Buddhist chaitya (hall). Named for a fort, not the goddess, the Durga is dedicated to Vishnu and was probably built in the seventh century.

The oldest temple is the Lad Khan, built about A.D. 450 and representing Hindu architecture in an embryonic stage, with the hall constructed first and the sanctum added later. The Suraya Naryana Temple, dedicated to the sun god, was built in the seventh or eighth century and contains an intriguing statue of the presiding deity surrounded by eight planets. Tap the stone in various places and it makes music. In the village, also see the Huchimalli Temple, one of the oldest structures, with excellent carvings, including Kartikeya, the war god, astride a peacock, chiseled into the ceiling. A short ride from the temples will take you to the Ravanaphad (or Brahmanical) Cave. A carved Nandi guards the approach. Stone steps lead into the rock-cut cave with the dancing form of Shiva and other lovely statues.

Badami

Badami, once the former second capital of the Chalukyas, is nestled between red sandstone hills. Here, cave temples were hewn out of solid rock, some as early as A.D. 550. Their setting is magical: carved into hills above a lovely reservoir with quaint, tiny temples dotting the edge. The four most important caves follow a set plan: a veranda with pillars, a hall with columns, and a small cell to enshrine the deity. Though the exteriors appear simple, with borders of grotesque dwarfs, the interiors are remarkably detailed.

The first cave, possibly the earliest, is dedicated to Shiva and burrows deep into the rock. Dwarfs decorate the front of the veranda. Inside you'll see a Nandi bull (with a human body) on the left, and on the right, a unique carving of Nataraja (Shiva) as the Cosmic Dancer with 18 hands (the only one of its kind in India). The hands are so well placed that any right hand matches up with any left hand and the carving strikes 81 dance poses. In the panel near the Nataraja, look for Shanmukha riding a peacock. Below this image is a carving of two boys that, on close inspection, creates the illusion of four. The columns and the ceiling are so artfully turned and executed that it is hard to believe that the rock was removed from around them; this cave looks like all the others—constructed, not dug out.

The second cave is the smallest and is dedicated to Vishnu, with its sanctuary depicting the god's various incarnations. You see Varaha (the boar), who rescued earth from a flood; Vishnu riding Garuda (an eagle); Vishnu as Trivikrama with one leg on the ground and the other kicked up in the air; plus Vishnu as Krishna depicted in scenes at the top of the wall.

Between the second and third caves is a path that leads to a rough excavation in which a Buddhist figure has been carved into the wall. If you follow the steps about two kilometers (about a mile), you'll reach the Badami Fort, with old granaries, a treasury, and the Malegitti Shivalaya Temple, dedicated to Shiva, with a Dravidian goporum.

The third cave, also dedicated to Vishnu, is considered the finest excavation. Just inside the veranda on the left wall is an enormous image of Vishnu as Trivikrama, similar to the one in the second cave, yet the tallest of its kind in India. On the opposite wall is another huge image of Vishnu with eight hands. If you stand just inside the cave with your back to the shrine, you'll see, on the panel above the entrance, an image of Garuda with the beak and wings of a bird but a human face. Stand up close, it looks serious; step back, it grins. Examine all the columns covered with couples (some of them are playfully sexy). Look for the traces of faded frescoes, the huge reliefs of Narasimha (the half-lion Vishnu incarnation) and Harihara (half-Shiva and half-Vishnu), and the image of Vishnu seated on a serpent. This is also the biggest cave, with a double row of pillars.

The final major cave is Jain and houses the only Jain temple in Badami. It was cut from the rock a hundred years after the others. Enshrined here are huge figures of Padmavati (the Jain saint) and Mahavira (the 24th tirthankara, or perfect soul).

Six kilometers (four miles) from Badami is the Banashankari Temple, originally built in the eighth century by the Chalukyas. Dedicated to a manifestation of Parvati, the current temple, constructed in the seventeenth century, has a black stone image of this goddess seated on a lion and trampling a demon to death. Out front is a large sacred pond, Harida Tirtha.

Pattadakal

The temples of Pattadakal show the evolution toward the high-towered, much-sculptured structure that is familiar in India. The sculpture, however, is not so much representative as decorative: pilasters, pillars, balconies, pierced work, and high relief of the faces of the towers. These temples are

Chalyukan or Dravidian, and the best examples in each group are the Papanatha and the Virupaksha. They are described below under Historic Sites.

Bijapur

Bijapur, "The City of Victory," is a walled, medieval Moslem city, due north of Badami, that boasts over 50 mosques, 20 tombs, and at least as many *mahals* (palaces). The architecture here is not the florid, overdecorated Oriental type often associated with Moslems, but Turkish—restrained and severe though grandiose in proportion.

The dominant building is the Gol Gumbaz, the vast mausoleum of Mohammed Adil Shah, who ruled his kingdom from Bijapur in the seventeenth century. His mausoleum was built in the mid-1600s around the same time as the Taj Mahal. The dome of the tomb is the second largest in the world: 38 meters (124 feet) in diameter, with St. Peter's in Rome outdoing it by a mere 5 meters (15 feet). The square monument has arched entranceways on each facade and an octagonal tiered turret at each angle. The inside is severely bare except for four tall pointed arches supporting the dome. The acoustics of the enclosed space make it a remarkable whispering gallery, where any sonic message, from the flicking of a match to a shout, is repeated 12 times.

Other monuments in Bijapur include the ornate tomb of Adil Shah's father; the Ibrahim Rauza, with its richly decorated walls and perforated stone windows; and the unfinished tomb of Ali Adil Shah. There are plenty of palaces: the Asar-I-Sharif, said to contain a hair of the Prophet Mohammed's beard; the Anand Mahal, where the harem lived; the Gagan Mahal, with its three magnificent arches; the Sat Manzil, a seven-story pleasure palace overlooking the city; and the Chini Mahal.

The Jama Masjid, started in 1557, is one of the finest mosques in India, remarkable for its harmonious proportions, its graceful minarets, the construction of the bulbous domes and the execution of the ornamental detail. Others are the Old Mosque, a converted Jain temple; the Andu Masjid, two-stories with a fluted dome; the miniature Makka; and the Mehtar Mahal, with its finely wrought gateway. Some of these buildings were sadly mutilated by Emperor Aurangzeb, but in spite of the ravages of time and men, Bijapur remains a splendid sight. The town is also notable for its many fine gardens.

If you're in Bijapur on Sunday, visit the Gandhi Market, where the nearby Lambanis set up shop in a center square selling colorful material and jewels. It's a photographer's paradise.

Bidar

Our last stop in Karnataka is Bidar, northeast of Bijapur. Bidar is a deceptive city. The modern area is uninteresting, but head straight to the area containing the old inner fort and the inner city, the former capital of the fifteenth-century Bahmani kings. Its remarkable ruins are a monument to the time of its glory.

Spend a morning wandering through the remains of the inner fort. See the beautiful Rangin Mahal (the Colorful Palace), with its small rooms and tile work; the Zanani Masjid, the oldest Moslem building in Bidar; the Gagan Mahal (Heavenly Palace), where you can meander down old stone steps into half-destroyed chambers and halls; the Royal Pavilion with more underground rooms; and the numerous other ancient constructions.

After seeing the fort, visit the nearby Bahamani Tombs of departed kings. Although not well maintained, they provide a sense of timeless grandeur. Wear good walking shoes and bring a flashlight.

PRACTICAL INFORMATION FOR KARNATAKA

WHEN TO GO. Karnataka, which is near-tropical, is at its best from mid-August to mid-April, when days are warm and nights are balmy. The monsoon arrives in June, with heavy downpours that turn to light rains by mid-August, when Karnataka is lush green.

HOW TO GET THERE. By Air. *Indian Airlines* connects Bangalore with over three daily flights from Madras; three daily flights from Bombay; 10 weekly flights from Delhi; a daily flight from Calcutta, Coimbatore, and Hyderabad; six weekly flights from Cochin; five weekly flights from Ahmedabad; four weekly flights from Goa and Trivandrum; and three weekly flights from Madurai, Pune, and Tiruchirappalli. It connects Mangalore with two daily flights from Bombay and four weekly flights from Madras. *Vayudoot* connects Bangalore with six weekly flights from Pondicherry, Puttaparthi, and Tirupati. It connects Belgaum with a daily flight from Bombay and three weekly flights from Madras and Tirupati. For Indian Airlines information, call 29769 in Bangalore; 23504 or 27207 in Mangalore. For Vayudoot information, call 29769 in Bangalore; in Belgaum contact Mayur World Travels, tel. 20864.

By Train. Most trains to Bangalore require an overnight journey. Be certain to reserve a berth as well as a sleeper or you could be asked to leave the train at bedtime. Travel second-class air-conditioned or first-class to get a reasonable night's rest. Daily trains from Bombay to Bangalore: *Udyan Express, Mahalakshmi Express, Sahyadhri Express* (24 hours). From Delhi to Bangalore: *Karnataka Express* (40 hours). Daily trains from Madras: *Bangalore Mail,* and *Brindavan Express* (six hours). In Bangalore, contact the Railway Station for inquiries, tel. 131, and for reservations, tel. 132.

By Bus. Buses are crowded and slow-going. They are not recommended.

By Hired Car with Driver. The cost of car with driver is about Rs. 4–Rs. 5 per km, plus a halt charge of Rs. 50–Rs. 100 per night. Hire a car with driver from one of the recommended tour operators listed below or one in the state from which you depart. Here are some important distances from Bangalore: Bombay, 1,100 km (682 mi.); Cochin, 578 km (358 mi.); Hyderabad, 566 km (351 mi.); Madras, 334 km (207 mi.); Ooty, 297 km (184 mi.); Panaji, 570 km (353 mi.); Trivandrum, 761 km (472 mi.).

TOURIST INFORMATION. There are three good sources of information on Karnataka. The *Government of India Tourist Office* has excellent brochures (KFC Bldg., 48 Church St., Bangalore 560001, tel. 579517). It's open Monday–Friday, 9:30 A.M.–6 P.M. and Saturday, 9 A.M.–1 P.M., closed Sunday. The head office of *Karnataka Tourism Department* (KTD) is at Cauvery Bhavan, 1st Floor, F Block, K. G. Rd., Bangalore 560009, tel. 215489. It's open Monday–Saturday, 10:30 A.M.–5 P.M., closed second Saturday and Sundays. It also has a counter at the airport (tel. 571467) that opens with arrivals, a counter at the City Railway Station (tel. 70068) that is open daily 7 A.M.–7 P.M., and an office at 64 St. Marks Rd. (tel. 213139) that is open during the same hours as the head office. The *Karnataka State Tourism Development Corporation* (KSTDC) takes reservations for its state-run hotels (10/4 Kasturba Rd., Bangalore 560001, tel. 212901–3); open Monday–Saturday, 10:30 A.M.–5 P.M., closed second Saturday and Sundays. For a KSTDC tour, reserve through its Transport Wing (Badami House, N. R. Square, Bangalore 560002, tel. 215869 or 215883); open daily 8 A.M.–9 P.M. KTD and KSTDC are also located in the following cities. Offices are open Monday–Saturday, 10:30 A.M.–5 P.M., closed second Saturday and Sundays, unless noted otherwise.

Badami. KSTDC, Hotel Mayura Chalukya, Ramdurg Rd., tel. 46.

Bijapur. *Tourist Bureau, Department of Tourism,* Hotel Mayura Adil Shahi, Anand Mahal Rd.; tel. 20359. KSTDC is also at the hotel; tel. 20934.

Hassan. *Tourist Bureau,* Department of Tourism, Vartha Bhavan, B. M. Rd.; tel. 8862.

Hospet (Hampi). *Tourist Counter,* Hampi Bazar, no phone; or *Tourist Bureau and KSTDC,* Transport Wing, Old Fire Station Bldg., Taluk Office Complex; tel. 8537.

Mangalore. *KSTDC,* Transport Wing, Hotel Indraprastha, opposite Kasturba Medical College; tel. 21692.

Mysore. *Tourist Bureau, Department of Tourism,* Old Exhibition Bldg., Irwin Rd., tel. 22096; or *KSTDC,* Hotel Mayura Hoysala, Jhansi Laxmibai Rd., tel. 23652. KSTDC also has a Transport Wing at Old Exhibition Bldg. (address above); tel. 23652.

FOREIGN CURRENCY EXCHANGE. Most Western-style hotels have money-exchange counters. Otherwise, ask your hotel to recommend a local bank. In Bangalore, the *State Bank of India* is at Almas Center, M. G. Rd., *ANZ Grindlays* is at Reheja Towers, M. G. Rd.; and *Thomas Cook* is at 55 M. G. Rd. State banks are open Monday–Friday, 10 A.M.–2 P.M.; Saturdays till noon. Thomas Cook is open Monday–Friday, 9:30 A.M.–1 P.M. and 2 P.M.–5 P.M., and Saturday, 9:30 A.M.–12:30 P.M.; closed Sunday.

ACCOMMODATIONS. In many large cities and popular tourist areas in Karnataka, excellent facilities exist. Other undervisited areas have few options, but what's there is adequate. For reservations at Karnataka Tourist Department (KTD) facilities, contact in advance the Directorate of Tourism (address above under Tourist Information). For reservations in KSTDC facilities, contact in advance in Bangalore (address above under Tourist Information). Prices are based on double occupancy and exclude taxes and service charges: *Deluxe,* over Rs. 2,000; *Expensive,* Rs. 1,200–Rs. 2,000; *Moderate,* Rs. 500–Rs. 1,200; *Inexpensive,* under Rs. 500. Most Western-style hotels take major credit cards.

AIHOLE

Inexpensive

Tourist Home. Aihole; tel. 41. Reservations: KTD, tel. 215489. 14 rooms—10 with Western-style toilets, 4 with Indian-style. This KTD facility offers clean rooms with fans and a modest decor. Its modesty is in keeping with its setting next to ancient temples. Room service and Indian- or Continental-cuisine meals provided on request. Rupees only.

BADAMI

Inexpensive

Hotel Mayura Chalukya. Ramdurg Rd., Badami; tel. 246. Reservations: KSTDC, tel. 212901. 10 rooms with bath. This bungalow, with an interior courtyard has clean rooms that are modestly furnished. Fans, room service, Indian-cuisine restaurant, bar. Rupees only.

Hotel Mukambika. Opposite Bus Stand, Badami; tel. 267. 7 rooms with bath. This simple two-story, Western-style hotel has clean rooms with overhead fans and good management. Multicuisine restaurant, bar, room service, car-rental arrangements. Rupees only.

BANGALORE

Deluxe

The Oberoi. 37/39 M. G. Rd., Bangalore 560001; tel. 585858, fax 585960. 130 rooms with bath. Scheduled to open at press time, this elegant hotel has a stunning lobby with green-marble floor, central fountain, and a bank of windows overlooking a landscaped garden and lawn where water cascades into a lotus pond. Spacious rooms have private balconies and handsome decor accenting either light blue or mauve pink. Air-conditioning, TV, room service, restaurants, bar, swimming pool, health club, business center, foreign-exchange and travel counter, courtesy airport shuttle, shop. AE, DC, MC, V.

Taj West End Hotel. Race Course Rd., Bangalore 560001; tel. 269281, fax 200010. 140 rooms with bath. A former 1920s British bungalow, this place has an exterior and public rooms that are decidedly Victorian but also have lush tropical gardens. Air-conditioned rooms are done up in a contemporary decor. Best rooms are on the second floor opening onto a veranda overlooking the pool. TV, room service, multicuisine restaurants, swimming pool, tennis courts, horseback riding and golfing arrangements, doctor, baby-sitters, foreign-exchange and travel counter, health club, business center, shopping arcade. AE, DC, MC, V.

Welcomgroup Windsor Manor. 25 Sankey Rd., Bangalore 560052; tel. 269898, fax 264941. 140 rooms with bath; 100 more under construction. This stately hotel was recently built but adheres impeccably to Indo-Gothic architecture. The exterior is strikingly white, with arched windows and wrought-iron touches. The magnificent lobby has a marble fountain beneath a domed skylight and massive teak pillars. Handsome air-conditioned rooms have modern furnishings with Victorian touches. TV, room service, multicuisine restaurants, bar, health club, swimming pool, golfing arrangements, business center, foreign-exchange and travel counter, nonsmoking rooms, doctor, shopping arcade. AE, DC, MC, V.

Expensive

Taj Gateway Hotel on Residency Road. 66 Residency Rd., Bangalore 560025; tel. 544545, fax 544030. 98 rooms with bath. This Western-style high rise has an attractive lobby and spacious rooms with contemporary furnishings. Air-conditioning, TV, room service, multicuisine restaurants, bar, swimming pool, health club, foreign-exchange and travel counter, business center, doctor, shops. AE, DC, MC, V.

Taj Residency. 41/3 Mahatma Gandhi Rd., Bangalore 560001; tel. 584444, fax 544748. 165 rooms with bath. A 10-story high rise, the Taj Residency has a spacious lobby and pretty, modern decor, and air-conditioned rooms with balconies. Best rooms are on the upper floors with a lake view. TV, room service, multicuisine restaurants, bar, swimming pool, health club, baby-sitters, business center, foreign-exchange and travel counter, doctor, bookshop. AE, DC, MC, V.

Moderate

Comfort Inn Ramanashree Bangalore. 16 Raja Ram Mohan Roy Rd., Bangalore 560025; tel. 235250, fax 544507. 67 rooms with bath. This new five-story hotel has an exterior glass elevator and a lobby with lots of polished granite. Rooms have a modern decor. Air-conditioning, TV, room service, projected rooftop restaurant, multicuisine restaurants, bar, foreign-exchange and travel counter, business center, doctor, nonsmoking floor, shop. Good value. AE, DC, MC, V.

Hotel Ashok. High Grounds, Bangalore 560001; tel. 269462. 181 rooms with bath. A high rise with an inviting marble lobby, the Ashok offers spacious air-conditioned rooms with a contemporary decor. Best rooms overlook the pool. Multicuisine restaurants, bar, TV, room service, swimming pool, golfing arrangements, tennis court, health club, bank, foreign-exchange counter, travel agency, doctor, shopping arcade. AE, DC, MC, V.

Inexpensive

Hotel Cauvery Continental. 11/37 Cunningham Rd., Bangalore 560052; tel. 266966. 59 rooms with bath. This simple Western-style hotel offers large rooms, with a clean institutional decor. Some rooms are air-conditioned. TV, room service, multicuisine restaurants, bar, foreign-exchange and travel counter, garden. AE, DC, MC, V.

BHIMESWARI

Deluxe

Cauvery Fishing Camp. Bhimeswari; no phone. Reservations: Jungle Lodge and Resorts Ltd., 2nd Floor, Shrungar Shopping Center, M. G. Rd., Bangalore, 560001; tel. 575195. Six tents with separate bathroom facilities. This excellent fishing resort has well-appointed safari-style tents set near the Cauvery River, on which you can enjoy great fishing from coracle boats (round animal-hide crafts). Meals included; multicuisine restaurant, bar, fishing equipment. Open December–March. AE, DC, MC, V.

BIJAPUR

Inexpensive

Hotel Mayura Adil Shahi. Anand Mahal Rd., Bijapur; tel. 934. Reservations: KSTDC; tel. 212901. 19 rooms with bath. This bungalow, with an interior court-yard and a separate annex, has clean, modestly furnished rooms. Overhead fans and mosquito nets, room service, multicuisine restaurant, bar, nearby tourist department office. Rupees only.

GOKARNA BEACH

Inexpensive

Tourist Cottages. Gokarna Beach; no phone. Reservations: KTD, tel. 215489. 4 cottages with bath. These cottages offer a valley view and are near a good beach for swimming. Rooms are clean, with a modest Western decor, and have small front porches. Fan, room service, Indian vegetarian-cuisine restaurant. Rupees only.

HASSAN

Moderate

Hotel Hassan Ashok. Bangalore-Mangalore Rd., Hassan 573201; tel. 68731. 46 rooms with bath. This three-story hotel offers reasonable rooms with a modern decor. Some rooms are air-conditioned. Room service, Indian- and Continental-cuisine restaurant, bar, health club, foreign-exchange counter, doctor, shopping arcade. AE, DC, MC, V.

HOSPET

Inexpensive

Malligai Tourist Home. 6/143 Jambunatha Rd., Hospet 583201; tel. 8101. 86 rooms with bath; 20 rooms under construction. This hotel has modestly appointed, very clean rooms. Best rooms are air-conditioned. Room service, multicuisine restaurant, bar, foreign-exchange counter, tour arrangements, doctor, shops. AE, DC, MC, V.

MANGALORE

Moderate

Welcomgroup Manjarun. Old Port Rd., Mangalore 575001; tel. 31791. 101 rooms with bath. This modern hotel, which overlooks the Gurpur River, has a spacious lobby and appealing contemporary-decor rooms. Best rooms have a view of the water. Air-conditioning, room service, TV, multicuisine restaurants, bar, foreign-exchange and travel counter, health club, swimming pool, doctor, secretarial services, shopping arcade. AE, DC, MC, V.

Inexpensive

Summer Sands Beach Resort. Chotamangalore, Ullal, Mangalore 574159; tel. 6400. 64 rooms with bath. Cottages in this beach resort, 10 km (six mi.) from Mangalore, offer lots of privacy and clean rooms with a simple Western decor. The best cottages face the beach. Some rooms are air-conditioned. Room service, multicuisine restaurant, bar, swimming pool, massages, foreign-exchange and travel counter, yoga. AE, DC, MC, V.

MANIPAL

Inexpensive

Valley View International. Manipal 576119; tel. 20285 or reserve through Welcomgroup Hotel. 70 rooms with bath. Set on a hill, this multistory hotel, which is under renovation, is a part of the Welcomgroup Graduate School of Hotel Administration. Air-conditioned rooms will be spacious and modern. TV, room service, multicuisine restaurants, bar, swimming pool, foreign-exchange and travel counter, yoga. AE, DC, MC, V.

MYSORE

Expensive

Ashok Lalitha Mahal Palace Hotel. Mysore 570011; tel. 27650. 54 rooms with bath. Situated just outside the city center, this 1920s palace of the former maharaja, now a hotel, is sumptuous—one of India's best treats. Its air-conditioned interior is Italian baroque. Painted walls are lavishly trimmed with ornate plaster moldings, huge pillars, and gorgeous domes. Best rooms are in the original structure and have appealing but not necessarily grand Victorian furnishings. Rooms in the new wing have a contemporary decor. TV, room service, multicuisine restaurant, bar, billiard room, health club, swimming pool, tennis courts, foreign-exchange and travel counter, baby-sitters, doctor, shopping arcade, helipad. AE, DC, MC, V.

Moderate

Quality Inn Southern Star Mysore. 13–14 Vinobha Rd., Mysore 570005; tel. 27217–9. 72 rooms with bath. This new Western-style high rise has a marble lobby with a large mural of Nandi (the sacred bull). Air-conditioned rooms are spacious, with a modern decor. Best rooms overlook the pool. TV, room service, restaurants, bar, swimming pool, health club, foreign-exchange and travel counter, business center, baby-sitters, doctor, shopping arcade. AE, DC, MC, V.

Inexpensive

Hotel Metropole. 5 Jhansi Lakshmi Bai Rd., Mysore 570005; tel. 20681. 20 rooms with bath. This lovely old guest house of the former maharaja is faultlessly maintained. Best rooms are on the upper floor off a sweeping veranda. Victorian furnishings are charming and evoke the 1940s. Most rooms are air-conditioned. Fans, TV, room service, multicuisine restaurant, bar, foreign-exchange and travel counter, doctor, shop. Good value. AE, DC, MC, V.

NAGARHOLE

Deluxe

Kabini River Lodge. Karpura, Nagarhole Wildlife Sanctuary. Reservations: Jungle Lodge and Resorts, 2nd Floor, Shrungar Shopping Center, M. G. Rd., Bangalore 560001; tel. 575195. 14 rooms with bath. Once the former vice-regal and maharaja's hunting lodge, this resort set in the sanctuary is wonderful. It is run by Colonel Wakefield and his staff, who are gracious and knowledgeable. Chances are you will see wildlife nearby. The ambience is peaceful; modern rooms have overhead fans and a rustic decor. Open-air multicuisine restaurant, room service, TV lounge, bar, jeep and elephant safaris, coracle rides on the nearby lake. Meals are included. AE, DC, MC, V.

SRIRANGAPATNA

Inexpensive

Hotel Mayura River View. Srirangapatna; tel. 2114. Reservations: KSTDC, tel. 212901. 8 rooms with bath. Four cottages, each with two units, make up this riverside complex. Cottages have clean rooms with a modern decor and a pleasant porch. There is a multicuisine restaurant and room service. Rupees only.

DINING OUT. Except for Bangalore, Mangalore, and Mysore, don't expect a lot of dining options. Bangalore is about as Western as you can get, with almost too many American-style fast-food reminders. Throughout Karnataka, you will find reasonable food, but limited menus. Besides the restaurants listed here, hotels also have restaurants. Breakfast is usually 8–10:30 A.M.; lunch, noon–3 P.M.; dinner, 7:30–11 P.M. Payment is normally in rupees unless the restaurant is connected to a Western-style hotel. The restaurants listed below are informal and, unless noted, are open for all three meals and don't require reservations. Prices are based on one person eating a three-course meal, excluding taxes, tip, or beverage: *Expensive,* Rs. 200–Rs. 300; *Moderate,* Rs. 100–Rs. 200; *Inexpensive,* under Rs. 100.

BANGALORE

Expensive

The Jockey Club. Taj Residency, 41/3 M. G. Rd.; tel. 584444. Belgian mirrors are set into carved teak walls; you're surrounded by paintings of Bangalore's derby winners. The lighting is always subdued, and at night a pianist adds to the elegant mood. The cuisine is Continental, including lobster benedictine and roast kid rack (rosemary flavored rack of lamb in a honey-and-sherry sauce). Save room for its famous desserts. Dinner reservations required. Open noon–3 P.M. and 7 P.M.– midnight. AE, DC, MC, V.

Paradise Island. Taj West End Hotel, Race Course Rd., tel. 269281. An open-air restaurant in a British gazebo surrounded by water and lush plantings, Paradise Island has an extensive multicuisine menu. At lunch it also offers a multicuisine buffet with the accent on Thai or Chinese dishes on alternating days. Dinner is à la carte. If you like things spicy, go for the *Thai kaeng ped gai* (chicken red curry); a less spicy favorite is *padh nahm mon hoi* (choose your cut of meat and its sautéed with bamboo shoots, mushrooms, and oyster sauce). Expect a Western band nightly. Dinner reservations advised. Open 12:30–3:30 P.M. and 7:30–11:30 P.M. AE, DC, MC, V.

Moderate

Chung Wah. 45/1 Residency Rd.; tel. 582662. A modern Oriental decor— wooden latticework, Chinese fans and paintings on the walls, and lanterns—defines this cozy restaurant, which offers most of China's cuisines. Two popular dishes are *huli* chicken (fried, sliced chicken simmered with soy sauce and onions) and deboned pomfret with a choice of mild-to-spicy sauces. Weekend dinner reservations advised. Open noon–3 P.M. and 7 P.M.–11 P.M. AE, DC, MC, V.

Karavalli. Taj Gateway Hotel. 66 Residency Rd.; tel. 544545. Set in a shady terrace and in an adjoining cottage, this restaurant features coastal cuisines from Goa, Kerala, and Karnataka's Mangalore. Its ambience is definitely southern: waiters dressed in dhotis, South Indian classical music playing in the background. Two regional specialties are: *kori gassi* (chicken pieces simmered in a coconut gravy) served with *neer dosa* (Karnataka-style crepe), and *kane bezule* (fish marinated in ground spices, then deep-fried). Dinner reservations advised. Open 12:30 P.M.–3 P.M. and 7:30 P.M.–midnight. AE, DC, MC, V.

Mandarin Room. Ashok Hotel, High Grounds; tel. 269462. A rooftop restaurant with a good view of Bangalore, Mandarin Room has a Chinese decor with the accent on green and gold. The chef prepares Szechuan and Cantonese dishes. Try the non-spicy chicken with bean curd, crisp lamb Peking-style, and the spicy shredded lamb in chili sauce. You can also dance to a good Western band. Reservations advised. Open 8 P.M.–midnight. AE, DC, MC, V.

Noodles. Comfort Inn Ramanashree, 16 Raja Ram Mohan Rd.; tel. 225152. Cozy, with dark wood walls, mirrored pillars, and recessed lighting, this popular new Chinese restaurant offers a free appetizer and serves Szechuan and Cantonese dishes. A pianist plays nightly. Try its special tofu stuffed pepper in hot garlic sauce or *tau fauchin yi* (pomfret steamed with local herbs, spices, and vegetables). Dinner reservations advised. Open noon–3 P.M. and 7:30 P.M.–11:30 P.M. AE, DC, MC, V.

Prince's. 1st Floor Curzon Complex, Brigade Rd.; tel. 580087. This elegant private restaurant is old-fashioned Victorian: etched glass lamps, carved rosewood furniture, a grandfather clock, even a menu styled like an old photo album. It offers multicuisine dishes, including a range of steaks and the popular Indian chicken *kalimirchiwalla* (chicken pieces simmered in black-pepper sauce). Dinner reservations advised. Open 11:30 A.M.–3 P.M. and 7:30 P.M.–11:30 P.M. AE, DC, MC, V.

Shogun. 45/3 Residency Rd.; tel. 581707. Expect a classy Oriental decor, with lots of pink and gray, and a bank of windows looking out at a small Japanese garden and pool. Come here for any Far Eastern cuisine. Try the unusual chicken taro nest (chicken coated in batter and deep-fried with mixed vegetables and served with a garlic sauce inside a crunchy fried-potato basket). Weekend dinner reservations advised. Open noon–3:30 P.M. and 7 P.M.–midnight. DC, MC, V.

Terrace Grill. Welcomgroup Windsor Manor, 25 Sankey Rd.; tel. 269898. Set on a terrace with wrought-iron chairs and tables, a nice breeze, lots of plants, and a red canopy overhead, you select a fresh cut of meat or the catch-of-the-day and it's grilled over charcoal. Also select your side dishes, enjoy a salad bar, and a complimentary pitcher of sangria. A guitarist entertains nightly. Reservations advised. Open 7 P.M.–11 P.M. AE, DC, MC, V.

Inexpensive

Amaravathi Restaurant. 45/3 Residency Rd.; tel. 585140. This restaurant offers Andhra Pradesh cuisine served on a banana leaf. Sit in a booth backed by teak lattice-wood screens. Expect subdued lighting, Hindi film music, and a crowd! It's most popular dishes are chicken *Amaravathi* (chicken pieces fried with chili and served in a mildly spicy gravy) and the unlimited *thali* (numerous portions of different dishes served until you say stop). Dinner reservations advised. Open 11 A.M.–11 P.M. DC, MC, V.

Mavalli Tiffin Rooms. Near Lalbagh, Lalbagh Rd.; tel. 220022. For a wonderful time and Indian vegetarian food, visit this Bangalore institution, established in 1924. Front rooms, with ceiling fans, are crowded with marble tables. The small back room is air-conditioned. You won't find better *dosas* (Indian-style stuffed crepes); and you can't beat the price (Rs. 5). You can also enjoy great sweets and superb coffee. You may have to wait for a table; but once the dhoti-clad bearer takes your order, it's fast food all the way. Open 6:30–11 A.M. and 3:30–7:30 P.M., closed Monday.

MANGALORE

Moderate

Embers. Welcomgroup Manjaran, Old Port Rd.; tel. 31791. At this poolside barbecue there's no menu. You choose your cut of meat or opt for the catch-of-the-day, then select the side dishes and create your own salad, while your main course is charcoal-grilled. Reservations advised. Open 7:30 P.M.–11:30 P.M. AE, DC, MC, V.

The Galley. Welcomgroup Manjarun, Old Port Rd.; tel. 31791. Granite walls are inset with mirrors and sailing-motif paintings; the mood is low-key. The chef offers Chinese, Continental, and Indian cuisines, including such regional dishes as Mangalorian prawn curry with *dosa* (Indian-style crepe) and prawn *sukka* (sautéed prawns in coconut and curry leaves). There's a luncheon buffet. Dinner reservations advised. Open 12:30 P.M.–3 P.M., and 7:30–midnight. AE, DC, MC, V.

Inexpensive

Sagar. University Rd. (10 km or 6 mi. from the heart of Mangalore); tel. 6916 or 6496. A signboard on the front of this extremely informal restaurant says: "Come to Where the Flavor Is." And the flavor here is Mangalorian-style fresh seafood. Don't expect a menu. Mr. Sudhakar, the owner, will come to your table on the lawn or inside a cozy thatched shack and tell you what's available. It could be squid, mussels, prawns, or pomfret. It will be spicy. Open 11 A.M.–3 P.M. and 6 P.M. until the food runs out. Extremely popular. Rupees only.

MYSORE

Moderate

Lalitha Mahal Palace Hotel Restaurant. Mysore; tel. 27650. Here you'll eat in the maharaja's former ballroom—a tour de force of Italian baroque-regal with stained-glass domes and sky-blue walls enhanced by ornate plaster moldings. You can also choose Chinese, Continental, or Indian dishes. Try the Mysore *thali* (assorted regional dishes served on a platter), the mutton *ulathiyathu* (mutton cooked with coconut, red chili, and curry leaves), or the *murgh tikka lovabdar* (boneless chicken simmered in tomato, yogurt, ginger, and green chili). There's a flutist at lunch and a sitarist or vina player at dinner to punctuate the ambience. Dinner reservations advised. Open 6–11 A.M., 12:30–3 P.M., and 8–11 P.M. AE, DC, MC, V.

Inexpensive

Jewel Rock. Hotel Maurya Palace, 2-3-7 Sri Harsha Rd.; tel. 35912. A cozy new restaurant, with soft lighting, checkered linen, lots of plants, it offers multicuisine fare. Its Chinese cuisine is the favorite, including nonspicy chicken in wine sauce (not on the menu) and shredded lamb with chilies. Open 11 A.M.–3 P.M. and 7 P.M.–11:30 P.M. V.

Sr Plaintain Leaf. 1979 Rajkamal Talkies Rd.; tel. 32217. Get ready for a kitsch, plastic decor and Hindi film songs. You can't tell the real plants from the fake ones. The chef offers Chinese and Indian dishes, with the unquestionably legitimate Andhra Pradesh dishes, the house favorites, which you eat off a banana leaf. No smoking allowed. Open 6 A.M.–11 P.M. Rupees only.

SWEETS AND TREATS. Bangalore. Stop at Chaatwalla (44/45 Residency Rd.) for *chaat* (spicy potato salad), *bhel puri* (puffed rice served with chutneys), and *pani puri* (small, fried bread filled with spicy water). Open 5 P.M.–midnight. Also visit Sreeraj Lassi Bar (Lavelle Rd.) for Bangalore's best *lassi* (yogurt drink), *kulfi* (Indian ice cream), and *paneer* (Indian cheese). Open 10 A.M.–11 P.M.

Bangalore-Mysore Road. About 10 km (6 mi.) beyond Maddur on the road from Bangalore to Mysore and opposite the KMF building, look for a white roadside stand with a signboard that says *Maddur Vadai.* Stop and enjoy its *vadai,* a deliciously crispy and spicy treat served with chutney.

HOW TO GET AROUND. From the Airport. Bangalore. At press time, the airport coach was not functioning. A taxi will take you to your hotel for about Rs. 150. **Belgaum.** A taxi into town will cost about Rs. 70. **Mangalore.** A taxi should cost about Rs. 100.

By Plane. *Indian Airlines* flies four times weekly between Bangalore and Mangalore; *Vayudoot* makes three weekly flights between Bangalore and Belgaum.

By Train. Numerous express trains run from Bangalore to Mysore. Other good trains connect Bangalore with Bijapur, Mangalore, and other important cities. In Bangalore, contact the Bangalore City Railway Station, tel. 131 for inquiries; call tel. 132 for reservations. In Mysore, contact the Mysore Railway Station, tel. 20100.

By Bus. KSTDC has a deluxe bus service that makes four daily trips in each direction between Mysore and Bangalore. It also makes an overnight trip in each direction between Mangalore and Bangalore. For information, contact KSTDC, Transport Wing (see Tourist Information, above).

By Hired Car with Driver. This is the best way to see Karnataka. Rates are about Rs. 4–Rs. 5 per km, with a halt charge of Rs. 50–Rs. 100 per night. Hire a car from one of the agencies listed below under Tour Operators.

By Taxi. This is a good option for travel outside a city. Taxis are not metered in Karnataka. Rates are the same as those for a hired car with driver. In Bangalore you can hire a tourist taxi for Rs. 200 for four hours.

By Auto Rickshaw. In congested cities, this is a convenient, quick way to travel. Rates: Rs. 4 for the first km; Rs. 1.50 per additional km. Set the fare in advance.

By Bike Rickshaw. An enjoyable way to travel, this should be cheaper than an auto rickshaw.

TOURS. *KSTDC* (see Tourist Information, above) conducts numerous tours from Bangalore, Hubli and Mysore to popular destinations within the state, including trips to Belur, Halebid, Hampi, Nagarhole, and Somnathpura. It also offers extensive statewide tours, such as a good trip to north Karnataka, and some interstate tours, which include Andhra Pradesh, Goa, and Tamil Nadu. Buses are usually deluxe and very comfortable, providing an inexpensive way to see much of the state if you don't have a rented car and driver. KSTDC also conducts the following city tours:

Bangalore Sightseeing Tour. Half-day tours departing at 7:30 A.M. and 2 P.M. Tippu's palace, Bull Temple, Lalbagh, Cauvery Handicrafts Emporium, Vidhana Soudha, Museum, and Ulsoor Lake. Rs. 45.

Mysore Sightseeing Tour (one day). Includes Somnathpura and Srirangapatna. Daily. Rs. 125.

TOUR OPERATORS. The following agencies can take care of all your travel needs, including car with driver:

Ashok Travels & Tours, Hotel Ashok, High Grounds, Bangalore 560001; tel. 261048.

Clipper Holidays, Madras Bank Rd., Bangalore 560001; tel. 217052–4.

Trade Wings, 48 Lavelle Rd., Bangalore 560001; tel. 214595–7.

Also check *Facts at Your Fingertips* for tour operators who offer special adventures in Karnataka.

SEASONAL EVENTS. Karnataka celebrates many festivals along with the rest of India; but the following events are particularly special. Actual dates are often determined by the lunar calendar; consult the India Tourist Office for details.

January. *Shankarnti.* This three-day festival celebrates the harvest. Unusually exuberant in rural areas, the final day honors the cow, which is worshiped, garlanded, and decorated to the hilt.

August/September. *Ganesha Chaturthi,* throughout Karnataka, is a three-day festival celebrating Ganesha with songs and dances in the hopes that paying tribute to this god will return blessings and especially good fortune.

September/October. Mysore and the rest of Karnataka observe *Dussera,* a 10-day festival that takes on tremendous pomp and pageantry. The festival celebrates the victory of the goddess Chamundeswari over the demon Mahishasura. While the maharaja no longer takes part, the rest of the city does. The palace is lit up and glows. On the 10th day there is a caparisoned elephant bearing the idol of the goddess, and a fantastic procession, including the camel corps, infantry, and cavalry.

November/December. *Kadalekaye Parishe.* This groundnut fair is held on the premises of the Bull Temple, Bangalore. Main event: who can consume the largest amount of groundnut. The temple bull is bedecked with a garland of groundnut to prevent him from ruining the local crops of this valuable product.

December. *Hampi–Vijaynagar Festival.* Hampi has a three-day festival of cultural shows, with Karnataka music and folk dances performed at the ruins. A beautiful event.

HISTORIC SITES. Karnataka is rich in historical sites. Indeed, some places are temple villages in themselves. A few of these are in close proximity to each other and can be visited in a half day. Such is the case of Aihole, Badami, and Pattadakal, as well as Belur and Halebid. We've grouped these villages together so that you can better organize your visits. Historic sites are generally free or have nominal entrance fees. They are open from sunrise to sunset unless noted otherwise.

AIHOLE-BADAMI-PATTADAKAL

Aihole alone has 125 temples dedicated to Hindu gods and goddesses. This temple village represents the cradle of Dravidian architecture. Aihole was founded by the first Chalukyan king around A.D. 450, and most of these temples are from A.D. 450 to A.D. 750. The simple towers of Aihole are precursors of the massive goporums in the south. See especially the temple of *Lad Khan,* possibly the oldest, the U-shaped *Durga Temple,* the *Suraya Naryana Temple,* the *Ravanaphad* (Brahmanical cave), and the *Huchimalli Temple.*

Badami. This second capital of the Chalukyas was founded by Pulakesin I around A.D. 550. Above the village, with stunning cave temples that date from the sixth century, is the old Badami Fort.

Pattadakal (22 km or 14 mi. from Badami). City founded by King Vikramaditya II in the eighth century and the site of the Chalukyan coronation ceremonies. The next stage in temple evolution after Aihole, with 10 temples constructed from the 600s to the 700s. The *Papanatha Temple* (A.D. 680) is the earliest example of pure Chalukyan style—a simple structure with plain pillars. The facades are decorated with themes from the *Ramayana.* The *Mallikarjuna Temple,* with Nandi standing out front, is decorated with scenes from the *Bhagvadgita.* The temple was constructed by a queen (Trilokya Mahadevi) of Vikramaditya II. The *Virupaksha Temple,* built in A.D. 740 by Lokamaha Devi, depicts scenes from the *Ramayana* and *Mahabharata.* See if you can find the carving that looks like an elephant from one side and a buffalo from the other.

BANGALORE

Bull Temple (five km or three mi. from Bangalore) is a monolithic bull built in the 1500s in the Dravidian style (5 meters [15 feet] high by 6 meters [20 feet] long) by Kempe Gowda, founder of Bangalore. Supposedly the iron plate on its head keeps the bull from growing.

Nandi Hills (59 km or 37 mi.) has 2,000-year-old Shiva temples, and is the former site of Tipu Sultan's summer palace. Walk up to Tipu's Drop, a 620-meter (2,000-foot) sheer cliff, where the condemned were pushed over the edge.

Tipu's Palace and Fort, just northwest of Lal Bagh, were originally built of mud in 1537 by Kempe Gowda; rebuilt in stone in the 1700s by Hyder Ali and embellished by his son Tipu Sultan. The palace was the summer residence of Tipu Sultan. Open 8 A.M.–6 P.M.

Vidhana Soudha, on the northern boundary of Cubbon Park, is an enormous white granite structure built in the neo-Dravidian style in 1956. On top sit three lions—India's national symbol. You can't go inside.

BELUR-HALEBID

Belur (39 km or 24 mi. from Hassan) is a former twelfth-century city under the Hoysala kings. *Belur Temple of Lord Channakeshava* (a Vishnu avatar and still a place of active worship) was begun in 1116 by Hoysala King Vishnuvardhana and completed 103 years later. Star-shaped and sitting on a platform, the squat temple is of soapstone. The guides are very informative, and Rs. 20 will make them very happy.

Halebid (16 km or 10 mi. from Belur) was started by the same king in 1121 after the construction of Belur began. It took 180 years of work. It has the same star-shaped patterns with a double shrine, again of soapstone, and a marvel of sculpture. Again, an informative guide (Rs. 20) will bring the gorgeous temple to life.

BIDAR

Bidar Fort, the former capital of the fifteenth-century Bahmani kings, is a creation that mixes Hindu and Moslem influences. There's a small museum as you enter, with an archaeological department. The hours are "iffy"—sort of 8 A.M.–4 P.M. Try to get a guide to show you around. The Karnataka Tourism Department has a good pamphlet on all the monuments within the fort and around Bidar. The pamphlet contains excellent information and is intelligently written, but it has no map. Bring a flashlight and good walking shoes and plan for plenty of time (two-three hours).

Bahamani Tombs are not far from the fort. Visit early in the day to see the interior paintings (best in the morning light). Again, a flashlight is a must. Buried here are eight former kings of Bidar. The tomb of Ahmed Shah-al-Wali Bahamani is 33 meters (107 feet) high and built on a square plane, with a dome that is three-quarters of an orb. No external decorations, but the interior was once quite colorful. You can still see remnants of intricate floral designs and calligraphy. Also, set into the dome are supposedly nine diamonds—but you'll need a powerful flashlight to see them. Also visit the tomb of Sultan Allauddin Shah II. It originally glittered, with the exterior covered with tilework, some of which still remains. Finally, visit the Chaukhandi of Hazrat Khalil-Ullah on the way to the Ashtur tombs. Steps lead up to the entrance of an octagonal structure that encloses another tomb. This building was also formerly covered with tilework. Notice the beautifully carved granite pillars and the entrance decorated with floral motifs. The *Baridi Tombs* are situated to the west of Bidar on Nanded Road. Usually Moslem tombs are closed on the western side, where a *mihrab* was built for saying prayers. Not so at the Tomb of Ali Barid (1542–1580). Legend claims that Ali Barid wanted his grave kept clean by the wind and sun, so it was kept open.

BIJAPUR

Bijapur has 50 mosques and 20 tombs. This Moslem-dominated city is best appreciated with a government-approved guide. The *Gol Gumbaz,* built in the mid-1600s, encloses the second-largest domed space in the world, with a wonderful whispering gallery that can only be appreciated early in the morning when children have not yet arrived. The inscription on the entrance arch states that this tomb houses the mortal remains of Mohammed Adil Shah, who, on his death, became "an inhabitant of Paradise and also a Particle of the Firmament."

The *Jama Masjid,* started in 1557, has lovely proportions, graceful minarets, and lovely bulbous domes, and is covered with ornamental detail. You can enter the courtyard, but only Moslems may enter the shrine itself. This is the largest mosque in the Deccan; 2,250 people can pray here, one to each painted block.

The *Ibrahim Rauza* has richly decorated walls and perforated stone windows. Built by Mohammed Adil Shah, it contains the tomb of his father, Ibrahim Adil Shah. Special acoustics enable the voice of the muezzin calling devotees to prayer to be heard from a mosque 62 meters (200 feet) away, though that same voice can't be heard outside the tomb. Try it.

HAMPI

Hampi, the ruins of the Vijayanagar empire, is also a place best appreciated with a government-approved guide, which can be arranged at the Hospet Tourist Bureau. A reasonable visit of the considerable ruins, spanning 24 kilometers (15 miles), requires a day. The grand flourish of this empire lasted from the fourteenth to the mid-sixteenth century. Do not miss seeing the *Virupaksha Temple* (visit early in the morning when the temple bells are rung and the monkeys come running to eat); the *Vithala Temple Complex,* with its renowned stone chariot; and the *Hazara Rama Temple Complex.*

MYSORE

Chamundi Hill is named after the royal family's patron goddess, Chamundeswari. See the 5-meter (16-foot) *Nandi,* constructed in the seventeenth century from a single granite boulder; the *Sri Chamundeswari Temple* dating from the twelfth century, with a richly carved tower constructed in the eighteenth century; and the *statue of Mahishasura,* built of mortar about 35 years ago (the goddess Chamundeswari killed this demon to bring peace to the country).

Lalitha Mahal Palace, now a hotel, was built in 1921 by the maharaja for his foreign guests. Beautiful interior and exterior. Have tea, at least.

Maharaja's Mysore Palace, built in 1857 on the former site of a former wooden palace that burned down, is one of the biggest palaces in India. The architecture is Indo-Saracenic, a synthesis of Hindu and Islamic design. On Sundays and holidays, the palace is illuminated with thousands of tiny lights. See the impressive Durbar Hall, with its ornate ceiling and huge "grandstand" awning. Also, the Kalyana Mandap (Marriage Hall), where women sat behind screened balconies; on the wall are lifelike paintings of the Dussehra procession. Plan at least an hour. Open 10:30 A.M.–5:30 P.M.

SRAVANABELGOLA

Here you'll find a colossal statue of the Jain saint, *Gomateswara*. The monolithic statue is 18 meters (57 feet) high and over a 1,000 years old. The statue's nakedness is symbolic of the saint's renunciation of worldly possessions.

SRINANGAPATNA

This is an island fortress and the capital of the Mysore raja from 1610 to 1799. Its most famous residents were Hyder Ali and Tipu Sultan. Visit the fortress with the mosque inside; the summer palace called *Daria Daulat Bagh;* and Tipu Sultan's mausoleum, the *Gumbaz* (both are outside the fort).

SRINGERI

Sringeri is an important Hindu center of pilgrimage. See St. Sankaracharya's monastery, created just at the start of the Vijayanagar empire, and the fourteenth-century *Vidya Shankara Temple,* with its 12 zodiac pillars arranged so that the sun's rays fall on the pillar that corresponds to that month.

TALKAD

Talkad's 30 temples lie beneath a strange stretch of sand dunes on the banks of the Cauvery River. Two main temples are the *Vaidyesvara,* a Dravidian temple of granite perhaps built in the fourteenth century, with later additions; and the beautiful *Kirtinarayana,* possibly erected in 1117 (an example of the Hoysalan style temple). The sand is a result of deforestation, the construction of a reservoir in the fourteenth century, and the yearly monsoon.

MUSEUMS AND GALLERIES. Entrance to these places is free or nominal in cost. **Bangalore.** *Government Museum,* set in Cubbon Park and established in 1887, is one of the oldest museums in India. It has exhibits in archaeology, ethnology, geology, art, and sculpture, and excavations from the Mohenjo-Daro ruins that date from 5000 B.C. Open 10 A.M.–5 P.M., closed Wednesday.

Venkatappa Art Gallery, Cubbon Park, exhibits the work of the court painter S. K. Venkatappa, who painted in the late 1800s. You can also see musical instruments that he designed. Open 10 A.M.–5 P.M., closed Wednesday.

Mysore. *Sri Jayachamarajendra Art Gallery,* in the Jaganmohan Palace, has various schools of Indian art, beautiful antique furniture, and decorated musical instruments. No picture-taking. Open daily 8 A.M.–5 P.M.

GARDENS AND ZOOS. Bangalore. *Cubbon Park,* laid out in 1864, has imposing Greco-Colonial-style buildings, including the Public Library, High Court, and Government Museum; plus an aquarium and a delightful toy train for children.

Lal Bagh. The name means red roses, which grow in abundance here. Designed by Hyder Ali in 1760 and added to by his son, Tipu Sultan, the garden has over 100 varieties of trees, thousands of flowers and plants. At the garden center is a stunning glass house reminiscent of the Crystal Palace in London. Its foundation stone was placed by Prince Albert of Wales in 1889. You'll also find a 3 billion-year-old rock called Peninsula Gneiss. Annual flower shows are held in January and August. Open 8 A.M.–6 P.M.

Mysore. The *Chamarajendra Zoological Gardens,* begun in 1892, has a large and varied collection of animals and birds in a natural habitat. Open 8:30 A.M.–5:30 P.M.

Brindavan Gardens, 19 km (12 mi.) from Mysore, stretch out in terraces below the Krishnarajasagar Dam. At night, garden lights twinkle, fountains play, and, yes, there's music. The lights actually respond rhythmically to the beat. Gardens are lit up for one hour on weekday nights and two hours on Sundays and holidays. Nominal entrance fee.

SPORTS AND OUTDOOR ADVENTURES. Karnataka is a perfect setting for outdoor adventures. Check *Facts at Your Fingertips* for tour operators who promote good trips in this state. **Beaches and Water Sports.** Karnataka's coastline is unspoiled, with good beaches north and south of Mangalore. Head north to Kaup (46 km or 28 mi.), where an idyllic stretch extends 10 km (six mi.) to Malpe. At Malpe, MANAS (Valley View International, Manipal 576119; tel. 20285) has set up a water-sports complex. You can waterski, windsurf, go kayaking, or parasail. You can also take lessons in these sports, arrange to take a backwater day cruise in an indigenous fishing boat, or hire a boat to go to St. Mary's Island, a beautiful hideaway with strange rock formations. North of Malpe are Marvanthe, Bilikerem, and Karwar beaches, which are also good for swimming. South of Mangalore, you can swim at nearby Ullal.

Golfing. The *Bangalore Golf Club,* designed by the British in 1876, has temporary memberships and equipment for hire. Call for details (tel. 266713 or 267121). You can also play golf at the Mysore Golf Club. Call for details (tel. 20743).

Horse Racing. The *Bangalore Turf Club* goes into high gear September–December and March–June. Call for details (tel. 262391). The season at the Mysore Race Club is August–October. Call for details (tel. 21675).

Wildlife Sanctuaries. *Bandipur Wildlife Sanctuary,* 80 km (50 mi.) south of Mysore, covers 689 sq km (427 sq mi.) adjoining the Mudumalai forest. Once the private preserve of the maharajas of Mysore, it offers good opportunities to see herds of bison, elephants, spotted deer, and, if you're lucky, a tiger or a leopard. There are observation platforms for viewing; and jeep rides and elephant safaris are available. For more details, contact the Mysore Tourist Office. The best time to visit is September–April.

Bannerghatta National Park, 22 km (14 mi.) from Bangalore, is a new park covering 104 km (64 mi.), with a variety of wildlife, a crocodile farm, and a snake park. It also has a "Lion Safari," where lions roam freely as visitors are transported through in vehicles. Open 9 A.M.–noon and 2–5 P.M., closed Tuesdays.

Nagarahole National Park, 96 km (60 mi.) south of Mysore, comprises 640 sq km (397 mi.) of forests and swamps that were once part of the exclusive preserve of the maharajas. It has at least 250 species of birds and numerous animals, including antelopes, bears, jungle cats, barking deer, wild dogs, elephants, langur, mongooses, panthers, porcupines, sambar, tigers, and lots of reptiles. Vehicle and guides are available. Numerous tribesmen also live here (the Jenu Kurubas and Betta Kurubas). You can also trek, with permission from the Chief Wildlife Warden, Aranya Bhavan, 18th Cross, Malleswaram, Bangalore, tel. 31993. Van, jeep, or minibus are available for game viewing drives. You can stay at the delightful Kabini River Lodge. The best season is October–March.

Ranganathittu Bird Sanctuary, 18 km (11 mi.) from Mysore, is made up of six islets in the Cauvery River. A large variety of birds (night herons, little cormorants, snakebirds, spoon bills), flying foxes, and reptiles. Boating is available. Accommodations are available; contact: KSTDC (address above). The best time to visit is June–September.

Yoga. *Kalpana* (Lalitha Mahal Palace Hotel, Mysore; tel. 27650) has yoga classes and gives ayurvedic, acupressure, Japanese shiatsu, or Thai massages. Open daily 9 A.M.–10 P.M. Rupees only. They also have a branch at Hotel Hassan Ashok; tel. 68731 for details. AE, MC, V.

SHOPPING. The skill of the old Karnataka craftsmen is still flourishing; inlaid furniture and sandalwood carvings are made in a variety of designs that delight the connoisseur. For hundreds of years, Karnataka has been the home of sandalwood. Statuettes and panels, beads, and pendants are executed in this delicately scented wood. Carved tables, screens, and dinner gongs are made in lovely designs. Its silks are also highly rated in India.

Bangalore. Visit these excellent fixed-price shops: *Natesan's Antiqarts* (64 Mahatma Gandhi Rd.) sells an unusual collection of high-quality stone, bronze, and wood antiquities; old paintings; and exquisite new artifacts, plus silver jewelry and precious stones. Merchandise is guaranteed and authorized for export. Open 10 A.M.–1 P.M. and 4 P.M.–7 P.M., closed Sundays. AE, DC, MC, V.

Priyadarshini Handlooms (45 M. G. Rd., Shop No. 8, KSHDC Complex) sells handloom and handblocked Karnataka silks by the meter. Open 10:30 A.M.–1:30

P.M. and 4 P.M.–7:30 P.M., closed Sundays. During festivals, it's open daily, 10 A.M.–8 P.M. AE, DC, MC, V.

Cauvery (49 Mahatma Gandhi Rd.), a state-run store, sells all of Karnataka's products: sandalwood handicrafts, terra-cotta, carved rosewood furniture, silk, leatherwork, jute products, lacquered toys, bidriwork, embossed bronze, soaps, perfumes, incense, and sachets. Open 10 A.M.–1:30 P.M. and 3–7:30 P.M., closed Sundays. AE, DC, MC, V.

Mysore. For good sandalwood and rosewood inlaid products, visit *Ganesh Industrial and Fine Art Works,* 532 Dhanavantri Rd. Open daily 9 A.M.–9 P.M. AE, DC, MC, V.

For silks by the meter, visit *K.S.F.C.* (Government Silk Factory Complex, Manandavai Rd.). The silks are excellent and the prices are good. Open 9:30 A.M.–8:30 P.M., closed Sundays. Rupees only.

Karnataka Cottage Emporium (Mysore Hotel Complex, opposite Lido Theater, 2729 Bangalore Nilgiri Rd.) also has a good selection of silks. Open daily 9 A.M.–9 P.M. AE, MC, V.

Handicrafts Sales Emporium and Kaveri Silk Emporium (Hotel Dasharath Complex, opposite Mysore Zoo) has a wide range of Karnataka handicrafts, silks, and other products. Open daily 9 A.M.–6 P.M. AE, DC, MC, V.

NIGHTLIFE AND BARS. Bangalore's most elegant bars are the *Jockey Club* (Taj Residency, 41/3 Mahatma Gandhi Rd.), with an exclusive club atmosphere, and the *Polo Bar* (The Oberoi, 37/39 M. G. Rd.), with its stained glass and magnificent views of the exterior gardens and cascading waterfall. Each is open 11 A.M.–midnight. Bangalore also has 200 pubs, with draft beer available from local breweries. Pubs are open daily, 11 A.M.–11 P.M. Two popular hangouts are the *Black Cadillac* (50 Residency Rd.) and the *Oaken Cask Pub* (45/3 Residency Rd.).

Mysore's best bar is at the *Lalitha Mahal Palace Hotel.* Though not palatial, the Victorian furnishings are comfy. The casual ambience feels right. Open 11 A.M.–11 P.M.

HYDERABAD AND ANDHRA PRADESH

India's Melting Pot

by
KATHLEEN COX

Andhra Pradesh is not on the itinerary of most Western visitors to India. It should be. The ancient Andhra culture reaches back into the great Indian epics: *Ramayana* and *Mahabharata*. Beautiful temples still stand from the earliest days of Hindu, Jain, and Buddhist worship, as do impressive Moslem forts, mosques, and palaces. A fine stretch of beach along the Bay of Bengal tempts you. Then there's Hyderabad, a fascinating city, with what many travelers regard as the liveliest market in all India.

If you're visiting Goa, Kerala, Madras, or any of southern India's many fascinating places, you'll find Andhra Pradesh on your route. Planes, trains, and buses from the north pass through Hyderabad on their way south. Spend four or five days in Hyderabad and its environs and enjoy the rich and varied culture, shopping, and delicious food.

Geographically, Andhra Pradesh includes fertile river systems in the north, the arid vastness of the Deccan plain, an extensive coastline along the Bay of Bengal, and the hilly Chitaur district of the south. Situated in central India, Andhra Pradesh has always been a melting pot. Here many great forces in Indian history clashed, mixed, and created the unique char-

433

acter of this region. Hindu, Jain, and Buddhist sites are within a few kilometers of one another. Moslem buildings are fashioned from the stones of Hindu structures, and mosques and Moslem palaces are decorated with Hindu motifs.

Andhra's history reaches back to the time of Emperor Ashoka (c. 230 B.C.), when this state marked the southern boundary of his great empire. At Ashoka's death, Satavahana, a local chieftain, established a dynasty that would endure for four centuries. The Ikshavaku rulers who succeeded the Satavahanas lasted only 57 years, yet it was during their reign that Buddhist culture flowered. The Buddhist monastery in Nagarjunakonda Valley was built at this time—a major center of learning for all Southeast Asia. The Pallavas of Tamil Nadu held sway over much of Andhra Pradesh for 3½ centuries until the Chalukyas supplanted them. Under successive Chalukyan kings, Andhra's Telegu culture came into its own. Each of India's major regions is fiercely proud of its language; yet all over India, Telegu is known for its gracefulness and intrinsic musical qualities.

In the thirteenth century, the Kakatyas undertook bold projects to control the great river systems of northern Andhra. Then, in the fourteenth century, Moslem armies of the Delhi sultanate swept through the Deccan Plateau and captured two Hindu princes in Warangal. The princes were brought to Delhi, converted to Islam, and sent south to establish a Moslem stronghold in Andhra and Karnataka. But the new religion had less hold than the wish for power.

In 1336, one of the two "converts" established the Vijayanagar kingdom, and for close to two centuries Vijayanagar rulers struggled for power with their Moslem counterparts—the Bahmanis, whose kingdom across the Krishna River included the fabled diamond mines of Golconda. Tension between ambitious Hindu and Moslem forces placed much of Andhra in a state of constant strife. But in years to come, these clashing elements would be reconciled and give rise to the region's vigorous mixed culture.

In 1518, Qutb Shahi broke away from the Bahmani kingdom and founded a dynasty responsible for the creation of Hyderabad and its memorable architecture. The dynasty ruled for 100 years until Aurangzeb's armies of the north conquered the area in 1687. Intrigue and treachery marked the next 40 years as the Mogul administration in Delhi tried in vain to maintain control over its new conquests in the Deccan. When Aurangzeb died in 1717, only seven years passed before Nizam-ul-Mulk took power and founded the Asafia dynasty, known for its fabulously rich rulers (Nizams), who controlled the region—India's largest and most important princely state—until independence in 1947.

EXPLORING ANDHRA PRADESH

When you visit Andhra Pradesh, expect variety in the scenery. The Eastern Ghats wind their hilly way along the eastern and northern borders; dense forests stretch along the east near the Bay of Bengal and farther west near Warangal. To the south is the Deccan Plateau, which lies across all India at this longitude, and two important rivers that flow toward the sea: the northern Godavari and the southern Krishna. Sleepy canals serve as inland waterways. The weather remains humid year-round, with relatively little variation in temperature. The environment is ideal for coconut palms, mango trees, and lush flowers. The world's third-largest artificial lake spills around the Nagarjunasagar Dam, a recently constructed gigantic hydroelectric project. Around Hyderabad City, huge granite boulders are strewn naturally on the bare plain as if by giants playing a game.

HYDERABAD

Today, Andhra Pradesh preserves vivid monuments from its complex past. There's no better place to begin than in Hyderabad. With upwards of 1½ million inhabitants, Hyderabad is India's fifth-largest city. Unlike so many of this nation's cultural attractions, Hyderabad doesn't have its origins in antiquity. The city derives its name from the romantic liaison of the Moslem ruler Quli Qutb Shahi—the fourth king of the Qutb Shahi dynasty that ruled from the forbidding fortress of Golconda. This king had a Hindu mistress named Bhagyamati (*bhagya* = lady luck; *mati* = harbinger). Early in his reign, he started building a new city because the Golconda stronghold had grown crowded and unhealthy. Six kilometers (3.6 miles) to the south by the river Musi he found a site, which he named Bhagyanagar—city of good luck—after his mistress. Here he erected a palace for her and named it Hydermahal. Later, in 1589, Bhagyanagar was renamed after this palace—and Hyderabad was born.

The diamond mines of Golconda gave the Nizams unlimited resources. Hyderabad is filled with magnificent structures—palaces that have been converted to public buildings, hotels, hospitals, universities, and museums.

The Heart of Hyderabad

The center of Hyderabad is defined by four great arches facing the cardinal points. Charkaman (*char* = four; *karman* = gate) was constructed by Quli Qutb Shahi in 1592, when Hyderabad was still coming into being. Within the area defined by these arches, you'll find Charminar and Mecca Masjid, the city's two most striking structures, as well as a teeming market filled with Hyderabad's well-known pearl and bangle shops.

Charminar is a rectangular granite edifice built in 1591. The building has elegant, tall arches and four minarets and is designed in the Indo-Saracenic style—which, like so much of Andhra culture, means it combines elements of both Moslem and Hindu art. The arches, domes, and minarets show Persian-Islamic influence, while various decorative motifs of leaves, petals, and flowers are done in Hindu style. At one time, an underground tunnel connected Charminar with Golconda Fort, some six kilometers (3.6 miles) away.

Walk through the Charminar Market and you'll understand why Hyderabad is a shopper's paradise. Here you can buy all kinds of fabrics, especially cotton prints and lightweight shirts and drawstring pants made from *khadi* cloth. Hyderabad is also famous for *nirmal* toys: wooden figurines of people and animals painted in bright lacquer. There's also *bidriware:* trays, vases, boxes, and other objects made from an alloy of zinc and copper that turns gun-metal black—in vivid contrast to the silver patterns traced across its surface. For Rs. 250–Rs. 600 you can buy a terrific example of this ancient craft. Ask someone to point you to *laad* (lacquer) bazaar, a bustling side street where bangles, pottery, nirmal toys, and bidriware are displayed in many stalls.

Best of all, Hyderabad is the unlikely world center for the pearl trade. Here in Charminar, in the heart of landlocked Andhra Pradesh, there are hundreds of shops dealing in pearl jewelry of all qualities and description. The pearls come from China and Japan; India's skilled jewelers and inexpensive labor make it a profitable enterprise. If you come looking for perfectly shaped natural pearls, you'll find them—but at no particular bargain. Instead, let the shopkeeper show you rice pearls, wheat pearls, flower pearls, seed pearls, and Chinese bean pearls in various shapes and sizes. For less than Rs. 600, you can buy an attractive triple-strand necklace of rice pearls. You can try to bargain, but prices are set according to weight, so unless you're making a fairly substantial purchase, don't expect the shopkeeper to knock more than 10 percent off the asking price. The two most respected shops are Mangatrai and Omprakash & Sons, both in the Charminar area. Just ask—everyone knows where they are. Mangatrai has a new air-conditioned shop outside the Charminar Market on Bashir Bagh, opposite Hotel Naragjuna, where you can see the jewelry being made. Prices are the same; you'll be more comfortable, but you'll miss the fun of buying pearls in the picturesque Moslem market.

Mecca Masjid is the second-largest mosque in India (after Jama Masjid in Old Delhi) and the seventh-largest mosque in the world. Its enormous colonnades are carved from single slabs of granite. Ten thousand people can gather under its double dome and in its vast courtyard for prayer. (Non-Moslems are welcome except during prayer services.)

Mecca Masjid is so named because soil was brought from the holy city of Mecca and mixed with Indian soil when construction was started in 1618. According to legend, completion of the mosque would herald the end of the Qutb Shahi dynasty. Aurangzeb's forces defeated the Qutb Shahi armies, bringing central India under the sway of the Delhi Moguls in 1687—the very year that construction of Mecca Masjid was finally completed.

Salar Jung Museum

The Salar Jung family served the Nizams of Hyderabad for five generations as prime ministers. In 1911, the last of the nizams, Mir Osman Ali Khan, appointed the youthful Mir Yousuf Ali Khan to serve him as Salar Jung III. But this new prime minister was more devoted to art and literature than to his administrative duties. Within three years, he resigned his post and spent the rest of his life amassing an eclectic collection of some 45,000 objects, ranging from ivory furniture and jewel-encrusted weapons to children's toys. When he died in 1949, he left his collection to the government of India. The museum is worth a visit.

The first room you enter is the Portrait Gallery. Here canvases depict the Nizam dynasty. If you have a guide, he or she will tell you with the utmost conviction that Mahboob Ali Khan, the sixth nizam, was so blessed that the mere mention of his name cured someone of the disastrous consequences of a poisonous snakebite.

At the far end of the room is a display case in which Salar Jung kept two dozen clay figurines, each modeled after one of his personal attendants. Possibly people of such great wealth and power too easily confused human lives with clay figures.

In other rooms, there are displays of magnificent silver and crystal pieces presented to Salar Jung by the British royal family, including a collection of stone sculptures from all over India: Chola, Pallava, Jain, and Buddhist art. In the gallery for wood carving you'll see elaborately carved furniture, plus a formidable representation of Garuda, the birdlike creature who is Lord Vishnu's mount (and the symbol of Indonesian Airlines.)

Two works of Western art draw the attention of curiosity seekers. *The Veiled Rebecca* by Benzoni, done in 1876, is a marble statue of a woman draped in a veil. It's more like a trick-or-treater done up as a ghost or a "wrapping" by the conceptual artist Christo. The second bizarre piece is *Mephistopheles and Margaretta,* a German work of the nineteenth century.

From the front, you'll stand face-to-face with Goethe's satanic tempter. From the other side, all you'll see is the virtuous Margaretta. Good and evil back-to-back.

Don't miss the eighteenth-century clock that presides over a covered courtyard. Children gather on benches to watch a mechanical blacksmith pound out the seconds on his anvil. On the hour, 10 soldiers file out of a sentry station to ring a brass bell the appropriate number of times. It's as much fun to watch the children as it is to watch the clock.

Golconda Fort

Eight kilometers (five miles) from the center of Hyderabad the ruins of Golconda Fort are sprawled for many acres over the top of a granite hill. The fort's origins go back to the thirteenth century, but it was rebuilt by the Qutb Shahi dynasty in 1525 and remained their seat of power for 162 years until Aurangzeb seized the fort after a ten-year siege.

At one time Golconda was the center of one of the world's great diamond markets, making it an object of curiosity for Marco Polo and the first European visitors of the thirteenth and fourteenth centuries. Golconda's riches provided extra incentive to the northern Moguls' dreams of expanding south. The Hope Diamond, the Orloff Diamond of Catherine the Great, and the British Crown's Kohinoor diamond all came from mines near the fort.

Climb the steep stone steps to a panoramic view of the city and the surrounding countryside. Move on to Qutb Shahi Tombs, where the seven rulers of the dynasty were laid to rest. Here, as at Charminar, you'll see Moslem architectural design joined with Hindu motifs in a style that's typical of Hyderabad. The dome and square base of the tombs are Moslem, as is the gallery of pointed arches. Hindu motifs include lotus leaves and buds, a chain and pendant design, projecting leaves, and cruciform capitals.

EXPLORING OUT OF HYDERABAD

Once you've seen Hyderabad, take in sights in the surrounding regions. Bidar Fort (see *Bangalore and Karnataka* chapter) is 132 kilometers (82 miles) northwest of the city and can be visited in a day's excursion. For those with two or three free days, an interesting tour can take in Warangal, Ramappa Temple, Nagarjunakonda, and Srisailam—a loop that will give you a vivid sampling of Hindu, Jain, Moslem, and Buddhist cultures.

Yadagirigutta and Mahavira Jain Temple

Warangal, your destination, is 140 kilometers (85 miles) north of Hyderabad on the Hanamkonda Road. There are two worthwhile stops along the way. When you are 69 kilometers (41 miles) out of Hyderabad, you'll pass through the town of Bhongir. A few kilometers more and you'll spot Yadagirigutta (in Telegu, *yada* means "shepherd"; *giri* and *Cutta* both mean "hill"), a small village perched at the foot of a rocky hill. Legend has it that Lord Vishnu revealed himself to the local saint, Yadava, by appearing in three forms of *narasimha* (*nara* = human; *simha* = lion). It is said that Lord Vishnu made this spot his abode, residing in a cave that in time became covered by thick forest. Many years later, Vishnu appeared to a local villager in a dream and guided him to the holy spot where the villager discovered a natural cave containing the three narasimha images. A temple was built to mark the sacred shrine for Hindu pilgrims.

It's worth a 30-minute detour to see *Lakshmi Narasimha Swamy Temple,* an unprepossessing structure built around the legendary cave that serves as sanctus sanctorum. Even if there weren't a temple, the trip would be worthwhile if only to climb the hill at Yadagirigutta for a view of the Deccan Plateau spreading majestically in every direction. In some respects it's evocative of sections of the American plains; yet the view remains distinctly Indian, with palm trees, simple huts, oxen, and busy villages dotting the great expanse.

Enter the temple and pass on to the inner sanctum, flanked by silver portals. Inside the holy cave, you'll see Lord Vishnu in his half-lion, half-human incarnation slaying the demon Kiranyakasipa. Give yourself time to stand back and watch the pilgrims file in. They have come hundreds of miles to pray in this sacred cave.

Most temples sell *prassadum* (god's gift)—food that pilgrims buy to take home to relatives and friends as a way of sharing their blessings. Here, for only one rupee, you can buy a delicious *pulihara,* a tasty mixture of rice, tamarind, and spices served on a coconut leaf. It is clean, nourishing food—a fine snack for less than a dime.

From here on to Warangal, look for toddy tapsters clambering up the palm trees with pots and tools slung over their shoulders and tied around their waist. Just 15 kilometers (nine miles) north of Yadagirigutta and 10 minutes off the main highway, you will come to Kolanupaka and the Mahavira Jain Temple, a pleasant cluster of small buildings that house magnificent sculptures of Jain *tirthankaras* (perfect souls). The temple is flanked by two elephant heads carved in bas-relief at the foot of the entrance. These are *dwarapalaka* (door guards) placed there to drive away visitors with evil intentions. Nevertheless, their spirit is far more one of *swagatham* (welcome) than of forbidding authority.

A few minutes inside this temple will reveal the power of Jain art. Sculptures of various Jain tirthankaras reside in closet-size niches, seated in the Buddha-like lotus posture. Yet these Jain figures appear more muscular and energetic than does the serene Buddha. Whereas the Buddha usually seems content to keep his position through all eternity, those broad-shouldered, barrel-chested deities look ready to jump up at any moment and do something unexpected.

In the far left corner of the main hall is a charming sculpture of the subdeity Sri Bumiya Ji and his son Sri Manibadr Ji that looks like an amiable pumpkin and child. To the right is Mahavira himself—the twenty-fourth and last Jain god—five feet high and solid jade! Mahavira's lips curl in a wide, radiant smile. You will see few works of art of any religion that are so generously concerned with the joy of existence.

In Jain temples, there are often several sculptural representations of deities, all of them virtually identical. But here, the sculptures are sharply individual. To Mahavira's right is Adeshwar, first of the Jain gods. The jewels in his forehead are valued at close to half a million dollars. And nearby is Shankeshwar, the second of the 24 gods—equally expressive, though less lavishly endowed.

All these gods have eerie, piercing eyes that literally bulge from their heads. Actually, each sculpture has a less startling set of eyes carved into the stone itself. What we see are called *chakshu* (spectacles) that have been added on to the deities to give them a startling, formidable presence. It makes us stop and take notice.

Warangal

Warangal, which includes the old town of Hanamkonda, was once the capital of the Kakatya kingdom that controlled two-thirds of present Andhra Pradesh for most of the twelfth and thirteenth centuries. Warangal is best known for its mighty fort that now lies in ruins. Even so, enough remains to suggest the scope and ambition of the Kakatya rulers.

Constructed between 1199 and 1261, Warangal Fort was surrounded by three walls. Driving through the Warangal area, you can still see traces of the outlying wall that once covered 127 kilometers (76 miles) to encircle this stronghold. The middle wall is still visible in most parts; a sloped earthen mound facing out on a broad moat. These two walls served to impede large invading forces. The inner wall, an imposing stone fortification, turns a daunting vertical face to the outside; on the inside, the wall is built in steps so the Kakatya defenders could rapidly mount the parapets to repel an attacking army. Marco Polo once passed through the triple-turning entrance and made his way to the dazzling royal court within.

When you arrive at the site of the Kakatya court, you'll see a rugged hill nearby. Actually, it's one enormous boulder. This was an ancient religious site, named, appropriately, *orunallu* (one stone). Centuries later, Moslem rulers inadvertently transformed the ancient Telegu to Warangal.

Though the Kakatya were ambitious builders, they were not completely practical. Their great buildings were erected on sand rather than stone foundations. In time, the great walls of Warangal Fort sank under their own weight; pillars tilted and fell, and the roof caved in. The awesome hall that Marco Polo visited is now a large field of broken columns and fractured statues. Goats graze among the solemn ruins. Still, it's a stirring sight.

Only the four grand entrance gates *(thorana)* remain standing. Each thorana is supported by four monolithic pillars rising nine meters (30 feet). Perched on the crossbars atop these pillars are pairs of *hamsa,* the emblematic bird of India's ancient kings. Somewhere between a swan and a fat duck, the hamsa's blue blood is made clear in a legend not unlike *The Princess and the Pea.* It is said that if equal parts of milk and water were mixed together in a bowl, the hamsa would sup at it and remove only the water, skillfully leaving the milk untouched. Apparently, milk was too thick for the hamsa's delicate blood. Today, these remarkable birds are extinct.

In 1323, the Kakatyas submitted to the overwhelming might of Tughlak Moslem invaders from Delhi. Sitab Khan was a military commander who was appointed district governor of the Warangal Fort area in the early fourteenth century. To celebrate his good fortune, he began to build Kush Mahal, which you can look at while you're exploring the fort.

The story of Kush Mahal is like a moral fable. *Kush Mahal* means "happy home," and for Sitab Khan, happiness came from pillaging Hindu religious sites to gather construction materials for his Moslem dream house. If you look carefully, high up on arches that once supported the ceiling, you can see stones carved with the Hindu lotus, Sitab Khan's way of boasting of the temples he dismantled. On other stones, you can make out the Moslem crescent moon. Lotus and crescent moon—united by conquest. But Sitab Khan never had the chance to enjoy the happy home that looting built. He died before its completion.

The 1,000 Pillar Temple in Warangal will introduce you to Chalukyan temple design. Instead of the soaring grandeur of Tamil Nadu temple construction, here we have low star-shaped buildings—intimate and cloistered—built on a series of platforms. This is a Shiva temple (the Kakatyas were great devotees of Shiva. As in virtually all Shiva temples of the south, there are three main architectural elements here:

• The *mandipam* is a formal entrance hall used for festivals, marriages, and celebrations. The mandipam here is dilapidated because of an inadequate foundation. The ceiling has fallen, and pillars tilt at crazy angles.

• Passing through the mandipam, you'll come to a small central courtyard presided over by a monolithic statue of *Nandi*. Nandi the bull is Shiva's vehicle—as much a part of the god's life and legend as Silver is to the Lone Ranger.

• Worshipers touch Nandi's flanks before entering the *temple* to pray at the Shiva *lingam* (phallic symbol). Each Hindu god is called by dozens of different names according to regional legends and language differences. Here Shiva is known as Rudresvara.

Many centuries ago, an underground passage connected this temple to Warangal Fort, some 11 kilometers (6.6 miles) away. It's exhausting just imagining the effort that went into tunneling through all that stone and rocky earth.

The well beside the temple is still working after over 800 years. Both the well and the temple were completed in 1163.

Only a few minutes from the 1,000 Pillar Temple is Bhadrakali Temple. It overlooks a broad, shallow lake where fishermen stand waist-deep in the silty water to cast their nets. The temple and its stone image of Kali (or Durga, as she is called elsewhere)—with her eight hands all brandishing weapons—require only a brief visit. Most interesting, perhaps, is the opportunity you'll have to get a vivid glimpse of Indian life, for this is a popular pilgrimage spot.

Indian villagers in the Warangal area use their minuscule savings to go on packaged bus tours that bring them to several such temples and holy shrines in a few days. The buses bring their own cooks, utensils, and food. It's likely that you'll encounter one of these groups resting or eating on the covered stone terrace just outside the inner temple.

Palampet

In Palampet, 64 kilometers (38 miles) from Warangal, Rudresvara Temple (popularly called Ramappa Temple) has some of the finest sculpture in India. The temple stands less than a kilometer away from Ramappa Dam, a mammoth wall of earth formed to link two chains of hills and thus create an artificial lake. Built by the Kakatyas in 1213, the dam clearly indicates the Kakatyas' strong belief that the gods meant for them to rule and control the land.

Like all Hindu temples, Rudresvara faces east, though now visitors approach it from its western porch, where the goporum is currently under restoration. Before entering the temple, examine the basalt obelisk in the courtyard. The Telegu inscription proudly proclaims the creation of Ramappa Lake and of the Shiva temple. The top of the obelisk is adorned with different images on each of its four faces: (1) the shiva lingam, (2) Ganesha, Shiva's beloved son, (3) Nandi, and (4) a double image of the sun (representing the Hindu faith) and the crescent moon (symbol of Moslem faith). The implication is that there's room on this planet for many religions, but the great god Shiva includes all faiths.

At one time, a canal diverted water from the nearby lake to form a shallow basin around the temple's outer wall—the architect's way of acknowledging that Hindu worshipers must bathe their feet before entering a temple.

Much of the pleasure this temple offers comes from the sculptural elements along the outer walls. The base of the temple has four layers of sculptured bands that wrap around the entire building. At the bottom is a procession of hundreds of elephants that represent the earthly power of the Kakatya dynasty. Only along the southwest wall is the procession interrupted to include a menagerie of snakes, birds, and other indigenous wildlife. Above the elephants is a row of open lotus blossoms, a sign of faith and, presumably, the divine favor shown to the Kakatyas. The third strip of sculpture depicts various aspects of social life. Each of the hundreds of panels is unique. There are images of dance, music, wrestling, social customs, worship, and sexual intercourse. Above these lively images of twelfth-century life is a second strip of lotus flowers to remind believers that transient life is surrounded by the eternal kingdom of god.

Charming as these representations are, probably more striking are the black-basalt human figures that peer down as brackets above the outer platform. Most other Hindu temples contain the repeated figures of Narasimha, the "human lion," perched triumphantly on an elephant's head. Here, an interesting feature has been added. Standing between the elephant's head and the squatting lion is a human form, further reminder that the Kakatyas saw themselves as wielding the combined qualities of these creatures—the elephant's brute strength and the lion's warriorlike ferocity.

Flanking the three entrances to the temple are the most notable sculptures to be found at Palampet: pairs of lively female figures, almost lifesize, carved from highly polished basalt. No matter what these women are doing, they seem to be dancing. Their simplicity, energy, and lithesome forms remind one of Matisse's dance panels, done near the end of his career. Beside the north porch, one of these women is caught in a crisis: a monkey has yanked her sari loose; with one hand she shoos away the mischievous creature, with the other, she tries to cover her private parts. Along the east porch, a woman hunter balances on one leg while an attendant removes a thorn from her foot. Also on the east porch is a dancing woman wearing the twelfth-century's version of platform shoes.

Inside the temple are more fine sculptures, though nothing is quite as impressive as the 12 figure brackets that stand outside. The four basalt pillars and the ceiling are crowded with scenes from the great religious epics. Particularly charming is a panel carved on the pillar to the right of the inner sanctum. Krishna, the playboy of the Hindu deities, has stolen all the clothing of a group of shepherd girls he saw bathing. The panel shows Krishna sitting merrily in a tree while the naked girls implore him to restore their clothes.

Even the most knowledgeable guide won't be able to account for all the legends and epics represented in this temple. Nevertheless, you'll be dazzled by the gaiety and sheer abundance of sculpture that makes Rudresvara Temple such an important site.

After you see the temple, you may want to stop at the Vanavihar Tourist Rest House for a snack or a cup of tea.

Less than one kilometer away and overlooking the lake, it is a lovely spot to relax before your return to Warangal.

Nagarjunakonda

A day's drive from Warangal (240 kilometers or 144 miles), or a shorter excursion from Hyderabad (144 kilometers or 86 miles), will bring you to the town of Nagarjunasagar, where one of the world's largest dams blocks the Krishna River. In 1926, excavations in the Nagarjunakonda

Valley uncovered relics from the early and middle stone age, as well as evidence of a great Buddhist civilization that flourished here during the third and fourth centuries. After Prime Minister Nehru set in motion the Nagarjunasaga Dam project in 1954, Indian archaeological teams devoted six hurried years to saving as many of the Buddhist treasures as they could. In 1960, the historic valley disappeared beneath the vast artificial lake created by the dam, but treasures from the Buddhist temples and learning center have been relocated and beautifully exhibited in the government museum set on Nagarjunakonda Island, 10 kilometers (six miles) from the dam.

At Anupa, five kilometers (three miles) from the dam, a *vihara* (Buddhist monastery) has been partially reconstructed from stones and pillars unearthed during excavations of the valley. This vihara was created by the Buddhist scholar Acharya (teacher) Nagarjuna, founder of the Madhyamika school of Mahayana Buddhism, as his instrument for teaching: a study center that attracted Buddhist scholars from as far away as Kashmir, Uttar Pradesh, Sri Lanka, and Southeast Asia. Here, Nagarjuna taught medicine, engineering, surgery, and astronomy, as well as pursued alchemical experiments in search of *amrit,* the heavenly herbal medicine said to produce immortality. (Legend has it that he succeeded and took a deep draught himself, a poetic way of saying that the spirit of the man lives on.) It's from Nagarjuna's teaching that Buddhism developed the doctrine of *Shunyata* (the void), the belief that we are surrounded by delusory forms and notions—that the truly enlightened reject illusion and experience all as a great, unchanging void.

The first thing you'll encounter as you approach the vihara site is a circular brick structure. This was once a *stupa,* an integral element in Buddhist worship that symbolizes the Buddha himself and his spiritual progress toward nirvana, beyond all concepts and forms. The stupa's parasol-like crown was divided into eight sections representing eight great precepts of the Buddha's teachings: (1) *Devatha:* devotion to God, to the Lord Buddha; (2) *Ghourva:* respect for one's guru or teacher; (3) *Ahimsa:* refusal to cause pain, injury, or physical punishment to one's fellow beings, which became an essential part of Gandhi's philosophy of nonviolence; (4) *Dharma:* obedience to sacred law; (5) *Moxa:* faith in salvation, striving for enlightenment; (6) *Araha:* renunciation of wealth and material needs; (7) *Kama:* renunciation of carnal desire; and (8) *Sanga:* commitment to the society of fellow Buddhists.

Turn from the remains of the eight-spoked stupa and you'll face a low brick wall that was once the main residential hall of the monastery. *Mahayana,* the form of Buddhism practiced by Nagarjuna, regards the Buddha as both a teacher and a god, whereas *Hinayana,* the older and more orthodox sect, regards the Buddha as supreme teacher but not as a god. Both branches of Buddhist thought were given separate meditation chambers at Nagarjuna's monastery. To the left is a meditation room, or *chaitya griha* (*chaitya* = idol; *griha* = house), where Mahayanas could meditate before an idol in the Buddha's image. To the right is an identical building, but it is a *stupa griha* (house with stupa), where Hinayanas could meditate on the Buddha's teachings without having to worship before a carved representation of the Buddha himself.

Just outside the door to the chaitya griha is a semicircular step ringed with a frieze of carved animal figures. This step, called "moonstone," symbolizes the Buddha's concept that life is a fragile bubble (the curved stone suggests the bubble shape), a reminder that our task in life is to seek enlightenment before the bubble bursts. A second function of the moonstone was to divert one's attention before entering the sacred space. When one's eyes were drawn down to the curved step and the animal figures, one was supposed to empty one's mind of evil thoughts. Otherwise, the intense act of meditating might accidentally concentrate the "evil eye" with such force that the entire shrine might shatter.

Nagarjunakonda Museum

A pleasant 20-minute boat ride leads to Nagarjunakonda Island and a gem of a museum. In the entrance gallery of the museum, on the wall to the right, are photographs of the excavations that unearthed the collection that is housed here. One series of photos shows several jars—terra-cotta, copper, silver, and gold—fashioned to fit inside each other in decreasing size. Inside the small gold jar, archaeologists found human bones, along with an inscription attesting that these were from the Buddha himself. The bones are not exhibited; they are kept in a secure vault on the island. But their very presence makes Nagarjunakonda a place of great importance to the Buddhist faithful.

At the entrance to the main exhibition hall, the visitor is greeted by a pair of chubby troll-like creatures. These are *Yaksha Padmanidhi* (*yaksha* = god of wealth; *padma* = lotus). Their heads are decorated with hanging lotus petals. A geyser of gold coins springs from the crown of each head, falling in a giant braid into each creature's left hand. It's an auspicious greeting: May you, too, be blessed with prosperity.

There are many appealing sculptures in this bright, spacious room. But if you want to learn a bit more about the Buddha's life, you can begin by studying the fourth display on the left wall, which is divided into five sections, each depicting a crucial stage in the story of the Buddha. Beginning on the far right of the panel you'll see the Buddha's birth (in 563 B.C.); his renunciation, when the Buddha left behind his wife, family, and earthly riches to seek enlightenment; Mara's attack, the temptation of sexuality and various negative emotional forces; the Buddha's first preaching at Sarnath; and the Buddha's death.

As with so many artists, the sculptor who created this five-part narrative appears to have lavished particular attention on the forces of temptation. Mara's attack is depicted in the middle section: the Buddha sits in the center of the scene while, to the right, sexual demons plot against him. To the left of the Buddha, Kama (sex) tries to tempt him, and just below Kama, wicked cherubs representing pride and miserliness await their chance to besiege him. On the far left of this group, pride (in a woman's form) glowers harshly; beneath her, a little demon, anger, joins the band of tempters. The Buddha, of course, remains divinely unperturbed.

It's impossible to spend more than a few moments in the exhibition hall without being drawn to the 3-meter (10-foot) statue of the Buddha that dominates the room. No need for description—it communicates without words.

The renunciation episode in the Buddha's life is narrated with economy and understated emotion in display No. 48, which hangs in the exhibition room connected to the main hall from the right. The story is told in three sections proceeding from the bottom to the top. As a young prince, Siddhartha Gautama (the Historic Buddha) led a cloistered life that was calculated to shield him from the harshness of the external world. The bottom bas-relief depicts the day Siddhartha explored the marketplace. The scenes of human misery and mortality—an old man, a diseased man, a corpse, and an ascetic who had renounced the world—disturbed him, and he understands the shallowness of his youthful vision of life. The middle section shows Siddhartha spending the night reflecting on what he has seen and vowing to pursue the ascetic's path. In the top section, he leaves his father's palace in search of enlightenment.

Though the museum is small, it's easy to enjoy several hours here and outside in the pleasant gardens. But make sure you arrange in town for a government guide to accompany you before you go. The Andhra Pradesh Tourist Department provides guides at no charge, and they'll bring these storytelling friezes to life. (The booking counter for the boat shuttle is near the dam. It costs 15 rupees round-trip. Try to book in advance at the government tourist department office.)

Amaravati

Another ancient Buddhist center, Amaravati, lies east of Nagarjunasagar on the right bank of the Krishna, a river inseparably linked with the history and culture of this region. Formerly an ancient Buddhist capital known as Dhyanakataka, Amaravati was a flourishing center of Buddhism in the second century B.C.—one of the four most important places of Buddhist worship in the country. Monasteries and a university brought devotees from as far away as China.

The ruins of the 2,000-year-old settlement are highly poetic, and much of the Buddhist culture is extremely elegant and remarkably well preserved. The stupa was originally the largest in the country. Although its size has been diminished (ravaged by the less spiritual), the richly carved panels and remaining friezes showing scenes of the life of the Buddha are beautiful and worth careful scrutiny.

Srisailam

Srisailam offers few of the conveniences that many Western travelers seek, but visitors who are willing to make a long day's excursion (from Hyderabad or Nagarjunasagar) or stay in a shabby government tourist house, will be rewarded by a firsthand look at the powerful emotion generated by Hindu worship.

Bharamarambha is the regional name for the goddess Durga (or Kali). Mallikarjunaswamy is the regional name for Shiva. Here Shiva and Durga exist in perpetual honeymoon—married anew every evening in a ceremony performed for thousands of pilgrims who flock here from all over India. This temple is particularly revered, for it holds one of the 12 *Jyotirlingas* in India. (*Jyoti* means "light"—in this case, spiritual light.) These 12 Jyotirlingas are said to have been formed by the divine force of nature itself.

In the central courtyard, a large map of India shows the location of the other 11 Jyotirlingas. These sacred places are scattered in every corner of the subcontinent.

This temple has no outstanding architectural or sculptural features, but its importance and popularity make it a memorable place in which to experience a Hindu prayer service. As you approach the temple, you'll see worshipers buying small baskets filled with coconut, fruits, and fragrant jasmine to offer the deity. Inside the low-ceilinged worship hall, devotees crowd along a metal railing, while a priest passes down the central aisle, chanting as he makes his way from the small Nandi statue toward the sanctus sanctorum, the small room that houses the sacred lingam. These quiet moments are merely a prelude to the actual ceremony. The priest enters the sanctus sanctorum and draws back a curtain to reveal the Jyotirlingam beneath a brass canopy covered with lotus blossoms. Instantly, an incredible clamor breaks forth. Drums, bells, curved horns, and brass gongs join in a deafening riot of sound. Numerous devotional candles are lit and passed over the lingam, as the Hindu faithful clasp their hands in prayer: wonder, reverence, and delight reflected in their faces.

This ceremony lasts for 10 minutes, after which the priest files past the worshipers once again, distributing jasmine flowers and collecting offerings. Worshipers are then invited into the sanctus sanctorum (non-Hindus can join them), where they kneel to kiss the lingam.

Note: It's best to attend the first prayer service at 5:45 A.M. to avoid the long lines that form by midmorning.

There are several other temples here and numerous other shrines in the Srisailam area, but nothing else leaves the lasting impression of this joyful ceremony.

The Bay of Bengal

Unless you're journeying between Calcutta or Bhubaneswar and Madras, this area is off the beaten path. Nevertheless, it offers several interesting attractions. Visakhapatnam, or Vizag, as it is commonly known, is a thriving seaport flanked by long stretches of excellent beach. Rama Krishna Mission Beach is one of the cleanest beaches on India's east coast. Mount Kailas, six kilometers (3.6 miles) away, overlooks another good beach.

From Vizag it's only a short trip (16 kilometers or 9.6 miles) to Simhachalam (Hill of the Lion), famous for its eleventh-century Narasimha Temple. Devotees flock to this dramatic hillside setting to celebrate Lord Vishnu's heroic defense of Prahlada, his follower. They smear the Vishnu image with sandal paste until it's unrecognizable. Once a year, on the third day of Vaisakha (April–May), the idol is cleansed in a ritual called Chandana Visarjana, during which Lord Vishnu is revealed. The temple is known for its many elegant sculptures.

Bheemunipatnam is 35 kilometers (21 miles) from Vizag by a road that runs along the beach. It is the site of a former Dutch trading settlement of the seventeenth century. A ruined fort remains, as well as Hollanders Green, the original Dutch cemetery. There's a good beach here. The spot hasn't been developed for supertourism, but if you're willing to live in a modest guest house, consider Bheemunipatnam as the place for a few days' retreat and relaxation.

Southeast Andhra Pradesh

The best approach to Tirupati in the hilly Chitaur district of southeast Andhra Pradesh is from Madras, in Tamil Nadu. Tirupati, with its temple of Lord Venkateshwara in nearby Tirumala, is visited by millions of pilgrims every year. It's a popular temple, in large part because a visit here is said to bring good fortune.

Fortune is very much a part of the temple's history. In the days of the Pallava and Chola dynasties, several rulers presented vast treasures at the hill temple. When Krishnadeva, the Raya king, visited the temple for the first time in 1513, he presented the deity with a jewel-studded crown, a necklace of pearls and precious stones, and 25 silver plates. Later that year, he returned to deliver a sword embedded with diamonds, rubies, and sapphires. The following year, glowing after a series of military victories, he buried the Lord's image in a pile of 30,000 gold coins.

This tradition of lavish offerings has made Tirumala the wealthiest temple in India. When you consider that India is a land of thousands of temples, this is no small distinction. Buses arrive from predawn until evening, conveying thousands of pilgrims who wait patiently for their chance to pray in the temple and make offerings to the treasury. (Those who administer the temple treasury have distributed the money to fund a university, research institutions, health care, and social welfare organizations.)

On arriving in Tirupati, many pilgrims choose to walk to Tirumala by rock steps that have been traveled for centuries. There is also a winding road that cuts into the hills, providing magnificent views as you make your way by bus or taxi to Tirumala. Non-Hindus are barred from witnessing some parts of the worship, but if you want that blessing of wealth and want to experience India in all its spiritual intensity, the pilgrims' path from Tirupati to Tirumala offers wealth of that sort, too.

PRACTICAL INFORMATION FOR

ANDHRA PRADESH

WHEN TO GO. From mid-October to late March is best. Temperature ranges from 60° F to 90° F with cooler evenings. Summer begins at the end of March, when temperatures climb above 100. The monsoon season is from June to August.

HOW TO GET THERE. By Air. *Indian Airlines* flies daily to Hyderabad from Bangalore, Bombay, Calcutta, Delhi, and Madras. It makes three flights a week to Hyderabad from Bhubaneswar and Nagpur. Indian Airlines also flies four times a week to Visakhapatam from Calcutta and Madras. *Vayudoot* flies into Hyderabad three times a week from Ahmedabad, Goa, Pune, and Vadodara. It also flies to Tirupati four times a week from Madras and three times a week from Bangalore and Belgaum. For Indian Airlines information in Hyderabad, call 844422 for inquiries or 236902 for reservations; in Visakhapatam call 64665. For Vayudoot information in Hyderabad, call 842855 for inquiries or 234717 for reservations; in Tirupati, contact Travel Express; tel. 21480.

By Bus. *Andhra Pradesh State Road Transport Corporation* (APSRTC) runs luxury coaches (many with loud, unceasing video sets blaring) to most important southern Indian cities: Bangalore, Madras, and Bombay, plus numerous tourist spots in the state. For details and fares in Hyderabad contact: APSRTC, Central Bus Stand, Gowliguda; tel. 44126. *Tiruvalluvar Transport Corporation* from Tamil Nadu runs deluxe coaches to and from Tirupati, as does APSRTC. In Madras, contact either at the Express Bus Stand; tel. 561835.

By Train. To Hyderabad (the station is actually at Secundrabad), daily trains from Bombay are *Hyderabad-Bombay Express* and *Minar Express;* from Delhi, *A. P. Express;* from Madras, *Madras-Hyderabad Express* and *Charminar Express;* from Bangalore, *Bangalore-Hyderabad Express.* To Visakhapatnam, there are numerous daily trains from Calcutta (Howrah Station). To Tirupati, two daily trains from Madras. Day trains are not hard to arrange. Sleepers with reserved berths (a must—don't just buy a sleeper ticket) require early reservations. For details and fares, contact Railway Inquiry at Hyderabad; tel. 131 or tel. 135 for reservations.

By Rented Car with Driver. Hyderabad is 566 km (351 mi.) from Bangalore, 735 km (458 mi.) from Bombay, and 704 km (436 mi.) from Madras. Hire a car from one of the agencies recommended below under Tour Operators. The rate is about Rs. 4 per km, with a halt charge of Rs. 50–Rs. 100 per night.

TOURIST INFORMATION. The *Government of India Tourist Office* is at 3–6–369/A/25 & 26 Sandozi Bldg., 2nd Floor, 26 Himayat Nagar, Hyderabad 500029; tel. 666877. It's open Monday–Friday, 9:15 A.M.–5:45 P.M., and Saturday, 9:15 A.M.–1 P.M.; closed Sunday. The main office for the *Andhra Pradesh Travel and Tourism Department* is at Gagan Vihar, 5th Floor, M. J. Rd., Hyderabad 500001; tel. 557531. Open Monday–Saturday, 10 A.M.–5 P.M., closed Sunday. These departments can help arrange excursions and will give you brochures and suggest hotels. Other tourist offices:

Hyderabad Airport, tel. 849844.

Nagarjunasagar. Tourist Information Officer, Hill Colony; tel. 3625. Open Monday–Saturday, 10 A.M.–5 P.M.

Tirupati/Tirumala. Tourist Information Officer, T. P. Area, Tirupati; tel. 4698. Open Monday–Saturday, 10 A.M.–5 P.M.

Visakhapatnam (Vizag). Tourist Information Office, Hotel Apsara Arcade, Visakhapatnam; tel. 63016. Open Monday–Saturday, 10 A.M.–5P.M.

Warangal. Tourist Information Officer, Tourist Rest House, Kazipet, Warangal; tel. 6201. Open Monday–Saturday, 10 A.M.–5 P.M. The Government of India also has a tourist office in Hyderabad at Sandozi Building Himayatnagar, Hyderabad 500029; tel. 66877. Open 9 A.M.–5 P.M., Monday–Saturday.

FOREIGN CURRENCY EXCHANGE. Most Western-style hotels have money-exchange counters. *Thomas Cook* is at 6–1–57 Nasir Arcade, Saifabad (tel. 237505) and is open Monday–Friday, 10 A.M.–5 P.M.; and Saturday, 10 A.M.–1 P.M. ANZ Grindlays (5–9–235 Abid Rd.; tel. 237505) or the *State Bank of India* are open Monday–Friday, 10 A.M.–2 P.M.; Saturdays till noon.

ACCOMMODATIONS. Hyderabad has a good range of hotels in all price categories. Throughout the rest of Andhra Pradesh, facilities exist, but not at the level or variety available in Hyderabad. Prices are based on double occupancy and exclude taxes and service charges: *Deluxe,* over Rs. 2,000; *Expensive,* Rs. 1,200–Rs. 2,000; *Moderate,* Rs. 500–Rs. 1,200; *Inexpensive,* under Rs. 500. Most Western-style hotels take major credit cards.

AMARAVATI

Inexpensive

Inspection Bungalow. Amaravati. Reservations: District Collector, Guntar, Andhra Pradesh; no phone. About 5 rooms with bath. For this price, clean is what you get. Very minimal. Catered simple meals are available at nominal cost. Rupees only.

HYDERABAD-SECUNDERABAD

Deluxe

The Krishna Oberoi. Road No. 1, Banjara Hills, Hyderabad 500034; tel. 222121, 842/223079. 265 rooms with bath. Set on nine acres overlooking Lake Hussain Sagar, the Krishna Oberoi is a striking blend of modern architecture tempered by strong Mogul influences. Beautiful fountains and formal gardens grace its front lawn. Rooms are elegant, with pastel decor. Air-conditioning, room service, TV, multicuisine restaurants, bar, swimming pool, health club, business center, foreign-exchange and travel counter, shopping arcade. AE, DC, MC, V.

Taj Gateway Hotel on Banjara Hill. Road No. 1, Banjara Hills, Hyderabad 500034; tel. 222222, fax 222218. 124 rooms with bath. This modern high rise overlooking a lake offers attractive contemporary-style rooms. Best rooms overlook Banjara Lake. Air-conditioning, room service, TV, multicuisine restaurants, bar, swimming pool, business center, foreign-exchange and travel counter, shops, doctor. AE, DC, MC, V.

Moderate

Hotel Golkarna. 10–1–124 Masab Tank, Hyderabad 500028; tel. 226001. 156 rooms with bath. This eight-story high rise has a marble lobby and spacious rooms with a modern decor. Air-conditioning, TV, room service, multicuisine restaurant, bar, foreign-exchange and travel counter, secretarial services, shops, doctor. AE, DC, MC, V.

Hotel Ritz. Hill Fort Palace, Hyderabad 500463; tel. 233571. 40 rooms with bath. Set on a hill, this small, older hotel was once the palace of a Hyderabadi *nizam* (prince) and has an interior courtyard, attractive lawns, and rooftop garden. Air-conditioned rooms aren't palatial or grand. Expect simple Western furnishings that are slightly worn around the edges. Room service, TV, multicuisine restaurant, bar, tennis, swimming pool, doctor, foreign-exchange and travel counter, bank, secretarial services. AE, DC, MC, V.

Quality Inn Green Park. Green Land Areas, Begumpet, Hyderabad 500016; tel. 224455. 156 rooms with bath. This new, modern hotel has an inviting lobby with ethnic touches. An exterior glass elevator leads to spacious rooms with a contemporary decor. Best rooms are even-numbered and overlook the front. Free breakfast and a "happy hour" drink, air-conditioning, TV, room service, multicuisine restaurants, bar, foreign-exchange and travel counter, secretarial services, courtesy airport shuttle, swimming pool by 1993. Excellent value. AE, DC, MC, V.

Inexpensive

Hotel Sarovar. 5–9–22 Secretariat Rd., Hyderabad 500004; tel. 237638. 77 rooms with bath. Set back from the road, this modern hotel has good-size clean rooms with simple Western decor. Best rooms are air-conditioned (also inexpensive); other rooms have fans. Room service, multicuisine restaurants, bar, car-rental service, shopping arcade, bank next door. Good value. MC, V.

NAGARJUNASAGAR

Inexpensive

Vijay Vihar Complex. Reservations: Asst. Manager, Tourist Guest House, V. V. Complex Nagarjunasagar; tel. 3625 or reserve through APTTDC (address below under Tours). 8 rooms with bath and 5 cottages. This government-run complex offers plain, minimal-decor rooms. Some rooms are air-conditioned. Room service, simple Indian and Continental restaurant. Rupees only.

VIJAYAWADA

Inexpensive

Hotel Kandhari International. Labbipet, M. G. Rd., Vijayawada 520010; tel. 471311. 73 rooms with bath. The city's best hotel, this place is modern, with clean air-conditioned rooms. Room service, TV, multicuisine restaurant, bar, doctor, foreign-exchange and travel counter, shopping arcade. AE, DC.

Hotel Mamata. Eluru Rd., opposite bus stand, Vijayawada 520002; tel. 61251. 63 rooms with bath. Right in town, this hotel has some air-conditioned rooms, which are best. The decor is modest modern. Room service, TV, Indian and Continental restaurant, bar. Rupees only.

VISAKHAPATNAM (VIZAG)

Expensive

Taj Hotel Sea Pearl. Beach Rd., Visakhapatnam 530023; no phone yet. Book your room through the Taj Hotel chain (see Group Hotels in *Facts at Your Fingertips*). About 95 rooms with bath. Closed for renovation at press time, this newly acquired Taj property will reopen by 1993. It will be Taj elegant. Best rooms will front the beach. Air-conditioning, TV, room service, multicuisine restaurants, bar, foreign-exchange and travel counter, secretarial services, excellent beach, possibly a swimming pool. AE, DC, MC, V.

Moderate

Park Hotel. Beach Rd., Visakhapatnam 530023; tel. 54181. 64 rooms with bath. On the beach, this modern hotel offers attractive rooms and a quiet location. Air-conditioning, room service, TV, multicuisine restaurant, foreign-exchange and travel counter, swimming pool, secretarial services, doctor. AE, DC, MC, V.

Inexpensive–Moderate

Dolphin Hotels Ltd., Dabagardens, Visakhapatnam; tel. 64811. 147 rooms with bath. This large hotel, also on the beach, has clean Western-style rooms. Best rooms are "superior" or "executive" and are very moderately priced. Standard rooms, which have a simpler decor, are inexpensive. Room service, TV, multicuisine restaurants, bar, foreign-exchange and travel counter, business center, swimming pool, baby-sitters, doctor, shopping arcade. AE, DC, MC, V.

Inexpensive

Ocean View Inn. Kirlampudi, Visakhaptnam; tel. 54828. 30 rooms with bath. This small beach hotel offers good service and pleasant, simple rooms. Best rooms are air-conditioned. Room service, TV, multicuisine restaurant. Rupees only.

WARANGAL

Inexpensive

Hotel Ashoka. Main Rd., Hanamkonda, Warangal; tel. 85491. 31 rooms with bath. This pleasant Western-style hotel is modest; but rooms are clean and comfortable. Amenities include air-conditioning, room service, multicuisine restaurant, bar. Rupees only.

DINING OUT. Andhra Pradesh cooking, especially in Hyderabad, reflects the same historical and cultural influences mentioned earlier in the chapter. Moslem and Hindu, north and south all come together to produce a wide selection of tasty dishes. Generally speaking, you're likely to eat better in Hyderabad than anywhere else in India, with the exception of Goa. Once you leave Hyderabad, options become extremely limited. On day excursions to popular destinations, be adventurous and just pick a crowded restaurant. Most likely, it'll be extremely informal; but a crowd is a safe indication that the food is good. Many accommodations, listed above, also have restaurants. Breakfast is usually 8–10:30; lunch, noon–3; dinner, 7:30–10. Payment is normally in rupees unless the restaurant is connected to a Western-style hotel. The restaurants listed below are informal and, unless noted, are open for all three meals and don't require reservations. Prices are based on one person eating a three-course meal, excluding taxes, tip, or beverage: *Deluxe,* over Rs. 300; *Expensive,* Rs. 200–Rs. 300; *Moderate,* Rs. 100–Rs. 200; *Inexpensive,* under Rs. 100.

HYDERABAD

Expensive

The Szechuan Garden. The Krishna Oberoi, Road No. 1, Banjara Hills; tel. 222121. Overlooking beautiful waterfalls and surrounded by a Chinese rock garden, the Szechuan Garden offers Szechuan cuisine. Try the murrel (local freshwater fish) steamed in chili sauce or the shredded lamb in a clay pot (cooked with vegetables in a chili-and-garlic sauce). Dinner reservations advised. Open 12:30–2:45 P.M. and 7:30–10:45 P.M. AE, DC, MC, V.

Moderate

Blue Fox. 3–6–199/1 Himayathnagar, Hyderabad; tel. 230448. The room is dimly lit; dark pillars are inlaid with mirrors. The food in this popular restaurant is multicuisine: Chinese, Continental, and Indian. The chef is known for his chicken Punjabi cooked in a tandoor, then simmered in a spicy gravy, and his *rogan josh* (mutton pieces simmered in a spicy gravy). Open 11 A.M.–11 P.M. AE, DC, MC, V.

Dakhni. Taj Gateway Hotel on Banjara Hill, Road No. 1, Banjara Hills; tel. 222222. Walls are white, with handsome paintings and dark-wood pillars. Upholstered chairs and settees, done up in soft pinks, are intimately placed around the room. The chef serves Andhra Pradesh and Deccan region specialties. This is a good place to order *haleem* (pounded wheat blended with spicy mutton and gravy) and spicy Andhra fried chicken. Reservations advised. Open 7:30 P.M.–12:30 A.M. AE, DC, MC, V.

Firdaus. The Krishna Oberoi, Road No. 1, Banjara Hills; tel. 222121. This restaurant evokes the elegance of the nizams, with waiters dressed in "sherwanis," embroidered "punka" fans gently swaying from the ceiling, and live *ghazel* performances nightly except Tuesday. The chef serves regal Hyderabadi cuisine. Specialties include *achaan gosht* (lamb cooked in pickled tomato masala paste) and *nizami handi* (vegetable-and-cottage cheese curry). Dinner reservations advised. Open 12:30–2:45 P.M. and 7:30–10:45 P.M. AE, DC, MC, V.

Kebab-E-Bahar. Taj Gateway Hotel on Banjara Hill, Road No. 1, Banjara Hills; tel. 222222. This outdoor restaurant is on the edge of the lake. Two popular dishes are *patthar-ka-gosht* (beaten lamb cooked on heated stones) and *murgh malai kebab* (boneless chicken marinated with cream and herbs, then cooked in the tandoor). Candlelit tables and taped Indian music create a soothing ambience. Reservations advised. Open 7 P.M.–midnight. AE, MC, V.

Once Upon a Time. Quality Inn Green Park, Green Lands Area, Begumpet, Hyderabad; tel. 224455. This new restaurant has stylish Indian touches: restored Burma teak "chettinad" pillars, Rajasthani "jharokas" (windows designed for women in purdah), and *Varanasi* brocade inset in the walls. It serves the princely cuisines of India. Two unusual dishes are *shan-e-murgh* (chicken-breast kebab stuffed with black cumin, Indian cheese, and pomegranate seeds that is either baked or steamed—your choice) and *labab-machli* (two fish fillets marinated with tangy chutney and steamed in a fresh banana leaf). Dinner reservations advised. Open noon–3 P.M. and 7 P.M.–midnight. AE, DC, MC, V.

Palace Heights. Triveni Complex, Abid Rd.; tel. 232898. This upper-floor restaurant in a modern high rise offers a great city view and elegant surroundings. Pictures of former nizams grace the walls. Antiques add a refined touch. Ask for a table by a window and choose from Continental, Chinese, and Indian cuisines. *Vegetable Manchuria* (deep-fried mixed vegetables with chopped garlic, ginger, and green chilies) and keba chicken (deep-fried chicken in a spicy batter) are local favorites. Dinner reservations advised. Open 11 A.M.–11 P.M. DC, MC, V.

Shogun Bar and Restaurant. 3–6–307 Central Chambers, Hyderguda, Hyderabad; tel. 243086. There's a small Japanese garden with water cascading over rocks visible through a bank of windows and two interior Japanese pavilions constructed in the interior of this restaurant, which features the cuisines of the Far East. Special dishes include *kong pou* fried crab (deep-fried crab cooked in Szechuan sauce) and Malyasian *satay* (chicken prepared in a peanut-flavored sauce). Dinner reservations advised. Open noon–3:30 P.M. and 7 P.M.–11 P.M. DC, MC, V.

Inexpensive

Amaravathi. 3–6–307 Central Chambers, Hyderguda, Hyderabad; tel. 243086. Eat spicy Andhra cuisine off a banana leaf in this casual restaurant, with booths, low lighting, and taped Hindi or Telegu songs. Try mutton *gongura* (mutton cubes simmered in a green leaf and spicy sauce) or the vegetable meal (unlimited portions of different vegetables cooked with Andhra spices). Open 11 A.M.–3:30 P.M. and 6:30 P.M.–10:30 P.M. DC, MC, V.

Parwaz Restaurant. Public Garden Rd., Nampally, Hyderabad; tel. 203301. Head upstairs to an informal air-conditioned, dimly lit room that is jammed with booths. Simple murals of Hyderabad are on the walls. Though the restaurant serves multicuisine fare, crowds come here for its popular dishes of Hyderabadi *biryani* (rice with chicken, fish, mutton, eggs, or vegetables). Open noon–midnight. Rupees only.

VIJAYAWADA

Moderate

Hotel Greenlands Restaurant. Bhavani Gardens; tel. 73081. This restaurant, with simple huts set on a lawn, serves Indian and Continental cuisines. Try the good curries or kebabs. Open 11 A.M.–2 P.M. and 6:30–11 P.M. Rupees only.

WARANGAL

Inexpensive

Classic Bar and Restaurant. Hotel Ashoka; tel. 85491. The restaurant is simple, with a slightly upscale Indian-style coffee-shop decor; but the food is the best in town. The Indian dishes are memorable, but the chef also prepares Continental and Chinese meals. Try the tasty mutton *do piaza* (mutton curry with onions) and chicken *masala* (chicken cooked in a spicy gravy). Just hope that this talented chef isn't snapped up by a big hotel chain. Open 12:30–3 P.M. and 7:30–10:30 P.M. Rupees only.

SWEETS AND TREATS. In Hyderabad, stop in at the *Kamat Hotel* (S. D. Rd., Secunderabad) for fresh fruit juices, locally popular curd rice, *Mysore pak* (a cake made with flour, sugar, and clarified butter), and other Indian snacks or sweets. Open daily 8 A.M.–10 P.M. *Shanbagh Hotel* (No. 3–6–354/A Basherbagh) is an upstairs air-conditioned eatery serving a range of popular *dosas* (Indian-style crepes) stuffed with various fillings, and other South Indian snacks. When the temperature soars, head to the *Alfa Hotel* (opposite Secunderabad Railway Station) and stand in line for great Iranian tea—a great thirst quencher. Open 7 A.M.–10 P.M.

HOW TO GET AROUND. By Plane. *Indian Airlines* flies daily between Hyderabad and Visakhapatnam. *Vaydudoot* has a daily flight connecting Hyderabad with Tirupati and six weekly flights between Hyderabad and Vijayawada.

From the Airport. Taxis into Hyderabad, Vizag, or Tirupati cost Rs. 50–Rs. 100. Regular bus service from the airport is much less, but it is also much less convenient.

By Rented Car with Driver. This is a good way to travel through the state. Here are some important distances from Hyderabad: Amaravati, 334 km (207 mi.); Nagarjunasagar, 150 km (93 mi.); Srisailam, 219 km (136 mi.); Tirupati, 580 km (360 mi.); Visakhapatnam, 667 km (414 mi.); Vijayawada, 271 km (168 mi.). Hire a car from one of the agencies recommended below under Tour Operators. Rates are about Rs. 4 per km with a halt charge of Rs. 50–100 per night.

By Taxi. Taxis are good for excursions on the outskirts of major cities. Drivers are loath to use the meter. Set the fare in advance. Use car-rental rates as your guide.

By Auto Rickshaw. In crowded cities, this is the easiest way to maneuver in congested streets. Rates are about Rs. 3.70 for the first km; Rs. 2 per additional km. If the driver claims a "broken" meter, set the fare in advance.

By Bus. There are local buses, too, throughout most of Andhra Pradesh, but they're a bit much to handle. Especially in Hyderabad, where you have to be a wild leaper to jump aboard.

TOURS. The *Andhra Pradesh Travel and Tourism Development Corporation* (APTTDC) is eager to help tourists visit the state. It has inexpensive government tours, in deluxe coaches, that will take you on the following excursions accompanied by a guide. For details and reservations, contact the head office of APTTDC (Yatri Niwas Hotel, Sardar Patel Rd., Secunderabad 500003; tel. 843943 or 843932), which is open daily 7 A.M.–7 P.M. It also has an office at Gagan Vihar (5th Floor, M. J. Rd., Hyderabad 500001; tel. 557531), which is open daily 8 A.M.–5 P.M.; and a counter at the airport (tel. 849844), which is open during flight arrivals.

Hyderabad City Sightseeing. Daily 8 A.M.–5 P.M. Rs. 45.

Nagarjunasagar. Daily tours 6 A.M.–9:30 P.M., one-way trips in either direction, and overnight package tours. Rs. 25 one-way; Rs. 48 round-trip; Rs. 10 for local sightseeing.

Mantralayam. Subject to demand, this tour leaves on Saturday at 10 A.M., returning on Sunday at 9 P.M. Tour to Raghavendra Swamy Temple, Alampur Temple, Pillalamarri. Rs. 150, including accommodation.

Srisailam. Subject to demand, this tour leaves on Saturday at 12 noon, returning on Saturday at 9 P.M. Rs. 150, including accommodation.

Vijayawada. Local sightseeing. Daily 8 A.M.–7 P.M. Rs. 45.

Tirupati-Tirumala. Every Friday at 4 P.M., returning Monday at 7 A.M. Rs. 275, including accommodation.

Visakhapatnam. City Sightseeing. Daily 8 A.M.–7 P.M. Rs. 45.

Statewide Tours. APTTDC offers a 15-day South India package tour that covers Andhra Pradesh, Tamil Nadu, Karnataka, and Kerala (covering 30 specific destinations). It leaves the second Saturday of every month. Rs. 1,800, including accommodation.

TOUR OPERATORS. For all your travel needs, including a car with driver, contact any of these reputable agencies:

Thomas Cook, 6–1–57 Nasir Arcade, Saifabad, Hyderabad 500004; tel. 231988.
Mercury Travels, 92 & 93 Suryakiran Bldg., S. D. Rd., Secunderabad 500003; tel. 830670.
Sita World Travels, Sita House, 3–5–874 Hyderguda 500029; tel. 233638.
Travel Corporation Ltd., 102 Regency House, 608 Somajiguda, Greenlands Rd., Hyderabad 500482; tel. 212722.
You can also rent a car with driver from APTTDC (address above).

SEASONAL EVENTS. Since most events are determined by the lunar calendar, contact the Government of India Tourist Office for details.
January. Throughout Andhra Pradesh, *Pongal* is a three-day harvest festival. The sun is worshiped on the first day, then cows and bullocks (painted and decorated) are fed *pongal,* a rice concoction, as part of a ceremony of thanksgiving. Processions and lots of happy celebration ensue.
March/April. A Moslem holy day, *Id-ul-Fitr* marks the end of Ramadan, a time of month-long fasting. Lots of feasting and celebrating.
April/May. Simhachalam observes the *Vaisakha Festival.* The sand-paste-covered image of Vishnu is cleansed in a ritual called *Chandana Visarjana* in which the actual image of Lord Vishnu is revealed before crowds of devotees.
August/September. *Muharram.* Muslims honor the martyrdom of Hussain, the grandson of the Prophet Mohammed. Processions of *tazias* (bamboo and paper replicas of the martyr's tomb at Karbala) are paraded through the streets.
September/October. *Dussehra,* a 10-day festival, celebrates the victory of good over evil. There are numerous events and noisy firecrackers.
October/November. *Diwali* marks the start of the Hindu New Year. Candles are lit on every house to welcome Lakshmi, the goddess of wealth.

HISTORIC SITES. Entrance to most places is free; where a donation is requested, a few rupees will suffice. Monuments are open sunrise to sunset, unless noted otherwise below.

AMARAVATI

Amaravati is a former Buddhist center that flourished in the second century B.C.—one of the four most important places of worship for Buddhists in India. Its stupa, which was originally the largest in India, is made of brick and covered with marble. Now largely in ruins, it's still a peaceful site.

HYDERABAD

Charminar, a beautiful granite structure with a slender minaret rising from each corner, was built in 1591 by Quli Qutb Shahi, the founder of Hyderabad. The arches face the cardinal points: north, south, east, and west. The rooms above the arches may have been used as a college. The structure was possibly built as an offering to drive away an epidemic that was destroying the population of the then new city.
Golconda Fort, six km (3.6 mi) from Charminar, is a thirteenth-century fort rebuilt by the Qutb Shahi kings in the sixteenth century and made their capital. It has great acoustics. A loud noise made under the dome of the front gate can be heard at the highest point in the fort. An ingenious water supply system—clay pipes and Persian wheels—carried water to roof gardens and palaces.
Mecca Masjid is the biggest mosque in South India. Ten thousand devotees can pray inside. Construction was started in 1614 by the sixth Qutb Shahi king, Abdullah Qutb Shah, and completed by the Mogul Emperor Aurangzeb. Colonnades and door arches were made from single slabs of granite.
Qutb Shahi Tombs are memorials for seven of the Qutb Shahi kings. Structures have a strange infusion of Hindu influence. Note the lotus leaves and buds.
Venkateswara Temple is a marble structure, dedicated to Lord Venkateswara and completed in 1976 by the Birla Foundation. An excellent fusion of northern and southern temple architecture. Workmen from all over India were involved, including some craftsmen who were supposedly descended from the artists who worked on the Taj Mahal. The idols were made by South Indian sculptors. Open to all, regardless of faith, 8 A.M.–noon; 4–8 P.M.

KOLANUPAKA

Mahavira Jain Temple is claimed to be 2,000 years old. Inside is a five-foot-high sculpture of Mahavira, the last of the Jain *tirthankaras* (perfect souls), built of solid jade. Another deity, Adeshwar (the first of the Jain tirthankaras) has jewels in his forehead valued at half a million dollars.

NAGARJUNAKONDA

Anupa, five km (three mi.) from Nagarjunakonda, is a Buddhist monastery reconstructed from excavated ruins of a lost city and an important Buddhist settlement dating from the third century. The original city was flooded by the Nagarjunasagar Dam, which created the world's third-largest artificial lake.

PALAMPET

Rudresvara Temple (also called Ramappa Temple), dedicated to Shiva, was constructed by the Kakatyas around A.D. 1234. This is a must-see if you're in the area. You'll find some of the best temple sculpture in India.

SRISAILAM

Bharamarambha Mallikarjunaswamy Temple contains a *Jyotirlangam,* which means "natural lingam created by a god" (one of 12 in India). The temple is enclosed in huge walls and gateways with bas-reliefs illustrating legends and avatars connected to Shiva. Parts of the temple complex date from the second century A.D. The daily *puja* (prayer service) is spectacular.

TIRUMALA/TIRUPATI

At Tirumala, *Sri Venkateshwara Temple* is the abode of the "Lord of the Seven Hills" and home of one of the richest temples in southern India. The shrine is an essential pilgrimage, a great example of early Dravidian art. Non-Hindus are allowed inside. The temple sits on a peak, with its several *goporums* (towers) visible during the ascent. The main door, or *vimana,* the cover of the sanctum sanctorum (inner shrine), and the temple flag post are covered in gold plate.

Chandragiri Fort, 11 km (6.6 mi.) from Tirupati, was important during the last days of the Vijayanagar Empire. Built in A.D. 1000, it features interesting remains of palaces and temples. Nearby, two palaces are used by members of the royal family.

Kalahasti, east of Tirupati, is another important pilgrimage center and old temple with inscriptions that connect it to the Cholas in the 1200s right through to the Vijayanagar Empire in the 1500s. The huge goporum was built in 1516. According to legend, the lingam inside the temple was worshiped by a spider (*sri*), a snake (*kala*), and an elephant (*hasti*), which obviously explains its name. The temple is dedicated to Vayudeva, the wind god.

At Simhachalam, 16 km (9.6 mi.) from Vizag, the eleventh-century *Narashima Temple* is dedicated to Lord Vishnu in his incarnation as Narasimha in the form of a boar. The pillars in the mandapas have beautiful carvings.

WARANGAL

One Thousand Pillar Temple in Warangal, capital of the Kakatya dynasty between the twelfth and thirteenth centuries, was constructed in 1163 by Rudra Deva in the Chalukyan style, with each pillar richly carved. A two-meter (six-foot) Nandi stands out front. This temple is dedicated to Shiva.

Warangal Fort covers an enormous area; constructed between 1199 and 1261 by the Kakatya rulers.

YADAGIRIGUTTA

Lakshmi Narasimha Swamy Temple is situated on top of a lovely hill offering a good view of the Deccan Plateau. The temple is built around a cave where Lord Vishnu supposedly lived. In the inner sanctum, flanked by silver doors, Lord Vishnu lies in his half-lion, half-human incarnation slaying the demon Kiranyakasipa.

MUSEUMS AND GALLERIES. Entrance is free or there is a nominal cost. **Amaravati.** *Archaeological Museum* holds Buddhist antiquities from the third century B.C. to A.D. twelfth century. Open 10 A.M.–5 P.M.; closed Monday.

Hyderabad. *Andhra Pradesh State Museum* in the Public Gardens was established in 1930. It features collections of weapons, bidriware, bronzes, miniatures, manuscripts, and sculpture and a prehistoric section complete with a mummy. Open daily except Mondays and official holidays, 10:30 A.M.–5 P.M.

Birla Museum in the Asmangadh Palace at Malakpet, near the TV tower, houses bronzes, sculptures, paintings, armor. Excellent miniatures from the Deccani, Mogul, and Rajasthani art schools. In fact, you'll find art from all over the world here. Very eclectic displays. For hours, contact Director, Birla Archaeological and Cultural Institute, tel. 558347.

Salar Jung Museum has 38 galleries of priceless art treasures amassed in the early 1900s by Yousuf Ali Khan, a.k.a. Nawab Salar Jung. A lonely man, he surrounded himself with every intricate notion of art: South Indian bronzes, miniatures from Shah Jahan's personal album, Nur Jahan's emerald and ruby dagger, and ivory furniture as well as Western Chippendale and Louis XIV furnishings, Persian carpets, even ordinary garden tools. A must-see, including the clock in the courtyard. Open daily except Fridays and official holidays, 9:30 A.M.–5:15 P.M.

Nagarjunasagar. *Nagarjunakonda Island Museum* is designed in the style of a Buddhist *vihara* (monastery) and is set on a hill. Here you can see the reconstructed relics of a third- and fourth-century Buddhist civilization: Buddhist stupas, actual relics of the Buddha, viharas, sacrificial altars, statues, even a peaceful garden. A boat takes you to the museum. Booking counter is near the dam. Rs. 15 per person. Departures 9 A.M. and 1 P.M.; return trips 1 and 4 P.M. Buy tickets *early!*— boats fill up fast. Museum is open 9 A.M.–4 P.M.; closed on Fridays. Admission free. For further details, call 3625 in Nagarjunasagar.

GARDENS AND ZOOS. *Lion Safari Park* and *Nehru Zoological Park* comprise 300 acres with almost 2,000 animals. Train and animal rides for kids. Also, see life-size fiberglass models of dinosaurs. Open 9 A.M.–5 P.M.; closed Mondays. Rs. 1 per person for minibus ride through the lion safari. *Osmansagar* and *Himayatsagar* are two nearby lakes with gardens. Lovely for walks and picnics. Open sunrise to sunset. The *Public Gardens* (*Bagh-e-aam*) is a beautiful public garden in the middle of Hyderabad containing plants from all over, a cypress garden, lotus pools, and a rose garden. Open sunrise to sunset.

SPORTS AND OUTDOOR ADVENTURES. Beaches. You'll find lovely beaches around Vishakapatnam that are just opening up for tourism. Beaches extend north and south along the Bay of Bengal and include *Mount Kailasa, Rama Krishna Beach, Waltair,* and *Bheemunipatnam Beach.* Lovely coves and long stretches of sand grace each of these.

Golfing. Temporary memberships and equipment are available at the *Secunderabad Club.* Call for details (tel. 76351).

Horse Races. Watch the races at the Malapet Race Course July–October and November–February. Call the *Hyderabad Race Club* for details (tel. 552491).

Sailing. Boats are available on Sagar Lake. Call the *Secunderabad Sailing Club* for details (tel. 75381).

SHOPPING. Bidriware work, made from a special alloy with its vivid contrast of dull black and lustrous white, is a distinctive craft of Hyderabad. Attractive novelties inlaid with pure silver wire in intricate designs are manufactured from this alloy, which resembles gun metal in composition. Bangles, buttons, cigarette cases, trays, cuff links, fruit bowls, and so forth are also made of this material. Nirmal toys are made of very light wood. Amusing specimens of animals painted with brilliant, metallike lacquer are manufactured for the delight of the children. Gold filigree work is another popular craft in this area. Ikat textiles (a process of tie-dye weaving) and other handloomed silks (all created in Pochampalli village) are also available.

If you appreciate fine carpets, look at the carpets of Warangal, which are famous and have won prizes in various international exhibitions. These carpets are of three kinds: silk, cotton, and woolen. Their designs conform to Persian patterns.

Hyderabad is also the center of India's pearl trade. Near Hyderabad's famous Charminar area, there is a row of small shops whose display cases gleam with treasures from the sea. Pearls of every shape and hue are polished and sorted according to quality (sheen, smoothness, and uniformity of roundness) before they are shipped throughout India.

Charminar Market itself is one of the best in India. It's fun, interesting, and teeming with tempting items to buy—fabrics, bangles, bidriware—all the crafts and handiwork for which Hyderabad is famous. It's a good place for bargaining, browsing, and getting a good look at India.

The following shops and bazaars offer the best examples of these products:

Mangatrai Pearls (22–6–191, Pathergatti, near Charminar Market and Basheer Bagh, opposite Hotel Nagarjuna) sells an astonishing range of pearls and can design jewelry on the spot. Open 10:30 A.M.–8 P.M., closed Sunday. AE, DC, MC, V.

Sanchay (Shop Nos. 21 & 22, Babukhan Estate, Basheer Bagh, Hyderabad) offers a carefully chosen selection of handloomed and handblocked silks and cottons from Andhra Pradesh, especially Pochampalli village. You'll find exquisite tussar silks, khadi silk, brocades, and ikat. Open 9:30 A.M.–9 P.M., closed Sunday. AE, DC, MC, V.

Lepakshi Handicrafts Emporium (Gunfoundry, Hyderabad) is run by the Andhra Pradesh government and has all the state's handicrafts and products under its roof. Open 10 A.M.–8 P.M., closed Sunday. AE, DC, MC, V.

You should also consider taking a lovely excursion to Pochampalli (60 km or 37 mi. south of Hyderabad on the road to Vijayawada). This village is home to the artisans who create some of India's loveliest silk. You can buy direct from their cooperative store. Open daily, 9 A.M.–7 P.M. Rupees only.

NIGHTLIFE AND BARS. Most of the better hotels in Hyderabad have bars, which are generally open 11 A.M.–11 P.M. The *Golconda Bar* in the Krishna Oberoi is elegant and offers good views of Husain Sagar Lake.

Pubs are also springing up in Hyderabad and serve multicuisine "finger food" along with draught beer from local distilleries and other alcoholic and nonalcoholic beverages. Here are two popular draws: *Oaken Cask* (3–6–307 Central Chambers, Hyderguda, Hyderabad) and *Pivot Club* (near Punjagutta "X" Rd., Begum Rd., Hyderabad). Pubs are open 11 A.M.–midnight.

For Indian dance and musical performances, contact *Ravindra Bharathi* (Public Garden Rd., Hyderabad; tel. 233672) or *Thyagaraja Gana Sabha* (Vivek Nagar Chikkadpally, Hyderabad; tel. 68241).

EASTERN REGION

CALCUTTA

City of Astonishments

by
LISA SAMSON and AMIT SHAH

Lisa Samson is a free-lance writer and photographer whose photographs have been published in India and the United States. She has lived in Southeast Asia and has traveled extensively there and in India.

Amit Shah is a free-lance writer whose work has been published in more than a dozen publications in the United States and in India.

You are always unprepared for Calcutta. You have tried to ready yourself for the grime, the filth, and the statistics of poverty that numb the most rational minds, and you were right to do so. They exist. Some time ago, a tourist brochure announced that "Calcutta assaults the senses like few other cities"; the burly, grimy, sweaty city is toiling, calculating, blind to suffering, and yet indispensable to the fabric of India.

You cannot remain objective about Calcutta. It is an intensely personal city, like New York, and you will not leave it without feeling a sense of bewilderment or coming under its bewitching spell. Revulsion is only for the ignorant. In Calcutta, you cannot hide from one of the largest cities in the world, a world of developing economies, of urban planning gone awry. For those who know its historic rise from obscurity in the 1700s to the beginning of its decline in the mid-1900s, Calcutta is a reminder of why and how the British Empire was created in India and what happened when the empire was dismantled.

Every day, hundreds of refugees pour across the Bangladesh border and make their way to Calcutta. Migrants from across India come to the fabled city. Yet despite the burgeoning population, Calcutta persists and surmounts.

Few visitors are prepared for Calcutta's inhabitants—the Bengalis— animated, laconic, intellectual, spirited, argumentative, anarchic, imaginative, and creative. They have dominated the city and have made it, for over 1½ centuries, the soul of India. They were among the first to react to the intellectual and political stimuli of the West and have produced, despite their sometimes desperate state, many of India's most respected filmmakers, writers, scientists, musicians, dancers, and philosophers. Blending the European humanism of the nineteenth century with the indigenous culture that was revived by Rabindranath Tagore, among others, Bengalis made the first organized efforts to oust the British in the early twentieth century. Ultimately, they broke away from Gandhian politics and chose terrorism (one of the reasons the British moved their capital from Calcutta to Delhi in 1911).

Leisurely Visit Advised

The city is a dynamo—exhausting and exhaustive. It is not an "easy" destination but an essential one if you want to claim that you have experienced India. Many Western travelers hurry through Calcutta and return home to spread misconceptions about India and this city on the flimsy basis of a short stay. A few years ago, graffiti (in English) splattered on a wall in Calcutta summed up the feelings of Indians about such tourists: "Calcutta Needs Development, Not Insults." In many ways, Calcutta represents India's essence: its economic and developmental pitfalls coupled with its imagination and tenacity.

The Calcutta metropolitan district covers 426 square kilometers (883 square miles) and has a population of over 12 million. It comprises two municipal corporation areas (Calcutta and Howrah), 32 municipalities, 62 nonmunicipal urban centers, and over 500 villages. By any count a huge cosmopolitan city, it sprang from three small fishing villages under the direction of the British East India Company.

A Bit of History

On August 24, 1690, Job Charnock, an agent for the East India Company, arrived in Sutanati, a cotton center in Bengal. That November, he bought three villages—Sutanati, Gobindpur, and Kali Kutta—for Rs. 1,300 from Sabarna Roy Choudhury, a local landowner. An undistinguished man by all historical accounts, Charnock won the hearts of Bengalis by a personal deed: He rescued a young Bengali widow about to be burned at the funeral pyre of her dead husband, as was the custom of *sati*, married her, and lived and died in Calcutta. His grave is at St. John's Church, off Dalhousie Square. Through Charnock's real estate acquisition, the British gained a foothold in what had been the Sultanate of Delhi under the Moguls. Thus began the great drama known as the British raj in India.

The English built Fort William—near what is now Benoy-Badal-Dinesh Bagh (BBD Bagh)—and consolidated their position till 1756, when Sirajud-Daula, the nawab of Bengal, attacked the garrison. Many of the British residents fled. Robert Clive, fighting in Madras at the time, raced back to retake the city in 1757, but not before a number of Englishmen died in an underground cellar where they had been imprisoned (near the pres-

1. National Library
2. Zoological Garden
3. St. Paul's Cathedral and Planetarium
4. Indian Museum
5. W. Bengal Tourist Office
6. General Post Office
7. Writers' Building
8. Howrah Station
9. Ashutosh Museum
10. Sealdah Station
11. Ferry Landing Stage
12. Victoria Memorial
13. Raj Bhavan
14. Govt. of India Tourist Office

CALCUTTA

0	1000	2000 Yards
0	1000	2000 Meters

N

BOTANICAL GARDENS

GRAND TRUNK ROAD SOUTH

Hooghly River

11

Eden Gardens

8

Howrah Bridge

Dakshineshwar Kali Temple →

Belur Math Shrine →

St. John's Church

STRAND ROAD SOUTH

6

Ochterlony Monument

13

BBD BAGH

OLD COURT HOUSE ST

7

STRAND ROAD NORTH

BENTINCK ST

5

Marble Palace

RABINDRA SARANI

MAHATMA GANDHI ROAD

L STREET

COLLEGE ST

LENIN SARANI

Nakhoda Mosque

CHITTARANJAN

9

RABINDRA SARANI

MACHUA BAZAR STREET

AVENUE

VIVEKA NANDA ROAD

BEADON STREET

SHAMBAZAR ST

BOSE ROAD

B.B. GANGULI STREET

BIDHAN

MIRZAPUR ST

SARANI

MOHAN SARANI

TO DUM-DUM AIRPORT →

ACHARYA

PRAFULLA CHANDRA ROAD

10

BELIAGATA ROAD

NARIKEL DANGA MAIN RD

RAJA DINENDRA ST

Parasnath Jain Temple

Circular Canal

MANIKTOLA MAIN RD

Digambar Jain Temple

ent-day general post office by Dalhousie Square). This prison became known as the infamous "Black Hole of Calcutta."

After Clive, the East India Company (John Company in local parlance) was no longer simply a group of traders but a government in power, levying and collecting taxes, making wars, and negotiating treaties. The stockholders in London lobbied Parliament to pass the Regulatory Act of 1773, which gave Calcutta supremacy over the other two English trading posts at Madras and Bombay. Parliament appointed a governor-general of British India based in Calcutta—Warren Hastings. Hastings, who represented the king and the crown government throughout British-held India, was paid by the East India Company, whose business interests and profits were of primary concern. The accumulation of profits, and the government machinery to ensure such projects, became the first order of British rule in India. Colonialism had reached a watershed through the acquisition of those three small villages along the muddy Hooghly River in Bengal.

Commercial and Political Hub

Throughout the nineteenth century, Bengal, with Calcutta as its capital, though difficult to govern, spread out from the eastern reaches of present-day Bangladesh. Because of the resurgent Bengali cultural nationalism, which fed the political nationalism of the late 1800s, Bengal became the commercial and political center of India and for the British east of the Suez Canal. The old pilgrim road that ran from the north (Chitpur Road) to the south (Kalighat) was named Chowringhee after the disciples of a hermit, Chowringheegiri. It became a fashionable boulevard facing the great *Maidan* (open space), with garden houses designed by Italian architects. In 1859, it was the first street in the city to have gas lamps. Today Chowringhee, renamed Jawaharlal (J. L.) Nehru Road, is the center of business and social life in Calcutta.

By 1905, the nationalist mood and the difficulty of governing the vast territory prompted Lord Curzon, the British viceroy, to partition Bengal into East and West, thereby splitting the nationalist forces. The Bengali response was so ferocious that a unified presidency was created again in 1912, but only after the capital of the raj was moved to Delhi and a new city, New Delhi, was designed by an English architect, Sir Edwin Lutyens. The commercial impact of this change in capitals was far less severe than the political impact.

World War II Ends Trade

But other developments occurred around the time of World War II that brought about the end of Calcutta's great economic trade—in cloth, silk, lacquer, indigo, rice, betelnut, tobacco, tea, and jute. After the partition of East Bengal between India and East Pakistan (now Bangladesh), the jute mills of Calcutta were cut off from their East Bengal source of raw material, and the demand for synthetic fibers began to overshadow that for jute. Seventeen million people were also uprooted in eastern India; fewer than 30 years later, during the 1972 Bangladesh War, another large migration began that has continued in a steady stream. Decay had begun to set in. After a period of postindependence reconstruction under the Congress party, the late 1960s brought Calcutta to a cathartic battle between the forces of change and the established, somewhat moribund, political forces.

One of the richest cities between Rome and Tokyo, in accumulated wealth and representations, Calcutta was once a leader of Indian exports, controlling 15 percent of the manufacturing industry, collecting over 30 percent of the national tax revenues and surpassing the rest of India in the manufacture of light machinery. In the late 1960s–early 1970s, Calcutta went into a depression of monumental proportions. Manufacturing plants closed because of labor disputes, schools and colleges couldn't offer examinations because of student strikes, transportation creaked, basic services were overtaxed, and political violence wrenched the city in a frightening rage that peaked in 1970.

Left Front in Control

In May 1977, the Congress party lost its grip on the political wheel of Bengal, and the Marxists (Communist party of West Bengal), with a coalition group, the Left Front, were elected by an overwhelming majority. Much is heard about the Left Front in Calcutta—their work was probably invented by a biblical Job. In power, they are pragmatists more than ideologues, and their balance sheet for the past decade has been mixed. The pressures from New Delhi (Congress), which controls the funds that could repair Calcutta's collapsing infrastructure and promote large-scale development, are enormous.

The Left Front's strategy of first consolidating its rural base in Bengal has worked, but in Calcutta, the politicization has practically crippled the legitimate functioning of public hospitals, government offices, and even the police. Some of the Left Front's gains are no mean achievements: doubling the rice production to the second state in India, increasing literacy in rural areas, providing health and legal benefits for sharecroppers, and decreasing the percentage of people below the poverty line. Living in a city with over 12 million people, 150,000 "pavement dwellers," power shortages, and huge population increases, Calcuttans hope for long-term investment projects and less short-term lectures by politicians and urban-development "experts." A poster, in English, summed up the feelings of many Calcuttans: Many say that Calcutta is a dead city. Yet, hundreds throng to Calcutta each day from neighboring states. Are they scavengers feeding on the mortal remains? No. They come in the hope for opportunities for a livelihood and survival. They do get them and settle down. They are not scavengers and Calcutta is very much alive.

EXPLORING CALCUTTA

Calcutta, unlike other metropolitan cities in India, is a relative newcomer, having sprouted from three fishing villages in the late seventeenth century. The course of British imperial history on the subcontinent is mirrored in Calcutta's own history and development.

If you come in by train, you're in for the experience of a lifetime. Howrah Station, situated on the west bank of the Hooghly River, is the major railway station in eastern India. A "permanent" population seems to reside on the platforms among the ferocious intensity of thousands on the move. This atmosphere extends to Howrah Bridge, a Calcutta landmark, which was built in 1941, a web of girders stretching 465 meters (1,500 feet) over the Hooghly. Passing over eight lanes of chaotic traffic that includes all manner of transportation—rickshaws, cars, scooters, bicycles, pushcarts, and animal-drawn carts—2 million people cross this single-span cantilevered bridge each day. Howrah, already a congested suburb of Calcutta, is becoming the fastest-growing population center in the metropolitan area.

A second Howrah Bridge, just south of the Maidan, opened in late 1992, but the approach roads are still under construction so the going is slow. Once over the bridge, you're near the Botanical Gardens. Spread over 270 acres and containing over 30,000 varieties of plants and trees, it is India's oldest (built in 1786). A 200-year-old banyan tree with over 600 branches taking root around the central tree creates a veritable forest—an awesome sight. Its circumference is 424 meters (1,367 feet). Tour buses race through these gardens, which, with the view of the Hooghly, are an ideal spot for picnicking. If you can, hire a car and go there early in the day to avoid the crush of humanity that clogs the narrow street in Shibour that leads to the gardens. The road is lined with jute mills, once Bengal's main export industry.

About 10 kilometers (6.2 miles) north of the gardens is Belur Math Shrine, the headquarters of the Ramakrishna Mission, a reform movement that has an impact far beyond Bengal. Ramakrishna Paramahansa, who died in 1886, forsook his Brahman status and preached the unity of religious faiths and an adherence to the altruistic values for all people. His disciple, Swami Vivekananda, established the mission in 1898. The Belur Math Shrine resembles a church, a temple, or a mosque, depending upon the angle from which it is viewed.

A short distance north is Dakshineshwar Kali Temple (1847), a major pilgrimage site to which devotees continue to flock to see the temples of Shiva, Kali, Radha, and Krishna. It was here that Ramakrishna received his spiritual vision; his room is a museum. Open till 10 P.M.

Either on the way north of the city or returning south from Belur, stop at Parasnath, one of Calcutta's most interesting Jain temples. Built in 1867 on Budree Das Temple Street and dedicated to Sitalnathji, the tenth of the 24 *tirthankaras* (perfect souls), it is a flamboyant structure filled with mirror-inlay pillars, stained-glass windows, marble floors in a floral design, a gilded dome, and chandeliers from nineteenth-century Paris and Brussels. In the garden, there are blocks of glass mosaics with European figures and statues that have been covered with silver paint. It is an unusual place of honor for the ascetic Jains. If you were lucky and beat the midday traffic back to the center of town, take a break to freshen up (without a doubt you will sweat in any season in Calcutta), have lunch (you might want to try one of the many brands of Indian beer—Bengal brews many of them), and when the midday heat abates a little, resume your sightseeing.

The Indian Museum (see Museum section, below), the Nehru Children's Museum, Victoria Memorial, and Birla Planetarium are all within a few kilometers.

The British came to Calcutta to trade, and they needed political stability and an infrastructure to manage the indigenous population. Toward this end, they brought in soldiers, priests, and clerks. Their legacies remain in Fort William, on the east bank of the Hooghly near Strand Road; the fort is an irregular octagon surrounded by a moat almost 16 meters (50 feet) wide. Built in 1773 and named after William III, it was said to be impregnable, a boast that has never been put to the test.

St. John's Church, built in 1787 and located at the intersection of Council House and K. S. Roy Road, is where Job Charnock, founder of Calcutta, is buried. In the garden, there is a monument to the victims of the "Black Hole" tragedy.

Nearby, St. Paul's Cathedral, with its soaring Gothic steeple, was built in 1847. Two earthquakes destroyed the previous steeples; the present one is a model of the one at Canterbury Cathedral. Florentine frescoes, the stained-glass western window, and a gold communion plate presented by Queen Victoria are of special interest. The hours of services are posted near the entrance gate.

Writers' Building, on one side of Dalhousie Square (BBD Bagh), built in 1780, housed the "writers" or clerks of the East India Company. It was synonymous with mind-numbing bureaucracy from its inception and is today the dreaded bottomless pit of the present government's paper mill. The Gothic structure, with rows of Ionic pillars and groups of statues, is evocative of a Victorian architecture that is a photographer's delight.

Another sight of interest in this city that blends Victorian order and the anarchic bustle of a developing country is the Ochterlony Monument (Shahid Minar) at the northern tip of the Maidan near the Park Street Metro entrance on J. L. Nehru Road. This 49-meter (158-foot) pillar, erected to commemorate Sir David Ochterlony's victories in nineteenth-century Nepal, is designed with a curious blend of Middle Eastern architecture. Its base is Egyptian, its pillar is Syrian, and its cupola is Turkish! It was the focal point for political rallies (much like Nelson's at London's Trafalgar Square). The Raj Bhawan (Government House), the residence of the governor and more or less a copy of Keddleston Hall in Derbyshire, is another such sight. Completed in 1802, it contains the throne of Tipu Sultan, the nemesis of the British, and a polished teak ballroom floor. Tourists are not allowed inside, however. While in this area, stroll through the green expanse of Eden Gardens, which has lakes for boating and a wooden pagoda from Burma.

Leaving the center of the city, go south past the Calcutta Racecourse and the Maidan, where English officers once hunted wild game but which is now the "green lung" of the city, with almost two square miles of open parkland. The original forests were cut down to provide a clear field of fire for Fort William. Near the racecourse are the Zoological Gardens, opened in 1876, with some of the best collections of reptiles and white tigers in India. The zoo also has a children's zoo and an aquarium; its attractive and easy to walk around. The air-conditioned snack bar, located near the entrance, is mobbed during the summer.

The Kali Temple at Kalighat is near a canal called Adiganga (the "real Ganga" because it is believed to be the original bed of the Hooghly). Built in 1809, the Kali is one of Hinduism's renowned pilgrimage sites, containing temples to Radha, Shiva, Krishna, and Kali. Human sacrifices were reputed to be common in the last century, but only goats are slaughtered now and offered to Kali with Ganges water and *bhang,* an uncultivated hemp.

Coming back north, there is Nakhoda Mosque, built in 1926, the largest Moslem mosque in Calcutta, modeled after Akbar's tomb at Sikandra (Agra). The mosque can accommodate 10,000 people.

The Agro-Horticultural Society's gardens are behind the National Library at Belvedere on Alipore Road. Founded in 1820, the gardens are in full bloom during December and January, and some flowers are out as late as early March. This is a soothing side trip.

At Muktaram Babu Street in Chorebagan (Thieves' Garden) is another site of historic interest, the famed Marble Palace, built in 1855 by Raja Rajendra Mullick. A member of Bengal's landed gentry, with lands in what is now Bangladesh (then East Bengal), Raja Mullick chose to spend his money in the "second city of the Empire"—Calcutta. Lavishly built of Italian marble, the palace's dark walls are covered with paintings, clocks, statues, crystal, and china. The palace is said to contain paintings by Gainsborough, Reynolds, and Reubens, and a statue by Michelangelo.

The grounds have aviaries and a family temple, as well as Roman fountains.

Calcutta's historical sights can keep you busy for days. Less well-known sights include Jorasanko Thakurbari at 5 Dwarkanath Tagore Lane, the house where Rabindranath Tagore lived and worked. Now Rabindra Bharati University, it actively fosters cultural activities. With its cupolas and balconies, Thakurbari (House of Tagores) was once known as a nerve center of intellectual life in Bengal. Today, part of it is a museum housing a splendid collection of Tagore memorabilia. Tagore and stalwarts, such as Michael Madhusudan Dutt, Bankim Chandra Chatterjee, Ishwar Chandra Vidyasagar, Raja Ram Monun Roy, Sarat Chandra Chatterjee, Sri Ramkrishna, and Swami Vivekananda, brought about a renaissance in Bengali cultural, social, and political life in the nineteenth and early twentieth centuries. To walk the Thakubari's lanes, made for pedestrians and palanquin bearers rather than cars and buses, is to "feel" the old city.

South Park Street Cemetery is a repository of British imperial history in Calcutta. Opened in 1767, the funereal obelisks are a testament to those participants in the British raj who made Calcutta their home. Among those whose graves are here are William Thackeray's father, Richmond; the linguist William Jones, founder of the Royal Asiatic Society; Colonel Charles Deare, who fought Tipu Sultan; and Anglo-Indian poet Louis Vivian Derozio. Bhowanipor Military Cemetery is the burial place of Charles Dickens's second son, Walter Landor Dickens, who died in Calcutta as a lieutenant.

PRACTICAL INFORMATION FOR CALCUTTA

WHEN TO GO. Calcutta is best visited between October and March, when temperatures are between 98° F and 45° F. From April to June and during the July and August monsoon, humidity can reach 100 percent. During the monsoon, rains invariably flood city thoroughfares and Calcutta's antiquated sewage and drainage system.

HOW TO GET THERE. By Air. Calcutta's international airport has flights connecting with Bangkok (Air India, Indian Airlines, and Thai Airways), Dhaka (Bangladesh Biman), Kathmandu (Indian Airlines and Royal Nepal Airlines), London (Air India), New York (Air India), Singapore (Singapore Airlines), and Tokyo (Air India). Indian Airlines has flights to Calcutta from Delhi (24 flights a week), Bombay and Guwahati (17 flights a week), Madras (14 flights a week), Bhubaneswar and Patna (10 flights a week), and a daily flight from Bangalore, Ranchi, Bagdogra, and Hyderabad. There are also six flights a week from Jorhat, four flights a week from Port Blair and Vishaskhaptam, and three flights a week from Jaipur, Nagpur, Lucknow, Raipur, and Varanasi. Vayudoot has three flights a week from Coochbihar and Shillong. Call Indian Airlines for information (tel. 262548) and reservations (tel. 263135). For Vayudoot information, call 433091 or 435316.

By Train. Howrah Station is the focal point of rail travel in the eastern region and the terminal for such folkloric trains as the *Delhi-Howrah Mail* (26 hours); *Air-conditioned Express* (same distance in 24 hours); the *Rajdhani Express* (fastest, in 22 hours); the *Calcutta Mail* (36 hours from Bombay); the *Gitanjali Express* and the *Howrah Express* (30 hours from Bombay); and the *Coromandel Express* (25 hours from Madras).

With computerization now available, you can purchase tickets at any of the following *Eastern Railway* booking offices: 14A Strand Rd., Calcutta 700 001 (near the GPO); 6 Fairlie Pl., Calcutta 700 001 (close to the Reserve Bank of India, a few blocks from the GPO). Tickets are also available at the railway stations (Howrah and Sealdah—the latter being the local commuter station in southern Calcutta) although the lines and the waiting periods can be daunting. *Southeastern Railway* tickets are available for all classes from Esplanade Mansions, Esplanade East (near Raj Bhavan or Governor's House). If you're traveling overnight, remember to reserve a sleeping berth. For railway inquiries, call 203535; for reservations, call 280370.

By Rented Car with Driver. India's oldest and most famous highway, the Grand Trunk Road, connects Delhi, Bombay, and Madras; but the closest major city, Madras, is a long journey—about 1,200 km (744 mi.). The *Automobile Association of Eastern India,* 13 Promothesh Barua Sarani, can provide road maps and vital information on gas stations, lodging, and detours enroute.

By Bus. *North Bengal State Transport Corporation* operates buses from Calcutta to North Bengal, various other parts of the state, Bihar, and Orissa. Booking offices are at Esplanade Bus Terminus, diagonally opposite the Central Cottage Industries Emporium at the hub of Calcutta's Chowringhee Road (J. L. Nehru Rd.).

TOURIST INFORMATION. The *Government of India Tourist Office* at 4 Shakespeare Sarani, Calcutta 700071 (tel. 221402) and the *West Bengal Tourist Information Center,* 3/2 BBD Bagh (East), Calcutta 700069 (tel. 288271) can provide you with all the information you require. The Government of India Tourist Office is open Monday–Friday, 9:30 A.M.–6 P.M.; Saturday till 1 P.M. The West Bengal Tourist Information Center is open Monday–Friday, 9 A.M.– 5:30 P.M.; and the first and third Saturdays till noon. The West Bengal Tourist Information Center has a free booklet, *Calcutta,* which lists the addresses and telephone numbers of airlines, trains, buses, ferries, travel agents, shipping companies, hotels, restaurants, medical services, banks, consulates, and tourist information counters for all other Indian states. The other guide to pick up, *Calcutta Briefs,* is sold at local bookstores (try Cambridge or Oxford on Park St.) for Rs. 30 (a little over a dollar) and includes information on shopping, local performances and art exhibits, and notes on Bengali cuisine. It is simple, informative, and amusing.

FOREIGN CURRENCY EXCHANGE. Most Western-style hotels have money-exchange counters. Otherwise, go to the *American Express* office, 21 Old Court House St.; *Bank of America,* 8 India Exchange Pl.; *Citibank,* Tata Center, 43 J. L. Nehru Rd.; *ANZ Grindlays,* 19 N. S. Rd.; the *State Bank of India,* 33 J. L. Nehru Rd. Banks are open Monday–Friday, 10–2; Saturday, 10–noon.

ACCOMMODATIONS. Prices are based on double occupancy and don't include taxes and service charges; *Deluxe,* over Rs. 2,000; *Expensive,* Rs. 1,200–Rs. 2,000; *Moderate,* Rs. 500–Rs. 1,200; *Inexpensive,* under Rs. 500. Most Western-style hotels accept major credit cards.

Deluxe

Oberoi Grand. 15 J. L. Nehru Rd., Calcutta 700013; tel. 292323, fax 291217. 250 rooms with bath. Impeccably maintained at the height of elegance, this Victorian landmark has spacious modern rooms; the best ones overlook the courtyard and pool. TV, air-conditioning, room service, restaurants, bar, pool, health club, shops, foreign-exchange and travel counter, business center. AE, DC, MC, V.

Taj Bengal. 34 B, Belvedere Rd., Alipore, Calcutta 700027; tel. 283939, fax 281766. 250 rooms with bath. Calcutta's newest hotel is elegant, with a handsome atrium lobby filled with palm trees, water channels, and Indian art and antiques. Air-conditioned rooms are done up in a contemporary decor with pretty floral bedspreads and drapes. Best rooms overlook the pool and offer a view of Victoria Memorial Hall. TV, room service, multicuisine restaurants, bar, swimming pool, health club, business center, foreign-exchange and travel counter, shopping arcade. AE, DC, MC, V.

Expensive

Hotel Airport Ashok. Calcutta Airport, Calcutta 700052; tel. 569111. 153 rooms with bath. This modern hotel with pleasant rooms is primarily for the traveler with just an overnight stop. TV, air-conditioning, room service, restaurants, bar, pool, health club, tennis courts, baby-sitters, doctor, shopping arcade, foreign-exchange and travel counter, courtesy airport shuttle. AE, DC, MC, V.

Park Hotel. 17 Park St., Calcutta 700016; tel. 297336, fax 298027. 155 rooms with bath. This Western-style hotel has small rooms with narrow beds. Best feature is its central location. TV, air-conditioning, room service, restaurants, pool, foreign-exchange and travel counter, business center, doctor. AE, DC, MC, V.

Moderate

Fairlawn Hotel. 13/A Sudder St., Calcutta 700016; tel. 444460. 20 rooms with bath. If you want old-fashioned charm, stay in this Calcutta landmark, built in 1801 on a side street. The rooms are furnished with chintz and memorabilia. In the hot months, ask for air-conditioning. Amenities include TV in a lovely upstairs sitting room, and a multicuisine restaurant. Meals included. AE, MC, V.

Great Eastern. 1 Old Court House St., Calcutta 700069; tel. 282331. 200 rooms with bath. Once Kipling's favorite hotel, Great Eastern is now run by the government. Though the management is wonderful, the hotel has lost its grandeur. The air-conditioned rooms are spacious and clean, however, and the location is ideal for Calcutta sightseeing. TV, room service, restaurants, bar, foreign-exchange and travel counter, shops. AE, DC, MC, V.

Lytton Hotel. 14 Sudder St., Calcutta 700016; tel. 291875, fax 291747. 69 rooms with bath. This unpretentious Western-style hotel has plain carpeted rooms with TV and air-conditioning. Restaurants, room service, bar. AE, DC, MC, V.

New Kenilworth. 1 & 2 Little Russell St., Calcutta 700071; tel. 228394. 110 rooms with bath. Popular with repeat visitors to Calcutta, this hotel has two attractive wings—one new and the other refurbished. The rooms are comfortable and spacious. TV, air-conditioning, room service, restaurants, travel counter, bookshop. AE, DC, MC, V.

Inexpensive

International Guest House. Ramakrishna Mission Institute of Culture, Golpark, Ballygunge, Calcutta; tel. 463431. Available here are decent, simple rooms, far from the city center in southern Calcutta. Rupees only.

YMCA. Chowringhee. J. L. Nehru Rd., Calcutta; tel. 233504. The deluxe section of this hostel, between Metro Cinema and the Grand Hotel, has air-conditioned rooms. Rupees only.

YWCA International Guest House. 1 Middleton Row, Calcutta, West Bengal; tel. 240260. Couples are permitted to stay in this simple, clean hostel. Rupees only.

DINING OUT. The passions of Calcuttans can be listed as politics, argument, *adda* (a spirited blend of gossip and intellectual discourse), cricket, and food. Bengali cuisine, with its accent on fish and prawn dishes, is fabulous. If you have the opportunity try these delicacies: freshwater fish (*macher jhol*); sweets, especially *sandesh* and *rossogolla; chingri* (prawns) in coconut sauce; fish in rich yogurt sauce (*doi maach*); smoked *hilsa*. Other cuisines that provide Calcutta with a pleasant flavor are Cantonese Chinese, Burmese, all manner of North Indian and South Indian food, and Continental Western food, as well as the movable feasts of roadside stalls at the southern end of the Maidan. *Daab* water, fresh coconut juice, fresh fruit juices, and *lassis* (yogurt and fruit drinks) are available during the summer near the Lighthouse Cinema, off Chowringhee (J. L. Nehru Rd.) on Humayun Place.

Most of the accommodations listed above also have restaurants. Breakfast is usually served 8–10:30; lunch is usually noon–3; and dinner, 7:30–11. The restaurants listed below are informal and don't require reservations unless noted. Dry days (no liquor) and meatless days (no red meat is served) are Thursdays. Prices are based on one person eating a three-course meal, excluding taxes, tip, or beverage: *Deluxe,* over Rs. 300; *Expensive,* Rs. 200–Rs. 300; *Moderate,* Rs. 100–Rs. 200; *Inexpensive,* under Rs. 100.

Deluxe

Chinoiserie. Taj Bengal, 34 B, Belvedere Rd., Alipore; tel. 283939. This elegant restaurant with an interior pavilion and handsome Chinese murals serves delicious Szechuan fare. Among its specialties are king prawns in pepper salt (fried prawns tossed in a mildly spicy sauce) and *tau su* chicken (fried chicken prepared in a wok with spices). Open noon–3 P.M. and 7–midnight. AE, DC, MC, V.

Ming Court. Oberoi Grand, 15 J. L. Nehru Rd.; tel. 292323. In this restaurant, elegance reigns supreme, with deep red pillars, silk-brocade robes framed on cool gray walls, and soft lighting. The Chinese cuisine, with a Szechuan emphasis, is equally refined. Try the prawns with oyster sauce or chicken in garlic sauce. Reservations advised. Open 12:30–2:30 P.M. and 8–midnight. AE, DC, MC, V.

Moghul Room. Oberoi Grand, 15 J. L. Nehru Rd.; tel. 292323. A sleek modern decor with lots of marble and Indian *ghazals* (musicians) nightly highlights the Moghul Room. The Indian cuisine, with the emphasis on Mughlai dishes, is superb. Dinner reservations advised. Open 12:30–2:30 P.M. and 8–11:30 P.M. AE, DC, MC, V.

Sonargaon. Taj Bengal, 34 B Belvedere Rd., Alipore; tel. 283939. The name of this restaurant means "golden village," and the restaurant itself is a replica of a rural home, complete with a courtyard, well, stringed cot mounted on the wall, and ethnic curios hung here and there. The cuisine is Indian; try the *kakori kebab* (minced lamb kebab) or *murg Wajid Ali* (stuffed, pounded chicken breasts marinated in saffron and cooked in a mildly spicy sauce). Reservations advised. Open 12:30 P.M.–3 P.M. and 7:30 P.M.–midnight. AE, DC, MC, V.

Expensive

Blue Fox. 55 Park St.; tel. 297948. This Calcutta landmark, popular with the smart set, is spacious and has high ceilings. It has a quiet decor in which to enjoy excellent Indian and Continental cuisines. The sizzlers and crab or lobster thermidor are excellent. Open 11 A.M.–10:30 P.M. Dinner reservations advised. DC.

Sky Room. 57 Park St.; tel. 294362. Extremely pretty, with upholstered chairs, crisp table linen, a ceiling with twinkling stars, and handsome murals, the Sky Room serves Indian and Continental dishes, with most people raving about the Western fare. Dinner reservations advised. Open 10:30 A.M.–midnight. Closed Tuesdays. Rupees only.

Moderate

Amber. 11 Waterloo St.; tel. 283018. An upstairs restaurant with subdued lighting, this popular eatery serves Continental and Indian cuisines, including especially tasty tandoori items. Open noon–4 P.M. and 7–11 P.M. Dinner reservations advised. AE, DC.

Bar-B-Q. 43 Park St.; tel. 299916. This popular upstairs restaurant, with an unexpected mix of German-chalet and Chinese decor, serves Cantonese and Szechuan dishes. Try the crispy fried chicken served with a mild "surprise" sauce, or the boneless chili chicken. Open noon–4 P.M. and 7–11 P.M. Weekend reservations advised. AE, DC, MC, V.

Peter Cat. 18 Park St.; tel. 298841. In this intimate restaurant, with white stucco walls, Tiffany-style lamps, and soft lighting, you can enjoy good Continental and Indian dishes, especially tandoori. Open 10 A.M.–midnight. Dinner reservations advised. DC, V.

Inexpensive

Aminia. 6 A, S. N. Banerjee Rd.; tel. 241318. This restaurant has a gigantic front room with overhead fans and taped Hindi music echoing off the walls; family rooms in the back have curtained booths. Waiters bustle around serving delicious tandoori chicken, biryani dishes, kebab, and great snacks. Open 10 A.M.–10 P.M. Rupees only.

Chung Wah. 13 A & B, Chittaranjan Ave.; tel. 277003. Popular and extremely informal, Chung Wah has been serving excellent Chinese dishes for 60 years. Popular choices are the delicious Szechuan prawns and the *yai chai* pork (steamed pork stuffed in cabbage leaves then garnished with a tangy sauce). Open 11 A.M.–11 P.M. Closed Thursdays. Rupees only.

Sabir's. 71 Biplabi Anukul Chunder St.; no phone. A large, plain room with about 50 tables and chairs and whirring overhead fans. Sabir's serves excellent North Indian fare. Try the good mutton biryani. Open 10 A.M.–10 P.M. Rupees only.

Suruchi. 89 Elliot Rd.; no phone. Popular and informal, this unpretentious restaurant, with rows of tables and overhead fans, serves a Bengali menu of fish and prawns. The menu changes daily, depending on the catch. Open Monday–Friday, 10 A.M.–8 P.M.; Saturday, 10 A.M.–3 P.M.; and Sunday, 10 A.M.–3 P.M. Rupees only.

Vineet. 1 Shakespeare Sarani; tel. 440788. This popular restaurant serves excellent vegetarian food (Continental, Chinese, and Indian) and has live Indian music at night. Open noon–3 P.M. and 7–11 P.M. DC.

SWEETS AND TREATS. Bengali sweets—*rosogollah, sandesh, rosomallai, gulab jamun, sitabhog, shorbhaja,* and *barfi,* to name a few—are available at a variety of places. Cool your feet and relax at *K. C. Das,* 11 Esplanade Rd. East; *Ganguram's* Chowringhee, near the Birla Planetarium; *Kathleen's Bakery,* 12 Free School St., which is unfortunately closed Thursdays; *Tulika's,* 41 J. L. Nehru Rd., which has great pizzas and sundaes; and *Flury's Swiss Confectionery,* 18 Park St.

After savoring some of the city's gastronomic delights, one last taste treat awaits you, *paan*—a concoction of betel nut and other items wrapped in a paan leaf that has been spread with lime paste. This after-dinner digestive is an acquired taste, but one worth trying, especially after a huge Indian meal.

Paan is prepared in many different ways. Ask for *mitha paan* (sweet paan), which has sweet condiments (no *masala* or spices) and mint. It will be given to you folded into a triangular shape that you pop whole into the back of your mouth. Next: chew! (Make your first bite a tentative one—sometimes the betel nut is so hard that you can do damage to fillings if you bite down too vigorously.)

Varieties of paan include one that contains *zarda,* a legal, mild narcotic. Restaurants will get it for you for a small tip. Paan shops are abundant in Calcutta, often selling cigarettes and soft drinks as well. We recommend the shop near Kwality's on Park Street, the one opposite the Waldorf restaurant on Park Street, and the one next door to the Amber restaurant.

HOW TO GET AROUND. From the Airport. The airport is 15 km (nine mi.) from the center of Calcutta. Only the Hotel Airport Ashok offers free pickup service. The airport coach (Rs. 15) goes to most of the better hotels and the city center; their counter is near the baggage-claim area. To go by taxi, the fare is about Rs. 90.

By Bus. Calcutta still operates over 225 separate public bus routes, over 25 "special" tram routes with carriages for women only, and over 50 minibus routes (buses that travel an express route). Fares, extremely inexpensive, are based on the distance traveled.

By Ferry Boat. There are ferries on the Hooghly River (as the Ganges is called in this area). Currently, eight ferry landings operate around metropolitan Calcutta, shuttling workers between Calcutta and Howrah. Ferries operate 8:15 A.M.–8 P.M. at 15-minute intervals, except on Sundays.

By Metro. Calcutta has a "first" in India in terms of mass transit. It is the *Metro,* the first subway on the subcontinent, built over a period of 15 years amid great controversy, long delays, and huge cost overruns. The butt of many a Bengali joke, it shuttles about 10,000 commuters each day over a 10-km (six-mi.) route from the eastern Tollygunge section to the Esplanade. Trains run 8 A.M.–9 P.M. daily and arrive promptly every 15 minutes, with announcements made in three languages (Hindi, Bengali, and English). The doors open without a fuss, and air-conditioned cars disgorge their occupants, who cannot believe that such an efficient system will remain so for long. In mid-1990, a 16-km (10-mi.) system was opened between Tollygunge and Dum Dum (near the airport). Many Calcuttans use the Metro as a tourist attraction, much like the beginning years of Washington, D.C.'s system. Ride it for pleasure and for a fast ride down Chowringhee (J. L. Nehru Rd.). The fare depends on the distance traveled; the minimum is Rs. 1.50.

By Taxi. Taxis have meters, but drivers won't use them. Ask your hotel for the appropriate fare, then negotiate.

By Auto Rickshaw. Again, don't expect meters to work. Fares should be cheaper than taxis.

By Bicycle Rickshaw. This is the cheapest way to get around. Negotiate the fare before you start; but have sympathy for the driver, who works hard for his rupees.

By Rented Car and Driver. For excursions around Calcutta, hire a car with driver from one of the recommended travel agencies (see Tour Operators, below). Rates are about Rs. 4–Rs. 5 per km, with a halt charge of Rs. 50–Rs. 100 per night.

For a complete and authoritative guide to all bus and tram routes in the city, we recommend the *Calcutta and Howrah Guide,* sold for less than $1 at, among other places, the Oxford Booksellers on Park Street, next door to Kwality Restaurant.

TOURS. The *West Bengal Government Tourist Office* at 3/2 BBD Bagh East, near Great Eastern Hotel (tel. 288271) offers numerous conducted and package tours. If you don't see printed information sheets at the office, ask; the tourist officers are helpful and informed. The ITDC at 4 Shakespeare Sarani (tel. 220901) also operates similar services. Tourist taxis are available from both locations. A full-day guided tour that takes in over 12 sights costs Rs. 45 (non-air-conditioned); Rs. 60 (air-conditioned).

From October to March, the West Bengal Tourist Office has a number of package tours (including meals and accommodations) via train, bus, and boat to North Bengal and the Sunderbans (the swampy delta region of the Bay of Bengal that has the largest population of Indian tigers). The prices for these tours, which run from two days to a week, are reasonable. The tours are worth investigating if you are short of time and have a limited budget.

During the festival of Durga Puja, this office also conducts excellent tours to traditional prayer services performed in some of Calcutta's older private homes. At night, they also offer a tour of the fabulous Durga Puja displays erected around the city. From April to August, they sponsor evening cruises on the Hooghly River.

TOUR OPERATORS. For all travel needs, contact *American Express,* 21 Old Court House St., tel. 236281; *Mercury Travels,* 46–C. J. L. Nehru Rd., tel. 223555, or *Travel Corporation of India,* 46–C. J. L. Nehru Rd., tel. 225469. *ITDC* (c/o Government of India Tourist Office, 4 Shakespeare Sarani, tel. 220901) also provides hired cars with driver. Most of these offices are open Monday–Saturday, 10 A.M.– 5 P.M.

SEASONAL EVENTS. Calcutta embodies Hindu India's "museum of festivals" and secular India's joy in celebrating its diverse cultures. There is a festival of some kind almost every week. Since the specific dates for most festivals each year are determined by the lunar calendar, consult the Government of India Tourist Office for details.

January/February. *Gango Sagar Mela.* During this Festival of the River Ganges, pilgrims from all over India celebrate the most important natural element in their mythology—the river, source of life, purifier, destroyer, and nurturer.

January/February. *Vasant Panchami.* This festival honors Saraswati, the goddess of learning and the arts, with immersion of her image into nearby rivers.

March. *Holi* or *Dol Jatra.* The festival of colors heralds the arrival of spring. Celebrants splatter each other with colored water. Wear old clothes.

April/May. *Baisak.* This festival celebrates the Bengali New Year.

June/July. Another interesting festival that occurs in the Calcutta area is the *Baul Festival* of song and prayer. The Bauls are wandering minstrels who worship Krishna and who, through their haunting songs, search for the divine in all of us. They carry on impromptu conversations with Krishna through their music as they travel from village to village through the winter and spring months. Baul music is being revived by individual groups in and around Calcutta in an effort to preserve it. Inquire at the tourist office for more information.

September/October. *Durga Puja.* This fabulous event, which is celebrated for three weeks, honors Kali, one of Durga's incarnations. Each neighborhood has its own separate shrine with elaborate clay figures, some over a full story high, on bamboo and straw skeletons, that are uniquely constructed by a group of artisans in north Calcutta at Kumartulli, near Chitpur Road. At the close of the festivities, these statues are taken by open flatbed trucks, with surging crowds guiding them through the streets, to the Hooghly (*Ma Ganga*—Mother Ganges) and floated away. If you take a tour of neighborhoods at night to see the different forms that this colorful and imaginative folk art takes, along with the panoply of neon lights, jatras, and music, you won't be disappointed.

October/November. *Diwali.* This Festival of Lights celebrates the return of Rama from his exile and his victory over Ravana, the demon, in the epic myth of the *Ramayana.* Almost all houses are lit with small terra-cotta oil lamps that ring the balconies and rooftop edges. Prayers are offered to Lakshmi, the goddess of wealth and prosperity, who is welcomed into households with crescendos of fire-crackers. At least for another year, good has triumphed over evil.

December. *Boro Deen.* This is the Bengali version of Christmas. The weeks before the holiday offer an opportunity to hear some of the city's excellent amateur choirs at churches such as St. Paul's Cathedral, to shop in the well-stocked stores, and to visit the traveling exhibits at fairs that are set up in the Maidan during this season.

HISTORIC SITES.
Entrance to most places is generally free; where a donation is requested, a few rupees will suffice. Most sites are open daily from sunrise to sun-set unless noted otherwise below.

Belur Math. Established in 1898, this is the center of the Ramakrishna Mission. Open daily 6:30 A.M.–noon and 3:30–7:30 P.M.

Botanical Gardens. This enormous garden, constructed in 1787, has over 30,000 varieties of plants and trees.

Dakshineshwar Temples. Built from 1847 to 1855, this complex with 13 temples, near the Vivekananda Bridge, is an important pilgrimage site.

Jorsanko House. Located at 5 Dwarkanath, this rambling house, the home of Rabindranath Tagore, suffered serious damage from heavy rain and was under ren-ovation at press time. You can, however, visit the nearby museum, which has won-derful family memorabilia. Open 10 A.M.–5 P.M.; Saturdays till 1:30 P.M.

Kalighat Kali Temple. This intriguing Hindu temple complex, built in 1809, is near Kalighat Road.

Marble Palace. Filled with outlandish whimsy and paintings, the Marble Palace, built in 1855, is set on a small estate with live birds and a melange of sculptures on Muktaram Babu Street. Closed Monday and Thursday; on other days it's open 10 A.M.–4 P.M. You supposedly need a pass to enter, but no one ever asks for it. Make a small donation to the obligatory guide.

Mother Theresa Homes. The headquarters of the Missionaries of Charity is at 54A, Lower Circular Road.

Nakhoda Mosque. The largest mosque in Calcutta, the Nakhoda, near Mahatma Gandhi Road, was built in 1926.

Ochterlony Monument. This pillar, erected in 1828, is at the northern end of the Maidan. To climb the spiral staircase you need prior permission from the Police Commissioner; consult the West Bengal Tourist Office.

Parasnath Jain Temple. Constructed in 1867 on Raja Dinendra Street, this mag-nificent structure has exquisite details and statues. Open daily 6 A.M.–noon and 3–7 P.M.

St. Andrew's Church. Built in 1847, this church is easy to spot. Soaring spires jut above J. L. Nehru Road.

St. John's Church. Erected in 1787, this beautiful church is on Kiron Sankar Roy Road.

Writers Building. This expansive Victorian structure, built in 1780, is on Dalhou-sie Square.

MUSEUMS AND GALLERIES.
Calcutta's cultural energy is ever present in the diversity and range of its museums, galleries, and constantly changing exhibits. From November to March, fairs and exhibitions dot the central Maidan. Most of the museums and galleries listed here are free. When donations are accepted, Rs. 5 will suffice.

Ashutosh Museum of Indian Art, College St., is a small museum, located in the Senate House of Calcutta University. It has an excellent and noteworthy collection of Bengal folk art, textiles, and terra-cotta clay models. The museum is open daily 10:30 A.M.–4:30 P.M. (Saturdays till 3 P.M.). It is closed Sundays and university holi-days.

The Asiatic Society, 1 Park St., founded in 1784, is a research center for Indology. The library contains 20,000 volumes of rare Sanskrit, Arabic, Persian, and Hindi manuscripts. It's open daily 10 A.M.–6 P.M.

Birla Academy of Art and Culture, 109 Southern Ave., houses contemporary paintings, graphic arts, and photographs. Open daily except Mondays 3–7 P.M.

Birla Planetarium, 97 J. L. Nehru Rd., near Victoria Memorial, is modeled on a Buddhist *stupa* (shrine) at Sanchi. Built in 1962, it was India's first planetarium and is one of the largest in the world. Daily programs are in English, Hindi, and

Bengali. Open Tuesday–Friday, 12:30 P.M.–6:30 P.M.; Saturday, 12:30 P.M.–8 P.M.; and Sunday, 10 A.M.–8 P.M.; closed Mondays.

Bungiya Sahitya Parishad, 243/1 Upper Circular Rd., has collections of paintings of the Bengal School, sculptures, coins, and rare books in Sanskrit and Bengali. Check with the tourist department for hours.

Gurusaday Museum of Bengal Folk Art, Bratacarigram, Thakurpukur, off Diamond Harbor Rd., about 19 km (12 mi.) from the city center, has exhibits of Bengali folk art, especially Kalighat *pat* (scrolls), similar to the mural-like Orissan palm-leaf paintings. Open Friday–Tuesday, 11:30 A.M.–4:30 P.M.; Wednesday until 1:30 P.M.; closed Thursdays.

The Indian Museum, 27 J. L. Nehru Rd., is the oldest in India and one of the largest and most comprehensive collections in Asia. It opened in 1878, after being under construction for three years. Known locally as *Jadu Ghar,* the "House of Magic," the museum has 36 galleries, including one of the best natural-history collections in the world. The archaeology section has a representative collection of antiquities from prehistoric times to the Mogul period, including relics from Mohenjo-Daro and Harappa, the oldest excavated Indus Valley civilizations. The southern wing includes the Bharhut and Gandhara rooms (Indian art from the second century B.C. to A.D. fifth century), the Gupta and Medieval galleries, and the Mogul gallery.

The museum also houses the largest collection of Indian coins in the world. To see this display, get permission from the museum information desk. Gems and jewelry are also on display. The art section is on the first floor and has a good collection of Indian textiles, carpets, wood, paper-mâché, and terra-cotta pottery. A gallery on the third floor contains exquisitely drawn Persian miniatures, Indian paintings, and Tibetan monastery banners. The anthropology section on the first floor is devoted to cultural anthropology. The museum is planning a major change to establish India's first comprehensive physical anthropology exhibit in a major museum. The geological section is the largest in Asia. Some interesting specimens on display are an Egyptian mummy donated in 1880 by an English seaman, a fossilized 200-million-year-old tree trunk, the lower jaw of a 26-meter (84-foot whale), and meteorites dating 50,000 years. Open daily 11 A.M.–5 P.M. Closed Mondays and public holidays.

Nehru Children's Museum, 94/1 J. L. Nehru Rd., adjoining St. Paul's Cathedral, has excellent exhibits for young and old that enliven mythology and history through the use of models and dolls. Open Tuesday–Sunday, 11 A.M.–7 P.M. Closed Mondays.

Victoria Memorial Hall Museum, J. L. Nehru Rd., was conceived in 1901 by Lord Curzon and constructed over a 20-year period. This "poor man's Taj Mahal" is designed in a mixture of Italian Renaissance and Saracenic architectural styles. Surrounded by spaciously laid-out gardens and Calcutta's great Maidan, Victoria Memorial houses an interesting collection of artifacts illustrating British roots in India. It includes Queen Victoria's writing desk and piano, pistols used by Warren Hastings, a governor-general, notebooks of Tipu Sultan, and prints, Indian miniature paintings, watercolors, and Persian books. Open daily 10:30 A.M.–4 P.M. except Mondays. Cameras are not allowed; you must leave them in the checkroom near the ticket booth.

Other museums and galleries of interest are *Academy of Fine Arts,* Cathedral Rd., next to St. Paul's Cathedral. Besides extensive galleries, plays are staged here daily. The galleries are open 3 P.M.–8 P.M., closed Mondays. *Philatelic and Postal History Museum,* next to the GPO at BBD Bagh; closed Sundays. *Ramakrishna Mission Institute of Culture,* Golpark, Ballygunge. *Birla Industrial and Technological Museum* at 19A Gurusaday Rd.; open 11 A.M.–5 P.M., closed Mondays. *Netaji Bhawan,* 38/2 Elgin Rd., originally the house where the nationalist Subhas Bose, Bengal's favorite son, lived and worked. Historical exhibits are on display; open 1:30 P.M.–4:30 P.M., closed Mondays. Other art centers include *Art and Prints Gallery,* 31 Park Mansion; *Calcutta Painters,* 37–C College Rd; *Society of Contemporary Artists,* 68/4 Purnadas Rd; *Rabindra Bharati Museum,* 6/4 Dwarkanath Tagore La.; and *Indian Society of Oriental Art,* 15 Park St.

For updated and current information on gallery offerings and museum exhibits, we recommend the Sunday edition of the *Telegraph* newspaper and *Calcutta: This Fortnight,* a free booklet available from the Government of India Tourist Office or the West Bengal Tourist Information Center.

PUBLIC LIBRARIES AND READING ROOMS. Calcutta has over 150 libraries (listed in *Calcutta and Howrah Guide,* Rs. 15, available at bookstores and newsstands). The *National Library* is at Belvedere, across from the Calcutta zoo, in the former viceregal residence. The biggest library in India, it contains over 8 million manuscripts in various languages. The reading rooms are quiet and restful. Open 8 A.M.–8 P.M. Here are a few other libraries with the best locations and facilities: *American Library (USIA),* 7 J. L. Nehru Rd.; *Asiatic Society,* 1 Park St.; *British Council,* 5 Shakespeare Sarani; and *Ramakrishna Mission Institute of Culture,* Golpark.

Recommended Reading. Two books are informative supplements to your visit: *Calcutta,* published by the West Bengal Tourist Office in conjunction with IBH Publishing, is available at Oxford Booksellers on Park Street. Its quirky, often amusing writing exhibits a loving feel for this chaotic yet mesmerizing city. Also available at Oxford is Geoffrey Moorhouse's *Calcutta* (New York: Holt, Rinehart, and Winston, 1985) and Dominique Lapierre's *City of Joy,* which are essential reading for anyone who visits this astonishing city.

GARDENS AND ZOOS. The *Botanical Gardens,* nine km (six mi.) from Calcutta, is the largest and oldest of its kind in India, with over 30,000 varieties of trees and plants. Take a ferry from Metiaburuz and picnic on the grounds. The garden is open 7 A.M.–5 P.M. *Eden Gardens,* located on the Maidan, was laid out in 1835 and has a pagoda hauled in from Burma. *Zoological Gardens* in Alipore, three km (two mi.) from Calcutta, was established in 1876 and is the largest zoo in India. Open daily 6:30 A.M.–5 P.M.

SPORTS AND OUTDOOR ADVENTURES. Calcuttans love sports, especially cricket. From November to February, the cricket season rules the day; work comes to a standstill, and Eden Gardens overflows. With television the motto has become, "If you can't play, watch." Matches of people with various levels of skill—from international test matches to backyard alley games—are fielded every day. Bengal's obsession with sports also includes **soccer,** which was, until recently, the best-loved sport. You always know when a divisional soccer match is in progress near the Maidan; the roar of the crowd is like a "cathartic release of emotion," according to one local observer.

Clubs were formed during British times to set off the rulers from the ruled, and clubs continue to be an arena for much of Calcutta's passion for sports. A new hierarchy has been established through membership dues, and **sports clubs** continue to flourish. You have to be a guest of a member to attend, or you can apply for temporary membership. There are over 100 such clubs in Calcutta. The *Calcutta Cricket Club,* at 19/1 Gurusaday Rd. (tel. 478721), was founded in 1792 and is the oldest cricket club outside England. The *Royal Calcutta Golf Club,* Golf Club Rd. (tel. 421352), is the oldest golf club in India.

Winter is also the time for **horse racing** and **polo.** The *Royal Calcutta Turf Club,* 11 Russell St. (tel. 291103), and the *Calcutta Polo Club,* 51 J. L. Nehru Rd. (tel. 442031), provide the organizational services for these two sports. The *Calcutta Racecourse,* built in 1819, is the scene of frenetic activity every Saturday, not just by the rich in box seats, but by ordinary racing enthusiasts perched atop the tallest tree branches on the outside of the track. Polo is played in sections of the Maidan.

Other sports include **rowing** at the *Lake* (tel. 462538) and *Bengal Rowing* (tel. 411751) clubs, both near Dhakuria Lake in Ballygunge; **horseback** riding at the Tollygunge Club (tel. 463141); **swimming** at the *Saturday Club,* 7 Wood St. (tel. 445411), and the *Calcutta Swimming Club,* 1 Strand Rd. (tel. 282894); **tennis** at the *Calcutta Cricket Club* (tel. 478721); and **squash** at the *Calcutta Racket Club* (tel. 441152), near St. Paul's Cathedral.

SHOPPING. During the winter, craft and textile exhibitions are often held on Calcutta's Maidan. Don't go when they first open (it sometimes takes a few days for all exhibitors to get set up) or too late, when goods have been picked over. Though the selection from other states is generally better in Bombay and Delhi, Bengal's crafts and fabrics are best bought in Calcutta.

Terra-cotta crafts from the Bankura, Birbhum, and Midnapore districts of West Bengal, especially brightly painted figurines of animals and dancers and bas-relief plaques of deities such as Krishna and Radha, make unusual gifts, but one must pack these fragile items carefully. From Krishnanagar come clay figurines in both realistic and stylized shapes. Pottery bowls, mugs, plates, and serving bowls, glazed a rich aqua blue, are beautiful. Perhaps the most delightful of the crafts from Bengal are the frequently whimsical *dokra* figures made of a mixture of clay and metal, usually cast in the lost-wax method. Shells are fashioned by shonkhari craftsmen into bangles, toe and finger rings, and exquisitely shaped demitasse spoons. Bell-metal work, bidri work, soapstone boxes and plates, and leather goods are some other indigenous crafts.

Textile buys are abundant in Calcutta. *Jamdani* weaving, a cotton fabric that is brocaded with cotton and *zari* (silver) threads is one of the more unusual weaves. Made on looms similar to the jamdani is the exquisite Baluchar brocaded silk from Murshidabad, with its deep purple or mauve background and ornately printed end pieces. For those who sew or have tailors back home, elegant Tussore silks are available by the meter.

You can purchase men's *kurtas* (loose thigh-length shirts) that are popular with both men and women for the quality and coolness of their handwoven cotton fabric (*khadi*) and the freedom of their design. Women find *salwar kameez* sets (loose dress-length tops worn with baggy pants that fit tightly at the ankle) especially comfortable, although they are not always as available readymade as are kurtas. These items are more easily found at Calcutta's bazaars than at village bazaars.

Kantha embroidery is a Bengali needlework specialty in which a quilted surface is embroidered with all manner of shapes, from the more usual birds, animals, and trees to abstract designs. Some of Calcutta's destitute women have been organized to make embroidered bedspreads and pillow covers that have plain or multihued floral designs on heavy cotton. Though the embroidery work in them is not as fine as that in Kashmiri woolen shawls, it is vigorous, cheerful, and appealing.

Shopping in bazaars around Calcutta can be either an exhilarating—if exhausting—experience or a lengthy test of wills. Parts of the famous *Sir Stuart Hogg Market,* better known as *New Market,* 19 Lindsay St., burned down a few years back, and many vendors have been relocated to J. L. Nehru Rd., across from the Grand Hotel. The New Market, which is over 110 years old, houses about 2,500 stores under one roof, selling cotton *tangail* saris, Bankura clay horses, Malda brassware, leather from Santiniketan, silk from Murshidabad, Khadi cloth, poultry, cheeses, nuts, and other foods. It is one of Calcutta's most extensive bazaars. The new location lacks the bustling charm of the original New Market, and most visitors will find the undamaged part of the old area a more intriguing place for poking around. The touts at the old New Market are often difficult to discourage. (No matter how insistent they are, do not change foreign currency with them, and if they show you around the shops, you should be aware that they usually get a percentage of whatever you spend.) Another good market is *Treasure Island,* just opposite Globe Cinema, near Hogg Market.

Other bazaar areas where Calcuttans go are *Gariahat,* 212, 214, and 216 Rash Behari Ave., *Barabazar,* in North Calcutta, and *Shyambazar,* 1A R. G. Kar Rd. On Sundays, traditionally the market day for Calcuttans, large wholesale markets spill from sidewalks into the streets in the North Calcutta area. At *Hathibagan,* 80, 81, and 82 Bidhan Sarani, even if one isn't interested in buying the goods being offered here—racing pigeons, parakeets, bright cotton children's clothes, inexpensive men's shirts and trousers, and plants—the energy and color are infectious. *Ultadanga Market,* 22 Ultadanga Rd., caters primarily to small retail businesses; both vendors and buyers are men, and few women are seen on the streets. Taxis line the side streets waiting to transport businessmen's large purchases.

Bargaining is essential at all markets. Transactions are cash only; credit cards are not accepted.

Some specialty markets are on or near Chitpur Rd., where there are shops that make musical instruments—sarods, sitars, harmoniums, *dholaks* (drums), and costumes for the traveling theatrical ensembles (*jatras*). At *Bowbazar,* the home of the jewelers' trade, one finds artisans who work in gold. Bentinck Street is known for its shoes and leather goods, and College Street, near the Ashutosh Museum, is the center for secondhand English and Bengali books. This street is packed tight with stalls overflowing with textbooks on every possible subject. Careful rummaging might turn up a first edition for a small price.

State-run emporiums lack the stimulating entrepreneurial energy of bazaar areas, but the quality of goods is usually better, and goods sell at fixed prices. Credit cards, usually American Express and Visa, are accepted in emporiums, such as *Central Cottage Industries Emporium* (7 J. L. Nehru Rd.). As the name implies, it has goods from all over India. Among other items, one can find colorful, intricate Mithila paintings from Bihar, beautiful hand-printed writing paper and envelopes, and wooden toys. Open Monday–Saturday, 10 A.M.–7 P.M. *Bengal Home Industries* (57 J. L. Nehru Rd.) sells Bengali handicrafts and items made in Bengal's cottage industries. Open Monday–Saturday, 10 A.M.–7 P.M.

Also on this road are *Cauvery* (Karnataka's state emporium), at No. 7; *Kashmir Government Art Emporium,* at No. 12, which sells this lovely northwestern state's renowned crafts, such as papier-mâché objects covered with intricate brushwork designs in silver and gold, finely woven textiles, richly embroidered woolen shawls, and silk and woolen carpets in traditional patterns; and *Rajasthali* (Rajasthan's state emporium), at No. 30E, offers silver jewelery and miniature paintings.

Two shops on Lindsay Street make convenient stops: *Handloom House,* at No. 2, where textiles by the yard and by the piece are available, and *Manjusha* (West Bengal Handicrafts Development Corporation), at No. 7/1D. Textiles are also available at *Khadi* Gramodyog Bhawan, 28 Chittaranjan Ave. At the *Assam Emporium,* 8 Russell St., one can get unusual baskets and honey from other northeast states. In south Calcutta, a new shopping center of emporiums has opened recently, the *CIT Market* on Dakhinapan near Dhakuria. Batik fabric, appliquéd silk salwars and pillow covers, and woolen shawls highlight the Gujarat emporium located here; and the *West Bengal Emporium* has a good selection of dokra figurines on the second floor. Most emporiums are open 9:30 A.M.–7 P.M., often take a lunch break 1 P.M.–3 P.M. and are closed on Sunday. Bazaars are generally open daily 9 A.M.–7 P.M.

Since Calcutta is cosmopolitan, it has some very special shops worth exploring. For lovely readymades for men or women or fabric by the meter, visit these stores:

Ananda, 13 Russell St.; open Monday–Friday, 10 A.M.–6:30 P.M. and Saturday till 2 P.M.

Take 'n Talk, 2 Russell St.; open Monday–Friday, 10 A.M.–7 P.M. and Saturday till 5 P.M.

Indian Silk House, College Street Market and 129 A Behari Ave.; open Monday, 2–7 P.M. and Tuesday–Saturday, 10 A.M.–7 P.M.

Kanishka, 2/1 Hindustan Rd., Gariahat; open Monday, 2–7 P.M. and Tuesday–Saturday, 10 A.M.–7 P.M.

For lovely linens and other household items, plus baby clothes and stuffed animals, visit *Good Companions,* 13 Russell St. All proceeds go to charity. Open Monday–Saturday, 10 A.M.–6 P.M. Rupees only.

For good jewelry, visit these reliable stores:

Ram Lakshman, 7 A Lindsey St.; open Monday–Friday, 10:30 A.M.–6:30 P.M. and Saturday till 2.

Satramdas, 12J Park St.; open Monday–Friday, 10 A.M.–7 P.M. and Saturday till 1 P.M.

P.C. Chandra, 127/1A B. B. Banguly St. and 49C Gariahat Rd.; open Monday 3–7 P.M. and Tuesday–Saturday 10:30 A.M.–7 P.M.

Calcutta is also the center of the tea trade in India. Tea auction houses flourish, as they have for almost 150 years. Packaged tea, loose or in teabags, is readily available at stores.

ENTERTAINMENT. Calcutta takes its sustenance from the fervent creativity of its artists. Throughout the years of political strife and population and economic disasters, and being browbeaten by the irritations and fatigue of daily life, Calcuttans have taken solace in the fact that their city has produced, and continues to produce, some of India's most imaginative cultural representatives. Rabindranath Tagore, the first Asian to be selected for the Nobel Prize for literature, wrote here. Tagore created a school of music, Rabindra Sangeet, whose two most famous expositions are the national anthems of India and Bangladesh. It was in Calcutta that filmmaker Satyajit Ray worked and brought a distinctively Bengali point of view of middle-class India to millions of viewers in the West. Here, too, Uday Shankar worked and brought Indian classical dance to the attention of the rest of the world, and Ravi Shankar, his younger brother, played sitar, to the joy of thousands the world over. It is here also that Bengali journals and broadsheets are sold for pennies on the street, poets hawk their poems on street corners, and theater, both traditional and modern, flourishes. Calcutta's entertainment possibilities are manifold.

To start out, look up *Calcutta: This Fortnight* (a free pamphlet from the West Bengal Tourist Office) and the Sunday edition of the *Telegraph* newspaper for daily listings of cultural and other entertainment news.

Dance. Besides the Bharat Natyam and Kathak, there are performances of the Manipuri and Odissi (Orissa) styles at the *Academy of Dance and Music,* 5 Dwarkanath Tagore La.; *Academy of Fine Arts,* Cathedral Rd., near the Birla Planetarium (tel. 444205); and at *Kala Mandir,* 48 Shakespeare Sarani (tel. 449086).

Two splendid versions of dance dramas or performance arts that are unique to Bengal are the *jatras* and *kavigan.* Jatra (folk theater) is enacted outside the traditional dramatic set. The audience sits in the open air and the actors and actresses sing or act their roles, while a small orchestra sits to one side of the performance space and accompanies the action. Taken traditionally from mythology or from old Bengali novels, jatras also address historical and political issues these days. The action here is broad and the scope of emotions is great. Although once considered an unsophisticated form of entertainment by urban Bengalis, the jatra has been enjoying a revival that has brought some of Bengal's most popular film actors and actresses to the stage. *Rabindra Bharati University,* 6/4 Dwarkanath Tagore La., once part of Tagore's residence, offers courses in jatra, and the university's performances are worth seeing. Watch the newspaper listings during the winter months for the performance times.

Kavigan is a stylized duet of poets who sing their responses in verse, *ex tempore,* on selected themes. Once immensely popular, it is a rare phenomenon now, though there are occasions that are advertised during the winter season.

Music. *Rabindra Sadan,* A. J. C. Bose Rd., near St. Paul's Cathedral (tel. 449937); *Kala Mandir* and *Ramakrishna Mission Institute of Culture,* Golpark; and *Mahajati Sadan,* 166 Chittaranjan Ave. are some of the major venues for the world-renowned maestros of Indian music. These include Niser Hussain Khan, Latafat Hussain Khan, and Girija Devi, who follow in the tradition of Bade Gulam Ali, and Allaudin Khan, whose disciple was Ravi Shankar. There is also a developed folk music school in Bengal, known as Puratani (of old times). The subgroups are Panchali, Ramprasadi, Kirtan, and Toppa.

Theater. Bengali theater is the fulcrum of much of the city's cultural activities. Watch for performances at *Kala Mandir,* 48 Shakespeare Sarani; *Rabindra Sadan,* A. J. Bose Rd., near St. Paul's Cathedral; *Star,* 79/34 Bidhan Sarani (tel. 551139); Biswaroopa, 2A Raj Kissen St. (tel. 553210); and *Rangana,* 153/2 Archarya Prafulla Chandra Rd. (tel. 556846). The groups to watch for are Bahuroopi, People's Little Theatre, and Drama Libraries-Museums.

Bars. Calcutta's independent bars are not sprightly places. The most attractive places for enjoying a nightcap are the Oberoi Grand and the Taj Bengal. Bars stay open until 11 P.M. or midnight and are closed on Thursdays.

WEST BENGAL AND BIHAR

Calcutta's "Suburbia" and Rural Neighbor

by
LISA SAMSON and AMIT SHAH

Calcutta's lack of "real" antiquities is sufficiently made up in the region surrounding it. After the British merged Bengal with Bihar under the Bengal presidency in 1765, the modern-day states of West Bengal, Bihar, and Orissa became one—the land of the bounty of the Ganges.

Like all great river deltas, Bengal was unquestionably a cradle of civilization. Ptolemy's geography mentions it as a seafaring nation. The Pala kings, who ruled from the eighth to the twelfth centuries, were patrons of the arts and learning; their artists traveled far south, even to Indonesia, and their religious scholars carried the Buddhist gospels to Tibet. During the Mogul period, Akbar conquered Bengal, but Bengal became virtually a separate kingdom under the independent nawab, Siraj-ud-Daula, who was routed in 1757 at Plassey, north of Calcutta, by Robert Clive through a series of treacherous conspiracies. The British thus won control over Bengal after the Dutch, the French, and the Portuguese had all made some efforts. The subsequent history of Bengal is synonymous with Calcutta and is outlined in that chapter of this guide.

Today, bounded by Sikkim and Bhutan in the north, by Assam and Bangladesh in the east, by the Bay of Bengal and Orissa in the south, and by Bihar and Neap in the west and northwest, West Bengal covers 87,617 square kilometers (54,446 square miles) and has a population of over 54 million, an increase of nearly 24 percent since 1971.

Many travelers to West Bengal go north into the Himalayas to Darjeeling or Kalimpong, two hill stations established by the British during the days of the raj. Once you leave Bagdogra, the northern gateway, the mountains dominate the landscape, towering above the waterfalls that thunder down ravines, the deep gorges sliced by fast-flowing rivers, and the terraced slopes of tea plantations. On clear days, Mount Kanchenjunga, the world's third-tallest peak, draws all eyes to its snow-clad pinnacles. No one may climb this mountain, the abode of Indra, the Hindu god of rain.

Darjeeling—Queen of the Himalayas

After the British acquired Darjeeling in 1835, crude huts of the original inhabitants gave way to manor houses, bungalows, and cottages with gingerbread trim. English-style gardens flowered everywhere. Tea gardens thrived in the perfect climate. By 1881, when a narrow-gauge Toy Train began to zigzag up the mountains, the hill station was completely anglicized. The British lived on the town's top ridge, and their workers lived on the hills below—a social and geographic stratification that exists today, with the Indian upper classes taking the place of the British.

From Chowrasta (The Mall), walk to Observatory Hill and the Mahakali Temple, a cave sacred to Shiva. Shiva's faithful bull, Nandi, guards the shrine along with two stone temple lions, your clue that this is also a solemn site for Buddhists—the location of a former monastery called Dorje Ling, which was destroyed in the nineteenth century by Nepalese Gurkhas. You'll see Buddhist prayer wheels, *chortens* (small shrines containing sacred relics), and prayer flags alongside bells for Hindus to clang to announce their arrival to Shiva. Pilgrims to the shrine first get a blessing from a Hindu priest who sits in the inner sanctum, then they receive a blessing from a Sikkimese Buddhist Lama. Then devotees of both religions circle the structure three times, spinning the prayer wheels, ringing the bells, and burning incense in the chortens.

From Chowrasta, walk down C. R. Das Road and visit the Bhutia Busty Monastery, which belongs to a Buddhist Red Hat Sect and was built in 1934 by a former *chogyal* (king) of Sikkim. On the way to the monastery you'll pass Step Aside, a modest museum commemorating the Indian nationalist leader Chittaranjan Das.

Head south to Lloyds Botanical Garden, which is set on Darjeeling's lowest ridge. Over 125 years old, this garden has over 2,000 species of orchids in its Orchid House. The terraced gardens have Sikkim spruce, geraniums, arum lilies, alpine plants, azaleas, rhododendrons, magnolias, and a variety of Himalayan conifers.

Another garden, The Shrubbery, planted by a former British governor of West Bengal, is at Jawahar Parbat (formerly Birch Hill) behind Raj Bhawan (Governor's House), northwest of the town square. From here you'll get a magnificent view of Mount Kanchenjunga and the Singla Valley.

The Himalayan Mountaineering Institute, on Jawahar Road West, is a unique contribution to mountaineering that India established after the first successful climb of Mount Everest in 1953. Tenzing Norgay, who made the climb with Sir Edmund Hillary, was the institute's first principal. The institute trains hundreds of mountaineers of all ages and nationalities. Its excellent museum has photographs and displays of equipment and notebooks from all the legendary climbs, successful and tragic, including memorabilia from Mallory's ill-fated attempt.

Ghoom

The Yiga-Choling Buddhist Monastery in Ghoom, eight kilometers (five miles) from Darjeeling, is the oldest *gompa* (shrine) in the area, established in 1850 by a famous Tibetan astrologer, Lama Sherap Gyansto. Currently, 25 Gelug (Yellow Hat) sect lamas are in residence. The small prayer hall, with crumbling but lovely wall frescoes, has an enormous gilded statue of Maitreya (Future Buddha) behind the front altar. You'll also see statues of Gyansto, Avolokitesvara (Buddha of Compassion), and Padmasambhava, the Indian mystic.

Tiger Hill, 11 kilometers (seven miles) from Darjeeling, is the place for a sunrise view of Mount Kanchenjunga. The golden glow of the rising sun changes the color of the snowcapped peaks to crimson, pink, and shining gold as you watch from the observation deck.

Kalimpong

Kalimpong, 52 kilometers (32 miles) from Darjeeling, is a tiny hill station with a central street lined by buildings built in the 1920s. Walks offer views of the Deola Hills to the north; the Durbindara Hills to the south; and, on a clear day, the plains of Nepal's Terai and the lofty summits of Kanchenjunga.

At Tripai Hills, three kilometers (two miles) from the center of town, visit the Tharpa Choling Monastery, built in 1937 and belonging to the Gelug sect that follows the Dalai Lama. A pavilion with a gigantic prayer wheel and walls covered with old frescoes leads to a prayer hall filled with more old frescoes and statues. On the left side of the front wall is a statue of Guru Padmasambhava, the Indian mystic. To the right is a statue of Nowang Kegang, the founder of the monastery. Behind the altar is a statue of Sakyamuni (Historic Buddha) surrounded by photos of the gurus of the Dalai Lama. To his right is a polished bronze statue of the Avolokitesvara (Buddha of Compassion). Exquisite *thang-kas* (religious paintings) brought from Tibet hang in the center of the hall along with prayer drums.

The Zongdogpalrifobrang Monastery, on Durpin Dara Hill at the other end of Kalimpong, also belongs to the Gelug. Stairs to the side of the monastery lead to the *Cherisi* (prayer chamber), covered with brightly painted frescoes. Here a replica of a celestial chorten that was destroyed by the Chinese in Lhasa dominates the room. It took the lamas two years to construct at a cost of Rs. 50,000. The statue of the Buddha to its right was originally in Lhasa. On the top floor is a tiny chamber containing 1,000 small statues of the Buddha. The walls of the main hall on the ground floor, where the daily prayer services are held, are covered with frescoes, and the front altar enshrines a large statue of the Buddha.

Exploring Southern West Bengal

In the district of Malda, 338 kilometers (210 miles) north of Calcutta, you'll find the ancient cities of Gour and Pandua. Former capitals of Bengal and important cities during the Mogul era, these cities have exquisite historic monuments, including Adina Masjid—one on the largest mosques in India.

Murshidabad, the capital of Bengal in the 1700s, is 209 kilometers (130 miles) north of Calcutta. Here you'll find more historic monuments, including the Katra Mosque and Hazarduari Palace, built in 1837 and known for its 1,000 doors. The palace contains firearms, china, and plates that are reputed to crack if poison is placed on them.

The seventeenth- and eighteenth-century capital of the Malla dynasties, Vishnupur is also the "terra-cotta capital" of West Bengal. Numerous historic building facades are covered with terra-cotta embellishments and depictions of legendary events.

Santiniketan, 136 kilometers (84 miles) northwest of Calcutta, is Rabindranath Tagore's "Abode of Peace," an open-air institution created in 1901 by the famous writer, painter, and philosopher. Here, in accordance with Tagore's philosophy, students learn the traditional arts of India's heritage in a setting that also reinforces man's relation with nature. In nearby Bakreswar, you can enjoy hot springs.

Diamond Harbour, a former Portuguese pirate stronghold 48 kilometers (30 miles) south of Calcutta, has a natural harbor and is an ideal picnic area. To the south, you'll find the Sunderbans, a jungle delta—approachable by boat—and the legendary home of the Bengal tiger. Bakkhali and Digha, 131 (81 miles) and 185 kilometers (115 miles) south of Calcutta, are West Bengal's most popular beach resorts.

Bihar

Bihar, bounded in the north by Nepal, east by West Bengal, south by Orissa, and west and southwest by Uttar Pradesh and Madhya Pradesh, was part of the great Magadh Empire from 500 B.C. to A.D. 500. Pataliputra (present-day Patna) was designated by Chandragupta Maurya as the empire's capital city. Maurya's grandson, Ashoka, later became the evangelist of Buddhism. During A.D. fourth and fifth centuries, Pataliputra formed part of the great Gupta Empire, which saw the revival of Hinduism. Factional and fractious battles denied Bihar a stable rule until the eighth century, when the Palas of Bengal won paramountcy. In 1193, Bihar was overrun by Moslem invaders and remained part of the sultanate in Delhi till the second half of the fourteenth century. In 1529, Babur, the first of the Moguls, wrested it from the Lodhi rulers and was eventually ousted by the English in 1765, more because of weak-kneed, indolent nawabs than because of British supremacy. In 1912, the British separated Bihar and Orissa from Bengal and divided the three into separate provinces in 1936.

Though rich in minerals, producing about 40 percent of the nation's mica, coal, copper, and iron ore, Bihar is still one of India's poorest states. Only 26 percent of its cultivatable lands are irrigated. Bihar, however, is amply endowed with important pilgrimage sites: Buddhist Bodhgaya, where Siddhartha Gautama (the Historic Buddha) attained enlightenment; and Gaya, a Hindu city second in importance to Varanasi. Bihar also has one of India's largest tribal populations, many of whom live in charming remote villages.

Exploring Southern Bihar

From West Bengal, the first stop in Bihar is Parasnath Hill. The site of numerous temples, this is the eastern center of Jain worship, and Parasnath, the 23rd tirthankara (perfect soul) is said to have gained nirvana on this hill.

Southwest of Parasnath is Ranchi, a busy industrial city and the summer capital of Bihar. From here, travelers can discover southern Bihar's beautiful countryside. Travel 45 kilometers (30 miles) northeast to Hundra Falls, one of the highest falls in Asia. Here, when the Subarnarekha River is at its postmonsoon highmark, the falls are spectacular. Ninety-five kilometers (60 miles) to the south is the quiet town of Hazirabagh and its nearby National Park. About 154 kilometers (95 miles) to the west is the small hill station of Netarhat, surrounded by forests and the Chotanagpur Plateau. This last journey takes you into the heart of a tribal area, where infrequent hamlets are marked by just a few roadside stalls. For miles, you'll pass a procession of fields and see the tribes as they turn up the soil with wooden plows pulled by bullocks or gather about their huddled homes of clay covered with dung and subtle decorations.

At Bodhgaya, 208 kilometers (129 miles) north of Ranchi, stands the peepal tree (the Bodhi tree) underneath which, 2,500 years ago, Siddhartha Gautama attained enlightenment and became the Buddha. The original Bodhi tree died, and saplings from it form the present tree. The Emperor Ashoka erected a shrine near the Bodhi tree that was replaced in the second century by the Mahabodhi Temple. The temple has been renovated many times, adding contours through the centuries. It shows the influence of various Buddhist countries, especially the curvilinear Burmese style. The surrounding railings are richly carved, and ornamented votive *stupas* (shrines) surround the main temple. The carvings are from the *Jataka* tales ("birth stories") and depict the Buddha's previous incarnations. The north side is flanked by the "jewel walk" or Chankramana—a raised platform with carved lotus flowers, where the Buddha is said to have paced back and forth, meditating and deliberating about whether he should reveal his wisdom and knowledge to the world. Bodhgaya is a pilgrimage spot for both Hindus and Buddhists. The Hindus consider the Buddha to be an incarnation of Vishnu. On the banks of the Niranjana River, where Siddhartha, a worldly young prince, came to seek the ultimate truth, modern-day visitors stand in awe, looking at and touching the relics and objects of veneration of one of the world's oldest religions. Near the Chankramana is the *Tibetan Monastery,* built in 1938. A two-meter- (six-foot-) high metal drum painted in golds and reds, the Dharma Chakra, or wheel of law, is the main object on view. For forgiveness of all past sins, turn the wheel three times, from left to right. There are also Chinese, Japanese, and Thai Buddhist temples here.

About 15 kilometers (nine miles) north of Bodhgaya is Gaya, a dusty little town at a major rail junction. Second only to Varanasi in sanctity for Hindus, Gaya attracts pilgrims from all over India, who come here after the deaths of their parents to offer *pindas* (funeral cakes) to the souls of the departed. This offering symbolically releases the dead from earthly bondage and is essential in Hindu ritual.

The center of the pilgrimage is the *Vishnupada Temple,* said to have been built over the footprints of Vishnu. Renovated in 1787, the structure is 30 meters (97 feet) high and has eight rows of sculpted pillars supporting the *mandapa* (hall). Non-Hindus are not allowed in the inner sanctum, but the exterior is well worth the visit. There's a banyan tree nearby under which the Buddha is said to have meditated for six years. One kilometer (half mile) away is *Bramanjuni Hill,* with 1,000 stone steps. Climb to the top and you'll see Gaya's rooftops and Bodhgaya's spires. On the Sone River at Baragaon, two kilometers (one mile) from Gaya, is the *Surya Temple,* dedicated to the Sun God, where pilgrims come to celebrate the Chhatha Vrata festival (see Seasonal Events, below).

About 50 kilometers (31 miles) from Gaya are the *Barabar Caves,* on which E. M. Forster based his Marabar Caves in *A Passage to India.* These are the earliest specimens of Buddhist rock-cut shrines, dating from 200 B.C.; two of them bear inscriptions of Emperor Ashoka. One hundred kilometers (62 miles) west of Gaya is *Sasaram* and one of the finest Moslem mausoleums. Sher Shah, the builder of the Grand Trunk Road, the oldest highway in India, is entombed here under a five-tiered hexagon with arches, latticework cupolas, and a 47-meter (150-foot) dome. It stands in the middle of a lake with fountains. Two other excursions from Gaya, to Rajgir (64 kilometers or 40 miles) and Nalanda (66 kilometers or 41 miles) complete this tour.

Rajgir is one of the ancient towns associated with Buddhism. It was here that the first Buddhist Council met after the Buddha attained enlightenment and where his teachings were written down. Lord Buddha spent 12 years here, as did Mahavira, the founder of the Jain religion. Today, it is a health spot known mainly for its hot springs. Besides the hot springs, you can see ruins from an aerial chair lift. The Japanese have built a new monastery, *Vishwa Shanti Stupa* (World Peace Stupa), whose four Buddha statues depict birth, death, enlightenment, and teaching. There are Burmese and Thai monasteries; *Venuvena,* the bamboo park where the Buddha and his disciples lived; and Jain and Hindu temples, among others. The *Cyclopean Wall,* originally (48 kilometers or 30 miles) of perfectly joined stones that girdled the city, is now in ruins. Also, there is the *Ajatshatru Fort,* built in the fifth century B.C. by a king whom the Buddha had cured of a plague of boils.

The most famous center of ancient Buddhist scholarship is Nalanda, the "place that confers the lotus" (*nalam*)—a symbol of spiritual learning. Between the fourth and twelfth centuries, Nalanda was one of the most celebrated university towns in India. The Chinese traveler-scholar Hiuen T'sang spent 12 years here in the early seventh century and recorded that there were 10,000 monks and students and 2,000 teachers. He also left detailed descriptions of the vigorous university life, where 9 million volumes of manuscripts were available for students from as far as Japan, Sumatra, Java, and Korea. In 1199, an Afghan marauder, Bhaktiar Khilji, torched the university and massacred its residents. Buddhism in India suffered a severe blow, and monks fled to caves or out of the country. Painstaking excavations have uncovered large areas of the university complex, including six temples and 11 monasteries. The most imposing is the *Sasiputa Stupa* (the Great Stupa), built by Ashoka to honor Ananda, the Buddha's first disciple. Also excavated is *Sarai Mound,* with frescoes of horses and elephants. Thai Buddhists have recently constructed a temple, *Wat Thai Nalanda,* here.

Exploring Northern Bihar

Traveling from the tranquillity of the Buddhist excavated sites to the ancient capital, Pataliputra (present-day Patna), is not an altogether pleasant experience. Patna, an overcrowded city of over 2 million on the banks of the Ganges, stretches for over 13 kilometers (eight miles). It is the logical jumping-off point for your travels in Bihar, since it is linked to all major Indian cities. While you are here, you should take a quick tour of the city. *Golghar,* a beehive-shaped building, previously a granary built in 1786 to store grain following a famine in 1770, is a squat, impressive structure, 27 meters (88 feet) high and 127 meters (410 feet) wide, with 4-meter (13-foot) walls. Two staircases lead to the top, from which you can see the Ganges and Patna over the rooftops. Harmandir Sahib is a shrine consecrating the birthplace of Guru Gobind Singh, the tenth and last Sikh guru. One of the holiest of Sikh shrines, it contains personal belongings of the guru and Sikh scriptures.

Gulzaribagh is the site of a former opium factory used by the British East India Company, which made hefty profits with this lucrative trade from China. It is now a printing office for the government. History buffs might want to visit the opium storage areas. About five kilometers (three miles) from the Patna Railway Station is Kumhrar, where excavations have unearthed relics of four continuous periods 600 B.C.–A.D. 600.

Moslem mosques in Patna are *Patherki Masjid* and *Shershahi Masjid,* the oldest in Patna, built in 1545. Other places of interest are the Bihar Institute of Handicrafts and Designs and Birla Mandir. Daily tours are operated by the Bihar State Tourism and ITDC. From Patna, trips can also be arranged for Nalanda, Rajgir, Gaya, Bodhgaya, and Vaishali.

PRACTICAL INFORMATION FOR

WEST BENGAL AND BIHAR

WHEN TO GO. Northern West Bengal. The most popular times to visit Darjeeling and Kalimpong are April–mid-June and mid-September–November. The monsoon rages in the summer; and winter is cold, but there's not much of a crowd in these snowy hill stations. **Southern West Bengal and Bihar.** These areas are ideal between October and March. The weather is dry and sunny and the mornings are crisp and pleasant. The average temperature ranges from 50° F to 85° F. The Chotanagpur Plateau and the Hararibagh region are slightly cooler because of their altitude and forestation.

HOW TO GET THERE.

By Air. *Indian Airlines* has daily flights into Bagdogra from Calcutta; and five weekly flights from Delhi and Guwahati in Assam. Foreign nationals planning to visit Darjeeling who fly into Bagdogra must register at the Foreigner's Registration Office at the airport upon arrival and departure. To get to Patna, Indian Airlines has 10 weekly flights from Calcutta, a daily flight from Delhi, three weekly flights from Lucknow, and two weekly flights from Bombay. Indian Airlines also has daily flights to Ranchi from Delhi and Calcutta. It has two weekly flights from Bombay. For Indian Airlines information in Bagdogra, call 20962; in Patna, 225554; and in Ranchi, 21841.

By Bus. Many buses connect Calcutta to destinations in Bihar and West Bengal. Buses leave from the Esplanade Terminus on Jawaharlal (J. L.) Nehru Rd. (Chowringhee) in Calcutta, diagonally opposite the Metro cinema hall. Go there in person; phones are unreliable in Calcutta. From Sikkim, the *Sikkim National Transport Service* runs frequent coaches (about Rs. 50 per person) between Gangtok and Darjeeling; a Restricted Area Permit is required. (See Travel Documents in *Facts at Your Fingertips.*) For departure times in Gangtok, contact *Sikkim Tourist Information Office* (tel. 2064). From Darjeeling, contact the *Darjeeling Gorkha Hill Council* (tel. 2524).

Numerous buses also make the two-day run between Kathmandu in Nepal and Patna in Bihar. In Nepal, contact the *Kathmandu Tourist Office* for details. In Patna, *Himalayan Tours and Travels* (New Market) offers an excellent one-way package to Kathmandu or a round-trip (with an open-date return) that includes lodging and breakfast on the road. (Rs. 400 each way.)

By Train. You can take a 12-hour train from Calcutta's Howrah Station to New Jalpaiguri, which is about 81 km (50 mi.) from Darjeeling. From New Jalpaiguri, a taxi to Darjeeling is about Rs. 500–Rs. 600 and takes about four hours. Bihar's capital, Patna, 10 hours from Calcutta, and Gaya are on the main lines of the railways between Delhi and Calcutta. From Calcutta, you can also go by train to Ranchi (about eight hours). Trains also connect Jamshedpur and north Bihar. Complete train information is available in Calcutta through *Eastern Railway Offices* at 14A Strand Rd., near the General Post Office (GPO); 6 Fairlie Pl., near Benoy-Bidal-Dinesh Bagh (BBD Bagh); and Southeastern Railway at Esplanade Mansion, near the Great Eastern Hotel. If you travel at night, remember to reserve a sleeping berth.

By Rented Car with Driver. From Calcutta, Ranchi is 456 km (283 mi.); Patna, 597 km (370 mi.); Gaya, 491 km (304 mi.); Bodhgaya, 540 km (335 mi.). Calcutta is 730 km (453 mi.) from Darjeeling. Travelers who have a Restricted Area Permit can also drive between Gangtok and Darjeeling, a six-hour excursion. Hire a car with driver from one of the travel agencies recommended in Calcutta, Sikkim, and below under Tour Operators.

TOURIST INFORMATION. West Bengal. Contact the *Government of India Tourist Office* ("Embassy," 4 Shakespeare Sarani, Calcutta 700071) or the *Regional Tourist Office of West Bengal* (Government of West Bengal, 3/2 B.B.D. Bagh, Calcutta 700069). Offices are also located at the Calcutta Airport and Howrah Railway Station; at the Bagdogra Airport; at the New Jalpaiguri Railway Station; and in Darjeeling (The *Darjeeling Gorkha Hill Council,* Silver Fir Bldg., The Mall, tel. 2524). Tourist offices are generally open Monday–Saturday, 10 A.M.–5 P.M.

Bihar. Contact the *Bihar Tourist Information Center,* Fraser Rd., Patna 800001, tel. 225295; open daily 10 A.M.–5 P.M. For government tours, accommodations, or car rentals, contact *Bihar State Tourism Development Corporation,* BSTDC, Birchand Patel Path, Patna 800001, tel. 225320; open daily 8 A.M.–8 P.M. Tourist Information Centers are also located at the Patna Airport, Patna Junction Railway Station, and Hotel Pataliputra Ashok in Patna. The *Government of India Tourist Office,* Paryatan Bhawan, Birchand Patel Path, Patna 800001, tel. 226721, is open Monday–Friday, 10 A.M.–5 P.M. Bihar Tourist Offices are also located in the following destinations (open 8 A.M.–8 P.M.): Bodhgaya, tel. 26; Hazaribagh, tel. 236; Nalanda, tel. 29; Pawapuri, no phone; Rajgir, Kund Market, tel. 226; Ranchi, Court Compound, Circular Rd., tel. 20426.

FOREIGN CURRENCY EXCHANGE. Most Western-style hotels have money-exchange counters. Otherwise, go to a branch of the *State Bank of India,* open Monday–Friday, 10 A.M.–2 P.M.; Saturdays till noon.

ACCOMMODATIONS. Prices are based on double occupancy and exclude taxes and service charges: *Deluxe,* over Rs. 2,000; *Expensive,* Rs. 1,200–Rs. 2,000; *Moderate,* Rs. 500–Rs. 1,200; *Inexpensive,* under Rs. 500. Most Western-style hotels take major credit cards.

WEST BENGAL

West Bengal Tourist Development Corporation (WBTDC) tourist lodges and bungalows can be booked three months in advance through WBTDC, Reservation Counter, 3/2 Benoy-Badal Dinesh Bagh (East), 1st Floor, Calcutta 700069, or through the Tourist Offices in Calcutta or Darjeeling (see addresses above). Reservations cannot be made on arrival at most lodges. For peace of mind, confirm bookings through Calcutta. Inquire about off-season discounts. WBTDC in Calcutta has a free booklet with detailed listings of over 40 lodges, which is updated regularly.

Bakkhali

Inexpensive

Bakkhali Tourist Lodge. Lakshmipur Prabartak, West Bengal. Reserve through WBTDC (address above). About 10 rooms with bath and 8 dormitories with shared bath. Simply furnished rooms are available in this lodge, shaded by casuarina groves; rooms open onto a deck that faces the beach. There is a restaurant. Breakfast and lunch included. Rupees only.

Darjeeling

Deluxe

Windamere Hotel. Darjeeling 734101; tel. and fax 2739. 27 rooms with bath. Situated near the uppermost ridge, this charming bungalow with cottages is surrounded by gardens. It's owned by an elegant Tibetan woman in her 80s. In its cozy drawing room warmed by a fireplace, Hook Cook met her future husband, the king of Sikkim. Cottages and upper-floor rooms are spacious, with lots of chintz. A fireplace will be blazing by the time you slip into bed, and your feet will be warmed by a hot-water bottle. Fixed-menu restaurant, bar, gardens, foreign-exchange and travel counter. Reserve well in advance. Meals included. AE, DC, MC, V.

Moderate

Central Hotel. Robertson Rd., Darjeeling 734101; tel. 2033. 52 rooms with bath. Recently renovated, this enormous hotel, which is on a lower ridge, dates from 1905. The large lobby retains its Old World aura. Although a separate annex has been added, rooms in the original building are preferable; they have fireplaces and a veranda offering mountain views. All rooms have simple Western-style furnishings. TV, room service, multicuisine restaurant, bar, foreign-exchange and travel counter, doctor. AE, DC, MC, V.

Hotel New Elgin. Darjeeling 734101; tel. 3314. 25 rooms with bath. This rambling 100-year-old bungalow is set on an upper ridge near the Mall. New rooms, complete with TVs, have been added through the years; but the older rooms are still the most pleasing and have an old-fashioned charm. All rooms have fireplaces and period furniture, and there is a cozy lobby and bar. There is a small garden. Multicuisine restaurant, bar, room service, travel counter, doctor on call, babysitters, library, cultural programs on request. Meals included. Discount mid-November–mid-March. AE, DC, MC, V.

Diamond Harbor

Inexpensive

Diamond Harbor Tourist Center. Diamond Harbor, West Bengal; tel. 46. Reserve through WBTDC (address above). About 20 rooms with bath and 3 dormitories with shared bath. From this lodge, with modestly decorated, clean rooms, you can take excursions to nearby fishing harbors. There is a good restaurant. Lunch and dinner included. Rupees only.

Digha

Inexpensive

Digha Tourist Lodge. Digha, West Bengal; tel. 55 and 56. Reserve through WBTDC (address above). About 15 rooms with bath, a dormitory with shared bath, and rustic cottages with bath. On the coast, near Orissa and overlooking the Bay of Bengal, this government-run resort offers modest rooms that add up to a bargain beach vacation. The lodge has a simple multicuisine restaurant. Rupees only.

Jaldapara Wildlife Sanctuary

Inexpensive

Hollong Forest Lodge. Madarihat, West Bengal; no phone. Reserve through WBTDC (address above). 7 rooms with bath. Inside the Jaldapara Sanctuary, this rustic lodge has modest rooms with an institutional decor. A caretaker can prepare plain meals. Rupees only.

Madarihat Tourist Lodge. Madarihat, West Bengal; tel. 30. Reserve through WBTDC (address above). 8 rooms with bath. One km (half mi.) from the Jaldapara Wildlife Sanctuary, this two-story lodge offers unadorned, clean rooms. Included are a restaurant and transportation to the park. Rupees only.

Kalimpong

Moderate

Himalayan Hotel. Upper Cart Rd., Kalimpong 734301; tel. 248. 10 rooms with bath (hot water by bucket). A short walk from the center of town, this secluded hotel is a former British residence built in the 1920s. The hotel features a mix of the East and the West—*thang-kas* share the walls with family memorabilia. Rooms are spotlessly clean, simply decorated, and have fireplaces. Ask for an upstairs room with mountain views. The dining room has an appealing attached sitting room. Meals included, beer available. Reserve well in advance. Rupees only.

Hotel Silver Oaks. Kalimpong 734301; tel. 296. 25 rooms with bath. This modern hotel, close to the main market, has an attractive lobby, beautiful gardens, and rooms with TV and and subdued decor. Ask for a room with a view of the Kanchenjunga range. Multicuisine restaurant, bar, room service, foreign-exchange and travel counter, baby-sitters, doctor on call. Meals included. DC, MC, V.

Inexpensive

Kalimpong Tourist Lodge. Kalimpong 734301; tel. 384. Reserve through WBTDC (address above). 7 rooms with bath. This handsome granite lodge, located about 3 km (2 mi.) from the heart of Kalimpong, was built in the 1930s and is set on seven acres of lawns and gardens. The upper-floor rooms offer the best views. The rooms are spacious, with mosquito netting and working fireplaces. TV, room service, restaurant, bar, and numerous terraces. Rupees only.

Malda

Inexpensive

Malda Tourist Lodge. Malda, West Bengal; tel. 2213. Reserve through WBTDC (address above). About 10 rooms with bath and a dormitory with shared bath. The decor here is institutional, but the rooms are clean. Some rooms are air-conditioned. Multicuisine restaurant. Dinner is included. Rupees only.

Murshidabad

Inexpensive

Berhampore Tourist Lodge. Berhampore, West Bengal; tel. 439. Reserve through WBTDC (address above). About 8 rooms with bath and a dormitory with shared bath. This lodge has some air-conditioned rooms and a restaurant. Rupees only.

Santiniketan

Inexpensive

Santiniketan Tourist Lodge. Bolpur, West Bengal; tel. 399. Reserve through WBTDC (address above). This comfortable lodge, which offers some air-conditioned rooms, is modestly furnished yet perfect for this small but frequently visited area. The lodge has an excellent restaurant. Two meals included. Rupees only.

Siliguri

Moderate

Hotel Sinclairs. Pradhan Nagar, Siliguri 734404; tel. 22674. 54 rooms with bath. This modern Western-style hotel has rooms with a simple modern decor. Multicuisine restaurants, bar, room service, swimming pool, TV, foreign-exchange and travel counter. DC.

Inexpensive

Mainak Tourist Lodge. Pradhan Nagar, Siliguri 734404; tel. 20986. Reserve through WBTDC (address above). About 15 rooms with bath. This Western-style lodge offers clean, reasonably decorated rooms; some are air-conditioned. Multicuisine restaurant, bar, TV in lounge, travel counter, doctor on call. Rupees only.

Sunderbans

Inexpensive

Sajnekhali Tourist Lodge. Sunderbans; no phone. Reserve through WBTDC (address above). 30 rooms with bath. Set in the Sunderbans, this rustic lodge, approachable by boat, has modestly furnished, clean rooms that are perfect for the location. There is also a restaurant. Rupees only.

Vishnupur

Inexpensive

Vishnupur Tourist Lodge. Vishnupur; tel. 13. Reserve through WBTDC (address above). About 8 rooms with bath and a dormitory with shared bath. There is a reasonable restaurant here; breakfast is included. Rupees only.

BIHAR

Bodhgaya

Moderate

Hotel Bodhgaya Ashok. Bodhgaya 824231; tel. 22708. 30 rooms with bath. This small Western-style hotel has a cozy lobby and air-conditioned rooms in a new wing and air-cooled rooms that open onto a lovely interior courtyard. All rooms are attractive, with modern decor. Multicuisine restaurant, room service, TV, bar, doctor, shopping arcade. AE, DC, MC, V.

Patna

Moderate–Expensive

Welcomgroup Maurya Patna. South Gandhi Maidan, Patna 800001; tel. 222061. 80 rooms with bath. This luxury high rise is modern and offers three room options. In expensive-priced rooms, you're paying only for more personalized service. All rooms are air-conditioned and have a contemporary decor. TV, room service, multicuisine restaurant, bar, swimming pool, foreign-exchange and travel counter, secretarial services, shopping arcade, golfing, terraces. AE, DC, MC, V.

Moderate

Pataliputra Ashok. Birchand Patel Path, Patna 800001; tel. 223467. 54 rooms with bath. While not as classy as the Maurya, this newly renovated hotel has an attractive lobby with a statue of the Buddha. Air-conditioned rooms are modern, with a cheery decor and TV. Multicuisine restaurant, room service, bar, foreign-exchange and travel counter, tourist office, shopping arcade, swimming pool. AE, DC, MC, V.

Rajgir

Expensive

Centaur Hokke Hotel. Rajgir 803116; tel. 231. 26 rooms with bath. Built by the Japanese, this luxury hotel has a redbrick exterior, stupa-shaped lobby, Buddhist prayer hall, and air-conditioned rooms (Western-style modern or sleek Japanese with sleeping mats on the floor). Indian- and Japanese-cuisine restaurant, bar, room service, doctor on call, Japanese hot baths, foreign-exchange counter, car rental, shops, table tennis. AE, DC.

Ranchi

Moderate

Hotel Ranchi Ashok. Doranda, Hinoo, Ranchi 834002; tel. 300037. 30 rooms with bath. This Western-style hotel has an attractive lobby and nice grounds. The spacious air-conditioned rooms have a pleasant modern decor and TV. Multicuisine restaurant, bar, room service, foreign-exchange counter, doctor on call. AE, DC, MC, V.

Inexpensive–Moderate

Hotel Yuvraj Palace. Doranda, Ranchi 834002; tel. 300805. 25 rooms with bath. This Western-style hotel has a spacious marble lobby and large deluxe rooms (moderately priced), with a separate sitting area, and smaller ordinary doubles (inexpensive). All rooms are furnished with a contemporary decor, air-conditioning, and TV. Indian- and Chinese-cuisine restaurant, bar, foreign-exchange and travel counter, doctor, courtesy airport shuttle service. DC, MC, V.

TOURIST BUNGALOWS. *Bihar State Tourism Development Corporation* has very inexpensive tourist bungalows, called *vihars,* scattered around the state. Rooms are clean, with unpretentious furnishings that include mosquito netting over the beds. To reserve in advance, contact Bihar State Tourism Development Corporation, Paryatan Bhawan, Birchand Patel Path, Patna 800001; tel. 225320. You can also reserve a room through the individual manager at each vihar. Rupees only.

Siddharth Vihar. Bodhgaya; no phone. 6 rooms with bath. Best rooms are air-conditioned. Meals can be supplied.

Prabhat Vihar. Netarhat; no phone. 8 rooms with bath. Simple meals available.

Kautilya Vihar. Patna; tel. 225411. 42 rooms with bath. Best rooms are air-conditioned. Indian- and Chinese-cuisine restaurant, bar.

Tourist Bungalow. Rajgir. Reserve through central office in Patna or Gautam Vihar, Rajgir; tel. 239. 32 rooms with bath. Best rooms in this new place are air-conditioned. Indian- and Chinese-cuisine restaurant.

Birsa Vihar. Ranchi; no phone. 20 rooms with bath. Indian- and Chinese-cuisine restaurant, bar, car-rental service, Bihar tour arrangements.

TREKKER'S HUTS. Rustic trekker's huts are available on trails in Manaybhanjang, Sandakphu, and Phalut, West Bengal. Bring a sleeping bag. For reservations, contact Assistant Director of Tourism, Darjeeling Gorkha Hill Council, Silver Fir Bldg., The Mall, Darjeeling 734001; tel. 2524. (Rs. 20 per bed.) Rupees only. There's also a rustic bungalow in Nilpara. Reserve through WBTDC, Reservation Counter, 3/2 Benoy-Badal-Dinesh Bagh (East), 1st Floor, Calcutta 700069.

DINING OUT. Many accommodations, listed above, have restaurants. Breakfast is usually served 7:30–10:30; lunch is usually noon–3; and dinner, 7:30–10. Payment is normally in rupees unless the restaurant is connected to a Western-style hotel. The restaurants listed below are informal and unless noted are open for all three meals and don't require reservations. Prices are based on one person eating a three-course meal, excluding taxes, tip, or beverage: *Moderate,* Rs. 100–200; *Inexpensive,* under Rs. 100.

WEST BENGAL

Darjeeling

Moderate

Central Hotel Restaurant. Central Hotel, Robertson Rd.; tel. 2033. This large restaurant, with banks of windows offering mountain views, has live entertainment during the peak season. The chef prepares fixed-menu meals, with a choice of Continental and Indian cuisines. Open 7:30 A.M.–9:30 A.M., 12:30 P.M.–2:30 P.M., and 7:30 P.M.–9:30 P.M. AE, DC, MC, V.

Glenary's. Nehru Rd.; tel. 3335. Darjeeling's most famous restaurant—dating back to British rule—has just been renovated. The large upstairs establishment has a large fireplace, tin ceiling, and lovely old bar. It offers good multicuisine choices. Open 8 A.M.–8:30 P.M. daily. AE, DC, MC, V.

Kanchan. Hotel New Elgin; tel. 3314. This restaurant is in an old Raj-style bungalow. The dining room has white furniture and a fireplace for extra warmth. The chef serves a wide range of tandoori and Indian dishes, plus Continental, Tibetan, and Nepali cuisines. Reservations advised. Open 7–9:30 A.M. 1–2:30 P.M., 7–9:30 P.M. AE, DC, V.

Windamere Hotel. Upper Ridge; tel. 2841. A lovely old restaurant with wonderful views, this dining room offers gracious service that matches its ambience—tablecloths, fresh flowers. The mixed menu includes mildly spiced Indian and Continental cuisines. Reservations required. Open 8–9:30 A.M., 1–2 P.M., 7–9:15 P.M. AE, DC, MC, V.

Inexpensive

Deveka's. Nehru Rd.; tel. 3057. Very informal and always crowded, this small eatery plays Western music and serves Chinese and Continental cuisines. Try the sliced chicken with mushrooms and vegetables. Open 7:30 A.M.–9 P.M. Rupees only.

Kalimpong

Inexpensive

Gompo's Restaurant and Bar. Just off Rishi Rd.; no phone. Set in the back of Gompo's Hotel, this casual restaurant, established in 1920, offers views of the valley and good Chinese, Tibetan, and Indian meals. Open 9 A.M.–9 P.M. Rupees only.

Kalimpong Park Hotel Restaurant. Tel. 304. This simple restaurant, with Buddhist symbols painted on the walls, serves Chinese, Indian or Tibetan meals. Open 11 A.M.–3 P.M. and 7 P.M.–9 P.M. DC, V.

BIHAR

Patna

Moderate

Amrapali. Kautilya Vihar; tel. 225411. The lighting at Amrapali is so subdued that you can barely see the Madhubani and Vaishali paintings that cover the walls. Hindi taped music sets an ethnic tone. The chef prepares Chinese, Indian, and Continental dishes. Specialties include chicken-leg kebab and tasty paneer butter masala (cheese cooked in a spicy curry). Open 7–11 A.M., noon–3 P.M. and 8–11 P.M. Rupees only.

Mumta Restaurant. Fraser Rd.; tel. 225888. This informal restaurant, with a bar in front and a family dining room in back, has very low lighting that offers an escape from Patna's intense heat and sun. You can order either Chinese or Indian cuisine. Especially good is the chicken butter masala (chicken pieces cooked in a spicy curry). Open noon–4 P.M. and 7–11 P.M. Rupees only.

Patliputra Ashok Restaurant. Birchand Patel Path; tel. 223467. This attractive restaurant with handsome chandeliers, mirrors on the ceiling and walls, and cedar pillars, serves Indian, Continental, and Chinese cuisines. Chinese is best, particularly the spicy garlic chicken or chicken capsicum and vegetables. Open 12:30–2:30 P.M. and 7:30–10:30 P.M. AE, DC, MC, V.

Vaishali. Welcomgroup Maurya Patna, South Gandhi Maidan; tel. 222061. Handsome Vaishali paintings adorn the pillars and walls of this restaurant, with a bank of windows overlooking the hotel swimming pool. You can enjoy good Continental, Chinese, and Indian cuisines. Try the *murgh mumtaz* (mildly spicy, boneless chicken cooked in a tandoor) or chicken stroganoff. Open 7:30–10:30 A.M., noon–2:45 P.M., and 8–11 P.M. AE, DC, MC, V.

Inexpensive

Rajasthan Restaurant. Fraser Rd.; tel. 22268. This popular eatery, with subdued lighting and booths and tables, serves delicious vegetarian fare—Chinese and Indian. Best bets are the fresh-cheese marshal cutlet (fried patty of cheese, potato, peas, and cashew nuts) and vegetable *malai kofta* (potato stuffed with cashew nuts and spices). Open noon–3:30 P.M. and 7–10:30 P.M.. Rupees only.

Ranchi

Moderate

Mithala. Hotel Ranchi Ashok, Doranda, Hinoo; tel. 300037. This pretty restaurant designed like a modern Bihari village home, with red tiles on the walls and thatched overhangs set above a bank of windows and a large Madhubani painting, serves Indian and Chinese cuisines. Specialties include *kebab-e-banu* (boneless chicken marinated in gram flour and masala spices and cooked in the tandoor) and *gosht saagwala* (spicy lamb pieces cooked with spinach in a rich gravy). Open 6–10 A.M., 12:30–2:45 P.M., and 7:30–10:30 P.M. AE, DC, MC, V.

Shafali. Hotel Yuvraj, Doranda; tel. 300805. This cozy restaurant, with light blue walls and white ceiling, has light Mogul touches such as arches set into the walls. There are live *ghazals* (romantic songs) Saturday nights. You can order Indian or Chinese cuisine. Try the *reshmi kebab* (boneless chicken cooked in a tandoor) or the Yuvraj special chicken (roasted chicken with spices). Open 10:30 A.M.–3:30 P.M. and 7:30–11 P.M. DC, MC, V.

Inexpensive

Kaveri Restaurant. Church Shopping Complex, Main Rd.; tel. 25193. in this popular restaurant, with subdued lighting and modern decor, you can have tasty Indian or Chinese vegetarian dishes. Their *paneer pasanda* (fried bread stuffed with cheese, vegetables, and fruit) is good, as is their *dosas* (stuffed crêpes). For dessert, enjoy their special *Kaveri* sweet (a cold milk-and-fruit pudding) or fresh *kulfi* (Indian ice cream). Open 10 A.M.–10 P.M. Rupees only.

SWEETS AND TREATS. West Bengal. *Penang Restaurant* on Laden La Rd., north of the Dhirdham Temple in Darjeeling is a hole-in-the-wall, with curtained booths, that serves the best Tibetan *momo* (dumplings) in Darjeeling. (Order beef; pork can be risky if it's undercooked.) Open daily 11 A.M.–7 P.M. *Glenary's Pastry Shop* on Nehru Rd. has good lemon tarts, cookies, cakes, and even fresh cheese. Open daily 7 A.M.–7 P.M. An unnamed bar next to Ravi Sales Corporation on Rishi Rd., Kalimpong, serves great *chang* (fermented millet) and momo. Sit in the tiny dark room crowded with tables. Let your chang brew 10 minutes after hot water is added, then sip it through the straw. Open from 9 A.M. to late at night.

Bihar. Visit the *Rajasthan Restaurant,* Fraser Rd., Patna, from 3:30 P.M. to 8 P.M., and have great vegetarian *samosa* (Indian fried dumplings) or tasty mixed *chat* (a yummy sweet-and-sour vegetable concoction). You can also get good ice cream and coffee. At *Maner,* 13 km (eight mi.) from Patna toward Sasaram, stop at a roadside stall and try the famous *ladu* sweets (little balls of butter, sugar, and ghee). On National Highway 31, 50 km (31 mi.) from Patna toward Rajgir, stop at *Mamta Hotel.* Sit outside or in the large interior hall and try *kheer* (a warm milk, rice, and sugar custard) or *kulfi* (Indian ice cream). Open 24 hours. At *Silao,* on the road six km (four mi.) from Nalanda toward Rajgir, stop for tasty *mita* (sweet) or *namkine* (salty) *khaja* (flaky pastry). It's delicious and freshly made in every stall.

HOW TO GET AROUND. West Bengal. From the Airport. To get from Bagdogra to Darjeeling, you can take the delightful narrow-gauge *Toy Train* from the nearby New Jalpaiguri Railroad Station. The train departs at 9:30 A.M. and arrives at 5 P.M., which, unfortunately, does not coincide with any flight arrivals and requires an overnight stay in Siliguri. Tickets cost about Rs. 200. You can also take the *West Bengal Tourist Department's Tourist Coach,* which has departures and arrivals coinciding with all flights (Rs. 55 for the four-hour drive), arrange for a hired car with driver, or take a taxi. The taxi or hired car with driver will cost about Rs. 500–Rs. 600 and takes about four hours.

By Rented Car with Driver. For excursions from Darjeeling to Kalimpong and its surrounding area, hire a car through your hotel or one of the recommended travel agencies in Darjeeling (see Tour Operators, below). Fares are usually determined by destination. For southern West Bengal, hire a car in Calcutta. Rates are about Rs. 4–Rs. 5 per km, with a halt charge of Rs. 50–Rs. 100 per night.

By Bus. The *North Bengal State Transport Corporation* runs buses throughout the state. For schedules and fares, contact the Booking Office: Calcutta, Esplanade Bus Terminus; Darjeeling, tel. 3133; Kalimpong, tel. 525.

By Taxi. Taxi fares should be about Rs. 4 per km.

By Bicycle Rickshaw and Auto Rickshaw. Both these modes of transport should be cheaper than a taxi, with a bicycle rickshaw the most economical.

Bihar. From the Airports. A taxi is your best bet at the Patna and Ranchi airports. Neither airport is far from town; fare should be about Rs. 50.

By Plane. *Indian Airlines* flies daily between Patna and Ranchi.

By Rented Car with Driver. Reasonably good roads connect Patna and Bodhgaya, a distance of 181 km (112 mi.), and Patna and Raxaul (on Nepal border), a distance of 290 km (180 mi.). Figure the cost of a rented car with driver at Rs. 4 per km, with an Rs. 50–Rs. 100 halt charge per night. Hire a car from one of the agencies listed below under Tour Operators.

By Bus. Avoid buses in this state; they're slow and crowded.

By Taxi. Taxis cost about Rs. 4 per km.

By Bicycle Rickshaw. Rates are about Rs. 2 per km—a delightful way to travel in Bodhgaya.

TOURS. West Bengal. The *West Bengal Tourist Bureau* runs a number of long-distance tours in air-conditioned coaches from Calcutta between September and March. Fares are reasonable. Inquire at 3/2 BBD Bagh (East) for complete information. The *Darjeeling Tourist Bureau* offers three tours by jeep in northern West Bengal: half-day sightseeing trips around Darjeeling; a day excursion to Kalimpong; or a two-day excursion to Gangtok via Kalimpong. At press time, fares were under review. For details, contact the Darjeeling Gorkha Hill Council (see address above).

Bihar. *The Bihar State Tourism Development Corporation* (Paryatan Bhawan, Birchand Patel Path, tel. 225320) offers the following tours by bus: Patna sightseeing, Rs. 30; Patna–Ranchi, Rs. 50; Ranchi–Patna, Rs. 50; Patna–Rajgir–Nalanda–Pawapuri–Patna, Rs. 40; Patna–Hazaribagh, Rs. 40; and Hazaribagh–Patna. Rs. 40.

TOUR OPERATORS. West Bengal. For hired car with driver and general travel needs, contact *ITDC,* c/o Government of India Tourist Office, 4 Shakespeare Sarani, Calcutta 700071, tel. 220901; *American Express,* 21 Old Court House St., Calcutta 700001, tel. 236281; *Mercury Travels,* 46–C. J. L. Nehru Rd., Calcutta 700071; tel. 223555, or *Travel Corporation of India,* 46–C. J. L. Nehru Rd., Calcutta 700071; tel. 225469. *Sherpa Sikkim Trekking Tour,* Dingpen Villa, 8 West Jawahar Rd., Darjeeling 734101; tel. 3478, fax 2603, offers ecologically sound treks in northern West Bengal and Sikkim. *Trek-Mate,* Pine Ridge Hotel, The Mall, Darjeeling 734101, tel. 2094 or 2074, sponsors treks in northern West Bengal and Sikkim, including customized treks, such as village stays or other theme-oriented adventures, and mountain expeditions. Also check *Facts at Your Fingertips* for tour operators that offer trips in West Bengal.

Bihar. *Travel Corporation of India* (Maurya Center, South Gandhi Maidan, Patna, 800001; tel. 231016) can arrange tours in Bihar and provide all travel assistance, including rented car with driver. You can also rent a car with driver from BSTDC (see address above under Tourist Information).

SEASONAL EVENTS. The specific dates for many events each year are determined by the lunar calendar; contact the Government of India Tourist Office for details.

WEST BENGAL

January. *Makar Sankranti.* This week-long Lepcha and Bhutia fair, which is held on the banks of the Teesta River near Kalimpong, celebrates their new year.

Mid-January. *Ganga Sagar Mela.* During this gigantic fair on Sagar Island, a 10-hour cruise south of Calcutta, throngs of Hindu devotees from all over India take a holy dip at the confluence of the Hooghly River and Bay of Bengal. Big event!

January/February. *Vasant Panchami.* This festival that honors Saraswati, the goddess of learning, is an important festival at Santniketan, Tagore's university.

Mid-February. *Losar.* Around the time of Losar, the Tibetan New Year, ritual *chaams* (dances) are performed in all the important Buddhist monasteries.

March. *Holi* or *Dol.* During this festival that marks spring's arrival, youngsters splash everyone with colored water. Wear washable clothes.

April. *Poyla Baisakh.* Bengalis celebrate their New Year.

June/July. *Id-ul-Fitr.* This Moslem holy day marks the end of Ramadan, a period of month-long fasting, with a big feast.

August/September. *Indrapuja.* In Vishnupur, Hindus celebrate this festival that pays tribute to Indra, the god of thunder.

September/October. *Durga Puja.* This Hindu festival, called Dussehra in most of India, is a 10-day celebration of Rama's victory over evil. It's visually breathtaking as well as deafening, with music and fireworks.

October/November. *Diwali.* Also called the Festival of Lights, this Hindu occasion honors Lakshmi, goddess of prosperity, and Kali, signifying strength and depicting the horrors that mortals have brought on themselves. Images of bamboo and clay, profusely and intricately adorned, are created throughout West Bengal.

December. *Paus Mela.* At Santiniketan and rural Bengal, Hindus energetically celebrate a fair that honors the Bengali month of Paus.

BIHAR

March/April. *Mahavira Jayanti.* This Jain festival is dedicated to Mahavira, the 24th tirthankara (perfect soul). It's a big event at Parasnath Hill.

May. *Buddha Jayanti.* Celebrated at Buddhist pilgrimage sites in Bihar, this festival commemorates the Buddha's birth, enlightenment, and death.

July. *Rath Yatra.* This is an especially important Hindu chariot festival at Jagannathour near Ranchi.

August. *Ganesh Chaturthi.* This harvest festival honors Ganesh, the plump and docile elephant-headed god. His image is brought into houses and stored for good luck.

November. *Sonepar Cattle Fair.* One of the largest of its kind in the world, this month-long fair has herdsmen from all over India walking their cattle into Sonepar to the fairgrounds on the banks of the Ganges. Decorated with colorful ribbons, horns festooned with garlands, and ankles circled with bells, cattle wade the river onto the shore, accompanied by the blowing of conch shells. This fair is at the heart of a rural tradition and shows that India is imaginative, vigorous, and alive.

November. *Chhatha Vrata.* About a week after Diwali, Bihar holds its most important annual event: a sun festival. The harvest season begins and the first crop is offered to the sun, the lord of the crops. The banks of the Ganges, at Patna, is the best place to witness this event.

HISTORIC SITES. Entrance to most places is generally free; where a donation is asked, a few rupees will suffice. Historic sites are open daily sunrise to sunset unless noted otherwise below.

WEST BENGAL

Darjeeling

Dhirdham Temple. Styled along the lines of the famous Pashupatinath Temple in Kathmandu, Nepal, and dedicated to Shiva, this temple (near the railway station) allows visits by non-Hindus, unlike the temple in Kathmandu.

Observatory Hill. Visit old shrines sacred to Buddhists and Hindus.

Tibetan Refugee Self-Help Center. Established after China took over Tibet, this center is home to over 600 refugees. Visit the handicraft and carpet factories, shops, training centers, gompa. The center also performs occasional cultural shows for the public. Consult the tourist department for a schedule of activities. Shops and factories are closed Sundays.

Yiga-Choling Monastery. This monastery in Ghoom, eight km (five mi.) from Darjeeling and built in 1850, has lovely frescoes and statues. But it's unlit, so bring a flashlight.

Kalimpong

Tharpa Choling Monastery. Built in 1937, this monastery has exquisite frescoes, *thang-kas* (paintings with a Buddhist theme), and statues. A flashlight will help you view them. Prayer ceremonies are held about 5 A.M. and 2 P.M.

Zongdogpalrifobrang Monastery. This monastery has great frescoes, statues, and a stunning replica of a celestial chorten. The original was destroyed by the Chinese in Lhasa.

Other Destinations

Malda. Adina Mosque. This fourteenth-century shrine is partially in ruins, but remaining details are worth a visit.

Murshidabad. Katra Mosque. Styled along the lines of the great Islamic mosque at Mecca, Katra contains the tomb of its builder, Murshid Kuli Khan.

Hazarduari Palace. Built by the Nawab Humayun Jah in 1837, this palace contains interesting exhibits of old firearms, crockery, and paintings. Open 9 A.M.–5 P.M.

Santiniketan. Santiniketan University. Conceived as an abode of peace, Tagore's unusual and delightful open-air university accepts visitors from 3–5 P.M. in summer and 2–4 P.M. in winter. Throughout the year Tuesday visiting hours are from 10 A.M.–noon.

BIHAR

Bodhgaya. This ancient seat of Buddhist learning where Siddhartha Gautama attained enlightenment has numerous important sites connected to the Historic Buddha. Be sure to see the *bodhi* (fig) tree, which is said to have grown from the original tree under which the Buddha meditated; the Mahabodhi temple, the most sacred Buddhist temple dedicated to Lord Buddha; the Animeshlochan Chaitya, where the Buddha stood after attaining enlightenment; Ratnagar (water tank), where he spent a week in contemplation; and Chankramana (Jewel Walk) where he strolled in meditation.

Gaya. Vishnupada Temple. Supposedly built over Vishnu's footprints, this temple, which was renovated in 1787, has beautifully sculpted pillars. An important pilgrimage site for Hindus, who believe that if they perform the last rituals for the deceased at Gaya, the dead will be absolved of all sins.

Parsanath Hill. On this hill, an extremely important Jain pilgrimage site, the 23rd tirthankara (perfect soul) gained enlightenment.

Patna. Golghar. This granary, built in 1786 after a great famine, offers excellent views of Patna. Open 10 A.M.–6 P.M.

Harmandir Sahib. This *gurdwara* (Sikhs' temple) is dedicated to Guru Gobind Singh, the tenth guru of the Sikhs, who was born in Patna in 1766.

Shershahi Masjid. Patna's oldest mosque, built in 1545, is an excellent example of Afghan architecture and dominates the city's skyline.

Rajgir. Gridhakuta (Vulture's Peak). On this bluff, the Buddha set in motion his second Wheel of Law and preached here to his disciples during the rainy season. To commemorate these events, the Japanese have built the Vishwa Shanti (Peace) Stupa. You can take a chair lift to the top 9:15 A.M.–1 P.M. and 2–5 P.M., except Thursdays.

Nalanda. Founded in the fifth century, this ancient international Buddhist university is still under excavation. The Buddha and Mahavira (founder of the Jain religion) visited this school. Numerous kings built monasteries and temples, including Emperor Ashoka and Kumaragupta of the Gupta dynasty. Today, it's still a great pilgrimage center.

Sasaram. Sher Shah Mausoleum. Set in a garden in the middle of a lake, this tomb—Bihar's finest—honors the sixteenth-century Moslem ruler who founded Patna. Nearby are the tombs of Sher Shah's father and son.

MUSEUMS AND GALLERIES. West Bengal. Ava Art Gallery. Hill Cart Rd., on the way to Ghoom (near Darjeeling), has a fine collection of embroidery and art. Open 8 A.M.–noon and 12:30–6:30 P.M. daily.

Himalayan Mountaineering Institute, on Birch Hill, Darjeeling, has excellent retrospective displays of equipment, photographs, and other memorabilia of Mount Everest and other twentieth-century Himalayan expeditions. Open daily 9 A.M.–5 P.M. in summer; 9 A.M.–4 P.M. in winter; closed 1–2 P.M. and all day Tuesdays. Fee.

Natural History Museum. Meadowbank Rd., Darjeeling, has 4,300 exhibits of the fauna of Darjeeling, Sikkim, Tibet, Bhutan, Nepal, and the Eastern Himalayan region. Very well presented. Open 10 A.M.–4 P.M. (Wednesdays from 1 P.M.); closed Thursdays.

Tenzing's House, on D. B. Giri, Darjeeling, was the home of the Sherpa who scaled Mount Everest with Edmund Hillary in 1953 and became the first to do so. Now a museum. Check with the tourist department for hours.

Bihar. Bodhgaya Site Museum, Bodhgaya, has a collection of archaeological exhibits excavated from the local area. Entrance is free to the museum, which has a fine collection of gold, bronze, and stone statues of Buddha. Open 10 A.M.–5 P.M., closed Fridays.

Nalanda Museum, Nalanda, has an excellent collection of Buddhist and Hindu relics that date from the seventh century. Also on display are the great seal of the twelfth-century university, panels depicting the avatars of Vishnu, stone and copper-plate inscriptions, and pottery. Open 10 A.M.–5 P.M., closed Fridays.

Jalan's Quila, Patna, has a rich collection of jade, Chinese paintings, and silver filigree work of the Mogul period. Prior permission is needed, since this is a private collection. Open 10:30 A.M.–4:30 P.M., closed Mondays.

Khuda Baksh Oriental Library, Patna, contains excellent Arabic and Persian manuscripts, Rajput and Mogul paintings, a tiny Quran that measures only one inch in width, and books rescued from the plunder of a university in Cordoba, Spain. Open 9 A.M.–5 P.M.

Patna Museum, Patna, has a good collection of metal and stone sculptures from the Maurya and Gupta periods, terra-cotta figurines and a 16-meter (52½-foot) fossilized tree that dates back 2,000 years. It also has a Tibetan section. Open 10:30 A.M.–4:30 P.M., closed Mondays.

GARDENS. In Darjeeling, *Lloyds Botanical Garden,* with plants from around the world and 2,000 species of orchids, is open 6 A.M.–5 P.M. Also visit the *Shrubbery,* an old garden with excellent views of the Himalayas. Same hours.

SPORTS AND OUTDOOR ADVENTURES. West Bengal. Fishing. In the area around Darjeeling, fishing is currently banned to increase the stocks.

Hot Springs. Bakreswar has numerous hot springs to enjoy.

Rafting. You can make a one- or two-day run on the Teesta and Rangit rivers September–May. Make all arrangements in advance. Contact Travel Corporation of India (see Tour Operators, above).

Swimming. Enjoy the beach resorts of Digha and Bakkhali in southern West Bengal.

Trekking. Treks in northern West Bengal may not exceed 15 days starting from arrival at Bagdogra or the railway station in Siliguri. Trekkers must also register with the Foreigner's Registration Office in Darjeeling before setting off to hike more than two days and they must also report their arrival at the Check Post at any destination. An excellent four- or five-day trek starts from Manaybhanjang, 26 km (16 mi.) from Darjeeling, and heads to Sandakphu village on the border of Nepal. You'll walk through rhododendron forests filled with birds, descend into tropical valleys, and climb to Sandakphu at 3,636 meters (11,929 feet). Here you have great views of Mt. Kanchenjunga and, if you're lucky, Mt. Everest. From Sandakphu, you'll walk through the Singlalila Range to Rimbak village, where a public bus can take you back to Darjeeling. You can extend this trek to six days and walk to Phalut on the border of West Bengal, Sikkim, and Bhutan. This trek is best March–April and October–mid-December, with the best visibility in November.

Wildlife Sanctuaries. At *Jalpaiguri,* 145 km (90 mi.) from Siliguri, is a sanctuary for bison, deer, elephants, tigers, leopards, barking deer, and Indian one-horned rhinoceroses. Lying below Bhutan and covering 93 sq. km (58 sq. mi.) of *terai* (sub-Himalayan forests), the sanctuary also has rich bird life that includes the lesser florican, great stone plover, and jungle fowl. The best viewing time is November–April. Elephant rides are available. For further information, contact the Tourist Bureau, Government of West Bengal, Hill Cart Rd., Siliguri 734401.

Sunderbans. These dense mangrove swamps in the delta region require a delightful three-hour trip by car through beautiful Bengali villages, then a four-hour boat cruise to the park area. Sunderbans, the "beautiful forest," has the largest population of tigers (200) in India. This extensive estuarine land has tigers swimming in its channels (only the lucky spot them), along with crocodiles, deer, and wild boar. The best time to visit is November–March. Contact the Regional Tourist Office of West Bengal in Calcutta (see address above under Tourist Information) for weekend excursions by coach and boat, details for permission to visit this sanctuary, and accommodation information.

Bihar. Wildlife Sanctuaries. *Palamau Tiger Reserve* (Betla Sanctuary) is the largest tiger reserve in Bihar and also home to elephants, panthers, wild boar, sambar (antlered Indian deer), pythons, and numerous birds. Palamau is 173 km (107 mi.) west of Ranchi. For accommodation on the edge of the sanctuary, you can reserve a room in a new BSTDC bungalow or in a forest lodge. Contact the Field Director, Project Tiger, Palamau Tiger Reserve, Daltonganj, Palamau District, Bihar. This park is most enjoyable September–March.

Hazaribagh Sanctuary. In the undulating forests of the Damodar Valley and once the private land of a local maharaja, this 182 sq. km (113 sq. mi.) reserve is home to tigers, sambar, leopards, wild boar, panthers, hyenas, and spotted deer. The sanctuary is 115 km (71 mi.) north of Ranchi. For further information, contact the Divisional Forest Officer, Hazaribagh, West Division, Hazaribagh, Bihar. The best time to visit is February–May.

SHOPPING. West Bengal. *Baluchar,* "figured muslin," as it is known in Bengal, is woven in the Murshidabad region of north Bengal and is one of the finest materials to emerge from Indian looms. Cotton fabrics are brocaded with *zari* (gold threads), and colors of deep purples and maroons highlight the weaving. Borders are ornamented with floral motifs and figurative works. Baluchar is a Moslem weaver's craft. In Murshidabad, the renowned Moslem center of pre-British Bengal, weavers under royal patronage made the town of Murshidabad synonymous with silk and cotton weaving. Murshidabad is also known for its gold and silver inlay work on wood, primarily as bases for hookahs (water pipes). Carved, painted, and stained ivory has long been an art form in Murshidabad, but it is illegal to import ivory into the United States.

Bengal's potters at Bankura, Birphum, and Midnapore make painted dolls, animal figures, and smooth, blue-glazed earthenware. Metalwork, *dokra* figures of metal and clay, soapstone carvings, bamboo crafts, and quilts are all found in bazaars. Little known to most tourists are *sholapith* toys. Sholapith is the core of a plant that grows wild in marshy areas, and delicate images of deities and flowers are fashioned from it. It is also commonly made into traditional headgear for weddings. Another Bengali craft is *shonkari* (shell craft), most often seen as bangles and toe rings.

If you visit Santiniketan or Vishnupur, you may come across the rural tradition of narrating stories with the aid of painted scrolls. As in Orissa, these *pats* are common in rural Bengal, with separate pieces depicting scenes of the story. In Calcutta, you can see them in a museum.

Vishnupur and Santiniketan also produce leather goods, bell metal wares, fine Tussar silks and terra-cotta figurines that are common in most Bengali households.

Darjeeling's crafts are different from those in the rest of Bengal. Nepalese and Tibetan brasswork and jewelry, gems, woodwork, carpets, and wool weavings are the mainstays. And, of course, you can buy the renowned Darjeeling tea directly from some of the tea estates after taking a tour to see their production methods.

In Darjeeling, visit *Habeen Mulliek and Son,* The Mall, for good curios. Open daily 9 A.M.–6:30 P.M. April 15–June 15 and September 15–November 15. The rest of the year, it's open Monday–Friday, 9 A.M.–6:30 P.M.; Saturday, 9 A.M.–2:30 P.M.; closed Sundays. AE, MC, V. For handmade Tibetan carpets, woolen sweaters, socks, and handicrafts, stop in at the *Tibetan Refugee Self-Help Center,* Lebong, (open Monday–Saturday, 8 A.M.–5 P.M.) and *N.P.A.A. Functional Literacy Shoppe* in Hayden Hall, Market Rd. (open Monday–Saturday, 9 A.M.–12:30 P.M. and 1:30 P.M.–5 P.M.) Both shops take rupees only.

In Kalimpong, visit *K. Shila Bhutia,* next to Christian Book Depot, Main Rd. Here you can buy handicrafts and handmade sweaters, caps, socks, baby clothes, and Nepali caps. It's open Monday–Saturday, 9:30 A.M.–4:30 P.M. Rupees only. Also stop at *Kazi Ratna Sakya & Bros.,* Rishi Rd., which has a good selection of Tibetan and Bhutanese curios, jewelry, and thang-kas. It's open daily 9 A.M.–6 P.M. Rupees only.

Bihar. Patna is well known for its wooden inlay work on metal, ivory, and stag horn. Artisans also use wood chips of unusual grain and color to decorate table tops, wall hangings, and trays.

Bihar has recently "discovered" a cottage industry that has become a lucrative and widely known art form—Madhubani paintings. The women painters of Mithila (for it is primarily the women who paint) in north Bihar create highly original paintings, previously done on mud walls but now done on paper and canvas. Growing out of myth and ritual, the forms are striking in their simplicity of execution and the complexity of their images.

In Patna, you can find all these products and the Madhubani paintings at the *Bihar State Handloom and Handicraft Emporium,* Apna Bazaar, near East Gandhi Maidan. Open 10 A.M.–5 P.M., closed Sundays. Rupees only.

NIGHTLIFE AND BARS. West Bengal. For intimacy, you can't beat the bar at the Windamere Hotel, Darjeeling, where 10 people means a crowd. The ambience creates good conversation. Glenary's, on Nehru Rd., has an open bar attached to its restaurant, which is popular with the year-round population in Darjeeling.

Bihar. Your best bet for a nightcap is in a Western-style hotel.

ORISSA

Natural and Spiritual Beauty

by
LISA SAMSON and AMIT SHAH

"Every standing tree is an ovation to life" is not an inscription on an ancient temple wall but a painted roadside sign put up by the Department of Forestry in the state of Orissa. The sign's ambiguous language testifies to one of Orissa's claims to fame: its abundant natural beauty. It also suggests the spiritual underpinnings, Buddhist and Hindu, that were the motivational factors for many of the man-made wonders to be seen here. Once a center of Buddhist learning and propagation, Orissa is one of Hinduism's most active pilgrimage sites. Some say that to see Orissa is to see India, and certainly, visitors to Orissa have much to choose from. In the temple cities of Bhubaneswar, Puri, and Konarak, you can see the unusual Orissan temple architecture, with its strange shapes and fabulous and frequently erotic sculptures. On the coast and in the north, west, and south, you can indulge, as ancient Orissans must have done, in the pleasures of nature.

For many years, Orissa has attracted tourists primarily to its three temple cities of Puri, Konarak, and Bhubaneswar. It is here that Hinduism's distinctive Orissan temple architecture reached its peak in the tenth century A.D. The state also has a large number of important Buddhist and Jain sites, such as the beautifully preserved rock edicts of Emperor Ashoka at Dhauli, which date from 261 B.C.; the first-century B.C. caves at Khandagiri, cut out and used by monks as meditation cells; and the ruins of the seventh-century Buddhist university at Ratnagiri-Lalitagiri. In these architectural monuments, you can trace the history of Orissa from its early Buddhist and Jain roots through the flourishing Orissan civilization between the fourth and thirteenth centuries, when the great Hindu temples were built. But there is much more to explore in Orissa.

In the past few years, Orissa has begun to develop other rich offerings for travelers: its fertile countryside, idyllic coastal towns, forested mountains, deep-cut gorges, varied waterways, and wildlife preserves. Orissa's unpopulated beaches, which stretch from Chandipur near the West Bengal border to Gopalpur-on-Sea; its hot springs at Atri and Taptapani; its wildlife preserves of Chilika Lake, Simlipal, and Ushakothi; and its Biological Park and Botanical Garden at Nandankanan (near Bhubaneswar) are just a few of the natural sights that are now popular with tourists.

Bounded by Bihar on the north, by West Bengal on the northeast, and by Andhra Pradesh and Madhya Pradesh on the south, Orissa consists of an extensive plateau in the interior that drops to a rich alluvial coastal plain crisscrossed by large rivers, including the great Mahanadi. The plateaus and hills in the north and south of the state have peaks that rise up to 1,676 meters (5,500 feet), at times creating spectacular waterfalls. Through the central part of the state, five rivers descend from higher reaches, cutting rocky gorges and creating fertile green valleys as they flow to the Bay of Bengal. Along the coast, which has beautiful isolated beaches, one also finds fertile land as one leaves the hills to the west and approaches the sandy stretches that adjoin the Bay. Rice paddies; cashew and mango groves; sugarcane fields; and jute, casuarina, and sal forests dot this primarily agricultural state of 31 million people. Though over 80 percent of the population cultivates rice, forests of sal, teak, sandal, and bamboo occupy 43 percent of the state's area. Historically slow to industrialize, Orissa now boasts a growing number of medium-sized industries based on minerals, sugar, glass, textiles, and handloom weaving that have begun to provide a secure economic base for this predominantly agricultural state. Steel plants at Rourkela, the Hirakud Dam Project on the Mahanadi River (one of the largest earth dams in the world), Asia's largest aluminum plant, and the profusion of high-tech companies around Bhubaneswar assure this state of steady growth into the twenty-first century.

Looking Backward

Orissa, known in earlier times as Kalinga, is noted in some of the most ancient Indian epics. Legend has it that Kalinga, one of the five sons of a sage, traveled as far as the hills of the Eastern Ghat and, looking down on the lovely countryside below him, decided to settle his people here, "where Nature abounds in wanton profusion." An early Kalinga king is believed to have sided with the Kauravas in the Mahabharata war, recorded in the great Indian epic of the same name. Part of the state is still called Kalinga by local people. Orissa was also known as Utkala ("land of arts and crafts"), a title that holds true today.

The recorded history of Orissa began in 261 B.C., with the edicts of the Mauryan Emperor Ashoka carved in rock at Dhauli, near Bhubaneswar. Ashoka, once known as Ashoka the Terrible, is said to have looked down from the hill at Dhauli to survey the plains of Kalinga strewn with the carnage of the Kalinga War that he had begun as conflicts of conquest. Horrified at what he saw, Ashoka repented for his deeds and converted to Buddhism, then the religion of Orissa. He actively propagated the Buddhist philosophy of nonviolence far beyond the borders of India. Soon after

Ashoka's death, Orissa reasserted its independence. In the first century B.C. Kharavela, the third Chedi king and perhaps the greatest king to rule Kalinga, extended his empire from near Agra in the north to Kanya Kumari in the south, bringing Jainism to Orissa.

It was during his reign that the Khandagiri and Udayagiri caves (near Bhubaneswar) were carved for Jain monks out of the rock faces of these hills, to be used as meditation cells. Many of these tiny cells are covered with friezes; the Hathi Gumpha (the Elephant Cave) at Udayagiri bears a Pali inscription carved in the rock that records Kharavela's reign. Some say that relics of Ashoka and Kharavela were preserved in Dhauli and Udayagiri and, therefore, that the hills that flank Bhubaneswar became sacred spots. After Kharavela, the Chedi dynasty of Kalinga declined, and Jainism was again replaced by Buddhism in about A.D. 100.

The zenith of Orissan civilization and architecture was reached between the fourth and thirteenth centuries, when the Kesari and Ganga kings brought Hinduism to this Buddhist land. The Lingaraj Temple at Bhubaneswar and the Jagganath Temple at Puri were constructed during the brilliant Kesari period. The Ganga kings ruled from the twelfth to the fifteenth century, during which time the magnificently engineered Sun Temple at Konarak was built on what were then coastal dunes. Moslem incursions into the state, prompted partly by a need to keep the Moslem armies equipped with war elephants that could be found in the Orissan wilds, culminated in the occupation of Orissa in 1568. The Afghans controlled Orissa until Akbar's Hindu general, Man Singh, annexed it for the Moguls in 1592. During their control, the Moslems destroyed many temples of the "idol worshipers." Of Bhubaneswar's 7,000 temples that once lined the banks of the sacred Bindusagar Lake, only about 500 are in some state of preservation today.

The Dutch came to Pipli, now a village of craftsmen near the coast, and the British East India Company came to Balasore near the West Bengal border in the seventeenth century. In 1751, the Moguls ceded Orissa to the Marathas, who held it until the British took it over in 1803. They did little to improve the economic condition of the country or of the people. After Indian independence, the modern state of Orissa was shaped by encompassing some 26 small kingdoms. Its move toward industrialization has involved some impressive strides in irrigation and energy production, and the capital, Bhubaneswar, is developing steadily in light industry and high-tech companies.

Tribes

Descendants of the people who lived in Orissa before the Aryan invasions over 3,000 years ago, the Adivasi tribals of Orissa are numerous. Over 60 tribes, each marked with its own culture, are concentrated in the forest and hill regions of the state, and many still live in much the same way that they have for thousands of years. Once forced back from their hereditary land into less fertile places, they are now protected by the Indian government under the Protection of Aboriginal Tribes regulations.

Many of the tribes, especially those in the northwestern industrialized area, are beginning to leave their traditional hunting and agricultural lifestyles to seek jobs in places like the iron fields. It is difficult to say how much longer these people, who have held on to their traditions through thousands of years of dynastic changes, will be able to continue passing them on to future generations.

EXPLORING ORISSA

The Temples

Bhubaneswar, Puri, and Konarak are famous for their stunning examples of Orissan temple architecture and for their spectacular religious celebrations. Many of the temples were constructed during the golden age of Orissan temple building, the eighth to the thirteenth centuries. Taken together, the Orissan shrines, especially those at Bhubaneswar, represent a coherent development of the Nagara style of Indo-Aryan architecture.

The Orissan temple consists almost entirely of a vaulting spire that thrusts upward in a pinnacle among much lower-replica turrets that seem like mere surface wall decorations. The temple contains the *jagamohan,* or porch, which is usually square with a pyramidal roof. Immediately following the jagamohan is the *deul,* the cubicle inner apartment that enshrines the deity and that is surmounted by the soaring tower. Sometimes one or two more halls—*natmandir* (the dancing hall) and *bhogmandir* (the hall of offerings)—are set in front of the porch.

The architecture of Orissan temples may seem strange and heavy, but the sculpture on these temples is graceful, often unashamedly erotic, and steeped in mythology. There is a musical, dancelike, animated quality to many of these sculptures. Beautifully detailed, the statues range from voluptuous, amorous couples to musicians; to fierce beasts; to historical scenes; to birds, flowers, and foliage, all of which alternately tease and soothe the viewer.

Bhubaneswar and Its Environs

The capital of Orissa since 1952, Bhubaneswar is known as the cathedral city of India and has over 500 temples in various stages of preservation. In Bhubaneswar and its immediate environs are presented a nearly 2,000-year panorama of Orissan art and history. From the third century B.C. to A.D. 1500 one can witness in the rock edicts of Dhauli, the caves at Khandagiri, the fort ruins at Sisulpalgarh, and the temples of Bhubaneswar a rarely preserved architectural record of the many dynasties that flourished and died out.

In Bhubaneswar the greatest of the temples, the Lingaraj, is off limits to non-Hindus. Its huge tower is visible from miles away, but the closest foreigners will get to it is a viewing stand erected during the period of the raj when Lord Curzon, the British viceroy, visited the temple. Other temples to visit are the ornate Parsurameswara, said to be the oldest surviving temple in the city; the Mukteswar, with the unmatched intricacy of its carved detail; the Rajarani, with its embracing couples; and the Brahmeswar.

Using Bhubaneswar as a base, you can travel easily into the surrounding countryside to explore the important Buddhist sites of Dhauli and Khandagiri or go farther afield to Konarak and Puri. The roads between the three major cities pass through Orissan villages with monochrome mud huts, decorated by women with complex rice-paste designs dedicated to Lakshmi, the goddess of wealth and beauty, along paddy fields green in the hot sun, past irrigation canals and ponds thick with water hyacinth, and—between Puri and Konarak on Marine Drive—past groves of casuarina, cashew, and mango, alongside the sea. Within minutes of leaving the fast-growing metropolitan area, you will see images of the rural Indian landscape that appear timeless. As wooden bullock carts creak under their loads of hay, and as farmers stand in watery ditches separating young rice shoots for replanting, and as children play among themselves with hand-made toys, you catch the continuation of the cycles of life, which thousands of years ago inspired the artisans who sculpted the temples of Orissa.

Ten kilometers (six miles) west of Bhubaneswar, the twin hills of Khandagiri and Udayagiri are worth a visit, especially for a short drive at dusk. You can see the mount at Dhauli and Bhubaneswar's rooftops from here. The caves and inscriptions are worth visiting more for their historical significance than for their artistic merit.

Dhauli, about six kilometers (four miles) southeast of Bhubaneswar, overlooks the Kalinga Plains. The irrigation canals, neatly lined palm trees, and the sculpted paddy fields offer a serene view of what was once the scene of tremendous bloodshed that finally persuaded Emperor Ashoka to convert to Buddhism in the third century B.C. This view, with its historical associations, is moving, and the rock edicts, in which Ashoka calls all men his children, are well preserved.

Konarak

The sleepy town of Konarak is home to one of India's most fabulous temples—the Sun Temple of "Black Pagoda," so named because of the dark patina that covered it over the centuries. Legend shrouds the Sun Temple. Constructed in the thirteenth century by King Narasimha, probably as much as a monument to himself as to honor Surya, the sun god, it is an architectural and engineering wonder. Built in the shape of Surya's chariot, with 24 huge chariot wheels and pulled by seven straining horses, this is a breathtaking temple. To see the temple lit at night and almost deserted in the early morning, stay overnight in one of the two simple government tourist lodges.

Puri

Puri is a coastal town that contains one of Hinduism's holiest sites. In the ninth century, the seer Sankaracharya designated Puri one of the four pilgrimage sites (dhams) for Hindus. Pious Hindus believe that a pilgrimage to Puri is an obligation and that if one stays here for three days and nights, one will gain freedom from the cycle of births and rebirths.

As you enter the tropical town with its pastel-colored ashrams and dharmasalas (rest houses), a religious aura intensifies, practically pulling you to its famous Jagannath Temple. Here, in the old quarter of Puri, open-air stalls sell religious souvenirs and trinkets. Pilgrims buy prasads (gifts) for the sacred deity, Lord Jagannath (an avatar of Krishna). Devotional songs blare out of speakers.

Jagannath is also the starting point for one of the most spectacular of India's temple fairs, Ratha Yatra, the Car Festival. Held in midsummer and attracting crushing hordes throughout the weeks of the celebration, the festival swells the already huge number of pilgrims to the Jagannath Temple to unbelievable proportions. Non-Hindus are not allowed to enter the Jagannath Temple, but you can see into the compound from nearby rooftops.

Buddhist Excavations

In addition to the rock edicts at Dhauli, there are other Buddhist sights of interest in Orissa. About 100 kilometers (62 miles) north of Bhubaneswar is the finest, the Ratnagiri-Lalitagiri complex, where Buddhists built Puspagiri, a university, in the seventh century. In A.D. 639, the Chinese pilgrim Hiuen-T'sang described Puspagiri in detail, stating that it was one of two Buddhist universities in Orissa. The ruins of sculptured portals and pagodas have been excavated and are in good condition.

Natural Beauties

Orissa's natural beauties are many, although few have the kind of Western accommodations that are available in Bhubaneswar and Puri. However, some of them are near areas with such accommodations and so can be visited in one day.

Near the West Bengal border is Chandipur, which has one of the best beaches in India. Here, the sea recedes five kilometers (three miles) each day at low tide. See it before it is unavailable for such casual visits. It's located in Balasore district and is in the middle of a raging controversy with the central government in New Delhi, which would like to set up a National Test Range for missiles, rockets, and pilotless target aircraft. The residents of Balasore have resisted the government's promises of relocation and compensation. This might not be an attractive locale for very long.

Simlipal Tiger Reserve in the center of Mayurbhanj, the northernmost district of Orissa, is breathtakingly beautiful. Aside from the wild animals (tigers, leopards, elephants, bison, and sambars) there are vast tracts of sal forest, cascading waterfalls, and lush grasslands. Popular with Bengalis and Biharis because it is near their borders, the reserve can be a busy place and one needs to book a stay here long in advance.

Ushakothi is another of Orissa's many wildlife sanctuaries. Located in the northwest corner of the state, it can be reached on National Highway 6 not too far from the huge Hirakud Dam.

Toshali Sands, between Puri and Konarak on Marine Drive, bills itself as Orissa's ethnic village resort. Its guests can enjoy the tranquil beauty of an almost deserted beach without having to be at the far reaches of civilization.

Chilika Lake, a huge lake on the coast south of Puri, is favored by many migratory birds and is a renowned sanctuary. However, check with local tourist officers about visiting the sanctuary. The practice shelling at the nearby military gunnery range drives birds away for weeks.

South of Chilika Lake is Gopalpur-on-Sea, a quiet seaside resort with good surf and sailing and a prewar quaintness. Like Toshali Sands, it offers a lovely beach without requiring that you forgo the creature comforts.

If your time is limited, Nandankanan Biological Park, near Bhubaneswar, is a lovely spot in which to see some of what the wilds of India have to offer. Wild animals found throughout India are kept here in their natural habitat. The park also boasts a botanical garden and a lake for boating.

Hot springs are located in various places throughout the state, but two can be visited in day trips. Taptapani, 64 kilometers (40 miles) from Gopalpur-on-Sea, is in a forest, and water from the spring is channeled into a nearby pond. Atri, a little over 40 kilometers (25 miles) from Bhubaneswar, has the additional attraction of the Temple of Lord Hatakeswar.

PRACTICAL INFORMATION FOR ORISSA

WHEN TO GO. The best time to visit Orissa is mid-September to April, when the weather is temperate. By mid-April, the temperature soars, reaching over 100 degrees at times. The monsoon generally arrives by June, and rain, tapering to periodic showers, can continue until September.

Note: When you prepare for your journey to Orissa, we recommend that you read Alistair Shearer's *The Traveler's Key to Northern India* (New York: Alfred A. Knopf, 1989), which contains two well-researched and illuminating chapters on Orissa's architectural history.

HOW TO GET THERE. By Air. *Indian Airlines* has daily flights to Bhubaneswar from Calcutta and Delhi. It has four weekly flights from Varanasi and five weekly flights from Bombay, Hyderabad, Madras, Nagpur, and Raipur. For Indian Airlines information in Bhubaneswar, call 400533.

By Train. The *Howrah-Puri Express, Jagannath Express,* and *Dhaulli Express* are first-class express trains that connect Bhubaneswar and Puri with Calcutta. The *Kalinga Utkal Express* and *Neelachal Express,* also first-class trains, connect Bhubaneswar and Puri with Delhi. In Bhubaneswar, contact the Bhubaneswar Railway Station, tel. 402233.

By Bus. A bus can get you to Orissa; but buses are normally crowded and often run nonstop video movies. Take the train.

By Rented Car with Driver. Good roads link Bhubaneswar with Calcutta, 480 km (298 mi.); and Visakhapatnam in Andhra Pradesh, 426 km (264 mi.). Hire a car from one of the tour operators listed below. Rates are about Rs. 4 per km, with a halt charge of Rs. 50–Rs. 100 per night.

TOURIST INFORMATION. For good brochures and information on accommodations, tours, and travel assistance, contact these agencies:

Department of Tourism, Government of Orissa, 5, Jayadev Marg, near Panthanivas, Bhubaneswar 751002; tel. 50099. Open 10 A.M.–5 P.M., closed Sundays and the second Saturday of each month. It also has a counter at the Bhubaneswar airport (tel. 404006) and at the railroad station (tel. 404715).

Orissa Tourist Offices are also located at these destinations:

Puri, Station Rd., tel. 3464. *Konarak,* Tourist Bungalow, tel. 221; Koraput, Koraput Club, tel. 2318; *Cuttack,* Arunodaya Market Bldg., Link Rd., tel. 23525. *Berhampur,* Station Rd., Berhampur, tel. 3226. *Rourkela,* U.G.I.E. Square, tel. 3923.

Orissa Tourism Development Corporation (OTDC), a government undertaking, conducts statewide tours, provides bookings in its OTDC accommodations, and rents cars with drivers. Its head office is at Panthanivas (Old Block), Lewis Rd., Bhubaneswar 751014; tel. 54727 for accommodations information and tel. 55515 for tours and car-rental information; fax 50477. The office is open daily, 8 A.M.–6 P.M. for tour bookings and car rentals; otherwise it follows the same working hours as the tourist office.

Government of India Tourist Office, B–21 Kalpana Area, Bhubaneswar 751014; tel. 54203. Open 10 A.M.–5 P.M., Monday–Friday. It also has a counter at the Bhubaneswar airport; no phone.

FOREIGN CURRENCY EXCHANGE. Most Western-style hotels have money-exchange counters. Otherwise, go to a branch of the *State Bank of India,* open Monday–Friday, 10 A.M.–2 P.M.; Saturdays till noon.

ACCOMMODATIONS. Good Western-style hotels in Cuttack, Puri, Gopalpur-on-Sea, and Bhubaneswar offer numerous amenities. In other areas, your best bet is to stay in one of the OTDC facilities listed below under Tourist Huts and Bungalows. Prices are based on double occupancy and exclude taxes and service charges:

Deluxe, over Rs. 2,000; *Expensive,* Rs. 1,200–Rs. 2,000; *Moderate,* Rs. 500–Rs. 1,200; *Inexpensive,* under Rs. 500. Most Western-style hotels take major credit cards.

BHUBANESWAR

Deluxe

The Oberoi. Nyapalli, Bhubaneswar 751013; tel. 56116, fax 56269. 70 rooms with bath. Bhubaneswar's majestic Lingaraj Temple was the model for this elegant luxury hotel. The lobby's lights are tucked inside huge brass temple bells. A balcony, guarded by carved temple lions, is mounted atop exquisite sandstone pillars. Air-conditioned rooms, overlooking either the pool or extensive landscaped gardens, have a modern decor and TV. Multicuisine restaurants, bar, room service, swimming pool, tennis court, business center, foreign-exchange and travel counter, baby-sitters, shops. AE, DC, MC, V.

Moderate

Hotel Kalinga Ashok. Gautam Nagar, Bhubaneswar 751014; tel. 53318. 64 rooms with bath. This modern hotel has spacious grounds and an inviting lobby with appealing Orissan touches, including a miniature replica of Puri's temple chariot tucked in the corner. Air-conditioned rooms have a simple Western-style decor and TV. Multicuisine restaurants, bar, room service, bank, foreign-exchange counter, shops. AE, DC, MC, V.

Hotel Prachi Bhubaneswar. 6 Janpath, Bhubaneswar 751001; tel. 52689. 48 rooms with bath. Its cheery lobby has a small shrine to Ganesh, the elephant-headed god, and Orissan touches. Air-conditioned rooms have a modest, modern decor and TV. Ask for a room overlooking the pool. Multicuisine restaurants, bar, room service, swimming pool, gardens, health club, foreign-exchange and travel counter, secretarial services, doctor, shops. AE, DC, MC, V.

Hotel Swosti. 103 Janpath, Bhubaneswar 751001; tel. 404178, fax 407524. 59 rooms with bath. A well-run Western-style hotel, the Swosti has a cozy lobby with Orissan *patta-chitra* (silk paintings). For maximum quiet, ask for a room in the back. All rooms are spacious and clean, with a contemporary decor, TV, and air-conditioning. Multicuisine restaurants, room service, bar, foreign-exchange and travel counter, business center, doctor, shop. AE, DC, MC, V.

The Kenilworth Bhubaneswar. 86/A–1 Gautam Nagar, Bhubaneswar 751014; tel. 54330. 72 rooms with bath. This Western-style high rise has an attractive lobby dominated by a large Orissan "lac" painting. Air-conditioned rooms are spacious, with a modern decor and TV. Best rooms overlook the pool. Room service, multicuisine restaurants, bar, small swimming pool, health club, foreign-exchange and travel counter, doctor, shops. AE, DC, MC, V.

CUTTACK

Inexpensive

Hotel Akbari Continental. Dolmundai, Haripur Rd., Cuttack 753001; tel. 25242. 45 rooms with bath. This Western-style high rise is Cuttack's best hotel. Its lobby has lots of marble, a water fountain, and sandstone pillars. Spacious, air-conditioned rooms are very clean, with a modest contemporary decor and TV. Best rooms overlook the back lawn. The service is excellent. Indian- and Chinese-cuisine restaurant, room service, bar, foreign-exchange counter, secretarial services, doctor. AE, DC, MC, V.

GOPALPUR-ON-SEA

Deluxe

Hotel Oberoi Palm Beach. Gopalpur-on-Sea, District Ganjam 761002; tel. 21. 20 rooms with bath. This one-story luxury 1920s bungalow has such an air of exclusivity that once you arrive, you won't want to leave. A sweeping veranda looks out on the beach and ocean. Tiered lawns lead down to the sand. Spacious rooms have a modern decor. Ask for a room with a good sea view. Indian and Continental restaurant, bar, room service, tennis court, yoga, foreign-exchange counter. AE, DC, MC, V.

PURI

Moderate

Hans Coco Palms. Swargadwar, Gourbarsahi, Puri 752001; tel. 2638, fax 0675/23165. 37 rooms with bath. This two-story hotel is on the beach at the edge of the city. Its lobby has an Orissan decor. Air-conditioned rooms, with balconies overlooking the sea, are spacious, with a modern decor. Room service, TV, multicuisine restaurant, bar, foreign-exchange and travel counter, doctor, shopping arcade. AE, DC, MC, V.

Hotel Nilachal Ashok. Adjoining Raj Bhavan, VIP Rd., Puri 752001; tel. 3639. Reservations can also be made through OTDC (see Tourist Information, above). 36 rooms with bath. This Western hotel, run by Ashok and OTDC, has lovely grounds and a spacious lobby, with interior wraparound verandas and a fountain surrounded by greens. It also has a good beach. But air-conditioned rooms, though spacious and clean, have an uninspired decor. Ask for an unobstructed beach view. TV, room service, Indian- and Continental-cuisine restaurant, bar, car-rental service, foreign-exchange counter, doctor. DC, MC, V.

Hotel South Eastern Railway Hotels. Puri 675256; tel. 2063. 35 rooms with bath. This former British bungalow, on the edge of Puri, overlooks the ocean. If you want an old-time ambience, stay here—the simple rooms in the newer wing are preferable. Sweeping verandas are ideal for relaxing. There's even a signboard reminding guests that quiet hours are 10 P.M.–6 A.M. and 2–4 P.M. A fixed-menu restaurant serves Indian dishes at lunch and Continental dishes at dinner. Room service, bar, billiards, library, beautiful grounds, beach, and travel agency. Meals included. Rupees only.

Toshali Sands. Konarak Marine Dr., Baliguali, Puri 752002; tel. 2888 (or, in Bhubaneswar, tel. 50074). 42 rooms with bath. This secluded resort is set on 12 beautifully landscaped acres and has an upscale Orissan village decor and ambience. Villas (also moderate in price) are best, with two spacious rooms. All rooms have cozy porches with terra-cotta sculptures. Modern interiors include Orissan handlooms and patta-chitra paintings. Air-conditioning, TV, room service, multicuisine restaurant, bar, doctor, foreign-exchange and travel counter, swimming pool, tennis court, health club, free transport to excellent beach, boating, bullock-cart rides, trekking, bicycling and fishing arrangements, cultural programs on request, shopping arcade. AE, DC, MC, V.

TOURIST HUTS AND BUNGALOWS. Throughout Orissa, OTDC has numerous bungalows, small hotels, and cottages that offer clean double or family rooms (with four beds), all of which have decent furnishings. Double rooms are under Rs. 300 (rupees only). To reserve a room, contact in advance the Divisional Manager (A & C), OTDC (see Tourist Information, above). For a double room, include one day's fee, Rs. 300, for each request.

Panthanivas Barkul-on-Chilika Lake. Balugaon, District Puri; tel. 240. 18 rooms with bath. Best rooms are air-conditioned. Restaurant, room service, bar, boating on Chilika Lake.

Panthanivas Chandipur. Chandipur, District Balasore 756001; tel. 2151. 10 rooms with bath. Best rooms are air-conditioned. Restaurant, room service, bar.

Panthanivas Tatapani. Tatapani, Gobindapur via Podamari, District Ganjam 761028; tel. 431. 5 rooms with bath. Best rooms are air-conditioned and have their own private sulfur baths. Restaurant, room service.

DINING OUT. In the major cities and resorts, you will find a variety of cuisines, with an emphasis on fresh seafood. Also try Orissan specialties, especially curries prepared with coconut milk and delicious eggplant and lady-finger vegetable dishes. Breakfast is usually 7:30–10:30; lunch, noon–3; dinner, 7–10. Payment is normally in rupees unless the restaurant is connected to a Western-style hotel. The restaurants listed below are informal and, unless noted, are open for all three meals and don't require reservations. Prices are based on one person eating a three-course meal, excluding taxes, tip, or beverage: *Moderate,* Rs. 100–Rs. 200; *Inexpensive,* under Rs. 100.

BHUBANESWAR

Moderate

Chandini. Oberoi Bhubaneswar, Nayapalli; tel. 56116. Its name means canopy, and in this elegant restaurant an antique chandini is suspended from the center of the ceiling, and paintings of Rajput heroes adorn the walls along with old daggers and mounted *gharokahs* (carved Indian bay windows). The cuisine is Indian and delicious, especially the *dahi machli* (fish cooked in creamy yogurt gravy) and *hari-machli* (fish marinated in spices and coriander, then fried). Reservations recommended. Open 7:30–11:30 P.M. AE, DC, MC, V.

Executive-Swosti. Hotel Swosti. 103 Janpath; tel. 404178. This cozy restaurant has a Japanese mural, mirrored pillars, upholstered chairs, and crisp table linen. The Indian cuisine is best, although the chef also prepares Continental and Chinese dishes. Try the delicious chicken butter masala (chicken cooked in spicy red gravy) or the exquisite tandoori prawns. For dessert, don't miss the fresh *kulfi* (Indian ice cream). Dinner reservations advised. Open 11 A.M.–3 P.M. and 7–11 P.M. AE, DC, MC, V.

Inexpensive

Hare Krishna Restaurant. Lalchand Market Complex; tel. 407186. This delightful upstairs restaurant has very subdued lighting; mirrored walls and ceiling; unobtrusive Hindi and Orissan taped music; and, best of all, a charming fountain in which Shiva is on top of Mount Kalash with the River Ganga flowing out of his hair. The cuisine is Indian or Chinese vegetarian and includes tasty "Keshaba's favorite" (vegetables sautéed in spicy tomato gravy) and "Makhan *chor* delight" (grated cheese and carrots simmered in a mild tomato gravy). Finish with *kheer* (sweet rice and milk pudding). Open 7:30 A.M.–10:30 P.M., with snacks served 3 P.M.–7 P.M. Rupees only.

CUTTACK

Moderate

Darvat. Hotel Akbari Continental, Dolmundai; tel. 25242. A visit to Cuttack should include a meal at this Indian and Chinese restaurant, one of Orissa's best. The decor is vaguely Mogul, with arches built into one wall, and Western, with lace curtains and chandeliers. At night there's often a *ghazal* singer. Favorite choices are the chicken 69 (marsala-coated chicken pieces cooked in a tandoor), chili chicken, and delicious Orissan specialties: navratan curry *korma* (mild curry made with cheese, vegetables, and cream), and *kalara* (unusual crispy-fried gourd with potatoes). Open 7–10 A.M., noon–3 P.M. and 7:30–11 P.M. AE, DC, MC, V.

PURI

Moderate

Phulpatna. Toshali Sands, Konarak Marine Dr.; tel. 2888. Phulpatna's walls and pillars are decorated with Orissan village designs, and the tablecloths are created from Orissan handlooms. The chef serves Chinese, Continental, and Indian cuisines, and, with a few hours' notice, Orissan specialties. Try the tandoori prawns, the Orissan *maccha* or *chingudi pattara poda* (fish or prawns wrapped in a banana leaf and roasted over charcoal), and ask for the special regional eggplant or *dahl* (lentils) dishes. Open 11:30 A.M.–3:30 P.M. and 7–11 P.M. AE, DC, MC, V.

Udichi Restaurant. Hans Coco Palms, Swargadwar, Gourbarsahi; tel. 2638. Here you'll find a good ocean view and Orissan decor—patta-chitra paintings and a colorfully decorated ceiling. You can choose from Chinese, Continental, and Indian dishes, including delicious regional favorites such as tasty fish curry or grilled fish along with fried *baigan* (eggplant) and exquisite *bhendi* (lady fingers). Open 7–10 A.M., noon–3 P.M., and 7:30–11 P.M. AE, DC, MC, V.

SWEETS AND TREATS. Bhubaneswar For good snacks and sweets, go to *Venus Inn* (217 Bapuji Nagar), a popular upstairs dining hall. The menu is an endless variety of *dosas* (Indian-style stuffed crepes) and *uttappams* (Indian-style pizzas). Sample the *rawa masala sada dosa* (slightly salty and sweet) or butter coconut uttappam, an Orissan specialty. For sweets, come early and have fresh *kassatta* (multiflavored ice cream mixed with cashew nuts). It's sold out by early afternoon. Open 6:30–11 A.M. and 3–9 P.M. for snacks.

HOW TO GET AROUND. From the Airport. Tourist taxis (white Ambassador cars) will take you to Bhubaneswar hotels for about Rs. 60–Rs. 100. The transfer from Bhubaneswar to Puri costs about Rs. 400–Rs. 500.

By Bus. Private buses travel to all parts of the state. They're inexpensive, but they do take time. For information, go the Central Bus Stand at Baramundar in Bhubaneswar on National Highway No. 5; tel. 400540.

By Rented Car with Driver. This is the best way to see Orissa. Here are some important distances from Bhubaneswar: Chilaka Lake, 130 km (81 mi.); Cuttack, 32 km (30 mi.); Konarak, 65 km (40 mi.); Puri, 62 km (38 mi.). Rates are about Rs. 4 per km, with a halt charge of Rs. 50–Rs. 100 per night. Hire a car from one of the agencies listed below under Tour Operators.

By Auto Rickshaw. Some auto rickshaws are available in larger cities; they should be cheaper than a tourist taxi. Fares are based on the destination. Set the fare in advance.

By Bicycle Rickshaw. The most leisurely way to travel, rickshaws are also the least expensive. Rates are determined by the destination. Bargain!

TOURS. OTDC (address above) conducts inexpensive tours by luxury bus.

Bhubaneswar Day Tour. 9 A.M.–5:30 P.M., Tuesday–Sunday. Departs from Panthanivas Tourist Bungalow. Rs. 55.

Bhubaneswar–Puri–Konarak Tour. 9 A.M.–6 P.M. daily. Departs from Panthanivas Tourist Bungalow. Rs. 70.

Sights Around Chandipur. 7 A.M.–1 P.M. daily. Departs from Chandipur Panthanivas. Rs. 48.

Puri–Chilika Lake. 6:30 A.M.–7 P.M. Monday, Wednesday, and Friday. Departs from Puri Panthabhavan. Rs. 80.

Puri–Konarak–Bhubaneswar Tour. 7 A.M.–7 P.M., Tuesday–Sunday. Departs from Puri Panthabhavan. Rs. 55.

Private Guides. The Government of India Tourist Office in Bhubaneswar (address above) provides good guides. For one–four people rates are about Rs. 80 for four hours; Rs. 100 for eight hours, not including lunch.

TOUR OPERATORS. The following agencies can take care of all your travel needs, including a hired car with driver:

Travel Wings, 14–C Janpath, Bapuji Nagar, Bhubaneswar 751009, tel. 400898. *Swosti Travels,* 103 Janpath, Bhubaneswar 751001; tel. 408738, fax 407524.

You can also rent a car with driver from OTDC (address above).

Swosti Travels (address above) and *Toshali Sands* (address under Puri in Accommodations, above) offer excellent tours and treks in Orissa that mainly concentrate on festivals, temples, tribal visits, handicrafts and textiles, and wildlife. Contact in advance.

SEASONAL EVENTS. Festivals in Orissa offer a good glimpse of this state's unique cultures and religious rituals. The specific dates for many events each year are determined by the lunar calendar; consult the Government of India Tourist Office for details.

January/February. *Magha Saptami.* Held at the Konarak Sun Temple, this event is Orissa's second-largest festival. Pilgrims from all over India take a sunrise ritual dip at the mouth of the Chandrabhaga River.

February/March. *Mahasivaratri.* Throughout Orissa, pilgrims flock to Shiva temples, especially the Lingara Temple in Bhubaneswar and Lord Loknath Temple in Puri, to honor Shiva. It's a joyous occasion, with intriguing rituals.

March/April. *Ashokastami.* During this car festival at Bhubaneswar, the image of Lord Lingaraj is taken from its inner sanctum in a mammoth chariot to the near-by Rameswar Shrine, then returns after four days. A big event.

Mid-April. *Chandan Yatra.* Honoring Lord Jagannath, this 21-day event features processions with devotees who carry images of deities to sacred tanks where they're rowed around in decorated boats. Especially colorful, with music and dances in Puri and Bhubaneswar.

May. *Snan Yatra.* In Puri, the images of Jagannath, Balabhadra, Subhadra, and Sudarsan are placed on a festive platform and given their annual ceremonial bath before they're put in seclusion for 15 days.

June. *Sitalsasthi.* This festival honors the marriage of Shiva and Parvati. A colorful wedding ceremony includes lavish processions with chariots carrying idols of the sacred couple. In Sambalpur, you can also see Odissi folk dances.

June/July. *Rath Yatra.* During Orissa's most sacred festival, Puri is crowded for seven days with celebrants. Lord Jagannath, Balabhadra (his brother), and Subhadra (his sister) are carried on spectacular chariots from their holy temple to Gundicha Mandira, another nearby shrine, to the Jagannath Temple in a similarly spectacular procession. At the end of these festivities the huge chariots are dismantled and their parts are sold to pilgrims. Because it is such a magnet for Hindu pilgrims, this festival is recommended if you want to experience the intensity of a particularly exhilarating, exhausting religious celebration.

November. *Konarak Dance Festival.* For five days, you can watch *Odissi* (classical Orissan dances) performed at the Sun Temple and attend a crafts fair during this wonderful event.

HISTORIC SITES. Entrance to most places is generally free; where a donation is requested, a few rupees will suffice. Although some of the Orissan temples, such as the Lingaraj Temple in Bhubaneswar and the Jagannath Temple in Puri, are closed to non-Hindus, others are accessible except for their inner sanctums. Signs indicating the restrictions are posted. Most sights are open sunrise to sunset.

BHUBANESWAR

The eleventh-century *Lingaraj Temple* is considered to be the ultimate in Orissan temple architecture. Closed to non-Hindus, its exterior carvings can be viewed from a raised platform on its periphery (bring binoculars and a few rupees as an "offering"). It is set in a huge walled-in compound that holds at least 70 smaller votive shrines. Like the great Jagannath Temple in Puri, the Lingaraj compound is a world in itself. Dating from about A.D. 1050, the Lingaraj Temple originally consisted only of the porch and shrine; the dancing hall and the hall of offering were added about a hundred years later. The curvilinear tower (*vimana*), built without mortar, rises to a height of 45 meters (147 feet). The tower is divided into vertical sections; at the top, just below the lineal spire, are figures of a lion crushing an elephant. The tower is hollow, and the top is reached by an interior staircase hewn out of walls that are two meters (seven feet) thick. The inner walls of the shrine, which have no adornment, house the *lingam* (phallic symbol) of Shiva. Outside, the sculpture is profuse, representing a high point of Hindu decorative art.

Near the Lingaraj Temple is one of Bhubaneswar's many sacred tanks (man-made ponds). The biggest of these tanks, *Bindusagar,* is surrounded by a stone embankment. Pilgrims believe that it is filled with water from every sacred stream and tank in India and can therefore wash away sins. It is said that 7,000 temples once stood on the shores of Bindusagar.

The eighth-century *Vaital Temple* near Bindusagar is one of the area's earlier temples. Unlike other temples in Bhubaneswar, its double-storied and barrel-shaped roof shows the influence of Buddhist rock architecture.

About one km (½ mi.) to the east of the northeast corner of the Lingaraj is "The Grove of the Perfect Being." In this mango grove are more than 20 temples, including the oldest surviving temple in the city, the *Parasurameswar;* the diminutive *Mukteswar,* considered the gem of Orissan architecture; the *Siddheswar;* and the

Kedareswar. The Parasurameswar was built in A.D. mid-600s and is decorated with sculpture that was executed with great vigor.

The *Mukteswar* (A.D. tenth century), called a "dream realized in sandstone" and the smallest temple in Bhubaneswar, bears very fine sculpture. An emaciated hermit teaching, a lady riding a rearing elephant, cobras darting their heads, and lions fighting are some of the themes represented. The most distinctive feature of the temple, its *torana* (arch gateway), shows the influence of Buddhist architecture and is intricately carved with peacocks and feminine figures in languorous positions.

Adjoining the Mukteswar is another of Bhubaneswar's many sacred tanks. Beyond it stands the *Kedareswar Temple,* with its eight-foot statue of Hanuman, the monkey god, and another of the goddess Durga standing on a lion. Northwest of the Mukteswar is the Siddheswar.

About one km (½ mi.) from the Lingaraj is the *Brahmeswar Temple* (A.D. eleventh century), built around the same time and sumptuously carved.

Standing by itself in green rice fields is the *Rajarani* (A.D. eleventh century), perhaps the most harmoniously proportioned temple in the city. So enchanting are its erotic sculptures that it has been suggested that it was built by some early Orissan king as a pleasure dome rather than as a temple.

AROUND BHUBANESWAR

Five km (three mi.) to the west of Bhubaneswar are the hills of Udayagiri and Khandagiri, with caves dating from the second century B.C. Used by Jain monks for meditation, many of the caves feature rough sculpture. In front of the *Hatigumpha Cave* is a Palli inscription of Kharavela, one of Orissa's early princes, which describes the events of his 13-year rule. The *Ranigumpha Cave* (Queen's Cave) and the *Ganesh Gumpha* are the most interesting. These three caves are located on Udayagiri, the hill to the right of the road. To the left is Khandagiri Hill and the *Ananta Cave,* with its veranda and decorated pilasters. From the top of this hill, you can look across the plains to Bhubaneswar and Dhauli.

DHAULI

In Dhauli, eight km (5 mi.) southeast of Bhubaneswar, Emperor Ashoka supposedly witnessed the carnage of the Kalinga War in 261 B.C. and resolved to put an end to such killing. His conversion to Buddhism, which began here, had profound effects on the propagation of Buddhism outside India. A huge elephant carved out of a large rock, representing the Buddha, Emperor Ashoka's "Rock Edicts" stating that all men are his children, a Hindu temple to Shiva, and the Buddhist Peace Pagoda are nearby. The elephant was built in the early 1970s by Japanese Buddhists.

KONARAK

Long ago, the thirteenth-century Sun Temple, built in the shape of the sun god's chariot and Orissa's most impressive temple, was even more spectacular than it is now. Today, only half the main temple and the audience hall approximate the Sun Temple's original shape. The original compound consisted of a dancing hall, an audience hall, and a tremendous tower that must have been 69 meters (227 feet) high if it conformed to traditional proportions of Indian temples. Part of the tower still existed as late as 1837, but it fell to ruin by 1869. Then the Audience Hall had to be filled with stone slabs and sealed off to prevent its collapse. The temple's location on sand, near the sea, which has since receded three kilometers (two miles) from the site, is majestic; but the salty air and the softness of the sand dunes have taken their toll.

The original architect, Sibai Santra, directed 1,200 workmen to lay the foundation of this temple, but the sand dunes on which it was being built did not provide him with much hope of success. Legend claims that when he failed in his attempts to raise the structure, he fell asleep on the nearby beach, crestfallen and dejected. When he awoke, an old woman offered him a plate of hot food. Seizing the plate, he dipped his fingers into the center of the steaming porridge and burned them. The woman chided him, saying, "My son, your manner of eating is like Sibai Santra's manner of building the temple. You must start from the edges and not in the center, as he throws stones into the middle." A wiser man, Sibai Santra started the construction again, and created his vision in stone.

The Sun Temple is constructed in the form of a huge chariot with 24 huge wheels pulled by seven straining horses. Every area of the temple is intricately carved with some of the most fantastic sculpture to be seen in India. Platforms, horses, colossal-sized elephants, pillars, and boundary walls of the main plinth are covered with mythical animals, whimsical depictions of daily life, war, trade, erotic sculptures of amorous dalliances—the panoply of a culture's finest instincts: its imagination, mythology, history, and knowledge of the life cycle. Each structural feature of the temple has a hidden meaning. The seven horses of the chariot represent the seven days of the week, the 24 wheels are the 24 fortnights of the Indian year, and the eight spokes of each wheel are the eight *pahars* into which the ancients divided day and night.

As was usual with temples of this period, both the spire, which was supported by the half-ruined structure (near the pagoda), and the audience hall, which remains, stood on a high plinth. Now that the hall has been blocked off, the entrance to the shrine is inaccessible. Three flights of steps lead up to it from the east, north, and south, and the main door on the west leads to the principal temple. The three-tiered roof, with space between each tier for closer inspection, is covered with elaborate carvings. The walls rise to about 14 meters (45 feet) before they begin to contract inward toward the flat ceiling.

To get a leisurely close-up look at the Sun Temple and its fabulous, intricate carvings, arrive between 7 and 8 A.M., before busloads of pilgrims and other tourists.

The Archaeological Survey of India provides a guide service, but be sure to ask the guide for an identification badge, since many less-informed free-lance guides are eager to take you around. At the entrance to the compound, vendors sell well-researched guidebooks to the Sun Temple and other Orissan monuments for a few rupees.

PURI

The Jagannath Temple, abode of Jagannath, lord of the universe and avatar of Krishna, is a majestic, tiered structure layered with carvings. Like the Lingaraj in Bhubaneswar, entry to the temple is prohibited to non-Hindus (so strictly is this rule enforced that former Prime Minister Indira Gandhi was refused admittance because she had married a Parsi and was thus outside the faith). You can view this imposing structure from the roof of the Raghunandan Library opposite the eastern gate of the temple. A few rupees' donation is expected. If the library is closed, the nearby Jaya Balia Lodge will let visitors climb to its roof. Binoculars are recommended. The temple, set in a compound surrounded by a wall, has the traditional porch and shrine, surmounted by a conical tower. The hall of offerings and the pillared hall of dance were added several centuries after the original temple was built in about 1030. As in Bhubaneswar, the compound is filled with smaller votive shrines.

Lord Jagannath's abode is a land of superlatives. Devotees lavish this holy city of Hinduism with their offerings: the temple kitchen, reportedly the largest kitchen in the world, feeds Mahaprasad, its unique steamed cuisine, to over 10,000 people daily. During festival times, this number multiplies to 25,000.

RATNAGIRI-LALITAGIRI

At Ratnagiri-Lalitagiri, the seat of Puspagiri, the A.D. seventh-century Buddhist University, excavations are gradually revealing a magnificent sight. Stupas, monasteries, and stone sculptures are in excellent condition.

MUSEUMS AND GALLERIES. Bhubaneswar. The *Orissa State Museum* has palm-leaf manuscripts and a few sculptures from temple ruins. Open 10 A.M.–noon and 2 P.M.–5 P.M., closed Mondays. The *Tribal Museum of Man* (Harijan & Tribal Research Institute) has ornaments, weapons, and dresses of Orissa's many tribes. Open 10 A.M.–5 P.M., closed Sundays.

Konarak. The *Archaeological Museum* (near the temple) features sculptures from the temple. Open 10 A.M.–5 P.M., closed Fridays.

SPORTS AND OUTDOOR ADVENTURES. Beaches. *Gopalpur-on-Sea,* an enchanting seaside resort, is located 13 km (eight mi.) from Berhampur. If you want seclusion, this is a quiet spot in which to spend a beach vacation.

Toshali Sands, located on Marine Drive between Konarak and Puri, is not on the beach, but guests at this resort have access to a nearly deserted beach a short distance away. Hotel shuttles provide transportation between the hotel and the beach.

Puri Beaches. The beach in the heart of Puri doesn't offer seclusion, but head to the edges of the city and you'll find good sand and surf.

Hot Springs. Atri. A holy place 42 km (26 mi.) from Bhubaneswar, this lovely hot spring is near the Temple of Hatakeswar.

Taptapani. 50 km (31 mi.) from Berhampur and a convenient excursion from Gopalpur-on-Sea, this hot sulfur spring is in a forest. The nearby panthanivas (travelers' lodge) has hot sulfur baths in two rooms.

Trekking. Tour operators (see above) now offer treks to Koraput, Orissa's intriguing tribal area. These operators will help you get the necessary permit to visit this area. If you plan to trek on your own, contact the tourist office in Koraput. Certain villages are off-limits. Tour operators also offer textile and handicraft-theme treks that take you through idyllic villages to the homes of artisans.

Wildlife Sanctuaries. Nandankanan. This lovely zoological park, situated in the Chandaka Forest 19 kilometers (12 miles) from Bhubaneswar, is highly recommended for wildlife enthusiasts on a tight schedule. Tigers, including the rare white tiger; lions; panthers; leopards; pelicans; peafowl; pythons; and gharial crocodiles are on exhibit in a biological park. Across the lake from this habitat park is a botanical garden. OTDC has a tour from Bhubaneswar that includes a visit to Nandankanan.

Simlipal. In the hilly Mayurbhanj district in northern Orissa is the less accessible Simlipal Forest. Here, you find the Simlipal National Park, also designated a Tiger Reserve, covering 2,750 sq. km (1,700 sq. mi.). Its valleys, gorges, waterfalls, vast grasslands, rivers and streams, and thickly wooded slopes, with their abundance of sal trees and orchids provide an excellent refuge for tigers. Tigers, elephants, Indian wolves, leopards, sambar and deer, hill mynas, peafowl, parakeets, and a variety of snakes all make their home here. Jeeps are necessary within the park and should be arranged for through the field director. You need permission to visit this park. Contact the Field Director, Simlipal Tiger Project, Baripada, District Mayurbhanj 757001, or the District Forest Office (also at Baripada). These offices can also arrange for a jeep and accommodations in forest rest houses. You can also stay just outside the park in an Orissa Tourist Department forest lodge. Reserve in advance (include an Rs. 150 deposit per night) through the Tourist Officer, Government of Orissa Tourist Office, Baripada, District Mayurbhang 757001; tel. 2710.

Chilika Lake. On the coast between Bhubaneswar and Gopalpur-on-Sea, Chilika Lake spreads over 1,100 sq. km (680 sq. mi.), making it the largest inland lake in India. Its brackish water, dotted with islands bearing such whimsical names as Honeymoon and Breakfast islands, is rich with marine life, and from November to March it is the temporary home of migrating birds—ducks, pelicans, golden plovers, cormorants, flamingoes, ospreys, and other birds from as far away as Siberia. Motorboats and kayaks are available through the OTDC at Barkul.

SHOPPING. Shopping can mean great side trips into the beautiful hidden Orissan villages that are home to master craftsmen. Visit Raghurajpur, about 12 km (7 mi.) from Puri on the way to Bhubaneswar. It's an idyllic village set back from the main road, with every dwelling owned by an artisan who creates stone and wood carvings, *patta-chitra* (finely wrought temple paintings), and *talapatra* (palm-leaf art). Expect to pay in rupees.

Pipli. This village, 16 km (10 mi.) southeast of Bhubaneswar, has stalls lining the street that are filled with gaily colored appliqué work. You name it, they make it—even great beach umbrellas. Also visit nearby homes where women create these products. Rupees only.

Bhubaneswar. In old Bhubaneswar, Sri Satya Badi Moharana, a renowned artisan, creates lovely stone carvings at reasonable prices (Bibhisena Colony, Lingaraj Rd.). Padmashree Raghunath Mohapatra (Sashanapada area of the old town) is another award-winning stone carver. His home, with a temple, is open for visits

8 A.M.–8 P.M. daily. Both craftsmen accept rupees only. To see other artisans in Bhubaneswar, contact the Orissa Tourist Office.

Sudarshan Arts and Crafts Village (CB–5 Nayapally, near Oberoi) sells beautiful stone carvings. Open daily 6 A.M.–noon and 2 P.M.–6 P.M. MC, V.

Odissika (265 Lewis Rd.) sells all of Orissa's handicrafts, including tribal products. Open daily 9:30 A.M.–1:30 P.M. and 2:30 P.M.–8:30 P.M. Rupees only.

Utkalika (Orissa State Handicrafts Emporium, Eastern Tower Market Building) sells great handicrafts. Open 9:30 A.M.–1 P.M. and 4–8:30 P.M., closed Sundays. V.

Orissan State Handloom W. C. S. Ltd. (Western Tower Market Bldg.) has good fabrics. Open 9 A.M.–12:30 P.M. and 4–8:30 P.M., closed Sundays.

Puri. *Utkalika* (Mahodadhi Market) is open 9 A.M.–1 P.M. and 5–9 P.M., closed Sundays. *Arts and Crafts Complex* (same market) is open 9 A.M.–12:30 P.M. and 4–8:30 P.M., closed Sundays. Government-run, fixed-price shops, they sell Orissan handicrafts and fabrics.

Sudarshan Crafts Museum (Station Rd.) sells beautiful stone carvings. Open daily 6:30 A.M.–noon and 2–8 P.M. MC, V.

Cuttack. This city is famous for its filigree jewelry. *Parekh Bros.* (Naya Sarak) has work in silver. Open 9:30 A.M.–8:30 P.M., closed Sundays. Rupees only. *Madhavji Jewellers* (Naya Sarak) has work in gold. Open 10 A.M.–1 P.M. and 3–8 P.M., closed Sundays. Rupees only.

ENTERTAINMENT AND NIGHTLIFE. *Odissi,* the classical dance form of Orissa, is perhaps the most lyrical Indian dance, with graceful gestures and postures. When you see a performance, it's as if the sculpted dancers on the Sun Temple at Konarak had suddenly come to life. In addition to classical Odissi dance, folk and tribal dances are still performed during festivals throughout Orissa. To find out about ongoing dance performances in Bhubaneswar, contact the Orissa Tourist Office or the College of Dance, Drama, and Music near Rabindra Mandap.

For a nightcap in Orissa, the best bar is at the Oberoi Hotel. Bars are generally open 11 A.M.–3 P.M. and 6:30–11 P.M.

ASSAM, MEGHALAYA, AND THE NORTHEAST STATES

Foothills of the Himalayas

by
LISA SAMSON and AMIT SHAH

Note: Due to continuing tensions and disturbances in Assam, the U.S. State Department advises deferring travel to this state.

The northeast states of Arunachal Pradesh, Assam, Manipur, Meghalaya, Mizoram, Nagaland, and Tripura are lush green and culturally rich areas of this diverse country. However, they have been troubled areas of India for many years, an Achilles' heel of sorts to the central government. Connected to the rest of the subcontinent by a narrow corridor of land, encompassing foothills of the Himalayas, marshy grasslands, and wild mountainous areas, these seven states are home to many of India's tribal peoples and the site of one of its ancient Hindu states.

Almost engulfed by Burma, Bangladesh, and China, the seven states have been all but inaccessible to foreign travelers for years. Political strife in the northeast, fueled by long-simmering internal disagreements or resulting from pressures brought about by conflicts in Bangladesh that overflow into India, erupt periodically into open conflict between disputing internal factions or against the central government.

As a result, regulations for access to these areas change frequently, making travel in this area somewhat of a gamble. At press time, only Assam,

512

Meghalaya, Arunachal Pradesh, and Manipur were open to foreign travel and all foreigners must obtain a Restricted Area Permit (see *Facts at Your Fingertips* and Practical Information, below). Before planning any trip to Assam, travelers should also check with the proper government agency in their home country (the State Department in the United States) to see if travel to this state is advised.

EXPLORING ASSAM

Through Assam winds the magnificent Brahmaputra River, its name meaning "son of Brahma," lord of the universe. It's an apt name. It provides life-nourishing water to irrigate the rich alluvial plain through which it runs as well as creating devastation during the monsoons, when rains have raised its crest to over 12 meters (40 feet) above its natural level. The river traverses east to west and makes Assam one of the most fertile areas of India. Rice grows in abundance here, but it is for tea that Assam is better known. Tea plantations abound in Assam, the low-lying green foliage of the tea plants dwarfed by the tall shade trees above them. At harvesttime, women with woven baskets strapped to their heads move slowly through the tea plants, picking the tender leaves, all the while seeming to swim through a waist-high sea of green. Tea grew wild in this area for centuries; the first organized tea estates were established by the British in the 1800s. Almost 800 such estates now blanket the hillsides of Assam, producing about 50 percent of India's tea.

Assam is not just a picture-postcard state continuing traditions of the raj, however. Rich oil fields were discovered in the area surrounding Digboi, where the first oil refinery in Asia was built and 50 percent of India's crude oil is now produced.

A Bit of History

Assam's ancient history, which is not well documented, is largely discussed in terms of the plains people, not the numerous tribes who populated the surrounding hills. In the thirteenth century, the Ahoms of Burma gained power in Upper Assam, gradually conquering the lands once ruled by the Kacharis. Moslem invaders in the 1500s were defeated by the Ahoms, but, in the 1600s, Lower Assam was ceded to Aurangzeb, the great Mogul emperor. A constant location of conflict, Assam came under the control of the East India Company in 1826 and remained under British control in one administrative guise or another until 1947. Since independence, conflict has continued. What was once Assam and the North East Frontier Agency (NEFA of Assam) has been restructured, creating the states of Nagaland (in 1963), Meghalaya (in 1972), and Mizoram (in 1987) from parts of Assam and Arunachal Pradesh (in 1987) from the NEFA.

Guwahati

Guwahati, the traditional capital of Assam (Dispur, part of Guwahati, is now the temporary capital), was called "Light of the East" and "City of Astrology." It sits on the southern bank of the Brahmaputra and is one of the few locations that is accessible to foreign travelers. Various religious and scholarly centers are found nearby. Hajo, 24 kilometers (15 miles) away, attracts Buddhists and Hindus, who come to worship the remains of the Buddha at the Hayagriba Madhab Temple, and Moslems who come to worship at the Pir Giyasuddin Aulia, believed to be one-quarter as holy as the great mosque in Mecca. Within Guwahati, the Nabagraha Shrine, with its inner sanctum a reflection of the solar system, was once a center of astrology and astronomy.

Guwahati's most famous shrine, however, is the tantric Kamakhya Temple, dedicated to the Hindu goddess Sati (also known as Kali or Shakti). Legend claims that after Sati's father insulted Shiva, her consort, Sati was so humiliated that she threw herself on a funeral pyre. Shiva took her body and circled the world, causing so much destruction that Vishnu, the Hindu god of creation, trailed after him and slowly hacked Sati's body into 51 pieces, which fell all over the Indian subcontinent. Her *yoni* (vagina), considered the source of all creation, fell on Nalachal Hill, which is said to represent Shiva's lingam. Kamakhya Temple commemorates their union. In time, Sati reappeared in a new manifestation, Parvati, who became Shiva's new consort.

The temple complex you see today—an assortment of beehive-shaped shrines commemorating the various manifestations of the Mother Goddess—represents renovations and remaining bits of temples first constructed in the thirteenth century by the Ahom dynasty. After it was destroyed by Moslems, a king of neighboring Cooch-Bihar restored the complex.

Long ago, kings sacrificed humans at this tantric temple. When this practice was banned, Kali, another manifestation of the Mother Goddess, had to make do with a goat, representing lust, or buffalo—bestial passion. Tantrics believe that the act of sacrifice destroys their own base instincts and also gives the sacrificed animal an opportunity for rebirth at a higher station.

Though non-Hindus are not permitted into the main shrine with its revered yoni, they can witness the purifications and sacrifices performed in the extensive complex. A door to the left of an old pavilion leads into the temple; a set of stairs descends to the sacred cave. The hallowed stone yoni, which is always dressed (covered with a cloth), is under a gold canopy inside the cave. Not even the special class of people allowed to clean the temple and purify the yoni set their eyes on the stone; they perform their tasks blindfolded.

Once you've circled the main complex, drive to the Bhubaneswari Devi Temple on a nearby foothill. Here, the Goddess Bhubaneswari, yet another manifestation of the Mother Goddess, is represented by a red slab of rock located under a canopy in a sunken dark chamber. Hindus say that the rock represents the abdomen of the goddess and, to protect her modesty, it's purposely difficult to see.

Manas and Kaziranga Wildlife Sanctuaries

What most attracts people to Assam, however, are the two great wildlife sanctuaries near Guwahati—Kaziranga and Manas. Swaying on top of an elephant, you can traverse the grasslands of these two splendid parks in the hopes of seeing some of the area's rare wildlife. Kaziranga, bounded by the Brahmaputra River and the Mikir Hills, is best known as the home of the largest population of Indian one-horned rhinoceroses. These massive beasts were mistaken for the legendary unicorns by Marco Polo, who proclaimed them "hideous." On the verge of extinction in the early 1900s, the rhinoceros population has increased steadily since 1908, when this sanctuary was set aside for them as a forest reserve. Not known for being sweet-tempered, the powerful rhinoceros creates vibrations in its wanderings that are an ample warning that it is not to be taken lightly. The elephants you ride through the parks, well acquainted with the moody rhinoceros, keep a respectful distance. Kaziranga also has wild elephants and water buffaloes—another impressive animal—sambar, swamp deer, bears, and a great variety of birds.

Manas Wildlife Sanctuary, a beautiful spot, watered by many rivers and streams, is an excellent place for those who are interested in fishing. Considered to be among the loveliest of India's wildlife sanctuaries, it was set up in 1928 as an original tiger reserve and is part of "Project Tiger." Sharing the riverine sanctuary with the tiger are one-horned rhinoceroses, wild buffaloes, sambar, and the unusual pygmy hogs and hispid hares. Manas has a great variety of birds; spectacular daily flights of great pied hornbill wing across the Manas River into neighboring Bhutan.

EXPLORING MEGHALAYA

India's decision at independence to keep foreigners out of Meghalaya was rooted in a bit of unfortunate history. To subdue headhunting tribals who lived within the hills, the British, during their rule, had divvied up this area among missionaries of various Christian faiths. While their choice of weapon—the Bible—did lead to pacification and, no doubt, saved a few heads, it also contributed to the destruction of the indigenous cultures.

Today, the Western missionaries are gone, but native itinerant preachers continue to spread the Word to non-Christian Meghalayans; and Meghalaya—part of India's "Bible Belt"—remains at a precarious crossroads, with traditional culture still facing extinction. In no other Indian state currently open to foreigners do travelers cross such cultural extremes. There's the capital, Shillong, very Western, with Western music, Western clothes, and Western problems like drugs and divorce. Travel one day to the east and you're in remote hill country, where many of the people have never seen foreigners, where *borangs* (tree houses) jut above the fields, where women, isolated in their villages, are apt to be bare breasted. The only statewide common symbol is the Christian cross. The British chose a powerful weapon.

Meghalaya has three racially distinct hill tribes, all of them matrilineal societies: the Khasis, who live primarily in the central Khasi Hills and trace their ancestry back to the Mon-Khmer of Cambodia; the Jaintias, also of Mon-Khmer descent, who live in the western Jaintia Hills; and the Garos of Tibeto-Burmese-stock who migrated from Tibet to the Garo Hills. All three show greater physical affinity with their original ancestry than with the rest of India.

Throughout the state, educated tribal women hold important positions in the government and business community. Bara Bazaar, the popular tribal market in Shillong, is run mainly by women. Though many marriages are still arranged, dowries don't exist; and the husband, not the wife, moves in with his spouse's family—which sets Meghalaya apart from Hindu and Moslem India.

Shillong

Set on a series of rolling hills, Shillong, the capital, is unlike any other Indian hill station. You won't find the traditional pedestrian mall on an upper ridge; you won't see billboards promoting the ideal honeymoon retreat. Instead, you will see evidence of Christianity: More pictures of Jesus than of Shiva are placed in homes and shops; church spires are everywhere.

Walk through Bara Bazaar, a produce market predominantly run by tribal women. Then get away from the bustle and explore the quiet, well-kept grounds of the Botanical Garden, or go boating on the adjacent Wards Lake.

Cherrapunjee

Cherrapunjee, 55 kilometers (34 miles) south of Shillong, is the wettest place on earth. Every year almost 450 inches of rain are dumped on this region. It is also an area studded with caves and beautiful waterfalls. The Nohkailikai Falls, the fourth-highest in the world, are near the village of Serrarim, about five kilometers (three miles) from Cherrapunjee. The falls, which plummet into an aquamarine pool, are named after Ka Likai, whose husband, a jealous stepfather, cooked her child and served it to her as an unnamed delicacy. Ka Likai soon discovered the child's fingers, which her husband had hidden in a basket of betel nut. She then leaped over the falls that now bear her name.

Garo Hills

Any visit to Meghalaya should include a trip east to the Garo tribal villages set in the Garo Hills. Not to be missed is the William Nagar Forest Reserve, about 220 kilometers (136 miles) from Shillong. This is the stomping ground of wild elephants and, with the Simsang River meandering through its borders, an angler's treat. Here you can also arrange to visit a typical Garo village—a work of art made of bamboo.

Usually the entrance to a Garo village is through a grove of jackfruit trees, which produce an important food staple. In the compound, even chickens have their own miniature bamboo homes—coops complete with ladders for easy access. Pigs are kept in tidy bamboo pens. The *nokpante* (thatch-covered pavilion), crowded with men who live here from age 12 until they marry, is in the central courtyard; and, in a nearby field, stands the village *borang* (bamboo watchtower), from which villagers watch for animals, wild or domesticated, that may wander into precious crops.

From the William Nagar Forest Reserve, you can also continue on to Tura, the district headquarters of the West Garo Hills, about 70 kilometers (43 miles) away. If it's Monday, plan to stop at Chinabat village, about 14 kilometers (eight miles) from the forest reserve, and walk through the festive weekly market. On Fridays, stop in Rongrem, closer to Tura. In these temporary bazaars you'll see Rajastanis, Punjabis, and northeastern tribal peoples selling everything from locally grown tobacco to exotic medicinal potions. You'll also get a good introduction to the Garo's fascinating culture.

Balpakram National Park

The Balpakram National Park, straddling the Bangladesh border, features prominently in Garo mythology as the land of their dead. Inaugurated in 1987, the park sits on a high plateau of thick jungle and forest—threaded with rivers feeding into small lakes—and is surrounded by a vast canyon. Here, you may see wild buffalo, bears, leopards, tigers, wild elephants, plus a large number of migrating birds: hornbills, peacocks, and Siberian ducks.

One last attraction is the nearby Siju Cave, on the bank of the Simsang River. This is one of the biggest caves in Meghalaya; and its interior, filled with stalactites, stalagmites, and bats, awaits thorough exploration.

PRACTICAL INFORMATION FOR
ASSAM AND MEGAHALAYA

WHEN TO GO. Assam. The best time to visit is September–June. The monsoon rages in the summer months. The best time to see animals in Manas Tiger Reserve is January–April; in Kaziranga National Sanctuary, from November–March. You can also plan a vacation around the Rongali Festival in April and Durga Puja in October.

Meghalaya. October–April is the best time to visit. There are torrential rains the rest of the year. In November, the Garo tribal people put on two of India's best festivals: Ka Pamblang Nongkrem and Wangala (for more information, see Seasonal Events, below).

RESTRICTED AREA PERMIT. To visit Assam and Meghalaya, you must have a Restricted Area Permit (see Travel Documents in *Facts at Your Fingertips*).

Assam. When you fill out the permit for Assam, list Guwahati and the two game parks (Manas and Kaziranga). As of this writing, the tourist department was trying to open up the cities of Sibsagar and Tezpur. Trip length is currently limited to a week for each destination; this is also under review. Ask the Government of India Tourist Bureau for the latest information. Travelers can also visit Assam as part of a tour group. (See Tour Operators, below. Also check the listings in *Facts at Your Fingertips*.)

Meghalaya. Ten-day trip permits are available for groups of four or more to Meghalaya. Individuals, however, should contact the Government of India Tourist Office in their home country to see if restrictions for individuals have been relaxed. You must plan your trip months in advance since it often takes 12 to 16 weeks to obtain the necessary clearance. Follow the procedure outlined in *Facts at Your Fingertips*. If you are told to designate specific destinations, list Shillong, Cherapungee, Tura in the Garo Hills, Jowai in the Jaintia Hills, and Nongstoin in the West Khasi Hills. For agencies that offer tours to Meghalaya, see Tour Operators, below. Also refer to the recommended listings in *Facts at Your Fingertips*. If your trip plans are flexible or geared to a major festival, chances are you'll get in. Your tour operator will also help you procure the obligatory Restricted Area Permit.

HOW TO GET THERE. Since the distances to Assam and Meghalaya are great, only air travel is recommended. To travel between the two states, you have many options. The distance from Guwahati to Shillong is about 103 km (64 mi.).

ASSAM

By Air. *Indian Airlines* has daily flights connecting New Delhi, Calcutta, and Bagdogra with Guwahati in Assam. Jorhat, the town nearest to the Kaziranga Wildlife Sanctuary, is connected by Indian Airlines to Calcutta and Guwahati. Guwahati is also connected to Imphal, the capital of Manipur. *Vayudoot* has two weekly flights from Calcutta to Guwahati.

For all flights, foreigners must show their permit to airport police on arrival and departure. For Indian Airlines information, call 231281 in Guwahati. For Vayudoot information, call 33194 or 82272 in Guwahati.

By Bus. Private and state-run deluxe buses make the trip to Shillong in about four hours. In Guwahati, contact *Assam State Transport Corporation* (ASTC) through the Assam Tourist Department, tel. 27102 or 24475. *Meghalaya Transport Road Service* (MTRC), Guwahati Airport; *Blue Hill Travels,* Brahmaputra Ashok

Hotel, tel. 41064, and Paltan Bazaar, tel. 31427; *Assam Valley Tours and Travels,* Paltan Bazaar, tel. 26133.

By Rented Car with Driver. You can hire a car from the Assam Tourist Department in Guwahati, Station Rd., tel. 27102. Rates are about Rs. 5 per km, with a halt charge of Rs. 50 per night. *Blue Hill Travels* in the Ashok Hotel also rents cars for about Rs. 6 per km, plus a halt charge of Rs. 100 per night.

MEGHALAYA

By Air. *Vayudoot* has four weekly flights from Umroi Airport near Shillong that connect Shillong and Calcutta. Otherwise, the closest airport is in Guwahati, Assam (see above). For Vayudoot information, call 26222 in Shillong.

By Bus. For trips from Shillong to Guwahati, contact *MRTC,* Jail Rd., Police Bazar, tel. 23206; or *Blue Hill Travels,* tel. 31427. MRTC can also make reservations for ASTC, Blue Hill Travels, and Assam Valley Tours and Travels.

By Taxi or Rented Car with Driver. Hire a car with driver from *Sheba Travels,* Police Bazar Point, Shillong 793001, tel. 23015 or 25020; The cost to Guwahati is about Rs. 600.

TOURIST INFORMATION. Assam. Contact the *Assam Directorate of Tourism,* Station Rd., Guwahati 781001 tel. 27102 or 24475; open Monday–Saturday, 10 A.M.–5 P.M., closed Sunday and second and fourth Saturdays of the month. It also has counters at the airport and railroad station, plus branch offices in important destinations.

Meghalaya. Contact the *Tourist Information Center,* MTC Bldg., Police Bazaar, Shillong 793001, tel. 26054. It's open March–October, Monday–Friday 10 A.M.–5 P.M.; otherwise Monday–Saturday, 10 A.M.–4 P.M. It's always closed Sunday and the second and fourth Saturdays of each month. The *Government of India Tourist Office* G. S. Rd., Police Bazar, Shillong 793001, tel. 25632. It's open Monday–Friday, 9:30 A.M.–5:30 P.M. and Saturday 9:30 A.M.–1 P.M., closed Sunday. The Meghalaya Tourist Department also has an office in Tura, Garo Hills, tel. 568.

FOREIGN CURRENCY EXCHANGE. Most Western-style hotels have money-exchange counters. Otherwise, go to a branch of the *State Bank of India,* open Monday–Friday 10 A.M.–2 P.M.; Saturdays till noon.

Assam. In Guwahati, the State Bank of India is on M. G. Rd. and *Grindlays Bank* is in Pan Bazar.

Meghalaya. In Shillong, the State Bank of India is on M. G. Rd. The Evening Branch State Bank of India (G. S. Rd.) is open Monday–Friday, 2 P.M.–6 P.M.; Saturday, 10 A.M.–noon.

ACCOMMODATIONS. Once you leave Guwahati and Shillong, you'll find limited accommodations and simple rooms. Prices are based on double occupancy and exclude taxes and service charges: *Moderate,* Rs. 500–Rs. 1,200; *Inexpensive,* under Rs. 500. Some Western-style hotels take traveler's checks and major credit cards.

ASSAM

Guwahati

Moderate

The Dynasty. Rahman Bldg., S. S. Rd., Guwahati 781001, tel. 40849 and 24353. 68 rooms with bath. Guwahati's newest hotel is centrally located in the middle of Fancy Bazaar, yet it's quiet once you step inside the marble lobby. Rooms are modern, with the accent on the West, not Assam. Ask for a city view with the Brahmaputra in the distance. Air-conditioning, TV, room service, restaurants, bar, foreign-exchange and travel counter, doctor. AE, DC, MC, V.

Hotel Brahmaputra Ashok. M. G. Rd., Guwahati 781001; tel. 41064 or 41065. 50 rooms with bath. Guwahati's stylish new hotel is on the Brahmaputra River near the center of town. Rooms are centrally air-conditioned and spacious, with contemporary Assamese touches and TV. The best rooms have a river view. Multicuisine restaurant, room service, bar, foreign-exchange and travel counter, house doctor. AE, DC, MC, V.

Inexpensive

Hotel Belle Vue. M. G. Rd., near Raj Bhavan, Box. 75, Guwahati 781001; tel. 40847. 45 rooms with bath. Guwahati's oldest hotel is away from the bustle on a hill overlooking the Brahmaputra River. The interior has a touch of whimsy: an elevator painted with a blue sky and clouds. Unfortunately, the rooms don't carry over the same flair: They're ordinary in decor. But all are carpeted, clean, and offer air-conditioning and TV, which make the hotel a good value. Corner rooms provide the best river views. Multicuisine restaurant, room service, house doctor, car rental, bar, foreign-exchange counter. AE, DC, MC, V.

Kaziranga

Moderate

Wild Grass. Reservations: Manju Barua, W. G. Resorts (Assam), Barua Bhavan, 107 M. C. Rd., Uzanbazar, Guwahati 781001, tel. 26827 or at the resort, tel. 437. 9 rooms with bath. At this new resort on the park's edge, you stay in a traditional Assamese bungalow with lovely lounges, verandas, and spacious, rustically decorated bedrooms. The best rooms overlook a stream that flows into the park. A lush jungle surrounds the grounds. The dining hall in a second bungalow serves Assamese cuisine. Swimming pool, wildlife safaris, tribal visits, boat cruises, fishing, restricted area permit and airport pickup arrangements, foreign-exchange counter. Discount May–October 15. AE.

Inexpensive

For reservations in the following three lodges at the Mihimukh entrance, contact the Deputy Director Tourism, Kaziranga National Park, P.O. Kaziranga Sanctuary, District Jorhat 785109; tel. 23 or 29. Apply at least two months in advance. Rupees only.

Kaziranga Forest Lodge. 24 rooms with bath. A concrete monolith on the edge of the jungle, this Western-style hotel doesn't fit into its environment. But the rooms are clean, adequately furnished, and have balconies. Multicuisine restaurant, bar, shop. Discount rates when park is closed.

Tourist Lodge No. 1. 5 rooms with bath. This attractive Assamese-style bungalow has cozy, simply furnished rooms with mosquito netting and fans. Upstairs rooms open onto a veranda. There is a dining room serving Indian and Continental food.

Tourist Lodge No. 2. 8 rooms with bath and a dormitory with shared bath. The rooms in this Assamese bungalow with a front veranda are plainly furnished. The beds are clean and have mosquito netting and fans.

Manas

For reservations, contact Reservation Authority, Field Director, Project Tiger, Barpeta Rd., Assam 781315; tel. 153 or 19. Reserve your room at least two months in advance. There are no restaurants in Manas: You must bring your own food and beverages. The caretaker at each lodge will cook your food for you for a small fee. Rupees only.

Inexpensive

Upper Bungalow. 7 rooms with baths. This lodge, on a hill overlooking the river, is typically Assamese and offers the best location. The rooms are spacious and have simple furnishings and overhead fans. The upper rooms open onto a veranda with great views.

Lower Bungalow. 2 rooms with bath. You can hear the river from this Assamese-style bungalow. The rooms are spacious and comfortable but have minimal furnishings and no overhead fan. There's a private front porch.

Cottages. 3 cottages with nearby shared bath. The cottages are near the lower bungalow. The rooms are small and sparse, but the linen is clean.

MEGHALAYA

Shillong

Moderate

Hotel Pinewood Ashok. European Ward, Shillong 793001; tel. 23116. 40 rooms with bath. On a hill above the center of Shillong, this is a charming 100-year-old bamboo-and-wood bungalow with cottages. The rooms are carpeted and comfortable and have fireplaces. The best ones open onto a veranda. Cottages, divided into suites, are less well appointed yet nicely located on the extensive grounds. TV, house doctor, room service, bar, coffee shop, multicuisine restaurant, billiard room. AE, DC, MC, V.

Hotel Polo Towers. Oakland Rd., Shillong 793001, tel. 22863, fax 23837. 58 rooms with bath. This new hotel, overlooking the golf course, has a fountain inside its marble lobby, and Western-style rooms. Air-conditioning, TV, room service, multicuisine restaurants, bar, foreign-exchange and travel counter, doctor. AE, DC, MC, V.

Thadlaskein Lake

Inexpensive

Orchid Inn. Thadlaskein Lake. Reservations: Director of Tourism, MTC Bldg., Police Bazar, Shillong 793001; tel. 26054. 6 rooms with bath. Renovated by the MTDC, this lakeside bungalow offers pleasant, simply furnished rooms. There is a multicuisine restaurant. Rupees only.

Tura

Inexpensive

Orchid Lodge. Tura, West Garo; tel. 568, or reserve through Director of Tourism (address above). 9 rooms with bath. This bungalow has clean rooms with overhead fans, multicuisine restaurant, room service, tourist office. Rupees only.

TOURIST HUTS AND BUNGALOWS. These simple accommodations are very inexpensive and accept only rupees. A caretaker will also prepare meals for a small fee.

Assam. Reservations: Assam Tourist Department, Guwahati 781001, tel. 27102. Patacharuchi has a two-room Assamese-style *Inspection Bungalow* with an inviting veranda. Each bedroom has a double bed with mosquito net and an attached bath and fastidiously clean dining room.

Meghalaya. Reservations: Deputy Commssioner, East Garo Hills, William Nagar. The new *Baghmara Circuit House* has about 5 furnished rooms with attached baths. Reservations: Sub-Divisional Officer (Civil), Baghmara, East Garo Hills. The *William Nagar Circuit House* has about 10 furnished rooms with attached baths.

DINING OUT. Breakfast is usually served 7–10; lunch is usually noon–3; and dinner, 7:30–9 or 10. Payment is normally in rupees unless the restaurant is connected to a Western-style hotel, in which case it may also accept credit cards. The restaurants listed below are informal and unless noted are open for all three meals and don't require reservations. Prices are based on one person eating a three-course meal, excluding taxes, tip, or beverage: *Moderate,* Rs. 100–Rs. 200; *Inexpensive,* under Rs. 100.

ASSAM

A specialty in Assam is the Assamese *thali*—assorted small portions of moderately spicy regional dishes, such as *pabha* (river fish simmered in mustard paste), *moricha* (a spinachlike green cooked in mustard oil), *roho* (fish in lemon or tomato sauce), *dahi* (lentils), and *omita* (fried papaya simmered with baking soda).

Guwahati

Moderate

Chopstick. The Dynasty, S. S. Rd., tel. 40849 and 24353. A modern restaurant, off the lobby, its done up in green and white decor and has subdued lighting. The chef prepares Indian and Chinese dishes, including crispy Szechuan prawns. Be advised: The portions are small. Open noon–3 P.M. and 7–9:30 P.M. AE, DC, MC, V.

Paradise. G.N.B. Rd.; tel. 26904. Guwahati's most popular restaurant, with an upscale chain-restaurant decor, serves the best Assamese cuisine in town. Try the delicious thali. Open 10 A.M.–3:30 P.M., 6:30–10 P.M. Serves beer until 7:30 P.M. Rupees only.

Ushaban. Hotel Brahmaputra Ashok, M. G. Rd.; tel. 41064. This cozy restaurant is modern Assamese, with white ceilings and lots of lacquered lattice. The chef cooks multicuisine dishes, including regional fare. You can also expect a special "health-conscious" menu. Reservations advised. Open 7:30–10:30 A.M., 12:30–2:30 P.M., 7:30–10:30 P.M. AE, DC, MC, V.

MEGHALAYA

Shillong

Moderate

Pinecone Restaurant. Hotel Pinewood Ashok; tel. 23116. This restaurant has a handsome rustic ambience and serves Chinese, Indian, and Continental cuisines. Try the shredded pork with fresh bamboo shoots or Indian butter chicken cooked in a spicy tomato gravy. Open 1–2:30 P.M., 8–10 P.M. AE, DC, MC, V.

Inexpensive

Dukan Jadoh Stall. Police Bazar; no phone. Try Khasi food at this tiny hangout. Don't expect much decor, just a laid-back ambience and fresh, regional dishes: *jadoh* (Khasi rice), *turembah* (fermented soy), or chicken dishes. Open 8 A.M.–9 P.M. Rupees only.

New World Restaurant. Police Bazar, tel. 22046. In this cozy, unpretentious bungalow with Chinese touches and a cane ceiling, you can choose from a range of Szechuan dishes. There's also a small room upstairs. Open 9 A.M.–8 P.M., closed last two Sundays of each month. Rupees only.

SWEETS AND TREATS. *The Orbit,* a tiny circular restaurant, revolves at the top of Hotel Kuber International, Hem Barua Rd., Fancy Bazaar in Guwahati, Assam, and serves tasty snacks and ice cream. Open 7 A.M.–11 P.M. In Shillong, Meghalaya, *Wards Lake Cafe* serves good snacks, coffee, and cold drinks. Open 9 A.M.–5:30 P.M.

HOW TO GET AROUND. Assam. From the Airport. The airport is 21 km (13 mi.) from Guwahati. A bus meets each plane from Calcutta, currently the afternoon flight, and goes to Guwahati for Rs. 15. A taxi costs about Rs. 175.

By Bus. *ASTC* (reservations through the Assam Tourist Department, tel. 27102 and 24475), *Blue Hill Travels* (Brahmaputra Ashok Hotel, tel. 41064, and Paltan Bazar, tel. 31427), and *Assam Valley Tours and Travels* (Paltan Bazar, tel. 26133) run daily trips to Manas Tiger Reserve and Kaziranga National Sanctuary.

By Taxi and Rented Car with Driver. For short excursions, hire a nonmetered taxi (about Rs. 5 per km). For longer excursions, arrange for a car with driver from the *Assam Tourist Department* in Guwahati (Station Rd., tel. 27102 and 24475), *Blue Hill Travels* (Brahmaputra Ashok Hotel, tel. 41064), and Rhino Travels (see Tour Operators, below).

By Rickshaw. For trips within Guwahati, take an auto rickshaw (about Rs. 3.50 per km) or use a bicycle rickshaw (Rs. 1.50 per km).

Meghalaya. From the Airport. The airport is 127 km (79 mi.) from Shillong. A taxi (Rs. 600) takes about three hours. Bargain. You can also take a Meghalaya Tourism Development Corporation (MTDC) bus, which leaves from the airport (Rs. 60) after the arrival of each Calcutta flight. The trip takes four hours. Umroi Airport is 35 km (22 mi.) from Shillong. Sheba Travels (see Tour Operators, below) runs a minibus (Rs. 35) between the airport and Shillong.

By Bus. *MTDC* runs deluxe buses on demand to Jowai, Cherrapunjee, Nongstoin, and Tura from the Bus Station, Jail Rd., Police Bazaar; tel. 23206. Most trips cost under Rs. 100. MRTC can also make reservations for similar trips offered by ASTC, Blue Hill Travels, and Assam Valley Tours and Travels.

By Taxi or Rented Car and Driver. If you hire a car with driver, the cost is determined by destination. From Shillong, a round-trip fare to Jowai or Cherrapunjee is Rs. 550; to Nongstoin, Rs. 800; to Tura, Rs. 2,500. Add Rs. 100 per overnight halt. Hire a car from *Sheba Travels* (see Tour Operators, below). For short excursions by taxi, rates are Rs. 6–Rs. 7 per km.

TOURS. Assam. The *Directorate of Tourism* (Station Rd., tel. 27102 or 24475) offers overnight tours by minibus from Guwahati to Kaziranga and Manas (Rs. 300). It also has a day trip to Shillong (about Rs. 125) and a Sunday river cruise on the Brahmaputra (Rs. 40).

Meghalaya. *MTDC* sponsors tours on demand by non-air-conditioned deluxe buses that cover local sightseeing around Shillong as well as trips to Cherrapunjee and Jaintia Hills. Tours depart from the Shillong Tourist Hotel and Bus Station on Jail Rd. For reservations, contact MTDC, Orchid Hotel, Polo Rd., Shillong 793001, tel. 24933.

TOUR OPERATORS. Assam. *Rhino Travels* (Nehru Rd., Pan Bazar, Guwahati 781001, tel. 40061) offers good general tours of Guwahati and surrounding areas, and can provide a car with driver. *Wild Grass Eco-Tours* (Manju Barua, W. G. Resorts, Barua Bhavan, 107 M. C. Rd., Uzanbazar, Guwahati 781001, tel. 26827) offers excellent ecological and cultural tours in and around Kaziranga National Park. Tours include fishing, bird-watching, wildlife safaris, river cruises in indigenous boats, tribal visits with music and dance programs, and a stay in its traditional bungalow resort. If you make arrangements months in advance, it can help procure the necessary Restricted Area Permit.

Meghalaya. Contact *Sheba Travels* (Police Bazar Point, Shillong 781003, tel. 23015 and 25020) for all travel needs: bookings, car with driver, guides, and customized tours.

SEASONAL EVENTS. Assam and Meghalaya celebrate numerous unique and splendid events. Since the lunar calendar determines the specific dates for many events, contact the Government of India Tourist Office for details.

ASSAM

Mid-April. *Rongali.* This week-long festival celebrates spring and the Assamese New Year. Women perform beautiful dances while men play traditional drums, horns, and flutes.

June. *Ambubashi Mela.* The Hindu Kamakhya Temple in Guwahati is closed for three days to symbolize the menstruation of the enshrined goddess, Kali. On the fourth day, the temple is reopened, and the goddess is given a sacred bath and redraped in her cloth.

October. *Durga Puja.* This important Hindu festival is a big event at the Kamakhya Shrine in Guwahati.

MEGHALAYA

April. *Khasi Spring Festival.* Khasi tribals perform the Shad Suk Mynsiem (Dance of Joyful Hearts) in Weiking on the outskirts of Shillong.

November. *Ka Pamblang Nongkrem* is a five-day knock-out Khasi ceremony with bejeweled Khasi virgins dancing and young men waging mock sword combats. On the final day, animals are sacrificed.

November/December. *Wangala* or the *Hundred Drums Festival.* During this terrific harvest celebration, Garo tribal people in elaborate feathered headpieces dance for four days to traditional accompaniment.

HISTORIC SITES. Entrance to most places is generally free; where a donation is requested, a few rupees will suffice. Important monuments are open daily sunrise to sunset unless noted otherwise below.

ASSAM AND ENVIRONS

Guwahati

Kamakhya Temple. This temple, with its swelling beehive shape that dominates Nilachal Hill, was first constructed in the thirteenth century and has been renovated numerous times. Dedicated to Kali, this is one of the most important tantric temples in India.

Umananda Shiva Temple. During the Shivratri festival, thousands of Hindus visit this temple on Peacock Island in the Brahmaputra River, dedicated to Shiva.

Nabagraha Shrine. Nabagraha, meaning nine planets, sits on Chitrashala Hill and was once the center of astronomical and astrological study.

Hayagriba Madhab Temple. In Hajo, on a hill 24 km (15 mi.) from Guwahati, this temple is sacred to Buddhists, who believe that it contains relics of the Buddha, and to Hindus, who come to honor Vishnu.

Pao Mecca. This mosque of Pir Giyasuddin Aulin, also in Haja, is believed by Moslems to have one-quarter of the sanctity of the holiest Moslem shrine in Mecca.

MEGHALAYA

Khasi Sacred Grove. In Mawplang, 25 km (16 mi.) from Shillong, a path leads to one of the few remaining Khasi sacred groves where Khasi tribal people still evoke the blessings of spirits. Everything is considered sacred; don't remove anything, not even a leaf.

Nartiang Village, Jantia Hills, has a hilltop filled with historic monoliths erected by Jantia tribal people from 1500 to 1835.

MUSEUMS AND GALLERIES. Assam. The *Assam State Museum's* collection includes costumes of Ahom kings, sculpture, pottery, coins, art, and archaeological artifacts. It is open 9:30 A.M.–3:30 P.M. Tuesday–Saturday, 9:30 A.M.–12:30 P.M. Sundays; closed Mondays. Guwahati also has many small museums. The following are open 10 A.M.–4 P.M. Monday–Friday, 10 A.M.–1 P.M. Saturdays, and are closed Sundays: *Assam Forest Museum, Assam Government Cottage Industries Museum,* which displays traditional crafts, and the *Anthropological Museum* (Department of Anthropology, Guwahati University, tel. 88248). The *Department of Historical and Antiquarian Research,* which has a collection of old manuscripts, and the *Museum of Animal Husbandry* at the Aassam Veterinary College are open 10 A.M.–4 P.M. Monday–Saturday; closed Sundays.

Meghalaya. *Meghalaya's State Museum* in Shillong includes anthropological, cultural, botanical, and wildlife exhibits. Open 10 A.M.–4:30 P.M. in summer and till 4 P.M. in winter. Closed Sundays and holidays.

GARDENS. Meghalaya. Shillong's *Botanical Garden* is a delightful, quiet place for a stroll. Open 9 A.M.–5 P.M.

SPORTS AND OUTDOOR ADVENTURES. Assam. Fishing. There's good fishing at *Manas Tiger Reserve* (permit costs Rs. 10 per day) from February to March. Bring your own rod and reel.

Wildlife Sanctuaries. *Kaziranga National Sanctuary,* open mid-October–mid-April, covers 430 sq. km (267 sq. mi.) of forests and grasslands and is the most famous home of the Indian one-horned rhinoceros. In 1908, when hardly a dozen of these powerful, armored animals lived in the area, Kaziranga was declared a forest reserve. Today, the rhinoceros, numbering close to 1,000, coexist with wild elephants, tigers, wild buffalos, sloth bear, jungle cats, leopards, langur, and barking deer. Gliding and darting over its *jheels* (swampy flats surrounded by shallow pools of water) are a rich variety of water birds, including ibis, purple herons, black-necked storks, egrets, ring-tailed fishing eagles, river terns, and pelicans. On arrival, visitors must stop at the Mihimukh Forest Range Office to pay nominal entrance fees and to make arrangements for jeep and elephant rides or excursions to a Karbi tribal village or a tea plantation.

Manas Tiger Reserve, open from October to May, covers 2,837 sq. km (1,759 sq. mi.) in the Himalayan foothills, bordering Bhutan. Manas is laced with many streams and rivers, which contribute to its reputation as one of India's most beautiful sanctuaries. The birds are exceptional. The early morning sight of large flocks of great pied hornbills crossing the river to feed in Bhutan is memorable. Manas has an abundance of water birds, such as the white-capped redstart, the merganser, egret, ruddy shelduck, cormorant, and a variety of ducks. Wildlife in the sanctuary includes tigers, Indian rhinoceros, golden langur, wild buffalos, elephants, swamp deer, rare pygmy hogs, and hispid hares. On arrival, visitors must show their permits at the Foreigner's Check Gate and stop at the Field Office to pay nominal park fees and to make arrangements for elephant rides, boat rentals, or fishing permits.

Meghalaya. Archery Contests. Daily, except Sunday, you can watch archery contests in Shillong's Polo Ground, a popular sport with Khasi people.

Caving. Meghalaya has a vast network of limestone caves open for exploration: Syndia in the Jaintia Hills, Siju in the Garo Hills, and Mawsmai near Cherrapunjee.

Fishing. At present, no license is required, and you must bring your own rod and reel. Best fishing is from February to November. You can fish at *Umiam Lake,* about 16 km (10 mi.) north of Shillong, and in and near *William Nagar Forest Reserve* and in *Balpakram National Park,* which are located in Garo Hills.

Golfing. Play golf at the *Shillong Golf Club* (tel. 3071), which is one of India's prettiest golf courses. Green fees are Rs. 30 per day; equipment is available at a nominal cost.

Wildlife Sanctuaries. *Balpakram National Park and Biosphere* is a new park on a vast plateau in Garo Hills, bordering Bangladesh. You can walk to lakes and see peacocks, pheasants, and hornbills, and you can count on seeing wild elephants. Park fees are under Rs. 50 per vehicle. Best time to visit is from November to February.

SHOPPING. Assam. Be sure to see this state's beautiful handwoven cottons and rare silks: *endi* (raw silk), *pat* (soft hand-dyed silk); *muga* (naturally golden, heavy silk). In Guwahati, you can also buy good tea and honey and products of bamboo, cane, jute, and brass. The following shops are open Monday–Saturday and take rupees only:

Government of Assam Emporium (G.N.B. Rd.), open April–September 10 A.M.–7 P.M., otherwise till 6, for excellent handicrafts and handlooms at reasonable fixed prices. *Jagaran Artfed Handloom House* (G.N.B. Rd.), open 10 A.M.–7 P.M., also government-run, offers a similar selection. *Purbashree Northeastern Handicrafts* and *Handlooms Development Corporation* (G.N.B. Rd.), open April–September 10 A.M.–2 P.M. and 3 P.M.–7 P.M., otherwise 10 A.M.–6 P.M., has handicrafts and handlooms from the northeastern states. For Assamese tea, try *Kamrupa* (G. S. Rd., Paltan Bazar) or *Kalpataru* (H. B. Rd., Pan Bazar), both open 10 A.M.–7 P.M. Traditional heavy hand-tooled brass products are at the *Assam Cooperative Bell Metal Manufacturing Society* (S.R.C.B. Rd., Fancy Bazar), open 8 A.M.–7 P.M. This is one of few shops that sell good "bell metal" tea cups, curry bowls, platters, and tumblers.

In Swalkuchi, the village of weavers not far from Guwahati, you can see the creation of *muga* and *pat* silks. Ask to visit the home of *Bogaram Baishya;* he'll show you his cottage industry and take you to others. Muga or pat is 30 percent cheaper here than in retail shops. Baishya can also make on order and ship.

Meghalaya. In Shillong, visit the *Meghalaya Handloom and Handicraft Development Corporation* (Jail Rd.), open 9 A.M.–7 P.M., closed Sundays, for wool-blend shawls, *jainsem* (traditional dresses), cotton fabric, carpets, and bamboo products. It takes rupees only. Shillong's *Pubashree Northeastern Handicrafts and Handlooms Development Corporation* (Jail Rd.), open weekdays 10 A.M.–1 P.M. and 3 P.M.–7 P.M., and Saturdays 10 A.M.–2 P.M., sells handicrafts from all the northeastern states at only a few rupees.

NIGHTLIFE AND BARS. Assam. With rare exceptions, you can drink only beer and only in hotel bars, open 11–11. Thursday and the first and last days of the month are "dry" days, when no beer is sold.

Meghalaya. The best bar is in Shillong's Hotel Pinewood, with a quiet ambience and rustic decor. It's open 10 A.M.–2 P.M., 6–10 P.M.

SIKKIM

Tiny State with Giant Vistas

by
KATHLEEN COX

There is a Sikkimese legend that goes something like this: Stars are the laughter of the Sikkimese that have risen far into the sky and frozen.

Something about this tiny state, one of India's newest, snuggled into the eastern Himalayas, makes you believe—or want to believe—in this legend. Perhaps it is the high altitude or the disconcerting lay of the land, which seems continually to rise or fall, never leveling out for any distance. Or perhaps it is the strange effect of witnessing ancient Buddhist religious rituals that are so bound up in the Sikkimese's daily life. The Sikkimese, despite the constant incursions into their country by aggressive neighbors, continue to exhibit a gaiety that gives credence to the legend.

Sikkim has always been vulnerable because it contains the best natural passes through the Himalayas and have therefore been the routes of choice for trade between India to the south and Lhasa, Tibet, to the north. For centuries, this tiny kingdom has been caught in a series of disputes over who should rule it. Since 1975, however, Sikkim has been the twenty-second state of India. Inside its tiny borders is an odd combination of forces; masses of Indian military troops remain perpetually on alert on the Tibetan border and a basically peaceful people go about their daily lives following the non-aggressive tenets of Mahayana Buddhism.

Sikkim is dominated by Kanchenjunga, the third-highest mountain in the world, which is revered by the Sikkimese as their presiding deity, the home of gods. In its shadow are other great beauties—forests thick with over 500 species of orchids, beautiful birds and butterflies, red pandas, blue sheep, rhododendrons, and blue poppies. In this naturally rich land, the people have been nurtured by Buddhism, which finds its expression in simple yet beautifully ornamented monasteries and shrines, and festivals that are filled with colorful dances.

Distinct ethnic groups share Sikkim. The Lepchas, or Rongkup (Children of Rong), originally lived in seclusion in North Sikkim. Although many have converted to Buddhism, most still worship many aspects of their physical surroundings—rainbows, clouds, rivers, and trees. Village priests preside over elaborate rituals, including animal sacrifices, to appease animist deities.

Tibetan Bhutias came into Sikkim in the seventeenth century with the first *chogyal* (king) and were members of a three-tiered hierarchy: the aristocracy, the landholding Kazi, and the commoners. Every Bhutia village has its prayer flags and *chortens* (small shrines containing relics); most families have a relative who has joined a monastery or nunnery. Every home has an altar room.

The Bhutias' culture dominates Sikkim. The national dress for women is the traditional *bhakhu,* a slim-fitting sleeveless robe—the epitome of elegance.

Nepalese immigrants are responsible for the introduction of terrace farming to Sikkim. Although most Nepalese are Hindu, you see few Hindu temples in Sikkim; often their faith incorporates Buddhist beliefs and practices, as it does in Nepal.

EXPLORING SIKKIM

Gangtok

Visit the Research Institute of Tibetology, founded by the Dalai Lama in 1957 and the most important Buddhist study center in India. It has rare Lepcha, Tibetan, and Sanskrit manuscripts, many donated by the Dalai Lama; numerous priceless statues, including one seven feet tall of Mahjushri and a small copper image of Avalokitesvara; and rare *thang-kas* (paintings with a Buddhist theme), some created on tapestry.

From here, a short walk leads to the Orchid Sanctuary, with numerous species in bloom during the winter months. Above the Tibetology is the Do-Drul Chorten, built in 1945 by the Venerable Trulsi Rimpoche, head of the Nyingmapa (Red) Sect. Surrounded by 108 prayer wheels, this chorten commemorates the Buddha's victory over evil. Nearby are two statues of Guru Padmasambhava. Also nearby is the Sheda Institute for Higher Ningmapa Studies, where young children train to become lamas or nuns. You are welcome to visit; the children are a delight.

In order to visit to Tsuklakhang, the royal gompa of the former chogyal of Sikkim, you must time your visit with a festival (see Seasonal Events, below). On a ridge above Gangtok, it's constructed in typical pagoda style. It was the most important monastery in Sikkim. The main hall has exquisitely carved and painted woodwork, frescoes, and precious Buddhist icons. Here kings were crowned and royal marriages were consecrated. Across the meadow sits the Royal Palace, also closed to the public.

Around Gangtok

Set on a mountain spur north of Gangtok, Enchey Monastery, built in 1840, is called the Palace of Solitude. This active monastery with 200 Nyingmapa monks has an interior that is an artistic celebration of the Buddhist faith. Old frescoes line the walls. Your eyes are drawn to the front altar and a gilded Lord Buddha, flanked by Avalokitesvara (Buddha of Compassion) and Guru Padmasambhava with his two consorts.

Phodang, north of Enchey, is a recently built monastery not far from the still-standing original *gompa* (shrine), which also contains old frescoes. Phodang belongs to the Kagyupa sect. If the sky is clear, you can get splendid views from this monastery.

A lovely drive 24 kilometers (15 miles) southwest of Gangtok takes you through rice fields and bamboo groves to Rumtek Monastery. When the Chinese occupied Tibet, His Holiness Gyalwa Karmapa, the 16th incarnation of the founder of the Karmapa sect of Tibet, took refuge in Sikkim. The chogyal of Sikkim gave him 75 acres to set up this monastery—a replica of the gompa at Chhofuk in Tibet.

Following the custom, before Gyalwa Karmapa died in 1982, he wrote a lengthy prophesy that described the 17th incarnation. In May 1988, the four head *rimpoches* (religious reincarnations) of the monastery discovered the document. At an auspicious time, they will locate the child it describes and bring him to Rumtek for his enthronement.

Rumtek contains numerous chambers (some not open to non-Buddhists). A courtyard leads to the entrance of the ornate main prayer hall. The throne, facing the assembly hall, is for His Holiness and has a photo of the 16th incarnation on its right. Steps behind the right of the exterior lead to the prestigious Nalanda Institute for Higher Studies and the Great Golden Reliquary, which contains the relics (bones and remnants of the cremated body) of the 16th Gyalwa Karmapa and a gold-plated chorten surrounded by statues of former Gyalwa Karmapas.

West Sikkim

The town of Rabangla, 65 kilometers (40 miles) from Gangtok, is the Gateway to West Sikkim. You'll traverse dark tropical forests with moss hanging from trees. The road winds, then descends, taking you past a small monastery (Yung Drum) studded with flags. Moments later, you'll round a sharp bend, and on a distant peak you'll see the Tashidang Monastery, its golden pinnacle catching the sun. Behind it looms the spectacular Mount Kanchenjunga, with clouds swirling around its crest.

Tashidang sits on a hill between the Rangit and Ratong rivers. It's an active monastery with about 60 monks from the Nyingmapa order. According to legend, Guru Padmasambhava shot an arrow into the air and where it fell—which was here—he vowed to pray. In 1642, one of the three lamas who consecrated the first chogyal built a *lhakhang* (shrine) venerating this sacred spot. In 1716, the main monastery was constructed.

Tashidang's exterior remains a lovely example of Sikkimese temple architecture; but its interior, including the old frescoes, needs repair. See the Thongwa Rangdol, reputed to contain the holy relics of Manjushri (Buddha of Transcendent Wisdom). Just the sight of it is said to cleanse the devotee of sin. Guru Padmasambhava is also credited with the creation of the *bumchu* (pot of holy water), which you can see during the Bumchu Celebration in February, when the sacred bumchu, which has a perpetual sweet aroma and has not been refilled since its discovery, is emptied of its holy contents. The amount of water determines Sikkim's prosperity in the new year.

At Geysing, farther west, a shortcut by jeep leads to Pemayangtse, Sikkim's most important monastery, with 200 Nyingmapa lamas. The original lhakhang, constructed in the mid-1600s by Lhatsun Chenpo, is the second-oldest monastery in Sikkim. Since then, the monastery has been renovated several times.

A gaily decorated entrance leads into the main assembly hall. Old frescoes cover the walls. Behind the front altar stands a large gold-covered clay statue of Guru Padmasambhava flanked by his two consorts—all of them protected by a wooden arch of Nagas (sacred serpents). To the right is a statue of Avalokitesvara with his disciples; a statue of the Buddha is to the left.

Steps on the right lead to upper floors. The first chamber, Guru Lhakhang, has frescoes and statues depicting Guru Padmasambhava. On the right wall near the statues, a fresco portrays the consecration of the first chogyal of Sikkim (he's on the left).

Interior walls of the other chamber on this floor are covered with 1,000 images of the Buddha; the room contains the holy scriptures and the main statue of Lord Buddha. A 6×9-meter (20×30-foot) thang-ka depicting the Buddha is kept in this room and unfurled only during the annual festival (usually in February).

On the third floor is the "must-see" chamber with its astonishing chorten. Three decades ago, Dungzin Rimpoche, now deceased, spent five years reconstructing a description of a vision of Sangthokpalri, the celestial palace of Guru Padmasambhava. The miniature palace takes into account the tiniest details: a combination of the whimsical and the serene.

PRACTICAL INFORMATION FOR SIKKIM

WHEN TO GO. The most popular time to visit is from mid-February to June and October to mid-December. Summer temperatures range from 68°F–76°F and winter temperatures fluctuate between 26°F and 50°F. As in other mountainous areas, it is recommended that you wear layered clothing that can ensure your comfort at a variety of altitudes, with their accompanying variation in temperature.

RESTRICTED AREA PERMIT. Because of Sikkim's sensitive border location, foreigners need a Restricted Area Permit to visit (see Travel Documents in *Facts at Your Fingertips*). A general permit is good for 15 days but does not allow for trekking. For a general permit, list Gangtok, Phodang, and the Rumtek and Pemayangtse monasteries. If you want to trek, you must apply for a trekking permit and be in a group with at least four people, as well as trek with a recognized travel agency. This permit, which can be processed within 24 hours on arrival in Gangtok, is also good for 15 days. For a trekking permit, list the above destinations, plus Dzongri. Once you have filled out your Restricted Area Permit, follow the guidelines in *Facts at Your Fingertips*. If you apply to a consular office or a mission in your home country, allow a few days for clearance. In India, the permit *should* be issued on the spot.

HOW TO GET THERE. By Air. Flying to Bagdogra Airport in northern West Bengal, 124 km (77 mi.) from Gangtok, the capital, is the best approach to Sikkim. Going by train to New Jalpaiguri, near Bagdogra, or in a bus or car takes a long time. *Indian Airlines* flies daily between Bagdogra and Calcutta; and it has five weekly flights between Bagdogra and Delhi and Bagdogra and Guwahati (Assam). Book well in advance, and reconfirm your ticket 72 hours before flight time. For information, call 3099 in Gangtok; 20962 in Bagdogra. At Bagdogra, foreigners must register their permit with the police.

By Bus. *Sikkim National Transport Service* (SNTS) runs luxury coaches between Darjeeling and Gangtok. Trip time is about six hours and costs about Rs. 65. In Gangtok, contact the *Sikkim Tourist Information Center,* tel. 2064. In Bagdogra, contact the *Sikkim Tourist Information Counter* at the airport. In Siliguri, near Bagdogra, contact the *Sikkim Tourist Information Center,* SNT Colony, tel. 24602. In Darjeeling, contact the *West Bengal Tourist Office,* tel. 2050.

By Taxi or Rented Car with Driver. The journey to Gangtok from Bagdogra or Darjeeling takes about four hours and costs about Rs. 1,000 per vehicle; from Kalimpong it takes about three hours and costs about Rs. 700. In West Bengal, hire a car from a recommended agency (see Tour Operators in West Bengal and Bihar chapter). In Gangtok, hire a car from the *Sikkim Tourist Information Center,* Mahatma Gandhi Marg, Gangtok, Sikkim 737101, tel. 2064. Some hotels also arrange car rentals. Figure about Rs. 400 per day (gas not included); also expect an Rs. 100 per night halt charge.

TOURIST INFORMATION. Contact the *Sikkim Tourist Information Center,* Mahatma Gandhi Marg, Gangtok, Sikkim 737101; tel. 2064. Open daily from mid-September to mid-November, 9 A.M.–5:30 P.M.; daily from April to June, 9 A.M.–6 P.M.; and Monday–Saturday from July to mid-September, 10 A.M.–4 P.M., closed Sunday and second Saturday of the month. There's also a counter at the Bagdogra Airport.

FOREIGN CURRENCY EXCHANGE. Most Western-style hotels have money-exchange counters. Otherwise, go to a branch of the *State Bank of India,* open Monday-Friday, 10 A.M.–2 P.M.; Saturday till noon. In Gangtok, the State Bank of India is on Mahatma Gandhi Marg.

ACCOMMODATIONS. Many hotels in Sikkim have appealing Buddhist touches. Prices are based on double occupancy and exclude taxes and service charges: *Moderate,* Rs. 500–Rs. 1,200; *Inexpensive,* under Rs. 500. Some Western-style hotels take major credit cards and traveler's checks.

GANGTOK

Moderate

Hotel Norkhill. Paljor Stadium Rd., Gangtok 737101; tel. 3186–7, fax 2707. 25 rooms with bath. Gangtok's oldest hotel, once owned by the king, is on a quiet ridge below the city. It has a lovely garden and lawn, and excellent views. Its exterior and public rooms are Sikkimese style. The rooms are simple, with small Buddhist and Sikkimese details. Ask for a room with a view and a tub. Fixed-menu restaurant (nonhotel guests must have reservations), bar, room service, baby-sitters, gift shop, library, house doctor, travel and foreign-exchange service, Sikkimese dances on request. Meals included. AE, DC, MC, V.

Hotel Tashi Delek. Mahatma Gandhi Marg, Gangtok 737101; tel. 2038 or 2991. 45 rooms with bath. Also centrally located, this hotel's public rooms feature Sikkimese decor in colors bright enough to warrant sunglasses. The bedrooms are simply decorated by comparison yet pleasant and clean. Ask for a mountain view. TV, multicuisine restaurant, bar, rooftop garden, baby-sitters, travel and foreign-exchange counter, small shopping arcade. AE, DC, MC, V.

Inexpensive

Hotel Mayur. Paljor Namgyal Stadium Rd., Gangtok 737101; tel. 2752 or 2825. 25 rooms with bath. Centrally located, this spiffy hotel has nicely furnished rooms and provides very good service. Some rooms have modern bathrooms with tubs or showers. Standard rooms are smaller and have simple decor. Ask for a room with mountain view. Multicuisine restaurant, bar, room service, house doctor, car rental, TV. Rupees only.

Hotel Tibet. Paljor Namgyal Stadium Rd., Gangtok 737101; tel. 2523 or 3468. 30 rooms with bath. Run by the Dalai Lama Charitable Trust, this hotel is centrally located and has wonderful Tibetan ambience. The best views are from rooms with tubs or showers. Multicuisine restaurant, room service, bar, car rental, foreign-exchange counter. AE, DC, MC, V.

PEMAYANGTSE

Inexpensive

Hotel Mount Pandim. Pemayangtse, Pelling, West Sikkim 737113; tel. 56. 25 rooms with bath. This government-run bungalow is set on a hill with great views and an attractive garden. The modestly furnished rooms are large; ask for one with a view. It may be necessary to insist on good service. Multicuisine restaurant, room service, bar, laundry, tour guide and car rental, doctor on call, library, gift shop. Meals included. Rupees only.

TOURIST HUTS AND BUNGALOWS. In West Sikkim, the government has put up simple trekkers' huts with rustic rooms or dormitories in delightful locations. Bring a sleeping bag and bug repellent. A caretaker will prepare plain meals for a modest fee. At present, trekkers' huts are at Pemayangtse, Barshey, Yoksum, Tsokha, and Dzongri. For reservations, contact the Assistant Manager, Hotel Mount Pandim, Pemayangtse, P.O. Pelling, West Sikkim; tel. 56.

DINING OUT. Expect good eating and a diversified cuisine in Gangtok: Tibetan, Indian, Chinese, Continental, and Sikkimese cuisines. Try Sikkimese sautéed bamboo shoots, nettle soup, and roast pork. If you like *momo* (Tibetan dumplings), order the beef or vegetable variety—pork is risky if undercooked. Sikkim also makes good local brews: cherry or musk brandy, wine, Teesta River white rum, juniper gin, *pan* (mixed nuts and leaves) liquor, and *chang* (fermented wine). Keep in mind that many accommodations listed above have restaurants. Breakfast is usually served 8–10:30; lunch is usually noon–3; and dinner, 7–9. Payment is normally in rupees unless the restaurant is connected to a Western-style hotel. The restaurants listed below are informal and, unless noted, are open for all three meals and don't require reservations. Prices are based on one person eating a three-course meal, excluding taxes, tip, or beverage: *Moderate,* Rs. 100–Rs. 200; *Inexpensive,* under Rs. 100.

GANGTOK

Moderate

Blue Poppy. Hotel Tashi Delek, Mahatma Gandhi Marg; tel. 2038. This delightful Sikkimese-style restaurant, with star cutouts on its blue ceiling, views of the mountains, and live music in season, serves good steaks, as well as Chinese, Indian, Sikkimese, and Continental fare. Open 8 A.M.–10 P.M. AE, DC, MC, V.

Blue Sheep. Next to Tourist Information Center on Mahatma Gandhi Marg; no phone. This informal upstairs restaurant is done up in modern Sikkimese style. The menu offers Indian, Continental, and the tasty Sikkimese fare, which is hard to find. There's an attached bar. Open 9–9. Rupees only.

Shaepi Restaurant. Hotel Mayur, Paljor Namgyal Stadium Rd.; tel. 2752. A modern hotel dining room, it has a bank of windows that provide great views. The chef offers a variety of Chinese items, plus Indian and Continental dishes. There's an attached bar. Open 7 A.M.–9 P.M. Rupees only.

Snow Lion. Hotel Tibet, Paljor Namgyal Stadium Rd.; tel. 2523. This peaceful restaurant is run by the Tibetan community. Snow Lion has soft lighting, Tibetan decor, and good views of Mount Kanchenjunga. Popular and informal, it serves Tibetan, Japanese, Chinese, Continental, and Indian food. Try the unusual *menyak polo* (special steamed vegetable dumplings). Open 7 A.M.–9:30 P.M. AE, DC, MC.

Inexpensive

House of Bamboo. Mahatma Gandhi Marg; no phone. Another upstairs restaurant, it's very informal, very Tibetan, and very cheap. You can also choose Chinese dishes. There's an attached bar. Open 8–8; closed during a full moon, half-moon, and on the Tibetan New Year. Rupees only.

SWEETS AND TREATS. *Risur Hotel & Bakery,* Deorali Bazaar, Gangtok, serves great *momo* (Tibetan dumplings) in its popular restaurant. Open 8–8, closed Tibetan holidays.

HOW TO GET AROUND. From the Airport. Taxis are always plentiful. Rates are about Rs. 1,000 for the four-hour journey. You can also go by SNTS bus for about Rs. 65; inquire at the airport Tourist Information Counter.

By Bus. *SNTS* runs buses to most places in Sikkim that are open to foreigners. For schedules and fares, contact its booking office just below the Tourist Information Center in Gangtok.

By Taxi. Taxis are unmetered and frequently pick up extra passengers. Rates are reasonable and are determined by the destination. Ask to see the rate card.

By Rented Car with Driver. In Gangtok, hire a car with driver from the *Manager of Transport,* Sikkim Tourist Information Center (address above), for about Rs. 400 per day (gas not included); also there's an Rs. 100 per night halt charge. This office plans to rent jeeps with drivers. Contact them for details. Some hotels also arrange car rentals.

TOURS. From Bagdogra, the *Sikkim Tourist Information Center* offers a six-night and seven-day Rhododendron Package Tour (Rs. 2,500 per person), which starts from Bagdogra and goes to Gangtok, Versay, and Gangtok. In Gangtok, it also conducts two daily local sightseeing tours to the Government of Cottage Industries, Deer Park, Do-Drul Chorten, Research Institute of Tibetology, Orchid Sanctuary, Enchey Monastery (10 A.M.–12:30 P.M.; by bus: Rs. 25); and around Gangtok to the Orchidarium, Rumtek Monastery, Tashi View Point, Phodang Monastery (1:15–4 P.M. by bus: Rs. 35). These same tours by car cost Rs. 200. No private guides are available in Gangtok.

TOUR OPERATORS. The *Sikkim Tourist Information Center* (address above) can arrange general tours in areas of this state that are open to foreigners and can also provide car and jeep rentals. For treks, mountaineering, yak safaris, river rafting, and fishing, contact: *Assistant Director Adventure, Department of Tourism,* Gangtok 737101; tel. 3425. *Himalventure Expeditions* (Hotel Norkhill, Gangtok 737101; tel. 3186, fax 2707) offers customized theme-oriented tours (butterflies, flora and fauna, culture and religion) and outdoor adventures, including rafting and high-altitude mountain treks and nature walks. Also check the listings under *Facts at Your Fingertips.* In Gangtok, many of the hotels also have travel counters that arrange car rentals or excursions.

SEASONAL EVENTS. Most of Sikkim's festivals are Buddhist celebrations with lamas, adorned in elaborate masks and ornate costumes, performing *chaams* (dances). Each chaam reenacts a legend connected to Buddhism that reaffirms the triumph of good over evil. Since the lunar calendar determines the specific dates for most events, contact the Sikkim Tourist Information Office or the Government of India Tourist Bureau for details.

February. *Losar.* The Tibetan New Year is celebrated with much pageantry at Pemayangste and Rumtek monasteries.

February. *Bumchu Ceremony.* During the Bumchu Ceremony at Tashidang Monastery, the sacred bumchu is shown to the public, and its contents are poured into 21 cups. The amount of water determines Sikkim's well-being for the next year.

May/June. *Saga Dawa.* During Saga Dawa, lamas, playing musical instruments and carrying holy books, lead huge processions at all the monasteries.

June. *Tse-Chu Chaams.* At Rumtek Monastery, lamas, dressed as the eight manifestations of Guru Padmasambhava, reenact his various triumphs.

August. *Drupka Tseshi.* Buddhists commemorate Lord Buddha's first teaching with ceremonial prayers at the Do-Drul Chorten in Gangtok.

August/September. *Pang Lhabsol.* At Tsuklakhang Monastery, costumed lamas perform ritual warrior dances.

October. *Autumn Festival.* The Sikkim Tourist Department sponsors a month-long festival in Gangtok that highlights Sikkim's culture.

November/December. *Kagyat Chaams.* Lamas at Tsuklakhang Monastery dance, then burn effigies—the triumph of good over evil. This colorful event ushers in Losar and celebrates the harvest.

December/January. *Drag-dMar Chaam.* At Enchey Monastery, lamas perform dances in honor of Guru Padmasambhava.

HISTORIC SITES. Entrance to many places is free; where a donation is requested, a few rupees will suffice. Most important sites are open daily from sunrise to sunset unless noted otherwise below.

GANGTOK AREA

Do-Drul Chorten. Near two statues of Guru Padmasambhava, this stupa was built in 1945 and is surrounded by prayer wheels.

Enchey Monastery. Just north of Gangtok, this gompa belongs to the Nyingma-pa Sect. Check with the tourist office for the timing of daily ceremonies.

Phodang Monastery. Located several km north of Gangtok, Phodang is one of Sikkim's five principal monasteries and one of the most beautiful.

Research Institute of Tibetology. This exquisite building and important Buddhist study center has precious religious icons and thang-kas. Remove your shoes before entering. Open Monday–Saturday, 10 A.M.–4 P.M.

Rumtek Monastery. Rumtek, southwest of Gangtok, is the state's largest monastery and belongs to the Karmapa sect. Also visit the adjoining Nalanda Institute for Higher Studies and Great Golden Reliquary, with holy relics, statues, and gold-plated chorten. Prayer services are around 4 A.M. and 6 P.M.; check with the tourist department.

Tsuklakhang. The royal monastery of the former chogyal of Sikkim is only open to the public on certain festival days (see above).

WESTERN SIKKIM

Dhubdi Monastery. An hour's climb from Yoksum, Dhubdi, also called the Hermit's Cell, is Sikkim's oldest monastery, with a simple altar, butter lamps, and a few icons. The views, however, are spectacular.

Pemayangtse Monastery. This is Sikkim's most important monastery, and it belongs to the Nyingmapa sect. Be sure to visit the exquisite upper-floor chambers. No photographs allowed.

Tashidang Monastery. This monastery also belongs to the Nyingmapa sect. Be sure to see the Thongwa Rangdol, which supposedly contains the holy relics of Manjushri (Buddha of Transcendent Wisdom).

GARDENS. *Orchid Sanctuary,* near the Institute of Tibetology in Gangtok, displays over 500 varieties of orchids. The best time to visit is April–May and December–January, when the orchids are in full bloom.

SPORTS AND OUTDOOR ADVENTURES. Climbing and Mountaineering. Climbers can attempt Rathong Peak, 6,797 meters (22,000 feet), and Kothang Peak, 6,148 meters (20,167 feet). All expeditions must be planned well in advance and cleared by the Home Department, Government of Sikkim, Sikkim 737101.

Fishing. Contact the tourist department in Gangtok for information regarding permits and locations. The season runs from mid-October until March. Bring your own equipment.

Hot Springs. From December to February, enjoy the hot springs at Phurchachu between Jorethang and Legship in western Sikkim.

Rafting. One- or two-day rafting trips from September to May on the Teesta River are now available. Contact the Assistant Director Adventure, Sikkim Tourism, Gangtok 737101 for details.

Trekking. The best treks are in western Sikkim, with the most popular season from mid-September to June. Trekking in the winter means cold nights and snow, but the temperature warms up by day, and you see numerous orchids at this time of year. Trekkers should also get in touch with the Assistant Director Adventure (address above) for specifics about new culture and nature treks. The Adventure Wing at the Sikkim Tourist Information Center (address above) rents sleeping bags and good tents. Here are two good treks, rated by degree of difficulty:

Rhododendron Trek. From the Soreng village in western Sikkim, you'll climb up to Bershay, 3,600 meters (12,000 feet), in the Singalila Range. This area is known as the Rhododendron belt, with about 40 different species of flowering trees. You'll walk through this forested area, also home to numerous birds, then descend to Dentam village, inhabited mainly by people of the Subba tribe. Continue down to the historic Pemayangtse Monastery. March through May is best. Four or five days. *Easy.*

Kanchenjunga Trek. Because this trek demands a lot of up- and-downhill walking, you should be physically fit. You will hike from Yoksum in western Sikkim through forests of rhododendron, orchid, pine, and magnolia to Bakhim village. The next day's walk will be more difficult, taking you through a village populated by gentle yak-herding Tibetans to the Dzongri outpost, with its views of Mt. Kanchenjunga. At Dzongri, altitude 4,030 meters (13,218 feet), you can ride a yak or hike up to Thangsing, altitude 3,930 meters (12,890 feet), at the base of Jopino Peak. From there, climb to Zimathang at 4,500 meters (14,760 feet). This excellent trek, with its terrific eastern Himalayan vistas, is just becoming popular. Seven to ten days. *Moderate.*

SHOPPING. In Gangtok, the *Government Institute of Cottage Industry* sells excellent wool carpets; new thang-kas; traditional clothes; handlooms in wool, silk, and cotton; jewelry; handbags; shawls; hand-knit sweaters; masks; wood carvings; and furniture. Open daily 9:30 A.M.–12:30 P.M. and 1–3:30 P.M. Fixed-price; rupees only. The *Tourist Department Gift Shop* (Mahatma Gandhi Marg) also sells good fixed-price handicrafts. Open mid-September–mid-November, daily 8:30 A.M.–6:30 P.M.; otherwise open 10 A.M.–5 P.M., closed Tuesday and government holidays. Rupees only. *Babu Kazi Sakya* (Mahatma Gandhi Marg) sells new and old traditional jewelry, curios, and handicrafts at fixed prices. Open 8 A.M.–7 P.M., closed Tuesday. Rupees only. Two good tailors make handsome traditional costumes: *Pema Seyden, Tibetan Tailor* (Lall Market Rd.) is open 7 A.M.–8 P.M., closed Tuesday. Pema will help you pick fabric in a nearby shop. *Lhasa Tailors* (Wangdi Children Park near Market Taxi Stand) is open 7 A.M.–8 P.M. Both are reliable, inexpensive, and will complete your order in two days. Rupees only. On Sunday, walk through *Lal Bazaar.* Bhutias and Lepchas in traditional clothes come from nearby villages to sell vegetables, spices, chickens, clothing, and trinkets. Begins around 8 A.M.

NIGHTLIFE AND BARS. Gangtok shuts down early unless there's a festival or *chaam* (dance) under way. Hotels and most restaurants have bars. Try the local brandies or chang—just remember that they're potent. *Snow Lion Bar* in the Hotel Tibet is cozy, with good views; open 10 A.M.–9:30 P.M. *Yak Bar* in the Hotel Tashi Delek is jazzy Sikkimese, with red brocade-draped booths and good views; open 10 A.M.–9 P.M.

ANDAMAN AND NICOBAR ISLANDS

Vacation Retreats in the Making

by
LISA SAMSON and AMIT SHAH

One descends from the heavens to Port Blair, Andaman Islands, as the monkey god, Hanuman, supposedly did in his valiant quest to rescue Sita, the lovely consort of Rama. The *Ramayana's* most mischievous character, Hanuman is said to have used these beautiful tropical islands as his bridge to Lanka, and his name has been lent to the Andaman Islands (from *Handuman*), the larger island group of this Union Territory. Only his pressing task of rescuing Sita can explain why this fun-loving, self-indulgent god didn't linger here, enjoying the invigorating sea breezes, the vast tracts of dense forests, and the stunning marine life found in coral beds that surround many of these islands. The modern-day traveler to India, having no such epic responsibilities, has good reason to stay here for a time to explore the natural beauty and historical sights of these islands.

The Andaman and Nicobar Islands (the territorial name of the two groups of islands) form the peaks of a submarine mountain range that stretches hundreds of miles into the Bay of Bengal, some 1,370 kilometers (850 miles) east of Madras, separating it from the Andaman Sea. Rising out of shimmering turquoise waters speckled a darker blue, where coral beds spread out from white sandy beaches, these islands hold the promise of evolving into one of India's most beautiful, relaxing vacation spots in the next decade. The islands, inaccessible to all but the aboriginal tribes for thousands of years and then used primarily as a penal colony by the British, are developing slowly. At present the changing policies that govern accessibility to the islands by foreign nationals place much of the islands' natural beauty off limits, but not so much that one shouldn't go now, before aspects of the fragile loveliness are altered.

Ptolemy, the Roman geographer, recorded the Andaman and Nicobar Islands in his first map of the world in the second century. I'Tsing, the Buddhist scholar, referred to the Nicobar Islands in the seventh century as the "land of naked people." And the adventurer Marco Polo inaccurately stated that the Andaman Islands were one large island. Though their existence has long been recorded, the reputed ferocity of some of the various aboriginal populations, the inhospitable environment, and the lack of "sweet" water on many of the islands long ensured their isolation from the rest of the world. Even today, only 38 islands of the 293 are inhabited and of these, many support only a diminishing number of tribes.

Inhabited by Aborigines

Until the 1600s, the various aboriginal tribes, which date from the Paleolithic Age, lived alone on the islands. Then the Mahrattas annexed the islands in the late seventeenth century and used them as a base to harass the British, Dutch, and Portuguese, who used this route for trade. The British attempted to establish a settlement in the Andamans in the late 1700s but were successful only after the Indian Mutiny in 1857, when they built a permanent penal colony at Port Blair. In the Nicobar Islands, France, Denmark, Austria, and Great Britain all had some vague rights at various periods from the seventeenth century onward.

The Danes in particular were tenacious in their attempts to occupy the islands until they relinquished them to the British in 1869. The Japanese controlled the Andaman and Nicobar Islands from 1942 till 1945. They allowed Subhas Chandra Bose, the Indian nationalist who formed the Indian National Army (INA), to fly the Indian flag for the first time. Bose had aligned with the Japanese to fight for Indian independence, but his group fell afoul of Japanese territorial ambitions, and the INA's tenure ended at Port Blair. From the time the Allies liberated the islands until Indian independence in 1947, they were again controlled by the British.

Once a Penal Colony

Arriving today in Port Blair, the capital, one finds none of the dread felt by the political activists and criminals who were deported here when the British used it as a penal colony. Known by them as Kala Pani, or "Black Waters," there is little now to indicate the brutalizing punishment that was meted out to these prisoners except what can be seen at the Cellular Jail, now a national museum, whose stark simplicity testifies to those bleak times.

Until press time, Port Blair, a relatively modern town for India, was the only metropolitan locale on this island chain that was accessible to foreign tourists. Today, the government is opening up more of the islands and foreigners will be allowed a 30-day stay in Havelock, Neil, Mayabunder, Rangat, Diglipur, and possibly other islands. It will take a while, however, for resorts to be developed.

India's history since its independence is also uniquely etched into the demographics of the Andamans. Displaced persons from East Bengal, evacuees from Burma, Indian emigrants from the former British Guiana, and, more recently, refugees from Bangladesh (formerly East Pakistan) have been relocated here. Any growth that has occurred in population over the past decades has been the result of emigration, not an increase in the aboriginal population.

Tribal Reserve Areas

The inaccessibility of the tribal population, preserved for thousands of years by their unwillingness to have contact with others, is now preserved by the Indian government under the Protection of Aboriginal Tribes regulations. Of the islands' six tribes, five are confined to their traditional habitation areas, which have been set aside by the government as "Special Primitive Tribal Reserve Areas." Contact with any of the tribes is completely restricted by the government, even to ethnologists.

In February 1987, a more remote tribal group with whom a government-sponsored party of local officials, sociologists, and anthropologists were trying to make contact, rebuffed the attempt by firing arrows with poison tips at the boat bearing the party. The existence of these ancient peoples, some of whom exist exactly as they did in the Stone Age, is an intriguing and provocative fact, but, in general, the closest you can come to their culture is a visit to the small but informative Anthropology Museum in Port Blair. Here you can learn of the Andamanese, Onges, Jarawas, and Sentinelese, who are the five Negrito tribes of the Andamans, and the Mongoloid tribes of the Nicobars, the Nicobarese and the Shompens.

As is true of much of what is accessible to tourists in these islands, you can get only a glimpse of the treasures that are here, but that glimpse alone is both fascinating and haunting.

Few Islands Accessible

If you come to the Andaman and Nicobar Islands expecting to see the spectacular natural beauty particular to such isolated, undeveloped tropical islands, you will not be disappointed as long as you get out of Port Blair. Port Blair also has appeal, however, with an unusual collection of museums and tourist sights. Although few of the hundreds of islands are accessible to foreign tourists, those that are offer some of the world's most spectacular coral reefs, guaranteed to dazzle and enchant even experienced divers. Here are the colors you dream of, spread out in warm, clear waters. The rich variety of marine life, from the vibrantly colored parrot fish to the shy seahorse, is mesmerizing. As schools of fish dart and glide through a background of intensely colored coral, you will understand the stories of divers who, becoming enraptured with such beauties, fail to remember their limited oxygen supply.

To experience the marine beauties of the islands, you must put up with some frustration at the limits placed on travel here. However, measured against the possibility of upsetting the fragile ecology of these islands in a rush to develop them too quickly, these are frustrations that you should take in stride. Currently, only trips are permitted to the coral-encircled islands of Jolly Buoy, Redskin, North and South Cinque, and some islands mentioned above. But the vivid colors, intriguing shapes, and the sometimes amusing, sometimes compelling activity of the myriad marine animals yield a surplus of memorable images on which you will reflect long after you return to the mainland.

Other water sports, such as windsurfing and sailing, can be enjoyed in the Andamans. They are all arranged through the larger hotels, since there is little evidence of a tourist industry here other than these hotels.

Cellular Jail

Sightseeing in the Andamans, though limited, offers some interesting finds. The primary attraction is the Cellular Jail, where thousands of men and women who fought for independence were interred, some of them for years, in tiny, spartan, isolated cells. Built by the British, it was completed in 1906 and part of it is still in use until the new local jail is completed.

Looking down from the central guard tower into the current prisoners' garden or walking through the grounds alongside some of the elderly Freedom Fighters who occasionally come back to visit, one senses how contemporary is this part of India's history, compared with what one sees on the mainland. Of the original seven wings of the jail, only three remain, the others having been destroyed in 1943 by an earthquake. A number of small museums are worth visiting for the information on the islands that they provide. In addition to the Anthropological Museum, there are the Marine and Forest Museums.

Rare Beauties Protected

The Andaman Islands are not a bustling, glamorous "resort" vacation spot like Thailand's Phuket. Rather, they are a peaceful vacation spot that offers outdoor activities associated with beach resorts but with restrictions to protect their rare beauty.

The fact that these islands aren't yet a developed tourist haven adds a great deal to their charm but is also the source of some irritation. The government has plans to expand the tourist facilities and is considering a variety of recommendations to take greater advantage of the islands' richness of botanical and marine life. Right now, however, tourists are set down in an environment that is uncluttered by the amenities of other island resorts. Although the hotel staffs are solicitous of your needs, you have a refreshing if sometimes frustrating feeling that to the rest of the islanders you just don't matter much. The sleepy, soothing atmosphere makes it a reviving spot to visit after the more boisterous encounters you will have had on the mainland.

PRACTICAL INFORMATION FOR
ANDAMAN AND NICOBAR ISLANDS

WHEN TO GO. The climate in the Andaman and Nicobar Islands is tropical and temperate, with temperatures varying between 62°F and 86°F throughout the year. Constant sea breezes bring relief even during hot spells. The relative humidity is 75 percent, and the annual rainfall, which is about 120 inches, is spread evenly over eight months, from mid-May to mid-September during the southwestern monsoons, and from early November to mid-December during the northeastern monsoons. The ideal time for vacationing here is mid-October–April, when conditions are optimum for enjoying water sports and the islands' natural beauty.

PERMITS. Foreign nationals need a permit to visit the Andamans; the Nicobar Islands are off-limits. Although you can obtain a permit from the Indian Mission or Consular offices in your home country, permits are also available on landing at Port Blair. Until the liberalized policy takes effect, hopefully in 1993, this permit is restricted to the Port Blair municipal area and the islands of Jolly Buoy, Redskin, Cinque, Neil, and Havelock. Night halts are only permitted in Port Blair and Havelock.

HOW TO GET THERE. By Air. *Indian Airlines* flies to Port Blair from Madras and Calcutta four times a week.

How to Get From the Airport. When you arrive in Port Blair, airline **vans** transport you from the plane to the edge of the runway, where there is a shed, a parking lot, and not much more. After claiming your luggage and getting your permit to visit the islands (if you haven't already done so), either take the **taxi** sent by individual hotels or hire one of the private taxis in the parking lot next to the arrival shed. Depending on where you are staying, the fare to hotels should be Rs. 50–Rs. 75. You'll have to do some bargaining, since taxis often do not run their meters.

By Ship. You can go by ship from Calcutta and Madras. The trip takes about three days. For information and reservations, contact the *Shipping Corporation of India* (SCI), 13 Strand Rd., Calcutta, 700001; SCI, Madras Port Trust, Old Warehouse Bldg., near Customs House, Rajaji Salai, Madras; 600006; and SCI, Aberdeen Bazaar, Port Blair 744101.

TOURIST INFORMATION. For information on the islands, contact these government offices:

Deputy Director, Information, Publicity & Tourism, Andaman & Nicobar Administration, Port Blair 744103; tel. 20694.

Tourist Information Center, Tourist Home, Port Blair 744103; tel. 2300.

Government of India Tourist Office, VIP Rd., Junglighat P.O., Port Blair 744103; tel. 21006. Open Monday–Friday, 8:30 A.M.–5 P.M.; Saturday till 1:30 P.M.

FOREIGN CURRENCY EXCHANGE. Most Western-style hotels have money-exchange counters. Otherwise, go to a branch of the *State Bank of India,* open Monday–Friday, 10 A.M.–2 P.M.; Saturdays till noon.

ACCOMMODATIONS. Since traveling to the Nicobar Islands is restricted, your stay must be prearranged when you apply for a permit. The Andaman Islands, however, have some lovely hotels—most with modern Western amenities and accoutrements. Even Indian-style hotels have a charming, relaxed atmosphere. Prices are based on double occupancy and exclude taxes and service charges: *Expensive,* Rs. 1,200–Rs. 2,000; *Moderate,* Rs. 500–Rs. 1,200; *Inexpensive,* under Rs. 500.

Expensive

Welcomgroup Bay Island. Marine Hill, Port Blair 744101; tel. 20881. 48 rooms with bath. This charming resort, built on a steep hill overlooking Ross Island and one km from the downtown area, was designed by Charles Correa, one of India's best architects. It is modeled after a cluster of tribal huts. Open breezeways connect the handsome lobby with each group of rooms, where furnishings are upscale-ethnic and comfy. Best rooms have a sea or bay view. Some rooms are air-conditioned. Good restaurant serving Burmese, Indian, and Continental cuisines, TV, room service, bar, doctor, swimming pool, fishing, snorkeling, and scuba-diving equipment and arrangements, bicycling, island cruises, foreign-exchange and travel counter. AE, DC, MC, V.

Moderate

Andaman Beach Resort. Corbyn's Cove, Port Blair 744101; tel. 21462. 54 rooms with bath. Operated by Travel Corporation of India, this resort, with lovely gardens, is seven km (four mi.) from the downtown area and overlooks a perfect beach. The lobby is cozy and tropical. Rooms have delightful bamboo furnishings and are whistle-clean. Some rooms are air-conditioned. There is a good restaurant serving Indian, Chinese, and Continental cuisines, plus a bar, diving equipment, scuba diving, snorkeling, windsurfing, tennis, foreign-exchange and travel counter. AE, DC, V.

Hotel Assiana. South Point, Port Blair 744101; tel. 21159 or 21165. 23 rooms with bath. This new five-story resort sits high over the sea, halfway between Corbyn's Cove and Marine Hill. Air-conditioned rooms have a modern-decor, with balconies that face the water. Some rooms have TV. Restaurant serving Indian, Chinese, and Continental cuisines, bar, room service, car-rental arrangements, doctor. Rupees only.

Inexpensive

Megapode Nest. Reservations: Deputy Director, Information, Publicity & Tourism, Port Blair 744101; tel. 20694. 10 rooms with bath. In this government-run facility, you'll find clean, air-conditioned rooms with simple decor. There is a restaurant serving simple meals. Rupees only.

DINING OUT. The best restaurants in Port Blair are part of the hotels, and they combine Indian, Chinese, Continental, and Burmese cuisines. Buffets are common for lunch and dinner. Because most food and drink are flown in from Calcutta and Madras, the prices are higher and fresh fruits are not always available. Prices are based on one person eating a three-course meal, excluding taxes, tip, or beverage: *Expensive* (Rs. 200–Rs. 300) at Andaman Beach Resort and Welcomgroup Bay Island; and *Moderate* (Rs. 100–Rs. 200) at Assiana.

HOW TO GET AROUND. From the Airport. After you arrive in Port Blair, obtain your permit if you have not already done so; then take a taxi to your hotel. Fare is about Rs. 50–Rs. 75.

By Boat. From the Fisheries Jetty, Port Blair, a ferry service runs three times a day around South Andaman Island. If you want to hire your own private launch, contact the *Marine Department or Oceanic Company,* M. G. Rd., Middle Point.

By Taxi. Taxis are available at all hotels for sightseeing around Port Blair. Rates are about Rs. 4.50 per km.

By Rented Car with Driver. Another alternative for local sightseeing is to make arrangements through your hotel. Figure about Rs. 100 per hour.

By Bike. This is a delightful and inexpensive way (about Rs. 25 per day) to move around Port Blair. Ask your hotel to recommend a rental shop in town.

TOURS. The Directorate of Information, Publicity, and Tourism conducts a daily bus tour around Port Blair and boat cruises in the harbor. Contact the Tourist Information Center or Directorate (addresses above).

TOUR OPERATORS. The better hotels can take care of all your island travel needs, including boat-cruise arrangements and a hired car with driver.

HISTORIC SITES. Monuments are either free or have a nominal fee.
Cellular Jail, just north of the Aberdeen Jetty, is now a national memorial to the Indian Freedom Fighters who were interred here by the British before independence. Built by the British between 1886 and 1906, its original design was a seven-winged building radiating out from a central guard tower. It contained 698 small cells in which prisoners were kept in solitary confinement. Today, to the right and left of the compound entrance, galleries hold photographs of many of these Freedom Fighters, grouped according to the incident for which they were imprisoned. Various prison artifacts, such as a device for holding prisoners when they were flogged, and information regarding food rations and work responsibilities, testify to the harsh treatment these "criminals" received. Within the compound, you can visit the gallows and the narrow whitewashed cells on the upper floors of the unoccupied wing on your right as you enter. Names of the Freedom Fighters are inscribed in stone at the top of the central guard tower. Open 9 A.M.–noon and 2–5 P.M., Monday–Saturday.
Chatham Saw Mill, Asia's oldest and one of its largest sawmills, gives informal tours to tourists. You get to follow the process that turns huge logs into finished planks of wood. Timber, brought in from the islands, is unloaded from boats, sawed into planks on large pre–World War II band saws, trimmed and planed, and then cured in huge temperature-controlled kilns. Once seasoned, the planks are sorted by grade and stored for shipment. You are also allowed to watch artisans in workshops turning premium-grade wood into furniture. Photographs not permitted.

MUSEUMS. The *Anthropological Museum* has extensive information on the islands' tribal peoples. You can see models of tribal villages, everyday tribal artifacts, and photographs of the various expeditions that have made contact, or, in some cases, failed to make contact, with the islands' six tribal groups. Powerful reminders of their cultural fragility are two photographs of a tribal couple, the first taken in their tribal dress, the second taken in Western attire. A small research library on the second floor has an extensive collection of books on the islands. The museum is open 9 A.M.–noon and 1–4 P.M., closed Saturdays.

Forest Museum, near Chatham Saw Mill, displays the variety of local woods and illustrates how each is put to use by the lumber industry. Dominating the two-room collection is a large tree fashioned out of pieces of all the tree varieties, from the velvety red padauk to the unusual marblewood. Open 8:30 A.M.–4 P.M. daily.

Marine Museum, near Marine Park, provides information on life under the sea. Any novice diver will appreciate the display of the coral that is found in the offshore waters. Open 8:30 A.M.–4 P.M., closed Sundays.

GARDENS AND ZOOS. *Marine Park,* a pleasant strip of land that runs along the sea, has modest, well-maintained topiary gardens.

Mini Zoo is home to some of the islands' unusual animal life and has a saltwater crocodile-rearing farm. Open 7 A.M.–noon and 1–5 P.M., closed Mondays.

SPORTS AND OUTDOOR ADVENTURES. The **coral beds** throughout the islands support some of the most spectacular underwater marine life in the world, and the multihued waters in which they are found are astonishingly clear and bathwater warm. From close to shore you can snorkel out to where the sea floor is covered with coral. Water temperatures range from 78°F on the surface to about 60°F at a depth of 40 meters (130 feet). There is good visibility to 16 meters (50 feet) below the surface; at a depth of 25 meters (80 feet), there is a visibility to about 5 meters (15 feet). Whether you snorkel from the surface or skin dive, the anemones, angelfish, sweetlips, parrot and squirrel fish, brain coral, and sea fan are vividly displayed in languid waters.

Coral beds are easily accessible at *Jolly Boy* and *Cinque* islands, both of which are uninhabited islands of great beauty. Convenient day trips can be arranged through the better hotels or the tour operator listed above. Since these islands are so isolated, have the hotel prepare a picnic lunch or take along food from shops in Port Blair. Drinking water and other beverages should also be taken.

The management of the *Andaman Beach Resort* is especially knowledgeable about the Islands' underwater attractions and is active in organizing **scuba-diving** and **snorkeling** expeditions. Although some snorkeling equipment is available through hotels and Island Travels, we recommend that you bring at least a well-fitting mask and snorkel. The much-advertised "glass-bottom" boat is no more than a motorized dinghy with a small plexiglass section through which passengers sitting in the middle of the boat can peer.

If **sunbathing** and **swimming** are of interest, the best spot near Port Blair is *Corbyn's Cove,* a peaceful spot at the southern end of Port Blair. The beach, like that of the other islands to which day trips are permitted, has clean white sand, gentle surf, and clear, warm waters. Ringing the crescent-shaped beach are tall palms that cast long shadows across the sands in the late afternoon.

SHOPPING. In Port Blair, the *Cottage Industries Emporium* (open 9 A.M.–1 P.M.; 1:30–5 P.M., closed Mondays and Fridays) has a sparse display of wood and shell items for sale in its sleepy showroom. Although shops near the *Aberdeen Bazaar* seem to carry only cheap "shell art" at first glance, you can find some beautiful shells in their natural state, such as mango shell, chambered nautilus, nancowry, spiney murex, and king shell if you poke around. Since tourism is only now becoming important to the islands' economy, local raw materials, such as the unusual varieties of woods, are rarely used in native crafts. When available, items of marblewood and padauk are beautiful and, in the case of the latter, a pleasure to touch. Hard bargaining and comparison shopping are suggested at these shops.

NIGHTLIFE AND BARS. The best places from which to watch the sunset, while sipping a drink, are the Welcomgroup Bay Island and the Andaman Beach Resort. Bars are generally open noon–2:30 P.M. and 6–10:30 P.M.

NEPAL

NEPAL

Nepal is the world's only declared Hindu nation, but its beliefs are actually a fusion of Hinduism, Buddhism, and remnants of animism. The amalgamation extends to the temples, festivals, and daily rituals celebrated by the faithful. Consider the most revered Hindu goddess in Nepal, the Royal Kumari (Living Goddess), who resides in a palace in Kathmandu and is honored as the incarnation of the goddess Kali, the wrathful consort of Shiva. Born a Buddhist, this young child became a Hindu goddess as soon as she was placed on the throne, and she now occupies a position of importance in Nepal second to that of the king.

As in India, Vishnu and Shiva in all their manifestations are the most popular Hindu gods. The king is considered a descendant of Vishnu; Shiva is the guardian of Nepal. Though the non-Hindu may be put off by animal sacrifice, it's an important practice in Nepal, and male edible animals are the exclusive offering. An understanding of the ritual of sacrifice places it in a proper context.

As defined by the Vedas, sacred Hindu texts, sacrifice is a symbolic act that allows the devotee to become one with God by means of the surrender of his ego and various negative traits. The death of a water buffalo represents the suppression of anger; a goat, lust; a sheep, stupidity; a duck, apathy; a chicken, fear. An egg is offered as a symbol of all five animals and of the creative process in its purest form.

Hindus believe an animal's death releases its spirit and allows for its rebirth at a higher plane. When an animal is presented to the temple priest, it's head, usually smeared with vermilion or henna (red is auspicious, a symbol of life), is first sprinkled with water, which makes it shake as if agreeing to its death. Should an animal fail to consent, it's not killed.

Hindus and Buddhists (the latter represent 6% of the population) also share each other's gods: Avalokitesvara (Buddha of Compassion) is wor-

Nepal

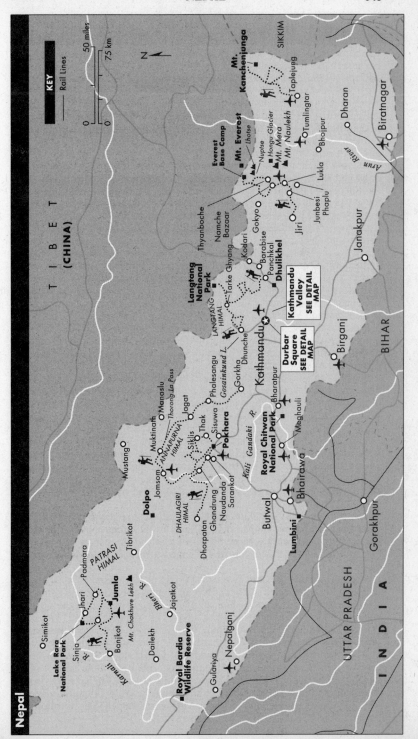

shiped by Hindus as a manifestation of Shiva; Ganesh, the elephant-headed god, and Sarasvati, Brahma's consort, are Hindu deities who often appear in Buddhist sanctuaries. Buddhism and Hinduism—tolerance and harmony. Nepal, which calls itself an international zone of peace, is exactly that. Its peoples get along very well.

Nepal's 18 million people represent numerous races and tribes, each living in different regions, wearing unique traditional dress (although they're slowly shedding them for Western garb), and speaking their own languages or dialects. Gorkhas, who include a variety of tribes—the Gurung, Magar, Rai, Limbu, and Sunwar—are either Buddhist or Hindu and reside primarily within the Annapurna district of central Nepal, where they usually farm or herd livestock.

Moving north into the remote mountains, the people are usually Buddhist and speak Tibetan dialects. Around Mt. Everest, you'll encounter the Sherpas—intrepid mountaineers and often the indispensable lifeline for a successful climbing or trekking expedition. In the towering peaks to the west of Mt. Everest and due north of Annapurna reside the Lo-pa (the people of the ancient kingdom of Mustang), yak traders whose high-perched homeland has just been opened to foreigners. Not far from the Lo-pa are the Thakali, successful traders and farmers. Inhabiting an even higher altitude near Mt. Dhaulagiri are the people of Dolpo, who cultivate barley. This is another area now open to foreign visitors.

The Newar, predominantly Hindu and claiming as ancestors the original inhabitants of Nepal, constitute the most important ethnic group in the Kathmandu Valley. On the valley fringe, you'll come across Buddhists called the Tamang, Tibetan for "Horse Trader," who once dealt in horses but now cultivate the land. In the tropical southern belt, called the Terai, are Hindu tribes, including the Tharu, who migrated north from the Tharu Desert in India's Rajasthan.

Nepal's topography is also diverse. The fertile plains of the Terai produce rice, wheat, and jute. The tiger still roams. Heat rages and rain pours in the summer, turning the wide belt a lush green. Dense elephant grass, which covers much of the protected sanctuary lands, grows so high it conceals the tallest tusker.

Throughout Nepal, over a 100 peaks soar over 6,098 meters (20,000 feet), many of them separated by plunging gorges, broken by windswept passes sliced by magnificent rivers. In the extreme north are the giants Everest ("Sagarmatha" to the Nepalese), 8,877 meters (29,108 feet); Kanchenjunga, 8,598 meters (28,208 feet); Lhotse, 8,511 meters (27,923 feet); and "little" Annapurna I, 8,091 meters (26,545 feet).

Central Nepal has undulating hills and valleys threaded by rivers that wind through the mountains to the Ganga in the Indian plains. Gentle slopes are covered with terraced fields. Villages and cities show off the indigenous talent that makes this small country a cornucopia of artistic delights.

Legends provide the only clue to the origin of Kathmandu Valley and the early history of the kingdom of Nepal. Hindus tell a story of Krishna, the popular incarnation of Vishnu, throwing a thunderbolt to break open a lake, known as Nagavosa—the abode of serpents (*naga* means "snake")—and now called Chorbar Gorge. When the water receded, Krishna's cowherds built a city that became the home of a dynasty.

Buddhists speak of Manjushri (Buddha of Transcendent Wisdom), who traveled into Nepal from China. He saw an enormous jewel-covered lotus, which emitted a powerful flame in the middle of this same lake. Divine revelation told him this was a manifestation of the Adibuddha (Supreme Buddha), called Swayambhu in Nepal. Manjushri decided that his followers should settle here. He took his sword and slit open a mountain, which drained the lake and created the valley. One part of the lotus became Swayambhunath, the other Pashupatinath, and the third became Boudanath—three important temples. A story, yes; but modern geologists do believe a lake once filled this valley.

Leaving mythology for recorded history, the earliest known inhabitants were Ahirs, or shepherd kings, most likely Tibeto-Burman migrants from northern India who occupied Kathmandu Valley as early as the eighth century B.C. The second wave of inhabitants were the Middle-Eastern Kirats, with a succession of kings who ruled for centuries. Before the sixth century B.C., the Shakyas, a Rajput clan from northern India, settled in the Terai. There they founded the city of Kapilvastu, which is renowned for its beauty and sophisticated culture. Prince Siddhartha Gautama, who became the Historic Buddha, was born in Lumbini in 563 BC.

History steps onto firmer ground with the next dynasty, the Licchavis, who most likely migrated from India and took control around A.D. 300. The Licchavis, who introduced the caste system to Nepal, also ushered in an age of prosperity. Art and architecture flourished. Palaces and temples, in the new and innovative pagoda-style design, cropped up in the valley. Though few buildings of this era survived, an excellent stone carving dating from the fifth century exists at the Changu Narayan Temple on a hilltop west of Kathmandu.

The thirteenth century saw the rise of the Malla dynasty, whose members were considered descendants of Vishnu. Great patrons of the arts, the Mallas constructed most of the beautiful temples and palaces of Kathmandu Valley. King Yaksha Malla, who ruled until 1482, extended the Malla domain into parts of Tibet and India, but he forgot to watch over his own backyard.

Family fighting left the dynasty vulnerable. In 1768 a Gorkha army, under the rule of Prithvi Narayan Shah, stormed across Nepal. Wary of the British, who had a firm hold on India, Prithvi Narayan Shah and his grandson, Bahadur Shah, conquered nearby rival kingdoms to create a buffer against the British threat, thus unifying Nepal.

In 1846 palace intrigues again erupted into a bloody massacre, which put an end to the Shah dynasty and marked the beginning of the Age of the Ranas. Acting as prime ministers, the Ranas ushered in a period of fragile peace, not to mention secrecy, since they closed Nepal's borders to outsiders. After World War II, fighting between the Ranas, helped along by pressure for meaningful reforms from a newly independent India, set in motion their downfall. In 1950 the titular king, Tribhuvan, took refuge in India. The Nepalese revolted against the Rana government. In 1951 King Tribhuvan returned to Nepal and recaptured the throne, putting an end to more than a century of Rana rule. In 1975 his grandson became King Birendra Bir Bikram Shah Dev.

For years King Birendra wielded nearly absolute power in matters of state until dissatisfaction and frustration led his people to demand a more representative and democratic form of government. In 1990, Nepalese workers, students, housewives, and even young children took to the streets to demand a multiparty system and democracy. Days of protest led to violence and the loss of lives, but finally King Birendra and his followers recognized that they were hopelessly outnumbered. The king dissolved the government and allowed the formation of a new constitution that restored the multiparty system and reduced the king's authority to that of a British-style constitutional monarch.

In May 1991, Nepal elected its first democratic government in three decades. While victorious, the Nepali Congress party, which won without a strong majority, must now placate the United Marxist-Leninist party if it intends to survive. This powerful communist minority has pledged to keep its eye on the politically moderate government to see how it addresses the severe problems that plague Nepal.

One of the world's poorest nations, its people have an average yearly income of only $170. The same rugged mountains that allowed many small kingdoms to develop over the years have inhibited economic progress. Lack of communication within the country is one of Nepal's greatest problems.

Only 2,170 kilometers (1,345 miles) of roads cut through the country, and these are not always passable. About 40 small airstrips have been opened in the country to provide many isolated regions with a direct link to Kathmandu. Still, much of the country remains remote and inaccessible. The majority of the Nepalese in these areas live a difficult life, one that has hardly changed over hundreds of years.

BEFORE YOU GO

GOVERNMENT TOURIST OFFICES. No government tourist office exists outside Nepal. The Nepalese embassies and consulates have some free brochures on Nepal (see Visas, below).

TOUR OPERATORS. General-Interest Tours. To arrange for a car or jeep with driver or a general tour, contact the following reliable agencies (*see* Telephones, *below,* for country and city codes):

Adventure Travel Nepal, a division of Tiger Tops (Box 3989, Durbar Marg, Kathmandu, tel. 223328, fax 221379).

Natraj Tours and Travels (Box 495, Ghantaghar, Durbar Marg, Kathmandu, tel. 222906, fax 227372).

Yeti Travels (Box 76, Durbar Marg, Kathmandu, tel. 221234, fax 226153).

Special-Interest Tours. The following companies offer great outdoor adventures. Their guides are excellent; service is tops. Most of them sponsor treks throughout Nepal, including the newly opened regions of Mustang and Manaslu. You can join a fixed-departure trip or let the companies custom-design a vacation. Make arrangements before you depart (see also Tour Operators in *Facts at Your Fingertips*).

Amadablam Trekking (Box 3035, Lazimpat, Kathmandu, tel. 410219, fax 416029) offers excellent, environmentally responsible treks, including trips to Mt. Dhaulagiri, Arun Valley, Dolpo, Mt. Kanchenjunga, Mustang, and around Mt. Manaslu. It also sponsors rafting runs, wildlife safaris in Royal Chitwan National Park, mountain climbing, long-distance mountain biking, and trips into Tibet.

Explorations (40 South 32nd St., Boulder, CO 80303, tel. 303/499–3314) is run by the chairman of the American Mountain Federation, Steve Matous, and his wife, Connie McDonald. They're fluent in Nepali, extremely knowledgeable about the country, and are involved in numerous projects to protect Nepal's culture and environment. The company specializes in customized trips and treks, especially to remote areas. It also arranged high-quality mountain expeditions. Just name a destination or tell the outfit your area of interest and a trip will be put together for you.

Himalayan Journeys (Box 989, Kanti Path, Kathmandu, tel. 226138, fax 227068 is also environmentally and culturally responsible. It arranges mountain expeditions and does all the standard treks, including those into eastern Nepal in Arun Valley and around Mt. Kanchenjunga, and to Dolpo, Mustang, Manaslu, and through the Rowaling Valley near Langtang, as well as one to Tibet.

Himalayan Mountain Bikes (Box 2769, Kathmandu Guest House, Kathmandu, tel. 413632 or 418733, fax 418479) offers three bike trips around Kathmandu Valley; biking trips combined with trekking to the Helambu area and its monasteries;

Terai trips with jungle safaris and rafting or kayaking; and triathalon adventures with biking, trekking, and rafting.

Himalayan River Exploration and **Mountain Travel Nepal,** part of Tiger Tops International (Box 170, Durbar Marg, Kathmandu, tel. 418491, fax 221379 for Himalayan River and tel. 41508, fax 419126 for Mountain Travel; also see Special-Interest Tours in *Facts at Your Fingertips* for its offices abroad) are the pioneers in Nepal rafting, trekking, mountaineering, and wildlife safaris. Mountain Travel sponsors all the standard treks, many theme-oriented or family treks, plus the "walk" to Lhasa and other new treks in Tibet. It also offers safaris in its classy resorts at Royal Chitwen National Park and Karnali, and a combination of biking, trekking, and rafting trips around Kathmandu Valley. Himalayan River arranges numerous white-water runs and safaris in its classy resorts at Royal Chitwen National Park and Karnali. It also offers a combination of biking, trekking, and rafting around Kathmandu Valley.

Osprey Waterways (contact through Himalayan Holidays, Box 5513, Kantipath, tel. 2289933, fax 272866) offers rafting runs, with a doctor on every trip, on these rivers: Trisuli, Sunkosi, Kali Gandaki, Bheri, Arun, Seti, Tamar, Tombakosi, Karnali, Bhotekosi. Trips range from two to 10 days. It also has special rafting excursions that focus on Nepal's culture, history, and geology.

Treks and Expeditions Services (Box 3057, Corner House, Kamal Pokhari, Kathmandu, tel. 412231) offers all the standard treks and mountaineering, plus crafts, cultural, or participatory religious walks and tours around Kathmandu and Annapurna. It also offers high-quality "teahouse" treks (all you need is a backpack) that patronize inns that respect the environment.

Nepal Mountaineering Association (Hattishar, Kathmandu, tel. 411525) offers two excellent courses in mountaineering. Apply months in advance.

WHEN TO GO. Nepal's peak season is September to December. Make all travel arrangements well in advance. Mountain views are excellent; temperatures are cool and comfortable. This season also coincides with some of the best festivals: Durga Puja, and Indra Jatra. It's also high season for trekking. Unless you go to a remote area, you'll see many hikers.

For trekkers and outdoor enthusiasts, December and January mean cold nights, some cloud cover, but comfortable daytime temperatures. Trekking can be hazardous; heavy snowfalls can leave you snowbound. February heralds the start of spring—a good chance to see animals, birds, and the mountains, with visibility improving until the onset of the June monsoon. In Kathmandu Valley, Pokhara, and the Terai, expect heavy cloud cover, rain, and steamy heat until October. Trekkers should be aware that the monsoon also brings leeches, but you can trek in higher altitudes where the monsoon doesn't penetrate. The best rafting season is September to June. The best time to visit Royal Chitwan National Park and Royal Bardia Wildlife Reserve is from October to June.

SEASONAL EVENTS. The lunar calendar determines most dates. Check with Nepal's embassy or consulate or your travel agent before you depart.

December or January. During the week-long Buddhist festival *Seto Macchendranath (Matyendranath) Snan,* devotees remove the sacred idol from its temple in Kathmandu.

January. *Prithvi Jayanti* honors King Prithvi Narayan Shah, the founder of modern Nepal, with parades.

February 18. A big parade in Kathmandu on *Tribhuvan Jayanti* (National Democracy Day) honors the late King Tribhuvan.

February. During *Shivaratri,* an important Hindu festival celebrating Shiva, pilgrims from India and Nepal attend a massive fair at Pashupatinath Temple near Kathmandu.

February or March. During the week-long *Losar* (Tibetan New Year), monks chant and perform ritual dances—a big event at Boudanath in Kathmandu.

February or March. *Holi,* an exuberant eight-day Hindu festival, ushers in spring and celebrates the victory of Narsingha (Vishnu) over the demon Hiranyakashipu, an important event depicted on statues throughout Nepal. Children throw red-colored water at anything that moves. Wear old clothes.

April. *Ghode Chatra* is celebrated with a horse race held at the Thundikhel Parade Ground.

April. A four-day festive Hindu and Buddhist celebration, *Seto Macchendranath Rath Jatra,* honors the White Macchendranath (Shiva to the Hindu, Avalokitesvara to the Buddhist), who is drawn in a gigantic chariot through the streets of Kathmandu to Hanuman Square.

April. One of Nepal's best festivals, *Red Macchendranath Jatra* is Patan's week-long chariot pageant honoring this god.

May. Buddhists celebrate *Buddha Jayanti* or *Baishakh Purnima,* which pays tribute to the Buddha's birthday, his enlightenment, and his death. Valuable old *thang-kas* (painted religious scrolls) are unfurled during ceremonies.

August. A carnival atmosphere surrounds *Gai Jatra,* which honors the sacred cow and recently deceased family members. Cows and teenagers in cow masks parade through the streets.

August or September. The night before *Krishna Jayanti* (Krishna's birthday), devotees celebrate at Hindu temples honoring Krishna, especially in Patan.

August or September. During *Teej,* Hindu women honor Parvati and Shiva and their own husbands with a fast and a ritual dip in the Bagmati River at Pashupatinath Temple near Kathmandu.

September. An eight-day festival dedicated to Indra, the Hindu god of rain, *Indra Jatra* honors his victory over the demon Vrita, who had cursed Nepal with a terrible drought. The festival begins with the sacrifice of a goat in Bhaktapur, then moves to Kathmandu, where devotees carry the Royal Kumari through the old city in her gold chariot. The huge mask of Bhairav (wrathful aspect of Shiva) is brought out for its annual viewing, and every night masked dancers perform in Hanuman Square.

October. Nepal's most important festival, *Durga Puja,* or *Dassan,* celebrates the victory of Durga, Shiva's consort, over the buffalo demon Mahishasur. Nawa Ratri, the first nine days, honor Durga in her nine manifestations. Devotees take ritual dips. On Kalratri, the eighth night, thousands of animals are sacrificed.

November. A five-day festival, *Tihar,* or *Diwali* (Festival of Lights), pays tribute to Yama, god of death. On the third day, candles illuminate the windows of every house in honor of Lakshmi, goddess of wealth and prosperity.

November. During *Mani Rimdu,* a Buddhist festival, lamas perform masked dances at monasteries near Mt. Everest.

December 15. *Mahendra Jayanti* (Constitution Day) celebrates the beginning of the Nepalese democracy.

December 28. *Shri Panch Ko Janma Divas* honors the birthday of the present king.

TAKING MONEY ABROAD. You can bring any amount of hard currency, including traveler's checks, into Nepal, but you must fill out a Currency Declaration Form when you arrive. There is an illegal black market in foreign-currency exchange. Convert your currency at Foreign Exchange Counters authorized by the Nepal Rastra Bank (State Bank of Nepal). A passport is required. Exchange currency in small amounts as needed because on departure, Nepal will reconvert only 15% of the total amount cashed, and only on presentation of an exchange receipt. Non-Indians who enter from India can't exchange Indian rupees for Nepalese currency.

The units of Nepalese currency are the rupee and paisa (100 paisas = 1 rupee). Paper money appears in rupees 1, 2, 5, 10, 50, 100, 500, and 1,000 denominations; coins are in 5, 10, 25, 50, and 100 denominations. At press time the rate of exchange was U.S. $1 = Rs. 42; £1 = Rs. 73. Carry lots of small denominations. Few taxi, rickshaw, and scooter drivers have change.

WHAT IT WILL COST. Nepal is no longer the great bargain it used to be. You can still buy a cup of tea for under 50¢, have a meal for $2–$3, and find acceptable lodging for less than $50 for two, but in Kathmandu and the wildlife sanctuaries, fancy accommodations mean fancy prices. To protect their profit margin against the frequent devaluation of the rupee, many hotels and tour operators fix the payment for lodging and the rental of a car or jeep with driver in U.S. dollars. Within Kathmandu Valley, a car costs about $75 per day (Rs. 3,150). Travel by car or jeep outside the valley is even more expensive, with night halt charges as high as $40 (Rs. 1,680). Often a flight to your destination is cheaper.

VISAS. Travelers need a tourist visa from the Nepalese consulate or embassy in their home country. You can obtain a 30-day tourist visa that's good for Kathmandu Valley, Pokhara, and other areas linked by highways. To get the visa, you'll need two passport photos and a valid passport. A single-entry visa is $20; double-entry, $40; multiple-entry, $80; the same fee applies to U.S., Canadian, and U.K. residents. If you apply in person, the visa will be ready in three working days. If you apply by mail, allow for a month. You can also wait and get a 30-day visa at any valid international entry point, but expect a long line if you do so at the Kathmandu Airport. You can extend this visa at the Central Immigration Office in Kathmandu or at any police office in Nepal. To extend it a second and (maximum) third month, you must fill out a visa application form, present your passport, a passport-size photo, and a foreign-exchange receipt proving that you've exchanged $20 for each day of the extension. The extended visa fee is $5 per week for the second month and $10 per week for the third.

Americans—Permanent Mission of the Kingdom of Nepal to the United Nations or **Royal Nepalese Consulate** (820 Second Ave., Suite 202, New York, NY 10017, tel. 212/370–4188); **Royal Nepalese Embassy** (2131 Leroy Pl. NW, Washington, DC 20008, tel. 202/667–4550).

Canadians—Royal Nepalese Consulate (310 Dupont St., Toronto, Ont., tel. 416/968–7252).

Britons—Royal Nepalese Embassy (12A Kensington Palace Gardens, London, W8 4QU, tel. 071/229–1594).

CUSTOMS AND DUTIES. On Arrival. Foreigners must fill out a disembarkation card and declare all baggage. Visitors can bring in personal effects, 200 cigarettes or 20 cigars, one bottle of distilled liquor or two bottles of beer, a pair of binoculars, a camera with 15 rolls of film, movie camera, video camera, portable radio, tape recorder, pocket calculator, portable typewriter, tent, sleeping bag, and rucksack.

On Departure. Foreigners must fill out an embarkation card and pay Rs. 450 airport tax. Don't export antiques (over 100 years old), animal skins, loose precious stones, drugs, or weapons. Get a certificate or stamp from the Department of Archaeology (National Archives Bldg., Ram Shah Path, Kathmandu) for any reasonably old item and be prepared to show it on departure.

TIME ZONE. Nepal is 15 minutes ahead of Indian standard time and five hours and 45 minutes ahead of Greenwich mean time.

STAYING HEALTHY. See Health Information in *Facts at Your Fingertips.* An international certificate of vaccination against yellow fever is required if you're arriving from certain specified countries in Africa and Central and South America.

RENTING CAR WITH DRIVER. The cost of a car is determined by your destination. Figure about $30 for three hours or a 60-kilometer (37-mile) round-trip. Hire a tourist taxi or car with driver only from a recommended agency (see Tour Operators, above).

ARRIVING AND DEPARTING

BY PLANE. Airport and Airlines. Only **Royal Nepal Airline (RNAC)** and **Lufthansa** fly into **Tribhuvan International Airport** from Europe (Frankfurt or London via Frankfurt). Other flights originate in Asia: **Thai Airways** from Bangkok; **Singapore Airlines** from Singapore; **PIA** from Karachi; **Biman Bangladesh Airlines** from Dhaka; **Indian Airlines** from Calcutta, Delhi, and Varanasi; **CAAC** (China) from Lhasa (Apr.–Nov.); **Dragon Air** from Hong Kong; **Druk Air** from Paro; **RNAC** from Bangkok, Bombay, Delhi, Calcutta, Colombo, Dhaka, Dubai via Karachi, Hong Kong, Lhasa, Rangoon, and Singapore. Reconfirm your ticket 72 hours before flight time. Arrive at the airport at least two hours before flight time. Planes are frequently overbooked, and Tribhuvan Airport can be a nightmare.

Flying Time. Plan on about a 2-hour flight from Delhi.

BY HIRED CAR WITH DRIVER OR TAXI. A road trip to Kathmandu from Delhi or Lhasa means a long journey, and getting through customs at the Nepal/India border is time-consuming. If this is the way you decide to travel, hire a car from one of the tour operators listed in the Delhi chapter. At press time, the road from Lhasa was blocked by an extensive landslide, which required a half-day walk on either side of the disaster.

STAYING IN NEPAL

CUSTOMS AND CULTURE. In Nepal, shoes are considered unclean. Remove them before you enter a Nepali house or temple. Follow the guidelines for visiting temples described under Customs and Culture in *Facts at Your Fingertips*. Also, it's discourteous to point your finger at a person or statue, to stand with your feet pointed at people or religious objects, or to sit in a position that forces others to step over you. In Kathmandu, beware of pickpockets. Watch your handbag, backpack, and camera, especially in crowded places.

GETTING AROUND. Roads are subject to landslides and washouts in much of Nepal. If you want to trek or mountaineer in remote northern areas, plan to fly to the nearest airport or airstrip. If you plan to visit Pokhara Valley or the Royal Chitwan National Park and Lumbini, you can fly or go by road, even during the monsoon, when landslides occur, but it can be slow going. You can also go to Chitwan by raft. For the Royal Bardia Wildlife Reserve in the western Terai, you should fly to Nepalganj, then do a five-hour trip by car. After a trek from Jumla in the northwest, you can raft to Bardia.

By Plane. RNAC, your only choice, flies between Kathmandu and numerous popular destinations (see Arriving and Departing in Kathmandu, below). Fares are reasonable; you must book early, especially in the peak season. Reconfirm each ticket at least 72 hours before departure and arrive at the airport 90 minutes in advance.

Special Fares. RNAC offers a 25% discount to students with a valid International Student Identity Card.

By Hired Car or Jeep with Driver. From Kathmandu, you can go by road to the border of Tibet in the north, west to Pokhara, and southwest to Lumbini and Royal Chitwan National Park. The recommended general-interest tour operators (see above), who can arrange for a hired car or jeep with driver, also offer standard packages to these destinations, with the cost determined by the length of stay. Make arrangements before you depart.

By Train. No trains exist in Nepal.

On Foot. You'll need a trekking permit to trek in Nepal. Go to the Central Immigration Office in Kathmandu or Pokhara and follow the same procedure as for a visa extension (see Visas, above). A trekking permit is also required for visits to Nepal's interior (any place not linked by major roads). If you plan to trek into two different areas, you'll need separate permits. The charge for individual trekkers going to the Dolpo or Mt. Kanchenjunga areas is $10 per week for the first four weeks; $15 for each additional week. For other areas, the permit is $5 for the first four weeks and $10 for each additional week. Total extendable trek time cannot exceed eight weeks. Permits to the newly opened areas of Mustang and Manaslu are more expensive and can only be obtained through a recognized Nepali trekking agency (see Special-Interest Tours, above). A 10-day permit for Mustang costs $700, with a $70 charge for each additional day. The permit for Manaslu costs $70 per week; the average trek there takes three weeks. The trekking permit also substitutes for a visa extension for all treks, but if you plan to trek longer than a month, you must also extend your visa. If you use a recommended tour operator, the staff will obtain the permit for you. Trekkers must also pay a $12 tax for trekking in the Annapurna Sanctuary in addition to a $12 entrance fee. Trekkers must also pay a $12 entrance fee to all other national parks.

TELEPHONES. Nepal's country code is 977. The city code for Kathmandu is 1; for Pokhara, 061. Telephone lines connect most major destinations in Nepal. In Kathmandu, you can make international calls at several international telephone offices in Thamel, including the **Central Telegraph Office** (across from the National Stadium on Kantipath; open 24 hours daily). If you phone from your hotel, expect a service charge. Phone calls must be paid for in local currency, except at Western-style hotels that accept credit cards. Local calls cost about Rs. 2.

Operators and Information. To book an international call, dial 186. For local telephone numbers, dial 197. There's no guarantee the operator will speak English, but if the person does, speak slowly.

Telegrams and FAX. You can send telegrams from some popular destinations, but the most expeditious office is Kathmandu's **Central Telegraph Office** (see address, above), open 24 hours daily. In Kathmandu, you can send a fax from many hotels and from **Inter-Continental Secretarial Services** (Thamel Chowk, tel. 410410), open daily 9 A.M.–11 P.M.

MAIL. Airmail letters weighing 10 grams to Canada and the United States cost Rs. 10; to England and Europe, Rs. 9. All aerograms and postcards cost Rs. 9.50 and Rs. 9, respectively.

TIPPING. The concept of tipping has arrived in Nepal. Follow the guidelines in *Facts at Your Fingertips.*

OPENING AND CLOSING TIMES. Nepal has numerous festivals during which government offices and banks shut down. Watch the calendar. Most commercial shops (not necessarily including bazaars) and government offices are closed on Saturday, the national day off, and government holidays. Hours are noted for each business establishment.

SHOPPING. Look for lovely thang-kas (painted Buddhist scrolls), statues, brass-work, masks, wood carvings, jewelry, beautiful wool sweaters, gloves, hats, and carpets. Antiques aren't allowed out of Nepal. With rare exceptions, bargain.

DINING. The standard fare is Nepali (not quite as spicy as Indian cuisine) and Tibetan (with lots of noodle and dumpling dishes). Kathmandu's restaurants offer a wide range of international cuisines and ambiences. Local and imported liquors are available. Expect an early dinner, even in Kathmandu; many restaurants shut down by 10 P.M.

Ratings. Prices, based on one person, excluding drinks, service, and taxes, are: *Deluxe,* over $10; *Expensive,* $7.50–$10; *Moderate,* $5–7.50; *Inexpensive,* under $5. Highly recommended restaurants are indicated by a star ★.

LODGING. Though Kathmandu, Pokhara, and Royal Chitwan National Park offer a range of options, from expensive Western-style hotels to budget lodges, expect few choices in other areas. In most Western-style hotels, rupees are accepted only on presentation of a foreign-exchange receipt; otherwise, foreign nationals must pay their hotel bills with foreign currency, traveler's checks, or credit cards.

Ratings. Prices, based on a standard double room, including taxes and excluding service charges, are: *Deluxe,* over $100; *Expensive,* $60–$100; *Moderate,* $25–$60; *Inexpensive,* under $25. Highly recommended hotels are indicated by a star ★.

CREDIT CARDS. Western-style hotels, travel agencies, and many shops accept American Express, Diners Club, MasterCard, and Visa credit cards. The following abbreviations are used: AE, American Express; DC, Diners Club; MC, Mastercard; and V, Visa.

KATHMANDU

In Kathmandu, ringed by the Himalayas, motorcycles roar down the streets. Nepali teens stroll along in jeans and T-shirts. Stalls display posters of Brooke Shields and Michael Jackson next to pictures of the Buddha and Shiva. But despite these signs of the West, Kathmandu's ancient temples, old palaces, and fifteenth-century homes still dominate the look of this city—a walker's paradise, with countless treasures to explore.

Kathmandu's buildings are more than beautiful—they are manifestations of Nepal's religious beliefs. To understand the essential principles tied to this faith is to increase your pleasure in this rich destination.

On many temples in Old Kathmandu, you'll see images of the male and female sexually united. This is an artistic rendering of the tantric concept that salvation comes from the union of the male and female forces. Shakti, the consort of Shiva, is an example of the female force. She has numerous manifestations. Like Shiva, she can be benign (as Parvati) or destructive (as Devi, Durga, and Kali). Kali represents the most terrifying form—black, half-naked, wearing a garland of human skulls; her red tongue hangs from her mouth.

Often you'll see Kali standing on a motionless Shiva. This image represents the universe, where everything is relative—static and dynamic. Shiva without Kali is incomplete, energyless.

Tantrics believe that through meditation, through a series of mysterious rituals, and, above all, through the mystical power of sexual union, you can reach nirvana. In this regard, they compare human existence to the lotus. The root comes from mud; the flower represents perfect beauty. You can't achieve nirvana without emerging from the dark.

A six-sided star on a temple represents the union of the female and male forces. The female triangle points down; the male triangle points up. Their union represents nirvana and the cosmos. The points on the male triangle also stand for Brahma, Vishnu, and Shiva—the Hindu trinity. The points on the female triangle symbolize the consorts Sarasvati, Lakshmi, and Parvati.

The pagoda style of Kathmandu's temples originated around 300 B.C. The two roofs represent the female triangle moving up to merge with the male. The stanchion in the center of each triangle points the way to enlightenment and stands above the temple's inner sanctum, which enshrines the sacred idol. The Nepalese flag has two triangles. The one on top with the crescent moon represents the female energy; the lower triangle with the sun is the male.

The erotic art on many Hindu temples also depicts the tantric division of the human body into seven *chakras* (centers of energy). One must master the sexual urge at the site of the lowest chakra before one can obtain enlightenment. Erotic art is always outside a shrine. Each female image stands for a vowel; each male represents a consonant. If you line up the figures on a temple, they spell out a prayer to the deity in the inner sanctum. Inside the shrine, you will usually find a carving of a lotus.

The swastika, a symbol associated so irrevocably with Nazism, confuses the Westerner who sees it on carvings, bronze statues, and thang-kas. "*Swastika*" is Sanskrit for "well-being" or "doing good for all." Its four arms stand for pure love, compassion, happiness, and indifference—the qualities that lead both Buddhists and Hindus to salvation.

Perhaps these four attributes explain how Kathmandu allowed itself to become a hippy paradise. In the 1960s, when the young flocked to India to find themselves, many were sidetracked when they heard that hashish and marijuana grew wild in Nepal. Years passed before the Nepalese realized that these foreigners brought problems and not the much-needed foreign currency. In 1973 Radio Nepal announced that shirtless foreigners with long beards, mustaches, and flip-flops couldn't get visas. Within a week, all the hippies were "reincarnated." There wasn't a beard in Kathmandu unless it was attached to a wandering *sadhu* (Hindu holy man). In 1975 the government banned trafficking in hashish and marijuana. The owners of land where the wild plants grew had to cut it before it reached three feet. That helped, but now there's a new imported problem: Twelve thousand Nepali children are addicted to heroin.

ARRIVING AND DEPARTING. By Plane. *Airport and Airlines.* From the domestic terminal near **Tribhuvan International Airport, RNAC** (Kanti Path, tel. 220757 or 214640) flies to Pokhara (two flights daily); Nepalganj—Royal Bardia Wildlife Reserve (over 10 weekly flights); Bhairawa—approach to Lumbini (daily flight); Maghauli—Royal Chitwan National Park (daily); Tumlingtar—gateway to Arun River (five weekly flights); Jumla (two weekly winter flights); Jomsom, north of Annapurna (one weekly winter flight); Lukla, near Everest and Khumbu (three daily winter flights, year-round flights under discussion); Taplejung—gateway to Kanchenjunga (two weekly winter flights). RNAC also arranges numerous charters, including one to Langtang, north of Kathmandu. Book all flights early. Reconfirm at least 72 hours before departure and arrive at the airport 90 minutes in advance.

Between Airport and City. The airport is eight kilometers (five miles) from Kathmandu. A few hotels provide courtesy airport service (see Lodging, below).

An airport bus (tel. 521064 or 522146) shuttles between the airport and New Road in Kathmandu. It runs daily 8 AM–10 PM and costs Rs. 15.

A taxi to Kathmandu should cost Rs. 150; negotiate.

GETTING AROUND. By Taxi. Taxis, with black-and-white licence plates, are inconvenient in Old Kathmandu. At night, expect to pay twice the normal fare. Call 224374 for night taxis. For longer excursions, insist that the driver use the meter or fix the fare beforehand. Offer half what he suggests; then increase your offer.

By Hired Car or Jeep with Driver. The cost is determined by your destination and length of stay. Hire a car or jeep with driver only from a recommended tour operator and make all peak-season arrangements before you depart.

By Tempo. A better option for the old city, *tempo* (auto rickshaw) rides should be cheaper than taxi rides.

By Bicycle Rickshaw. A wonderful way to travel through the old city, especially at night, a bicycle rickshaw should be cheaper than a tempo.

By Bicycle. With the exception of walking, bicycling is the nicest way to get around Kathmandu and the surrounding valley. Be prepared for crowds in the old city and for hard pedaling on hills beyond the city limits. Many recommended hotels rent bicycles (see Lodging, below). Shops in Thamel and on Freak Street also supply bikes. Figure Rs. 20 per day.

ADDRESSES AND NUMBERS. Tourist Information. The **Tourist Information Center** has a counter (tel. 470537) at the International Airport and an office (tel. 220818) on New Road, near Durbar Square, that is open Sunday–Thursday 9–6 and Friday 9–4. Ask for a free copy of the *Nepal Traveler,* which has useful information and maps.

Emergencies. The **American Embassy** (Pani Pokhari, tel. 411179 or 412718) is open weekdays 8–12:30 and 1:30–5. There is no Canadian embassy or consulate. The **British Embassy** (Lainchaur, tel. 411789) is open weekdays 9–1 and 3–6. For medical emergencies, ask your hotel to recommend a clinic or private physician. In Kathmandu, the **Nepal International Clinic** (Durbar Marg, tel. 412842), with its English-speaking staff, is open Sunday–Friday 9:30–5 and for emergencies on Saturday.

Travel Agencies. Most of the indigenous adventure outfits (see Before You Go, above) and a few overseas outfits (see *Facts at Your Fingertips*) have offices in Kathmandu. To hire a guide or car with driver or to arrange excursions, use the following travel agencies. They are open daily 9:30–6. **Adventure Travel Nepal** (Durbar Marg, tel. 223328), **Natraj Tours and Travels** (Ghantaghar, Durbar Marg, tel. 222906), and **Yeti Travels** (Durbar Marg, tel. 221234).

Bookstores. Good bookstores with English-language publications are located throughout Thamel and on Rani Pokharai near Durbar Marg. **Tiwari's Pilgrim's Book House** (near Kathmandu Guest House, Thamel), open daily 8 AM–10 PM, has excellent books on the Himalayas. **Tibet Book Store** (Keshar Mahal, Tridevi Marg, Thamel), open Sunday–Friday 9–9, specializes in Buddhism.

Banks. American Express is on Jamal Tol, off Durbar Marg (tel. 225020) and is open Sunday–Friday 8–8 and Saturday 9:30–5. Grindlay's Bank (Kantipath) is open Sunday–Friday 10–2:30; its branch in Thamel is open Sunday–Friday 10–6. Nepal state banks are open Sunday–Thursday 10–2:30, Friday 10–2. Outside Kathmandu and Pokhara, carry sufficient rupees. Credit cards and traveler's checks aren't accepted in small villages.

Post Office. The **General Post Office** is at Sundhara (near Bhimsen Tower on lower Kanti Path) and is open in winter, Sunday–Friday 10–4; summer, Sunday–Friday 10–5; closed Saturday and government holidays.

GUIDED TOURS. The travel agencies listed above (see *Tour Operators* in Before You Go, above) conduct half-day tours by car, minibus, or bus to Bhaktapur (Bhadgaon), Pashupatinath, and Boudanath or to Kathmandu City, Patan (Lalitpur), and Swayambunath; morning tours to Dakshin Kali; and overnight trips to Dhulikhel for a good view of the sunrise or sunset over the Himalayas. During the peak season, book your tour as soon as you arrive.

Private Guides. These same operators can supply excellent guides.

HIGHLIGHTS FOR FIRST-TIME VISITORS. Don't miss Old Kathmandu, Patan, Bhaktapur, and Swayambunath Temple or a sightseeing flight on the Nepalese side of Mt. Everest.

EXPLORING OLD KATHMANDU

Walk you must—preferably without a guide. Before you visit the famous monuments that crowd Durbar Square, spend a few hours wandering through the maze of narrow lanes *(gallis)* in **Old Kathmandu.** The typical Newari house was built as early as 1400. Notice the door sills studded with bits of metal; each year a new piece is added to ward off evil spirits.

Step through low portals that lead into *chowks* (courtyards), and most likely you'll discover a small Hindu shrine or Buddhist *chaitya* (small stupa). Houses abutting the courtyard are connected. Public courtyards are often owned by an extended family. Since one chowk often leads to another, see how long you can avoid stepping back into a main street.

Now head to **Durbar Square** and start your historical and cultural tour of Old Kathmandu, once called Kantipur, "City of Bliss." Many historians believe Kathmandu acquired its present name from the three-story **Kashthamandap,** a wooden temple at the southwest corner of the square. Built in 1596, it was restored in 1934 after an earthquake. Legend says it was built from a single tree as ransom for a kidnapped god—a remarkable claim, given its 21-meter (68-foot) width and 20-meter (60-foot) height. This and all other attractions mentioned here are best visited between sunrise and sunset. Inquire at the Tourist Information Center for times of special events or religious services. Admission is free, but donations are gladly accepted.

In the morning, Hindus come to the Kashthamandap and leave offerings at the nearby pagoda-style **Maru Ganesh** shrine. *Maru* means "nonexistent" and may refer to the unusual lack of a spire on the gilded roof. Ganesh is an important Hindu god who has the head of an elephant, and his vehicle is the tiny, cunning rat.

The son of Shiva and Parvati, Ganesh has a brother, Kumari, the god of war. One day Shiva held a contest to see which son could circle the universe first. Ku-

Durbar Square

mari, tasting victory, flew off. Sad, fat Ganesh discussed his predicament with his rat, who told him to circle his parents and tell them they were the universe. Shiva was so impressed, he blessed Ganesh with the title "God of Auspicious Beginnings." The faithful start each day with an offering to Ganesh, and each king of Nepal comes to this temple to make a gift before he's crowned.

Behind this temple stands the white stucco **Kumari Chowk,** the profusely decorated palace of the Kumari (Living Goddess), built in 1757. The young girl who lives here is not allowed to smile; her feet never touch ground. She leaves her palace only when she's honored in a festival, and then she travels in a gold chariot.

Candidates for the post of the Royal Kumari must be about five years old and a member of the Buddhist Sakya sect. Royal Kumari's horoscope must be compatible with that of the king. Her body must be flawless and conform to 32 requirements, including no body odors, perfect white teeth with no gaps, a small tongue, and the voice of a sparrow. The would-be Kumari must also witness, without flinching, the midnight sacrifice of 108 goats and 108 buffalo (108 is a sacred number for Hindus), and she must spend the night in the temple with the carcasses. Only then is she named the Kumari—a title she keeps until she reaches puberty or cuts herself. If she sheds any blood, her reign is over.

Across the square from Kumari Chowk stands the **Gaddi Baithak,** a neo-Grecian building constructed in 1908. Today the government uses the building, which contains the king's throne, for state functions. Opposite the Gaddi Baithak is the three-tiered **Maju Deval,** a Shiva temple built in 1690. The supporting beams have cornices with animal heads, and the roof struts are covered with erotic carvings.

Statues of Shiva and Parvati peer down from an upper window in the two-story 1790 **Shiva Parvati Temple.** It's a rare domestic-style temple, resembling a house. Most other temples have a pagoda design, which was eventually copied in China and Japan.

Behind the Shiva Parvati Temple is **Hanuman Dhoka Square,** the cultural and religious center of Old Kathmandu. Hanuman Dhoka means "Gate of Hanuman," the monkey god of Ramayana fame, an obedient servant who performed herculean tasks on behalf of the other gods. The Malla dynasty's kings put Hanuman's image on their battle flags and in 1672 placed his statue outside the **Royal Palace.** Since its installation, Hanuman's statue, dressed in a red cloak, has been the object of devotion, with gobs of mustard oil and red powder dabbed on its surface by the faithful.

Before entering the Royal Palace, notice the two guardian lions near Hanuman. Shiva (the male force) sits on one side and Shakti (the female force) sits on the other. Just inside the Royal Palace, you'll come to a statue of Narsingha (an avatar, or manifestation, of Vishnu) killing the demon Hiranyakashipu, who tortured his son for worshiping this Hindu god. Vishnu turned himself into Narsingha, half-man and half-lion; stretched the demon across his lap; and tore open its stomach with his claws. This image appears throughout the valley.

The palace, much of it off-limits, wraps around several courtyards, with the Golden Door leading into **Nasal Chowk,** where coronations take place. A gilded fish on a pole at the northern end is an avatar of Vishnu and can swim through the world's waters. It is an auspicious sign that represents peace, prosperity, and transcendental wisdom. On the eastern side of this courtyard is a small whitewashed shrine that contains a statue of Nasaleshwar (Dancing Shiva), which gives the square its name.

The nine-story **Basantapur Tower** was added to the complex in the seventeenth century. There is a good view of Kathmandu from here. Also visible is the unusual round-roofed pagoda, **Pancha Mukhi Hanuman Temple,** dedicated to the monkey god, at the opposite end of the courtyard.

When you leave the palace, notice the huge golden mask on a wall hidden behind a carved wood screen. This is **Seto (White) Bhairav,** a wrathful aspect of Shiva, placed here by a rana in 1769 to protect his kingdom from evil and ignorance. During the Indra Jatra festival, the screen is opened. A big pot of *chang* (rice beer) is placed behind the mask's mouth, and the faithful suck the chang through a long bamboo straw—a gift from Seto Bhairav.

Atop a pillar near the Seto Bhairav is a bronze **statue of King Pratap Malla,** sitting on a lotus-shape pedestal and surrounded by his four sons. Erected in 1670, all the images kneel piously facing the **Degu Taleju Temple,** which was once the Malla's private shrine. This is the tallest shrine in Hanuman Dhoka, and its gilded roofs rise above the square. Its sacred idol, Taleju, is a manifestation of Parvati and was the guardian deity of the dynasty.

On a plinth near the pillar is the multitiered, seventeenth-century **Jaganath Temple,** dedicated to Jaganath (Krishna) and Guheshwari (Parvati), with erotic carvings on its wood struts. Nearby is **Krishna Mandir** (Krishna Temple), an octagonal temple built in the 1600s, with a typical Nepalese first floor and a white plaster northern Indian-style second floor.

On the north wall of the square is the revered seventeenth-century **bas relief of Kalo (black) Bhairav,** a dreaded aspect of Shiva, with fangs and a necklace of human skulls, trampling his father-in-law, who had insulted him. This image reminds devotees of the inevitability of justice. Legend claims that it once served as a lie detector: Anyone who stood before it and spoke dishonestly bled to death. Nearby is the seventeenth-century temple **Indrapur,** with an open balcony on the second tier. Though dedicated to Indra (the god of rain, who saved Nepal from a destructive drought), the inner sanctum contains a lingam, or phallus, symbol of Shiva.

The famous sixteenth-century **Taleju Temple,** guarded by a pair of stone lions, is east of Indrapur and is also dedicated to the guardian goddess. The four-story temple has a gold pinnacle and a gold umbrella atop its gilded roofs. Large bronze faces of the goddess Taleju gaze from upper-floor windows. Except for during the ninth day of the autumn Durga Puja festival, the interior is off-limits to everyone except the royal family and a few priests.

Walk along **Makhan Tole,** a street heading diagonally northeast of Hanuman Dhoka Square, to the first of three small squares, **Indra Chowk.** Four stone dragons on a second-story balcony guard the tile-covered **Akash Bhairav Temple,** dedicated to a wrathful aspect of Shiva—another example of a domestic-style temple. Non-Hindus can go inside but are not allowed into the inner sanctum, which contains a silver head of Yalambar, a king whom legend claims Krishna beheaded during the Great Battle described in the Hindu epic *Mahabharata.* The head of the fallen king, whose eyes look up to the sky (the meaning of "Akash") was enshrined here and soon assumed the status of a god, called Akash Bhairav.

In the second square, **Khel Tole,** and set behind a massive gate guarded by two dragons and a small Buddha on a pillar, is one of Nepal's holiest and most ornate temples, **Seto Macchendranath Temple.** Inside are bronze statues of the goddess Tara holding a lotus and a Classical Greek–style statue of a woman. The temple has metal banners hanging from the pinnacle of the gilded roof. Called *dhvajas,* these banners, which decorate many temples, provide a pathway to heaven. Behind the gilded doorway is the inner sanctum, with a simple cotton doll-like image of the White Macchendranath. Buddhists revere this idol as Avalokitesvara; Hindus, as a manifestation of Shiva.

Numerous small temples crowd **Asan Tole,** the third and busiest of the squares. The most interesting is the three-story **Annapurna Temple,** dedicated to this benign aspect of Durga. Hindus say this goddess lived in the Indian plains and longed to see the mountain named in her honor. A priest offered to take her to Kathmandu. She turned herself into a *kalash* (sacred vessel), and he placed her here by a tree. Parts of the tree and kalash are enshrined in the inner sanctum.

On **Bangemudha Square,** west of Asan Tole, try to find **Vaisha Dev** (Toothache Tree), with hundreds of coins nailed into its boulder-shape trunk, which protrudes from the side wall of a corner shop. Bits of metal hammered in by sufferers hoping for relief nearly obliterate the tree and its golden statue of the deity.

Walk south (back toward Hanuman Square) on the narrow road that faces Vaisha Dev to the intersection of Nara Devi Tole. Turn right and walk about a minute to **Yitum Bahal,** a courtyard on the left. One of the oldest courtyards in Kathmandu, the fourteenth-century Yitum Bahal has a *peepal* tree (fig tree) that has grown around a chaitya. To the right is a sixteenth-century portal with a handsome carving of the Buddha on the *torana* (carved crest).

Inside a nearby courtyard is **Hum Bahal,** a former monastery (*bahal*) that surrounds a Buddhist shrine. To your left is an unusual chaitya with four standing bodhisattvas. On the right, examine the carved metal plates with images of Guru Mapa, a demon who ate disobedient children. One depicts his mask; another shows him enjoying a meal. The monastery is now a school, and from the children's behavior, it seems that Guru Mapa remains a powerful disciplinarian.

Time Out

For apple pie, brownies, or cappuccino, stop at **Helena's** (Thamel), open daily 7:30 A.M.–10 P.M., or **La Cimbali** (Thahity Kwabahal, Thamel), open daily 8:30 A.M.–10 P.M. For ice cream, go to **Nirula's** (Durbar Marg), open daily 10 AM–10:30 P.M.

SHOPPING. The **Kashmiri Bead Bazaar,** open daily 9–7, is behind Indra Chowk. It's run by Kashmiri Moslems who sell fine glass beads from Belgium, Czechoslovakia, and Japan. Sit on a platform and pick out strands, which the shopkeeper will quickly make into a necklace. One of the best bead shops is No. 388. Be sure to bargain; they don't accept credit cards. For good thang-kas, visit **Mannie's Art** (Sakya Arcade, Durbar Marg, tel. 2237115), open Sunday–Friday 9:30–7:30. No bargaining here; he accepts American Express, Diners Club, MasterCard, and Visa credit cards.

For old artwork and curios, visit these shops on Durbar Marg and bargain: **Ritual Art Gallery** (tel. 223410), open Sunday–Friday 10–6, no credit cards; **Treasure Art Concern** (Annapurna Arcade, Shop No. 5), open Sunday–Friday 10–7:30, accepts Diners Club, MasterCard, and Visa. In Thamel, don't miss **Zambalha Tibetan-Bhutanese Handicrafts** (12/902 Thamel), open Sunday–Friday 9–1 and 3–8; accepts American Express, MasterCard, and Visa. This shop sells excellent Tibetan and Bhutanese handicrafts and gorgeous textiles, especially the traditional raw silk scarves, shawls, blankets, and vests.

For stylish clothing and lovely handknit sweaters, stop at **Roof of the World—D. D. Tibetan Boutique** (Kantipath, tel. 220349), open Sunday–Friday 9:30–7, no credit cards. You'll also find good woolen handknits in countless other shops in Thamel and on Freak Street.

Finally, the following shops sell handknits and handicrafts, with all proceeds going to help needy rural villages and the destitute: **Kumbeshwar Technical School** (near the Kumbeshwar Temple in Lalitpur), open Sunday–Thursday 9–5 and Friday 9–1; **Mahaguthi Shop** (Durbar Marg, near the Annapurna Coffee Shop), open

Sunday–Friday 10–6; **Dhukuti** (Himthai Plaza, Thamel), open daily 11–7; **Tibetan Refugee Center** (Tibetan Camp, Jawalakhel, tel. 522414), open Sunday–Friday 8:30–noon and 1–5. All of these cooperatives sell at fixed prices, and none takes credit cards.

OUTDOOR ADVENTURES. Bicycling. Bikes are available for hire (see Getting Around, above). Himalayan Mountain Bikes (tel. 413632 or 418733) offers good trips around Kathmandu Valley.

Fishing. Fish along the Sunkosi River (Oct.–Mar.). Bring your own equipment. No license is required.

Golfing. Play at the Royal Golf Course (tel. 472836) near the airport. Clubs are available.

Hiking. There are many great hikes right outside of Kathmandu. A trekking map of Kathmandu Valley, available at most Kathmandu bookstores, will show good hiking routes. Or, pick a destination, bring a canteen and packed lunch, then have a taxi drop you at the starting point of these day-long walks;

Mt. Pulchoki. It's 2,762 meters (9,062 feet) high and about 16 kilometers (10 miles) southeast of Kathmandu. Visit mountaintop shrines, then follow the trail down the mountain through rhododendron forests to the nearby Godavar Botanical Gardens—a lovely place to picnic. Catch a taxi back to Kathmandu.

Changu Narayan. Take a taxi to Bhaktapur. Walk about six kilometers (three miles) north from Bhaktapur's Durbar Square to Changu Narayan, a historic temple set on a hill (see Excursions, below).

Physical Fitness. The Kathmandu Physical Fitness Center (across from the Ambassador Hotel, tel. 412473) offers aerobic dance classes, massages, and weight training and has saunas and Jacuzzis.

Rafting. Though rafting is possible year-round on the Sunkosi River (east of Kathmandu) and the crowded Trisuli River (west of Kathmandu), the September to November period offers the best white water. Short trips (under four days) can be arranged on arrival. Longer trips should be arranged in advance. Use an agency listed under *Tour Operators* in *Before You Go,* above, or in *Facts at Your Fingertips.*

Sunkosi. The 10-day journey to Chattra on the Sunkosi is considered one of the best runs in the world. You start at Dolalghat on the road to Tibet. Almost immediately you'll encounter rapids, which take you by fishing villages, through gorges with bats clinging to cliffs and monkeys scampering through the trees.

Trisuli. Trips on the Trisuli are less rigorous and can last from three to seven days. A typical run starts at Benighat, west of Kathmandu, where two days of fairly mild rapids take you to the Trisuli gorge and challenging white water.

Sightseeing Flight. An hour-long flight Sunday–Friday (Sept.–May) gives you the mountaineer's glimpse of Everest and other peaks 6,000–8,000 meters (19,680–26,240 feet) high. Before you depart, book through a recommended tour operator or through RNAC.

Trekking (up to a week). Many special-interest tour operators offer a good three-day trek around the Kathmandu Valley, ideal in the spring when flowers are in bloom. You'll walk through villages, terraced fields, and forests, and see cultural monuments.

DINING OUT. Kathmandu's private restaurants offer many cuisines: Thai, German, Indian, Japanese, Tibetan, fast-food American, Nepalese (less spicy than Indian), and Newari, a spicy cuisine that was developed by the valley's original inhabitants, the Newers. All of the restaurants listed below are excellent. Though some restaurants import beef from Calcutta, generally you'll be munching on "buff" (as in buffalo). Dress is casual unless stated otherwise.

INDIAN AND NEPALESE

Naachghar. A formal restaurant set in a neo-Grecian palace, it has Italian-marble and parquet floors, gray walls with ornate plaster moldings, Belgian chandeliers, and a painted ceiling. Nepalese classical music and Indian *ghazels* (romantic ballads) are performed evenings and accompany traditional specialties, including *banel tareko* (fried wild boar), *charako achhar* (shredded marinated chicken), *hansko sekua* (grilled marinated duck), and *dhukur tareko* (grilled marinated dove). *Yak*

& Yeti Hotel, Durbar Marg, tel. 413999. Dinner reservations advised. AE, MC, V. Open 6:30 P.M.–11 P.M. Moderate.

Ghar-E-Kabob. The Mogul decor at Ghar-E-Kabob, together with the ghazels that are performed nightly, create the perfect ambience for the Indian cuisine served here. Try reshmi kebab (minced chicken with herbs and spices roasted over charcoal) or tangri masaledar (drumsticks served with a spicy tomato sauce). Hotel de L'Annapurna, Durbar Marg, tel. 221711. Dinner reservations advised. AE, DC, MC, V. Open noon–3, 7–11. Expensive.

★ **Thayabhu Newari Restaurant and Bar.** This new restaurant with upscale Newari decor—white stucco walls, painted mandalas, brick floors—offers traditional Newari and Nepalese cuisines. Choose a fixed-menu meal, la dugu chatanmari (Newari pizza), or momocha (Newari steamed dumplings). Lazimpat Plaza (near Hotel Shanker), tel. 411570. Dinner reservations advised. AE, MC. Open noon–10. Expensive.

★ **Bhanchha Ghar.** This century-old Nepalese home is now a restaurant, with a relaxing bar on the top floor. The dining rooms, with white brick walls and black window frames, are cozy and the Nepalese cuisine can be ordered from a fixed menu or à la carte. Try the kukhura ko sekuwa (marinated chicken grilled over charcoal) or khasi ko bhutuwa (marinated mutton cooked in a special oil), Kamaladi Ganeshthan, tel. 225172. Dinner reservations advised. AE. Open noon–10. Expensive.

CHINESE

Arniko Room. Scheduled for renovation, Arniko Room will have an upscale Chinese decor, with private dining areas available. The menu will offer Szechuan, Cantonese, and possibly Japanese and Thai dishes. The chef will continue to offer his popular jade chicken (chicken and spinach dumplings) and smoked lamb sesame with mushrooms. Hotel de L'Annapurna, Durbar Marg, tel. 221711. Dinner reservations advised. AE, DC, MC, V. Open noon–3, 7–11. Expensive.

Ras Rang. Eat in its cozy Newari interior with a large brass fireplace or outside on the lawn. Choose from good Hakka, Cantonese, and Szechuan specialties. Across from Hotel Ambassador, tel. 416086. Dinner reservations advised. AE, MC, V. Open 12:30–3, 5–10:30. Inexpensive.

JAPANESE

Fuji Restaurant. Set back from the road, this restaurant, in an old brick palace, is approached via a wood footbridge over a pond. Eat inside at a table or counter, on cushions, on the veranda, or in the garden. Try the norimaki (vegetable sushi) or sukiyaki (beef fillet). Kantipath (across from the American Embassy), tel. 225272. Dinner reservations advised. No credit cards. Open 11:30–10. Moderate.

THAI

★ **Himthai Restaurant and Bar.** Eat Thai cuisine in a garden or upstairs in a former palace, where the simple decor includes old Thai horoscopes on the wall and statues. Try kai pad bai krapas (fried chicken and rice with basil leaves) or pai pad King Kap Taokio (fried prawns with ginger in bean sauce). Himthai Plaza, Thamel, tel. 229230. Dinner reservations advised. No credit cards. Open 11–10. Moderate.

CONTINENTAL

Kokonor. Enhanced by dim lighting and soft piano music, Kokonor offers French cuisine and an array of fish dishes and mixed grills. Hotel Shangril-La, Lazimpat, tel. 412999. Dinner reservations advised. AE, MC, V. Open 6:30 P.M.–11. Deluxe.

Rumdoodle. This famous hangout, with the best bar in town and good food, has a casual "mountaineering" motif. A tent hangs from the ceiling. Walls have "Yeti" footprints autographed by the Himalayan greats—Sir Edmund Hillary and Reinhold Messner. Expect a crowd in season. Thamel, near Kathmandu Guest House, no phone. AE, V. Open noon–10. Inexpensive–Moderate.

ACCOMMODATIONS. In the high season, reserve well in advance. Prices are for a standard double room, including taxes and excluding service charges.

Deluxe

★ **Hotel de L'Annapurna.** This old three-story hotel, now under Taj management, was under renovation at press time. Its lobby is lovely, and the spacious rooms will have a subdued, elegant decor. The best rooms front the garden and pool. *Durbar Marg, tel. 221711, fax 225236. For reservations abroad see Group Hotels under Staying in India in Facts at Your Fingertips. 140 rooms with bath. Facilities: air-conditioning, TV, room service, 4 restaurants, bar, health club, pool, tennis and billiards, shopping arcade, foreign-exchange and travel counter. AE, DC, MC, V.*

Hotel Shanker. The nineteenth-century former palace and birthplace of the present queen is opulent, with numerous attractive sitting rooms—some evoke Versailles, others are traditional Nepalese with brick and wood trim. A few bedrooms have painted ceilings and other Rococo touches. The garden and enormous front lawn are ideal for relaxing. The downside: In peak season, service can be indifferent; don't be afraid to complain. *Near the Royal Palace on Lalimpat, Reservations: Box 350, Kathmandu, tel. 410151. 94 rooms with bath. Facilities: room service, air-conditioning, 3 restaurants, bar, travel and foreign-exchange counter, shopping arcade, pool. AE, MC, V.*

Soaltee Oberoi. On a ridge 10 minutes from Durbar Square, this Western-style hotel is decorated in attractive Newari style with lots of brick and wood trim. Rooms in the Himalayan Wing are large, with ethnic touches; rooms in the older Garden Wing are quieter but less spacious. *Tahachal, tel. 272555, fax 272205. For reservations abroad, see Hotel Groups in Facts at Your Fingertips. 300 rooms with bath. Facilities: air-conditioning, 4 restaurants, bar, room service, TV, baby-sitters, pool, tennis court, health club, foreign-exchange and travel counter, shopping arcade, casino, courtesy bus to airport and Kathmandu. AE, DC, MC, V.*

★ **Yak & Yeti.** This eighteenth-century palace, with an additional wing under construction, is quiet and elegant. The best rooms face the garden and pool. *Durbar Marg, tel. 413999, fax 227782; in Canada, tel. 800/668–8355, fax 416/480–2770. Reservations abroad: Utell International in New Jersey, tel. 201/902–7800, fax 201/902–7738; in London, tel. 081/995–8211, fax 081/995–2474. 111 rooms with bath. Facilities: air-conditioning, TV, room service, 3 restaurants, bar, pool, tennis court, health club, baby-sitters, shopping arcade, foreign-exchange and travel counter. AE, MC, V.*

Expensive

★ **Dwarika's Kathmandu Village Hotel.** The only hotel in Nepal to have received the coveted Pacific Area Travel Association Heritage Award for cultural conservation efforts, this series of guest houses is in a shady compound with brick terraces; each room has carved antique windows and traditional furnishings. *Reservations: Box 459, Battisputali, Kathmandu, tel. 470770, fax 225131. 32 rooms with bath. Facilities: dining room, library, bar, foreign-exchange and travel counter, bike rentals. AE, MC, V.*

Hotel Himalaya. On a hill 10 minutes from Durbar Square, Himalaya is modern and streamlined, with a marble interior that highlights an enclosed Japanese rock garden and sleek, understated decor in the rooms. *Reservations: Box 2141, Sahid Sukra Marg, Lalitpur (Patan), tel. 523900. 100 rooms with bath. Facilities: air-conditioning, room service, 2 restaurants, bar, free center-city shuttle service, foreign-exchange and travel counter, shopping arcade, pool, tennis court. AE, MC, V.*

Hotel Shangri-La. A handsome Newari hotel in the diplomatic enclave, the decor has lots of brick, stucco, and wood trim. The rooms are cheery. The best rooms overlook the garden. *Reservations: Box 655, Lazimpat, Kathmandu, tel. 412999, fax 414184. 82 rooms with bath. Facilities: room service, air-conditioning, 3 restaurants, bar, free airport and center-city shuttle service, pool, foreign-exchange and travel counter, shopping arcade. AE, MC, V.*

Moderate

★ **Summit Hotel.** About three kilometers (two miles) from Durbar Square, this popular two-story hotel has lovely gardens and lawns and excellent views of the mountains and valley. The cheery rooms have traditional touches—especially those in the Himalayan wing. The best views are from upstairs, overlooking the lawn and pool. The management is excellent. *Reservations: Box 1406, Kupondole Heights, Kathmandu, tel. 521894. 37 rooms with bath. Facilities: room service, air-conditioning, pool, restaurants, terrace bar, bike rentals, bar, foreign-exchange and travel counter. AE, MC, V.*

Inexpensive

★ **Kathmandu Guest Hotel.** This popular Kathmandu institution, in the heart of Thamel, caters to the traveler on a budget. The best rooms are those in the newer wing and upstairs with a veranda that overlooks a spacious lawn and garden. Lower-price rooms in the older wing are simpler but clean. Reserve well in advance. *Reservations: Thamel, Kathmandu, tel. 413632, fax 417133. 120 rooms with bath. Facilities: room service, restaurant, rooftop garden, foreign-exchange and travel counter. AE, MC.*

Tibet Guest House. This three-story hotel has a modest lobby with a few simple Buddhist hangings and helpful management. The rooms are simple, with adequate furnishings. *Box 1132, Chhetrapati, Thamel, Kathmandu, tel. 214383. 37 rooms with bath. Facilities: room service, fans, roof garden, bike and motorbike rentals, travel counter. No credit cards.*

THE ARTS. Theater. The New Himalchuli Cultural Group performs traditional Nepalese dances daily in the Cultural Hall in the Hotel Shanker compound. *Tel. 410151 for reservations. Admission: Rs. 100. Open Oct.–Mar., 6:30–7:30; Apr.–Sept., 7–8.*

The Everest Cultural Society performs classical and folk dances daily next to Hotel de L'Annapurna. *Tel. 220676 for reservations. Admission: Rs. 100. Open 6:30 P.M.–7:30 P.M.*

NIGHTLIFE. Bars. The best bars are at **Rumdoodle** (open 4–10), **Hotel Shanker,** and the **Thayabhu Newari Restaurant and Bar.** Most bars close around 11 P.M.

Casino Nepal. Foreigners flying into Kathmandu get Rs. *200* worth of free coupons upon presentation of a passport and used airline ticket. (The offer expires seven days after arrival.) The entrance makes it look like a dive, but downstairs is pure Las Vegas. *Next door to Soaltee Oberoi Hotel. Open 24 hours.*

EXCURSION FROM KATHMANDU TO SWAYAMBUNATH

On a hill east of Old Kathmandu stands **Swayambunath,** literally "Place of the Self-born," or, as called affectionately by the Nepalese, the Monkey Temple, after the swarms of critters who scavenge for food left by devotees. To reach the top, walk up the 365 steps (benches are located at frequent intervals) on the east side of the hill. You can also drive up the road from the southwest.

After walking through a colorful arch, you'll head up the steps past statues of the Dhyani Buddhas (Five Cosmic Buddhas) and their animal vehicles, small chaityas (small, stupa-shaped monuments), the footprints of Manjushri, Tibetan refugees, pilgrims, and those monkeys. Watch your belongings; these animals are fast.

At the top, crowds of pilgrims circle the 2,000-year-old Swayambunath and its monastery, which belongs to the Nyingma (Old Sect). The large white hemisphere is made of brick and earth; it's called *garbha* (womb) and represents the cosmos. Unlike most important stupas, no sacred relic is concealed inside the solid structure. On top, the gilded copper spire consists of 13 concentric circles—the steps to enlightenment, which is symbolized by the intricate metal umbrella above. Below the all-knowing eyes that look out in each cardinal direction is a simple figure that reminds the devout that the Buddha is the only way to salvation.

Start your tour of the complex at the large seventeenth-century *vajra* (thunderbolt) that belonged to the Hindu god Indra and symbolizes boundless power. It is placed on a plinth, or square base, that is decorated with the 12 animals of the Tibetan calendar. The small shrine in front of the vajra contains the first of the five Dhyani Buddhas whose temples encircle the large stupa: Aksobhya (Undisturbed Buddha and Buddha of the East), with his right fingers touching the earth. His vehicle, the elephant, is carved into the base.

Kathmandu Valley

From here, walk clockwise around Swayambunath. The next Buddha you'll come across is Vairocana (Buddha of Resplendent Light and the Buddha Supreme and Eternal), who is shown holding his hands up like a teacher. His consort, Mamki, is in the shrine to his right. Ratansambhava (Buddha of Precious Birth and Buddha of the South) has his palm open, and a horse, his vehicle, is carved into his pedestal. Pandara, his consort, is in the shrine just before the meditating Amitabha (Buddha of Boundless Light and Buddha of the West). Tara, his consort, is enshrined next to Amoghasiddhi (Buddha of Infallible Power and Buddha of the North), who holds his right hand up and has the winged Garuda, his vehicle, set in his base. Lochana, his consort, brings you back to vajra.

At Swayambunath, you'll see symbols of the five elements—air, water, fire, ether, earth—that make up the cosmos. Behind Amoghasiddhi is the Nagapur Temple honoring water. Behind Mamki is the Vasupur Temple, which symbolizes the earth. In the left corner near the Pandara Shrine, the Vayupur Temple represents the air. From here, leave the main courtyard and walk west of the Buddhist library to Agnipur, a temple honoring fire. On its right, a path leads to Shantipur, the ether temple near an enormous statue of Sakyamuni.

This same courtyard has an ornate nineteenth-century Hindu temple, Hariti Devi, dedicated to the goddess Hariti, who is responsible for both averting smallpox and ensuring fertility. Worshiped by Hindus and Buddhists, the temple has gilded roofs and a wall of prayer wheels. Its arch is covered with snakes, protecting the enshrined deity, who is surrounded by children. Beams are carved with animal heads. On Saturday, the temple is crowded with those who come to ask special favors.

Finally, near the Hariti Devi, see the pillared pavilion with chiseled images of the Green and White Tara and a peacock, Amitabha's vehicle, facing the shrine that honors this Dhyani Buddha. In this same area, you will find the National Museum. It has good collections of antique stone and bronze statues, wood carvings, thang-kas, weapons, and beautifully illustrated old books, as well as natural-science displays. *Three km (two mi.) from the old city. Walk, rent a bike, or take an auto rickshaw or taxi. Plan 4 hrs round-trip if you walk. Museum admission: Rs. 4; Rs.*

8 with camera. Open Wed.–Mon. 10–3:30. Temple open sunrise–sunset. You can attend a service in the early morning or later afternoon; check for times with the Kathmandu Tourist Information Center.

EXCURSION FROM KATHMANDU TO PASHUPATINATH AND BOUDANATH

Dedicated to Shiva, Pashupatinath (Temple of Living Beings) is the oldest and most sacred Hindu temple in Nepal. It is set on the banks of the sacred Bagmati River, a tributary of the Ganges, or Ganga. The original temple was supposedly constructed in the 1400s; much of the present complex was built in 1696. Pashupatinath is an important cremation site, since the ashes sprinkled on the water flow down to the Ganga.

During Shivaratri (Feb. or Mar.), pilgrims from all over India and Nepal flock here; throughout the year, devotees come here for ritual baths or bring cows, goats, and dogs to the shrine. The animals are not sacrificed, but honored with a *tika* (red dot on the forehead), which gives them the right to live undisturbed within the complex, as befits the temple's name.

Although the main temple is open only to Hindus, you can get a good look from the far side of the narrow river. Cross the bridge; as you climb the path, take the first set of stairs on the left. At the end of the terrace, notice the head of Shiva (its nose is missing) carved on a fifth- or sixth-century lingam.

From this terrace, you can see the walls and the intricate metalwork of the silver doors surrounding the lower level of two-tiered Pashupatinath, which is crowned with gilded roofs. Within the building is a huge Shiva lingam, and outside stands an equally large gilded bull, Nandi, Shiva's mount. Continue up the path, accompanied by as many monkeys as wandering sadhus, and look at the numerous old shrines and small stone lingams.

Returning to the far side of the river, head left along the bank to the cremation site; be discreet about photos. At the end of the walkway, look at the seventh-century head of the Buddha. Its presence supports the theory that this temple was also a Buddhist shrine—built on a sacred spot where one of the legendary lotus flowers came to rest.

Now drive northeast to **Boudanath Temple.** Dating from A.D. 600, Boudanath is the second-largest stupa in Asia and the most important Tibetan Buddhist center outside Tibet. Once again, the all-knowing eyes of the Buddha peer from the top of the white brick-and-earth hemisphere, dedicated to Boudanath (Buddha of Wisdom), with an unknown relic—some believe it's a tooth of the Buddha—interred during construction.

As with most Buddhist structures, the stupa's base is shaped like a mandala, symbolizing the universe and serving as an aid to meditation. The five elements appear in its design and are symbolized in the colors of the prayer flags: the base—earth, yellow flag; the dome—water, blue flag; the central tower—fire, red flag; crescent—light, pale blue flag; flame on top—ether, white flag. Thirteen rings wrap around the dome from base to pinnacle, symbolizing the steps to enlightenment, or "Bodhi," hence the stupa's name. Prayer wheels encircle its base.

On your left as you walk clockwise, a huge prayer wheel encloses a shrine covered with 1,000 Buddhas. Beyond this structure is a new monastery, with an enormous gold-painted Buddha seated in meditation. *Pashupatinath is 5 km (3 mi.) and Boudanath is 8 km (5 mi.) northeast of Kathmandu. Take a taxi to each site and plan 3 hours for this excursion. Visit both sunrise–sunset.*

EXCURSION FROM KATHMANDU TO LALITPUR (PATAN)

Tibetan traders once called Patan "Ye Rang" (Eternity Itself). It is the oldest of the three ancient city-kingdoms in Kathmandu Valley that were ruled by the Mallas, who created most of the old structures. Patan is five kilometers (three miles) south of Kathmandu, and you should plan four hours for this excursion. Rent a car with a guide for about $20 or take a taxi for Rs. 40.

Patan is still populated by Newars, two-thirds of them Buddhist—talented artisans who continue to turn out traditional fine arts. As in Kathmandu and Bhaktapur, a fusion prevails between Hinduism and Buddhism. Also as in those cities, it has a Durbar Square and a maze of winding lanes.

As you walk down the main street of Patan toward Durbar Square, you'll see the first of the old structures built during the Malla dynasty, a small white-domed **Shiva temple** guarded by Nandi. The next building of note is the octogonal-shape 1637 **Krishna Mandir** of black stone, topped with a gold dome. Guarded by lions, symbols of power, its facade is carved with battle scenes from the *Ramayana* and *Mahabharata*. Its design is influenced by the Indian shikhara-style temple, with graceful finials adorning the peaked roofs. Inside the shrine stands a black stone image of Krishna with his two consorts, Radha and Rukmani. The second story has sculptures of the nine incarnations of Vishnu. The third story has an image of Shiva.

On a pillar in front of the Krishna Mandir is a large bronze statue of Vishnu's vehicle, **Garuda**, half man and half eagle, erected in 1647 to mark the completion of the temple. Garuda sits on a lotus pedestal and is one of Nepal's finest sculptures.

Across from the pillar is the **Royal Palace**, three buildings set around courtyards. Before you enter the first courtyard, notice three statues on the right front wall: Ganesh, Narsingha ripping open the demon Hiranyakashipu, and Hanuman wearing his familiar red coat and with his hand raised.

The entrance to **Sundari Chowk** (Magnificent Courtyard), constructed in the 1620s, is between Narsingha and Ganesh. The ground-floor rooms surrounding the courtyard were formerly stables, storehouses, and the barracks of the guards. The upper floors were the living quarters of the royal family. In the courtyard, you'll see the **Taleju Temple,** which contains an image of the patron deity of the king—Taleju Bhavani.

The **Tusa Hiti** (Royal Bath) is an exquisite Newari creation, with a gold water-spout depicting Narayan (Vishnu) and his consort, Lakshmi, astride Garuda. It's a sacrilege to put your feet on the naga encircling the tank or to step into the basin. A stone Garuda faces this royal bath.

Access to the **Mul Chowk** (Main Courtyard), completed in 1660 by Shrinivasa Malla, is to the left of the exterior of the palace. Its two temples are dedicated to the goddess Taleju. On the right of one temple door, Yamuna (Goddess of the Sacred Yamuna River) stands on a tortoise, her vehicle. To the left, the goddess Ganga is poised on top of a *makara* (hybrid crocodile-elephant), her vehicle.

The entranceway to the **Mani Keshab Narayan Chowk,** the third courtyard that was completed around 1734, is called the Golden Gate. It is another Patan treasure, with three carved windows and a dazzling torana covered with images of Shiva and Parvati directly above the gate. In the center window is an image of Vishnu.

Near a gigantic bell in Durbar Square is the eighteenth-century **Hari Shankar Temple,** which you can identify by its three roofs and two stone elephants. It's dedicated to Shiva and Vishnu.

The nearby freestanding pillar has a statue of the late-seventeenth-century King Yoga Narenda, who sits on his throne with his two wives nearby. Over his head is a large cobra with a bird perched on its head. According to legend, this king was kidnapped by the king of Bhaktapur and later killed. But while Narenda was still alive, he sent word to his people that he would continue to live until the bird on the statue flew away, the two elephants guarding the Hari Shankar Temple walked off to drink from a nearby tap, and a statue of a man with a gun fired it once. To this day, people leave Narenda plates of food and prepare his *hookah* (water pipe).

The **Char Narayan Temple,** dedicated to Vishnu and built possibly as early as 1566, has two stone lions—Ajaya and Vijaya—on the front steps heading to the first plinth where two more lions guard the passage up to the second platform leading to the inner sanctum, which contains a lingam supported by four images of Narayan. Erotic carvings on the roof struts apparently depict 84 different positions for sexual intercourse.

Dedicated to Bhim, one of the Pandava brothers of *Mahabharata* fame, the **Bhimsen Temple,** with a gold roof and a gold *dhvaja* (banner), sits at the end of Durbar Square. Guarded by lions, it is constructed in typical Newari style—three stories with numerous roofs, all resting on an elevated plinth. The animals that stand on the lower roof are more symbols of power. Elaborately carved balconies have images of Shiva, Parvati, and Ganesh.

Patan's most handsome structure is **Hiranya Varna Mahavihar** (Golden Temple), a three-story golden pagoda dedicated to Avalokitesvara and built in the thirteenth century with periodic later additions. To get to this temple, turn left on the road next to the Bhimsen Temple. At the next wide lane, turn right. When you come to a passageway guarded by lions, turn left and head toward a gate with an image of Buddha.

You must remove your shoes before you step into the courtyard to examine the small shrine with ornate silver doors and a gilded roof. Inside, you can see numerous statues and chaityas. This is an active monastery, with lamas living in the surrounding rooms. Their main prayer hall is up a flight of stairs to the right as you enter (circle around the structure clockwise to enter). Here they pray before an altar filled with statues and surrounded by frescoes and thang-kas.

From the Golden Temple, head down to the river and see the **Khumbeshwar Temple.** The bottom two tiers of this five-story, pagoda-style Shiva temple topped in gold date from the fourteenth century, making it one of the oldest temples in the country. The top three tiers were added in the seventeenth century. The setting is pastoral, with goats, chickens, and ducks wandering around, women washing clothes, and children bathing in pools. The temple is covered with carvings associated with Shiva.

Inside the courtyard is a gold Nandi on a brick pedestal. Two lions guard the inner sanctum, with its multiheaded image of Shiva dressed in orange and covered in sandalwood paste. Around the complex are other shrines with statues of Vishnu, Surya (the Sun God), Ganesh, and the goddess Baglamukhi (Goddess of Poisons), who protects devotees from black magic. The nearby grassy courtyard is a grazing ground for Nandi.

When you leave this temple to return to Durbar Square, instead of retracing your steps, go left and walk along the side of the temple. At the next lane, turn right to a lane that leads past more stupas and temples. When you reach Durbar Square, head to **Mahabouddha** (Temple of 1,000 Buddhas). Walk to the far end of the Royal Palace, turn left, and pass through the brass and copper market. A road to the right leads to this well-known temple, concealed behind a painted archway that leads to a courtyard. The tall pyramid-shape, Indian-influenced temple, built of red brick and terra-cotta, crowds the tiny space.

Originally constructed in 1585 as a replica of the temple of Bodh Gaya, where the Historic Buddha attained his enlightenment, the structure was extensively damaged by the earthquake of 1934 and rebuilt—a replica of a replica. Each brick has a tiny image of the Buddha in his meditation pose or of important scenes in his life. All the oil lamps are dedicated to Maya Devi (Sakyamuni's mother).

When you head back to Durbar Square, turn left and see the **Temple of Rato (Red) Macchendranath,** or Matsyendranath (a manifestation of Shiva). Constructed in 1408, it's worshiped by both Hindus and Buddhists. The dark red wood image of Macchendranath, whom many call the guardian deity of Patan, is taken out of the temple and paraded through the city on a huge chariot during the festival of Red Macchendranath Matsyendranath Jatra.

Nearby is the **Minanath Temple,** with an image of Avalokitesvara, whom Buddhists consider to be a brother of Matsyendranath. The small bronze image of Minanath, which is adorned with clothes, is taken out during the annual procession in his honor.

EXCURSION FROM KATHMANDU TO BHAKTAPUR (BHADGAON)

This excursion to Bhaktapur, 13 kilometers (eight miles) east of Kathmandu, will take about four hours. Rent a car with a guide for about $38 or take a taxi and bargain!

Raja Ananda Malla supposedly created **Bhaktapur** around A.D. 889, designing his kingdom in the shape of Shiva's conch shell; other sources claim that it was Shiva's drum. Today the original shape is impossible to detect. Still, Bhaktapur's beauty and ancient character remain intact, to a large extent because of extensive renovation by the West German government, which is actively involved in the restoration of Nepal's ancient monuments.

A large gate flanked by statues of Bhairav and Hanuman leads to Durbar Square. To your left, behind two ornate stone lions, are seventeenth-century statues of

Bhairav and the goddess Ugrachandi, a manifestation of Durga. Surrounded by female attendants, the goddess is shown killing the buffalo-headed demon, Mahishasur. Legend claims that the king who ordered the construction of these statues was so delighted by the craftsmanship that he had the sculptor's hands chopped off so they couldn't be duplicated.

To your right, as you face Durga, you will see another pair of stone lions that guard the entrance to the **National Art Museum,** formerly the Royal Palace, which extends nearly the length of Durbar Square. Its collection of paintings, statuary, and thang-kas spans the thirteenth to nineteenth centuries. Most pieces depict Hindu and Buddhist tantric deities. Statues of Hanuman Bhairav (a hybrid deity with four hands who stands on a demon) and Narsingha Narayan (a manifestation of Vishnu) stand behind the lions on either side of the door. *Admission: Rs. 4. Open Wed.–Mon. 10:30–5.*

The main entrance to the Royal Palace is through Nepal's most famous **Golden Gate** (actually copper and gold), which has in the center an image of the goddess Taleju, with three heads and numerous arms. It was constructed in 1745 by King Ranjit Malla, who put the now-famous image of wrestlers along the bottom edge. Facing the gate is a bronze statue of King Bhupatindra Malla, seated with his hands together in a gesture of devotion to the goddess. To his right is the royal residence, the famous Durbar Hall, or Palace of 55 Windows, which was constructed in 1427. Renovated in the seventeenth century, each balcony has carved windows that become increasingly more ornate at each ascending level. The wood carvings are considered the best in Nepal.

Walk through the Golden Gate to the entrance of **Taleju Chowk.** Inside the courtyard (closed to non-Hindus) is the **Taleju Temple.** Look for a wood pole in the open area. During Dassan festivities, the army sacrifices 108 water buffalo—each one killed with one strike of the knife. The blood is given to the goddess; the meat is distributed to government employees.

Return to Durbar Square and look for two large bells. The smaller of the two is the **Bell of the Barking Dogs.** Its ring triggers croons from canines. Hemmed in by the bells is the **Vatsala Temple,** dedicated to Shiva and constructed in 1737. Behind the Vatsala Temple is the oldest temple in Bhaktapur, the two-story **Pashupatinath Temple,** which some historians claim was constructed in 1492, although others say 1682. It is a replica of the famous Pashupatinath Temple in Kathmandu.

Head down a short street behind the Pashupatinath to **Taumadhi Tole** (Taumadhi Square). The square is dominated by the tallest temple in Nepal, the **Nyatapola.** Built in 1708, this is one of the finest examples of Nepal's pagoda-style temples. Five platforms lead up to the temple with its five-tiered roof. On each platform stands a set of guardians, with each pair supposedly 10 times stronger than the pair below. At the bottom are the pair of famous wrestlers, Jaya and Pata, who were 10 times stronger than ordinary men. The deity enshrined inside, the tantri goddess Siddhi Lakshmi, is the strongest of all. Since the temple was never officially inaugurated, its doors have never been opened.

The large **Bhairavanath Temple,** dedicated to Bhairav, is also on Taumadhi Tole. It's worshiped by Hindus and Buddhists. Constructed in stages from 1617 to 1718, it is often the scene of sacrifices. Don't be surprised if you see animal heads and inflated intestines hanging from its beams.

Head north from Taumadhi Tole back to the edge of Durbar Square; then turn right and see the **Dattatreya Square,** which contains buildings with intricately carved windows. The Peacock Windows, carved in 1492, that grace the **Pujari Math** Hindu monastery are considered among the finest examples of Newari wood carving. Pujari Math stands beside the three-story **Dattatreya Temple.** A legend asserts that the wood for this temple came from the trunk of a single tree in 1458. This date makes it one of the oldest temples in the valley. Statues standing out front are the famous Bhaktapur wrestlers. Inside is the **National Woodworking Museum,** which houses an exquisite collection of this artwork. Opposite the monastery is the **Brass and Bronze Museum,** which houses a collection of Nepalese brass and bronze work dating from the eighteenth century. *Admission: Rs. 4. Open Wed.–Mon. 10:30–4.*

EXCURSION FROM KATHMANDU TO DAKSHIN KALI

A trip to Dakshin Kali is best taken by hired car with driver; the cost is about $25 and you should plan two hours for the trip. The best times to visit the temple are Tuesday or Saturday morning, when the traditional sacrifices are offered. **Dakshin Kali,** 22 kilometers (14 miles) south of Kathmandu, is dedicated to Kali, the black goddess of destruction, and was built 300 years ago by a Malla king whose people were dying from a cholera epidemic. In a dream, Kali told him to build a temple for her in Dakshin, south of his kingdom, and then to sacrifice 108 buffalo. The king obeyed Kali's command, and the epidemic ended.

A sacrifice at Dakshin Kali is a highly charged event, full of activity. Follow the lane from the hillside parking area past stalls selling Nepalese fast food, including *khuwa* (sweet-milk-and-cheese curd served on a large leaf); vendors offering handicrafts and garlands; and, no doubt, at least one praying Shivite sadhu in an orange dhoti, his face smeared with ash. Go under an arch and take the steps leading down to a bridge that crosses over a stream. From here, you see two groups of pilgrims—men and women—lining up for the temple, plus numerous others bathing, picnicking, and washing their animals by the stream.

The temple is designed as a female tantric triangle, point aimed at the ground. Lion figures, vehicles of the goddess, guard the temple. A Bhairav idol stands under the canopy. On the side wall is a Ganesh idol. On the left side of the main temple entrance is the idol Dakshin Kali, with eight arms, lifting her body onto Shiva, who lies motionless.

The priest, nearly hidden, sits inside the inner sanctum and sprinkles holy water on each animal as it's presented to him. The temple butcher grabs the squawking animal, usually a chicken or rooster, walks over to the image of Kali and Shiva on the side wall, and lops off the head. Blood drenches the statue red. He hands the headless creature to its owner and dabs a speck of its blood onto his own forehead, sanctifying himself. In front of the temple, in the midst of the ruckus and surging crowds, holy men sitting under a covered pavilion read aloud from holy scriptures.

EXCURSION FROM KATHMANDU TO CHANGU NARAYAN

Changu Narayan is 13 kilometers (eight miles) west of Kathmandu. The excursion will take three hours if you travel by taxi. You can also do a delightful day walk to Changu Narayan from Bhaktapur.

This excursion requires a 20-minute walk up a steep hill to great vistas and the site of **Changu Narayan,** a Hindu temple complex set in a courtyard and dedicated to Narayan (Vishnu). Many call it the most beautiful group of temples in Kathmandu Valley.

Historians believe the original temple was constructed in the third or fourth century and restored in 1708 after a fire. Changu Narayan also celebrates Garuda, "Changu" in Nepali. Once when Garuda was fighting with a snake-god who prevented his son from worshiping Vishnu, Vishnu intervened to restore peace. To prove his friendship, the snake wrapped himself around Garuda's neck. Vishnu jumped aboard, and the three of them flew off to this hill, where a statue of the trio remains.

In the courtyard, elephants flank the entrance to the two-story temple. Oil lamps and bells hang from the lower tiled roof. Birds are perched on each corner. Roof struts are carved with colorfully painted deities, animals, and erotic images. The finely wrought portal has a gilded overhead torana depicting Vishnu with his consorts. His symbols—conch shell, lotus, disc, and mace—appear repeatedly. A fifth-or sixth-century statue of Garuda kneels out front.

Nearby is the sole surviving monument from the reign of the Licchavis—a stone pillar with an inscription that dates from the fourth century. To the left of the temple stands the black statue commemorating the legendary flight—an image duplicated on Nepal's Rs. 10 note. Finally, notice the sculpture of Vishnu in all his incarnations—one of the finest examples of sixth-century art in the subcontinent.

EXCURSION FROM KATHMANDU TO DHULIKHEL

For the best view of the northeastern Himalayas, including 12 peaks over 6,098 meters (20,000 feet), head east to **Dhulikhel** in the foothills of Panchkhal Valley, 34 kilometers (21 miles) east of Kathmandu. Hire a car with driver. The cost for a half-day trip is about $62. You'll drive along the Chinese Highway, which leads to Tibet, passing by Bhaktapur and through the village of Banepa, a former city-kingdom.

Once you climb a low pass, you'll enter the valley and the village of Dhulikhel, with a main square surrounded by temples. You can stay at the **Dhulikhel Mountain Resort.** Thatched cottages (two doubles in each) have mountain views or overlook lovely gardens and lawns. *Reservations: Box 3203, Durbar Marg, Kathmandu, tel. 220031. 40 rooms with bath (shower). Facilities: good multicuisine restaurant, bar, cultural programs on request; arrangements for trekking, camping, rafting, hikes. AE. Deluxe, including full board.*

POKHARA

Until the mid-1900s **Pokhara** bustled only in the winter, when Tibetans from the north arrived with their mule trains to barter salt and raw yak wool for grain. In 1959, after the Chinese seized Tibet, their route was closed. But by then, new arrivals had discovered the valley.

Now Pokhara is busy during the other three seasons as well, due mainly to the rapid increase of tourism and trekking in the area. The area around Lake Phewa resembles the Thamel area of Kathmandu, with streets lined with small shops selling Tibetan and Nepalese wares, and inexpensive hotels and restaurants that cater to Western palates. With its views of the Annapurna and Machhapuchhare mountains, large lake, and relaxed pace, Pokhara is where many tourists come to get away from the crowded frenzy of Kathmandu and where trekkers collapse after days or even weeks of hiking in the outlying areas.

Though the advent of tourism sped up the arrival of electricity, an airport, new roads, and improved social services, it also increased the cost of necessities for local villagers. The creation of teahouses on popular trekking routes also made trekking too easy by eliminating the need for camping gear and food portage. Trails are now overburdened.

Visitors who want to trek near Pokhara should heed the advice of conservationists and avoid Annapurna, especially during the peak season. Consider instead the new destination of **Dolpo,** northwest of Pokhara. An ancient kingdom and the site of the sacred Crystal Mountain, it is a land of deep river gorges and jagged, barren peaks and the home of Buddhists who ride ponies and herd yak and sheep. To visit this area, contact a travel agency listed in Before You Go above, or a tour operator listed in *Facts at Your Fingertips.*

ADDRESSES AND NUMBERS. Tourist Information. Nepal's **Tourist Office** (across from the airport, tel. 20028) is open Sunday–Friday 10–5.

Emergencies. The nearest embassies are in Kathmandu. Turn to your hotel for the name of a reliable doctor. As a last resort, Pokhara has two hospitals: Gandaki Zonal Hospital (Ramghat) and Shining Hospital (northern edge of Pokhara). In Jomsom (see the Around Annapurna trek, below), the government has a small clinic.

Travel Agencies. For outdoor adventures contact, if you are planning in advance, the Special-Interest Tour Groups in *Before You Go* or the Special-Interest Tours in *Facts at Your Fingertips.* For excursions by car, make arrangements through the recommended hotels.

Bookstores. Small shops near Phewa Lake sell new and secondhand English-language books.

Banks. Rastriya Banijva Bank Exchange Counter at Ratnapuri is open daily 7–7.

Post Office. Post offices are at **Pardi** and near the **Mahendra Bridge** and are open Sunday–Friday 10–5.

ARRIVING AND DEPARTING. By Plane. *Airports and Airline* From Kathmandu, **RNAC** (in Pokhara, tel. 20040) makes two daily flights to Pokhara (year-round) and one weekly winter flight to Jomsom (north of Annapurna and gateway to Dolpo). Reserve your ticket in advance. Reconfirm 72 hours before departure; arrive at the airport 90 minutes in advance.

Between Airport and City. The airport is on the southern edge of Pokhara. A taxi to most hotels is about Rs. 60. Hotel New Crystal offers a free shuttle service.

By Hired Car with Driver. The cost of a two-night excursion by car with driver from Kathmandu to Pokhara is about $250 round-trip. For longer trips, expect to pay an additional $70 per day. Hire a car only from a recommended travel agency in Kathmandu (see above) or from your hotel in Pokhara (see below).

By Taxi. A taxi should cost about Rs. 5,000 to Pokhara. Set the fare in advance, and bargain!

GETTING AROUND. By Taxi. Taxis are unmetered. Ask your hotel for reasonable fares.

By Bicycle. Bicycles cost Rs. 30 per day. Flat stretches and quiet streets make pedaling easy. Biking into the hilly valley is more rigorous (see Outdoor Adventures, below).

By Bus. Buses are only recommended for the seasoned traveler. Even deluxe buses are crowded, slow, and uncomfortable. If you're up to the experience, expect to pay around Rs. 400 (one-way).

OUTDOOR ADVENTURES. Biking. Himalayan Mountain Bikes (see Tour Operators in *Before You Go*) offers mountain-bike trips combined with trekking around Pokhara Valley. Arrange before you depart.

Boating. Paddle around Phewa Lake.

Fishing. Fish for trout along Mardi Khola River, east of Pokhara. No license required; bring equipment.

Hikes. *Sarankot:* Head to the hilltop Bhindyabasani Temple in Pokhara and follow the trail through rural villages to Sarankot, the ruins of an eighteenth-century fort, with beautiful mountain views. Plan for about eight hours round-trip; bring a picnic lunch.

Regnas and Rupa Lakes. Drive to the village of Sisuwa, 15 kilometers (nine miles) east of Pokhara and hike through Nepalese hamlets to the village of Panchbhaiya, with views of the Himalayas and the two beautiful lakes in a tropical valley. Plan six hours and bring a picnic lunch.

Hot Springs. From November to May, trek about a week (see Trekking, below) or take a two-day pony ride to the base of Macchapuchhre and enjoy the hot springs at Diprang Bridge.

Horseback Riding. Contact New Hotel Crystal (see Lodging, below) to arrange horseback-riding trips.

Swimming. Swim only in tame meandering rivers and at Begnas and Rupa lakes.

Trekking (up to a week):

Siklis. This six-day trek, offered by Tiger Mountains, is demanding, with lots of up-and-down climbing, but you'll meet few trekkers and get fabulous views of all the great peaks. You'll pass through farming land and tiny settlements to a mountain ridge above the village of Kalikathan. Descend to a lush valley and the Madi Khola River, then climb through a scrub forest to the village of Thak. During the next two days you'll climb to an altitude of 2,250 meters (7,380 feet), passing through rhododendron forests to Siklis village, populated by the Buddhist Gurung. You'll descend through forests and mountain pastures to Pokhara. The trek is available November–May.

Macchapuchhre. This seven-day trek, also offered by Tiger Mountains, involves rugged climbing. You'll head north of Pokhara through rhododendron forests to high pastures—altitude 3,660 meters (12,000 feet)—until you reach the base of Macchapuchhre, at 6,997 meters (22,950 feet). The return route leads to hot springs at Diprang Bridge, then through the rugged Seti Khola River's gorge back to Pokhara. This trek is made November–May.

Trekking (over a week):

Around Annapurna. To trek in the Annapurna Sanctuary, you must pay a $12 entrance fee at the Pokhara Airport or through your tour operator. This rigorous 24- to 26-day trip (Mar.–Nov.), commonly called the Annapurna Circuit, takes you around the massif. Most trekking companies start the hike at the old city of **Gorkha**, the site of the eighteenth-century palace of King Prithvi Narayan Shah, who was responsible for the unification of Nepal. From here you'll walk through the Marsyangdi Valley, threaded by a river and terraced with rice fields and mango groves. The trail winds up slopes to hilltop Buddhist Gurung villages. Following the Khudi Khola River's canyon, you'll climb to old villages that are Tibetan in appearance. At times the trail is gouged out of rock; then suddenly you'll veer into a forest that opens into a mountaintop meadow before you descend into the Manangbhot Valley, hemmed in at the south by numerous mountains, including the Annapurnas. To the west lies the glacier-fed Tilicho Lake. From here, it's an arduous climb to the Thorong La Pass, at 5,396 meters (17,700 feet), where you may see the *bharal* (blue sheep) scampering along distant cliffs. From the pass, you'll see the entire Annapurna Range and the Dolpo district to the west before descending to Muktinath. This 2,000-year-old sacred grove is revered by Buddhists and Hindus, who flock here in August to the small Jawala Mai Temple, dedicated to Vishnu and enshrining a mysterious water that burns with a blue flame caused by natural-gas seepage. On a rock north of the shrine, Buddhists claim that footprints imbedded in the surface belong to Guru Padmasambhava, who introduced Buddhism to Tibet. From here, it's on to the Kali Gondaki Gorge, home of the Thakalis, who used to control the salt trade route between Nepal and Tibet. You'll enter forests and bamboo groves and pass rice paddies as the trek comes to an end.

Annapurna Sanctuary Trek. This moderately difficult 14- to 16-day trek (Mar.–Nov.) avoids high altitudes but keeps you surrounded by mountains. Our recommended companies try hard to avoid the overused teahouse route; they start the trip south of Pokhara, then head to Panchase Lekh (Black Mountain) before joining the main route that heads through rhododendron forests to Poon Hill, with its majestic views of Macchapuchhre, Annapurna, Dhaulagiri, and the Kali Gondaki Valley. You'll cross the Deorali Pass, at 2,522 meters (8,275 feet), which leads to the Kyumnu Khola River (good for swimming) and the last village, before you enter the sacred sanctuary—home of the Hindu goddesses Annapurna and Gangapurna. You'll climb to the Hinko Cave, then on to the Macchapuchhre Base Camp and deeper into the Annapurna Sanctuary. The descent is through rhododendron and bamboo forests to the Madi Khola Valley and Ghandrung, a wealthy Gurung village. After Ghandrung, it's a steep descent to the Madi Khola River, then a steep climb up to the village of Landrung, before you head down through meadows and back to Pokhara.

Dhorpatan. This moderate 23-day trek (Mar.–Nov.) is an excellent alternative to "Around Annapurna." You'll get views of all the great mountains and walk along a beautiful ridge leading into Dhorpatan. The trek begins at Sarankot, above Pokhara, where you will follow the ridge northwest to the village of Naudanda. Sharing the trail with mule trains, you'll head through Gurung villages, then descend into a pine forest and follow the Modi Khola River. A moderate up-and-down trail leads into the Kali Gondaki and Mayangi Khola valleys, with lovely river campsites. Again, the trail climbs sharply, taking you past hamlets still unaccustomed to foreigners to the Jaja La Ridge, at 3,414 meters (11,200 feet). You'll descend into the Dhorpatan Valley—alpine beautiful with shepherd's huts huddled around its rim and the Dhauligiri Range in front of you. This is the year-round home of Tibetan refugees, and the summer home of Nepalese shepherds. From Dhorpatan, you'll proceed to the mountains and glaciers that drain into the Gusung Khola. You'll climb another pass, 4,573 meters (15,000 feet) high, where you may see bharal and pheasants. To return to Pokhara, the trek follows the concluding days of the Annapurna Sanctuary trek.

Dolpo. This strenuous 20- to 30-day trek (May–Oct.) offers a great combination of beautiful vistas, wildlife, and glimpses of local culture. Heading northwest of Pokhara, you'll follow an old trade route from Dhorpatan through flat-roofed villages, crossing high passes—some over 3,500 meters (11,000 feet). The trek takes you along streams at the bottom of gorges and on top of forested ridges. Finally, you'll reach the former kingdom of Dolpo, with its revered Phoksundo Lake. Set against a desolate rocky mountain landscape, this turquoise lake is part of the Shey Phoksundo National Park, which is home to the rare snow leopard. From here, the trek continues west through remote hamlets, inhabited by followers of Bonism, the early religion of Tibet. The trek ends at Jumla. Some companies do this trip in reverse.

Macchapucchre Sanctuary. This 14-day trek (Mar.–Nov.) is also a good alternative to "Around Annapurna." From Sarankot, you'll climb through beautiful grazing country, retracing the end of the Annapurna Sanctuary trek until the middle of the second day. Then you leave the main trail and make a steep climb before descending into the Mardi Khola Valley and wading across the Mardi River. Getting to Odane Hill requires a difficult climb to a ridge and through forests of rhododendron and, finally, great views of Annapurna and Macchapucchre and a glimpse of Dhaulagiri. The next day is rough. You'll travel a narrow trail along a gorge to the sanctuary, at 4,054 meters (13,300 feet)—an open plateau, with astonishing views of the south side of the Annapurna Range. You'll relax and recoup for two days, then climb to 4,634 meters (15,200 feet) to see the Macchapucchre Glaciers. From here you'll start your descent; you'll pass scattered hamlets, then reach Diprang Bridge, where you can jump into hot springs before heading on to Puran Chaur, just outside Pokhara.

Lamjung Himal. This difficult 14-day trek (year-round) starts after an arduous day-long drive to Phalesangu village. You'll trek along the Marsyangdi River, picking up a trail that goes through farms and villages before you start the climb up slopes and through forests to the Buddhist Gurung village of Ghanpokhara. The hike continues along a ridge through rhododendron and bamboo forests filled with birds. The next day is tough, with a climb up to the Telbrong Danga Ridge, but there are incredible views that stay with you until you cross the Namun Pass, at 3,506 meters (11,500 feet). You'll descend through forests, past waterfalls, then climb to the Rambrong Danda River, which has excellent views of the Annapurna Range. From here you'll climb to Thulo Lake, at 4,024 meters (13,200 feet), then descend a mountain-goat trail to Jagat, the first village you'll see after nine days of trekking. You will walk through the Madi Valley, with great views of Dhauligiri, before reaching the Gurung village of Syang. Two days later you'll reach Pokhara.

DINING OUT. All restaurants are casual and multicuisine, unless noted. From October to March, make dinner reservations. Prices are per person, including taxes and excluding drinks and service.

Fishtail Restaurant. This is a cozy place in which to dine, with a fireplace in the middle of the circular room. The bar is nearby. Though waiters push the fixed menu, you can eat à la carte, either Nepalese or Continental. There's a performance of Nepalese folk dances nightly from October to March. *Fishtail Lodge, tel. 20071. AE, DC, MC, V. Open 7–9:30, noon–2, 7–9:30. Moderate.*

New Crystal Restaurant. On the second floor of the New Hotel Crystal, this restaurant was under renovation at press time. It will serve multicuisine dishes, including a good mixed grill and chicken butter masala (chicken in a spicy tomato sauce). *Nagdhunga, tel. 20035. AE, DC, MC, V. Open 7–9:30, noon–2:30, 7–9:30. Moderate.*

Solo. Solo is unpretentious, with a few antique Buddhist urns and thang-kas and good views of the mountains. Try the tasty soups and curries. *Dragon Hotel, Pardi, tel. 20391. MC, V. Open 7–10, noon–3, 6–10. Inexpensive–Moderate.*

Himalchuli Restaurant. A spacious *khar ko jhupadi* (thatched hut), Himalchuli is very informal. The menu is hearty multinational fare, including pizza and Mexican cuisine. *Pardi Damside, Phewa Lake, tel. 20189. AE, V. Open Sept.–June, daily 5:30 AM–11 PM; June–Sept., daily 7 A.M.–10 P.M. Inexpensive.*

ACCOMMODATIONS. Prices are for a standard double room or cottage, including taxes and excluding service charges.

Pokhara Mountain Lodge. At press time, Tiger Tops was constructing a Gurung-style village on a ridge east of Pokhara. The lodge, which won't be completed until the end of 1993, will offer the same excellent service available at other Tiger Top resorts. Specific details about the lodge and its facilities were not available at press time. Contact the Tiger Tops offices abroad (see Tour Operators in *Facts at Your Fingertips*) for the latest information. *Deluxe.*

Fishtail Lodge. Space-age-style Fishtail Lodge is secluded in landscaped gardens on Phewa Lake island. The rooms are in modular units; the best ones have mountain views. *Box 10, Pokhara, tel. 20071, or reserve through Hotel de L'Annapurna (see Hotel de L'Annapurna in Kathmandu, above). 50 rooms with bath (shower). Facilities: air-conditioning, fans, restaurant, bar, cultural programs in season, travel and foreign-exchange counter. AE, DC, MC, V. Expensive.*

Dragon Hotel. In a quiet neighborhood away from the lake and center of town, modest Dragon Hotel offers excellent service and simple, clean rooms. There are great views of the mountains from the roof terrace. *Box 15, Pardi, Lakeside, Pokhara, tel. 20391. 22 rooms with bath. Facilities: room service, restaurant, bar, cultural performances in season, air-conditioning, fans, foreign exchange and travel counter. MC, V. Moderate.*

New Hotel Crystal. Set on sweeping lawns, this large, two-story hotel was undergoing a complete renovation at press time. Good-size rooms will have a modest Western decor, some with mountain views. *Box 234, Nagdhunga, Pokhara, tel. 20035, or reserve in Kathmandu: Chha 199 Jyatha Tole, Box 1253, tel. 227932, fax 228028. 69 rooms with bath; 23 more under construction. Facilities: air-conditioning, room service, restaurant, bar, cultural programs, doctor, foreign-exchange and travel counter, trekking, biking, fishing, horseback-riding arrangements. AE, DC, MC, V. Moderate.*

Hotel Tragopan. Near Phewa Lake, this new four-story hotel offers good service and comfortable Western-style rooms. Newer rooms, called deluxe (but moderately priced), are spacious and include TV. Front rooms have the best mountain views. *Pokhara, tel. 21708. 36 rooms with bath. Facilities: air-conditioning, fans, TV, room service, bar, restaurants, foreign-exchange and travel counter. AE, MC, V. Inexpensive–Moderate.*

NIGHTLIFE. Bars. The best bar is at **Fishtail Lodge,** with its island setting. It's open daily 11–11.

Theater. Four hotels sponsor nightly cultural programs (Oct.–Mar.): **Dragon Hotel** (tel. 20391 for details), **Fishtail Lodge** (6:30–7:30, Rs. 55 for nonguests), **New Hotel Crystal** (7–8 in the bar; Rs. 35), and **Hotel Mount Annapurna** (near the airport, tel. 22027 for details).

THE TERAI

A trip south to the Terai takes you from the mountains to the heat of the Indo-Gangetic Plains and groves of bamboo and banana trees jutting above rice paddies. The slow-paced Terai is home to the Tharu, former nomads who migrated from the Thar Desert in India during the twelfth century to escape conversion to the Moslem religion. First the women came, accompanied by male servants who served as helpers and later became the women's lovers. Today women still rule the roost. Even the man designated the village chieftain must bow to their power. When his wife serves him his meal, she kicks it to him across the mud floor.

Their dark complexions make the Tharu easy to recognize. Many of the men wear a loincloth—ancient garb that contrasts with the modern black umbrellas that shield their exposed bodies from the sun. The women usually wear white saris and heavy silver ornaments on their ankles, wrists, and necks; gold adorns their ears and noses. Women also tattoo their legs. In the past, these markings discouraged Moslems, who were offended by the practice. Now it's primarily an artistic embellishment. Around their neck or wrist, many Tharu also wear a white thread—a symbol of purity—and a black thread—to ward off evil spirits.

In the Terai, you can visit the **Royal Chitwan National Park,** southwest of Kathmandu, and the **Royal Bardia Wildlife Reserve** in the extreme west of Nepal. The town of **Lumbini** is midway between the two parks, a destination that has minimal lodging but important cultural significance; it is the birthplace of Sakyamuni, the Historic Buddha. To the extreme northeast is the Arun River, an excellent rafting alternative to Trisuli and Seti Khola. Travelers who head to Chitwan in December should try to see the annual five-day elephant polo match held at Tiger Tops. For details, write to the World Elephant Polo Association (Box 242, Kathmandu) or contact Tiger Tops (see Travel Agencies under Addresses and Numbers, below).

ADDRESSES AND NUMBERS. Tourist Information. Three **Tourist Informa-tion Centers** are in the Terai, none at convenient locations: **Birgunj** (tel. 2083); **Janakpur** (tel. 20755); and **Bhairawa** (on the way to Lumbini, tel. 1304).

Emergencies. The nearest embassies are in Kathmandu. Small government hos-pitals are at **Bharatpur** (near Chitwan), **Nepalganj** (near Lumbini and the approach to Bardia), and **Biratnagar** (near the Arun River). If you're staying at Chitwan or Bardia, ask your lodge for assistance.

Travel Agencies. Lodges in Chitwan and Bardia can make all travel arrange-ments. **Tiger Tops** runs a summer package to Tharu village in Chitwan that includes an excellent day excursion to Lumbini (see Tours Operators in *Facts at Your Fingertips*).

Banks. There are banks in Nepalganj and other towns. They are out of the way if you are going to a game park. Bring sufficient rupees.

ARRIVING AND DEPARTING. By Plane. *Airports and Airline.* From Kath-mandu, **RNAC** flies daily to Maghauli, Bharatpur (Chitwan), and Bhairawa (ap-proach to Lumbini). RNAC makes over 10 weekly flights to Nepalganj (Bardia) and five weekly flights to Tumlingtar (gateway to Arun River). On trips to Bardia, once you arrive at Nepalganj, you can get to Tiger Tops by jeep or raft (see Outdoor Adventures, below).

By Hired Car with Driver. For trips to Chitwan, the recommended lodges have numerous packages that offer transportation by car or raft. (See Outdoor Adven-tures, below.) The recommended tour operators in Kathmandu arrange an over-night excursion to Lumbini for about $375. In high season, make all arrangements before you depart. All recommended lodges at Chitwan offer packages that cover the cost of surface transportation.

OUTDOOR ADVENTURES. Biking. Himalayan Mountain Bikes (see Tour Op-erators in *Before You Go*) offers bike trips in the Terai, with rafting and a jungle safari.

Fishing. Fish for *mahseer* (Himalayan river fish) along the Karnali River. Equip-ment available through Tiger Tops.

Rafting. *Chitwan:* To raft to Chitwan, lodges offer a one- to three-day trip (Sept.–May; Tiger Tops also rafts in the summer). From the Kali Gandaki River, south of Kathmandu, you'll leave the forested hills and enter the Terai plains and the Seti Khola River. You'll pass Hindu shrines and villages, then float into the park to see wild animals. Osprey Waterways (see Tour Operators in *Before You Go*) of-fers a seven-day run on the Kali Gandaki (Oct.–Nov. and Feb.–mid-Apr.) and a three-day run on the Seti Khola (Oct.–Nov. and Mar.–June).

Bardia. To raft from Nepalganj to Bardia (a three-day trip), you'll start at the Bheri River, with its rapids that lead to a narrow gorge, broken by an occasional valley with small villages. On the final day, you'll reach the confluence of the Bheri and Karnali rivers and then enter a final narrow canyon that opens into the Terai and the wildlife reserve (Oct.–Nov. and Feb.–mid-Apr.).

Arun River. This river in the east has rafting runs rated moderate to difficult and trips averaging about five days. The tropical terrain is lush and remote (Oct.–Nov. and Feb.–mid-Apr.).

For all trips, make arrangements in advance. In Chitwan or Bardia, you can ar-range your trip through a lodge in the sanctuaries, or if you prefer to tent, some outdoor-adventure outfits now offer rafting trips with their own private campsites (see *Before You Go* above, or *Facts at Your Fingertips).*

Swimming. Swim at the game parks, but watch out for the freshwater crocodiles.

ROYAL CHITWAN NATIONAL PARK

Bordering the Rapti River, the Royal Chitwan National Park was once the private playground and hunting preserve of Nepal's Rana prime ministers. In 1962 King Mahendra turned the area into a wildlife sanctuary. Only 22 tigers and 100 rhinoc-eroses had survived the hunter's gun. Eleven years later, Chitwan was declared a national park. Today, it's closely guarded by armed forces who keep out poachers. Even the Tharu are restricted to one annual two-week harvesting of the elephant grass they use for thatching.

By 1987, 100 tigers and over 400 rhinoceroses were spotted in the park. The sanctuary is also home to leopards and other jungle cats, elephants, buffalo, sloth bear, gaur (wild oxen), wild boar, langur and rhesus monkeys, freshwater dolphins, freshwater crocodiles, pythons, and king cobras, plus over 350 species of birds, including giant hornbills, peacocks, and eagles. Chitwan has been called the best sanctuary in Asia, and its excellent accommodations, beautiful vistas, and the splendid wildlife justify the claim.

The best way to explore the park is from a four-wheel-drive vehicle, on the back of an elephant, in a dugout canoe cruising quietly down the Rapti River, or from the cover of a *machan* (watchtower) built deep in the forest. Unlike Africa, where animals roam in herds, most of the protected species in Chitwan rarely move in large groups. The elusive tiger is a nocturnal hunter. Your best chance of a sighting is early morning or early evening, when numerous lodges arrange excursions. Also, remember to wear neutral-color clothes.

DINING OUT AND ACCOMMODATIONS. To get the most of the park, you should stay a minimum of three days and two nights. Rates include full board (with a fixed multicuisine menu), elephant safaris, nature walks, bird-watching, canoeing, and jeep rides. All lodges have bars, but drinks are extra. Exceptions or additions are noted with each option. Prices are per person in a standard double room, tent, or cottage, including taxes and excluding service charges. Most prices are deluxe.

Chitwan Jungle Lodge. Nine kilometers (about six miles) inside the park and four kilometers (three miles) from the river, this lodge offers a popular two-night package by road from Kathmandu or Pokhara for about $250 per person. You can also raft a day for an additional $50 per person. Stay in thatched clay huts with attractive furnishings. Swimming is possible in the nearby river, and you can visit Tharu villages. At night, you'll eat in a roundhouse and can attend lectures by naturalists or watch cultural programs. *Reservations: Box 1281, Durbar Marg, Kathmandu, tel. 228918, fax 227567. 32 rooms with shower. AE. Closed June–Aug.*

Gaida Wildlife Camp. Also in the park, Gaida offers cottages and tents. Each thatched cottage, built on stilts, has two double rooms and a veranda overlooking the Dungla River. The nearby lodge serves good food; the bar is well stocked. At night you can attend cultural programs and wildlife lectures. Safari-style tents (cheaper) are located farther in the jungle. Gaida offers a three-day package ($250 per person) or a four-day package that includes one day of rafting (about $325 per person). *Reservations: Box 2056, Durbar Marg, Kathmandu, tel. 220940, fax 227292. 23 rooms with bath; 10 tents with nearby bath. AE, DC. Closed June–Aug.*

Hotel Elephant Camp. At the edge of the park by the Rapti River, this modest resort has great service and a pleasant ambience. Thatched cottages, most with four double rooms, are nicely decorated. It also offers less expensive tents with cots. The National Park Museum and its park elephants are nearby, as are some Tharu villages. Elephant Camp offers two three-day packages: by road from Kathmandu ($180 per person) or with a day of rafting ($220 per person). *Box 4729, Durbar Marg, Kathmandu, tel. 213976. 6 cottages with showers; 10 tents with shared bathrooms. AE, DC, MC, V.*

★ **Temple Tiger Jungle Lodge and Camp.** This new resort is nine kilometers (six miles) inside the park in a remote area and offers fancy tents. A library, large roundhouse, and cots are constructed with local materials and create an ethnic ambience. Set on high ground, it also offers mountain views and opportunities to spot wildlife. Road transportation is $140 per person; $70 each for two people. The cost for tent accommodation is $150 per person per night. *Box 3968, Kantipath, Kathmandu, tel. 225780; or reserve in the U.S. (Ste. 306, 24843 Del Prado, Dana Pt., CA 92629, tel. 800–359–9319). 20 tents with separate bath. AE, MC, V. Closed July–Aug.*

Tiger Tops. Set deep within the park, Tiger Tops has attractive rooms in the Jungle Lodge. (The best views are on the upper floor.) You can also stay in a fancy safari-style tent, with separate showers and bathrooms. Or stay in a typical longhouse of timber, reed, and clay in the Tharu Safari Resort, just outside the park, and see Tharu cultural programs, observe the Tharu lifestyle, and enjoy a new swimming pool. You can also design a package that includes all three. Tiger Tops offers two special packages: a three-day deluxe rafting trip down to Chitwan (Oct.–May, $890 per person) and a five-day excursion with two days of rafting, two days at Tharu, and a trip to Lumbini (May–Sept., $770 per person). It also offers a three-day package from Kathmandu (by car or plane) and will make pickups from Pokhara. Reserve well in advance. *Reservations: Box 242, Durbar Marg, Kathmandu, tel. 222706, fax 414075; or through the Tiger Tops offices abroad (see Tour Operators in* Facts at Your Fingertips*). 20 rooms with bath in the lodge, 10 tents with nearby bath, 12 rooms with bath at Tharu. Cost for lodge: $250 per night; tented camp: $180; Tharu Village: $110. Camp and lodge are closed mid-June–mid-Sept. AE, MC, V.*

EXCURSION FROM CHITWAN TO LUMBINI

Lumbini is 136 kilometers (83 miles) from Chitwan. You can arrange an excursion with Tiger Tops and do the trip in a day. You can also fly into Bhairawa or make a two-day car excursion to Lumbini from Kathmandu (use a recommended travel agent).

Lord Buddha was born around 563 B.C. at this isolated spot near the Indian border. In 1895 a German archaeologist discovered an inscribed pillar honoring Lumbini as the birthplace of Sakyamuni, left behind by north India's Emperor Ashoka in 250 B.C. The discovery triggered other archaeological excavations, currently assisted by the United Nations. Since then, Lumbini has become one of the holiest destinations for Buddhists.

Today Ashoka's pillar marks the formal Royal Garden at Lumbini as the birthplace of Siddhartha Gautama, the prince who later became Sakyamuni, the Enlightened One. Behind the pillar is the Maya Temple, a third-century brick shrine, which honors the Buddha's mother, Maya Devi. Inside, fine stone carvings portray the birth of the Buddha. Maya Devi bathed in the nearby brick *ghat* (temple tank) before giving birth. Not far from these remains, foreign Buddhist sects have built *gompas* (monasteries) and shrines, including the Dharma Swami Maharaj Buddhavihar, a Tibetan monastery with a golden statue of the Buddha. In Bhairawa, two simple Western-style hotels offer reasonable but clean rooms with attached bathrooms and decent restaurants: Hotel Himalaya Inn and Lumbini Garden Guest House. Both are inexpensive and neither accepts credit cards.

ROYAL BARDIA WILDLIFE RESERVE

In the western Terai, the Royal Bardia Wildlife Reserve is a vast stretch of sal forest. The Karnali River threads through it, bordered by Tharu villages. You can see black buck and swamp deer, wild boars, otters, monkeys, and many species of birds. The lucky will see wild elephants, the solitary tiger, freshwater crocodiles, and freshwater dolphins.

DINING OUT AND ACCOMMODATIONS. Rates include full board, park activities, and taxes, but not alcoholic drinks or service charges. Prices are per person in a standard double room or tent and are deluxe.

Tiger Tops Karnali Lodge and Tented Camp. The lodge is on a grassy plain outside the jungle. The rooms have an attractive ethnic-style decor, and the attached bathrooms are modern. Tucked in the forest and overlooking the Karnali River, the tented camp (cheaper) has secluded safari-style tents. In both facilities, you can go on nature walks, take a jeep, ride an elephant, embark on a river cruise, visit Tharu villages, and go fishing. *Reservations: Box 242, Durbar Marg, Kathmandu, tel. 222706, fax 414075; or through the Tiger Tops offices abroad (see Tour Operators in* Facts at Your Fingertips). *10 rooms with bath, 14 tents with nearby bath. AE, MC, V.*

EVEREST AND NORTHEAST NEPAL

Mt. Everest. The highest in the world, at 8,877 meters (29,028 feeet), this renowned mountain is visually spectacular, as well as surrounded by fascinating history and legends. Look at it from one angle and jagged pinnacles jut up like daggers and glaciers mirror the heavens; look at it from another direction and black rock contrasts with icy slopes and snow massifs. Wild animals roam craggy cliffs.

Sightings of Everest's most famous inhabitant, the Yeti—which means "wild man of the mountain," not "abominable snowman"—date from the fourteenth century, when Asian travelers reported seeing enormous, hairy, foul-smelling creatures that attacked men, kidnapped women, and drank yak blood. Eric Shipton, the famous twentieth-century mountaineer, took a photograph of his foot next to a gigantic snowprint with an extended big toe. Scientific expeditions have attempted to track the elusive Yeti, a far more difficult quest than climbing the peak that is the creature's supposed home.

According to devout Buddhists, the successful ascent made by Sir Edmund Hillary and Tenzing Norgay was not the first. A shaman priest challenged Guru Padmasambhava (the eighth-century Indian mystic who brought Buddhism to Tibet) to a race to Everest's summit. The guru waited for the first rays of the sun, which carried him and his chair of wisdom to the top. The priest never appeared, lost en route astride his magical drums, now heard in the periodic claps of thunder that crash around the mountain—his drums calling out for their master. As for Padmasambhava, he left behind his chair as a symbol of power and casually ambled down the mountain.

When Hillary and Norgay made their ascent, they paid their respects to this giant, called Sagarmatha (Mother Goddess of the Universe) by the Nepalese and Chomolungma (Mother Goddess of the Winds) by the Tibetans. Norgay, a Buddhist, buried a small parcel of sweets as an offering. Hillary added a crucifix.

Today's climbers and trekkers have left behind less touching souvenirs. In 1987 Sir Edmund announced, "Everest is a junkpile." Fully 75% of the forest cover at the base of the mountain is gone. Many local Sherpas, who used to revere the trees, now prefer the money they make selling bundled firewood to trekkers. By the year 2,000, if the current rate of deforestation persists, visitors to Sagarmatha will see not the mountain's massive forest mantle but barren slopes.

A trip to Everest means accommodations in trekker's huts, dormitories, or the lodges used by private trekking outfits; or in the classy and very expensive **Everest View Hotel,** a 30-minute walk from Namche Bazaar. *Reserve well in advance: Box 1694, Durbar Marg, Kathmandu, tel. 224854, fax 227289. 12 rooms with bath. Facilities: room service, restaurant, bar, sun terrace, shop, pressure chamber, sightseeing, trekking, and flight arrangements to Namche. Meals included. Closed June–Sept. AE. Deluxe.*

When you choose your trek, the agency will determine where you will stay and will supply all basic food and tents and, most likely, sleeping bags. Kathmandu and Namche are the best places in which to buy extra supplies. Other villages have minimal provisions. Trekkers heading into the Everest area, declared the Sagarmatha National Park in 1976, must pay a $12 entrance fee at the Visitors Center in Namche. Trekkers crowd the route to Everest from Lukla during the fall, so plan this trip for between December and March. Trekking outfits also offer a trip to Sherpa villages and monasteries; the same advice applies.

Or, consider a new option. The Nepalese government has opened **Mt. Kanchenjunga,** the third-highest peak in the world. To visit this area to the east of Everest, you must trek with an authorized trekking agent (see the outdoor adventure outfits listed in *Before You Go,* above).

ADDRESSES AND NUMBERS. Tourist Information. There are no sources of information in the Everest area. Get information in Kathmandu.

Emergencies. The nearest embassies are in Kathmandu. The hospital Sir Edmund Hillary founded, primarily for villagers, is at **Kunde.** The **Himalayan Rescue Association** has a clinic at Pheriche (open Oct.–May), and the government runs small hospitals at **Jiri** and **Phaplu.**

Banks. Bring sufficient rupees from Kathmandu. There are few banks in this area.

ARRIVING AND DEPARTING. By Plane. *Airport and Airline.* From Kathmandu, RNAC makes three daily winter flights to Lukla (near Everest and Khumbu) and two weekly winter flights to Taplejung (gateway to Kanchenjunga). Book all flights early. Reconfirm at least 72 hours before departure and arrive at the airport 90 minutes in advance.

OUTDOOR ADVENTURES. Biking. Contact Himalayan Mountain Bikes (Box 2769, Kamal Pokhari, Kathmandu, tel. 413632 or 418733 for details about mountain-bike trips combined with trekking around Everest.

Climbing and Mountaineering. Expeditions to Everest are booked through the year 2000. If you're determined to climb a peak in this area, contact the recommended special-interest tour operators who offer scheduled-departure expeditions, usually to Island Peak, altitude 5,600 meters (18,368 feet), southeast of Everest (see Tour Operators in *Before You Go* above).

Trekking. For all treks in the Everest area, you must be physically fit and prepared for high altitudes, especially if you fly into Lukla. Recommended trekking season is October to May.

Trekking (over a week):

Sherpa Villages and Monasteries. Popular in the autumn, this moderately difficult 10- to 24-day trek goes through a series of villages around Khumbu Valley. The accent is on culture and monasteries, yet the views are spectacular. Longer versions take you on a wider circle, which allows for more variety of terrain, yet the altitude never exceeds 4,115 meters (13,500 feet). This trek is less crowded after the autumn peak season.

"Walk in" from Jiri to the Everest base. This trek takes 20 to 30 days, depending on side trips. You'll start in the Hindu-Buddhist world of Nepal's hill people. From their lush verdant terrain of rhododendron forests and bamboo groves, you'll cross the Kharubas Pass, at 2,713 meters (8,900 feet), and descend to a region dominated by Buddhism. Villages have gompas, mani walls (to protect the village), and prayer flags. At Junbesi, you can visit Nepal's largest monastery, Thubten Chholing, the present seat of the Tulshi Rimpoche, who was one of two abbots who presided over the Rongbuk Gompa in Tibet until he fled the Chinese invasion. Cross the Tragsindo La Pass, at 3,072 meters (10,076 feet), and then Khari La Pass, at about 3,900 meters (12,792 feet), which leads to Lukla and Namche and offers good views of Everest and surrounding peaks. Now it's on to the Everest Base Camp. The mountains are rough and dark, with upper slopes caked with glaciers and snow. You climb steep ridges, with the Buddhist mantra "Om Mani Padme Hum" ("Hail to the jewel in the lotus") carved into the surfaces. You'll traverse the Changri Glacier, strewn with rubble and frozen daggers of ice, then head higher into yak grazing lands. Local people, accustomed to the altitude, pass by with ease as you trudge along. Kala Pattar, or "Black Rock," 5,545 meters (18,188 feet), provides a close-up view of the famous peak—the moment to remember. The entire South Face, the West Ridge, and the pass leading into Tibet loom defiantly before you. From here you'll circle back to Lukla.

Lukla to Everest Base Camp. Besides the "walk-in," many companies also offer a 20-day trek from Lukla to the base.

Lukla to Gokyo Peak and Everest Base Camp. This 20-day trek follows a trail along the Dudh Kosi River to its source near the Gokyo Lakes. From here you can climb up Gokyo Peak, 5,483 meters (17,984 feet), and have wonderful views of nearby giants: Cho Oyu, Everest, Lhotse, and Makalu. After crossing the Chyugima La Pass, at 5,422 meters (17,783 feet), you'll head into the Everest Base Camp and on to Kala Pattar.

All these treks are popular in the autumn; however, the low-altitude regions of the "walk-in" up to Lukla don't get as much traffic.

Kanchenjunga. This strenuous trek to the world's third-highest peak requires 28 to 33 days. After a flight to Biratnagar in Nepal's east, you'll head north through rhododendron forests that soon offer a glimpse of Mt. Kanchenjunga. The trek takes you through pastoral villages, up and down terraced hills, and along rivers winding through gorges. The trail turns rugged as you climb higher into the Himalayas, where the views are spectacular. You'll visit Buddhist monasteries and villages rarely seen by foreigners. You'll pass waterfalls and possibly encounter yak herders on the trail, which finally leads to the sacred Mt. Kanchenjunga and its gigantic field of glaciers. Recommended trekking season is Oct.–Nov.

JUMLA AND NORTHWEST NEPAL

Because it's in an area long closed to foreigners, not many have heard of **Jumla** or Nepal's largest body of water, Lake Rara, tucked in the northwest. This lake, at an elevation of 2,980 meters (9,777 feet), is the showpiece of Lake Rara National Park, which is considered by many to be the prettiest park in Nepal. The lake is idyllic, encircled by pine slopes, with white peaks in the distance.

The distant Himalayas form a ridge—a natural barrier that guards what was the summer capital of the Mallas, rulers of Nepal in the fourteenth century. The land is reminiscent of the American West, with wide, rough valleys dotted with scrub and occasional huddled settlements of houses with flat stone roofs. This area, compared with the rest of Nepal, is sparsely populated. Its people are unaccustomed to foreigners. There are no tourist hotels or restaurants, few phones, and few roads. You will be camping exclusively. Once trekkers start coming in large numbers, though, this situation will change.

ADDRESSES AND NUMBERS. Tourist Information. Get all your information in Kathmandu; there are no services here.

Emergencies. The nearest embassies are in Kathmandu. The government has a small hospital at **Jumla** and a dispensary in **Gumgarhi** at Rara Lake.

Banks. Bring sufficient rupees from Kathmandu. There are no convenient places to change money in this area.

ARRIVING AND DEPARTING. By Plane *Airport and Airline.* **RNAC** makes two weekly flights to the Jumla airstrip from Kathmandu and four weekly flights from Nepalganj. Book all flights early. Reconfirm at least 72 hours before departure; arrive at the airport 90 minutes in advance.

OUTDOOR ADVENTURES. This is such a new destination that adventures are just being developed.

Hot Springs. Tatopani, three hours west of Jumla, has good hot springs.

Trekking. Though you can get some provisions in Jumla, you should bring supplies from Kathmandu or Nepalganj.

Trekking (over a week):

Lake Rara National Park. This fairly easy eight-day trek with two overnights at the lake takes you to the park and back to Jumla. You'll follow the Chaudbise Khola River, pass through pine forests, and head up to the Ghurchi Lagna Pass, at 3,545 meters (11,627 feet), with good views of the snow-covered Patrasi range. You'll cross footbridges, one suspended 2,743 meters (8,997 feet) above the water. You'll traverse steep slopes until you reach the hilltop hamlet of Jhari, at 2,500 meters (8,200 feet), where you will see the lake spread out in the valley below. On the return trip to Jumla, the highlight is the climb to the top of Ghorosain, altitude 5,351 meters (17,548 feet), with good views of much of Nepal's northwest. From here you'll head to the village of Sinja, where you can visit a temple on a hill and the ruins of Lamathada, the old capital of the Mallas. The last two days are for the descent into Jumla.

Trekking and Rafting:

Trek to Karnali River and **Run to Bardia Wildlife Reserve.** This 20-day trip (six days of trekking, 12 days of rafting, two days in the Royal Bardia Reserve in the Terai) begins in Jumla. You'll follow the Tila River west past mud houses surrounded by rice paddies. At Tatopani, three hours west of Jumla, you can enjoy hot springs. You'll walk through rhododendron forests, follow a ridge over a pass, altitude 1,212 meters (4,000 feet), and descend to Banjkot village at the confluence of the Tila and Karnali rivers. From here you'll run the rapids to Bardia, camping on beaches, swimming in the water, and visiting temples and villages not far from the bank. The landscape turns tropical, with cultivated paddies, terraced slopes, and occasional Tharu villages and their thatched clay homes. (For a description of your destination, Bardia, see the Terai section, above). This trip is best from mid-November to mid-December or mid-February to June.

LANGTANG VALLEY AND HELAMBU

Glaciers, high-altitude lakes, imposing mountains, and proximity to Kathmandu and the Tibetan Plateau make **Langtang** and these valleys a popular trekking alternative to Everest or Annapurna, especially for the visitor who is short on time. In this area, 75 kilometers (47 miles) north of Kathmandu, you're surrounded by gigantic peaks, including Langtang Lirung, altitude 7,246 meters, (23,771 feet), the highest mountain in this area. Huge glaciers sprawl down mountain slopes, spread across high valley floors, and empty into the sacred Gosainkund Lake. As in neighboring Everest, the people who inhabit Langtang are Sherpas. Their handsome villages and gompas add a peaceful touch to the formidable landscape.

In 1976, to preserve the beauty of Langtang Valley and Gosainkund, Nepal turned the area into its second-largest national park, a protected area for the endangered musk deer, Himalayan *thar* (wild goat), pandas, and the elusive snow leopard.

Trekkers who plan to visit this area should bring all necessary supplies and provisions. The entrance fee to the national park is $12.

ADDRESSES AND NUMBERS. Tourist Information. There is no tourist information office in this area. Get whatever information you need in Kathmandu.

Emergencies. The nearest embassies are in Kathmandu. At press time, no hospitals or clinics existed.

Banks. Bring sufficient rupees from Kathmandu. There are no convenient places to change money in this area.

ARRIVING AND DEPARTING. The only flights into Langtang are by prearranged **RNAC** charters. Most people trek in from the village of Dhunche, a five-hour drive north of Kathmandu, or walk in from Panchkhal, a village on the road from Kathmandu to Tibet.

OUTDOOR ADVENTURES. Trekking (over a week):
Helambu Trek. This moderately difficult 9- to 13-day trek starts from Panchkhal, 52 kilometers (32 miles) north of Kathmandu. You follow the Indravati Khola River and ascend to Taramarang village, then up to Tarke Ghyang, at 2,560 meters (8,397 feet), the biggest Sherpa village in Helambu, tucked under towering mountains. At its monastery, lamas perform masked dances on the March full moon. From Tarke Ghyang, trekkers have two choices. One option is a 13-day trek over the Ganja La Pass, 5,122 meters (16,767 feet), and through villages to a view of the Langtang glaciers tumbling down from Langtang Lirung. The second nine-day route affords great panoramas of the Jugal Himal and its tallest peak, altitude 6,989 meters (22,930 feet). You'll then proceed to Shermathang village and monastery, encircled by alpine hills, then head back to Taramarang.

Lantang, Gosainkund, and Helambu. This 25-day trek starts from Dhunche, north of Kathmandu. You'll follow the Trisuli River north (an old caravan route to Tibet), then head east through a dense forest and into a gorge that opens into the alpine Langtang Valley. This trek includes most of the villages visited on the shorter treks described above and takes you to Gosainkund Lake, altitude 4,380 meters (14,366 feet), encircled by craggy peaks. You'll walk through evergreen forests and alpine meadows, by cascading waterfalls, and up barren slopes. All treks can be done year-round, but the Ganja La Pass is open only from May to October.

HINDI-ENGLISH VOCABULARY

Although English is the lingua franca of India and is spoken by almost everyone who has received a high-school education, you may find yourself in a position where no one understands your English (although this is highly unlikely unless you stray far from the usual tourist paths). Because there are more than a dozen major languages and hundreds of dialects, we are quoting only a few expressions of courtesy in Hindi, understood in most parts of India, together with the more current terms in art and architecture, religion, etc., that you will come across in this volume. They are largely of Sanskrit origin, the sacred language of the Indo-Aryans. Some are from Arabic and Persian.

You know more words of Indian origin than you realize: These words entered the English vocabulary during the presence of the East India Company and during subsequent British rule, spread wherever English is spoken, and were eventually absorbed into other languages.

Various

atcha	(ach-*cha*)	O.K.
bagh	(ba*gh*)	a garden
baksheesh	(baksh*eesh*)	a tip, a reward
dhoti	(dhoetee)	white skirtlike garment worn by men
ha (nasal)	(ha)	yes
howdah	(how-d*ah*)	the seat fixed on an elephant's back. It usually accommodates two in front and two behind.
ji	(jee)	a respectful suffix (Gandhi*ji*); also used as an address (ha-ji—yes sir).
mahout	(*ma* hoot)	elephant driver
maidan	(*ma*-eh-*dan*)	open ground
mehrbani se	(may-her-banee-say)	please
nahin	(na*heen*)	no
namastey	(na-ma-stay)	word for all greetings
nawab	(*na* wab)	title given to important Moslem land-owners
ram-ram	(*ram-ram*)	equivalent of "hello"
sahib	(sa*heeb*)	master
Shri (or Sri); Shrimatee	((Shree /Shree-ma-*tee*)	Mr; Mrs
shukriya	(sh*oo* kree ya)	thank you
wallah	(wal-*lah*)	a fellow (rickshaw wallah)

Art-Architecture

chaitya	(*cha*-eet-ya)	a Buddhist prayer hall
dravida	(dra-*vee-da*)	Southern or Dravidian style of architecture
dvarapala	(Varapala)	door guardian statue
ghazal	(*gha*-zal)	poetry set to music, originating from Persia and now usually sung in Urdu
geet	(geet)	light popular song
ghats	(*gha* ts)	terraces on a sacred river bank (also mountains)

gopurum	(go-poo-ram)	tower over gate of South Indian temple complex
gurudwara	(goo-rood-wara)	Sikh temple
jagamohan	(jag-mohan)	in Orissan architecture an enclosed porch preceding the sanctuary
Kathakali	(katha-kalee)	classic dance form of Kerala
mandir	(mandeer)	Hindu temple
mandapa	(mandapa)	main hall
Manipuri	(maneepooree)	classical dance form of Manipur (Assam)
mithuna	(meethoonaa)	statues of amorous couples
Nagara style	(Nagaara)	the Northern or Indo-Aryan type of temple characterized by the tower
stupa	(stewpaa)	Buddhist sacred mound
sitar	(seetaar)	stringed instrument with movable frets, played by plucking the strings
torana	(towrana)	gateway of a temple enclosure
vihara	(*vee* har)	a Buddhist monastery

Religion

ahimsa	(a-heem-saa)	nonviolence, harmlessness
apsara	(aapsaaraa)	a damsel of Indra's heaven
ashram	(*aash* raam)	residence of a spiritual teacher
avatar	(ahvatar)	one of the various incarnations of a god or goddess
Bodhisattva	(Bodheesatt*v*a)	potential Buddha who before final enlightenment ministers to humanity
Brahma	(Bramma)	the creator of all things in Hindu Trinity
Brahman	(Br*a*m-m*a*n; nasal "n" pronounced)	the first, or priestly, class in Hinduism
Buddha	(B*oo* dha)	Prince Siddhartha, born on the Nepalese border about 563 B.C. Buddha means "the Enlightened One"
Devi	(Day*v*ee)	Parvati, consort to Siva in her benevolent form
dharma	(Dh*a* rm*aa*)	path of conduct
dharmachakra	(dhar*m*a chakra)	the Buddhist Wheel of the Law, an ancient solar symbol
Durga	(Doorg*a*)	Parvati, consort of Siva in her form as a destroyer of evil
guru	(gooroo)	spiritual teacher
hatha yoga	(haatha yog)	the mystic path of physical exercise
hinayana	(heenayana)	"small vehicle": early Buddhism with emphasis on the doctrine rather than on worship
Jainism	(Ja-ay-nee-sum)	a religion founded by Mahavira in the 6th century B.C. preaching solicitude for all life
jatakas	(Ja-ta-kas)	tales about the Buddha in his previous incarnations
Kali	(Kalee)	the goddess Parvati in her terrible form
kirtan	(*keer* tan)	religious songs
Krishna	(Kreesh-*na*)	hero of the epic Mahabharata. One of Vishnu's incarnations
Kshatriya	(sh*a* t-ree-y*a*)	the second, or warrior, caste in Hinduism
Lakshmi	(laksh-mee)	Goddess of wealth and beauty, the consort of Vishnu

lingam	(leengum)	sacred symbol of Siva
mahayana	(maha-yeah-na)	"great vehicle"; later from Buddhism, with emphasis on Buddha's divinity
mantra	(*man* tra)	a word or sentence used as an invocation
maya	(ma-yeah)	escape from material reality, an illusion
moksha	(mawksha)	release from all material desires
mudra	(moodra)	ritual gestures denoting mystic powers
Nandi	(Nandee)	the sacred bull, Siva's vehicle
Nirvana	(Neervana)	eternal bliss
Pariahs	(paree-ahs)	the untouchables or outcasts of Hinduism (this practice is now banned in India)
Parvati	(Parvatee)	consort of Siva
prana	(pran; nasal "n" pronounced)	Breath of Life, sustaining the body
puja	(pooja)	prayer service performed before a god's image
Puranas	(pooranas)	Hindu mythology; there are eighteen Puranas and a number of epics, which include the *Ramayana* and the *Mahabharata*
Rama	(Raam)	incarnation of Vishnu and hero of the *Ramayana*
rishi	(reeshee)	Hindu sage
sadhu	(sadhoo)	a celibate holy man
samadhi	(samad*hee*)	the deepest form of yoga meditation
samsara	(saamsaaraa)	the cycle of life and rebirth
Saraswati	(Sa-ras-wa-tee)	Goddess of wisdom
Siva or Shiva	(Seeva or Sheeva)	God of the Hindu Trinity—the destructive and creative aspect
Sudra	(soodra)	the fourth main caste in Hinduism (farmers and artisans mostly)
sutra	(sootra)	a sacred text
swami	(swam-ee)	a teacher of certain branches of Hinduism
tandava	(tan-da-va)	Siva's cosmic dance, symbolic of his function of creation and destruction
Tirthankara	(Teerthankara)	one of the twenty-four Jain patriarchs who attained perfection
Trimurti	(Tree-moor-tee)	physical shape of the Hindu Trinity (Brahma, Vishnu, Siva)
twice-born		a term used to denote high-caste Hindus, who are said to have a second birth when invested with the sacred thread of their caste
Vedanta	(Vay-dan-ta)	an inquiry into the aim of all knowledge; a metaphysic of intuition
Vedas	(Vay-das)	the four most ancient Hindu scriptures
Vishnu	(Veesh-noo)	the Preserver of Mankind in the Hindu Trinity
yoga	(yog*a*)	a discipline of meditation by which the powers of man over himself are developed
yogi	(yog*ee*)	a follower of yoga

INDEX

INDEX

INDIA

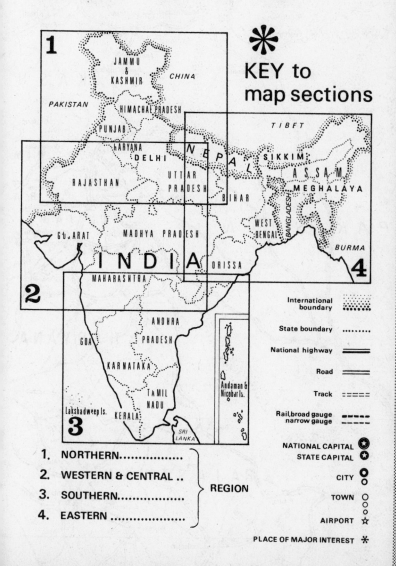

KEY to map sections

1	JAMMU & KASHMIR, CHINA, PAKISTAN, HIMACHAL PRADESH, PUNJAB, HARYANA, DELHI, RAJASTHAN, UTTAR PRADESH
	NEPAL, TIBET, SIKKIM, ASSAM, MEGHALAYA, BIHAR, WEST BENGAL, BANGLADESH, BURMA
	GUJARAT, MADHYA PRADESH, INDIA, ORISSA, MAHARASHTRA
2	
3	GOA, ANDHRA PRADESH, KARNATAKA, TAMIL NADU, KERALA, Lakshadweep Is., Andaman & Nicobar Is., SRI LANKA
4	

International boundary	⋯⋯
State boundary	⋯⋯
National highway	━━
Road	──
Track	═══
Rail, broad gauge / narrow gauge	▬▬ / ───
NATIONAL CAPITAL	⊛
STATE CAPITAL	⊛
CITY	◖
TOWN	○○○
AIRPORT	☆
PLACE OF MAJOR INTEREST	✳

1. **NORTHERN**.................
2. **WESTERN & CENTRAL** ..
3. **SOUTHERN**................. } **REGION**
4. **EASTERN** ....

NORTHERN REGION 1

0 miles 100 200
0 km 100 200 300

Karakoram Pass

K H

Leh

MIR

CHINA

LAHAUL

Manali SPITI

A CHAL

Kullu

DESH

Narkanda

SHIMLA

Gangotri

Yamunotri Kedarnath

Chakrata

Mussoorie Badrinath

Tehri Joshimath

Dehra Dun

Rishikesh Nanda Devi

Haridwar Pindari Glacier

Saharanpur Lansdowne

Ranikhet Almora

Ramnagar NainItal

Meerut CORBETT NAT. PARK

Rampur

Moradabad

DELHI

Bareilly

Aligarh

Shahjahanpur

Brindaban

Mathura UTTAR PRADESH

Bharatpur

Agra

Fatehpur Sikri Kanauj Faizabad

Dholpur Gorakhpur

Kanpur LUCKNOW

Gwalior

R. Ganga

Datia

R. Yamuna Sarnath

Shivpuri Varanasi

Jhansi Allahabad Ramnagar

Orchha

TIBET

H i m a l a y a s

N E P A L

Lumbini

3 SOUTHERN REGION

0 miles · 100 · 200

0 k n · 100 · 200 · 300

4 EASTERN REGION

0 miles 100 200
0 km 100 200 300

T I
H
I
M
A
L
A
Y
A
N E P A L
Mt Everest 29028
Kanchenjunga 28209
SIKKIM
GANGTOK
B
KATHMANDU
Darjeeling
Kalimpong
Kurseong
Siliguri
Bagdogra

UTTAR
Faizabad
Gorakhpur
PRADESH
Vaisali
Sarnath
Varanasi
PATNA
R. Ganga
Bhagalpur
Allahabad
Rajnagar
Nalanda
Rajgir
Gaur
BAN
Mirzapur
Sasaram
Gaya
Bodhgaya
Murshidabad
Berhampur
B I H A R
Parasnath
Santiniketan
Plassey
Daltonganj
Hazaribagh
Asansol
Krishnagar
Ranchi
WEST
CALCUTTA
Netarhat
BENGAL
Howrah
MADHYA
Jamshedpur
PRADESH
Rourkela
Bilaspur
Khiching
Baripada
Jaleswar
Jharsuguda
Doogarh
Balasore
Hirakud Dam
Sambalpur
Bhadrak
Rajpur
Angul
Talcher
Jajpur
R. Mahanadi
Sonepur
Dhenkanal
Cuttack
Bay
Bolangir
BHUBANESWAR
Titlagarh
Puri
Konarak
O R I S S A
L. Chilika
Berhampur
Gopalpur on Sea

Fodor's Travel Guides

U.S. Guides

Alaska

Arizona

Boston

California

Cape Cod, Martha's
Vineyard, Nantucket

The Carolinas & the
Georgia Coast

Chicago

Disney World & the
Orlando Area

Florida

Hawaii

Las Vegas, Reno,
Tahoe

Los Angeles

Maine, Vermont,
New Hampshire

Maui

Miami & the Keys

New England

New Orleans

New York City

Pacific North Coast

Philadelphia & the
Pennsylvania Dutch
Country

San Diego

San Francisco

Santa Fe, Taos,
Albuquerque

Seattle & Vancouver

The South

The U.S. & British
Virgin Islands

The Upper Great
Lakes Region

USA

Vacations in New York
State

Vacations on the
Jersey Shore

Virginia & Maryland

Waikiki

Washington, D.C.

Foreign Guides

Acapulco, Ixtapa,
Zihuatanejo

Australia & New
Zealand

Austria

The Bahamas

Baja & Mexico's
Pacific Coast Resorts

Barbados

Berlin

Bermuda

Brazil

Budapest

Budget Europe

Canada

Cancun, Cozumel,
Yucatan Penisula

Caribbean

Central America

China

Costa Rica, Belize,
Guatemala

Czechoslovakia

Eastern Europe

Egypt

Euro Disney

Europe

Europe's Great Cities

France

Germany

Great Britain

Greece

The Himalayan
Countries

Hong Kong

India

Ireland

Israel

Italy

Italy's Great Cities

Japan

Kenya & Tanzania

Korea

London

Madrid & Barcelona

Mexico

Montreal &
Quebec City

Morocco

The Netherlands
Belgium &
Luxembourg

New Zealand

Norway

Nova Scotia, Prince
Edward Island &
New Brunswick

Paris

Portugal

Rome

Russia & the Baltic
Countries

Scandinavia

Scotland

Singapore

South America

Southeast Asia

South Pacific

Spain

Sweden

Switzerland

Thailand

Tokyo

Toronto

Turkey

Vienna & the Danube
Valley

Yugoslavia

Special Series

Fodor's Affordables

Affordable Europe

Affordable France

Affordable Germany

Affordable Great
Britain

Affordable Italy

**Fodor's Bed &
Breakfast and
Country Inns Guides**

California

Mid-Atlantic Region

New England

The Pacific Northwest

The South

The West Coast

The Upper Great
Lakes Region

Canada's Great
Country Inns

Cottages, B&Bs and
Country Inns of
England and Wales

The Berkeley Guides

On the Loose in
California

On the Loose in
Eastern Europe

On the Loose in
Mexico

On the Loose in the
Pacific Northwest &
Alaska

**Fodor's Exploring
Guides**

Exploring California

Exploring Florida

Exploring France

Exploring Germany

Exploring Paris

Exploring Rome

Exploring Spain

Exploring Thailand

Fodor's Flashmaps

New York

Washington, D.C.

Fodor's Pocket Guides

Pocket Bahamas

Pocket Jamaica

Pocket London

Pocket New York
City

Pocket Paris

Pocket Puerto Rico

Pocket San Francisco

Pocket Washington,
D.C.

Fodor's Sports

Cycling

Hiking

Running

Sailing

The Insider's Guide
to the Best Canadian
Skiing

**Fodor's Three-In-Ones
(guidebook, language
cassette, and phrase
book)**

France

Germany

Italy

Mexico

Spain

**Fodor's
Special-Interest
Guides**

Cruises and Ports
of Call

Disney World & the
Orlando Area

Euro Disney

Healthy Escapes

London Companion

Skiing in the USA
& Canada

Sunday in New York

**Fodor's Touring
Guides**

Touring Europe

Touring USA:
Eastern Edition

Touring USA:
Western Edition

**Fodor's Vacation
Planners**

Great American
Vacations

National Parks of the
West

**The Wall Street
Journal Guides to
Business Travel**

Europe

International Cities

Pacific Rim

USA & Canada

I hoped Ms. Sims wouldn't notice my math homework wasn't there.

But of course teachers always notice that sort of thing.

"Babette," she said, looking over the top of her glasses right at me. "Where is your arithmetic homework?"

"I don't have it," I said.

"Why not?" asked Ms. Sims.

"Well, I did it," I said. "But I asked my mom to check it for me. She stuck it in the script she's reading. She's going to be in a new play, you know. Anyway, she took it with her this morning by accident. It was stuck between the pages. I'll bring it tomorrow."

Ms. Sims got this squishy look on her face. Her mouth got all pinched together—sort of like a raisin. She was about to say something when Susie yelled, "Your mother isn't an actress! That's just another one of your dumb stories."

The Real Deal About Third Grade

Leslie McGuire

Illustrated by Dave Henderson

SCHOLASTIC INC.
New York Toronto London Auckland Sydney
Mexico City New Delhi Hong Kong Buenos Aires

ISBN-13: 978-0-545-01859-3
ISBN-10: 0-545-01859-5

12 11 10 9 8 7 6 5 4 3 2 1   8 9 10 11 12 13/0

Printed in the U.S.A.   40

This edition first printing, September 2008

*To Kathy J. with appreciation
for all your beautiful gifts.*

The Real Deal About Third Grade

Chapter 1

"*I* love October," I said as I walked out onto the playground with my friends. "It makes me think of France."

I was going out for lunchtime recess with Ellen Winston, Marybeth Hughes, and John Boles. They stared at me as I spoke. I could see that they did not believe me about France. I decided I had better say a few more things—just to make the story better. But first, I suppose I should tell you who I am. My name is Babette Simpson. I am the most interesting person in Southside Elementary School.

"My parents took me to France last year," I said. "They took me so I wouldn't feel so sad."

"What did you feel sad about?" asked Marybeth.

"Well, I don't like to talk about it much," I said. Then I looked down at my feet. "You see, that was the year my pony died."

"Oh, no, Babette," said Marybeth. "That's so-o-o horribly sad!"

"Gee, Babette," said Ellen. "What happened to your pony?"

Just then Susie Alton walked past us. Her nose was in the air. Susie's nose is always in the air. That's because she is so stuck up. She was with Warren Peach. Susie and Warren are both in my class. Susie thinks she is the prettiest girl in the world because she has long, blonde hair. I don't agree. Warren thinks he is the smartest boy in the world, but I don't agree with that either.

"Her name isn't Babette," Susie said with a nasty giggle. "Her real name is Jane."

I stuck my tongue out at Susie. Susie stuck her tongue out, too.

Susie knows my real name because she was in my second-grade class last year. Now, she's telling everyone in my third-grade class that my name isn't really Babette. I mean, what difference does it make to her? None.

I know the real reason she tells my real name. It's because Susie is a total rat.

My parents named me Jane. What a boring name. I have been looking for a better name for a long time. This year I finally decided that Babette is perfect.

Even Ms. Sims, our third-grade teacher, calls me Babette. Ms. Sims is nice. She is very tall, and sort of thin. She has reddish hair and she wears glasses.

It only took me a day to get Ms. Sims to call me Babette. All I had to do was not answer when Ms. Sims called me Jane. Then I would remind her that my name is Babette.

Of course, the first few times Ms. Sims forgot. She called me Jane again. But by the end of the day, she only forgot my name a few times. By the end of September, Ms. Sims seemed to have forgotten that my name was anything else but Babette. I wonder if she crossed out "Jane" and wrote "Babette" on her seating plan.

By the end of September everyone else in the class was calling me Babette, too. Everyone except Susie Alton and Warren Peach. But I don't really mind. I just don't answer them.

"See you later, *Jane*," Warren called.

I glared after Susie and Warren. Then I went on with my story.

"My pony's name was Blaze, and he was the most beautiful pony in the whole world," I said. "He once saved my life in a flood. But he got this terrible sickness from eating rose bushes. Then he died. I cried for a month."

Marybeth looked very sad. I felt bad about saying the part about eating rose bushes. Marybeth has a big soft spot for animals. But it made the story better, so I put it in anyway.

"Where did you get a pony?" asked John. He looked suspicious.

"My dad gave him to me," I said, looking gloomy.

"You must be rich," said Ellen Winston.

"My dad is rich," I said. Then I looked even gloomier. "But my parents are divorced, you know."

Ellen looked embarrassed, but John looked sort of interested. His parents are getting a divorce, too. I know because my mom told me.

"My dad is a really famous football player," I said.

"Neato!" said John. "What position does he play?"

"He's a quarterback," I said.

"I thought you told me he was something else," said Marybeth. "Didn't you say he was a tight end?"

I couldn't remember ever having said that. But Marybeth looked puzzled. Maybe I *had* said it once. My problem is I really can't remember what any of those football players are called.

"You must have gotten mixed up," I said quickly. "Quarterbacks are the smart ones."

John frowned. I guess he thinks all football players are smart.

Anyway, I guess I should tell you that most of the kids at school—except for my friends—think I lie a lot. But I don't lie. I just make up stories. You would make up stories, too, if you got as bored as I do. I mean, Southside Elementary School is not a very exciting place.

The kids are boring. No one ever has an exciting story to tell.

The school building is boring, too. It's got four "wings." Don't ask me why they call them wings. They sure don't look like wings. If they did, the building would be a lot more interesting.

First and second grades are in one wing. Third and fourth grades take up another wing. Fifth and sixth grades are in the third wing. Kindergarten and the art and music rooms fill the fourth wing.

There is a big, flat playground in back. All the grown-ups say a flat playground is good because it has lots of running space. But what good is running space if there is nothing interesting to run to?

The town I live in is pretty boring, too. It's called Greatdale, but I don't think it's so great. They should have called it Dulldale.

My mom and I live in an apartment. The only place in our apartment that isn't dull is my bedroom. I put lots of posters all over my walls. They are pictures of things I like to look at. I have posters of frozen lakes, Paris, the Amazon rain forest, and cute puppies. I even have one of kittens dressed up to look like a rock band.

My mom and dad are divorced. My mom works at a bank. She is a very nice mom. But I wish her job sounded more interesting. Banks are boring.

Anyway, I like to make up stories so things seem more exciting around here.

After listening to me for a while, Ellen and Marybeth and John decided to play on the swings. I would have gone, too, but there weren't enough swings for all of us. I decided to go sit under a tree.

Then I saw Marty Degan at one side of the playground. Marty collects rocks. He's always walking around looking at the ground. I decided that he might like to hear some good stories while he looked for rocks. After all, it must get pretty boring for Marty. All he does is stare at the ground.

"Hi, Babette," Marty said—once he noticed me walking with him. Sometimes it takes Marty a while to notice stuff.

"Find any good rocks?" I asked.

"Only one," said Marty.

He reached into his pocket and pulled out a gray rock that had some sparkly stuff on it.

"What's so good about it?" I asked.

"It's pyrite," said Marty. "Fool's gold is what they call it sometimes."

"Wow!" I said. "That's gold?"

"No," said Marty. "It just sparkles like gold."

"Too bad," I said. "Is there a lot of that stuff in the playground?"

"Yep," said Marty. "But sometimes it's hard to find. Mostly it's under the ground."

"You mean you have to dig for it?" I asked.

"Yeah," said Marty.

"That might make a neat story," I said. "You could say you'd discovered gold in the playground. All the kids would start digging for it."

Marty didn't say anything. Maybe he didn't want all the other kids digging for his favorite kind of rock.

The bell rang. It was time to go back inside.

Ms. Sims said we were going to do some arithmetic problems. She handed out the work sheets. That's when I realized I had forgotten to do my math homework. I tried to race through the problems. If I got done early, I would have time to do the homework from last night.

But before I knew it, Ms. Sims had started collecting the math homework. I had finished the work sheet. But I only had two of the homework problems done.

"Now, boys and girls," said Ms. Sims. "Before we go over the work sheet, I'd like you to pass your homework to the front."

All the kids—except me—took out their homework. Then they passed it forward.

Ms. Sims walked along the front row and collected the homework papers.

I hoped she wouldn't notice mine wasn't

in there. But of course teachers always notice that sort of thing.

"Babette," she said, looking over the top of her glasses right at me. "Where is your arithmetic homework?"

"I don't have it," I said.

"Why not?" asked Ms. Sims.

"Well, I did it," I said. "But I asked my mom to check it for me. She stuck it in the script she's reading. She is going to be in a new play, you know. Anyway, she took it with her this morning by accident. It was stuck between the pages. I'll bring it tomorrow."

Ms. Sims got this squishy look on her face. Her mouth got all pinched together— sort of like a raisin. She was about to say something when Susie yelled, "Your mother isn't an actress! That's just another one of your dumb stories."

Everyone started to laugh. But I didn't care.

"She is, too," I said loudly.

"She is not," said Susie. "She works at the bank. I see her there all the time!"

"Lots of actresses work at other jobs

between plays," I said. "They get jobs as waitresses, or taxi drivers, or anything."

"Now, class," said Ms. Sims. "Quiet, please!"

She gave me another one of those squishy looks. Sometimes I think Ms. Sims doesn't believe my stories. But she never says anything. Whatever the look meant, it didn't matter. She had a hard time getting the class to be quiet. By the time things settled down, she had forgotten about my math homework. So I guess I should have thanked Susie for picking on me. It gave Ms. Sims another problem to worry about.

Karen Wiggs, who sits next to me, started scribbling in her notebook. Then she passed the notebook to me. It said: "Liar, liar, chicken frier."

Have you ever heard anything so dumb?

I guess some kids don't like me because I make up so many stories. But I don't care. Who wants a bunch of dull friends like them?

Chapter 2

Well, things stayed pretty boring until just before Thanksgiving. Then we went on this really great class trip. Ms. Sims took the whole class to the Museum of Natural History. That's in New York City. I wish my mom and I lived there. It sure is an exciting city.

We took the school bus to the museum. That was the only boring part. It is bad enough to have to ride the school bus to go home. But the ride home only lasts half an hour. The ride to the city took one and a half hours. But it was worth it anyway.

I sat next to Marty Degan. Nobody else wanted to sit with me. I didn't really want to sit next to them either. Besides, Marty is pretty okay. At least he's okay when he isn't looking for rocks.

We got on the highway. Even Ms. Sims knew this part was going to be boring. She said that we should all start singing songs. We sang "Michael, Row the Boat Ashore" and then we sang "Ninety-Nine Bottles of Milk on the Wall." I always thought that song was supposed to be about beer. I guess Ms. Sims thought that third graders shouldn't be singing songs about beer, so she changed it.

But then the bus driver started to get cranky. I heard him tell Ms. Sims that the noise was driving him crazy. He couldn't keep the bus on the road when it was that noisy. So we had to stop singing. That was okay with me. The singing was starting to make me crazy, too. Besides, I don't like sitting in school buses that are driving off the road.

When the singing stopped, I had a chance

to talk to Marty. I told him about how I got all A's last year. That's not *exactly* true. But I *could* have gotten all A's. I'm very smart, but homework is totally boring. So I don't always do it very carefully.

"That's really nice," said Marty.

"I also have this great doll collection," I said. "There are hundreds and hundreds of dolls in it."

I really *do* have a doll collection. My Aunt Sally gave it to me. There aren't exactly hundreds of dolls in it. But there are at least twenty-five.

"Wow," said Marty. "You have more dolls than I have rocks."

I guess he kind of liked the idea that I collected stuff, too.

"There are dolls from every country in my collection," I said.

Well, *almost* every country.

"I didn't even know there *were* hundreds of different countries," said Marty.

"There are *thousands* of different countries," I answered. "My Aunt Sally traveled all over the world. She went to Peru on a donkey. She went to Alaska on a dog sled."

"That sounds uncomfortable," said Marty. "Did she bring back any rocks?"

"Not that I know of," I said. I was getting kind of bored with that story. All Marty could think about was rocks.

"Last year I went to summer camp in Europe," I said.

"Oh yeah?" said Marty. "Where?"

"Yugoslavia," I said.

"I hear there are great boulder fields in Yugoslavia," said Marty.

See what I mean? Marty is really nice. But all he can think about is rocks!

Just then, things started to get interesting. We went over a bridge. We were finally in the city. I looked out of the window. There were lots of tall buildings and strange people all over the place.

And it was really noisy! Cars were honking. Trucks were screeching. I got a little worried about the bus driver. But he seemed to be doing all right. Maybe it was just singing that drove him crazy. If car noises drove him crazy he wouldn't last long as a bus driver, would he?

Anyway, as I was looking at all the sights,

I suddenly saw a really neat theater. It had a marquee out in front with light bulbs all around the edges. A big sign said, "Starting Next Week! *Southern Express*! All-Star Cast!"

"Hey look, Ms. Sims!" I said. "That's my mom's new play!"

Nobody even turned around to look. Snooty Susie turned up her nose.

"Her mom works at a bank," she said.

"Only during the day," I explained.

Marty was still looking out the window. He was smiling.

"I wonder why everyone in class isn't more excited about my mom's play?" I asked Marty. "After all, it isn't every day that you know someone who's going to be acting in a real play."

"Maybe kids don't know a lot about plays and stuff," he said.

I sighed. "I guess you're right."

We finally got to the museum. It was great to get off the bus. I felt like my legs were going to turn into pretzels after sitting in that school bus for so long.

The museum was neat. There was so much interesting stuff in there, I could have stayed for a year! Unfortunately, we had only a few hours.

We saw the dinosaurs, and the Hall of the Fishes. They had this giant whale hanging from the ceiling. John Boles asked Ms. Sims how come the whale didn't smell. Can you believe it? He actually thought the whale was real!

All Warren Peach could say was, "When is lunch?"

We also went to the part of the museum that had all these neat gems and rocks. I thought Marty was going to move in. Ms. Sims had to practically drag him out of there. It was a good thing we went to the rock room right before lunch. If Marty hadn't been hungry, he probably never would have left.

After lunch we saw some great animals that had been stuffed. They were in glass displays that showed where they lived and what the trees and stuff looked like. It was like taking a trip to Africa. That made me think of a few good stories.

There was one room that had elephants up on a platform. The big one in front looked like he was about to run right out the front door!

"My father shot that elephant when he was on safari in Africa," I said.

Ms. Sims just looked at me. Then Susie got in on the act.

"There's just another one of Jane's dumb lies," said Susie. "The sign right here says this elephant was shot in 1910. Your father wasn't even born in 1910."

I had to think quickly.

"What I meant to say is that my grandfather shot that elephant," I said. I looked down my nose at Susie. She thought she was so smart. But I am smarter. "It was just a slip of the tongue."

Well, that kept *her* quiet for a while.

The bus ride back home was worse than the one going into the city. That's because I knew we were headed back to Greatdale.

But when I got home, Samantha Peters and Jimmy Taggart were sitting on our front lawn, waiting for me.

Samantha is in second grade, and Jimmy is in first. Samantha has bright, carrot-red hair and millions of freckles. Jimmy has lost

his front teeth, and the new ones aren't in yet. He also wears huge glasses. I like them a lot. They are kind of my best friends. They believe *all* my stories.

"How was the museum?" Samantha asked. Her eyes were all round and blue. "I wish my class would go."

"We have to wait until we're in the third grade," said Jimmy, looking sad. After all, he had to wait two years for third grade. I guess two years seemed like a very long time to him.

I started telling them all about the planetarium. While I was describing how you could sign up to be in a spaceship that goes to Jupiter, some kids rode by on bicycles.

"Weird Jane!" they yelled.

"My name is Babette!" I yelled back.

"You only hang out with little kids because they believe your lies!" they shouted.

Samantha looked like she might cry, and Jimmy stuck his tongue out.

Who cares, I thought. At least Samantha and Jimmy are pretty smart for little kids. I decided to make the museum trip really interesting for them.

"The stuffed elephants were great, and so were the dinosaurs," I said. "But it was a pretty scary trip."

"How come?" asked Jimmy.

"Well, just as we were leaving the museum," I said, lowering my voice, "this bunch of guys wearing weird masks to hide their faces came up to us. They made the bus driver take us to a deserted warehouse."

"Omigosh!" said Samantha. Her mouth was as round as a donut.

"How did you get away?" asked Jimmy. His glasses had fallen down low on his nose.

"They made us all get out of the bus," I said. "But I saw a subway entrance right by the door to the warehouse. I told Ms. Sims to get all the kids down into the subway."

"Didn't the bad guys follow you?" asked Jimmy. He pushed his glasses up his nose.

"They couldn't," I said. "I led all the kids into the tunnel. It was so dark down there, they couldn't find us."

"Weren't you scared?" asked Samantha.

Her voice was so squeaky, she sounded like a mouse.

"Of course not," I said. "I just led the class underground through the tunnel until we ended up in the basement of the police station."

"Wow!" said Jimmy. "And then the police arrested the kidnappers?"

"Of course," I said.

"How did you know how to get to the police station if you were underground?" asked Samantha. She had a funny look on her face—like maybe she didn't believe me.

"It was easy," I said. "You see, a long time ago I memorized a map of the New York City sewer and subway system. I knew exactly where I was going."

"Wow!" said Jimmy. "How did you do that?"

"It was in the encyclopedia. I've read the encyclopedia from A to Z," I said. "I happen to be an awesome reader."

"Wow!" said Jimmy.

"Wow!" said Samantha.

Just then, I saw my mom coming up the

walk to our apartment. She looked tired. She's really pretty, for a mom. She has curly brown hair and big, blue eyes. But she was wearing a very boring suit. They make her wear boring clothes at the bank.

"Hi, Samantha. Hi, Jimmy," she called out.

Then she came up and gave me a kiss. "How was your day at school, honey?" she asked.

"Neat," I said. "We had a great time at the museum."

"Well, come inside and tell me all about it," said my mom. She started up the steps.

"I'll be right in," I said.

"Are you going to tell her about the kidnappers?" whispered Jimmy.

"Naw," I said. "That kind of stuff upsets parents. I don't think she could take it."

"Why couldn't she take it?" asked Jimmy.

"She has a heart problem from having had a bad fever," I said. "She was really sick when she was a little girl."

"Wow!" said Samantha, looking at my mom as the door closed behind her. "That's terrible."

"I have to go inside now," I said. "I'm a little tired from running around all day. Besides, I should wash my hands. Sewers aren't the cleanest places in the world, you know."

Chapter 3

*I*t really is true that I'm an awesome reader. What isn't true is the part about reading the encyclopedia from A to Z. Not that I don't read the encyclopedia a lot. I do. I just never read it from start to finish.

I read a lot of grown-up books, though. I like books about romance in the deep South, or during the Civil War. You can learn a lot of history reading grown-up books.

Unfortunately, I also mess up on my schoolwork a lot because I read too much.

Sometimes I think grown-ups have it backward. I mean, the reason they send you to school is so you will learn how to read. But if you already know how to read, you end up reading so much you don't have time to do your homework. Then you get bad grades in school. Then everyone gets mad at you because you are doing the very thing they sent you to school to learn how to do. This doesn't make sense.

Anyway, it was right before Christmas vacation that the trouble started. Ms. Sims asked me to stay inside for a few minutes during recess. She was holding an envelope in her hand.

"Babette, I'm worried about your homework," she said after all the kids had left.

I looked at my feet. *Uh-oh*, I thought.

"You do very well on the work I give you during the day," said Ms. Sims. "But you haven't handed in any homework for three days now."

"I keep forgetting to bring it in," I said. "But I really do it!"

"Did you remember to bring it in today?"

she asked. She took off her glasses and put them on the desk.

"I'm afraid I didn't do my homework last night," I said. "We had to visit my grandmother in the hospital. She had a heart attack."

My grandmother didn't have a heart attack, but she hadn't been looking very good lately. She *could* have had a heart attack.

"You always have some excuse, Babette," said Ms. Sims. "I am tired of so many excuses and so little work."

"I promise I'll do the homework every night from now on," I said.

I meant it, too. I really don't like it when Ms. Sims gets upset with me.

Then Ms. Sims handed me the envelope. A great big "uh-oh" was forming in my stomach. I knew that envelope would make my life miserable.

I didn't want to take that envelope home, but what could I do? I couldn't hand it back to her. That sort of thing just doesn't work with teachers. I put it in my backpack. I knew I would figure out what to do with it later.

"You can go to recess now," said Ms. Sims.

I walked slowly through the door and almost ran into Ellen Winston. Ellen, Marybeth, and John had been listening the whole time!

Remember the museum trip kidnapping story I told Samantha and Jimmy? Well, Samantha told Ellen's little sister, Kathy. Kathy told everyone in her second grade class. Next thing you know, all the kids in *my* class were laughing at me on the playground. Even Ellen, Marybeth, and John joined in singing, "Liar, liar, chicken frier." They turned out to be just like all the other kids around here. Boring.

Now they were giggling at me because I had gotten into trouble. I ignored them and went outside.

Usually the school day goes by very, very slowly. Today it zipped by as if it were wearing roller skates and going downhill. Before I knew it, it was time to get on the bus and go home. "You're gonna be in tr-r-o-u-b-b-b-l-e!" sang Susie Alton all the way home—right in my ear, too. Ellen or Marybeth or John must have told her about the envelope.

At least she was saying something else besides, "Her name isn't Babette. It's Jane."

My backpack was very heavy as I got off the bus. It was heavy because of that dumb note. But it was also heavy because it was the day I go to the library.

Luckily for me, the library is only three blocks from my house. That way I can go by myself. My mother is very busy. If I had to wait for my mother to take me, I would wait a long time.

I can go to the library whenever I want. But usually I only go once a week.

I like the library a lot. The ceiling is very high. There are big, tall windows with lots of little panes in them. It is always quiet at the library. It also smells good. It smells like books, and glue, and the shavings from inside the pencil sharpener.

Every week when I go to the library I check out two grown-up books. The next week I bring them back and check out two more. Miss Fredericks, the librarian, doesn't seem to care that I only take out grown-up books. I think she doesn't believe that I really read them.

Miss Fredericks is very pretty. She has curly hair, and she wears lots of eye shadow and big, dangly earrings. She looks very fancy for a librarian.

I started coming to the library when I was in kindergarten. By the time I finished first grade, I had read all the picture books they had. Last year, I finished all the books for kids in the third and fourth grade. I even read all of the books for older kids. Well, maybe not *all* of them, but at least all of the interesting ones. I had to move up to the adult section.

Whenever I bring my books back, Miss Fredericks always says the same thing.

"Did you enjoy them?" she asked as I walked in the door and put the books on the return desk.

She always smiles at me the same way, too. It's as if she thinks I'm very cute, but a big show-off. I *am* very cute. But I don't show off at all. Can I help it if I happen to be a good reader?

"They were really good," I said. "I liked the one about the Revolutionary War the best. It was about this lady who really liked Patrick Henry. Patrick Henry was an important man during the American Revolution. He said, 'Give me liberty or give me death.' But the lady who liked him got into lots of trouble. It turned out okay in the end."

Miss Fredericks laughed—very quietly of course. You have to be very quiet in the library. Then she patted my head as if I were a baby, or maybe a small dog.

"Are you planning to take out more books today?" she asked.

"You bet," I said.

"Why not look for something in the children's section?" she said. "You might find some books that are much more interesting for you."

"I've already read them all," I said. "But thanks for the suggestion."

Miss Fredericks smiled and shook her

head. She just started working at the library last summer. If she had been here for a while, she'd know that I've already read everything in the children's section.

I went over to a reading table and opened my backpack. I took out the dumb envelope from Ms. Sims. I thought it might be a good idea to read what she'd written to my mother before my mother read it.

But the envelope was sealed!

I sat down in one of the chairs to think. Christmas vacation was a few days away. If my mother didn't have a chance to talk to Ms. Sims for a couple of days, it would be too late. Then school would be closed for two and a half weeks. By that time, Ms. Sims would forget all about it. Right?

I decided to rip the letter up and throw it away. I made up my mind that I would do so much homework that Ms. Sims would be totally buried in pieces of paper that had my handwriting on them. She would forget there ever was a time when I *didn't* do homework. She would pray that I would *stop* doing homework, there would be so much of it!

I was going to get up and leave without checking out another book. But then I decided to see if there was anything new on the grown-up shelves. I had read most of the books up to "L." They arranged the fiction section by the author's last name. Of course, I didn't read every single book from A to L. Some of them looked pretty boring—even for grown-up books.

My eye caught a neat-looking cover. It showed a lady wearing a red ball gown. She looked very scared. The title was *Wild Flowers*. It sounded pretty exciting. I decided to take it out. I figured maybe if I took out just one book instead of two, I could stay out of trouble.

While the librarian was checking out my book I remembered I hadn't told her any good stories lately.

"My mom is opening in a new play next week," I said.

"Oh really?" said Miss Fredericks. She didn't even look up. "Which play is that?"

"It's called *Southern Express*. It has an all-star cast," I said. "Of course."

"Of course," said Miss Fredericks.

She handed me my book, and smiled sweetly.

"Are you going to be in the play, too?"

"They don't let little kids in plays like that," I said. "This play is in the big city, you know. It's not like in a church basement or something."

"I see," said Miss Fredericks. "Well, enjoy your book, dear."

I figured Miss Fredericks didn't know much about plays, either. Marty Degan was wrong about kids in Greatdale not knowing much about plays. *Nobody* in Greatdale knows much about plays.

As soon as I got outside the library, I ripped up the note from Ms. Sims. I looked around to make sure nobody from my class was hiding behind a tree or anything. The coast was clear. I dropped the pieces in the trash.

Chapter 4

Christmas vacation came and went. My plan worked for a while. I did my homework every night, and I only read one book a week. Ms. Sims must have forgotten about talking to my mother. She didn't send any more notes home.

January came and went, too. I was really doing a good job on my homework. I decided that Ms. Sims must have thought my mom had read the note and gotten mad at me. Maybe she thought my mom was

standing over me every night with a baseball bat, making sure I did my homework.

Actually, my mom would never stand
over me with a baseball bat. My mom and
I get along really well. When she sees my
report cards, she never makes a fuss about
the bad grades. Once she told me that she
realizes how hard it is to be a child growing
up in a single-parent household.

My mom reads all these books about feeling better about yourself and how not to
make your children upset about themselves,
either. I guess her theory is that you should
just say nice things to your kids all the time.
That way, they get to like hearing nice
things. Then they try really hard to be nice
all the time. I think it's a good theory.

I was pretty good about doing the homework all through January and February. If
I had a box of gold stars, I'd give myself
fifty gold stars for good behavior for two
months.

But by the beginning of March my life
got so boring I couldn't stand it another
second. Finally, I broke down and went to
the library. I took out four books! Ms. Sims

was lucky I even showed up for school that week.

After a week of not seeing any homework, Ms. Sims gave me another note to take home. But giving me the note didn't work. I just threw it away again.

Throwing the notes away turned out not to be good enough. One day in the middle of March, Ms. Sims asked me why my mother was not calling her to set up a conference.

"Babette," she said, "I haven't heard from your mother. Is there something wrong?"

"No, nothing is wrong," I said slowly. "My aunt and uncle from Switzerland came to visit us right after New Year's. They were supposed to leave last week."

"Have they gone home yet?" said Ms. Sims. She looked a little annoyed.

"Not yet," I said. "They just love Great-dale. My mother is starting to worry that they might move in with us."

Ms. Sims's face got that squishy look that means she doesn't believe me.

"I can't understand it at all," I went on.

"I hear Switzerland is one of the best countries in the world. Why would anyone want to live in Greatdale when he could live in Geneva?"

"Well, America is a wonderful and exciting place," said Ms. Sims. She had gotten sidetracked. I can usually get her mind onto another subject very quickly. This time was no different.

"More exciting than Switzerland?" I asked. I looked amazed, as if such a thing just couldn't happen.

Ms. Sims got going. "Of course it is. America has wonderful theater, beautiful countryside, and very interesting and lively people. Your relatives probably just love the energy in this country."

"You're probably right," I said.

Then the lunch bell rang. I left as quickly as I could.

I thought the story about the relatives from Switzerland would help, but it didn't for long. Even though I handed in my homework, two days later Ms. Sims started again.

"Have your relatives from Switzerland

gone home yet?" Ms. Sims asked when I came in from recess.

"Yes, they left yesterday," I said.

"Good," said Ms. Sims. "Then I should be hearing from your mother shortly. Parent/Teacher Night is next Monday."

But Parent/Teacher Night came and went. My mom didn't show up. I guess I forgot to give her the flyer about it.

"I expected to see your mother last night," said Ms. Sims after Parent/Teacher Night was over. "What happened?"

"My mother sprained her ankle and the doctors think maybe she tore a ligament," I said. "All she can do is hobble to the car and back. She's in a lot of pain."

"Oh dear," said Ms. Sims. She looked upset. "How did that happen?"

"She slipped on the ice," I said. "It's the fault of the people who own our apartment building. They should have cleared the ice from the steps. Her boss at the theater says she should sue."

"Oh dear," said Ms. Sims. "I certainly hope she feels better soon."

"Me, too," I said.

Then the next day, Ms. Sims said she'd called my mom at home, but no one answered the phone.

"Are you sure your mother's ankle is sprained, young lady?" she said. "Or is this just one of your stories?"

"It's a miracle," I said. "Her ankle is cured. The doctors can't believe it. It's as if she never fell down at all."

"What a relief," said Ms. Sims. But she was squinting at me. I decided she wasn't buying the story. I had to think of something fast.

"Yes, it *is* a relief," I said. "Because Mom just went into rehearsal for her new play. They're opening in a month, and she has to be in the city every night and every weekend for two months."

By this time, it was almost April. I figured a month of rehearsals would move this conference up until May. Then being in the play would probably mean my mom would be busy for a year at least! Maybe for the rest of the time I was in school!

Ms. Sims called me outside the classroom. I guess she wanted to have another talk.

But as soon as I stepped outside, bells started clanging like crazy. There was a fire drill—thank goodness. By the time we all got back, we had to go to assembly, and then it was time to go home. I was saved, but not for long.

The next day, Ms. Sims didn't let me go to lunch with everyone else.

"Now, Babette," she said. "I realize things are hard for you."

"They are," I said.

"But it's very important for me to talk with your mother. I'm worried about you. I would feel awful if I let your schoolwork slide to the point of no return."

What was that supposed to mean? How can you get to a point of no return in schoolwork? Schoolwork just keeps returning—day after day, week after week.

"I feel I wouldn't be doing my job if I let this go on," said Ms. Sims. "I was sure your mother would come in on Parent/Teacher Night. I added a special note for her on the flyer."

"She really tried to make it," I said, "but . . ."

Ms. Sims didn't let me finish.

"I'm going to have to call your mother at work and speak to her personally," she said.

I gulped. This was going to be difficult. But then I had an idea!

"I wouldn't do that if I were you," I said. "They're having a big problem down at the bank."

"Oh really?" said Ms. Sims. "Now what would that be?"

"Well, you see, the bank president is suspected of having embezzled—that means stolen—all the bank's money. He and everyone who works at the bank are under house arrest. They can't leave until the police and the FBI and the IRS finish questioning them. My mom is really mad. She has to go to rehearsals and they may have to change the opening date of the play because she's the star—"

"Babette!" yelled Ms. Sims. "I have had about enough of your stories!"

I shut my mouth.

"Young lady, you are not going out for recess today—or for the rest of the term, either," she said sternly. "You will eat lunch in the classroom, and you will clean erasers every day until the end of the year. And I am going to call your mother tonight at home and tell her exactly what you've been up to!"

Then she handed me two chalk-filled erasers and said, "Get to work!"

I hate cleaning erasers. You want to talk about boring? Cleaning erasers is even worse than having kids yell, "Liar, liar, chicken frier." Yeccch!

Chapter 5

Well, there I was, me and about five hundred grubby erasers. Well, maybe not five hundred, but it sure *felt* like five hundred.

"And I want to see every eraser clean as a whistle by the time I get back," Ms. Sims said, looking at me over the top of her glasses. "No excuses."

"What about my lunch?" I asked.

"You may eat your lunch at your desk," she said.

I was about to say I didn't bring my

lunch. I thought maybe I could tell Ms. Sims I had to buy lunch in the cafeteria. But then I realized I didn't have any money to buy a school lunch with. I was just going to have to eat the peanut butter and jelly sandwich my mother made for me.

Ms. Sims walked out the door. She said she was going to the teachers' lounge to calm her nerves.

I sat down at my desk and got out my lunch. I wished I had something to read. I always like to read a book when I eat by myself. It keeps me from getting bored. But the grown-up book I had from the library was at home. It's a mystery written by a lady named Agatha Christie.

It was the first grown-up mystery I had ever read. I really liked it. There were a lot more books by her in the library. I couldn't wait to read them all! Anyway, just as I was biting into my sandwich and wishing I had someone to talk to, Susie Alton came running through the door.

She was someone to talk to. Sort of. But someone else would have been a lot better.

"What's wrong?" asked Susie. "Did you do something *really* bad this time?"

"I never do anything bad," I said with my mouth full.

My mother always tells me I shouldn't talk with my mouth full because it's rude. I don't like being rude. But since Susie was rude first, I figured it was okay in this case.

"Then why are you eating lunch in the classroom?" she asked.

"My knee hurts too much to walk on it," I said.

"What happened?" she asked. She had her hands on her hips and her head tilted way over to the side. She looked like a parakeet. I bet her mother does that all the time, and that's why she does it. "Did you fall off Mount Everest on a hiking trip or something?"

"No," I said, swallowing another mouthful. "I hurt my knee in a car accident in France last summer. Every now and then it bothers me."

"I bet," said Susie with a sniff.

"So what are *you* doing in the classroom during lunch?" I asked. "I thought kids weren't allowed in here without a teacher's permission."

"Ms. Anderson gave me permission," Susie said in her snootiest voice. "I left my lunch money in my backpack."

"That sounds like a story to me," I said in *my* snootiest voice.

"Well, it isn't," said Susie.

She stomped over to her desk and reached into her backpack. Susie's desk is next to mine. As she unzipped the backpack, a little book fell out onto the floor. It opened to a page with a drawing on it. The drawing was of a baby chewing a rattle.

Susie didn't notice it falling. So I reached down and picked it up. There were lots of drawings of babies in it. There were a couple of drawings of a dog, too.

Suddenly Susie saw me looking at it. "Hey!" she said, snatching it from me. "Give that back. It's mine!"

"What is it?" I asked.

"It's my sketchbook," Susie said, turning red.

"Now *you're* making up a story," I said with a sniff. "You probably took it from somebody."

"I did not!" she said loudly. Then she stuffed it back into her backpack.

"You can't draw that well," I said. "I bet you couldn't draw a picture as good as this if you had art lessons for ninety years!"

The drawings were really, really good. They were almost like photographs. That's how I knew she was making up a story.

"Who cares what you think?" she said. "They are pictures of my little brother."

"I never heard you say anything about a little brother," I said, taking a bite of my sandwich. "You don't even *have* a little brother."

"I do, too," she yelled, turning redder. "My dad and his new wife just had a baby."

"Right," I said. "And this is their dog, I suppose."

"Yes, it is," she said, looking really mad.

"If you can draw pictures this good, how come you never draw in class?"

"There's nothing good to draw in class,"

Susie said. That was true, but it still sounded like a story to me.

"I say you took it from somebody else," I said. "But who cares?"

Susie just gave me a snooty, red-faced look. I bet she was red-faced because she was making up a dumber story than even I had ever made up.

"Who cares whether you believe me or not?" she said loudly. Then she left with her lunch money.

I was glad to be by myself. Being alone is better than being with Susie Alton any day. I figured I had better hurry up and eat or else I would never get to the erasers. But just as I finished my box of juice, Ms. Sims came back in the room.

Uh–oh, I thought. Now I'm really in for it.

"I haven't finished them yet!" I said. Ms. Sims hadn't even asked.

"I have homework papers to go over," said Ms. Sims. "Besides, I wanted to have a little talk with you."

Double uh-oh, I thought. I have noticed that whenever a grown-up wants to have a "little talk," it's never a good thing. I have also noticed that the best way to handle a "little talk" is not to talk at all. But that only works if the grown-up doesn't ask you any questions.

So, of course, that was the first thing Ms. Sims did.

"Can you just tell me the *real* reason why you don't do your homework, Babette?" said Ms. Sims.

She sat at her desk and got comfortable. She folded her hands in front of her and got that "I'll just wait until you're ready to tell me the truth" look on her face. I could see there was no point in telling her any stories. She probably wouldn't like them anyway.

"It's boring," I said.

"Boring?" said Ms. Sims. "Why do you think that? After all, teachers and parents work very hard to make things interesting for the students."

"I know," I said. "But everything is still boring."

"Sometimes in life, people have to do things that they don't like," said Ms. Sims.

"Just because something is dull doesn't mean that you can simply refuse to do it."

"I know," I said. I could feel a long lecture coming on.

"Are there any special problems at home?" Ms. Sims asked. "Is there something happening between your parents that you don't want to talk about? Is that the reason you don't do your homework?"

I tried to think if there was anything I could say, but there wasn't. Things at home were just fine.

"Everything is okay," I said. "I just get bored at school. The work isn't that interesting."

"Everyone gets bored with work," said Ms. Sims. "Even I get bored with work. Some days I would much rather play tennis, or sail a boat. But I come to school every day and do my job anyway."

That was pretty surprising. It never crossed my mind that teachers would rather do something else besides teach. I always figured they didn't have anything better to do. Maybe Ms. Sims was more exciting than I thought.

"But it's so hard to keep my mind on schoolwork," I said finally.

"What do you do that's more interesting at home?" asked Ms. Sims. "Do you watch television?"

"I read books," I said.

"If you like to read, why don't you read what I give you for homework?" asked Ms. Sims.

"Because what you give us to read for homework is *really* boring," I said.

This was not going well. Ms. Sims was looking grouchier by the minute.

"Perhaps you can help me make it more interesting," said Ms. Sims. "I thought *Pepito's Burro* was a very good story. What, in your opinion, is wrong with it?"

"It isn't that there's anything wrong with that story, Ms. Sims," I said. "It's just that it's so short. And it's also kind of simple, if you know what I mean."

"Not exactly," she said. "You mean the words are too simple for you?"

"That, too," I said. "But also, Pepito doesn't do much. Nothing happens to him. He just has a little burro. So what?"

"And what books do you read that are more interesting?" said Ms. Sims.

"I just finished a neat book called *A High Wind in Jamaica*," I said. "And now I'm in the middle of a really good mystery by Agatha Christie. It's about a murder on this train called the Orient Express. Nobody can get off the train, so the murderer is someplace in there with all the good guys. . . ."

Ms. Sims looked at me as if I had just turned into a giant lizard or something.

"What did you like about *A High Wind in Jamaica*?" asked Ms. Sims.

"I liked how all these little kids were able to drive a whole ship full of pirates totally crazy," I said. "I like it when kids turn out to be tougher than grown-ups."

Ms. Sims smiled. "I liked that book, too," she said. "Kids are stronger than most adults think they are, aren't they?"

After that, we talked about all the books I've been reading. It turned out that Ms.

Sims had read a lot of the same books. It was the weirdest conversation I'd ever had with a grown-up.

It was so strange that I totally forgot to tell Ms. Sims that Susie Alton had taken somebody's drawing notebook. Not that I'm a tattletale. I just thought it might be a good idea to get someone else in trouble for a change.

Then Ms. Sims said the weirdest thing of all.

"I have a great idea, Babette," she said. "Instead of giving you the same homework that I give the rest of the class, I'm going to give you something different."

Here's where I get into major big trouble, I thought. I scrunched my face up and waited for the bomb to drop.

"I want you to write a book of your own," said Ms. Sims. "Every night, instead of the usual reading homework, I want you to go home and write a grown-up story that's very, very long."

"You mean with chapters and everything?" I gulped.

"Exactly," said Ms. Sims. "After all, I can

tell from the crazy stories you've been telling me all year that you have a wonderful imagination."

She said this with a funny, crooked smile. Then the smile got bigger.

"But I think you should know that it's wrong to make up stories to get out of doing work," she said. "So there is one other little problem we need to take care of."

I wondered why she was smiling. I wasn't smiling at all. Here I had been thinking I was off the hook. But Ms. Sims wasn't letting me off at all. She was probably going to make me wiggle a lot more before she was done.

"I still want to talk to your mother—and soon, Babette," she said. "So I'm going to call her in for a parent/teacher conference anyway."

"But I really will do my homework," I said. I did *not* want my mom to talk to Ms. Sims.

"Don't worry, dear," she said. "Your mom won't be angry."

That's what she thought.

"What about the erasers?" I asked as the bell rang.

"Don't worry about them," said Ms. Sims. "You have a lot of work to do. You can't waste your time cleaning erasers when you have a novel to write!"

◆ Chapter 6 ◆

I started writing my novel on April 10th. It was the night of my mom's parent/teacher conference with Ms. Sims.

It took more than a week for Ms. Sims and my mom to get together. That's because my mom *was* busy—she really *did* have a play to rehearse for. Of course, it wasn't a big hit show in the city. But it was still a real play.

You see, my mom always wanted to be an actress. So she tried out for a part in a play that the little theater group in town was putting on in the church basement.

Well, she got the part! Maybe she'll be a big movie star someday.

While my mom and Ms. Sims were trying to figure out when to meet, I was trying to figure out what to write a novel about.

That part was a lot harder than I'd thought it would be. I have read every book ever written. Well, not *every* book, but a lot of books. But reading someone else's book is pretty easy. Figuring out how to write one yourself is not so easy at all.

The stories I make up to keep from getting bored are pretty good. But they're awfully short. Novels are two hundred pages long! I don't know how writers make their books so long.

I thought about all the books I had ever read. I thought about what I liked best about each book.

I like history books, but to write one you have to know what was going on in the old days. You have to know what people wore, and what kind of houses and machines they had then. If I wanted to write a book like that, I would actually have to read some real history books! That's the same as doing homework! Ms. Sims is very sneaky, you know.

That left the love stories or the mysteries. I didn't feel like writing a love story. They have people going to all these fancy restaurants, and taking planes to Europe, and stuff like that.

The fanciest restaurant I was ever in was Nell's Steak House on Route 43. It was nice, but it sure wasn't very romantic. And I've never been in an airplane in my life. You have to have done something in order to write about it, I think.

That left writing a mystery. Now, I think mysteries are great, but murder mysteries are the best. The problem is, I don't know anything about guns, or knives, or poisons, or getaway cars, either.

So what *do* I know about? I only know about one thing, and that's Southside Elementary School. That's not much.

After thinking for a week, I still hadn't decided what to write about. I was feeling really gloomy about it one day on the playground. I sat on the swings and watched all the kids run around. Then I started to think about the kids and what they always did. You see, each kid has some kind of interesting, weird habit.

Marty Degan collects rocks. John Boles asks a zillion questions. Karen Wiggs sniffles all day long. Warren Peach always says he's hungry. The more I thought about them, the more interesting each kid got.

Suddenly, I thought about what would happen if we were all stuck together on an island someplace—sort of like the *Swiss Family Robinson*. I wondered if any of our habits would come in handy on the island. Maybe I wasn't looking at people right. Maybe rock collecting *could* actually be helpful sometimes.

That's when it came to me!

I would write a book about the whole class going on a long trip—maybe to Disney World. Then the tour boat gets hijacked by some bad guys. And we drive them all crazy with our weird singing, noise-making, backtalking, and whining about being hungry all the time. Finally, the hijackers put us off on some deserted island in the Florida Keys because they can't stand having us around for another second. And we all manage to survive and build shelters and stuff until we get rescued!

I went right back to the classroom. I made notes all during math. I made notes during assembly. I even made notes on the bus home. I forgot all about the parent/teacher conference until I got home. Then I saw the note my mom had left on the refrigerator.

It said, "Seeing Ms. Sims tonight after work. Be home later. Eat the leftover meatloaf if you're hungry. Love, Mom."

Whoops! This was the big night. Suddenly, I felt awful. I wished I had done my homework like a regular kid. I wondered if my mom would be mad at me. Or worse, she might be worried about me. She had enough things to worry about without having to worry about me, too.

But just when I was beginning to get upset about upsetting my mom, I remembered something that I wanted to put in my book. It was neat how easy it was to forget about my own problems when I had something really fun to think about—like writing!

I decided I would make Warren Peach the pest who drives the hijackers totally off the deep end. All Warren ever does is ask about food. That could drive even the worst criminal crazy.

As I was making notes, I remembered that Ms. Sims should be in the book, too. After all, why would the whole class go on a trip without their teacher?

I decided she had to get sick, or something. If Ms. Sims couldn't take care of us, we would have to figure out a way to take care of ourselves and her, too.

I just couldn't wait another second. I got out the nice new notebook Ms. Sims had given me to start my novel in. On the first page I wrote, "THE WORST CLASS TRIP EVER, Chapter One."

Then I started writing. I couldn't write fast enough to keep up with the story inside my head. It was like a movie running right behind my eyes. I was afraid I would forget how I wanted it to go, so I grabbed a scrap of paper and made some more notes.

I called myself Amber in the story. I got to the part where I noticed these really weird looking men on the boat. They were wearing long raincoats, which was totally dumb in Florida in June. Their coats were all lumpy. I said to Marty Degan (who I called Tex in the story) that unless those guys had a really great rock collection under their coats, I would be willing to bet they were carrying submachine guns.

Just then the door slammed.

My mom was home.

I looked up and noticed that it was dark outside already. When I looked at the clock, I saw that it was almost seven-thirty! I had been writing for three and a half hours, nonstop. I had even forgotten to get hungry. I hadn't even worried about what Ms. Sims was saying to my mom. I had forgotten everything but the story!

But now I remembered everything. I was hungry and I didn't really want to talk to my mom about the parent/teacher conference.

Before I could escape into the bathroom or the closet, Mom came into my room.

"Oh, Janey, you sweet little thing!" she said, giving me a kiss on the head.

I guess I don't have to tell you that my mom doesn't call me Babette.

"Hi, Mom," I said, looking glum.

"Ms. Sims is very nice," said my mom. "And she thinks a lot of you, too."

I almost fell off my chair. "She does?" I said.

"Oh, yes," Mom said. "And I'm going to call you Babette from now on. I never knew you didn't like to be called Janey."

I felt pretty bad right then. After all, my mom had named me Jane. I didn't want to tell her I thought her idea of a good name was dumb.

"It will be like having a stage name," she said warmly. "Lots of actresses have them. Maybe you can help me think up a good stage name for myself, too."

"You mean, for when you get famous?" I said.

"Of course," said my mom. "Now come into the kitchen with me while I make some dinner."

Here comes the bad part, I thought as I

77

helped her chop carrots for a salad. This is when she tells me what a rotten kid I am.

But that isn't what happened at all.

"Ms. Sims says that you are a gifted child," Mom said as she stuck the meatloaf in the microwave. "Please get out the knives and forks."

My mom does that a lot. She tells you a story all broken up with chores, and complaints, and stories about something else.

"She says she feels that you may need special teaching, or perhaps you should skip ahead a grade."

"I don't want to get skipped ahead," I said. "I'm already the littlest kid in the third grade. In the fourth grade, I'd look like a midget."

"Don't worry," said Mom. "I told her the same thing. But she still thinks you might need something extra because you are bored with third-grade work."

Well, I knew that. I just didn't know that anyone else did.

"And she told me you are writing a book!" said Mom. "I would love to see what you've written so far! Actually, I'm a little hurt that you didn't tell me about it."

"I didn't start writing it until tonight," I said. "Besides, I thought you would be mad at me for not doing my homework."

"Ms. Sims says that many gifted children don't do homework, and they get bad grades for that reason," said my mom. "She says they are so far ahead of everyone in the class, they get bored. And then they get lost in their own thoughts."

Well, *that* certainly was true.

"Ms. Sims told me that Albert Einstein— who was the smartest scientist ever, and won the Nobel prize for physics—got a c in physics when he was in school!" said my mom with a laugh. "Does that make you feel better?"

It sure did.

After dinner, Mom read my story. I told her what was going to happen next. She liked it!

"I think you should show Ms. Sims what you've written," she said as she tucked me into bed. "I don't want her to think you aren't doing anything at all for homework, you know."

The next day, I handed the notebook to Ms. Sims right before lunch.

"So you finally did some homework?" Marty asked as we went outside for lunch.

"No, that was my novel," I answered.

John Boles was walking right behind us. He heard what I said. So he butted in, of course.

"Kids don't write novels," he said.

"Ms. Sims asked me to write a novel instead of doing the homework all the rest of you do," I said. "I just gave her the first chapter."

"Liar, liar, chicken frier," John yelled. Then he ran off and told Marybeth, who told Susie, who told Warren, who told the whole world. Soon, all the kids in the class were laughing and pointing at me. There were probably some kids laughing and pointing who *weren't* in our class.

Finally, Marybeth came over with Susie.

"This is the biggest lie Jane has ever told," said Susie.

"Is it bigger than the story about her

father being a football star?" asked Marybeth.

"Yes. It's even bigger than the one she told about her mom acting in a Broadway play," said Susie. "It's bigger because we can prove that this story is a lie."

Then she and Marybeth walked off, giggling.

Marty looked upset. "Don't listen to them, Babette," he said. "I believe you."

"It's true about the novel, Marty," I said. "But it makes no difference if you tell people the truth or not. They still don't believe you. So why should I bother?"

"Maybe it's like that fable," said Marty.

"What fable?" I said, stomping off to the edge of the playground. I didn't want to be around those creepy kids anymore.

Marty shuffled after me. He was looking at the ground. Only this time he wasn't looking for rocks.

"Remember that story about the little boy who cried wolf?" he said. Marty looked up. His face was bright red.

"You mean the one where the kid makes up so many stories about the wolf eating the sheep, that when the wolf finally shows up nobody believes him?" I said.

"That's the one," said Marty. "Maybe it's like that."

"Well, I'll show them!" I said.

When we got back inside from recess, Ms. Sims was waiting for me.

"This is wonderful, Babette," she said. "Would it embarrass you to read it aloud to the class?"

"Not at all," I said. "As a matter of fact, I'd like to read the whole book to the class as I write it."

"That's a great idea," said Ms. Sims.

"I want their suggestions," I said sweetly. But that wasn't what I wanted at all.

I wanted to prove that this time, I was telling the truth. And besides, it might be fun to see how everyone felt when they figured out that *they* were the crazy, annoying kids I was writing about!

Chapter 7

*T*he next morning, Ms. Sims stood in front of the class. She waited until we were quiet. Then she said, "As some of you may know, Babette has been working on a special project. She's writing a book, and she wants to share it with you."

Warren started to laugh. Ms. Sims stared at him and he stopped.

"Why don't you come up to the front of the classroom, Babette," she said.

I stood up and walked to the front of

the class with my first chapter. I cleared my throat, took a deep breath, and started to read:

It was supposed to be a class trip like any other one—except, of course, that Mrs. Ripley's third–grade class was going to Disney World.

Mrs. Ripley was checking for lunches, sweatshirts, and permission slips when suddenly a loud voice popped up from the back of the bus.

"I don't have my lunch," said Eldridge.

"Why not?" asked Mrs. Ripley.

"I ate it on the way to school," said Eldridge.

"Why on earth did you do that?" asked Mrs. Ripley. She looked at the chubby boy over the top of her glasses.

"I was hungry," said Eldridge.

"Well, then you won't be hungry at lunchtime, will you?" said Mrs. Ripley.

"Yes, I will," said Eldridge. "I'm hungry right now!"

The kids in class started to laugh.

"That sounds just like Warren," said John Boles.

"Please don't interrupt," said Ms. Sims. But she was smiling, too. I wondered if she had figured out the truth.

I continued reading. By the time I got to the end of the chapter, everyone was all excited about the book.

Ms. Sims decided I should read the class a chapter each week from THE WORST CLASS TRIP EVER for the rest of the school year.

The kids could hardly wait to hear what was going to happen next. Some of the kids—mainly Warren Peach—actually pestered me in the playground to tell them what was going to happen next. Warren wanted to know before everyone else did.

At the end of every chapter I left the kids on the edge of a new and crazy and dangerous disaster. I had hurricanes, bad guys, wild pigs, and poisoned water holes. You name it, I stuck it in there.

I had lots of funny things happen in my book, too. Like when Karen Wiggs got lost in the jungle and we couldn't find her for two days. Marty and I tracked her down by following the sound of her sniffling!

But the funny things that happened were not just in the story, either. For one thing, I had planned to give each kid in the class a strange habit. It was going to be their weird habits that ended up saving us all, of course.

I was hoping that even though I'd changed everyone's names, they wouldn't catch on to who they were too quickly.

Well, the first surprise was that they all got it right away! Of course, with the easy ones like Marty Degan and Warren Peach, everyone figured it out in a second. Then the rest of the kids in the class guessed that they were probably in the story, too. So they started looking for themselves. By Chapter Two—when the class was driving the hijackers out of their minds—they all figured it out.

I thought the kids might be mad, but they loved it. They thought it was a great joke that their oddball acts were actually better weapons than guns and knives.

Not only that, but they started giving me ideas for the story. Marybeth sent me a zillion notes during math class.

"Why don't you have Marty go rock collecting on top of a volcano? Then I could save him before the volcano erupts."

The next note was even sillier. *"Why not have everyone get trapped in an underground water cavern? We could discover a family of mermaids!"*

During recess Marybeth came up to me. I could tell she wanted to give me some more ideas.

"If you're so good at coming up with ideas," I said to Marybeth, "why don't you write a book of your own?"

"Maybe I will!" she said. I think she was mad at me.

It turned out that she actually *did* write one over summer vacation. Nobody saw Marybeth for the whole two months.

But the very best part of all was Susie Alton.

By the time I was up to Chapter Four it was the end of May and practically the end of school. Susie came up to me on the playground.

"I want you to look at something," she said.

I was about to tell her to take a long walk off a short plank, but she looked sort of funny. For one thing, her cheeks were all red. For another, she didn't have that snooty look on her face. She was even smiling an almost regular smile.

"Sure," I said. "But I only have a minute."

She held out her sketchbook to me.

"Why are you showing me this?" I asked.

"Never mind," said Susie. She started to take it back. But I snatched it away from her. I figured she was about to show me another bunch of drawings done by a grown-up. Then she would confess that I had been right about her all along. She was just pretending to be able to draw. I could hardly wait to catch Susie Alton making up a big lie.

I opened the sketchbook. On the first page there was a picture of all the kids in our class at the gates to Disney World. There were Warren Peach, Marybeth Hughes, Ellen Winston, me, and John Boles—and, of course, Ms. Sims. The next picture showed everyone getting on the tour boat. The two guys with the long, lumpy overcoats were looking at us. Ms. Sims looked grouchy and hot.

In the next picture, all of us stood lined up against the boat cabin. The lumpy guys were holding machine guns on us. The captain and Ms. Sims had their hands up in the air. They looked really scared. Ms. Sims's glasses hung off one ear. Warren Peach was yanking on the sleeve of one of the bad guys. This was the part where Warren kept saying, "When is lunch?"

These pictures were great!

"You did these?" I asked as I flipped through a few more. But I knew the answer.

"Uh-huh," said Susie, looking sort of snooty, but still red-faced.

The rest of the pictures matched the story, right up through Chapter Four.

"When did you draw them?" I asked.

"I did some of them while you were reading out loud to us," Susie said. "But most of them I drew at home, from what I remembered."

"I bet," I said. I tried to sound like I didn't think they were so great.

Actually, I was really pleased. But I didn't want to tell Susie that. After all, I'd accused her of lying about being able to draw. These pictures looked like a grown-up's work, but Susie was the only person who could have done them.

The only grown-ups who had heard the story were Ms. Sims and my mom. Neither of them could draw at all. Susie had just proved she was telling the truth.

Of course, I had been proving for the last month that I was telling the truth about writing a real novel.

So there we were. I wasn't a liar anymore. And Susie wasn't a liar either. We were artists! How neat!

"Let's go inside and show your drawings to Ms. Sims," I said, still holding on to the sketchbook.

Susie tried to grab the book back. "No! They're not good enough to show her yet."

"Sure they are," I said. "I think Ms. Sims will really like them."

We walked back inside together. Ms. Sims was sitting at her desk correcting papers. She glanced up from her desk when we entered the room. "Ms. Sims," I said, "we have something to show you."

Susie walked slowly to the front of the classroom and handed her the sketchbook. Her face was bright red.

Ms. Sims spent a long time studying the pictures. Then she looked up at Susie. "Your drawings are excellent, Susie."

Susie smiled. And I did, too. I was really glad Ms. Sims liked the pictures.

Ms. Sims thought for a minute. Then she said, "I have an idea. Why don't you put the drawings and the story together? Then we can make photocopies. That way, all of the class can have their own copy of the story to remember our third-grade year."

"That's great!" I cried. "All I have to do now is finish it!"

And I did—or I should say, *we* did. We finished it just before the last day of school.

With Susie drawing pictures right along

with me, I got really excited. I began thinking about what each part of the story should *look* like. I wanted to write good scenes for Susie to draw.

Of course, that meant Susie and I had to talk to each other a lot.

And guess what?

Susie and I are best friends now.

It turns out that she's just like me. I mean, her mom and dad are divorced, too. But it's worse for her. Her dad got married again and actually started a whole new family! At least my mom and dad have the sense to keep it simple.

And Susie was snooty to me because she thought *I* was stuck up. I guess I *was* acting stuck up, too.

Having a best friend was great. We worked, and we talked, and we played together all the time. And I didn't have to make up even one story! The truth could actually be pretty interesting, too.

By the time the last day of school came in June, the book was done and so were all the pictures.

I got everyone off the island. I got the

bad guys arrested. We had already started driving the Coast Guard crazy on the boat that rescued us in the last chapter.

In the book, Ms. Sims was very grateful to all of us. She promised that since we had saved her life—I had her step on a piece of coral and get poisoned—she would never give us any homework again.

We said she could give us all the homework she wanted, but that she wasn't allowed to give anyone a lower grade than a B +.

All we wanted, we said, was another chance to take a trip to Disney World!

So here we are, Susie and I and the rest of the class, headed for fourth grade. We'll be rich and famous by then, I'm sure. You see, I sent a copy of the book to this famous Hollywood director. Maybe he'll want to make it into a movie. And he'll want everyone in the class to be in it. I can just see Susie and me riding to school next year in a limousine.

I feel sort of sorry for our fourth-grade teacher.

Wouldn't you?